Little Oxford Thesaurus

THIRD EDITION

Edited by
Maurice Waite

OXFORD
UNIVERSITY PRESS

OXFORD

UNIVERSITY PRESS

Great Clarendon Street, Oxford OX2 6DP

Oxford University Press is a department of the University of Oxford.
It furthers the University's objective of excellence in research, scholarship,
and education by publishing worldwide in

Oxford New York

Auckland Cape Town Dar es Salaam Hong Kong Karachi
Kuala Lumpur Madrid Melbourne Mexico City Nairobi
New Delhi Shanghai Taipei Toronto

With offices in

Argentina Austria Brazil Chile Czech Republic France Greece
Guatemala Hungary Italy Japan Poland Portugal Singapore
South Korea Switzerland Thailand Turkey Ukraine Vietnam

Oxford is a registered trade mark of Oxford University Press
in the UK and in certain other countries

Published in the United States
by Oxford University Press Inc., New York

© Oxford University Press 2002, 2006

Database right Oxford University Press (makers)

First edition 1995
Second edition 2002
Third edition 2006

British Library Cataloguing in Publication Data

Data available

Library of Congress Cataloging in Publication Data

Data available

ISBN 978-0-19-861449-4
ISBN 978-0-19-920299-7 (US edn)

10 9 8 7 6 5 4 3 2

Typeset in Frutiger and Parable
by Interactive Sciences Ltd, Gloucester
Printed in China by The Hanway Press/Phoenix Offset

Contents

Preface

Everyone occasionally finds that the right word will not come to them, and that is when a good thesaurus is essential.

You may have a word in mind but you know that it is not the right word because it does not accurately express what you want to say. In short, you want to find out how you can express something better.

Or perhaps you need to find alternatives when you wish to avoid using the same word again and again when speaking or writing.

Or you might be looking for a more modern or more formal equivalent that would be better suited to your audience and purpose.

The word *thesaurus* comes from Greek, meaning 'storehouse' or 'treasure'. A thesaurus will open up to you the vast riches of the English language by giving you lists of words with similar meaning (called 'synonyms'), providing an array of choices as well as ways of pinpointing the right word.

In addition, the new section in the centre pages of this book provides you with still further sources of vocabulary: handy lists of animals, clothes, foods, plants, forms of transport, and many other categories, to help with vocabulary-building and puzzle-solving.

Whether for everyday quick reference, essays, reports, creative writing, or crosswords and puzzle-solving, the *Little Oxford Thesaurus* is the perfect companion for all your writing needs.

Guide to the thesaurus entry

example of use, to help distinguish different senses

headword

words meaning the opposite of the headword; most have entries of their own, where a wider choice will be found

cheerful adjective **1** *he arrived looking cheerful:* **happy,** jolly, merry, bright, sunny, joyful, in good/high spirits, buoyant, cheery, animated, smiling, good-humoured; informal chipper, chirpy, full of beans. **2** *a cheerful room:* **pleasant,** attractive, agreeable, bright, sunny, friendly, welcoming.
OPPOSITES sad, gloomy.

numbered sense of the headword

core synonym— the closest synonym to the headword

part of speech of the headword

everywhere adverb **all over,** all around, in every nook and cranny, far and wide, near and far, high and low, {here, there, and everywhere}, the world over, worldwide; informal all over the place; Brit. informal all over the shop; N. Amer. informal all over the map.
OPPOSITES nowhere.

brackets around a phrase, to avoid confusion

label indicating the specialist field in which the following synonym is used

infant noun baby, newborn, young child, tiny tot, little one; Medicine neonate; Scottish & N. English bairn, wean; informal tiny, sprog.

label indicating the level or style of English in which the following synonyms are used (*see opposite for explanations*)

label indicating the region of the world in which the following synonyms are used (*see opposite for abbreviations*)

Guide to the thesaurus entry

root noun **1** *the root of the problem:* **source**, origin, cause, reason, basis, foundation, bottom, seat. **2** (roots) **origins**, beginnings, family, birth, heritage.
verb *he rooted around in the cupboard:* **rummage**, hunt, search, rifle, delve, forage, dig, nose, poke.
■ **root something out** eradicate, eliminate, weed out, destroy, wipe out, stamp out, abolish, end, put a stop to.

form of the headword for which synonyms are given

phrase for which synonyms are given

seldom adverb **rarely**, infrequently, hardly (ever), scarcely (ever); informal once in a blue moon.
OPPOSITES often.

brackets to show more than one possibility: *hardly* and *hardly ever*

Most of the synonyms are part of standard English, but some are used only in certain styles or situations. These are grouped at the end of their sense and have labels in front of them:

informal, e.g. *swig*: normally only used in speech or informal writing.

formal, e.g. *dwelling*: normally only used in writing, such as official documents.

literary, e.g. *wondrous*.

historical, e.g. *serfdom*: only used today to refer to things that are no longer part of modern life.

archaic, e.g. *apothecary*: not in use today except for old-fashioned effect.

Synonyms are also labelled if they are exclusively or mainly British (abbreviated to Brit.), Northern English (N. English), Scottish, North American (N. Amer.), Australian (Austral.), or New Zealand (NZ).

Note on trademarks and proprietary status

This thesaurus includes some words which have, or are asserted to have, proprietary status as trademarks or otherwise. Their inclusion does not imply that they have acquired for legal purposes a non-proprietary or general significance, nor any other judgement concerning their legal status. In cases where the editorial staff have some evidence that a word has proprietary status this is indicated by the label trademark, but no judgement concerning the legal status of such words is made or implied thereby.

abandon verb **1** *he abandoned his wife:* **desert,** leave, turn one's back on, cast aside, finish with, jilt, throw over; informal walk/run out on, dump, ditch; literary forsake. **2** *she had abandoned painting:* **give up,** stop, have done with; informal pack in, quit; Brit. informal jack in. **3** *they abandoned the car:* **leave (behind),** vacate, dump, quit, evacuate, discard, jettison. **4** *the party abandoned those policies:* **renounce,** relinquish, dispense with, discard, give up, drop; informal ditch, scrap, junk; formal forswear.
OPPOSITES keep, continue, retain.
noun *with reckless abandon:* **uninhibitedness,** recklessness, lack of restraint, lack of inhibition.
OPPOSITES self-control.

abate verb *the storm had abated:* **subside,** die down/away/out, lessen, ease (off), let up, decrease, diminish, fade, weaken.
OPPOSITES intensify.

abatement noun **1** *the storm still rages with no sign of abatement:* **subsiding,** dying down/away/out, lessening, easing (off), let-up. **2** *noise abatement:* **reduction,** control.

abbreviate verb **shorten,** reduce, cut, contract, condense, compress, abridge.
OPPOSITES lengthen, expand.

abbreviation noun **short form,** contraction, acronym, initialism.

abdicate verb **resign,** retire, stand down, step down, renounce the throne.

abdomen noun **stomach,** belly, gut, middle; informal tummy, guts; Austral. informal bingy.

abdominal adjective **gastric,** intestinal, stomach, duodenal, visceral, coeliac, ventral.

abduct verb **kidnap,** carry off, seize, capture, run away/off with; informal snatch.

aberration noun **anomaly,** deviation, abnormality, irregularity, variation, freak, oddity, peculiarity, curiosity, mistake.

abhor verb **hate,** detest, loathe, despise, regard with disgust, shudder at; formal abominate.
OPPOSITES love, admire.

abhorrent adjective **hateful,** detestable, loathsome, abominable, repellent, repugnant, repulsive, revolting, disgusting, horrible, horrid, horrifying, awful, heinous.
OPPOSITES admirable.

abide verb **1** (informal) *I can't abide smoke:* **stand,** bear; Brit. informal stick. **2** *one memory will abide:* **continue,** remain, survive, last, persist, live on.
■ **abide by** comply with, obey, observe, follow, keep to, adhere to, stick to, go along with, heed, accept.

abiding adjective **enduring,** lasting, everlasting, perpetual, eternal, unending, permanent.
OPPOSITES short-lived, ephemeral.

ability noun **1** *the ability to read:* **capacity,** capability, power,

a

faculty, facility, wherewithal, means. **2** *leadership ability:* **talent,** skill, aptitude, expertise, savoir faire, prowess, accomplishment, competence, proficiency, flair, gift, knack, genius; informal know-how.
OPPOSITES inability.

able adjective **1** *able to resume his duties:* **capable of,** competent to, up to, fit to, in a position to, allowed to, free to. **2** *an able student:* **intelligent,** clever, talented, skilful, skilled, accomplished, gifted, proficient, apt, adroit, adept, capable, competent.
OPPOSITES incompetent, incapable.

abnormal adjective **unusual,** uncommon, atypical, untypical, unrepresentative, irregular, anomalous, deviant, aberrant, freak, strange, odd, peculiar, bizarre, weird, unnatural, perverted, twisted, warped; informal funny, freaky, kinky.
OPPOSITES normal, typical, common.

abnormality noun **oddity,** strangeness, irregularity, anomaly, deviation, aberration, deformity, defect, malformation.
OPPOSITES normality.

abolish verb **put an end to,** get rid of, scrap, cancel, end, remove, dissolve, stop, ban; informal do away with, ditch.
OPPOSITES retain, create.

abolition noun **scrapping,** ending, cancellation, dissolution, removal.
OPPOSITES retention, creation.

abominable adjective **loathsome,** detestable, hateful, obnoxious, despicable, contemptible, disgusting, revolting, repellent, repulsive,

repugnant, abhorrent, reprehensible, atrocious, foul, vile, wretched, horrible, awful, dreadful, appalling, nauseating; informal terrible, shocking, God-awful; Brit. informal beastly.
OPPOSITES good, admirable.

abort verb **1 miscarry,** have a miscarriage, terminate. **2** *the crew aborted the take-off:* **halt,** stop, end, call off, abandon, discontinue, terminate, arrest; informal pull the plug on.

abortion noun **termination,** miscarriage.

abortive adjective **unsuccessful,** failed, vain, ineffective, ineffectual, unproductive.
OPPOSITES successful, fruitful.

abound verb **1** *cafes abound in the narrow streets:* **be plentiful,** be abundant, be numerous, be thick on the ground; informal grow on trees, be two/ten a penny. **2** *a stream which abounded with trout:* **be full of,** overflow with, teem with, be packed with, be crowded with; informal be stuffed with, be chock-a-block with.

about preposition *a book about Greece:* **regarding,** concerning, referring to, with regard to, with respect to, relating to, on, touching on, dealing with, on the subject of.
adverb **1** *there were babies crawling about:* **around,** here and there, to and fro, back and forth, in all directions. **2** *he was about somewhere:* **near,** nearby, around, hereabouts, in the vicinity, in the neighbourhood. **3** *about £15,000:* **approximately,** roughly, around, in the region of, circa, of the order of, or so, or thereabouts, more or less; Brit. getting on for; N. Amer. informal in

the ballpark of.

above preposition **1** over, higher (up) than, on top of, on. **2** *those above the Colonel*: **superior to,** senior to, over, higher (up) than, more powerful than, in charge of, commanding.
opposites below.
adverb **overhead,** on/at the top, high up, on high, up above, (up) in the sky.
■ **above all** most importantly, most of all, chiefly, primarily, first and foremost, essentially, in essence, at bottom; informal at the end of the day, when all is said and done.

abrasion noun **1** *he had abrasions to his forehead*: **graze,** cut, scrape, scratch, gash, laceration. **2** *the metal is resistant to abrasion*: **erosion,** wearing away/down.

abrasive adjective **1** *abrasive kitchen cleaners*: **rough,** coarse, harsh, scratchy. **2** *her abrasive manner*: **curt,** brusque, sharp, harsh, rough.
opposites gentle, friendly.

abridge verb **shorten,** cut (down), edit, abbreviate, condense, compress, truncate, prune, summarize, precis; (abridged) concise.
opposites extend.

abroad adverb **overseas,** out of the country, to/in foreign parts, to/in a foreign country/land.

abrupt adjective **1** *an abrupt halt*: **sudden,** rapid, quick, unexpected, unanticipated, unforeseen, precipitate. **2** *an abrupt manner*: **curt,** brusque, blunt, short, rude, sharp, terse, brisk, unceremonious.
opposites gradual, gentle.

absence noun **1** *his absence from the office*: **non-attendance,** absenteeism, truancy, leave, holiday, vacation, sabbatical. **2** *the absence of activity*: **lack,** want, non-existence, unavailability, scarcity, shortage, dearth.
opposites presence.

absent adjective **1** *she was absent from work*: **away,** off, out, elsewhere, off duty, on holiday, on leave; informal AWOL.
2 *symptoms were absent*: **non-existent,** lacking, missing. **3** *an absent look*: **distracted,** preoccupied, inattentive, vague, absorbed, dreamy, faraway, blank, empty, vacant.
opposites present, attentive, alert.
■ **absent oneself** stay away, be absent, go away, leave, withdraw.

absent-minded adjective **forgetful,** distracted, scatterbrained, preoccupied, inattentive; informal with a mind/ memory like a sieve.

absolute adjective **1** *absolute silence* | *an absolute disgrace*: **complete,** total, utter, out-and-out, outright, perfect, pure, thorough, unqualified, unreserved, downright, unmitigated, sheer. **2** *absolute power*: **unlimited,** unrestricted, unrestrained, infinite, total, supreme, unconditional. **3** *an absolute ruler*: **autocratic,** dictatorial, all-powerful, omnipotent, supreme.
opposites partial, qualified, limited, democratic.

absolutely adverb **completely,** totally, utterly, perfectly, entirely, wholly, fully, quite, thoroughly, unreservedly, definitely, certainly, unquestionably, undoubtedly, without (a) doubt, without question, in every way/respect,

one hundred per cent.
OPPOSITES partially.

absorb verb **1** *a material which absorbs water:* **soak up**, suck up, draw up/in, take up/in, mop up. **2** *she was absorbed in her book:* **engross**, captivate, occupy, preoccupy, engage, rivet, grip, hold, immerse, involve, enthral, spellbind, fascinate.

absorbent adjective **spongy**, sponge-like, porous, permeable.

absorbing adjective **fascinating**, interesting, captivating, gripping, engrossing, compelling, compulsive, enthralling, riveting, spellbinding; informal unputdownable.
OPPOSITES boring.

absorption noun **1** *the absorption of water:* **soaking up**, sucking up. **2** *her total absorption in the music:* **involvement**, immersion, raptness, preoccupation, captivation, fascination, enthralment.

abstain verb **1** *he abstained from wine:* **refrain**, desist, forbear, give up, renounce, avoid, eschew, forgo, go/do without, refuse, decline; informal cut out. **2** *one member abstained:* **not vote**, decline to vote.

abstemious adjective **moderate**, restrained, temperate, self-disciplined, self-restrained, sober, austere, ascetic, puritanical, spartan.
OPPOSITES self-indulgent.

abstinence noun **self-denial**, self-restraint, teetotalism, temperance, sobriety, abstemiousness.

abstract adjective *abstract concepts:* **theoretical**, conceptual, intellectual, metaphysical, philosophical, academic.
OPPOSITES actual, concrete.
noun *an abstract of her speech:* **summary**, synopsis, precis, résumé, outline; N. Amer. wrap-up.

abstruse adjective **obscure**, arcane, esoteric, rarefied, recondite, difficult, hard, cryptic, over/above one's head, incomprehensible, unfathomable, impenetrable.

absurd adjective **irrational**, illogical, inappropriate, ridiculous, ludicrous, farcical, comical, stupid, foolish, silly, pointless, senseless, preposterous; informal crazy, cockeyed; Brit. informal barmy, daft.
OPPOSITES reasonable, sensible.

abundance noun **plenty**, plethora, profusion, exuberance, riot, superabundance.
OPPOSITES lack, scarcity.

abundant adjective **plentiful**, copious, ample, profuse, large, huge, great, bumper, prolific, overflowing, teeming, superabundant; informal galore.
OPPOSITES scarce, sparse.

abuse verb **1** *the judge abused his power:* **misuse**, exploit, take advantage of. **2** *he was accused of abusing women:* **mistreat**, maltreat, ill-treat, molest, beat, sexually abuse, interfere with. **3** *the referee was abused by players:* **insult**, be rude to, swear at, shout at.
noun **1** *the abuse of power:* **misuse**, exploitation. **2** *the abuse of women:* **mistreatment**, maltreatment, ill-treatment, molestation, beating, sexual abuse. **3** *torrents of abuse:*

insults, expletives, swear
words, swearing, name-calling,
invective.

abusive adjective **1** *abusive
language:* **insulting,** rude,
offensive, derogatory,
slanderous, libellous. **2** *an
abusive husband:* **violent,**
brutal, cruel, harsh, oppressive.
OPPOSITES polite, kind.

abysmal adjective (informal)
terrible, dreadful, awful,
frightful, atrocious, disgraceful,
lamentable; informal rotten,
appalling, pathetic, pitiful,
woeful, useless, lousy, dire,
poxy, the pits; Brit. informal
chronic, shocking.

academic adjective **1** *an
academic institution:*
educational, scholastic. **2** *his
academic turn of mind:*
scholarly, learned, literary,
intellectual, bookish, studious.
3 *only of academic interest:*
theoretical, hypothetical,
notional, speculative,
conjectural, irrelevant, beside
the point.
noun *a group of academics:*
scholar, intellectual, don,
professor, man/woman of
letters, thinker; informal egghead;
Brit. informal boffin.

academy noun **educational
institution,** school, college,
university, institute.

accelerate verb **1** *the car
accelerated:* **speed up,** go faster,
gain momentum, increase
speed, pick up speed, gather
speed. **2** *sunlight accelerates
growth:* **hasten,** quicken, speed
up, further, advance, expedite;
informal crank up.
OPPOSITES decelerate, delay.

acceleration noun speeding up,
quickening, hastening.

accent noun **1** *a Scottish accent:*

pronunciation, intonation,
enunciation, articulation,
inflection. **2** *the accent is on
comfort:* **emphasis,** stress,
priority, importance,
prominence.

accept verb **1** *he accepted a pen
as a present:* **receive,** take, get,
obtain, acquire, pick up. **2** *just
accept what you're told:* **go
along with,** believe, respect,
abide by, defer to, put up with,
give in to, resign oneself to;
informal buy, swallow.
OPPOSITES refuse, reject.

acceptable adjective
satisfactory, adequate,
reasonable, fair, good enough,
sufficient, tolerable, passable.
OPPOSITES unacceptable.

acceptance noun **1** *the
acceptance of an award:*
receipt, receiving, taking. **2** *his
acceptance of her ideas:* **respect,**
acknowledgement, belief,
toleration, consent, agreement,
assent, compliance,
acquiescence.

accepted adjective **recognized,**
acknowledged, established,
traditional, orthodox, agreed,
approved, customary, normal,
standard.
OPPOSITES unorthodox.

access noun **1** *the building has a
side access:* **entrance,** entry,
approach, path, drive, way in.
2 *they were denied access to the
stadium:* **admission,**
admittance, entry.

accessible adjective
approachable, attainable,
reachable, obtainable, available,
understandable,
comprehensible, intelligible;
informal get-at-able.

accessory noun **1** *a car
accessory:* **extra,** add-on,
addition, supplement,

a

attachment. **2** *an accessory to murder:* **accomplice,** abetter, collaborator, co-conspirator, henchman, associate.

accident noun **1** *an accident at work:* **mishap,** misadventure, disaster, tragedy, catastrophe, calamity. **2** *a road accident:* **crash,** collision, smash, bump, derailment; N. Amer. wreck; informal smash-up, pile-up; Brit. informal shunt. **3** *we met by accident:* **chance,** fate, fortune, luck, good luck, fluke, coincidence.

accidental adjective **1** *accidental death:* **chance,** coincidental, unexpected, incidental, fortuitous, serendipitous. **2** *accidental damage:* **unintentional,** unintended, unplanned, inadvertent, unwitting.
OPPOSITES predictable, intentional.

acclaim verb *the booklet has been acclaimed by teachers:* **praise,** applaud, cheer, commend, approve, welcome, hail.
OPPOSITES criticize.
noun *she has won widespread acclaim:* **praise,** applause, tributes, approval, admiration, congratulations, commendation.
OPPOSITES criticism.

acclimatize verb **adjust,** adapt, get used, familiarize oneself, find one's feet, get one's bearings; N. Amer. acclimate.

accommodate verb **1** *refugees were accommodated in army camps:* **lodge,** house, put up, billet, board. **2** *the cottages accommodate six people:* **hold,** take, have room for, sleep, seat. **3** *we tried to accommodate her:* **help,** assist, oblige, cater for, fit

in with, satisfy.

accommodating adjective **obliging,** cooperative, helpful, amenable, hospitable, flexible.

accommodation noun **housing,** homes, lodging(s), (living) quarters, rooms, billet, shelter, a roof over one's head; informal digs, pad; formal residence, dwelling.

accompaniment noun **1** *a musical accompaniment:* **backing,** support, background, soundtrack. **2** *the wine makes a superb accompaniment to cheese:* **complement,** addition, adjunct, accessory, companion.

accompany verb **1** *the driver accompanied her to the door:* **go with,** travel with, keep someone company, partner, escort, show, see, usher, conduct. **2** *an illness accompanied by nausea:* **go along with,** occur with, go together with, attend, be linked with. **3** *he accompanied the choir on the piano:* **back,** play along with, support.

accomplice noun **partner in crime,** abetter, accessory, collaborator, co-conspirator, henchman, associate.

accomplish verb **achieve,** succeed in, realize, attain, manage, bring off, carry through, execute, effect, perform, complete.

accomplished adjective **expert,** skilled, skilful, masterly, virtuoso, master, consummate, talented, gifted, able, capable; informal mean, nifty, crack, ace.

accomplishment noun **1** *a remarkable accomplishment:* **achievement,** success, act, deed, exploit, effort, feat, coup. **2** *her many accomplishments:* **talent,** skill, gift, ability.

accord verb 1 *the national assembly accorded him more power:* **give,** grant, present, award, confer on, bestow on. 2 *his views accorded with mine:* **correspond,** agree, tally, match, concur, be in harmony, be in tune.
OPPOSITES withhold, disagree, differ.
noun 1 *a peace accord:* **pact,** treaty, agreement, settlement, deal, entente, protocol. 2 *the two sides failed to reach accord:* **agreement,** consensus, unanimity, harmony.
OPPOSITES disagreement.
■ **of one's own accord** voluntarily, of one's own free will, of one's own volition, by choice, willingly, freely, readily.

account noun 1 *his account of the incident:* **description,** report, version, story, statement, explanation, tale, chronicle, history, record, log. 2 *the firm's accounts:* **financial record,** ledger, balance sheet, financial statement; (**accounts**) books. 3 *his background is of no account:* **importance,** import, significance, consequence, value.
■ **account for 1** they must account for the delay: **explain,** answer for, give reasons for, justify. **2** *excise duties account for over half the price:* **constitute,** make up, comprise, represent, be responsible for, produce.

accountability noun **responsibility,** liability, answerability.

accountable adjective **responsible,** liable, answerable, to blame.

accumulate verb **gather,** collect, amass, stockpile, pile up, build up, store (up), hoard, lay in/up, increase, accrue, run up.
OPPOSITES disperse.

accumulation noun **mass,** build-up, pile, collection, stock, store, stockpile, hoard.

accuracy noun **correctness,** precision, exactness, fidelity, truth, truthfulness, authenticity, realism.

accurate adjective 1 *accurate information:* **correct,** precise, exact, right, factual, literal, faithful, true, truthful, on the mark, authentic, realistic; Brit. informal spot on, bang on; N. Amer. informal on the money, on the button. 2 *an accurate shot:* **well aimed,** on target, unerring, deadly, true.

accusation noun **allegation,** charge, indictment, impeachment, claim, assertion, imputation.

accuse verb 1 *four people were accused of assault:* **charge with,** indict for, impeach for. 2 *you accused the companies of causing job losses:* **blame for,** hold responsible for, condemn for, criticize for, denounce for; informal point the finger at.
OPPOSITES absolve, exonerate.

accustom verb **adapt,** adjust, acclimatize, habituate, familiarize, become reconciled, get used to, come to terms with, learn to live with; N. Amer. acclimate.

accustomed adjective **customary,** established, habitual, usual, normal, regular, routine.

ache noun **pain,** twinge, pang, soreness, tenderness, irritation, discomfort, burning, cramp.
verb *my legs were aching:* **hurt,** be sore, be painful, be tender,

a

burn, be in pain.

achieve verb attain, reach, realize, bring off, pull off, accomplish, carry through, fulfil, complete; informal wrap up, swing.

achievement noun **1** *the achievement of high growth:* **attainment**, realization, accomplishment, fulfilment, implementation, completion. **2** *they were proud of their achievement:* **feat**, exploit, triumph, coup, accomplishment, act, action, deed, effort, work, handiwork.

acid adjective **1** *an acid flavour:* **sour**, acidic, tart, sharp, vinegary. **2** *acid remarks:* **sharp**, sharp-tongued, sarcastic, scathing, cutting, biting, stinging, caustic; informal bitchy, catty.
OPPOSITES alkali, sweet, kind.

acknowledge verb **1** *he acknowledges his unfitness for the role:* **admit**, accept, grant, allow, concede, confess, recognize. **2** *he did not acknowledge Colin:* **greet**, salute, address, nod to, wave to, say hello to. **3** *few people acknowledged my letters:* **answer**, reply to, respond to.
OPPOSITES reject, deny, ignore.

acquaint verb familiarize, make aware of, inform of, advise of; informal fill in on, clue in on.

acquaintance noun **1** *a business acquaintance:* **contact**, associate, colleague. **2** *my acquaintance with George:* **association**, relationship. **3** *some acquaintance with the language:* **familiarity with**, knowledge of, experience of, awareness of, understanding of, grasp of.

acquire verb get, obtain, come by, receive, collect, gain, buy, earn, win, come into, secure, pick up; informal get one's hands on, get hold of, land, bag, score.
OPPOSITES lose.

acquisition noun **1** *a new acquisition:* **purchase**, addition, investment, possession; informal buy. **2** *the acquisition of funds:* **obtaining**, collection, gaining, earning, winning, securing.

acquit verb **1** *the jury acquitted her:* **clear**, exonerate, find innocent, absolve, discharge, free, release; informal let off (the hook). **2** *the boys acquitted themselves well:* **behave**, conduct oneself, perform, act.
OPPOSITES convict.

act verb **1** *the Government must act:* **take action**, take steps, take measures, move. **2** *Alison began to act oddly:* **behave**, conduct oneself, react. **3** *I'll act as lookout:* **function**, work, serve, operate. **4** *he acted in a film:* **perform**, play, appear. noun **1** *acts of kindness:* **deed**, action, gesture, feat, exploit. **2** *the act will raise taxes:* **law**, decree, statute, bill, edict, ruling, order. **3** *a comedy act:* **performance**, turn, routine, number, sketch. **4** *it was all an act:* **pretence**, show, front, facade, masquerade, charade, pose; informal a put-on.

acting adjective temporary, interim, caretaker, pro tem, provisional, stopgap; N. Amer. informal pinch-hitting.
OPPOSITES permanent.

action noun **1** *their actions are inexcusable:* **deed**, act, undertaking, exploit, behaviour, conduct, activity. **2** *the need for local action:* **measures**, steps, activism, campaigning, pressure. **3** *the action of hormones:* **operation**, working, effect, influence, process, power. **4** *he died in action:* **battle**, combat, hostilities, fighting, active service. **5** *a civil action:* **lawsuit**, suit, case, prosecution, litigation, proceedings.

activate verb **start (up)**, switch on, turn on, set going, trigger (off), set off, energize.
OPPOSITES switch off.

active adjective **1** *she kept active:* **busy**, mobile, lively, vigorous; informal on the go, full of beans. **2** *an active member of the union:* **hard-working**, industrious, tireless, energetic. **3** *the watermill was active until 1960:* **working**, operative, functioning, operational, in action, in operation, in force; informal (up and) running.
OPPOSITES listless, inactive.

activity noun **1** *there was a lot of activity:* **action**, bustle, movement, life; informal toing and froing, comings and goings. **2** *a leisure activity:* **pursuit**, occupation, hobby, pastime, recreation, diversion, venture, undertaking, enterprise, project, scheme.
OPPOSITES inactivity.

actor, actress noun **performer**, player, thespian, star, starlet; Brit. informal luvvy.

actual adjective **real**, true, genuine, authentic, confirmed, definite, hard, concrete; informal real live.
OPPOSITES imaginary.

actually adverb **really**, in (actual) fact, in point of fact, as a matter of fact, in reality, in truth, if truth be told, to tell the truth.

acute adjective **1** *acute food*

shortages: **severe**, dire, terrible, grave, serious, desperate. **2** *acute pain:* **excruciating**, sharp, severe, stabbing, agonizing, racking, searing. **3** *his acute mind:* **quick**, astute, shrewd, sharp, keen, penetrating, razor-sharp, quick-witted, agile, nimble, intelligent, canny, discerning, perceptive.
OPPOSITES mild, dull.

adamant adjective **unshakeable**, unwavering, unswerving, immovable, resolute, resolved, determined, firm, dead set.

adapt verb **1** *the policy can be adapted:* **modify**, alter, change, adjust, remodel, reorganize, customize, tailor; informal tweak. **2** *he adapts well to new surroundings:* **adjust**, conform, acclimatize, accommodate.

add verb **1** *the porch was added later:* **attach**, append, tack on, join on. **2** *they added the figures up:* **total**, count (up), reckon up, tally; Brit. tot up.
OPPOSITES subtract.
■ **add to** increase, augment, magnify, amplify, enhance, intensify, heighten, deepen, exacerbate, aggravate, compound, reinforce. ■ **add up to** amount to, come to, run to, make, total, equal, number.

addict noun **1** *a heroin addict:* **abuser**; informal junkie, druggy, -head, freak; N. Amer. informal hophead. **2** (informal) *skiing addicts:* **enthusiast**, fan, lover, devotee, aficionado; informal buff, freak, nut, fanatic.

addicted adjective **dependent**, obsessed, fixated, fanatical, passionate, a slave to; informal hooked.

addiction noun **dependency**, dependence, habit, obsession, infatuation, passion, love, mania, enslavement.

addictive adjective
habit-forming, compulsive; Brit. informal **moreish.**

addition noun **1** *the addition of extra rooms:* **adding,** inclusion, incorporation, introduction. **2** *a useful addition:* **add-on,** extra, adjunct, appendage, supplement, rider.
OPPOSITES subtraction, removal, essential.
■ **in addition.** See ADDITIONALLY.

additional adjective **extra,** added, supplementary, further, more, spare, other, new, fresh.

additionally adverb **also,** in addition, besides, too, as well, on top (of that), furthermore, moreover, into the bargain, to boot, to say nothing of.

address noun **1** *officers called at the address:* **house,** flat, apartment, home; formal residence, dwelling. **2** *his address to Parliament:* **speech,** lecture, talk, presentation, dissertation, sermon.
verb *he addressed his audience:* **speak to,** talk to, give a talk to, make a speech to, hold forth to.

adept adjective **expert,** proficient, accomplished, skilful, practised, masterly, consummate.
OPPOSITES inept.

adequate adjective **1** *adequate financial resources:* **sufficient,** enough. **2** *an adequate service:* **satisfactory,** acceptable, passable, reasonable, tolerable, fair, average, not bad, all right, middling; informal OK.
OPPOSITES insufficient, inadequate.

adhere verb **stick,** cling, bond, hold.
■ **adhere to** abide by, stick to,

hold to, comply with, conform to, follow, obey, heed, observe, respect, uphold, fulfil.

adjacent adjective **adjoining,** neighbouring, next-door, abutting.
■ **adjacent to** next to, by the side of, bordering on, beside, alongside, touching.

adjoining adjective **connecting,** connected, interconnecting, bordering, abutting, attached, adjacent, neighbouring, next-door.

adjourn verb **1** *the hearing was adjourned:* **suspend,** break off, discontinue, interrupt, recess. **2** *sentencing was adjourned until June 9:* **postpone,** put off/back, defer, delay, hold over.

adjust verb **1** *he adjusted the brakes:* **modify,** alter, regulate, tune, fine-tune, balance, tailor, customize, rearrange, change, reshape; informal **tweak. 2** *Kate had adjusted to her new life:* **adapt,** become accustomed, get used, accommodate, acclimatize, habituate oneself, assimilate, come to terms with, blend in with, fit in with; N. Amer. acclimate.

adjustable adjective **alterable,** adaptable, modifiable, variable, multiway, versatile.

administer verb **1** *the union is administered by an executive:* **manage,** direct, control, operate, regulate, coordinate, conduct, handle, run, organize, govern, steer. **2** *the crew administered first aid:* **dispense,** issue, give out, provide, apply, offer, distribute, deliver, hand out, deal out, dole out.

administration noun **1** *the administration of the company:* **management,** direction, control, conduct, operation, running, coordination, governance, supervision, regulation. **2** *the Labour administration:* **government**, regime, executive, cabinet, authority, directorate, council, leadership, management, term of office, incumbency.

administrative adjective **managerial**, executive, operational, organizational, supervisory, directorial, governmental, regulatory.

administrator noun **manager**, director, executive, controller, official, coordinator, supervisor.

admirable adjective **commendable**, praiseworthy, laudable, creditable, exemplary, worthy, deserving, respectable, worthwhile, good, sterling, fine.
OPPOSITES deplorable.

admiration noun **respect**, approval, appreciation, (high) regard, esteem, recognition.
OPPOSITES scorn.

admire verb **1** *I admire your courage:* **respect**, think highly of, hold in high regard, rate highly, esteem, prize, approve of. **2** *Simon had admired her for a long time:* **adore**, love, worship, be taken with, be attracted to; informal carry a torch for, have a thing about.
OPPOSITES despise.

admirer noun **fan**, devotee, enthusiast, aficionado, supporter, adherent, follower, disciple.

admission noun **1** *an admission of liability:* **confession**, acknowledgement, acceptance, concession, disclosure, divulgence. **2** *free admission:* **admittance**, entry, entrance, access, entrée, acceptance, initiation.

admit verb **1** *Paul admitted that he was angry:* **confess**, acknowledge, concede, grant, accept, allow, reveal, disclose, divulge. **2** *he admitted the offence:* **confess (to)**, plead guilty to, own up to. **3** *he was admitted to the college:* **let in**, accept, receive, initiate, take on.
OPPOSITES deny, exclude.

admittance noun **entry**, admission, entrance, access, entrée.
OPPOSITES exclusion.

adolescence noun **teenage years**, teens, youth, later childhood.

adolescent noun **teenager**, youth, juvenile; informal teen, teeny-bopper.
adjective **teenage**, young, immature, childish, juvenile, infantile, puerile; informal teen.
OPPOSITES mature.

adopt verb **take on**, embrace, take up, espouse, assume, follow, choose, endorse, approve.
OPPOSITES abandon.

adore verb **love**, be devoted to, dote on, cherish, treasure, prize, think the world of, admire, look up to, revere, worship.
OPPOSITES hate.

adorn verb **decorate**, embellish, array, ornament, enhance.
OPPOSITES disfigure.

adrift adjective **1** *adrift in a strange country:* **lost**, off course, drifting, disorientated, confused, (all) at sea, rootless, unsettled. **2** (informal) *the hook has come adrift:* **loose**, free, detached, unsecured, unfastened.

adult adjective **1** *an adult woman:* **mature**, grown-up, fully grown, fully developed, of age. **2** *an adult movie:* **(sexually) explicit,** pornographic, obscene, dirty, erotic, sexy; informal porn, porno, naughty, blue, X-rated.

advance verb **1** *the battalion advanced rapidly:* **move forward,** press on, push on, attack, make progress, make headway, gain ground. **2** *the move advanced his career:* **promote,** further, forward, help, aid, assist, boost. **3** *technology has advanced:* **progress,** develop, evolve, make strides, move forward (in leaps and bounds), move on. **4** *a relative advanced him some money:* **lend,** loan, put up, come up with; Brit. informal sub.
OPPOSITES retreat, hinder, regress.
noun **1** *the army's advance:* **progress,** (forward) movement, attack. **2** *a significant medical advance:* **breakthrough,** development, step forward, (quantum) leap.
adjective *advance warning:* **early,** prior.
■ **in advance** beforehand, before, ahead of time, earlier, previously, in readiness.

advanced adjective **1** *advanced manufacturing techniques:* **state-of-the-art,** modern, up to date, up to the minute, cutting-edge, new, the latest, pioneering, innovative, sophisticated. **2** *an advanced course:* **higher-level,** higher, tertiary.
OPPOSITES primitive, elementary.

advantage noun **1** *they have the advantage:* **upper hand,** edge, lead, sway, whip hand, superiority, dominance, supremacy. **2** *the advantage of* belonging to a union: **benefit,** value, good/strong point, asset, plus, bonus, boon, blessing, virtue, profit, good.
OPPOSITES disadvantage.

advantageous adjective **1** *an advantageous position:* **superior,** dominant, powerful, fortunate, lucky, favourable. **2** *the arrangement is advantageous to both sides:* **beneficial,** of benefit, helpful, of assistance, useful, of value, profitable, in someone's interests.
OPPOSITES disadvantageous.

adventure noun **1** *her adventures in Italy:* **exploit,** escapade, undertaking, experience, incident. **2** *in search of adventure:* **excitement,** thrills, action, stimulation, risk, danger.

adventurous adjective **1** *an adventurous traveller:* **daring,** intrepid, bold, fearless, brave; informal gutsy. **2** *adventurous activities:* **risky,** dangerous, perilous, hazardous, exciting.
OPPOSITES cautious, safe, predictable.

adversary noun **opponent,** rival, enemy, antagonist, challenger, contender, competitor, opposition, competition; literary foe.
OPPOSITES ally, supporter.

adverse adjective **1** *adverse weather:* **unfavourable,** inclement, bad, poor, untoward. **2** *the drug's adverse side effects:* **harmful,** dangerous, injurious, detrimental. **3** *an adverse response:* **hostile,** unfavourable, antagonistic, unfriendly, negative.
OPPOSITES favourable, auspicious, beneficial.

advertise verb **publicize,** make

public, announce, broadcast, proclaim, trumpet, promote; informal push, plug, hype; N. Amer. informal ballyhoo, flack.

advertisement noun **announcement**, commercial, promotion, blurb, write-up; informal ad, push, plug, puff; Brit. informal advert.

advice noun **guidance**, counselling, counsel, help, direction, recommendations, guidelines, suggestions, hints, tips, pointers.

advise verb **1** *her grandmother advised her about marriage*: **counsel**, give guidance, guide, offer suggestions, give hints/tips/pointers. **2** *he advised caution*: **recommend**, advocate, suggest, urge. **3** *you will be advised of our decision*: **inform**, notify, give notice, apprise, warn.

adviser noun **counsellor**, aide, mentor, guide, consultant, confidant, confidante, guru.

advocate noun **champion**, upholder, supporter, backer, promoter, proponent, campaigner, lobbyist; N. Amer. booster.
OPPOSITES critic.
verb **recommend**, champion, uphold, support, back, promote, campaign for, urge, subscribe to, speak for, argue for, lobby for.
OPPOSITES oppose, advise against.

affair noun **1** *it was a strange affair*: **event**, incident, episode, case, matter, business. **2** *what you do is your affair*: **business**, concern, matter, responsibility; Brit. informal lookout. **3** (**affairs**) *financial affairs*: **transactions**, activities, dealings, undertakings, ventures,

business. **4** *his affair with Anthea was over*: **relationship**, romance, fling, dalliance, liaison, involvement, amour; informal hanky-panky; Brit. informal carry-on.

affect¹ verb **1** *this affected our decision*: **influence**, have an effect on, have an impact on, act on, change, alter, modify. **2** *he was visibly affected by the experience*: **move**, touch, hit (hard), make an impression on, upset, trouble, distress, disturb, shake (up).

affect² verb *he affected an air of boredom*: **put on**, assume, take on, adopt, feign.

affectation noun **pretension**, pretentiousness, affectedness, artificiality, posturing, airs (and graces); Brit. informal side.

affection noun **fondness**, love, liking, tenderness, warmth, devotion, caring, attachment, friendship.

affectionate adjective **fond**, loving, adoring, devoted, caring, tender, warm, friendly, demonstrative; informal touchy-feely, lovey-dovey.
OPPOSITES cold.

affiliate verb **associate**, unite, combine, join (up), join forces, link up, ally, align, amalgamate, merge.

affinity noun **empathy**, rapport, sympathy, accord, harmony, similarity, relationship, bond, closeness, understanding; informal chemistry.
OPPOSITES aversion, dislike, dissimilarity.

affirm verb **declare**, state, assert, proclaim, pronounce, attest, swear.
OPPOSITES deny.

affirmative adjective **positive**, assenting, consenting,

a

approving, favourable.
OPPOSITES negative.

afflict verb **trouble,** burden, distress, beset, harass, worry, oppress, torment, plague.

affluent adjective **wealthy,** rich, prosperous, well off, well-to-do, of means; informal well heeled, rolling in it, made of money, loaded.
OPPOSITES poor.

afford verb **1** *I can't afford a new car:* **pay for,** find the money for, run to, stretch to, stand, manage. **2** *can you afford the time?* **spare,** allow oneself. **3** *the terrace affords beautiful views:* **give,** offer, supply, provide, furnish, yield.

afraid adjective **1** *they ran away because they were afraid:* **frightened,** scared, terrified, fearful, nervous, petrified, intimidated, cowardly, faint-hearted; informal scared stiff; N. Amer. informal spooked. **2** *don't be afraid to ask awkward questions:* **reluctant,** hesitant, unwilling, slow, shy. **3** *I'm afraid I'm late:* **sorry.**
OPPOSITES brave, confident, glad.

after preposition **following,** subsequent to, at the end of, in the wake of.

aftermath noun **consequences,** after-effects, results, repercussions, upshot.

afterwards adverb **later,** later on, subsequently, then, next, after this/that, in due course.

again adverb **once more,** another time, afresh, anew.

against preposition **1** *most delegates were against the motion:* **opposed to,** in opposition to, hostile to, antagonistic towards, unsympathetic to, at odds with, in disagreement with; informal

anti, agin. **2** *swimming against the tide:* **counter to,** contrary to, in the opposite direction to, resisting. **3** *she leaned against the wall:* **touching,** in contact with, up against, abutting, on.
OPPOSITES in favour of, with.

age noun **1** *her hearing deteriorated with age:* **old age,** maturity, advancing years, elderliness, seniority. **2** *the Elizabethan age:* **era,** epoch, period, time.
verb **1** *Cabernet Sauvignon ages well:* **mature,** mellow, ripen, soften, season, weather. **2** *the experience has aged her:* **make old,** wear out, weather. **3** *she has aged a lot:* **grow old,** decline, wither, fade.

agency noun **business,** organization, company, firm, office, bureau.

agenda noun **programme,** schedule, to-do list, timetable, plan.

agent noun **1** *the sale was arranged through an agent:* **representative,** intermediary, negotiator, go-between, proxy, broker, emissary, envoy, spokesperson; informal rep. **2** *a CIA agent:* **spy,** secret agent, operative, mole; N. Amer. informal spook, G-man.

aggravate verb **1** *the new law could aggravate the situation:* **worsen,** make worse, exacerbate, inflame, compound. **2** (informal) *you'll only aggravate him!* **annoy,** antagonize, irritate, exasperate, nettle, provoke, get on someone's nerves; Brit. rub up the wrong way; informal needle, hack off, get someone's goat, get up someone's nose; Brit. informal wind up; N. Amer. informal tick off.

OPPOSITES alleviate, improve, placate.

aggregate noun **total,** sum, grand total, combined score.

aggression noun **1** *an act of aggression:* **hostility,** belligerence, force, violence, attack. **2** *he played with unceasing aggression:* **confidence,** self-confidence, boldness, determination, forcefulness, vigour, energy, dynamism, commitment.

aggressive adjective
1 *aggressive behaviour:* **violent,** confrontational, antagonistic, pugnacious. **2** *aggressive foreign policy:* **warmongering,** warlike, warring, belligerent, bellicose, hawkish, militaristic, expansionist; informal gung-ho. **3** *an aggressive promotional drive:* **assertive,** forceful, vigorous, energetic, dynamic, audacious; informal in-your-face, feisty.
OPPOSITES peaceable, peaceful, laid-back.

agile adjective **1** *she was as agile as a monkey:* **nimble,** lithe, supple, acrobatic. **2** *an agile mind:* **alert,** sharp, acute, shrewd, astute, perceptive, quick.
OPPOSITES stiff, clumsy, dull.

agitate verb **1** *any mention of Clare agitates my grandmother:* **upset,** fluster, ruffle, disconcert, unnerve, disquiet, disturb, distress, unsettle; informal rattle, faze. **2** *agitate the solution:* **shake,** whisk, beat, stir.

agonizing adjective **excruciating,** painful, acute, harrowing, torturous.

agony noun **suffering,** torture, pain, torment, anguish.

agree verb **1** *I agree with you:* concur, see eye to eye, be in sympathy, be as one, be unanimous. **2** *they agreed to a ceasefire:* **consent,** assent, acquiesce; formal accede. **3** *the plan and the drawing do not agree:* **match (up),** correspond, conform, coincide, fit, tally, be consistent; informal square. **4** *they agreed a price:* **settle,** decide on, arrive at, negotiate, shake hands on.
OPPOSITES differ, reject, contradict.

agreeable adjective **1** *an agreeable atmosphere:* **pleasant,** pleasing, enjoyable, pleasurable, nice, appealing, relaxing, friendly, congenial. **2** *an agreeable man:* **likeable,** amiable, affable, pleasant, nice, friendly, good-natured, sociable, genial. **3** *we should get together, if you're agreeable:* **willing,** amenable, in agreement.
OPPOSITES unpleasant.

agreement noun **1** *all heads nodded in agreement:* **accord,** concurrence, consensus, assent, acceptance, consent, acquiescence. **2** *an agreement on imports:* **contract,** treaty, pact, accord, settlement, understanding, bargain. **3** *there is some agreement between the two datasets:* **correspondence,** consistency, compatibility, accord, similarity, resemblance, likeness.
OPPOSITES discord, dissimilarity.

agricultural adjective **farm,** farming, agrarian, rural, rustic, countryside.
OPPOSITES urban.

agriculture noun **farming,** cultivation, husbandry, agribusiness, agronomy.

aid noun **1** *with the aid of his*

colleagues: **assistance,** support, help, backing, cooperation.
2 *humanitarian aid:* **relief,** assistance, support, subsidy, funding, donations, grants; historical alms.
OPPOSITES hindrance.
verb **help,** assist, support, encourage, further, boost, promote, facilitate.
OPPOSITES hinder.

aide noun **assistant,** helper, adviser, supporter, right-hand man/woman, adjutant, deputy, second (in command), lieutenant.

ailing adjective **1** *his ailing mother:* **ill,** sick, sickly, poorly, weak, in poor/bad health, infirm. **2** *the country's ailing economy:* **failing,** weak, poor, tottering, fragile, unstable.
OPPOSITES healthy.

ailment noun **illness,** disease, disorder, affliction, malady, complaint, infirmity; informal bug, virus.

aim verb **1** *he aimed the rifle:* **point,** direct, train, sight, line up. **2** *she aimed at the target:* **take aim,** fix on, zero in on, draw a bead on. **3** *this food is aimed at children:* **target,** intend, direct, design, tailor, market, pitch. **4** *we aim to give you good service:* **intend,** mean, hope, want, plan, propose.
noun *our aim is to develop top gymnasts:* **objective,** goal, end, target, design, desire, intention, intent, plan, purpose, ambition, aspiration, wish, dream, hope.

aimless adjective **purposeless,** directionless, undirected, random.
OPPOSITES purposeful.

air noun **1** **breeze,** draught, wind, gust/puff of wind. **2** *an air of*

defiance: **look,** appearance, impression, aspect, manner, tone, feel, atmosphere, mood.
verb **1** *a chance to air your views:* **express,** voice, make public, articulate, declare. **2** *the room needs airing:* **ventilate,** freshen, refresh, cool.

airless adjective **stuffy,** close, stifling, suffocating, oppressive, unventilated.
OPPOSITES airy.

airy adjective **spacious,** uncluttered, light, bright, well ventilated, fresh.
OPPOSITES poky, stuffy.

aisle noun **passage,** passageway, lane, path, gangway, walkway.

akin adjective **similar,** related, close, near, comparable, equivalent, connected, alike, analogous.
OPPOSITES unlike.

alarm noun **1** *the girl spun round in alarm:* **fear,** anxiety, apprehension, distress, agitation, consternation, fright, panic. **2** *a fire alarm:* **warning,** danger signal, siren, bell, detector, sensor.
OPPOSITES calmness, composure.
verb *the news alarmed her:* **frighten,** scare, panic, unnerve, distress, agitate, upset, disconcert, shock, disturb; informal rattle, spook; Brit. informal put the wind up.
OPPOSITES reassure.

alarming adjective **frightening,** unnerving, shocking, worrying, upsetting, disconcerting, disturbing; informal scary.
OPPOSITES reassuring.

alcoholic adjective **intoxicating,** strong, hard, stiff, fermented, brewed, distilled.
noun **drunkard,** dipsomaniac, drunk, heavy drinker, problem

drinker, alcohol-abuser; informal boozer, alky, dipso, soak, wino; Austral./NZ informal hophead.

alert adjective **1** *an alert sentry:* **vigilant,** watchful, attentive, observant, wide awake, on the lookout, on one's guard/toes; informal keeping one's eyes open/peeled. **2** *mentally alert:* **quick-witted,** sharp, bright, quick, perceptive, on one's toes; informal on the ball, quick on the uptake, all there, with it.
OPPOSITES inattentive, dull.
noun **1** *a state of alert:* **vigilance,** watchfulness, attentiveness, alertness. **2** *a flood alert:* **warning,** notification, notice, siren, alarm, signal.
verb *police were alerted:* **warn,** notify, forewarn, put on one's guard; informal tip off.

alien adjective **foreign,** unfamiliar, unknown, peculiar, exotic, strange.
OPPOSITES native, familiar.
noun **1** *an illegal alien:* **foreigner,** non-native, immigrant, émigré, stranger. **2** *the alien's spaceship crashed:* **extraterrestrial,** ET; informal little green man.

alienate verb **isolate,** distance, estrange, cut off, turn away, drive apart, set at variance/odds, drive a wedge between.

alienation noun **isolation,** detachment, estrangement, separation.

alight adjective *the stable was alight:* **burning,** ablaze, on fire, in flames, blazing.

align verb **1** *the desks are aligned with the wall:* **line up,** straighten, even up, arrange, coordinate. **2** *he aligned himself with the workers:* **ally,** affiliate, associate, side, join forces, team up, band together, throw in

one's lot.

alike adjective *all the doors looked alike:* **similar,** (much) the same, indistinguishable, identical, uniform, interchangeable; informal much of a muchness.
OPPOSITES different.
adverb *great minds think alike:* **similarly,** the same, correspondingly, analogously, identically.
OPPOSITES differently.

alive adjective **1** *the synagogue has kept the Jewish faith alive:* **active,** in existence, functioning, in operation, operative, on the map. **2** *teachers need to be alive to their pupils' needs:* **alert,** awake, aware, conscious, mindful, heedful, sensitive, familiar.
OPPOSITES dead, unaware.

allay verb **reduce,** diminish, decrease, lessen, alleviate, ease, relieve, soothe, soften, calm.
OPPOSITES increase, intensify.

allegation noun **claim,** assertion, charge, accusation, contention.

allege verb **claim,** assert, charge, accuse, contend.

alleged adjective **reported,** supposed, so-called, claimed, professed, purported, ostensible, unproven.
OPPOSITES confirmed.

allegiance noun **loyalty,** faithfulness, fidelity, obedience, adherence, devotion.
OPPOSITES disloyalty, treachery.

alleviate verb **ease,** relieve, take the edge off, deaden, dull, lessen, reduce, moderate, allay, soothe, help, soften.
OPPOSITES aggravate.

alley noun **passage,** passageway, alleyway, backstreet, lane, path,

a

pathway, walk.

alliance noun association, union, league, confederation, federation, coalition, marriage, cooperation.

allied adjective associated, united, related, connected, interconnected, linked, cooperating, in league, affiliated, combined, coupled, married.
OPPOSITES unrelated, independent.

allocate verb allot, assign, set aside, earmark, consign, distribute, apportion, share out, dole out, give out.

allocation noun 1 *the efficient allocation of resources:* allotment, assignment, distribution, sharing out, doling out, giving out. 2 *our annual allocation of funds:* allowance, allotment, consignment, quota, share, ration; informal cut; Brit. informal whack.

allow verb 1 *the police allowed him to go home:* permit, let, enable, authorize, give leave, license, entitle, consent to, assent to, acquiesce in, agree to, approve; informal give the go-ahead to, give the thumbs up to, OK, give the green light to; formal accede to. 2 *allow an hour or so for driving:* set aside, allocate, allot, earmark, designate, reserve.
OPPOSITES prevent, forbid.

allowance noun 1 *your baggage allowance:* allocation, allotment, quota, share, ration, grant, limit. 2 *her father gave her an allowance:* payment, pocket money, contribution, grant, handout, subsidy, maintenance.

all right adjective 1 *the tea was all right:* satisfactory, acceptable, adequate, passable, reasonable; informal so-so, OK. 2 *are you all right?* unhurt, uninjured, unharmed, in one piece, safe (and sound), alive and well; informal OK. 3 *it's all right for you to go:* permissible, permitted, allowed, acceptable, legal, lawful, authorized, approved, in order; informal OK, legit, cool.
OPPOSITES unsatisfactory, hurt, forbidden.
adverb *the system works all right:* satisfactorily, adequately, fairly well, passably, acceptably, reasonably, well, fine; informal OK.
OPPOSITES unsatisfactorily.

ally noun *a political ally:* associate, colleague, friend, confederate, partner, supporter.
OPPOSITES enemy, opponent.
verb *the Catholic powers allied with Philip II:* unite, combine, join (up), join forces, band together, team up, collaborate, side, align oneself.
OPPOSITES split.

almost adverb nearly, (just) about, practically, virtually, all but, as good as, close to, not quite; informal pretty nearly/much/well; literary well-nigh, nigh on.

alone adjective & adverb 1 *she was alone in the house:* by oneself, on one's own, apart, solitary, single, solo; Brit. informal on one's tod. 2 *she felt terribly alone:* lonely, isolated, deserted, abandoned, friendless.
OPPOSITES accompanied, loved.
adverb *he travelled alone:* by oneself, on one's own, solo, singly, independently, unaccompanied, without help.
OPPOSITES in company.

a

also adverb too, as well, besides, in addition, additionally, furthermore, further, moreover, into the bargain, on top (of that), what's more, to boot.

alter verb 1 *Eliot was persuaded to alter the passage:* **change,** adjust, adapt, amend, modify, revise, rework, redo, transform; informal tweak. 2 *the situation has altered:* **change,** become different, undergo a (sea) change, evolve, move on.
OPPOSITES preserve, stay the same.

alternate verb 1 *rows of trees alternate with dense shrub:* **be interspersed,** follow one another, take turns, take it in turns, oscillate, see-saw. 2 *we could alternate the two groups:* **rotate,** swap, exchange, interchange.
adjective 1 *she attended on alternate days:* **every other,** every second, alternating. 2 (N. Amer.) *an alternate plan.* See **ALTERNATIVE** adjective sense 1.

alternative adjective 1 *an alternative route:* **different,** other, second, substitute, replacement, standby, emergency, reserve, backup, auxiliary, fallback; N. Amer. alternate. 2 *an alternative lifestyle:* **unorthodox,** unconventional, nonconformist, radical, revolutionary, avant-garde; informal offbeat, way-out.
noun *we have no alternative:* **(other) option,** (other) choice, substitute, replacement.

altogether adverb 1 *he wasn't altogether happy:* **completely,** totally, entirely, absolutely, wholly, fully, thoroughly, utterly, perfectly, one hundred per cent, in all respects. 2 *we*

have five offices altogether: **in all,** all told, in total.

always adverb 1 *he's always late:* **every time,** all the time, without fail, consistently, invariably, regularly, habitually, unfailingly. 2 *she's always complaining:* **continually,** continuously, constantly, forever, all the time, day and night; informal 24-7. 3 *the place will always be dear to me:* **forever,** for good, for evermore, for ever and ever, until the end of time, eternally.
OPPOSITES never, seldom, sometimes.

amalgamate verb **combine,** merge, unite, join, fuse, blend, meld.
OPPOSITES separate.

amass verb **gather,** collect, assemble, accumulate, stockpile, hoard.
OPPOSITES disperse.

amateur noun 1 *the crew were all amateurs:* **non-professional,** non-specialist, layman, layperson, dilettante, dabbler. 2 *what a bunch of amateurs:* **incompetent,** bungler; Brit. informal bodger, cowboy, clown.
OPPOSITES professional, expert.
adjective **non-professional,** unpaid, non-specialist, lay, dilettante.

amateurish adjective **incompetent,** inept, inexpert, amateur, clumsy, bumbling; Brit. informal bodged.

amaze verb **astonish,** astound, surprise, stun, stagger, nonplus, shock, startle, stop someone in their tracks, leave open-mouthed, dumbfound; informal bowl over, flabbergast; Brit. informal knock for six; (**amazed**) thunderstruck, at a loss for words, speechless; Brit. informal gobsmacked.

amazement noun
astonishment, surprise, shock, speechlessness, awe, wonder.

amazing adjective astonishing, astounding, surprising, stunning, staggering, breathtaking, awesome, awe-inspiring, sensational, remarkable, spectacular, stupendous, phenomenal, extraordinary, incredible, unbelievable; informal mind-blowing; literary wondrous.

ambassador noun envoy, emissary, representative, diplomat, minister, consul, attaché.

ambiguous adjective vague, unclear, ambivalent, equivocal, inconclusive, enigmatic, cryptic. OPPOSITES clear.

ambition noun 1 *young people with ambition:* drive, determination, enterprise, initiative, eagerness, motivation, a sense of purpose; informal get-up-and-go. 2 *her ambition was to become a model:* aspiration, desire, dream, intention, goal, aim, objective, plan.

ambitious adjective 1 *an ambitious politician:* aspiring, determined, motivated, energetic, committed, purposeful, power-hungry; informal go-ahead, go-getting. 2 *an ambitious task:* challenging, exacting, demanding, formidable, difficult, hard, tough. OPPOSITES laid-back, easy.

ambush verb surprise, waylay, trap, ensnare, attack, jump on, pounce on; N. Amer. bushwhack.

amend verb revise, alter, change, modify, adapt, adjust, edit, rewrite, redraft, rephrase, reword.

amends
■ **make amends for** make up for, atone for, make good.
■ **make amends to** compensate, recompense, indemnify, make it up to.

amenity noun facility, service, resource, convenience, comfort.

amnesty noun pardon, reprieve, forgiveness, release, discharge; informal let-off.

amount noun quantity, number, total, aggregate, sum, quota, size, mass, weight, volume.
■ **amount to 1** *the bill amounted to £50:* add up to, come to, run to; Brit. tot up to. **2** *their actions amounted to conspiracy:* constitute, comprise, be tantamount to.

ample adjective 1 *there is ample time for discussion:* enough, sufficient, adequate, plenty of, more than enough. **2** *an ample supply of wine:* plentiful, abundant, copious, profuse, lavish, liberal, generous; informal galore. **3** *his ample tunic:* spacious, full, capacious, roomy, voluminous, loose-fitting, baggy, sloppy. OPPOSITES insufficient, meagre, tight.

amuse verb 1 *her annoyance simply amused him:* make someone laugh, entertain, delight, divert, cheer (up), please, charm, tickle; informal crack up; Brit. informal crease up. **2** *he amused himself by writing poetry:* occupy, engage, busy, absorb, engross, entertain. OPPOSITES bore.

amusement noun 1 *the cause of much amusement:* mirth, merriment, hilarity, glee, delight. **2** *I read the book for* *amusement:* **entertainment,** pleasure, leisure, relaxation, fun, enjoyment, interest. **3** *a range of amusements:* **activity,** entertainment, diversion, pastime, recreation, game, sport.

amusing adjective **funny,** comical, humorous, light-hearted, jocular, witty, droll, entertaining, diverting; informal rib-tickling.
OPPOSITES solemn, boring.

analogy noun **similarity,** parallel, correspondence, likeness, resemblance, correlation, relation, comparison.
OPPOSITES dissimilarity.

analyse verb **examine,** inspect, survey, study, scrutinize, investigate, probe, explore, evaluate.

analysis noun **examination,** inspection, study, scrutiny, investigation, exploration, evaluation.

analytical, analytic adjective **systematic,** logical, scientific, methodical, precise, meticulous, rigorous, investigative, enquiring.
OPPOSITES unsystematic.

anarchy noun **lawlessness,** disorder, chaos, pandemonium, riot, revolution.
OPPOSITES government, order.

anatomy noun **structure,** make-up, composition, constitution, form, body, physique.

ancestor noun **forefather,** forebear, predecessor, antecedent, progenitor, parent, grandparent.
OPPOSITES descendant.

ancient adjective **1** *ancient civilizations:* **early,** prehistoric, primeval, primordial, primitive. **2** *an ancient custom:* **old,** age-

old, archaic, antediluvian, time-honoured. **3** *I feel positively ancient:* **antiquated,** decrepit, antediluvian, geriatric; informal out of the ark; Brit. informal past its/one's sell-by date.
OPPOSITES recent, contemporary, young.

anecdote noun **story,** tale, urban myth, narrative, reminiscence; informal yarn.

angelic adjective **innocent,** pure, virtuous, saintly, cherubic, adorable.

anger noun **annoyance,** vexation, temper, indignation, rage, fury, wrath, outrage.
OPPOSITES pleasure, good humour.
verb **annoy,** irk, vex, enrage, incense, infuriate, rile, outrage.
OPPOSITES pacify, placate.

angle noun **1** *an angle of 33°:* **gradient,** slope, slant, inclination. **2** *right in the angle of the roof:* **corner,** point, fork, nook, crook, edge. **3** *consider the problem from a different angle:* **perspective,** point of view, viewpoint, standpoint, position, aspect, slant, direction, approach, tack.
verb *Anna angled her camera upwards:* **tilt,** slant, twist, swivel, lean, tip, turn.

angry adjective **furious,** irate, vexed, irked, enraged, seething, infuriated, in a temper, fuming, outraged, cross; informal (hopping) mad, up in arms, foaming at the mouth, steamed up, in a paddy; Brit. informal shirty; N. Amer. informal sore, teed off, ticked off; Austral./NZ informal ropeable, snaky.
OPPOSITES pleased, good-humoured.
■ **get angry** lose one's temper, go berserk, flare up; informal go

a

mad/crazy/wild, go bananas, hit the roof, go through the roof, go up the wall, see red, go off the deep end, fly off the handle, blow one's top, blow a fuse/gasket, lose one's rag, flip (one's lid), have a fit, foam at the mouth, explode, go ballistic; Brit. informal go spare, do one's nut; N. Amer. informal flip one's wig, blow one's lid/stack.

anguish noun agony, pain, torment, torture, suffering, distress, woe, misery, sorrow, heartache.
OPPOSITES happiness.

animal noun 1 creature, beast, (living) thing; (animals) wildlife, fauna. 2 *the man was an animal:* beast, brute, monster, devil, fiend; informal swine, bastard, pig.

animate verb *the forces animating community life:* enliven, energize, invigorate, liven up, inspire, fire, rouse, excite, move.
OPPOSITES depress.
adjective *an animate being:* living, alive, live, breathing, sentient.
OPPOSITES inanimate.

animated adjective lively, spirited, energetic, full of life, excited, enthusiastic, eager, alive, vigorous, vibrant, vivacious, exuberant, ebullient, bouncy, bubbly, perky; informal bright-eyed and bushy-tailed, full of beans, bright and breezy, chirpy, chipper.
OPPOSITES lethargic, lifeless.

animosity noun hostility, antipathy, antagonism, enmity, resentment, ill feeling/will, bad blood.
OPPOSITES goodwill, friendship.

annihilate verb destroy, obliterate, eradicate, wipe out, wipe off the face of the earth; informal rub out, snuff out.
OPPOSITES create.

announce verb make public, make known, report, declare, state, give out, publicize, broadcast, publish, advertise, circulate, proclaim, release.

announcement noun 1 *an announcement by the Minister:* statement, declaration, proclamation, pronouncement, bulletin, communiqué; N. Amer. advisory. 2 *the announcement of the decision:* declaration, notification, reporting, publishing, broadcasting.

annoy verb irritate, bother, vex, make cross, exasperate, irk, anger, antagonize, nettle; Brit. rub up the wrong way; informal aggravate, peeve, miff, rile, needle, get (to), bug, hack off; Brit. informal wind up, nark, get on someone's wick; N. Amer. informal tee off, tick off, burn up, rankle, gravel.
OPPOSITES please, gratify.

annoyance noun irritation, exasperation, vexation, indignation, anger, displeasure, chagrin.

annual adjective yearly, once-a-year, year-long, twelve-month.

annually adverb yearly, once a year, each year, per annum.

annul verb declare invalid, declare null and void, nullify, invalidate, void, repeal, revoke.
OPPOSITES restore, enact.

anomaly noun oddity, peculiarity, abnormality, irregularity, inconsistency, aberration, quirk.

anonymous adjective 1 *an anonymous donor:* unnamed, nameless, unidentified, unknown, incognito. 2 *an anonymous letter:* unsigned,

unattributed.
OPPOSITES known.

answer noun **1** *her answer was
unequivocal:* **reply,** response,
rejoinder, reaction, retort,
riposte; informal comeback. **2** *the
answer to this problem:*
solution, remedy, way out,
explanation.
OPPOSITES question.
verb *Steve was about to answer:*
reply, respond, rejoin, retort,
riposte.
■ **answer for** *he will answer for
his crime:* pay for, be punished
for, suffer for, make amends
for.

antagonistic adjective **hostile,**
opposed, antipathetic, ill-
disposed, resistant, in
disagreement; informal anti.
OPPOSITES pro.

antagonize verb **provoke,**
intimidate, alienate, anger,
annoy.
OPPOSITES pacify, disarm.

anthem noun **hymn,** song,
chorale, chant, psalm, canticle.

anticipate verb **1** *the police did
not anticipate trouble:* **expect,**
foresee, predict, be prepared
for, bargain on, reckon on;
N. Amer. informal figure on. **2** *we
eagerly anticipated his arrival:*
look forward to, await, long
for, can't wait for.

anticipation noun **expectation,**
expectancy, prediction, hope,
excitement, suspense.

anticlimax noun **let-down,**
disappointment, comedown,
non-event, disillusionment; Brit.
damp squib; informal washout.

antics plural noun **capers,** pranks,
larks, high jinks, skylarking,
horseplay, clowning; Brit. informal
monkey tricks.

antidote noun **remedy,** cure,
solution, countermeasure,

corrective.

antipathy noun **hostility,**
antagonism, animosity,
aversion, animus, distaste,
hatred, abhorrence, loathing.
OPPOSITES affinity, liking.

antiquated adjective **outdated,**
outmoded, outworn, behind the
times, old-fashioned,
anachronistic; informal out of the
ark; N. Amer. informal horse-and-
buggy, clunky.
OPPOSITES modern, up to date.

antique noun **collector's item,**
museum piece, period piece,
bygone, antiquity.
adjective *antique furniture:*
antiquarian, old, collectable,
vintage, classic.
OPPOSITES modern.

antisocial adjective **1** *antisocial
behaviour:* **objectionable,**
offensive, unacceptable,
disruptive, rowdy. **2** *I'm feeling
a bit antisocial:* **unsociable,**
unfriendly, uncommunicative,
reclusive.
OPPOSITES acceptable, sociable.

anxiety noun **worry,** concern,
apprehension, unease, fear,
disquiet, doubts, nervousness,
nerves; informal butterflies (in
one's stomach), the jitters,
collywobbles.
OPPOSITES confidence.

anxious adjective **1** *I'm anxious
about her:* **worried,** concerned,
apprehensive, fearful, uneasy,
disturbed, fretful, agitated,
nervous, on edge, worked up,
jumpy; informal uptight, with
butterflies in one's stomach,
jittery, twitchy; N. Amer. informal
antsy, squirrelly, in a twit;
Austral./NZ informal toey. **2** *she was
anxious for news:* **eager,** keen,
itching, impatient.
OPPOSITES confident,
unconcerned.

a

apart
■ **apart from** except for, but for, aside from, with the exception of, excepting, excluding, bar, barring, besides, other than; informal outside of.

apartment noun **1** *a rented apartment:* **flat,** suite, penthouse; Austral. home unit; N. Amer. informal crib. **2** *the royal apartments:* **suite (of rooms),** rooms, quarters, accommodation.

apathetic adjective **uninterested,** indifferent, unconcerned, unmoved, uninvolved, unemotional, lukewarm, lethargic; informal couldn't-care-less.
OPPOSITES interested, enthusiastic, involved.

apathy noun **indifference,** lack of interest, lack of enthusiasm, lack of concern, lack of involvement, unconcern, lethargy.
OPPOSITES enthusiasm, interest, concern.

aperture noun **opening,** hole, gap, slit, slot, vent, crevice, chink, crack; technical orifice.

apologetic adjective **sorry,** regretful, contrite, remorseful, penitent, repentant.
OPPOSITES unrepentant.

apologize verb **say sorry,** express regret, ask forgiveness, ask for pardon, eat humble pie.

apology noun **regrets,** expression of regret.
■ **apology for** travesty of, poor imitation of, poor substitute for, pale shadow of; informal excuse for.

appal verb **horrify,** shock, dismay, distress, outrage, scandalize, disgust, revolt, sicken, nauseate, offend, make someone's blood run cold.

appalling adjective **1** *an appalling crime:* **horrific,** shocking, horrible, terrible, awful, dreadful, ghastly, hideous, horrendous, frightful, atrocious, abominable, outrageous. **2** (informal) *your schoolwork is appalling:* **dreadful,** terrible, atrocious, deplorable, hopeless, lamentable; informal rotten, crummy, woeful, useless, lousy, abysmal, dire; Brit. informal chronic, shocking.

apparatus noun **1** *laboratory apparatus:* **equipment,** gear, tackle, mechanism, appliance, device. **2** *the apparatus of government:* **system,** machinery, framework, structure, organization.

apparent adjective **1** *their relief was all too apparent:* **evident,** plain, obvious, clear, manifest, visible, discernible, unmistakable. **2** *his apparent lack of concern:* **seeming,** ostensible, outward, superficial.
OPPOSITES unclear, real.

apparently adverb **seemingly,** evidently, ostensibly, outwardly.

appeal verb **ask,** request, call, plead, entreat, beg, implore.
■ **appeal to** attract, interest, fascinate, please, tempt, lure, draw; informal float someone's boat.
noun **1** *an appeal for help:* **plea,** request, entreaty, cry, call. **2** *the cultural appeal of the island:* **attraction,** allure, charm, fascination, magnetism, pull.

appealing adjective **attractive,** engaging, alluring, enchanting, captivating, bewitching, fascinating, tempting, enticing, irresistible, charming; Brit. informal tasty.

OPPOSITES disagreeable, off-putting.

appear verb **1** become visible, come into view/sight, materialize. **2** *differences were beginning to appear:* be revealed, emerge, surface, manifest itself, become apparent/evident, come to light, arrive, arise, crop up, show up. **3** *they appeared completely devoted:* seem, look, give the impression of being, come across as, strike someone as.
OPPOSITES vanish.

appearance noun **1** *her dishevelled appearance:* look, air, aspect, looks, mien, expression, behaviour. **2** *an appearance of respectability:* impression, air, (outward) show, semblance, illusion, facade, front, pretence. **3** *the appearance of these symptoms:* occurrence, manifestation, emergence, arrival, development, materialization.

appease verb placate, conciliate, pacify, mollify, reconcile, win over; informal sweeten.
OPPOSITES provoke, inflame.

appendix noun supplement, addendum, postscript, codicil, coda, epilogue, afterword, tailpiece.

appetite noun **1** hunger, taste, palate. **2** *my appetite for learning:* desire, liking, hunger, thirst, longing, yearning, passion, enthusiasm, keenness, eagerness; informal yen.

applaud verb **1** *the audience applauded:* clap, give a standing ovation, put one's hands together; informal give someone a big hand. **2** *police have applauded the decision:* praise,

commend, salute, welcome, celebrate, approve of.
OPPOSITES boo, criticize.

applause noun clapping, (standing) ovation, cheering.

appliance noun device, machine, instrument, gadget, contraption, apparatus, mechanism, contrivance, labour-saving device; informal gizmo.

applicable adjective relevant, appropriate, pertinent, apposite, material, fitting, suitable, apt.
OPPOSITES inappropriate, irrelevant.

applicant noun candidate, interviewee, contender, entrant, claimant, petitioner, prospective student/employee, job-seeker.

application noun **1** *an application for an overdraft:* request, appeal, petition, approach, claim, demand. **2** *the application of anti-inflation policies:* implementation, use, exercise, employment, execution, enactment. **3** *the job requires a great deal of application:* hard work, diligence, industry, effort, commitment, dedication, devotion, perseverance, persistence, concentration.

apply verb **1** *300 people applied for the job:* bid, put in, try, audition, seek, solicit, claim, request, ask, petition. **2** *the Act did not apply to Scotland:* be relevant, pertain, relate, concern, affect, involve, cover, touch, deal with, have a bearing on. **3** *countries apply their own national rules:* implement, put into practice, introduce. **4** *she applied some ointment:* put on, rub in/on, work in, spread,

a

smear on, slap on. **5** *steady pressure should be applied:* **exert**, administer, use, exercise, employ, utilize, bring to bear.
■ **apply oneself** work hard, exert oneself, make an effort, be industrious, show dedication, buckle down, persevere, persist, concentrate; informal put one's back in it, knuckle down, get stuck in.

appoint verb **nominate**, name, designate, install, commission, engage, co-opt, select, choose, elect, vote in.
OPPOSITES reject.

appointed adjective **1** *at the appointed time:* **scheduled**, arranged, prearranged, specified, agreed, designated, allotted, set, fixed. **2** *a well appointed room:* **furnished**, decorated, fitted out, supplied.

appointment noun **1** *a six o'clock appointment:* **meeting**, engagement, interview, consultation, session. **2** *the appointment of directors:* **nomination**, naming, designation, installation, commissioning, engagement, co-option, selection, choosing, election. **3** *he held an appointment at the university:* **job**, post, position, situation, place, office.

appraisal noun **assessment**, evaluation, estimation, judgement, summing-up, consideration.

appreciate verb **1** *I'm not appreciated here:* **value**, admire, respect, think highly of, think much of, be grateful for, be glad of. **2** *we appreciate the problems:* **recognize**, realize, know, be aware of, be conscious of, be sensitive to, understand, sympathize with. **3** *a home will*

appreciate in value: **increase**, gain, grow, rise, go up, soar.
OPPOSITES disparage, depreciate, decrease.

appreciation noun **1** *her appreciation of literature:* **knowledge**, awareness, enjoyment, love, feeling, discrimination, sensitivity. **2** *he showed his appreciation:* **gratitude**, thanks, gratefulness. **3** *an appreciation of the value of teamwork:* **acknowledgement**, recognition, realization, knowledge, awareness, consciousness, understanding. **4** *an appreciation of the professor's work:* **review**, critique, criticism, analysis, assessment, evaluation, judgement; Brit. informal crit. **5** *the appreciation of the euro against the pound:* **increase**, gain, growth, rise, inflation, escalation.
OPPOSITES ingratitude, unawareness, depreciation, decrease.

appreciative adjective **1** *we are appreciative of all your efforts:* **grateful**, thankful, obliged, indebted. **2** *an appreciative audience:* **admiring**, enthusiastic, approving, complimentary.
OPPOSITES ungrateful, disparaging.

apprehension noun **1** *he was filled with apprehension:* **anxiety**, worry, unease, nervousness, nerves, misgivings, disquiet, concern, trepidation. **2** *the apprehension of a criminal:* **arrest**, capture, seizure, detention.
OPPOSITES confidence.

apprehensive adjective **anxious**, worried, uneasy, nervous, concerned, agitated.

OPPOSITES confident.

apprentice noun trainee, learner, probationer, novice, beginner, starter, pupil, student; N. Amer. tenderfoot; informal rookie; N. Amer. informal greenhorn.
OPPOSITES veteran, master, expert.

approach verb **1** *she approached the altar:* **move towards,** near, come near, close in on, close with, gain on. **2** *she approached him about a pay rise:* **speak to,** talk to, sound out, make a proposal to, proposition. **3** *he approached the problem in the best way:* **tackle,** address, manage, set about, go about, start work on.
OPPOSITES leave.
noun **1** *the traditional British approach:* **method,** procedure, technique, modus operandi, style, way, strategy, tactic, system, means, line of action. **2** *he considered an approach to the High Court:* **proposal,** submission, application, appeal, plea, request. **3** *the dog barked at the approach of any intruder:* **advance,** arrival, appearance. **4** *the approach to the castle:* **driveway,** drive, road, path, entry, way.

approachable adjective **1** *students found the staff approachable:* **friendly,** welcoming, pleasant, agreeable, sympathetic, congenial. **2** *the island is approachable by boat:* **accessible,** reachable, attainable; informal get-at-able.
OPPOSITES aloof, inaccessible.

appropriate adjective *this isn't the appropriate time:* **suitable,** proper, fitting, apt, right, convenient, opportune, relevant, apposite.

OPPOSITES inappropriate.
verb *the barons appropriated church lands:* **seize,** commandeer, expropriate, usurp, take over, hijack, steal; informal swipe, rip off, nab; Brit. informal pinch, nick.

approval noun **1** *their proposals went to the ministry for approval:* **acceptance,** agreement, consent, assent, permission, rubber stamp, sanction, blessing, endorsement, ratification, authorization; informal the go-ahead, the green light, the OK, the thumbs up. **2** *Lily looked at him with approval:* **favour,** liking, appreciation, admiration, regard, esteem, respect.
OPPOSITES refusal, disapproval.

approve verb **agree to,** accept, consent to, assent to, give one's blessing to, bless, ratify, sanction, endorse, authorize, validate, pass; informal give the go-ahead to, give the green light to, give the OK to, give the thumbs-up to.
OPPOSITES refuse.
■ **approve of** agree with, hold with, endorse, support, be in favour of, favour, think well of, like, take kindly to, admire.

approximate adjective **estimated,** rough, imprecise, inexact, broad, loose; N. Amer. informal ballpark.
OPPOSITES precise.
■ **approximate to** roughly equal, come near/close to, approach, border on, verge on, resemble, be similar to.

approximately adverb **roughly,** about, around, circa, round about, more or less, nearly, almost, approaching; Brit. getting on for; informal pushing;

a

N. Amer. informal **in the ballpark of.**
OPPOSITES precisely.

apt adjective **1** *a very apt description:* **suitable,** fitting, appropriate, relevant, apposite; Brit. informal spot on. **2** *they are apt to be a bit slipshod:* **inclined,** given, likely, liable, prone. **3** *an apt pupil:* **bright,** quick, clever, sharp, smart, able, gifted, talented.
OPPOSITES inappropriate, unlikely, slow.

arbitrary adjective **random,** unpredictable, capricious, subjective, whimsical, wanton, motiveless, irrational, groundless, unjustified.
OPPOSITES reasoned, democratic.

arbitration noun **adjudication,** judgement, mediation, conciliation, intervention.

arbitrator noun **adjudicator,** arbiter, judge, referee, umpire, mediator, go-between.

arc noun **curve,** arch, bow, curl, crescent, semicircle, half-moon.

arch noun *a stone arch:* **archway,** vault, span.
verb *she arched her eyebrows:* **curve,** arc, bend, bow, crook, hunch.

architect noun **designer,** planner, originator, author, creator, founder, inventor.

architecture noun **1** *modern architecture:* **building,** planning, design, construction. **2** *computer architecture:* **structure,** construction, organization, layout, design, build, make-up; informal set-up.

archive noun **1** *the family archives:* **records,** papers, documents, files, annals, chronicles, history. **2** *the National Sound Archive:* **record office,** registry, repository, museum, library.

verb *the videos are archived for future use:* **file,** log, catalogue, document, record, register, store.

ardent adjective **passionate,** fervent, zealous, wholehearted, intense, enthusiastic, keen, eager, avid, committed, dedicated.
OPPOSITES apathetic.

arduous adjective **tough,** difficult, hard, heavy, laborious, onerous, taxing, strenuous, back-breaking, demanding, challenging, punishing, gruelling; informal killing; Brit. informal knackering.
OPPOSITES easy.

area noun **1** *an inner-city area:* **district,** zone, region, sector, quarter, locality, neighbourhood; informal neck of the woods; Brit. informal manor; N. Amer. informal turf. **2** *the dining area:* **space,** section, part, place, room. **3** *specific areas of knowledge:* **field,** sphere, realm, domain, sector, province, territory.

arena noun **1** *an ice-hockey arena:* **stadium,** amphitheatre, ground, field, ring, rink, pitch, court; N. Amer. bowl, park. **2** *the political arena:* **scene,** sphere, realm, province, domain, forum, territory, world.

argue verb **1** *they argued that the government was to blame:* **claim,** maintain, insist, contend, assert, hold, reason, allege. **2** *the children are always arguing:* **quarrel,** disagree, dispute, row, squabble, bicker, have words, cross swords.

argument noun **1** *he had an argument with Tony:* **quarrel,** disagreement, squabble, dispute, altercation; informal slanging match; Brit. informal row, barney. **2** *an argument for the existence of God:* **reasoning,** justification, explanation, case, defence, vindication, evidence, reasons, grounds.

arise verb **1** *many problems arose:* **come about,** happen, occur, come into being, emerge, crop up, come to light, become apparent, appear, turn up, surface, spring up. **2** *injuries arising from defective products:* **result,** stem, originate, proceed, follow, ensue, be caused by.

aristocrat noun **nobleman,** noblewoman, lord, lady, peer (of the realm), patrician; informal aristo; Brit. informal toff, nob.
OPPOSITES commoner.

aristocratic adjective **noble,** titled, upper-class, blue-blooded, high-born; informal upper crust, top drawer; Brit. informal posh.
OPPOSITES common.

arm verb **equip,** provide, supply, furnish, issue, fit out.

armaments plural noun **arms,** weapons, weaponry, firearms, guns, ordnance, artillery, munitions, materiel.

armoured adjective **armour-plated,** steel-plated, ironclad, bulletproof, bombproof, reinforced, toughened.

arms plural noun **weapons,** weaponry, firearms, guns, ordnance, artillery, armaments, munitions.

army noun **1** **armed force,** military force, land force(s), military, soldiery, infantry, militia, troops, soldiers. **2** *an army of tourists:* **crowd,** swarm, horde, mob, gang, throng, mass, flock, herd, pack.

aroma noun **smell,** odour, fragrance, scent, perfume,

bouquet, nose.

aromatic adjective **fragrant,** scented, perfumed, fragranced.

around preposition **1** *the hills around the city:* **surrounding,** enclosing, on all sides of. **2** *around three miles:* **approximately,** about, round about, circa, roughly, more or less, nearly, almost, approaching; Brit. getting on for; N. Amer. informal in the ballpark of.
OPPOSITES precisely.

arouse verb **1** *they had aroused suspicion:* **provoke,** trigger, stir up, kindle, engender, cause. **2** *his ability to arouse the masses:* **stir up,** whip up, rouse, galvanize, electrify, stimulate, inspire, fire up, inflame, agitate, incite. **3** *she was aroused from sleep:* **wake (up),** awaken, bring to/round, rouse.
OPPOSITES allay, pacify.

arrange verb **1** *she arranged the flowers in a vase:* **set out,** order, lay out, position, present, display, exhibit, group, sort, organize. **2** *they hoped to arrange a meeting:* **organize,** fix (up), plan, schedule, contrive, determine, agree. **3** *he arranged the piece for a full orchestra:* **adapt,** set, score, orchestrate.

arrangement noun **1** *the arrangement of the furniture:* **positioning,** presentation, grouping, organization, alignment. **2** *the arrangements for my trip:* **preparation,** plan, provision, planning. **3** *we had an arrangement:* **agreement,** deal, understanding, bargain, settlement, pact. **4** *an arrangement of Beethoven's symphonies:* **adaptation,** orchestration, scoring, interpretation.

array noun **range,** collection,

a

selection, assortment, variety, arrangement, line-up, display, exhibition.
verb **arrange**, assemble, group, order, range, place, position, set out, lay out, spread out, display, exhibit.

arrest verb **1** *police arrested him for murder:* **detain**, apprehend, seize, capture, take into custody; informal pick up, pull in, collar; Brit. informal nick. **2** *the spread of the disease can be arrested:* **stop**, halt, check, block, curb, prevent, obstruct.
OPPOSITES release, start.
noun **detention**, apprehension, seizure, capture.

arresting adjective **striking**, eye-catching, conspicuous, impressive, imposing, spectacular, dramatic, breathtaking, stunning, awe-inspiring.
OPPOSITES inconspicuous.

arrival noun **1** *they awaited Ruth's arrival:* **coming**, appearance, entrance, entry, approach. **2** *the arrival of democracy:* **emergence**, appearance, advent, coming, dawn, onset.
OPPOSITES departure, end.

arrive verb **1** *more police arrived:* **come**, turn up, get here/there, make it, appear; informal show (up), roll in/up, blow in. **2** *virtual reality had arrived:* **emerge**, appear, surface, dawn, be born, come into being, arise.
OPPOSITES depart, leave.

arrogant adjective **haughty**, conceited, self-important, cocky, supercilious, condescending, full of oneself, overbearing, proud; informal high and mighty, too big for one's boots.

OPPOSITES modest.

art noun **1** *he studied art:* **fine art**, design, artwork, aesthetics. **2** *the art of writing:* **skill**, craft, technique, knack, aptitude, talent, flair, mastery, expertise.

article noun **1** *household articles:* **object**, thing, item, piece, artefact, device, implement. **2** *an article in The Times:* **report**, account, story, essay, feature, item, piece (of writing), column, commentary. **3** *the crucial article of the treaty:* **clause**, section, paragraph, head, point, item.

articulate adjective *an articulate speaker:* **eloquent**, fluent, effective, persuasive, lucid, expressive, silver-tongued.
OPPOSITES unintelligible.
verb *they were unable to articulate their emotions:* **express**, voice, vocalize, put in words, communicate, state.

artificial adjective **1** *artificial flowers:* **synthetic**, fake, imitation, mock, ersatz, man-made, manufactured, plastic; informal pretend. **2** *an artificial smile:* **insincere**, feigned, false, unnatural, contrived, put-on, forced, laboured, hollow; informal pretend, phoney.
OPPOSITES natural, genuine.

artistic adjective **1** *he's very artistic:* **creative**, imaginative, inventive, expressive, sensitive, perceptive, discerning. **2** *artistic dances:* **aesthetic**, beautiful, stylish, ornamental, graceful, subtle, expressive.
OPPOSITES unimaginative.

ascent noun **1** *the ascent of the Matterhorn:* **climbing**, scaling, conquest. **2** *the ascent grew steeper:* **slope**, incline, gradient.
OPPOSITES descent, drop.

ascertain verb **find out**,

discover, get to know, work out, make out, fathom (out), learn, deduce, divine, establish, determine; informal figure out.

ashamed adjective **1** *she felt ashamed that she had hit him:* **sorry,** shamefaced, sheepish, guilty, contrite, remorseful, regretful, mortified, humiliated. **2** *he was ashamed to admit it:* **reluctant,** loath, unwilling, afraid, embarrassed.
OPPOSITES proud, pleased.

ask verb **1** *he asked what time we opened:* **enquire,** want to know, question, interrogate, quiz. **2** *they'll ask a few questions:* **put (forward),** pose, raise, submit. **3** *do ask for advice:* **request,** demand, seek, solicit, apply, petition, call, appeal.
OPPOSITES answer.

asleep adjective **sleeping,** napping, dozing, drowsing; informal snoozing, dead to the world; humorous in the land of Nod.
OPPOSITES awake.

aspect noun **1** *every aspect of life:* **feature,** facet, side, characteristic, particular, detail. **2** *from every aspect:* **point of view,** position, standpoint, viewpoint, perspective, angle, slant. **3** *his face had a sinister aspect:* **appearance,** look, air, mien, demeanour, expression.

aspiration noun **desire,** hope, dream, wish, longing, yearning, aim, ambition, expectation, goal, target.

aspire
■ **aspire to** desire, aim for, hope for, dream of, long for, yearn for, set one's heart on, wish for, want, seek, set one's sights on.

aspiring adjective **would-be,** hopeful, budding, potential, prospective; informal wannabe.

assassin noun **murderer,** killer, gunman, executioner; informal hit man.

assassinate verb **murder,** kill, eliminate, liquidate, execute; N. Amer. terminate; informal hit.

assault verb *he assaulted a police officer:* **attack,** hit, strike, beat up, thump; informal wallop, belt, clobber, lay into, rough up; Austral. informal quilt.
noun **1** *he was charged with assault:* **violence,** battery; Brit. grievous bodily harm, GBH, actual bodily harm, ABH. **2** *an assault on the city:* **attack,** strike, onslaught, offensive, charge, push, thrust, raid.

assemble verb **1** *a crowd had assembled:* **gather,** collect, get together, congregate, convene, meet, muster, rally. **2** *he assembled the suspects:* **bring/ call together,** gather, collect, round up, marshal, muster. **3** *how to assemble the kite:* **construct,** build, erect, set up, put together, connect.
OPPOSITES disperse, dismantle.

assembly noun **1** *an assembly of dockers:* **gathering,** meeting, congregation, convention, council, rally, group, crowd; informal get-together. **2** *car assembly:* **construction,** manufacture, building, fabrication, erection.

assert verb **1** *she asserts that hysteria is universal:* **declare,** maintain, contend, argue, claim, insist. **2** *you should assert your rights:* **insist on,** stand up for, uphold, defend, press/push for.

assertion noun **declaration,** contention, statement, claim, opinion, protestation.

assertive adjective **confident,** self-confident, bold, decisive,

a

forceful, insistent, determined, commanding, pushy; informal feisty.
OPPOSITES timid.

assess verb **1** *the committee's power is hard to assess:* **evaluate,** judge, gauge, rate, estimate, appraise, weigh up; informal size up. **2** *the damage was assessed at £5 billion:* **value,** calculate, work out, determine, cost, price, estimate.

assessment noun **1** *a teacher's assessment of the pupil's abilities:* **evaluation,** judgement, rating, estimation, appraisal, opinion. **2** *some assessments valued the estate at £2 million:* **valuation,** calculation, costing, pricing, estimate.

asset noun **1** **benefit,** advantage, blessing, good/strong point, strength, forte, virtue, recommendation, attraction, resource. **2** (**assets**) **property,** resources, estate, holdings, funds, valuables, possessions, effects, belongings.
OPPOSITES liability.

assign verb **1** *a young doctor was assigned the task:* **allocate,** allot, give, set, charge with, entrust with. **2** *she was assigned to a new post:* **appoint,** promote, delegate, nominate, commission, post, co-opt; Military detail. **3** *we assign large sums of money to travel budgets:* **earmark,** designate, set aside, reserve, appropriate, allot, allocate.

assignation noun **rendezvous,** date, appointment, meeting.

assignment noun **task,** job, duty, mission, errand, undertaking, exercise, project, homework.

assist verb **1** **help,** aid, lend a (helping) hand to, support, back (up), work with. **2** *the aim was to assist cashflow:* **facilitate,** aid, ease, promote, boost, speed, benefit, encourage, further.
OPPOSITES hinder.

assistance noun **help,** aid, a (helping) hand, support, backing, reinforcement.
OPPOSITES hindrance.

assistant noun **helper,** aide, deputy, second (in command), number two, right-hand man/ woman, PA, mate, auxiliary, attendant; informal sidekick, gofer; Brit. informal dogsbody, skivvy.

associate verb **1** *the colours that we associate with fire:* **link,** connect, relate, bracket, identify, equate. **2** *I was forced to associate with them:* **mix,** keep company, mingle, socialize, go around, have dealings; informal hobnob, hang out/around/round.
OPPOSITES avoid.
noun *a business associate:* **partner,** colleague, co-worker, workmate, collaborator, comrade, ally; informal crony.

associated adjective **related,** connected, linked, similar, corresponding, attendant, accompanying, incidental.
OPPOSITES unrelated.

association noun **1** *a trade association:* **alliance,** consortium, coalition, union, league, guild, syndicate, federation, confederation, cooperative, partnership. **2** *the association between man and environment:* **relationship,** relation, interrelation, connection, interconnection, link, bond, interdependence.

assorted adjective **various,** miscellaneous, mixed, varied, diverse, different, sundry.
OPPOSITES uniform.

assortment noun **variety,** mixture, array, mix, miscellany, selection, medley.

assume verb **1** *I assumed he wanted me to keep the book:* **presume,** suppose, take it (as given), take for granted, take as read, conclude, infer, think, fancy, believe, understand, gather; N. Amer. figure. **2** *he assumed a Southern accent:* **affect,** adopt, put on. **3** *they are to assume more responsibility:* **accept,** shoulder, bear, undertake, take on/up. **4** *he assumed control of their finances:* **seize,** take (over), appropriate, wrest, usurp.
OPPOSITES know, drop, give up.

assumed adjective **false,** fictitious, fake, bogus, invented, made-up; informal pretend, phoney.
OPPOSITES genuine.

assumption noun **presumption,** supposition, inference, conjecture, belief.
OPPOSITES knowledge.

assurance noun **1** *you have my assurance:* **promise,** word (of honour), pledge, vow, oath, undertaking, guarantee, commitment. **2** *her calm assurance:* **confidence,** self-confidence, self-assurance, self-possession, nerve, poise; informal cool. **3** *life assurance:* **insurance,** indemnity, protection, security, cover.
OPPOSITES self-doubt, nervousness.

assure verb **1** *we must assure him of our loyal support:* **reassure,** convince, satisfy, persuade. **2** *I assure you all is* *well:* **promise,** guarantee, swear, confirm, certify, vow. **3** *he wants to assure a favourable vote:* **ensure,** secure, guarantee, seal, clinch; informal sew up.
OPPOSITES avoid.

assured adjective **1** *an assured performance:* **confident,** self-confident, self-assured, self-possessed, poised, composed, imperturbable, unruffled; informal unflappable, together. **2** *an assured supply of weapons:* **guaranteed,** certain, sure, secure, reliable, dependable; informal sure-fire.
OPPOSITES nervous, uncertain.

astonish verb **amaze,** astound, stagger, startle, stun, confound, dumbfound, nonplus, take aback, leave open-mouthed; informal flabbergast, bowl over; Brit. informal knock for six.

astonishing adjective **amazing,** astounding, staggering, surprising, breathtaking, remarkable, extraordinary, incredible, unbelievable, phenomenal; informal mind-boggling.
OPPOSITES unremarkable.

astound verb **amaze,** astonish, stagger, surprise, startle, stun, confound, dumbfound, take aback, leave open-mouthed; informal flabbergast, bowl over; Brit. informal knock for six.

astounding adjective **amazing,** astonishing, staggering, surprising, breathtaking, remarkable, extraordinary, incredible, unbelievable, phenomenal; informal mind-boggling.
OPPOSITES unremarkable.

astute adjective **shrewd,** sharp, acute, quick, clever, intelligent, bright, smart, canny,

a

perceptive; informal quick on the uptake.
OPPOSITES stupid.

asylum noun *political asylum:* **refuge**, sanctuary, shelter, protection, immunity, a safe haven.

athletic adjective **muscular**, fit, strapping, well built, strong, sturdy, powerful, brawny, burly.
OPPOSITES puny.

atmosphere noun **1 air**, sky; literary the heavens. **2** *a relaxed atmosphere:* **spirit**, ambience, air, mood, feel, feeling, character, tone, aura, quality; informal vibe.

atrocious adjective **1** *atrocious cruelties:* **wicked**, cruel, brutal, barbaric, vicious, monstrous, vile, inhuman, fiendish. **2** *the weather was atrocious:* **appalling**, dreadful, terrible, miserable; informal abysmal, dire, rotten, lousy; Brit. informal shocking.
OPPOSITES admirable, superb.

atrocity noun **1** *a number of atrocities:* **outrage**, horror, violation, abuse, massacre. **2** *scenes of hardship and atrocity:* **wickedness**, cruelty, brutality, barbarity, viciousness, savagery, inhumanity.
OPPOSITES humanity.

attach verb **1** *a weight is attached to the cord:* **fasten**, fix, join, secure, stick. **2** *they attach importance to research:* **ascribe**, assign, attribute, accredit, impute. **3** *the medical officer attached to HQ:* **assign**, appoint, allocate, second.
OPPOSITES detach.

attached
■ **attached to** fond of, devoted to, keen on; informal mad about.

attachment noun **1** *a strong attachment to his mother:* **bond**, closeness, devotion, loyalty, fondness for, love for, affection for, feeling for, sympathy for. **2** *the shower had a massage attachment:* **accessory**, fitting, extension, add-on.

attack verb **1** *Chris was brutally attacked:* **assault**, beat up, set upon, mug; N. Amer. beat up on; informal work over, rough up; Brit. informal duff up. **2** *the French attacked the fort:* **strike at**, assault, charge, pounce on, raid, storm. **3** *the clergy attacked government policies:* **criticize**, censure, condemn, disparage; informal knock, slam, lay into; Brit. informal slate, slag off, rubbish.
OPPOSITES defend, praise.
noun **1** *an attack on their home:* **assault**, onslaught, offensive, strike, blitz, raid, charge, invasion. **2** *an attack on his leadership:* **criticism**, censure, condemnation, disparagement; Brit. informal slating. **3** *an asthmatic attack:* **fit**, seizure, spasm, convulsion, paroxysm, bout, episode.
OPPOSITES defence, praise.

attacker noun **assailant**, assaulter, mugger, aggressor, raider, invader.
OPPOSITES defender, victim.

attain verb **achieve**, accomplish, reach, obtain, gain, secure, get, win, earn, realize, fulfil; informal clinch, bag, wrap up.

attempt verb *I attempted to answer the question:* **try**, strive, aim, venture, endeavour, seek, have a go.
noun *an attempt to reach the summit:* **try**, effort, endeavour, venture, bid, go; informal crack, shot, stab.

attend verb **1** *they attended a carol service:* **be present at**, sit in on, take part in, appear at,

turn up at, visit, go to; informal show up at. **2** *the children were not attending:* **pay attention,** listen, be attentive, concentrate.
OPPOSITES miss, take no notice.
■ **attend to something** deal with, see to, look after, manage, organize, sort out, handle, take care of, tackle. ■ **attend to someone** care for, look after, minister to, see to, tend, treat, help.

attendance noun **1** *you requested the attendance of a doctor:* **presence,** appearance, attention. **2** *their gig attendances grew:* **audience,** turnout, house, gate, crowd; Austral. informal muster.
OPPOSITES absence.

attendant noun *a royal attendant:* **assistant,** aide, companion, steward, equerry, escort, servant, retainer, valet, maid.
adjective *new discoveries and the attendant excitement:* **accompanying,** associated, related, connected, resulting, consequent.

attention noun **1** *the issue needs further attention:* **consideration,** contemplation, deliberation, thought, study, observation, mind, investigation, action. **2** *he tried to attract the attention of a policeman:* **awareness,** notice, scrutiny, eye, gaze. **3** *medical attention:* **care,** treatment, relief, aid, assistance.

attentive adjective **1** *an attentive pupil:* **alert,** perceptive, observant, acute, aware, heedful, focused, studious, diligent, conscientious, earnest. **2** *the most attentive of husbands:*

considerate, conscientious, thoughtful, kind, caring, solicitous, understanding, sympathetic.
OPPOSITES inattentive.

attic noun **loft,** roof space, garret.

attitude noun **1** *you seem ambivalent in your attitude:* **view,** viewpoint, outlook, perspective, stance, standpoint, position, approach, opinion. **2** *an attitude of prayer:* **position,** posture, pose, stance.

attract verb **1** *he was attracted by her smile:* **entice,** appeal to, tempt, lure, allure, charm, win, woo, captivate; informal turn on. **2** *electrical equipment attracts dust:* **draw,** pull, suck.
OPPOSITES repel, put off.

attraction noun **1** *she had lost her attraction:* **appeal,** attractiveness, pull, desirability, fascination, allure, charisma, charm. **2** *the town's attractions:* **entertainment,** activity, diversion, amenity, service. **3** *magnetic attraction:* **pull,** draw, force.
OPPOSITES repulsion.

attractive adjective
1 good-looking, beautiful, pretty, handsome, lovely, stunning, striking, arresting, gorgeous, prepossessing, fetching; Scottish & N. English bonny; informal drop-dead gorgeous; Brit. informal fit; N. Amer. informal cute; Austral./NZ informal spunky. **2** *an attractive career:* **appealing,** inviting, tempting, pleasing, interesting.
OPPOSITES unattractive, ugly, uninviting.

attribute verb *they attributed their success to him:* **ascribe,** assign, accredit, credit, put down, chalk up, pin on.

a

noun *the attributes of a top player:* **quality,** characteristic, trait, feature, element, aspect, property, sign, hallmark, mark.

audible adjective **perceptible,** discernible, detectable, clear, distinct.
OPPOSITES inaudible, faint.

audience noun **1** *the audience applauded:* **spectators, listeners,** viewers, onlookers, crowd, throng, gallery, congregation, turnout. **2** *an audience with the Pope:* **meeting,** interview, consultation, conference, hearing, reception.

augment verb **increase,** add to, supplement, enhance, build up, raise, up, hike up, enlarge, swell, expand, extend; informal jack up.
OPPOSITES decrease, reduce.

august adjective **distinguished,** respected, eminent, venerable, illustrious, prestigious, renowned, celebrated, honoured, acclaimed, esteemed.
OPPOSITES lowly, obscure, disreputable.

aura noun **atmosphere,** ambience, air, quality, character, mood, feeling; informal vibe.

auspicious adjective **favourable,** promising, encouraging, fortunate, opportune, timely, advantageous, good.
OPPOSITES inauspicious, unfavourable.

austere adjective **1** *an austere man:* **severe,** stern, strict, harsh, dour, grim, cold, frosty, unfriendly. **2** *an austere life:* **spartan,** frugal, ascetic, puritanical, abstemious, strict, simple, hard. **3** *an austere building:* **plain,** simple, basic, functional, unadorned, bleak,

bare, clinical.
OPPOSITES easy-going, friendly, luxurious, extravagant, ornate.

authentic adjective **1** *an authentic document:* **genuine,** real, bona fide, true, legitimate; informal pukka, kosher; Austral./NZ informal dinkum. **2** *an authentic depiction of the situation:* **accurate,** factual, true, truthful, reliable, trustworthy, honest, faithful.
OPPOSITES fake, inaccurate, unreliable.

authenticate verb **verify,** validate, prove, substantiate, corroborate, confirm, support, back up.
OPPOSITES disprove.

author noun **1** *modern Canadian authors:* **writer,** novelist, poet, playwright, columnist, reporter, wordsmith; informal scribe, scribbler. **2** *the author of the peace plan:* **creator,** originator, founder, father, architect, designer, producer.

authoritarian adjective **strict,** autocratic, dictatorial, despotic, tyrannical, domineering, imperious, illiberal, undemocratic; informal bossy.
OPPOSITES democratic, liberal.
noun **disciplinarian,** autocrat, dictator, despot, tyrant.
OPPOSITES democrat, liberal.

authoritative adjective **1** *authoritative information:* **reliable,** dependable, trustworthy, accurate, authentic, valid. **2** *the authoritative edition:* **definitive,** most reliable, best, authorized, approved. **3** *his authoritative manner:* **commanding,** masterful, assertive, self-assured, self-confident.
OPPOSITES unreliable, timid.

authority noun **1** *a rebellion against those in authority:* **power,** command, control, charge, dominance, jurisdiction, rule; informal clout. **2** *the authority to arrest drug traffickers:* **right,** authorization, power, mandate, prerogative, licence. **3** *the money was spent without parliamentary authority:* **permission,** authorization, consent, sanction, assent, agreement, approval, clearance; informal the go-ahead. **4** *the authorities:* **officials,** officialdom, government, administration, establishment, police; informal the powers that be. **5** *an authority on coins:* **expert,** specialist, professional, master, connoisseur, pundit, doyen(ne), guru.
OPPOSITES amateur, ignoramus.

authorize verb **1** *they authorized further action:* **permit,** sanction, allow, approve, consent to, assent to; informal give the go-ahead to, OK. **2** *the troops were authorized to fire:* **empower,** give authority, mandate, commission, entitle.
OPPOSITES forbid.

authorized adjective **approved,** sanctioned, accredited, recognized, licensed, certified, official, legal, legitimate.
OPPOSITES unauthorized, unofficial.

automatic adjective **1** *automatic garage doors:* **mechanized,** powered, mechanical, automated, computerized, electronic, robotic. **2** *an automatic reaction:* **instinctive,** involuntary, unconscious, reflex, knee-jerk, subconscious, spontaneous, impulsive, unthinking, mechanical; informal gut. **3** *the automatic choice:* **inevitable,** unavoidable, inescapable, only possible.
OPPOSITES manual, conscious, deliberate.

autonomous adjective **self-governing,** independent, sovereign, free.
OPPOSITES dependent, repressed.

autonomy noun **self-government,** self-rule, home rule, self-determination, independence, sovereignty, freedom.
OPPOSITES dependence, repression.

auxiliary adjective **additional,** supplementary, extra, reserve, backup, emergency, fallback, second.
OPPOSITES primary, regular.

available adjective **1** *refreshments will be available:* **obtainable,** accessible, to/at hand, to be had, on sale, untaken, unsold; informal up for grabs, on tap. **2** *I'll see if he's available:* **free,** unoccupied, on duty, contactable.
OPPOSITES unavailable, taken, busy.

avalanche noun *an avalanche of enquiries:* **barrage,** flood, deluge, torrent, wave.
OPPOSITES trickle.

avant-garde adjective **experimental,** modern, cutting-edge, progressive, unorthodox, unconventional; informal edgy, offbeat, way-out.
OPPOSITES conservative, established.

avarice noun **greed,** acquisitiveness, covetousness, materialism.
OPPOSITES generosity.

average noun *the national average:* **mean,** median, mode, norm, standard, rule, par.

a

adjective **1** *the average temperature:* **mean,** median, modal. **2** *a woman of average height:* **ordinary,** standard, normal, typical, regular.
OPPOSITES abnormal, unusual.
■ **on average** normally, usually, ordinarily, generally, typically, for the most part, as a rule, by and large, overall, on the whole.

averse adjective **opposed,** hostile, antagonistic, resistant, disinclined, reluctant, loath; informal anti.
OPPOSITES keen.

aversion noun **dislike,** hatred, loathing, abhorrence, distaste, antipathy, hostility, reluctance, disinclination.
OPPOSITES liking.

avert verb **1** *she averted her gaze:* **turn aside,** turn away, shift, redirect. **2** *an attempt to avert political chaos:* **prevent,** avoid, stave off, ward off, head off, forestall.
OPPOSITES bring about, allow.

avid adjective **keen,** eager, enthusiastic, ardent, passionate, zealous, devoted.
OPPOSITES apathetic.

avoid verb **1** *I avoid situations that cause me stress:* **keep away from,** steer clear of, give a wide berth to. **2** *he avoids responsibility:* **evade,** dodge, sidestep, escape, run away from; informal duck, wriggle out of, get out of. **3** *book early to avoid disappointment:* **prevent,** preclude, stave off, forestall, head off, ward off. **4** *he should avoid drinking alcohol:* **refrain from,** abstain from, desist from, steer clear of.
OPPOSITES confront, face up to, seek out, cause, allow, continue, insist on.

await verb **1** *Peter was awaiting news:* **wait for,** expect, look forward to, anticipate. **2** *many dangers await them:* **be in store for,** lie ahead of, lie in wait for, be waiting for, be round the corner.

awake verb *she awoke early:* **wake up,** wake, awaken, waken, stir, come to, come round, rouse, call.
adjective **1** *she was still awake:* **sleepless,** wide awake, restless, insomniac. **2** *too few are awake to the dangers:* **aware of,** conscious of, mindful of, alert to.
OPPOSITES asleep, oblivious.

awaken verb **1** See AWAKE verb. **2** *he had awakened strong emotions in her:* **arouse,** bring out, trigger, stir up, stimulate, kindle, revive.
OPPOSITES suppress.

award verb *the society awarded him a medal:* **give,** grant, accord, confer on, bestow on, present to, decorate with.
noun **1** *an award for long service:* **prize,** trophy, medal, decoration, reward; informal gong. **2** *an award of £1,500:* **grant,** scholarship, endowment; Brit. bursary.

aware adjective **1** *she is aware of the dangers:* **conscious of,** mindful of, informed about, acquainted with, familiar with, alive to, alert to; informal wise to, in the know about. **2** *environmentally aware:* **sensitive,** enlightened, knowledgeable, (well) informed; informal clued up; Brit. informal switched-on.
OPPOSITES unaware, ignorant.

awareness noun **consciousness,** recognition, realization, perception, understanding, grasp, appreciation, knowledge, familiarity.

away adverb *we'll be away for two weeks:* **elsewhere,** abroad, gone, off, out, absent, on holiday, on vacation.

awe noun **wonder,** wonderment, admiration, reverence, respect, fear, dread.

awesome adjective **breathtaking,** awe-inspiring, magnificent, amazing, stunning, staggering, imposing, formidable, intimidating; informal mind-boggling, mind-blowing, brilliant.
OPPOSITES unimpressive.

awful adjective **1** *the place smelled awful:* **disgusting,** terrible, dreadful, ghastly, horrible, vile, foul, revolting, repulsive, repugnant, sickening, nauseating; informal gross; Brit. informal beastly. **2** *an awful book:* **dreadful,** terrible, frightful, atrocious, lamentable; informal crummy, pathetic, rotten, woeful, lousy, appalling, abysmal, dismal, dire; Brit. informal rubbish. **3** *an awful accident:* **serious,** bad, terrible, dreadful, shocking. **4** *I feel awful:* **ill,** unwell, sick, nauseous; Brit. off colour, poorly; Brit. informal grotty, ropy; Scottish informal wabbit, peely-wally; Austral./NZ informal crook.
OPPOSITES delightful, excellent, well.

awfully adverb **1** (informal) *an awfully nice man:* **very,** extremely, really, immensely, exceedingly, thoroughly, dreadfully, terrifically, terribly, exceptionally, remarkably, extraordinarily; N. English right; informal seriously, majorly; Brit. informal jolly, dead, well; N. Amer. informal real, mighty, awful; informal, dated frightfully. **2** *we played awfully:* **terribly,** dreadfully, atrociously, appallingly; informal abysmally, pitifully, diabolically.

awkward adjective **1** *the box was awkward to carry:* **difficult,** tricky, cumbersome, unwieldy; Brit. informal fiddly. **2** *you're being really awkward:* **unreasonable,** uncooperative, unhelpful, difficult, obstructive, contrary, obstinate; Brit. informal bloody-minded, bolshie; N. Amer. informal balky. **3** *an awkward time:* **inconvenient,** inappropriate, inopportune, difficult. **4** *he put her in a very awkward position:* **embarrassing,** uncomfortable, unenviable, delicate, tricky, problematic, troublesome, humiliating, compromising; informal sticky. **5** *she felt awkward when alone with him:* **uncomfortable,** uneasy, tense, nervous, edgy, self-conscious, embarrassed. **6** *his awkward movements:* **clumsy,** ungainly, uncoordinated, graceless, inelegant, gauche, gawky, stiff, unskilful, inept, blundering; informal ham-fisted, cack-handed; Brit. informal all (fingers and) thumbs.
OPPOSITES easy, amenable, convenient, at ease, graceful, dexterous.

axe noun **hatchet,** chopper, cleaver, adze.
verb **1** *the show was axed:* **cancel,** withdraw, drop, scrap, cut, discontinue, end; informal ditch, dump, pull the plug on. **2** *500 staff were axed:* **dismiss,** make redundant, lay off, get rid of; informal sack, fire.
OPPOSITES start, launch, recruit.

axle noun **shaft,** spindle, rod.

b

Bb

babble verb **prattle**, rattle on, gabble, chatter, jabber, twitter, burble, blather; informal yatter, blabber, jaw, gas, shoot one's mouth off; Brit. informal witter, rabbit, chunter, natter, waffle.

baby noun **infant**, newborn, child; Scottish & N. English bairn; technical neonate; informal sprog, tot; literary babe.
adjective *baby carrots:* **miniature,** mini, little, toy, pocket, midget, dwarf; Scottish wee; N. Amer. vest-pocket; informal teeny, teensy, tiddly, bite-sized; Brit. informal titchy; N. Amer. informal little-bitty.
OPPOSITES large.

babyish adjective **childish,** infantile, juvenile, puerile, immature.
OPPOSITES mature.

back noun **1 spine,** backbone, spinal column, vertebral column. **2** *the back of the house:* **rear;** Nautical stern. **3** *the back of the queue:* **end,** tail end, rear end; N. Amer. tag end. **4** *the back of a postcard:* **reverse,** other side, underside; informal flip side.
OPPOSITES front, bow, head, face.
adverb **1** *he pushed his chair back:* **backwards,** behind one, to one's rear, rearwards, away. **2** *a few months back:* **ago,** earlier, previously, before.
OPPOSITES forward, ahead.
verb **1** *companies backed the scheme generously:* **sponsor,** finance, fund, subsidize, underwrite; informal pick up the bill for. **2** *most people backed the idea:* **support,** endorse, sanction, approve of, give one's

blessing to, smile on, favour, advocate, promote, champion; informal throw one's weight behind. **3** *he backed the horse at 33–1:* **bet on,** gamble on, stake money on. **4** *he backed away:* **reverse,** draw back, step back, pull back, retreat, withdraw.
OPPOSITES oppose, advance.
adjective **1** *the back seats:* **rear,** rearmost, hind, hindmost, posterior. **2** *a back copy:* **past,** old, previous, earlier.
OPPOSITES front, future.
■ **back down** give in, concede defeat, surrender, yield, submit, climb down. ■ **back out of** renege on, withdraw from, pull out of, fail to honour.
■ **back something up** substantiate, corroborate, confirm, support, bear out, endorse, lend weight to. ■ **back someone up** support, stand by, side with, take someone's part.

backer noun **1** *our financial backers:* **sponsor,** investor, underwriter, financier, patron, benefactor; informal angel. **2** *the backers of the proposition:* **supporter,** defender, advocate, promoter; N. Amer. booster.

backfire verb *Bernard's plan backfired on him:* **rebound,** boomerang, come back, fail; informal blow up in someone's face.

background noun **1** *a background of trees:* **backdrop,** backcloth, surrounding(s), setting, scene. **2** *students from different backgrounds:* **social circumstances,** family circumstances, environment,

class, culture, tradition. **3** *her nursing background:* **experience**, record, history, past, training, education.
OPPOSITES foreground.

backing noun **1** *he has the backing of his colleagues:* **support**, endorsement, approval, blessing. **2** *financial backing:* **sponsorship**, finance, funding, subsidy, patronage.

backlash noun **adverse reaction**, counterblast, repercussion, comeback, retaliation, reprisal.

backup noun *troops will provide backup:* **help**, support, assistance, aid, reserve, reinforcements.
adjective *a backup supply:* **reserve**, spare, substitute, replacement, standby, fallback, emergency.

backward adjective **1** *a backward look:* **rearward**, towards the rear, behind one, reverse. **2** *the decision was a backward step:* **retrograde**, regressive, for the worse, in the wrong direction, downhill, negative. **3** *economically backward:* **underdeveloped**, undeveloped, primitive. **4** *he was not backward in displaying his talents:* **hesitant**, reticent, reluctant, shy, diffident, timid.
OPPOSITES forward, progressive, advanced, confident.

backwards adverb **towards the rear**, rearwards, behind one.
OPPOSITES forwards.

bad adjective **1** *bad workmanship:* **unsatisfactory**, substandard, poor, inferior, second-rate, second-class, inadequate, deficient, imperfect, defective, faulty, shoddy, negligent; informal crummy, rotten, pathetic, useless, woeful, lousy; Brit.

informal duff, rubbish. **2** *the alcohol had a bad effect:* **harmful**, damaging, detrimental, injurious, hurtful, destructive. **3** *the bad guys:* **wicked**, evil, sinful, criminal, immoral, corrupt; informal crooked, bent. **4** *you bad girl!* **naughty**, badly behaved, disobedient, wayward, wilful, defiant, unruly, undisciplined. **5** *bad news:* **unpleasant**, disagreeable, unwelcome, unfavourable, unfortunate, grim, distressing, gloomy. **6** *a bad time to arrive:* **unfavourable**, inauspicious, inopportune, unfortunate, disadvantageous, inappropriate, unsuitable. **7** *a bad accident:* **serious**, severe, grave, critical, acute. **8** *the meat's bad:* **rotten**, off, decayed, putrid, rancid, curdled, sour, mouldy. **9** *a bad knee:* **injured**, wounded, diseased; Brit. informal **gammy**, knackered; Austral./NZ informal crook.
OPPOSITES good, quality, beneficial, virtuous, well behaved, welcome, favourable, slight, fresh, healthy.

badge noun **1** **brooch**, pin, emblem, crest, insignia; N. Amer. button. **2** *a badge of success:* **sign**, symbol, indication, signal, mark, hallmark, trademark.

badger verb **pester**, harass, hound, harry, nag, bother, go on at; informal hassle, bug.

badly adverb **1** *the job had been badly done:* **poorly**, unsatisfactorily, inadequately, incorrectly, faultily, defectively, shoddily, amateurishly, carelessly, negligently, incompetently, inexpertly. **2** *try not to think badly of me:* **unfavourably**, ill, critically,

b

disapprovingly. **3** *stop behaving badly:* **naughtily,** disobediently, wilfully, mischievously. **4** *he had been badly treated:* **cruelly,** wickedly, unkindly, harshly, shamefully, unfairly, unjustly, wrongly. **5** *it turned out badly:* **unfavourably,** unsuccessfully, adversely, unfortunately. **6** *some of the victims are badly hurt:* **severely,** seriously, gravely, acutely, critically.
OPPOSITES well, properly, humanely, fairly, favourably, slightly.

bad-tempered adjective **irritable,** irascible, tetchy, testy, grumpy, grouchy, crotchety, in a (bad) mood, cantankerous, curmudgeonly, ill-tempered, ill-humoured, peevish, cross, fractious, pettish, crabby; informal **snappish,** on a short fuse; Brit. informal shirty, stroppy, ratty; N. Amer. informal cranky, ornery; Austral./NZ informal snaky.
OPPOSITES good-humoured, affable.

baffle verb **puzzle,** perplex, bewilder, mystify, confuse; informal flummox, stump, beat, fox.
OPPOSITES enlighten.

bag noun **suitcase,** case, valise, holdall, grip.
verb **1** *locals bagged the most fish:* **catch,** land, capture, trap, net, snare. **2** *he bagged seven medals:* **get,** secure, obtain, acquire, pick up, win, achieve; informal land, net.

baggage noun **luggage,** suitcases, cases, bags.

baggy adjective **loose,** roomy, generously cut, sloppy, full, voluminous.
OPPOSITES tight.

bail noun *he was released on bail:* **surety,** security, indemnity,

bond, guarantee, pledge.
■ **bail out** *the pilot bailed out:* eject, parachute to safety. ■ **bail someone/something out** rescue, save, relieve, finance, help (out), aid.

bait noun *was she the bait to lure him into a trap?* **enticement,** lure, decoy, snare, trap, inducement, siren, carrot, attraction; informal come-on.
verb *he was baited at school:* **taunt,** tease, goad, pick on, torment, persecute; informal needle; Brit. informal wind up.

balance noun **1** *I tripped and lost my balance:* **stability,** equilibrium, steadiness, footing. **2** *political balance in broadcasting:* **fairness,** justice, impartiality, parity, equity, evenness, uniformity, comparability. **3** *the balance of the rent:* **remainder,** outstanding amount, rest, residue, difference.
OPPOSITES instability, bias.
verb **1** *she balanced the book on her head:* **steady,** stabilize, poise, level. **2** *he balanced his radical remarks with more familiar declarations:* **counterbalance,** balance out, offset, counteract, compensate for, make up for. **3** *their income and expenditure do not balance:* **correspond,** agree, tally, match up, coincide. **4** *you need to balance cost against benefit:* **weigh (up),** compare, evaluate, consider, assess.

bald adjective **1** *a bald head:* **hairless,** smooth, shaven, depilated. **2** *a bald statement:* **plain,** simple, direct, blunt, unadorned, unvarnished; informal upfront.
OPPOSITES hairy, vague.

ball noun **sphere,** globe, orb,

globule, spheroid.

ballot noun **vote,** poll, election, referendum, show of hands, plebiscite.

ban verb **1** *smoking was banned:* **prohibit,** forbid, veto, proscribe, outlaw, make illegal, bar. **2** *Gary was banned from the playground:* **exclude,** bar, banish, expel, eject, evict, drive out, force out; informal kick out.
OPPOSITES permit, admit.
noun **1** *a ban on smoking:* **prohibition,** veto, bar, proscription, moratorium, injunction. **2** *a ban from league football:* **exclusion,** bar, banishment, expulsion, ejection, eviction.
OPPOSITES permission, admission.

banal adjective **unoriginal,** unimaginative, trite, hackneyed, clichéd, commonplace, stereotyped, overused, stale, boring, obvious; informal corny.
OPPOSITES original.

band[1] noun *a band round his wrist:* **loop,** wristband, headband, ring, hoop, circlet, belt, sash, girdle, strap, strip, tape, circle.

band[2] noun **1** *a band of robbers:* **gang,** group, mob, pack, troop, troupe, company, set, party, crew, body, team; informal bunch. **2** *the band played on:* **group,** pop group, ensemble, orchestra; informal combo.

bandage noun **dressing,** covering, plaster, compress, gauze, lint.
verb *she bandaged my knee:* **bind,** dress, cover, strap (up).

bandit noun **robber,** thief, raider, mugger, pirate, outlaw, hijacker, looter, gangster; literary brigand; historical rustler,

highwayman.

bang noun **1** *the door slammed with a bang:* **thud,** thump, bump, crack, crash, smack, boom, blast, clap, report, explosion. **2** *a bang on the head:* **blow,** knock, thump, bump, hit, smack, crack; informal bash, whack.
verb **1** *he banged the table with his fist:* **hit,** strike, beat, thump, hammer, knock, rap, pound, thud, punch, bump, smack, crack, slap, slam; informal bash, whack, clobber, clout, wallop. **2** *fireworks banged in the air:* **thud,** thump, bump, crack, crash, boom, pound, explode, detonate, burst, blow up.

banish verb **1** *he was banished for his crime:* **exile,** expel, deport, eject, repatriate, transport, extradite, evict, throw out, exclude, shut out, ban. **2** *he tried to banish his fear:* **dispel,** dismiss, disperse, scatter, dissipate, drive away, chase away, shut out.
OPPOSITES admit, cause, induce.

bank[1] noun **1** *the banks of Lake Michigan:* **edge,** shore, side, embankment, levee, margin, verge, brink. **2** *a grassy bank:* **slope,** rise, incline, gradient, ramp, mound, pile, heap, ridge, hillock, knoll, bar, shoal, mass, drift. **3** *a bank of switches:* **array,** row, line, tier, group, series.
verb **1** *they banked up the earth:* **pile up,** heap up, stack up, amass. **2** *the aircraft banked:* **tilt,** lean, tip, slant, incline, angle, list, camber, pitch.
OPPOSITES level, spread out, level out.

bank[2] noun **store,** reserve, stock, stockpile, supply, pool, fund, cache, hoard, deposit.

b

verb *I banked the money:* **deposit,** pay in, save.
OPPOSITES withdraw.

bankrupt adjective **insolvent,** ruined; Brit. in administration, in receivership; informal **bust,** broke, belly up, wiped out.
OPPOSITES solvent.

banner noun **1** *students waved banners:* **placard,** sign, poster, notice. **2** *banners fluttered above the troops:* **flag,** standard, ensign, colour(s), pennant, banderole.

banquet noun **feast,** dinner; informal **spread,** blowout; Brit. informal **nosh-up,** slap-up meal.
OPPOSITES snack.

baptize verb **1** *he was baptized as a baby:* **christen. 2** *they were baptized into the church:* **admit,** initiate, enrol, recruit. **3** *he was baptized Enoch:* **name,** call, dub.

bar noun **1** *an iron bar:* **rod,** stick, pole, batten, shaft, rail, spar, strut, crosspiece, beam. **2** *a bar of chocolate:* **block,** slab, cake, tablet, wedge, ingot. **3** *your drinks are on the bar:* **counter,** table, buffet. **4** *she had a drink in a bar:* **inn,** tavern, hostelry; Brit. **pub,** public house; Brit. informal **local,** boozer. **5** *a bar to promotion:* **obstacle,** impediment, hindrance, obstruction, block, hurdle, barrier.
OPPOSITES aid.

verb **1** *they have barred the door:* **bolt,** lock, fasten, secure, block, barricade, obstruct. **2** *I was barred from entering:* **prohibit,** debar, preclude, forbid, ban, exclude, obstruct, prevent, hinder, block.
OPPOSITES open, admit, allow.

barbarian noun **1** *the city was besieged by barbarians:* **savage,** heathen. **2** *you arrogant barbarian!* **brute,** beast, philistine, boor, yahoo, oaf, lout; Brit. informal **yob.**

barbaric adjective **1** *barbaric crimes:* **cruel,** brutal, barbarous, brutish, savage, vicious, wicked, ruthless, vile, inhuman. **2** *barbaric cultures:* **uncultured,** uncivilized, barbarian, philistine, boorish, loutish; Brit. informal **yobbish.**
OPPOSITES civilized.

bare adjective **1** *he was bare to the waist:* **naked,** unclothed, undressed, uncovered, stripped, with nothing on, nude; informal **without a stitch on,** in the altogether; Brit. informal **starkers;** Scottish informal **in the scud;** N. Amer. informal **buck naked. 2** *the room was bare:* **empty,** unfurnished, clear, undecorated, unadorned. **3** *the bare facts:* **basic,** essential, fundamental, plain, straightforward, simple, unembellished, pure, stark, bald, cold, hard.
OPPOSITES dressed, furnished, decorated, embellished.

barely adverb **hardly,** scarcely, only just, narrowly, by the skin of one's teeth, by a hair's breadth; informal **by a whisker;** Brit. informal **at a push.**
OPPOSITES easily.

bargain noun **1** *I'll make a bargain with you:* **agreement,** arrangement, understanding, deal, contract, pact. **2** *this binder is a bargain at £1.98:* **good value;** informal **good buy,** cheap buy, snip, steal, giveaway.
OPPOSITES rip-off.

verb **haggle,** negotiate, discuss terms, deal, barter.

■ **bargain for/on** expect, anticipate, be prepared for, allow for, plan for, reckon with, envisage, foresee, predict, count on, reckon on; N. Amer. informal figure on. ■ **into the bargain** in addition, as well, also, besides, on top, to boot, for good measure.

bark¹ verb **1** *the dog barked:* **woof**, yap. **2** *'Okay, outside!' he barked:* **shout**, snap, bawl, yell, roar, bellow, thunder; informal holler.
OPPOSITES whisper.

bark² noun *the bark of a tree:* **rind**, skin, peel, covering.

barracks plural noun **garrison**, camp, encampment, depot, billet, quarters, fort, cantonment.

barrage noun **1** *an artillery barrage:* **bombardment**, gunfire, shelling, salvo, volley, fusillade; historical broadside. **2** *a barrage of criticism:* **deluge**, stream, storm, torrent, onslaught, flood, spate, tide, avalanche, hail, blaze. **3** *a barrage across the river:* **dam**, barrier, weir, dyke, embankment, wall.

barrel noun **cask**, keg, butt, vat, tun, drum, hogshead, firkin.

barren adjective **unproductive**, infertile, unfruitful, sterile, arid, desert.
OPPOSITES fertile.

barricade noun *a barricade across the street:* **barrier**, roadblock, blockade, obstacle, obstruction.
verb *they barricaded the building:* **seal up**, close up, block off, shut off/up, defend, protect, fortify, occupy.

barrier noun **1** **fence**, railing, barricade, hurdle, bar, blockade, roadblock. **2** *a barrier to international trade:* **obstacle**, obstruction, hurdle, stumbling block, bar, impediment, hindrance, curb.

barter verb **1** *they bartered grain for salt:* **trade**, swap, exchange, sell. **2** *you can barter for souvenirs:* **haggle**, bargain, negotiate, deal.

base¹ noun **1** *the base of the tower:* **foundation**, bottom, foot, support, stand, pedestal, plinth. **2** *the system uses existing technology as its base:* **basis**, foundation, bedrock, starting point, source, origin, root(s), core, key component. **3** *the troops returned to their base:* **headquarters**, camp, site, station, settlement, post, centre.
OPPOSITES top.
verb **1** *he based his idea on a movie:* **found**, build, construct, form, ground; (**be based on**) derive from, spring from, stem from, depend on. **2** *the company was based in London:* **locate**, situate, position, install, station, site.

base² adjective *base motives:* **sordid**, ignoble, low, mean, immoral, unscrupulous, unprincipled, dishonest, dishonourable, shameful.
OPPOSITES noble.

bashful adjective **shy**, reserved, diffident, inhibited, retiring, reticent, reluctant, shrinking, timid, nervous.
OPPOSITES bold, confident.

basic adjective **1** *basic human rights:* **fundamental**, essential, vital, primary, principal, cardinal, elementary, intrinsic, central, pivotal, critical, key, focal. **2** *basic cooking facilities:* **plain**, simple, unsophisticated, straightforward, adequate, spartan, stark, severe, austere, limited, meagre, rudimentary, patchy, sketchy, minimal, crude, makeshift; informal bog-standard.

b

b

OPPOSITES secondary, unimportant, elaborate.

basically adverb **fundamentally,** essentially, first and foremost, primarily, at heart, at bottom, intrinsically, inherently, principally, chiefly, above all, mostly, mainly, on the whole, by and large; informal at the end of the day.

basics plural noun **fundamentals,** essentials, first principles, foundations, preliminaries, groundwork, essence, basis, core; informal nitty-gritty, brass tacks, nuts and bolts, ABC.

basin noun **bowl,** dish, pan.

basis noun **1** *the basis of his method:* **foundation,** support, base, reasoning, rationale, defence, reason, grounds, justification. **2** *the basis of discussion:* **starting point,** base, point of departure, beginning, premise, fundamental point/ principle, cornerstone, core, heart. **3** *on a part-time basis:* **footing,** condition, status, position, arrangement.

bask verb **laze,** lie, lounge, relax, sprawl, loll.

bass adjective **low,** deep, resonant, sonorous, rumbling, booming, resounding.
OPPOSITES high.

batch noun **group,** quantity, lot, bunch, cluster, raft, set, collection, bundle, pack, consignment, shipment.

bathe verb **1** *I bathed in the pool:* **swim,** take a dip. **2** *they bathed his wounds:* **clean,** wash, rinse, wet, soak. **3** *the room was bathed in light:* **flood,** cover, envelop, fill, wash, pervade, suffuse.

baton noun **1** *the conductor's baton:* **stick,** rod, staff, wand. **2** *police batons:* **truncheon,**

club, cudgel, stick, mace, shillelagh; N. Amer. nightstick, blackjack; Brit. informal cosh.

batter verb **beat up,** hit repeatedly, pummel, pound, rain blows on, buffet, belabour, thrash; informal knock about/ around, lay into, do over.

battle noun **1** *he was killed in the battle:* **fight,** engagement, armed conflict, clash, struggle, skirmish, fray, war, campaign, crusade, warfare, combat, action, hostilities; informal scrap, dogfight, shoot-out. **2** *a legal battle:* **conflict,** clash, struggle, disagreement, argument, dispute.
OPPOSITES peace.
verb **fight,** combat, contend with, resist, withstand, stand up to, confront, war, feud, struggle, strive, work.

battlefield noun **battleground,** field of battle, field of operations, combat zone, lines, front, theatre of war.

bawl verb **1** *'Come on!' he bawled:* **shout,** yell, roar, bellow, screech, scream, shriek, bark, thunder; informal yammer, holler. **2** *the children continued to bawl:* **cry,** sob, weep, wail, whine, howl; Scottish informal greet.
OPPOSITES whisper.

bay¹ noun *ships were anchored in the bay:* **cove,** inlet, gulf, sound, bight, basin, fjord.

bay² noun *there was a bay let into the wall:* **alcove,** recess, niche, nook, opening, inglenook.

bazaar noun **1** *a Turkish bazaar:* **market,** marketplace, souk, mart. **2** *the church bazaar:* **fête,** fair, fund-raiser, charity event; Brit. jumble sale, bring-and-buy sale, car boot sale; N. Amer. tag sale.

beach noun **sands**, seaside, seashore, coast; literary strand.
verb *they beached the boat:* **land,** ground, strand, run ashore.

beacon noun **signal**, light, fire, danger signal, bonfire, lighthouse.

bead noun **1** *a string of beads:* **ball,** pellet, pill, globule, sphere, spheroid, orb, round; (**beads**) necklace, rosary, chaplet. **2** *beads of sweat:* **droplet,** drop, drip, blob, pearl, dot.

beaker noun **cup**, tumbler, glass, mug, drinking vessel.

beam noun **1** *an oak beam:* **plank,** timber, joist, rafter, lintel, spar, girder, support. **2** *a beam of light:* **ray,** shaft, stream, streak, flash, gleam, glint. **3** *the beam on her face:* **grin,** smile.
OPPOSITES frown.
verb **1** *the signal is beamed out:* **broadcast,** transmit, relay, disseminate, direct, send, aim. **2** *the sun beamed down:* **shine,** radiate, glare, gleam. **3** *he beamed broadly:* **grin,** smile, smirk.
OPPOSITES frown.

bear verb **1** *she was bearing a box:* **carry,** bring, transport, move, convey, take, fetch; informal tote. **2** *the bag bore my name:* **display,** be marked with, show, carry, exhibit. **3** *will it bear his weight?* **support,** withstand, sustain, stand, take, carry, hold up, cope with, handle. **4** *she bore no grudge:* **harbour,** foster, entertain, cherish, nurse. **5** *I can't bear sport:* **endure,** tolerate, put up with, stand, abide, countenance, stomach; informal

hack, swallow; Brit. informal stick, wear, be doing with; formal brook. **6** *she bore a son:* **give birth to,** bring forth, deliver, have, produce, spawn. **7** *a shrub that bears berries:* **produce,** yield, give, provide, supply.
■ **bear fruit** yield results, succeed, be effective, be profitable, work; informal pay off, do the trick. ■ **bear something out** confirm, corroborate, substantiate, endorse, vindicate, give credence to, support, justify, prove. ■ **bear up** remain cheerful, cope, manage, get by, muddle through. ■ **bear with** be patient with, make allowances for, tolerate, put up with, endure.

bearer noun **1** *a lantern-bearer:* **carrier,** porter. **2** *the bearer of bad news:* **bringer,** messenger, agent, conveyor, emissary.

bearing noun **1** *a man of military bearing:* **posture,** stance, carriage, gait; Brit. deportment. **2** *a rather regal bearing:* **demeanour,** manner, air, aspect, attitude, style. **3** *this has no bearing on the matter:* **relevance,** pertinence, connection, import, significance. **4** *a bearing of* 015°: **direction,** orientation, course, trajectory, heading, tack, path. **5** (**bearings**) **orientation,** sense of direction, whereabouts, location, position.
OPPOSITES irrelevance.

beast noun **1** *the beasts of the forest:* **animal,** creature, brute; N. Amer. informal critter. **2** *he is a cruel beast:* **monster,** brute, savage, barbarian, animal, swine, ogre, fiend, sadist, demon, devil.

beat verb **1** **hit**, strike, batter, thump, bang, hammer, punch,

b

knock, thrash, pound, pummel, slap, rain blows on, assault; informal wallop, belt, bash, whack, clout, clobber. **2** *her heart was still beating:* throb, pulse, pulsate, pump, palpitate, pound, thump, thud, hammer, drum. **3** *the eagle beat its wings:* flap, flutter, thrash, wave, vibrate. **4** *beat the cream into the mixture:* whisk, mix, blend, whip. **5** *the team they need to beat:* defeat, conquer, vanquish, trounce, rout, overpower, overcome; informal lick, thrash, whip. **6** *he beat the record:* exceed, surpass, better, improve on, eclipse, transcend, top, trump, cap.
noun **1** *the song has a good beat:* rhythm, pulse, metre, time, measure, cadence, stress, accent. **2** *the beat of hooves:* pounding, banging, thumping, thudding, hammering, crashing. **3** *the beat of her heart:* pulse, pulsation, vibration, throb, palpitation, reverberation, pounding, thump, thud, hammering, drumming. **4** *a policeman on his beat:* circuit, round, route, path.
■ **beat someone/something off** repel, fight off, fend off, stave off, repulse, drive away/back, push back. ■ **beat someone up** assault, attack, mug; informal knock about/around, do over, work over, rough up; Brit. informal duff someone up; N. Amer. informal beat up on.

beautiful adjective attractive, pretty, handsome, good-looking, fetching, lovely, charming, graceful, elegant, appealing, winsome, ravishing, gorgeous, stunning, glamorous; Scottish & N. English bonny; informal tasty, knockout, drop-dead gorgeous; Brit. informal smashing;

N. Amer. informal cute, foxy; Austral./ NZ informal beaut, spunky.
OPPOSITES ugly.

beauty noun **1** attractiveness, prettiness, good looks, loveliness, appeal, winsomeness, charm, grace, elegance, exquisiteness, glamour; Scottish & N. English bonniness. **2** *she is a beauty:* belle, vision, goddess, picture, Venus; informal babe, looker, lovely, stunner, knockout, bombshell, bit of all right.
OPPOSITES ugliness, hag, boot.

because conjunction since, as, seeing that, in view of the fact that, in that.
■ **because of** on account of, as a result of, as a consequence of, owing to, due to, thanks to, by virtue of; formal by reason of.

beckon verb **1** *the guard beckoned to Benny:* gesture, signal, wave, gesticulate, motion. **2** *the countryside beckons you:* entice, invite, tempt, lure, charm, attract, draw, call.

become verb **1** *she became rich:* grow, get, turn, come to be, get to be. **2** *he became a tyrant:* turn into, change into, transform into, be converted into. **3** *he became Foreign Secretary:* be appointed, be assigned as, be nominated, be elected. **4** *the dress becomes her:* suit, flatter, look good on, set off; informal do something for.
■ **become of** happen to, be the fate of, be the lot of, overtake.

becoming adjective flattering, fetching, attractive, pretty, elegant, handsome, well-chosen, stylish, fashionable, tasteful.

bed noun **1** couch, berth, billet, cot; informal the sack. **2** *a flower*

bed: **patch,** plot, border, strip.
3 *built on a bed of stones:* **base,** foundation, footing, support, basis.
verb *the tiles are bedded in mortar:* **embed,** set, fix, insert, inlay, implant, bury, plant.
■ **go to bed** retire; informal hit the sack, hit the hay, turn in.

bedraggled adjective
dishevelled, disordered, untidy, unkempt, tousled; N. Amer. informal mussed.
OPPOSITES neat.

before preposition **1** *he dressed up before going out:* **prior to,** previous to, earlier than, preparatory to, in advance of, ahead of, pre-.... **2** *he appeared before the judge:* **in front of,** in the presence of. **3** *death before dishonour:* **in preference to,** rather than, sooner than.
OPPOSITES after.
adverb *previously,* before now/ then, until now/then, up to now/then, earlier, formerly, hitherto, in the past.
OPPOSITES afterwards, later.

beforehand adverb **in advance,** in readiness, ahead of time, before, before now/then, earlier (on), previously, already, sooner.
OPPOSITES afterwards.

beg verb **1** *he begged on the streets:* **ask for money,** seek charity; informal sponge, cadge, scrounge, bum. **2** *we begged for mercy:* **plead for,** request, ask for, appeal for, call for, sue for, solicit, seek. **3** *he begged her not to go:* **implore,** entreat, plead with, appeal to, pray to, call on, petition; literary beseech.

beggar noun **tramp,** vagrant, vagabond, mendicant; N. Amer. hobo; informal scrounger, sponger, cadger, freeloader; Brit. informal dosser; N. Amer. informal bum; Austral./NZ informal bagman.

begin verb **1** *we began work:* **start,** commence, set about, go about, embark on, launch into, get down to, take up, initiate, set in motion, get going, get off the ground, lead off, institute, inaugurate, open; informal get cracking on, kick off. **2** *when did the illness begin?* **appear,** arise, become apparent, spring up, crop up, turn up, come into existence, originate, start, commence, develop.
OPPOSITES finish, end, disappear.

beginner noun **novice,** learner, starter, (raw) recruit, newcomer, tyro, fresher, probationer; N. Amer. tenderfoot; informal rookie, new kid (on the block), newie; N. Amer. informal greenhorn.
OPPOSITES expert, veteran.

beginning noun **1** *the beginning of socialism:* **start,** commencement, creation, birth, inception, conception, origination, origin, genesis, emergence, rise, dawn, launch, onset, outset, day one; informal kick-off. **2** *the beginning of the article:* **opening,** start, commencement, first part, introduction, preamble.
OPPOSITES end, conclusion.

behalf
■ **on behalf of/on someone's behalf 1** *I am writing on behalf of my client:* **as a representative of,** as a spokesperson for, for, in the name of, in place of, on the authority of. **2** *a campaign on behalf of cycling:* **in the interests of,** in support of, for, for the benefit of, for the good of, for the sake of.

behave verb **1** *she behaved badly:* **act,** conduct oneself,

acquit oneself. **2** *the children behaved themselves:* **act correctly,** be good, be well behaved, conduct oneself well.
OPPOSITES misbehave.

behaviour noun **1** *his behaviour was inexcusable:* **conduct,** actions, doings, manners, ways, deportment, bearing, etiquette. **2** *the behaviour of these organisms:* **functioning,** action, performance, operation, working, reaction, response.

behind preposition **1** *he hid behind a tree:* **at the back/rear of,** beyond, on the far/other side of; N. Amer. in back of. **2** *a guard ran behind him:* **after,** following, at the back/rear of, hard on the heels of, in the wake of. **3** *you are behind the rest of the class:* **less advanced than,** slower than, weaker than. **4** *he was behind the bombings:* **responsible for,** at the bottom of, the cause of, the perpetrator of, the organizer of, to blame for, guilty of. **5** *they have the nation behind them:* **supporting,** backing, for, on the side of, in agreement with; informal rooting for.
OPPOSITES in front of, ahead of, against.
adverb **1** *a man followed behind:* **after,** afterwards, at the back/ end, in the rear. **2** *I looked behind:* **over one's shoulder,** towards the back/rear, backwards. **3** *we're behind, so don't stop:* **running late,** behind schedule, behindhand, not on time. **4** *he was behind with his subscription:* **in arrears,** overdue, late, unpunctual, behindhand.
OPPOSITES in front, ahead, in advance.

being noun **1** *she is warmed by his very being:* **existence,** living, life, reality, lifeblood, vital force. **2** *God is alive in the being of man:* **soul,** spirit, nature, essence, psyche, heart, bosom, breast. **3** *an enlightened being:* **creature,** life form, organism, living thing, individual, person, human.

belated adjective **late,** overdue, behindhand, delayed, tardy, unpunctual.
OPPOSITES early, punctual.

beleaguered adjective **1** *the beleaguered garrison:* **besieged,** blockaded, surrounded, encircled, hemmed in, under attack. **2** *a beleaguered government:* **troubled,** harassed, hard-pressed, in difficulties, under pressure, in a tight corner; informal up against it.

belief noun **1** *it's my belief that age is irrelevant:* **opinion,** view, conviction, judgement, thinking, idea, theory. **2** *belief in God:* **faith,** trust, reliance, confidence, credence. **3** *traditional beliefs:* **ideology,** principle, ethic, tenet, doctrine, teaching, dogma, creed, credo.
OPPOSITES disbelief, doubt.

believe verb **1** *I don't believe you:* **trust,** have confidence in, consider honest, consider truthful. **2** *do you believe that story?* **accept,** be convinced by, give credence to, credit, trust, put confidence in; informal swallow, buy, go for. **3** *I believe he worked for you:* **think,** be of the opinion that, have an idea that, imagine, assume, presume, take it, understand, gather; informal reckon, figure.
OPPOSITES doubt.

■ **believe in** have faith in, trust in, have every confidence in, cling to, set (great) store by, value, be convinced by, be persuaded by; informal swear by, rate.

believer noun disciple, follower, supporter, adherent, devotee, upholder, worshipper.
OPPOSITES infidel, sceptic.

belittle verb disparage, denigrate, run down, deprecate, play down, trivialize, minimize; informal do down, pooh-pooh.
OPPOSITES praise, magnify.

belligerent adjective **1** *a belligerent stare:* **hostile,** aggressive, threatening, antagonistic, pugnacious, bellicose, truculent, confrontational, contentious, militant, combative; informal spoiling for a fight; Brit. informal stroppy, bolshie; N. Amer. informal scrappy. **2** *the belligerent states:* **warring,** combatant, fighting, battling.
OPPOSITES peaceable, neutral.

bellow verb roar, shout, bawl, thunder, boom, bark, yell, shriek, howl, scream; informal holler.
OPPOSITES whisper.

belly noun stomach, abdomen, paunch, middle, midriff, girth; informal tummy, gut, insides.

belong verb **1** *the house belongs to his mother:* **be owned by,** be the property of, be held by, be in the hands of. **2** *I belong to a union:* **be a member of,** be in, be affiliated to, be allied to, be associated with. **3** *the garden belongs to the flat:* **be part of,** be attached to, go with. **4** *she doesn't belong here:* **fit in,** be suited to; informal go, click.

belongings plural noun possessions, effects, worldly goods, chattels, property; informal gear, tackle, kit, things, stuff,

bits and pieces; Brit. informal clobber.

beloved adjective *her beloved brother:* **darling,** dear, precious, adored, cherished, treasured, prized, valued, idolized.
OPPOSITES hated.
noun *he watched his beloved:* **sweetheart,** love, darling, dearest, lover, girlfriend, boyfriend; informal steady, baby, angel, honey, pet.

below preposition **1** *the water rushed below them:* **beneath,** under, underneath, lower than. **2** *the sum is below average:* **less than,** lower than, under, not as much as, smaller than. **3** *a captain is below a major:* **lower than,** under, inferior to, subordinate to.
OPPOSITES above, over, more than.
adverb **1** *I could see what was happening below:* **further down,** lower down, underneath, beneath. **2** *the statements below:* **underneath,** following, further on, at a later point.
OPPOSITES above.

belt noun **1** **sash,** girdle, band, strap, cummerbund. **2** *the commuter belt:* **region,** strip, stretch, zone, area, district, sector, territory.

bemused adjective bewildered, confused, puzzled, perplexed, baffled, mystified, nonplussed, dumbfounded, at sea, at a loss; informal flummoxed, bamboozled, fazed.

bench noun **1** *he sat on a bench:* **seat,** form, pew, stall, settle. **2** *a laboratory bench:* **workbench,** worktop, counter.

benchmark noun standard, point of reference, guide, guideline, norm, touchstone, yardstick, barometer, model, gauge, criterion, specification.

bend verb **1** *the frames can be bent to fit your face:* **curve**, crook, flex, angle, hook, bow, arch, buckle, warp, contort, distort, deform, twist. **2** *the highway bent to the left:* **turn**, curve, incline, swing, veer, fork, change course, curl, loop. **3** *he bent down to tie his shoe:* **stoop**, bow, crouch, hunch, lean down/over.
OPPOSITES straighten.
noun *a bend in the road:* **curve**, turn, corner, kink, angle, arc, twist.
OPPOSITES straight.

beneath preposition **1** *we sat beneath the trees:* **under**, underneath, below, at the foot of, at the bottom of, lower than. **2** *the rank beneath theirs:* **inferior to**, below, lower than, subordinate to. **3** *such an attitude was beneath her:* **unworthy of**, unbecoming to, degrading to.
OPPOSITES above.
adverb *sand with rock beneath:* **underneath**, below, further down, lower down.
OPPOSITES above.

benefactor noun **patron**, supporter, backer, sponsor, donor, contributor; informal **angel**.

beneficial adjective **advantageous**, favourable, helpful, useful, of assistance, valuable, profitable, rewarding, gainful.
OPPOSITES disadvantageous.

beneficiary noun **recipient**, payee, heir, heiress, inheritor.

benefit noun **1** *for the benefit of others:* **good**, sake, welfare, well-being, advantage, comfort, ease, convenience, help, aid, assistance, service. **2** *the benefits of working for a large firm:* **advantage**, profit, plus point, boon, blessing, reward; informal **perk**. **3** *state benefit:* **social security payment**, welfare, charity; informal **the dole**; Scottish informal **the broo**.
OPPOSITES detriment, disadvantage.
verb **1** *the deal benefited them both:* **be advantageous to**, be beneficial to, profit, do good to, be of service to, serve, be useful to, be helpful to, aid. **2** *they may benefit from drugs:* **profit**, gain, reap reward, make the most of, exploit, turn to one's advantage, put to good use.
OPPOSITES disadvantage, harm, suffer.

benevolent adjective **kind**, kindly, kind-hearted, good-natured, compassionate, caring, altruistic, humanitarian, philanthropic.
OPPOSITES unkind.

benign adjective **1** *a benign grandfatherly role:* **kindly**, kind, warm-hearted, good-natured, friendly, genial, tender-hearted, gentle, sympathetic, compassionate, caring, well disposed, benevolent. **2** *a benign climate:* **mild**, temperate, gentle, balmy, soft, pleasant, favourable, healthy. **3** (Medicine) *a benign tumour:* **harmless**, non-malignant, non-cancerous.
OPPOSITES unkind, unhealthy, hostile, malignant.

bent adjective **1** **twisted**, crooked, warped, contorted, deformed, misshapen, out of shape, bowed, arched, curved, angled, hooked, kinked; N. Amer. informal **pretzeled**. **2** *a mob bent*

on violence: **intent,** determined, set, insistent, resolved.
OPPOSITES straight.
noun *an artistic bent:* **inclination,** leaning, tendency, talent, gift, flair, aptitude, facility, skill.

bequeath verb **leave,** will, hand down, pass on, entrust, make over, grant, transfer, give, bestow on, confer on.

bequest noun **legacy,** estate, inheritance, endowment, settlement.

bereavement noun **death in the family,** loss, passing (away), demise.

berserk adjective **mad,** crazy, insane, out of one's mind, hysterical, frenzied, crazed, demented, maniacal, manic, frantic, raving, wild, out of control, amok, on the rampage; informal off one's head, off the deep end, ape, bananas, bonkers; Brit. informal spare; N. Amer. informal postal.

berth noun **1** *a 4-berth cabin:* **bunk,** bed, cot, couch, hammock. **2** *the vessel left its berth:* **mooring,** dock, pier, jetty, quay.
verb *the ship berthed in London:* **dock,** moor, land, tie up, make fast.

beside preposition **alongside,** by/ at the side of, next to, parallel to, abreast of, adjacent to, next door to, neighbouring.
■ **beside oneself** distraught, overcome, out of one's mind, frantic, desperate, distracted, at one's wits' end, frenzied, hysterical.

besides preposition *who did you ask besides Mary?* **in addition to,** as well as, over and above, on top of, apart from, other than, aside from, not counting,

excluding, leaving aside; N. Amer. informal outside of.
adverb **1** *there's a lot more besides:* **in addition,** as well, too, also, into the bargain, on top of that, to boot. **2** *besides, he's a man:* **furthermore,** moreover, further; informal what's more.

besiege verb **1** *the army besieged Leith:* **lay siege to,** beleaguer, blockade. **2** *he was besieged by fans:* **surround,** mob, harass, pester, badger. **3** *we were besieged with requests:* **overwhelm,** bombard, inundate, deluge, flood, swamp, snow under.

best adjective **1** *the best hotel in Paris:* **finest,** premier, greatest, top, foremost, leading, pre-eminent, supreme, superlative, unrivalled, second to none, without equal, unsurpassed, unparalleled, unbeatable, optimum, ultimate, incomparable, record-breaking; informal star, number-one, a cut above the rest, top-drawer. **2** *do whatever you think best:* **most advantageous,** most useful, most suitable, most fitting, most appropriate, most advisable.
OPPOSITES worst.
adverb **1** *the best-dressed man:* **to the highest standard,** in the best way. **2** *the food he liked best:* **most,** to the highest/ greatest degree. **3** *this is best done at home:* **most appropriately,** most suitably, most fittingly, most usefully, most advantageously, most sensibly, most prudently, most wisely.
OPPOSITES worst, least.
noun *only the best will do:* **finest,** choicest, top, cream, choice, prime, elite, crème de la

b

crème, flower, jewel in the crown; informal tops, pick of the bunch.
OPPOSITES worst.

bestow verb confer on, grant, accord, afford, endow someone with, present, award, give, donate, entrust with, vouchsafe.

bet verb 1 *he bet £10 on the favourite:* **wager,** gamble, stake, risk, venture, hazard, chance; Brit. informal punt, have a flutter. 2 (informal) *I bet it was your idea:* **be certain,** be sure, be convinced, be confident, expect, predict, guess.
noun 1 *a £20 bet:* **wager,** gamble, stake, ante; Brit. informal punt, flutter. 2 (informal) *your best bet is to go early:* **option,** choice, alternative, course of action, plan.

betray verb 1 *he betrayed his own brother:* **be disloyal to,** be unfaithful to, break faith with, play someone false, inform on/against, give away, denounce, sell out, stab in the back; informal split on, rat on, stitch up, do the dirty on, sell down the river; Brit. informal grass on, shop, sneak on; N. Amer. informal rat out, drop a/the dime on, finger; Austral./NZ informal dob in, point the bone at. 2 *he betrayed a secret:* **reveal,** disclose, divulge, tell, give away, leak, bring out into the open.
OPPOSITES be loyal to, keep.

betrayal noun **disloyalty,** treachery, bad faith, breach of faith, breach of trust, faithlessness, duplicity, deception, double-dealing, stab in the back, double-cross, sell-out.
OPPOSITES loyalty.

better adjective 1 *better*

facilities: **superior,** finer, of higher quality, preferable; informal a cut above, streets ahead, head and shoulders above, ahead of the pack/field. 2 *there couldn't be a better time:* **more advantageous,** more suitable, more fitting, more appropriate, more useful, more valuable, more desirable. 3 *are you better?* **healthier,** fitter, stronger, well again, cured, healed, recovered, recovering, on the road to recovery, on the mend.
OPPOSITES worse, inferior.
adverb 1 *I played better today:* **to a higher standard,** in a superior way, more effectively. 2 *this may suit you better:* **more,** to a greater degree/extent. 3 *the money could be better spent:* **more wisely,** more sensibly, more suitably, more fittingly, more advantageously, more usefully.
verb 1 *he bettered the record:* **surpass,** improve on, beat, exceed, top, cap, trump, eclipse. 2 *refugees who want to better their lot:* **improve,** ameliorate, raise, advance, further, lift, upgrade, enhance.
OPPOSITES worsen.

between preposition 1 *Philip stood between his parents:* **in the middle of,** with one on either side, among; archaic betwixt. 2 *the bond between her and her mother:* **connecting,** linking, joining, uniting, allying.

beware verb **watch out,** look out, mind out, be alert, keep your eyes open/peeled, keep an eye out, take care, be careful, be cautious, watch your step, guard against.

bewilder verb **baffle,** mystify,

bemuse, perplex, puzzle, confuse; informal flummox, faze, stump, beat.
OPPOSITES enlighten.

beyond preposition **1** *beyond the trees:* **on the far side of,** on the other side of, further away than, behind, past, after. **2** *beyond six o'clock:* **later than,** past, after. **3** *inflation beyond 10 per cent:* **greater than,** more than, exceeding, in excess of, above, upwards of. **4** *little beyond food was provided:* **apart from,** except, other than, besides; informal outside of; formal save.

bias noun *he accused the media of bias:* **prejudice,** partiality, favouritism, unfairness, one-sidedness, discrimination, leaning, tendency, inclination.
OPPOSITES impartiality.
verb *this may have biased the result:* **prejudice,** influence, colour, sway, predispose, distort, skew, slant.

biased adjective **prejudiced,** partial, partisan, one-sided, bigoted, discriminatory, distorted, warped, twisted, skewed.
OPPOSITES impartial.

bid verb *United bid £1 million for the striker:* **offer,** put up, tender, proffer, propose.
noun **1** *a bid of £3,000:* **offer,** tender, proposal. **2** *a bid to cut crime:* **attempt,** effort, endeavour, try; informal crack, go, shot, stab.

bidding noun **command,** order, direction, instruction, decree, injunction, demand, beck and call.

big adjective **1** *a big building:* **large,** sizeable, substantial, great, huge, immense, enormous, extensive, colossal, massive, vast, gigantic, giant, spacious; informal jumbo, whopping, thumping, bumper, mega; Brit. informal whacking, ginormous; formal commodious. **2** *a big man:* **well built,** sturdy, brawny, burly, broad-shouldered, muscular, bulky, hulking, strapping, hefty, tall, huge, fat, stout; informal hunky, beefy. **3** *my big brother:* **grown-up,** adult, mature, grown, elder, older. **4** *a big decision:* **important,** significant, major, momentous, weighty, far-reaching, key, vital, crucial. **5** *that was big of you:* **generous,** kind, kindly, caring, compassionate, loving.
OPPOSITES small, little, younger, minor, mean.

bigoted adjective **prejudiced,** biased, partial, one-sided, sectarian, discriminatory, opinionated, dogmatic, intolerant, narrow-minded, blinkered, illiberal.
OPPOSITES open-minded.

bill noun **1** *a bill for £6:* **invoice,** account, statement, list of charges; humorous the damage; N. Amer. check; N. Amer. informal tab. **2** *a parliamentary bill:* **draft law,** proposal, measure. **3** *she was top of the bill:* **programme,** line-up; N. Amer. playbill. **4** (N. Amer.) *a $10 bill:* **banknote,** note; US informal greenback. **5** *he had been posting bills:* **poster,** advertisement, notice, announcement, flyer, leaflet, handbill; informal ad; Brit. informal advert.
verb **1** *please bill me for the work:* **invoice,** charge, debit. **2** *the concert went ahead as billed:* **advertise,** announce, schedule, programme, timetable; N. Amer. slate. **3** *he was billed as the new Sean*

Connery: **describe,** call, style, label, dub, promote, talk up; informal **hype.**

billow noun *billows of smoke*: **cloud,** mass.
verb **1** *her dress billowed around her*: **puff up/out,** balloon (out), swell, fill (out). **2** *smoke billowed from the chimney*: **swirl,** spiral, roll, undulate, eddy, pour, flow.

bind verb **1** *they bound her hands*: **tie up,** fasten together, secure, make fast, attach, rope, lash, tether. **2** *Shelley bound up the wound*: **bandage,** dress, cover, wrap, strap up, tape up. **3** *the edges are bound in a contrasting colour*: **trim,** hem, edge, border, fringe. See also **BOUND¹.**
OPPOSITES untie.

binding adjective **irrevocable,** unalterable, inescapable, unbreakable, contractual, compulsory, obligatory, mandatory, incumbent.

binge noun (informal) **bout,** spell, fling, spree, orgy, drinking bout; informal **bender, session;** Scottish informal **skite;** N. Amer. informal **jag, toot.**

birth noun **1** childbirth, delivery, nativity. **2** *the birth of science*: **beginning(s),** emergence, genesis, dawn, dawning, rise, start. **3** *he is of noble birth*: **ancestry,** lineage, blood, descent, parentage, family, extraction, origin, stock.
OPPOSITES death, end.
■ **give birth to** have, bear, produce, be delivered of, bring into the world; N. Amer. **birth;** informal **drop.**

bit noun **piece,** portion, section, part, chunk, lump, hunk, fragment, scrap, shred, crumb, grain, speck, spot, drop, pinch, dash, morsel, mouthful, bite, sample, iota, jot, whit, atom, particle, trace, touch, suggestion, hint, tinge; informal **smidgen, tad.**
OPPOSITES lot.

bite verb **1** **chew,** sink one's teeth into, munch, crunch, champ. **2** *my boots failed to bite*: **grip,** hold, get a purchase. **3** *the measures begin to bite*: **take effect,** work, act, have results.
noun **1** *he took a bite at his sandwich*: **chew,** munch, nibble, gnaw, nip, snap. **2** *he ate it in two bites*: **mouthful,** piece, bit, morsel. **3** *the appetizer had a fiery bite*: **piquancy,** pungency, spiciness, tang, zest; informal **kick, punch, zing.**

biting adjective **1** *biting comments*: **vicious,** harsh, cruel, savage, cutting, sharp, bitter, scathing, caustic, acid, acrimonious, spiteful, venomous; informal **bitchy, catty. 2** *the biting wind*: **freezing,** icy, arctic, bitter, piercing, penetrating, raw.
OPPOSITES mild, pleasant, warm.

bitter adjective **1** *bitter coffee*: **sharp,** acid, acrid, tart, sour, vinegary. **2** *a bitter row*: **acrimonious,** hostile, angry, rancorous, spiteful, vicious, vitriolic, savage, ferocious, nasty. **3** *a bitter woman*: **resentful,** embittered, aggrieved, spiteful, jaundiced, sullen, sour. **4** *a bitter wind*: **freezing,** icy, arctic, biting, piercing, penetrating, raw.
OPPOSITES pleasant, sweet, amicable, magnanimous, content, mild, warm.

bitterness noun **1** *the bitterness of the medicine*: **sharpness,** acidity, tartness, sourness. **2** *there was no bitterness*

between them: **acrimony,** hostility, anger, antipathy, antagonism, enmity, animus, friction, rancour, vitriol, venom, nastiness, bad blood. **3** *his bitterness grew:* **resentment,** rancour, indignation, grudge, spite, sullenness, sourness, pique.
OPPOSITES sweetness, pleasantness, goodwill, magnanimity, contentment.

bizarre adjective **strange,** peculiar, odd, funny, fantastic, curious, outlandish, eccentric, unconventional, unorthodox; informal weird, wacky, oddball, way out, freaky; N. Amer. informal wacko.
OPPOSITES normal.

black adjective **1** *a black horse:* **dark,** pitch-black, jet-black, ebony, inky. **2** *the blackest day of the war:* **tragic,** dark, disastrous, calamitous, catastrophic, cataclysmic, fateful. **3** *Mary was in a black mood:* **miserable,** unhappy, sad, wretched, heartbroken, grief-stricken, sorrowful, anguished, desolate, despairing, disconsolate, downcast, dejected, gloomy; informal blue. **4** *black humour:* **macabre,** cynical, unhealthy, ghoulish, weird, morbid, gruesome; informal sick.
OPPOSITES white, bright, happy.
■ **black out** faint, lose consciousness, pass out, swoon.

blacklist verb **boycott,** ostracize, avoid, embargo, ignore, refuse to employ.

blackmail noun *he was accused of blackmail:* **extortion,** demanding money with menaces, threats, intimidation.
verb **1** *he was blackmailing the murderer:* **extort money from,**

threaten, hold to ransom, intimidate. **2** *she blackmailed me into working for her:* **coerce,** pressure, force, dragoon; informal lean on, twist someone's arm.

blame verb **1** *he always blames others:* **hold responsible,** hold accountable, condemn, accuse, find/consider guilty. **2** *they blame youth crime on unemployment:* **attribute to,** ascribe to, impute to, lay at the door of, put down to; informal pin.
OPPOSITES absolve.
noun *he was cleared of all blame:* **responsibility,** guilt, accountability, liability, culpability, fault.

blameless adjective **innocent,** guiltless, above reproach, unimpeachable, in the clear, exemplary; informal squeaky clean.
OPPOSITES blameworthy.

bland adjective **1** *a bland film:* **uninteresting,** dull, boring, tedious, monotonous, ordinary, run-of-the-mill, drab, dreary, unexciting, lacklustre, flat, stale, trite. **2** *bland food:* **tasteless,** flavourless, plain, insipid, weak, watery, thin, wishy-washy.
OPPOSITES interesting, tangy.

blank adjective **1** *a blank sheet of paper:* **empty,** unmarked, unused, clear, free, bare, clean, plain. **2** *a blank face:* **expressionless,** deadpan, wooden, stony, impassive, glazed, fixed, lifeless, inscrutable.
OPPOSITES full, marked, expressive.
noun *fill in the blanks:* **space,** gap.

blanket noun *a blanket of cloud:* **covering,** layer, coating, carpet,

cloak, mantle, veil, pall, shroud.
verb *snow blanketed the mountains:* **cover,** coat, carpet, cloak, shroud, swathe, envelop.

blast noun **1** *the blast from the bomb:* **shock wave,** pressure wave. **2** *Friday's blast killed two people:* **explosion,** detonation, discharge, burst. **3** *a blast of cold air:* **gust,** rush, gale, squall, flurry. **4** *the shrill blast of the trumpets:* **blare,** wail, roar, screech, shriek, hoot, honk, beep.
verb **1** *bombers were blasting airfields:* **blow up,** bomb, blow (to pieces), dynamite, explode. **2** *guns were blasting away:* **fire,** shoot, blaze, let fly, discharge. **3** *he blasted his horn:* **honk,** beep, toot, sound. **4** *radios blasting out pop music:* **blare,** boom, roar, thunder, bellow, pump, shriek, screech.

blatant adjective **flagrant,** glaring, obvious, undisguised, open, shameless, barefaced, unashamed, brazen.
OPPOSITES inconspicuous, shamefaced.

blaze noun **1** **fire,** flames, conflagration, inferno, holocaust. **2** *a blaze of light:* **glare,** flash, burst, flare, streak, radiance, brilliance, beam, glitter.
verb **1** *the fire blazed merrily:* **burn,** be alight, be on fire, be in flames. **2** *headlights blazed:* **shine,** flash, flare, glare, gleam, glitter, glisten. **3** *soldiers blazed away:* **fire,** shoot, blast, let fly.

bleach verb **turn white,** whiten, turn pale, blanch, lighten, fade.
OPPOSITES darken.

bleak adjective **1** *a bleak landscape:* **bare,** exposed, desolate, stark, desert, lunar, open, empty, windswept. **2** *the future is bleak:* **unpromising,** unfavourable, dim, gloomy, black, grim, discouraging, disheartening, depressing.
OPPOSITES lush, promising.

bleary adjective **blurry,** unfocused, fogged, clouded, misty, watery.
OPPOSITES clear.

blend verb **1** *blend the ingredients until smooth:* **mix,** mingle, combine, merge, amalgamate, stir, whisk, fold in. **2** *the new buildings blend with the older ones:* **harmonize,** go (well), fit (in), be in tune, be compatible, coordinate, match, complement, suit.
noun *a blend of bananas and ginger:* **mixture,** mix, combination, compound, amalgam, fusion, alloy.

bless verb **1** *the Cardinal blessed the memorial plaque:* **consecrate,** sanctify, dedicate to God, make holy; formal hallow. **2** *the gods blessed us with magical voices:* **endow,** bestow, furnish, give, favour, confer on. **3** *the government refused to bless the undertaking:* **sanction,** consent to, endorse, agree to, approve, back, support; informal give the green light to, OK.
OPPOSITES curse, trouble, oppose.

blessed adjective **holy,** sacred, hallowed, consecrated, sanctified, ordained, canonized, beatified.
OPPOSITES cursed.

blessing noun **1** *a blessing from the priest:* **benediction,** dedication, consecration, grace, invocation, intercession. **2** *she gave the plan her blessing:* **sanction,** endorsement, approval, consent, assent, agreement, backing, support;

informal the green light, OK. **3** *it was a blessing they didn't have far to go:* **advantage,** godsend, boon, benefit, help, bonus, plus, stroke of luck, windfall.
OPPOSITES condemnation, affliction.

blight noun **1** *potato blight:* **disease,** canker, infestation, fungus, mildew, mould. **2** *the blight of aircraft noise:* **curse,** scourge, affliction, plague, menace, misfortune, bane, trouble, nuisance, pest.
OPPOSITES blessing.
verb *scandal blighted his career:* **ruin,** wreck, spoil, mar, frustrate, disrupt, undo, scotch, destroy, shatter, devastate, demolish; informal mess up, foul up, put paid to, put the kibosh on, stymie; Brit. informal scupper.

blind adjective **1** **sightless,** unsighted, visually impaired, unseeing. **2** *blind acceptance of conventional opinion:* **uncritical,** unreasoned, unthinking, unquestioning, mindless, undiscerning, indiscriminate. **3** *she was blind to the realities of her position:* **unaware of,** oblivious to, ignorant of, unmindful of, heedless of, insensible to, indifferent to.
OPPOSITES sighted, discerning, mindful.
noun *a window blind:* **screen,** shade, sunshade, curtain, awning, canopy, louvre, jalousie, shutter.

blindly adverb **1** *he ran blindly upstairs:* **impetuously,** impulsively, recklessly, heedlessly. **2** *they blindly followed US policy:* **uncritically,** unquestioningly, unthinkingly, mindlessly, indiscriminately.
OPPOSITES cautiously, critically,
selectively.

bliss noun **joy,** happiness, pleasure, delight, ecstasy, elation, rapture, euphoria.
OPPOSITES misery.

blitz noun **bombing,** air raid, air strike, bombardment, barrage, attack, assault.

bloated adjective **swollen,** distended, bulging, inflated, dilated.
OPPOSITES shrunken.

blob noun **1** *a blob of cold gravy:* **drop,** droplet, globule, bead, bubble. **2** *a blob of ink:* **spot,** dab, blotch, blot, dot, smudge; informal splodge.

bloc noun **group,** alliance, coalition, federation, confederation, league, union, axis, association.

block noun **1** *a block of cheese:* **chunk,** hunk, lump, wedge, cube, brick, slab, piece. **2** *an apartment block:* **building,** complex, structure, development. **3** *a block to development:* **obstacle,** bar, barrier, impediment, hindrance, check, hurdle.
OPPOSITES aid.
verb **1** *weeds can block ditches:* **clog,** stop up, choke, plug, bung up, obstruct, gum up, dam up, congest, jam. **2** *picket lines blocked access to the factory:* **hinder,** hamper, obstruct, impede, inhibit, halt, stop, bar, check, prevent, fend off, hold off, repel.
OPPOSITES clear, aid, allow.
■ **block something out** keep out, exclude, stop, conceal, blot out, obliterate.

blockage noun **obstruction,** stoppage, block, jam, congestion.

blonde, blond adjective **fair,** light, yellow, flaxen, golden.

OPPOSITES dark.

blood noun **1 lifeblood,** gore, vital fluid. **2** *a woman of noble blood:* **ancestry,** lineage, descent, parentage, family, birth, extraction, origin, stock.

bloodshed noun **slaughter,** massacre, killing, wounding, carnage, butchery, bloodletting, bloodbath.

bloodthirsty adjective **murderous,** homicidal, violent, vicious, barbarous, barbaric, savage, brutal, cut-throat.

bloody adjective **1** *his hands were all bloody:* **bloodstained,** blood-soaked, gory, bleeding. **2** *a bloody civil war:* **vicious,** ferocious, savage, fierce, brutal, cruel, murderous, gory.
OPPOSITES clean, bloodless.

bloom verb **1** *the geraniums bloomed:* **flower,** blossom, open, mature. **2** *the children bloomed in the Devonshire air:* **flourish,** thrive, prosper, burgeon; informal be in the pink.
OPPOSITES wither, fade, decline.

blossom noun *pink blossoms:* **flower,** bloom, bud.
verb **1** *the snowdrops have blossomed:* **bloom,** flower, open, mature. **2** *the whole region had blossomed:* **develop,** grow, mature, progress, evolve, burgeon, flourish, thrive, prosper, bloom.
OPPOSITES wither, fade, decline.

blot noun **1** *an ink blot:* **patch,** dab, smudge, blotch, mark, dot, spot; Brit. informal splodge. **2** *the only blot on a clean campaign:* **blemish,** taint, stain, blight, flaw, fault. **3** *a blot on the landscape:* **eyesore,** monstrosity, carbuncle, mess; informal sight.

■ **blot something out 1** *clouds were starting to blot out the*

stars: conceal, hide, obscure, exclude, obliterate, shadow, eclipse. **2** *he urged her to blot out the memory:* erase, blank out, wipe out, eradicate.

blow¹ verb **1** *the icy wind blew around us:* **gust,** puff, flurry, blast, roar, bluster, rush, storm. **2** *his ship was blown on to the rocks:* **sweep,** carry, toss, drive, push, force. **3** *leaves blew across the road:* **drift,** flutter, waft, float, glide, whirl, move. **4** *he blew a smoke ring:* **exhale,** puff. **5** *he blew a trumpet:* **sound,** blast, toot, play, pipe, trumpet.
■ **blow something out** extinguish, put out, snuff, douse, quench, smother. ■ **blow up** *a lorryload of shells blew up:* explode, detonate, go off, ignite, erupt. ■ **blow something up 1** *they blew the plane up:* explode, detonate, bomb, blast, destroy. **2** *blow up the balloons:* inflate, pump up, fill up, puff up, swell, expand.

blow² noun **1** *a blow on the head:* **knock,** bang, hit, punch, thump, smack, crack, rap; informal whack, bash, clout, wallop. **2** *losing his wife must have been a blow:* **upset,** disaster, setback, misfortune, disappointment, calamity, catastrophe, thunderbolt, bombshell, shock, surprise, jolt.

blue adjective sky-blue, azure, cobalt, sapphire, navy, ultramarine, aquamarine, cyan.

blueprint noun **1** *blueprints of the aircraft:* **plan,** design, diagram, drawing, sketch, layout. **2** *a blueprint for similar measures in other countries:* **model,** plan, template, pattern, example, guide, prototype, pilot.

bluff¹ noun *this offer was*

b

denounced as a bluff: **trick,** deception, fraud, ruse, pretence, sham, fake, hoax, charade; informal put-on.
verb 1 *they are bluffing to hide their guilt:* **pretend,** sham, fake, feign, lie, hoax, pose. **2** *I managed to bluff the board into believing me:* **deceive,** delude, mislead, trick, fool, hoodwink, dupe, hoax; informal con, kid, have on.

bluff² adjective *a bluff man:* **plain-spoken,** straightforward, blunt, direct, no-nonsense, frank, open, candid, forthright, unequivocal; informal upfront.
OPPOSITES guarded, secretive.

blunder noun *he shook his head at his blunder:* **mistake,** error, gaffe, slip, oversight, faux pas; informal slip-up, boo-boo; Brit. informal clanger, boob; N. Amer. informal blooper.
verb 1 *the government admitted it had blundered:* **make a mistake,** err, miscalculate, bungle, trip up; informal slip up, screw up, blow it, goof; Brit. informal boob. **2** *she blundered down the steps:* **stumble,** lurch, stagger, flounder, grope.

blunt adjective **1** *a blunt knife:* **dull,** worn. **2** *the leaf is broad with a blunt tip:* **rounded,** flat, stubby. **3** *a blunt message:* **straightforward,** frank, plain-spoken, candid, direct, bluff, forthright, unequivocal, brusque, abrupt, curt, bald, brutal, harsh, stark; informal upfront.
OPPOSITES sharp, pointed, subtle.
verb *age hasn't blunted my passion for life:* **dull,** deaden, dampen, numb, take the edge off, weaken, allay, diminish, lessen.
OPPOSITES intensify.

blur verb **1** *she felt tears blur her vision:* **cloud,** fog, obscure, dim, make hazy, make fuzzy, soften, dull, numb, deaden, mute. **2** *the digits on the screen blurred:* **become fuzzy,** become dim, become hazy, become vague.
OPPOSITES sharpen, focus.
noun *a blur on the horizon:* **indistinct shape,** smudge, haze, cloud, mist.

blurred adjective **indistinct,** fuzzy, hazy, misty, foggy, faint, unclear, vague, indefinite, unfocused.
OPPOSITES sharp, clear.

blurt
■ **blurt something out** burst out with, exclaim, call out, divulge, disclose, reveal, betray, let slip, give away; informal blab, let on, spill the beans.

blush verb *Joan blushed at the compliment:* **redden,** go pink, go red, flush, colour, burn up.
noun *the darkness hid her blush:* **flush,** rosiness, redness, pinkness, bloom, high colour, glow.

blustery adjective **stormy,** gusty, blowy, windy, squally, wild.
OPPOSITES calm.

board noun **1** *a wooden board:* **plank,** beam, panel, slat, batten, timber. **2** *the board of directors:* **committee,** council, panel, directorate, commission.
verb 1 *he boarded the aircraft:* **get on,** go aboard, enter, mount, ascend, embark, catch. **2** *a number of students boarded with them:* **lodge,** live, reside, stay, be housed; N. Amer. room; informal put up.

boast verb **1** *his mother had been boasting about him:* **brag,** crow, swagger, swank, gloat, show off; informal talk big, lay it on thick; Austral./NZ informal skite.

b

2 *the hotel boasts a fine restaurant:* **have**, possess, own, enjoy, pride oneself/itself on, offer.
OPPOSITES hush up.
noun **1** *the government's main boast seemed undone:* **brag**, exaggeration, overstatement; informal swank; Austral./NZ informal skite. **2** *the hall is the boast of the county:* **pride**, joy, pride and joy, apple of someone's eye, wonder, delight.

boastful adjective **bragging**, swaggering, bumptious, puffed up, full of oneself, cocky, conceited, arrogant; informal swanky, big-headed.
OPPOSITES modest.

bob verb **move up and down**, bounce, toss, skip, dance, wobble, jiggle, joggle, jolt, jerk.

bodily adjective *bodily sensations:* **physical**, corporeal, corporal, mortal, material, tangible, concrete, real, actual.
OPPOSITES spiritual, mental.
adverb *he hauled her bodily from the van:* **forcefully**, forcibly, violently, completely, entirely.

body noun **1** *the human body:* **figure**, frame, form, physique, anatomy, skeleton. **2** *he was hit by shrapnel in the head and body:* **torso**, trunk. **3** *the bodies were put in the fire:* **corpse**, carcass, skeleton, remains; informal stiff; Medicine cadaver. **4** *the body of the article:* **main part**, core, heart, hub. **5** *the representative body of the employers:* **association**, organization, assembly, delegation, committee, executive, company, society, corporation, group.

bog noun **marsh**, swamp, mire, quagmire, morass, slough, fen, wetland.

■ **bog someone/something down** mire, stick, entangle, ensnare, embroil, hamper, hinder, impede, obstruct, swamp, overwhelm.

bogus adjective **fake**, spurious, false, fraudulent, sham, counterfeit, forged, feigned; informal phoney, pretend.
OPPOSITES genuine.

boil[1] verb *the soup is boiling:* **simmer**, bubble, stew, seethe, froth, foam.

boil[2] noun *a boil on her neck:* **swelling**, spot, pimple, blister, gathering, pustule, carbuncle, abscess.

boisterous adjective **lively**, animated, exuberant, spirited, noisy, loud, rowdy, unruly, wild, uproarious, unrestrained, uninhibited, uncontrolled, rough, disorderly, riotous; informal rumbustious.
OPPOSITES restrained.

bold adjective **1** *bold adventurers:* **daring**, intrepid, brave, courageous, valiant, fearless, dauntless, audacious, daredevil, adventurous, heroic, plucky; informal gutsy, spunky. **2** *a bold pattern:* **striking**, vivid, bright, strong, eye-catching, prominent, gaudy, lurid, garish.
OPPOSITES timid, pale, faint.

bolster verb **strengthen**, reinforce, boost, fortify, support, buoy up, shore up, maintain, help, augment, increase.
OPPOSITES undermine.

bolt noun **1** *the bolt on the door:* **bar**, lock, catch, latch, fastener. **2** *nuts and bolts:* **pin**, rivet, peg, screw.
verb **1** *he bolted the door:* **lock**, bar, latch, fasten, secure. **2** *the lid was bolted down:* **pin**, rivet, peg, screw, fasten, fix. **3** *Anna*

bolted from the room: **dash,** dart, run, sprint, hurtle, rush, fly, shoot; informal tear, scoot, leg it. **4** *he bolted his breakfast:* **gobble,** gulp, wolf, guzzle, devour; informal demolish, polish off, shovel down; N. Amer. informal scarf, snarf.

bomb noun **explosive,** incendiary (device), missile, projectile.
verb *their headquarters were bombed:* **blow up,** blast, shell, blitz, strafe, pound, bombard, attack, assault, destroy, demolish.

bombard verb **1** *gun batteries bombarded the islands:* **shell,** pound, blitz, strafe, bomb, batter, blast, pelt. **2** *we were bombarded with information:* **swamp,** inundate, flood, deluge, snow under, overwhelm.

bonanza noun **windfall,** godsend, blessing, bonus, stroke of luck; informal jackpot.

bond noun **1** *the women forged a close bond:* **friendship,** relationship, fellowship, partnership, association, affiliation, alliance, attachment. **2** *I've broken my bond:* **promise,** pledge, vow, oath, word (of honour), guarantee, assurance, agreement, contract, pact, deal.
verb *the extensions are bonded to your hair:* **join,** fasten, fix, affix, attach, secure, bind, stick, fuse.

bonus noun **1** *the extra work's a real bonus:* **extra,** plus, benefit, advantage, boon, blessing, godsend, stroke of luck, attraction. **2** *she's on a good salary and she gets a bonus:* **gratuity,** handout, gift, present, reward, prize, incentive; informal perk, sweetener.
OPPOSITES disadvantage.

bony adjective **skinny,** thin, lean, gaunt, spare, skin and bone, skeletal, emaciated, underweight.
OPPOSITES plump.

book noun **1** *he published his first book in 1610:* **volume,** tome, publication, title, novel, treatise, manual. **2** *he scribbled in his book:* **notepad,** notebook, pad, exercise book, logbook, ledger, journal, diary; Brit. jotter, pocketbook; N. Amer. scratch pad.
verb **1** *she booked a table at the restaurant:* **reserve,** prearrange, order; informal bag. **2** *we booked a number of events in the Festival:* **arrange,** programme, schedule, timetable, line up, lay on; N. Amer. slate.
■ **book in** register, check in, enrol.

booklet noun **pamphlet,** brochure, leaflet, tract; N. Amer. folder, mailer.

boom noun **1** *the boom of the waves on the rocks:* **roar,** rumble, thunder, crashing, drumming, pounding, echoing, resonance, reverberation. **2** *an unprecedented boom in sales:* **increase,** growth, advance, boost, escalation, improvement, upsurge, upturn.
OPPOSITES slump.
verb **1** *thunder boomed overhead:* **roar,** rumble, thunder, crash, roll, clap, explode, bang, resound, blare, echo, resonate, reverberate. **2** *a voice boomed at her:* **shout,** yell, bellow, roar, thunder, bawl; informal holler. **3** *the market continued to boom:* **flourish,** thrive, prosper, burgeon, progress, improve, pick up, expand.
OPPOSITES whisper, slump.

boorish adjective **coarse,**

b

uncouth, rude, vulgar, uncivilized, unrefined, rough, thuggish, loutish, Neanderthal; Brit. informal yobbish; Austral. informal ocker.
OPPOSITES refined.

boost verb *they used advertising to boost sales:* **increase**, raise, escalate, improve, strengthen, inflate, push up, promote, advance, foster, stimulate, encourage, facilitate, help, assist, aid; informal hike, bump up.
OPPOSITES decrease.
noun **1** *a boost to one's morale:* **uplift**, lift, spur, encouragement, help, inspiration, stimulus, fillip; informal shot in the arm. **2** *a boost in sales:* **increase**, expansion, upturn, upsurge, rise, escalation, improvement, advance, growth, boom; informal hike.
OPPOSITES decrease.

boot verb **kick**, punt, tap, propel, drive, knock.

booth noun **1** *booths for different traders:* **stall**, stand, kiosk. **2** *a phone booth:* **cubicle**, kiosk, box, enclosure, cabin.

booty noun **loot**, plunder, haul, spoils, ill-gotten gains, pickings; informal swag.

border noun **1** *the border of a medieval manuscript:* **edge**, margin, perimeter, circumference, periphery, rim, fringe, verge, sides. **2** *the French border:* **frontier**, boundary, borderline, perimeter.
verb **1** *the fields were bordered by hedges:* **surround**, enclose, encircle, edge, fringe, bound, flank. **2** *the straps are bordered with gold braid:* **edge**, fringe, hem, trim, pipe, finish. **3** *the*

forest bordered Broadmoor: **adjoin**, abut, be next to, be adjacent to, touch.
■ **border on** verge on, approach, come close to, be comparable to, approximate to, be tantamount to.

bore¹ verb *bore a hole:* **drill**, pierce, perforate, puncture, punch, tunnel, burrow, mine, dig, gouge, sink.

bore² verb *the television news bored Philip:* **weary**, pall on, tire, fatigue, send to sleep, leave cold; informal turn off.
OPPOSITES interest.
noun *you can be such a bore:* **tedious person/thing**, tiresome person/thing, bother, nuisance, pest, annoyance, trial, thorn in one's flesh/side; informal drag, pain (in the neck), headache, hassle.

boredom noun **tedium**, ennui, apathy, weariness, dullness, monotony, repetitiveness, flatness, dreariness.
OPPOSITES interest, excitement.

boring adjective **tedious**, dull, dreary, monotonous, repetitive, uneventful, unimaginative, characterless, featureless, colourless, lifeless, uninteresting, unexciting, lacklustre, humdrum, mind-numbing, soul-destroying, wearisome, tiresome; informal deadly; Brit. informal samey; N. Amer. informal dullsville.
OPPOSITES interesting, exciting.

borrow verb **1** *we borrowed a lot of money:* **loan**, lease, hire; informal cadge, scrounge, bum, touch someone for; N. Amer. informal mooch; Austral./NZ informal bludge. **2** *adventurous chefs borrow foreign techniques:* **adopt**, take on, acquire, embrace.

OPPOSITES lend.

boss (informal) noun *the boss of a large company:* **head,** chief, principal, director, president, chief executive, chair, manager, supervisor, foreman, overseer, controller, employer, owner, proprietor; Brit. informal gaffer, governor; N. Amer. informal head honcho.

verb *you have no right to boss me about:* **order about/around,** dictate to, bully, push around/ about, call the shots, lay down the law; informal bulldoze, walk all over, railroad.

bossy adjective (informal) **domineering,** pushy, overbearing, imperious, officious, authoritarian, dictatorial; informal high and mighty.

OPPOSITES submissive.

bother verb 1 *no one bothered her:* **disturb,** trouble, inconvenience, pester, badger, harass, molest, plague; informal hassle, bug; N. English informal mither; N. Amer. informal ride. **2** *the incident was too small to bother about:* **mind,** care, worry, concern oneself, trouble oneself. **3** *there was something bothering him:* **worry,** trouble, concern, perturb, disturb, disquiet; informal rattle.

noun 1 *I don't want to put you to any bother:* **trouble,** effort, exertion, inconvenience, fuss, pains; informal hassle. **2** *the food was such a bother to cook:* **nuisance,** pest, palaver, rigmarole, job, trial, bind, bore, drag, inconvenience, trouble; informal hassle, headache, pain (in the neck). **3** *a spot of bother in the public bar:* **disorder,** fighting, trouble, disturbance, commotion, uproar; informal hoo-

ha, aggro, argy-bargy, kerfuffle.

bottom noun 1 *the bottom of the stairs:* **foot,** lowest part, base, foundation. **2** *the bottom of the car:* **underside,** underneath, undersurface, underbelly. **3** *the bottom of Lake Ontario:* **floor,** bed, depths. **4** *the bottom of his garden:* **farthest point,** far end, extremity. **5** (Brit.) *I've got a tattoo on my bottom:* **buttocks,** rear (end), rump, seat; informal behind, backside; Brit. informal bum, botty, jacksie; N. Amer. informal butt, fanny; humorous posterior.

OPPOSITES top, surface.

adjective *she sat on the bottom step:* **lowest,** last, bottommost.

OPPOSITES top.

bounce verb 1 *the ball bounced:* **rebound,** spring back, ricochet; N. Amer. carom. **2** *William bounced down the stairs:* **bound,** leap, jump, spring, bob, hop, skip, gambol, trip, prance.

noun 1 *the pitch's uneven bounce:* **springiness,** resilience, elasticity, give. **2** *she had lost her bounce:* **vitality,** vigour, energy, vivacity, liveliness, animation, sparkle, verve, spirit; informal get-up-and-go, pep, zing.

bound¹ adjective 1 *he raised his bound ankles:* **tied,** restrained, fixed, fastened, secured. **2** *she seemed bound to win:* **certain,** sure, very likely, destined. **3** *bound by the Official Secrets Act:* **constrained,** obliged, compelled, required, obligated. **4** *religion and morality are bound up with one another:* **connected,** linked, tied, united, allied, interdependent.

OPPOSITES free, unlikely, independent.

bound² verb *Louis came*

bounding down the stairs: leap, jump, spring, vault, bounce, hop, skip, dance, prance, gambol, gallop.

bound³ verb **1** *corporate freedom is bounded by law:* **limit**, restrict, confine, circumscribe, demarcate, delimit. **2** *the heath is bounded by a hedge:* **enclose**, surround, encircle, circle, border, close in/off, hem in. **3** *the garden was bounded by Mill Lane:* **border**, adjoin, abut, be next to, be adjacent to.

boundary noun **1** *the boundary between Israel and Jordan:* **border**, frontier, borderline, partition. **2** *the boundary between art and advertising:* **dividing line**, division, borderline, cut-off point. **3** *the boundary of his estate:* **limits**, confines, bounds, margins, edges, fringes, border, periphery, perimeter.

bouquet noun **1** *her bridal bouquet:* **posy**, nosegay, spray, corsage, buttonhole, garland, wreath, arrangement. **2** *the Chardonnay has a fine bouquet:* **aroma**, nose, smell, fragrance, perfume, scent, odour.

bourgeois adjective **middle-class**, conservative, conformist, conventional, propertied, provincial, suburban, small-town.
OPPOSITES proletarian.

bout noun **1** *a bout of exercise:* **spell**, period, stretch, stint, session, burst, flurry, spurt. **2** *a coughing bout:* **attack**, fit, spasm. **3** *he is fighting only his fifth bout:* **contest**, fight, match, round, competition, meeting, encounter.

bow¹ verb **1** *the officers bowed:* **nod**, bend, stoop, bob, curtsy,

kneel, genuflect. **2** *the mast quivered and bowed:* **bend**, buckle, curve, flex, deform. **3** *the government bowed to foreign pressure:* **give in**, submit, yield, surrender, succumb, capitulate.
noun *a perfunctory bow:* **nod**, bob, obeisance, curtsy, genuflection.

bow² noun *the bow of the tanker:* **prow**, front, stem, nose, head.

bowels plural noun **1** *a disorder of the bowels:* **intestines**, entrails, viscera, innards, digestive system; Medicine gut; informal guts, insides. **2** *the bowels of the ship:* **interior**, inside, core, belly, depths, recesses; informal innards.

bowl¹ verb *he bowled a hundred or so balls:* **throw**, pitch, hurl, toss, lob, fling, roll, launch, propel; informal chuck, sling, bung.

bowl² noun **dish**, basin, pot, crock, vessel, receptacle.

box¹ noun **1** **carton**, pack, packet, case, crate, chest, coffer, casket. **2** *a telephone box:* **booth**, cubicle, compartment, kiosk, cabin, hut.
verb *Muriel boxed up his clothes:* **pack**, package, parcel, encase, bundle, crate.

box² verb *he began boxing professionally:* **fight**, prizefight, spar, battle, brawl; informal scrap.

boxer noun **fighter**, pugilist, prizefighter; informal bruiser, scrapper.

boy noun **lad**, youth, young man, stripling; Scottish & N. English laddie; derogatory brat. See also CHILD.

boycott verb *they boycotted the election:* **shun**, snub, spurn, avoid, abstain from, reject, veto.

boyfriend | brave

OPPOSITES support.

noun *a boycott on the use of tropical timbers:* **ban,** veto, embargo, prohibition, sanction, restriction, avoidance, rejection.

boyfriend noun lover, sweetheart, beloved, darling, partner; informal fella, flame, fancy man; N. Amer. informal squeeze.

brace noun *the aquarium is supported by wooden braces:* **prop,** strut, stay, support, bracket.

verb **1** *the plane's wing is braced by rods:* **support,** shore up, prop up, hold up, buttress, reinforce. **2** *he braced his hand on the railing:* **steady,** secure, stabilize, poise, fix. **3** *brace yourself for disappointment:* **prepare,** get ready, gear up, nerve, steel, fortify; informal psych oneself up.

bracing adjective **invigorating,** refreshing, stimulating, energizing, exhilarating, restorative, rejuvenating.

bracket noun **1** *each speaker is fixed on a bracket:* **support,** prop, stay, batten, rest, mounting, rack, frame. **2** *a higher tax bracket:* **group,** category, grade, classification, division.

brag verb **boast,** crow, swagger, swank, bluster, gloat, show off, blow one's own trumpet, sing one's own praises; informal talk big.

brain noun **intelligence,** intellect, brainpower, cleverness, wit(s), reasoning, wisdom, judgement, understanding, sense; informal nous, grey matter; N. Amer. informal smarts.

brake noun **curb,** check,

restraint, constraint, control, limit.

OPPOSITES accelerator.

verb **slow (down),** decelerate, reduce speed.

OPPOSITES accelerate.

branch noun **1** *the branches of a tree:* **bough,** limb, arm, offshoot, twig. **2** *the judicial branch of government:* **division,** subdivision, section, subsection, department, unit, sector, wing. **3** *the corporation's New York branch:* **office,** bureau, agency, subsidiary.

verb **1** *the place where the road branches:* **fork,** divide, split, bifurcate. **2** *narrow paths branched off the road:* **diverge,** deviate, split off, fan out, radiate.

brand noun **1** *a new brand of margarine:* **make,** line, label, marque, trade name, trademark, proprietary name. **2** *her particular brand of humour:* **type,** kind, sort, variety, class, category, genre, style, ilk; N. Amer. stripe.

verb **1** *the letter M was branded on each animal:* **mark,** stamp, burn, sear. **2** *the scene was branded on her brain:* **engrave,** stamp, etch, imprint. **3** *the media branded us as communists:* **stigmatize,** mark out, denounce, discredit, vilify, label.

brandish verb **flourish,** wave, shake, wield, swing, swish.

brash adjective **1** *a brash man:* **self-assertive,** pushy, cocky, self-confident, arrogant, bold, audacious, brazen. **2** *brash colours:* **garish,** gaudy, loud, flamboyant, showy, tasteless; informal flashy, tacky.

OPPOSITES meek, subdued.

brave adjective **courageous,**

intrepid, bold, plucky, heroic,
fearless, daring, audacious,
dauntless, valiant; informal game,
gutsy.
OPPOSITES cowardly.
verb *fans braved freezing
temperatures:* **endure,** put up
with, bear, withstand, weather,
suffer, face, confront, defy.
OPPOSITES succumb to.

bravery noun **courage,** boldness,
heroism, intrepidity, nerve,
daring, fearlessness, audacity,
pluck, valour; informal guts; Brit.
informal bottle; N. Amer. informal
moxie.

brawl noun **fight,** skirmish,
scuffle, tussle, fray, melee,
fracas, fisticuffs; informal scrap,
set-to; Brit. informal punch-up.

brawny adjective **strong,**
muscular, muscly, well built,
powerful, strapping, burly,
sturdy; informal beefy, hulking.
OPPOSITES puny, weak.

breach noun **1** *a breach of the
regulations:* **contravention,**
violation, infringement,
infraction, transgression. **2** *a
breach in the sea wall:* **break,**
rupture, split, crack, fracture,
opening, gap, hole, fissure.
OPPOSITES observance.
verb **1** *the river breached its
banks:* **break (through),** burst,
rupture. **2** *the changes breached
union rules:* **break,** contravene,
violate, infringe, defy, disobey,
flout.

breadth noun **1** *a breadth of 100
metres:* **width,** broadness,
thickness, span, diameter. **2** *the
breadth of his knowledge:*
range, extent, scope, depth,
reach, compass, scale.

break verb **1 shatter,** smash,
crack, snap, fracture, fragment,
splinter, split, burst; informal
bust. **2** *the coffee machine has*

broken: **stop working,** break
down, give out, go wrong,
malfunction, crash; informal go
kaput, conk out; Brit. informal pack
up. **3** *traders who break the law:*
violate, contravene, infringe,
breach, defy, flout, disobey.
4 *the film broke box-office
records:* **beat,** surpass, exceed,
better, cap, top, outdo, outstrip.
5 *he tried to break the news
gently:* **reveal,** disclose, divulge,
impart, tell, announce, release.
OPPOSITES repair, obey.
noun **1** *the magazine has been
published without a break since
1950:* **stop,** interruption,
interval, gap, disruption,
stoppage, cessation. **2** *let's have
a break:* **rest,** respite, recess,
pause, interval, intermission;
informal breather, time out. **3** *a
break in the wall:* **gap,** opening,
space, hole, breach, chink,
crack, fracture, fissure, tear,
split.
■ **break down 1** *his van broke
down.* See **BREAK** verb sense 2.
2 *pay negotiations broke down:*
fail, collapse, founder, fall
through. **3** *Vicky broke down,
sobbing loudly:* burst into tears,
lose control, be overcome, go to
pieces; informal crack up, lose it.
■ **break something down
1** *police broke the door down:*
knock down, kick down, smash
in, pull down, tear down,
demolish. **2** *the information can
be broken down:* analyse,
categorize, classify, sort,
itemize, organize, divide,
separate, split. ■ **break
something off 1** *I broke off a
branch from the tree:* snap off,
pull off, sever, detach. **2** *they
threatened to break off
diplomatic relations:* end,
terminate, stop, cease, call a
halt to, suspend, discontinue;

informal **pull the plug on.** ■ **break out 1** *he broke out of the detention centre:* escape, abscond, flee, get free. **2** *fighting broke out:* flare up, start suddenly, erupt, burst out. ■ **break up 1** *the meeting broke up:* end, finish, stop, terminate, adjourn; N. Amer. recess. **2** *the crowd began to break up:* disperse, scatter, disband, part company. **3** *Danny and I broke up last year:* split up, separate, part (company), divorce. ■ **break something up 1** *police tried to break up the crowd:* disperse, scatter, disband. **2** *I'm not going to let you break up my marriage:* wreck, ruin, destroy.

breakdown noun **1** *the breakdown of the negotiations:* **failure**, collapse, disintegration, foundering. **2** *she suffered a breakdown:* **nervous breakdown**, collapse. **3** *a breakdown of the computer system:* **malfunction**, failure, crash. **4** *a breakdown of the figures:* **analysis**, itemization, classification, examination, investigation, explanation.

break-in noun **burglary**, robbery, theft, raid, breaking and entering; informal smash-and-grab.

breakthrough noun **advance**, development, step forward, success, improvement, discovery, innovation, revolution.
OPPOSITES setback.

breast noun **1** *the curve of her breasts:* **bosom(s)**, bust; informal boobs, knockers. **2** *her heart was hammering in her breast:* **chest**, bosom, front.

breath noun **inhalation**, gulp of air, puff, gasp, exhalation; Medicine respiration.

breathe verb **1** *she breathed deeply:* **inhale**, exhale, respire, draw breath, puff, pant, blow, gasp, wheeze; Medicine inspire, expire. **2** *'Together at last,' she breathed:* **whisper**, murmur, purr, sigh.

breathless adjective **1** *Will arrived breathless:* **out of breath**, panting, puffing, gasping, wheezing, winded; informal out of puff. **2** *the crowd were breathless with anticipation:* **eager**, agog, open-mouthed, excited, on the edge of one's seat, on tenterhooks.

breathtaking adjective **spectacular**, magnificent, awe-inspiring, awesome, astonishing, amazing, stunning, thrilling; informal sensational, out of this world.
OPPOSITES run-of-the-mill.

breed verb **1** *elephants breed readily in captivity:* **reproduce**, produce offspring, procreate, multiply, mate. **2** *she was born and bred in the village:* **bring up**, rear, raise, nurture. **3** *the political system bred discontent:* **cause**, produce, bring about, give rise to, arouse, stir up, generate, foster.
OPPOSITES stifle.
noun **1** *a breed of cow:* **variety**, stock, strain, race, species. **2** *a new breed of journalist:* **type**, kind, sort, variety, class, genre, generation.

breeding noun **(good) manners**, gentility, refinement, cultivation, polish, urbanity; informal class.

breeze noun **gentle wind**, puff of air, gust, draught; literary zephyr.

breezy adjective **1** *a breezy day:* **windy**, fresh, brisk, blowy, blustery, gusty. **2** *his breezy* *manner:* **jaunty,** cheerful, cheery, brisk, carefree, easy, casual, relaxed, informal, light-hearted; informal upbeat.

brew verb **1** *this beer is brewed in Frankfurt:* **ferment,** make. **2** *I'll brew some tea:* **prepare,** infuse, make; Brit. informal mash. **3** *there's trouble brewing:* **develop,** loom, be imminent, be on the horizon, be in the offing, be just around the corner.
noun **1** *home brew:* **beer,** ale. **2** *a hot reviving brew:* **drink,** beverage. **3** *a rich brew of myths and distortion:* **mixture,** mix, blend, combination, amalgam, cocktail.

bribe verb *they tried to bribe the police:* **buy off,** pay off, suborn; informal grease someone's palm, keep someone sweet, square; Brit. informal nobble.
noun *he accepted a bribe:* **inducement;** informal backhander, pay-off, kickback, sweetener.

bribery noun **corruption;** N. Amer. payola; informal palm-greasing, graft, hush money.

brief adjective **1** *a brief account:* **concise,** succinct, short, pithy, compact, thumbnail, potted. **2** *a brief visit:* **short,** flying, fleeting, hasty, hurried, quick, cursory, perfunctory, temporary, short-lived.
OPPOSITES lengthy.
noun **1** *my brief is to reorganize the project:* **instructions,** directions, directive, remit, mandate. **2** *a barrister's brief:* **case,** summary, argument, contention, dossier.
verb *employees were briefed about the decision:* **inform,** tell, update, notify, advise, prepare, prime, instruct; informal fill in, put in the picture.

briefing noun **1** *a press briefing:* **conference,** meeting, interview. **2** *this briefing explains the systems:* **information,** rundown, guidance, instructions, directions, guidelines.

briefly adverb **1** *tell me as briefly as you can:* **concisely,** succinctly. **2** *Henry paused briefly:* **momentarily,** temporarily, fleetingly. **3** *briefly, the plot is as follows:* **in short,** in brief, in a word, in a nutshell, in essence.

briefs plural noun **underpants,** pants, knickers, bikini briefs; N. Amer. shorts; informal panties; Brit. informal kecks.

brigade noun **squad,** team, group, band, party, crew, force, outfit.

bright adjective **1** *the bright surface of the metal:* **shining,** brilliant, dazzling, glaring, sparkling, flashing, glittering, gleaming, glowing, luminous, shiny, glossy. **2** *a bright morning:* **sunny,** cloudless, clear, fair, fine. **3** *bright colours:* **vivid,** brilliant, intense, strong, vibrant, bold, gaudy, lurid, garish. **4** *a bright young graduate:* **clever,** intelligent, quick-witted, smart, canny, astute, perceptive, ingenious; informal brainy.
OPPOSITES dull, cloudy, dark, stupid.

brighten verb **1** *sunshine brightened the room:* **illuminate,** light up, lighten. **2** *the sky brightened:* **become lighter,** grow brighter, lighten. **3** *Sarah brightened up:* **cheer up,** perk up, rally, feel heartened; informal buck up.

brilliance noun **1** *the brilliance of the sunshine:* **brightness,**

vividness, intensity, sparkle, glitter, blaze, luminosity, radiance. **2** *a philosopher of great brilliance:* **genius,** intelligence, talent, ability, prowess, skill, expertise, aptitude, flair, wisdom, intellect. **3** *the brilliance of Paris:* **splendour,** magnificence, grandeur, resplendence, glory. OPPOSITES dullness, stupidity, simplicity, lowliness.

brilliant adjective **1** *a shaft of brilliant light:* **bright,** shining, blazing, dazzling, vivid, intense, glaring, luminous, radiant. **2** *a brilliant student:* **clever,** bright, intelligent, smart, able, talented, gifted, skilful, astute; informal **brainy. 3** *his brilliant career:* **superb,** glorious, illustrious, impressive, remarkable, exceptional. OPPOSITES dim, stupid, undistinguished.

bring verb **1** *he brought over a tray:* **fetch,** carry, bear, take, convey, transport, shift. **2** *Philip brought his bride to his mansion:* **escort,** conduct, guide, lead. **3** *the wind brought rain:* **cause,** produce, create, generate, precipitate, occasion, provoke, lead to, give rise to, result in.

■ **bring something about/on.** See **BRING** sense 3. ■ **bring something in** introduce, launch, inaugurate, initiate, institute. ■ **bring something off** achieve, accomplish, bring about, succeed in, pull off, carry off, manage. ■ **bring something out** launch, establish, begin, start, found, set up, market, publish, issue. ■ **bring someone up** rear, raise, nurture, look after. ■ **bring something up** mention, raise, broach, introduce, air, suggest.

brink noun **1** *the brink of the crater:* **edge,** verge, margin, rim, lip, border, boundary. **2** *two countries on the brink of war:* **verge,** threshold, point, edge.

brisk adjective **1** *a brisk pace:* **quick,** rapid, fast, swift, speedy, hurried, energetic, lively; informal **nippy. 2** *his tone became brisk:* **no-nonsense,** businesslike, decisive, brusque, abrupt, short, sharp, curt, blunt, terse; informal **snappy.** OPPOSITES leisurely.

bristle noun **1** *the bristles on his chin:* **hair,** whisker; (bristles) stubble, five o'clock shadow. **2** *a hedgehog's bristles:* **spine,** prickle, quill, barb. verb **1** *the hair on the back of his neck bristled:* **rise,** stand up, stand on end. **2** *she bristled at his tone:* **take offence,** bridle, take umbrage, be offended. **3** *the roof bristled with antennae:* **be crowded,** be full, be packed, be jammed, be covered, overflow; informal **be thick,** be chock-full.

brittle adjective **breakable,** fragile, crisp, crumbly, delicate. OPPOSITES flexible, solid.

broach verb **bring up,** raise, introduce, mention, touch on, air.

broad adjective **1** *a broad expanse of prairie:* **wide,** extensive, vast, immense, great, spacious, expansive, sizeable, sweeping. **2** *a broad range of opportunities:* **comprehensive,** inclusive, extensive, wide, all-embracing, unlimited. **3** *this report gives a broad outline:* **general,** non-specific, rough, approximate, basic, loose, vague. OPPOSITES narrow, limited,

b

detailed.

broadcast verb **1** *the show will be broadcast worldwide:* **transmit,** relay, air, beam, show, televise, screen. **2** *the result was broadcast far and wide:* **report,** announce, publicize, advertise, make public, proclaim, spread, circulate.
noun *a live broadcast:* **transmission,** programme, show, telecast, production, screening.

broaden verb **1** *her smile broadened:* **widen,** expand, stretch (out), spread. **2** *the government tried to broaden its political base:* **expand,** enlarge, extend, widen, swell, increase, add to, develop.
OPPOSITES narrow, restrict.

broad-minded adjective **liberal,** tolerant, freethinking, indulgent, progressive, permissive, unshockable, unprejudiced, unbiased.
OPPOSITES intolerant.

brochure noun **booklet,** prospectus, catalogue, pamphlet, leaflet, circular, mailshot; N. Amer. folder.

broken adjective **1** *smashed,* shattered, fragmented, splintered, crushed, snapped, in bits, in pieces, cracked, split, fractured; informal in smithereens. **2** *his video's broken:* **faulty,** damaged, defective, not working, malfunctioning, out of order, broken down, down; informal kaput, bust, acting up; Brit. informal knackered. **3** *a night of broken sleep:* **interrupted,** disturbed, fitful, disrupted, discontinuous, intermittent. **4** *she spoke in broken English:* **halting,** hesitating, disjointed,

faltering, imperfect.
OPPOSITES whole, working, uninterrupted, fluent, perfect.

broker noun **dealer,** agent, middleman, intermediary, mediator, factor, liaison, stockbroker.
verb **arrange,** organize, orchestrate, work out, settle, clinch, negotiate, mediate.

brood noun *she looked after her brood well:* **offspring,** young, family, litter, clutch, progeny.
verb *he does brood a lot:* **think,** ponder, contemplate, meditate, ruminate, muse, worry, fret, agonize.

brook noun **stream,** rill; N. English beck; Scottish & N. English burn; N. Amer. & Austral./NZ creek.

brotherly adjective **fraternal,** friendly, comradely, affectionate, amicable, kind, devoted, loyal.

brow noun **1** **forehead,** temple. **2** *the brow of the hill:* **summit,** peak, top, crest, crown, head, pinnacle, apex.

brown adjective **1** *brown eyes:* **hazel,** chocolate, coffee, brunette, sepia, mahogany, tan, café au lait, caramel, chestnut. **2** *his face was brown from the sun:* **tanned,** suntanned, bronzed.
verb *the grill browns food evenly:* **grill,** toast, singe, sear, barbecue, sauté.

browse verb **look round/over,** scan, skim, glance, peruse, thumb, leaf, flick, dip into.

bruise noun *a bruise on her forehead:* **contusion,** bump, swelling, lump, mark, injury, welt.
verb **1** *her face was badly bruised:* **contuse,** injure, mark, discolour, make black and blue. **2** *every one of the apples is*

bruised: **mark,** discolour, blemish, damage, spoil.

brush¹ noun **1** *a dustpan and brush:* **broom,** sweeper, besom, whisk. **2** *he gave the seat a brush with his hand:* **clean,** sweep, wipe, dust. **3** *a brush with the law:* **encounter,** clash, confrontation, conflict, altercation, incident; informal run-in, to-do; Brit. informal spot of bother.
verb **1** *he spent his day brushing the floors:* **sweep,** clean, buff, polish, scrub. **2** *she brushed her hair:* **groom,** comb, neaten, tidy, smooth, arrange, curry. **3** *she felt his lips brush her cheek:* **touch,** stroke, caress, skim, sweep, graze, contact, kiss.
■ **brush something aside** disregard, ignore, dismiss, shrug off, wave aside, reject, spurn, laugh off, make light of; informal pooh-pooh. ■ **brush up (on)** revise, read up, go over, improve, polish up, enhance, hone, perfect; informal bone up on; Brit. informal swot up (on).

brush² noun **undergrowth,** scrub, brushwood, shrubs, bushes; N. Amer. underbrush, chaparral.

brusque adjective **curt,** abrupt, blunt, short, sharp, brisk, peremptory, gruff.
OPPOSITES polite.

brutal adjective **1** *a brutal attack:* **savage,** cruel, vicious, ferocious, barbaric, wicked, murderous, bloodthirsty, cold-blooded, callous, heartless, merciless, sadistic. **2** *brutal honesty:* **harsh,** unforgiving, pitiless, frank, blunt, tough, hard, bleak, disagreeable.
OPPOSITES gentle, kind.

bubbly adjective **1** *bubbly water:* **fizzy,** sparkling, effervescent, gassy, aerated, carbonated, frothy, foamy. **2** *she was bubbly and full of life:* **vivacious,** animated, ebullient, lively, high-spirited, bouncy, merry, happy, cheerful, sunny; informal chirpy.
OPPOSITES still, listless.

buckle noun *a belt buckle:* **clasp,** clip, catch, hasp, fastener.
verb **1** *he buckled the belt round his waist:* **fasten,** do up, hook, secure, clasp, clip. **2** *the front axle buckled:* **bend,** warp, twist, distort, contort, deform, crumple, collapse, give way.
OPPOSITES unbuckle, straighten.

budding adjective **promising,** up-and-coming, rising, in the making, aspiring, future, fledgling, developing.

budge verb **1** *the horses wouldn't budge:* **move,** shift, stir, go. **2** *I couldn't budge the door:* **dislodge,** shift, move, stir, reposition.

budget noun **1** *your budget for the week:* **financial plan,** forecast. **2** *the defence budget:* **allowance,** allocation, quota, funds, resources, capital.
verb *we have to budget £7,000 for the work:* **allocate,** allot, allow, earmark, designate, set aside.

buff¹ verb *he buffed the glass:* **polish,** burnish, shine, smooth, rub.

buff² noun (informal) *a film buff:* **enthusiast,** fan, devotee, lover, admirer, expert, aficionado, authority; informal freak, nut, addict.

buffer noun **cushion,** bulwark, shield, barrier, guard, safeguard.

buffet¹ noun **1** *a sumptuous buffet:* **cold table,** self-service meal, smorgasbord. **2** *a station buffet:* **cafe,** cafeteria, snack bar, canteen, restaurant.

buffet² verb *rough seas buffeted the coast:* **batter,** pound, lash, strike, hit.

bug noun **1** (informal) *a stomach bug:* **illness,** disease, sickness, disorder, upset, ailment, infection, virus; Brit. informal lurgy. **2** *bugs were crawling everywhere:* **insect,** minibeast; informal creepy-crawly, beastie. **3** *the bug planted on his phone:* **listening device,** hidden microphone, wire, wiretap, tap. **4** *the program developed a bug:* **fault,** error, defect, flaw, virus; informal glitch, gremlin.
verb *her conversations were bugged:* **eavesdrop on,** spy on, tap, monitor.

build verb **construct,** erect, put up, assemble, make, create, fashion, model, shape.
OPPOSITES demolish, dismantle.
noun *a man of slim build:* **physique,** frame, body, figure, form, shape, stature, proportions; informal vital statistics.
■ **build up** increase, grow, mount up, intensify, strengthen. ■ **build something up 1** *he built up his stamina:* boost, strengthen, increase, improve, augment, raise, enhance, swell. **2** *I have built up a collection of prints:* accumulate, amass, collect, gather.

building noun **structure,** construction, edifice, erection, property, premises, establishment.

build-up noun **increase,** growth, expansion, enlargement, escalation, accumulation, development.

bulbous adjective **bulging,** round, fat, rotund, swollen, distended, bloated.

bulge noun *a bulge under his jacket:* **swelling,** bump, lump, hump, protrusion.
verb *the veins in his neck bulged:* **swell,** stick out, project, protrude, stand out, puff out, balloon (out), fill out, distend.

bulk noun **1** *the sheer bulk of the bags:* **size,** volume, dimensions, proportions, mass, scale. **2** *the bulk of entrants were British:* **majority,** mass, generality, main part, lion's share, preponderance.
OPPOSITES minority.

bulky adjective **unwieldy,** cumbersome, unmanageable, awkward, ponderous, outsize, oversized; informal hulking.
OPPOSITES manageable, handy.

bullet noun **ball,** shot, pellet; informal slug; (bullets) lead.

bulletin noun **1** *a news bulletin:* **report,** dispatch, story, flash, statement, announcement, message, communication, communiqué. **2** *the society's monthly bulletin:* **newsletter,** news-sheet, proceedings, newspaper, magazine, gazette, review.

bully noun *the school bully:* **persecutor,** oppressor, tyrant, tormentor, intimidator, bully boy, thug.
verb **1** *the others bully him:* **persecute,** oppress, tyrannize, browbeat, intimidate, dominate; informal push around/about. **2** *she was bullied into helping:* **coerce,** pressure, press, push, prod, browbeat, dragoon, strong-arm; informal bulldoze, railroad, lean on.

bump noun **1** *I landed with a bump:* **jolt,** crash, smash,

smack, crack, bang, thud, thump; informal whack, wallop. **2** *I was woken by a bump*: **bang,** crack, boom, clang, knock, thud, thump, clunk, crash, smash. **3** *a bump in the road*: **hump,** lump, ridge, bulge, knob. **4** *a bump on his head*: **swelling,** lump, bulge, injury, contusion.
verb **1** *cars bumped into each other*: **hit,** crash, smash, slam, bang, knock, run, plough, ram, collide with, strike; N. Amer. impact. **2** *a cart bumping along the road*: **bounce,** jolt, jerk, rattle, shake.

bumper adjective **exceptional,** large, abundant, rich, bountiful, good, plentiful, record, successful; informal whopping.
OPPOSITES meagre.

bumpy adjective **1** *a bumpy road*: **uneven,** rough, rutted, pitted, potholed, lumpy, rocky. **2** *a bumpy ride*: **bouncy,** rough, uncomfortable, jolting, lurching, jerky, jarring, bone-shaking.
OPPOSITES smooth.

bunch noun **1** *a bunch of flowers*: **bouquet,** posy, nosegay, spray, wreath, garland. **2** *a bunch of keys*: **cluster,** clump, knot, group.
verb *the runners bunched up behind him*: **cluster,** huddle, gather, congregate, collect, amass, group, crowd.
OPPOSITES scatter.

bundle noun *a bundle of clothes*: **bunch,** roll, clump, wad, parcel, sheaf, bale, pile, stack, heap, mass; informal load, wodge.
verb **1** *she bundled up her things*: **tie,** pack, parcel, wrap, swathe, roll, fold, bind.
2 (informal) *he was bundled into a van*: **push,** shove, thrust, throw, propel, jostle, manhandle.

bungle verb **mishandle,** mismanage, mess up, spoil, ruin; informal blow, botch, fluff, make a hash of, screw up; Brit. informal make a pig's ear of, cock up; N. Amer. informal goof up.
OPPOSITES carry off.

bungling adjective **incompetent,** blundering, amateurish, inept, unskilful, clumsy, awkward, bumbling; informal ham-fisted, cack-handed.
OPPOSITES competent.

buoy noun **float,** marker, beacon.

buoyant adjective **1** *a buoyant substance*: **floating,** floatable. **2** *a buoyant mood*: **cheerful,** cheery, happy, light-hearted, carefree, joyful, bubbly, bouncy, sunny; informal upbeat.
OPPOSITES gloomy.

burden noun *a financial burden*: **responsibility,** onus, obligation, liability, trouble, care, problem, worry, strain.
verb *avoid burdening them with guilt*: **oppress,** trouble, worry, weigh down, harass, upset, distress, haunt, afflict.

bureau noun **1** *an oak bureau*: **desk,** writing table, secretaire. **2** *the intelligence bureau*: **department,** agency, office, division, branch, section, station, unit.

bureaucracy noun **1** *the ranks of the bureaucracy*: **civil service,** government, administration, establishment, system, powers that be, authorities. **2** *unnecessary bureaucracy*: **red tape,** rules and regulations, protocol, officialdom, paperwork.

burgeon verb **grow,** increase, rocket, mushroom, expand, escalate, swell, boom, flourish, thrive, prosper.

b

b

burglar noun **housebreaker,** robber, thief, raider, looter, cat burglar.

burglary noun **1** *a sentence for burglary:* **housebreaking,** breaking and entering, theft, stealing, robbery, larceny, looting, pillaging. **2** *a series of burglaries:* **break-in,** theft, robbery, raid; informal smash-and-grab; N. Amer. informal heist.

burgle verb **rob,** loot, steal from, pillage.

burial noun **funeral,** interment, committal, inhumation, entombment.
OPPOSITES exhumation.

burly adjective **strapping,** well built, strong, muscular, muscly, hefty, sturdy, brawny; informal hunky, beefy.
OPPOSITES puny.

burn verb **1** *the coal was burning:* **be on fire,** be alight, blaze, go up (in smoke), be in flames, smoulder, glow. **2** *he burned the letters:* **set fire to,** set alight, set light to, kindle, ignite, touch off, incinerate, cremate; informal torch. **3** *I burned my dress with the iron:* **scorch,** singe, sear, char, blacken, brand.

burning adjective **1** *burning coals:* **on fire,** blazing, flaming, fiery, glowing, red-hot, smouldering. **2** *a burning desire:* **intense,** passionate, deep-seated, profound, strong, ardent, fervent, urgent, fierce, consuming. **3** *burning issues:* **important,** crucial, critical, vital, essential, pivotal, urgent, pressing, compelling.

burrow noun *a rabbit's burrow:* **warren,** tunnel, hole, dugout, lair, set, den, earth.
verb *rabbits burrowed among the roots:* **tunnel,** dig, excavate, mine, bore, channel.

burst verb **1** *one balloon burst:* **split (open),** rupture, break, tear. **2** *a shell burst:* **explode,** blow up, detonate, go off. **3** *smoke burst through the hole:* **gush,** erupt, surge, rush, stream, flow, pour, spurt, jet. **4** *he burst into the room:* **charge,** plunge, barge, plough, hurtle, career, rush, dash, tear.
noun **1** *a burst in the tyre:* **rupture,** puncture, breach, split, blowout. **2** *mortar bursts:* **explosion,** detonation, blast, eruption, bang. **3** *a burst of gunfire:* **volley,** salvo, barrage, hail, rain. **4** *a burst of activity:* **outbreak,** eruption, flare-up, blaze, attack, fit, rush, storm, surge, spurt.

bury verb **1** *the dead were buried:* **inter,** lay to rest, entomb. **2** *she buried her face in her hands:* **hide,** conceal, cover, enfold, cup, sink. **3** *the bullet buried itself in the wood:* **embed,** sink, implant, submerge, lodge.
OPPOSITES exhume.

bush noun **1** *a rose bush:* **shrub,** thicket; (**bushes**) undergrowth, shrubbery. **2** *the bush:* **wilds,** wilderness, backwoods; N. Amer. backcountry; Austral./NZ outback, backblocks; N. Amer. informal boondocks.

bushy adjective **thick,** shaggy, curly, fuzzy, bristly, fluffy, woolly.
OPPOSITES sleek, wispy.

business noun **1** *she has to smile in her business:* **work,** occupation, profession, career, employment, job, position. **2** *who do you do business with?* **trade,** commerce, dealing, traffic, dealings, transactions, negotiations. **3** *her own*

business: **firm,** company, concern, enterprise, venture, organization, operation, undertaking; informal outfit.
4 *none of your business:* **concern,** affair, responsibility, duty. **5** *an odd business:* **affair,** matter, case, circumstance, situation, event, incident.

businessman, businesswoman noun **executive,** entrepreneur, industrialist, merchant, dealer, trader, manufacturer, tycoon, employer, broker, buyer, seller, tradesman, retailer, supplier.

bust noun **1** *her large bust:* **bosom,** breasts, chest; informal boobs, knockers; N. Amer. informal bazooms. **2** *a bust of Caesar:* **sculpture,** carving, effigy, statue, head and shoulders.

bustle verb *people bustled about:* **rush,** dash, hurry, scurry, scuttle, scamper, scramble; informal scoot, beetle, buzz.
noun *the bustle of the market:* **activity,** action, liveliness, excitement, tumult, commotion, hubbub, whirl; informal toing and froing.

bustling adjective **busy,** crowded, swarming, teeming, humming, buzzing, hectic, lively.
OPPOSITES leisurely, deserted.

busy adjective **1** *they are very busy at the moment:* **hard at work,** involved, rushed off one's feet, hard-pressed, on the job; informal on the go, hard at it; Brit. informal on the hop. **2** *I'm sorry, she is busy:* **unavailable,** engaged, occupied, absorbed, engrossed, immersed, preoccupied, working; informal tied up. **3** *a busy day:* **hectic,** active, lively, full, eventful, energetic, tiring.

OPPOSITES idle, free, quiet.
verb *he busied himself with paperwork:* **occupy,** involve, engage, concern, absorb, engross, immerse, distract, divert.

but conjunction **1** *he stumbled but didn't fall:* **however,** nevertheless, nonetheless, even so, yet, still. **2** *I am clean but you aren't:* **whereas,** conversely.
preposition *everyone but him:* **except (for),** apart from, other than, besides, aside from, with the exception of, bar.
■ **but for** except for, if it were not for, barring, notwithstanding.

butt[1] verb *she butted him:* **ram,** headbutt, bump, poke, prod, push, shove, thrust.
■ **butt in** interrupt, intrude, break in, cut in, interfere, put one's oar in; informal poke one's nose in; Brit. informal chip in.

butt[2] noun *the butt of a joke:* **target,** victim, object, dupe, laughing stock.

butt[3] noun **1** *the butt of a gun:* **stock,** end, handle, hilt, haft. **2** *a cigarette butt:* **stub,** end, stump; informal fag end, dog end.
verb *the shop butts up against the house:* **adjoin,** abut, be next to, be adjacent to, border (on), neighbour.

buttocks plural noun **bottom,** rear (end), rump, seat; informal behind, backside; Brit. informal bum, botty, jacksie; N. Amer. informal butt, fanny; humorous posterior.

buy verb *they bought a new house:* **purchase,** acquire, obtain, get, pick up, snap up, invest in; informal get hold of, score.
OPPOSITES sell.
noun (informal) *a good buy:*

purchase, deal, bargain, investment, acquisition.

buzz noun **1** *the buzz of the bees:* **hum,** murmur, drone. **2** *an insistent buzz from her control panel:* **tone,** purr, ring, warble, note, beep, alarm, warning.

by preposition **1** *I broke it by forcing the lid:* **through,** as a result of, because of, by dint of, by means of, with the help of, by virtue of. **2** *be there by midday:* **no later than,** in good time for, before. **3** *a house by the lake:* **next to,** beside, alongside, by/at the side of, adjacent to.

adverb *people hurried by:* **past,** on, along.

bypass noun ring road, detour, diversion, alternative route; Brit. relief road.

verb **1** *bypass the farm:* **go round,** go past, make a detour round, avoid. **2** *the system had been bypassed:* **ignore,** sidestep, avoid, evade, escape, elude, skirt, dodge, circumvent, get round, go over the head of, pass over; informal short-circuit, duck.

bystander noun onlooker, passer-by, observer, spectator, eyewitness.

Cc

cab noun taxi, taxi cab; Brit. minicab, hackney carriage; N. Amer. hack.

cabin noun **1** *a ship's cabin:* **berth,** stateroom, compartment. **2** *a cabin by the lake:* **hut,** log cabin, shanty, shack, chalet; Scottish bothy; N. Amer. cabana.

cabinet noun cupboard, bureau, chest of drawers.

cable noun **1** *a thick cable moored the ship:* **rope,** cord, line; Nautical hawser; N. Amer. choker. **2** *electric cables:* **wire,** lead, cord, power line; Brit. flex.

cache noun hoard, store, stockpile, stock, supply, reserve, arsenal; informal stash.

cafe noun snack bar, cafeteria, coffee bar/shop, tea room/shop, bistro, brasserie; N. Amer. diner, lunchroom.

cafeteria noun self-service restaurant, canteen, cafe,

buffet, refectory, mess hall.

cage noun *the lion's cage:* **enclosure,** pen, pound, coop, hutch, birdcage, aviary.

verb *they were caged up like animals:* **confine,** shut in/up, pen, coop up, enclose.

cagey adjective (informal) **secretive,** guarded, tight-lipped, reticent, evasive; informal playing one's cards close to one's chest.

OPPOSITES open.

cajole verb persuade, wheedle, coax, talk into, prevail on; informal sweet-talk, soft-soap.

cake noun **1** *cream cakes:* **bun,** pastry, gateau, slice. **2** *a cake of soap:* **bar,** tablet, block, slab, lump, wedge.

verb *boots caked with mud:* **coat,** encrust, plaster, cover.

calculate verb **1** *the interest is calculated daily:* **compute,** work out, reckon, figure, add up/ together, count up, tally; total;

Brit. **tot up. 2** *his words were calculated to wound her:* **intend,** mean, design.

calculated adjective **deliberate,** premeditated, planned, pre-planned, preconceived, intentional, intended.
OPPOSITES unintentional, rash.

calculating adjective **cunning,** crafty, wily, sly, scheming, devious, disingenuous.
OPPOSITES ingenuous, innocent.

calculation noun **1** *the calculation of the overall cost:* **computation,** reckoning, adding up, counting up, working out, figuring; Brit. totting up. **2** *political calculations:* **assessment,** judgement, forecast, projection, prediction.

calendar noun *my social calendar:* **schedule,** programme, diary, timetable, agenda.

calibre noun **1** *a man of his calibre:* **quality,** merit, distinction, stature, excellence, ability, expertise, talent, capability. **2** *rugby of this calibre:* **standard,** level, quality. **3** *the calibre of a gun:* **bore,** diameter, gauge.

call verb **1** *'Wait for me!' she called:* **cry out,** shout, yell, sing out, chant, exclaim; informal holler. **2** *Mum called me in the morning:* **wake (up),** awaken, rouse; Brit. informal knock up. **3** *I'll call you tomorrow:* **phone,** telephone, give someone a call; Brit. ring (up), give someone a ring; informal call up; Brit. informal give someone a bell, get someone on the blower; N. Amer. informal get someone on the horn. **4** *Rose called a taxi:* **summon,** send for, order. **5** *he called at Ashgrove Cottage:* **pay a visit to,** visit, call/drop/look

in on, drop/stop by, pop into, nip over to. **6** *the prime minister called a meeting:* **convene,** summon, assemble. **7** *they called their daughter Hannah:* **name,** christen, baptize, designate, style, term, dub. **8** *I would call him a friend:* **describe as,** regard as, look on as, think of as, consider to be.

noun **1** *I heard calls from the auditorium:* **cry,** shout, yell, chant, exclamation; informal holler. **2** *the call of the barn owl:* **cry,** song. **3** *I'll give you a call tomorrow:* **phone call,** telephone call; Brit. ring; informal buzz; Brit. informal bell. **4** *a call for party unity:* **appeal,** request, plea. **5** *there's no call for that kind of language:* **need,** necessity, reason, justification, excuse. **6** *there's no call for expensive wine here:* **demand,** desire, market. **7** *the call of the Cairngorms:* **attraction,** appeal, lure, allure, pull, draw.

■ **call for 1** *this calls for a celebration:* **require,** need, necessitate, make necessary, demand, be grounds for, justify, warrant. **2** *he called for an enquiry:* **ask for,** request, seek, apply for, appeal for, demand, insist on, order. ■ **call something off** **cancel,** abandon, scrap, drop, axe; informal scrub; N. Amer. informal redline. ■ **call someone up** (informal) *Roland called me up.* See **CALL** verb sense 3. **2** *they called up the reservists:* **enlist,** recruit, conscript; US draft.

calling noun **profession,** occupation, vocation, career.

callous adjective **heartless,** unfeeling, uncaring, cold, cold-hearted, hard, as hard as nails, hard-hearted, insensitive,

unsympathetic.
OPPOSITES kind, compassionate.
calm adjective **1** *she seemed very calm:* **relaxed,** serene, tranquil, unruffled, unperturbed, unflustered, untroubled, unexcitable, unemotional, phlegmatic, composed; informal unflappable, laid-back. **2** *the night was calm:* **windless,** still, quiet, tranquil, smooth.
OPPOSITES excited, nervous, stormy.
noun **1** *his usual calm deserted him:* **composure,** coolness, calmness, self-possession, sangfroid, serenity, tranquillity; informal cool, unflappability.
2 *calm prevailed:* **tranquillity,** stillness, quiet, peace.
■ **calm down 1** *I tried to calm him down:* soothe, pacify, placate, mollify; Brit. quieten (down); Austral. square off. **2** *she forced herself to calm down:* compose oneself, recover/regain one's composure, control oneself, pull oneself together, simmer down, cool down/off, take it easy; Brit. quieten down; informal get a grip, keep one's shirt on; N. Amer. informal decompress.
camouflage noun *the stripes act as camouflage:* **disguise,** mask, screen, cover, cloak, front, facade, blind, concealment, subterfuge.
verb *I used cement to camouflage the hole:* **disguise,** hide, conceal, mask, screen, cover (up).
camp noun **1** *an army camp:* **campsite,** encampment, camping ground, bivouac, base, settlement. **2** *the liberal and conservative camps:* **faction,** wing, group, lobby, caucus, bloc.

campaign noun **1** *Napoleon's Russian campaign:* **operation(s),** manoeuvre(s), offensive, attack, war, battle, crusade. **2** *the campaign to reduce vehicle emissions:* **effort,** drive, push, struggle, movement, crusade, operation, strategy.
verb *they are campaigning for political reform:* **fight,** battle, push, press, strive, struggle, lobby, agitate.
cancel verb **1** *the match was cancelled:* **call off,** abandon, scrap, drop, axe; informal scrub; N. Amer. informal redline. **2** *his visa has been cancelled:* **annul,** invalidate, declare null and void, void, revoke, rescind, retract, withdraw.
■ **cancel out** neutralize, negate, nullify, wipe out, balance (out), make up for, compensate for, offset.
OPPOSITES arrange, confirm, reinstate, issue.
cancer noun **(malignant) growth,** tumour.
candid adjective **frank,** forthright, direct, blunt, open, honest, truthful, sincere; informal upfront; N. Amer. informal on the up and up.
OPPOSITES guarded.
candidate noun **applicant,** contender, competitor, entrant, claimant, nominee, interviewee, examinee, possible; Brit. informal runner.
canny adjective **shrewd,** astute, smart, sharp, discerning, discriminating, perceptive.
OPPOSITES foolish.
canopy noun **awning,** shade, sunshade, covering.
canvass verb **1** *he's canvassing for the Green Party:* **campaign,** electioneer. **2** *they promised to*

canvass all members: **poll,** question, survey, interview, consult.

canyon noun **ravine,** gorge, gully, chasm, abyss, gulf; N. Amer. gulch, coulee.

cap noun **1** *a white plastic cap:* **lid,** top, stopper, cork, bung; N. Amer. stopple. **2** *a cap on spending:* **limit,** ceiling, curb, check.
verb **1** *mountains capped with snow:* **top,** crown, cover, coat, tip. **2** *budgets will be capped:* **limit,** restrict, curb, control, peg.

capability noun **ability,** capacity, power, potential, competence, aptitude, faculty, skill, talent, flair; informal know-how.
OPPOSITES inability.

capable adjective **able,** competent, effective, proficient, accomplished, experienced, skilful, talented, gifted; informal useful.
OPPOSITES incompetent.

capacity noun **1** *the capacity of the freezer:* **volume,** size, dimensions, measurements, proportions. **2** *his capacity to inspire trust.* See **CAPABILITY. 3** *in his capacity as Commander-in-Chief:* **role,** function, position, post, job, office.

cape[1] noun *a woollen cape:* **cloak,** mantle, poncho.

cape[2] noun *the ship rounded the cape:* **headland,** promontory, point, head, horn, mull, peninsula.

capital noun **money,** finance(s), funds, cash, wherewithal, means, assets, wealth, resources.

capitalism noun **private enterprise,** free enterprise, the free market, private ownership.
OPPOSITES communism.

capitalize
■ **capitalize on** take advantage of, profit from, make the most of, exploit, develop; informal cash in on.

capitulate verb **surrender,** give in, yield, concede defeat, give up (the struggle), submit, lay down one's arms, throw in the towel/sponge.
OPPOSITES resist, hold out.

capricious adjective **fickle,** volatile, unpredictable, temperamental, erratic, wayward, whimsical, flighty, faddish.
OPPOSITES consistent.

capsule noun **1** *he swallowed a capsule:* **pill,** tablet, lozenge, pastille; informal tab. **2** *a space capsule:* **module,** craft, probe.

captain noun **1** *the ship's captain:* **commander,** master; informal skipper. **2** *the team captain:* **leader,** head, chief; informal boss, skipper.

caption noun **title,** heading, legend, description.

captivate verb **enthral,** charm, enchant, bewitch, fascinate, beguile, entrance, delight, attract, allure.
OPPOSITES repel, bore.

captive noun **prisoner,** convict, detainee, hostage, prisoner of war, internee.
adjective **confined,** caged, incarcerated, locked up, jailed, imprisoned, interned, detained.
OPPOSITES free.

captivity noun **imprisonment,** incarceration, confinement, detention, internment.
OPPOSITES freedom.

capture verb **1** *Mark Dawes was captured in Moscow:* **catch,** apprehend, seize, arrest. **2** *guerrillas have captured*

several towns: **occupy,** invade, conquer, seize, take.
OPPOSITES release, abandon, liberate.
noun *he tried to avoid capture:* **arrest,** seizure.

car noun **1** *he drove up in his car:* **motor,** motor car, automobile; informal **wheels;** N. Amer. informal auto. **2** *the dining car:* **carriage,** coach; Brit. **saloon.**

carcass noun **corpse,** dead body, remains; Medicine **cadaver;** informal stiff.

care noun **1** *the care of the child:* **safe keeping,** supervision, custody, charge, protection, responsibility, guardianship. **2** *she chose her words with care:* **discretion,** caution, sensitivity, thought, regard, consideration. **3** *the cares of the day:* **worry,** anxiety, trouble, concern, stress, pressure, strain.
OPPOSITES neglect, carelessness.
verb *the teachers didn't care about our work:* **be concerned,** worry (oneself), trouble/concern oneself, bother, mind, be interested; informal give a damn/hoot.
■ **care for 1** *he cares for his children:* love, be fond of, be devoted to, treasure, adore, dote on, think the world of, worship. **2** *the hospice cares for the terminally ill:* look after, take care of, tend, attend to, minister to, nurse.

career noun *a business career:* **profession,** occupation, vocation, calling, life's work, employment.
verb *they careered down the hill:* **hurtle,** rush, shoot, race, speed, charge, hare, fly; informal belt, tear; Brit. informal bucket.

carefree adjective **unworried,** untroubled, blithe, nonchalant,
happy-go-lucky, free and easy, easy-going, relaxed; informal laid-back.
OPPOSITES troubled.

careful adjective **1** *be careful when you go up the stairs:* **cautious,** alert, attentive, watchful, vigilant, wary, on one's guard, circumspect. **2** *careful with money:* **prudent,** thrifty, economical, sparing, frugal. **3** *careful consideration of the facts:* **attentive,** conscientious, painstaking, meticulous, diligent, assiduous, scrupulous, methodical.
OPPOSITES careless, extravagant, casual.

careless adjective **1** *careless motorists:* **inattentive,** negligent, heedless, irresponsible, impetuous, reckless. **2** *careless work:* **shoddy,** slapdash, slipshod, scrappy, slovenly, sloppy, negligent, lax, slack, disorganized, hasty, hurried. **3** *a careless remark:* **thoughtless,** insensitive, indiscreet, unguarded, incautious, inadvertent.
OPPOSITES careful, attentive, meticulous, deliberate, calculated.

caress verb **stroke,** touch, fondle, brush, feel, skim.

caretaker noun **janitor,** attendant, porter, custodian, concierge; N. Amer. superintendent.
adjective *the caretaker manager:* **temporary,** acting, provisional, substitute, interim, stand-in, fill-in, stopgap; N. Amer. informal pinch-hitting.
OPPOSITES permanent.

cargo noun **freight,** load, haul, consignment, delivery, shipment, goods, merchandise.

carnage noun slaughter, massacre, murder, butchery, bloodbath, bloodletting, holocaust.

carnival noun festival, fiesta, fête, fair, gala, Mardi Gras.

carp verb complain, find fault, quibble, grumble, grouse, whine; informal nit-pick, gripe, moan, bitch, whinge.
OPPOSITES praise.

carpenter noun woodworker, joiner, cabinetmaker; Brit. informal chippy.

carriage noun 1 a railway carriage: coach, car; Brit. saloon. 2 a horse and carriage: wagon, coach. 3 an erect carriage: posture, bearing, gait; Brit. deportment.

carry verb 1 she carried the box into the kitchen: convey, transfer, transport, move, take, bring, bear, fetch; informal cart, hump, lug. 2 satellites carry the signal over the Atlantic: transmit, conduct, relay, communicate, convey, beam, send. 3 a resolution was carried: approve, pass, accept, endorse, ratify. 4 his voice carried across the quay: be audible, travel, reach, be heard.
OPPOSITES reject.
■ carry on continue, keep (on), go on, persist in; informal stick with/at. ■ carry something out 1 they carried out an operation: conduct, perform, execute, implement. 2 I carried out my promise: keep, honour, fulfil, observe, abide by, comply with, adhere to, stick to.

carton noun box, package, cardboard box, case, container, pack, packet.

cartoon noun 1 a cartoon of the Prime Minister: caricature, parody, lampoon, satire; informal take-off, send-up. 2 he was reading cartoons: comic strip, comic, graphic novel. 3 we watched Yogi Bear cartoons: cartoon film, animated film, animation.

cartridge noun cassette, magazine, canister, case, container.

carve verb 1 he carved horn handles: sculpt, cut, hew, whittle, chisel, shape, fashion. 2 I carved my initials on the tree: engrave, incise, score, cut. 3 he carved the roast chicken: slice, cut up, chop.
■ carve something up divide, break up, partition, apportion, subdivide, split up, share out.

case¹ noun 1 a classic case of overreaction: instance, example, occurrence, occasion, demonstration, illustration. 2 is that the case? situation, position, state of affairs, circumstances, conditions, facts; Brit. state of play; informal score. 3 the officers on the case: assignment, job, project, investigation, exercise. 4 he lost his case: lawsuit, legal action, trial, legal proceedings, litigation. 5 the case against animal testing: argument, defence, justification, vindication, exposition, thesis.

case² noun 1 a cigarette case: container, box, canister, holder. 2 a seed case: casing, cover, sheath, envelope, sleeve, jacket, shell. 3 (Brit.) she threw some clothes into a case: suitcase, travel bag, valise; (cases) luggage, baggage. 4 a glass display case: cabinet, cupboard.

cash noun 1 a wallet stuffed with cash: money, currency, bank notes, coins, change; N. Amer. bills; informal dough, loot; Brit.

informal dosh, brass; N. Amer. informal dinero. **2** *a lack of cash:* **finance,** money, resources, funds, assets, means, wherewithal.

cashier noun **clerk,** teller, banker, treasurer, bursar, purser.

cast verb **1** *he cast the stone into the stream:* **throw,** toss, fling, pitch, hurl, lob; informal chuck, sling, bung. **2** *she cast a fearful glance over her shoulder:* **direct,** shoot, throw, fling, send. **3** *each citizen cast a vote:* **register,** record, enter, file. **4** *the fire cast a soft light:* **emit,** give off, throw, send out, radiate.
5 *printing type was cast by hand:* **mould,** fashion, form, shape, forge.
noun **1** *a cast of his hand:* **mould,** die, matrix, shape, casting, model. **2** *the cast of 'Hamlet':* **actors,** performers, players, company, troupe, dramatis personae, characters.

caste noun **class,** rank, level, order, stratum, echelon, status.

castle noun **fortress,** fort, stronghold, fortification, keep, citadel, palace, chateau, tower.

casual adjective **1** *a casual attitude to life:* **unconcerned,** uncaring, indifferent, lackadaisical, nonchalant, offhand, flippant, easy-going, free and easy, blithe, carefree, devil-may-care; informal laid-back. **2** *a casual remark:* **offhand,** spontaneous, unthinking, unconsidered, impromptu, throwaway, unguarded; informal off-the-cuff. **3** *a casual glance:* **cursory,** perfunctory, superficial, passing, fleeting. **4** *a casual acquaintance:* **slight,** superficial. **5** *casual work:* **temporary,** freelance, irregular,

occasional. **6** *a casual meeting changed his life:* **chance,** accidental, unplanned, unintended, unexpected, unforeseen. **7** *a casual shirt:* **informal,** leisure, everyday; informal sporty. **8** *the inn's casual atmosphere:* **relaxed,** friendly, informal, easy-going, free and easy; informal laid-back.
OPPOSITES serious, premeditated, careful, good, permanent, planned, formal.

casualty noun **victim,** sufferer, fatality, death, loss, wounded person, injured person.

cat noun **feline,** tomcat, tom, kitten; informal pussy (cat), puss, kitty; Brit. informal moggie, mog.

catalogue noun *a library catalogue:* **directory,** register, index, list, listing, record, schedule, archive, inventory.
verb *the collection is fully catalogued:* **classify,** categorize, index, list, archive, record, itemize.

catastrophe noun **disaster,** calamity, cataclysm, ruin, tragedy, fiasco, debacle.

catch verb **1** *he caught the ball:* **seize,** grab, snatch, grasp, grip, clutch, intercept, trap, receive, get. **2** *we've caught the thief:* **capture,** seize, apprehend, arrest, take prisoner, trap, snare, net; informal nab, collar; Brit. informal nick. **3** *her heel caught in a hole:* **become trapped,** become entangled, snag, jam, wedge, lodge, get stuck. **4** *they were caught siphoning petrol:* **discover,** find, come across, stumble on, chance on, surprise. **5** *he caught malaria:* **contract,** go/come down with, be taken ill with, develop, pick up.
OPPOSITES drop, miss, release.

catch noun **1** *he inspected the catch:* **haul,** net, bag, yield. **2** *he slipped the catch:* **latch,** lock, fastener, clasp, hasp. **3** *there must be a catch:* **snag,** disadvantage, drawback, stumbling block, hitch, complication, problem, trap, trick.
■ **catch on** (informal) **1** *radio soon caught on:* **become popular,** take off, boom, flourish, thrive. **2** *I caught on fast:* **understand,** comprehend, learn, see the light; informal cotton on, latch on.

catching adjective (informal) **infectious,** contagious, communicable; dated infective.
OPPOSITES non-infectious.

catchy adjective **memorable,** unforgettable, haunting, appealing, popular.
OPPOSITES forgettable.

categorical adjective **unqualified,** unconditional, unequivocal, absolute, explicit, unambiguous, definite, direct, emphatic, positive, out-and-out.
OPPOSITES qualified, equivocal.

category noun **class,** classification, group, grouping, bracket, heading, set, type, sort, kind, grade, order, rank.

cater
■ **cater for 1** *we cater for vegetarians:* **provide (food) for,** feed, serve, cook for. **2** *a resort catering for older holidaymakers:* **serve,** provide for, meet the needs/wants of, accommodate. **3** *he seemed to cater for all tastes:* **take into account/consideration,** allow for, consider, bear in mind, make provision for, have regard for.

cattle plural noun **cows,** oxen, herd, livestock.

cause noun **1** *the cause of the fire:* **source,** root, origin, beginning(s), starting point, originator, author, creator, agent. **2** *there is no cause for alarm:* **reason,** grounds, justification, call, need, necessity, occasion, excuse. **3** *the cause of human rights | a good cause:* **principle,** ideal, belief, conviction, object, aim, objective, purpose, charity.
verb *this disease can cause blindness:* **bring about,** give rise to, lead to, result in, create, produce, generate, engender, spawn, bring on, precipitate, prompt, provoke, trigger, make happen, induce, inspire, promote, foster.

caution noun **1** *proceed with caution:* **care,** attention, alertness, circumspection, discretion, prudence. **2** *a first offender may receive a caution:* **warning,** admonishment, injunction, reprimand, rebuke; informal telling-off, dressing-down; Brit. informal ticking-off.
verb **1** *advisers cautioned against tax increases:* **advise,** warn, counsel, urge. **2** *he was cautioned by the police:* **warn,** admonish, reprimand; informal tell off; Brit. informal tick off.

cautious adjective **careful,** attentive, alert, judicious, circumspect, prudent, tentative, guarded.
OPPOSITES reckless.

cave noun **cavern,** grotto, pothole, chamber, gallery, hollow.

cavity noun **space,** chamber, hollow, hole, pocket, gap, crater, pit.

cease verb **come/bring to an end,** come/bring to a halt, end, halt, stop, conclude, terminate, finish, wind up, discontinue,

suspend, break off.
OPPOSITES start, continue.

celebrate verb 1 *they were celebrating their wedding anniversary*: **commemorate**, observe, mark, keep, honour, remember. 2 *let's all celebrate!* **enjoy oneself**, make merry, have fun, have a good time, have a party; N. Amer. step out; informal party, whoop it up, have a ball. 3 *the priest celebrated mass*: **perform**, observe, officiate at, preside at.

celebrated adjective **acclaimed**, admired, highly rated, esteemed, exalted, vaunted, eminent, great, distinguished, prestigious, illustrious, notable.
OPPOSITES unsung.

celebration noun 1 *the celebration of his 50th birthday*: **commemoration**, observance, marking, keeping. 2 *a cause for celebration*: **merrymaking**, jollification, revelry, revels, festivities; informal partying. 3 *a birthday celebration*: **party**, function, gathering, festivities, festival, fête, carnival, jamboree; informal do, bash, rave; Brit. informal rave-up. 4 *the celebration of the Eucharist*: **performance**, observance, officiation, solemnization.

celebrity noun 1 *his celebrity grew*: **fame**, prominence, renown, stardom, popularity, distinction, prestige, stature, repute, reputation. 2 *a sporting celebrity*: **famous person**, VIP, personality, big name, household name, star, superstar; informal celeb, megastar.
OPPOSITES obscurity, nonentity.

cell noun 1 *a prison cell*: **room**, cubicle, chamber, dungeon, compartment, lock-up.

2 *terrorist cells*: **unit**, squad, detachment, group.

cellar noun **basement**, vault, crypt.

cement noun **adhesive**, glue, fixative, gum, paste; N. Amer. mucilage; N. Amer. informal stickum.

cemetery noun **graveyard**, churchyard, burial ground, necropolis, garden of remembrance, mass grave; Scottish kirkyard.

censor verb *letters home were censored*: **cut**, edit, expurgate, sanitize, clean up, ban, delete.

censure verb *he was censured for his conduct*: **condemn**, criticize, attack, reprimand, rebuke, admonish, upbraid, reproach.
OPPOSITES defend, praise.
noun *a note of censure*: **condemnation**, criticism, attack, reprimand, rebuke, admonishment, reproof, disapproval, reproach.
OPPOSITES approval, praise.

central adjective 1 *occupying a central position*: **middle**, centre, halfway, midway, mid. 2 *central London*: **inner**, innermost, middle, mid. 3 *their central campaign issue*: **main**, chief, principal, primary, foremost, key, crucial, vital, essential, basic, fundamental, core; informal number-one.
OPPOSITES side, extreme, outer, subordinate.

centralize verb **concentrate**, consolidate, amalgamate, condense, unify, focus.
OPPOSITES devolve.

centre noun *the centre of the town*: **middle**, nucleus, heart, core, hub.
OPPOSITES edge.
verb *the story centres on a*

doctor: **focus,** concentrate, pivot, revolve, be based.

ceremonial adjective **formal,** official, state, public, ritual, ritualistic, stately, solemn.
OPPOSITES informal.

ceremony noun **1** *a wedding ceremony:* **rite,** ritual, observance, service, event, function, formality. **2** *the new Queen was proclaimed with due ceremony:* **pomp,** protocol, formalities, niceties, decorum, etiquette.

certain adjective **1** *I'm certain he's guilty:* **sure,** confident, positive, convinced, in no doubt, satisfied. **2** *it is certain that more changes are in the offing:* **unquestionable,** sure, definite, beyond question, indubitable, undeniable, indisputable. **3** *they are certain to win:* **sure,** bound, destined. **4** *certain defeat:* **inevitable,** assured, unavoidable, inescapable, inexorable. **5** *there is no certain cure for this:* **reliable,** dependable, foolproof, guaranteed, sure, infallible; informal sure-fire.
OPPOSITES doubtful, unlikely, possible.

certainly adverb **definitely,** surely, assuredly, unquestionably, beyond/ without question, undoubtedly, without doubt, indubitably, undeniably, irrefutably, indisputably.
OPPOSITES possibly.

certainty noun **1** *she knew with certainty that it was true:* **confidence,** sureness, conviction, assurance. **2** *he accepted defeat as a certainty:* **inevitability,** foregone conclusion; informal sure thing; Brit. informal (dead) cert.

OPPOSITES doubt, possibility.

certificate noun **guarantee,** document, authorization, authentication, accreditation, credentials, testimonial.

certify verb **1** *the aircraft was certified as airworthy:* **verify,** guarantee, attest, validate, confirm, endorse. **2** *a certified hospital:* **accredit,** recognize, license, authorize, approve.

cessation noun **end,** termination, halt, finish, stoppage, conclusion, winding up, pause, suspension.
OPPOSITES start, resumption.

chain noun **1** *he was held in chains:* **fetters,** shackles, irons, manacles, handcuffs; informal cuffs, bracelets. **2** *a chain of events:* **series,** succession, string, sequence, train, course.
verb *she chained her bicycle to the railings:* **secure,** fasten, tie, tether, hitch, restrain, shackle, fetter, manacle, handcuff.

chairman, chairwoman noun **chair,** chairperson, president, chief executive, leader, master of ceremonies, MC.

challenge noun **1** *he accepted the challenge:* **dare,** provocation, offer. **2** *a challenge to his leadership:* **opposition,** confrontation, stand, dispute, test. **3** *it was proving quite a challenge:* **problem,** difficult task, test, trial.
OPPOSITES cinch.
verb **1** *we challenged their statistics:* **question,** dispute, take issue with, call into question. **2** *he challenged me to deny it:* **dare,** defy, invite, throw down the gauntlet to. **3** *changes that would challenge them:* **test,** tax, strain, make demands on, stretch.

challenging adjective

champion noun **1** *the world champion:* **winner,** title-holder, gold medallist, prizewinner; informal **champ,** number one. **2** *a champion of change:* **advocate,** proponent, promoter, supporter, defender, upholder, backer; N. Amer. **booster.**
verb *championing the rights of tribal peoples:* **advocate,** promote, defend, uphold, support, espouse, stand up for, campaign for, lobby for, fight for.
OPPOSITES oppose.

chance noun **1** *there was a chance he might be released:* **possibility,** prospect, probability, likelihood, risk, threat, danger. **2** *I gave her a chance to answer:* **opportunity,** opening, occasion, window; N. Amer. & Austral./NZ **show;** Brit. informal look-in. **3** *Nigel took an awful chance:* **risk,** gamble, leap in the dark. **4** *pure chance:* **accident,** coincidence, fate, destiny, providence, happenstance, good fortune, luck, fluke.
OPPOSITES certainty.
adjective *a chance discovery:* **accidental,** fortuitous, fluky, coincidental.
OPPOSITES planned.
■ **by chance** by accident, fortuitously, accidentally, coincidentally, unintentionally, inadvertently.

change verb **1** *this could change Britain | things have changed:* **alter,** make/become different, adjust, adapt, amend, modify, revise, vary, transform, metamorphose, evolve. **2** *he's changed his job:* **exchange,** substitute, swap, switch, replace, alternate.
OPPOSITES preserve, keep.
noun **1** *a change of plan:* **alteration,** modification, variation, revision, amendment, adjustment, adaptation, metamorphosis, transformation, evolution. **2** *a change of government:* **replacement,** exchange, substitution, swap, switch.

channel noun **1** *the English Channel:* **strait(s),** sound, narrows, passage. **2** *the water ran down a channel:* **duct,** gutter, conduit, trough, sluice, drain. **3** *a channel of communication:* **means,** medium, instrument, mechanism, agency, vehicle, route, avenue.
verb *many countries channel their aid through charities:* **convey,** transmit, conduct, direct, relay, pass on, transfer.

chant noun **shout,** cry, call, slogan, chorus, refrain.
verb **shout,** chorus, repeat, call.

chaos noun **disorder,** disorganization, confusion, mayhem, bedlam, pandemonium, havoc, turmoil, anarchy, lawlessness; Brit. a **shambles;** informal all hell broken loose.
OPPOSITES order.

chaotic adjective **disorderly,** disorganized, in confusion, in turmoil, topsy-turvy, anarchic, lawless; Brit. informal **shambolic.**

chap noun (Brit.) **man,** boy, individual, character; informal **fellow,** guy, geezer; Brit. informal **bloke,** lad; N. Amer. informal **dude,** hombre.

chapter noun **1** *the first chapter of the book:* **section,** part, division, topic, stage, episode.

2 *a new chapter in our history:* **period,** phase, page, stage, epoch, era.

character noun **1** *a forceful character | the character of a town:* **personality,** nature, quality, disposition, temperament, mentality, make-up, spirit, identity, tone, feel. **2** *a woman of character:* **integrity,** honour, moral strength/fibre, strength, backbone, resolve, grit, will power; informal **guts;** Brit. informal **bottle. 3** *a stain on his character:* **reputation,** (good) name, standing, position, status. **4** (informal) *a bit of a character:* **eccentric,** oddity, crank, original, individualist, madcap, nonconformist; informal **oddball. 5** *a boorish character:* **person,** man, woman, soul, creature, individual, customer; informal **cookie;** Brit. informal **bod, guy. 6** *written in Cyrillic characters:* **letter,** figure, symbol, mark, device, sign, hieroglyph.

characteristic noun *interesting characteristics:* **attribute,** feature, quality, property, trait, aspect, idiosyncrasy, peculiarity, quirk.
adjective *his characteristic eloquence:* **typical,** usual, normal, distinctive, representative, particular, special, peculiar, idiosyncratic. OPPOSITES abnormal.

characterize verb **1** *the period was characterized by scientific advancement:* **distinguish,** mark, typify, set apart. **2** *the women are characterized as prophets of doom:* **portray,** depict, present, represent, describe, categorize, class, brand.

charade noun **pretence,** act, masquerade, show, facade, pantomime, farce, travesty, mockery, parody.

charge verb **1** *he didn't charge much:* **ask,** demand, bill, invoice. **2** *two men were charged with murder:* **accuse,** indict, arraign, prosecute, try, put on trial; N. Amer. **impeach. 3** *they charged him with reforming the system:* **entrust,** burden, encumber, saddle, tax. **4** *the cavalry charged the tanks:* **attack,** storm, assault, assail, descend on; informal **lay into,** tear into. **5** *we charged into the crowd:* **rush,** storm, stampede, push, plough, launch oneself, go headlong; informal **steam;** N. Amer. informal **barrel. 6** *charge your glasses!* **fill (up),** top up, load (up), arm.
noun **1** *all customers pay a charge:* **fee,** payment, price, rate, tariff, fare, levy. **2** *he pleaded guilty to the charge:* **accusation,** allegation, indictment, arraignment; N. Amer. **impeachment. 3** *an infantry charge:* **attack,** assault, offensive, onslaught, drive, push. **4** *the child was in her charge:* **care,** protection, safe keeping, control, custody, hands.

charisma noun **charm,** presence, (force of) personality, strength of character, (animal) magnetism, appeal, allure.

charismatic adjective **charming,** magnetic, compelling, inspiring, captivating, mesmerizing, appealing, alluring, glamorous.

charitable adjective **1** *charitable activities:* **philanthropic,** humanitarian, altruistic, benevolent, non-profit-making.

C

2 *charitable people:* **generous,** open-handed, munificent. **3** *he was charitable in his judgements:* **magnanimous,** generous, liberal, tolerant, sympathetic, understanding, lenient, indulgent, forgiving. OPPOSITES commercial, mean, harsh.

charity noun **1** *an AIDS charity:* **voluntary organization,** charitable institution, fund, trust, foundation. **2** *we don't need charity:* **aid,** financial assistance, welfare, relief, donations, handouts, gifts, largesse; historical alms. **3** *his actions are motivated by charity:* **philanthropy,** humanitarianism, altruism, public-spiritedness, social conscience, benevolence. **4** *show a bit of charity:* **goodwill,** compassion, consideration, concern, kindness, sympathy, indulgence, tolerance, leniency. OPPOSITES business, misanthropy, intolerance.

charm noun **1** *people were captivated by her charm:* **appeal,** attraction, fascination, beauty, loveliness, allure, seductiveness, magnetism, charisma; informal pulling power. **2** *magical charms:* **spell,** incantation, formula; N. Amer. mojo, hex. **3** *a lucky charm:* **talisman,** trinket, amulet, mascot, fetish.
verb **1** *he charmed them with his singing:* **delight,** please, win (over), attract, captivate, lure, fascinate, enchant, beguile. **2** *he charmed his mother into agreeing:* **coax,** cajole, wheedle; informal sweet-talk, soft-soap.

charming adjective **delightful,** pleasing, endearing, lovely, adorable, appealing, attractive, good-looking, alluring, winning, fetching, captivating, enchanting, entrancing. OPPOSITES repulsive.

chart noun *check your ideal weight on the chart:* **graph,** table, diagram, plan, map; Computing graphic.
verb **1** *the changes were charted accurately:* **plot,** tabulate, graph, record, register, represent. **2** *the book charted his progress:* **follow,** trace, outline, describe, detail, record, document.

charter noun **1** *a Royal charter:* **authority,** authorization, sanction, dispensation, permit, licence, warrant. **2** *the UN Charter:* **constitution,** code, principles.
verb *they chartered a bus:* **hire,** lease, rent, book.

chase verb **1** *the dogs chased the fox:* **pursue,** run after, follow, hunt, track, trail; informal tail. **2** *she chased away the donkeys:* **drive,** send, scare; informal send packing. **3** *she chased away all thoughts of him:* **dispel,** banish, dismiss, drive away, shut out, put out of one's mind.
noun *they gave up the chase:* **pursuit,** hunt, trail.

chat noun *I popped in for a chat:* **talk,** conversation, gossip; informal jaw, gas, confab; Brit. informal natter, chinwag.
verb *they chatted with the guests:* **talk,** gossip; informal gas, jaw, chew the rag/fat; Brit. informal natter, have a chinwag; N. Amer. informal shoot the breeze/bull; Austral./NZ informal mag.

chatter verb *they chattered excitedly:* **prattle,** chat, gossip, jabber, babble; informal yatter; Brit.

informal natter, chunter, rabbit on.
noun *she tired him with her chatter:* **prattle,** chat, gossip, patter, jabber, babble; informal chit-chat, yattering; Brit. informal nattering, chuntering, rabbiting on.

chatty adjective **talkative,** communicative, effusive, gossipy, loquacious, voluble; informal mouthy, gabby.
OPPOSITES taciturn.

cheap adjective **1** *cheap tickets:* **inexpensive,** low-priced, low-cost, economical, competitive, affordable, reasonable, budget, economy, bargain, cut-price, reduced, discounted; informal dirt cheap. **2** *plain without looking cheap:* **poor-quality,** second-rate, substandard, inferior, vulgar, shoddy, trashy, tawdry, cheap and nasty; informal rubbishy, cheapo, junky, tacky, kitsch; Brit. informal naff, duff, ropy, grotty; N. Amer. informal two-bit, dime-store. **3** *a cheap remark:* **despicable,** contemptible, immoral, unscrupulous, unprincipled, cynical.
OPPOSITES expensive, superior, kind.

cheat verb **swindle,** defraud, deceive, trick, dupe, hoodwink, double-cross, gull; informal diddle, rip off, con, pull a fast one on; N. Amer. informal sucker, goldbrick; Austral. informal rort.
noun **swindler,** fraudster, confidence trickster, double-dealer, double-crosser, fraud, fake, charlatan; informal con artist; N. Amer. informal bunco artist, gold brick; Austral. informal shicer.

check verb **1** *troops checked all vehicles:* **examine,** inspect, look at/over, scrutinize, study, investigate, probe, look into, enquire into; informal check out, give something a/the once-over. **2** *he checked that the gun was cocked:* **make sure,** confirm, verify. **3** *two defeats checked their progress:* **halt,** stop, arrest, bar, obstruct, foil, thwart, curb, block.
noun **1** *a check of the records:* **examination,** inspection, scrutiny, perusal, study, investigation, test, check-up; informal once-over. **2** *a check on the abuse of authority:* **control,** restraint, constraint, curb, limitation.
■ **check in** register, book in, report. ■ **check out** pay the bill, settle up, leave.

cheek noun **impudence,** impertinence, insolence, rudeness, disrespect; informal brass neck, lip, mouth, chutzpah; Brit. informal backchat; N. Amer. informal sass, nerviness, back talk.
OPPOSITES respect, politeness.

cheeky adjective **impudent,** impertinent, insolent, rude, disrespectful; informal brass-necked, lippy, mouthy, fresh; N. Amer. informal sassy, nervy.
OPPOSITES respectful, polite.

cheer verb **1** *they cheered their team:* **applaud,** hail, salute, shout for, clap, put one's hands together for; informal holler for, give someone a big hand; N. Amer. informal ballyhoo. **2** *the bad weather did little to cheer me:* **raise/lift someone's spirits,** brighten, buoy up, hearten, gladden, perk up, encourage; informal buck up.
OPPOSITES boo, depress.
noun *the cheers of the crowd:* **hurrah,** hurray, whoop, bravo,

shout; (**cheers**) acclaim, applause, ovation.
OPPOSITES boo.

■ **cheer up** perk up, brighten up, rally, revive, bounce back, take heart; informal buck up.

■ **cheer someone up.** See CHEER verb sense 2.

cheerful adjective **1** *he arrived looking cheerful:* **happy,** jolly, merry, bright, sunny, joyful, in good/high spirits, buoyant, cheery, animated, smiling, good-humoured; informal chipper, chirpy, full of beans. **2** *a cheerful room:* **pleasant,** attractive, agreeable, bright, sunny, friendly, welcoming.
OPPOSITES sad, gloomy.

chemist noun **pharmacist,** dispenser; N. Amer. druggist; archaic apothecary.

cherish verb **1** *a woman he could cherish:* **adore,** love, dote on, be devoted to, revere, think the world of, care for, look after, protect, keep safe. **2** *I cherish her letters:* **treasure,** prize, hold dear. **3** *they cherished dreams of glory:* **harbour,** entertain, nurse, cling to, foster.
OPPOSITES hate, disdain.

chest noun **1** *a wound in the chest:* **breast,** upper body, torso, trunk, front. **2** *an oak chest:* **box,** case, casket, crate, trunk, coffer, strongbox.

chew verb **munch,** champ, chomp, crunch, gnaw, bite, masticate.

chic adjective **stylish,** smart, elegant, sophisticated, fashionable; informal trendy; Brit. informal swish; N. Amer. informal kicky, tony.
OPPOSITES unfashionable.

chief noun **1** *a Highland chief:* **leader,** chieftain, head, ruler, master, commander. **2** *the chief of the central bank:* **head,** chief executive, chief executive officer, president, chairman, chairwoman, principal, governor, director, manager; informal boss, (head) honcho; Brit. informal gaffer, guv'nor.
adjective **1** *the chief rabbi:* **head,** leading, principal, premier, highest, supreme, arch. **2** *their chief aim:* **main,** principal, primary, prime, first, cardinal, central, key, crucial, essential; informal number-one.
OPPOSITES subordinate, minor.

chiefly adverb **mainly,** in the main, primarily, principally, predominantly, mostly, for the most part, usually, typically, commonly, generally, on the whole, largely.

child noun **youngster,** baby, infant, toddler, minor, juvenile, junior, descendant; Scottish & N. English bairn; informal kid, kiddie, nipper, tiny, tot; derogatory brat.

childbirth noun **labour,** delivery, birthing; archaic confinement.

childhood noun **youth,** early years/life, infancy, babyhood, boyhood, girlhood, minority.
OPPOSITES adulthood.

childish adjective *childish behaviour:* **immature,** babyish, infantile, juvenile, puerile, silly.
OPPOSITES mature.

childlike adjective *childlike curiosity:* **youthful,** innocent, unsophisticated, naive, trusting, artless, unaffected, uninhibited, natural, spontaneous.
OPPOSITES adult.

chill noun **1** *a chill in the air:* **coldness,** chilliness, coolness, nip. **2** *he had a chill:* **cold,** dose of flu, fever. **3** *a chill ran down my spine:* **shiver,** frisson.

OPPOSITES warmth.

verb *his quiet tone chilled Ruth:* **scare,** frighten, petrify, terrify, alarm, make someone's blood run cold; informal scare the pants off; Brit. informal put the wind up.
OPPOSITES warm.

adjective *a chill wind:* **cold,** chilly, cool, fresh, wintry, frosty, icy, arctic, bitter, freezing; informal nippy; Brit. informal parky.

chilly adjective 1 *the weather had turned chilly:* **cold,** cool, crisp, fresh, wintry, frosty, icy; informal nippy; Brit. informal parky. **2** *a chilly reception:* **unfriendly,** unwelcoming, cold, cool, frosty; informal stand-offish.
OPPOSITES warm.

china noun crockery, dishes, plates, cups and saucers, tableware, porcelain, dinnerware, dinner service, tea service.

chink noun *a chink in the curtains:* **gap,** crack, space, hole, aperture, fissure, cranny, cleft, split, slit.

chip noun 1 *wood chips:* **fragment,** sliver, splinter, shaving, shard, flake. **2** *a chip in the glass:* **nick,** crack, scratch. **3** *gambling chips:* **counter,** token; N. Amer. check.
verb 1 *the teacup was chipped:* **nick,** crack, scratch. **2** *chip off the old plaster:* **cut,** hack, chisel, carve, hew, whittle.

choice noun 1 *freedom of choice:* **selection,** choosing, picking, pick, preference, decision, say, vote. **2** *you have no other choice:* **option,** alternative, course of action. **3** *an extensive choice:* **range,** variety, selection, assortment.
adjective *choice plums:* **superior,** first-class, first-rate, prime,

premier, grade A, best, finest, select, quality, top, top-quality, high-grade, prize; informal A1, top-notch.
OPPOSITES inferior.

choke verb 1 *Christopher started to choke:* **gag,** retch, cough, fight for breath. **2** *she had been choked to death:* **suffocate,** asphyxiate, smother, stifle, strangle, throttle; informal strangulate. **3** *the guttering was choked with leaves:* **clog (up),** bung up, stop up, block, obstruct.

choose verb 1 *we chose a quiet country hotel:* **select,** pick (out), opt for, plump for, settle on, prefer, decide on, fix on, elect, adopt. **2** *I'll stay as long as I choose:* **wish,** want, desire, please, like.

chop verb cut (up), cube, dice, hew, split, fell; N. Amer. hash.
■ **chop something off** cut off, sever, lop, shear.

chore noun task, job, duty, errand, burden; informal hassle.

christen verb 1 *she was christened Sara:* **baptize,** name, give the name of, call. **2** *a group who were christened 'The Magic Circle':* **call,** name, dub, style, term, label, nickname.

chronicle noun *a chronicle of the region's past:* **record,** account, history, annals, archive(s), log, diary, journal.
verb *the events have been chronicled:* **record,** write down, set down, document, report.

chubby adjective plump, tubby, flabby, rotund, portly, chunky; Brit. informal podgy; N. Amer. informal zaftig, corn-fed.
OPPOSITES skinny.

chuck verb (informal) **1** *he chucked the letter on to the table:* **throw,** toss, fling, hurl, pitch, cast, lob;

informal sling, bung; Austral. informal hoy; NZ informal bish. **2** *I chucked the rubbish:* **throw away/out,** discard, dispose of, get rid of, dump, bin, jettison; informal ditch, junk; N. Amer. informal trash. **3** *I've chucked my job:* **give up,** leave, resign from; informal quit, pack in; Brit. informal jack in. **4** *Mary chucked him for another guy:* **leave,** finish with, break off with, jilt; informal dump, ditch, give someone the elbow; Brit. informal give someone the push.

chuckle verb **laugh,** chortle, giggle, titter, snigger.

chum noun (informal) **friend,** companion, playmate, classmate, schoolmate, workmate; informal pal, crony; Brit. informal mate; N. Amer. informal buddy.

OPPOSITES enemy, stranger.

chunk noun **lump,** hunk, wedge, block, slab, square, nugget, brick, cube; informal wodge; N. Amer. informal gob.

churlish adjective **rude,** ill-mannered, discourteous, impolite, inconsiderate, surly, sullen.

OPPOSITES polite.

churn verb **disturb,** stir up, agitate, beat.

cinema noun **1** *the local cinema:* **the movies,** the pictures; N. Amer. movie theatre/house; informal the flicks. **2** *British cinema:* **films,** film, movies, pictures, motion pictures.

circa preposition **approximately,** (round) about, around, in the region of, roughly, something like, or so, or thereabouts, more or less; informal as near as dammit; N. Amer. informal in the ballpark of.

OPPOSITES exactly.

circle noun **1** *a circle of gold stars:* **ring,** band, hoop, circlet, halo, disc. **2** *her circle of friends:* **group,** set, crowd, band, company, clique, coterie, club, society; informal gang, bunch.

verb **1** *seagulls circled above:* **wheel,** revolve, rotate, whirl, spiral. **2** *satellites circling the earth:* **go round,** travel round, circumnavigate, orbit. **3** *the abbey was circled by a wall:* **surround,** encircle, ring, enclose.

circuit noun **1** *two circuits of the track:* **lap,** turn, round, circle. **2** (Brit.) *a racing circuit:* **track,** racetrack, course, route, stadium.

circular adjective *a circular room:* **round,** ring-shaped.

noun **leaflet,** pamphlet, handbill, flyer, advertisement, notice.

circulate verb **1** *the news was widely circulated:* **spread,** communicate, disseminate, make known, make public, broadcast, publicize, distribute. **2** *they circulated among the guests:* **socialize,** mingle, mix, wander, stroll.

circumstances plural noun **situation,** conditions, state of affairs, position, the lie of the land, (turn of) events, factors, facts, background, environment, context.

cite verb **1** *cite the passage in full:* **quote,** reproduce, excerpt. **2** *he cited the case of Leigh v. Gladstone:* **refer to,** allude to, instance, specify, mention, name.

citizen noun **1** *a British citizen:* **subject,** national, passport holder. **2** *the citizens of Edinburgh:* **inhabitant,** resident, native, townsman, townswoman, taxpayer, people; formal denizen.

city noun **town,** municipality, metropolis, conurbation, urban area; Scottish burgh; informal big smoke; N. Amer. informal burg.

civic adjective **municipal,** city, town, urban, metropolitan, public, community.

civil adjective **1** *a civil marriage:* **secular,** non-religious, lay. **2** *civil aviation:* **non-military,** civilian. **3** *he behaved in a civil manner:* **polite,** courteous, well mannered, gentlemanly, chivalrous, ladylike.
OPPOSITES religious, military, rude.

civilization noun **1** *a higher stage of civilization:* **human development,** advancement, progress, enlightenment, culture, refinement, sophistication. **2** *ancient civilizations:* **culture,** society, nation, people.

civilize verb **enlighten,** improve, educate, instruct, refine, cultivate, socialize.

civilized adjective **1** *civilized society:* **advanced,** developed, sophisticated, enlightened, educated, cultured, cultivated. **2** *civilized behaviour:* **polite,** courteous, well mannered, civil, refined, polished.
OPPOSITES unsophisticated, rude.

claim verb **1** *he claimed that she was lying:* **assert,** declare, profess, protest, maintain, insist, contend, allege. **2** *you can claim compensation:* **request,** ask for, apply for, demand.
noun **1** *her claim that she was robbed:* **assertion,** declaration, profession, protestation, insistence, contention, allegation. **2** *a claim for*

damages: **application,** request, demand.

clamour noun **noise,** din, racket, rumpus, uproar, shouting, commotion, hubbub; informal hullabaloo; Brit. informal row.

clamp verb **fasten,** secure, fix, attach, clench, grip, hold, press, clasp, screw, bolt.

clan noun **family,** house, dynasty, tribe.

clap verb *the audience clapped:* **applaud,** give someone a round of applause, put one's hands together; informal give someone a (big) hand; N. Amer. informal give it up.
noun **1** *everybody gave him a clap:* **round of applause,** handclap; informal hand. **2** *a clap of thunder:* **crack,** peal, crash, bang, boom.

clarify verb **make clear,** shed/throw light on, illuminate, elucidate, explain, interpret, spell out, clear up.
OPPOSITES confuse.

clarity noun **1** *the clarity of his explanation:* **lucidity,** precision, coherence, transparency, simplicity. **2** *the clarity of the image:* **sharpness,** clearness, crispness, definition. **3** *the clarity of the water:* **transparency,** clearness, limpidity, translucence.
OPPOSITES vagueness, blurriness, cloudiness.

clash noun **1** *clashes between armed gangs:* **fight,** battle, confrontation, skirmish, engagement, encounter, conflict. **2** *clashes in parliament:* **argument,** altercation, confrontation, quarrel, disagreement, dispute; informal run-in, slanging match. **3** *the clash of cymbals:* **crash,** clang, bang.

c

verb **1** *protesters clashed with police:* **fight,** battle, confront, skirmish, contend, come to blows. **2** *the prime minister clashed with union leaders:* **disagree,** differ, wrangle, dispute, cross swords, lock horns, be at loggerheads. **3** *the dates clash:* **conflict,** coincide, overlap. **4** *she clashed the cymbals together:* **bang,** strike, clang, crash.

clasp verb *Ruth clasped him to her:* **grasp,** grip, clutch, hold, squeeze, seize, grab, embrace, hug.
noun **1** *a gold clasp:* **fastener,** catch, clip, pin, buckle. **2** *his tight clasp:* **grasp,** grip, squeeze, embrace, hug.

class noun **1** *a new class of drug:* **kind,** sort, type, variety, genre, category, grade, rating, classification. **2** *mixing with people of her own class:* **group,** grouping, rank, stratum, level, echelon, status, caste.
verb *the 12-seater is classed as a commercial vehicle:* **classify,** categorize, group, grade, order, rate, bracket, designate, label, rank.

classic adjective **1** *the classic work on the subject:* **definitive,** authoritative, outstanding, first-rate, first-class, best, finest, excellent, superior, masterly. **2** *a classic example of Norman design:* **typical,** archetypal, quintessential, model, representative, perfect, prime, textbook. **3** *a classic look:* **timeless,** traditional, simple, elegant, understated.
OPPOSITES insignificant, second-rate, atypical, ephemeral.
noun *a classic of the genre:* **definitive example,** model, epitome, paradigm, exemplar,

masterpiece.

classification noun **categorization,** classifying, grouping, grading, ranking, organization, sorting, codification.

classify verb **categorize,** group, grade, rank, order, organize, sort, type, codify, bracket.

classy adjective (informal) **stylish,** high-class, superior, exclusive, chic, elegant, smart, sophisticated; Brit. upmarket; N. Amer. high-toned; informal posh, ritzy, plush, swanky; Brit. informal swish.

clause noun **section,** paragraph, article, passage, subsection, chapter, condition, proviso, rider.

claw noun **1** *a bird's claw:* **talon,** nail. **2** *a crab's claw:* **pincer,** nipper.
verb *her fingers clawed his shoulders:* **scratch,** lacerate, tear, rip, scrape, dig into.

clean adjective **1** *keep the wound clean:* **washed,** scrubbed, cleansed, cleaned, laundered, spotless, unstained, unsullied, unblemished, immaculate, pristine, disinfected, sterilized, sterile, aseptic, decontaminated. **2** *a clean sheet of paper:* **blank,** empty, clear, plain, unused, new, pristine, fresh, unmarked. **3** *clean air:* **pure,** clear, fresh, unpolluted, uncontaminated.
OPPOSITES dirty, polluted, used.
verb *Dad cleaned the windows:* **wash,** cleanse, wipe, sponge, scrub, mop, rinse, scour, swab, shampoo, launder, dry-clean.
OPPOSITES dirty.

cleanse verb **1** *the wound was cleansed:* **clean (up),** wash, bathe, rinse, disinfect. **2** *cleansing the environment of* *traces of lead:* **rid,** clear, free, purify, purge.

clear adjective **1** *clear instructions:* **understandable,** comprehensible, intelligible, plain, uncomplicated, explicit, lucid, coherent, simple, straightforward, unambiguous, clear-cut. **2** *a clear case of harassment:* **obvious,** evident, plain, sure, definite, unmistakable, manifest, indisputable, unambiguous, patent, incontrovertible, visible, conspicuous, overt, blatant, glaring. **3** *clear water:* **transparent,** limpid, translucent, crystal clear. **4** *a clear sky:* **bright,** cloudless, unclouded, blue, sunny, starry. **5** *the road was clear:* **unobstructed,** passable, open, unrestricted, unhindered. **OPPOSITES** vague, disputed, cloudy, obstructed.
verb **1** *the smoke had cleared:* **disappear,** go away, stop, die away, fade, wear off, lift, settle, evaporate, dissipate, decrease, lessen, shift. **2** *they cleared the table:* **empty,** unload, strip. **3** *clearing drains:* **unblock,** unstop. **4** *staff cleared the building:* **evacuate,** empty, leave. **5** *Karen cleared the dirty plates:* **remove,** take away, carry away, tidy away/up. **6** *I cleared the bar at my first attempt:* **go over,** pass over, sail over, jump (over), vault (over), leap (over). **7** *he was cleared by the court:* **acquit,** declare innocent, find not guilty, absolve, exonerate; informal let off (the hook).
■ **clear something up 1** *clear up the garden:* **tidy (up),** put in order, straighten up, clean up, fix. **2** *we've cleared up the problem:* **solve,** resolve,

straighten out, find an/the answer to, get to the bottom of, explain; informal crack, figure out, suss out.

clearance noun **1** *slum clearance:* **removal,** clearing, demolition. **2** *you must have Home Office clearance:* **authorization,** permission, consent, approval, leave, sanction, licence, dispensation; informal the go-ahead. **3** *there is plenty of clearance:* **space,** room (to spare), headroom, margin, leeway.

clear-cut adjective **definite,** distinct, precise, specific, explicit, unambiguous, unequivocal, black and white. **OPPOSITES** vague.

clearly adverb **1** *write clearly:* **intelligibly,** plainly, distinctly, comprehensibly, legibly, audibly. **2** *clearly, substantial changes are needed:* **obviously,** evidently, patently, unquestionably, undoubtedly, without doubt, plainly, undeniably.

cleft noun **split,** crack, fissure, crevice.

clench verb **grip,** grasp, grab, clutch, clasp, clamp, hold tightly, seize, squeeze.

clergyman, clergywoman noun **priest,** cleric, minister, preacher, chaplain, padre, father, pastor, vicar, rector, parson, curate; Scottish kirkman.

clever adjective **1** **intelligent,** bright, smart, astute, quick-witted, shrewd, talented, gifted, capable, able, competent; informal brainy. **2** *a clever scheme:* **ingenious,** canny, cunning, crafty, artful, slick, neat. **3** *she was clever with her hands:* **skilful,** dexterous, adroit, adept, deft,

nimble, handy, skilled, talented, gifted.
OPPOSITES stupid.

cliché noun **platitude,** hackneyed phrase, commonplace, banality, truism, stock phrase; informal old chestnut.

client noun **customer,** buyer, purchaser, shopper, patient, patron; Brit. informal punter.

cliff noun **precipice,** rock face, crag, bluff, ridge, escarpment, scar, scarp.

climate noun **1** *a mild climate:* **(weather) conditions,** weather. **2** *the political climate:* **atmosphere,** mood, spirit, ethos, feeling, ambience, environment.

climax noun *the climax of his career:* **peak,** pinnacle, height, high point, top, zenith, culmination.
OPPOSITES anticlimax, nadir.

climb verb **1** *we climbed the hill:* **ascend,** mount, scale, scramble up, clamber up, shin up, conquer. **2** *the plane climbed:* **rise,** ascend, go up, gain height, soar, rocket. **3** *the road climbs steeply:* **slope (upwards),** rise, go uphill, incline.
OPPOSITES descend.
■ **climb down** back down, retreat, give in, backtrack, eat one's words, eat humble pie, do a U-turn; N. Amer. informal eat crow.

clinch verb **1** *he clinched the deal:* **secure,** settle, conclude, close, confirm, seal, finalize; informal sew up. **2** *these findings clinched the matter:* **settle,** decide, determine, resolve. **3** *they clinched the title:* **win,** secure.
OPPOSITES lose.

cling verb *rice grains cling together:* **stick,** adhere, hold.
■ **cling (on) to** hold on, clutch, grip, grasp, clasp, hang on, embrace, hug.

clinical adjective **1** *he seemed so clinical:* **detached,** impersonal, dispassionate, indifferent, uninvolved, distant, remote, aloof, cold. **2** *the room was very clinical:* **plain,** stark, austere, spartan, bleak, bare, functional, basic, institutional.
OPPOSITES emotional, luxurious.

clip¹ noun *the clip on his briefcase:* **fastener,** clasp, hasp, catch, hook, buckle, lock.
verb *he clipped the pages together:* **fasten,** attach, fix, join, pin, staple, tack.

clip² verb **1** *I clipped the hedge:* **trim,** prune, cut, snip, crop, shear, lop. **2** *his lorry clipped a van:* **hit,** strike, graze, glance off, nudge, scrape.
noun **1** *a film clip:* **extract,** excerpt, snippet, fragment, trailer. **2** *I gave the dog a clip:* **trim,** cut, crop, haircut, shear.

cloak noun **1** *the cloak over his shoulders:* **cape,** robe, wrap, mantle. **2** *a cloak of secrecy:* **cover,** veil, mantle, shroud, screen, blanket.
verb *a peak cloaked in mist:* **conceal,** hide, cover, veil, shroud, mask, obscure, cloud, envelop, swathe, surround.

clog verb **block,** obstruct, congest, jam, choke, bung up, plug, stop up.

close¹ adjective **1** *the town is close to Leeds:* **near,** nearby, adjacent, neighbouring, adjoining, abutting, at hand. **2** *a very close match:* **even,** neck and neck. **3** *close friends:* **intimate,** dear, bosom, close-knit, inseparable, devoted, faithful, special, firm. **4** *a close*

resemblance: **noticeable,** marked, distinct, pronounced, strong. **5** *a close examination:* **careful,** detailed, thorough, minute, searching, painstaking, meticulous, rigorous. **6** *the weather was close:* **humid,** muggy, stuffy, airless, heavy, sticky, sultry, stifling.
OPPOSITES far, distant, one-sided, slight, cursory, fresh.

close² verb **1** *she closed the door:* **shut,** pull to, push to, slam. **2** *close the hole:* **block,** stop up, plug, seal, bung up, clog up, choke, obstruct. **3** *he closed the meeting:* **end,** conclude, finish, terminate, wind up. **4** *the factory is to close:* **shut down,** close down, cease production, cease trading, be wound up, go out of business; informal fold, go to the wall, go bust. **5** *he closed a deal:* **clinch,** settle, secure, seal, confirm, pull off, conclude, finalize; informal wrap up.
OPPOSITES open, start.
noun *the close of the talks:* **end,** finish, conclusion.
OPPOSITES beginning.

cloth noun **1** *a maker of cloth:* **fabric,** material, textile(s). **2** *a cloth to wipe the table:* **rag,** wipe, duster, flannel; Austral. washer.

clothe verb **dress,** attire, robe, garb, costume, swathe, deck (out), turn out, fit out, rig (out); informal get up.

clothes plural noun **clothing,** garments, attire, garb, dress, wear, costume, wardrobe; informal gear, togs; Brit. informal clobber; N. Amer. informal threads.

clothing noun. See CLOTHES.

cloud noun *a cloud of exhaust smoke:* **mass,** billow, pall, mantle, blanket.

verb *anger clouded my judgement:* **confuse,** muddle, obscure.

cloudy adjective **1** *a cloudy sky:* **overcast,** dark, grey, black, leaden, murky, gloomy, sunless, starless. **2** *cloudy water:* **murky,** muddy, milky, dirty, turbid.
OPPOSITES clear, sunny.

clown noun **1** *the class clown:* **joker,** comedian, comic, wag, wit, jester, buffoon. **2** *bureaucratic clowns:* **fool,** idiot, dolt, ass, ignoramus; informal moron, numbskull, halfwit, fathead; Brit. informal prat, berk, twit, twerp.
verb *Harvey clowned around:* **fool around/about,** play the fool, play about/around, monkey about/around, joke; informal mess about/around, lark (about/around); Brit. informal muck about/around.

club¹ noun **1** *a canoeing club:* **society,** association, group, circle, league, guild, union. **2** *the city has great clubs:* **nightclub,** bar; informal disco. **3** *the top club in the league:* **team,** squad, side.

club² noun *a wooden club:* **stick,** cudgel, truncheon, bludgeon, baton, mace, bat; N. Amer. blackjack, nightstick; Brit. informal cosh.
verb *he was clubbed with an iron bar:* **hit,** beat, strike, cudgel, bludgeon, batter; informal clout, clobber; Brit. informal cosh.

clue noun **hint,** indication, sign, signal, pointer, lead, tip, evidence.

clump noun **1** *a clump of trees:* **cluster,** thicket, group, bunch. **2** *a clump of earth:* **lump,** clod, mass, chunk.

clumsy adjective **1** *she was terribly clumsy:* **awkward,**

C

uncoordinated, ungainly, graceless, lumbering, inelegant, inept, unskilful, accident-prone, all fingers and thumbs; informal cack-handed, ham-fisted, butterfingered; N. Amer. informal klutzy. **2** *a clumsy contraption:* **unwieldy,** cumbersome, bulky, awkward.
OPPOSITES graceful, handy.

cluster noun *clusters of berries:* **bunch,** clump, mass, knot, group, clutch, huddle, crowd.
verb *they clustered around the television:* **congregate,** gather, collect, group, assemble, huddle, crowd.

clutch verb **grip,** grasp, clasp, cling to, hang on to, clench, hold, grab, snatch.

clutter noun **disorder,** chaos, disarray, untidiness, mess, confusion, litter, rubbish, junk.
verb **litter,** mess up, be strewn, be scattered, cover, bury.

coach[1] noun **1** *a journey by coach:* **bus. 2** *a railway coach:* **carriage,** wagon; N. Amer. car.

coach[2] noun *a football coach:* **instructor,** trainer, teacher, tutor, mentor, guru.
verb *he coached Richard in maths:* **instruct,** teach, tutor, school, educate, drill, train.

coalition noun **alliance,** union, partnership, bloc, federation, league, association, confederation, consortium, syndicate, amalgamation, merger.

coarse adjective **1** *coarse blankets:* **rough,** scratchy, prickly, wiry, harsh. **2** *coarse manners:* **uncouth,** oafish, loutish, boorish, rude, impolite, ill-mannered, vulgar, common, rough. **3** *a coarse remark:* **vulgar,** crude, rude, off colour, lewd, smutty, indelicate.
OPPOSITES soft, refined, polite.

coast noun *the west coast:* **shore,** coastline, seashore, seaboard, shoreline, seaside.
verb *the car coasted down a hill:* **freewheel,** cruise, taxi, drift, glide, sail.

coat noun **1** *a dog's coat:* **fur,** hair, wool, fleece, hide, pelt, skin. **2** *a coat of paint:* **layer,** covering, coating, skin, film, deposit.
verb *the tube was coated with wax:* **cover,** surface, plate, spread, daub, smear, plaster.

coax verb **persuade,** wheedle, cajole, get round, inveigle, manoeuvre; informal sweet-talk, soft-soap, twist someone's arm.

cocky adjective **arrogant,** conceited, overconfident, swollen-headed, self-important, egotistical, presumptuous, boastful.
OPPOSITES modest.

code noun **1** *a secret code:* **cipher. 2** *a strict social code:* **convention,** etiquette, protocol, ethic. **3** *the penal code:* **law(s),** rules, regulations, constitution, system.

coerce verb **pressure,** press, push, constrain, force, compel, oblige, browbeat, bully, threaten, intimidate, dragoon, twist someone's arm; informal railroad, steamroller, lean on.

coherent adjective **logical,** reasoned, rational, sound, cogent, consistent, lucid, articulate, intelligible.
OPPOSITES muddled.

coil verb **wind,** loop, twist, curl, spiral, twine, wrap.

coin verb **invent,** create, make up, conceive, originate, think up, dream up.

coincide verb **1** *the events coincided:* **occur**

simultaneously, happen together, co-occur, coexist. **2** *their interests do not always coincide:* **tally,** correspond, agree, accord, match up, be compatible, dovetail, mesh; informal square.
OPPOSITES differ.

coincidence noun accident, chance, providence, happenstance, fate, luck, fortune, fluke.

coincidental adjective accidental, chance, fluky, random, fortuitous.

cold adjective **1** *a cold day:* chilly, chill, cool, freezing, icy, wintry, frosty, bitter, raw; informal nippy; Brit. informal parky. **2** *a cold reception:* unfriendly, inhospitable, unwelcoming, cool, frigid, frosty, distant, formal, stiff.
OPPOSITES hot, warm.

collaborate verb **1** *they collaborated on the project:* cooperate, join forces, work together, combine, pool resources, club together. **2** *they collaborated with the enemy:* fraternize, conspire, collude, cooperate, consort.

collaborator noun **1** *his collaborator on the book:* co-worker, partner, associate, colleague, confederate, assistant. **2** *a wartime collaborator:* sympathizer, traitor, quisling, fifth columnist.

collapse verb **1** *the roof collapsed:* cave in, fall in, subside, fall down, give (way), crumple, crumble, disintegrate. **2** *he collapsed last night:* faint, pass out, black out, lose consciousness. **3** *she collapsed in tears:* break down, go to pieces, be overcome; informal crack up. **4** *peace talks collapsed:* break down, fail, fall through, fold, founder; informal flop, fizzle out.
noun **1** *the collapse of the roof:* cave-in, disintegration. **2** *the collapse of the talks:* breakdown, failure.

colleague noun co-worker, fellow worker, workmate, teammate, associate, partner, collaborator, ally, confederate.

collect verb **1** *he collected up the rubbish:* gather, accumulate, assemble, amass, stockpile, pile up, heap up, store (up), hoard, save. **2** *a crowd soon collected:* gather, assemble, meet, muster, congregate, convene, converge. **3** *I must collect the children:* fetch, pick up, go/come and get, call for, meet.
OPPOSITES distribute, disperse, deliver.

collected adjective calm, cool, self-possessed, self-controlled, composed, poised, serene, tranquil, relaxed; informal laid-back.
OPPOSITES excited, hysterical.

collection noun **1** *a collection of stolen items:* hoard, pile, heap, stock, store, stockpile, accumulation, reserve, supply, bank, pool, fund; informal stash. **2** *a collection of shoppers:* group, crowd, body, gathering, knot, cluster. **3** *a collection of short stories:* anthology, selection, compendium, compilation, miscellany. **4** *a collection for famine relief:* appeal; informal whip-round.

collective adjective common, shared, joint, combined, mutual, communal, pooled, united, allied, cooperative, collaborative.
OPPOSITES individual.

C

collide verb crash, hit, strike, run into, bump into.

collision noun crash, accident, smash; N. Amer. wreck; informal pile-up; Brit. informal shunt.

colloquial adjective informal, conversational, everyday, familiar, popular, casual, idiomatic, slangy, vernacular.
OPPOSITES formal.

colonize verb settle (in), people, populate, occupy, take over, invade.

colony noun territory, dependency, protectorate, satellite, settlement, outpost, province.

colossal adjective huge, massive, enormous, gigantic, giant, mammoth, vast, immense, monumental, mountainous; informal monster, whopping, humongous; Brit. informal ginormous.
OPPOSITES tiny.

colour noun 1 *the lights changed colour:* **hue,** shade, tint, tone, coloration. 2 *oil colour:* **paint,** pigment, colourant, dye, stain.
verb 1 *the wood was coloured blue:* **tint,** dye, stain, tinge. 2 *the experience coloured her outlook:* **influence,** affect, taint, warp, skew, distort.

colourful adjective 1 *a colourful picture:* **brightly coloured,** vivid, vibrant, brilliant, radiant, gaudy, garish, multicoloured; informal jazzy. 2 *a colourful account:* **vivid,** graphic, lively, animated, dramatic, fascinating, interesting, stimulating, scintillating, evocative.
OPPOSITES drab, plain, boring.

column noun 1 *arches supported by massive columns:* **pillar,** post, support, upright, pier, pile. 2 *a column in the paper:* **article,** piece, feature. 3 *we walked in a column:* **line,** file, queue, procession, convoy; informal crocodile.

comb verb 1 *she combed her hair:* **groom,** brush, untangle, smooth, straighten, neaten, tidy, arrange. 2 *police combed the area:* **search,** scour, explore, sweep.

combat noun *he was killed in combat:* **battle,** fighting, action, hostilities, conflict, war, warfare.
verb *they tried to combat the disease:* **fight,** battle, tackle, attack, counter, resist.

combination noun mixture, mix, blend, fusion, amalgamation, amalgam, merger, marriage, synthesis.

combine verb 1 *he combines comedy with tragedy:* **mix,** blend, fuse, amalgamate, integrate, merge, marry. 2 *teachers combined to tackle the problem:* **unite,** collaborate, join forces, get together, team up.

come verb 1 *come and listen:* **approach,** advance, draw close/ closer, draw near/nearer. 2 *they came last night:* **arrive,** get here/there, make it, appear, turn up, materialize; informal show (up), roll up. 3 *they came to a stream:* **reach,** arrive at, get to, come across, run across, happen on, chance on, come upon, stumble on, end up at; informal wind up at. 4 *she comes from Belgium:* **be from,** be a native of, hail from, live in, reside in. 5 *attacks came without warning:* **happen,** occur, take place, come about, fall, crop up.
OPPOSITES go, leave.
■ **come about** happen, occur, take place, transpire, fall, arise.

■ **come across** meet, run into, run across, come upon, chance on, stumble on, happen on, discover, encounter, find; informal bump into. ■ **come on** progress, develop, shape up, take shape, come along, turn out, improve.

comeback noun return, recovery, resurgence, rally, upturn; Brit. fightback.

comedian noun **1** *a famous comedian:* **comic**, comedienne, funny man/woman, humorist, stand-up; N. Amer. tummler. **2** *Dad was such a comedian:* **joker**, wit, wag, comic, clown; informal laugh, hoot.

comedy noun *the comedy in their work:* **humour**, fun, hilarity, funny side, laughs, jokes.
OPPOSITES tragedy.

comfort noun **1** *travel in comfort:* **ease**, repose, luxury, prosperity. **2** *words of comfort:* **consolation**, condolence, sympathy, commiseration, support, reassurance, cheer.
OPPOSITES discomfort.
verb *a friend tried to comfort her:* **console**, support, reassure, soothe, calm, cheer, hearten.
OPPOSITES distress, depress.

comfortable adjective **1** *a comfortable lifestyle:* **pleasant**, affluent, well-to-do, luxurious, opulent. **2** *a comfortable room:* **cosy**, snug, warm, pleasant, agreeable, homely; informal comfy. **3** *comfortable clothes:* **loose**, casual; informal comfy.
OPPOSITES hard, spartan, restricting.

comforting adjective soothing, reassuring, calming, heartening, cheering.
OPPOSITES upsetting.

comic adjective humorous, funny, amusing, hilarious, comical, zany, witty.
OPPOSITES serious.
noun comedian, comedienne, funny man/woman, humorist, wit, joker.

comical adjective **1** *he could be quite comical:* **funny**, humorous, droll, witty, amusing, entertaining; informal wacky. **2** *they look comical in those suits:* **silly**, absurd, ridiculous, laughable, ludicrous, preposterous, foolish; informal crazy.
OPPOSITES serious, sensible.

coming adjective *the coming election:* **forthcoming**, imminent, impending, approaching.
noun *the coming of spring:* **approach**, advance, advent, arrival, appearance, emergence.

command verb **1** *he commanded his men to retreat:* **order**, tell, direct, instruct, call on, require. **2** *Jones commanded a tank squadron:* **be in charge of**, be in command of, head, lead, control, direct, manage, supervise, oversee; informal head up.
noun **1** *officers shouted commands:* **order**, instruction, direction. **2** *he had 160 men under his command:* **authority**, control, charge, power, direction, dominion, guidance, leadership, rule, government, management, supervision, jurisdiction. **3** *a brilliant command of English:* **knowledge**, mastery, grasp, comprehension, understanding.

commander noun leader, head, chief, overseer, director, controller; informal boss, skipper, head honcho; Brit. informal gaffer, guv'nor.

commanding adjective

C

C

dominant, controlling, superior, powerful, advantageous, favourable.
OPPOSITES disadvantageous, weak.

commemorate verb celebrate, remember, recognize, acknowledge, observe, mark, pay tribute to, pay homage to, honour, salute.

commence verb begin, inaugurate, start, initiate, launch into, open, get the ball rolling, get going, get under way, get off the ground, set about, embark on; informal kick off.
OPPOSITES conclude.

commend verb **1** *we should commend him:* **praise**, compliment, congratulate, applaud, salute, honour, sing the praises of, pay tribute to. **2** *I commend her to you without reservation:* **recommend**, endorse, vouch for, speak for, support, back.
OPPOSITES criticize.

commendable adjective **admirable**, praiseworthy, creditable, laudable, meritorious, exemplary, honourable, respectable.
OPPOSITES reprehensible.

comment noun **1** *their comments on her appearance:* **remark**, observation, statement, pronouncement, judgement, reflection, opinion, view. **2** *a great deal of comment:* **discussion**, debate, interest. **3** *a comment in the margin:* **note**, annotation, commentary, footnote, gloss, explanation.
verb **1** *they commented on the food:* **remark on**, speak about, talk about, discuss, mention. **2** *'It will soon be night,' he commented:* **remark**, observe,

say, state, note, point out.

commentary noun **1** *the test match commentary:* **narration**, description, report, review, voice-over. **2** *textual commentary:* **explanation**, elucidation, interpretation, analysis, assessment, review, criticism, notes, comments.

commentator noun **1** *a sports commentator:* **reporter**, narrator, journalist, newscaster. **2** *a political commentator:* **analyst**, pundit, critic, columnist, leader-writer, opinion-former, monitor, observer.

commerce noun trade, trading, business, dealing, buying and selling, traffic, trafficking.

commercial adjective **1** *a vessel built for commercial purposes:* **trade**, trading, business, mercantile, sales. **2** *a commercial organization:* **profit-making**, materialistic, mercenary.
OPPOSITES non-profit-making.

commission noun **1** *the dealer's commission:* **percentage**, share, premium, fee, bonus, royalty; informal cut, rake-off, slice; Brit. informal whack. **2** *a commission to design a monument:* **contract**, engagement, assignment, booking, job. **3** *an independent commission:* **committee**, board, council, panel, body.
verb **1** *he was commissioned to paint a portrait:* **engage**, contract, book, employ, hire, recruit, take on, retain, appoint. **2** *they commissioned a sculpture:* **order**.

commit verb **1** *he committed a murder:* **carry out**, do, perpetrate, engage in, execute, accomplish, be responsible for; informal pull off. **2** *she was*

committed to their care:
entrust, consign, assign,
deliver, hand over. **3** *the judge
committed him to prison:*
consign, send, confine.

commitment noun **1** *the
pressure of his commitments:*
responsibility, obligation, duty,
liability, engagement, tie. **2** *her
commitment to her students:*
dedication, devotion,
allegiance, loyalty. **3** *he made a
commitment:* **promise,** vow,
pledge, undertaking.

committed adjective **devoted,**
dedicated, staunch, loyal,
faithful, devout, firm, steadfast,
unwavering, passionate, ardent,
sworn.
OPPOSITES apathetic.

common adjective **1** *a common
occurrence:* **frequent,** regular,
everyday, normal, usual,
ordinary, familiar, standard,
commonplace. **2** *a common
belief:* **widespread,** general,
universal, popular, mainstream,
prevalent, rife, established,
conventional, accepted. **3** *the
common people:* **ordinary,**
normal, average, unexceptional,
typical, simple. **4** *the common
good:* **collective,** communal,
shared, community, public,
popular, general. **5** *she's so
common:* **uncouth,** vulgar,
coarse, rough, uncivilized,
unsophisticated, unrefined,
inferior, plebeian; informal
plebby.
OPPOSITES unusual, rare,
individual, refined.

commonplace adjective. See
COMMON sense 1.

common sense noun **good
sense,** native wit, good
judgement, level-headedness,
prudence, wisdom; informal horse
sense, nous; Brit. informal

common; N. Amer. informal **smarts.**
OPPOSITES stupidity.

commotion noun **disturbance,**
uproar, disorder, confusion,
rumpus, fuss, furore, hue and
cry, stir, storm, chaos, havoc,
pandemonium.

communal adjective **1** *a
communal kitchen:* **shared,**
joint, common. **2** *they farm on
a communal basis:* **collective,**
cooperative, community.
OPPOSITES private, individual.

communicate verb **1** *they
communicate daily:* **liaise,** be in
touch, be in contact, have
dealings, talk, speak. **2** *he
communicated the news to his
boss:* **convey,** tell, relay,
transmit, impart, pass on,
report, recount, relate. **3** *the
disease is communicated easily:*
transmit, spread, transfer, pass
on.

communication noun **1** *there
was no communication between
them:* **contact,** dealings,
relations, connection,
correspondence, dialogue,
conversation. **2** *an official
communication:* **message,**
statement, announcement,
report, dispatch, bulletin,
disclosure, communiqué, letter,
correspondence.

communicative adjective
forthcoming, expansive,
expressive, unreserved, vocal,
outgoing, frank, open, candid,
talkative, chatty.
OPPOSITES uncommunicative.

communist noun & adjective
collectivist, Bolshevik, Marxist,
Maoist, Soviet; informal, derogatory
Commie, red.

community noun **society,**
population, populace, people,
public, residents, inhabitants,
citizens.

compact[1] adjective **1** *extremely compact rugs:* **dense,** tightly packed, compressed, thick, tight, firm, solid. **2** *a very compact phone:* **neat,** small, handy, petite. **3** *her tale is compact and readable:* **concise,** succinct, condensed, brief, pithy, to the point, short and sweet; informal snappy.
OPPOSITES loose, bulky, lengthy.
verb *the rubbish is then compacted:* **compress,** condense, pack down, tamp (down), flatten.

compact[2] noun *the warring states signed a compact:* **treaty,** pact, accord, agreement, contract, bargain, deal, settlement.

companion noun comrade, fellow ..., partner, associate, escort, compatriot, confederate, friend; informal pal, chum, crony; Brit. informal mate; N. Amer. informal buddy.

company noun **1** *an oil company:* **firm,** business, corporation, establishment, agency, office, house, institution, concern, enterprise, consortium, syndicate; informal outfit. **2** *I enjoy his company:* **companionship,** fellowship, society, presence. **3** *a company of infantry:* **unit,** section, detachment, corps, squad, platoon.

comparable adjective **1** *comparable incomes:* **similar,** close, near, approximate, equivalent, proportionate. **2** *nobody is comparable with him:* **equal to,** as good as, in the same league as, on a level with, a match for.
OPPOSITES incomparable.

compare verb **1** *we compared the two portraits:* **contrast,** balance, set against, weigh up. **2** *he was compared to Wagner:* **liken,** equate, class with, bracket with. **3** *the porcelain compares with Dresden china:* **be as good as,** be comparable to, bear comparison with, be the equal of, match up to, be on a par with, be in the same league as, come close to, rival.

comparison noun *there's no comparison between them:* **resemblance,** likeness, similarity, correspondence.

compartment noun bay, locker, recess, alcove, cell, cubicle, pod, pigeonhole, cubbyhole.

compass noun scope, range, extent, reach, span, breadth, ambit, limits, parameters, bounds.

compassion noun sympathy, empathy, understanding, fellow feeling, pity, care, concern, sensitivity, kindness.
OPPOSITES indifference, cruelty.

compassionate adjective sympathetic, understanding, pitying, caring, sensitive, warm, loving, kind.
OPPOSITES unsympathetic, uncaring.

compatible adjective well matched, (well) suited, like-minded, in tune, in harmony, in keeping, consistent, consonant; informal on the same wavelength.
OPPOSITES incompatible.

compel verb force, pressure, coerce, dragoon, press, push, oblige, require, make; informal lean on, railroad, put the screws on.

compelling adjective **1** *a compelling performance:* **enthralling,** captivating, gripping, riveting, spellbinding, mesmerizing, absorbing. **2** *a compelling argument:*

C

convincing, persuasive, cogent, irresistible, powerful, strong.
OPPOSITES boring, weak.

compensate verb **1** *we agreed to compensate him for his loss:* **recompense,** repay, pay back, reimburse, remunerate, indemnify. **2** *his flair compensated for his faults:* **balance (out),** counterbalance, counteract, offset, make up for, cancel out.

compensation noun **recompense,** repayment, reimbursement, remuneration, redress, amends, damages; N. Amer. informal comp.

compete verb **1** *they competed in a tennis tournament:* **take part,** participate, be a contestant, play, enter, go in for. **2** *they had to compete with other firms:* **contend,** vie, battle, jockey, go head to head, pit oneself against, challenge, take on.

competence noun **1** *my technical competence:* **ability,** capability, proficiency, accomplishment, expertise, skill, prowess; informal know-how. **2** *the competence of the system:* **adequacy,** suitability, fitness.
OPPOSITES incompetence.

competent adjective **1** *a competent carpenter:* **able,** capable, proficient, adept, accomplished, skilful, skilled, expert. **2** *the court was not competent to hear the case:* **fit,** suitable, suited, appropriate, qualified, empowered, authorized.
OPPOSITES incompetent, unfit.

competition noun **1** *Stephanie won the competition:* **contest,** tournament, championship. **2** *I'm not interested in competition:* **rivalry,** competitiveness, conflict; informal keeping up with the Joneses. **3** *we must stay ahead of the competition:* **opposition,** rivals, other side, field, enemy; informal other guy.

competitive adjective **1** *a competitive player:* **ambitious,** zealous, keen, combative, aggressive; informal go-ahead. **2** *a highly competitive industry:* **ruthless,** aggressive, fierce, cut-throat; informal dog-eat-dog. **3** *competitive prices:* **reasonable,** moderate, keen, low, cheap, budget, bargain, rock-bottom, bargain-basement.
OPPOSITES apathetic, exorbitant.

competitor noun **1** *the competitors in the race:* **contestant,** contender, challenger, participant, entrant, player. **2** *our European competitors:* **rival,** challenger, opponent, competition, opposition.
OPPOSITES partner, teammate, ally.

compile verb **assemble,** put together, make up, collate, compose, organize, arrange, gather, collect.

complacency noun **smugness,** self-satisfaction, self-congratulation, self-regard.

complacent adjective **smug,** self-satisfied, self-congratulatory, resting on one's laurels.

complain verb **protest,** grumble, whine, bleat, carp, cavil, grouse, make a fuss, object, find fault; informal whinge, gripe, moan, bitch.

complaint noun **1** *they lodged a complaint:* **protest,** objection, grievance, grouse, grumble, criticism; informal gripe, whinge.

2 *a kidney complaint:* disorder, disease, illness, sickness, ailment, infection, condition, problem, upset, trouble.

complement noun **1** *the perfect complement to the food:* **accompaniment,** companion, addition, supplement, accessory, finishing touch. **2** *a full complement of lifeboats:* **amount,** contingent, capacity, allowance, quota.
OPPOSITES contrast.
verb *this sauce complements the dessert:* **accompany,** go with, round off, set off, suit, harmonize with, enhance, complete.
OPPOSITES contrast with.

complementary adjective **harmonious,** compatible, corresponding, matching, reciprocal.
OPPOSITES incompatible.

complete adjective **1** *the complete text:* **entire,** whole, full, total, uncut, unabridged, unexpurgated. **2** *their research was complete:* **finished,** ended, concluded, completed; informal wrapped up, sewn up. **3** *a complete fool:* **absolute,** utter, out-and-out, total, downright, prize, perfect, unqualified, unmitigated, sheer; N. Amer. full-bore.
OPPOSITES partial, unfinished.
verb **1** *he had to complete his training:* **finish,** end, conclude, finalize, wind up; informal wrap up. **2** *the outfit was completed with a veil:* **finish off,** round off, top off, crown, cap. **3** *complete the application form:* **fill in/out,** answer.

completely adverb **totally,** entirely, wholly, thoroughly, fully, utterly, absolutely, perfectly, downright.

complex adjective **1** *a complex structure:* **compound,** composite, multiplex. **2** *a complex situation:* **complicated,** involved, intricate, convoluted, elaborate, difficult; Brit. informal fiddly.
OPPOSITES simple.
noun **1** *a complex of roads:* **network,** system, nexus, web. **2** (informal) *he had a complex about losing his hair:* **obsession,** fixation, preoccupation, neurosis; informal hang-up, thing.

complexion noun **1** *a pale complexion:* **skin,** skin colour/tone, colouring. **2** *governments of all complexions:* **kind,** nature, character, colour, persuasion, outlook.

complicate verb **make (more) difficult,** make complicated, mix up, confuse, muddle, compound.
OPPOSITES simplify.

complicated adjective **1** *a complicated stereo system:* **compound,** composite, multiplex. **2** *a long and complicated saga:* **involved,** intricate, complex, convoluted, elaborate, difficult; Brit. informal fiddly.
OPPOSITES simple, straightforward.

complication noun **difficulty,** problem, obstacle, hurdle, stumbling block, snag, catch, hitch; Brit. spanner in the works; informal headache.

compliment noun *an unexpected compliment:* **tribute,** accolade, commendation, pat on the back; (**compliments**) praise, acclaim, admiration, flattery, congratulations.
OPPOSITES criticism, insult.
verb *they complimented him on*

his performance: **praise,** pay tribute to, flatter, commend, acclaim, applaud, salute, congratulate.
OPPOSITES criticize.

complimentary adjective
1 *complimentary remarks:* **flattering,** appreciative, congratulatory, admiring, approving, favourable, glowing. **2** *complimentary tickets:* **free (of charge),** gratis, donated, courtesy; informal on the house.
OPPOSITES critical.

comply verb **obey,** observe, abide by, adhere to, conform to, follow, respect, go along with.
OPPOSITES disobey.

component noun **part,** piece, bit, element, constituent, ingredient, unit, module.

compose verb **1** *a poem composed by Shelley:* **write,** devise, make up, think up, produce, invent, pen, author. **2** *how to compose a photograph:* **organize,** arrange, construct, set out. **3** *the congress is composed of ten senators:* **make up,** constitute, form, comprise.
■ **compose oneself calm down,** control oneself, regain one's composure, pull oneself together, steady oneself; informal get a grip.

composed adjective **calm,** collected, cool (as a cucumber), self-possessed, poised, serene, relaxed, at ease, unruffled, unperturbed; informal unflappable, together, laid-back.
OPPOSITES excited.

composition noun **1** *the composition of the council:* **make-up,** constitution, configuration, structure, formation, anatomy, organization. **2** *a literary composition:* **work (of art),** creation, opus, piece. **3** *the composition of a poem:* **writing,** creation, formulation, compilation. **4** *a school composition:* **essay,** paper, study, piece of writing; N. Amer. theme. **5** *the composition of the painting:* **arrangement,** layout, proportions, balance, symmetry.

compound noun *a compound of two materials:* **amalgam,** blend, mixture, mix, alloy.
adjective *a compound substance:* **composite,** complex, multiple.
OPPOSITES simple.
verb **1** *soap compounded with disinfectant:* **mix,** combine, blend. **2** *his illness compounds their problems:* **aggravate,** exacerbate, worsen, add to, augment, intensify, heighten, increase.
OPPOSITES separate, alleviate.

comprehend verb **understand,** grasp, see, take in, follow, make sense of, fathom; informal work out, figure out, get.

comprehensible adjective **intelligible,** understandable, accessible, self-explanatory, clear, plain, straightforward.
OPPOSITES opaque.

comprehension noun **understanding,** grasp, mastery, conception, knowledge, awareness.
OPPOSITES ignorance.

comprehensive adjective **inclusive,** all-inclusive, complete, thorough, full, extensive, all-embracing, blanket, exhaustive, detailed, sweeping, wholesale, broad, wide-ranging.
OPPOSITES limited.

compress verb **1** *it is coconut compressed into a slab:* **squeeze,** press, squash, crush, compact.

2 *the material has been compressed into 17 pages:* **shorten,** abridge, condense, abbreviate, contract, telescope, summarize, precis.
OPPOSITES expand, pad out.

comprise verb **1** *the country comprises twenty states:* **consist of,** be made up of, be composed of, contain. **2** *this breed comprises half the herd:* **make up,** constitute, form, account for.

compromise noun *they reached a compromise:* **agreement,** understanding, settlement, terms, deal, trade-off, bargain, middle ground.
OPPOSITES intransigence.
verb **1** *we compromised:* **meet each other halfway,** come to an understanding, make a deal, make concessions, find a happy medium, strike a balance. **2** *his actions could compromise his reputation:* **undermine,** weaken, damage, harm, jeopardize, prejudice.

compulsion noun **1** *he is under no compulsion to go:* **obligation,** pressure, coercion. **2** *a compulsion to tell the truth:* **urge,** impulse, need, desire, drive, obsession, fixation, addiction.

compulsive adjective **1** *a compulsive desire:* **irresistible,** uncontrollable, compelling, overwhelming. **2** *compulsive eating:* **obsessive,** obsessional, addictive, uncontrollable. **3** *a compulsive liar:* **inveterate,** chronic, incorrigible, incurable, hopeless, persistent, habitual; informal pathological. **4** *it's compulsive viewing:* **fascinating,** compelling, gripping, riveting, engrossing, enthralling, captivating.

compulsory adjective **obligatory,** mandatory, required, requisite, necessary, binding, enforced, prescribed.
OPPOSITES optional.

compute verb **calculate,** work out, reckon, determine, evaluate, add up, total.

comrade noun **companion,** friend, colleague, associate, partner, ally; Brit. informal mate; N. Amer. informal buddy.

conceal verb **1** *clouds concealed the sun:* **hide,** screen, cover, obscure, block out, blot out, mask. **2** *he concealed his true feelings:* **keep secret,** hide, disguise, mask, veil, bottle up; informal keep a/the lid on.
OPPOSITES reveal, confess.

concede verb **1** *I had to concede that I'd overreacted:* **admit,** acknowledge, accept, allow, grant, recognize, own, confess, agree. **2** *he eventually conceded the title:* **surrender,** yield, give up, relinquish, hand over.
OPPOSITES deny, retain.

conceit noun **vanity,** pride, arrogance, egotism, self-importance, narcissism, self-admiration.
OPPOSITES humility.

conceited adjective **vain,** proud, arrogant, egotistic, self-satisfied, self-important, narcissistic, full of oneself; informal big-headed, stuck-up.

conceive verb **1** *the project was conceived in 1977:* **think up,** think of, dream up, devise, formulate, design, create, develop. **2** *I could hardly conceive what it must be like:* **imagine,** envisage, visualize, picture, grasp, appreciate.

concentrate verb **1** *the government concentrated its efforts on staying in power:*

focus, direct, centre. **2** *she concentrated on the film:* **focus on**, pay attention to, keep one's mind on, be absorbed in, be engrossed in, be immersed in. **3** *troops concentrated on the horizon:* **collect**, gather, congregate, converge, mass, rally.
OPPOSITES disperse.

concentrated adjective **1** *a concentrated effort:* **strenuous**, concerted, intensive, all-out, intense. **2** *a concentrated solution:* **condensed**, reduced, undiluted, strong.
OPPOSITES half-hearted, diluted.

concentration noun **close attention**, attentiveness, application, single-mindedness, absorption.
OPPOSITES inattention.

concept noun **idea**, notion, conception, abstraction, theory, hypothesis.

conception noun **1** *the fertility treatment resulted in conception:* **pregnancy**, fertilization, impregnation, insemination. **2** *the product's conception:* **inception**, genesis, origination, creation, invention, beginning, origin. **3** *his original conception:* **plan**, idea, notion, scheme, project, proposal, intention, aim.

concern verb **1** *the report concerns the war:* **be about**, deal with, cover, relate to, pertain to. **2** *that doesn't concern you:* **affect**, involve, be relevant to, apply to, have a bearing on, impact on. **3** *one thing still concerns me:* **worry**, disturb, trouble, bother, perturb, unsettle.
noun **1** *a voice full of concern:* **anxiety**, worry, disquiet, apprehensiveness, unease,

misgiving. **2** *his concern for others:* **care**, consideration, solicitude, sympathy. **3** *housing is the concern of the council:* **responsibility**, business, affair, duty, job; informal bailiwick; Brit. informal lookout. **4** *issues of concern to women:* **interest**, importance, relevance, significance. **5** *a publishing concern:* **firm**, business, company, enterprise, operation, corporation; informal outfit.
OPPOSITES indifference.

concerned adjective **1** *her mother looked concerned:* **worried**, anxious, upset, troubled, uneasy, bothered. **2** *all concerned parties:* **interested**, involved, affected, implicated.
OPPOSITES unconcerned.

concerning preposition **about**, regarding, relating to, with reference to, referring to, with regard to, as regards, touching, in connection with, re, apropos.

concession noun **1** *the government made several concessions:* **compromise**, accommodation, trade-off, sop. **2** *tax concessions:* **reduction**, cut, discount, deduction, rebate; informal break. **3** *a logging concession:* **right**, privilege, licence, permit, franchise, warrant.

concise adjective **succinct**, pithy, brief, abridged, condensed, abbreviated, compact, potted.
OPPOSITES lengthy.

conclude verb **1** *the meeting concluded at ten:* **finish**, end, draw to a close, stop, cease. **2** *he concluded the press conference:* **bring to an end**, close, wind up, terminate; informal wrap up. **3** *an attempt to conclude a deal:* **settle**, clinch,

finalize, tie up. **4** *I concluded that he was rather unpleasant:* **deduce,** infer, gather, judge, decide, surmise; N. Amer. figure.
OPPOSITES begin.

conclusion noun **1** *the conclusion of his speech:* **end,** ending, finish, close. **2** *the conclusion of a trade agreement:* **settlement,** clinching, completion, arrangement. **3** *his conclusions have been verified:* **deduction,** inference, interpretation, judgement, verdict.
OPPOSITES beginning.

concrete adjective **1** *concrete objects:* **solid,** material, real, physical, tangible. **2** *concrete proof:* **definite,** specific, firm, positive, conclusive, precise.
OPPOSITES abstract, imaginary.

condemn verb **1** *he condemned the suspended players:* **censure,** criticize, denounce; informal slam; Brit. informal slate, slag off. **2** *his illness condemned him to a lonely life:* **doom,** destine, damn, sentence.
OPPOSITES praise.

condemnation noun censure, criticism, denunciation; informal flak, a bad press.

condense verb abridge, compress, summarize, shorten, cut, abbreviate, edit.
OPPOSITES expand.

condition noun **1** *check the condition of your wiring:* **state,** shape, order; Brit. informal nick. **2** *they lived in appalling conditions:* **circumstances,** surroundings, environment, situation. **3** *she was in tip-top condition:* **fitness,** health, form, shape. **4** *a liver condition:* **disorder,** problem, complaint, illness, disease. **5** *a condition of employment:* **stipulation,**

constraint, prerequisite, precondition, requirement, term, proviso.
verb *our minds are conditioned by habit:* **train,** teach, educate, guide, accustom, adapt, habituate, mould.

conditional adjective **qualified,** dependent, contingent, with reservations, limited, provisional, provisory.

condone verb **disregard,** accept, allow, let pass, turn a blind eye to, overlook, forget, forgive, pardon, excuse.
OPPOSITES condemn.

conduct noun **1** *they complained about her conduct:* **behaviour,** actions, deeds, doings, exploits. **2** *the conduct of the elections:* **management,** running, direction, control, supervision, regulation, administration, organization, coordination, handling.
verb **1** *the election was conducted lawfully:* **manage,** direct, run, administer, organize, coordinate, orchestrate, handle, carry out/ on. **2** *he was conducted through the corridors:* **escort,** guide, lead, usher, steer. **3** *aluminium conducts heat:* **transmit,** convey, carry, channel.
■ **conduct oneself** behave, act, acquit oneself, bear oneself.

confer verb **1** *she conferred a knighthood on him:* **bestow on,** present to, grant to, award to, decorate with. **2** *she went to confer with her colleagues:* **consult,** talk, speak, converse, have a chat, deliberate.

conference noun meeting, congress, convention, seminar, discussion, council, forum, summit.

confess verb **1** *he confessed that*

he had done it: **admit,**
acknowledge, reveal, disclose,
divulge, own up; informal come
clean. **2** *they could not make
him confess:* **own up,** plead
guilty, accept the blame; informal
come clean. **3** *I confess I don't
know:* **acknowledge,** admit,
concede, grant, allow, own.
OPPOSITES deny.

confide verb reveal, disclose,
divulge, impart, declare,
vouchsafe, tell, confess.

confidence noun **1** *I have little
confidence in these figures:*
trust, belief, faith, credence.
2 *she's brimming with
confidence:* **self-assurance,** self-
confidence, self-possession,
assertiveness, self-belief,
conviction.
OPPOSITES distrust, doubt.

confident adjective **1** *we are
confident that business will
improve:* **sure,** certain, positive,
convinced, in no doubt,
satisfied. **2** *a confident girl:*
self-assured, assured, self-
confident, positive, assertive,
self-possessed.

confidential adjective private,
personal, intimate, quiet,
secret, sensitive, classified,
restricted; informal hush-hush.

confine verb **1** *they were
confined in the house:* **enclose,**
incarcerate, imprison, intern,
hold captive, cage, lock up,
coop up. **2** *he confined his
remarks to the weather:*
restrict, limit.

confirm verb **1** *records confirm
the latest evidence:*
corroborate, verify, prove,
substantiate, justify, vindicate,
bear out. **2** *he confirmed that
help was on the way:* **affirm,**
reaffirm, assert, assure
someone, repeat. **3** *his*

*appointment was confirmed by
the President:* **ratify,** approve,
endorse, validate, sanction,
authorize.
OPPOSITES contradict, deny.

confiscate verb impound,
seize, commandeer, requisition,
appropriate, expropriate,
sequester.
OPPOSITES return.

conflict noun **1** *industrial
conflicts:* **dispute,** quarrel,
squabble, disagreement, clash,
feud, discord, friction, strife,
antagonism, hostility. **2** *the
Vietnam conflict:* **war,**
campaign, fighting,
engagement, struggle,
hostilities, warfare, combat. **3** *a
conflict between work and home
life:* **clash,** incompatibility,
friction, mismatch, variance,
contradiction.
OPPOSITES agreement, peace,
harmony.
verb *their interests sometimes
conflict:* **clash,** be incompatible,
be at odds, differ, diverge,
disagree, collide.

conflicting adjective
contradictory, incompatible,
inconsistent, irreconcilable,
contrary, opposite, opposing,
clashing.

conform verb **1** *visitors have to
conform to our rules:* **comply
with,** abide by, obey, observe,
follow, keep to, stick to, adhere
to, uphold, heed, accept, go
along with. **2** *they refuse to
conform:* **fit in,** behave
(oneself), toe the line, obey the
rules; informal play by the rules.
OPPOSITES flout, rebel.

confound verb baffle, bewilder,
mystify, bemuse, perplex,
puzzle, confuse, dumbfound,
throw; informal flabbergast,
flummox.

confront verb **1** *Martin confronted the burglar:* **challenge,** square up to, face (up to), come face to face with, meet, accost, stand up to, tackle. **2** *the problems that confront us:* **face,** plague, bother, trouble, beset, threaten. **3** *they must confront these issues:* **tackle,** address, face, get to grips with, grapple with. **4** *she confronted him with the evidence:* **present,** face.
OPPOSITES evade.

confrontation noun **conflict,** clash, fight, battle, encounter, head-to-head; informal set-to, run-in, dust-up, showdown.

confuse verb **1** *don't confuse students with too much detail:* **bewilder,** baffle, mystify, bemuse, perplex, puzzle, nonplus; informal flummox, faze. **2** *the authors have confused the issue:* **complicate,** muddle, blur, obscure, cloud. **3** *some confuse strokes with heart attacks:* **mix up,** muddle up, mistake for.
OPPOSITES enlighten, simplify.

confused adjective **1** *they are confused about what is going on:* **puzzled,** bemused, bewildered, perplexed, baffled, mystified; informal flummoxed. **2** *her confused elderly mother:* **disorientated,** bewildered, muddled, addled, befuddled, demented, senile. **3** *a confused recollection:* **vague,** unclear, indistinct, imprecise, blurred, hazy, dim. **4** *a confused mass of bones:* **disorderly,** disorganized, untidy, jumbled, mixed up, chaotic, topsy-turvy, tangled; informal higgledy-piggledy; Brit. informal shambolic.
OPPOSITES clear, lucid, precise, neat.

confusing adjective **puzzling,** baffling, perplexing, bewildering, mystifying, ambiguous, misleading, inconsistent, contradictory.

confusion noun **1** *there is confusion about the new system:* **uncertainty,** doubt, ignorance. **2** *she stared in confusion:* **bewilderment,** bafflement, perplexity, puzzlement, befuddlement. **3** *her life was in utter confusion:* **disorder,** disarray, chaos, mayhem, turmoil, muddle, mess; informal shambles.
OPPOSITES certainty, order.

congenial adjective **1** *very congenial people:* **sociable,** convivial, hospitable, genial, personable, agreeable, friendly, amiable. **2** *a congenial environment:* **pleasant,** agreeable, enjoyable, pleasurable, relaxing, welcoming, hospitable, favourable.
OPPOSITES unsociable, unpleasant.

congested adjective **blocked,** clogged, choked, jammed, obstructed, crowded, overcrowded, overflowing, packed; informal snarled up, gridlocked.
OPPOSITES clear.

congratulate verb **compliment,** wish someone happiness, pay tribute to, pat on the back, take one's hat off to, praise, applaud, salute, honour.
OPPOSITES criticize.

congratulations plural noun **best wishes,** compliments, greetings, felicitations.

congregate verb **assemble,** gather, collect, come together, convene, rally, muster, meet, cluster, group.

conjure verb 1 *he conjured a cigarette out of the air:* **produce,** magic, summon. 2 *the picture that his words conjured up:* **bring to mind,** call to mind, evoke, summon up, suggest.

connect verb 1 *electrodes were connected to the device:* **attach,** join, fasten, fix, link, hook (up), secure, hitch, stick. 2 *customs connected with Easter:* **associate,** link, couple, identify, relate to.
OPPOSITES detach.

connection noun 1 *the connection between commerce and art:* **link,** relationship, relation, interconnection, interdependence, association, bond, tie, tie-in, correspondence. 2 *he has the right connections:* **contact,** friend, acquaintance, ally, colleague, associate, relation.

conquer verb 1 *the Franks conquered the Visigoths:* **defeat,** beat, vanquish, triumph over, overcome, overwhelm, overpower, overthrow, subdue, subjugate. 2 *Peru was conquered by Spain:* **seize,** take (over), appropriate, capture, occupy, invade, annex, overrun. 3 *the first men to conquer Mount Everest:* **climb,** ascend, scale. 4 *the way to conquer fear:* **overcome,** get the better of, control, master, deal with, cope with, rise above; *informal* lick.
OPPOSITES lose to, lose, give in to.

conquest noun 1 *the conquest of the Aztecs:* **defeat,** overthrow, subjugation. 2 *their conquest of the territory:* **seizure,** takeover, capture, occupation, invasion, annexation. 3 *the conquest of Everest:* **ascent,** climbing.

conscience noun **sense of right and wrong,** morals, standards, values, principles, ethics, beliefs, scruples, qualms.

conscientious adjective **diligent,** industrious, punctilious, painstaking, dedicated, careful, meticulous, thorough, attentive, hard-working, rigorous, scrupulous, religious.
OPPOSITES casual.

conscious adjective 1 *the patient was conscious:* **aware,** awake; *informal* with us. 2 *a conscious decision:* **deliberate,** purposeful, knowing, considered, calculated, wilful, premeditated.
OPPOSITES unaware, unconscious.

consecutive adjective **successive,** succeeding, in succession, running, in a row, straight; *informal* on the trot.

consensus noun 1 *there was consensus among delegates:* **agreement,** unanimity, harmony, accord, unity, solidarity. 2 *the consensus was that they should act:* **general opinion,** common view.
OPPOSITES disagreement.

consent noun *the consent of all members:* **agreement,** assent, acceptance, approval, permission, authorization, sanction; *informal* go-ahead, green light, OK.
OPPOSITES dissent.
verb *she consented to surgery:* **agree,** assent, submit, allow, sanction, approve, go along with.
OPPOSITES forbid, refuse.

consequence noun 1 *a consequence of inflation:* **result,** upshot, outcome, effect, repercussion, ramification,

product, end result. **2** *the past is of no consequence:* **importance,** import, significance, account, value, concern.
OPPOSITES cause.

consequently adverb **as a result,** as a consequence, so, thus, therefore, accordingly, hence, for this/that reason, because of this/that.

conservation noun **preservation,** protection, safe keeping, husbandry, upkeep, maintenance, repair, restoration.

conservative adjective **1** *the conservative wing of the party:* **right-wing,** reactionary, traditionalist. **2** *the conservative trade-union movement:* **traditionalist,** old-fashioned, dyed-in-the-wool, hidebound, unadventurous, reactionary, set in one's ways; informal stick in the mud. **3** *a conservative suit:* **conventional,** sober, modest, sensible, restrained; informal square.
OPPOSITES socialist, radical, ostentatious.

conserve verb *fossil fuel should be conserved:* **preserve,** protect, save, safeguard, keep, look after, sustain, husband.
OPPOSITES squander.

consider verb **1** *Isabel considered her choices:* **think about,** contemplate, reflect on, mull over, ponder, deliberate on, chew over, meditate on, ruminate on, evaluate, weigh up, appraise, take account of, bear in mind; informal size up. **2** *I consider him irresponsible:* **deem,** think, believe, judge, rate, count, find, regard as, hold to be, reckon to be, view as, see as. **3** *he considered the painting:*

look at, contemplate, observe, regard, survey, examine, inspect.

considerable adjective **sizeable,** substantial, appreciable, significant, plentiful, goodly; informal tidy.
OPPOSITES paltry.

considerably adverb **greatly,** (very) much, a great deal, a lot, lots, significantly, substantially, appreciably, markedly, noticeably; informal plenty.

considerate adjective **attentive,** thoughtful, solicitous, kind, unselfish, caring, polite, sensitive.

consideration noun **1** *your case needs careful consideration:* **thought,** deliberation, reflection, contemplation, examination, inspection, scrutiny, analysis, discussion, attention. **2** *his health is the prime consideration:* **factor,** issue, matter, concern, aspect, feature. **3** *firms should show more consideration:* **attentiveness,** concern, care, thoughtfulness, solicitude, understanding, respect, sensitivity.

considering preposition **bearing in mind,** taking into consideration, taking into account, in view of, in the light of.

consist
■ **consist of** be composed of, be made up of, be formed of, comprise, include, contain.

consistent adjective **1** *consistent opinion-poll evidence:* **constant,** regular, uniform, steady, stable, even, unchanging. **2** *her injuries were consistent with a knife attack:* **compatible,** in tune, in line, corresponding to, conforming to.

OPPOSITES irregular, incompatible.

consolation noun comfort, solace, sympathy, pity, commiseration, relief, encouragement, reassurance.

console verb comfort, sympathize with, commiserate with, show compassion for, help, support, cheer (up), hearten, encourage, reassure, soothe.
OPPOSITES upset.

consolidate verb 1 *we consolidated our position in the market:* **strengthen,** secure, stabilize, reinforce, fortify. 2 *consolidate the results into an action plan:* **combine,** unite, merge, integrate, amalgamate, fuse, synthesize.

conspicuous adjective obvious, evident, apparent, visible, noticeable, clear, plain, marked, patent, blatant.
OPPOSITES inconspicuous.

conspiracy noun plot, scheme, intrigue, plan, collusion, ploy.

conspire verb 1 *they admitted conspiring to steal cars:* **plot,** scheme, intrigue, manoeuvre, plan. 2 *circumstances conspired against them:* **combine,** unite, join forces, work together.

constant adjective 1 *constant noise:* **continuous,** persistent, sustained, ceaseless, unceasing, perpetual, incessant, never-ending, eternal, endless, non-stop. 2 *a constant speed:* **consistent,** regular, steady, uniform, even, invariable, unvarying, unchanging. 3 *a constant friend:* **faithful,** loyal, devoted, true, fast, firm, unswerving.
OPPOSITES intermittent, variable, fickle.

constitute verb 1 *farmers constituted 10 per cent of the population:* **comprise,** make up, form, account for. 2 *this constitutes a breach of copyright:* **amount to,** be tantamount to, be equivalent to, represent. 3 *the courts were constituted in 1875:* **establish,** inaugurate, found, create, set up.

constitution noun 1 *the chemical constitution of the dye:* **composition,** make-up, structure, construction, arrangement, configuration, formation, anatomy. 2 *she has the constitution of an ox:* **health,** condition, strength, stamina, build, physique.

constraint noun 1 *financial constraints:* **restriction,** limitation, curb, check, restraint, control. 2 *they were able to talk without constraint:* **inhibition,** uneasiness, embarrassment, self-consciousness, awkwardness.
OPPOSITES freedom, ease.

constrict verb narrow, tighten, compress, contract, squeeze, strangle.
OPPOSITES expand, dilate.

construct verb 1 *a bridge constructed by the army:* **build,** erect, put up, set up, assemble, fabricate. 2 *he constructed a faultless argument:* **create,** formulate, form, put together, devise, compose, work out, frame.
OPPOSITES demolish.

construction noun 1 *the station was a spectacular construction:* **structure,** building, edifice, work. 2 *you put such a sordid construction on it:* **interpretation,** explanation, analysis, reading, meaning; informal take.

constructive adjective **useful,** helpful, productive, positive, practical, valuable, profitable, worthwhile.
OPPOSITES unhelpful.

consult verb **1** *you need to consult a solicitor:* **seek advice from,** ask, call (on), turn to; informal pick someone's brains. **2** *the government must consult with interested parties:* **confer,** talk things over, communicate, deliberate, compare notes. **3** *she consulted her diary:* **refer to,** look at, check.

consultant noun **adviser,** expert, specialist, authority.

consultation noun **1** *the need for further consultation with industry:* **discussion,** dialogue, debate, negotiation, deliberation. **2** *a 30-minute consultation:* **meeting,** talk, discussion, interview, examination, audience, hearing.

consume verb **1** *vast amounts of food and drink were consumed:* **eat,** devour, swallow, gobble up, wolf down, guzzle, drink. **2** *natural resources are being consumed at an alarming rate:* **use (up),** expend, deplete, exhaust, spend. **3** *the fire consumed fifty houses:* **destroy,** demolish, lay waste, raze, devastate, gut, ruin, wreck. **4** *Carolyn was consumed with guilt:* **eat up,** devour, grip, overwhelm, absorb, obsess, preoccupy.

consumer noun **buyer,** purchaser, customer, shopper, user.

contact noun **1** *have you had any contact with him?* **communication,** correspondence, connection, relations, dealings, touch. **2** *he had many contacts in Germany:* **connection,** link, acquaintance, associate, friend.
verb *he should contact the police:* **get in touch with,** communicate with, approach, notify, speak to, write to, come forward; informal get hold of.

contain verb **1** *the boat contained four people:* **hold,** carry, enclose, accommodate. **2** *the archive contains much unpublished material:* **include,** comprise, incorporate, involve, consist of, be made up of, be composed of. **3** *he must contain his anger:* **restrain,** control, curb, rein in, suppress, stifle, swallow, bottle up, keep in check.
OPPOSITES vent.

container noun **receptacle,** vessel, holder, repository.

contaminate verb **pollute,** taint, poison, stain, adulterate, defile, debase, corrupt.
OPPOSITES purify.

contemplate verb **1** *she contemplated her image in the mirror:* **look at,** gaze at, stare at, view, regard, examine, inspect, observe, survey, study, eye. **2** *he contemplated his fate:* **think about,** ponder, reflect on, consider, mull over, muse on, dwell on, deliberate over, meditate on, ruminate on, chew over. **3** *he was contemplating legal action:* **consider,** think about, have in mind, intend, plan, propose.

contemporary adjective **1** *contemporary sources:* **of the time,** contemporaneous, concurrent, coexisting. **2** *contemporary society:* **modern,** present-day, present, current. **3** *a very contemporary design:* **modern,** up to date, up to the minute, fashionable,

recent; informal trendy.
opposites older, newer, former, old-fashioned.

contempt noun scorn, disdain, derision, disgust, disrespect.
opposites respect.

contemptuous adjective scornful, disdainful, derisive, mocking, sneering, scoffing, condescending, dismissive.
opposites respectful.

contend verb 1 *three groups were contending for power:* compete, vie, battle, tussle, struggle, jostle, strive. 2 *he contends that the judge was wrong:* assert, maintain, hold, claim, argue, insist, allege.
■ contend with cope with, struggle with, grapple with, deal with, take on, handle.

content[1] adjective *she seemed content with life:* satisfied, contented, pleased, fulfilled, happy, glad, at ease.
opposites dissatisfied.
verb *her reply seemed to content him:* satisfy, comfort, gratify, gladden, please, soothe, placate, appease, mollify.

content[2] noun 1 *foods with a high fibre content:* amount, proportion, level. 2 (contents) *the contents of a vegetarian sausage:* constituents, ingredients, components. 3 *the content of the essay:* subject matter, theme, argument, thesis, message, substance, material, ideas.

contented adjective. See CONTENT[1] adjective.

contentious adjective 1 *a contentious issue:* controversial, debatable, disputed, open to debate, moot, vexed. 2 *contentious people:* quarrelsome, argumentative, confrontational; Brit. informal stroppy.

contest noun 1 *a boxing contest:* competition, match, tournament, game, bout. 2 *the contest for the party leadership:* fight, battle, tussle, struggle, competition, race.
verb 1 *he intended to contest the seat:* compete for, contend for, vie for, fight for. 2 *a system where parties contest elections:* compete in, take part in, fight, enter. 3 *we contested the decision:* oppose, challenge, take issue with, question, call into question, object to.
opposites accept.

contestant noun competitor, participant, player, contender, candidate, entrant.

context noun circumstances, conditions, frame of reference, factors, state of affairs, situation, background, scene, setting.

contingency noun eventuality, possibility, chance event, incident, occurrence, accident, emergency.

continual adjective 1 *continual breakdowns:* frequent, repeated, constant, recurrent, recurring, regular. 2 *continual pain:* constant, continuous, unremitting, unrelenting, chronic, uninterrupted, unbroken.
opposites occasional, temporary.

continue verb 1 *he was unable to continue with his job:* carry on, proceed, pursue, go on, keep on, persist, persevere, keep at; informal stick at. 2 *discussions continued throughout the year:* go on, carry on, last, extend, run on, drag on. 3 *we are keen to continue this relationship:*

C

maintain, keep up, sustain, keep going, keep alive, preserve. **4** *his willingness to continue in office:* **remain,** stay, carry on, keep going. **5** *we continued our conversation after supper:* **resume,** pick up, take up, carry on with, return to, revisit.
OPPOSITES stop, break off, leave.

continuous adjective **continual,** persistent, sustained, ceaseless, unceasing, perpetual, incessant, never-ending, eternal, endless, non-stop.
OPPOSITES intermittent.

contort verb **twist,** bend out of shape, distort, misshape, warp, buckle, deform.

contract noun *a legally binding contract:* **agreement,** arrangement, commitment, settlement, understanding, compact, covenant, deal, bargain.
verb **1** *the market began to contract:* **shrink,** diminish, reduce, decrease, dwindle, decline. **2** *her stomach muscles contracted:* **tighten,** tense, flex, constrict, draw in. **3** *the company was contracted to build the stadium:* **engage,** take on, hire, commission, employ. **4** *she contracted German measles:* **catch,** pick up, come/go down with, develop.
OPPOSITES expand, relax, lengthen.

contraction noun **1** *the contraction of the industry:* **shrinking,** shrinkage, decline, decrease, diminution, dwindling. **2** *the contraction of muscles:* **tightening,** tensing, flexing. **3** *'goodbye' is a contraction of 'God be with you':* **abbreviation,** short form, shortening.

OPPOSITES expansion, relaxation, lengthening.

contradict verb **1** *he contradicted the government's account:* **deny,** refute, rebut, dispute, challenge, counter. **2** *nobody dared contradict him:* **argue with,** go against, challenge, oppose.
OPPOSITES confirm, agree with.

contradiction noun **1** *the contradiction between his faith and his lifestyle:* **conflict,** clash, disagreement, inconsistency, mismatch. **2** *a contradiction of his statement:* **denial,** refutation, rebuttal, countering.
OPPOSITES agreement, confirmation.

contradictory adjective **inconsistent,** incompatible, irreconcilable, opposed, opposite, contrary, conflicting, at variance.

contrary adjective **1** *contrary views:* **opposite,** opposing, contradictory, clashing, conflicting, antithetical, incompatible, irreconcilable. **2** *she was sulky and contrary:* **perverse,** awkward, difficult, uncooperative, obstinate, pig-headed, intractable; Brit. informal bloody-minded, stroppy; N. Amer. informal balky.
OPPOSITES compatible, accommodating.
noun *in fact, the contrary is true:* **opposite,** reverse, converse, antithesis.

contrast noun **1** *the contrast between rural and urban trends:* **difference,** dissimilarity, disparity, divergence, variance, distinction, comparison. **2** *Jane was a complete contrast to Sarah:* **opposite,** antithesis, foil,

complement.
OPPOSITES similarity.
verb **1** *a view which contrasts with his earlier opinion:* **differ,** be at variance, be contrary, conflict, be at odds, disagree, clash. **2** *people contrasted her with her sister:* **compare,** juxtapose, measure, distinguish, differentiate.
OPPOSITES resemble, liken.

contribute verb **give,** donate, put up, grant, provide, supply; informal chip in; Brit. informal stump up.
■ **contribute to** play a part in, be instrumental in, have a hand in, be conducive to, make for.

contribution noun **gift,** donation, offering, present, handout, grant, subsidy.

contributor noun **donor,** benefactor, supporter, backer, patron, sponsor.

contrive verb **1** *they contrived a plan:* **create,** engineer, manufacture, devise, concoct, construct, fabricate, hatch. **2** *Lomax contrived to bump into him:* **manage,** find a way, engineer a way, arrange, succeed in.
OPPOSITES fail.

contrived adjective **forced,** strained, laboured, overdone, unnatural, artificial, false, affected.
OPPOSITES natural.

control noun **1** *China retained control over the region:* **power,** authority, command, dominance, sway, management, direction, leadership, rule, government, sovereignty, supremacy. **2** *strict import controls:* **limit,** limitation, restriction, restraint, check, curb, regulation. **3** *her control deserted her:* **self-control,** self-

restraint, composure, calm; informal cool.
verb **1** *one family controlled the company:* **run,** manage, direct, preside over, supervise, command, rule, govern, lead, dominate. **2** *she struggled to control her temper:* **restrain,** keep in check, curb, hold back, suppress, repress. **3** *public spending was controlled:* **limit,** restrict, curb, cap.

controversial adjective **disputed,** contentious, moot, debatable, arguable, vexed.

controversy noun **dispute,** disagreement, argument, debate, contention, quarrel, war of words, storm; Brit. informal row.

convene verb **1** *he convened a secret meeting:* **summon,** call, order. **2** *the committee convened for its final session:* **assemble,** gather, meet, come together; formal foregather.
OPPOSITES disperse.

convenience noun **1** *the convenience of the arrangement:* **advantage,** benefit, expedience, suitability. **2** *for convenience, the handset is wall-mounted:* **ease of use,** usefulness, utility, accessibility, availability.
OPPOSITES inconvenience.

convenient adjective **1** *a convenient time:* **suitable,** favourable, advantageous, appropriate, opportune, timely, expedient. **2** *a convenient shop:* **nearby,** handy, well situated, practical, useful, accessible.
OPPOSITES inconvenient.

convention noun **1** *social conventions:* **custom,** usage, practice, tradition, etiquette, protocol. **2** *a convention signed by 74 countries:* **agreement,** accord, protocol, pact, treaty. **3** *the party's biennial* convention: **conference,** meeting, congress, assembly, gathering.

conventional adjective
1 *conventional wisdom:* **orthodox,** traditional, established, accepted, received, prevailing. **2** *a conventional railway:* **normal,** standard, regular, ordinary, usual, traditional, typical. **3** *a very conventional woman:* **conservative,** traditional, conformist, old-fashioned; informal square, stick-in-the-mud. **4** *a conventional piece of work:* **unoriginal,** formulaic, predictable, unadventurous.
OPPOSITES unorthodox, unconventional, original.

converge verb *here the lines converge:* **meet,** intersect, cross, connect, link up, join, merge.
OPPOSITES diverge.
■ **converge on** meet at, arrive at, close in on, bear down on, descend on, approach, move towards.

conversation noun **discussion,** talk, chat, gossip, tête-à-tête, exchange, dialogue; Brit. informal chinwag, natter.

conversion noun **1** *the conversion of waste into energy:* **change,** transformation, metamorphosis. **2** *the conversion of the building:* **adaptation,** alteration, modification, redevelopment.

convert verb **1** *plants convert the sun's energy into chemical energy:* **change,** turn, transform, metamorphose. **2** *the factory was converted into flats:* **adapt,** turn, change, alter, modify, redevelop. **3** *they sought to convert sinners:* **win over,** claim, redeem, save, reform, re-educate, proselytize, evangelize.

convey verb **1** *taxis conveyed guests to the station:* **transport,** carry, bring, take, fetch, move. **2** *he conveyed the information to me:* **communicate,** pass on, impart, relate, relay, transmit, send. **3** *it's impossible to convey how I felt:* **express,** communicate, get across/over, put across/over, indicate.

convict verb **find guilty,** sentence.
OPPOSITES acquit.
noun **prisoner,** inmate, criminal, offender, felon; informal jailbird, con, (old) lag.

conviction noun **1** *his political convictions:* **beliefs,** opinions, views, persuasion, ideals, position, stance, values. **2** *she spoke with conviction:* **assurance,** confidence, certainty.
OPPOSITES diffidence.

convince verb **1** *he convinced me that I was wrong:* **assure,** persuade, satisfy, prove to. **2** *I convinced her to marry me:* **persuade,** induce, prevail on, talk into, talk round, win over, coax, cajole, inveigle.

convincing adjective **1** *a convincing argument:* **persuasive,** powerful, strong, forceful, compelling, cogent, plausible, irresistible, telling. **2** *a convincing 5–0 win:* **resounding,** emphatic, decisive, conclusive.
OPPOSITES unconvincing, narrow.

cool adjective **1** *a cool breeze:* **chilly,** chill, cold, bracing, brisk, crisp, fresh; informal nippy; Brit. informal parky. **2** *a cool response to the suggestion:* **unenthusiastic,** lukewarm, tepid, indifferent, uninterested, apathetic. **3** *David seemed*

distinctly cool: **unfriendly,** distant, remote, aloof, cold, chilly, frosty, unwelcoming; informal stand-offish. **4** *his ability to keep cool in a crisis:* **calm,** collected, composed, self-possessed, poised, serene, relaxed, at ease, unruffled, unperturbed; informal unflappable, together, laid-back.
OPPOSITES warm, enthusiastic, friendly, excited.
noun **1** *the cool of the evening:* **chill,** chilliness, coldness, coolness. **2** (informal) *Ken lost his cool:* **self-control,** control, composure, self-possession, calmness, aplomb, poise.
OPPOSITES warmth.
verb *cool the sauce in the fridge:* **chill,** refrigerate, freeze.
OPPOSITES warm.

cooperate verb **1** *police and social services cooperated:* **collaborate,** work together, pull together, join forces, team up, unite, combine, pool resources. **2** *he was happy to cooperate:* **assist,** help, lend a hand, be of service, do one's bit; informal play ball.

cooperation noun
1 *cooperation between management and workers:* **collaboration,** joint action, combined effort, teamwork, give and take, compromise.
2 *thank you for your cooperation:* **assistance,** help.

cooperative adjective **1** *a cooperative effort:* **collaborative,** collective, combined, joint, shared, united, concerted. **2** *pleasant and cooperative staff:* **helpful,** eager to help, obliging, accommodating, willing.

coordinate verb organize, arrange, order, synchronize, bring together, orchestrate.

cope verb **1** *she couldn't cope on her own:* **manage,** survive, look after oneself, fend for oneself, shift for oneself, get by/through, hold one's own. **2** *his inability to cope with the situation:* **deal with,** handle, manage, address, face (up to), confront, tackle, get to grips with.

copy noun **1** *a copy of the report:* **duplicate,** facsimile, photocopy; trademark Xerox. **2** *a copy of a sketch by Leonardo da Vinci:* **replica,** reproduction, imitation, likeness, forgery, fake, counterfeit.
verb **1** *each form had to be copied:* **duplicate,** photocopy, xerox, photostat, reproduce.
2 *portraits copied from originals:* **reproduce,** replicate, forge, fake, counterfeit. **3** *their sound was copied by a lot of jazz players:* **imitate,** reproduce, emulate, mimic; informal rip off.

cord noun string, thread, line, rope, cable, wire, twine, yarn.

cordon noun barrier, line, chain, ring, circle.
■ **cordon something off** close off, seal off, fence off, separate off, isolate, enclose, encircle, surround.

core noun **1** *the earth's core:* **centre,** interior, middle, nucleus. **2** *the core of the argument:* **heart,** nucleus, nub, kernel, meat, essence, crux, pith, substance; informal nitty-gritty.
OPPOSITES edge, periphery.

corner noun **1** *the cart lurched round the corner:* **bend,** curve, turn, junction; Brit. hairpin bend. **2** *a charming corner of*

C

Italy: **district,** region, area, quarter; informal neck of the woods.

verb 1 *he was eventually cornered by police dogs:* **surround,** trap, hem in, pen in, cut off. 2 *crime syndicates have cornered the stolen car market:* **gain control of,** take over, dominate, monopolize, capture; informal sew up.

corporation noun **company,** firm, business, concern, operation, conglomerate, group, chain, multinational.

corpse noun **dead body,** carcass, remains; informal stiff; Medicine cadaver.

correct adjective 1 *the correct answer:* **right,** accurate, exact, true, perfect. 2 *correct behaviour:* **proper,** right, decent, respectable, decorous, suitable, appropriate, accepted. OPPOSITES wrong, improper.
verb *correct any mistakes:* **rectify,** right, put right, set right, amend, remedy, repair, reform, cure.

correction noun **rectification,** righting, amendment, repair, remedy, cure.

correctly adverb 1 *the questions were answered correctly:* **accurately,** right, perfectly, exactly, precisely. 2 *she behaved correctly at all times:* **properly,** decorously, with decorum, decently, fittingly, appropriately, well.
OPPOSITES wrongly, improperly.

correspond verb 1 *the setting corresponds with the number on the dial:* **be consistent,** correlate, agree, accord, coincide, tally, tie in, match; informal square. 2 *a rank corresponding to a British sergeant:* **be equivalent,** be analogous, be comparable, equate. 3 *Debbie and I corresponded for years:* **exchange letters,** write, communicate.

correspondence noun 1 *there is some correspondence between the two variables:* **parallel,** correlation, agreement, consistency, conformity, similarity, resemblance, comparability. 2 *his private correspondence:* **letters,** messages, mail, post, communication.

correspondent noun **reporter,** journalist, columnist, writer, contributor, commentator.

corresponding adjective **equivalent,** related, parallel, matching, comparable, analogous.

corrupt adjective 1 *a corrupt official | corrupt practices:* **dishonest,** unscrupulous, criminal, fraudulent, illegal, unlawful; informal crooked; Brit. informal bent. 2 *he is utterly corrupt:* **immoral,** depraved, degenerate, debauched, vice-ridden, perverted, dissolute. OPPOSITES honest, ethical, pure.
verb **deprave,** pervert, lead astray, debauch, defile, pollute, sully.

corruption noun 1 *political corruption:* **dishonesty,** unscrupulousness, double-dealing, fraud, misconduct, bribery, venality; N. Amer. payola; informal graft, sleaze. 2 *his fall into corruption:* **immorality,** depravity, vice, degeneracy, perversion, debauchery, wickedness, evil, sin.
OPPOSITES honesty, morality, purity.

cosmetic adjective **superficial,** surface, skin-deep, outward,

external.
OPPOSITES fundamental.

cosmopolitan adjective **1** *the student body has a cosmopolitan character:* **multicultural,** multiracial, international, worldwide, global. **2** *a very cosmopolitan chap:* **sophisticated,** cultivated, cultured, worldly, suave, urbane.

cost noun **1** *the cost of the equipment:* **price,** fee, tariff, fare, toll, levy, charge, payment, value, rate, outlay; humorous damage. **2** *the human cost of the conflict:* **sacrifice,** loss, toll, harm, damage, price. **3** (**costs**) *we need to cover our costs:* **expenses,** outgoings, overheads, expenditure, spend, outlay.
verb **1** *the chair costs £186:* **be priced at,** sell for, be valued at, fetch, come to, amount to; informal set someone back, go for. **2** *the proposal has not yet been costed:* **price,** value, put a price/value/figure on.

costly adjective **1** *costly machinery:* **expensive,** dear, high-cost, overpriced; informal steep, pricey. **2** *a costly mistake:* **catastrophic,** disastrous, calamitous, ruinous, damaging, harmful, deleterious.
OPPOSITES cheap.

costume noun clothes, garments, outfit, ensemble, dress, clothing, attire, garb, uniform, livery; formal apparel.

cosy adjective **1** *a cosy country cottage:* **snug,** comfortable, warm, homely, welcoming, safe, sheltered, secure; informal comfy. **2** *a cosy chat:* **intimate,** relaxed, informal, friendly.

cottage noun lodge, chalet, cabin, shack, shanty; (in Russia)

dacha; Scottish bothy; Austral. informal weekender.

cough verb *he coughed loudly:* **hack,** hawk, bark, clear one's throat.
noun *a loud cough:* **bark,** hack; informal frog in one's throat.

council noun **1** *the town council:* **authority,** government, administration, executive, chamber, assembly; Brit. corporation. **2** *the Schools Council:* **committee,** board, commission, assembly, panel, synod.

counsel noun **1** *his wise counsel:* **advice,** guidance, counselling, recommendations, suggestions, direction. **2** *the counsel for the defence:* **barrister,** lawyer; Scottish advocate; N. Amer. attorney, counselor(-at-law).
verb *he counselled the team to withdraw:* **advise,** recommend, advocate, encourage, warn, caution, guide.

count verb **1** *she counted the money again:* **add up,** reckon up, total, tally, calculate, compute; Brit. tot up. **2** *250 employees, not counting overseas staff:* **include,** take into account/consideration, take account of, allow for. **3** *I count it a privilege to be asked:* **consider,** think, feel, regard, look on as, view as, hold to be, judge, deem. **4** *it's your mother's feelings that count:* **matter,** be important, be of consequence, be significant, signify, carry weight, rate.
■ **count on/upon** rely on, depend on, bank on, be sure of, have confidence in, believe in, put one's faith in, take for granted, take as read.

counter verb **1** *workers countered accusations of*

dishonesty with claims of oppression: **respond to,** parry, hit back at, answer. **2** *the second argument is more difficult to counter:* **oppose,** dispute, argue against/with, contradict, challenge, contest.
OPPOSITES support.

■ **counter to** against, in opposition to, contrary to, at variance with, in defiance of, in conflict with, at odds with.

counterpart noun **equivalent,** opposite number, peer, equal, parallel, complement, analogue, match, twin, mate, fellow.

countless adjective **innumerable,** numerous, untold, legion, numberless, limitless, incalculable; informal umpteen; N. Amer. informal gazillions of.
OPPOSITES few.

country noun **1** *foreign countries:* **nation,** state, kingdom, realm, land, territory, province. **2** *the country took to the streets:* **people,** public, population, populace, citizens, nation; Brit. informal Joe Public. **3** *thickly forested country:* **terrain,** land, territory, landscape, countryside, scenery, surroundings, environment. **4** *she hated living in the country:* **countryside,** provinces, rural areas, backwoods, hinterland; Austral./NZ outback, bush, back country; informal sticks.

countryside noun. See COUNTRY senses 3, 4.

county noun **shire,** province, territory, region, district, area.

coup noun **1** *a violent military coup:* **takeover,** coup d'état, overthrow, palace revolution, rebellion, uprising. **2** *a major publishing coup:* **success,** triumph, feat, masterstroke, accomplishment, achievement, scoop.

couple noun **1** *a couple of girls:* **pair,** duo, twosome, two, brace. **2** *a honeymoon couple:* **husband and wife,** twosome, partners, lovers; informal item.
verb **1** *hope is coupled with a sense of loss:* **combine,** accompany, mix, incorporate, ally, add to. **2** *a cable is coupled to one of the wheels:* **connect,** attach, join, fasten, fix, link, secure, hook (up).
OPPOSITES detach.

coupon noun **voucher,** token, ticket, slip; N. Amer. informal rain check.

courage noun **bravery,** pluck, valour, fearlessness, nerve, daring, audacity, boldness, grit, heroism, gallantry; informal guts; Brit. informal bottle.
OPPOSITES cowardice.

courageous adjective **brave,** plucky, fearless, intrepid, valiant, heroic, undaunted, dauntless; informal gutsy, have-a-go.
OPPOSITES cowardly.

course noun **1** *the island was not far off our course:* **route,** way, track, path, line, trail, trajectory, bearing, heading. **2** *the best course to adopt:* **procedure,** plan (of action), course of action, practice, approach, technique, policy, strategy, tactic. **3** *a waterlogged course:* **racecourse,** racetrack, track. **4** *a French course:* **programme/course of study,** curriculum, syllabus, classes, lectures, studies. **5** *a course of antibiotics:* **programme,** series, sequence, system, schedule, regime.
verb *tears coursed down her*

cheeks: **flow,** pour, stream, run, rush, gush, cascade, flood, roll.
■ **of course** naturally, as you would expect, needless to say, as a matter of course, obviously, it goes without saying.

court noun **1** *the court found him guilty:* **court of law,** law court, bench, bar, tribunal, assizes. **2** *the King's court:* **household,** retinue, entourage, train, courtiers, attendants.
verb **1** *he was courting a girl from the village:* **woo,** go out with, date, go steady with. **2** *an editor who was courted by politicians:* **cultivate,** flatter, curry favour with, wine and dine; informal butter up. **3** *he was courting public attention:* **seek,** pursue, go after, strive for, solicit. **4** *he's often courted controversy:* **risk,** invite, attract, bring on oneself.

courteous adjective **polite,** well mannered, civil, respectful, well behaved, gracious, obliging, considerate.
OPPOSITES rude.

courtesy noun **politeness,** good manners, civility, respect, grace, consideration, thought.

cove noun **bay,** inlet, fjord.

cover verb **1** *she covered her face with a towel:* **protect,** shield, shelter, hide, conceal, mask. **2** *his car was covered in mud:* **cake,** coat, encrust, plaster, smother. **3** *snow covered the fields:* **blanket,** carpet, coat, shroud, smother. **4** *a course covering all aspects of the business:* **deal with,** consider, take in, include, involve, incorporate, embrace.
OPPOSITES reveal.
noun **1** *a protective cover:* **covering,** sleeve, wrapping, wrapper, envelope, sheath, housing, jacket, casing, cowling, canopy. **2** *a manhole cover:* **lid,** top, cap. **3** *a book cover:* **binding,** jacket, dust jacket, dust cover, wrapper. **4** *a thick cover of snow:* **coating,** coat, covering, layer, carpet, blanket, film, sheet, veneer, crust, skin, cloak, mantle, veil, pall, shroud. **5** *panicking onlookers ran for cover:* **shelter,** protection, refuge, sanctuary.

coward noun **mouse,** baby; informal **chicken,** scaredy-cat, yellow-belly, sissy; Brit. informal big girl's blouse; N. Amer. informal pantywaist, pussy; Austral./NZ informal sook.
OPPOSITES hero.

cowardly adjective **faint-hearted,** lily-livered, spineless, craven, timid, timorous, fearful; informal yellow, chicken, gutless, yellow-bellied.
OPPOSITES brave.

cower verb **cringe,** shrink, flinch, crouch, blench.

coy adjective **demure,** shy, modest, bashful, diffident, self-effacing, shrinking.
OPPOSITES brazen.

crack noun **1** *a crack in the glass:* **split,** break, chip, fracture, rupture. **2** *a crack between two rocks:* **space,** gap, crevice, fissure, cleft, cranny, chink. **3** *the crack of a rifle:* **bang,** report, explosion, detonation, clap, crash. **4** *a crack on the head:* **blow,** bang, hit, knock, rap, bump, smack, slap; informal bash, whack, clout.
verb **1** *the glass cracked in the heat:* **break,** split, fracture, rupture, snap. **2** *he finally cracked:* **break down,** give way, cave in, go to pieces, give in, yield, succumb. **3** *she cracked*

him across the forehead: **hit,** strike, smack, slap, beat, thump, knock, rap; informal bash, whack, clobber, clout, clip. **4** (informal) *the code proved hard to crack:* **decipher,** interpret, decode, break, solve.

cradle noun **1** *the baby's cradle:* **crib,** Moses basket, cot, carrycot. **2** *the cradle of democracy:* **birthplace,** fount, fountainhead, source, spring, origin.
verb *she cradled his head in her arms:* **hold,** support, cushion, pillow, nurse, rest.

craft noun **1** *the historian's craft:* **activity,** occupation, trade, profession, work, line of work, job. **2** *she used craft and diplomacy:* **cunning,** craftiness, guile, wiliness, artfulness, deviousness, slyness, trickery, duplicity, dishonesty, deceit, deceitfulness, deception, intrigue, subterfuge, wiles, ploys, ruses, schemes, tricks. **3** *a sailing craft:* **vessel,** ship, boat, aircraft, spacecraft.

craftsman, craftswoman noun **artisan,** artist, skilled worker, technician, expert, master.

crafty adjective **cunning,** wily, sly, artful, devious, tricky, scheming, calculating, shrewd, canny, dishonest, deceitful.
OPPOSITES open, honest.

cram verb **1** *wardrobes crammed with clothes:* **fill,** stuff, pack, jam, fill to overflowing, overload, crowd, throng. **2** *they all crammed into the car:* **crowd,** pack, pile, squash. **3** *he crammed his clothes into a suitcase:* **push,** thrust, shove, force, ram, jam, stuff, pack, pile, squash, squeeze. **4** *most of the students are cramming for*

exams: **revise**; informal swot, mug up, bone up.

cramp noun *stomach cramps:* **spasm,** pain, shooting pain, twinge, pang, convulsion.
verb *tighter rules will cramp economic growth:* **hinder,** impede, inhibit, hamper, constrain, hamstring, interfere with, restrict, limit, slow.

cramped adjective **1** *cramped accommodation:* **poky,** uncomfortable, confined, restricted, constricted, small, tiny, narrow, crowded, congested. **2** *cramped handwriting:* **small,** crabbed, illegible, unreadable, indecipherable.
OPPOSITES spacious, flamboyant.

crash verb **1** *the car crashed into a tree:* **smash into,** collide with, be in collision with, hit, strike, ram, cannon into, plough into, meet head-on; N. Amer. impact. **2** *he crashed his car:* **smash,** wreck; Brit. write off; N. Amer. informal total. **3** *a tree crashed to the ground:* **fall,** drop, plummet, plunge, sink, dive, tumble. **4** (informal) *his company crashed:* **collapse,** fold, fail, go under, go bankrupt; informal go bust, go to the wall.
noun **1** *a crash on the motorway:* **accident,** collision, smash; N. Amer. wreck; informal pile-up; Brit. informal shunt. **2** *a loud crash:* **bang,** smash, smack, crack, bump, thud. **3** *the crash of her company:* **collapse,** failure, liquidation, bankruptcy.

crate noun packing case, chest, tea chest, box, container.

crater noun **hollow,** bowl, basin, hole, cavity, depression, dip; Geology caldera.

crave verb **long for,** yearn for, hanker after, desire, want, hunger for, thirst for, pine for; informal be dying for.

craving noun longing, yearning, desire, hankering, hunger, thirst, appetite.

crawl verb 1 *they crawled under the table:* creep, worm one's way, go on all fours, wriggle, slither, squirm. 2 (informal) *I'm not crawling to him:* grovel, kowtow, pander, toady, bow and scrape, fawn; informal suck up, lick someone's boots.

craze noun fad, fashion, trend, vogue, enthusiasm, mania, passion, rage; informal thing.

crazy adjective (informal) 1 *a crazy old man:* mad, insane, out of one's mind, deranged, demented, crazed, lunatic, unbalanced, unhinged; informal mental, off one's head, round the bend; Brit. informal barmy, crackers, barking (mad), potty, round the twist. 2 *a crazy idea:* stupid, foolish, idiotic, silly, absurd, ridiculous, ludicrous, preposterous; informal cockeyed; Brit. informal barmy, daft. 3 *he's crazy about her:* passionate, very keen, enamoured, infatuated, smitten, enthusiastic, fanatical; informal wild, mad, nuts; Brit. informal potty.
OPPOSITES sane, sensible, apathetic.

cream noun 1 *skin cream:* lotion, ointment, moisturizer, cosmetic, salve, rub. 2 *the cream of the world's photographers:* best, finest, pick, flower, crème de la crème, elite.
OPPOSITES dregs.
adjective *a cream dress:* off-white, creamy, ivory.

creamy adjective smooth, thick, velvety, rich, buttery.

OPPOSITES lumpy.

crease noun 1 *trousers with creases:* fold, line, ridge, furrow, groove, corrugation. 2 *creases at the corners of her eyes:* wrinkle, line, crinkle, pucker, crow's foot.
verb *her skirt was creased:* crumple, wrinkle, crinkle, line, scrunch up, rumple.

create verb 1 *she has created a work of stunning originality:* produce, generate, bring into being, make, fashion, build, construct. 2 *regular socializing creates a good team spirit:* bring about, give rise to, lead to, result in, cause, breed, generate, engender, produce. 3 *the governments planned to create a free-trade zone:* establish, found, initiate, institute, constitute, inaugurate, launch, set up. 4 *she was created a life peer:* appoint, make.
OPPOSITES destroy, abolish.

creation noun 1 *the creation of a government:* establishment, formation, foundation, initiation, institution, inauguration, constitution, setting up. 2 *the whole of creation:* the world, the universe, the cosmos, nature, the natural world. 3 *Dickens's literary creations:* work, work of art, production, opus, achievement, concoction, invention; informal brainchild.
OPPOSITES abolition, destruction.

creative adjective inventive, imaginative, innovative, experimental, original, artistic, inspired, visionary.
OPPOSITES unimaginative.

creativity noun inventiveness, imagination, innovation,

originality, artistry, inspiration, vision.

creator noun **maker,** producer, author, designer, deviser, originator, inventor, architect.

creature noun **animal,** beast, brute, living thing, living being; N. Amer. informal critter.

credentials plural noun **1** *a biologist with impeccable credentials:* **suitability,** eligibility, attributes, qualifications, record, experience, background. **2** *examine the credentials of all callers:* **documents,** identity papers, ID, passport, testimonial, reference, certification.

credibility noun **plausibility,** believability, credence, trustworthiness, reliability, dependability, integrity.

credible adjective **believable,** plausible, conceivable, persuasive, convincing, tenable, probable, possible, feasible, reasonable.

credit noun *he got the credit for the work:* **praise,** commendation, acclaim, acknowledgement, recognition, kudos, glory, respect, appreciation.
verb (Brit.) *you wouldn't credit it!* **believe,** accept, give credence to, trust, have faith in.
■ **credit someone with something** ascribe something to someone, attribute something to someone.

creed noun **1** *people of many creeds:* **faith,** religion, belief, religious persuasion. **2** *his political creed:* **beliefs,** principles, articles of faith, ideology, credo.

creek noun **inlet,** bay, estuary, fjord; Scottish firth.

creep verb **tiptoe,** steal, sneak, slink, edge, inch, skulk, prowl.

creepy adjective (informal) **frightening,** eerie, disturbing, sinister, weird, menacing, threatening; informal spooky, scary.

crest noun **1** *the bird's crest:* **tuft,** comb, plume, crown. **2** *the crest of the hill:* **summit,** peak, top, ridge, pinnacle, brow, crown, apex. **3** *the Duke's crest:* **insignia,** emblem, coat of arms, arms, badge, device, regalia.

crevice noun **crack,** fissure, cleft, chink, cranny, slit, split.

crew noun **1** *the ship's crew:* **company,** complement, sailors, hands. **2** *a film crew:* **team,** squad, company, unit, party, gang.

crime noun **1** *kidnapping is a serious crime:* **offence,** unlawful act, illegal act, felony, violation, misdemeanour. **2** *the increase in crime:* **lawbreaking,** delinquency, wrongdoing, criminality, misconduct, illegality, villainy, vice.

criminal noun *a convicted criminal:* **lawbreaker,** offender, villain, delinquent, felon, culprit; informal crook; Austral./NZ informal crim.
adjective **1** *criminal conduct:* **unlawful,** illegal, illicit, lawless, delinquent, corrupt; informal crooked; Brit. informal bent. **2** (informal) *a criminal waste of money:* **deplorable,** shameful, reprehensible, disgraceful, inexcusable, outrageous, scandalous.
OPPOSITES lawful, reasonable.

cripple verb **1** *the accident crippled her:* **disable,** paralyse, immobilize, incapacitate, handicap. **2** *the company had been crippled by the recession:*

damage, weaken, hamper, paralyse, ruin, destroy, wipe out, bring to a standstill, put out of action, put out of business.
OPPOSITES assist.

crippled adjective **disabled,** paralysed, incapacitated, (physically) handicapped, lame, immobilized, bedridden, confined to a wheelchair; euphemistic physically challenged.

crisis noun **1** *the current economic crisis:* **emergency,** disaster, catastrophe, calamity, meltdown, predicament, plight, dire straits. **2** *the situation had reached a crisis:* **critical point,** turning point, crossroads, head, moment of truth; informal crunch.

crisp adjective **1** *crisp bacon:* **crunchy,** crispy, brittle, breakable, dry. **2** *a crisp autumn day:* **invigorating,** brisk, fresh, refreshing, exhilarating. **3** *crisp white bedlinen:* **smooth,** fresh, ironed, starched.
OPPOSITES soft, sultry, crumpled.

criterion noun **standard,** measure, gauge, test, benchmark, yardstick, touchstone, barometer.

critic noun **1** *a literary critic:* **reviewer,** commentator, analyst, judge, pundit, expert. **2** *critics of the government:* **detractor,** attacker, fault-finder; informal knocker.

critical adjective **1** *a highly critical report:* **disapproving,** disparaging, scathing, fault-finding, judgemental, negative, unfavourable, censorious; informal nit-picking, picky. **2** *the situation is critical:* **serious,** grave, precarious, touch-and-go, in the balance, desperate, dire,

acute, life-and-death. **3** *the choice of materials is critical:* **crucial,** vital, essential, all-important, paramount, fundamental, key, pivotal.
OPPOSITES complimentary, safe, unimportant.

criticism noun **1** *she was stung by his criticism:* **fault-finding,** censure, condemnation, disapproval, disparagement; informal flak, a bad press, panning; Brit. informal stick. **2** *literary criticism:* **evaluation,** assessment, appraisal, appreciation, analysis, critique, judgement, commentary.
OPPOSITES praise.

criticize verb **find fault with,** censure, condemn, attack, disparage, denigrate, run down; informal knock, pan, pull to pieces; Brit. informal slag off, slate, rubbish; N. Amer. informal pummel, trash; Austral./NZ informal bag.
OPPOSITES praise.

crook noun (informal). See CRIMINAL noun.

crooked adjective **1** *narrow, crooked streets:* **winding,** twisting, zigzag, meandering, tortuous, serpentine. **2** *a crooked spine:* **bent,** twisted, misshapen, deformed, malformed, contorted, warped, bowed, distorted. **3** *the picture over the bed looked crooked:* **lopsided,** askew, awry, off-centre, out of true, at an angle, slanting, squint; Scottish agley; Brit. informal skew-whiff, wonky. **4** (informal) *a crooked deal:* **dishonest,** criminal, illegal, unlawful, nefarious, fraudulent, corrupt; informal shady; Brit. informal bent.
OPPOSITES straight, legal, honest.

crop noun *some farmers lost their entire crop:* **harvest,** yield,

fruits, produce, vintage.
verb **1** *she's had her hair cropped:* **cut,** clip, trim, shear, shave, lop off, chop off, hack off, dock. **2** *a flock of sheep were cropping the turf:* **graze on,** browse on, feed on, nibble, eat.

■ **crop up** happen, occur, arise, turn up, pop up, emerge, materialize, surface, appear, come to light.

cross noun **1** *we all have our crosses to bear:* **burden,** trouble, worry, trial, affliction, curse, misfortune, woe; informal hassle, headache. **2** *a cross between a yak and a cow:* **mixture,** blend, combination, amalgam, hybrid, cross-breed, mongrel.
verb **1** *they crossed the hills on foot:* **travel across,** traverse, negotiate, navigate, cover. **2** *the two roads cross:* **intersect,** meet, join, connect. **3** *no one dared cross him:* **oppose,** resist, defy, obstruct, contradict, argue with, stand up to. **4** *the breed was crossed with Friesian:* **hybridize,** cross-breed, interbreed, cross-fertilize, cross-pollinate.
adjective *Jane was getting cross:* **angry,** annoyed, irate, irritated, in a bad mood, put out; informal hot under the collar, peeved; Brit. informal shirty, ratty; N. Amer. informal sore, ticked off; Austral./NZ informal ropeable, snaky.
OPPOSITES pleased.

■ **cross something out** delete, strike out, score out, cancel, obliterate.

crouch verb **squat,** bend (down), hunker down, hunch over, stoop, duck, cower.

crow verb **boast,** brag, blow one's own trumpet, swagger, swank, gloat.

crowd noun **1** *a crowd gathered:* **throng,** horde, mass, multitude, host, army, swarm, mob, rabble; informal gaggle. **2** *they're a nice crowd:* **group,** set, circle, clique; informal gang, bunch, crew, lot. **3** *the final attracted a capacity crowd:* **audience,** spectators, listeners, viewers, house, turnout, attendance, gate, congregation.
verb **1** *reporters crowded round her:* **cluster,** flock, swarm, mill, throng, huddle, gather, assemble, congregate, converge. **2** *the guests crowded into the dining room:* **surge,** throng, push, jostle, elbow one's way, squeeze, pile, cram. **3** *the quayside was crowded:* **throng,** pack, jam, cram, fill.

crowded adjective **packed,** full, filled to capacity, full to bursting, congested, overflowing, teeming, swarming, thronged, populous, overpopulated, busy; informal jam-packed, stuffed, chock-a-block, chock-full, bursting at the seams, full to the gunwales, wall-to-wall, mobbed; Austral./NZ informal chocker.
OPPOSITES deserted.

crown noun **1** *the royal crown:* **coronet,** diadem, tiara, circlet. **2** *loyal servants of the Crown:* **monarch,** sovereign, king, queen, emperor, empress, monarchy, royalty. **3** *the crown of the hill:* **top,** crest, summit, peak, pinnacle, tip, brow, apex.
verb **1** *the building is crowned by a balustrade:* **top,** cap, tip, head, surmount. **2** *a teaching post at Harvard crowned his career:* **round off,** cap, be the climax of, be the culmination of, top off, complete.

crucial adjective **1** *negotiations*

were at a crucial stage: **pivotal,** critical, key, decisive, life-and-death. **2** *confidentiality is crucial:* **all-important,** of the utmost importance, of the essence, critical, paramount, essential, vital.
OPPOSITES insignificant, unimportant.

crude adjective **1** *crude oil:* **unrefined,** unpurified, unprocessed, untreated, coarse, raw, natural. **2** *a crude barricade:* **primitive,** simple, basic, homespun, rudimentary, rough and ready, improvised. **3** *crude jokes:* **vulgar,** rude, dirty, naughty, smutty, indecent, obscene, coarse; informal blue.
OPPOSITES refined, sophisticated, clean.

cruel adjective **1** *a cruel man:* **brutal,** savage, inhuman, barbaric, vicious, sadistic, monstrous, callous, ruthless, merciless, heartless, unkind, inhumane. **2** *her death was a cruel blow:* **harsh,** severe, bitter, heartbreaking, heart-rending, painful, agonizing, traumatic.
OPPOSITES compassionate.

cruelty noun brutality, savagery, inhumanity, barbarity, viciousness, sadism, callousness, ruthlessness.

cruise noun *a cruise down the Nile:* (**boat**) **trip,** voyage, sail.
verb **1** *she cruised across the Atlantic:* **sail,** voyage. **2** *a taxi cruised past:* **drive slowly,** drift, sail; informal mosey, tootle; Brit. informal pootle.

crumb noun fragment, bit, morsel, particle, speck, scrap, shred, atom, trace, mite, jot, ounce; informal smidgen, tad.

crumble verb **1** *the plaster was*

crumbling: **disintegrate,** fall apart, fall to pieces, collapse, decompose, break up, decay, become dilapidated. **2** *crumble the cheese with your fingers:* **break up,** crush, fragment. **3** *party unity began to crumble:* **collapse,** deteriorate, degenerate, fail.

crumple verb **1** *she crumpled the note in her fist:* **crush,** scrunch up, screw up, squash, squeeze. **2** *his trousers were dirty and crumpled:* **crease,** wrinkle, crinkle, rumple. **3** *her resistance crumpled:* **collapse,** give way, cave in, go to pieces, break down, crumble.
OPPOSITES flatten out, iron, hold.

crunch verb munch, chomp, champ, bite into, crush, grind, break, smash.

crusade noun *a crusade against crime:* **campaign,** drive, push, movement, effort, struggle, battle, war, offensive.
verb *he has crusaded for hopeless causes:* **campaign,** fight, battle, strive, struggle, agitate, lobby.

crush verb **1** *essential oils are released when the herbs are crushed:* **squash,** squeeze, press, pulp, mash, mangle, pulverize. **2** *your dress will get crushed:* **crease,** crumple, rumple, wrinkle, scrunch up. **3** *crush the biscuits with a rolling pin:* **pulverize,** pound, grind, break up, smash, crumble. **4** *the new regime crushed all opposition:* **suppress,** put down, quell, stamp out, repress, subdue, extinguish. **5** *Alan was crushed by her words:* **demoralize,** deflate, flatten, squash, devastate, shatter, mortify, humiliate.
OPPOSITES allow, promote,

C

encourage.

noun *the crush of people:* **crowd,** throng, horde, swarm, press, mob.

crust noun **covering,** layer, coating, surface, topping, sheet, film, skin, shell, scab.

cry verb **1** *Mandy started to cry:* **weep,** shed tears, sob, wail, snivel, whimper; Scottish greet; informal blub, blubber; Brit. informal grizzle. **2** *'Wait!' he cried:* **call,** shout, exclaim, sing out, yell, bawl, bellow, roar; informal holler.
OPPOSITES laugh, whisper.

noun call, shout, exclamation, yell, bawl, bellow, roar; informal holler.

■ **cry off** (informal) back out, pull out, cancel, withdraw, change one's mind; informal get cold feet, cop out.

cuddle verb **1** *she picked up the baby and cuddled her:* **hug,** embrace, clasp, hold in one's arms. **2** *the pair were kissing and cuddling:* **embrace,** hug, caress, pet, fondle; informal canoodle, smooch. **3** *I cuddled up to him:* **snuggle,** nestle, curl, nuzzle.

cudgel noun **club,** truncheon, bludgeon, baton, shillelagh, mace; N. Amer. blackjack, nightstick; Brit. informal cosh.
verb **club,** bludgeon, beat, batter, bash; Brit. informal cosh.

cue noun **signal,** sign, indication, prompt, reminder.

culminate verb **come to a climax,** come to a head, climax, end, finish, conclude, build up to, lead up to.

culpable adjective **to blame,** guilty, at fault, in the wrong, answerable, accountable, responsible.
OPPOSITES innocent.

culprit noun **guilty party,**

offender, wrongdoer, miscreant, criminal, lawbreaker, felon, delinquent; informal baddy, crook.

cult noun **1** *a religious cult:* **sect,** group, movement. **2** *the cult of youth in Hollywood:* **obsession,** fixation, idolization, devotion, worship, veneration.

cultivate verb **1** *the peasants cultivated the land:* **farm,** work, till, plough, dig. **2** *they cultivated basic food crops:* **grow,** raise, rear, tend, plant, sow. **3** *Tessa tried to cultivate her:* **woo,** court, curry favour with, ingratiate oneself with; informal get in someone's good books. **4** *he wants to cultivate his mind:* **improve,** better, refine, educate, develop, enrich.

cultivated adjective. See CULTURED.

cultural adjective **1** *cultural differences:* **social,** lifestyle, sociological, anthropological, racial, ethnic. **2** *cultural achievements:* **aesthetic,** artistic, intellectual, educational, civilizing.

culture noun **1** *a lover of culture:* **the arts,** high art. **2** *a man of culture:* **education,** cultivation, enlightenment, discernment, discrimination, taste, refinement, sophistication. **3** *Afro-Caribbean culture:* **civilization,** society, way of life, lifestyle, customs, traditions, heritage, values. **4** *a corporate culture of greed and envy:* **philosophy,** ethic, outlook, approach, rationale.

cultured adjective **cultivated,** artistic, enlightened, civilized, educated, well read, learned, discerning, discriminating, refined, sophisticated; informal arty.

OPPOSITES ignorant.

cunning adjective **1** *a cunning scheme:* **crafty,** wily, artful, devious, sly, scheming, canny, dishonest, deceitful. **2** *a cunning plan:* **clever,** ingenious, imaginative, enterprising, inventive, creative, original, inspired, brilliant.
OPPOSITES open, honest, stupid.
noun **1** *his political cunning:* **guile,** craftiness, deviousness, trickery, duplicity. **2** *it took cunning just to survive:* **ingenuity,** imagination, inventiveness, enterprise, creativity, brilliance.

curator noun **custodian,** keeper, conservator, guardian, caretaker.

curb noun *a curb on imports:* **restraint,** restriction, check, brake, rein, control, limit.
verb *a plan to curb consumer spending:* **restrain,** hold back, keep in check, control, rein in, contain; informal keep a lid on.

cure verb **1** *he was cured of the disease:* **heal,** restore to health, make well/better. **2** *economic equality cannot cure all social ills:* **rectify,** remedy, put/set right, right, fix, mend, repair, solve, sort out, eliminate, end. **3** *some farmers cured their own bacon:* **preserve,** smoke, salt, dry, pickle.
noun *a cure for cancer:* **remedy,** medicine, medication, antidote, treatment, therapy.

curiosity noun **1** *his evasiveness roused my curiosity:* **interest,** inquisitiveness, attention, prying; informal nosiness. **2** *the shop is full of curiosities:* **oddity,** curio, novelty, rarity.

curious adjective **1** *she was curious to know what had happened:* **intrigued,** interested, eager, inquisitive. **2** *her curious behaviour:* **strange,** odd, peculiar, funny, unusual, bizarre, weird, eccentric, extraordinary, abnormal, anomalous.
OPPOSITES uninterested, normal.

curl verb **1** *smoke curled up from his cigarette:* **spiral,** coil, wreathe, twirl, swirl, wind, curve, twist (and turn), snake, corkscrew. **2** *Ruth curled her arms around his neck:* **wind,** twine, entwine, wrap.
noun **1** *the tangled curls of her hair:* **ringlet,** corkscrew, kink, lock. **2** *a curl of smoke:* **spiral,** coil, twirl, swirl, twist, corkscrew.

curly adjective **wavy,** curling, curled, frizzy, kinky, corkscrew.
OPPOSITES straight.

currency noun **1** *foreign currency:* **money,** legal tender, cash, banknotes, notes, coins; N. Amer. bills. **2** *a term which has gained new currency:* **popularity,** circulation, exposure, acceptance, prevalence.

current adjective **1** *current events:* **contemporary,** present-day, modern, topical, live, burning. **2** *the idea is still current:* **prevalent,** common, accepted, in circulation, popular, widespread. **3** *a current driving licence:* **valid,** usable, up to date. **4** *the current prime minister:* **incumbent,** present, in office, in power, reigning.
OPPOSITES past, out of date, former.
noun **1** *a current of air:* **flow,** stream, draught, jet, tide. **2** *the current of human life:* **course,** progress, progression, flow, tide, movement.

curse noun **1** *she'd put a curse on him:* **jinx**; N. Amer. hex. **2** *the curse of unemployment:* **affliction**, burden, misery, ordeal, evil, scourge. **3** *muffled curses:* **swear word**, expletive, oath, profanity, four-letter word, dirty word, obscenity; informal cuss word.
verb **1** *she was cursed with feelings of inadequacy:* **afflict**, trouble, plague, bedevil. **2** *he cursed loudly:* **swear**, take the Lord's name in vain; informal cuss, turn the air blue, eff and blind.

cursed adjective **damned**, doomed, ill-fated, ill-starred; informal jinxed.

cursory adjective **brief**, hasty, hurried, rapid, passing, perfunctory, desultory, casual.
OPPOSITES thorough.

curt adjective **terse**, brusque, abrupt, clipped, blunt, short, sharp.
OPPOSITES expansive.

curtail verb **1** *policies designed to curtail spending:* **reduce**, cut, cut down, decrease, trim, restrict, limit, curb, rein in/back; informal slash. **2** *his visit was curtailed:* **shorten**, cut short, truncate.
OPPOSITES increase, extend.

curve noun *the curves of the river:* **bend**, turn, loop, arc, arch, bow, curvature.
verb *the road curved back on itself:* **bend**, turn, loop, wind, meander, snake, arc, arch.

curved adjective **bent**, arched, bowed, rounded, crescent.
OPPOSITES straight.

cushion noun *a cushion against inflation:* **protection**, buffer, shield, defence, bulwark.
verb **1** *residents are cushioned from the outside world:* **protect**, shield, shelter, cocoon. **2** *to cushion the blow, pensions were increased:* **soften**, lessen, diminish, mitigate, alleviate, take the edge off, dull, deaden.

custody noun *custody of the child:* **care**, guardianship, charge, supervision, safe keeping, responsibility, protection.
■ **in custody** in prison, in jail, imprisoned, incarcerated, under lock and key, on remand; informal behind bars, doing time, inside; Brit. informal banged up.

custom noun **1** *his unfamiliarity with local customs:* **tradition**, practice, usage, way, convention, formality, ritual, mores. **2** *it was his custom to sleep in a chair:* **habit**, practice, routine, way; formal wont.

customary adjective **usual**, traditional, normal, conventional, habitual, familiar, accepted, accustomed, routine, established, time-honoured, prevailing.
OPPOSITES unusual.

customer noun **consumer**, buyer, purchaser, patron, client, shopper; Brit. informal punter.

cut verb **1** *he cut his finger:* **gash**, slash, lacerate, slit, wound, scratch, graze, nick. **2** *cut the pepper into small pieces:* **slice**, chop, dice, cube, carve; N. Amer. hash. **3** *the name had been cut into the stone:* **carve**, engrave, incise, etch, score, chisel, whittle. **4** *the government will cut expenditure:* **reduce**, cut back/down on, decrease, lessen, mark down, discount, lower; informal slash. **5** *the text has been substantially cut:* **shorten**, abridge, condense, abbreviate, truncate, edit, censor. **6** *you need to cut ten lines per page:*

delete, remove, take out, excise.

noun 1 *a cut on his jaw:* **gash,** slash, laceration, incision, wound, scratch, graze, nick. **2** *a cut of beef:* **piece,** joint, fillet, section. **3** (informal) *they want their cut:* **share,** portion, quota, percentage; informal slice of the cake). **4** *a cut in interest rates:* **reduction,** cutback, decrease, lessening; N. Amer. rollback. **5** *the cut of his jacket:* **style,** design, line, fit.

cutback noun **reduction,** cut, decrease, economy, saving; N. Amer. rollback.
OPPOSITES increase.

cute adjective **endearing,** adorable, lovable, sweet, lovely, appealing, engaging, delightful, dear; informal twee; Brit. informal dinky.
OPPOSITES hateful, ugly.

cutting noun *a newspaper cutting:* **clipping,** article, piece, column, paragraph.
adjective *a cutting remark:* **hurtful,** wounding, barbed, scathing, caustic, sarcastic, snide, spiteful, malicious, cruel; informal bitchy; Brit. informal sarky; N. Amer. informal snarky.
OPPOSITES friendly, warm.

cycle noun **1** *the cycle of birth, death, and rebirth:* **circle,** round, pattern, rhythm, loop. **2** *a cycle of three plays:* **series,** set, sequence, succession, run.

cynic noun **sceptic,** doubter, doubting Thomas, pessimist, prophet of doom.
OPPOSITES idealist, optimist.

cynical adjective **sceptical,** doubtful, distrustful, suspicious, disbelieving, pessimistic, negative, world-weary, disillusioned, disenchanted, jaundiced.
OPPOSITES idealistic, optimistic.

Dd

dab verb *she dabbed disinfectant on the cut:* **pat,** press, touch, swab, daub, wipe.
noun *a dab of glue:* **drop,** spot, smear, splash, bit.

dabble verb **toy with,** dip into, flirt with, tinker with, play with.

daft adjective (Brit. informal) **1** *a daft idea:* **absurd,** preposterous, ridiculous, ludicrous, idiotic, stupid, foolish; informal crazy; Brit. informal barmy. **2** *he's really daft:* **stupid,** idiotic, empty-headed, unhinged, insane, mad; informal thick, dim, dopey; Brit. informal barmy, crackers. **3** *she's daft about him:* **infatuated,** smitten, besotted; informal crazy, mad, nuts; Brit. informal potty.
OPPOSITES sensible, sane.

daily adjective *a daily event:* **everyday,** day-to-day.
adverb *the museum is open daily:* **every day,** once a day, day after day.

dainty adjective **1** *a dainty china cup:* **delicate,** fine, elegant, exquisite. **2** *a dainty eater:* **fastidious,** fussy, particular; informal choosy, picky; Brit. informal faddy.
OPPOSITES unwieldy, undiscriminating.

dam noun **barrage,** barrier, wall, embankment, barricade,

obstruction.
verb **block (up)**, obstruct, bung up, close, hold back.

damage noun **1** *did the thieves do any damage?* **harm**, destruction, vandalism, injury, ruin, devastation. **2** (**damages**) **compensation**, recompense, restitution, redress, reparation(s); N. Amer. informal comp.
verb *the parcel had been damaged:* **harm**, injure, deface, spoil, impair, vandalize, ruin, destroy, wreck; N. Amer. informal trash.
OPPOSITES repair.

damaging adjective **harmful**, detrimental, injurious, hurtful, destructive, ruinous, deleterious.
OPPOSITES beneficial.

damn verb **condemn**, censure, criticize, attack, denounce.
OPPOSITES bless, praise.

damning adjective **incriminating**, implicating, damaging, condemnatory, conclusive, irrefutable.

damp adjective *her hair was damp:* **moist**, humid, muggy, clammy, sweaty, dank, wet, rainy, drizzly, showery, misty, foggy, dewy.
OPPOSITES dry.
noun *the damp in the air:* **moisture**, liquid, wet, wetness, dampness, humidity.
OPPOSITES dryness.

dampen verb **1** *the rain dampened her face:* **moisten**, damp, wet, soak. **2** *nothing could dampen her enthusiasm:* **lessen**, decrease, diminish, reduce, moderate, cool, suppress, stifle, inhibit.
OPPOSITES dry, heighten.

dance verb **1** *he danced with her:* **trip**, sway, twirl, whirl,

pirouette, gyrate; informal bop, trip the light fantastic; N. Amer. informal get down. **2** *the girls danced round me:* **caper**, cavort, frolic, skip, prance, gambol, leap, hop, bounce.
noun *the school dance:* **ball**; N. Amer. prom, hoedown; informal disco, rave, hop, bop.

danger noun **1** *an element of danger:* **peril**, hazard, risk, jeopardy. **2** *he is a danger to society:* **menace**, hazard, threat, risk. **3** *a serious danger of fire:* **possibility**, chance, risk, probability, likelihood.
OPPOSITES safety.

dangerous adjective **1** *a dangerous animal:* **menacing**, threatening, treacherous. **2** *dangerous wiring:* **hazardous**, perilous, risky, unsafe, unpredictable, precarious, insecure; informal dicey, hairy; Brit. informal dodgy.
OPPOSITES harmless, safe.

dangle verb **1** *a chain dangled from his belt:* **hang**, swing, droop, wave, trail, stream. **2** *he dangled the keys:* **wave**, swing, jiggle, brandish, flourish.

dank adjective **damp**, musty, chilly, clammy.
OPPOSITES dry.

dapper adjective **smart**, spruce, trim, debonair, neat, well dressed, elegant; informal snappy, natty; N. Amer. informal spiffy, fly.
OPPOSITES scruffy.

dare verb **1** *nobody dared to say a word:* **be brave enough**, have the courage, venture, have the nerve, risk, take the liberty of; N. Amer. take a flyer; informal stick one's neck out. **2** *she dared him to go:* **challenge**, defy, invite, bid, provoke, goad.
noun *she accepted the dare:*

challenge, invitation, wager, bet.

daring adjective *a daring attack:* **bold,** audacious, intrepid, fearless, brave, heroic, dashing; informal **gutsy.**
OPPOSITES cowardly, timid.
noun *his sheer daring:* **boldness,** audacity, temerity, fearlessness, bravery, courage, pluck; informal **nerve, guts;** Brit. informal **bottle;** N. Amer. informal **moxie.**
OPPOSITES cowardice.

dark adjective **1** *a dark night:* **dingy,** gloomy, shadowy, murky, poorly lit, grey, inky, black. **2** *dark hair:* **brunette,** dark brown, sable, jet-black, ebony. **3** *dark skin:* **swarthy,** dusky, olive, black, ebony. **4** *dark thoughts:* **gloomy,** dismal, negative, downbeat, bleak, grim, fatalistic, black. **5** *a dark look:* **angry,** forbidding, threatening, ominous, moody, brooding, sullen, scowling, glowering. **6** *dark deeds:* **evil,** wicked, sinful, bad, iniquitous, ungodly, vile, foul, monstrous; informal **dirty,** crooked, shady.
OPPOSITES bright, light, blonde, pale, white, happy, friendly, good.
noun *walking in the dark:* **night,** night-time, darkness, nightfall, blackout.
OPPOSITES light, day.

darken verb *grow dark,* make dark, blacken, grow dim, cloud over, lour.
OPPOSITES lighten.

darkness noun **1** *lights shone in the darkness:* **dark,** blackness, gloom, dimness, murk, shadow, shade. **2** *darkness fell:* **night,** night-time, dark. **3** *the forces of darkness:* **evil,** wickedness, sin, ungodliness, the Devil.

darling noun **1** *good night, darling:* **dear,** dearest, love, sweetheart, beloved; informal **honey,** angel, pet, sweetie, baby, poppet. **2** *the darling of the media:* **favourite,** idol, hero, heroine; Brit. informal **blue-eyed boy/girl.**
OPPOSITES bugbear, villain.
adjective **1** *his darling wife:* **dear,** dearest, precious, beloved. **2** *a darling little hat:* **adorable,** charming, cute, sweet, enchanting, dear, delightful; Scottish & N. English **bonny.**
OPPOSITES ugly.

dart verb **1** *Karl darted across the road:* **dash,** rush, tear, shoot, sprint, bound, scurry, scamper; informal **scoot,** whip. **2** *he darted a glance at her:* **direct,** cast, throw, shoot, send, flash.

dash verb **1** *he dashed home:* **rush,** race, run, sprint, career, charge, shoot, hurtle, hare, fly, speed, zoom; informal **tear,** belt; Brit. informal **bomb;** N. Amer. informal **barrel. 2** *he dashed the glass to the ground:* **hurl,** smash, fling, slam, throw, toss, cast; informal **chuck,** sling; N. Amer. informal **peg. 3** *her hopes were dashed:* **shatter,** destroy, wreck, ruin, demolish, scotch, frustrate, thwart; informal **put paid to;** Brit. informal **scupper.**
OPPOSITES dawdle, raise.
noun **1** *a dash for the door:* **rush,** race, run, sprint, bolt, dart, leap, charge, bound. **2** *a dash of salt:* **pinch,** touch, sprinkle, taste, spot, drop, dab, splash; informal **smidgen,** tad. **3** *he led off with such dash:* **verve,** style, flamboyance, gusto, zest, elan, flair, vigour, panache; informal **pizzazz,** oomph.

dashing adjective **1** *a dashing pilot:* **debonair,** devil-may-care, raffish, flamboyant, swashbuckling. **2** *he looked very dashing:* **stylish,** smart, elegant, dapper, spruce, trim, debonair; informal **natty;** N. Amer. informal spiffy.

data noun **facts,** figures, statistics, details, particulars, information.

date noun **1** *at a later date:* **day,** occasion, time, year, age, period, era, epoch. **2** *a lunch date:* **appointment,** meeting, engagement, rendezvous, commitment. **3** (informal) *a date for tonight:* **partner,** escort, girlfriend, boyfriend.
verb **1** *the best films don't date:* **age,** grow old, become dated, show its age, be of its time. **2** *assign a date to,* put a date on. **3** (informal) *he's dating Jill:* **go out with,** take out, go with, see; informal go steady with.
■ **date from** be from, originate in, come from, belong to, go back to.

dated adjective **old-fashioned,** outdated, outmoded, unfashionable, passé, behind the times, archaic, obsolete, antiquated; informal old hat, out of the ark.
OPPOSITES modern.

daunting adjective **intimidating,** forbidding, challenging, formidable, unnerving, disconcerting, discouraging, disheartening, demoralizing, dismaying, scary, frightening, alarming.
OPPOSITES inviting, reassuring.

dawdle verb **1** *they dawdled over breakfast:* **linger,** take one's time, be slow, waste time, dally; informal dilly-dally. **2** *Ruth dawdled home:* **amble,** stroll, trail, dally, move at a snail's pace; informal mosey, tootle; Brit.

informal **pootle.**
OPPOSITES hurry.

dawn noun **1** *we got up at dawn:* **daybreak,** sunrise, first light, daylight, cockcrow, first thing; N. Amer. sunup. **2** *the dawn of civilization:* **beginning,** start, birth, inception, genesis, emergence, advent, appearance, arrival, rise, origin.
OPPOSITES dusk, end.
verb **1** *Thursday dawned crisp and sunny:* **begin,** break, arrive, emerge. **2** *a bright new future has dawned:* **begin,** start, commence, be born, appear, arrive, emerge, arise, rise, unfold, develop. **3** *the reality dawned on him:* **become evident,** register, cross someone's mind, suggest itself, occur, come, strike, hit.
OPPOSITES end.

day noun **1** *I stayed for a day:* **twenty-four hours.** **2** *enjoy the beach during the day:* **daytime,** daylight, waking hours. **3** *the leading architect of the day:* **period,** time, date, age, era, generation.
OPPOSITES night.

daze verb *she was dazed by the revelations:* **dumbfound,** stupefy, stun, shock, stagger, bewilder, take aback, nonplus; informal **flabbergast;** Brit. informal knock for six.
noun *she is in a daze:* **stupor,** trance, haze, spin, whirl, muddle, jumble.

dazzle verb **1** *she was dazzled by the headlights:* **blind,** confuse, disorient. **2** *I was dazzled by the exhibition:* **overwhelm,** overcome, impress, move, stir, touch, awe, overawe; informal bowl over, blow away, knock out.

dead adjective **1** *my parents are*

dead: passed on/away, departed, late, lost, perished, fallen, killed, lifeless, extinct; informal six feet under, pushing up daisies; formal deceased. **2** *a dead issue/language:* **obsolete,** extinct, defunct, disused, abandoned, superseded, vanished, archaic, ancient. **3** *the phone was dead:* **not working,** out of order, inoperative, inactive, broken, defective; informal kaput, conked out, on the blink, bust; Brit. informal knackered. **4** *a dead town:* **boring,** uninteresting, unexciting, uninspiring, dull, flat, quiet, sleepy, slow, lifeless; informal one-horse; N. Amer. informal dullsville.
OPPOSITES alive, live, living, working, lively.
adverb **1** *he was dead serious:* **completely,** absolutely, totally, utterly, deadly, perfectly, entirely, quite, thoroughly.
2 *flares were seen dead ahead:* **directly,** exactly, precisely, immediately, right, straight, due.

deadline noun **time limit,** finishing date, target date, cut-off point.

deadlock noun **stalemate,** impasse, checkmate, stand-off, standstill, gridlock.

deadly adjective **1** *these drugs can be deadly:* **fatal,** lethal, mortal, life-threatening, noxious, toxic, poisonous.
2 *deadly enemies:* **mortal,** irreconcilable, implacable, bitter, sworn. **3** *his aim is deadly:* **unerring,** unfailing, perfect, true, accurate; Brit. informal spot on.
OPPOSITES harmless, inaccurate.

deafening adjective **ear-splitting,** thunderous,

crashing, uproarious, almighty, booming.
OPPOSITES low, soft.

deal noun *completion of the deal:* **agreement,** understanding, pact, bargain, covenant, contract, treaty, arrangement, compromise, settlement, terms.
verb **1** *how to deal with difficult children:* **cope with,** handle, manage, treat, take care of, take charge of, take in hand, sort out, tackle, take on, control. **2** *the article deals with advances in biochemistry:* **concern,** be about, have to do with, discuss, consider, cover, tackle, explore, investigate, examine. **3** *the company deals in high-tech goods:* **trade in,** buy and sell, purvey, supply, market, traffic in. **4** *the cards were dealt:* **distribute,** give out, share out, divide out, hand out, pass out, pass round, dispense, allocate.

dealer noun **trader,** merchant, salesman/woman, seller, vendor, purveyor, pedlar, distributor, supplier, shopkeeper, retailer, wholesaler, tradesman, tradesperson; Brit. stockist.

dear adjective **1** *a dear friend:* **beloved,** precious, close, intimate, bosom. **2** *her pictures were too dear to part with:* **precious,** treasured, valued, prized, cherished, special.
3 *such a dear man:* **endearing,** adorable, lovable, appealing, engaging, charming, captivating, lovely, delightful, sweet, darling. **4** *rather dear meals:* **expensive,** costly, high-priced, overpriced, exorbitant, extortionate; Brit. over the odds; informal pricey.
OPPOSITES disagreeable, cheap.

noun *don't worry, my dear:* **darling,** dearest, love, beloved, sweetheart, precious; informal sweetie, sugar, honey, baby, pet, poppet.

dearly adverb *I love him dearly:* **very much,** a great deal, greatly, deeply, profoundly.

dearth noun **lack,** scarcity, shortage, shortfall, deficiency, insufficiency, inadequacy, absence.

OPPOSITES surfeit.

death noun **1** *her father's death:* **dying,** demise, end, passing, loss of life; formal decease. **2** *the death of their dream:* **end,** finish, termination, extinction, extinguishing, collapse, destruction.

OPPOSITES life, birth, start.

deathly adjective **deathlike,** ghostly, ghastly, ashen, white, pale, pallid.

debacle noun **fiasco,** failure, catastrophe, disaster.

debate noun *a debate on the reforms:* **discussion,** argument, dispute, talks.
verb **1** *MPs will debate our future:* **discuss,** talk over/through, talk about, thrash out, argue, dispute. **2** *he debated whether to call her:* **consider,** think over/about, chew over, mull over, weigh up, ponder, deliberate.

debris noun **ruins,** remains, rubble, wreckage, detritus, refuse, rubbish, waste, scrap, flotsam and jetsam.

debt noun **1** *he couldn't pay his debts:* **bill,** account, dues, arrears, charges. **2** *his debt to the author:* **indebtedness,** obligation, gratitude, appreciation.

decay verb **1** *the corpses had decayed:* **decompose,** rot,

putrefy, go bad, go off, spoil, fester, perish. **2** *the cities continue to decay:* **deteriorate,** degenerate, decline, go downhill, slump, slide, go to rack and ruin, go to seed; informal go to the dogs.
noun **1** *signs of decay:* **decomposition,** putrefaction, rot. **2** *the decay of American values:* **deterioration,** degeneration, decline, weakening, crumbling, disintegration, collapse.

deceit noun **deception,** deceitfulness, duplicity, double-dealing, lies, fraud, cheating, trickery.

OPPOSITES honesty.

deceitful adjective **dishonest,** untruthful, insincere, false, disingenuous, untrustworthy, unscrupulous, unprincipled, two-faced, duplicitous, fraudulent, double-dealing; informal sneaky, tricky, crooked; Brit. informal bent.

OPPOSITES honest.

deceive verb **trick,** cheat, defraud, swindle, hoodwink, hoax, dupe, take in, mislead, delude, fool; informal con, pull the wool over someone's eyes; N. Amer. informal sucker, goldbrick; Austral. informal rort.

decency noun **1** *standards of taste and decency:* **propriety,** decorum, good taste, respectability, morality, virtue, modesty. **2** *he didn't have the decency to tell me:* **courtesy,** politeness, good manners, civility, consideration, thoughtfulness.

decent adjective **1** *a decent burial:* **proper,** correct, right, appropriate, suitable, respectable, decorous, modest, seemly, accepted; informal pukka.

2 *a job with decent pay:*
satisfactory, reasonable, fair,
acceptable, adequate, sufficient,
not bad, all right, tolerable,
passable, suitable; informal OK.
3 (Brit. informal) *a very decent
chap:* **kind,** generous,
thoughtful, considerate,
obliging, courteous, polite, well
mannered, neighbourly,
hospitable, pleasant, agreeable,
amiable.
OPPOSITES indecent,
unsatisfactory, unpleasant.

deception noun **1** *they obtained
money by deception:* **deceit,**
duplicity, double-dealing, fraud,
cheating, trickery, guile, bluff,
lying, pretence, treachery. **2** *it
was all a deception:* **trick,** sham,
fraud, pretence, hoax, ruse,
scheme, dodge, cheat, swindle;
informal con, set-up, scam.

deceptive adjective **misleading,**
confusing, illusory, distorted,
ambiguous.

decide verb **1** *she decided to
become a writer:* **resolve,**
determine, make up one's
mind, choose, opt, plan, aim,
intend, have in mind, set one's
sights on. **2** *research to decide a
variety of questions:* **settle,**
resolve, determine, work out,
answer; informal sort out. **3** *the
court is to decide the case:*
adjudicate, arbitrate, judge,
pronounce on, give a verdict
on, rule on.

decidedly adverb **distinctly,**
clearly, markedly, obviously,
noticeably, unmistakably,
patently, manifestly, definitely,
positively.

decision noun **1** *they came to a
decision:* **resolution,**
conclusion, settlement, choice,
option, selection. **2** *the judge's
decision:* **verdict,** finding,

ruling, judgement,
adjudication, sentence.

decisive adjective **1** *a decisive
man:* **resolute,** firm, strong-
minded, strong-willed,
determined, purposeful. **2** *the
decisive factor:* **deciding,**
conclusive, determining, key,
pivotal, critical, crucial.
OPPOSITES indecisive.

declaration noun **1** *they issued
a declaration:* **announcement,**
statement, communication,
pronouncement, proclamation;
N. Amer. advisory. **2** *a declaration
of faith:* **assertion,** profession,
affirmation, acknowledgement,
revelation, disclosure,
confirmation, testimony,
avowal, protestation.

declare verb **1** *she declared her
political principles:* **announce,**
proclaim, state, reveal, air,
voice, articulate, express, vent,
set forth, publicize, broadcast.
2 *he declared that they were
guilty:* **assert,** profess, affirm,
maintain, state, contend, argue,
insist.

decline verb **1** *she declined all
invitations:* **turn down,** reject,
brush aside, refuse, rebuff,
spurn, repulse, dismiss, pass up,
say no; informal give something a
miss. **2** *the number of traders
has declined:* **decrease,** reduce,
lessen, diminish, dwindle,
contract, shrink, fall off, tail
off, drop, fall, go down.
3 *standards steadily declined:*
deteriorate, degenerate, decay,
crumble, collapse, slump, slip,
slide, go downhill, worsen;
informal go to the dogs.
OPPOSITES accept, increase, rise,
improve.
noun **1** *a decline in profits:*
reduction, decrease, downturn,
downswing, diminution, ebb,

d

d

drop, slump, plunge. **2** *habitat decline:* **deterioration,** degeneration, degradation, shrinkage, erosion.
OPPOSITES rise, improvement.

decor noun decoration, furnishing, colour scheme.

decorate verb **1** *the door was decorated with a wreath:* **ornament,** adorn, trim, embellish, garnish, furnish, enhance. **2** *he started to decorate his home:* **paint, wallpaper,** paper, refurbish, renovate, redecorate; informal do up, give something a facelift, give something a makeover. **3** *he was decorated for courage:* **give a medal to,** honour, cite, reward.

decoration noun **1** *a ceiling with rich decoration:* **ornamentation,** adornment, trimming, embellishment, beautification. **2** *a Christmas tree decoration:* **ornament,** bauble, trinket, knick-knack. **3** *a decoration won on the battlefield:* **medal,** award, prize; Brit. informal gong.

decorative adjective **ornamental,** fancy, ornate, attractive, pretty, showy.
OPPOSITES functional.

decrease verb **1** *pollution levels decreased:* **lessen,** reduce, drop, diminish, decline, dwindle, fall off, plummet, plunge.
2 *decrease the amount of fat in your body:* **reduce,** lessen, lower, cut, deplete, minimize; informal slash.
OPPOSITES increase.
noun *a decrease in crime:* **reduction,** drop, decline, downturn, cut, cutback, diminution.
OPPOSITES increase.

decree noun **1** *a presidential*

decree: **order,** command, commandment, edict, proclamation, law, statute, act. **2** *a court decree:* **judgement,** verdict, adjudication, finding, ruling, decision.
verb *he decreed that a stadium should be built:* **order,** direct, command, rule, dictate, pronounce, proclaim, ordain.

dedicate verb **1** *she dedicated her life to the sick:* **devote,** commit, pledge, give (up), sacrifice, set aside. **2** *the book is dedicated to his wife:* **inscribe,** address, offer. **3** *a chapel dedicated to St Jude:* **devote,** assign, bless, consecrate, sanctify.

dedicated adjective **1** *a dedicated supporter:* **committed,** devoted, staunch, firm, steadfast, loyal, faithful. **2** *a dedicated rail link:* **specialized,** custom-built, customized, purpose-built, exclusive.
OPPOSITES half-hearted, general-purpose.

dedication noun **1** *sport requires dedication:* **commitment,** devotion, loyalty, allegiance, application, resolve, conscientiousness, perseverance, persistence. **2** *the book has a dedication to his wife:* **inscription,** message.
OPPOSITES apathy.

deduct verb **subtract,** take away, take off, debit, dock, stop; informal knock off.
OPPOSITES add.

deduction noun **1** *the deduction of tax:* **subtraction,** removal, debit. **2** *gross pay, before deductions:* **stoppage,** tax, expenses, rebate, discount, concession. **3** *she was right in her deduction:* **conclusion,**

inference, supposition, hypothesis, assumption, presumption, suspicion.

deed noun **1** *heroic deeds:* act, action, feat, exploit, achievement, accomplishment, endeavour. **2** *mortgage deeds:* **document**, contract, instrument.

deep adjective **1** *a deep ravine:* **cavernous**, yawning, gaping, huge, extensive, bottomless, fathomless. **2** *deep affection:* **intense**, heartfelt, wholehearted, deep-seated, sincere, genuine, earnest, enthusiastic, great. **3** *a deep sleep:* **sound**, heavy. **4** *a deep thinker:* **profound**, serious, intelligent, intellectual, learned, wise, scholarly. **5** *he was deep in concentration:* **rapt**, absorbed, engrossed, preoccupied, immersed, lost, gripped. **6** *a deep mystery:* **obscure**, complex, mysterious, unfathomable, opaque, abstruse, esoteric, enigmatic. **7** *his deep voice:* **low-pitched**, low, bass, rich, resonant, booming, sonorous. **8** *a deep red:* **dark**, intense, rich, strong, vivid.
OPPOSITES shallow, superficial, light, high, shrill.

deepen verb **1** *his love for her had deepened:* **grow**, increase, intensify, strengthen; informal step up. **2** *they deepened the hole:* **dig out**, dig deeper, excavate.

deeply adverb profoundly, greatly, enormously, extremely, strongly, intensely, keenly, acutely, thoroughly, completely, entirely, seriously, gravely; informal majorly.

defeat verb **1** *the army which defeated the Scots:* **beat**, conquer, win against, triumph over, get the better of, vanquish, rout, trounce, overcome, overpower; informal lick, thrash. **2** *this defeats the original point of the plan:* **thwart**, frustrate, foil, ruin, scotch, derail; informal put paid to, stymie; Brit. informal scupper.
noun *a crippling defeat:* **loss**, conquest, rout; informal thrashing, hiding, drubbing, licking.
OPPOSITES victory.

defect noun *he spotted a defect in my work:* **fault**, flaw, imperfection, deficiency, deformity, blemish, mistake, error.

defective adjective **faulty**, flawed, imperfect, unsound, inoperative, malfunctioning, out of order, broken; informal on the blink; Brit. informal duff.
OPPOSITES perfect, working, intact.

defence noun **1** *the defence of the fortress:* **protection**, guarding, security, fortification, resistance. **2** *more spending on defence:* **armaments**, weapons, weaponry, arms, the military, the armed forces. **3** *the prisoner's defence:* **justification**, vindication, explanation, mitigation, excuse, alibi, denial, rebuttal, plea, pleading, argument, case.
OPPOSITES attack, prosecution.

defend verb **1** *a fort built to defend Ireland:* **protect**, guard, safeguard, secure, shield, fortify, watch over. **2** *he defended his policy:* **justify**, vindicate, explain, argue for, support, back, stand by, make a case for, stick up for.
OPPOSITES attack, criticize.

defender noun **1** *defenders of*

the environment: **protector,** guardian, guard, custodian. **2** *a defender of colonialism:* **supporter,** upholder, backer, champion, advocate, apologist.

defensive adjective **1** *troops in defensive positions:* **defending,** protective, guarding. **2** *a defensive response:* **self-justifying,** oversensitive, prickly, paranoid, neurotic; informal **twitchy.**

defer verb **postpone,** put off, delay, hold over/off, put back, shelve, suspend; N. Amer. **table;** informal **put on ice,** put on the back burner.

defiance noun **resistance,** opposition, non-compliance, disobedience, insubordination, rebellion, disregard, contempt, insolence.
OPPOSITES obedience.

defiant adjective **disobedient,** resistant, obstinate, uncooperative, non-compliant, recalcitrant, insubordinate; Brit. informal **stroppy, bolshie.**
OPPOSITES cooperative.

deficiency noun **1** *a vitamin deficiency:* **lack,** insufficiency, shortage, inadequacy, deficit, shortfall, scarcity, dearth. **2** *the team's big deficiency:* **defect,** fault, flaw, failing, weakness, shortcoming, limitation.
OPPOSITES surplus, sufficiency, strength.

deficit noun **shortfall,** deficiency, shortage, debt, arrears, loss.
OPPOSITES surplus.

definite adjective **specific,** explicit, express, precise, exact, clear, clear-cut, unambiguous, certain, sure, positive, conclusive, decisive, firm, unequivocal, unmistakable, proven, decided, marked,

distinct, identifiable.
OPPOSITES vague, ambiguous, indeterminate.

definitely adverb **certainly,** surely, for sure, unquestionably, without doubt, undoubtedly, undeniably, clearly, positively, absolutely, unmistakably.

definition noun **1** *the definition of 'intelligence':* **meaning,** sense, interpretation, explanation, description. **2** *the definition of the picture:* **clarity,** sharpness, focus, crispness, resolution.

definitive adjective **1** *a definitive decision:* **conclusive,** final, unqualified, absolute, categorical, positive, definite. **2** *the definitive guide:* **authoritative,** best, ultimate, classic, standard, recognized, accepted, exhaustive.
OPPOSITES provisional, average.

deflect verb **divert,** turn away, draw away, distract, fend off, parry, stave off.

defraud verb **swindle,** cheat, rob, deceive, dupe, hoodwink, double-cross, trick; informal **con,** do, sting, diddle, rip off, shaft, pull a fast one on, put one over on, sell a pup to; N. Amer. informal **sucker,** snooker, stiff; Austral. informal **pull a swifty on.**

defy verb **disobey,** flout, disregard, ignore, break, violate, contravene, breach, challenge, confront.
OPPOSITES obey.

degenerate adjective *her degenerate brother:* **corrupt,** perverted, decadent, dissolute, dissipated, debauched, immoral, unprincipled, disreputable.
OPPOSITES upright, pure.
verb *their quality of life had*

degenerated: **deteriorate,** decline, slip, slide, go downhill; informal go to the dogs.
OPPOSITES improve.

degrade verb **demean,** debase, humiliate, humble, belittle, mortify, dehumanize, brutalize.
OPPOSITES dignify.

degree noun **level,** standard, grade, stage, mark, amount, extent, measure, intensity, strength, proportion.

dejected adjective **downcast,** downhearted, despondent, disconsolate, dispirited, crestfallen, disheartened, depressed; informal down in the mouth, down in the dumps.
OPPOSITES cheerful.

delay verb **1** *we were delayed by the traffic:* **detain,** hold up, make late, slow up/down, bog down, hinder, hamper, impede, obstruct. **2** *don't delay:* **linger,** drag one's feet, hold back, dawdle, waste time, stall, hesitate, dither, shilly-shally; informal dilly-dally. **3** *he may delay the cut in interest rates:* **postpone,** put off, defer, hold over, adjourn, reschedule.
OPPOSITES assist, hurry, advance.
noun **1** *drivers will face lengthy delays:* **hold-up,** wait, interruption, stoppage. **2** *the delay of his trial:* **postponement,** deferral, adjournment.

delegate noun *trade union delegates:* **representative,** envoy, emissary, commissioner, agent, deputy.
verb *she must delegate routine tasks:* **assign,** entrust, pass on, hand on/over, turn over, devolve.

delegation noun **1** *the delegation from South Africa:* **deputation,** mission,

commission, contingent, legation. **2** *the delegation of tasks to others:* **assignment,** entrusting, devolution.

delete verb **remove,** cut (out), take out, edit out, excise, cancel, cross out, strike out, obliterate, rub out, erase.
OPPOSITES add.

deliberate adjective **1** *a deliberate attempt to provoke him:* **intentional,** calculated, conscious, intended, planned, wilful, premeditated. **2** *small, deliberate steps:* **careful,** cautious, measured, regular, even, steady. **3** *a deliberate worker:* **methodical,** systematic, careful, painstaking, meticulous, thorough.
OPPOSITES accidental, hasty, careless.
verb *she deliberated on his words:* **think about/over,** ponder, consider, contemplate, reflect on, muse on, meditate on, ruminate on, mull over; N. Amer. think on.

deliberately adverb **1** *he deliberately hurt me:* **intentionally,** on purpose, purposely, by design, knowingly, wittingly, consciously, wilfully. **2** *he walked deliberately down the aisle:* **carefully,** cautiously, slowly, steadily, evenly.

deliberation noun **thought,** consideration, reflection, contemplation, discussion.

delicacy noun **1** *the delicacy of the fabric:* **fineness,** delicateness, fragility, thinness, lightness, flimsiness. **2** *the delicacy of the situation:* **difficulty,** trickiness, sensitivity, ticklishness, awkwardness. **3** *treat this matter with delicacy:* **care,**

d

sensitivity, tact, discretion, diplomacy, subtlety. **4** *an Australian delicacy:* **treat**, luxury, speciality.

delicate adjective **1** *delicate embroidery:* **fine**, intricate, dainty. **2** *a delicate shade of blue:* **subtle**, soft, muted, pastel, pale, light. **3** *delicate china cups:* **fragile**, frail. **4** *his wife is very delicate:* **sickly**, unhealthy, frail, feeble, weak. **5** *a delicate issue:* **difficult**, tricky, sensitive, ticklish, awkward, touchy, embarrassing; informal sticky, dicey. **6** *the matter required delicate handling:* **careful**, sensitive, tactful, diplomatic, discreet, kid-glove, subtle. **7** *a delicate mechanism:* **sensitive**, light, precision.
OPPOSITES coarse, lurid, strong, robust, clumsy, crude.

delicious adjective delectable, mouth-watering, appetizing, tasty, flavoursome; informal scrumptious; N. Amer. informal nummy.
OPPOSITES unpalatable.

delight verb *her manners delighted him:* **charm**, enchant, captivate, entrance, thrill, entertain, amuse, divert; informal send, tickle pink, bowl over.
OPPOSITES dismay, disgust.
noun *she squealed with delight:* **pleasure**, happiness, joy, glee, excitement, amusement, bliss.
OPPOSITES displeasure.
■ **delight in** love, relish, savour, adore, lap up, take pleasure in, enjoy, revel in.

delighted adjective pleased, glad, happy, thrilled, overjoyed, ecstatic, elated, on cloud nine, walking on air, in seventh heaven, jumping for joy; enchanted, charmed; amused, diverted; gleeful, cock-a-hoop; informal over the moon, tickled pink, as pleased as Punch, on top of the world, as happy as Larry; Brit. informal chuffed; N. English informal made up; Austral. informal wrapped.

delightful adjective **1** *a delightful evening:* **lovely**, enjoyable, amusing, entertaining. **2** *the delightful Sally:* **charming**, enchanting, captivating, bewitching, appealing, sweet, endearing, cute.

deliver verb **1** *the parcel was delivered to his house:* **bring**, take, convey, carry, transport, send, distribute, dispatch, ship. **2** *the court delivered its verdict:* **state**, utter, give, read, broadcast, pronounce, announce, declare, proclaim, hand down, return. **3** *she delivered a blow to his head:* **administer**, deal, inflict, give; informal land.

delivery noun **1** *the delivery of the goods:* **conveyance**, carriage, transportation, transport, distribution, dispatch, shipping. **2** *we get several deliveries a day:* **consignment**, load, shipment. **3** *her delivery was stilted:* **speech**, pronunciation, enunciation, articulation, elocution.

delusion noun misapprehension, misconception, false impression, misunderstanding, mistake, error, misconstruction, illusion, fantasy, fancy.

demand noun **1** *I give in to her demands:* **request**, call, command, order, dictate. **2** *the demands of a young family:* **requirement**, need, claim, commitment, imposition. **3** *the*

big demand for such toys: **market,** call, appetite, desire.
verb **1** *workers demanded wage increases:* **call for,** ask for, request, push for, seek, claim. **2** *Harvey demanded that I tell him the truth:* **order,** command, enjoin, require, insist. **3** *'Where is she?' he demanded:* **ask,** enquire. **4** *an activity demanding detailed knowledge:* **require,** need, necessitate, call for, involve, entail. **5** *they demanded complete anonymity:* **insist on,** stipulate, expect, look for.

demanding adjective **1** *a demanding task:* **difficult,** challenging, taxing, exacting, tough, hard, onerous, formidable, arduous, gruelling, back-breaking, punishing. **2** *a demanding child:* **nagging,** trying, tiresome, hard to please. OPPOSITES easy.

demeaning adjective **degrading,** humiliating, shameful, undignified, menial; informal infra dig.

demise noun **1** *her tragic demise:* **death,** dying, passing, end. **2** *the demise of the Ottoman Empire:* **end,** break-up, disintegration, fall, downfall, collapse, overthrow. OPPOSITES birth.

democratic adjective **elected,** representative, parliamentary, popular, egalitarian, self-governing.

demolish verb **1** *they demolished a block of flats:* **knock down,** pull down, tear down, destroy, flatten, raze to the ground, dismantle, level, bulldoze, blow up. **2** *he demolished her credibility:* **destroy,** ruin, wreck, overturn, explode, drive a coach and

horses through; informal shoot full of holes. OPPOSITES build, strengthen.

demonstrate verb **1** *his findings demonstrate that boys commit more crimes:* **show,** indicate, establish, prove, confirm, verify. **2** *she demonstrated various drawing techniques:* **show,** display, present, illustrate, exemplify. **3** *his work demonstrated an analytical ability:* **reveal,** manifest, indicate, signify, signal, denote, show, display, exhibit. **4** *they demonstrated against the Government:* **protest,** march, parade, picket, strike.

demonstration noun **1** *a demonstration of carving:* **exhibition,** presentation, display. **2** *his paintings are a demonstration of his talent:* **manifestation,** indication, sign, mark, proof, testimony. **3** *an anti-racism demonstration:* **protest,** march, rally, mass lobby, sit-in, sit-down strike; informal demo.

demoralized adjective **dispirited,** disheartened, downhearted, dejected, downcast, low, depressed, dismayed, daunted, discouraged.

demure adjective **modest,** reserved, shy, unassuming, decorous, decent, proper. OPPOSITES brazen.

den noun **1** *the wolves' den:* **lair,** burrow, hole, shelter, hiding place, hideout. **2** *sulking in his den:* **study,** studio, workshop, retreat, sanctuary, hideaway; informal hidey-hole.

denial noun **1** *the reports met with a denial:* **contradiction,** rebuttal, repudiation,

d

refutation, disclaimer. **2** *the denial of insurance to certain people:* **refusal,** withholding.

denomination noun **1** *a Christian denomination:* **religious group,** sect, cult, movement, persuasion, order, creed, school, church.
2 *banknotes in a number of denominations:* **value,** unit, size.

denote verb **indicate,** be a mark of, signify, signal, designate, symbolize, represent.

denounce verb **1** *the pope denounced his critics:* **condemn,** attack, censure, decry, stigmatize, deprecate, disparage, revile, damn. **2** *he was denounced as a traitor:* **expose,** betray, inform on, incriminate, implicate, cite, accuse.
OPPOSITES praise.

dense adjective **1** *a dense forest:* **thick,** crowded, compact, solid, tight, overgrown, impenetrable, impassable. **2** *dense smoke:* **thick,** heavy, opaque, murky. **3** (informal) *they were dense enough to believe me:* **stupid,** brainless, foolish, slow, simple-minded, empty-headed, idiotic; informal thick, dim; Brit. informal daft.
OPPOSITES sparse, thin, clever.

dent noun *a dent in his car:* **knock,** indentation, dint, depression, hollow, crater, pit; N. Amer. informal ding.
verb *Jamie dented his car:* **knock,** dint, mark; N. Amer. informal ding.

deny verb **1** *the report was denied by witnesses:* **contradict,** rebut, repudiate, refute, challenge, contest. **2** *he denied the request:* **refuse,** turn down, reject, rebuff, decline, veto,

dismiss; informal give the thumbs down to.
OPPOSITES confirm, allow, accept.

depart verb **1** *James departed after lunch:* **leave,** go away, withdraw, absent oneself, quit, exit, decamp, retreat, retire, make off; informal make tracks, take off, split; Brit. informal sling one's hook. **2** *the budget departed from the norm:* **deviate,** diverge, digress, stray, veer, differ, vary.
OPPOSITES arrive, stick to.

department noun **division,** section, sector, unit, branch, wing, office, bureau, agency, ministry.

departure noun **1** *he tried to delay her departure:* **leaving,** going, leave-taking, withdrawal, exit. **2** *a departure from normality:* **deviation,** divergence, digression, shift, variation. **3** *an exciting departure for film-makers:* **change,** innovation, novelty.

depend verb **1** *her career depends on this reference:* **be dependent on,** hinge on, hang on, rest on, rely on. **2** *my family depends on me:* **rely on,** lean on, count on, bank on, trust (in), pin one's hopes on.

dependent adjective **1** *she is dependent on drugs:* **addicted,** reliant; informal hooked. **2** *he is ill and dependent:* **reliant,** needy, helpless, infirm, invalid, incapable, debilitated, disabled.
OPPOSITES independent.
■ **dependent on 1** conditional on, contingent on, based on, subject to, determined by, influenced by. **2** reliant on, relying on, counting on, sustained by.

depict verb **1** *the painting depicts the Last Supper:*

portray, show, represent, picture, illustrate, reproduce, render. **2** *the process depicted by Darwin's theory:* **describe,** detail, relate, present, set forth, set out, outline.

deplete verb reduce, decrease, diminish, exhaust, use up, consume, expend, drain, empty. OPPOSITES augment.

deplore verb **1** *we deplore violence:* **abhor,** find unacceptable, frown on, disapprove of, take a dim view of, take exception to, condemn, denounce. **2** *he deplored their lack of flair:* **regret,** lament, mourn, bemoan, bewail, complain about, grieve over, sigh over.
OPPOSITES applaud, rejoice at.

deploy verb **1** *forces were deployed at strategic points:* **position,** station, post, place, install, locate, base. **2** *she deployed all her skills:* **use,** utilize, employ, take advantage of, exploit, call on.

deport verb expel, banish, extradite, repatriate.
OPPOSITES admit.

depose verb overthrow, unseat, dethrone, topple, remove, supplant, displace, oust.

deposit noun **1** *a thick deposit of ash:* **layer,** covering, coating, blanket, accumulation, sediment. **2** *a copper deposit:* **seam,** vein, lode, layer, stratum, bed. **3** *they paid a deposit:* **down payment,** advance payment, prepayment, instalment, retainer, security.
verb **1** *she deposited her books on the table:* **put down,** place, set down, unload, rest, drop; informal dump, park, plonk; N. Amer. informal plunk. **2** *the silt deposited by flood water:* **leave**

(behind), precipitate, dump, wash up, cast up. **3** *the gold was deposited at the bank:* **lodge,** bank, house, store, stow.

depot noun **1** *the bus depot:* **terminal,** terminus, station, garage, headquarters, base. **2** *an arms depot:* **storehouse,** warehouse, store, repository, depository, cache, arsenal, armoury, dump.

depress verb **1** *the news depressed him:* **sadden,** dispirit, cast down, get down, dishearten, demoralize, crush, weigh down on. **2** *new economic policies depressed sales:* **slow down,** weaken, impair, inhibit, restrict. **3** *imports will depress farm prices:* **reduce,** lower, cut, cheapen, discount, deflate, diminish, depreciate, devalue. **4** *depress each key in turn:* **press,** push, hold down, tap.
OPPOSITES cheer, boost, raise, lift.

depressed adjective **1** *he felt lonely and depressed:* **sad,** unhappy, miserable, gloomy, dejected, downhearted, downcast, down, despondent, dispirited, low, morose, dismal, desolate; informal blue, down in the dumps, down in the mouth. **2** *a depressed economy:* **weak,** inactive, flat, slow, slack, sluggish, stagnant. **3** *a depressed area:* **poverty-stricken,** poor, disadvantaged, deprived, needy, distressed, run down.
OPPOSITES cheerful, strong, prosperous.

depressing adjective dismal, sad, unhappy, sombre, gloomy, grave, bleak, black, melancholy, dreary, grim, cheerless.

depression noun **1** *she ate to*

ease her depression:
unhappiness, sadness,
melancholy, melancholia,
misery, sorrow, gloom,
despondency, low spirits. **2** *an
economic depression:* **recession,**
slump, decline, downturn. **3** *a
depression in the ground:*
hollow, indentation, dent,
cavity, dip, pit, crater, basin,
bowl.

deprivation noun
1 *unemployment and
deprivation:* **poverty,**
impoverishment, privation,
hardship, destitution, need,
want. **2** *deprivation of political
rights:* **dispossession,**
withholding, withdrawal,
removal, seizure.
OPPOSITES prosperity, granting.

deprive verb **dispossess,** strip,
divest, relieve, rob, cheat out
of.

deprived adjective
disadvantaged,
underprivileged, poverty-
stricken, impoverished, poor,
destitute, needy.
OPPOSITES privileged.

depth noun **1** *the depth of the
caves:* **deepness,** drop, height.
2 *the depth of his knowledge:*
extent, range, scope, breadth,
width. **3** *her lack of depth:*
profundity, wisdom,
understanding, intelligence,
discernment, penetration,
insight, awareness. **4** *depth of
colour:* **intensity,** richness,
vividness, strength, brilliance.
OPPOSITES triviality.

deputy noun **second in
command,** number two,
assistant, aide, proxy, stand-in,
replacement, substitute,
representative, reserve.

derelict adjective *a derelict
building:* **dilapidated,**
ramshackle, run down,
tumbledown, in ruins, falling
down, disused, abandoned,
deserted.
noun *the derelicts who survive
on the streets:* **tramp,** vagrant,
down and out, homeless
person, drifter, beggar, outcast;
informal dosser, bag lady.

derision noun **mockery,**
ridicule, jeers, sneers, taunts,
disdain, disparagement,
denigration, insults.

derogatory adjective
disparaging, disrespectful,
demeaning, critical, pejorative,
negative, unfavourable,
uncomplimentary, unflattering,
insulting, defamatory,
slanderous, libellous.
OPPOSITES complimentary.

descend verb **1** *the plane started
descending:* **go down,** come
down, drop, fall, sink, dive,
plummet, plunge, nosedive.
2 *she descended the stairs:*
climb down, go down, come
down, shin down, slide down.
3 *the road descends to a village:*
slope, dip, slant, go down, fall
away. **4** *she saw Leo descend
from the bus:* **alight,** disembark,
get down, get off, dismount.
OPPOSITES climb, board.
■ **descend on** flock to, besiege,
surround, take over, invade,
swoop on, occupy.

descent noun **1** *the plane began
its descent:* **dive,** drop, fall,
plunge, nosedive. **2** *a steep
descent:* **slope,** incline, dip,
drop, gradient. **3** *his descent
into alcoholism:* **decline,** slide,
fall, degeneration,
deterioration. **4** *she is of Italian
descent:* **ancestry,** parentage,
ancestors, family, extraction,
origin, derivation, birth,

lineage, stock, blood, roots, origins.

describe verb **1** *he described his experiences:* **report,** recount, relate, narrate, tell of, set out, detail, give a rundown of. **2** *she described him as a pathetic figure:* **portray,** depict, paint, define, characterize, call, label, class, brand. **3** *the pen described a circle:* **mark out,** delineate, outline, trace, draw.

description noun **1** *a description of my travels:* **account,** report, narrative, story, portrayal, portrait, sketch, details. **2** *the description of oil as 'black gold':* **designation,** labelling, naming, dubbing, characterization, definition, classification, branding. **3** *vehicles of every description:* **sort,** variety, kind, type.

desert[1] verb **1** *his wife deserted him:* **abandon,** leave, jilt, leave high and dry, leave in the lurch, leave behind, strand, maroon; informal walk/run out on, dump, ditch; literary forsake. **2** *soldiers deserted in droves:* **abscond,** defect, run away, decamp, flee, turn tail, take French leave; Military go AWOL.

desert[2] noun *an African desert:* **wasteland,** wastes, wilderness, dust bowl.

deserted adjective **1** *a deserted wife:* **abandoned,** jilted, cast aside, neglected, stranded, marooned, forlorn; literary forsaken. **2** *a deserted village:* **empty,** uninhabited, unoccupied, abandoned, evacuated, desolate, lonely, godforsaken.
OPPOSITES cherished, populous.

deserve verb merit, earn, warrant, rate, justify, be worthy of, be entitled to.

deserved adjective well earned, merited, warranted, justified, rightful, due, fitting, just, proper.

deserving adjective *a deserving cause:* **worthy,** commendable, praiseworthy, admirable, estimable, creditable.

design noun **1** *a design for the offices:* **plan,** blueprint, drawing, sketch, outline, map, plot, diagram, draft. **2** *a Celtic design:* **pattern,** motif, device, style, theme, layout.
verb **1** *they designed a new engine:* **invent,** create, think up, come up with, devise, formulate, conceive; informal dream up. **2** *this paper is designed to provoke discussion:* **intend,** aim, mean.

designate verb **1** *some firms designate a press officer:* **appoint,** nominate, delegate, select, choose, pick, elect, name, identify, assign. **2** *the rivers are designated 'Sites of Special Scientific Interest':* **classify,** class, label, tag, name, call, term, dub.

desirable adjective **1** *a desirable location:* **attractive,** sought-after, in demand, popular, enviable; informal to die for, must-have. **2** *it is desirable that they should meet:* **advantageous,** advisable, wise, sensible, recommended, beneficial, preferable. **3** *a very desirable woman:* **(sexually) attractive,** beautiful, pretty, appealing, seductive, alluring, irresistible; informal sexy.
OPPOSITES unattractive, unwise, ugly.

desire noun **1** *a desire to see the world:* **wish,** want, aspiration, yearning, longing, craving,

hankering, hunger; informal yen, itch. **2** *his eyes glittered with desire:* **lust,** passion, sensuality, sexuality, libido, lasciviousness, lechery.
verb *they desired peace:* **want,** wish for, long for, yearn for, crave, hanker after, be desperate for, be bent on, covet, aspire to.

desolate adjective **1** *desolate moorlands:* **bleak,** stark, bare, dismal, grim, wild, inhospitable, deserted, uninhabited, godforsaken, abandoned, empty, isolated, remote. **2** *she is desolate:* **miserable,** despondent, depressed, disconsolate, devastated, despairing, inconsolable.
OPPOSITES populous, joyful.

despair noun **desperation,** anguish, unhappiness, despondency, depression, misery, wretchedness, hopelessness.
OPPOSITES hope, joy.
verb **lose hope,** give up, lose heart, be discouraged, be despondent, be demoralized.

despatch verb & noun. See DISPATCH.

desperate adjective **1** *a desperate look:* **despairing,** hopeless, anguished, distressed, wretched, desolate, forlorn, distraught, at one's wits' end, at the end of one's tether. **2** *a desperate attempt to escape:* **last-ditch,** last-gasp, eleventh-hour, do-or-die, final, frantic, frenzied, wild. **3** *a desperate shortage of teachers:* **grave,** serious, critical, acute, urgent, pressing, drastic, extreme.

desperation noun **hopelessness,** despair, distress, anguish, agony, torment, misery.

despise verb **detest,** hate, loathe, abhor, deplore, scorn, disdain, deride, sneer at, revile, spurn, shun.
OPPOSITES adore, respect.

despite preposition **in spite of,** notwithstanding, regardless of, in the face of, in the teeth of, undeterred by, for all, even with.

destined adjective **1** *he is destined to lead a troubled life:* **fated,** ordained, predestined, doomed, meant, intended. **2** *computers destined for Pakistan:* **heading,** bound, en route, scheduled, headed.

destiny noun **1** *master of his own destiny:* **future,** fate, fortune, doom, lot. **2** *she was sent by destiny:* **fate,** providence, God, the stars, luck, fortune, chance, karma.

destroy verb **1** *their offices were destroyed by bombing:* **demolish,** knock down, level, raze to the ground, fell, blow up. **2** *traffic would destroy the conservation area:* **spoil,** ruin, wreck, blight, devastate, wreak havoc on. **3** *the horse had to be destroyed:* **kill,** put down, put to sleep, slaughter, cull. **4** *we had to destroy the enemy:* **annihilate,** wipe out, obliterate, eliminate, eradicate, liquidate, exterminate; informal take out; N. Amer. informal waste.
OPPOSITES build, preserve, spare.

destruction noun **1** *the destruction caused by allied bombers:* **devastation,** carnage, ruin, chaos, wreckage. **2** *the destruction of the countryside:* **wrecking,** ruining, annihilation, obliteration, elimination, eradication,

devastation. **3** *the destruction of cattle:* **killing,** slaughter, putting down, extermination, culling.
OPPOSITES preservation.

destructive adjective **devastating,** ruinous, damaging, harmful, detrimental, injurious, hurtful, deleterious.

detach verb **disconnect,** separate, unfasten, disengage, uncouple, isolate, remove, loose, unhitch, unhook, free, pull off, cut off, break off, split off, sever.
OPPOSITES attach, join.

detached adjective **1** *a detached collar:* **disconnected,** separated, separate, unfastened, disengaged, uncoupled, unhitched, isolated, loosened, unhooked, free, severed, cut off. **2** *a detached observer:* **dispassionate,** disinterested, objective, outside, neutral, unbiased, impartial.

detachment noun **1** *she looked on with detachment:* **objectivity,** dispassion, disinterest, neutrality, impartiality. **2** *a detachment of soldiers:* **unit,** squad, detail, troop, contingent, task force, party, platoon.

detail noun **1** *the picture is correct in every detail:* **particular,** respect, feature, characteristic, specific, aspect, fact, point, element. **2** *that's just a detail:* **triviality,** technicality, nicety, fine point. **3** *a guard detail:* **unit,** detachment, squad, troop, contingent, outfit, task force, party, platoon.
verb *the report details our objections:* **describe,** relate, catalogue, list, spell out,

itemize, identify, specify.

detailed adjective **comprehensive,** full, complete, thorough, exhaustive, all-inclusive, elaborate, minute, precise, itemized, blow-by-blow.
OPPOSITES general.

detain verb **1** *they were detained for questioning:* **hold,** take into custody, confine, imprison, intern, arrest, apprehend, seize; informal pick up; Brit. informal nick. **2** *don't let me detain you:* **delay,** hold up, make late, keep, slow up/down, hinder.
OPPOSITES release.

detect verb **1** *I detected a note of urgency in her voice:* **notice,** perceive, discern, become aware of, note, make out, spot, recognize, identify, catch, sense. **2** *they are responsible for detecting fraud:* **discover,** uncover, turn up, unearth, dig up, root out, expose. **3** *the hackers were detected:* **catch,** hunt down, track down, find out, expose, reveal, unmask, smoke out.

detective noun **investigator,** police officer; informal private eye, sleuth; N. Amer. informal gumshoe.

detention noun **custody,** imprisonment, incarceration, internment, captivity, remand, arrest, quarantine.
OPPOSITES release.

deter verb **1** *the high cost deterred many:* **discourage,** dissuade, put off, scare off, dishearten, demoralize, daunt, intimidate. **2** *the presence of a caretaker deters crime:* **prevent,** stop, avert, stave off, ward off.
OPPOSITES encourage.

deteriorate verb **worsen,** decline, degenerate, fail, go downhill, wane.

OPPOSITES improve.

determination noun
resolution, resolve, will power, strength of character, dedication, single-mindedness, perseverance, persistence, tenacity, staying power, doggedness; informal guts.

determine verb 1 *chromosomes determine the sex of the embryo:* control, decide, regulate, direct, dictate, govern. 2 *he determined to sell up:* resolve, decide, make up one's mind, choose, elect, opt. 3 *the rent shall be determined by an accountant:* specify, set, fix, decide on, settle, establish, ordain, prescribe, decree. 4 *determine the composition of the fibres:* ascertain, find out, discover, learn, establish, calculate, work out; informal figure out.

determined adjective resolute, purposeful, adamant, single-minded, unswerving, unwavering, persevering, persistent, tenacious, dedicated, dogged.
OPPOSITES irresolute.

deterrent noun disincentive, discouragement, damper, curb, check, restraint, inhibition.
OPPOSITES incentive.

detest verb hate, abhor, loathe, regard with disgust, be unable to bear, have an aversion to, find intolerable, disdain, despise.
OPPOSITES love.

devastate verb 1 *the city was devastated by an earthquake:* destroy, ruin, wreck, lay waste, ravage, demolish, raze to the ground, level, flatten. 2 *he was devastated by the news:* shatter, shock, stun, daze, dumbfound, traumatize, distress; informal

knock sideways; Brit. informal knock for six.

devastation noun destruction, ruin, desolation, wreckage, ruins.

develop verb 1 *the industry developed rapidly:* grow, expand, spread, advance, progress, evolve, mature. 2 *a plan was developed:* initiate, instigate, set in motion, originate, invent, form. 3 *children should develop their talents:* expand, augment, broaden, supplement, reinforce, enhance, refine, improve, polish, perfect. 4 *a row developed:* start, begin, emerge, erupt, break out, arise, break, unfold.
OPPOSITES shrink, regress.

development noun 1 *the development of the firm:* evolution, growth, expansion, enlargement, spread, progress. 2 *there have been a number of developments:* event, change, circumstance, incident, occurrence. 3 *a housing development:* estate, complex, site.

deviate verb diverge, digress, drift, stray, veer, swerve, get sidetracked, branch off, differ, vary.

device noun 1 *a device for measuring pressure:* implement, gadget, utensil, tool, appliance, apparatus, instrument, machine, mechanism, contrivance, contraption; informal gizmo. 2 *an ingenious legal device:* ploy, tactic, move, stratagem, scheme, plot, trick, ruse, manoeuvre.

devil noun 1 *God and the Devil:* Satan, Beelzebub, Lucifer, the Prince of Darkness; informal Old

Nick. **2** *they drove out the devils:* **evil spirit**, demon, fiend. **3** *he was a devil:* **brute**, beast, monster, fiend, villain, sadist, barbarian, ogre.

devious adjective **1** *the devious ways in which they bent the rules:* **underhand**, dishonest, crafty, cunning, conniving, scheming, sneaky, furtive; informal **crooked**, shady; Brit. informal **dodgy**. **2** *a devious route:* **circuitous**, roundabout, indirect, meandering, tortuous. OPPOSITES open, honest, direct.

devise verb **conceive**, think up, dream up, work out, formulate, concoct, hatch, contrive, design, invent, coin; informal **cook up**.

devoid
■ **devoid of** empty of, free of, bereft of, lacking, deficient in, without, wanting in; informal minus.

devote verb **dedicate**, allocate, assign, allot, commit, give (over), consign, pledge, set aside, earmark, reserve.

devoted adjective **dedicated**, committed, devout, loyal, faithful, true, staunch, steadfast, fond, loving.

devotee noun **enthusiast**, fan, lover, aficionado, admirer, supporter, disciple; informal **buff**, freak, nut, fanatic.

devotion noun **1** *wifely devotion:* **loyalty**, fidelity, commitment, allegiance, dedication, fondness, love, care. **2** *a life of devotion:* **piety**, spirituality, godliness, holiness, sanctity.

devour verb **1** *he devoured his meal:* **gobble**, guzzle, gulp down, bolt, wolf; informal **polish off**; Brit. informal **scoff**. **2** *flames devoured the house:* **consume**, engulf, envelop.

devout adjective **dedicated**, devoted, committed, loyal, sincere, fervent, pious, reverent, God-fearing, dutiful, churchgoing.

diagnose verb **identify**, determine, distinguish, recognize, interpret, detect, pinpoint.

diagnosis noun **1** *the diagnosis of coeliac disease:* **identification**, detection, recognition, determination, discovery, pinpointing. **2** *the results confirmed his diagnosis:* **opinion**, judgement, verdict, conclusion.

diagonal adjective **crosswise**, crossways, slanting, slanted, oblique, angled, cornerways, cornerwise.

diagram noun **drawing**, representation, plan, outline, figure, chart, graph.

dialogue noun **conversation**, talk, discussion, chat, tête-à-tête, exchange, debate, conference, consultation; informal **confab**.

diary noun **1** *he put the date in his diary:* **appointment book**, engagement book, personal organizer; trademark **Filofax**. **2** *her World War II diaries:* **journal**, memoir, chronicle, log, logbook, history, annal, record; N. Amer. **daybook**.

dictate verb **1** *his attempts to dictate policy:* **prescribe**, lay down, impose, set down, order, command, decree, ordain, direct. **2** *choice is often dictated by availability:* **determine**, control, govern, decide, influence, affect.
■ **dictate to** give orders to, order about/around, lord it over; informal **boss about/around**, push about/around.

d

dictator noun autocrat, despot, tyrant, absolute ruler.
OPPOSITES democrat.

dictatorial adjective domineering, autocratic, authoritarian, oppressive, imperious, overweening, overbearing, peremptory; informal bossy, high-handed.

dictionary noun lexicon, glossary, vocabulary.

die verb 1 *her father died last year:* **pass away,** pass on, perish; informal give up the ghost, kick the bucket, croak; Brit. informal snuff it, peg out; N. Amer. informal buy the farm. 2 *the wind had died:* **lessen,** subside, drop, ease (off), let up, moderate, abate, fade, peter out, wane, ebb. 3 (informal) *the engine died:* **fail,** cut out, give out, break down, stop; informal conk out, go kaput; Brit. informal pack up.
OPPOSITES live, intensify.

diet noun 1 *a healthy diet:* **food,** nutrition, eating habits. 2 *she's on a diet:* **dietary regime,** regimen, restricted diet, fast, abstinence.
OPPOSITES binge.
verb *I began dieting again:* **be on a diet,** slim, lose weight, watch one's weight; N. Amer. reduce; N. Amer. informal slenderize.
OPPOSITES binge.

differ verb 1 *the second set of data differed from the first:* **contrast with,** be different to, vary from, deviate from, conflict with, run counter to, be at odds with, contradict. 2 *the two sides differed over this issue:* **disagree,** conflict, be at variance/odds, be in dispute, not see eye to eye.
OPPOSITES resemble, agree.

difference noun 1 *the difference between the two sets of data:* **dissimilarity,** contrast, distinction, differentiation, variance, variation, divergence, disparity, contradiction. 2 *we've had our differences:* **disagreement,** difference of opinion, dispute, argument, quarrel; Brit. informal row. 3 *I'll pay the difference:* **balance,** remainder, rest.
OPPOSITES similarity.

different adjective 1 *people with different lifestyles:* **dissimilar,** unlike, contrasting, differing, varying, disparate, poles apart, incompatible, mismatched; informal like chalk and cheese. 2 *suddenly everything in her life was different:* **changed,** altered, transformed, new, unfamiliar, unknown, strange. 3 *two different occasions:* **distinct,** separate, individual, independent. 4 (informal) *try something different:* **unusual,** out of the ordinary, unfamiliar, novel, new, fresh, original, unconventional, exotic.
OPPOSITES similar, normal, related, ordinary.

difficult adjective 1 *a very difficult job:* **laborious,** strenuous, arduous, hard, tough, demanding, punishing, gruelling, back-breaking, exhausting, tiring; informal hellish, killing, no picnic. 2 *a difficult problem:* **hard,** complicated, beyond one, puzzling, baffling, problematic, thorny, ticklish. 3 *a difficult child:* **troublesome,** tiresome, trying, exasperating, awkward, demanding, contrary, uncooperative, fussy.
OPPOSITES easy, simple, cooperative, accommodating.

difficulty noun 1 *the difficulty*

of balancing motherhood with a career: **strain,** trouble, problems, struggle, laboriousness, arduousness; informal hassle, stress. **2** *practical difficulties:* **problem,** complication, snag, hitch, obstacle, hurdle, stumbling block; Brit. spanner in the works; informal headache. **3** *Charles got into difficulties:* **trouble,** predicament, plight, hard times.
OPPOSITES ease.

dig verb **1** *she began to dig the soil:* **turn over,** work, break up. **2** *he dug a hole:* **excavate,** dig out, quarry, hollow out, scoop out, bore, burrow, mine. **3** *Winnie dug her elbow into his ribs:* **poke,** prod, jab, stab, shove, ram, push, thrust, drive, stick. **4** *he'd been digging into my past:* **delve,** probe, search, enquire, look, investigate, research.
noun **1** *a dig in the ribs:* **poke,** prod, jab, stab, shove, push. **2** (informal) *they're always making digs at each other:* **snide remark,** cutting remark, jibe, taunt, sneer, insult; informal wisecrack, put-down.
■ **dig something up** exhume, disinter, unearth.

digest verb *Liz digested this information:* **assimilate,** absorb, take in, understand, comprehend, grasp.
noun *a digest of their findings:* **summary,** synopsis, abstract, precis, résumé, summation.

dignified adjective **stately,** noble, majestic, distinguished, regal, imposing, impressive, grand, solemn, formal, ceremonious, decorous, sedate.

dignity noun **1** *the dignity of the Crown:* **stateliness,** nobility, majesty, impressiveness, grandeur, magnificence, ceremoniousness, formality, decorum, propriety, respectability, worthiness, integrity, solemnity, gravitas. **2** *little regard for human dignity:* **self-respect,** pride, self-esteem, self-worth.
OPPOSITES informality.

dilemma noun **quandary,** predicament, catch-22, vicious circle, plight, conflict; informal fix, tight spot/corner; (in a dilemma) between the devil and the deep blue sea, between a rock and a hard place.

dilute verb **1** *strong bleach can be diluted with water:* **make weaker,** water down, thin, doctor, adulterate; informal cut. **2** *the original plans have been diluted:* **weaken,** moderate, tone down, water down, compromise.
OPPOSITES concentrate, beef up.

dim adjective **1** *the dim light:* **faint,** weak, feeble, soft, pale, dull, subdued, muted. **2** *long dim corridors:* **dark,** badly lit, dingy, dismal, gloomy, murky. **3** *a dim figure:* **indistinct,** ill-defined, vague, shadowy, nebulous, blurred, fuzzy. **4** *dim memories:* **vague,** imprecise, imperfect, unclear, indistinct, sketchy, hazy. **5** (informal) *I'm awfully dim.* See STUPID.
OPPOSITES bright, distinct, clear.
verb **1** *the lights were dimmed:* **turn down,** lower, soften, subdue. **2** *memories have dimmed:* **fade,** dwindle, dull.
OPPOSITES brighten.

dimension noun **1** *the dimensions of the room:* **size,** measurements, proportions, extent, length, width, breadth, depth. **2** *the cultural*

d

dimensions of the problem: **aspect,** feature, element, angle, facet, side.

diminish verb **1** *the pain will gradually diminish:* **decrease,** lessen, decline, reduce, subside, dwindle, fade, slacken off, let up. **2** *new legislation diminished the courts' authority:* **reduce,** decrease, lessen, curtail, cut, limit, curb.
OPPOSITES increase.

din noun **noise,** racket, rumpus, cacophony, hubbub, uproar, commotion, clangour, clatter, clamour; informal hullabaloo; Brit. informal row.
OPPOSITES silence.

dine verb **eat,** have dinner, have lunch; dated sup.

dinner noun **main meal,** lunch, evening meal, supper, feast, banquet; Brit. tea.

dip verb **1** *he dipped a rag in the water:* **immerse,** submerge, plunge, dunk, bathe, sink. **2** *the sun dipped below the horizon:* **sink,** set, drop, fall, descend. **3** *the president's popularity has dipped:* **decrease,** fall, drop, fall off, decline, diminish, dwindle, slump, plummet, plunge. **4** *the road dipped:* **slope down,** descend, go down, drop (away), fall away.
OPPOSITES rise, increase.
noun **1** *a dip in the pool:* **swim,** bathe, paddle. **2** *the hedge at the bottom of the dip:* **slope,** incline, decline, descent, hollow, depression, basin. **3** *a dip in sales:* **decrease,** fall, drop, downturn, decline, falling-off, slump, reduction.
■ **dip into 1** draw on, use, spend. **2** browse through, skim through, look through, flick through.

diplomacy noun **1** *diplomacy*
failed to win them independence: **statesmanship,** statecraft, negotiation(s), discussion(s), talks. **2** *Jack's quiet diplomacy:* **tact,** tactfulness, sensitivity, discretion.

diplomat noun **ambassador,** attaché, consul, chargé d'affaires, envoy, emissary.

diplomatic adjective **tactful,** sensitive, subtle, delicate, polite, discreet, judicious, politic.
OPPOSITES tactless.

dire adjective **terrible,** dreadful, appalling, frightful, awful, grim, sore, alarming, acute, grave, serious, urgent, pressing, wretched, desperate, parlous.

direct adjective **1** *the most direct route:* **straight,** short, quick. **2** *a direct flight:* **non-stop,** through, unbroken, uninterrupted. **3** *he is very direct:* **frank,** candid, straightforward, open, blunt, plain-spoken, outspoken, forthright, no-nonsense, matter-of-fact; informal upfront.
verb **1** *an economic elite directed the nation's affairs:* **manage,** govern, run, administer, control, conduct, handle, be in charge of, preside over, lead, head, rule. **2** *was that remark directed at me?* **aim,** target, address to, intend for, mean for, design for. **3** *a man in uniform directed them to the hall:* **give directions,** show the way, point someone in the direction of. **4** *the judge directed the jury to return a not guilty verdict:* **instruct,** tell, command, order, require.

direction noun **1** *a northerly direction:* **way,** route, course, line, bearing, orientation. **2** *his direction of the project:*

running, management, administration, conduct, handling, supervision, superintendence, command, rule, leadership. **3** *explicit directions about nursing care:* **instruction**, order, command, rule, regulation, requirement.

directive noun **instruction**, direction, command, order, injunction, decree, dictum, edict.

directly adverb **1** *they flew directly to New York:* **straight**, as the crow flies. **2** *directly after breakfast:* **immediately**, right (away), straight (away), without delay, promptly. **3** *the houses directly opposite:* **exactly**, right, immediately, diametrically; informal bang. **4** *she spoke simply and directly:* **frankly**, candidly, openly, bluntly, forthrightly, without beating around the bush.

director noun **manager**, head, chief, principal, leader, governor, president, chair, chief executive; informal boss, gaffer.

dirt noun **1** *his face was streaked with dirt:* **grime**, filth, muck, dust, mud; Brit. informal gunge. **2** *a dirt road:* **earth**, soil, clay, ground.

dirty adjective **1** *a dirty sweatshirt | dirty water:* **soiled**, grimy, grubby, filthy, mucky, stained, unwashed, greasy, muddy, dusty, polluted, contaminated, foul, unhygienic; Brit. informal manky, grotty. **2** *a dirty joke:* **obscene**, indecent, rude, naughty, vulgar, smutty, coarse, crude, filthy, off colour, pornographic, explicit, X-rated; informal blue; euphemistic adult. **3** *a dirty look:* **malevolent**, hostile, black, angry, disapproving. OPPOSITES clean, friendly.

verb *the dog had dirtied her dress:* **soil**, stain, muddy, blacken, mess (up), mark, spatter, smudge, smear, splatter, sully, pollute, foul. OPPOSITES clean.

disability noun **handicap**, incapacity, impairment, infirmity, defect, abnormality, condition, disorder, affliction.

disable verb **1** *an injury that could disable somebody for life:* **incapacitate**, put out of action, debilitate, handicap, cripple, lame, maim, immobilize, paralyse. **2** *the bomb squad disabled the device:* **deactivate**, defuse, disarm, make safe.

disabled adjective **handicapped**, incapacitated, infirm, crippled, lame, paralysed, immobilized, bedridden; euphemistic physically challenged, differently abled. OPPOSITES able-bodied.

disadvantage noun **1** *that's the disadvantage of this scheme:* **drawback**, snag, downside, fly in the ointment, catch, nuisance, handicap, trouble, informal minus. **2** *she did nothing to his disadvantage:* **detriment**, prejudice, harm, loss, hurt. OPPOSITES advantage.

disagree verb **1** *no one disagreed with him:* **be of a different opinion**, not see eye to eye, take issue, challenge, contradict, differ, dissent, be in dispute, clash. **2** *their accounts disagree:* **differ**, be dissimilar, be different, be at variance/odds, vary, contradict each other, conflict. **3** *the spicy food disagreed with her:* **make ill**, make unwell, sicken, upset. OPPOSITES agree.

disagreement noun **dissent**, difference of opinion, controversy, discord, division,

dispute, quarrel.
OPPOSITES agreement.

disappear verb **1** *the mist had disappeared:* **vanish**, be lost to view/sight, recede, fade away, melt away, clear. **2** *this way of life has disappeared:* **die out**, cease to exist, end, go, pass away, pass into oblivion, perish, vanish.
OPPOSITES materialize, arise.

disappoint verb **let down,** fail, dissatisfy, upset, dismay, sadden, disenchant, disillusion, shatter someone's illusions.
OPPOSITES delight.

disappointed adjective **upset,** saddened, let down, displeased, dissatisfied, disheartened, downhearted, discouraged, crestfallen, disenchanted, disillusioned; informal choked, cut up; Brit. informal gutted, as sick as a parrot.
OPPOSITES delighted.

disappointment noun **1** *she tried to hide her disappointment:* **sadness,** sorrow, regret, dismay, displeasure, dissatisfaction, disenchantment, disillusionment. **2** *the trip was a disappointment:* **let-down,** non-event, anticlimax; Brit. damp squib; informal washout.
OPPOSITES delight, pleasant surprise.

disapproval noun **disfavour,** objection, dislike, dissatisfaction, distaste, displeasure, criticism, censure, condemnation, denunciation.
OPPOSITES approval.

disapprove
∎ **disapprove of** object to, have a poor opinion of, take exception to, dislike, take a dim view of, look askance at, frown on, be against, not believe in, deplore,

censure, condemn, denounce.

disarm verb **1** *the militia refused to disarm:* **lay down one's arms,** demobilize, disband, demilitarize. **2** *police disarmed the bomb:* **defuse,** disable, deactivate, make safe. **3** *the warmth in his voice disarmed her:* **win over,** charm, persuade, soothe, mollify, appease, placate.
OPPOSITES arm, antagonize.

disarmament noun **demilitarization,** demobilization, disbandment, decommissioning, arms reduction, arms limitation.
OPPOSITES arming.

disarming adjective **winning,** charming, irresistible, persuasive, soothing, conciliatory, mollifying.
OPPOSITES infuriating.

disarray noun **disorder,** confusion, chaos, untidiness, disorganization, a mess, a muddle, a shambles.
OPPOSITES tidiness.

disaster noun **1** *a railway disaster:* **catastrophe,** calamity, cataclysm, tragedy, act of God, accident. **2** *a string of personal disasters:* **misfortune,** mishap, misadventure, setback, reversal, stroke of bad luck, blow. **3** (informal) *the film was a disaster:* **failure,** fiasco, catastrophe; informal flop, washout, dead loss.
OPPOSITES success.

disastrous adjective **catastrophic,** calamitous, cataclysmic, tragic, devastating, ruinous, terrible, awful.

disbelief noun **incredulity,** incredulousness, scepticism, doubt, cynicism, suspicion, distrust, mistrust.
OPPOSITES belief.

discard verb **dispose of**, throw away/out, get rid of, toss out, jettison, dispense with, scrap, reject, drop; informal ditch, bin, junk; Brit. informal get shot of; N. Amer. informal trash.
OPPOSITES keep.

discharge verb **1** *he was discharged from service:* **dismiss**, eject, expel, throw out, make redundant, release, let go; Military cashier; informal sack, fire. **2** *he was discharged from prison:* **release**, free, let out. **3** *oil is routinely discharged from ships:* **release**, eject, let out, pour out, give off, dump. **4** *he accidentally discharged a pistol:* **fire**, shoot, let off, set off, loose off, trigger, launch. **5** *the ferry was discharging passengers:* **unload**, offload, put off, remove. **6** *they discharged their duties efficiently:* **carry out**, perform, execute, conduct, fulfil, complete.
OPPOSITES recruit, imprison, take on.
noun **1** *his discharge from the service:* **dismissal**, release, removal, ejection, expulsion; Military cashiering; informal the sack, the boot. **2** *her discharge from prison:* **release**. **3** *a discharge of diesel oil into the river:* **leak**, leakage, emission, release, outflow. **4** *a watery discharge from the eyes:* **emission**, secretion, excretion, suppuration, pus. **5** *the discharge of their duties:* **carrying out**, performance, execution, conduct, fulfilment, accomplishment, completion.

disciple noun **follower**, adherent, believer, admirer, devotee, acolyte, apostle, supporter, advocate.

discipline noun **1** *parental discipline:* **control**, regulation, direction, order, authority, strictness. **2** *he maintained discipline among his men:* **good behaviour**, order, control, obedience. **3** *sociology is a fairly new discipline:* **field (of study)**, branch of knowledge, subject, area, speciality.
verb **1** *she had disciplined herself to ignore the pain:* **train**, drill, teach, school, coach. **2** *he was disciplined by the management:* **punish**, penalize, bring to book, reprimand, rebuke; Brit. informal carpet.

disclose verb **1** *the information must not be disclosed:* **reveal**, make known, divulge, tell, impart, communicate, pass on, release, make public, broadcast, publish. **2** *surgery disclosed a growth:* **uncover**, reveal, show, bring to light.
OPPOSITES keep secret, conceal.

discomfort noun **1** *discomfort caused by indigestion:* **pain**, aches and pains, soreness, aching, twinge, pang, throb, cramp. **2** *the discomforts of life at sea:* **inconvenience**, difficulty, problem, trial, tribulation, hardship. **3** *Thomas noticed her discomfort:* **embarrassment**, discomfiture, unease, awkwardness, discomposure, confusion, nervousness, distress, anxiety.

discontent noun **dissatisfaction**, disaffection, grievances, unhappiness, displeasure, resentment, envy, restlessness, unrest, unease.
OPPOSITES satisfaction.

discontented adjective **dissatisfied**, disgruntled, disaffected, unhappy, aggrieved, displeased, resentful, envious, restless,

discount noun *a 10 per cent discount:* **reduction**, deduction, markdown, price cut, concession, rebate.
verb **1** *I discounted the rumours:* **disregard**, pay no attention to, take no notice of, dismiss, ignore, overlook; informal pooh-pooh. **2** *the price is heavily discounted:* **reduce**, mark down, cut, lower; informal knock down.
OPPOSITES believe, increase.

discourage verb **1** *we want to discourage children from smoking:* **dissuade**, deter, put off, talk out of. **2** *she was discouraged by his hostile tone:* **dishearten**, dispirit, demoralize, disappoint, put off, unnerve, daunt, intimidate. **3** *he sought to discourage further speculation:* **prevent**, deter, stop, avert, inhibit, curb.
OPPOSITES encourage.

discover verb **1** *firemen discovered a body:* **find**, locate, come across/upon, stumble on, chance on, uncover, unearth, turn up. **2** *I discovered the truth:* **find out**, learn, realize, ascertain, work out, recognize; informal figure out; Brit. informal twig.

discovery noun **1** *the discovery of the body:* **finding**, location, uncovering, unearthing. **2** *the discovery that she was pregnant:* **realization**, recognition, revelation, disclosure. **3** *he failed to take out a patent on his discoveries:* **find**, finding, breakthrough, innovation.

discredit verb **1** *an attempt to discredit him:* **bring into disrepute**, disgrace, dishonour, blacken the name of, put/show in a bad light, compromise,
smear, tarnish; N. Amer. slur. **2** *that theory has been discredited:* **disprove**, invalidate, explode, refute; informal debunk.
OPPOSITES honour, prove.
noun *to his discredit:* **dishonour**, disgrace, shame, humiliation, ignominy.
OPPOSITES honour, glory.

discreet adjective **tactful**, circumspect, diplomatic, judicious, sensitive, careful, cautious, strategic.

discrepancy noun **difference**, disparity, variation, deviation, divergence, disagreement, inconsistency, mismatch, conflict.
OPPOSITES correspondence.

discretion noun **1** *you can rely on his discretion:* **tact**, diplomacy, delicacy, sensitivity, good sense, prudence, circumspection. **2** *at the discretion of the council:* **choice**, option, preference, disposition, pleasure, will, inclination.
OPPOSITES tactlessness.

discriminate verb **1** *he cannot discriminate between fact and opinion:* **differentiate**, distinguish, draw a distinction, tell the difference, tell apart, separate. **2** *policies that discriminate against women:* **be biased**, be prejudiced, treat differently, treat unfairly, put at a disadvantage, victimize, pick on.

discriminating adjective **discerning**, perceptive, judicious, selective, tasteful, refined, sensitive, cultivated, cultured.
OPPOSITES indiscriminate.

discrimination noun **1** *racial discrimination:* **prejudice**, bias, bigotry, intolerance,

favouritism, partisanship. **2** *a man with no discrimination:* **discernment,** judgement, perceptiveness, (good) taste, refinement, sensitivity, cultivation.
OPPOSITES impartiality.

discuss verb **1** *I discussed the matter with my wife:* **talk over,** talk about, talk through, debate, confer about. **2** *chapter three discusses this topic:* **examine,** explore, study, analyse, go into, deal with, consider, tackle.

discussion noun **1** *a long discussion with her husband:* **conversation,** talk, dialogue, conference, debate, exchange of views, consultation, deliberation; informal confab. **2** *see Chapter 7 for a detailed discussion:* **examination,** exploration, study, analysis, treatment, consideration.

disdain noun *she looked at him with disdain:* **contempt,** scorn, derision, disrespect, condescension, superciliousness, hauteur, haughtiness.
OPPOSITES respect.
verb *she disdained exhibitionism:* **scorn,** deride, regard with contempt, sneer at, look down one's nose at, look down on, despise.
OPPOSITES value.

disease noun **illness,** sickness, ill health, infection, ailment, malady, disorder, condition, problem; informal bug, virus; Brit. informal lurgy.
OPPOSITES health.

diseased adjective **unhealthy,** ill, sick, unwell, ailing, infected, septic, rotten, bad.

disgrace noun **1** *he brought disgrace on the family:*

dishonour, shame, discredit, ignominy, disrepute, infamy, scandal, stigma, humiliation, loss of face. **2** *the unemployment figures are a disgrace:* **scandal,** discredit, reproach, stain, blemish, blot, outrage, affront.
OPPOSITES honour, credit.
verb *you have disgraced the family name:* **shame,** bring shame on, dishonour, discredit, stigmatize, taint, sully, tarnish, stain, blacken.
OPPOSITES honour.

disgraceful adjective **shameful,** scandalous, contemptible, dishonourable, discreditable, disreputable, reprehensible, blameworthy, unworthy, ignoble.
OPPOSITES admirable.

disgruntled adjective **dissatisfied,** discontented, aggrieved, resentful, displeased, unhappy, disappointed, annoyed; informal hacked off, browned off; Brit. informal cheesed off, narked; N. Amer. informal sore, ticked off.
OPPOSITES contented.

disguise verb **camouflage,** conceal, hide, cover up, mask, screen, veil, paper over.
OPPOSITES expose.

disgust noun **1** *the sight filled her with disgust:* **revulsion,** repugnance, aversion, distaste, abhorrence, loathing, hatred. **2** *the audience walked out in disgust:* **disapproval,** displeasure, indignation, annoyance, anger, fury, outrage, contempt, resentment.
OPPOSITES delight.
verb **1** *they were disgusted by the violence:* **revolt,** repel, repulse, sicken, horrify, appal, turn someone's stomach; N. Amer.

d

informal **gross out. 2** *Toby's behaviour disgusted her:* **displease,** dissatisfy, arouse the disapproval of, annoy, anger, outrage, scandalize, offend, affront, dismay.
OPPOSITES delight.

disgusting adjective **1** *the food was disgusting:* **revolting,** repulsive, sickening, nauseating, stomach-turning, off-putting; N. Amer. vomitous; informal sick-making. **2** *I find racism disgusting:* **outrageous,** objectionable, abhorrent, repellent, loathsome, offensive, appalling, shocking, horrifying, scandalous, monstrous, detestable; informal gross, sick.
OPPOSITES delightful.

dish noun **1** *a china dish:* **bowl,** plate, platter, salver, pot. **2** *vegetarian dishes:* **recipe,** meal, course, fare.
■ **dish something out** distribute, dispense, issue, hand out/round, give out, pass round, deal out, dole out, allocate.

dishonest adjective **fraudulent,** cheating, underhand, devious, treacherous, unfair, dirty, criminal, illegal, unlawful, false, untruthful, deceitful, lying; informal crooked, shady, sharp; Brit. informal bent; Austral./NZ informal shonky.
OPPOSITES honest.

disintegrate verb **break up,** crumble, break apart, fall apart, fall to pieces, collapse, fragment, shatter, splinter.

disinterested adjective *disinterested advice:* **unbiased,** unprejudiced, impartial, neutral, detached, objective, dispassionate.

dislike verb *a man she had always disliked:* **find distasteful,** regard with

distaste, be averse to, have an aversion to, hate, disapprove of, object to, take exception to.
OPPOSITES like.
noun *she viewed the other woman with dislike:* **distaste,** aversion, disfavour, antipathy, disgust, abhorrence, hatred.
OPPOSITES liking.

dismal adjective **1** *a dismal look:* **gloomy,** glum, melancholy, morose, doleful, woebegone, forlorn, dejected, downcast. **2** *dismal weather:* **dim,** dingy, dark, gloomy, dreary, drab, dull.
OPPOSITES cheerful, bright.

dismantle verb **take apart,** take to pieces/bits, pull to pieces, disassemble, break up, strip (down).
OPPOSITES build.

dismay noun *to his dismay:* **alarm,** distress, concern, surprise, consternation, disquiet.
OPPOSITES pleasure, relief.
verb *he was dismayed by the answer:* **concern,** distress, disturb, worry, alarm, disconcert, take aback, unnerve, unsettle.
OPPOSITES encourage, please.

dismiss verb **1** *the president dismissed five ministers:* **give someone their notice,** discharge, lay off, make redundant; informal sack, fire. **2** *the guards were dismissed:* **send away,** let go, release. **3** *don't dismiss the idea so lightly:* **reject,** deny, repudiate, spurn. **4** *she dismissed the thought:* **banish,** set aside, put out of one's mind.
OPPOSITES appoint, keep on, entertain, dwell on.

disobedient adjective **naughty,** insubordinate, defiant, unruly, wayward, badly behaved, delinquent, rebellious, mutinous, troublesome, wilful. OPPOSITES obedient.

disobey verb **defy**, go against, flout, contravene, infringe, transgress, violate, disregard, ignore, pay no heed to.

disorder noun **1** *he hates disorder:* **untidiness**, mess, disarray, chaos, confusion, clutter, jumble, a muddle, a shambles. **2** *incidents of public disorder:* **unrest**, disturbance, turmoil, mayhem, violence, fighting, fracas, rioting, lawlessness, anarchy, breach of the peace. **3** *a blood disorder:* **disease**, infection, complaint, condition, affliction, malady, sickness, illness, ailment. OPPOSITES order, tidiness, peace.

disorderly adjective **1** *a disorderly desk:* **untidy**, disorganized, messy, cluttered, in disarray; informal like a bomb's hit it, higgledy-piggledy; Brit. informal shambolic. **2** *disorderly behaviour:* **unruly**, riotous, disruptive, troublesome, lawless. OPPOSITES tidy, peaceful.

dispatch verb **1** *all the messages were dispatched:* **send (off)**, post, mail, forward. **2** *the business was dispatched in the morning:* **deal with**, finish, conclude, settle, discharge, perform. **3** *the good guy dispatched a host of villains:* **kill**, put to death, massacre, wipe out, exterminate, eliminate, murder, assassinate, execute. noun *the latest dispatch from the front:* **message**, report, communication, communiqué, bulletin, statement, letter, news, intelligence.

dispel verb **banish**, drive away/ off, chase away, scatter, eliminate, dismiss, allay, ease, quell. OPPOSITES form, give rise to.

dispense verb **1** *servants dispensed the drinks:* **distribute**, pass round, hand out, dole out, dish out, share out. **2** *the soldiers dispensed summary justice:* **administer**, deliver, issue, deal out, mete out. **3** *dispensing medicines:* **prepare**, make up, supply, provide.
■ **dispense with 1** *let's dispense with the formalities:* **waive**, omit, drop, leave out, forgo, do away with; informal give something a miss. **2** *he dispensed with his crutches:* **get rid of**, throw away/out, dispose of, discard; informal ditch, scrap, dump, chuck out/away; Brit. informal get shot of.

disperse verb **1** *the crowd began to disperse | police dispersed the demonstrators:* **break up**, split up, disband, scatter, leave, go their separate ways, drive away/off, chase away. **2** *the fog finally dispersed:* **dissipate**, dissolve, melt away, fade away, clear, lift. **3** *the seeds are dispersed by birds:* **scatter**, distribute, spread, disseminate. OPPOSITES assemble, form, gather.

displace verb **1** *roof tiles were displaced by gales:* **dislodge**, dislocate, move out of place/ position, shift. **2** *English displaced the local language:* **replace**, take the place of, supplant, supersede. OPPOSITES replace.

display verb **1** *the Crown Jewels are displayed in London:* **exhibit**, show, arrange, array, present, lay out, set out. **2** *the* *play displays his many theatrical talents:* **show off,** parade, highlight, reveal, showcase. **3** *she displayed a vein of sharp humour:* **manifest,** show evidence of, reveal, demonstrate, show.

OPPOSITES conceal.

noun 1 *a display of dolls:* **exhibition,** exposition, array, arrangement, presentation, demonstration, spectacle, show, parade. **2** *his display of concern:* **manifestation,** expression, show, proof, demonstration, evidence.

displease verb **annoy,** irritate, anger, incense, irk, vex, nettle, put out, upset, exasperate.

dispose
■ **dispose of** throw away/out, get rid of, discard, jettison, scrap; informal dump, junk, ditch, chuck (out/away); Brit. informal get shot of; N. Amer. informal trash.

disposition noun **1** *a nervous disposition:* **temperament,** nature, character, constitution, make-up, mentality. **2** *the disposition of the troops:* **arrangement,** positioning, placement, configuration, set-up, line-up, layout.

disprove verb **refute,** prove false, rebut, debunk, give the lie to, demolish; informal shoot full of holes, blow out of the water.

dispute noun **1** *a subject of dispute:* **debate,** discussion, argument, controversy, disagreement, dissent, conflict. **2** *they have settled their dispute:* **quarrel,** argument, altercation, squabble, falling-out, disagreement, difference of opinion, clash; Brit. informal row.

OPPOSITES agreement.

verb **1** *George disputed with him:* **debate,** discuss, exchange views, quarrel, argue, disagree, clash, fall out, wrangle, bicker, squabble. **2** *they disputed his proposals:* **challenge,** contest, question, call into question, quibble over, contradict, argue about, disagree with, take issue with.

OPPOSITES accept.

disregard verb *Annie disregarded the remark:* **ignore,** take no notice of, pay no attention to, discount, overlook, turn a blind eye to, shut one's eyes to, gloss over, brush off/aside, shrug off.

OPPOSITES heed.

noun *blithe disregard for the rules:* **indifference,** non-observance, inattention, heedlessness, neglect, contempt.

OPPOSITES attention.

disrupt verb **interrupt,** disturb, interfere with, play havoc with, upset, unsettle, obstruct, impede, hold up, delay.

disruptive adjective **troublesome,** disturbing, upsetting, unsettling, unruly, badly behaved, rowdy, disorderly, undisciplined, unmanageable, uncontrollable, uncooperative.

OPPOSITES well behaved.

dissatisfaction noun **discontent,** disaffection, disquiet, unhappiness, disappointment, disgruntlement, displeasure, vexation, annoyance, irritation.

dissatisfied adjective **discontented,** disappointed, disaffected, displeased, disgruntled, aggrieved, unhappy.

OPPOSITES contented.

dissent verb **disagree,** differ, demur, be at variance/odds, take issue, protest, object.
OPPOSITES agree, conform.
noun **disagreement,** difference of opinion, argument, dispute, resistance, objection, protest, opposition.
OPPOSITES agreement, conformity.

dissident noun **dissenter,** objector, protester, rebel, revolutionary, subversive, agitator, refusenik.
OPPOSITES conformist.
adjective **dissenting,** opposing, objecting, protesting, rebellious, revolutionary, subversive, nonconformist.
OPPOSITES conformist.

dissociate verb **separate,** detach, disconnect, sever, cut off, divorce, isolate, alienate.
OPPOSITES relate.

dissolve verb **1** *sugar dissolves in water:* **break down,** liquefy, melt, deliquesce, disintegrate. **2** *the crowd dissolved:* **disperse,** disband, break up, scatter. **3** *the assembly was dissolved:* **disband,** bring to an end, end, terminate, discontinue, close down, wind up/down, suspend, adjourn. **4** *their marriage was dissolved:* **annul,** nullify, void, invalidate, revoke.

dissuade verb **discourage,** deter, prevent, divert, stop, talk out of, persuade against, advise against, argue out of.
OPPOSITES encourage.

distance noun **1** *they measured the distance:* **interval,** space, span, gap, extent, length, range, reach. **2** *a mix of warmth and distance:* **aloofness,** remoteness, detachment, unfriendliness, reserve, reticence, formality; informal stand-offishness.
OPPOSITES proximity, friendliness.

distant adjective **1** *distant parts of the world:* **faraway,** far-off, far-flung, remote, out of the way, outlying. **2** *the distant past:* **remote,** bygone, ancient, prehistoric. **3** *a distant memory:* **vague,** faint, dim, indistinct, sketchy, hazy. **4** *father was always very distant:* **aloof,** reserved, remote, detached, unapproachable, unfriendly; informal stand-offish. **5** *a distant look in his eyes:* **distracted,** absent, faraway, detached, vague.
OPPOSITES near, recent, clear, close, friendly, alert.

distinct adjective **1** *two distinct categories:* **discrete,** separate, different, unconnected, distinctive, contrasting. **2** *the tail has distinct black tips:* **clear,** well defined, unmistakable, easily distinguishable, recognizable, visible, obvious, pronounced, prominent, striking.
OPPOSITES overlapping, similar, indefinite.

distinction noun **1** *distinctions that we observed:* **difference,** contrast, variation, division, differentiation, discrepancy. **2** *a painter of distinction:* **merit,** worth, greatness, excellence, quality, repute, renown. **3** *he had served with distinction:* **honour,** credit, excellence, merit.
OPPOSITES similarity, mediocrity, dishonour.

distinctive adjective **distinguishing,** characteristic, typical, individual, particular, peculiar, unique, exclusive, special.

OPPOSITES common.

distinctly adverb **1** *there's something distinctly odd about him:* **decidedly,** markedly, definitely, unmistakably, manifestly, patently. **2** *Laura spoke quite distinctly:* **clearly,** plainly, intelligibly, audibly.

distinguish verb **1** *he can distinguish reality from fantasy:* **differentiate,** tell apart, discriminate between, tell the difference between. **2** *he could distinguish shapes in the dark:* **discern,** see, perceive, make out, detect, recognize, identify. **3** *this is what distinguishes history from other disciplines:* **separate,** set apart, make distinctive, make different, single out, mark off.

distinguished adjective **eminent,** famous, renowned, prominent, well known, esteemed, respected, illustrious, acclaimed, celebrated.
OPPOSITES unknown, obscure.

distorted adjective **1** *a distorted face:* **twisted,** warped, contorted, buckled, deformed, malformed, misshapen, disfigured, crooked, out of shape. **2** *a distorted version:* **misrepresented,** perverted, twisted, falsified, misreported, misstated, garbled, inaccurate, biased, prejudiced.
OPPOSITES normal, straight, honest.

distract verb **divert,** sidetrack, draw away, lead astray, disturb, put off.

distracted adjective **preoccupied,** inattentive, vague, abstracted, absent-minded, faraway, in a world of one's own, troubled, harassed,

worried; informal miles away, not with it.
OPPOSITES attentive.

distraction noun **1** *a distraction from the real issues:* **diversion,** interruption, disturbance, interference. **2** *frivolous distractions:* **amusement,** entertainment, diversion, recreation, pastime, leisure pursuit.

distraught adjective **distressed,** frantic, fraught, overcome, overwrought, beside oneself, out of one's mind, desperate, hysterical, worked up, at one's wits' end; informal in a state.
OPPOSITES calm.

distress noun **1** *she concealed her distress:* **anguish,** suffering, pain, agony, torment, heartache, heartbreak, sorrow, sadness, unhappiness. **2** *a ship in distress:* **danger,** peril, difficulty, trouble, jeopardy, risk.
OPPOSITES happiness, safety.
verb *he was distressed by the trial:* **upset,** pain, trouble, worry, perturb, disturb, disquiet, agitate, torment.
OPPOSITES comfort.

distribute verb **1** *the proceeds were distributed among his creditors:* **give out,** deal out, dole out, dish out, hand out/round, share out, divide out/up, parcel out. **2** *the newsletter is distributed free:* **circulate,** issue, deliver, disseminate, publish.
OPPOSITES gather in, pool.

distribution noun **1** *the distribution of aid:* **giving out,** dealing out, doling out, handing out/round, issuing, allocation, sharing out, dividing up/out, parcelling out. **2** *centres of food distribution:* **supply,**

delivery, dispersal, transportation.
OPPOSITES gathering in, pooling, collection.

district noun area, region, quarter, sector, zone, territory, locality, neighbourhood, community.

distrust noun *distrust of Soviet intentions:* mistrust, suspicion, wariness, chariness, scepticism, doubt, cynicism, misgivings, qualms.
OPPOSITES trust.
verb *the Army distrusted the peace process:* mistrust, be suspicious of, be wary of, be chary of, regard with suspicion, suspect, be sceptical of, doubt, be unsure of/about, have misgivings about.
OPPOSITES trust.

disturb verb 1 *somewhere where we won't be disturbed:* interrupt, intrude on, butt in on, barge in on, distract, disrupt, bother, trouble, pester, harass. 2 *don't disturb his papers:* move, rearrange, mix up, interfere with, mess up, muddle. 3 *he wasn't disturbed by the allegations:* perturb, trouble, concern, worry, upset, fluster, disconcert, dismay, alarm, distress, unsettle.
OPPOSITES calm, reassure.

disturbance noun 1 *a disturbance to local residents:* disruption, distraction, interference, inconvenience, upset, annoyance, irritation, intrusion. 2 *disturbances in the town centre:* riot, fracas, brawl, street fight, free-for-all, commotion, disorder.
OPPOSITES order.

disturbed adjective 1 *disturbed sleep:* disrupted, interrupted, fitful, intermittent, broken.

2 *disturbed children:* troubled, distressed, upset, distraught, unbalanced, unstable, disordered, dysfunctional, maladjusted, neurotic, unhinged; informal screwed up.
OPPOSITES uninterrupted, well adjusted, sane.

ditch noun trench, trough, channel, dyke, drain, gutter, gully, watercourse.

dive verb 1 *they dived into the clear water | the plane was diving towards the ground:* plunge, nosedive, jump, plummet, fall, drop, pitch. 2 *they dived for cover:* leap, jump, lunge, throw/fling oneself, go headlong, duck.
noun 1 *a dive into the pool:* plunge, nosedive, jump, fall, drop, swoop. 2 *a sideways dive:* lunge, spring, jump, leap.

diverge verb 1 *the two roads diverged:* separate, part, fork, divide, split, bifurcate, go in different directions. 2 *areas where our views diverge:* differ, be different, be dissimilar, disagree, be at variance/odds, conflict, clash.
OPPOSITES converge, agree.

diverse adjective various, sundry, varied, varying, miscellaneous, assorted, mixed, diversified, divergent, different, differing, distinct, unlike, dissimilar.
OPPOSITES similar.

diversion noun 1 *the diversion of the river:* re-routing, redirection, deflection, deviation, divergence. 2 *traffic diversions:* detour, deviation, alternative route. 3 *the noise created a diversion:* distraction, disturbance, smokescreen; informal red herring. 4 *a city full of diversions:* entertainment, amusement, pastime, delight, fun, recreation, pleasure.

diversity noun **variety,** miscellany, assortment, mixture, mix, range, array, multiplicity, variation, diverseness, difference. OPPOSITES uniformity.

divert verb **1** *a plan to divert Siberia's rivers:* **re-route,** redirect, change the course of, deflect, channel. **2** *he diverted her from her studies:* **distract,** sidetrack, disturb, draw away, put off. **3** *the story diverted them:* **amuse,** entertain, distract, delight, enchant, interest, fascinate, absorb, engross, rivet, grip.

divide verb **1** *he divided his kingdom into four:* **split (up),** cut up, carve up, dissect, bisect, halve, quarter. **2** *a curtain divided her cabin from the galley:* **separate,** segregate, partition, screen off, section off, split off. **3** *the stairs divide at the mezzanine:* **diverge,** separate, part, branch (off), fork, split (in two). **4** *Jack divided the cash:* **share out,** ration out, parcel out, deal out, dole out, dish out, distribute. **5** *he aimed to divide his opponents:* **disunite,** drive apart, drive a wedge between, break up, split (up), separate, isolate, alienate. OPPOSITES unify, converge, collect, unite.

divine[1] adjective **1** *a divine being:* **godly,** angelic, heavenly, celestial, holy. **2** *divine worship:* **religious,** holy, sacred, sanctified, consecrated, blessed, devotional. OPPOSITES mortal, infernal.

divine[2] verb *Fergus divined how afraid she was:* **guess,** surmise,

deduce, infer, discern, discover, perceive; informal figure (out); Brit. informal suss.

division noun **1** *the division of the island | cell division:* **dividing (up),** breaking up, break-up, carving up, splitting, dissection, partitioning, separation. **2** *the division of his estates:* **sharing out,** dividing up, parcelling out, dishing out, allocation, allotment, splitting up, carving up. **3** *the division between nomadic and urban cultures:* **dividing line,** divide, boundary, border, demarcation line, gap, gulf. **4** *each class is split into nine divisions:* **section,** subsection, subdivision, category, class, group, grouping, set. **5** *an independent division of the executive:* **department,** branch, arm, wing. **6** *the causes of social division:* **disunity,** disunion, conflict, discord, disagreement, alienation, isolation. OPPOSITES unification, unity.

divorce noun **1** *she wants a divorce:* **dissolution,** annulment, decree nisi, separation. **2** *a growing divorce between the church and people:* **separation,** division, split, disunity, alienation, schism, gulf. OPPOSITES unity. verb **1** *her parents have divorced:* **split up,** get a divorce, separate, end one's marriage. **2** *religion cannot be divorced from morality:* **separate,** divide, detach, isolate, alienate, set apart, cut off.

divulge verb **disclose,** reveal, tell, communicate, pass on, publish, give away, let slip. OPPOSITES conceal.

dizzy adjective **giddy,** light-headed, faint, unsteady, shaky, muzzy, wobbly; informal woozy.

do verb **1** *she does most of the work:* **carry out,** undertake, discharge, execute, perform, accomplish, achieve, bring about, engineer; informal pull off. **2** *they can do as they please:* **act,** behave, conduct oneself. **3** *regular coffee will do:* **suffice,** be adequate, be satisfactory, fill/fit the bill, serve. **4** *a portrait I am doing:* **make,** create, produce, work on, design, manufacture.
■ **do away with** *they want to do away with the old customs:* abolish, get rid of, eliminate, discontinue, stop, end, terminate, drop, abandon, give up; informal scrap. ■ **do without** forgo, dispense with, abstain from, refrain from, eschew, give up, cut out, renounce, manage without.

dock[1] noun *his boat was moored at the dock:* **harbour,** marina, port, wharf, quay, pier, jetty, landing stage.
verb *the ship docked:* **moor,** berth, put in, tie up, anchor.

dock[2] verb **1** *they docked the money from his salary:* **deduct,** subtract, remove, debit, take off/away; informal knock off. **2** *workers had their pay docked:* **reduce,** cut, decrease. **3** *the dog's tail was docked:* **cut off,** cut short, shorten, crop, lop.

doctor noun **physician,** medical practitioner, general practitioner, GP, clinician, consultant; informal doc, medic.
verb **1** *he doctored Stephen's drink:* **adulterate,** tamper with, lace; informal spike. **2** *the reports have been doctored:* **falsify,** tamper with, interfere with, alter, change, forge, fake; Brit. informal fiddle.

doctrine noun **creed,** credo, dogma, belief, teaching, ideology, tenet, maxim, canon, principle.

document noun *a legal document:* **paper,** certificate, deed, form, contract, agreement, report, record.
verb *its history is well documented:* **record,** register, report, log, chronicle, authenticate, verify.

dodge verb **1** *he could easily dodge the two coppers:* **elude,** evade, avoid, escape, run away from, lose, shake (off); informal give someone the slip. **2** *the minister tried to dodge the debate:* **avoid,** evade, get out of, back out of, sidestep; informal duck, wriggle out of. **3** *she dodged into a telephone booth:* **dart,** bolt, dive, slip.
noun *a clever dodge | a tax dodge:* **ruse,** ploy, scheme, tactic, stratagem, subterfuge, trick, hoax, cheat, deception, fraud; informal scam; Brit. informal wheeze; Austral. informal lurk, rort.

dog noun **hound,** canine, man's best friend; informal pooch, mutt; Austral. informal bitzer.
verb *the scheme was dogged by bad weather:* **plague,** beset, bedevil, blight, trouble.

dogged adjective **tenacious,** determined, resolute, stubborn, obstinate, purposeful, persistent, persevering, single-minded, tireless.
OPPOSITES half-hearted, tentative.

dogmatic adjective **opinionated,** assertive, insistent, emphatic, adamant, doctrinaire, authoritarian, imperious, dictatorial, uncompromising.

d

dole
∎ **dole something out** deal out, share out, divide up, allocate, distribute, dispense, hand out, give out, dish out.

domain noun **1** *they extended their domain:* **realm**, kingdom, empire, dominion, province, territory, land. **2** *the domain of art:* **field**, area, sphere, discipline, province, world.

domestic adjective **1** *domestic commitments:* **family**, home, household. **2** *she was not at all domestic:* **domesticated**, homely, home-loving. **3** *small domestic animals:* **pet**, tame, domesticated, household. **4** *the domestic car industry:* **national**, state, home, internal.

dominant adjective **1** *the dominant classes:* **ruling**, governing, controlling, presiding, commanding. **2** *he has a dominant personality:* **assertive**, authoritative, forceful, domineering, commanding, controlling, pushy. **3** *the dominant issues in psychology:* **main**, principal, prime, chief, primary, central, key, crucial, core.
OPPOSITES subservient, subsidiary.

dominate verb **1** *the Russians dominated Iran in the nineteenth century:* **control**, influence, command, be in charge of, rule, govern, direct. **2** *the village is dominated by the viaduct:* **overlook**, command, tower above/over, loom over.

domination noun **control**, power, command, authority, dominion, rule, supremacy, superiority, ascendancy, sway.

don verb put on, get dressed in, dress (oneself) in, get into, slip into/on, change into.

donate verb give, contribute, gift, subscribe, grant, present, endow.

donation noun gift, contribution, subscription, present, handout, grant, offering.

donor noun giver, contributor, benefactor, benefactress, subscriber, supporter, backer, patron, sponsor.
OPPOSITES beneficiary.

doom noun *prepare to meet your doom:* **destruction**, downfall, ruin, extinction, annihilation, death, nemesis.
verb *they were doomed to die:* **destine**, fate, predestine, preordain, mean, condemn, sentence.

doomed adjective ill-fated, ill-starred, cursed, jinxed, damned.

dope verb **1** *the horse was doped:* **drug**, tamper with, interfere with, sedate; Brit. informal nobble. **2** *they doped his drink:* **add drugs to**, tamper with, adulterate, lace; informal spike, doctor.

dose noun *a dose of medicine:* **measure**, portion, draught, dosage.
verb *he dosed himself with vitamins:* **drug**, fill (up), pump, prime, load, stuff, cram.

dot noun *a pattern of dots:* **spot**, speck, fleck, speckle, full stop, decimal point.
verb **1** *spots of rain dotted his shirt:* **spot**, fleck, mark, spatter. **2** *restaurants are dotted around the site:* **scatter**, pepper, sprinkle, strew, spread.

dote
∎ **dote on** adore, love dearly, be devoted to, idolize, treasure, cherish, worship.

double adjective *a double garage:* **dual**, duplex, twin, binary,

duplicate, coupled, matching, twofold, in pairs.
OPPOSITES single.
noun *it must be her double:* **lookalike,** twin, clone, duplicate, exact likeness, replica, copy, facsimile, Doppelgänger; informal spitting image, dead ringer.

doubt noun **1** *there was some doubt as to the caller's identity:* **uncertainty,** confusion, controversy. **2** *a weak leader racked by doubt:* **indecision,** hesitation, uncertainty, insecurity, hesitancy, vacillation. **3** *there is doubt about their motives:* **scepticism,** distrust, mistrust, suspicion, cynicism, wariness, reservations, misgivings, suspicions.
OPPOSITES certainty, conviction, trust.
verb *they doubted my story:* **disbelieve,** distrust, mistrust, suspect, be suspicious of, have misgivings about.
OPPOSITES trust.
■ **in doubt 1** *the outcome is in doubt:* **doubtful,** uncertain, unconfirmed, unknown, undecided, unresolved, in the balance, up in the air; informal iffy. **2** *if you are in doubt, ask for advice:* irresolute, hesitant, doubtful, unsure, uncertain, in two minds, undecided, in a quandary/dilemma. ■ **no doubt** doubtless, undoubtedly, indubitably, without (a) doubt, unquestionably, undeniably, clearly, plainly, obviously, patently.

doubtful adjective **1** *I was doubtful about going:* **hesitant,** in doubt, unsure, uncertain, in two minds, in a quandary, in a dilemma. **2** *it is doubtful whether he will come:* **in doubt,**

uncertain, open to question, unsure, debatable, up in the air. **3** *the whole trip is looking rather doubtful:* **unlikely,** improbable. **4** *they are doubtful of the methods used:* **distrustful,** mistrustful, suspicious, wary, chary, leery, sceptical. **5** *this decision is of doubtful validity:* **questionable,** arguable, debatable, controversial, contentious.
OPPOSITES confident, certain, probable, trusting.

doubtless adverb **undoubtedly,** no doubt, unquestionably, indisputably, undeniably, certainly, surely, of course.

douse verb **1** *a mob doused the thieves with petrol:* **drench,** soak, saturate, wet. **2** *a guard doused the flames:* **extinguish,** put out, quench, smother.

downfall noun **ruin,** ruination, undoing, defeat, overthrow, destruction, annihilation, end, collapse, fall, crash, failure.
OPPOSITES rise.

downgrade verb **demote,** reduce, relegate.
OPPOSITES promote.

downright adjective *downright lies:* **complete,** total, absolute, utter, thorough, out-and-out, outright, sheer, arrant, pure.
adverb *that's downright dangerous:* **thoroughly,** utterly, positively, profoundly, really, completely, totally, entirely.

drab adjective **1** *a drab interior:* **colourless,** grey, dull, washed out, dingy, dreary, dismal, cheerless, gloomy, sombre. **2** *a drab existence:* **uninteresting,** dull, boring, tedious, monotonous, dry, dreary.
OPPOSITES bright, cheerful, interesting.

draft noun **1** *the first draft of his*

speech: **version**, sketch, attempt, effort, outline, plan. **2** *a banker's draft:* **cheque**, order, money order, bill of exchange.

drag verb *she dragged the chair backwards:* **haul**, pull, tug, heave, lug, draw, trail.
noun **1** *the drag from the parachute:* **pull**, resistance, tug. **2** (informal) *work can be a drag:* **bore**, nuisance, bother, trouble, pest, annoyance, trial; informal pain (in the neck), bind, headache, hassle.

drain verb **1** *a valve for draining the tank:* **empty (out)**, void, clear (out), evacuate, unload. **2** *drain off any surplus liquid:* **draw off**, extract, siphon off, pour out, pour off, bleed, tap, filter, discharge. **3** *the water drained away to the sea:* **flow**, pour, trickle, stream, run, rush, gush, flood, surge, leak, ooze, seep, dribble. **4** *more people would just drain our resources:* **use up**, exhaust, deplete, consume, expend, get through, sap, milk, bleed. **5** *he drained his drink:* **drink (up/down)**, gulp (down), guzzle, quaff, swallow, finish off, toss off; informal sink, down, swig, swill (down), knock back.
OPPOSITES fill.
noun **1** *the drain filled with water:* **sewer**, channel, ditch, culvert, duct, pipe, gutter. **2** *a drain on the battery:* **strain**, pressure, burden, load, demand.

drama noun **1** *a television drama:* **play**, show, piece, theatrical work, stage show, dramatization. **2** *he is studying drama:* **acting**, the theatre, the stage, dramatic art, stagecraft, dramaturgy. **3** *she liked to*

create a drama: **incident**, scene, spectacle, crisis, disturbance, row, commotion, excitement, thrill, sensation, dramatics, theatrics, histrionics.

dramatic adjective **1** *dramatic art:* **theatrical**, thespian, stage, dramaturgical. **2** *a dramatic increase:* **considerable**, substantial, significant, remarkable, extraordinary, exceptional, phenomenal. **3** *there were dramatic scenes in the city:* **exciting**, stirring, action-packed, sensational, spectacular, startling, unexpected, tense, gripping, riveting, thrilling, hair-raising, lively. **4** *dramatic headlands:* **striking**, impressive, imposing, spectacular, breathtaking, dazzling, sensational, awesome, awe-inspiring, remarkable. **5** *a dramatic gesture:* **exaggerated**, theatrical, ostentatious, actressy, stagy, showy, melodramatic.
OPPOSITES insignificant, boring, unremarkable, unimposing, restrained.

dramatize verb **1** *the novel was dramatized for television:* **turn into a play/film**, adapt (for the stage/screen). **2** *the tabloids dramatized the event:* **exaggerate**, overdo, overstate, hyperbolize, magnify, amplify, inflate, sensationalize, embroider, colour, aggrandize, embellish, elaborate; informal blow up (out of all proportion).

drape verb **wrap**, cover, envelop, shroud, wind, swathe, festoon, hang.

drastic adjective **extreme**, serious, desperate, radical, far-reaching, momentous, substantial.
OPPOSITES moderate.

draught noun **1** *the draught made Robin shiver:* **current of air,** wind, breeze, gust, puff, waft. **2** *a draught of beer:* **gulp,** drink, swallow, mouthful; informal swig.

draw verb **1** *he drew the house:* **sketch,** outline, rough out, illustrate, render, represent, trace, portray, depict. **2** *she drew her chair in to the table:* **pull,** haul, drag, tug, heave, lug, tow; informal yank. **3** *the train drew into the station:* **move,** go, come, proceed, progress, pass, drive, inch, roll, glide, cruise, sweep. **4** *he drew his gun:* **pull out,** take out, produce, fish out, extract, withdraw, unsheathe. **5** *she drew huge audiences:* **attract,** win, capture, catch, engage, lure, entice, bring in.
noun **1** *she won the Christmas draw:* **raffle,** lottery, sweepstake, sweep, tombola, ballot. **2** *the match ended in a draw:* **tie,** dead heat, stalemate. **3** *the draw of central London:* **attraction,** lure, allure, pull, appeal, temptation, charm, fascination.
■ **draw on call** on, have recourse to, turn to, look to, exploit, use, employ, utilize, bring into play. ■ **draw something out** prolong, protract, drag out, spin out, string out, extend, lengthen. ■ **draw something up** compose, formulate, frame, write down, draft, prepare, think up, devise, work out, create, invent, design.

drawback noun **disadvantage,** snag, downside, stumbling block, catch, hitch, pitfall, fly in the ointment, weak spot/point, weakness, imperfection; informal minus.
OPPOSITES benefit.

drawing noun **sketch,** picture, illustration, representation, portrayal, depiction, diagram, outline.

dread verb *I used to dread going to school:* **fear,** be afraid of, worry about, be anxious about, shudder at the thought of.
OPPOSITES look forward to.
noun *she was filled with dread:* **fear,** apprehension, trepidation, anxiety, panic, alarm, terror, disquiet, unease.
OPPOSITES confidence.

dreadful adjective **1** *a dreadful accident:* **terrible,** frightful, horrible, grim, awful, horrifying, shocking, distressing, appalling, harrowing, ghastly, fearful, horrendous, tragic. **2** *a dreadful meal:* **very bad,** frightful, shocking, awful, abysmal, atrocious, disgraceful, deplorable; informal woeful, rotten, lousy, ropy; Brit. informal duff, rubbish. **3** *you're a dreadful flirt:* **outrageous,** shocking, real, awful, terrible, inordinate, incorrigible, quite a.
OPPOSITES pleasant, wonderful, excellent, no.

dream noun **1** *she went around in a dream:* **daydream,** reverie, trance, daze, stupor. **2** *he realized his childhood dream:* **ambition,** aspiration, hope, goal, aim, objective, intention, desire, wish, daydream, fantasy. **3** *he's an absolute dream:* **delight,** joy, marvel, wonder, gem, treasure, beauty, vision.
OPPOSITES alertness, nightmare, horror.
verb **1** *I dreamed of making the Olympic team:* **fantasize,** daydream, wish, hope, long, yearn, hanker. **2** *she's always dreaming:* **daydream,** be in a

d

trance, be lost in thought, be preoccupied, be abstracted, stare into space, be in cloud cuckoo land.

■ **dream something up** think up, invent, concoct, devise, hatch, come up with.

dreary adjective **dull,** uninteresting, tedious, boring, unexciting, unstimulating, uninspiring, soul-destroying, monotonous, uneventful.
OPPOSITES exciting.

drench verb **soak,** saturate, wet through, douse, steep, flood, drown.

dress verb **1** *he dressed quickly:* **put on clothes,** clothe oneself, get dressed. **2** *she was dressed in a suit:* **clothe,** attire, deck out; informal get up. **3** *she enjoyed dressing the tree:* **decorate,** trim, adorn, arrange, prepare. **4** *they dressed his wounds:* **bandage,** cover, bind, wrap.
OPPOSITES undress.
noun **1** *a long blue dress:* **frock,** gown, robe, shift. **2** *full evening dress:* **clothes,** clothing, garments, attire, costume, outfit; informal **get-up;** Brit. informal clobber.

dribble verb **1** *the baby started to dribble:* **drool,** slaver, slobber. **2** *rainwater dribbled down her face:* **trickle,** drip, roll, run, drizzle, ooze, seep, leak.

drift verb **1** *his raft drifted down the river:* **be carried,** be borne, float, bob, glide, coast, waft. **2** *the guests drifted away:* **wander,** meander, stray, stroll, dawdle, float, roam. **3** *don't allow your attention to drift:* **stray,** digress, wander, deviate, be diverted. **4** *snow drifted over the path:* **pile up,** bank up, heap up, accumulate, gather, amass.

noun **1** *a drift from the country to urban areas:* **movement,** shift, flow, transfer, gravitation. **2** *he caught the drift of her thoughts:* **gist,** meaning, sense, significance, thrust, import, tenor, intention, direction. **3** *a drift of deep snow:* **pile,** heap, bank, mound, mass, accumulation.

drill noun **1** *military drill:* **training,** instruction, coaching, teaching, (physical) exercises; informal square-bashing. **2** *Estelle knew the drill:* **procedure,** routine, practice, programme, schedule, method, system.
verb **1** *drill the piece of wood:* **bore,** pierce, puncture, perforate. **2** *a sergeant drilling new recruits:* **train,** instruct, coach, teach, discipline, exercise.

drink verb **1** *she drank her coffee:* **swallow,** gulp (down), quaff, guzzle, imbibe, sip, drain; informal swig, down, knock back. **2** *he never drank:* **drink alcohol,** tipple, indulge, carouse; informal hit the bottle, booze; Brit. informal bevvy.
noun **1** *cocoa is a nice drink:* **beverage,** liquid refreshment; Brit. informal bevvy. **2** *she turned to drink:* **alcohol,** intoxicating liquor, spirits; informal booze, the hard stuff, the bottle, grog. **3** *she took a drink of wine:* **swallow,** gulp, mouthful, draught, sip; informal swig, slug.

drip verb **1** *there was a tap dripping:* **dribble,** leak. **2** *sweat dripped from his chin:* **drop,** dribble, trickle, run, splash, sprinkle, leak.
noun *a bucket caught the drips:* **drop,** dribble, spot, trickle, splash.

drive verb **1** *I can't drive a car:*

operate, handle, manage, pilot, steer, work. **2** *he drove to the police station:* **go by car,** motor. **3** *I'll drive you to the airport:* **run,** chauffeur, give someone a lift, take, ferry, transport, convey. **4** *the engine drives the front wheels:* **power,** propel, move, push. **5** *he drove a nail into the boot:* **hammer,** screw, ram, sink, plunge, thrust, knock. **6** *she was driven to crime:* **force,** compel, prompt, precipitate, oblige, coerce, pressure, spur, prod.
noun **1** *an afternoon drive:* **excursion,** outing, trip, jaunt, tour, ride, run, journey; informal spin. **2** *she lacked the drive to succeed:* **motivation,** ambition, single-mindedness, willpower, dedication, doggedness, tenacity, enthusiasm, zeal, commitment, energy, vigour; informal get-up-and-go. **3** *an anti-corruption drive:* **campaign,** crusade, movement, effort, push, initiative.

droop verb **hang down,** wilt, dangle, sag, flop, sink, slump, drop.

drop verb **1** *Eric dropped the box:* **let fall,** let go of, lose one's grip on, release. **2** *a plane dropped out of the sky:* **fall,** descend, plunge, plummet, dive, sink, dip, tumble. **3** *the exchange rate dropped:* **decrease,** lessen, reduce, fall, decline, dwindle, sink, slump. **4** *let's drop this pretence:* **abandon,** give up, discontinue, finish with, renounce, reject, forgo, relinquish, dispense with, leave out; informal dump, pack in, quit.
OPPOSITES rise, increase, keep.
noun **1** *a drop of water:* **droplet,** blob, globule, bead. **2** *it needs a drop of oil:* **small amount,**

little, bit, dash, spot, dribble, sprinkle, trickle, splash, mouthful; informal smidgen, tad. **3** *a small drop in profits:* **decrease,** reduction, decline, fall-off, downturn, slump. **4** *I walked to the edge of the drop:* **cliff,** precipice, slope, descent, incline.
OPPOSITES flood, increase.
■ **drop off** fall asleep, doze (off), nap, drowse; informal nod off, drift off, snooze, take forty winks. ■ **drop out** leave, go up, withdraw, retire, pull out, abandon something, fall by the wayside; informal quit, pack something in, jack something in.

drug noun **1** *drugs prescribed by doctors:* **medicine,** medication, remedy, cure, antidote. **2** *she was under the influence of drugs:* **narcotic,** stimulant, hallucinogen; informal dope, gear.
verb **1** *he was drugged:* **anaesthetize,** poison, knock out; informal dope. **2** *she drugged his coffee:* **tamper with,** lace, poison; informal dope, spike, doctor.

drum noun *a drum of radioactive waste:* **canister,** barrel, cylinder, tank, bin, can.
verb **1** *she drummed her fingers on the desk:* **tap,** beat, rap, thud, thump, tattoo, thrum. **2** *the rules were drummed into us at school:* **instil,** drive, din, hammer, drill, implant, ingrain, inculcate.
■ **drum something up** round up, gather, collect, summon, attract, canvass, solicit, petition.

drunk adjective **intoxicated,** inebriated, drunken, tipsy, under the influence; informal tight, merry, plastered, sloshed,

pickled, tanked (up), ratted; Brit.
informal legless, paralytic, Brahms
and Liszt, trolleyed, tiddly;
N. Amer. informal loaded, trashed,
sauced.
OPPOSITES sober.
noun **drunkard,** inebriate; informal
boozer, soak, wino, alky.
OPPOSITES teetotaller.

dry adjective **1** *the dry desert:*
arid, parched, waterless,
dehydrated, desiccated,
withered, shrivelled, wizened.
2 *a dry debate:* **dull,**
uninteresting, boring,
unexciting, tedious, dreary,
monotonous, unimaginative,
sterile; informal deadly. **3** *a dry
sense of humour:* **wry,** subtle,
laconic, ironic, sardonic,
sarcastic, cynical.
OPPOSITES wet, moist,
interesting, lively, broad.
verb **1** *the sun dried the ground:*
parch, scorch, bake, sear,
dehydrate, desiccate, wither,
shrivel. **2** *he dried the dishes:*
wipe, towel, rub dry, drain.
OPPOSITES wet, moisten.

dual adjective **double,** twofold,
duplex, binary, twin, matching,
paired, coupled.
OPPOSITES single.

dub verb **name,** call, nickname,
label, christen, term, tag.

dubious adjective **1** *I was rather
dubious about the idea:*
doubtful, uncertain, unsure,
hesitant, sceptical, suspicious;
informal iffy. **2** *a dubious
businessman:* **suspicious,**
suspect, untrustworthy,
unreliable, questionable; informal
shady; Brit. informal dodgy.
OPPOSITES certain, trustworthy.

duck verb **1** *he ducked behind the
wall:* **bob down,** bend down,
stoop, crouch, squat, hunch
down, hunker down. **2** (informal)

*they cannot duck the issue
forever:* **shirk,** dodge, evade,
avoid, elude, escape, sidestep.

duct noun **tube,** channel, canal,
vessel, conduit, pipe, outlet,
inlet, flue, shaft, vent.

due adjective **1** *their fees were
due:* **owing,** owed, payable,
outstanding, overdue, unpaid,
unsettled. **2** *the chancellor's
statement is due today:*
expected, anticipated,
scheduled for, awaited,
required. **3** *a little respect is
due:* **deserved,** merited,
warranted, justified, owing,
appropriate, fitting, right,
rightful, proper. **4** *he drove
without due care:* **proper,**
correct, suitable, appropriate,
adequate, sufficient.
noun *members have paid their
dues:* **fee,** subscription, charge,
payment, contribution, levy.
adverb *due north:* **directly,**
straight, exactly, precisely,
dead.
■ **due to 1** *her death was due to
an infection:* attributable to,
caused by, because of, down to.
2 *the train was cancelled due to
staff shortages:* because of,
owing to, on account of, as a
consequence of, as a result of,
thanks to.

duel noun **1** *he was killed in a
duel:* **single combat,** fight,
confrontation, head-to-head;
informal shoot-out. **2** *a snooker
duel:* **contest,** match, game,
meet, encounter, clash.

dull adjective **1** *a dull novel:*
uninteresting, boring, tedious,
monotonous, unimaginative,
uneventful, characterless,
featureless, colourless, lifeless,
unexciting, uninspiring, flat,
bland, stodgy, dreary; informal
deadly; N. Amer. informal dullsville.

2 *a dull morning:* **overcast,** cloudy, gloomy, dark, dismal, dreary, sombre, grey, murky, sunless. **3** *dull colours:* **drab,** dreary, sombre, dark, subdued, muted. **4** *a dull sound:* **muffled,** muted, quiet, soft, faint, indistinct, stifled. **5** *the chisel became dull:* **blunt,** worn. **6** *a rather dull child:* **unintelligent,** stupid, slow, brainless, mindless, foolish, idiotic; informal dense, dim, half-witted, thick.
OPPOSITES interesting, bright, resonant, sharp, clever.
verb *the pain was dulled by drugs:* **lessen,** decrease, diminish, reduce, dampen, blunt, deaden, allay, ease.
OPPOSITES intensify.

duly adverb **1** *the document was duly signed:* **properly,** correctly, appropriately, suitably, fittingly. **2** *he duly arrived to collect Alice:* **at the right time,** on time, punctually.

dumb adjective **1** *she stood dumb while he shouted:* **mute,** speechless, tongue-tied, silent, at a loss for words. **2** (informal) *he is not as dumb as you'd think:* **stupid,** unintelligent, ignorant, dense, brainless, foolish, slow, dull, simple; informal thick, dim; Brit. informal daft.
OPPOSITES talkative, clever.

dummy noun *a shop-window dummy:* **mannequin,** model, figure.
adjective *a dummy attack:* **simulated,** practice, trial, mock, make-believe; informal pretend.
OPPOSITES real.

dump noun **1** *take the rubbish to the dump:* **tip,** rubbish dump, dumping ground, recycling centre. **2** (informal) *the house is a dump:* **hovel,** slum; informal hole, pigsty.

verb **1** *he dumped his bag on the table:* **put down,** set down, deposit, place, shove, unload, drop, throw down; informal stick, park, plonk; Brit. informal bung. **2** *they will dump asbestos at the site:* **dispose of,** get rid of, throw away/out, discard, bin, jettison; informal ditch, junk.

dune noun **bank,** mound, hillock, hummock, knoll, ridge, heap, drift.

duplicate noun *a duplicate of the invoice:* **copy,** photocopy, facsimile, reprint, replica, reproduction, clone; trademark Xerox, photostat.
adjective *duplicate keys:* **matching,** identical, twin, corresponding, equivalent.
verb **1** *she will duplicate the newsletter:* **copy,** photocopy, photostat, xerox, reproduce, replicate, reprint, run off. **2** *a feat difficult to duplicate:* **repeat,** do again, redo, replicate.

durable adjective **1** *durable carpets:* **hard-wearing,** wear-resistant, heavy-duty, tough, long-lasting, strong, sturdy, robust. **2** *a durable peace:* **lasting,** long-lasting, long-term, enduring, persistent, abiding, permanent, undying, everlasting.
OPPOSITES delicate, short-lived.

duration noun **length,** time, period, term, span, extent, stretch.

dusk noun **twilight,** nightfall, sunset, sundown, evening, close of day, semi-darkness, gloom; literary gloaming.
OPPOSITES dawn.

dust noun *the desk was covered in dust:* **dirt,** grime, grit, powder, particles.
verb **1** *she dusted her*

mantelpiece: **wipe,** clean, brush, sweep. **2** *dust the cake with icing sugar:* **sprinkle,** scatter, powder, dredge, sift, cover.

dusty adjective **1** *the floor was dusty:* **dirty,** grimy, grubby, mucky, unswept. **2** *dusty sandstone:* **powdery,** crumbly, chalky, granular, soft, gritty.
OPPOSITES clean, hard, smooth.

duty noun **1** *a misguided sense of duty:* **responsibility,** obligation, commitment, allegiance, loyalty. **2** *it was his duty to attend the king:* **job,** task, assignment, mission, function, role. **3** *the duty was raised on alcohol:* **tax,** levy, tariff, excise, toll, rate.

dwarf noun **1 small person,** person of restricted growth, midget, pygmy. **2** *the wizard captured the dwarf:* **gnome,** goblin, hobgoblin, troll, imp, elf, brownie, leprechaun.
adjective *dwarf conifers:* **miniature,** toy, pocket, baby, pygmy; informal mini.
OPPOSITES giant.
verb **1** *the buildings dwarf the trees:* **dominate,** tower over, loom over, overshadow. **2** *her*

progress was dwarfed by her sister's success: **overshadow,** outshine, surpass, exceed, outclass, outstrip, outdo, top.

dwindle verb **diminish,** decrease, reduce, lessen, shrink, wane.
OPPOSITES increase.

dye noun *a blue dye:* **colouring,** dyestuff, pigment, tint, stain, wash.
verb *the gloves were dyed:* **colour,** tint, pigment, stain, wash.

dying adjective **1** *his dying aunt:* **terminally ill,** at death's door, on one's deathbed, fading fast, not long for this world. **2** *a dying art form:* **declining,** vanishing, fading, waning; informal on the way out. **3** *her dying words:* **final,** last.
OPPOSITES thriving, first.

dynamic adjective **energetic,** spirited, active, lively, vigorous, forceful, high-powered, aggressive, enterprising; informal go-getting, go-ahead.
OPPOSITES lackadaisical.

dynasty noun **family,** house, line, lineage, regime, empire.

Ee

each adverb *they gave a tenner each:* **apiece,** per person, per head, per capita.

eager adjective **1** *small eager faces:* **keen,** enthusiastic, avid, ardent, highly motivated, committed, earnest. **2** *we were eager for news:* **anxious,** impatient, longing, yearning, wishing, hoping; informal itching, dying.

OPPOSITES apathetic.

early adjective **1** *early copies of the book:* **advance,** initial, preliminary, first. **2** *an early death:* **untimely,** premature, unseasonable. **3** *early man:* **primitive,** ancient, prehistoric, primeval. **4** *an early response:* **prompt,** timely, quick, speedy.
OPPOSITES late, timely, modern.
adverb **1** *get your application in*

early: **in advance,** in good time, ahead of schedule, with time to spare, before the last moment. **2** *she was widowed very early:* **prematurely,** before the usual time, too soon, ahead of schedule.
OPPOSITES late.

earmark verb **set aside,** keep (back), reserve, designate, assign, allocate.

earn verb **1** *they earned £20,000:* **be paid,** take home, gross, receive, get, make, collect, bring in; informal pocket, bank. **2** *he has earned their trust:* **deserve,** merit, warrant, justify, be worthy of, gain, win, secure, obtain.
OPPOSITES lose.

earnest adjective **1** *he is dreadfully earnest:* **serious,** solemn, grave, sober, humourless, staid, intense. **2** *earnest prayer:* **devout,** heartfelt, wholehearted, sincere, impassioned, fervent, intense.
OPPOSITES frivolous, half-hearted.

earnings plural noun **income,** pay, wages, salary, stipend, remuneration, fees, revenue, yield, profit, takings, proceeds.

earth noun **1** *the moon orbits the earth:* **world,** globe, planet. **2** *a trembling of the earth:* **land,** ground, terra firma, floor. **3** *he ploughed the earth:* **soil,** clay, dust, dirt, loam, ground, turf.

earthly adjective **worldly,** temporal, mortal, human, material, carnal, fleshly, bodily, physical, corporeal, sensual.
OPPOSITES extraterrestrial, heavenly.

ease noun **1** *he defeated them all with ease:* **effortlessness,** no trouble, simplicity. **2** *his ease of*

manner: **naturalness,** casualness, informality, composure, nonchalance, insouciance. **3** *a life of ease:* **affluence,** wealth, prosperity, luxury, plenty, comfort, enjoyment, well-being.
OPPOSITES difficulty, formality, hardship.
verb **1** *the alcohol eased his pain:* **relieve,** alleviate, soothe, moderate, dull, deaden, numb. **2** *the rain eased off:* **let up,** abate, subside, die down, slacken off, diminish, lessen. **3** *work helped to ease her mind:* **calm,** quieten, pacify, soothe, comfort, console. **4** *he eased out the cork:* **slide,** slip, squeeze, guide, manoeuvre, inch, edge.
OPPOSITES aggravate, intensify, unsettle.

easily adverb **effortlessly,** comfortably, simply, without difficulty, readily, without a hitch.

easy adjective **1** *the task was very easy:* **uncomplicated,** undemanding, effortless, painless, trouble-free, simple, straightforward, elementary, plain sailing; informal a piece of cake, child's play, a cinch. **2** *an easy target:* **vulnerable,** susceptible, defenceless, naive, gullible, trusting. **3** *Vic's easy manner:* **natural,** casual, informal, unceremonious, unreserved, unaffected, easy-going, amiable, affable, genial, good-humoured, carefree, nonchalant, unconcerned; informal laid-back. **4** *an easy life:* **quiet,** tranquil, serene, peaceful, untroubled, contented, relaxed, comfortable, secure, safe; informal cushy. **5** *an easy pace:* **leisurely,** unhurried, comfortable, undemanding,

easy-going, gentle, sedate, moderate, steady.
OPPOSITES difficult, formal, hard, demanding.

eat verb **1** *we ate a hearty breakfast:* **consume,** devour, swallow, partake of, munch, chomp; informal tuck into, put away. **2** *we ate at a local restaurant:* **have a meal,** feed, snack, breakfast, lunch, dine; informal graze.

ebb verb **1** *the tide ebbed:* **recede,** go out, retreat. **2** *his courage began to ebb:* **diminish,** dwindle, wane, fade (away), peter out, decline, flag.
OPPOSITES flow, increase.

eccentric adjective *eccentric behaviour:* **unconventional,** abnormal, anomalous, odd, strange, peculiar, weird, bizarre, outlandish, idiosyncratic, quirky; informal oddball, kooky, cranky.
OPPOSITES conventional.
noun *he was something of an eccentric:* **oddity,** free spirit, misfit; informal oddball, weirdo.

echo noun *a faint echo of my shout:* **reverberation,** reflection, ringing, repetition, repeat.
verb **1** *his laughter echoed round the room:* **reverberate,** resonate, resound, reflect, ring, vibrate. **2** *Bill echoed Rex's words:* **repeat,** restate, reiterate, imitate, parrot, mimic, reproduce, recite.

eclipse verb **outshine,** overshadow, surpass, exceed, outclass, outstrip, outdo, transcend.

economic adjective **1** *economic reform:* **financial,** monetary, budgetary, fiscal, commercial. **2** *the firm cannot remain economic:* **profitable,** moneymaking, lucrative, remunerative, fruitful, productive.
OPPOSITES unprofitable.

economical adjective **1** *an economical car:* **cheap,** inexpensive, low-cost, budget, economy, cut-price, bargain. **2** *a very economical shopper:* **thrifty,** provident, prudent, sensible, frugal.
OPPOSITES expensive, spendthrift.

economize verb **save (money),** cut costs, cut back, make cutbacks, retrench, scrimp.

economy noun **1** *the nation's economy:* **wealth,** financial resources, financial system, financial management. **2** *one can combine good living with economy:* **thrift,** thriftiness, prudence, careful budgeting, saving, restraint, frugality.
OPPOSITES extravagance.

ecstasy noun **rapture,** bliss, joy, elation, euphoria, rhapsodies.
OPPOSITES misery.

ecstatic adjective **enraptured,** elated, euphoric, rapturous, joyful, overjoyed, blissful; informal over the moon, on top of the world.

eddy noun *eddies at the river's edge:* **swirl,** whirlpool, vortex.
verb *the snow eddied around her:* **swirl,** whirl, spiral, wind, twist.

edge noun **1** *the edge of the lake:* **border,** boundary, extremity, fringe, margin, side, lip, rim, brim, brink, verge, perimeter. **2** *she had an edge in her voice:* **sharpness,** severity, bite, sting, sarcasm, malice, spite, venom. **3** *they have an edge over their rivals:* **advantage,** lead, head start, the whip hand, the upper hand, dominance.

OPPOSITES middle, kindness, disadvantage.

verb 1 *poplars edged the orchard:* **border,** fringe, skirt, surround, enclose, encircle, bound. **2** *a frock edged with lace:* **trim,** decorate, finish, border, fringe. **3** *he edged closer to the fire:* **creep,** inch, work one's way, ease oneself, sidle, steal.
OPPOSITES stride.

edit verb **correct,** check, copy-edit, improve, polish, modify, adapt, revise, rewrite, reword, shorten, condense, cut, abridge.

edition noun **issue,** number, volume, printing, impression, publication, programme, version.

educate verb **teach,** school, tutor, instruct, coach, train, inform, enlighten.

educated adjective **informed,** literate, schooled, tutored, well read, learned, knowledgeable, enlightened, intellectual, academic, erudite, scholarly, cultivated, cultured.
OPPOSITES uneducated.

education noun **1** *the education of young children:* **teaching,** schooling, tuition, tutoring, instruction, coaching, training, guidance, enlightenment. **2** *a woman of some education:* **learning,** knowledge, literacy, scholarship, enlightenment.

educational adjective **1** *an educational establishment:* **academic,** scholastic, learning, teaching, pedagogic. **2** *an educational experience:* **instructive,** instructional, educative, informative, illuminating, enlightening; formal edifying.

eerie adjective **uncanny,** sinister, ghostly, unnatural, unearthly, supernatural, other-worldly, strange, abnormal, weird, freakish; informal creepy, scary, spooky.

effect noun **1** *the effect of these changes:* **result,** consequence, upshot, outcome, repercussions, end result, aftermath. **2** *the effect of the drug:* **impact,** action, effectiveness, power, potency, strength, success. **3** *the dead man's effects:* **belongings,** possessions, worldly goods, chattels, property; informal things, stuff; Brit. informal clobber.
OPPOSITES cause.

verb *they effected many changes:* **achieve,** accomplish, carry out, manage, bring off, execute, conduct, engineer, perform, do, cause, bring about, produce.

effective adjective **1** *an effective treatment:* **successful,** effectual, potent, powerful, helpful, beneficial, advantageous, valuable, useful. **2** *an effective argument:* **convincing,** compelling, strong, forceful, persuasive, plausible, credible, logical, reasonable, cogent. **3** *the new law will be effective from next week:* **operative,** in force, in effect, valid, official, legal, binding. **4** *Korea was under effective Japanese control:* **virtual,** practical, essential, actual.
OPPOSITES ineffective, weak, invalid, theoretical.

efficiency noun **1** *we need reforms to bring efficiency:* **economy,** productivity, cost-effectiveness, organization, order, orderliness, regulation. **2** *I compliment you on your efficiency:* **competence,** capability, ability, proficiency, expertise, skill, effectiveness.
OPPOSITES inefficiency, incompetence.

e

efficient adjective **1** *efficient techniques:* **economic,** productive, effective, cost-effective, streamlined, organized, methodical, systematic, orderly. **2** *an efficient secretary:* **competent,** capable, able, proficient, skilful, skilled, effective, productive, organized, businesslike.
OPPOSITES inefficient, incompetent.

effort noun **1** *an effort to work together:* **attempt,** try, endeavour; informal shot, stab, bash. **2** *a fine effort:* **achievement,** accomplishment, feat, undertaking, enterprise, work, result, outcome. **3** *the job requires little effort:* **exertion,** energy, work, application; informal elbow grease; Brit. informal graft.

eject verb **1** *the volcano ejected ash:* **emit,** spew out, discharge, give off, send out, belch, vent. **2** *the pilot had time to eject:* **bail out,** escape. **3** *they were ejected from the hall:* **expel,** throw out, remove, oust, evict, banish; informal kick out.
OPPOSITES admit.

elaborate adjective **1** *an elaborate plan:* **complicated,** complex, intricate, involved, detailed. **2** *an elaborate plasterwork ceiling:* **ornate,** decorated, embellished, adorned, ornamented, fancy, fussy, busy.
OPPOSITES simple, plain.
verb *both sides refused to elaborate on their reasons:* **expand on,** enlarge on, add to, flesh out, develop, fill out, amplify.

elastic adjective **1** *elastic material:* **stretchy,** elasticated, springy, flexible, pliable, supple. **2** *an elastic concept of nationality:* **adaptable,** flexible, adjustable, accommodating, variable, fluid, versatile.
OPPOSITES rigid.

elder adjective *his elder brother:* **older,** senior, big.
noun *the church elders:* **leader,** patriarch, father.

elderly adjective **aged,** old, ageing, long in the tooth, grey-haired, in one's dotage; informal getting on, over the hill.
OPPOSITES youthful.

elect verb **1** *a new president was elected:* **vote in,** vote for, return, cast one's vote for, choose, pick, select. **2** *she elected to stay behind:* **choose,** decide, opt, prefer, vote.

election noun **ballot,** vote, poll; Brit. by-election; US primary.

electric adjective *the atmosphere was electric:* **exciting,** charged, electrifying, thrilling, dramatic, dynamic, stimulating, galvanizing.

electrify verb **excite,** thrill, stimulate, arouse, rouse, inspire, stir (up), exhilarate, galvanize, fire (with enthusiasm), fire someone's imagination, invigorate, animate; N. Amer. light a fire under.

elegance noun **1** *he was attracted by her elegance:* **style,** grace, taste, sophistication, refinement, dignity, poise. **2** *the elegance of the idea:* **neatness,** simplicity.

elegant adjective **1** *an elegant black outfit:* **stylish,** graceful, tasteful, sophisticated, classic, chic, smart, poised, cultivated, polished, cultured. **2** *an elegant solution:* **neat,** simple.
OPPOSITES inelegant.

element noun **1** *an essential*

element of the local community: **component,** constituent, part, section, portion, piece, segment, aspect, factor, feature, facet, ingredient, strand, detail, member. **2** *there is an element of truth in this stereotype:* **trace,** touch, hint, smattering, soupçon. **3** (**elements**) *I braved the elements:* **weather,** climate, weather conditions.

elementary adjective **1** *an elementary astronomy course:* **basic,** rudimentary, preparatory, introductory. **2** *a lot of the work is elementary:* **easy,** simple, straightforward, uncomplicated, undemanding, painless, child's play, plain sailing; informal a piece of cake.
OPPOSITES advanced, difficult.

elevate verb **1** *we need a breeze to elevate the kite:* **raise,** lift (up), raise up/aloft, hoist, hike up, haul up. **2** *he was elevated to Secretary of State:* **promote,** upgrade, move up, raise; informal kick upstairs.
OPPOSITES lower, demote.

elevated adjective **1** *an elevated motorway:* **raised,** overhead, in the air, high up. **2** *elevated language:* **lofty,** grand, exalted, fine, sublime, inflated, pompous, bombastic. **3** *his elevated status:* **high,** high-ranking, lofty, exalted, grand, noble.
OPPOSITES sunken, everyday, lowly.

elicit verb **obtain,** draw out, extract, bring out, evoke, induce, prompt, generate, trigger, provoke.

eligible adjective **1** *those eligible to vote:* **entitled,** permitted, allowed, qualified, able. **2** *an eligible bachelor:* **desirable,** suitable, available, single,

unmarried, unattached.

eliminate verb **1** *a policy that would eliminate inflation:* **remove,** get rid of, put an end to, do away with, end, stop, eradicate, destroy, stamp out. **2** *he was eliminated from the title race:* **knock out,** exclude, rule out, disqualify.

elite noun **best,** pick, cream, crème de la crème, flower, high society, beautiful people, aristocracy, ruling class.
OPPOSITES dregs.

eloquent adjective **articulate,** fluent, expressive, persuasive, well expressed, effective, lucid, vivid.
OPPOSITES inarticulate.

elusive adjective **1** *her elusive husband:* **difficult to find,** slippery. **2** *an elusive quality:* **indefinable,** intangible, impalpable, fugitive, fleeting, transitory, ambiguous.

embargo noun *an embargo on oil sales:* **ban,** bar, prohibition, stoppage, veto, moratorium, restriction, block, boycott.
verb *arms sales were embargoed:* **ban,** bar, prohibit, stop, outlaw, blacklist, restrict, block, boycott.
OPPOSITES allow.

embark verb **board (ship),** go on board, go aboard; informal hop on, jump on.
OPPOSITES disembark.
■ **embark on** begin, start, undertake, set out on, take up, turn one's hand to, get down to, enter into, venture into, launch into, plunge into, engage in.

embarrass verb **humiliate,** shame, put someone to shame, abash, mortify, fluster, discomfit; informal show up.
embarrassed adjective

humiliated, mortified, red-faced, blushing, abashed, shamed, ashamed, shamefaced, self-conscious, uncomfortable, discomfited, disconcerted, flustered; informal with egg on one's face.

embarrassing adjective **humiliating,** shameful, mortifying, ignominious, awkward, uncomfortable, compromising; discomfiting; informal cringeworthy, cringe-making, toe-curling.

embarrassment noun **1** *he was scarlet with embarrassment:* **humiliation,** mortification, shame, shamefacedness, awkwardness, self-consciousness, discomfort, discomfiture. **2** *his current financial embarrassment:* **difficulty,** predicament, plight, problem, mess; informal bind, pickle, fix.

emblem noun **symbol,** representation, token, image, figure, mark, sign, crest, badge, device, insignia, coat of arms, shield, logo, trademark.

embody verb **1** *Gradgrind embodies the spirit of industrial capitalism:* **personify,** manifest, symbolize, represent, express, epitomize, stand for, typify, exemplify. **2** *the changes embodied in the Act:* **incorporate,** include, contain.

embrace verb **1** *he embraced her warmly:* **hug,** take/hold in one's arms, hold, cuddle, clasp to one's bosom, squeeze, clutch, enfold. **2** *most western European countries have embraced the concept:* **welcome,** welcome with open arms, accept, take on board, take up, take to one's heart, adopt, espouse. **3** *the faculty embraces a wide range of disciplines:* **include,** take in, comprise, contain, incorporate, encompass, cover, subsume. noun *a fond embrace:* **hug,** cuddle, squeeze, clinch, caress.

emerge verb **1** *a policeman emerged from the alley:* **come out,** appear, come into view, become visible, surface, materialize, issue, come forth. **2** *several unexpected facts emerged:* **become known,** become apparent, be revealed, come to light, come out, turn up, transpire, unfold, turn out, prove to be the case.

emergence noun **appearance,** arrival, coming, materialization, advent, inception, dawn, birth, origination, start, development.

emergency noun *a military emergency:* **crisis,** disaster, catastrophe, calamity, plight; informal panic stations. adjective **1** *an emergency meeting:* **urgent,** crisis, extraordinary. **2** *emergency supplies:* **reserve,** standby, backup, fallback.

emigrate verb **move abroad,** move overseas, leave one's country, migrate, relocate, resettle. OPPOSITES immigrate.

eminent adjective **illustrious,** distinguished, renowned, esteemed, pre-eminent, notable, noted, noteworthy, great, prestigious, important, outstanding, celebrated, prominent, well known, acclaimed, exalted. OPPOSITES unknown.

emission noun **discharge,** release, outpouring, outflow, outrush, leak.

emit verb **1** *hydrocarbons emitted from vehicle exhausts:*

discharge, release, give out/off, pour out, radiate, leak, ooze, disgorge, eject, belch, spew out, exude. **2** *he emitted a loud cry:* **utter**, voice, let out, produce, give vent to, come out with.
OPPOSITES absorb, stifle.

emotion noun **1** *she was good at hiding her emotions:* **feeling**, sentiment, reaction, response, instinct, intuition, heart.
2 *overcome by emotion, she turned away:* **passion**, strength of feeling.

emotional adjective **1** *an emotional young man:* **passionate**, hot-blooded, ardent, fervent, excitable, temperamental, demonstrative.
2 *he paid an emotional tribute to his wife:* **poignant**, moving, touching, affecting, powerful, stirring, emotive, impassioned, dramatic; *informal* tear-jerking.
OPPOSITES cold, clinical.

emphasis noun **1** *the curriculum gave more emphasis to reading and writing:* **prominence**, importance, significance, value, stress, weight, accent, attention, priority. **2** *the emphasis is on the word 'little':* **stress**, accent, weight, beat.

emphasize verb **stress**, underline, highlight, focus attention on, point up, lay stress on, draw attention to, spotlight, foreground.
OPPOSITES understate.

emphatic adjective **forceful**, firm, vehement, wholehearted, energetic, vigorous, direct, insistent, certain, definite, out-and-out, decided, categorical, unqualified, unconditional, unequivocal, unambiguous, absolute, explicit, downright, outright, clear.
OPPOSITES hesitant.

empire noun **1** *the Ottoman Empire:* **kingdom**, realm, domain, territory, commonwealth, power. **2** *a worldwide shipping empire:* **business**, firm, company, corporation, multinational, conglomerate, group, consortium, operation.

employ verb **1** *she employed a chauffeur:* **hire**, engage, recruit, take on, sign up, appoint, retain. **2** *Sam was employed in carving a stone figure:* **occupy**, engage, involve, keep busy, tie up. **3** *the team employed subtle psychological tactics:* **use**, utilize, make use of, apply, exercise, practise, put into practice, exert, bring into play, bring to bear, draw on, resort to, turn to, have recourse to.
OPPOSITES dismiss.

employed adjective **working**, in work, in employment, holding down a job, earning, salaried, waged.
OPPOSITES unemployed.

employee noun **worker**, member of staff, blue-collar worker, white-collar worker, workman, labourer, (hired) hand; (**employees**) personnel, staff, workforce.

employment noun **work**, labour, service, job, post, position, situation, occupation, profession, trade, business, line of work.

empower verb **1** *the act empowered Henry to punish heretics:* **authorize**, entitle, permit, allow, license, enable. **2** *movements to empower the poor:* **emancipate**, unshackle, set free, liberate, enfranchise.
OPPOSITES forbid.

empty adjective **1** *an empty*

e

house: **vacant,** unoccupied, uninhabited, bare, clear, free. **2** *an empty threat:* **meaningless,** hollow, idle, vain, futile, worthless, useless, ineffectual. **3** *without her my life is empty:* **futile,** pointless, purposeless, worthless, meaningless, valueless, of no value, aimless, senseless.
OPPOSITES full, occupied, serious, worthwhile.
verb **1** *I emptied the dishwasher:* **unload,** unpack, clear, evacuate, drain. **2** *he emptied out the contents of the case:* **remove,** take out, extract, tip out, pour out.
OPPOSITES fill, replace.

emulate verb imitate, copy, mirror, echo, follow, model oneself on, take a leaf out of someone's book.

enable verb allow, permit, let, equip, empower, make able, fit, authorize, entitle, qualify.
OPPOSITES prevent.

enact verb **1** *the government enacted an environmental protection bill:* **make law,** pass, approve, ratify, validate, sanction, authorize. **2** *they are to enact a nativity play:* **act out,** perform, appear in, stage, mount, put on, present.
OPPOSITES repeal.

enchanting adjective captivating, charming, delightful, adorable, lovely, attractive, appealing, engaging, fetching, irresistible, fascinating.

enclose verb **1** *tall trees enclosed the garden:* **surround,** circle, ring, encircle, bound, close in, wall in. **2** *please enclose a stamped addressed envelope:* **include,** insert, put in, send.

enclosure noun compound, pen, fold, stockade, ring, paddock, yard, run, coop; N. Amer. corral.

encompass verb include, cover, embrace, incorporate, take in, contain, comprise, involve, deal with.

encounter verb **1** *we encountered a slight problem:* **experience,** run into, meet, come up against, face, be faced with, confront, suffer. **2** *I encountered a girl I used to know:* **meet,** run into, come across/upon, stumble across/on, chance on, happen on; informal bump into.
noun **1** *an unexpected encounter:* **meeting,** chance meeting. **2** *a violent encounter between police and demonstrators:* **battle,** fight, clash, scuffle, confrontation, struggle; informal run-in, scrap.

encourage verb **1** *the players were encouraged by the crowd:* **hearten,** cheer, buoy up, uplift, inspire, motivate, spur on, stir, fire up, stimulate, embolden; informal buck up. **2** *she encouraged him to go:* **persuade,** coax, urge, press, push, pressure, prod. **3** *the Government was keen to encourage local businesses:* **support,** back, promote, further, foster, nurture, cultivate, strengthen, stimulate.
OPPOSITES discourage, dissuade, hinder.

encouragement noun **1** *she needed a bit of encouragement:* **support,** cheering up, inspiration, motivation, stimulation, morale-boosting. **2** *they required no encouragement to get back to work:* **persuasion,** coaxing, urging, prodding, prompting,

inducement, incentive, carrot.
3 *the encouragement of foreign investment:* **support,** backing, sponsorship, promotion, furtherance, fostering, nurture, cultivation, stimulation.

end noun **1** *the end of the novel:* **conclusion,** termination, ending, finish, close, resolution, climax, finale, culmination, denouement. **2** *the end of the road:* **extremity,** limit, edge, border, boundary, periphery, point, tip, head, top, bottom. **3** *wealth is not an end in itself:* **aim,** goal, purpose, objective, object, target, intention, aspiration, wish, desire, ambition.
OPPOSITES beginning, means.
verb **1** *the show ended with a wedding scene:* **finish,** conclude, terminate, close, stop, cease, culminate, climax. **2** *she ended their relationship:* **break off,** call off, bring to an end, put an end to, stop, finish, terminate, discontinue, cancel.
OPPOSITES begin.

endanger verb **jeopardize,** risk, put at risk, put in danger, be a danger to, threaten, compromise, imperil.
OPPOSITES safeguard.

endearing adjective **charming,** appealing, attractive, engaging, winning, captivating, enchanting, cute, sweet, delightful, lovely.

endeavour verb *the company endeavoured to expand:* **try,** attempt, seek, strive, struggle, labour, toil, work.
noun **1** *an endeavour to build a more buoyant economy:* **attempt,** try, bid, effort. **2** *an extremely unwise endeavour:* **undertaking,** enterprise, venture, exercise, activity,

exploit, deed, act, action, move.

ending noun **end,** finish, close, conclusion, resolution, summing-up, denouement, finale.
OPPOSITES beginning.

endless adjective **1** *a woman with endless energy:* **unlimited,** limitless, infinite, inexhaustible, boundless, unbounded, ceaseless, unending, everlasting, constant, continuous, interminable, unfailing, perpetual, eternal. **2** *we played endless games:* **countless,** innumerable, numerous, a multitude of; informal umpteen, no end of; literary myriad.
OPPOSITES limited, few.

endorse verb **support,** back, agree with, approve (of), favour, subscribe to, recommend, champion, uphold, sanction.
OPPOSITES oppose.

endorsement noun **support,** backing, approval, seal of approval, agreement, recommendation, patronage, sanction.

endow verb **1** *Henry II endowed the hospital:* **finance,** fund, pay for, subsidize, sponsor. **2** *he was endowed with great strength:* **provide,** supply, furnish, equip, favour, bless, grace.

endowment noun **gift,** present, grant, funding, award, donation, contribution, subsidy, sponsorship, bequest, legacy.

endurance noun **1** *she pushed him beyond endurance:* **toleration,** tolerance, forbearance, patience, acceptance, resignation, stoicism. **2** *an endurance test:* **resistance,** durability, permanence, longevity, strength, toughness, stamina, staying power, fortitude.

endure verb **1** *he endured much pain:* **undergo,** go through, live through, experience, cope with, deal with, face, suffer, tolerate, put up with, brave, bear, withstand. **2** *our love will endure:* **last,** live, live on, go on, survive, abide, continue, persist, remain.
OPPOSITES fade.

enemy noun **opponent,** adversary, rival, antagonist, combatant, challenger, competitor, opposition, competition, the other side; literary foe.
OPPOSITES friend, ally.

energetic adjective **1** *an energetic woman:* **active,** lively, dynamic, spirited, animated, bouncy, bubbly, sprightly, tireless, indefatigable, enthusiastic; informal full of beans. **2** *energetic exercises:* **vigorous,** strenuous, brisk, hard, arduous, demanding, taxing, tough, rigorous. **3** *an energetic advertising campaign:* **forceful,** vigorous, aggressive, hard-hitting, high-powered, all-out, determined, bold, intensive; informal in-your-face.
OPPOSITES lethargic, gentle, half-hearted.

energy noun **vitality,** vigour, strength, stamina, animation, spirit, verve, enthusiasm, zest, exuberance, dynamism, drive; informal punch, bounce, oomph, go, get-up-and-go.

enforce verb **1** *the sheriff enforced the law:* **impose,** apply, administer, carry out, implement, bring to bear, put into effect. **2** *they cannot enforce cooperation:* **force,** compel, coerce, exact.

engage verb **1** *tasks which engage children's interest:* **capture,** catch, arrest, grab, draw, attract, gain, hold, grip, absorb, occupy. **2** *he engaged a secretary:* **employ,** hire, recruit, take on, enrol, appoint. **3** *the chance to engage in a wide range of pursuits:* **participate in,** join in, take part in, partake in/of, enter into, embark on. **4** *infantry units engaged the enemy:* **attack,** fall on, take on, clash with, encounter, meet, fight, do battle with.
OPPOSITES lose, dismiss.

engagement noun **1** *a business engagement:* **appointment,** meeting, arrangement, commitment, date, assignation, rendezvous. **2** *Britain's engagement in open trading:* **participation,** involvement. **3** *the first engagement of the war:* **battle,** fight, clash, confrontation, encounter, conflict, skirmish, action, hostilities.

engaging adjective **charming,** attractive, appealing, pleasing, pleasant, agreeable, likeable, lovable, sweet, winning, fetching; Scottish & N. English bonny.
OPPOSITES unappealing.

engine noun **motor,** generator, machine, turbine.

engineer noun **1** *a structural engineer:* **designer,** planner, builder. **2** *a repair engineer:* **mechanic,** repairer, technician, maintenance man, operator, driver, controller.
verb *he engineered a takeover deal:* **bring about,** arrange, pull off, bring off, contrive, manoeuvre, negotiate, organize, plan, mastermind.

engraving noun **etching,** print,

plate, picture, illustration, inscription.

engulf verb **swamp**, inundate, flood, deluge, immerse, swallow up, submerge, bury, envelop, overwhelm.

enhance verb **improve**, add to, strengthen, boost, increase, intensify, heighten, magnify, amplify, inflate, build up, supplement, augment.
OPPOSITES diminish.

enjoy verb **1** *he enjoys playing the piano:* **like**, be fond of, take pleasure in, be keen on, delight in, relish, revel in, adore, lap up, savour, luxuriate in, bask in; informal get a thrill out of.
2 *she had always enjoyed good health:* **benefit from**, be blessed with, be favoured with, be endowed with, possess, own, boast.
OPPOSITES dislike, lack.
■ **enjoy oneself** have fun, have a good time, make merry, celebrate, revel; informal party, have a whale of a time, let one's hair down.

enjoyable adjective **entertaining**, amusing, delightful, pleasant, congenial, convivial, agreeable, pleasurable, satisfying.
OPPOSITES disagreeable.

enjoyment noun **pleasure**, fun, entertainment, amusement, recreation, relaxation, happiness, merriment, joy, satisfaction, liking.

enlarge verb **1** *they enlarged the scope of their research:* **extend**, expand, grow, add to, amplify, augment, magnify, build up, stretch, widen, broaden, lengthen, elongate, deepen, thicken. **2** *the lymph glands had enlarged:* **swell**, distend, bloat, bulge, dilate, blow up, puff up.

OPPOSITES reduce, shrink.
■ **enlarge on** elaborate on, expand on, add to, flesh out, add detail to, develop, fill out, embellish, embroider.

enlighten verb **inform**, tell, make aware, open someone's eyes, illuminate; informal put someone in the picture.

enlightened adjective **informed**, aware, sophisticated, liberal, open-minded, broad-minded, educated, knowledgeable, civilized, refined, cultured.
OPPOSITES benighted.

enlightenment noun **insight**, understanding, awareness, education, learning, knowledge, illumination, awakening, instruction, teaching, open-mindedness, broad-mindedness, culture, refinement, cultivation, civilization.

enlist verb **1** *he enlisted in the Royal Engineers:* **join up**, enrol, sign up, volunteer, register. **2** *he was enlisted in the army:* **recruit**, call up, enrol, sign up, conscript, mobilize; US draft. **3** *he enlisted the help of a friend:* **obtain**, engage, secure, win, get.
OPPOSITES discharge, demobilize.

enormity noun **1** *the enormity of his crimes:* **wickedness**, vileness, heinousness, baseness, depravity, outrageousness. **2** *the enormity of the task:* **immensity**, hugeness, size, extent, magnitude.

enormous adjective **huge**, vast, immense, gigantic, giant, massive, colossal, mammoth, tremendous, extensive, mighty, monumental, mountainous; informal mega, monster, whopping; Brit. informal ginormous.

e

OPPOSITES tiny.

enough determiner *they had enough food:* **sufficient**, adequate, ample, abundant, the necessary; informal plenty of.
OPPOSITES insufficient.
▸ pronoun *there's enough for everyone:* **sufficient**, plenty, an adequate amount, as much as necessary, a sufficiency, an ample supply, one's fill.

enquire, inquire verb 1 *I enquired about training courses:* **ask**, make enquiries. 2 *the commission is to enquire into the payments:* **investigate**, probe, look into, research, examine, explore, delve into; informal check out.

enquiry, inquiry noun 1 *telephone enquiries:* **question**, query. 2 *an enquiry into alleged security leaks:* **investigation**, probe, examination, exploration, inquest, hearing.

enrage verb **anger**, infuriate, incense, madden, inflame, antagonize, provoke; informal drive mad/crazy, make someone see red, make someone's blood boil.
OPPOSITES placate.

enraged adjective **furious**, infuriated, irate, incensed, raging, incandescent, fuming, seething, beside oneself; informal mad, livid, foaming at the mouth.
OPPOSITES calm.

enrich verb **enhance**, improve, better, add to, augment, supplement, complement, refine.
OPPOSITES spoil.

enrol verb 1 *they both enrolled for the course:* **register**, sign on/up, put one's name down, apply, volunteer, enter, join. 2 *280 new members were*

enrolled: **accept**, admit, take on, sign on/up, recruit, engage.

ensemble noun 1 *a Bulgarian folk ensemble:* **group**, band, company, troupe, cast, chorus, corps; informal combo. 2 *the buildings present a charming provincial ensemble:* **whole**, unit, body, set, collection, combination, composite, package. 3 *a pink and black ensemble:* **outfit**, costume, suit; informal get-up.

ensue verb **result**, follow, develop, succeed, emerge, arise, proceed, stem.

ensure verb 1 *ensure that the surface is completely clean:* **make sure**, make certain, see to it, check, confirm, establish, verify. 2 *legislation to ensure equal opportunities for all:* **secure**, guarantee, assure, certify.

entail verb **involve**, necessitate, require, need, demand, call for, mean, imply, cause, give rise to, occasion.

enter verb 1 *police entered the house:* **go into**, come into, get into, set foot in, gain access to. 2 *a bullet entered his chest:* **penetrate**, pierce, puncture, perforate. 3 *they entered the Army at eighteen:* **join**, enrol in/for, enlist in, volunteer for, sign up for. 4 *she entered a cookery competition:* **go in for**, register for, enrol for, sign up for, compete in, take part in, participate in. 5 *the cashier entered the details in a ledger:* **record**, write, put down, take down, note, jot down, register, log. 6 *please enter your password:* **key (in)**, type (in), tap in.
OPPOSITES leave.

enterprise noun 1 *a joint*

enterprise: **undertaking,** endeavour, venture, exercise, activity, operation, task, business, project, scheme. **2** *a woman with enterprise:* **initiative,** resourcefulness, imagination, ingenuity, inventiveness, originality, creativity. **3** *a profit-making enterprise:* **business,** company, firm, venture, organization, operation, concern, establishment; informal outfit.

enterprising adjective **resourceful,** entrepreneurial, imaginative, ingenious, inventive, creative, adventurous; informal go-ahead.
OPPOSITES unimaginative.

entertain verb **1** *he wrote stories to entertain them:* **amuse,** please, charm, cheer, interest, engage, occupy. **2** *he entertains foreign visitors:* **receive,** play host/hostess to, invite (round/over), throw a party for, wine and dine, feed. **3** *I would never entertain such an idea:* **consider,** contemplate, think of, hear of, countenance.
OPPOSITES bore, reject.

entertainment noun **amusement,** pleasure, leisure, recreation, relaxation, fun, enjoyment, interest.

enthusiasm noun **keenness,** eagerness, passion, fervour, zeal, zest, gusto, energy, vigour, fire, spirit, interest, commitment, devotion; informal get-up-and-go.
OPPOSITES apathy.

enthusiast noun **fan,** devotee, supporter, follower, aficionado, lover, admirer; informal buff.

enthusiastic adjective **keen,** eager, avid, ardent, fervent, passionate, zealous, excited, wholehearted, committed,

devoted, fanatical, earnest.
OPPOSITES apathetic.

entice verb **tempt,** lure, attract, appeal to, invite, persuade, beguile, coax, woo, lead on, seduce; informal sweet-talk.

entire adjective **whole,** complete, total, full.

entirely adverb **1** *that's entirely out of the question:* **absolutely,** completely, totally, wholly, utterly, quite, altogether, thoroughly. **2** *a gift entirely for charitable purposes:* **solely,** only, exclusively, purely, merely, just, alone.

entitle verb **1** *this pass entitles you to visit the museum:* **qualify,** make eligible, authorize, allow, permit, enable, empower. **2** *a chapter entitled 'Comedy and Tragedy':* **name,** title, call, label, designate, dub.

entity noun **being,** creature, individual, organism, life form, body, object, article, thing.

entrance[1] noun **1** *the main entrance:* **entry,** way in, access, approach, door, portal, gate, opening, mouth, foyer, lobby, porch; N. Amer. entryway. **2** *the entrance of Mrs Knight:* **appearance,** arrival, entry, coming. **3** *he was refused entrance:* **admission,** admittance, (right of) entry, entrée, access.
OPPOSITES exit, departure.

entrance[2] verb *I was entranced by her beauty:* **enchant,** bewitch, beguile, captivate, mesmerize, hypnotize, spellbind, transfix, enthral, engross, absorb, fascinate, stun, electrify, charm, delight; informal bowl over, knock out.

entrant noun **competitor,** contestant, contender,

e

participant, candidate, applicant.

entrust verb **1** *he was entrusted with the task:* **charge,** give someone the responsibility for, present. **2** *the powers entrusted to the Home Secretary:* **assign,** confer on, bestow on, vest in, delegate, give, grant, vouchsafe.

entry noun **1** *my moment of entry:* **appearance,** arrival, entrance, coming. **2** *the entry to the flats:* **entrance,** way in, access, approach, door, portal, gate, entrance hall, foyer, lobby; N. Amer. entryway. **3** *he was refused entry:* **admission,** admittance, entrance, access. **4** *entries in the cash book:* **item,** record, note, memo, memorandum. **5** *data entry:* **recording,** archiving, logging, documentation, capture. **6** *we must pick a winner from the entries:* **submission,** entry form, application.
OPPOSITES departure, exit.

envelop verb **surround,** cover, enfold, engulf, encircle, cocoon, sheathe, swathe, enclose, cloak, veil, shroud.

environment noun **1** *the hospital environment:* **situation,** setting, milieu, background, backdrop, context, conditions, ambience, atmosphere. **2** *the impact of pesticides on the environment:* **the natural world,** nature, the earth, the ecosystem, the biosphere, Mother Nature, wildlife, flora and fauna, the countryside.

environmentalist noun **conservationist,** ecologist, nature-lover, green; informal eco-warrior, tree-hugger.

envisage verb **1** *it was envisaged that the hospital would open soon:* **foresee,** predict, forecast, anticipate, expect, think likely. **2** *I cannot envisage what the future holds:* **imagine,** contemplate, picture, conceive of, think of.

envoy noun **ambassador,** emissary, diplomat, representative, delegate, spokesperson, agent, intermediary, mediator; informal go-between.

envy noun *feelings of envy:* **jealousy,** covetousness, resentment, bitterness.
verb **1** *I admired and envied her:* **be envious of,** be jealous of, be resentful of. **2** *we envied her lifestyle:* **covet,** desire, aspire to, wish for, want, long for, yearn for, hanker after, crave.

epidemic noun **1** *an epidemic of typhoid:* **outbreak,** plague, pandemic. **2** *a joyriding epidemic:* **spate,** rash, wave, eruption, plague, outbreak, craze, upsurge.

episode noun **1** *the best episode of his career:* **incident,** event, occurrence, chapter, experience, occasion, interlude, adventure, exploit. **2** *the final episode of the series:* **instalment,** chapter, passage, part, portion, section, programme, show. **3** *an episode of illness:* **period,** spell, bout, attack, phase; informal dose.

equal adjective **1** *lines of equal length:* **identical,** uniform, alike, like, the same, matching, equivalent, corresponding. **2** *equal treatment before the law:* **impartial,** non-partisan, fair, just, equitable, unprejudiced, non-discriminatory. **3** *an equal contest:* **evenly matched,** even, balanced, level; informal level pegging, neck and neck.

OPPOSITES different, discriminatory.
noun *they did not treat him as their equal:* **equivalent,** peer, fellow, like, counterpart, match, parallel.
verb **1** *two plus two equals four:* **be equal to,** be equivalent to, be the same as, come to, amount to, make, total, add up to. **2** *he equalled the world record:* **match,** reach, parallel, be level with.

equality noun **fairness,** equal rights, equal opportunities, impartiality, even-handedness, justice.

equate verb **1** *he equates criticism with treachery:* **identify,** compare, bracket, class, associate, connect, link, relate. **2** *moves to equate supply and demand:* **equalize,** balance, even out/up, level, square, tally, match.

equilibrium noun **balance,** stability, poise, symmetry, harmony.
OPPOSITES imbalance.

equip verb **1** *the boat was equipped with a flare gun:* **provide,** furnish, supply, issue, kit out, stock, provision, arm. **2** *the course will equip them for the workplace:* **prepare,** qualify, ready, suit, train.

equipment noun **apparatus,** paraphernalia, tools, utensils, implements, hardware, gadgetry, things; informal stuff, gear.

equivalent adjective *a degree or equivalent qualification:* **comparable,** corresponding, commensurate, similar, parallel, analogous.
noun *Denmark's equivalent of the Daily Mirror:* **counterpart,** parallel, alternative, analogue,

twin, opposite number.

era noun **age,** epoch, period, time, date, day, generation.

eradicate verb **eliminate,** get rid of, remove, obliterate, extinguish, exterminate, destroy, annihilate, kill, wipe out.

erase verb **1** *they erased his name:* **delete,** rub out, wipe off, blank out, expunge, excise, remove, obliterate. **2** *the data had been erased:* **wipe,** kill, delete, record over, format.

erect adjective **upright,** straight, vertical, perpendicular, standing (on end), bristling, stiff.
OPPOSITES bent, flat.
verb **build,** construct, put up, assemble, put together, fabricate, raise.
OPPOSITES demolish, dismantle, lower.

erode verb **wear away/down,** abrade, grind down, crumble, weather, undermine, weaken, deteriorate, destroy.

erosion noun **wearing away,** abrasion, attrition, weathering, dissolution, deterioration, disintegration, destruction.

erotic adjective **sexually arousing,** sexually stimulating, titillating, suggestive, pornographic, sexually explicit; informal blue, X-rated; euphemistic adult.

errand noun **task,** job, chore, assignment, mission.

erratic adjective **unpredictable,** inconsistent, changeable, variable, inconstant, irregular, fitful, unstable, varying, fluctuating, unreliable.
OPPOSITES consistent.

error noun **mistake,** inaccuracy, miscalculation, blunder, slip, oversight, misconception, delusion, misprint; Brit. informal boob.

erupt verb 1 *the volcano erupted:* **give out lava,** become active, explode. 2 *fighting erupted:* **break out,** flare up, start.

eruption noun 1 *a volcanic eruption:* **discharge,** explosion, lava flow, pyroclastic flow. 2 *an eruption of violence:* **outbreak,** flare-up, upsurge, outburst, explosion, wave, spate.

escalate verb 1 *prices have escalated:* **increase rapidly,** soar, rocket, shoot up, spiral; informal go through the roof. 2 *the dispute escalated:* **grow,** develop, mushroom, increase, heighten, intensify, accelerate. OPPOSITES plunge, subside.

escape verb 1 *he escaped from prison:* **run away/off,** get out, break out, break free, bolt, make one's getaway, slip away; Brit. informal do a runner. 2 *he escaped his pursuers:* **get away from,** elude, avoid, dodge, shake off; informal give someone the slip. 3 *they escaped injury:* **avoid,** evade, elude, cheat, sidestep, circumvent, steer clear of, shirk. 4 *lethal gas escaped:* **leak (out),** spill (out), seep (out), discharge, flow (out), pour (out).
noun 1 *his escape from prison:* **getaway,** breakout, flight. 2 *a gas escape:* **leak,** spill, seepage, discharge, outflow, outpouring.

escort noun *a police escort:* **guard,** bodyguard, protector, minder, attendant, chaperone, entourage, retinue, protection, convoy.
verb 1 *he was escorted home by the police:* **conduct,** accompany, guide, usher, shepherd, take. 2 *he escorted her in to dinner:*

accompany, partner, take, bring.

especially adverb 1 *work poured in, especially from Kent:* **mainly,** mostly, chiefly, particularly, principally, largely, primarily. 2 *a committee formed especially for the purpose:* **expressly,** specially, specifically, exclusively, just, particularly, explicitly. 3 *he is especially talented:* **exceptionally,** particularly, specially, unusually, extraordinarily, uncommonly, uniquely, remarkably, outstandingly; informal seriously, majorly.

essay noun **article,** composition, paper, dissertation, thesis, discourse, study, assignment, treatise, piece, feature; N. Amer. theme.

essence noun 1 *the very essence of economics:* **nature,** heart, core, substance, basis, principle, quintessence, soul, spirit, reality; informal nitty-gritty. 2 *essence of ginger:* **extract,** concentrate, elixir, juice, oil.

essential adjective 1 *it is essential to remove the paint:* **crucial,** key, vital, indispensable, all-important, critical, imperative. 2 *the essential simplicity of his style:* **basic,** inherent, fundamental, quintessential, intrinsic, underlying, characteristic, innate, primary.
OPPOSITES unimportant, incidental.
noun 1 *an essential for broadcasters:* **necessity,** prerequisite; informal must. 2 *the essentials of the job:* **fundamentals,** basics, rudiments, first principles, foundations, essence, basis, core, kernel, crux; informal nitty-

gritty, nuts and bolts.

establish verb **1** *they established an office in Moscow:* **set up**, start, initiate, institute, found, create, inaugurate. **2** *evidence to establish his guilt:* **prove**, demonstrate, show, indicate, determine, confirm.

establishment noun **1** *the establishment of a democracy:* **foundation**, institution, formation, inception, creation, installation, inauguration. **2** *a dressmaking establishment:* **business**, firm, company, concern, enterprise, venture, organization, operation; informal outfit. **3** *educational establishments:* **institution**, place, premises, institute. **4** *they dare to poke fun at the Establishment:* **the authorities**, the powers that be, the system, the ruling class.

estate noun **1** *the Balmoral estate:* **property**, grounds, garden(s), park, parkland, land(s), territory. **2** *a housing estate:* **area**, development, complex; Scottish scheme. **3** *a coffee estate:* **plantation**, farm, holding, forest, vineyard; N. Amer. ranch. **4** *he left an estate worth £610,000:* **assets**, capital, wealth, riches, holdings, fortune, property, effects, possessions, belongings.

esteem noun *she was held in high esteem:* **respect**, admiration, acclaim, appreciation, recognition, honour, reverence, estimation, regard.
verb *such ceramics are highly esteemed:* **respect**, admire, value, regard, appreciate, like, prize, treasure, revere.

estimate verb **1** *estimate the cost:* **calculate roughly**, approximate, guess, evaluate, judge. **2** *we estimate it to be worth £50,000:* **consider**, believe, reckon, deem, judge, rate.
noun *an estimate of the cost:* **rough calculation**, approximation, estimation, guess, costing, quotation, valuation, evaluation; informal guesstimate.

etch verb **engrave**, carve, inscribe, incise, score, mark, scratch, scrape.

etching noun **engraving**, print, plate.

eternal adjective **1** *eternal happiness:* **everlasting**, never-ending, endless, perpetual, undying, immortal, abiding, permanent, enduring. **2** *eternal vigilance:* **constant**, continual, continuous, perpetual, sustained, uninterrupted, unbroken, non-stop, round-the-clock.
OPPOSITES transient, intermittent.

eternity noun **1** *the memory will remain for eternity:* **ever**, all time, perpetuity. **2** (informal) *I waited an eternity for you:* **a long time**, an age, ages, a lifetime, hours, years, forever.

ethical adjective **1** *an ethical dilemma:* **moral**. **2** *ethical investment:* **morally correct**, right-minded, principled, good, moral, just, honourable, fair.
OPPOSITES unethical.

ethics plural noun **morals**, morality, values, principles, ideals, standards (of behaviour).

ethnic adjective **racial**, race-related, national, cultural, folk, tribal, ethnological.

euphoria noun **elation**, happiness, joy, delight, glee,

excitement, exhilaration, jubilation, exultation, ecstasy, bliss, rapture.
OPPOSITES misery.

evacuate verb 1 *local residents were evacuated:* **remove,** move out, take away. 2 *they evacuated the building:* **leave,** vacate, abandon, move out of, quit, withdraw from, retreat from, flee. 3 *police evacuated the area:* **clear,** empty.

evade verb 1 *they evaded the guards:* **elude,** avoid, dodge, escape (from), steer clear of, sidestep, lose, leave behind, shake off; informal give someone the slip. 2 *he evaded the question:* **avoid,** dodge, sidestep, bypass, skirt round; informal duck.
OPPOSITES confront.

evaluate verb **assess,** judge, gauge, rate, estimate, appraise, weigh up; informal size up.

evaporate verb 1 *the water evaporated:* **vaporize,** dry up. 2 *the feeling has evaporated:* **end,** pass (away), fizzle out, peter out, wear off, vanish, fade, disappear, melt away.
OPPOSITES condense, materialize.

evasive adjective **equivocal,** prevaricating, elusive, ambiguous, non-committal, vague, unclear, oblique.

even adjective 1 *an even surface:* **flat,** smooth, uniform, level, plane. 2 *an even temperature:* **uniform,** constant, steady, stable, consistent, unvarying, unchanging, regular. 3 *the score was even:* **level,** drawn, tied, all square, neck and neck; Brit. level pegging; informal even-steven(s).
OPPOSITES bumpy, irregular, unequal.

evening noun **dusk,** twilight, nightfall, sunset, sundown, night.

event noun 1 *an annual event:* **occurrence,** happening, incident, affair, occasion, phenomenon, function, gathering; informal do. 2 *a team event:* **competition,** contest, tournament, match, fixture, race, game, sport, discipline.

eventful adjective **busy,** action-packed, full, lively, active, hectic.
OPPOSITES dull.

eventual adjective **final,** ultimate, resulting, ensuing, consequent, subsequent.

eventually adverb **in the end,** in due course, by and by, in time, after a time, finally, at last, ultimately, in the long run, at the end of the day, one day, some day, sometime, sooner or later.

ever adverb 1 *the best I've ever done:* **at any time,** at any point, on any occasion, under any circumstances, on any account, until now. 2 *he was ever the optimist:* **always,** forever, eternally. 3 *an ever increasing rate of crime:* **continually,** constantly, always, endlessly, perpetually, incessantly.

everlasting adjective **eternal,** endless, never-ending, perpetual, undying, abiding, enduring, infinite.
OPPOSITES transient, occasional.

every determiner 1 *he exercised every day:* **each,** each and every, every single. 2 *we make every effort to satisfy our clients:* **all possible,** the utmost.
OPPOSITES no.

everybody pronoun **everyone,** every person, each person, all, one and all, all and sundry, the whole world, the public.

OPPOSITES nobody.

everyday adjective **1** *the everyday demands of a baby:* **daily,** day-to-day, ongoing. **2** *everyday drugs like aspirin:* **commonplace,** ordinary, common, usual, regular, familiar, conventional, routine, run-of-the-mill, standard, stock, household, domestic; Brit. common or garden.
OPPOSITES unusual.

everyone pronoun. See EVERYBODY.

everything pronoun every single thing, each thing, the (whole) lot, all; informal the works.
OPPOSITES nothing.

everywhere adverb all over, all around, in every nook and cranny, far and wide, near and far, high and low, {here, there, and everywhere}, the world over, worldwide; informal all over the place; Brit. informal all over the shop; N. Amer. informal all over the map.
OPPOSITES nowhere.

evidence noun **1** *evidence of his infidelity:* **proof,** confirmation, verification, substantiation, corroboration. **2** *the court accepted her evidence:* **testimony,** witness statement, declaration, submission; Law deposition, affidavit. **3** *evidence of a struggle:* **signs,** indications, marks, traces, suggestions, hints.

evident adjective obvious, apparent, noticeable, conspicuous, visible, discernible, clear, plain, manifest, patent; informal as clear as day.

evidently adverb **1** *he was evidently upset:* **obviously,** clearly, plainly, unmistakably, manifestly, patently. **2** *evidently, she believed him:* **seemingly,** apparently, as far as one can tell, from all appearances, on the face of it, it seems, it appears.

evil adjective **1** *an evil deed:* **wicked,** bad, wrong, immoral, sinful, vile, iniquitous, villainous, vicious, malicious, malevolent, demonic, diabolical, fiendish, dark, monstrous. **2** *an evil spirit:* **harmful,** bad, malign. **3** *evil weather:* **unpleasant,** disagreeable, nasty, horrible, foul, filthy, vile.
OPPOSITES good, benign, pleasant.
noun **1** *the evil in our midst:* **wickedness,** badness, wrongdoing, sin, sinfulness, immorality, vice, iniquity, corruption, villainy. **2** *nothing but evil will result:* **harm,** pain, misery, sorrow, suffering, trouble, disaster, misfortune, woe.
OPPOSITES good.

evoke verb bring to mind, put one in mind of, conjure up, summon (up), invoke, elicit, induce, kindle, awaken, arouse.

evolution noun **1** *the evolution of Bolshevism:* **development,** progress, rise, expansion, growth. **2** *his interest in evolution:* **natural selection,** Darwinism, adaptation, development.

evolve verb develop, progress, advance, grow, expand, spread.

exact adjective **1** *an exact description:* **precise,** accurate, correct, faithful, close, true, literal, strict, perfect. **2** *an exact record keeper:* **careful,** meticulous, painstaking, punctilious, conscientious,

e

scrupulous.
OPPOSITES inaccurate, careless.
verb **1** *he exacted certain promises:* **demand,** require, impose, extract, compel, force, wring. **2** *they exacted a terrible vengeance on him:* **inflict,** impose, administer, mete out, wreak.

exacting adjective **demanding,** stringent, testing, challenging, arduous, laborious, taxing, gruelling, punishing, hard, tough.
OPPOSITES easy, easy-going.

exactly adverb **1** *it's exactly as I expected:* **precisely,** entirely, absolutely, completely, totally, just, quite, in every respect. **2** *write it out exactly:* **accurately,** precisely, unerringly, faultlessly, perfectly, faithfully.

exaggerate verb **overstate,** overemphasize, overestimate, inflate, embellish, embroider, elaborate, overplay, dramatize; Brit. informal blow out of all proportion.
OPPOSITES understate.

examination noun **1** *artefacts spread out for examination:* **scrutiny,** inspection, perusal, study, investigation, consideration, analysis. **2** *a medical examination:* **inspection,** check-up, assessment, appraisal, test, scan. **3** *a school examination:* **test,** exam, assessment; N. Amer. quiz.

examine verb **1** *they examined the bank records:* **inspect,** scrutinize, investigate, look at, study, appraise, analyse, review, survey; informal check out. **2** *students were examined after a year:* **test,** quiz, question, assess, appraise.

example noun **1** *a fine example of Chinese porcelain:* **specimen,** sample, instance, case, illustration. **2** *we must follow their example:* **precedent,** lead, model, pattern, ideal, standard. **3** *he was hanged as an example to others:* **warning,** lesson, deterrent, disincentive.

excavate verb **unearth,** dig up, uncover, reveal, disinter, exhume, dig out, quarry, mine.

exceed verb **be more than,** be greater than, be over, go beyond, top, surpass.

excel verb **shine,** be excellent, be outstanding, be skilful, be talented, stand out, be second to none.

excellence noun **distinction,** quality, superiority, brilliance, greatness, calibre, eminence.

excellent adjective **very good,** superb, outstanding, exceptional, marvellous, wonderful, splendid; informal terrific, fantastic.
OPPOSITES inferior.

except preposition **excluding,** not including, excepting, except for, omitting, not counting, but, besides, apart from, aside from, barring, bar, other than; informal outside of.
OPPOSITES including.

exception noun **anomaly,** irregularity, deviation, special case, peculiarity, abnormality, oddity.

exceptional adjective **1** *the drought was exceptional:* **unusual,** abnormal, atypical, out of the ordinary, rare, unprecedented, unexpected, surprising. **2** *her exceptional ability:* **outstanding,** extraordinary, remarkable, special, phenomenal, prodigious.

OPPOSITES normal, average.

excerpt noun **extract**, part, section, piece, portion, snippet, clip, citation, quotation, quote, line, passage, fragment.

excess noun **1** *an excess of calcium:* **surplus**, surfeit, over-abundance, superabundance, superfluity, glut. **2** *the excess is turned into fat:* **extra**, surplus, remainder, rest, residue. **3** *a life of excess:* **overindulgence**, intemperance, immoderation, profligacy, extravagance, self-indulgence.
OPPOSITES lack, restraint.
adjective *excess oil:* **surplus**, superfluous, redundant, unwanted, unneeded, excessive, extra.

excessive adjective **1** *excessive alcohol consumption:* **immoderate**, intemperate, overindulgent, unrestrained, uncontrolled, extravagant. **2** *the cost is excessive:* **exorbitant**, extortionate, unreasonable, outrageous, uncalled for, inordinate, unwarranted, disproportionate; informal over the top.

exchange noun **1** *the exchange of ideas:* **interchange**, trade, trading, swapping, traffic, trafficking. **2** *a brief exchange:* **conversation**, dialogue, chat, talk, discussion.
verb *we exchanged shirts:* **trade**, swap, switch, change.

excite verb **1** *the prospect of a holiday excited me:* **thrill**, exhilarate, animate, enliven, rouse, stir, stimulate, galvanize. **2** *his clothes excited envy:* **provoke**, stir up, rouse, arouse, kindle, trigger, spark off, incite, cause.
OPPOSITES bore.

excitement noun **1** *the*

excitement of seeing a leopard in the wild: **thrill**, pleasure, delight, joy; informal buzz. **2** *excitement in her eyes:* **exhilaration**, elation, animation, enthusiasm, eagerness, anticipation.

exciting adjective **thrilling**, exhilarating, stirring, rousing, stimulating, intoxicating, electrifying, invigorating, gripping, compelling, powerful, dramatic.

exclaim verb **cry out**, declare, proclaim, blurt out, call out, shout, yell.

exclude verb **1** *women were excluded from the club:* **keep out**, deny access to, shut out, bar, ban, prohibit. **2** *the clause excluded any judicial review:* **rule out**, preclude. **3** *the price excludes postage:* be **exclusive of**, not include.
OPPOSITES admit, include, allow for.

exclusive adjective **1** *an exclusive club:* **select**, chic, high-class, elite, fashionable, stylish, elegant, premier; Brit. upmarket; informal posh, classy; Brit. informal swish. **2** *a room for your exclusive use:* **sole**, unshared, unique, individual, personal, private. **3** *prices exclusive of VAT:* **not including**, excluding, leaving out, omitting, excepting.
OPPOSITES shared, inclusive.

excursion noun **outing**, trip, jaunt, expedition, journey, tour, day trip, day out, drive, run; informal spin.

excuse verb **1** *please excuse me:* **forgive**, pardon. **2** *such conduct cannot be excused:* **justify**, defend, condone, forgive, overlook, disregard, ignore, tolerate, explain, mitigate. **3** *she*

e

was excused from her duties: **let off,** release, relieve, exempt, absolve, free.
OPPOSITES punish, blame, condemn.
noun **1** *that's no excuse for stealing:* **justification,** defence, reason, explanation, mitigating circumstances, mitigation. **2** *an excuse to get away:* **pretext,** pretence; Brit. get-out; informal story, alibi.

execute verb **1** *he executed a series of financial deals:* **carry out,** accomplish, bring off/about, implement, achieve, complete, engineer; informal pull off. **2** *he was finally executed:* **put to death,** kill, hang, behead, electrocute, shoot.

execution noun **1** *the execution of the plan:* **implementation,** carrying out, performance, accomplishment, bringing off/about, attainment, realization. **2** *public execution:* **killing,** capital punishment, the death penalty.

executive adjective *executive powers:* **administrative,** managerial, decision-making, law-making, governing, controlling.
noun **1** *the company's chief executive:* **director,** manager, senior official, administrator; informal boss, exec, suit. **2** *the future role of the executive:* **administration,** management, directorate, government, authority.

exemplary adjective **perfect,** ideal, model, faultless, flawless, impeccable, irreproachable.
OPPOSITES deplorable.

exemplify verb **typify,** epitomize, be an example of, be representative of, symbolize, illustrate, demonstrate.

exempt adjective **free,** not liable, not subject, immune, excepted, excused, absolved.
OPPOSITES subject to.
verb **excuse,** free, release, exclude, grant immunity, spare, absolve; informal let off.
OPPOSITES oblige.

exemption noun **immunity,** exception, dispensation, indemnity, exclusion, freedom, release, relief, absolution.

exercise noun **1** *exercise improves your heart:* **physical activity,** a workout, working out, movement, training. **2** *translation exercises:* **task,** piece of work, problem, assignment, practice. **3** *a military exercise:* **manoeuvre,** operation, deployment.
verb **1** *she exercised every day:* **work out,** do exercises, train. **2** *he must learn to exercise patience:* **use,** employ, make use of, utilize, practise, apply. **3** *the problem continued to exercise him:* **concern,** occupy, worry, trouble, bother, disturb, prey on someone's mind.

exert verb **bring to bear,** apply, use, utilize, deploy.
■ **exert oneself** work hard, labour, toil, make an effort, endeavour, slog away, push oneself.

exhaust verb **1** *the effort had exhausted him:* **tire out,** wear out, overtire, fatigue, weary, drain; informal take it out of one, shatter; Brit. informal knacker; N. Amer. informal poop, tucker out. **2** *the country has exhausted its reserves:* **use up,** get through, consume, finish, deplete, spend, empty, drain; informal blow.
OPPOSITES invigorate, replenish.

exhaustion noun **tiredness,** overtiredness, fatigue,

weariness.

exhibit verb 1 *the paintings were exhibited in Glasgow:* **display,** show, put on display, unveil, present. 2 *Luke exhibited signs of jealousy:* **show,** reveal, display, manifest, indicate, demonstrate, express. noun *an exhibit at the British Museum:* **item,** piece, artefact, display, collection.

exhibition noun 1 *a photography exhibition:* **display,** show, showing, presentation, exposition. 2 *a convincing exhibition of concern:* **display,** show, demonstration, manifestation, expression.

exhilarating adjective **thrilling,** exciting, invigorating, stimulating, intoxicating, electrifying.

exile noun 1 *his exile from his homeland:* **banishment,** expulsion, deportation, eviction, isolation. 2 *political exiles:* **expatriate,** émigré, deportee, displaced person, refugee.

exist verb 1 *animals that existed long ago:* **live,** be alive, be, be present. 2 *the liberal climate that now exists:* **prevail,** occur, be found, be in existence, be the case. 3 *she had to exist on a low income:* **survive,** subsist, live, support oneself, manage, make do, get by, scrape by, make ends meet.

existence noun 1 *the industry's continued existence:* **survival,** continuation. 2 *her suburban existence:* **way of life,** life, lifestyle, situation.
■ **in existence** existing, alive, surviving, remaining, extant, existent, in circulation, current.

exit noun 1 *a fire exit:* **way out,** door, escape route, egress.

2 *take the second exit:* **turning,** turn-off, junction. 3 *his sudden exit:* **departure,** leaving, withdrawal, going, retreat, flight, exodus, escape.
OPPOSITES entrance, arrival.
verb *the doctor had just exited:* **leave,** go out, depart, withdraw, retreat.
OPPOSITES enter.

exotic adjective 1 *exotic birds:* **foreign,** non-native, alien, tropical. 2 *exotic places:* **foreign,** faraway, far-off, far-flung, distant. 3 *Linda's exotic appearance:* **striking,** colourful, eye-catching, unusual, unconventional, extravagant, outlandish.
OPPOSITES native, nearby, conventional.

expand verb 1 *metals expand when heated:* **enlarge,** increase in size, swell, lengthen, stretch, spread, thicken, fill out. 2 *the company is expanding:* **grow,** enlarge, increase in size, extend, augment, broaden, widen, develop, diversify, build up, branch out, spread.
OPPOSITES contract.
■ **expand on** elaborate on, enlarge on, go into detail about, flesh out, develop.

expansion noun 1 *expansion and contraction:* **enlargement,** swelling, lengthening, elongation, stretching, thickening. 2 *the expansion of the company:* **growth,** increase in size, enlargement, extension, development, diversification, spread.
OPPOSITES contraction.

expect verb 1 *I expect she'll be late:* **suppose,** presume, imagine, assume, surmise; informal guess, reckon; N. Amer. informal figure. 2 *a 10 per cent* rise was expected: **anticipate,** envisage, await, look for, hope for, look forward to, contemplate, bargain for/on, predict, forecast. **3** we expect total loyalty: **require,** ask for, call for, want, insist on, demand.

expectation noun **1** her expectations were unrealistic: **supposition,** assumption, presumption, conjecture, calculation, prediction, hope. **2** tense with expectation: **anticipation,** expectancy, eagerness, excitement, suspense.

expedition noun journey, voyage, tour, safari, trek, mission, quest, hike, trip.

expel verb throw out, bar, ban, debar, drum out, banish, exile, deport, evict; informal chuck out.
OPPOSITES admit.

expense noun cost, expenditure, spending, outlay, outgoings, payment, price, charge, fees, overheads, tariff, bill.
OPPOSITES income, profit.

expensive adjective costly, dear, high-priced, overpriced, exorbitant, extortionate; informal steep, stiff, pricey.
OPPOSITES cheap.

experience noun
1 qualifications and experience: skill, practical knowledge, understanding, background, track record, history; informal know-how. **2** an enjoyable experience: incident, occurrence, event, happening, episode, adventure. **3** his first experience of business: involvement in, participation in, contact with, acquaintance with, exposure to.
verb they experience daily harassment: **undergo,** go

through, encounter, face, meet, come across, come up against.

experienced adjective knowledgeable, skilful, skilled, expert, proficient, trained, competent, capable, seasoned, practised, mature, veteran.
OPPOSITES inexperienced.

experiment noun the calculations were confirmed by experiment: **test,** investigation, trial, examination, observation, research, assessment, evaluation, appraisal, analysis, study.
verb they experimented with new ideas: **carry out experiments,** test, trial, try out, assess, appraise, evaluate.

experimental adjective **1** the experimental stage: **exploratory,** investigational, trial, test, pilot, speculative, tentative, preliminary. **2** experimental music: **new,** innovative, creative, radical, avant-garde, alternative, unorthodox, unconventional, cutting-edge.

expert noun specialist, authority, pundit, maestro, virtuoso, master, wizard, connoisseur, aficionado; informal ace, pro, hotshot; Brit. informal dab hand; N. Amer. informal maven.
OPPOSITES amateur.
adjective skilful, skilled, adept, accomplished, experienced, practised, knowledgeable, talented, masterly, virtuoso; informal ace, crack, mean.
OPPOSITES incompetent.

expertise noun skill, prowess, proficiency, competence, knowledge, ability, aptitude, capability; informal know-how.

expire verb **1** my contract has expired: **run out,** become invalid, become void, lapse, end, finish, stop, terminate.

2 *the spot where he expired:* die, pass away, breathe one's last; informal kick the bucket, croak; Brit. informal snuff it, peg out; N. Amer. informal buy the farm.

explain verb **1** *he explained the procedure:* **describe**, make clear, spell out, put into words, define, elucidate, expound, clarify, throw light on. **2** *that could explain his behaviour:* **account for**, give a reason for, excuse.

explanation noun **1** *an explanation of his theory:* **clarification**, description, statement, interpretation, definition, commentary. **2** *I owe you an explanation:* **account**, reason, justification, answer, excuse, defence, vindication.

explicit adjective **1** *explicit instructions:* **clear**, plain, straightforward, crystal clear, precise, exact, specific, unequivocal, unambiguous, detailed. **2** *sexually explicit material:* **graphic**, candid, full-frontal, uncensored.
OPPOSITES vague, tasteful, decent.

explode verb **1** *a bomb has exploded:* **blow up**, detonate, go off, burst, erupt. **2** *exploding an atomic device:* **detonate**, set off, let off, discharge. **3** *he just exploded:* **lose one's temper**, blow up; informal fly off the handle, hit the roof, blow one's top; Brit. informal go spare; N. Amer. informal blow one's lid/stack.
4 *the city's exploding population:* **increase rapidly**, mushroom, snowball, escalate, burgeon, rocket. **5** *exploding the myths about men:* **disprove**, refute, rebut, repudiate, debunk, give the lie to; informal shoot full of holes, blow out of the water.
OPPOSITES shrink.

exploit verb **1** *we should exploit this opportunity:* **utilize**, make use of, turn/put to good use, make the most of, capitalize on, benefit from; informal cash in on. **2** *exploiting the workers:* **take advantage of**, abuse, impose on, treat unfairly, misuse, ill-treat; informal walk (all) over.
noun *his exploits brought him notoriety:* **feat**, deed, act, adventure, stunt, escapade, achievement.

exploitation noun taking advantage, abuse, misuse, ill-treatment, unfair treatment, oppression.

exploration noun investigation, study, survey, research, inspection, examination, scrutiny, observation.

explore verb **1** *exploring Iceland:* **travel through**, tour, survey, scout, reconnoitre. **2** *they explored the possibilities:* **investigate**, look into, consider, examine, research, survey, scrutinize, study, review; informal check out.

explosion noun **1** *Ed heard the explosion:* **detonation**, eruption, bang, blast, boom. **2** *an explosion of anger:* **outburst**, flare-up, outbreak, eruption, storm, rush, surge, fit, paroxysm. **3** *a population explosion:* **sudden increase**, mushrooming, snowballing, escalation, multiplication, burgeoning, rocketing.

explosive adjective **1** *explosive gases:* **volatile**, inflammable, flammable, combustible, incendiary. **2** *Marco's explosive temper:* **fiery**, stormy, violent, volatile, passionate,

e

tempestuous, turbulent, touchy, irascible. **3** *an explosive situation:* **tense,** highly charged, overwrought, dangerous, perilous, hazardous, sensitive, delicate, unstable, volatile.
OPPOSITES inert, cool, stable.
noun *stocks of explosives:* **bomb,** charge, incendiary (device).

expose verb **1** *at low tide the rocks are exposed:* **reveal,** uncover, lay bare. **2** *he was exposed to radiation:* **lay open,** subject, put at risk of, put in jeopardy of, leave unprotected from. **3** *they were exposed to new ideas:* **introduce to,** bring into contact with, make aware of, familiarize with, acquaint with. **4** *he was exposed as a liar:* **uncover,** reveal, unveil, unmask, detect, find out, denounce, condemn; informal blow the whistle on.
OPPOSITES cover, protect from, insulate from, protect.

exposure noun **1** *suffering from exposure:* **frostbite,** cold, hypothermia. **2** *the exposure of a banking fraud:* **uncovering,** revelation, disclosure, unveiling, unmasking, discovery, detection. **3** *we're getting a lot of exposure:* **publicity,** advertising, public attention, media interest; informal hype.

express¹ verb **communicate,** convey, indicate, show, demonstrate, reveal, put across/over, get across/over, articulate, put into words, voice, give voice to, state, air, give vent to.
■ **express oneself** communicate one's thoughts/opinions/views, put thoughts into words, speak one's mind, say what's on one's mind.

express² adjective **rapid,** swift, fast, high-speed, non-stop, direct.
OPPOSITES slow.

express³ adjective **1** *it was his express wish:* **explicit,** clear, direct, plain, distinct, unambiguous, categorical. **2** *his express purpose was to do aid work:* **sole,** specific, particular, special, specified.
OPPOSITES vague, implied.

expression noun **1** *the free expression of their views:* **utterance,** uttering, voicing, declaration, articulation. **2** *an expression of sympathy:* **indication,** demonstration, show, exhibition, token, communication, illustration. **3** *a sad expression:* **look,** appearance, air, manner, countenance. **4** *a well-known expression:* **idiom,** phrase, term, proverb, saying, adage, maxim. **5** *put more expression into it:* **emotion,** feeling, spirit, passion, intensity, style.

expressive adjective **1** *an expressive shrug:* **eloquent,** meaningful, demonstrative, suggestive. **2** *an expressive song:* **emotional,** passionate, poignant, moving, stirring, emotionally charged.
OPPOSITES undemonstrative, inexpressive.

expulsion noun **1** *expulsion from the party:* **removal,** debarment, dismissal, exclusion, ejection, banishment, eviction. **2** *the expulsion of waste:* **discharge,** ejection, excretion, voiding, evacuation, elimination, passing.
OPPOSITES admission.

exquisite adjective **1** *exquisite antiques:* **beautiful,** lovely, elegant, fine, delicate, fragile, dainty, subtle. **2** *exquisite taste:* **discriminating**, discerning, sensitive, fastidious, refined.

extend verb **1** *we've extended the kitchen:* **expand**, enlarge, increase, lengthen, widen, broaden. **2** *the garden extends to the road:* **continue**, carry on, stretch, reach. **3** *we have extended our range:* **widen**, expand, broaden, augment, supplement, increase, add to, enhance, develop. **4** *extending the life of parliament:* **prolong**, lengthen, increase, stretch out, protract, spin out, string out. **5** *he extended a hand:* **hold out**, reach out, hold forth, stretch out, offer, give, proffer. **6** *we wish to extend our thanks:* **offer**, proffer, give, accord. OPPOSITES reduce, shorten, withdraw.

■ **extend to** include, take in, incorporate, encompass.

extension noun **1** *they are planning an extension:* **addition**, add-on, adjunct, annex, wing. **2** *an extension of our knowledge:* **expansion**, increase, enlargement, widening, broadening, deepening, augmentation, enhancement, development, growth. **3** *an extension of opening hours:* **prolongation**, lengthening, increase. OPPOSITES restriction, shortening.

extensive adjective **1** *extensive grounds:* **large**, sizeable, substantial, considerable, ample, great, vast. **2** *extensive knowledge:* **comprehensive**, thorough, exhaustive, broad, wide, wide-ranging, catholic.

extent noun **1** *two acres in extent:* **area**, size, expanse, length, proportions,

dimensions. **2** *the full extent of her illness:* **degree**, scale, level, magnitude, scope, size, reach, range.

exterior adjective *the exterior surface:* **outer**, outside, outermost, outward, external. OPPOSITES interior.
noun *a beautiful exterior:* **outside**, external surface, outward appearance, facade. OPPOSITES interior.

external adjective **1** *an external wall:* **outer**, outside, outermost, outward, exterior. **2** *an external examiner:* **outside**, independent, visiting. OPPOSITES internal.

extinct adjective **1** *an extinct species:* **vanished**, lost, gone, died out, wiped out, destroyed. **2** *an extinct volcano:* **inactive**. OPPOSITES living, dormant.

extinction noun **dying out**, disappearance, vanishing, extermination, destruction, elimination, eradication, annihilation.

extra adjective **additional**, more, added, supplementary, further, auxiliary, ancillary, subsidiary, secondary.
adverb **exceptionally**, particularly, specially, especially, extremely.
noun **addition**, supplement, bonus, adjunct, addendum, add-on.

extract verb **1** *he extracted the cassette:* **take out**, draw out, pull out, remove, withdraw, release, extricate. **2** *they extracted a confession:* **wrest**, exact, wring, screw, squeeze, obtain by force, extort. **3** *the roots are crushed to extract the juice:* **squeeze out**, press out, obtain. OPPOSITES insert.

e

e
f

noun **1** *an extract from his article:* **excerpt,** passage, citation, quotation. **2** *an extract of ginseng:* **distillation,** distillate, concentrate, essence, juice.

extraordinary adjective **1** *an extraordinary coincidence:* **remarkable,** exceptional, amazing, astonishing, astounding, sensational, stunning, incredible, unbelievable, phenomenal; informal **fantastic. 2** *extraordinary speed:* **very great,** tremendous, enormous, immense, prodigious, stupendous, monumental.
OPPOSITES unremarkable, tiny.

extravagant adjective **1** *an extravagant lifestyle:* **spendthrift,** profligate, wasteful, prodigal, lavish. **2** *extravagant praise:* **excessive,** immoderate, exaggerated, gushing, unrestrained, effusive, fulsome. **3** *decorated in an extravagant style:* **ornate,** elaborate, fancy, over-elaborate, ostentatious, exaggerated; informal **flashy.**
OPPOSITES thrifty, moderate, plain.

extreme adjective **1** *extreme danger:* **utmost,** (very) great, greatest (possible), maximum, great, acute, enormous, severe,

serious. **2** *extreme measures:* **drastic,** serious, desperate, dire, radical, far-reaching, draconian; Brit. swingeing. **3** *extreme views:* **radical,** extremist, immoderate, fanatical, revolutionary, subversive, militant. **4** *extreme sports:* **dangerous,** hazardous, risky, high-risk, adventurous; informal white-knuckle. **5** *the extreme north-west:* **furthest,** farthest, utmost, remotest, ultra-.
OPPOSITES slight, moderate, safe, near.
noun *the two extremes:* **opposite,** antithesis, side of the coin, (opposite) pole, limit, extremity, contrast.

extremely adverb **very,** exceptionally, especially, extraordinarily, tremendously, immensely, hugely, supremely, highly, mightily; informal awfully, terribly, seriously; Brit. informal jolly; N. Amer. informal mighty.
OPPOSITES slightly.

extremist noun **fanatic,** radical, zealot, fundamentalist, hardliner, militant, activist.
OPPOSITES moderate.

eye verb **look at,** observe, view, gaze at, stare at, regard, contemplate, survey, scrutinize, consider, glance at, watch; informal check out, size up; N. Amer. informal eyeball.

Ff

fable noun **parable,** allegory, myth, legend, story.
fabric noun **1** *the finest fabrics:* **cloth,** material, textile. **2** *the fabric of society:* **structure,** construction, make-up,

organization, framework, essence.

fabulous adjective **1** *fabulous salaries:* **stupendous,** prodigious, phenomenal, exceptional, fantastic,

breathtaking, staggering, unthinkable, unimaginable, incredible, undreamed of.
2 (informal) *we had a fabulous time.* See **EXCELLENT**.

facade noun **1** *a half-timbered facade:* **front**, frontage, face, elevation, exterior, outside. **2** *a facade of bonhomie:* **show**, front, appearance, pretence, simulation, affectation, act, charade, mask, veneer.

face noun **1** *a beautiful face:* **countenance**, physiognomy, features, profile. **2** *her face grew sad:* **expression**, look, appearance, countenance. **3** *he made a face:* **grimace**, scowl, wince, frown, pout. **4** *a cube has six faces:* **side**, aspect, surface, plane, facet, wall, elevation.
verb **1** *the hotel faces the sea:* **look out on**, front on to, look towards, look over/across, overlook, be opposite (to).
2 *you'll have to face the truth:* **accept**, get used to, adjust to, learn to live with, cope with, deal with, come to terms with, become resigned to. **3** *the problems facing our police force:* **beset**, worry, trouble, confront, torment, plague, bedevil. **4** *he faced the challenge:* **brave**, face up to, encounter, meet (head-on), confront. **5** *a wall faced with flint:* **cover**, clad, veneer, surface, dress, laminate, coat, line.

facelift noun **renovation**, redecoration, refurbishment, revamp, makeover.

facet noun **aspect**, feature, side, dimension, strand, component, element.

facilitate verb **make easy/easier**, ease, make possible, smooth the way for, enable,

assist, help (along), aid, promote, hasten, speed up.
OPPOSITES impede.

facility noun **1** *car-parking facilities:* **provision**, space, means, equipment. **2** *the camera has a zoom facility:* **feature**, setting, mode, option. **3** *a wealth of local facilities:* **amenity**, resource, service. **4** *a medical facility:* **establishment**, centre, station, location, premises, site, post, base.

fact noun **1** *a fact we cannot ignore:* **reality**, actuality, certainty, truth, verity, gospel. **2** *every fact was double-checked:* **detail**, particular, finding, point, factor, feature, characteristic, aspect; (**facts**) information, data.
OPPOSITES lie, fiction.

faction noun **1** *a faction of the Liberal Party:* **clique**, coterie, caucus, bloc, camp, group, grouping, splinter group. **2** *the council was split by faction:* **infighting**, dissent, dispute, discord, strife, conflict, friction, argument, disagreement, disunity, schism.
OPPOSITES agreement, unity.

factor noun **element**, part, component, ingredient, strand, constituent, feature, facet, aspect, characteristic, consideration, influence, circumstance.

factory noun **works**, plant, yard, mill, facility, workshop, shop.

factual adjective **truthful**, true, accurate, authentic, historical, genuine, true-to-life, correct, exact.
OPPOSITES fictitious.

faculty noun **1** *the faculty of speech:* **power**, capability, capacity, facility; (**faculties**) senses, wits, reason,

f

intelligence. **2** *the arts faculty:* **department**, school.

fad noun craze, vogue, trend, fashion, mode, mania, rage.

fade verb **1** *the paintwork has faded:* **become pale**, become bleached, become washed out, lose colour, discolour.
2 *sunlight had faded the picture:* **bleach**, wash out, make pale, blanch. **3** *the afternoon light began to fade:* **(grow) dim**, grow faint, fail, dwindle, die away, wane, disappear, vanish, decline, melt away.
4 *Communism was fading away:* **decline**, die out, diminish, decay, crumble, collapse, fail.
OPPOSITES brighten, grow.

fail verb **1** *the scheme had failed:* **be unsuccessful**, fall through, fall flat, collapse, founder, backfire, miscarry, come unstuck; informal flop, bomb. **2** *he failed his examination:* **be unsuccessful in**, not make the grade; informal flunk. **3** *his friends had failed him:* **let down**, disappoint, desert, abandon, betray, be disloyal to.
4 *the ventilation system has failed:* **break (down)**, stop working, cut out, crash, malfunction, go wrong; informal conk out; Brit. informal pack up.
5 *Ceri's health was failing:* **deteriorate**, degenerate, decline, fade. **6** *900 businesses are failing a week:* **collapse**, crash, go under, go bankrupt, cease trading, be wound up; informal fold, go bust.
OPPOSITES succeed, pass, work, improve, thrive.

failing noun fault, shortcoming, weakness, imperfection, deficiency, defect, flaw, frailty.
OPPOSITES strength.

failure noun **1** *the failure of the*

escape attempt: lack of success, defeat, collapse, foundering.
2 *the scheme had been a failure:* **fiasco**, debacle, catastrophe, disaster; informal flop, washout, dead loss. **3** *she was a failure:* **loser**, underachiever, ne'er-do-well, disappointment; informal no-hoper. **4** *a failure on my part:* **negligence**, dereliction, omission, oversight. **5** *the failure of the heating system:* **breaking down**, breakdown, malfunction, crash. **6** *company failures:* **collapse**, crash, bankruptcy, insolvency, liquidation, closure.
OPPOSITES success.

faint adjective **1** *a faint mark:* **indistinct**, vague, unclear, indefinite, ill-defined, imperceptible, pale, light, faded. **2** *a faint cry:* **quiet**, muted, muffled, stifled, feeble, weak, low, soft, gentle. **3** *a faint possibility:* **slight**, slender, slim, small, tiny, remote, vague.
4 *I suddenly felt faint:* **dizzy**, giddy, light-headed, unsteady; informal woozy.
OPPOSITES clear, loud, strong.
verb *he nearly fainted:* **pass out**, lose consciousness, black out, keel over, swoon.
noun *a dead faint:* **blackout**, fainting fit, loss of consciousness, coma, swoon.

faintly adverb **1** *Maria called his name faintly:* **indistinctly**, softly, gently, weakly, in a whisper. **2** *he looked faintly bewildered:* **slightly**, vaguely, somewhat, quite, fairly, rather, a little, a bit, a touch, a shade.
OPPOSITES loudly, extremely.

fair¹ adjective **1** *the courts were generally fair:* **just**, equitable, honest, impartial, unbiased, unprejudiced, neutral, even-

handed. **2** *fair weather:* **fine,** dry, bright, clear, sunny, cloudless. **3** *fair hair:* **blond(e),** yellow, golden, flaxen, light. **4** *fair skin:* **pale,** light, pink, white, creamy. **5** *a fair achievement:* **reasonable,** passable, tolerable, satisfactory, acceptable, respectable, decent, all right, good enough, pretty good.
OPPOSITES unfair, inclement, dark, poor.

fair² noun **1** *a country fair:* **fête,** gala, festival, carnival. **2** *an antiques fair:* **market,** bazaar, exchange, sale. **3** *an art fair:* **exhibition,** display, show, exposition.

fairly adverb **1** *we were treated fairly:* **justly,** equitably, impartially, without bias, without prejudice, even-handedly, equally. **2** *in fairly good condition:* **reasonably,** passably, tolerably, adequately, moderately, quite, relatively, comparatively; informal **pretty. 3** *he fairly hauled her along the street:* **positively,** really, simply, actually, absolutely.
OPPOSITES unfairly.

fairy noun **sprite,** pixie, elf, imp, brownie, puck, leprechaun.

faith noun **1** *our faith in him:* **trust,** belief, confidence, conviction, reliance. **2** *she died for her faith:* **religion,** belief, creed, church, persuasion, ideology, doctrine.
OPPOSITES mistrust.

faithful adjective **1** *his faithful assistant:* **loyal,** constant, true, devoted, staunch, steadfast, dedicated, committed, trusty, dependable, reliable. **2** *a faithful copy:* **accurate,** precise, exact, true, strict, realistic, authentic.
OPPOSITES disloyal, inaccurate.

fake noun **1** *the sculpture was a fake:* **forgery,** counterfeit, copy, pirated copy, sham, fraud, hoax, imitation; informal **phoney,** rip-off. **2** *that doctor is a fake:* **charlatan,** quack, sham, fraud, impostor; informal **phoney.**
adjective **1** *fake banknotes:* **counterfeit,** forged, fraudulent, sham, pirated, false, bogus; informal **phoney,** dud. **2** *fake diamonds:* **imitation,** artificial, synthetic, simulated, reproduction, replica, ersatz, man-made, dummy, false, mock; informal **pretend. 3** *a fake accent:* **feigned,** faked, put-on, assumed, invented, affected.
OPPOSITES genuine, real, authentic.
verb **1** *the certificate was faked:* **forge,** counterfeit, falsify, copy, pirate. **2** *he faked a yawn:* **feign,** pretend, simulate, put on, affect.

fall verb **1** *bombs began to fall:* **drop,** descend, plummet, plunge, sink, dive, tumble, cascade. **2** *he tripped and fell:* **topple over,** tumble over, fall down/over, collapse. **3** *the water level began to fall:* **subside,** recede, drop, retreat, fall away, go down, sink. **4** *inflation will fall:* **decrease,** decline, diminish, fall off, drop off, lessen, dwindle, plummet, plunge, slump, sink. **5** *those who fell in the war:* **die,** perish, lose one's life, be killed, be slain, be lost; informal **bite the dust,** buy it. **6** *the town fell to the barbarians:* **surrender,** yield, submit, give in, capitulate, succumb, be taken, be overwhelmed. **7** *Easter falls on 23rd April:* **occur,** take place, happen, come about.
OPPOSITES rise.

f

noun **1** *an accidental fall:* **tumble,** trip, spill, topple. **2** *a fall in sales:* **decline,** fall-off, drop, decrease, cut, dip, reduction, slump; informal **crash.** **3** *the fall of the Roman Empire:* **downfall,** collapse, failure, decline, destruction, overthrow, demise. **4** *the fall of Berlin:* **surrender,** capitulation, yielding, submission, defeat. **5** *a steep fall down to the ocean:* **descent,** slope, slant.
OPPOSITES rise.

■ **fall back** retreat, withdraw, back off, draw back, pull back, move away. ■ **fall back on** resort to, turn to, look to, call on, have recourse to. ■ **fall for** (informal) **1** *she fell for John:* fall in love with, take a fancy to, be smitten by, be attracted to. **2** *she won't fall for that trick:* be deceived by, be duped by, be fooled by, be taken in by; informal go for, buy, swallow. ■ **fall out** quarrel, argue, row, fight, squabble, bicker. ■ **fall through** fail, be unsuccessful, come to nothing, miscarry, go awry, collapse, founder, come to grief.

false adjective **1** *a false report:* **incorrect,** untrue, wrong, inaccurate, untruthful, fictitious, fabricated, invented, made up, trumped up, counterfeit, forged, fraudulent. **2** *a false friend:* **disloyal,** faithless, unfaithful, untrue, inconstant, treacherous, double-crossing, deceitful, dishonest, duplicitous. **3** *false pearls:* **fake,** artificial, imitation, synthetic, simulated, reproduction, replica, ersatz, man-made, dummy, mock; informal **pretend.**
OPPOSITES correct, faithful, genuine.

falter verb **hesitate,** delay, drag one's feet, stall, waver, vacillate, be indecisive, be irresolute; Brit. hum and haw; informal sit on the fence.

fame noun **renown,** celebrity, stardom, popularity, prominence, distinction, esteem, eminence, repute.
OPPOSITES obscurity.

familiar adjective **1** *a familiar task:* **well known,** recognized, accustomed, everyday, day-to-day, habitual, customary, routine. **2** *are you familiar with the subject?* **acquainted,** conversant, versed, knowledgeable, well informed, au fait; informal well up on. **3** *he is too familiar with the teachers:* **overfamiliar,** presumptuous, disrespectful, forward, bold, impudent, impertinent.
OPPOSITES unfamiliar, formal.

familiarity noun **1** *a familiarity with politics:* **acquaintance with,** awareness of, knowledge of, experience of, insight into, understanding of, comprehension of. **2** *she was affronted by his familiarity:* **overfamiliarity,** presumption, forwardness, boldness, cheek, impudence, impertinence, disrespect. **3** *our familiarity allows us to tease each other:* **closeness,** intimacy, friendliness, friendship.

family noun **1** *I met his family:* **relatives,** relations, (next of) kin, clan, tribe; informal **folks.** **2** *she is married with a family:* **children,** little ones, youngsters; informal **kids.** **3** *the cat family:* **species,** order, class, genus, phylum.

famine noun **1** *a nation threatened by famine:* **food**

shortage, hunger, starvation, malnutrition. **2** *the cotton famine:* **shortage,** scarcity, lack, dearth, deficiency, insufficiency, shortfall, drought.
OPPOSITES plenty.

famous adjective **well known,** prominent, famed, popular, renowned, noted, eminent, distinguished, celebrated.
OPPOSITES unknown.

fan noun **enthusiast,** devotee, admirer, lover, supporter, follower, disciple, adherent; informal buff.

fanatic noun **extremist,** militant, dogmatist, bigot, zealot, radical, diehard; informal maniac.

fancy verb **1** (Brit. informal) *I fancied a change of scene:* **wish for,** want, desire, long for, yearn for, crave, thirst for, hanker after, dream of, covet. **2** (Brit. informal) *she fancied him:* **be attracted to,** find attractive, be infatuated with, be taken with; informal have a crush on, carry a torch for. **3** *I fancied I could see lights:* **imagine,** believe, think, be under the impression; informal reckon.
adjective *fancy clothes:* **elaborate,** ornate, ornamental, decorative, embellished, intricate, ostentatious, showy, flamboyant, lavish, expensive; informal flashy, snazzy, posh, classy; Brit. informal swish.
OPPOSITES plain.
noun **1** *a passing fancy:* **whim,** foible, urge, whimsy, fascination, fad, craze, enthusiasm, passion, caprice. **2** *a flight of fancy:* **fantasy,** dreaming, imagination, delusion, creativity.

fantastic adjective **1** *a fantastic notion:* **fanciful,** extravagant, extraordinary, irrational, wild, absurd, far-fetched, unthinkable, implausible, improbable, unlikely; informal crazy. **2** *fantastic shapes:* **strange,** weird, bizarre, outlandish, grotesque, surreal, exotic. **3** (informal) *a fantastic car:* **marvellous,** wonderful, sensational, outstanding, superb, excellent; informal terrific, fabulous; Brit. informal brilliant; Austral./NZ informal bonzer.
OPPOSITES rational, ordinary, indifferent.

fantasy noun **1** *a mix of fantasy and realism:* **imagination,** fancy, invention, make-believe, creativity, vision, daydreaming, reverie. **2** *his fantasy about being famous:* **dream,** daydream, pipe dream, fanciful notion, wish, fond hope, delusion; informal pie in the sky.
OPPOSITES realism.

far adverb **1** *far from the palace:* **a long way,** a great distance, a good way, afar. **2** *her charm far outweighs any flaws:* **much,** considerably, markedly, greatly, significantly, substantially, appreciably, by a long way, by a mile, easily.
OPPOSITES near, barely.
adjective **1** *far places:* **distant,** faraway, far-off, remote, out of the way, far-flung, outlying. **2** *the far side:* **further,** opposite.
OPPOSITES near.

farce noun **mockery,** travesty, parody, sham, pretence, charade, joke; informal shambles.
OPPOSITES tragedy.

fare noun **1** *we paid the fare:* **price,** cost, charge, fee, toll, tariff. **2** *they eat simple fare:* **food,** meals, cooking, cuisine.

f

verb *how are you faring?* **get on,** get along, cope, manage, do, survive; informal make out.

farewell exclamation *farewell, Patrick!* **goodbye,** so long, adieu, au revoir, ciao; informal bye, cheerio, see you (later); Brit. informal ta-ta, cheers.
noun *an emotional farewell:* **goodbye,** adieu, leave-taking, parting, departure, send-off.

farming noun **agriculture,** cultivation, husbandry; Brit. crofting.

fascinating adjective **interesting,** captivating, engrossing, absorbing, enchanting, enthralling, spellbinding, riveting, engaging, compelling, compulsive, gripping, charming, attractive, intriguing, diverting, entertaining.

fascination noun **interest,** preoccupation, passion, obsession, compulsion, allure, lure, charm, attraction, appeal, pull, draw.

fashion noun **1** *the fashion for tight clothes:* **vogue,** trend, craze, rage, mania, fad, style, look, convention; informal thing. **2** *the world of fashion:* **clothes,** clothing design, couture; informal the rag trade. **3** *in a sensible fashion:* **manner,** way, method, style, approach.
verb *fashioned from clay:* **construct,** build, make, manufacture, cast, shape, form, mould, sculpt, forge, hew, carve.

fashionable adjective **in vogue,** in fashion, popular, up to date, up to the minute, modern, all the rage, trendsetting, stylish, chic; informal trendy, classy, cool; N. Amer. informal tony.
OPPOSITES unfashionable.

fast¹ adjective **1** *a fast pace:* **speedy,** quick, swift, rapid, high-speed, accelerated, express, blistering, breakneck, hasty, hurried; informal nippy, scorching, supersonic; Brit. informal cracking. **2** *make the rope fast:* **secure,** fastened, tight, firm, closed, shut, immovable. **3** *fast friends:* **loyal,** devoted, faithful, firm, steadfast, staunch, true, boon, bosom, inseparable.
OPPOSITES slow, loose, temporary.
adverb **1** *she drove fast:* **quickly,** rapidly, swiftly, speedily, briskly, at full tilt, hastily, hurriedly, in a hurry; informal double quick, nippily; N. Amer. informal lickety-split. **2** *his wheels were stuck fast:* **securely,** firmly, tight. **3** *he's fast asleep:* **deeply,** sound, completely.
OPPOSITES slowly, loosely, lightly.

fast² verb *we must fast and pray:* **eat nothing,** refrain from eating, go without food, go hungry, starve oneself, go on hunger strike.
OPPOSITES eat.
noun *a five-day fast:* **period of fasting,** period of abstinence, hunger strike, diet.
OPPOSITES feast.

fasten verb **1** *he fastened the door:* **bolt,** lock, secure, make fast, chain, seal. **2** *they fastened splints to his leg:* **attach,** fix, affix, clip, pin, tack, stick, join. **3** *he fastened his horse to a tree:* **tie (up),** tether, hitch, truss, fetter, lash, anchor, strap, rope.
OPPOSITES unlock, remove, untie.

fat adjective **1** *a fat man:* **obese,** overweight, plump, stout, chubby, portly, flabby, paunchy,

pot-bellied, corpulent; informal tubby; Brit. informal podgy. **2** *fat bacon:* **fatty**, greasy, oily. **3** *a fat book:* **thick**, big, chunky, substantial, long.
OPPOSITES thin, slim, lean.
noun **1** *whale fat:* **blubber**, fatty tissue, adipose tissue, cellulite. **2** *eggs in sizzling fat:* **oil**, grease, lard, suet, butter, margarine.

fatal adjective **1** *a fatal disease:* **deadly**, lethal, mortal, death-dealing, terminal, incurable, untreatable, inoperable. **2** *a fatal mistake:* **disastrous**, devastating, ruinous, catastrophic, calamitous, dire.
OPPOSITES harmless, beneficial.

fate noun **1** *what has fate in store for me?* **destiny**, providence, the stars, chance, luck, serendipity, fortune. **2** *my fate was in their hands:* **future**, destiny, outcome, end, lot. **3** *a similar fate would befall Harris:* **death**, demise, end, sentence.
verb *she was fated to face the same problem:* **predestine**, preordain, destine, mean, doom.

father noun **1** informal **dad**, daddy, pop, pa, old man. **2** *the father of democracy:* **originator**, initiator, founder, inventor, creator, author, architect.
verb **sire**, spawn, breed, give life to.

fatigue noun **tiredness**, weariness, exhaustion.
OPPOSITES energy.
verb **tire out**, exhaust, wear out, drain, weary, overtire; informal knock out, take it out of; Brit. informal knacker.
OPPOSITES invigorate.

fatty adjective **greasy**, fat, oily, creamy, rich.
OPPOSITES lean.

fault noun **1** *he has his faults:* **defect**, failing, imperfection, flaw, blemish, shortcoming, weakness, vice. **2** *engineers have located the fault:* **defect**, flaw, imperfection, bug, error, mistake, inaccuracy; informal glitch. **3** *it was not my fault:* **responsibility**, liability, culpability, guilt; informal
OPPOSITES strength.
verb *you can't fault their commitment:* **find fault with**, criticize, attack, condemn; informal knock; Brit. informal slag off.
■ **at fault** to blame, blameworthy, culpable, responsible, guilty, in the wrong.

faulty adjective **1** *a faulty electric blanket:* **malfunctioning**, broken, damaged, defective, not working, out of order; informal on the blink, acting up; Brit. informal playing up. **2** *her logic is faulty:* **defective**, flawed, unsound, inaccurate, incorrect, erroneous, wrong.
OPPOSITES working, sound.

favour noun **1** *will you do me a favour?* **good turn**, service, good deed, act of kindness, courtesy. **2** *she looked on him with favour:* **approval**, approbation, goodwill, kindness, benevolence.
OPPOSITES disservice, disapproval.
verb **1** *the party favours electoral reform:* **advocate**, recommend, approve of, be in favour of, support, back, champion, campaign for, press for, lobby for, promote; informal push for. **2** *Robyn favours loose clothes:* **prefer**, go for, choose, opt for, select, pick, plump for. **3** *Father always favoured George:* **prefer**, be biased

f

towards, indulge, like more/
better. **4** *the conditions
favoured the other team:*
benefit, be to the advantage of,
help, assist, aid, be of service
to.
OPPOSITES oppose, dislike,
hinder.
■ **in favour of** on the side of,
pro, for, giving support to,
approving of, sympathetic to.

favourable adjective **1** *a
favourable review:* **approving,**
positive, complimentary, full of
praise, flattering, glowing,
enthusiastic, kind, good; informal
rave. **2** *conditions are
favourable:* **advantageous,**
beneficial, in one's favour,
good, right, suitable,
appropriate, auspicious,
promising, encouraging. **3** *a
favourable reply:* **positive,**
affirmative, assenting,
approving, encouraging,
reassuring.
OPPOSITES critical,
disadvantageous, negative.

favourite adjective **favoured,**
preferred, chosen, choice, best-
loved, dearest, pet.
noun **first choice,** pick,
preference, pet, darling, the
apple of one's eye; informal
golden boy, teacher's pet; Brit.
informal blue-eyed boy/girl; N.
Amer. informal fair-haired boy/girl.

fear noun **1** *she felt fear at
entering the house:* **terror,**
fright, fearfulness, horror,
alarm, panic, trepidation, dread,
anxiety, angst, apprehension,
nervousness. **2** *a fear of heights:*
phobia, aversion, antipathy,
dread, nightmare, horror,
terror; informal hang-up.
verb **1** *she feared her husband:*
be afraid of, be fearful of, be
scared of, be apprehensive of,

dread, live in fear of, be
terrified of. **2** *I fear you may be
right:* **suspect,** be afraid, have a
sneaking suspicion, be inclined
to think, have a hunch.
■ **fear for** worry about, feel
anxious about, feel concerned
about, have anxieties about.

fearful adjective **1** *they are
fearful of being overheard:*
afraid, scared, frightened,
scared stiff, scared to death,
terrified, petrified, nervous,
apprehensive, uneasy, anxious,
timid; informal jittery. **2** *a fearful
accident:* **terrible,** dreadful,
awful, appalling, frightful,
ghastly, horrific, horrible,
shocking, gruesome.
OPPOSITES unafraid.

fearless adjective **brave,**
courageous, bold, audacious,
intrepid, valiant, plucky, heroic,
daring, unafraid; informal gutsy.
OPPOSITES timid, cowardly.

feasible adjective **practicable,**
practical, workable, achievable,
attainable, realizable, viable,
realistic, possible; informal
doable.
OPPOSITES impracticable.

feast noun *a wedding feast:*
banquet, dinner, treat; informal
spread; Brit. informal beanfeast,
slap-up meal.
verb *they feasted on lobster:*
gorge, dine, binge; (**feast on**)
devour, consume, partake of,
eat one's fill of; informal stuff
one's face with, pig out.

feat noun **achievement,**
accomplishment, coup,
triumph, undertaking,
enterprise, venture, exploit,
operation, exercise, endeavour,
effort.

feather noun **plume,** quill;
(**feathers**) plumage, down.

feature noun **1** *a feature of*

Indian music: **characteristic**, attribute, quality, property, trait, hallmark, aspect, facet, factor, ingredient, component, element. **2** *her delicate features:* **face**, countenance, physiognomy; informal mug; Brit. informal mush, phizog. **3** *she made a feature of her sculptures:* **centrepiece**, special attraction, highlight, focal point, focus, conversation piece. **4** *a series of short features:* **article**, piece, item, report, story, column.
verb **1** *Radio 3 is featuring a week of live concerts:* **present**, promote, make a feature of, spotlight, highlight, showcase, foreground. **2** *she is to feature in a new movie:* **star**, appear, participate.

federation noun
confederation, confederacy, association, league, alliance, coalition, union, syndicate, guild, consortium.

fee noun **payment**, wage, salary, price, charge, bill, tariff, rate; (**fees**) remuneration, dues, earnings, pay; formal emolument.

feeble adjective **1** *old and feeble:* **weak**, weakened, debilitated, enfeebled, frail, decrepit, infirm, delicate, sickly, ailing, unwell, poorly. **2** *a feeble argument:* **ineffective**, unconvincing, implausible, unsatisfactory, poor, weak, flimsy, lame. **3** *he's too feeble to stand up to her:* **cowardly**, faint-hearted, spineless, timid, timorous, fearful, unassertive, weak, ineffectual; informal sissy, chicken; Brit. informal wet. **4** *a feeble light:* **faint**, dim, weak, pale, soft, subdued, muted.
OPPOSITES strong, well, brave.

feed verb **1** *a large family to

feed: **cater for**, provide for, cook for, dine, nourish. **2** *cows feeding:* **eat**, graze, browse, crop. **3** *she fed secrets to the Russians:* **supply**, provide, give, deliver, furnish, issue, leak.
noun *animal feed:* **fodder**, food, provender.

feel verb **1** *she felt the fabric:* **touch**, stroke, caress, fondle, finger, paw, handle. **2** *she felt a breeze on her back:* **perceive**, sense, detect, discern, notice, be aware of, be conscious of. **3** *he will not feel any pain:* **experience**, undergo, go through, bear, endure, suffer. **4** *he felt his way towards the door:* **grope**, fumble, scrabble. **5** *he feels that he should go:* **believe**, think, consider it right, be of the opinion, hold, maintain, judge; informal reckon, figure.
noun **1** *the feel of the paper:* **texture**, finish, touch, consistency. **2** *the feel of the house:* **atmosphere**, ambience, aura, mood, feeling, air, impression, spirit; informal vibes. **3** *a feel for languages:* **aptitude**, knack, flair, bent, talent, gift, ability.

feeling noun **1** *a feeling of nausea:* **sensation**, sense. **2** *I had a feeling I would win:* **(sneaking) suspicion**, notion, inkling, hunch, intuition, funny feeling, fancy, idea. **3** *the strength of her feeling:* **love**, affection, fondness, tenderness, warmth, emotion, passion, desire. **4** *public feeling:* **mood**, (tide of) opinion, attitude, sentiment, emotion, belief, views, consensus. **5** *show some feeling:* **compassion**, sympathy, empathy, fellow feeling, concern, pity, sorrow, commiseration. **6** *he had hurt _her feelings:_ **sensibilities,** sensitivities, self-esteem, pride. **7** _my feeling is that it is true:_ **opinion,** belief, view, impression, intuition, instinct, hunch, estimation, guess. **8** _a feeling of peace:_ **atmosphere,** ambience, aura, air, mood, impression, spirit; informal **vibes.** **9** _a remarkable feeling for language:_ **aptitude,** knack, flair, bent, talent, feel, gift, ability.

fell verb **1** _the dead trees had to be felled:_ **cut down,** chop down, hack down, saw down, clear. **2** _she felled him with one punch:_ **knock down,** knock to the ground, floor, strike down, knock out; informal **deck,** flatten, lay out.

fellow noun **1** (informal) _he's a decent sort of fellow:_ **man,** boy, person, individual, character; informal **guy,** lad; Brit. informal **chap,** **bloke;** N. Amer. informal **dude.** **2** _he exchanged glances with his fellows:_ **companion,** friend, comrade, partner, associate, co-worker, colleague; informal **pal,** **buddy;** Brit. informal **mate.**

fellowship noun **1** _a community bound together in fellowship:_ **companionship,** comradeship, camaraderie, friendship, sociability, solidarity. **2** _the church fellowship:_ **association,** organization, society, club, league, union, guild, alliance, fraternity, brotherhood.

feminine adjective **womanly,** ladylike, soft, gentle, tender, delicate, pretty.
OPPOSITES masculine.

fence noun **barrier,** paling, railing, enclosure, barricade, stockade.
verb **1** _they fenced off the meadow:_ **enclose,** surround, encircle. **2** _he fenced in his_

chickens: **confine,** pen in, coop up, shut in/up, enclose, surround; N. Amer. corral.

fend
■ **fend someone/something off** ward off, head off, stave off, hold off, repel, repulse, resist, fight off. ■ **fend for oneself** take care of oneself, look after oneself, shift for oneself, cope alone, stand on one's own two feet.

ferocious adjective **1** _ferocious animals:_ **fierce,** savage, wild, predatory, ravening, aggressive, dangerous. **2** _a ferocious attack:_ **brutal,** vicious, violent, bloody, barbaric, savage, frenzied.
OPPOSITES gentle, mild.

ferry verb **transport,** convey, carry, run, ship, shuttle.

fertile adjective **1** _the soil is fertile:_ **productive,** fruitful, fecund, rich, lush. **2** _a fertile imagination:_ **creative,** inventive, innovative, visionary, original, ingenious, prolific.
OPPOSITES barren, uncreative.

fertilizer noun **plant food,** dressing, manure, muck, compost.

festival noun **celebration,** festivity, fête, fair, gala, carnival, fiesta, jamboree, feast day, holiday, holy day.

festive adjective **jolly,** merry, joyous, joyful, happy, jovial, light-hearted, cheerful, jubilant, celebratory, holiday, carnival.

fetch verb **1** _he went to fetch a doctor:_ **go and get,** go for, call for, summon, pick up, collect, bring, carry, convey, transport. **2** _the land could fetch millions:_ **sell for,** bring in, raise, realize, yield, make, command; informal go for.

fetching adjective **attractive,**

feud | field

appealing, sweet, pretty, lovely, delightful, charming, captivating, enchanting; Scottish & N. English bonny; Brit. informal fit.

feud noun *a long-standing feud:* **vendetta**, conflict, quarrel, row, rivalry, hostility, strife.
verb *feuding families:* **quarrel**, fight, clash, argue, squabble, dispute.

fever noun **1** *he developed fever:* **feverishness**, high temperature; Medicine pyrexia; informal temperature. **2** *World Cup fever:* **excitement**, mania, frenzy, agitation, passion.

few determiner *police are revealing few details:* **not many**, hardly any, scarcely any, a small number of, a handful of, a couple of, one or two.
OPPOSITES many.
adjective *comforts here are few:* **scarce**, scant, meagre, sparse, in short supply, thin on the ground, few and far between.
OPPOSITES plentiful.

fiasco noun **failure**, disaster, catastrophe, debacle, farce, mess; informal flop, washout, shambles; Brit. informal cock-up; N. Amer. informal snafu; Austral./NZ informal fizzer.
OPPOSITES success.

fibre noun **thread**, strand, filament, wisp, yarn.

fickle adjective **capricious**, flighty, giddy, changeable, volatile, mercurial, erratic, unpredictable, unreliable, unsteady.
OPPOSITES constant.

fiction noun **1** *the traditions of British fiction:* **novels**, stories, literature, creative writing. **2** *this is an absolute fiction:* **fabrication**, invention, lie, fib, tall story, untruth, falsehood, fantasy, nonsense.

OPPOSITES non-fiction, fact.

fictitious adjective **false**, fake, fabricated, bogus, spurious, assumed, affected, adopted, invented, made up; informal pretend, phoney.
OPPOSITES genuine.

fiddle (informal) noun *a VAT fiddle:* **fraud**, swindle, confidence trick; informal racket, scam.
verb **1** *he fiddled with a beer mat:* **fidget**, play, toy, finger, handle. **2** *he fiddled with the dials:* **adjust**, tinker, play about/ around, fool about/around, meddle, interfere, tamper; informal tweak, mess about/ around; Brit. informal muck about/ around. **3** *fiddling the figures:* **falsify**, manipulate, massage, rig, distort, misrepresent, doctor, tamper with, interfere with; informal fix, cook (the books).

fidelity noun **1** *fidelity to her husband:* **faithfulness**, loyalty, constancy, allegiance, commitment, devotion. **2** *the fidelity of the reproduction:* **accuracy**, exactness, precision, correctness, strictness, closeness, authenticity.
OPPOSITES disloyalty, inaccuracy.

field noun **1** *a large ploughed field:* **meadow**, pasture, paddock, grassland. **2** *a football field:* **pitch**, ground; Brit. informal park. **3** *the field of biotechnology:* **area**, sphere, discipline, province, department, domain, territory, branch, subject. **4** *your field of vision:* **scope**, range, sweep, reach, extent. **5** *she is well ahead of the field:* **competitors**, entrants, competition, applicants, candidates, runners.
verb **1** *she fielded the ball:* **catch**, stop, retrieve, return, throw

f

back. **2** *fielding a great team:* **send out,** play, put up, assemble, offer. **3** *he fielded some awkward questions:* **deal with,** handle, cope with, answer, reply to, respond to.

fierce adjective **1** *a fierce black mastiff:* **ferocious,** savage, vicious, aggressive. **2** *fierce competition:* **aggressive,** cut-throat, keen, intense, strong, relentless. **3** *fierce jealousy:* **intense,** powerful, vehement, passionate, impassioned, fervent, ardent. **4** *a fierce wind:* **powerful,** strong, violent, forceful, stormy, howling, raging, tempestuous.
OPPOSITES gentle, mild.

fiery adjective **1** *a fiery blast:* **burning,** blazing, flaming, on fire, ablaze. **2** *a fiery red:* **bright,** brilliant, vivid, intense, rich. **3** *her fiery spirit:* **passionate,** impassioned, excitable, spirited, quick-tempered, volatile, explosive, impetuous.

fight verb **1** *two men were fighting:* **brawl,** exchange blows, scuffle, grapple, wrestle; informal scrap; Brit. informal have a punch-up; N. Amer. informal rough-house; Austral./NZ informal stoush. **2** *he fought in Vietnam:* **do battle,** serve one's country, go to war, take up arms, engage, meet, clash, skirmish. **3** *a war fought for freedom:* **wage,** engage in, conduct, prosecute, undertake. **4** *they are always fighting:* **quarrel,** argue, row, bicker, squabble, fall out; informal scrap. **5** *fighting against injustice:* **campaign,** strive, battle, struggle, contend, crusade, agitate, lobby, push, press. **6** *they will fight the decision:* **oppose,** contest,

confront, challenge, appeal against, combat, dispute. **7** *Don fought the urge to cry:* **repress,** restrain, suppress, stifle, smother, hold back, fight back, keep in check, curb, choke back; informal keep the lid on, cork up.

noun **1** *a fight outside a club:* **brawl,** scuffle, disturbance, fisticuffs, fracas, melee, skirmish, clash; informal scrap, dust-up; Brit. informal punch-up; N. Amer. informal rough house; Austral./NZ informal stoush. **2** *a heavyweight fight:* **boxing match,** bout, match, contest. **3** *the fight against terrorism:* **battle,** engagement, conflict, struggle, war, campaign, crusade, action, hostilities. **4** *a fight with my girlfriend:* **argument,** quarrel, squabble, row, wrangle, disagreement, falling-out, dispute; informal tiff, spat, scrap; Brit. informal barney, ding-dong. **5** *their fight for control of the company:* **struggle,** battle, campaign, push, effort. **6** *she had no fight left in her:* **will,** resistance, spirit, pluck, grit, strength, backbone, determination, resolution, resolve.

fighter noun **1** *a guerrilla fighter:* **soldier,** fighting man/woman, warrior, combatant, serviceman, servicewoman; (**fighters**) troops, personnel, militia. **2** *the fighter was knocked to the ground:* **boxer,** pugilist, prizefighter, wrestler.

figure noun **1** *the figure for April:* **statistic,** number, quantity, amount, level, total, sum; (**figures**) data, statistics, information. **2** *the second figure was 9:* **digit,** numeral, character, symbol. **3** *he can't put a figure on it:* **price,** cost,

amount, value, valuation. **4** *her petite figure*: **shape**, outline, form, silhouette, proportions, physique, build, frame. **5** *a figure of authority*: **person**, personage, individual, character, personality, celebrity. **6** *geometrical figures*: **shape**, pattern, design, motif. **7** *figure 1 shows an ignition circuit*: **diagram**, illustration, drawing, picture, plate.
verb *he figures in many myths*: **feature**, appear, be featured, be mentioned, be referred to.
■ **figure something out** (informal) work out, fathom, puzzle out, decipher, make sense of, think through, get to the bottom of, understand, comprehend, see, grasp, get the hang of; informal twig, crack; Brit. informal suss out.

file¹ noun **1** *he opened the file*: **folder**, portfolio, binder. **2** *we have files on all of you*: **dossier**, document, record, report, data, information, documentation, archives.
verb **1** *file the documents correctly*: **categorize**, classify, organize, put in order, order, arrange, catalogue, store, archive. **2** *two women have filed a civil suit*: **bring**, press, lodge.

file² noun *a file of boys*: **line**, column, row, queue, string, chain, procession; Brit. informal crocodile.
verb *we filed out into the park*: **walk in a line**, queue, march, parade, troop.

file³ verb *she filed her nails*: **smooth**, buff, rub down, polish, shape, scrape, abrade, rasp, manicure.

fill verb **1** *he filled a bowl*: **fill up**, top up, charge. **2** *guests filled the room*: **crowd into**, throng, pack (into), occupy, squeeze

into, cram (into). **3** *he began filling his shelves*: **stock**, pack, load, supply, replenish. **4** *fill all the holes with putty*: **block up**, stop (up), plug, seal, caulk. **5** *the perfume filled the room*: **pervade**, permeate, suffuse, penetrate, infuse. **6** *the person who fills this vacancy*: **occupy**, hold, take up.
OPPOSITES empty, clear, leave.

filling noun *filling for cushions*: **stuffing**, padding, wadding, filler, contents.
adjective *a filling meal*: **substantial**, hearty, ample, satisfying, square, heavy, stodgy.

film noun **1** *a film of sweat*: **layer**, coat, coating, covering, cover, skin, patina, tissue. **2** *Emma was watching a film*: **movie**, picture, feature film, motion picture, video, DVD. **3** *she would like to work in film*: **cinema**, movies, the pictures, films, the silver screen, the big screen.
verb **1** *he filmed the next scene*: **photograph**, record on film, shoot, capture on film, video. **2** *his eyes had filmed over*: **cloud**, mist, haze, blur.

filter noun *a carbon filter*: **strainer**, sifter, sieve, gauze, mesh, net.
verb **1** *the farmers filter the water*: **sieve**, strain, sift, clarify, purify, refine, treat. **2** *the rain had filtered through her jacket*: **seep**, percolate, leak, trickle, ooze, leach.

filthy adjective **1** *the room was filthy*: **dirty**, mucky, grimy, foul, squalid, sordid, soiled, stained, polluted, contaminated, unwashed. **2** *filthy jokes*: **obscene**, rude, vulgar, dirty, smutty, improper, coarse,

f

bawdy, lewd; informal blue. **3** *he was in a filthy mood:* **bad,** foul, irritable, grumpy, grouchy, cross; informal **snappy**; Brit. informal shirty, stroppy; N. Amer. informal cranky, ornery.
OPPOSITES clean, pleasant.

final adjective **1** *the final year of study:* **last,** closing, concluding, finishing, end, ultimate, eventual. **2** *their decisions are final:* **irrevocable,** unalterable, absolute, conclusive, irrefutable, incontrovertible, indisputable, unchallengeable, binding.
OPPOSITES first, provisional.

finale noun **climax,** culmination, end, ending, finish, close, conclusion, termination, denouement.
OPPOSITES opening.

finally adverb **1** *she finally got married:* **eventually,** ultimately, in the end, after a long time, at (long) last, in the long run, in the fullness of time. **2** *finally, attach the ribbon:* **lastly,** last, in conclusion. **3** *this should finally dispel that myth:* **conclusively,** irrevocably, decisively, definitively, for ever, for good, once and for all.

finance noun **1** *he knows about finance:* **financial affairs,** money matters, economics, commerce, business, investment. **2** *short-term finance:* **funds,** money, capital, cash, resources, assets, reserves, funding.
verb *a project financed by grants:* **fund,** pay for, back, capitalize, endow, subsidize, invest in, sponsor; N. Amer. informal bankroll.

financial adjective **monetary,** money, economic, pecuniary, fiscal, banking, commercial,

business, investment.

find verb **1** *I found the book I wanted:* **locate,** spot, pinpoint, unearth, obtain, search out, track down, root out, come across/upon, run across/into, chance on, happen on, stumble on, encounter; informal bump into. **2** *they found a cure for rabies:* **discover,** invent, come up with, hit on. **3** *you'll find that it's a lively area:* **discover,** become aware, realize, observe, notice, note, learn. **4** *I find this strange:* **consider,** think, feel to be, look on as, view as, see as, judge, deem, regard as. **5** *he was found guilty:* **judge,** deem, rule, declare, pronounce.
OPPOSITES lose.
noun **1** *an archaeological find:* **discovery,** acquisition. **2** *this table is a real find:* **bargain,** godsend, boon, catch, asset; informal good buy.
■ **find something out** discover, become aware of, learn, detect, discern, observe, notice, note, get/come to know, realize, bring to light; informal figure out, cotton on, tumble; Brit. informal twig, suss.

fine¹ adjective **1** *fine wines:* **good,** choice, select, prime, quality, special, superior, of distinction, premium, classic, vintage. **2** *a fine piece of work:* **excellent,** first-class, first-rate, great, exceptional, outstanding, splendid, magnificent, exquisite, superb, wonderful, superlative; informal A1, topnotch. **3** *a fine fellow:* **worthy,** admirable, praiseworthy, laudable, upright, upstanding, respectable. **4** *that's fine, but it's not enough:* **all right,** acceptable, suitable, good (enough), passable, satisfactory, adequate, reasonable, tolerable;

informal OK. **5** *I feel fine:* **good,** well, healthy, all right, (fighting) fit, blooming, thriving, in good shape/ condition; informal OK, great, in the pink. **6** *a fine day:* **fair,** dry, bright, clear, sunny, cloudless. **7** *fine clothes:* **elegant,** stylish, expensive, smart, chic, fashionable, fancy, sumptuous, lavish, opulent; informal flashy. **8** *a fine mind:* **keen,** quick, alert, sharp, bright, brilliant, astute, clever, intelligent. **9** *fine china:* **delicate,** dainty, thin, light, fragile. **10** *fine hair:* **thin,** light, delicate, wispy, flyaway. **11** *a fine point:* **sharp,** keen, acute, razor-sharp. **12** *fine material:* **sheer,** light, lightweight, thin, flimsy, diaphanous, filmy, see-through. **13** *fine sand:* **fine-grained,** powdery, dusty, ground, crushed. **14** *fine details:* **intricate,** delicate, detailed, elaborate, meticulous. **15** *a fine distinction:* **subtle,** ultra-fine, nice, hair-splitting.
OPPOSITES everyday, poor, contemptible, ill, dull, wet, coarse.

fine² noun *heavy fines:* **financial penalty,** forfeit, damages, sanction, fee, excess charge.

finger noun **digit.**
verb *she fingered her brooch:* **touch,** feel, handle, stroke, rub, caress, fondle, toy with, play (about/around) with, fiddle with.

finish verb **1** *Pam finished her work:* **complete,** end, conclude, terminate, wind up, round off; informal wrap up, sew up, polish off. **2** *Hitch finished his dinner:* **consume,** eat, devour, drink, finish off, polish off, gulp (down), use (up), exhaust,

empty, drain, get through; informal down. **3** *the programme has finished:* **end,** come to an end, stop, conclude, come to a close, cease. **4** *finished in a black lacquer:* **coat,** surface, texture.
OPPOSITES start.
noun **1** *the finish of filming:* **end,** ending, completion, conclusion, close, termination, finale, denouement. **2** *a shiny finish:* **surface,** texture, coating, covering, lacquer, glaze, veneer, gloss, patina, sheen, lustre.
OPPOSITES start.
■ **finish someone/something off 1** *the hunters finished them off:* **kill,** execute, terminate, exterminate, liquidate, get rid of; informal wipe out, bump off, dispose of; N. Amer. informal waste. **2** *financial difficulties finished us off:* **overwhelm,** overcome, defeat, get the better of, bring down; informal drive to the wall.

fire noun **1** *a fire broke out:* **blaze,** conflagration, inferno, flames, burning, combustion. **2** *he lacked their fire:* **dynamism,** energy, vigour, animation, vitality, exuberance, zest, elan, passion, zeal, spirit, verve, vivacity, enthusiasm; informal go, get-up-and-go, oomph. **3** *machine-gun fire:* **gunfire,** firing, shooting, bombardment, shelling, volley, salvo, hail.
verb **1** *howitzers firing shells:* **launch,** shoot, discharge, let fly with. **2** *someone fired a gun:* **shoot,** discharge, let off, set off. **3** (informal) *he was fired:* **dismiss,** discharge, give someone their notice, lay off, let go; informal sack. **4** *the story fired my imagination:* **stimulate,** stir up, excite, awaken, rouse, inflame, animate, inspire, motivate.
■ **catch fire** ignite, catch light,

f

burst into flames, go up in flames. ■ **set on fire** ignite, light, set fire to, set alight.

firm[1] adjective **1** *the ground is fairly firm:* **hard**, solid, unyielding, resistant, compacted, compressed, dense, stiff, rigid, set. **2** *firm foundations:* **secure**, stable, steady, strong, fixed, fast, tight, immovable, rooted, stationary, motionless. **3** *I was very firm | a firm supporter:* **resolute**, determined, decided, resolved, steadfast, adamant, emphatic, insistent, single-minded, wholehearted, unfaltering, unwavering, unflinching, unswerving, unbending, committed. **4** *firm friends:* **close**, good, boon, intimate, inseparable, dear, special, constant, devoted, loving, faithful, long-standing, steady, steadfast. **5** *firm plans:* **definite**, fixed, settled, decided, cut-and-dried, established, confirmed, agreed.
OPPOSITES soft, unstable, irresolute, indefinite.

firm[2] noun *an accountancy firm:* **business**, company, concern, enterprise, organization, corporation, conglomerate, office, bureau, agency, consortium; informal outfit, operation.

first adjective **1** *the first chapter:* **earliest**, initial, opening, introductory. **2** *first principles:* **fundamental**, basic, rudimentary, primary, key, cardinal, central, chief, vital, essential. **3** *our first priority:* **foremost**, principal, highest, greatest, paramount, top, main, overriding, central, core; informal number-one. **4** *first prize:* **top**, best, prime, premier, winner's,

winning.
OPPOSITES last.
adverb **1** *the room they had first entered:* **at first**, to begin with, first of all, at the outset, initially. **2** *I'd like to eat first:* **before anything else**, now. **3** *she wouldn't go—she'd die first!* **rather**, sooner, in preference.
OPPOSITES last, later.
noun *that's a first:* **novelty**, innovation, departure, break with tradition.

fish verb **1** *some people were fishing in the lake:* **go fishing**, angle, trawl. **2** *she fished for her purse:* **search**, delve, look, hunt, grope, fumble, ferret, rummage.
■ **fish someone/something out** pull out, haul out, remove, extricate, extract, retrieve, rescue, save.

fit[1] adjective **1** *a fit subject for a book:* **suitable**, appropriate, suited, apposite, fitting, good enough, apt, -worthy. **2** *not fit to look after children:* **competent**, able, capable, ready, prepared, equipped. **3** *tanned and fit:* **healthy**, well, in good health, in (good) shape, in trim, in good condition, fighting fit, athletic, muscular, strapping, strong, robust, hale and hearty.
OPPOSITES unsuitable, incapable, unfit.
verb **1** *having carpets fitted:* **lay**, install, put in, position, place, fix, arrange. **2** *cameras fitted with autofocus:* **equip**, provide, supply, fit out, furnish. **3** *they fitted the slabs together:* **join**, connect, piece together, attach, unite, link. **4** *a sentence that fits his crime:* **be appropriate to**, suit, match, correspond to, tally with, go with, accord with.

5 *an MSc fits you for a scientific career:* **qualify,** prepare, make ready, train.
■ **fit in** conform, be in harmony, blend in, be in line, be assimilated.

fit² noun **1** *an epileptic fit:* **convulsion,** spasm, paroxysm, seizure, attack. **2** *a fit of the giggles:* **outbreak,** outburst, attack, bout, spell. **3** *mum would have a fit:* **tantrum,** frenzy; informal paddy, heart attack; N. Amer. informal blowout.

fitness noun **1** *polo requires tremendous fitness:* **good health,** strength, robustness, vigour, athleticism, toughness, stamina. **2** *his fitness for active service:* **suitability,** capability, competence, ability, aptitude, readiness, preparedness.

fitting noun **1** *a light fitting:* **attachment,** part, piece, component, accessory, apparatus. **2** *bathroom fittings:* **furnishings,** furniture, fixtures, fitments, equipment.
adjective *a fitting conclusion:* **apt,** appropriate, suitable, apposite, fit, proper, right, seemly, correct.
OPPOSITES unsuitable.

fix verb **1** *signs were fixed to lamp posts:* **fasten,** attach, affix, secure, connect, couple, link, install, stick, glue, pin, nail, screw, bolt, clamp, clip. **2** *his words are fixed in my memory:* **stick,** lodge, embed. **3** *his eyes were fixed on the ground:* **focus,** direct, level, point, train. **4** *he fixed my car:* **repair,** mend, put right, get working, restore. **5** *Jim fixed it for us to see the show:* **arrange,** organize, contrive, manage, wangle; informal swing, wangle. **6** (informal) *Laura was fixing her hair:*

arrange, put in order, adjust, style, groom, comb, brush; informal do. **7** (informal) *I'll fix supper:* **prepare,** cook, make, get; informal rustle up; Brit. informal knock up. **8** *let's fix a date:* **decide on,** select, choose, settle, set, arrange, establish, allot, designate, name, appoint, specify. **9** (informal) *the fight was fixed:* **rig,** tamper with, skew, influence; informal fiddle.
OPPOSITES remove.
noun (informal) **1** *they are in a bit of a fix:* **predicament,** plight, difficulty, awkward situation, corner, tight spot, mess; informal pickle, jam, hole, scrape, bind. **2** *the result was a fix:* **fraud,** swindle, trick, charade, sham; informal set-up, fiddle.

fixed adjective **predetermined,** set, established, arranged, specified, decided, agreed, determined, confirmed, prescribed, definite, defined, explicit, precise.

fizz verb *the mixture fizzed like mad:* **bubble,** sparkle, effervesce, froth.
noun **1** *the fizz in champagne:* **bubbles,** sparkle, fizziness, effervescence, gassiness, froth. **2** *the fizz of the static:* **crackle,** buzz, hiss, white noise.

fizzy adjective **sparkling,** effervescent, carbonated, gassy, bubbly, frothy.
OPPOSITES still, flat.

flag¹ noun *the Irish flag:* **banner,** standard, ensign, pennant, streamer, colours; Brit. pendant.
verb *flag the misspelt words:* **indicate,** identify, point out, mark, label, tag, highlight.
■ **flag someone/something down** hail, wave down, stop, halt.

flag² verb **1** *they were flagging towards the finish:* **tire,** grow

tired, weaken, grow weak, wilt, droop. **2** *my energy flags in the afternoon:* **fade,** decline, wane, ebb, diminish, decrease, lessen, dwindle.
OPPOSITES revive.

flagrant adjective **blatant,** glaring, obvious, conspicuous, barefaced, shameless, brazen, undisguised.

flair noun **1** *a flair for publicity:* **aptitude,** talent, gift, instinct, ability, facility, knack, skill. **2** *she dressed with flair:* **style,** elegance, panache, dash, elan, poise, taste; informal class.

flake noun *a flake of paint:* **sliver,** wafer, shaving, paring, chip, fragment, scrap, shred. verb *the paint was flaking off:* **peel (off),** chip, blister, come off.

flamboyant adjective **1** *her flamboyant personality:* **ostentatious,** exuberant, confident, lively, animated, vibrant, vivacious. **2** *a flamboyant cravat:* **colourful,** bright, vibrant, vivid, dazzling, bold, showy, gaudy, garish, loud; informal jazzy, flashy.
OPPOSITES restrained.

flame noun **1** *a sheet of flames:* **fire,** blaze, conflagration, inferno. **2** (informal) *an old flame:* **sweetheart,** boyfriend, girlfriend, lover, partner.
■ **in flames** on fire, burning, alight, flaming, blazing.

flank noun **1** *the horse's flanks:* **side,** haunch, quarter, thigh. **2** *the southern flank of the Eighth Army:* **side,** wing, sector, face, aspect.
verb *the garden is flanked by two rivers:* **edge,** bound, line, border, fringe.

flap verb **1** *the mallards flapped their wings:* **beat,** flutter,

agitate, vibrate, wag, thrash, flail. **2** *the flag flapped in the breeze:* **flutter,** wave, fly, blow, swing, ripple, stir.
noun **1** *a few flaps of its wing:* **beat,** stroke, flutter, movement. **2** (informal) *in a flap:* **panic,** fluster; informal state, stew, tizzy; N. Amer. informal twit.

flare noun **1** *the flare of the match:* **blaze,** flame, flash, burst, flicker. **2** *a flare set off by the crew:* **signal,** beacon, rocket, light, torch, maroon.
verb **1** *the match flared:* **blaze,** flash, flare up, flame, burn, flicker. **2** *her nostrils flared:* **spread,** splay, broaden, widen, dilate.

flash verb **1** *a torch flashed:* **shine,** flare, blaze, gleam, glint, sparkle, burn, blink, wink, flicker, shimmer, twinkle, glimmer, glisten. **2** (informal) *flashing his money about:* **show off,** flaunt, flourish, display, parade. **3** *racing cars flashed past:* **zoom,** streak, tear, shoot, dash, dart, fly, whistle, hurtle, rush, bolt, race, speed, career; informal belt, zap; Brit. informal bomb, bucket; N. Amer. informal barrel.
noun *a flash of light:* **flare,** blaze, burst, gleam, glint, sparkle, flicker, shimmer, twinkle, glimmer.

flashy adjective (informal) **ostentatious,** flamboyant, showy, conspicuous, extravagant, expensive, vulgar, tasteless, brash, garish, loud, gaudy; informal snazzy, fancy, swanky, flash, glitzy.
OPPOSITES understated.

flat¹ adjective **1** *a flat roof:* **level,** horizontal. **2** *the sea was flat:* **calm,** still, glassy, smooth, placid, like a millpond. **3** *plane*

the wood completely flat: **smooth,** even, plane. **4** *a flat wooden box:* **shallow,** low, low-sided. **5** *his voice was flat:* **monotonous,** toneless, droning, boring, dull, tedious, uninteresting, unexciting. **6** *the market was flat:* **slow,** inactive, sluggish, slack, quiet, depressed. **7** (Brit.) *a flat battery:* **run down,** dead, used up, expired. **8** *a flat tyre:* **deflated,** punctured, burst, blown. **9** *a flat fee:* **fixed,** set, invariable, regular, constant. **10** *a flat denial:* **outright,** direct, absolute, definite, positive, straight, plain, explicit.
OPPOSITES sloping, vertical, rough, uneven, curved, tall, animated, lively, charged, new, inflated, variable, equivocal.
adverb *she lay flat on the floor:* **stretched out,** outstretched, spreadeagled, sprawling, prone, prostrate.

flat² noun *a two-bedroom flat:* **apartment,** suite, penthouse, rooms.

flatten verb **1** *Tom flattened the crumpled paper:* **make/become flat,** even out, smooth out, level. **2** *the cows flattened the grass:* **squash,** compress, press down, crush, compact, trample. **3** *tornadoes can flatten buildings in seconds:* **demolish,** raze (to the ground), tear down, knock down, destroy, wreck, devastate.
OPPOSITES crumple, raise, build.

flatter verb **1** *it amused him to flatter her:* **compliment,** praise, express admiration for, fawn on, humour, wheedle, blarney; informal sweet-talk, soft-soap, butter up, play up to. **2** *I was flattered to be asked:* **honour,** gratify, please, delight; informal

tickle pink. **3** *a hairstyle that flattered her:* **suit,** become, look good on, go well with; informal do something for.
OPPOSITES insult, offend.

flattering adjective **1** *flattering remarks:* **complimentary,** praising, favourable, admiring, appreciative, fulsome, honeyed, obsequious, ingratiating, sycophantic. **2** *it was very flattering to be nominated:* **pleasing,** gratifying, an honour. **3** *her most flattering dress:* **becoming,** enhancing.
OPPOSITES unflattering.

flattery noun **praise,** adulation, compliments, blandishments, honeyed words, fawning, blarney; informal sweet talk, soft soap, buttering up, toadying.

flaunt verb **show off,** display, make a great show of, put on show/display, parade, draw attention to, brag about, crow about, vaunt; informal flash.

flavour noun **1** *the flavour of basil:* **taste,** savour, tang, smack. **2** *salami can give extra flavour:* **flavouring,** seasoning, taste, tang, relish, bite, piquancy, spice. **3** *a strong international flavour:* **character,** quality, feel, feeling, ambience, atmosphere, air, mood, tone, spirit. **4** *this excerpt will give you a flavour of the report:* **impression,** suggestion, hint, taste.
verb *spices for flavouring food:* **season,** spice (up), add piquancy to, ginger up, enrich, infuse.

flaw noun **defect,** blemish, fault, imperfection, deficiency, weakness, weak spot/point, failing; Computing bug; informal glitch.
OPPOSITES strength.

flawed adjective **1** *a flawed mirror:* **faulty,** defective, unsound, imperfect, blemished, broken, cracked, scratched; Brit. informal duff. **2** *the findings were flawed:* **unsound,** distorted, inaccurate, incorrect, erroneous, fallacious.
OPPOSITES flawless.

flee verb **run (away/off),** run for it, make off, take off, take to one's heels, make a break for it, bolt, beat a (hasty) retreat, make a quick exit, escape; informal beat it, clear off/out, skedaddle, scram; Brit. informal scarper; N. Amer. informal light out; Austral./NZ informal shoot through.

fleet noun **navy,** naval force, (naval) task force, armada, flotilla, squadron, convoy.

fleeting adjective **brief,** short-lived, quick, momentary, cursory, transient, ephemeral, passing, transitory.
OPPOSITES lasting.

flesh noun **1** *his smooth, white flesh:* **tissue,** skin, body, muscle, fat. **2** *strip the flesh from the bone:* **meat,** muscle. **3** *a fruit with juicy flesh:* **pulp,** marrow, meat. **4** *the pleasures of the flesh:* **the body,** human nature, physicality, sensuality, sexuality.

flexibility noun **1** *the flexibility of wood:* **pliability,** suppleness, elasticity, stretchiness, springiness, spring, resilience, bounce; informal give. **2** *the flexibility of an endowment loan:* **adaptability,** adjustability, versatility, open-endedness, freedom, latitude. **3** *the flexibility shown by the local authority:* **willingness to compromise,** accommodation, give and take, amenability, cooperation, tolerance.

OPPOSITES rigidity, inflexibility, intransigence.

flexible adjective **1** *flexible tubing:* **bendy,** pliable, supple, pliant, plastic, elastic, stretchy, springy, resilient, bouncy. **2** *a flexible arrangement:* **adaptable,** adjustable, variable, versatile, open-ended, open. **3** *the need to be flexible towards tenants:* **accommodating,** amenable, willing to compromise, cooperative, tolerant.
OPPOSITES rigid, inflexible, intransigent.

flick noun *a flick of the wrist:* **jerk,** snap, flip, whisk.
verb **1** *he flicked the switch:* **click,** snap, flip, jerk, throw. **2** *the horse flicked its tail:* **swish,** twitch, wave, wag, waggle, shake.
■ **flick through** thumb (through), leaf through, flip through, skim, scan, look through, browse through, dip into, glance at/through.

flicker verb **1** *the lights flickered:* **glimmer,** flare, dance, gutter, twinkle, sparkle, wink, flash. **2** *his eyelids flickered:* **flutter,** quiver, tremble, shiver, shudder, jerk, twitch.

flight noun **1** *the history of flight:* **aviation,** flying, air transport, aeronautics. **2** *a flight to Rome:* **plane trip/journey,** air trip/journey, service. **3** *the flight of the ball:* **trajectory,** path (through the air), track, orbit. **4** *a flight of birds:* **flock,** swarm, cloud, throng. **5** *his headlong flight from home:* **escape,** getaway, hasty departure, exit, exodus, breakout, bolt, disappearance; Brit. informal flit.

flimsy adjective **1** *a flimsy*

building: **insubstantial,** fragile, frail, rickety, ramshackle, makeshift, jerry-built, shoddy. **2** *a flimsy dress:* **thin,** light, fine, filmy, floaty, diaphanous, sheer, delicate, gossamer, gauzy. **3** *flimsy evidence:* **weak,** feeble, poor, inadequate, insufficient, thin, unsubstantial, unconvincing, implausible.
OPPOSITES sturdy, thick, sound.

flinch verb **1** *he flinched at the noise:* **wince,** start, shudder, quiver, jerk. **2** *he never flinched from his duty:* **shrink from,** recoil from, shy away from, dodge, evade, avoid, duck, baulk at.

fling verb *he flung the axe into the river:* **throw,** hurl, toss, sling, launch, pitch, lob; informal chuck, heave.
noun **1** *a birthday fling:* **good time,** party, spree, fun and games; informal binge, bash, night on the town. **2** *she had a brief fling with him:* **affair,** love affair, relationship, romance, liaison, entanglement, involvement.

flippant adjective frivolous, facetious, tongue-in-cheek, disrespectful, irreverent, cheeky; informal flip, saucy; N. Amer. informal sassy.
OPPOSITES serious, respectful.

flirt noun *Anna was quite a flirt:* **tease,** coquette, heartbreaker.
■ flirt with **1** *he liked to flirt with her:* **tease,** lead on, toy with. **2** *those who flirt with fascism:* dabble in, toy with, trifle with, play with, tinker with, dip into, scratch the surface of.

float verb **1** *oil floats on water:* **stay afloat,** stay on the surface, be buoyant, be buoyed up. **2** *the*

balloon floated in the air: **hover,** levitate, be suspended, hang, defy gravity. **3** *a cloud floated across the moon:* **drift,** glide, sail, slip, slide, waft. **4** *the company was floated on the Stock Exchange:* **launch,** offer, sell, introduce.
OPPOSITES sink, drop, rush, take private.

floating adjective **1** *floating voters:* **uncommitted,** undecided, undeclared, wavering; informal sitting on the fence. **2** *a floating population:* **unsettled,** transient, temporary, migrant, wandering, nomadic, migratory, itinerant.
OPPOSITES committed, decided, settled.

flock noun **1** *a flock of sheep:* **herd,** drove. **2** *a flock of birds:* **flight,** swarm, cloud, gaggle, skein.
verb **1** *people flocked around her:* **gather,** collect, congregate, assemble, converge, mass, crowd, throng, cluster, swarm. **2** *tourists flock to the place:* **stream,** go in large numbers, swarm, crowd, troop.

flog verb whip, thrash, lash, scourge, birch, cane, beat.

flood noun **1** *a severe flood:* **inundation,** deluge, torrent, overflow, flash flood; Brit. spate. **2** *a flood of tears:* **gush,** outpouring, torrent, rush, stream, surge, cascade. **3** *a flood of complaints:* **succession,** series, string, barrage, volley, battery, avalanche, torrent, stream, storm.
OPPOSITES trickle.
verb **1** *the town was flooded:* **inundate,** swamp, deluge, immerse, submerge, drown, engulf. **2** *the river could flood:* **overflow,** burst its banks, brim

over, run over. **3** *cheap goods flooding the market:* **glut,** swamp, saturate. **4** *refugees flooded in:* **pour,** stream, flow, surge, swarm, pile, crowd.
OPPOSITES drain, starve, trickle.

floor noun **1** *he sat on the floor:* **ground,** flooring. **2** *the second floor:* **storey,** level, deck, tier, stage.
verb **1** *he floored his attacker:* **knock down,** knock over, fell; informal deck, lay out. **2** (informal) *the question floored him:* **baffle,** defeat, confound, perplex, puzzle, disconcert; informal throw, beat, stump; N. Amer. informal buffalo.

flop verb **1** *he flopped into a chair:* **collapse,** slump, crumple, sink, drop. **2** *his hair flopped over his eyes:* **hang (down),** dangle, droop, sag, loll.
3 (informal) *the play flopped:* **be unsuccessful,** fail, fall flat, founder; informal bomb; N. Amer. informal tank.
OPPOSITES spring, succeed.
noun (informal) *the play was a flop:* **failure,** disaster, fiasco, debacle, catastrophe; Brit. damp squib; informal washout, also-ran; N. Amer. informal clinker.
OPPOSITES success.

floppy adjective **limp,** flaccid, slack, flabby, relaxed, drooping, droopy, loose, flowing.
OPPOSITES erect, stiff.

flounder verb **1** *floundering in the water:* **struggle,** thrash, flail, twist and turn, splash, stagger, stumble, reel, lurch, blunder. **2** *she floundered, not knowing what to say:* **struggle,** be out of one's depth, be confused; informal scratch one's head, be flummoxed, be fazed, be floored.

flourish verb **1** *ferns flourish in*

the shade: **grow,** thrive, prosper, do well, burgeon, increase, multiply, proliferate, run riot. **2** *the arts flourished:* **thrive,** prosper, bloom, be in good health, be vigorous, be in its heyday, make progress, advance, expand; informal go places. **3** *he flourished a sword:* **brandish,** wave, shake, wield, swing, display, show off.
OPPOSITES die, wither, decline.

flout verb **defy,** refuse to obey, disobey, break, violate, fail to comply with, fail to observe, contravene, infringe, breach, commit a breach of, transgress against, ignore, disregard; informal cock a snook at.
OPPOSITES observe.

flow verb **1** *the water flowed down the channel:* **pour,** run, course, circulate, stream, swirl, surge, sweep, gush, cascade, roll, rush, trickle, seep, ooze, dribble. **2** *many questions flow from today's announcement:* **result,** proceed, arise, follow, ensue, stem, originate, emanate, spring.
noun *a good flow of water:* **movement,** motion, current, circulation, stream, swirl, surge, gush, rush, spate, tide, trickle, ooze.

flower noun & verb **bloom,** blossom.

fluctuate verb **vary,** change, shift, alter, waver, swing, oscillate, alternate, rise and fall.

fluent adjective **articulate,** eloquent, silver-tongued, communicative, natural, effortless.
OPPOSITES inarticulate.

fluid noun *the fluid seeps up the tube:* **liquid,** solution, liquor, gas, vapour.

OPPOSITES solid.

adjective 1 *a fluid substance:*
free-flowing, runny, liquid,
liquefied, melted, molten,
gaseous. **2** *he stood up in one
fluid movement:* **smooth,**
fluent, flowing, effortless, easy,
continuous, graceful, elegant.
OPPOSITES solid, jerky.

flurry noun **1** *a flurry of snow:*
swirl, whirl, eddy, shower,
gust. **2** *a flurry of activity:*
burst, outbreak, spurt, fit,
spell, bout, rash, eruption.
OPPOSITES dearth.

flush verb **1** *she flushed in
embarrassment:* **blush,** redden,
go pink, go red, go crimson, go
scarlet, colour (up). **2** *flushing
toxins from the body:* **rinse,**
wash, sluice, swill, cleanse,
clean; Brit. informal sloosh. **3** *they
flushed out the snipers:* **drive,**
chase, force, dislodge, expel.
OPPOSITES pale.

noun *a flush crept over her face:*
blush, colour, rosiness,
pinkness, ruddiness, bloom.
OPPOSITES pallor.

flutter verb **1** *butterflies
fluttered around:* **flit,** hover,
dance. **2** *a tern was fluttering
its wings:* **flap,** beat, quiver,
agitate, vibrate. **3** *she fluttered
her eyelashes:* **flicker,** bat.
4 *flags fluttered:* **flap,** wave,
ripple, undulate, quiver, fly.
5 *her heart fluttered:* **beat
irregularly,** palpitate, miss/skip
a beat, quiver.

fly verb **1** *a bird flew overhead:*
wing, glide, soar, wheel, take
wing, take to the air. **2** *they
flew to Paris:* **travel by plane/
air,** jet. **3** *we flew in supplies:*
transport (by plane/air),
airlift, lift, jet, drop, parachute.
4 *he can fly a plane:* **pilot,**
operate, control, manoeuvre,

steer. **5** *the ship was flying a
French flag:* **display,** show,
exhibit. **6** *flags flew in the town:*
flutter, flap, wave. **7** *doesn't
time fly?* **go quickly,** fly by/past,
pass swiftly, rush past.

foam noun *the foam on the
waves:* **froth,** spume, surf,
spray, fizz, effervescence,
bubbles, head, lather, suds.
verb *the water foamed:* **froth,**
fizz, effervesce, bubble, lather,
ferment, boil, seethe.

focus noun **1** *a focus of
community life:* **centre,** focal
point, central point, centre of
attention, hub, pivot, nucleus,
heart, cornerstone, linchpin.
2 *the main focus of this chapter:*
subject, theme, concern,
subject matter, topic, point,
essence, gist.
verb *he focused his binoculars on
the tower:* **bring into focus,**
aim, point, turn.
■ **focus on** concentrate, centre,
zero in, zoom in, address
oneself to, pay attention to,
pinpoint, revolve around.

fog noun **mist,** smog, murk,
haze; informal pea-souper.

foil[1] verb *the escape attempt was
foiled:* **thwart,** frustrate, stop,
defeat, block, prevent, obstruct,
hinder, snooker, scotch; informal
put paid to; Brit. informal scupper.
OPPOSITES assist.

foil[2] noun *the wine was a perfect
foil to pasta:* **contrast,**
complement, antithesis.

fold verb **1** *I folded the cloth:*
double, crease, turn, bend,
tuck, pleat. **2** *the firm folded
last year:* **fail,** collapse, founder,
go bankrupt, cease trading, be
wound up, be shut (down);
informal crash, go bust, go under,
go to the wall, go belly up.
noun *there was a fold in the*

paper: **crease,** knife-edge, wrinkle, crinkle, pucker, furrow, pleat.

folk noun (informal) **1** *the local folk:* **people,** individuals, {men, women, and children}, (living) souls, citizenry, inhabitants, residents, populace, population. **2** *my folks live in Hull:* **relatives,** relations, family, people; informal peeps.

follow verb **1** *we'll let the others follow:* **come behind,** come after, go behind, go after, walk behind. **2** *people who follow the band around:* **accompany,** go along with, go around with, travel with, escort, attend; informal tag along with. **3** *the police followed her everywhere:* **shadow,** trail, stalk, track; informal tail. **4** *follow the instructions:* **obey,** comply with, conform to, adhere to, stick to, keep to, act in accordance with, abide by, observe. **5** *I couldn't follow what he said:* **understand,** comprehend, take in, grasp, fathom, see; informal make head or tail of, figure out; Brit. informal suss out. **6** *he follows Manchester United:* **be a fan of,** be a supporter of, support, watch, keep up with.
OPPOSITES lead, flout, misunderstand.

follower noun **1** *a follower of Christ:* **disciple,** apostle, defender, champion, believer, worshipper. **2** *followers of Scottish football:* **fan,** enthusiast, admirer, devotee, lover, supporter, adherent.
OPPOSITES leader, opponent.

following noun *his devoted following:* **admirers,** supporters, backers, fans, adherents, devotees, public, audience.

OPPOSITES opposition.
adjective **1** *the following day:* **next,** ensuing, succeeding, subsequent. **2** *the following questions:* **below,** underneath, these.
OPPOSITES preceding, above.

folly noun **foolishness,** foolhardiness, stupidity, idiocy, lunacy, madness, rashness, recklessness, irresponsibility.
OPPOSITES wisdom.

fond adjective **1** *she was fond of dancing:* **keen on,** partial to, enthusiastic about, attached to, attracted to; informal into. **2** *his fond father:* **adoring,** devoted, doting, loving, caring, affectionate. **3** *a fond hope:* **unrealistic,** naive, foolish, over-optimistic, absurd, vain.
OPPOSITES indifferent, uncaring, realistic.

fondle verb **caress,** stroke, pat, pet, finger, tickle, play with.

food noun **nourishment,** sustenance, nutriment, fare, cooking, cuisine, foodstuffs, refreshments, meals, provisions, rations; informal eats, grub.

fool noun **1** *acting like a fool:* **idiot,** ass, halfwit, blockhead, dunce, simpleton; informal nincompoop, clod, dimwit, dummy, fathead, numbskull; Brit. informal nitwit, twit, clot, berk, prat, pillock, wally, dork, twerp, charlie; Scottish informal nyaff, balloon; N. Amer. informal schmuck, turkey; Austral./NZ informal drongo, nong, galah, boofhead. **2** *she made a fool of me:* **laughing stock,** dupe, gull; informal stooge, sucker, mug, fall guy; N. Amer. informal sap.
OPPOSITES genius.
verb **1** *he'd been fooled:* **deceive,** trick, hoax, dupe, take in,

mislead, delude, hoodwink, bluff, gull; informal bamboozle, take for a ride, have on; N. Amer. informal sucker; Austral. informal pull a swifty on. **2** *I'm not fooling, I promise:* **pretend,** make believe, put on an act, act, sham, fake, joke, jest; informal kid; Brit. informal have someone on.

foolish adjective **stupid,** idiotic, mindless, unintelligent, thoughtless, imprudent, unwise, ill-advised, rash, reckless, foolhardy; informal dumb, dim, dim-witted, half-witted, thick, hare-brained; Brit. informal barmy, daft; Scottish & N. English informal glaikit; N. Amer. informal dumb-ass, chowderheaded.
OPPOSITES sensible, wise.

footing noun **1** *a solid financial footing:* **basis,** base, foundation. **2** *on an equal footing:* **standing,** status, position, condition, arrangement, basis, relationship, terms.

forbid verb **prohibit,** ban, outlaw, make illegal, veto, proscribe, embargo, bar, debar, rule out.
OPPOSITES permit.

forbidding adjective **threatening,** ominous, menacing, sinister, brooding, daunting.
OPPOSITES inviting.

force noun **1** *he pushed with all his force:* **strength,** power, energy, might, effort. **2** *they used force to achieve their aims:* **coercion,** compulsion, constraint, duress, pressure, oppression, harassment, intimidation, violence; informal arm-twisting. **3** *the force of the argument:* **power,** weight, effectiveness, validity, strength, significance, influence, authority; informal punch. **4** *a peacekeeping force:* **body,** group, outfit, party, team, detachment, unit, squad.
verb **1** *he was forced to pay:* **compel,** coerce, make, constrain, oblige, impel, drive, pressure, press-gang, bully; informal lean on, twist someone's arm. **2** *the door had to be forced:* **break open,** knock/smash/break down, kick in. **3** *water was forced through a hole:* **propel,** push, thrust, shove, drive, press, pump.
■ in force **1** *the law is now in force:* **effective,** in operation, operative, valid, current, binding. **2** *her fans were out in force:* in great numbers, in hordes/droves, in their hundreds/thousands.

forced adjective **1** *forced repatriation:* **enforced,** compulsory, obligatory, mandatory, involuntary, imposed, required. **2** *a forced smile:* **strained,** unnatural, artificial, false, feigned, simulated, contrived, laboured, affected, hollow; informal phoney, pretend, put on.
OPPOSITES voluntary, natural.

forceful adjective **1** *a forceful personality:* **dynamic,** energetic, assertive, authoritative, vigorous, powerful, strong, pushy; informal in-your-face, go-ahead, feisty. **2** *a forceful argument:* **convincing,** cogent, compelling, strong, powerful, persuasive, coherent.
OPPOSITES weak, submissive, unconvincing.

forecast verb *they forecast record profits:* **predict,** prophesy, foretell, foresee.
noun *a gloomy forecast:* **prediction,** prophecy,

prognostication, prognosis.

foreign adjective **alien,** overseas, non-native, imported, distant, external, far-off, exotic, strange.
OPPOSITES domestic, native.

foreigner noun **alien,** non-native, stranger, outsider, immigrant, settler, newcomer, incomer.
OPPOSITES native, national.

foremost adjective **leading,** principal, premier, prime, top, greatest, best, supreme, pre-eminent, outstanding, most important, most notable; N. Amer. ranking; informal number-one.
OPPOSITES minor.

foresee verb **anticipate,** expect, envisage, predict, forecast, foretell, prophesy.

foretell verb **predict,** forecast, prophesy, foresee, anticipate, envisage, warn of.

forever adverb **1** *their love would last forever:* **for always,** evermore, for ever and ever, for good, for all time, until the end of time, eternally; N. Amer. forevermore; informal until the cows come home. **2** *he was forever banging into things:* **always,** continually, constantly, perpetually, incessantly, endlessly, persistently, repeatedly, regularly; informal 24-7.
OPPOSITES never, occasionally.

forfeit verb **lose,** be deprived of, surrender, relinquish, sacrifice, give up, renounce, forgo.
OPPOSITES retain.
noun **penalty,** sanction, punishment, penance, fine, confiscation, loss, forfeiture, surrender.

forge verb **1** *he forged a huge sword:* **hammer out,** beat out, fashion. **2** *they forged a partnership:* **build,** construct,

form, create, establish, set up. **3** *he forged her signature:* **fake,** falsify, counterfeit, copy, imitate; informal pirate.

forged adjective **fake,** false, counterfeit, imitation, copied, pirate, bogus; informal phoney, dud.
OPPOSITES genuine.

forgery noun **fake,** counterfeit, fraud, imitation, replica, copy, pirate copy; informal phoney.

forget verb **1** *he forgot where he was:* **fail to remember,** be unable to remember. **2** *I never forget my briefcase:* **leave behind,** fail to take/bring, travel/leave home without. **3** *I forgot to close the door:* **neglect,** fail, omit.
OPPOSITES remember.

forgive verb **1** *she would not forgive him:* **pardon,** excuse, exonerate, absolve. **2** *you must forgive his rude conduct:* **excuse,** overlook, disregard, ignore, make allowances for, turn a blind eye to, condone, indulge, tolerate.
OPPOSITES blame, resent.

forgiveness noun **pardon,** absolution, exoneration, indulgence, clemency, mercy, reprieve, amnesty; informal let-off.
OPPOSITES mercilessness, punishment.

fork verb **split,** branch, divide, separate, part, diverge, go in different directions, bifurcate.

form noun **1** *the form of the landscape:* **shape,** configuration, formation, structure, construction, arrangement, appearance, exterior, outline, format, layout, design. **2** *the human form:* **body,** shape, figure, frame, physique, anatomy; informal vital statistics.

3 *the infection takes different forms:* **manifestation,** appearance, embodiment, incarnation, semblance, shape, guise. **4** *sponsorship is a form of advertising:* **kind,** sort, type, class, category, variety, genre, brand, style. **5** *you have to fill in a form:* **questionnaire,** document, coupon, slip. **6** *what form is your daughter in?* **class,** year; N. Amer. grade. **7** *in good form:* **condition,** fettle, shape, health; Brit. informal nick.

verb **1** *formed from mild steel:* **make,** construct, build, manufacture, fabricate, assemble, put together, create, fashion, shape. **2** *he formed a plan:* **formulate,** devise, conceive, work out, think up, lay, draw up, put together, produce, fashion, concoct, forge, hatch; informal dream up. **3** *they formed a company:* **set up,** establish, found, launch, create, institute, start, inaugurate. **4** *a mist was forming:* **materialize,** come into being/existence, emerge, develop, take shape, gather, accumulate, collect, amass. **5** *his men formed themselves into a line:* **arrange,** draw up, line up, assemble, organize, sort, order. **6** *these parts form an integrated whole:* **comprise,** make, make up, constitute, compose, add up to.
OPPOSITES dissolve, disappear.

formal adjective **1** *a formal dinner:* **ceremonial,** ritualistic, ritual, conventional, traditional, stately, solemn, elaborate. **2** *a very formal manner:* **aloof,** reserved, remote, detached, unapproachable, stiff, stuffy, ceremonious, correct, proper; informal stand-offish. **3** *formal permission:* **official,** legal, authorized, approved, certified, endorsed, sanctioned, licensed, recognized.
OPPOSITES informal, friendly, casual, colloquial, unofficial.

formality noun **1** *the formality of the occasion:* **ceremony,** ritual, protocol, decorum, solemnity. **2** *his formality was off-putting:* **aloofness,** reserve, remoteness, detachment, unapproachability, stiffness, stuffiness, correctness; informal stand-offishness. **3** *we keep the formalities to a minimum:* **official procedure,** bureaucracy, red tape, paperwork. **4** *the interview is just a formality:* **routine,** routine practice, normal procedure.
OPPOSITES informality, friendliness.

format noun **design,** style, appearance, look, form, shape, size, arrangement, plan, structure, scheme, composition, configuration.

formation noun **1** *the formation of the island:* **emergence,** genesis, development, evolution, shaping, origin. **2** *the formation of a new government:* **establishment,** setting up, institution, foundation, creation, inauguration. **3** *fighters flying in a V formation:* **configuration,** arrangement, grouping, pattern, array, alignment, order.
OPPOSITES destruction, disappearance, dissolution.

former adjective **1** *the former bishop:* **one-time,** erstwhile, sometime, ex-, previous, preceding, earlier, prior, last. **2** *in former times:* **earlier,** old, past, bygone, olden, long ago, gone by, long past, of old. **3** *the*

former view: **first-mentioned,** first.
OPPOSITES future, current, latter.

formerly adverb **previously,** earlier, before, until now/then, once, once upon a time, at one time, in the past.

formidable adjective **1** *a formidable beast:* **intimidating,** forbidding, alarming, frightening, awesome, fearsome, threatening. **2** *a formidable pianist:* **accomplished,** masterly, virtuoso, expert, impressive, powerful, terrific, superb; informal tremendous, nifty, crack, ace, wizard, magic, mean, wicked, deadly.
OPPOSITES pleasant-looking, comforting, poor.

formula noun **1** *a legal formula:* **form of words,** set expression, phrase, saying. **2** *a peace formula:* **recipe,** prescription, blueprint, plan, policy, method, procedure.

formulate verb **1** *the miners formulated a plan:* **devise,** conceive, work out, think up, lay, draw up, form, concoct, contrive, forge, hatch, prepare, develop. **2** *how Marx formulated his question:* **express,** phrase, word, define, specify, put into words, frame, couch, put, articulate, say.

fort noun **fortress,** castle, citadel, bunker, stronghold, fortification, bastion.

forte noun **strength,** strong point, speciality, strong suit, talent, skill, gift; informal thing.
OPPOSITES weakness.

forthcoming adjective
1 *forthcoming events:* **coming,** upcoming, approaching, imminent, impending, future.
2 *no reply was forthcoming:*

available, on offer, offered.
3 *he was not very forthcoming:* **communicative,** talkative, chatty, expansive, expressive, frank, open, candid.
OPPOSITES past, current, unavailable, uncommunicative.

fortify verb **1** *measures to fortify the building:* **strengthen,** secure, barricade, protect. **2** *I'll have a drink to fortify me:* **invigorate,** strengthen, energize, enliven, animate, vitalize; informal pep up, buck up.
OPPOSITES weaken, sedate, subdue.

fortitude noun **courage,** bravery, endurance, resilience, mettle, strength of character, backbone, grit; informal guts; Brit. informal bottle.
OPPOSITES faint-heartedness.

fortress noun **fort,** castle, citadel, bunker, stronghold, fortification.

fortunate adjective **1** *he was fortunate enough to survive:* **lucky,** favoured, blessed, blessed with good luck, in luck; Brit. informal jammy. **2** *in a fortunate position:* **favourable,** advantageous, happy.
OPPOSITES unfortunate, unfavourable.

fortunately adverb **luckily,** by good luck, by good fortune, as luck would have it, happily, mercifully, thankfully.

fortune noun **1** *fortune favoured him:* **chance,** accident, coincidence, serendipity, destiny, providence; N. Amer. happenstance. **2** *a change of fortune:* **luck,** fate, destiny, predestination, the stars, karma, lot. **3** *an upswing in Sheffield's fortunes:* **circumstances,** state of affairs, condition, position, situation.

4 *he made his fortune in steel:* **wealth,** money, riches, assets, resources, means, possessions, property, estate.

forum noun **meeting,** assembly, gathering, rally, conference, seminar, convention, symposium.

forward adverb **1** *the traffic moved forward:* **ahead,** forwards, onwards, onward, on, further. **2** *the winner stepped forward:* **towards the front,** out, forth, into view, up. **3** *from that day forward:* **onward,** onwards, on, forth, for ever. OPPOSITES backwards, back. adjective **1** *a forward movement:* **onward,** advancing. **2** *the Red Army's forward bridgehead:* **front,** advance, foremost, leading. **3** *forward planning:* **future,** forward-looking, for the future, anticipatory. **4** *the girls were very forward:* **bold,** brazen, cheeky, shameless, familiar, overfamiliar, presumptuous; informal fresh. OPPOSITES backward, rear, shy. verb **1** *my mother forwarded your letter:* **send on,** post on, redirect, readdress, pass on. **2** *the goods were forwarded by sea:* **send,** dispatch, transmit, carry, convey, deliver, ship.

foster verb **1** *he fostered the arts:* **encourage,** promote, further, nurture, help, aid, assist, support, back. **2** *they fostered two children:* **bring up,** rear, raise, care for, take care of, look after, provide for. OPPOSITES suppress, neglect.

foul adjective **1** *a foul smell:* **disgusting,** revolting, repulsive, repugnant, abhorrent, loathsome, offensive, sickening, nauseating; informal ghastly, gruesome, gross. **2** *foul*

drinking water: **contaminated,** polluted, infected, tainted, impure, filthy, dirty, unclean. **3** *foul language:* **vulgar,** crude, coarse, filthy, dirty, obscene, indecent, naughty, offensive; informal blue. OPPOSITES pleasant, clean. verb **1** *the river had been fouled:* **dirty,** pollute, contaminate, poison, taint. **2** *the trawler had fouled its nets:* **tangle up,** entangle, snarl, catch, entwine. OPPOSITES clean up, disentangle.

found verb **establish,** set up, start, begin, get going, institute, inaugurate, launch. OPPOSITES dissolve.

foundation noun **1** *the foundations of the wall:* **footing,** foot, base, substructure, underpinning. **2** *there was no foundation for the claim:* **justification,** grounds, evidence, basis. **3** *an educational foundation:* **endowed institution,** charitable body, funding agency.

founder[1] noun *the founder of modern physics:* **originator,** creator, (founding) father, architect, developer, pioneer, author, inventor, mastermind.

founder[2] verb **1** *the ship foundered:* **sink,** go to the bottom, go down, be lost at sea. **2** *the scheme foundered:* **fail,** be unsuccessful, fall flat, fall through, collapse, backfire, meet with disaster; informal flop, bomb. OPPOSITES be raised, succeed.

fountain noun **1** *a fountain of water:* **jet,** spray, spout, spurt, cascade, water feature. **2** *a fountain of knowledge:* **source,** fount, well, reservoir, fund, mine.

f

foyer noun entrance hall, hallway, entry, porch, reception area, atrium, concourse, lobby, anteroom; N. Amer. entryway.

fraction noun **1** *a fraction of the population:* **tiny part**, fragment, snippet, snatch. **2** *he moved a fraction closer:* **tiny amount**, little, bit, touch, soupçon, trifle, mite, shade, jot; informal smidgen, tad.
OPPOSITES whole.

fracture noun **break**, crack, split, rupture, fissure.
verb **break**, crack, split, rupture, snap, shatter, fragment, splinter.

fragile adjective **1** *fragile vases:* **breakable**, delicate, brittle, flimsy, dainty, fine. **2** *the fragile ceasefire:* **tenuous**, shaky, insecure, vulnerable, flimsy. **3** *she is still very fragile:* **weak**, delicate, frail, debilitated, ill, unwell, poorly, sickly.
OPPOSITES sturdy, durable, robust.

fragment noun **1** *meteorite fragments:* **piece**, bit, particle, speck, chip, shard, sliver, splinter, flake. **2** *a fragment of conversation:* **snatch**, snippet, scrap, bit.
verb *explosions caused the chalk to fragment:* **break up**, crack open, shatter, splinter, fracture, disintegrate, fall to pieces, fall apart.

fragrance noun **1** *the fragrance of spring flowers:* **sweet smell**, scent, perfume, bouquet, aroma, nose. **2** *a daring new fragrance:* **perfume**, scent, eau de toilette.

fragrant adjective **sweet-scented**, sweet-smelling, scented, perfumed, aromatic.
OPPOSITES smelly.

frail adjective **1** *a frail old lady:* weak, delicate, feeble, infirm, ill, unwell, sickly, poorly. **2** *a frail structure:* **fragile**, easily damaged, delicate, flimsy, insubstantial, unsteady, unstable, rickety.
OPPOSITES strong, robust.

frame noun **1** *a tubular metal frame:* **framework**, structure, substructure, skeleton, casing, chassis, shell. **2** *his tall, slender frame:* **body**, figure, form, shape, physique, anatomy, build.
verb **1** *he had the picture framed:* **mount**, set in a frame. **2** *those who frame the regulations:* **formulate**, draw up, draft, shape, compose, put together, form, devise.
■ **frame of mind** mood, state of mind, humour, temper, disposition.

framework noun **1** *a metal framework:* **frame**, structure, skeleton, chassis, support, scaffolding. **2** *the framework of society:* **structure**, shape, fabric, order, scheme, system, organization, anatomy; informal make-up.

frank adjective **1** *he was quite frank with me:* **candid**, direct, forthright, plain, straight, to the point, matter-of-fact, open, honest; informal upfront. **2** *she looked at Sam with frank admiration:* **open**, undisguised, unconcealed, naked, unmistakable, clear, obvious, transparent, patent, evident.
OPPOSITES evasive, disguised.

frankly adverb **1** *frankly, I'm not interested:* **to be frank**, to be honest, to tell the truth, in all honesty. **2** *he stated the case quite frankly:* **candidly**, directly, plainly, straightforwardly, forthrightly, openly, honestly, without beating about the bush, bluntly.

frantic adjective **panic-stricken,** panicky, beside oneself, at one's wits' end, distraught, overwrought, worked up, frenzied, frenetic, fraught, feverish, desperate; informal in a state, tearing one's hair out; Brit. informal having kittens, in a flat spin.
OPPOSITES calm.

fraternity noun **1** *a spirit of fraternity:* **brotherhood,** fellowship, kinship, friendship, mutual support, solidarity, community. **2** *the teaching fraternity:* **profession,** community, trade, set, circle. **3** (N. Amer.) *a college fraternity:* **society,** club, association, group.

fraud noun **1** *he was arrested for fraud:* **deception,** sharp practice, cheating, swindling, trickery, embezzlement, deceit, double-dealing, chicanery. **2** *social security frauds:* **swindle,** racket, deception, trick, cheat, hoax; informal scam, con, rip-off, sting, fiddle; N. Amer. informal hustle. **3** *they exposed him as a fraud:* **impostor,** fake, sham, charlatan, swindler, fraudster, confidence trickster; informal phoney.

fraudulent adjective **dishonest,** cheating, swindling, corrupt, criminal, deceitful, double-dealing, duplicitous; informal crooked, shady, dirty; Brit. informal bent, dodgy; Austral./NZ informal shonky.
OPPOSITES honest.

frayed adjective **1** *a frayed collar:* **worn,** threadbare, tattered, ragged, the worse for wear; informal tatty; N. Amer. informal raggedy. **2** *his frayed nerves:* **strained,** fraught, tense, edgy, stressed.

freak noun **1** *a genetically engineered freak:* **aberration,** abnormality, oddity, monster, monstrosity, mutant, chimera. **2** *the accident was a freak:* **anomaly,** aberration, rarity, oddity, one-off, fluke, twist of fate. **3** (informal) *a bunch of freaks:* **oddity,** eccentric, misfit, crank; informal oddball, weirdo, nut; Brit. informal nutter; N. Amer. informal wacko, kook. **4** (informal) *a fitness freak:* **enthusiast,** fan, devotee, lover, aficionado; informal nut, fanatic, addict, maniac.
adjective *a freak storm:* **unusual,** anomalous, aberrant, atypical, unrepresentative, irregular, exceptional, isolated.
OPPOSITES normal.

free adjective **1** *admission is free:* **free of charge,** without charge, for nothing, complimentary, gratis; informal for free, on the house. **2** *free of any pressures:* **without,** unencumbered by, unaffected by, clear of, rid of, exempt from, not liable to, safe from, immune to, excused. **3** *I'm free this afternoon:* **unoccupied,** not busy, available, off duty, off work, on holiday, on leave, at leisure, with time to spare. **4** *bathroom's free:* **vacant,** empty, available, unoccupied, not in use. **5** *a free nation:* **independent,** self-governing, self-determining, sovereign, autonomous, democratic. **6** *the killer is still free:* **on the loose,** at liberty, at large, loose, unrestrained. **7** *you are free to leave:* **able,** in a position, allowed, permitted. **8** *the free flow of water:* **unobstructed,** unimpeded, unrestricted,

f

unhampered, clear, open. **9** *she was free with her money:* **generous,** liberal, open-handed, unstinting.
OPPOSITES chargeable, busy, occupied, captive, confined, obstructed, mean.
verb **1** *the hostages were freed:* **release,** set free, let go, liberate, set loose, untie. **2** *victims were freed by firefighters:* **extricate,** release, get out, cut free, pull free, rescue.
OPPOSITES confine, trap.

freedom noun **1** *a desperate bid for freedom:* **liberty,** liberation, release, deliverance. **2** *the fight for freedom:* **independence,** self-government, self-determination, self-rule, home rule, sovereignty, autonomy, democracy. **3** *freedom from political accountability:* **exemption,** immunity, dispensation, impunity. **4** *patients have more freedom to choose who treats them:* **right,** entitlement, privilege, prerogative, discretion, latitude, elbow room, licence, free rein, a free hand, carte blanche.
OPPOSITES captivity, subjection, liability, obligation.

freely adverb **1** *may I speak freely?* **openly,** candidly, frankly, directly, without beating about the bush, without mincing one's words. **2** *they gave their time and labour freely:* **voluntarily,** willingly, readily, of one's own accord, of one's own free will, without being told to.

freeze verb **1** *the stream had frozen:* **ice over,** ice up, solidify. **2** *she froze in horror:* **stop dead in one's tracks,** stand (stock) still, go rigid, become motionless, become paralysed. **3** *the prices of basic foodstuffs were frozen:* **fix,** hold, peg, set, limit, restrict, cap.
OPPOSITES thaw.

freezing adjective **1** *a freezing wind:* **icy,** bitter, chill, frosty, glacial, arctic, wintry, sub-zero, raw, biting. **2** *you must be freezing:* **frozen,** numb with cold, chilled to the bone/marrow.
OPPOSITES balmy, hot.

freight noun **goods,** cargo, merchandise.

frenzied adjective **frantic,** wild, frenetic, hectic, feverish, fevered, mad, crazed, manic, furious, uncontrolled.
OPPOSITES calm.

frenzy noun **hysteria,** madness, mania, delirium, wild excitement, fever, lather, passion, panic, fury, rage.

frequent adjective *frequent complaints:* **recurrent,** recurring, repeated, periodic, continual, habitual, regular, successive, numerous, several.
OPPOSITES occasional.
verb *he frequented chic clubs:* **visit,** patronize, spend time in, visit regularly, haunt; informal hang out at.
OPPOSITES avoid.

frequently adverb **often,** all the time, habitually, regularly, customarily, routinely, again and again, repeatedly, recurrently, continually; N. Amer. oftentimes.
OPPOSITES infrequently.

fresh adjective **1** *a fresh approach:* **new,** modern, original, novel, different, innovative. **2** *fresh food:* **recently made,** just picked, crisp, raw, natural, unprocessed.

3 *feeling fresh after a sleep:* **refreshed,** rested, restored, energetic, vigorous, invigorated, lively, sprightly, bright, alert, bouncing, perky; informal full of beans, bright-eyed and bushy-tailed. **4** *a fresh breeze:* **strong,** brisk, bracing, invigorating, chilly, cool; informal nippy; Brit. informal parky. **5** *the night air was fresh:* **cool,** crisp, refreshing, invigorating, pure, clean, clear. **6** (informal) *he's getting too fresh:* **impudent,** impertinent, insolent, presumptuous, forward, cheeky, disrespectful, rude; informal mouthy, saucy, lippy; N. Amer. informal sassy.
OPPOSITES stale, old, used, cooked, preserved, processed, tired, light, warm, sultry, respectful.

fret verb **worry,** be anxious, distress oneself, upset oneself, concern oneself, agonize, lose sleep.

friction noun **1** *lubrication reduces friction:* **rubbing,** chafing, grating, rasping, scraping, resistance, drag, abrasion. **2** *friction between father and son:* **discord,** disagreement, dissension, dispute, conflict, hostility, animosity, antipathy, antagonism, resentment, acrimony, bitterness, bad feeling.
OPPOSITES harmony.

friend noun **companion,** comrade, confidant, confidante, familiar, intimate, soul mate, playmate, playfellow, ally, associate; informal pal, chum; Brit. informal mate; N. Amer. informal buddy, amigo, compadre, homeboy.
OPPOSITES enemy.

friendly adjective **1** *a friendly woman:* **amiable,** companionable, sociable, gregarious, comradely, neighbourly, hospitable, easy to get on with, affable, genial, cordial, warm, affectionate, convivial; Scottish couthy; informal chummy, pally; Brit. informal matey; N. Amer. informal buddy-buddy. **2** *friendly conversation:* **amicable,** cordial, pleasant, easy, relaxed, casual, informal, unceremonious, close, intimate, familiar.
OPPOSITES unfriendly, hostile.

friendship noun **1** *lasting friendships:* **relationship,** attachment, association, bond, tie, link, union. **2** *ties of friendship:* **friendliness,** affection, camaraderie, comradeship, companionship, fellowship, closeness, affinity, unity, intimacy.
OPPOSITES hostility.

fright noun **1** *she was paralysed with fright:* **fear,** terror, horror, alarm, panic, dread, trepidation, dismay, nervousness. **2** *the experience gave everyone a fright:* **scare,** shock, surprise, turn, jolt, start.
OPPOSITES pleasant surprise.

frighten verb **scare,** startle, alarm, terrify, petrify, shock, chill, panic, unnerve, intimidate; informal spook; Brit. informal put the wind up.
OPPOSITES reassure.

frightful adjective **horrible,** horrific, ghastly, horrendous, awful, dreadful, terrible, nasty; informal horrid.

fringe noun **1** *the city's northern fringe:* **edge,** border, margin, extremity, perimeter, periphery, rim, limits, outskirts. **2** *blue curtains with a yellow fringe:*

edging, border, trimming, frill, flounce, ruffle.
OPPOSITES middle.
adjective *fringe theatre:* **alternative,** avant-garde, experimental, innovative, left-field, radical, off-Broadway.
OPPOSITES mainstream.

frivolous adjective **flippant,** glib, facetious, joking, jokey, light-hearted, fatuous, inane; informal flip.
OPPOSITES serious.

front noun **1** *the front of the boat:* **fore,** foremost part, forepart, nose, head, bow, prow, foreground. **2** *a shop front:* **frontage,** face, facing, facade, window. **3** *the front of the queue:* **head,** beginning, start, top, lead. **4** *a brave front:* **appearance,** air, face, manner, exterior, veneer, (outward) show, act, pretence. **5** *the shop was a front for his real business:* **cover,** blind, disguise, facade, mask, cloak, screen, smokescreen, camouflage.
OPPOSITES back.
adjective **leading,** lead, first, foremost.
OPPOSITES back, last.
■ **in front** ahead, to/at the fore, at the head, up ahead, in the lead, leading, coming first, at the head of the queue; informal up front.

frontier noun **border,** boundary, borderline, dividing line, perimeter, limit, edge.

frosty adjective **1** *a frosty morning:* **cold,** freezing, frozen, icy, bitter, chill, wintry, arctic; informal nippy; Brit. informal parky. **2** *a frosty reception:* **unfriendly,** cold, frigid, icy, glacial, inhospitable, unwelcoming, forbidding, hostile, stony.
OPPOSITES warm, friendly.

frown verb **scowl,** glower, glare, lour, make a face, look daggers, give someone a black look, knit one's brows; informal give someone a dirty look.
OPPOSITES smile.
■ **frown on** disapprove of, take a dim view of, take exception to, object to, look askance at, not take kindly to.

fruitful adjective **productive,** constructive, useful, worthwhile, helpful, beneficial, valuable, rewarding, advantageous.
OPPOSITES barren, futile.

frustrate verb **1** *his plans were frustrated:* **thwart,** defeat, foil, block, stop, counter, spoil, check, forestall, scotch, derail, snooker; informal stymie; Brit. informal scupper. **2** *the delays frustrated him:* **exasperate,** infuriate, discourage, dishearten, disappoint.
OPPOSITES further, satisfy.

frustration noun **1** *he clenched his fists in frustration:* **exasperation,** annoyance, anger, vexation, irritation, disappointment, dissatisfaction. **2** *the frustration of his plans:* **thwarting,** defeat, prevention, foiling, blocking, spoiling, forestalling, derailment, obstruction.

fudge verb **evade,** avoid, dodge, skirt, duck, gloss over, cloud, hedge, beat about the bush, equivocate.

fuel verb **1** *power stations fuelled by coal:* **power,** fire, drive, run. **2** *the rumours fuelled people's anxiety:* **fan,** feed, stoke up, inflame, intensify, stimulate, encourage, provoke, incite, sustain.

fugitive noun **escapee,** runaway, deserter, absconder, refugee.

fulfil verb **1** *he fulfilled a lifelong ambition:* **achieve**, attain, realize, make happen, succeed in, bring to completion, bring to fruition, satisfy. **2** *she failed to fulfil her duties:* **carry out**, perform, accomplish, execute, do, discharge, conduct. **3** *they fulfilled the criteria:* **meet**, satisfy, comply with, conform to, fill, answer.

fulfilled adjective **satisfied**, content, contented, happy, pleased, at peace.
OPPOSITES discontented.

full adjective **1** *her glass was full:* **filled**, brimming, brimful, packed, loaded, crammed, crowded, bursting, overflowing, congested; informal jam-packed, wall-to-wall, chock-a-block, chock-full, awash. **2** *I'm full:* **replete**, full up, satisfied, sated, satiated; informal stuffed. **3** *a full life:* **eventful**, interesting, exciting, lively, action-packed, busy, active. **4** *a full list of facilities:* **comprehensive**, thorough, exhaustive, all-inclusive, all-encompassing, all-embracing, in-depth, complete, entire, whole, unabridged, uncut. **5** *at full speed:* **maximum**, top. **6** *a full figure:* **plump**, rounded, buxom, shapely, ample, curvaceous, voluptuous; informal busty, curvy, well endowed; N. Amer. informal zaftig. **7** *a full skirt:* **loose-fitting**, loose, baggy, voluminous, roomy, capacious, billowing.
OPPOSITES empty, hungry, uneventful, selective, low, thin, tight.

fully adverb **completely**, entirely, wholly, totally, perfectly, quite, altogether, thoroughly, in all respects, (up) to the hilt.

OPPOSITES partly, nearly.

fumble verb **grope**, fish, scrabble, feel.

fume noun *toxic fumes:* **smoke**, vapour, gas, exhaust, pollution.
verb *Ella was fuming at his arrogance:* **be furious**, seethe, be livid, be incensed, boil, be beside oneself, spit; informal foam at the mouth, see red.

fumigate verb **disinfect**, purify, sterilize, sanitize, decontaminate, cleanse, clean out.
OPPOSITES soil.

fun noun **1** *I joined in with the fun:* **enjoyment**, entertainment, amusement, pleasure, jollification, merrymaking, recreation, leisure, relaxation, a good time; informal living it up, a ball. **2** *she's full of fun:* **merriment**, cheerfulness, jollity, joviality, high spirits, mirth, laughter, hilarity, light-heartedness, levity. **3** *he became a figure of fun:* **ridicule**, derision, mockery, scorn, contempt.
OPPOSITES boredom, misery, respect.
adjective (informal) *a fun evening:* **enjoyable**, entertaining, amusing, pleasurable, pleasant, agreeable, convivial.
■ **make fun of** tease, poke fun at, ridicule, mock, laugh at, parody, caricature, satirize; informal take the mickey out of, send up; N. Amer. informal goof on.

function noun **1** *the main function of the machine:* **purpose**, task, use, role. **2** *my function was to train the recruits:* **responsibility**, duty, role, province, activity, assignment, task, job, mission. **3** *a function attended by local dignitaries:* **social event**, party,

social occasion, affair, gathering, reception, soirée; N. Amer. levee; informal do, bash.
verb **1** *the system had ceased to function:* **work,** go, run, be in working/running order, operate. **2** *the museum functions as an education centre:* **act,** serve, operate, perform, do duty.

functional adjective **1** *a small functional kitchen:* **practical,** useful, utilitarian, workaday, serviceable, no-frills. **2** *the machine is now fully functional:* **working,** in working order, functioning, in service, in use, going, running, operative; informal up and running.

fund noun **1** *an emergency fund:* **collection,** kitty, reserve, pool, purse, savings, coffers. **2** *short of funds:* **money,** cash, wealth, means, assets, resources, savings, capital, reserves, the wherewithal; informal dosh; Brit. informal lolly.
verb *we were funded by the Treasury:* **finance,** pay for, back, capitalize, subsidize, endow, invest in, sponsor; N. Amer. informal bankroll.

fundamental adjective **basic,** underlying, core, rudimentary, root, primary, prime, cardinal, principal, chief, key, central, vital, essential.
OPPOSITES secondary, incidental.

fundamentally adverb **essentially,** in essence, basically, at heart, at bottom, deep down, profoundly, primarily, above all.

funeral noun **burial,** interment, entombment, committal, laying to rest, cremation.

funny adjective **1** *a very funny film:* **amusing,** humorous, witty, comic, comical, hilarious, hysterical, riotous, uproarious, farcical; informal rib-tickling, priceless. **2** *a funny coincidence:* **strange,** peculiar, odd, weird, bizarre, curious, freakish, quirky, unusual. **3** *there's something funny about him:* **suspicious,** suspect, dubious, untrustworthy, questionable; informal fishy; Brit. informal dodgy.
OPPOSITES unfunny, serious, unsurprising, trustworthy.

furious adjective **1** *he was furious when we told him:* **very angry,** enraged, infuriated, irate, incensed, fuming, ranting, raving, seething, beside oneself, outraged; informal hopping mad, wild, livid. **2** *a furious debate:* **fierce,** heated, passionate, fiery, tumultuous, turbulent, tempestuous, violent, stormy, acrimonious.
OPPOSITES pleased, calm.

furnish verb **1** *the bedrooms are elegantly furnished:* **fit out,** appoint, equip; Brit. informal do out. **2** *they furnished us with waterproofs:* **supply,** provide, equip, issue, kit out; informal fix up.

furore noun **commotion,** uproar, outcry, fuss, upset, brouhaha, stir; informal to-do, hoo-ha, hullabaloo.

further adverb *further, it gave him an alibi.* See FURTHERMORE.
adjective *further information:* **additional,** more, extra, supplementary, new, fresh.
OPPOSITES existing.
verb *attempts to further his career:* **promote,** advance, forward, develop, facilitate, aid, assist, help, boost, encourage.
OPPOSITES impede.

furthermore adverb **moreover,** further, what's more, also, additionally, in addition, besides, as well, too, on top of that, into the bargain.

furthest adjective **most distant,** remotest, farthest, furthermost, farthermost, outer, outermost, extreme.
OPPOSITES nearest.

furtive adjective **surreptitious,** secretive, secret, clandestine, hidden, covert, conspiratorial, cloak-and-dagger, sneaky; informal shifty.
OPPOSITES open.

fury noun **1** *she exploded with fury:* **rage,** anger, wrath, outrage. **2** *the fury of the storm:* **ferocity,** violence, turbulence, tempestuousness, savagery, severity, intensity, vehemence, force.
OPPOSITES pleasure.

fuss noun **1** *what's all the fuss about?* **commotion,** excitement, stir, confusion, disturbance, brouhaha, uproar, furore, storm in a teacup; informal hoo-ha, to-do, song and dance, performance. **2** *he didn't put up too much of a fuss:* **protest,** complaint, objection, argument, row. **3** *they settled in with very little fuss:* **trouble,** bother, inconvenience, effort, exertion, labour; informal hassle.
verb *he was still fussing about his clothes:* **worry,** fret, be agitated, be worked up, make a big thing out of, make a

mountain out of a molehill; informal flap, be in a tizzy.

fussy adjective **1** *he's very fussy about what he eats:* **particular,** finicky, fastidious, hard to please, faddish; informal pernickety, choosy, picky; Brit. informal faddy; N. Amer. informal persnickety. **2** *a fussy bridal gown:* **over-elaborate,** ornate, fancy, busy, cluttered.

futile adjective **fruitless,** vain, pointless, useless, ineffectual, forlorn, hopeless.
OPPOSITES useful.

future noun **1** *plans for the future:* **time to come,** what lies ahead. **2** *her future lay in acting:* **destiny,** fate, fortune, prospects, chances.
OPPOSITES past.
adjective **1** *a future date:* **later,** to come, following, ensuing, succeeding, subsequent, coming. **2** *his future wife:* **to be,** destined, intended, planned, prospective.
OPPOSITES previous, past.

fuzzy adjective **1** *her fuzzy hair:* **frizzy,** fluffy, woolly, downy. **2** *a fuzzy picture:* **blurred,** indistinct, unclear, out of focus, misty. **3** *a fuzzy concept:* **unclear,** imprecise, unfocused, nebulous, vague, hazy, loose, woolly.
OPPOSITES straight, smooth, sharp, clear.

f

Gg

gadget noun device, appliance, apparatus, instrument, implement, tool, utensil, contrivance, contraption, machine, mechanism, invention; informal gizmo.

gag[1] verb 1 *the government tried to gag its critics:* silence, muzzle, suppress, stifle, censor, curb, restrain. 2 *the stench made her gag:* retch, heave.

gag[2] noun (informal) *he told a few gags:* joke, quip, jest, witticism; informal crack, wisecrack, one-liner.

gain verb 1 *he gained a scholarship:* obtain, get, secure, acquire, come by, procure, attain, achieve, earn, win, capture; informal land. 2 *they stood to gain from the deal:* profit, make money, benefit, do well out of. 3 *she gained weight:* put on, increase in, build up. 4 *they were gaining on us:* catch up (with), catch, reduce someone's lead, narrow the gap.
OPPOSITES lose, fall behind.
noun 1 *his gain from the deal:* profit, earnings, income, yield, return, reward, advantage, benefit; informal take. 2 *weight gain:* increase, addition, rise, increment, advance.
OPPOSITES loss.

gala noun festival, fair, fête, carnival, pageant, jubilee, jamboree, celebration.

gale noun 1 *a howling gale:* high wind, blast, squall, storm, tempest, hurricane, tornado, cyclone, whirlwind, typhoon. 2 *gales of laughter:* peal, howl, hoot, shriek, scream, roar, fit, paroxysm.

gamble verb 1 *he started to gamble:* bet, place a bet, wager, hazard; Brit. informal punt, have a flutter. 2 *investors are gambling that the pound will fall:* take a chance, take a risk; N. Amer. take a flyer; informal stick one's neck out; Brit. informal chance one's arm.
noun *I took a gamble:* risk, chance, leap in the dark, speculation, lottery, pot luck.

game noun 1 *the children invented a new game:* pastime, diversion, entertainment, amusement, distraction, recreation, sport, activity. 2 *we lost the game:* match, contest, fixture, meeting, tie, clash.
adjective *are you game?* willing, prepared, ready, disposed, interested, eager, keen, enthusiastic.

gang noun 1 *a gang of teenagers:* band, group, crowd, pack, horde, throng, mob, herd, swarm, troop; informal bunch, gaggle, load. 2 *a gang of workmen:* crew, team, group, squad, shift, detachment, unit.

gangster noun hoodlum, racketeer, thug, villain, criminal, Mafioso; informal mobster, crook, tough; N. Amer. informal hood.

gaol noun. See JAIL.

gap noun 1 *a gap in the shutters:* opening, aperture, space, breach, chink, slit, crack, crevice, cleft, cavity, hole. 2 *a gap between meetings:* pause, intermission, interval, interlude, break, breathing space, breather, respite; N. Amer. recess. **3** *a gap in our records:* **omission**, blank. **4** *the gap between rich and poor:* **chasm**, gulf, separation, contrast, difference, disparity, divergence, imbalance.

gape verb **1** *she gaped at him in astonishment:* **stare**, stare open-mouthed, goggle, gaze, ogle; informal **rubberneck**; Brit. informal gawp. **2** *a jacket which gaped at every seam:* **open**, yawn, part, split.

gaping adjective **wide**, broad, vast, wide open, yawning, cavernous.

garish adjective **gaudy**, lurid, loud, harsh, showy, glittering, brash, tasteless, vulgar; informal flashy.
OPPOSITES drab, subdued, tasteful.

garment noun **item/article of clothing**; (**garments**) clothes, clothing, dress, garb, wardrobe, costume; N. Amer. attire; Brit. informal clobber; N. Amer. informal threads.

garnish verb **decorate**, adorn, ornament, trim, dress, embellish.
noun **decoration**, adornment, ornament, embellishment, enhancement, finishing touch.

garrison noun **1** *the English garrison had left:* **troops**, forces, militia, soldiers, force, detachment, unit. **2** *forces from three garrisons:* **base**, camp, station, barracks, fort, command post.
verb *troops were garrisoned in York:* **station**, post, deploy, base, site, place, billet.

gash noun **cut**, laceration, slash, slit, split, wound, injury.
verb **cut**, lacerate, slash, slit, split, wound, injure.

gasp verb **1** *I gasped in surprise:* catch/draw in one's breath, gulp. **2** *he fell on the ground, gasping:* **pant**, puff, puff and blow, wheeze, breathe hard/heavily, choke, fight for breath.
noun *he could speak only between gasps:* **gulp**, pant, puff.

gate noun **barrier**, turnstile, gateway, doorway, entrance, exit, door, portal; N. Amer. entryway.

gather verb **1** *we gathered in the hotel lobby:* **congregate**, assemble, meet, collect, get together, convene, muster, rally, converge. **2** *he gathered his family:* **summon**, call together, bring together, assemble, convene, rally, round up, muster, marshal. **3** *they gathered the crops:* **harvest**, reap, crop, pick, pluck, collect. **4** *I gather he's a footballer:* **understand**, believe, be led to believe, conclude, infer, assume, take it, surmise, hear, learn, discover. **5** *her dress was gathered at the waist:* **pleat**, pucker, tuck, fold, ruffle.
OPPOSITES disperse.

gathering noun **assembly**, meeting, convention, rally, council, congress, congregation, audience, crowd, group, throng, mass; informal get-together.

gaudy adjective **garish**, lurid, loud, glaring, harsh, showy, glittering, ostentatious, tasteless; informal flashy, tacky.
OPPOSITES drab, tasteful.

gauge noun *the temperature gauge:* **meter**, measure, indicator, dial, scale, display.
verb **1** *astronomers can gauge the star's brightness:* **measure**, calculate, compute, work out, determine, ascertain, count, weigh, quantify, put a figure on. **2** *it is hard to gauge how*

effective the ban was: **assess,** evaluate, determine, estimate, form an opinion of, appraise, weigh up, judge, guess; informal size up.

gay adjective **homosexual,** lesbian; informal queer, pink.
OPPOSITES heterosexual.

gaze verb **stare,** gape, look fixedly, goggle, eye, scrutinize, ogle; informal rubberneck; Brit. informal gawp; N. Amer. informal eyeball.
noun **stare,** gape, fixed look, regard, scrutiny.

gear noun **1** *fishing gear:* **equipment,** apparatus, paraphernalia, tools, utensils, implements, instruments, rig, tackle; Brit. informal clobber. **2** (informal) *I'll pick up my gear from my hotel:* **belongings,** possessions, effects, paraphernalia, bits and pieces; informal things, stuff, kit; Brit. informal clobber, gubbins. **3** (informal) *the best designer gear:* **clothes,** clothing, garments, outfits, attire, garb, wardrobe; informal togs; Brit. informal clobber, kit; N. Amer. informal threads.

gem noun **1** *rubies and other gems:* **jewel,** precious stone, semi-precious stone; informal rock. **2** *a musical gem:* **masterpiece,** classic, treasure, prize, find; informal one in a million, the bee's knees.

general adjective **1** *suitable for general use:* **widespread,** common, extensive, universal, wide, popular, public, mainstream. **2** *a general pay increase:* **comprehensive,** overall, across the board, blanket, global, universal, mass, wholesale. **3** *the general practice:* **usual,** customary, habitual, traditional, normal,

conventional, typical, standard, regular, accepted, prevailing, routine, established, everyday. **4** *a general description:* **broad,** rough, loose, approximate, unspecific, vague, imprecise, inexact.
OPPOSITES restricted, localized, exceptional, detailed.

generally adverb **1** *summers were generally hot:* **normally,** in general, as a rule, by and large, mainly, mostly, for the most part, predominantly, on the whole, usually. **2** *the idea was generally accepted:* **widely,** commonly, extensively, universally, popularly.

generate verb **create,** make, produce, engender, spawn, precipitate, prompt, provoke, trigger, spark off, stir up, induce.

generation noun **1** *people of the same generation:* **age,** age group, peer group. **2** *the next generation of computers:* **crop,** batch, wave, range.

generosity noun **liberality,** lavishness, magnanimity, bounty, munificence, open-handedness, largesse, unselfishness, altruism, charity.
OPPOSITES meanness, selfishness.

generous adjective **1** *she is generous with money:* **liberal,** lavish, magnanimous, giving, open-handed, bountiful, unselfish, ungrudging, free. **2** *a generous amount of fabric:* **plentiful,** copious, ample, liberal, large, abundant.
OPPOSITES mean, selfish, meagre.

genesis noun **origin,** source, root, beginning, start.

genius noun **1** *the world knew of his genius:* **brilliance,** intelligence, intellect, ability, cleverness, brains. **2** *he has a*

g

genius for organization: **talent,** gift, flair, aptitude, facility, knack, ability, expertise, capacity, faculty. **3** *he is a genius:* **brilliant person,** gifted person, mastermind, Einstein, intellectual, brain, prodigy; informal **egghead, bright spark;** Brit. informal **brainbox, clever clogs;** N. Amer. informal **brainiac.**
OPPOSITES stupidity, dunce.

genre noun **category,** class, classification, group, set, type, sort, kind, variety.

gentle adjective **1** *his manner was gentle:* **kind,** tender, sympathetic, considerate, understanding, compassionate, humane, mild, placid, serene. **2** *a gentle breeze | gentle music:* **light,** soft, quiet, low, slow. **3** *a gentle slope:* **gradual,** slight, easy, slow, imperceptible.
OPPOSITES brutal, strong, loud, steep.

genuine adjective **1** *a genuine Picasso:* **authentic,** real, actual, original, bona fide, true; informal **pukka, the real McCoy, the real thing, kosher;** Austral./NZ informal **dinkum. 2** *a very genuine person:* **sincere,** honest, truthful, straightforward, direct, frank, candid, open, natural; informal **straight, upfront.**
OPPOSITES bogus, insincere.

germ noun **1** *this detergent kills germs:* **microbe,** microorganism, bacillus, bacterium, virus; informal **bug. 2** *the germ of an idea:* **start,** beginnings, seed, embryo, bud, root, origin, source.

gesture noun **1** *a gesture of surrender:* **signal,** sign, motion, indication, gesticulation. **2** *a symbolic gesture:* **action,** act, deed, move.

verb *he gestured to her:* **signal,** motion, gesticulate, wave, indicate, give a sign.

get verb **1** *where did you get that hat?* **obtain,** acquire, come by, receive, gain, earn, win, be given; informal **get hold of, score. 2** *your tea's getting cold:* **become,** grow, turn, go. **3** *get the children from school:* **fetch,** collect, go/come for, call for, pick up, bring, deliver, convey. **4** *did the police get him?* **capture,** catch, arrest, apprehend, seize; informal **collar, grab, pick up;** Brit. informal **nick. 5** *she got flu:* **contract,** develop, go down with, catch, fall ill with. **6** *I didn't get what he said:* **hear,** catch, make out, follow, take in. **7** *I don't get the joke:* **understand,** comprehend, grasp, see, fathom, follow. **8** *we got there early:* **arrive,** reach, make it, turn up, appear, present oneself, come along; informal **show up. 9** *we got her to agree:* **persuade,** induce, prevail on, influence, talk into. **10** *I'll get supper:* **prepare,** get ready, cook, make; informal **fix, rustle up;** Brit. informal **knock up.**
OPPOSITES give, shake off.
■ **get something across** communicate, get over, impart, convey, transmit, make clear, express. ■ **get along** be friendly, be compatible, get on, agree, see eye to eye; informal **hit it off.**
■ **get away** escape, run away/off, break free, bolt, flee, make off, take off, decamp; informal **skedaddle, scarper;** Brit. informal **do a bunk, do a runner.** ■ **get by** manage, cope, survive, exist, subsist, muddle through/along, scrape by, make ends meet, make do; informal **make out.** ■ **get out of** evade, dodge, shirk, avoid, escape, sidestep; informal

g

wriggle out of. ■ **get round someone** cajole, persuade, wheedle, coax, prevail on, win over, bring round, sway, inveigle; informal sweet-talk, butter up. ■ **get up** get out of bed, rise, stir, rouse oneself; informal surface.

ghastly adjective **1** *a ghastly murder:* **terrible,** frightful, horrible, grim, awful, horrifying, shocking, appalling, horrendous, monstrous. **2** (informal) *a ghastly building:* **unpleasant,** objectionable, disagreeable, distasteful, awful, terrible, dreadful, frightful, detestable, vile; informal horrible, horrid.
OPPOSITES pleasant.

ghost noun **spectre,** phantom, wraith, spirit, presence, apparition; informal spook.

ghostly adjective **supernatural,** unearthly, spectral, phantom, unnatural, eerie, weird, uncanny; informal spooky.

giant noun **colossus,** mammoth, monster, leviathan, ogre.
OPPOSITES dwarf.
adjective **huge,** colossal, massive, enormous, gigantic, mammoth, vast, immense, monumental, mountainous, titanic, towering, gargantuan; informal mega, monster, whopping; Brit. informal ginormous.
OPPOSITES miniature.

giddy adjective **1** *she felt giddy:* **dizzy,** light-headed, faint, unsteady, wobbly, reeling; informal woozy. **2** *she was young and giddy:* **flighty,** silly, frivolous, skittish, irresponsible, scatty; informal dizzy.
OPPOSITES steady, sensible.

gift noun **1** *he gave the staff a gift:* **present,** handout, donation, offering, bonus, award, endowment; informal prezzie. **2** *a gift for music:* **talent,** flair, aptitude, facility, knack, bent, ability, skill, capacity, faculty.

gifted adjective **talented,** skilled, accomplished, expert, able, proficient, intelligent, clever, bright, brilliant, precocious; informal crack, ace.
OPPOSITES inept.

gigantic adjective **huge,** enormous, vast, giant, massive, colossal, mammoth, immense, monumental, mountainous, gargantuan; informal mega, monster, whopping, humongous; Brit. informal ginormous.
OPPOSITES tiny.

giggle verb & noun **titter,** snigger, chuckle, chortle, laugh.

girl noun **young woman,** young lady, miss; Scottish & N. English lass, lassie; Irish colleen; informal chick; Brit. informal bird; N. Amer. informal gal, broad, dame, babe; Austral./NZ informal sheila.

girlfriend noun **sweetheart,** lover, partner, significant other, girl, woman; informal steady; Brit. informal bird; N. Amer. informal squeeze.

give verb **1** *he gave them £2,000:* **donate,** contribute, present with, award, grant, bestow, hand (over). **2** *can I give him a message?* **convey,** pass on, impart, communicate, transmit, send, deliver, relay. **3** *he gave his life for them:* **sacrifice,** give up, relinquish, devote, dedicate. **4** *he gave a party:* **organize,** arrange, lay on, throw, host, hold, have. **5** *Dominic gave a bow:* **perform,** execute, make, do. **6** *she gave a shout:* **utter,** let out, emit, produce, make.

OPPOSITES receive, take.
■ **give someone away** betray, inform on; informal split on, rat on; Brit. informal grass on, shop; N. Amer. informal finger; Austral./NZ informal dob in. ■ **give in/up** capitulate, concede defeat, admit defeat, give up, surrender, yield, submit. ■ **give something off** emit, produce, send out, throw out, discharge, release. ■ **give something up** stop, cease, discontinue, desist from, abstain from, cut out, renounce, forgo; informal quit; Brit. informal jack in.

glad adjective **1** *I'm really glad you're coming:* **pleased,** happy, delighted, thrilled; informal over the moon; Brit. informal chuffed; N. English informal made up. **2** *I'd be glad to help:* **willing,** eager, happy, pleased, delighted, ready, prepared.
OPPOSITES dismayed, reluctant.

gladly adverb **with pleasure,** happily, cheerfully, willingly, readily, eagerly, delighted, ungrudgingly.

glamorous adjective **1** *a glamorous woman:* **beautiful,** elegant, chic, stylish, fashionable. **2** *a glamorous lifestyle:* **exciting,** glittering, glossy, colourful, exotic; informal glitzy, jet-setting.
OPPOSITES dowdy, dull.

glamour noun **1** *she had undeniable glamour:* **beauty,** allure, elegance, chic, style, charisma, charm, magnetism. **2** *the glamour of TV:* **allure,** attraction, fascination, charm, magic, romance, excitement, thrill; informal glitz, glam.

glance verb **1** *Rachel glanced at him:* **look briefly,** look quickly, peek, peep. **2** *I glanced through the report:* **read quickly,** scan,

skim, leaf, flick, flip, thumb, browse.
OPPOSITES study.
noun *a glance at his watch:* **peek,** peep, brief look, quick look.

glare verb *she glared at him:* **scowl,** glower, look daggers, frown, lour; informal give someone a dirty look.
noun **1** *a cold glare:* **scowl,** glower, angry stare, frown, black look; informal dirty look. **2** *the glare of the lights:* **blaze,** dazzle, shine, beam, brilliance.

glaring adjective **1** *glaring lights:* **dazzling,** blinding, blazing, strong, harsh. **2** *a glaring omission:* **obvious,** conspicuous, unmistakable, inescapable, unmissable, striking, flagrant, blatant.
OPPOSITES soft, inconspicuous.

glaze verb *pastry glazed with caramel:* **cover,** coat, varnish, lacquer, polish.
noun *a cake with an apricot glaze:* **coating,** topping, varnish, lacquer, polish.

gleam verb *a light gleamed:* **shine,** glint, glitter, shimmer, glimmer, sparkle, twinkle, flicker, wink, glisten, flash.
noun *a gleam of light:* **flash,** glimmer, glint, shimmer, twinkle, sparkle, flicker, beam, ray, shaft.

glide verb **1** *a gondola glided past:* **slide,** slip, sail, float, drift, flow. **2** *seagulls gliding over the waves:* **soar,** wheel, plane, fly.

glimpse noun *a glimpse of her face:* **brief/quick look,** glance, sight, sighting, peek, peep.
verb *he glimpsed a figure:* **catch sight of,** sight, spot, notice, discern, spy, pick out, make out.

glitter verb *crystal glittered in*

g

the candlelight: **sparkle,** twinkle, glint, shimmer, glimmer, wink, flash, shine. noun *the glitter of light on the water:* **sparkle,** twinkle, glint, shimmer, glimmer, flicker, flash.

global adjective **1** *the global economy:* **worldwide,** international, world, intercontinental, universal. **2** *a global view of the problem:* **comprehensive,** overall, general, all-inclusive, all-encompassing, universal, broad.

gloom noun **1** *she peered into the gloom:* **darkness,** dark, murk, shadows, shade. **2** *his gloom deepened:* **despondency,** depression, dejection, melancholy, unhappiness, sadness, misery, woe, despair. OPPOSITES light, happiness.

gloomy adjective **1** *a gloomy room:* **dark,** shadowy, murky, sunless, dim, dingy. **2** *Joanna looked gloomy:* **despondent,** depressed, downcast, downhearted, dejected, dispirited, disheartened, demoralized, crestfallen, glum, melancholy; informal down in the mouth, down in the dumps. **3** *gloomy forecasts about the economy:* **pessimistic,** depressing, downbeat, disheartening, disappointing, unfavourable, bleak, black. OPPOSITES bright, cheerful, optimistic.

glorious adjective **wonderful,** marvellous, magnificent, superb, sublime, spectacular, lovely, fine, delightful; informal stunning, fantastic, terrific, tremendous, sensational, heavenly, divine, gorgeous, fabulous, awesome.

OPPOSITES undistinguished, horrid.

glory noun **1** *a sport that won him glory:* **honour,** distinction, prestige, fame, renown, kudos, eminence, acclaim, praise, celebrity, recognition. **2** *a house restored to its former glory:* **magnificence,** splendour, grandeur, majesty, greatness, nobility, opulence, beauty, elegance. OPPOSITES shame, obscurity, modesty. verb *we gloried in our independence:* **delight,** triumph, revel, rejoice, exult, relish, savour, be proud of; informal get a kick out of.

gloss noun *the gloss of her hair:* **shine,** sheen, lustre, gleam, patina, polish, brilliance, shimmer. ■ **gloss over** conceal, cover up, hide, disguise, mask, veil, play down, minimize, understate.

glossy adjective **shiny,** gleaming, lustrous, brilliant, glistening, glassy, polished, lacquered, glazed. OPPOSITES dull.

glow verb **1** *lights glowed in the windows:* **shine,** gleam, glimmer, flicker, flare. **2** *a fire glowed in the hearth:* **smoulder,** burn. noun *the glow of the fire:* **radiance,** light, gleam, glimmer.

glowing adjective **1** *glowing coals:* **bright,** radiant, incandescent, luminous, smouldering. **2** *his glowing cheeks:* **rosy,** pink, red, ruddy, flushed, blushing, burning. **3** *glowing colours:* **vivid,** vibrant, bright, brilliant, rich, intense, radiant. **4** *a glowing report:* **complimentary,**

favourable, enthusiastic, admiring, rapturous, fulsome; informal rave.
OPPOSITES dead, pale, drab, damning.

glue noun *a tube of glue:* adhesive, gum, paste, cement; N. Amer. mucilage; N. Amer. informal stickum.
verb *the planks were glued together:* stick, gum, paste, fix, seal, cement.

glum adjective gloomy, downcast, dejected, despondent, crestfallen, disheartened, depressed, doleful, miserable; informal fed up, down in the dumps.
OPPOSITES cheerful.

go verb **1** *he's gone into town:* travel, move, proceed, make one's way, journey, advance, progress, pass. **2** *the road goes to London:* lead, stretch, reach, extend. **3** *it's time to go:* leave, depart, take oneself off, go away, withdraw, absent oneself, exit, set off, start out, get under way, be on one's way; Brit. make a move; informal make tracks. **4** *all our money had gone:* be used up, be spent, be exhausted, be consumed. **5** *his hair had gone grey:* become, get, turn, grow. **6** *everything went well:* turn out, work out, develop, progress, result, end (up); informal pan out. **7** *those colours don't go:* match, harmonize, blend, be complementary, coordinate, be compatible. **8** *my car won't go:* function, work, run, operate.
OPPOSITES arrive, come, return, clash, malfunction.
noun (informal) **1** *here, have a go:* try, attempt, effort, bid; informal shot, stab, crack. **2** *whose go is it?* turn, opportunity, chance,

stint, spell, time.
■ **go down 1** *the ship went down:* sink, founder. **2** *interest rates are going down:* decrease, get lower, fall, drop, decline, plummet, plunge, slump. ■ **go in for** take part in, participate in, engage in, get involved in, join in, enter into, undertake, practise, pursue, espouse, adopt, embrace. ■ **go into** investigate, examine, enquire into, look into, research, probe, explore, delve into, consider, review, analyse. ■ **go off 1** *the bomb went off:* explode, detonate, blow up. **2** (Brit.) *the milk's gone off:* go bad, go stale, go sour, turn, spoil, go rancid. ■ **go on 1** *the lecture went on for hours:* last, continue, carry on, run on, proceed, endure, persist, take. **2** *she went on about the sea:* talk at length, ramble, rattle on, chatter, prattle; Brit. informal witter, rabbit. **3** *I'm not sure what went on:* happen, take place, occur, transpire; N. Amer. informal go down. ■ **go out 1** *the lights went out:* be turned off, be extinguished, stop burning. **2** *he's going out with Kate:* see, take out, be someone's boyfriend/girlfriend, be in a relationship with; informal date, go with. ■ **go over** See GO THROUGH 3. ■ **go through 1** *the terrible things she has gone through:* undergo, experience, face, suffer, live through, endure. **2** *he went through Susie's bag:* search, look, hunt, rummage, rifle. **3** *I went through the report:* examine, study, scrutinize, inspect, look over, scan, check.

goal noun objective, aim, end, intention, plan, purpose, target, ambition, aspiration.

g

gobble verb guzzle, bolt, gulp, devour, wolf; informal tuck into, put away, demolish; Brit. informal scoff; N. Amer. informal scarf (down/up).

god noun deity, goddess, divine being, divinity, immortal.

golden adjective blonde, yellow, fair, flaxen.
OPPOSITES dark.

gone adjective 1 *I wasn't gone long*: **away**, absent, off, out, missing. **2** *those days are gone*: **past**, over (and done with), no more, done, finished, ended, forgotten. **3** *the milk's all gone*: **used up**, consumed, finished, spent, depleted.
OPPOSITES present, here.

good adjective 1 *a good product*: **fine**, superior, excellent, superb, outstanding, magnificent, exceptional, marvellous, wonderful, first-rate, first-class, quality; informal great, ace, terrific, fantastic, fabulous, class, awesome, wicked; Brit. informal brilliant. **2** *a good person*: **virtuous**, righteous, upright, upstanding, moral, ethical, principled, law-abiding, blameless, honourable, decent, respectable, trustworthy; informal squeaky clean. **3** *the children are good at school*: **well behaved**, obedient, dutiful, polite, courteous, respectful. **4** *a good driver*: **capable**, able, proficient, adept, adroit, accomplished, skilful, talented, masterly, expert; informal mean, wicked, nifty; N. Amer. informal crackerjack. **5** *a good friend*: **close**, intimate, dear, bosom, special, best, firm, loyal. **6** *we had a good time*: **enjoyable**, pleasant, agreeable, pleasurable, delightful, lovely, amusing. **7** *it was good of you to come*: **kind**, generous, charitable, gracious, noble, altruistic, unselfish. **8** *a good time to call*: **convenient**, suitable, appropriate, fitting, fit, opportune, timely, favourable. **9** *milk is good for you*: **wholesome**, healthy, nourishing, nutritious, beneficial. **10** *good food*: **tasty**, appetizing, flavoursome, palatable, succulent; informal scrumptious, scrummy, yummy; Brit. informal moreish; N. Amer. informal nummy. **11** *a good reason*: **valid**, genuine, authentic, legitimate, sound, bona fide, convincing, compelling. **12** *good weather*: **fine**, fair, dry, bright, clear, sunny, cloudless, calm, warm, mild.
OPPOSITES bad, wicked, naughty, unenjoyable, mean, inconvenient, disgusting.
noun **1** *issues of good and evil*: **virtue**, righteousness, goodness, morality, integrity, honesty, truth, honour. **2** *it's for your own good*: **benefit**, advantage, profit, gain, interest, welfare, well-being.
OPPOSITES wickedness, disadvantage.
■ **for good** forever, permanently, for always, (for) evermore, for ever and ever; N. Amer. forevermore; informal for keeps.

goodbye exclamation **farewell**, adieu, au revoir, ciao, adios; Austral./NZ hooray; informal bye, bye-bye, so long, see you (later); Brit. informal cheerio, cheers, ta-ta.

goodness noun **1** *he had some goodness in him*: **virtue**, good, righteousness, morality, integrity, rectitude, honesty, honour, decency, respectability, nobility, worth, merit. **2** *his goodness towards us:* **kindness,** humanity, benevolence, tenderness, warmth, affection, love, goodwill, sympathy, compassion, care, concern, understanding, generosity, charity.

goods plural noun **merchandise,** wares, stock, commodities, produce, products, articles.

goodwill noun **kindness,** compassion, goodness, benevolence, consideration, charity, decency, neighbourliness.
OPPOSITES hostility.

gorge noun **ravine,** canyon, gully, defile, couloir, chasm, gulf; S. English **chine**; N. English **gill**; N. Amer. **gulch, coulee.**
■ **gorge oneself stuff oneself,** guzzle, overindulge; informal **pig oneself, stuff one's face.**

gorgeous adjective **1** *a gorgeous girl:* **good-looking,** attractive, beautiful, pretty, handsome, lovely, stunning; Scottish & N. English **bonny**; informal **fanciable, tasty, hot**; Brit. informal **fit**; N. Amer. informal **cute, foxy. 2** *a gorgeous view:* **spectacular,** splendid, superb, wonderful, grand, impressive, awe-inspiring, awesome, stunning, breathtaking; informal **sensational, fabulous, fantastic. 3** *gorgeous uniforms:* **resplendent,** magnificent, sumptuous, luxurious, elegant, dazzling, brilliant.
OPPOSITES ugly, dreary, drab.

gossip noun **1** *tell me all the gossip:* **news,** rumours, scandal, hearsay; informal **dirt, buzz**; Brit. informal **goss**; N. Amer. informal **scuttlebutt. 2** *they went for a gossip:* **chat,** talk, conversation, chatter, heart-to-heart, tête-à-

tête; informal **jaw, gas**; Brit. informal **natter, chinwag**; N. Amer. informal **gabfest**; Austral./NZ informal **yarn. 3** *she's such a gossip:* **gossip-monger,** busybody, scandalmonger, rumour-monger, muckraker.
verb **1** *she gossiped about his wife:* **talk,** whisper, tell tales; informal **dish the dirt. 2** *people sat around gossiping:* **chat,** talk, converse, discuss things; informal **gas, chew the fat, jaw**; Brit. informal **natter, chinwag**; N. Amer. informal **shoot the breeze.**

gourmet noun **gastronome,** epicure, epicurean, connoisseur; informal **foodie.**

govern verb **1** *he governs the province:* **rule,** preside over, control, be in charge of, command, run, head, manage, oversee, supervise. **2** *the rules governing social behaviour:* **determine,** decide, control, constrain, regulate, direct, rule, dictate, shape, affect.

government noun **administration,** executive, regime, authority, council, powers that be, cabinet, ministry.

governor noun **leader,** ruler, chief, head, administrator, principal, director, chairman, chairwoman, chair, superintendent, commissioner, controller; informal **boss.**

gown noun **dress,** frock, robe, habit, costume.

grab verb **seize,** grasp, snatch, take hold of, grip, clasp, clutch, catch.

grace noun **1** *the grace of a ballerina:* **elegance,** poise, finesse, polish, fluency, suppleness. **2** *he had the grace to apologize:* **courtesy,** decency, (good) manners, politeness,

respect, tact. **3** *he fell from grace:* **favour,** approval, approbation, acceptance, esteem, regard, respect.
OPPOSITES awkwardness, effrontery, disfavour.
verb *a mosaic graced the floor:* **adorn,** embellish, decorate, ornament, enhance.

graceful adjective **elegant,** fluid, fluent, easy, polished, supple.

gracious adjective **courteous,** polite, civil, well-mannered, tactful, diplomatic, kind, considerate, thoughtful, obliging, accommodating, hospitable.
OPPOSITES ungracious.

grade noun **1** *hotels within the same grade:* **category,** class, classification, ranking, quality, grouping, group, bracket. **2** *his job is of the lowest grade:* **rank,** level, standing, position, class, status, order, echelon. **3** (N. Amer.) *the best grades in the school:* **mark,** score, assessment, evaluation, appraisal. **4** (N. Amer.) *the fifth grade:* **year,** form, class.
verb *eggs are graded by size:* **classify,** class, categorize, bracket, sort, group, arrange, pigeonhole, rank, evaluate, rate, value.

gradient noun **slope,** incline, hill, rise, ramp, bank; N. Amer. grade.

gradual adjective **1** *a gradual transition:* **slow,** steady, measured, unhurried, cautious, piecemeal, step-by-step, bit-by-bit, progressive, continuous. **2** *a gradual slope:* **gentle,** moderate, slight, easy.
OPPOSITES abrupt, steep.

gradually adverb **slowly,** steadily, slowly but surely, cautiously, gently, gingerly, piecemeal, bit by bit, by degrees, progressively, systematically.
OPPOSITES abruptly.

graft noun *a skin graft:* **transplant,** implant.
verb **1** *graft a bud onto the stem:* **splice,** join, insert, fix. **2** *tissue is grafted on to the cornea:* **transplant,** implant.

grain noun **1** *fields of grain:* **cereal. 2** *a grain of corn:* **kernel,** seed. **3** *grains of sand:* **granule,** particle, speck, bit, scrap, crumb, fragment, morsel. **4** *a grain of truth:* **trace,** hint, tinge, suggestion, shadow, soupçon, ounce, iota, jot, scrap, shred; informal smidgen. **5** *the grain in paper:* **texture,** weave, pattern.

grand adjective **1** *a grand hotel:* **magnificent,** imposing, impressive, awe-inspiring, splendid, resplendent, majestic, monumental, palatial, stately; Brit. upmarket; N. Amer. upscale; informal fancy, posh; Brit. informal swish. **2** *a grand scheme:* **ambitious,** bold, epic, big, extravagant. **3** *a grand old lady:* **august,** distinguished, illustrious, eminent, venerable, dignified, proud. **4** (informal) *you're doing a grand job:* **excellent,** marvellous, splendid, first-class, first-rate, wonderful, outstanding; informal superb, terrific, great, super; Brit. informal brilliant.
OPPOSITES humble, small-scale, poor.

grandeur noun **splendour,** magnificence, glory, resplendence, majesty, greatness, stateliness, pomp, ceremony.

grant verb **1** *he granted them leave of absence:* **allow,** permit,

accord, afford. **2** *he granted them £20,000:* **give,** award, bestow on, confer on, present with, endow with. **3** *I grant that the difference is slight:* **admit,** accept, concede, allow, appreciate, recognize, acknowledge, confess.
OPPOSITES refuse, deny.
noun *a grant from the council:* **award,** bursary, endowment, scholarship, allowance, subsidy, contribution, handout, donation, gift.

graphic adjective **1** *a graphic representation:* **visual,** pictorial, illustrative, diagrammatic. **2** *a graphic account:* **vivid,** explicit, detailed, realistic, descriptive, powerful, colourful, lurid, shocking.
OPPOSITES vague.

grapple verb **1** *the police grappled with him:* **wrestle,** struggle, tussle, scuffle, battle. **2** *grappling with addiction:* **deal,** cope, get to grips, tackle, confront, face.

grasp verb **1** *she grasped his hand:* **grip,** clutch, clasp, clench, squeeze, catch, seize, grab, snatch. **2** *he grasped the important points:* **understand,** comprehend, take in, see, apprehend, assimilate, absorb; informal get, take on board; Brit. informal twig.
OPPOSITES release, overlook.
noun **1** *his grasp on her hand:* **grip,** hold, squeeze. **2** *a prize lay within their grasp:* **reach,** scope, power, range, sights. **3** *a grasp of history:* **understanding,** comprehension, awareness, grip, knowledge, mastery, command.

grasping adjective **greedy,** acquisitive, avaricious,

rapacious, mercenary, materialistic; informal tight-fisted, tight, money-grubbing; N. Amer. informal grabby.

grate verb **1** *grate the cheese:* **shred,** pulverize, mince, grind, crush, crumble. **2** *her bones grated together:* **grind,** rub, rasp, scrape, jar, creak.

grateful adjective **thankful,** appreciative, indebted, obliged, in someone's debt, beholden.

gratitude noun **thanks,** gratefulness, thankfulness, appreciation, indebtedness, recognition, acknowledgement.

grave[1] noun *an unmarked grave:* **tomb,** burial place, last resting place, vault, mausoleum, sepulchre.

grave[2] adjective **1** *a grave matter:* **serious,** important, weighty, profound, significant, momentous, critical, urgent, pressing, dire, terrible, dreadful. **2** *Jackie looked grave:* **solemn,** serious, sober, unsmiling, grim, sombre, dour.
OPPOSITES trivial, light-hearted.

graveyard noun **cemetery,** churchyard, burial ground, necropolis, garden of remembrance; Scottish kirkyard.

gravity noun **1** *the gravity of the situation:* **seriousness,** importance, significance, weight, consequence, magnitude, acuteness, urgency, dreadfulness. **2** *the gravity of his demeanour:* **solemnity,** seriousness, sobriety, severity, grimness, sombreness, dourness.
OPPOSITES triviality, light-heartedness.

graze[1] verb *the deer grazed:* **feed,** eat, crop, nibble, browse.

graze[2] verb **1** *he grazed his arm:* **scrape,** skin, scratch, chafe,

g

scuff, rasp. **2** *his shot grazed the bar:* **touch,** brush, shave, skim, kiss, scrape, clip, glance off.
noun *grazes on the skin:* **scratch,** scrape, abrasion.

grease noun oil, fat, lubricant.

greasy adjective **oily,** fatty, buttery, slippery, slick, slimy, slithery; informal slippy.
OPPOSITES fat-free, clean, dry.

great adjective **1** *they showed great interest:* **considerable,** substantial, significant, serious, exceptional, extraordinary. **2** *a great expanse of water:* **large,** big, extensive, expansive, broad, wide, vast, immense, huge, enormous, massive; informal humongous, whopping; Brit. informal ginormous. **3** *great writers:* **prominent,** eminent, distinguished, illustrious, celebrated, acclaimed, admired, esteemed, renowned, notable, famous, well known, leading, top, major. **4** *a great castle:* **magnificent,** imposing, impressive, awe-inspiring, grand, splendid, majestic. **5** *a great sportsman:* **expert,** skilful, skilled, adept, accomplished, talented, fine, masterly, master, brilliant, virtuoso, marvellous, outstanding, first-class, superb; informal crack, class. **6** *a great fan of rugby:* **keen,** eager, enthusiastic, devoted, ardent, fanatical, passionate, dedicated, committed. **7** *we had a great time:* **enjoyable,** delightful, lovely, excellent, marvellous, wonderful, fine, splendid; informal terrific, fantastic, fabulous, super, cool; Brit. informal brilliant.
OPPOSITES little, small, minor, modest, poor, apathetic, half-hearted, miserable.

greatly adverb very much,

extremely, considerably, substantially, significantly, markedly, seriously, materially, enormously, vastly, immensely, tremendously, mightily; informal majorly.
OPPOSITES slightly.

greatness noun **1** *a woman destined for greatness:* **eminence,** distinction, celebrity, fame, prominence, renown, importance. **2** *his greatness as a writer:* **brilliance,** genius, prowess, talent, expertise, mastery, artistry, skill, proficiency, flair.

greed, greediness noun **1** *human greed:* **avarice,** acquisitiveness, covetousness, materialism, mercenariness; informal money-grubbing. **2** *her mouth watered with greed:* **gluttony,** hunger, voracity, self-indulgence; informal piggishness. **3** *their greed for power:* **desire,** appetite, hunger, thirst, craving, longing, yearning, hankering; informal itch.
OPPOSITES generosity, temperance, indifference.

greedy adjective **1** *a greedy eater:* **gluttonous,** ravenous, voracious; informal piggish, piggy. **2** *his greedy manager:* **avaricious,** acquisitive, covetous, grasping, materialistic, mercenary; informal money-grubbing; N. Amer. informal grabby.

green adjective **1** olive green, pea green, emerald green, lime green, avocado, pistachio, bottle green, Lincoln green, jade, sea green. **2** *a green island:* **verdant,** grassy, leafy. **3** *Green issues:* **environmental,** ecological, conservation, eco-. **4** *a green alternative to diesel:* **environmentally friendly,** eco-

g

friendly. **5** *the new supervisor was very green:* **inexperienced,** callow, raw, unseasoned, untried, naive, innocent, unworldly; informal wet behind the ears.
OPPOSITES barren, experienced.

greet verb **1** *she greeted Hank cheerily:* **say hello to,** address, salute, hail, welcome, meet, receive. **2** *the decision was greeted with outrage:* **receive,** respond to, react to, take.

greeting noun **1** *he shouted a greeting:* **hello,** salutation, welcome, reception. **2** *birthday greetings:* **best wishes,** good wishes, congratulations, compliments, regards, respects.
OPPOSITES farewell.

grey adjective **1** silvery, gunmetal, slate, charcoal, smoky. **2** *a grey day:* **cloudy,** overcast, dull, sunless, murky. **3** *her face looked grey:* **pale,** wan, ashen, pasty, pallid, colourless. **4** *his grey existence:* **characterless,** colourless, nondescript, flat, bland, dull, boring, tedious, monotonous. **5** *a grey area:* **ambiguous,** doubtful, unclear, uncertain, indefinite, debatable.
OPPOSITES sunny, ruddy, exciting, certain.

grief noun **sorrow,** misery, sadness, anguish, pain, distress, heartache, heartbreak, agony, woe, desolation.
OPPOSITES joy.

grievance noun **complaint,** objection, grumble, grouse, ill feeling, bad feeling, resentment; informal gripe.

grieve verb **1** *she grieved for her father:* **mourn,** sorrow, cry, sob, weep. **2** *it grieved me to leave her:* **sadden,** upset, distress, pain, hurt, wound, break

someone's heart.
OPPOSITES rejoice, please.

grim adjective **1** *his grim expression:* **stern,** forbidding, uninviting, unsmiling, dour, formidable. **2** *grim secrets:* **dreadful,** ghastly, horrible, terrible, awful, appalling, frightful, shocking, grisly, gruesome, depressing, distressing, upsetting. **3** *a grim hovel:* **bleak,** dismal, dingy, wretched, miserable, depressing, cheerless, joyless, gloomy, uninviting.
OPPOSITES amiable, pleasant, cheerful.

grin verb & noun **smile,** beam, smirk.
OPPOSITES frown, scowl.

grind verb **1** *the ore is ground into powder:* **crush,** pound, pulverize, mill, crumble. **2** *one stone grinds against another:* **rub,** grate, scrape. **3** *the edge of the knife is then ground:* **sharpen,** whet, hone, put an edge on, mill, machine, polish, smooth.
noun *the daily grind:* **drudgery,** toil, labour, donkey work, exertion, chores, slog.

grip verb **1** *she gripped the edge of the table:* **grasp,** clutch, clasp, take hold of, clench, cling to, grab, seize, squeeze. **2** *we were gripped by the drama:* **engross,** enthral, absorb, rivet, spellbind, fascinate, mesmerize.
OPPOSITES release.
noun **1** *a tight grip:* **grasp,** hold. **2** *the wheels lost their grip on the road:* **traction,** purchase, friction, adhesion. **3** *in the grip of an obsession:* **control,** power, hold, stranglehold, clutches, influence.

gripping adjective **engrossing,** enthralling, absorbing, riveting,

captivating, spellbinding, fascinating, compelling, thrilling, exciting, action-packed, dramatic.
OPPOSITES boring.

groan verb **1** *she groaned and rubbed her stomach:* **moan,** cry. **2** *they groan about everything:* **complain,** grumble, moan, mutter; informal grouse, bellyache, bitch, whinge. **3** *the tree groaned:* **creak,** grate, rasp.
noun **1** *a groan of anguish:* **moan,** cry. **2** *she listens to all their moans and groans:* **complaint,** grumble, grievance, moan, muttering; informal grouse, gripe, whinge. **3** *the groan of the timbers:* **creaking,** creak, grating, grinding.

groom verb **1** *she groomed her pony:* **curry,** brush, clean, rub down. **2** *his hair was carefully groomed:* **brush,** comb, arrange, do; informal fix. **3** *groomed for stardom:* **prepare,** prime, condition, coach, train, drill, teach, school.
noun *the bride and groom:* **bridegroom.**

groove noun **furrow,** channel, trench, trough, rut, gutter, canal, hollow, indentation.

grope verb **fumble,** scrabble, fish, ferret, rummage, feel, search, hunt.

gross adjective **1** (informal) *the place smelled gross:* **disgusting,** repulsive, revolting, foul, nasty, obnoxious, sickening, nauseating, stomach-churning. **2** *a gross distortion of the truth:* **thorough,** complete, utter, out and out, shameful, serious, unacceptable, flagrant, blatant, obvious, barefaced, shameless, brazen. **3** *gross income:* **total,** full, overall, combined, before deductions, before tax.

OPPOSITES pleasant, slight, acceptable, net.
verb *he grosses over a million a year:* **earn,** make, bring in, take, get, receive; informal rake in.

grotesque adjective **1** *a grotesque creature:* **misshapen,** deformed, distorted, twisted, monstrous, hideous, freakish, unnatural, abnormal, strange; informal weird. **2** *a grotesque exaggeration:* **outrageous,** monstrous, shocking, appalling, preposterous, ridiculous, ludicrous, unbelievable, incredible.
OPPOSITES normal, sensible.

ground noun **1** *she collapsed on the ground:* **floor,** earth, terra firma; informal deck. **2** *soggy ground:* **earth,** soil, turf, land, terrain. **3** *the team's home ground:* **stadium,** pitch, field, arena, track; Brit. informal park. **4** *the mansion's grounds:* **estate,** gardens, park, land, property, surroundings, territory. **5** *grounds for dismissal:* **reason,** cause, basis, foundation, justification, rationale, argument, occasion, excuse, pretext.
verb **1** *the religious life must be grounded on the law:* **base,** found, establish, root, build, form. **2** *she was well grounded in the classics:* **teach,** instruct, coach, tutor, educate, school, train, drill.

group noun **1** *the exhibits are in three groups:* **category,** class, classification, grouping, cluster, set, batch, type, sort, kind, variety, family. **2** *a group of tourists:* **crowd,** party, body, band, company, gathering, congregation, assembly, collection, cluster, clump, knot, flock, pack, troop, gang; informal bunch. **3** *a folk group:* **band,** ensemble, act; informal line-up, combo, outfit.

verb 1 *patients were grouped according to age:* **categorize,** classify, class, catalogue, sort, bracket, pigeonhole. **2** *chairs were grouped in fours:* **assemble,** collect, organize, place, arrange, range, line up, lay out.

grow verb **1** **enlarge,** get bigger, get larger, get taller, expand, increase in size, extend, spread, swell, multiply, snowball, mushroom, balloon, build up, mount up, pile up. **2** *flowers grew among the rocks:* **sprout,** germinate, spring up, develop, bud, bloom, flourish, thrive, run riot. **3** *he grew vegetables:* **cultivate,** produce, propagate, raise, rear, farm. **4** *Leonora grew bored:* **become,** get, turn, begin to be.
OPPOSITES shrink, decline.

grown-up adjective *she has two grown-up daughters:* **adult,** mature, of age, fully grown, independent.
OPPOSITES under age.
noun *she wanted to be treated like a grown-up:* **adult,** woman, man, grown man/woman.
OPPOSITES child.

growth noun **1** *population growth:* **enlargement,** increase in size, expansion, extension, swelling, multiplication, mushrooming, snowballing, rise, escalation, build-up, development. **2** *a growth on his jaw:* **tumour,** malignancy, cancer, lump, swelling.
OPPOSITES shrinkage, decline.

grubby adjective **dirty,** grimy, filthy, mucky, unwashed, stained, soiled; informal cruddy, yucky; Brit. informal **manky;** Austral./ NZ informal scungy.
OPPOSITES clean.

grudge noun **grievance,** resentment, bitterness, rancour, ill will, animosity, antipathy, antagonism; informal a chip on one's shoulder.

gruelling adjective **exhausting,** tiring, taxing, draining, demanding, exacting, difficult, arduous, strenuous, back-breaking, punishing, crippling; informal murderous; Brit. informal knackering.

gruesome adjective **grisly,** ghastly, frightful, horrid, horrifying, hideous, horrible, grim, awful, dreadful, terrible, horrific; informal sick, sick-making, gross.
OPPOSITES pleasant.

grumble verb **complain,** grouse, whine, mutter, carp, make a fuss; informal moan, bellyache, bitch, whinge; N. English informal mither.
noun **complaint,** grouse, grievance, protest; informal grouch, moan, whinge, beef, gripe.

grumpy adjective **bad-tempered,** crabby, tetchy, touchy, irascible, cantankerous, curmudgeonly, surly, fractious; informal grouchy; Brit. informal ratty; N. Amer. informal cranky, ornery.
OPPOSITES good-humoured.

guarantee noun **1** *a one-year guarantee:* **warranty. 2** *a guarantee that the hospital will stay open:* **promise,** assurance, word (of honour), pledge, vow, oath, commitment. **3** *a guarantee for loans:* **collateral,** security, surety, bond.
verb **1** *I guarantee he will accept:* **promise,** swear, pledge, vow, give one's word, give an assurance, give an undertaking.

2 *he agreed to guarantee the loan:* **underwrite,** stand surety.

guard verb *troops guarded the bridge:* **protect,** defend, shield, secure, cover, mind, stand guard over, watch, keep an eye on.
noun **1** *border guards:* **sentry,** sentinel, nightwatchman, protector, defender, guardian, lookout, watch. **2** *a prison guard:* **warder,** warden, keeper, jailer; informal screw. **3** *a metal guard:* **cover,** shield, screen, fender, bumper, buffer.

guarded adjective **cautious,** careful, circumspect, wary, chary, reluctant, non-committal; informal cagey.

guardian noun **protector,** defender, preserver, custodian, warden, guard, keeper, curator, caretaker, steward, trustee.

guerrilla noun **rebel,** irregular, partisan, freedom fighter, revolutionary, terrorist.

guess verb **1** *he guessed that she was about 40:* **estimate,** reckon, judge, speculate, conjecture, hypothesize, surmise. **2** (informal) *I guess I owe you an apology:* **suppose,** think, imagine, expect, suspect, dare say; informal reckon.
noun *my guess was right:* **hypothesis,** theory, conjecture, surmise, estimate, belief, opinion, supposition, speculation, suspicion, impression, feeling.

guest noun **1** *we have guests:* **visitor,** caller, company. **2** *hotel guests:* **client,** customer, resident, boarder, lodger, patron, diner, holidaymaker, tourist.
OPPOSITES host, staff.

guidance noun **1** *she looked to him for guidance:* **advice,** counsel, instruction, suggestions, tips, hints, pointers, guidelines. **2** *under the guidance of an expert:* **direction,** control, leadership, management, supervision.

guide noun **1** *our guide took us back to the hotel:* **escort,** attendant, courier, leader, usher. **2** *the techniques given serve as a guide:* **outline,** template, example, exemplar, model, pattern, guideline, yardstick, precedent. **3** *a guide to Paris:* **guidebook,** travel guide, companion, handbook, manual, directory, A to Z, instructions, directions; informal bible.
verb **1** *he guided her to her seat:* **lead,** conduct, show, usher, shepherd, direct, steer, pilot, escort. **2** *the chairman guides the meeting:* **direct,** steer, manage, conduct, run, be in charge of, govern, preside over, supervise, oversee. **3** *he was always there to guide me:* **advise,** counsel, direct.

guild noun **association,** society, union, league, organization, company, fellowship, club, order, lodge.

guilt noun **1** *the proof of his guilt:* **culpability,** blameworthiness, responsibility. **2** *a terrible feeling of guilt:* **remorse,** shame, regret, contrition, self-reproach, a guilty conscience.
OPPOSITES innocence, shamelessness.

guilty adjective **1** *the guilty party:* **culpable,** to blame, at fault, in the wrong. **2** *I still feel guilty about it:* **ashamed,** guilt-ridden, conscience-stricken, remorseful, sorry, contrite, repentant, penitent, regretful,

rueful, shamefaced.
OPPOSITES innocent,
unrepentant.

gulf noun **1** *our ship sailed into the gulf:* **bay**, inlet, cove, bight, fjord, estuary, sound; Scottish firth. **2** *a gulf between rich and poor:* **gap**, divide, separation, difference, contrast.

gulp verb **1** *she gulped her juice:* **swallow**, quaff, swill down; informal swig, down, knock back. **2** *he gulped down the rest of his meal:* **gobble**, guzzle, devour, bolt, wolf; informal shovel down; Brit. informal scoff. **3** *Jenny gulped back her tears:* **choke back**, fight/hold back, suppress, stifle, smother.
OPPOSITES sip, nibble, let out.
noun *a gulp of cold beer:* **mouthful**, swallow, draught; informal swig.

gum noun *stuck down with gum:* **glue**, adhesive, paste, cement; N. Amer. **mucilage**; N. Amer. informal stickum.
verb *the receipts were gummed in:* **stick**, glue, paste, cement, attach.

gun noun **firearm**, side arm, handgun, weapon; informal shooter; N. Amer. informal piece, shooting iron.

gunman noun **armed criminal**, assassin, sniper, terrorist, gunfighter; informal hit man, gunslinger; N. Amer. informal shootist.

guru noun **1** *a Hindu guru and mystic:* **spiritual teacher**, tutor, sage, mentor, spiritual leader, master. **2** *a management guru:* **expert**, authority, pundit, leading light, master, specialist.
OPPOSITES disciple.

gush verb **surge**, stream, spout, spurt, jet, rush, pour, spill, cascade, flood; Brit. informal sloosh.
noun **surge**, stream, spout, spurt, jet, rush, outpouring, spill, outflow, cascade, flood, torrent.

gushing, gushy adjective **effusive**, overenthusiastic, extravagant, fulsome, lavish; informal over the top.
OPPOSITES restrained.

gust noun **flurry**, blast, puff, blow, rush, squall.

gut noun **1** *an ache in his gut:* **stomach**, belly, abdomen, paunch, intestines; informal tummy, insides, innards. **2** (informal) *Nicola has a lot of guts:* **courage**, bravery, backbone, nerve, pluck, spirit, daring, grit, fearlessness, determination; Brit. informal bottle; N. Amer. informal moxie.
adjective (informal) *a gut feeling:* **instinctive**, intuitive, deep-seated, involuntary, spontaneous, unthinking.
verb **1** *gut the sardines:* **clean (out)**, disembowel, draw. **2** *builders had gutted the old place:* **strip**, empty, devastate, lay waste, ravage, ruin, wreck.

gutter noun **drain**, trough, trench, ditch, sluice, sewer, channel, conduit, pipe.

guy noun (informal) **man**, fellow; informal lad; Brit. informal chap, bloke; N. Amer. informal dude, hombre.

guzzle verb **1** *he guzzled his burger:* **gobble**, bolt, wolf, devour; informal tuck into, shovel down; Brit. informal scoff; N. Amer. informal scarf. **2** *she guzzled down the orange juice:* **gulp down**, quaff, swill; informal knock back, swig, down.

g

Hh

habit noun **1** custom, practice, routine, way. **2** (informal) *his cocaine habit*: **addiction**, dependence, craving, fixation.

hack verb **cut**, chop, hew, lop, saw, slash.

haggle verb **barter**, bargain, negotiate, wrangle.

hail¹ noun *a hail of bullets*: **barrage**, volley, shower, stream, salvo.

hail² verb **1** *a friend hailed him*: **call out to**, shout to, address, greet, say hello to, salute. **2** *he hailed a cab*: **flag down**, wave down. **3** *critics hailed the film as a masterpiece*: **acclaim**, praise, applaud. **4** *Rick hails from Australia*: **come**, be, be a native of.

hair noun **1** **head of hair**, shock of hair, mane, mop, locks, tresses, curls. **2** **hairstyle**, haircut; informal hairdo. **3** **fur**, wool, coat, fleece, mane.

hairdresser noun **hairstylist**, coiffeur, coiffeuse, barber.

hairy adjective **1** *animals with hairy coats*: **shaggy**, bushy, long-haired, woolly, furry, fleecy. **2** *his hairy face*: **bearded**, unshaven, stubbly, bristly; formal hirsute. **3** (informal) *a hairy situation*: **risky**, dangerous, perilous, hazardous, tricky; informal dicey; Brit. informal dodgy.
OPPOSITES short-haired, smooth-haired, shaven, safe.

halfway adjective *the halfway point*: **midway**, middle, mid, central, centre, intermediate.
adverb *halfway down the passage*: **midway**, in the middle, in the centre, part of the way.

hall noun **1** **entrance hall**, hallway, entry, entrance, lobby, foyer, vestibule. **2** *the village hall*: **assembly room**, meeting room, chamber, auditorium, theatre, house.

halt verb **1** *halt at the barrier*: **stop**, come to a halt, come to a stop, come to a standstill, pull up, draw up. **2** *a strike has halted production*: **bring to a stop**, put a stop to, suspend, arrest, check, curb, stem, staunch, block, stall.
OPPOSITES start, continue, restart.
noun **1** *a bus screeched to a halt*: **stop**, standstill. **2** *a halt in production*: **stoppage**, break, pause, interval, interruption.
OPPOSITES start, resumption.

halting adjective **hesitant**, faltering, hesitating, stumbling, stammering, stuttering, broken, imperfect.
OPPOSITES fluent.

hammer verb **1** *hammered metal*: **beat**, forge, shape, form, mould, fashion. **2** *he hammered the nail in*: **batter**, bang, pummel, pound, knock, thump.

hamper verb **hinder**, obstruct, impede, inhibit, interfere, slow down, hold up, interfere with, handicap, hamstring.
OPPOSITES help.

hand noun **1** **fist**, palm; informal paw, mitt. **2** *written in his own hand*: **handwriting**, writing, script. **3** *a factory hand*: **worker**, employee, workman, labourer, operative, craftsman,

roustabout.
verb *hand me a spanner:* **pass,** give, present, let someone have.

handbook noun manual, instructions, ABC, A to Z, companion, guide, guidebook.

handcuff verb *he was handcuffed:* **manacle,** shackle, clap/put someone in irons; informal **cuff.**
noun (handcuffs) manacles, shackles, irons; informal **cuffs,** bracelets.

handful noun few, small number, small amount, small quantity, sprinkling, smattering, one or two, some, not many.
OPPOSITES lot.

handicap noun 1 disability, infirmity, defect, impairment, affliction. **2** *a handicap to industrial competitiveness:* **impediment,** hindrance, obstacle, barrier, constraint, disadvantage, stumbling block.
OPPOSITES benefit, advantage.
verb *handicapped by lack of funding:* **hamper,** impede, hinder, impair, hamstring, restrict, constrain.
OPPOSITES help.

handle verb 1 *handle the vase carefully:* **hold,** pick up, grasp, grip, lift, finger. **2** *a car which is easy to handle:* **control,** drive, steer, operate, manoeuvre. **3** *she handled the job well:* **deal with,** manage, tackle, take care of, look after, take charge of, attend to, see to, sort out. **4** *the traders handled imported goods:* **trade in,** deal in, buy, sell, supply, peddle, traffic in.
noun *a knife handle:* **grip,** haft, hilt, stock, shaft.

handsome adjective 1 *a handsome man:* **good-looking,** attractive, striking; informal hunky, dishy, tasty, fanciable; Brit. informal fit; N. Amer. informal cute. **2** *a handsome woman:* **striking,** imposing, prepossessing, good-looking, attractive. **3** *a handsome profit:* **substantial,** considerable, sizeable, princely, generous, lavish, ample, bumper; informal tidy, whopping; Brit. informal ginormous.
OPPOSITES ugly, meagre.

handy adjective 1 *a handy gadget:* **useful,** convenient, practical, neat, easy to use, user-friendly, helpful. **2** *keep your credit card handy:* **ready,** to hand, within reach, accessible, readily available, nearby, at the ready. **3** *he's handy with a needle:* **skilful,** skilled, dexterous, deft, adept, proficient.
OPPOSITES useless, unwieldy, inconvenient, inept.

hang verb 1 *lights hung from the trees:* **be suspended,** dangle, swing, sway, hover, float. **2** *hang the picture at eye level:* **suspend,** put up, pin up, display. **3** *the room was hung with streamers:* **decorate,** adorn, drape, festoon, deck out. **4** *he was hanged for murder:* **send to the gallows,** execute, lynch; informal string up.

hanker verb yearn, long, wish, hunger, thirst, lust, ache; informal itch.

happen verb 1 *remember what happened last time:* **occur,** take place, come about, develop, result, transpire; N. Amer. informal go down. **2** *they happened to be in London:* **chance,** have the good/bad luck.

happening noun occurrence, event, incident, episode, affair.

happily adverb 1 cheerfully,

contentedly, cheerily, merrily, joyfully. **2** *I will happily do as you ask:* **gladly,** willingly, readily, freely. **3** *happily, we arrived just in time:* **fortunately,** luckily, thankfully, mercifully, as luck would have it.
OPPOSITES unhappily.

happiness noun **pleasure,** contentment, satisfaction, cheerfulness, merriment, joy, well-being.
OPPOSITES unhappiness.

happy adjective **1 cheerful,** cheery, merry, joyful, jovial, jolly, carefree, in good spirits, in a good mood, pleased, contented, content, satisfied. **2** *we will be happy to advise you:* **glad,** pleased, delighted, more than willing. **3** *a happy coincidence:* **fortunate,** lucky, timely, convenient.
OPPOSITES unhappy, unwilling, unfortunate.

harass verb **persecute,** intimidate, hound, pester, bother; informal hassle, bug; N. Amer. informal ride.

harassed adjective **stressed,** hard-pressed, careworn, worried, troubled; informal hassled.
OPPOSITES carefree.

harassment noun **persecution,** intimidation, victimization, trouble, bother; informal hassle.

harbour noun **port,** dock, haven, marina, mooring, wharf, anchorage, waterfront.
verb **1** *he is harbouring a dangerous criminal:* **shelter,** conceal, hide, shield, protect, give asylum to. **2** *Rose harboured a grudge against him:* **bear,** hold, nurse, foster.

hard adjective **1** *hard ground:* **firm,** solid, rigid, stiff, unbreakable, unyielding, compacted, tough, strong. **2** *hard physical work:* **arduous,** strenuous, tiring, exhausting, back-breaking, gruelling, heavy, laborious, demanding; Brit. informal knackering. **3** *hard workers:* **industrious,** diligent, assiduous, conscientious, energetic, keen, enthusiastic, indefatigable. **4** *a hard problem:* **difficult,** puzzling, complicated, intricate, thorny, problematic. **5** *times are hard:* **harsh,** grim, austere, difficult, bad, bleak, tough. **6** *a hard blow:* **forceful,** heavy, strong, sharp, violent, powerful.
OPPOSITES soft, easy, lazy, gentle.
adverb **1** *George pushed her hard:* **forcefully,** roughly, heavily, sharply, violently. **2** *they worked hard:* **diligently,** industriously, assiduously, conscientiously, energetically, doggedly; informal like mad, like crazy. **3** *she looked hard at me:* **closely,** intently, critically, carefully, searchingly.
OPPOSITES gently, lazily, casually.

harden verb **1** *this glue hardens in four hours:* **solidify,** set, stiffen, thicken. **2** *their suffering had hardened them:* **toughen,** desensitize, inure, season, train, numb.
OPPOSITES soften.

hardened adjective *a hardened criminal:* **inveterate,** seasoned, habitual, chronic, compulsive, confirmed, incorrigible.

hardly adverb **scarcely,** barely, only just, just.
OPPOSITES fully, easily.

hardship noun **difficulty,** privation, destitution, poverty, austerity, need, distress, suffering, adversity.
OPPOSITES prosperity, ease.

hardware noun **equipment,** apparatus, gear, paraphernalia, tackle, kit, machinery.

hardy adjective **robust,** healthy, fit, strong, sturdy, tough, rugged.
OPPOSITES delicate.

harm noun *it won't do you any harm:* **injury,** damage, mischief.
OPPOSITES good.
verb **1** *he's never harmed anybody:* **hurt,** injure, lay a finger on, mistreat, ill-treat. **2** *this could harm his prospects:* **damage,** spoil, affect, undermine, ruin.
OPPOSITES heal, help.

harmful adjective **damaging,** injurious, detrimental, dangerous, unhealthy, unwholesome, hurtful, destructive, hazardous.
OPPOSITES beneficial.

harmless adjective **1** *a harmless substance:* **safe,** innocuous, gentle, mild, non-toxic. **2** *he seems harmless enough:* **inoffensive,** innocuous, gentle.
OPPOSITES harmful, objectionable.

harmony noun **1** *musical harmony:* **tunefulness,** euphony, melodiousness, unison. **2** *the villagers live together in harmony:* **accord,** agreement, peace, friendship, fellowship, cooperation, understanding, rapport, unity.
OPPOSITES dissonance, disagreement.

harrowing adjective **distressing,** traumatic, upsetting, shocking, disturbing, painful, agonizing.

harry verb **harass,** hound, torment, pester, worry, badger, nag, plague; informal hassle, bug.

harsh adjective **1** *a harsh voice:* **grating,** rasping, strident, raucous, discordant. **2** *harsh*

colours: **glaring,** loud, garish, gaudy, lurid. **3** *his harsh treatment of captives:* **cruel,** savage, barbarous, merciless, inhumane, ruthless. **4** *they took harsh measures to end the crisis:* **severe,** stringent, firm, stiff, stern, rigorous. **5** *harsh words:* **rude,** discourteous, unfriendly, sharp, bitter, unkind, critical, disparaging. **6** *harsh conditions:* **austere,** grim, spartan, hard, inhospitable. **7** *a harsh winter:* **cold,** freezing, icy, bitter, hard, severe, bleak.
OPPOSITES soft, subdued, kind, mild, friendly, comfortable.

harvest noun *a poor harvest:* **crop,** yield, vintage, produce.
verb *he harvested the wheat:* **gather,** bring in, reap, pick, collect.

hassle (informal) noun *parking is such a hassle:* **inconvenience,** bother, nuisance, trouble, annoyance, irritation, fuss; informal aggravation, headache, pain in the neck.
verb *don't hassle me!* **harass,** pester, be on at, badger, hound, bother, nag, torment; informal bug; N. English informal mither.

hasten verb **1** *we hastened back:* **hurry,** rush, dash, race, fly, speed; informal zip; N. Amer. informal hightail. **2** *chemicals can hasten ageing:* **speed up,** bring on, precipitate, advance.
OPPOSITES dawdle, delay.

hasty adjective **hurried,** rash, impetuous, impulsive, reckless, precipitate, spur-of-the-moment.
OPPOSITES considered.

hate verb **1** *they hate each other:* **loathe,** detest, despise, dislike, abhor, shrink from, be unable to bear/stand. **2** *I hate to bother*

h

you: **be sorry,** be reluctant, be loath.
OPPOSITES love.
noun *feelings of hate:* **hatred,** loathing, abhorrence, abomination, aversion, disgust.
OPPOSITES love.

hatred noun. See HATE noun.

haul verb *she hauled the basket upstairs:* **drag,** pull, heave, lug, hump.
noun *the thieves' haul:* **booty,** loot, plunder, spoils, stolen goods; informal swag.

haunt verb *the sight haunted me:* **torment,** disturb, trouble, worry, plague, prey on.
noun *a favourite haunt of artists:* **meeting place,** stamping ground, spot, venue; informal hang-out; N. Amer. stomping ground.

haunted adjective **1** *the church is haunted:* **possessed,** cursed, jinxed, eerie. **2** *his haunted eyes:* **tormented,** anguished, tortured, obsessed, troubled, worried.

haunting adjective **evocative,** affecting, stirring, powerful, poignant, memorable.

have verb **1** *he had a new car:* **own,** be in possession of, be blessed with, boast, enjoy. **2** *the flat has five rooms:* **comprise,** consist of, contain, include, incorporate, be composed of, be made up of. **3** *they had tea:* **eat,** drink, take. **4** *let's have a party:* **organize,** hold, give, throw, put on, lay on. **5** *I have to get up at six:* **must,** be obliged to, be required to, be compelled to, be forced to, be bound to.
■ **have someone on** (Brit. informal) play a trick on, play a joke on, pull someone's leg; Brit. informal wind someone up; N. Amer. informal put someone on. ■ **have**

something on be wearing, be dressed in, be clothed in, be decked out in.

haven noun **refuge,** retreat, shelter, sanctuary, oasis.

havoc noun **chaos,** mayhem, bedlam, pandemonium, a shambles.

hazard noun **danger,** risk, peril, menace, jeopardy, threat.

hazardous adjective **risky,** dangerous, unsafe, perilous, fraught with danger, high-risk; informal dicey; Brit. informal dodgy.
OPPOSITES safe, certain.

haze noun **mist,** fog, cloud, vapour.

head noun **1** *her head hit the wall:* **skull,** cranium; informal nut. **2** *he had to use his head:* **brain(s),** brainpower, intellect, intelligence, grey matter; Brit. informal loaf; N. Amer. informal smarts. **3** *she had a head for business:* **aptitude,** talent, gift, capacity. **4** *the head of the church:* **leader,** chief, controller, governor, superintendent, commander, captain, director, manager, principal, president; informal boss; Brit. informal gaffer, guv'nor. **5** *the head of the queue:* **front,** beginning, start, top.
OPPOSITES back.
adjective *the head waiter:* **chief,** principal, leading, main, first, top, highest.
verb *a team headed by a manager:* **command,** control, lead, manage, direct, supervise, superintend, oversee, preside over.
■ **head someone/something off 1** *he went to head off the visitors:* **intercept,** divert, redirect, re-route, turn away. **2** *they headed off an argument:* **forestall,** avert, stave off, nip in

the bud, prevent, avoid, stop.

headache noun **1** *I've got a headache:* **sore head,** migraine, hangover. **2** (informal) *it was a real headache:* **problem,** worry, hassle, pain in the neck, bind.

heading noun **title,** caption, legend, rubric, headline.

heady adjective **1** *heady wine:* **potent,** intoxicating, strong. **2** *the heady days of my youth:* **exhilarating,** exciting, stimulating, thrilling, intoxicating.
OPPOSITES weak, boring.

heal verb **1** *he heals the sick:* **cure,** make better, restore to health, treat. **2** *his knee had healed:* **get better,** be cured, recover, mend. **3** *we tried to heal the rift:* **put right,** repair, resolve, settle; informal patch up.
OPPOSITES worsen, aggravate.

health noun **1** *he was restored to health:* **well-being,** fitness, good condition, strength, robustness, vigour. **2** *poor health:* **condition,** physical shape, constitution.
OPPOSITES illness.

healthy adjective **1** *a healthy baby:* **well,** fit, in good shape, in fine fettle, in tip-top condition, strong, fighting fit. **2** *a healthy diet:* **wholesome,** good for one, health-giving, nutritious, nourishing, invigorating, sanitary, hygienic.
OPPOSITES unhealthy.

heap noun *a heap of boxes:* **pile,** stack, mound, mountain.
verb *she heaped logs on the fire:* **pile (up),** stack (up), make a mound of.

hear verb **1** *she could hear voices:* **make out,** catch, get, perceive, overhear. **2** *they heard that I had moved:* **learn,** find out, discover, gather, glean. **3** *a jury heard the case:* **try,** judge, adjudicate on.

hearing noun **1** *she moved out of hearing:* **earshot,** hearing distance. **2** *I had a fair hearing:* **chance to speak,** opportunity to be heard. **3** *he gave evidence at the hearing:* **trial,** court case, enquiry, inquest, tribunal.

heart noun **1** *he poured out his heart:* **emotions,** feelings, sentiments, soul, mind. **2** *he has no heart:* **compassion,** sympathy, humanity, feeling(s), empathy, understanding, soul, goodwill. **3** *they lost heart:* **enthusiasm,** spirit, determination, resolve, nerve; Brit. informal bottle. **4** *the heart of the city:* **centre,** middle, hub, core. **5** *the heart of the matter:* **essence,** crux, core, nub, root, meat, substance, kernel; informal nitty-gritty.
OPPOSITES edge.
■ **at heart** deep down, basically, fundamentally, essentially, in essence, intrinsically. ■ **by heart** from memory, off pat, word for word, verbatim, parrot-fashion, word-perfect. ■ **take heart** be encouraged, be heartened, be comforted, be consoled.

heartily adverb **1** *we heartily welcome the changes:* **wholeheartedly,** warmly, profoundly, eagerly, enthusiastically. **2** *they were heartily sick of them:* **thoroughly,** completely, absolutely, exceedingly, downright; N. Amer. quite; informal seriously; Brit. informal jolly; N. Amer. informal real, mighty.

hearty adjective **1** *a hearty character:* **exuberant,** jovial, ebullient, cheerful, lively, loud, animated, vivacious, energetic, spirited. **2** *hearty*

congratulations: **wholehearted,** heartfelt, sincere, genuine, real. **3** *a hearty woman of sixty-five:* **robust,** healthy, hardy, fit, vigorous, sturdy, strong. **4** *a hearty meal:* **substantial,** large, ample, satisfying, filling, generous.
OPPOSITES introverted, half-hearted, frail, light.

heat noun **1** *a plant sensitive to heat:* **warmth,** hotness, high temperature. **2** *he took the heat out of the dispute:* **passion,** intensity, vehemence, fervour, excitement, agitation, anger.
OPPOSITES cold, apathy.
verb **1** *the food was heated:* **warm (up),** reheat, cook, keep warm. **2** *the pipes expand as they heat up:* **get hot,** get warm, warm up; Brit. informal hot up.
OPPOSITES cool.

heated adjective **1** *a heated argument:* **vehement,** passionate, impassioned, animated, lively, acrimonious, angry, bitter, furious, fierce. **2** *Robert grew heated as he spoke:* **excited,** animated, worked up, wound up, keyed up; informal het up.

heaven noun **1** *the good will have a place in heaven:* **paradise,** the hereafter, the next world, the afterworld, nirvana, Zion, Elysium. **2** *a good book is my idea of heaven:* **bliss,** ecstasy, rapture, contentment, happiness, delight, joy, paradise.
OPPOSITES hell, misery.

heavenly adjective **1** *heavenly choirs:* **divine,** holy, celestial, angelic. **2** *a heavenly body:* **celestial,** cosmic, stellar, sidereal. **3** (informal) *a heavenly morning:* **delightful,** wonderful, glorious, sublime, exquisite,

beautiful, lovely, gorgeous, enchanting; informal **divine,** super, fantastic, fabulous.
OPPOSITES mortal, infernal, terrestrial, dreadful.

heavily adverb **1** *Dad walked heavily:* **laboriously,** slowly, ponderously, awkwardly, clumsily. **2** *we were heavily defeated:* **decisively,** conclusively, roundly, soundly, utterly, completely, thoroughly. **3** *he drank heavily:* **excessively,** immoderately, copiously, intemperately. **4** *the area is heavily planted with trees:* **densely,** closely, thickly. **5** *I became heavily involved:* **deeply,** extremely, greatly, exceedingly, tremendously, profoundly.
OPPOSITES easily, narrowly, moderately, thinly, slightly.

heavy adjective **1** *a heavy box:* **weighty,** hefty, substantial, ponderous, solid, dense. **2** *a heavy blow to the head:* **forceful,** hard, strong, violent, powerful, mighty, sharp, severe. **3** *heavy work:* **strenuous,** hard, physical, difficult, arduous, demanding, back-breaking, gruelling. **4** *heavy fighting:* **intense,** fierce, relentless, severe, serious. **5** *a heavy meal:* **substantial,** filling, stodgy, rich, big.
OPPOSITES light.

hectic adjective **frantic,** frenetic, frenzied, feverish, manic, busy, active, fast and furious.
OPPOSITES leisurely.

heed verb *heed the warnings:* **pay attention to,** take note of, take note of, listen to, consider, take to heart, take into account, obey, adhere to, abide by, observe.
OPPOSITES disregard.

noun *he paid no heed:* **attention,** notice, note, regard, thought.

hefty adjective **1** *a hefty young man:* **burly,** sturdy, strapping, bulky, strong, muscular, big, solid, well built; informal hulking, beefy. **2** *a hefty kick:* **powerful,** violent, hard, forceful. **3** *a hefty fine:* **substantial,** sizeable, considerable, stiff, large, heavy; informal whopping.
OPPOSITES slight, feeble, light, small.

height noun **1** *the height of the wall:* **tallness,** stature, elevation, altitude. **2** *mountain heights:* **summit,** top, peak, crest, crown, tip, cap, pinnacle. **3** *the height of their fame:* **highest point,** peak, zenith, pinnacle, climax.
OPPOSITES width, depth, nadir.

heighten verb **intensify,** increase, enhance, add to, augment, boost, strengthen, deepen, magnify, reinforce.
OPPOSITES reduce.

heir, heiress noun **successor,** next in line, inheritor, beneficiary, legatee.

hell noun **1** *the underworld,* the netherworld, eternal damnation, perdition, hellfire, fire and brimstone, the Inferno, Hades. **2** *he made her life hell:* **misery,** torture, agony, purgatory, torment, a nightmare.
OPPOSITES heaven, bliss.

help verb **1 assist,** aid, abet, lend a hand (to), give assistance to, come to the aid of, be of service to, do someone a favour, do someone a service, do someone a good turn, rally round, pitch in. **2** *this credit card helps cancer research:* **support,** contribute to, give money to, donate to, promote,

boost, back. **3** *sore throats are helped by lozenges:* **relieve,** soothe, ease, alleviate, improve, lessen. **4** *he could not help laughing:* **resist,** avoid, refrain from, keep from, stop.
OPPOSITES hinder, impede, worsen.
noun **1** *this could be of help:* **assistance,** aid, support, succour, benefit, use, advantage, service. **2** *help for his eczema:* **relief,** alleviation, improvement, healing.
OPPOSITES hindrance, aggravation.

helper noun **assistant,** aide, deputy, auxiliary, supporter, second, mate, right-hand man/woman, attendant.

helpful adjective **1** *the staff are very helpful:* **obliging,** of assistance, supportive, accommodating, cooperative, eager to please. **2** *we found your comments helpful:* **useful,** beneficial, valuable, constructive, informative, instructive. **3** *a helpful new tool:* **handy,** useful, convenient, practical, easy-to-use, serviceable; informal neat, nifty.
OPPOSITES unhelpful, useless.

helping noun **portion,** serving, piece, slice, share, plateful; informal dollop.

helpless adjective **dependent,** incapable, powerless, paralysed, defenceless, vulnerable, exposed, unprotected.
OPPOSITES independent.

hence adverb **consequently,** as a consequence, for this reason, therefore, so, accordingly, as a result, that being so.

herd noun **drove,** flock, pack, fold, swarm, mass, crowd, horde.

hereditary adjective **1** *a*

hereditary right: **inherited,** bequeathed, handed down, passed down, family, ancestral. **2** *a hereditary disease:* **genetic,** inborn, inherited, inbred, innate, in the family, in the blood, in the genes.
OPPOSITES acquired, infectious.

heritage noun **1** *Europe's cultural heritage:* **tradition,** history, past, background, culture, customs. **2** *his Greek heritage:* **ancestry,** lineage, descent, extraction, parentage, roots, heredity.

hero noun **1** *a sporting hero:* **star,** superstar, megastar, idol, celebrity, favourite, darling; informal celeb. **2** *the hero of the film:* **main character,** starring role, male protagonist, (male) lead, leading man; informal good guy.
OPPOSITES loser, supporting role, villain.

heroic adjective **brave,** courageous, valiant, intrepid, bold, fearless, daring; informal gutsy, spunky.
OPPOSITES cowardly.

heroine noun **1** *a sporting heroine:* **star,** superstar, megastar, idol, celebrity, favourite, darling; informal celeb. **2** *the film's heroine:* **main character,** female protagonist, lead, leading lady, prima donna, diva.
OPPOSITES loser, supporting role.

heroism noun **bravery,** courage, valour, daring, fearlessness, pluck; informal guts, spunk; Brit. informal bottle; N. Amer. informal moxie.
OPPOSITES cowardice.

hesitant adjective **1** *she is hesitant about buying:* **uncertain,** undecided, unsure, doubtful, dubious, nervous,

ambivalent, in two minds; Brit. havering, humming and hawing; informal iffy. **2** *a hesitant child:* **timid,** diffident, shy, bashful, insecure.
OPPOSITES certain, decisive, confident.

hesitate verb **1** *she hesitated, unsure of what to say:* **pause,** delay, wait, stall, be uncertain, be unsure, be doubtful, be indecisive, vacillate, waver; Brit. haver; informal dilly-dally. **2** *don't hesitate to ask:* **be reluctant,** be unwilling, be disinclined, scruple, have misgivings about, have qualms about, think twice about.
OPPOSITES plunge in.

hidden adjective **1** *a hidden camera:* **concealed,** secret, invisible, unseen, camouflaged. **2** *a hidden meaning:* **obscure,** unclear, concealed, cryptic, mysterious, secret, covert, abstruse, deep.
OPPOSITES visible, obvious.

hide verb **1** *he hid the money:* **conceal,** secrete, put out of sight, cache; informal stash. **2** *they hid in an air vent:* **conceal oneself,** secrete oneself, take cover, lie low, go to ground; informal hole up. **3** *clouds hid the moon:* **obscure,** block out, blot out, obstruct, cloud, shroud, veil, eclipse. **4** *he could not hide his dislike:* **conceal,** keep secret, cover up, keep quiet about, bottle up, suppress, disguise, mask; informal keep a/the lid on.
OPPOSITES flaunt, reveal, emerge, betray.

hideaway noun **retreat,** refuge, hiding place, hideout, safe house, den, bolt-hole; informal hidey-hole.

hideous adjective **1** *a hideous face:* **ugly,** repulsive, repellent,

unsightly, revolting, grotesque.
2 *hideous cases of torture:*
horrific, terrible, appalling,
awful, dreadful, frightful,
horrible, horrendous,
horrifying, shocking, sickening,
gruesome, ghastly.
OPPOSITES beautiful, pleasant.

hiding noun (informal) **beating,**
thrashing, whipping, drubbing;
informal **licking,** belting, pasting,
walloping.

hierarchy noun **ranking,** order,
pecking order, grading, ladder,
scale.

high adjective **1** *a high mountain:*
tall, lofty, towering, giant, big,
multi-storey, high-rise,
elevated. **2** *a high position in
the government:* **high-ranking,**
leading, top, prominent, senior,
influential, powerful,
important, exalted; N. Amer.
ranking. **3** *high prices:* **inflated,**
excessive, unreasonable,
expensive, exorbitant,
extortionate, informal steep, stiff.
4 *a high voice:* **high-pitched,**
shrill, piercing, squeaky,
penetrating, soprano, treble,
falsetto. **5** (informal) *high on
drugs:* **intoxicated,** befuddled,
delirious, hallucinating; informal
high as a kite, stoned, wrecked,
off one's head.
OPPOSITES low, short, lowly,
deep.
adverb *a jet flew high overhead:*
at a great height, high up, way
up, at altitude, in the sky, aloft,
overhead, to a great height.
OPPOSITES low.

highlight noun *the highlight of
his career:* **high point,** climax,
peak, pinnacle, height, zenith,
summit, focus, feature.
OPPOSITES low point.
verb *he has highlighted
shortcomings in the plan:*

spotlight, call attention to,
focus on, underline, show up,
bring out, accentuate, accent,
stress, emphasize.
OPPOSITES play down.

highly adverb **very,** extremely,
immensely, thoroughly,
decidedly, exceptionally,
extraordinarily; N. English right;
informal **awfully,** terribly,
seriously; Brit. informal dead, jolly;
N. Amer. informal real, mighty,
awful.
OPPOSITES slightly.

hijack verb **commandeer,** seize,
take over, appropriate,
expropriate.

hike noun **1** *a hike across
country:* **walk,** trek, tramp,
trudge, slog, march, ramble. **2** *a
price hike:* **increase,** advance,
boom.
OPPOSITES reduction.
verb **1** *they hiked across Europe:*
walk, trek, tramp, trudge, slog,
march, ramble, backpack. **2** *they
hiked the price:* **increase,** raise,
up, put up, push up; informal jack
up, bump up.
OPPOSITES reduce.

hilarious adjective **very funny,**
hysterical, uproarious, rib-
tickling; informal side-splitting,
priceless, a scream, a hoot.
OPPOSITES unfunny, serious.

hill noun **high ground,** hillock,
hillside, rise, mound, knoll,
hummock, fell, mountain;
Scottish brae.

hinder verb **hamper,** impede,
inhibit, thwart, foil, delay,
interfere with, slow down, hold
back, hold up, restrict,
handicap, hamstring.
OPPOSITES ease.

hint noun **1** *a hint that he would
leave:* **clue,** inkling, suggestion,
indication, sign, signal,
intimation. **2** *handy hints about*

h

painting: **tip,** suggestion, pointer, guideline, recommendation. **3** *a hint of garlic:* **trace,** touch, suspicion, suggestion, dash, soupçon; informal smidgen, tad.
verb *what are you hinting?* **imply,** insinuate, intimate, suggest, refer to, drive at, mean; informal get at.

hire verb **1** *we hired a car:* **rent,** lease, charter. **2** *they hire workers locally:* **employ,** engage, recruit, appoint, take on, sign up.
OPPOSITES dismiss.

hiss verb **1** *the escaping gas hissed:* **fizz,** whistle, wheeze. **2** *the audience hissed:* **jeer,** catcall, whistle, hoot.
OPPOSITES cheer.
noun **1** *the hiss of steam:* **fizz,** whistle, wheeze. **2** *the speaker received hisses:* **jeer,** catcall, whistle, abuse, derision.
OPPOSITES cheer.

historic adjective **significant,** notable, important, momentous, memorable, groundbreaking; informal earth-shattering.
OPPOSITES insignificant.

historical adjective **1** *historical evidence:* **documented,** recorded, chronicled, authentic, factual, actual. **2** *historical figures:* **past,** bygone, ancient, old, former.
OPPOSITES anecdotal, contemporary.

history noun **1** *my interest in history:* **the past,** former times, the olden days, yesterday, antiquity. **2** *a history of the Civil War:* **chronicle,** archive, record, report, narrative, account, study. **3** *she gave details of her history:* **background,** past, life story,

experiences, record.

hit verb **1** **strike,** beat, punch, thump, thrash; informal whack, wallop, bash, clout, belt; Brit. informal stick one on; N. Amer. informal slug; Austral./NZ informal dong, quilt. **2** *a car hit the barrier:* **crash into,** run into, smash into, knock into, bump into, plough into, collide with, meet head-on. **3** *the tragedy hit her hard:* **devastate,** affect badly, upset, shatter, crush, traumatize; informal knock sideways; Brit. informal knock for six.
noun **1** **blow,** thump, punch, knock, bang; informal whack, wallop, bash, clout, belt; N. Amer. informal slug; Austral./NZ king-hit. **2** *he directed many big hits:* **success,** sell-out, winner, triumph, sensation, best-seller; informal smash hit, chart-topper, crowd-puller.
OPPOSITES failure.
■ **hit back** retaliate, respond, reply, react, counter. ■ **hit it off** (informal) get on (well), get along, be compatible, be on the same wavelength, see eye to eye, take to each other; informal click. ■ **hit on/upon** discover, come up with, think of, conceive of, dream up, invent, devise.

hitch verb **1** *she hitched the blanket around her:* **pull,** lift, raise; informal yank. **2** *Tom hitched the pony to his cart:* **harness,** yoke, couple, fasten, connect, attach.
noun *it went without a hitch:* **problem,** difficulty, snag, setback, obstacle, complication; informal glitch, hiccup.

hoard noun *a secret hoard:* **cache,** stockpile, store, collection, supply, reserve; informal stash.

verb *they hoarded their rations:* **stockpile**, store up, put aside, put by, lay by, set aside, cache, save, squirrel away; informal salt away.
OPPOSITES squander.

hoax noun **practical joke**, prank, trick, deception, fraud; informal con, spoof, wind-up, scam.

hobby noun **pastime**, leisure activity, sideline, diversion, relaxation, recreation, amusement.

hoist verb *we hoisted the mainsail:* **raise**, lift, haul up, heave up, winch up, pull up, elevate.
OPPOSITES lower.
noun *a mechanical hoist:* **crane**, winch, pulley, windlass.

hold verb **1** *she held a suitcase:* **clasp**, clutch, grasp, grip, clench, cling to, hold on to, embrace, hug, squeeze. **2** *he was being held by police:* **detain**, imprison, lock up, keep behind bars, confine, intern. **3** *the tank held 250 gallons:* **take**, contain, accommodate, fit, have room for. **4** *the court held that there was no evidence:* **maintain**, consider, take the view, believe, think, feel, deem, be of the opinion, rule, decide; informal reckon. **5** *they held a meeting:* **convene**, call, summon, conduct, organize, run.
OPPOSITES release.
noun **1** *she kept a hold on my hand:* **grip**, grasp, clasp, clutch. **2** *Tom had a hold over his father:* **influence**, power, control, dominance, authority, sway. **3** *the military tightened their hold on the capital:* **control**, grip, power, stranglehold.

holder noun **1** *the licence holder:* **bearer**, owner, possessor, keeper. **2** *a knife holder:* **container**, receptacle, case, cover, housing, sheath.

hold-up noun **1** *a hold-up in production:* **delay**, setback, hitch, snag, difficulty, problem, glitch, hiccup, traffic jam, tailback; informal snarl-up. **2** *a bank hold-up:* **robbery**, raid, armed robbery, mugging; informal stick-up; N. Amer. informal heist.

hole noun **1** *a hole in the roof:* **opening**, aperture, gap, space, vent, chink, breach, crack, rupture, puncture. **2** *a hole in the ground:* **pit**, crater, depression, hollow, cavern, cave, chamber. **3** *the badger's hole:* **burrow**, lair, den, earth, sett.

holiday noun **vacation**, break, rest, recess, time off, leave, day off, festival, feast day.

hollow adjective **1** *a hollow tube:* **empty**, hollowed out, void. **2** *hollow cheeks:* **sunken**, deep-set, concave, depressed, recessed. **3** *a hollow promise:* **insincere**, hypocritical, feigned.
OPPOSITES solid, chubby, convex, sincere.
noun **1** *a hollow under the tree:* **hole**, pit, cavity, crater, trough, depression, indentation, dip. **2** *the village lay in a hollow:* **valley**, vale, dale, dell.
OPPOSITES rise.
verb *hollowed out of rock:* **gouge**, scoop, dig, cut, excavate, channel.

holy adjective **1** *holy men:* **saintly**, godly, pious, religious, devout, God-fearing, spiritual. **2** *a holy place:* **sacred**, consecrated, hallowed, sanctified, venerated, revered.
OPPOSITES sinful, irreligious, cursed.

homage noun **respect**, honour,

reverence, worship, admiration, esteem, adulation, tribute.
OPPOSITES contempt.

home noun **1** *they fled their homes:* **residence,** house, accommodation, property, quarters, lodgings, address, place; informal pad; formal abode, dwelling. **2** *I am far from my home:* **homeland,** native land, home town, birthplace, roots, fatherland, mother country, motherland. **3** *a home for the elderly:* **institution,** hospice, shelter, refuge, retreat, asylum, hostel.
adjective *the UK home market:* **domestic,** internal, local, national.
OPPOSITES foreign, international.

homeless adjective **of no fixed abode,** without a roof over one's head, on the streets, vagrant, sleeping rough, destitute.

homely adjective **1** (Brit.) *a homely atmosphere:* **cosy,** comfortable, snug, welcoming, friendly; informal comfy. **2** (N. Amer.) *she's rather homely:* **unattractive,** plain, unprepossessing, ugly; Brit. informal no oil painting.
OPPOSITES uncomfortable, attractive.

homicide noun *murder,* manslaughter, killing, slaughter, butchery, assassination.

honest adjective **1** *an honest man:* **upright,** honourable, principled, virtuous, decent, law-abiding, trustworthy, scrupulous. **2** *I haven't been honest with you:* **truthful,** sincere, candid, frank, open, forthright, straight; informal upfront.
OPPOSITES dishonest.

honestly adverb **1** *he earned the*

money honestly: **fairly,** lawfully, legally, legitimately, honourably, decently, ethically; informal on the level. **2** *we honestly believe this:* **sincerely,** genuinely, truthfully, truly, wholeheartedly, to be honest, to be frank, in all honesty, in all sincerity.
OPPOSITES dishonestly.

honesty noun **1** *I can attest to his honesty:* **integrity,** uprightness, honour, righteousness, virtue, goodness, probity, trustworthiness. **2** *they spoke with honesty about their fears:* **sincerity,** candour, frankness, directness, truthfulness, truth, openness, straightforwardness.
OPPOSITES dishonesty, insincerity.

honorary adjective **1** *an honorary doctorate:* **titular,** nominal, in name only, unofficial, token. **2** (Brit.) *an honorary treasurer:* **unpaid,** unsalaried, voluntary, volunteer.
OPPOSITES paid.

honour noun **1** *a man of honour:* **integrity,** honesty, uprightness, morality, principles, high-mindedness, decency, probity, scrupulousness, fairness, justness. **2** *a mark of honour:* **distinction,** privilege, glory, kudos, cachet, prestige. **3** *our honour is at stake:* **reputation,** good name, character, repute, image, standing, status. **4** *the honour of meeting the Queen:* **privilege,** pleasure, compliment.
OPPOSITES unscrupulousness, shame.
verb **1** *we should honour our parents:* **respect,** esteem, admire, look up to, value,

cherish, revere, venerate. **2** *they were honoured at a special ceremony:* **applaud,** acclaim, praise, salute, recognize, celebrate, pay tribute to. **3** *he honoured the contract:* **fulfil,** observe, keep, obey, heed, follow, carry out, keep to, abide by, adhere to, comply with, conform to, be true to.
OPPOSITES scorn, disgrace, disobey, break.

honourable adjective **1** *an honourable man:* **honest,** moral, principled, righteous, decent, respectable, virtuous, good, upstanding, upright, noble, fair, trustworthy, law-abiding. **2** *an honourable career:* **illustrious,** distinguished, eminent, great, glorious, prestigious.
OPPOSITES crooked, deplorable.

hook noun **1** *she hung her jacket on the hook:* **peg,** nail. **2** *the dress has six hooks:* **fastener,** clasp, hasp, clip.
verb **1** *they hooked baskets onto the ladder:* **attach,** hitch, fasten, fix, secure, hang, clasp. **2** *he hooked a large pike:* **catch,** land, net, take, bag.

hooked adjective **1** *a hooked nose:* **curved,** hook-shaped, aquiline, angular, bent. **2** (informal) *hooked on cocaine:* **addicted to,** dependent on. **3** (informal) *he is hooked on crosswords:* **keen on,** enthusiastic about, addicted to, obsessed with, fanatical about; informal mad about.
OPPOSITES straight.

hooligan noun **lout,** thug, tearaway, vandal, ruffian, troublemaker; Austral. larrikin; informal tough, bruiser; Brit. informal yob, yobbo, lager lout; Scottish informal ned.

hoop noun **ring,** band, circle,

wheel, circlet, loop.

hop verb & noun **jump,** bound, spring, bounce, skip, leap, prance, caper.

hope noun **1** *I had high hopes:* **aspiration,** desire, wish, expectation, ambition, aim, plan, dream. **2** *a life filled with hope:* **optimism,** expectation, confidence, faith, belief.
OPPOSITES pessimism.
verb **1** *he's hoping for a medal:* **expect,** anticipate, look for, be hopeful of, dream of. **2** *we're hoping to address this issue:* **aim,** intend, be looking, have the intention, have in mind, plan.

hopeful adjective **1** *he remained hopeful:* **optimistic,** full of hope, confident, positive, buoyant, bullish. **2** *hopeful signs:* **promising,** encouraging, heartening, reassuring, favourable, optimistic.
OPPOSITES pessimistic, discouraging.

hopefully adverb **1** *he rode on hopefully:* **optimistically,** full of hope, confidently, buoyantly, expectantly. **2** *hopefully it should finish soon:* **all being well,** if all goes well, God willing, with luck, touch wood, fingers crossed.

hopeless adjective **1** *a hopeless case:* **forlorn,** beyond hope, lost, irreparable, irreversible, incurable, impossible, futile. **2** *hopeless at maths:* **bad,** poor, awful, terrible, dreadful, appalling, atrocious, incompetent; informal pathetic, useless, lousy, rotten; Brit. informal rubbish.
OPPOSITES competent.

hopelessly adverb **utterly,** completely, irretrievably, impossibly, extremely, totally.

h

horde noun **crowd,** mob, pack, gang, troop, army, swarm, mass, throng.

horizontal adjective **level,** flat, parallel.
OPPOSITES vertical.

horrible adjective **1** *a horrible murder:* **dreadful,** awful, terrible, shocking, appalling, horrifying, horrific, horrendous, grisly, ghastly, gruesome, harrowing, unspeakable. **2** (informal) *a horrible little man:* **nasty,** horrid, disagreeable, obnoxious, hateful, odious, objectionable, insufferable.
OPPOSITES pleasant, agreeable.

horrific adjective **dreadful,** horrendous, horrible, terrible, atrocious, horrifying, shocking, appalling, harrowing, hideous, grisly, ghastly, sickening.

horrify verb **shock,** appal, outrage, scandalize, offend, disgust, revolt, nauseate, sicken.

horror noun **1** *children screamed in horror:* **terror,** fear, fright, alarm, panic. **2** *to her horror she found herself alone:* **dismay,** consternation, alarm, distress, disgust, shock.
OPPOSITES delight, satisfaction.

horse noun **mount,** charger, cob, nag, hack, colt, stallion, mare, filly; N. Amer. bronco; Austral./NZ moke, yarraman; informal gee-gee.

hospitable adjective **welcoming,** friendly, sociable, cordial, gracious, accommodating, warm.
OPPOSITES inhospitable.

hospitality noun **friendliness,** neighbourliness, sociability, welcome, warmth, kindness, cordiality, generosity.

host noun *the host of a TV series:* **presenter,** compère, anchor, anchorman, anchorwoman, announcer.
OPPOSITES guest.
verb *the show is hosted by Angus:* **present,** introduce, compère, front, anchor.

hostage noun **captive,** prisoner, detainee, internee.

hostile adjective **1** *a hostile attitude:* **unfriendly,** unkind, unsympathetic, antagonistic, aggressive, confrontational, belligerent. **2** *hostile conditions:* **unfavourable,** adverse, bad, harsh, grim, inhospitable, forbidding. **3** *they are hostile to the idea:* **opposed,** averse, antagonistic, ill-disposed, unsympathetic, antipathetic, against; informal anti.
OPPOSITES friendly, favourable, in favour.

hostility noun **1** *he glared at her with hostility:* **antagonism,** unfriendliness, malevolence, venom, hatred, aggression, belligerence. **2** *their hostility to the present regime:* **opposition,** antagonism, animosity, antipathy. **3** *a cessation of hostilities:* **fighting,** armed conflict, combat, warfare, war, bloodshed, violence.

hot adjective **1** *hot food:* **heated,** piping, sizzling, roasting, boiling, scorching, scalding, red-hot. **2** *a hot day:* **very warm,** balmy, summery, tropical, scorching, searing, blistering, sweltering; informal boiling, baking, roasting. **3** *a hot chilli:* **spicy,** peppery, fiery, strong, piquant, powerful. **4** *the competition was hot:* **fierce,** intense, keen, competitive, cut-throat, ruthless, aggressive, strong. **5** (informal) *she is hot on local history:* **knowledgeable**

about, well informed about, au fait with, up on, well versed in; informal clued up about.
OPPOSITES cold, mild, weak.

hotel noun inn, motel, boarding house, guest house, bed and breakfast, B & B, hostel.

hotly adverb **vehemently,** vigorously, strenuously, fiercely, heatedly.
OPPOSITES calmly.

hound verb **pursue,** chase, stalk, harry, harass, pester, badger, torment.

house noun **1** residence, home; formal dwelling. **2** *the house of Stewart:* **family,** clan, tribe, dynasty, line, bloodline, lineage. **3** *a printing house:* **firm,** business, company, corporation, enterprise, establishment, institution, concern, organization, operation; informal outfit. **4** *the country's upper house:* assembly, legislative body, chamber, council, parliament, congress, senate.
verb **1** *we can house twelve adults:* **accommodate,** give someone a roof over their head, lodge, quarter, board, billet, take in, sleep, put up. **2** *this panel houses the main switch:* **contain,** hold, store, cover, protect, enclose.

household noun *the household was asleep:* **family,** house, occupants, clan, tribe; informal brood.
adjective *household goods:* **domestic,** family, everyday, workaday.

housing noun **1** *a housing development:* **houses,** homes, residences, accommodation, living quarters; formal dwellings. **2** *the housing for the equipment:* **casing,** covering,

case, cover, holder, fairing, sleeve.

hovel noun **shack,** slum, shanty, hut; informal dump, hole.

hover verb **1** *helicopters hovered overhead:* **hang,** be poised, be suspended, float, fly, drift. **2** *a servant hovered nearby:* **wait,** linger, loiter.

however adverb **nevertheless,** nonetheless, even so, but, for all that, despite that, in spite of that.

howl noun **1** *the howl of a wolf:* **baying,** cry, bark, yelp. **2** *a howl of anguish:* **wail,** cry, yell, yelp, bellow, roar, shout, shriek, scream, screech.
verb **1** *dogs howled in the distance:* **bay,** cry, bark, yelp. **2** *a baby started to howl:* **wail,** cry, yell, bawl, bellow, shriek, scream, screech, caterwaul; informal holler.

hub noun **centre,** core, heart, focus, focal point, nucleus, kernel, nerve centre.
OPPOSITES periphery.

huddle verb **1** *they huddled together:* **crowd,** cluster, gather, bunch, throng, flock, collect, group, congregate. **2** *he huddled beneath the sheets:* **curl up,** snuggle, nestle, hunch up.
OPPOSITES disperse.
noun *a huddle of passengers:* **group,** cluster, bunch, collection; informal gaggle.

hue noun **colour,** shade, tone, tint, tinge.

hug verb *they hugged each other:* **embrace,** cuddle, squeeze, clasp, clutch, hold tight.
noun *there were hugs as we left:* **embrace,** cuddle, squeeze, bear hug.

huge adjective **enormous,** vast, immense, massive, colossal, prodigious, gigantic,

h

gargantuan, mammoth,
monumental, giant, towering,
mountainous; informal mega,
monster, astronomical; Brit.
informal ginormous.
OPPOSITES tiny.

hugely adverb **extremely,** very,
tremendously, exceptionally,
immensely, extraordinarily,
vastly; informal terrifically,
awfully, terribly, seriously; Brit.
informal dead, jolly; N. Amer. informal
real, mighty, awful.

hull noun *the ship's hull:*
framework, body, shell, frame,
skeleton, structure.

hum verb **1** *the engine was
humming:* **purr,** drone,
murmur, buzz, whirr, throb.
2 *the workshops are humming:*
be busy, be active, be lively,
buzz, bustle, be a hive of
activity, throb.
noun *a low hum of conversation:*
murmur, drone, purr, buzz.

human adjective **1** *they're only
human:* **mortal,** flesh and
blood, fallible, weak, frail,
imperfect, vulnerable, physical,
bodily, fleshly. **2** *his human
side:* **compassionate,** humane,
kind, considerate,
understanding, sympathetic.
OPPOSITES infallible, inhuman.
noun *the link between humans
and animals:* **person,** human
being, Homo sapiens, man,
woman, individual, mortal,
(living) soul, earthling;
(**humans**) the human race,
humanity, humankind,
mankind, man, people.

humane adjective
compassionate, kind,
considerate, understanding,
sympathetic, tolerant,
forbearing, forgiving, merciful,
humanitarian, charitable.
OPPOSITES cruel.

humanitarian adjective **1** *a
humanitarian act:*
compassionate, humane,
unselfish, altruistic, generous.
2 *a humanitarian organization:*
charitable, philanthropic,
public-spirited, socially
concerned, welfare, aid.
OPPOSITES selfish, commercial.
noun **philanthropist,** altruist,
benefactor, social reformer,
good Samaritan, do-gooder.

humanity noun **1** *humanity
evolved from the apes:*
humankind, mankind, man,
people, the human race, Homo
sapiens. **2** *he praised them for
their humanity:* **compassion,**
brotherly love, fellow feeling,
humaneness, kindness,
consideration, understanding,
sympathy, tolerance.

humble adjective **1** *she was very
humble:* **meek,** deferential,
respectful, submissive, self-
effacing, unassertive, modest,
unassuming, self-deprecating;
Scottish mim. **2** *a humble
background:* **lowly,** poor,
undistinguished, mean,
common, ordinary, simple. **3** *my
humble abode:* **modest,** plain,
simple, ordinary, little.
OPPOSITES proud, illustrious,
grand.
verb *it humbled him to ask for
help:* **humiliate,** demean, lower,
degrade, debase, mortify,
shame.

humid adjective **muggy,** close,
sultry, sticky, steamy, clammy,
heavy.
OPPOSITES dry, fresh.

humiliate verb **embarrass,**
mortify, humble, shame,
disgrace, chasten, deflate,
crush, squash, demean, take
down a peg or two; informal show

up, put down, cut down to size; N. Amer. informal make someone eat crow.
OPPOSITES dignify.

humiliating adjective **embarrassing,** mortifying, humbling, ignominious, inglorious, shaming, undignified, chastening, demeaning, degrading, deflating.

humiliation noun **embarrassment,** mortification, shame, indignity, ignominy, disgrace, dishonour, degradation, discredit, loss of face, blow to one's pride.
OPPOSITES honour.

humility noun **modesty,** humbleness, meekness, respect, deference, diffidence, unassertiveness.
OPPOSITES pride.

humorous adjective **amusing,** funny, comic, comical, entertaining, diverting, witty, jocular, light-hearted, hilarious, uproarious, riotous, farcical.
OPPOSITES serious.

humour noun **1** *the humour of the situation:* **comedy,** funny side, hilarity, absurdity, ludicrousness, satire, irony. **2** *the stories are spiced with humour:* **jokes,** jests, quips, witticisms, funny remarks, wit, comedy; informal gags, wisecracks. **3** *his good humour was infectious:* **mood,** temper, disposition, spirits.
OPPOSITES seriousness.
verb *she was always humouring him:* **indulge,** accommodate, pander to, cater to, give in to, go along with, flatter, mollify, placate.
OPPOSITES stand up to.

hunch noun **feeling,** guess,

suspicion, impression, inkling, idea, notion, fancy, intuition; informal gut feeling.

hunger noun **1** *she was faint with hunger:* **lack of food,** starvation, malnutrition, undernourishment. **2** *a hunger for news:* **desire,** craving, longing, yearning, hankering, appetite, thirst; informal itch.
■ **hunger after/for** desire, crave, long for, yearn for, pine for, ache for, hanker after, thirst for, lust for; informal itch for, be dying for, be gagging for.

hungry adjective **1** *I was really hungry:* **ravenous,** starving, starved, famished, malnourished, undernourished, underfed; informal peckish. **2** *they are hungry for success:* **eager,** keen, avid, longing, yearning, aching, greedy, craving, desirous of, hankering after; informal itching, dying, gagging.
OPPOSITES full.

hunk noun **chunk,** wedge, block, slab, lump, square, gobbet; Brit. informal wodge.

hunt verb **1** *they hunted deer:* **chase,** stalk, pursue, course, track, trail. **2** *police are hunting for her:* **search,** seek, look high and low, scour the area.
noun **1** *the thrill of the hunt:* **chase,** pursuit. **2** *a police hunt:* **search,** quest.

hurdle noun **obstacle,** difficulty, problem, barrier, bar, snag, stumbling block, impediment, obstruction, complication, hindrance.

hurl verb **throw,** toss, fling, launch, pitch, cast, lob; informal chuck, sling, bung.

hurricane noun **cyclone,** typhoon, tornado, storm, windstorm, whirlwind, gale,

tempest; Austral. willy-willy;
N. Amer. informal twister.

hurried adjective **1** *hurried
glances:* **quick,** fast, swift,
rapid, speedy, brisk, cursory,
perfunctory, brief, short,
fleeting. **2** *a hurried decision:*
hasty, rushed, precipitate, spur-
of-the-moment.
OPPOSITES slow, considered.

hurry verb **1** *hurry or you'll be
late:* **be quick,** hurry up, hasten,
speed up, run, dash, rush, race,
scurry, scramble, scuttle, sprint;
informal get a move on; Brit. informal
get one's skates on; N. Amer.
informal get a wiggle on. **2** *she
hurried him out:* **hustle,** hasten,
push, urge, usher.
OPPOSITES dawdle, delay.
noun *in all the hurry, we forgot:*
rush, haste, speed, urgency,
hustle and bustle.
OPPOSITES ease.

hurt verb **1** *my back hurts:* **be
painful,** ache, be sore, be
tender, smart, sting, burn,
throb; informal be agony. **2** *Dad
hurt his leg:* **injure,** wound,
damage, disable, bruise, cut,
gash, graze, scrape, scratch.
3 *his words hurt her:* **distress,**
pain, wound, sting, upset,
sadden, devastate, grieve,
mortify.
OPPOSITES comfort.
noun *all the hurt he had caused:*
distress, pain, suffering, grief,
misery, anguish, upset, sadness,
sorrow.
OPPOSITES joy.
adjective **1** *my hurt hand:*
injured, wounded, bruised,
grazed, cut, gashed, sore,
painful, aching. **2** *Anne's hurt
expression:* **pained,** aggrieved,
offended, distressed, upset, sad,
mortified; informal miffed.
OPPOSITES unhurt, pleased.

hurtful adjective **upsetting,**
distressing, wounding, unkind,
cruel, nasty, mean, malicious,
spiteful.

hush verb *he tried to hush her:*
silence, quieten (down), shush,
gag, muzzle; informal shut up.
noun *a hush descended:* **silence,**
quiet, stillness, peace, calm,
tranquillity.
OPPOSITES noise.
■ **hush something up** keep
secret, conceal, hide, suppress,
cover up, keep quiet about,
sweep under the carpet.

hut noun **shack,** shanty, cabin,
shelter, shed, lean-to, hovel;
Scottish bothy; N. Amer. cabana.

hybrid noun *a hybrid of a goose
and a swan:* **cross,** cross-breed,
mixture, blend, combination,
composite, fusion, amalgam.
adjective *hybrid roses:*
composite, cross-bred,
interbred, mixed, blended,
compound.

hygiene noun **cleanliness,**
sanitation, sterility, purity,
disinfection.

hygienic adjective **sanitary,**
clean, germ-free, disinfected,
sterilized, sterile, antiseptic,
aseptic.
OPPOSITES insanitary.

hypocritical adjective
sanctimonious, pious, self-
righteous, holier-than-thou,
superior, insincere, two-faced.

hysteria noun **frenzy,**
feverishness, hysterics,
agitation, mania, panic, alarm,
distress.
OPPOSITES calm.

hysterical adjective **1** *Janet
became hysterical:*
overwrought, overemotional,
out of control, frenzied, frantic,
wild, beside oneself, manic,

delirious; informal in a state.
2 *the film was hysterical:*
(informal) **very funny**, hilarious,
uproarious, rib-tickling; informal
side-splitting, priceless, a
scream, a hoot.
OPPOSITES calm, unfunny,
serious.

Ii

icy adjective **1** *icy roads:* **iced**
(over), frozen, frosty, slippery,
treacherous; literary rimy. **2** *an
icy wind:* **freezing**, chill, biting,
bitter, raw, arctic. **3** *an icy
voice:* **unfriendly**, hostile,
forbidding, cold, chilly, frosty,
stern.

idea noun **1** *the idea of death:*
concept, notion, conception,
thought. **2** *our idea is to open a
new shop:* **plan**, scheme, design,
proposal, proposition,
suggestion, aim, intention,
objective, goal. **3** *Liz had
various ideas on the subject:*
thought, theory, view, opinion,
feeling, belief. **4** *I had an idea
this might happen:* **sense**,
feeling, suspicion, fancy,
inkling, hunch, notion. **5** *an
idea of the cost:* **estimate**,
approximation, guess,
conjecture; informal guesstimate.

ideal adjective *ideal flying
weather:* **perfect**, faultless,
exemplary, classic, model,
ultimate, theoretical, utopian.
OPPOSITES bad, real.
noun **1** *an ideal to aim at:*
model, pattern, exemplar,
example, perfection, epitome,
last word. **2** *liberal ideals:*
principle, standard, value,
belief, conviction.

identical adjective **(exactly) the
same**, indistinguishable, twin,
duplicate, interchangeable,
alike, matching.

OPPOSITES different.

identification noun **1** *the
identification of the suspect:*
recognition, singling out,
pinpointing, naming. **2** *early
identification of problems:*
determination, establishment,
ascertainment, discovery,
diagnosis. **3** *may I see your
identification?* **ID**, papers,
documents, credentials, card,
pass, badge.

identify verb **1** *Gail identified
her attacker:* **recognize**, pick
out, spot, point out, pinpoint,
put one's finger on, name. **2** *I
identified four problem areas:*
determine, establish, ascertain,
make out, discern, distinguish.
3 *we identify sport with
glamour:* **associate**, link,
connect, relate. **4** *Peter
identifies with the team
captain:* **empathize**,
sympathize, understand, relate
to, feel for.

identity noun **individuality**,
self, personality, character,
originality, distinctiveness,
uniqueness.

idiot noun **fool**, ass, halfwit,
blockhead, dunce, simpleton;
informal nincompoop, clod,
dimwit, dummy, fathead,
numbskull; Brit. informal nitwit,
twit, clot, berk, prat, pillock,
wally, dork, twerp, charlie;
Scottish informal nyaff, balloon; N.
Amer. informal schmuck, turkey;

h

i

Austral./NZ informal drongo, nong,
galah, boofhead.
OPPOSITES genius.

idle adjective **1** *an idle fellow:*
lazy, indolent, slothful, work-
shy. **2** *I was bored with being
idle:* **unemployed,** jobless, out
of work, redundant,
unoccupied; Brit. informal on the
dole. **3** *their idle hours:*
unoccupied, spare, empty,
unfilled. **4** *idle remarks:*
frivolous, trivial, trifling,
minor, insignificant,
unimportant, empty,
meaningless, vain.
OPPOSITES industrious,
employed, busy, serious.

idol noun **1** *an idol in a shrine:*
icon, effigy, statue, figurine,
totem. **2** *the pop world's latest
idol:* **hero,** heroine, star,
superstar, icon, celebrity,
darling; informal pin-up, heart
throb.

if conjunction **1** *if the weather is
fine, we can walk:* **provided,**
providing, on condition that,
presuming, supposing,
assuming, as long as, in the
event that. **2** *if I go out she gets
nasty:* **whenever,** every time.
3 *I wonder if he noticed:*
whether, whether or not.
OPPOSITES unless.

ignite verb **1** *moments before the
petrol ignited:* **catch fire,** burst
into flames, explode. **2** *a
cigarette ignited the fumes:*
light, set fire to, set alight,
kindle.
OPPOSITES go out, extinguish.

ignorance noun **1** *their
attitudes are based on
ignorance:* **lack of knowledge,**
lack of education,
unenlightenment. **2** *his
ignorance of economics:*
unfamiliarity with,

incomprehension, inexperience,
innocence.
OPPOSITES education,
knowledge.

ignorant adjective **1** *an ignorant
country girl:* **uneducated,**
unschooled, illiterate,
uninformed, unenlightened,
inexperienced, unsophisticated.
2 *ignorant of working-class life:*
unaware, unconscious,
unfamiliar, unacquainted,
uninformed.
OPPOSITES educated,
knowledgeable.

ignore verb **1** *he ignored her:*
take no notice of, pay no
attention to, snub, look right
through, cold-shoulder.
2 *doctors ignored her
instructions:* **disregard,** take no
account of, fail to observe,
disobey, defy, overlook, brush
aside.
OPPOSITES acknowledge, obey.

ill adjective **1** *she was feeling
rather ill:* **unwell,** sick, poorly;
informal under the weather,
rough; Brit. informal grotty; Austral./
NZ informal crook. **2** *the ill effects
of smoking:* **harmful,** damaging,
detrimental, deleterious,
adverse, injurious, destructive,
dangerous.
OPPOSITES well, beneficial.
noun *the ills of society:* **problem,**
trouble, difficulty, misfortune,
trial, tribulation; informal
headache, hassle.
adverb **1** *he can ill afford the
loss:* **barely,** scarcely, hardly,
only just. **2** *we are ill prepared:*
inadequately, insufficiently,
poorly, badly.
OPPOSITES easily, well.

illegal adjective **unlawful,** illicit,
illegitimate, criminal,
fraudulent, corrupt, dishonest,
outlawed, banned, forbidden,

prohibited, proscribed, unlicensed, unauthorized; informal crooked, shady; Brit. informal bent, dodgy.
OPPOSITES legal.

illegible adjective **unreadable**, indecipherable, unintelligible.

illicit adjective **illegal**, unlawful, criminal, outlawed, banned, forbidden, prohibited, proscribed, unlicensed, unauthorized, improper, disapproved of.
OPPOSITES legal, approved.

illness noun **sickness**, poor health, disease, ailment, disorder, complaint, malady, affliction, infection; informal bug, virus.
OPPOSITES health.

illuminating adjective **informative**, enlightening, revealing, explanatory, instructive, helpful, educational.
OPPOSITES confusing.

illumination noun **light**, lighting, radiance, gleam, glow, glare.

illusion noun **1** *I had no illusions:* **delusion**, misapprehension, misconception, false impression, mistaken impression, fantasy, dream, fancy. **2** *the illusion of depth:* **appearance**, impression, semblance. **3** *it's just an illusion:* **mirage**, hallucination, apparition, figment of the imagination, trick of the light.

illustrate verb **1** *the photographs that illustrate the text:* **decorate**, ornament, accompany, support, explain, elucidate, clarify; informal get across/over. **2** *this can be illustrated through a brief example:* **demonstrate**, show,

exemplify, bring home.

illustration noun **1** *the illustrations in children's books:* **picture**, drawing, sketch, figure, plate, image, print. **2** *an illustration of such a dilemma:* **example**, sample, case, instance, exemplification, demonstration.

image noun **1** *images of the Queen:* **likeness**, depiction, portrayal, representation, painting, picture, portrait, drawing, photograph. **2** *the image of this country as a democracy:* **conception**, impression, idea, perception, notion. **3** *his public image:* **persona**, profile, face.

imaginary adjective **unreal**, non-existent, fictional, pretend, make-believe, invented, made-up, illusory.
OPPOSITES real.

imagination noun **1** *in your imagination:* **mind's eye**, fancy. **2** *she lacked imagination:* **creativity**, vision, inventiveness, resourcefulness, ingenuity, originality.

imaginative adjective **creative**, visionary, inventive, resourceful, ingenious, original, innovative.

imagine verb **1** *you can imagine the scene:* **visualize**, envisage, picture, see in the mind's eye, dream up, think up/of, conceive. **2** *I imagine he was at home:* **assume**, presume, expect, take it (as read), suppose.

imitate verb **1** *other artists have imitated his style:* **copy**, emulate, follow, echo, ape, parrot; informal rip off. **2** *he could imitate Winston Churchill:* **mimic**, do an impression of, impersonate; informal take someone off.

imitation noun **1** *an imitation of a sailor's hat:* copy, simulation, reproduction, replica, forgery. **2** *learning by imitation:* emulation, copying. **3** *a perfect imitation of Francis:* impersonation, impression, caricature; informal take-off, spoof.
▶ adjective *imitation ivory:* artificial, synthetic, mock, fake, simulated, man-made, manufactured, ersatz, substitute.
OPPOSITES real.

immaculate adjective **1** *an immaculate white shirt:* clean, spotless, shining, shiny, gleaming. **2** *immaculate condition:* perfect, pristine, mint, flawless, faultless, unblemished; informal tip-top, A1. **3** *his immaculate record:* unblemished, spotless, impeccable, unsullied, untarnished; informal squeaky clean.
OPPOSITES dirty, damaged, sullied.

immediate adjective **1** *the UN called for immediate action:* instant, instantaneous, prompt, swift, speedy, rapid, quick. **2** *their immediate concerns:* current, present, urgent, pressing. **3** *our immediate neighbours:* nearest, close, next-door, adjacent, adjoining.
OPPOSITES delayed.

immediately adverb **1** *you must decide immediately:* straight away, at once, right away, instantly, now, directly, forthwith, there and then. **2** *I sat immediately behind him:* directly, right, exactly, precisely, squarely, just, dead; informal slap bang; N. Amer. informal smack dab.

OPPOSITES sometime, later, somewhere.

immense adjective huge, vast, massive, enormous, gigantic, colossal, monumental, towering, giant, mammoth; informal monster, whopping (great); Brit. informal ginormous.
OPPOSITES tiny.

immerse verb **1** *the metal was immersed in acid:* dip, submerge, dunk, duck, sink. **2** *Elliot was immersed in his work:* absorb, engross, occupy, engage, involve, bury, preoccupy; informal lose.

immigrant noun newcomer, settler, incomer, migrant, non-native, foreigner, alien.
OPPOSITES native.

imminent adjective near, close (at hand), impending, approaching, coming, forthcoming, on the way, expected, looming.
OPPOSITES distant.

immoral adjective wicked, bad, wrong, unethical, unprincipled, unscrupulous, dishonest, corrupt, sinful, impure.
OPPOSITES ethical, pure.

immortal adjective **1** *our immortal souls:* undying, deathless, eternal, everlasting, imperishable, indestructible. **2** *an immortal children's story:* timeless, perennial, classic, time-honoured, enduring, evergreen.
OPPOSITES mortal, ephemeral.

immune adjective resistant, not subject, not liable, not vulnerable, protected from, safe from, secure against.
OPPOSITES susceptible, liable.

immunity noun **1** *immunity to malaria:* resistance, protection, defence. **2** *immunity from prosecution:* exemption,

impact | implement

exception, freedom.
3 *diplomatic immunity:*
indemnity, privilege,
prerogative, licence, exemption,
impunity, protection.
OPPOSITES susceptibility,
liability.

impact noun **1** *the force of the
impact:* **collision,** crash, smash,
bump, knock. **2** *the job losses
will have a major impact:*
effect, influence, consequences,
repercussions, ramifications.
verb **1** *an asteroid impacted the
earth:* **crash into,** smash into,
collide with, hit, strike, smack
into, bang into. **2** *interest rates
have impacted on spending:*
affect, influence, hit, have an
effect, make an impression.

impair verb **weaken,** damage,
harm, have a negative effect
on, undermine, diminish,
reduce, lessen, decrease.
OPPOSITES improve, enhance.

impart verb **communicate,** pass
on, convey, transmit, relay,
relate, tell, make known,
report, announce.

impartial adjective **unbiased,**
unprejudiced, neutral, non-
partisan, disinterested,
detached, dispassionate,
objective.
OPPOSITES biased, partisan.

impasse noun **deadlock,** dead
end, stalemate, stand-off,
standstill.

impatient adjective **1** *Melissa
grew impatient:* **restless,**
agitated, nervous, anxious.
2 *they are impatient to get back
home:* **anxious,** eager, keen;
informal itching, dying. **3** *an
impatient gesture:* **irritated,**
annoyed, angry, tetchy, snappy,
cross, curt, brusque.
OPPOSITES patient, reluctant,
calm.

impeccable adjective **flawless,**
faultless, unblemished,
spotless, stainless, perfect,
exemplary, irreproachable;
informal squeaky clean.
OPPOSITES imperfect.

impede verb **hinder,** obstruct,
hamper, hold back/up, delay,
interfere with, disrupt, retard,
slow (down).
OPPOSITES facilitate.

imperative adjective **vital,**
crucial, critical, essential,
pressing, urgent.
OPPOSITES unimportant.

imperfect adjective **faulty,**
flawed, defective, inferior,
second-rate, substandard,
damaged, blemished, torn,
broken, cracked, scratched; Brit.
informal duff.
OPPOSITES perfect.

impertinent adjective **rude,**
insolent, impolite, ill-
mannered, disrespectful,
impudent, cheeky,
presumptuous, forward.
OPPOSITES polite, respectful.

impetuous adjective **impulsive,**
rash, hasty, reckless, foolhardy,
imprudent, ill-considered,
spontaneous, impromptu, spur-
of-the-moment.
OPPOSITES considered, cautions.

implant verb **1** *the collagen is
implanted under the skin:*
insert, embed, bury, inject,
transplant, graft. **2** *he
implanted the idea in my mind:*
instil, inculcate, introduce,
plant, sow.
OPPOSITES excise, banish.

implement noun *garden
implements:* **tool,** utensil,
instrument, device, apparatus,
gadget, contraption, appliance;
informal gizmo.
verb *the cost of implementing
the new law:* **execute,** apply,

i

put into effect/action, put into practice, carry out/through, perform, enact, fulfil.
OPPOSITES abolish, cancel.

implicate verb **1** *he had been implicated in a financial scandal:* **incriminate,** involve, connect, embroil, enmesh. **2** *viruses are implicated in the development of cancer:* **involve in,** concern with, associate with, connect with.

implication noun **1** *he was smarting at their implication:* **suggestion,** inference, insinuation, innuendo, intimation, imputation. **2** *important political implications:* **consequence,** result, ramification, repercussion, reverberation, effect. **3** *his implication in the murder:* **incrimination,** involvement, connection, entanglement, association.
OPPOSITES exoneration.

implore verb **plead with,** beg, entreat, appeal to, ask, request, call on, exhort, urge.

imply verb **1** *are you implying he is mad?* **insinuate,** suggest, infer, hint, intimate, give someone to understand, make out. **2** *the forecast traffic increase implies more roads:* **involve,** entail, mean, point to, signify, presuppose.

impolite adjective **rude,** bad-mannered, ill-mannered, discourteous, uncivil, disrespectful, insolent, impudent, impertinent, cheeky; informal lippy.
OPPOSITES polite.

import verb *the UK imports iron ore:* **bring in,** buy in, ship in.
OPPOSITES export.
noun **1** *a matter of great import:* **importance,** significance, consequence, momentousness, magnitude, substance, weight, note, gravity, seriousness. **2** *the full import of her words:* **meaning,** sense, essence, gist, drift, message, thrust, substance, implication.
OPPOSITES insignificance.

importance noun **1** *an event of immense importance:* **significance,** momentousness, moment, import, consequence, note, weight, seriousness, gravity. **2** *she had an exaggerated sense of her own importance:* **status,** eminence, prestige, worth, influence, power, authority.
OPPOSITES insignificance.

important adjective **1** *an important meeting:* **significant,** consequential, momentous, of great import, major, valuable, necessary, crucial, vital, essential, pivotal, decisive, far-reaching, historic. **2** *he was an important man:* **powerful,** influential, well-connected, high-ranking, prominent, eminent, notable, distinguished, esteemed, respected, prestigious.
OPPOSITES unimportant, insignificant.

impose verb **1** *he imposed his ideas on everyone:* **foist,** force, inflict, press, saddle someone with. **2** *new taxes will be imposed:* **levy,** charge, apply, enforce, set, establish, institute, introduce, bring into effect.
OPPOSITES abolish.
■ **impose on** take advantage of, exploit, take liberties with, bother, trouble, disturb, inconvenience, put out, put to trouble.

imposing adjective **impressive,** striking, dramatic, spectacular,

commanding, arresting, awesome, formidable, splendid, grand, majestic.
OPPOSITES modest.

imposition noun 1 *the imposition of an alien culture:* **imposing,** foisting, forcing, inflicting. 2 *the imposition of VAT:* **levying,** charging, application, enforcement, enforcing, setting, establishment, introduction. 3 *it would be no imposition:* **burden,** encumbrance, liberty, bother, worry; informal hassle.
OPPOSITES abolition.

impossible adjective 1 *the winds made fishing impossible:* **out of the question,** impracticable, non-viable, unworkable. 2 *an impossible dream:* **unattainable,** unachievable, unobtainable, hopeless, impracticable, unworkable. 3 *food shortages made life impossible:* **unbearable,** intolerable, unendurable. 4 (informal) *an impossible woman:* **unreasonable,** difficult, awkward, intolerable, unbearable, exasperating, maddening, infuriating.
OPPOSITES possible, attainable, bearable, reasonable.

impound verb **confiscate,** appropriate, take possession of, seize, commandeer, expropriate, requisition, take over.
OPPOSITES release.

impress verb *Hazel had impressed him mightily:* **make an impression on,** have an impact on, influence, affect, move, stir, rouse, excite, inspire, dazzle, awe.
OPPOSITES disappoint.

■ **impress something upon someone** emphasize to, stress to, bring home to, instil in, inculcate into, drum into.

impression noun 1 *he got the impression she was hiding something:* **feeling,** sense, fancy, (sneaking) suspicion, inkling, intuition, hunch, notion, idea. 2 *a favourable impression:* **opinion,** view, image, picture, perception, reaction, judgement, verdict, estimation. 3 *school made a profound impression on me:* **impact,** effect, influence. 4 *the lid had left a circular impression:* **indentation,** dent, mark, outline, imprint. 5 *he did a good impression of their science teacher:* **impersonation,** imitation, caricature; informal take-off.

impressive adjective **magnificent,** majestic, imposing, splendid, spectacular, grand, awe-inspiring, stunning, breathtaking.
OPPOSITES unimpressive.

imprint verb *patterns can be imprinted in the clay:* **stamp,** print, impress, mark, emboss. noun *her feet left imprints on the floor:* **impression,** print, mark, stamp, indentation.

imprison verb **incarcerate,** send to prison, jail, lock up, put away, intern, detain, hold prisoner, hold captive; informal send down; Brit. informal bang up.
OPPOSITES release.

improbable adjective 1 *it seemed improbable that the hot weather would continue:* **unlikely,** doubtful, dubious, debatable, questionable, uncertain. 2 *an improbable exaggeration:* **unconvincing,** unbelievable, implausible, unlikely.
OPPOSITES probable, believable.

improper adjective **1** *it is improper for police to accept gifts:* **unacceptable,** unprofessional, irregular, unethical, dishonest. **2** *it was improper for young ladies to drive a young man home:* **unseemly,** unfitting, unbecoming, unladylike, ungentlemanly, inappropriate, indelicate, indecent, immodest, indecorous, immoral. **3** *an extremely improper poem:* **indecent,** risqué, suggestive, naughty, dirty, filthy, vulgar, crude, rude, obscene, lewd; informal blue, raunchy, steamy.
OPPOSITES acceptable, decent, clean.

improve verb **1** *ways to improve the service:* **make better,** ameliorate, upgrade, refine, enhance, boost, build on, raise. **2** *communications improved:* **get better,** advance, progress, develop, make headway, make progress, pick up, look up, move forward. **3** *the patient is improving:* **recover,** get better, recuperate, rally, revive, be on the mend.
OPPOSITES worsen, deteriorate.

improvement noun **advance,** development, upgrade, refinement, enhancement, betterment, amelioration, boost, augmentation, rally, recovery, upswing.

improvise verb **1** *she was improvising in front of the cameras:* **extemporize,** ad-lib; informal speak off the cuff, play it by ear, busk it, wing it. **2** *she improvised a sandpit:* **contrive,** devise, throw together, cobble together, rig up; informal whip up, rustle up; Brit. informal knock up.

impulse noun **1** *she had an impulse to hide:* **urge,** instinct, drive, compulsion, itch, whim, desire, fancy, notion. **2** *a man of impulse:* **spontaneity,** impetuosity, recklessness, rashness.
OPPOSITES forethought.

impulsive adjective **1** *he had an impulsive nature:* **impetuous,** spontaneous, hasty, passionate, emotional. **2** *an impulsive decision:* **impromptu,** snap, spontaneous, unpremeditated, spur-of-the-moment.
OPPOSITES cautious, premeditated.

inaccurate adjective **inexact,** imprecise, incorrect, wrong, erroneous, faulty, imperfect, defective, unreliable, false, mistaken, untrue; Brit. informal adrift.
OPPOSITES accurate.

inactivity noun **inaction,** inertia, idleness, non-intervention, negligence, apathy, indolence, laziness, slothfulness.
OPPOSITES action.

inadequate adjective **1** *inadequate water supplies:* **insufficient,** deficient, poor, scant, scarce, sparse, in short supply, paltry, meagre. **2** *he's a bit inadequate:* **incapable,** incompetent, immature; informal not up to scratch.
OPPOSITES adequate.

inadvertently adverb **accidentally,** by accident, unintentionally, by mistake, mistakenly, unwittingly.
OPPOSITES intentionally.

inappropriate adjective **unsuitable,** unfitting, unseemly, unbecoming, improper, out of place/keeping, inapposite; informal out of order.
OPPOSITES appropriate.

inaudible adjective **unclear,** indistinct, faint, muted, soft, low, muffled, whispered, muttered, murmured, mumbled.

inaugurate verb **1** *he inaugurated a new policy:* **initiate,** begin, start, institute, launch, get going, get under way, establish, bring in, usher in; informal kick off. **2** *the new President will be inaugurated:* **install,** instate, swear in, invest, ordain, crown.
OPPOSITES terminate, abolish, dismiss.

incapable adjective **incompetent,** inept, inadequate, ineffective, ineffectual, unfit, unqualified, unequal to the task; informal not up to it.
OPPOSITES competent.

incense verb **enrage,** infuriate, anger, madden, outrage, exasperate, antagonize, provoke; informal make someone see red; N. Amer. informal burn someone up.
OPPOSITES placate, please.

incensed adjective **enraged,** furious, infuriated, irate, raging, incandescent, fuming, seething, beside oneself, outraged; informal mad, hopping mad, wild, livid.
OPPOSITES pleased.

incentive noun **inducement,** motivation, motive, reason, stimulus, spur, impetus, encouragement, carrot; informal sweetener.
OPPOSITES deterrent.

incident noun **1** *incidents in his youth:* **event,** occurrence, episode, happening, affair, business, adventure, exploit, escapade. **2** *police investigating another incident:* disturbance, commotion, clash, confrontation, accident, shooting, explosion, scene, situation. **3** *the journey was not without incident:* **excitement,** adventure, drama, crisis, danger.

incidental adjective **1** *incidental details:* **secondary,** subsidiary, minor, peripheral, background, by-the-by, unimportant, insignificant, tangential. **2** *an incidental discovery:* **chance,** accidental, random, fluky, fortuitous, serendipitous, coincidental, unlooked-for.
OPPOSITES essential.

incidentally adverb
1 *incidentally, I haven't had a reply yet:* **by the way,** by the by, in passing, speaking of which; informal as it happens. **2** *the infection was discovered incidentally:* **by chance,** by accident, accidentally, fortuitously, by a fluke, by happenstance.

incite verb **1** *he was arrested for inciting racial hatred:* **stir up,** whip up, encourage, stoke up, fuel, kindle, inflame, instigate, provoke, excite, trigger, spark off. **2** *she incited him to commit murder:* **provoke,** encourage, urge, goad, spur on, egg on, drive, prod, prompt; informal put up to.
OPPOSITES discourage, deter.

inclination noun **tendency,** propensity, leaning, predisposition, predilection, impulse, bent, liking, taste, penchant, preference.
OPPOSITES aversion.

incline verb **1** *his prejudice inclines him to overlook obvious facts:* **predispose,** lead, make, dispose, prejudice, prompt, induce. **2** *I incline to the*

i

opposite view: **tend,** lean, swing, veer, gravitate, be drawn, prefer, favour, go for. **3** *he inclined his head:* **bend,** bow, nod, bob, lower, dip.
noun *a steep incline:* **slope,** gradient, pitch, ramp, bank, ascent, rise, hill, dip, descent; N. Amer. grade.

inclined adjective **1** *I'm inclined to believe her:* **disposed,** minded, of a mind. **2** *she's inclined to gossip:* **prone,** given, in the habit of, liable, apt.

include verb **1** *activities include drama and music:* **incorporate,** comprise, encompass, cover, embrace, take in, number, contain. **2** *include the cost of repairs:* **allow for,** count, take into account, take into consideration. **3** *include your address:* **add,** insert, put in, append, enter.
OPPOSITES exclude, leave out.

inclusive adjective **all-in,** comprehensive, overall, full, all-round, umbrella, catch-all, all-encompassing.
OPPOSITES exclusive, limited.

income noun **earnings,** salary, wages, pay, remuneration, revenue, receipts, takings, profits, proceeds, yield, dividend; N. Amer. take.
OPPOSITES expenditure, outgoings.

incoming adjective **1** *incoming flights:* **arriving,** approaching, inbound, inward, returning, homeward. **2** *the incoming president:* **new,** next, future, ... elect, ... designate.
OPPOSITES outward, outgoing.

incompatible adjective **mismatched,** unsuited, poles apart, irreconcilable, inconsistent, conflicting, opposed, opposite,

contradictory, at odds, at variance.
OPPOSITES well matched, harmonious, consistent.

incompetent adjective **inept,** unskilled, inexpert, amateurish, unprofessional, bungling, blundering, clumsy; informal useless, not up to it.
OPPOSITES competent.

incomplete adjective **1** *the manuscript is still incomplete:* **unfinished,** uncompleted, partial, half-finished. **2** *incomplete information:* **deficient,** insufficient, partial, sketchy, fragmentary, scrappy, bitty.
OPPOSITES completed, full.

incomprehensible adjective **unintelligible,** impenetrable, unclear, indecipherable, unfathomable, abstruse, difficult, involved; Brit. informal double Dutch.
OPPOSITES intelligible, clear.

inconsistent adjective
1 *inconsistent behaviour:* **erratic,** changeable, unpredictable, variable, unstable, fickle, unreliable, volatile; informal up and down. **2** *he had done nothing inconsistent with his morality:* **incompatible,** conflicting, at odds, at variance, irreconcilable, out of keeping, contrary to.
OPPOSITES consistent.

inconvenience noun **1** *we apologize for any inconvenience caused:* **trouble,** bother, problems, disruption, difficulty, disturbance; informal aggravation, hassle. **2** *his early arrival was clearly an inconvenience:* **nuisance,** trouble, bother, problem; informal headache, pain, pain in the neck, hassle.

verb *I don't want to inconvenience you:* **trouble**, bother, put out, put to any trouble, disturb, impose on.

inconvenient adjective **awkward**, difficult, inopportune, badly timed, unsuitable, inappropriate, unfortunate.
OPPOSITES convenient.

incorporate verb **1** *the region was incorporated into Moldavian territory:* **absorb**, include, subsume, assimilate, integrate, swallow up. **2** *the model incorporates advanced features:* **include**, contain, embrace, build in, offer, boast. **3** *incorporate the salt and the butter:* **blend**, mix, combine, fold in, stir in.
OPPOSITES partition, separate.

incorrect adjective **1** *an incorrect answer:* **wrong**, erroneous, mistaken, untrue, false. **2** *incorrect behaviour:* **inappropriate**, unsuitable, unacceptable, improper, unseemly; informal out of order.
OPPOSITES correct.

increase verb **1** *demand is likely to increase:* **grow**, get bigger, get larger, enlarge, expand, swell, rise, climb, mount, intensify, strengthen, extend, spread, widen. **2** *higher expectations will increase user demand:* **add to**, make larger, make bigger, augment, supplement, top up, build up, extend, raise, swell, inflate, intensify, heighten; informal up, bump up.
OPPOSITES decrease, reduce.
noun *the increase in size | an increase in demand:* **growth**, rise, enlargement, expansion, extension, increment, gain, addition, augmentation, surge;

informal hike.
OPPOSITES decrease.

incredible adjective **1** *I find his story incredible:* **unbelievable**, unconvincing, far-fetched, implausible, improbable, inconceivable, unimaginable. **2** *an incredible feat of engineering:* **wonderful**, marvellous, spectacular, remarkable, phenomenal, prodigious, breathtaking; informal fantastic, terrific.
OPPOSITES believable, unremarkable.

incur verb **bring upon oneself**, expose oneself to, lay oneself open to, run up, earn, sustain, experience.

indecent adjective **1** *indecent photographs:* **obscene**, dirty, filthy, rude, naughty, vulgar, smutty, pornographic; informal blue; euphemistic adult. **2** *indecent haste:* **unseemly**, improper, unbecoming, inappropriate.

independence noun **1** *the struggle for American independence:* **self-government**, self-rule, home rule, self-determination, sovereignty, autonomy. **2** *the adviser's independence:* **impartiality**, neutrality, disinterestedness, detachment, objectivity.
OPPOSITES dependence, partiality.

independent adjective **1** *an independent country:* **self-governing**, self-ruling, self-determining, sovereign, autonomous, non-aligned. **2** *two independent groups verified the results:* **separate**, different, unconnected, unrelated, discrete. **3** *an independent school:* **private**, non-state-run, private-sector, fee-paying, privatized,

deregulated, denationalized.
4 *independent advice:*
impartial, unbiased,
unprejudiced, neutral,
disinterested, uninvolved,
detached, dispassionate,
objective, non-partisan, with no
axe to grind.
OPPOSITES dependent, related,
state, public, biased.

independently adverb **alone**,
on one's own, separately,
individually, unaccompanied,
solo, unaided, unassisted,
without help, by one's own
efforts, under one's own steam,
single-handedly.

index noun **list**, listing,
inventory, catalogue, register,
directory, database.

indicate verb **1** *sales indicate a*
growing market: **point to,** be a
sign of, be evidence of,
demonstrate, show, testify to,
be symptomatic of, denote,
mark, signal, reflect, signify,
suggest, imply. **2** *the president*
indicated his willingness to use
force: **state,** declare, make
known, communicate,
announce, put on record.
3 *please indicate your choice of*
prize on the form: **specify,**
designate, stipulate, show.

indication noun **sign**, signal,
indicator, symptom, mark,
demonstration, pointer, guide,
hint, clue, omen, warning.

indicator noun **measure**, gauge,
meter, barometer, guide, index,
mark, sign, signal.

indictment noun **charge**,
accusation, arraignment,
prosecution, citation, summons;
N. Amer. impeachment.

indifference noun **detachment**,
lack of concern, disinterest,
lack of interest, nonchalance,
boredom, unresponsiveness,

impassivity, coolness.
OPPOSITES concern.

indifferent adjective **1** *an*
indifferent shrug: **detached**,
unconcerned, uninterested,
uncaring, casual, nonchalant,
offhand, unenthusiastic,
unimpressed, unmoved,
impassive, cool. **2** *an indifferent*
performance: **mediocre,**
ordinary, average, middle-of-
the-road, uninspired,
undistinguished, unexceptional,
pedestrian, forgettable,
amateurish; informal no great
shakes, not up to much.
OPPOSITES enthusiastic, brilliant.

indignant adjective **aggrieved,**
affronted, displeased, resentful,
angry, annoyed, offended,
exasperated; informal peeved,
irked, put out; Brit. informal
narked; N. Amer. informal sore.
OPPOSITES content.

indirect adjective **1** *an indirect*
effect: **incidental,** secondary,
subordinate, ancillary,
collateral, concomitant,
contingent. **2** *an indirect route:*
roundabout, circuitous,
meandering, winding, tortuous.
3 *an indirect attack:* **oblique,**
implicit, implied.
OPPOSITES direct.

individual adjective
1 *exhibitions devoted to*
individual artists: **single,**
separate, discrete, independent,
lone. **2** *he had his own*
individual style of music:
unique, characteristic,
distinctive, distinct, particular,
idiosyncratic, peculiar,
personal, special. **3** *a highly*
individual apartment: **original,**
exclusive, different, unusual,
novel, unorthodox, out of the
ordinary.
OPPOSITES multiple, shared,

ordinary.

noun *a rather stuffy individual:* **person,** human being, soul, creature, character; informal type, sort, customer.

individually adverb **separately,** singly, one by one, one at a time, independently.
OPPOSITES together.

induce verb **1** *the pickets induced many workers to stay away:* **persuade,** convince, prevail upon, get, make, prompt, encourage, cajole into, talk into. **2** *these activities induce a feeling of togetherness:* **bring about,** cause, produce, create, give rise to, generate, engender.
OPPOSITES dissuade, prevent.

indulge verb **1** *Sally indulged her passion for chocolate:* **satisfy,** gratify, fulfil, feed, yield to, give in to. **2** *she did not like her children to be indulged:* **pamper,** spoil, overindulge, coddle, mollycoddle, cosset, pander to, wait on hand and foot.
■ **indulge in** carry out, become involved in, participate in, commit, yield to.■ **indulge oneself** treat oneself, splash out; informal go to town, splurge.

indulgence noun **1** *the indulgence of all his desires:* **satisfaction,** gratification, fulfilment. **2** *indulgence contributed to his ill-health:* **self-gratification,** self-indulgence, overindulgence, intemperance, excess, lack of restraint, extravagance, hedonism. **3** *they viewed holidays as an indulgence:* **extravagance,** luxury, treat, non-essential, extra, frill. **4** *her indulgence left him spoilt:* **pampering,** coddling,

mollycoddling, cosseting. **5** *his parents view his lapses with indulgence:* **tolerance,** forbearance, understanding, compassion, sympathy, leniency.
OPPOSITES asceticism, intolerance.

indulgent adjective **generous,** permissive, easy-going, liberal, tolerant, forgiving, forbearing, lenient, kind, kindly, soft-hearted.
OPPOSITES strict.

industrialist noun **manufacturer,** factory owner, captain of industry, magnate, tycoon.

industry noun **1** *British industry:* **manufacturing,** production, construction, trade, commerce. **2** *the publishing industry:* **business,** trade, field, line of business, profession. **3** *the kitchen was a hive of industry:* **activity,** energy, effort, endeavour, hard work, industriousness, diligence, application.

ineffective adjective **1** *an ineffective scheme:* **unsuccessful,** unproductive, unprofitable, ineffectual. **2** *an ineffective president:* **ineffectual,** inefficient, inadequate, incompetent, incapable, unfit, inept; informal useless, hopeless.
OPPOSITES effective.

inefficient adjective **1** *an inefficient worker:* **ineffective,** ineffectual, incompetent, inept, disorganized, unprepared. **2** *inefficient processes:* **uneconomical,** wasteful, unproductive, time-wasting, slow, unsystematic.
OPPOSITES efficient.

inequality noun **imbalance,**

i

inequity, inconsistency, disparity, discrepancy, dissimilarity, difference, bias, prejudice, discrimination, unfairness.
OPPOSITES equality.

inevitable adjective
unavoidable, inescapable, inexorable, assured, certain, sure.
OPPOSITES avoidable.

inevitably adverb **unavoidably**, necessarily, automatically, naturally, as a matter of course, of necessity, inescapably, certainly, surely; informal like it or not.

inexpensive adjective **cheap**, affordable, low-cost, economical, competitive, reasonable, budget, economy, bargain, cut-price, reduced.
OPPOSITES expensive.

inexperienced adjective
inexpert, untrained, unqualified, unskilled, unseasoned, naive, new, callow, immature; informal wet behind the ears, wide-eyed.
OPPOSITES experienced.

infamous adjective **notorious**, disreputable, scandalous.
OPPOSITES reputable.

infancy noun **beginnings**, early days, early stages, emergence, dawn, outset, birth, inception.
OPPOSITES end.

infant noun **baby**, newborn, young child, tiny tot, little one; Medicine neonate; Scottish & N. English bairn, wean; informal tiny, sprog.

infect verb **1** *they can infect their children:* **pass infection to**, contaminate. **2** *nitrates were infecting rivers:* **contaminate**, pollute, taint, foul, poison.

infection noun **1** *a kidney infection:* **disease**, virus, illness, ailment, disorder, sickness;

informal bug. **2** *the infection in his wounds:* **contamination**, poison, inflammation, germs; Medicine sepsis.

infectious adjective **1** *infectious diseases:* **communicable**, contagious, transmittable, transmissible, transferable; informal catching. **2** *her laughter is infectious:* **irresistible**, compelling, contagious; informal catching.

inferior adjective **1** *she regards him as inferior:* **second-class**, lower-ranking, subordinate, junior, minor, lowly, humble, menial, beneath one. **2** *inferior accommodation:* **second-rate**, substandard, low-grade, unsatisfactory, shoddy, poor; informal crummy, lousy.
OPPOSITES superior, luxury.
noun *how dare she treat him as an inferior?* **subordinate**, junior, underling, minion.
OPPOSITES superior.

infertility noun **barrenness**, sterility, childlessness.
OPPOSITES fertility.

infested adjective **overrun**, swarming, teeming, crawling, alive, plagued.

infiltrate verb **penetrate**, insinuate oneself into, worm one's way into, sneak into, slip into, creep into, invade.

infiltrator noun **spy**, secret agent, plant, intruder, interloper, subversive, informer, mole, fifth columnist; N. Amer. informal spook.

infinite adjective **1** *the universe is infinite:* **boundless**, unbounded, unlimited, limitless, never-ending, incalculable, untold. **2** *in infinite combinations:* **countless**, uncountable, innumerable, numberless,

immeasurable.
OPPOSITES finite, limited.

inflame verb **1** *his opinions inflamed his rival:* **enrage**, incense, anger, madden, infuriate, exasperate, provoke, antagonize; informal make someone see red. **2** *he inflamed a sensitive situation:* **aggravate**, exacerbate, intensify, worsen, compound.
OPPOSITES placate, calm.

inflamed adjective **swollen**, red, hot, burning, itchy, sore, painful, tender, infected.

inflate verb **1** *inflate the balloon:* **blow up**, pump up, fill, puff up/out, dilate, distend, swell, bloat. **2** *the demand inflated prices:* **increase**, raise, boost, escalate, put up; informal hike up, jack up.
OPPOSITES deflate, lower.

inflated adjective **1** *inflated prices:* **high**, sky-high, excessive, unreasonable, outrageous, exorbitant, extortionate; Brit. over the odds; informal steep. **2** *an inflated opinion of himself:* **exaggerated**, immoderate, overblown, overstated.
OPPOSITES low, modest.

inflict verb **1** *he inflicted an injury on Frank:* **give**, administer, deal out, mete out, cause someone something, exact, wreak. **2** *I won't inflict my views on my children:* **impose**, force, thrust, foist.
OPPOSITES spare.

influence noun **1** *the influence of parents on their children:* **effect**, impact, control, spell, hold, magic. **2** *a bad influence on young girls:* **example to**, role model for, inspiration to. **3** *political influence:* **power**, authority, sway, leverage, weight, pull; informal clout.
verb **1** *bosses can influence our careers:* **affect**, have an impact on, determine, guide, control, shape, govern, decide, change, alter. **2** *an attempt to influence the jury:* **sway**, bias, prejudice, suborn, pressurize, coerce, intimidate; informal lean on; Brit. informal nobble.

influential adjective **powerful**, controlling, important, authoritative, leading, significant, instrumental, guiding.

inform verb **1** *she informed him that she was ill:* **tell**, notify, apprise, advise, impart to, communicate to, let someone know, brief, enlighten, send word to. **2** *he informed on two colleagues:* **betray**, give away, denounce, incriminate, report; informal rat, squeal, split, tell, blow the whistle, snitch; Brit. informal grass, shop; N. Amer. informal finger; Austral./NZ informal dob in.

informal adjective **1** *an informal discussion:* **unofficial**, casual, relaxed, easy-going, low-key. **2** *informal language:* **colloquial**, vernacular, idiomatic, popular, familiar, everyday; informal slangy, chatty. **3** *informal clothes:* **casual**, relaxed, comfortable, everyday, sloppy, leisure; informal comfy.
OPPOSITES formal, official, literary, smart.

information noun **facts**, particulars, details, figures, statistics, data, knowledge, intelligence; informal info, gen.

informative adjective **instructive**, illuminating, enlightening, revealing, explanatory, factual, educational, edifying.

informed adjective

knowledgeable, enlightened, educated, briefed, up to date, up to speed, in the picture, in the know, au fait; informal clued up.
OPPOSITES ignorant.

infuriate verb **enrage,** incense, provoke, anger, madden, exasperate; informal make someone see red; Brit. informal wind up.
OPPOSITES please.

ingenious adjective **inventive,** creative, imaginative, original, innovative, pioneering, resourceful, enterprising, inspired, clever.
OPPOSITES unimaginative.

ingredient noun **constituent,** component, element, item, part, strand, unit, feature, aspect, attribute.

inhabit verb **live in,** occupy, settle, people, populate, colonize.

inhabitant noun **resident,** occupant, occupier, settler, local, native; (**inhabitants**) population, populace, people, public, community, citizenry, townsfolk, townspeople.

inhale verb **breathe in,** draw in, suck in, sniff in, drink in, gasp.
OPPOSITES exhale.

inherit verb **1** *she inherited the farm:* **be left,** be bequeathed, be willed, come into. **2** *Richard inherited the title:* **succeed to,** assume, take over.
OPPOSITES leave.

inheritance noun **legacy,** bequest, endowment, birthright, heritage, patrimony.

inhibit verb **impede,** hinder, hamper, hold back, discourage, interfere with, obstruct, slow down, retard.
OPPOSITES assist, allow.

inhibited adjective **reserved,**

reticent, guarded, self-conscious, insecure, withdrawn, repressed, undemonstrative, shy, diffident, bashful; informal uptight.
OPPOSITES uninhibited.

initial adjective **beginning,** opening, commencing, starting, first, earliest, primary, preliminary, preparatory, introductory, inaugural.
OPPOSITES final.

initially adverb **at first,** at the start, at the outset, in/at the beginning, to begin with, to start with, originally.

initiate verb **1** *the government initiated the scheme:* **begin,** start (off), commence, institute, inaugurate, launch, instigate, establish, set up. **2** *he was initiated into a religious cult:* **introduce,** admit, induct, install, swear in, ordain, invest.
OPPOSITES finish, expel.

initiative noun **1** *employers are looking for initiative:* **enterprise,** resourcefulness, inventiveness, imagination, ingenuity, originality, creativity. **2** *he has lost the initiative:* **advantage,** upper hand, edge, lead, start. **3** *a recent initiative on recycling:* **scheme,** plan, strategy, measure, proposal, step, action.
OPPOSITES apathy.

inject verb **1** *he injected the codeine:* **administer,** take; informal shoot (up), mainline, fix. **2** *troops were injected with the vaccine:* **inoculate,** vaccinate. **3** *a pump injects air into the valve:* **insert,** introduce, feed, push, force, shoot. **4** *he injected new life into the team:* **introduce,** instil, infuse, imbue, breathe.

injection noun **1** *injections*

against diphtheria: **inoculation,** vaccination, immunization, booster; informal **jab,** shot. **2** *a cash injection:* **addition,** introduction, investment, dose, infusion, insertion.

injunction noun **order,** ruling, direction, directive, command, instruction, mandate.

injure verb **1** *he injured his foot:* **hurt,** wound, damage, harm, disable, break; Medicine traumatize; Brit. informal knacker. **2** *a libel injured her reputation:* **damage,** mar, spoil, ruin, blight, blemish, tarnish, blacken.
OPPOSITES boost.

injured adjective **1** *his injured arm:* **hurt,** wounded, damaged, sore, bruised, broken, fractured; Medicine traumatized; Brit. informal gammy. **2** *an injured tone:* **upset,** hurt, wounded, offended, reproachful, pained, aggrieved.
OPPOSITES healthy.

injury noun **1** *minor injuries:* **wound,** bruise, cut, gash, scratch, graze; Medicine trauma, lesion. **2** *they escaped without injury:* **harm,** hurt, damage, pain, suffering. **3** *injury to his feelings:* **offence,** abuse, injustice, disservice, affront, insult.

injustice noun **1** *the injustice of the world:* **unfairness,** one-sidedness, inequity, bias, prejudice, discrimination, intolerance, exploitation, corruption. **2** *his sacking was an injustice:* **wrong,** offence, crime, sin, outrage, scandal, disgrace, affront.
OPPOSITES justice, just deserts.

inland adjective **interior,** inshore, internal, upcountry.
OPPOSITES coastal.

inlet noun **1** *a rocky inlet:* **cove,** bay, bight, creek, estuary, fjord, sound; Scottish firth. **2** *an air inlet:* **vent,** flue, shaft, duct, channel, pipe.

inmate noun **1** *the inmates of the hospital:* **patient,** inpatient, resident, occupant. **2** *prison inmates:* **prisoner,** convict, captive, detainee, internee.

inner adjective **1** *inner London:* **central,** downtown, innermost. **2** *the inner gates:* **internal,** interior, inside, innermost. **3** *the inner meaning:* **hidden,** secret, deep, underlying, veiled, esoteric.
OPPOSITES outer, apparent.

innocence noun **1** *he protested his innocence:* **guiltlessness,** blamelessness. **2** *she took advantage of his innocence:* **naivety,** credulity, inexperience, gullibility, ingenuousness.

innocent adjective **1** *he was entirely innocent:* **guiltless,** blameless, clean, irreproachable, honest, upright, law-abiding. **2** *innocent fun:* **harmless,** innocuous, safe, inoffensive. **3** *innocent foreign students:* **naive,** ingenuous, trusting, credulous, impressionable, easily led, inexperienced, unsophisticated, artless.
OPPOSITES guilty, dangerous, worldly.

innovation noun **change,** alteration, upheaval, reorganization, restructuring, novelty, departure.

innovative adjective **original,** new, novel, fresh, unusual, experimental, inventive, ingenious, pioneering, groundbreaking, revolutionary, radical.

i

inquest noun enquiry, investigation, probe, examination, review, hearing.

inquire, inquiry See ENQUIRE, ENQUIRY.

insane adjective **1** *she was declared insane:* **mad,** of unsound mind, certifiable, psychotic, schizophrenic, unhinged; informal crazy, (stark) raving mad, bonkers, loony, round the bend; Brit. informal crackers, off one's trolley; N. Amer. informal nutso, out of one's tree; Austral./NZ informal bushed. **2** *an insane suggestion:* **stupid,** idiotic, nonsensical, absurd, ridiculous, ludicrous, preposterous; informal crazy, mad; Brit. informal daft, barmy.
OPPOSITES sane, sensible.

insect noun bug; informal creepy-crawly; Brit. informal minibeast.

insecure adjective **1** *an insecure young man:* **unconfident,** uncertain, unsure, doubtful, diffident, hesitant, self-conscious, anxious, fearful. **2** *insecure windows:* **unprotected,** unguarded, vulnerable, unsecured. **3** *an insecure footbridge:* **unstable,** rickety, wobbly, shaky, unsteady, precarious.
OPPOSITES confident, secure, stable.

insecurity noun lack of confidence, uncertainty, self-doubt, diffidence, hesitancy, nervousness, self-consciousness, anxiety, worry, unease.

insert verb put, place, push, thrust, slide, slip, load, fit, slot, install; informal pop, stick, bung.
OPPOSITES extract, remove.

inside noun **1** *the inside of the volcano:* **interior,** centre, core, middle, heart, bowels. **2** (informal) *my insides are out of order:* **stomach,** gut, bowels, intestines; informal tummy, belly, guts.
OPPOSITES outside.
adjective **1** *his inside pocket:* **inner,** interior, internal, innermost. **2** *inside information:* **confidential,** classified, restricted, privileged, private, secret, exclusive; informal hush-hush.
OPPOSITES outside, public.
adverb *she ushered me inside:* **indoors,** within, in.
OPPOSITES outside.

insight noun **1** *your insight has been invaluable:* **intuition,** perception, understanding, comprehension, appreciation, judgement, vision, imagination; informal nous, savvy. **2** *an insight into the government:* **understanding of,** appreciation of, introduction to; informal eye-opener.
OPPOSITES stupidity.

insignificant adjective **unimportant,** trivial, trifling, negligible, inconsequential, of no account, paltry, petty, insubstantial; informal piddling.
OPPOSITES significant.

insincere adjective false, fake, hollow, artificial, feigned, pretended, put-on, disingenuous, hypocritical, cynical; informal phoney, pretend.
OPPOSITES sincere.

insist verb **1** *be prepared to insist:* **stand firm,** stand one's ground, be resolute, be determined, hold out, persist, be emphatic, lay down the law, not take no for an answer; informal stick to one's guns, put one's foot down. **2** *she insisted that they pay up:* **demand,** command, order, require. **3** *he* insisted that he knew nothing: **maintain,** assert, protest, swear, declare, repeat.

insistent adjective **1** *Tony's insistent questioning:* **persistent,** determined, tenacious, unyielding, dogged, unrelenting, inexorable. **2** *an insistent buzzing:* **incessant,** constant, unremitting.

inspect verb **examine,** check, scrutinize, investigate, vet, test, monitor, survey, study, look over; informal check out, give something a/the once-over.

inspection noun **examination,** check-up, survey, scrutiny, exploration, investigation; informal once-over, going-over.

inspector noun **examiner,** scrutineer, investigator, surveyor, assessor, supervisor, monitor, watchdog, ombudsman, auditor.

inspiration noun **1** *she's an inspiration to others:* **stimulus,** motivation, encouragement, influence, spur. **2** *his work lacks inspiration:* **creativity,** invention, innovation, ingenuity, imagination, originality, insight, vision. **3** *she had a sudden inspiration:* **bright idea,** revelation; informal brainwave; N. Amer. informal brainstorm.

inspire verb **1** *the landscape inspired him to write:* **stimulate,** motivate, encourage, influence, move, spur, energize, galvanize. **2** *the film inspired a musical:* **give rise to,** lead to, bring about, prompt, spawn, engender. **3** *Charles inspired awe in her:* **arouse,** awaken, prompt, induce, ignite, trigger, kindle, produce, bring out.

inspired adjective **outstanding,** wonderful, marvellous, excellent, magnificent, exceptional, first-class, virtuoso, superlative; informal tremendous, superb, awesome, out of this world; Brit. informal brilliant. **OPPOSITES** uninspired.

inspiring adjective **inspirational,** encouraging, heartening, uplifting, stirring, rousing, electrifying, moving. **OPPOSITES** uninspiring.

instability noun **1** *the instability of political life:* **unreliability,** uncertainty, unpredictability, insecurity, volatility, capriciousness, changeability, mutability. **2** *emotional instability:* **volatility,** unpredictability, variability, inconsistency. **OPPOSITES** steadiness.

install verb **1** *a photocopier was installed in the office:* **put,** place, station, site, insert. **2** *they installed a new president:* **swear in,** induct, inaugurate, invest, appoint, ordain, consecrate, anoint, enthrone, crown. **3** *she installed herself behind the table:* **ensconce,** position, settle, seat, plant, sit (down); informal plonk, park. **OPPOSITES** remove.

instalment noun **1** *they paid by monthly instalments:* **payment,** tranche, repayment, part payment, planned payment, regular payment. **2** *the book was published in instalments:* **part,** episode, chapter, issue, programme, section, volume.

instance noun **example,** occasion, occurrence, case, illustration, sample.

instant adjective **1** *instant access to your money:* **immediate,** instantaneous, on-the-spot, prompt, swift, speedy, rapid, quick; informal snappy. **2** *instant*

i

meals: **prepared,** pre-cooked, microwaveable, convenience. OPPOSITES delayed.

noun 1 *come here this instant!* **moment,** minute, second. **2** *it all happened in an instant:* **flash,** trice, moment, minute, (split) second, twinkling of an eye, no time (at all); informal jiffy.

instantly adverb **immediately,** at once, straight away, right away, instantaneously, forthwith, there and then, here and now, this/that minute, this/that second.

instead adverb **as an alternative,** in lieu, alternatively, rather, on second thoughts; N. Amer. alternately. OPPOSITES as well.
■ **instead of** as an alternative to, as a substitute for, as a replacement for, in place of, in lieu of, in preference to, rather than.

instinct noun **1** *some instinct told me to be careful:* **inclination,** urge, drive, compulsion, intuition, feeling, sixth sense, nose. **2** *a good instinct for acting:* **talent,** gift, ability, aptitude, skill, flair, feel, knack.

instinctive adjective **intuitive,** natural, instinctual, innate, inborn, inherent, unconscious, subconscious, automatic, reflex, knee-jerk; informal gut. OPPOSITES learned.

institute noun **organization,** establishment, institution, foundation, centre, academy, school, college, university, society, association, federation, body.
verb **set up,** inaugurate, found, establish, organize, initiate, set in motion, get under way, get

off the ground, start, launch. OPPOSITES abolish, end.

institution noun **1** *an academic institution:* **establishment,** organization, institute, foundation, centre, academy, school, college, university, society, association, body. **2** *they spent their lives in institutions:* **(residential) home,** hospital, asylum, prison. **3** *the institution of marriage:* **practice,** custom, convention, tradition.

institutional adjective **organized,** established, bureaucratic, conventional, procedural, formal, formalized, systematic, systematized, structured, regulated. OPPOSITES free and easy.

instruct verb **1** *the union instructed them to strike:* **order,** direct, command, tell, mandate. **2** *nobody instructed him in how to operate it:* **teach,** coach, train, educate, tutor, guide, school, show.

instruction noun **1** *obey my instructions:* **order,** command, directive, direction, decree, injunction, mandate, commandment. **2** *read the instructions:* **directions,** handbook, manual, guide, advice, guidance. **3** *he gave instruction in self defence:* **tuition,** teaching, coaching, schooling, lessons, classes, lectures, training, drill, guidance.

instructor noun **trainer,** coach, teacher, tutor, adviser, counsellor, guide.

instrument noun **1** *a wound made with a sharp instrument:* **implement,** tool, utensil, device, apparatus, gadget. **2** *cockpit instruments:* **gauge,**

meter, indicator, dial, display.
3 *an instrument of learning:*
agent, agency, cause, channel,
medium, means, vehicle.

instrumental
■ **be instrumental in** play a part
in, contribute to, be a factor in,
have a hand in, promote,
advance, further.

insufficient adjective
inadequate, deficient, poor,
scant, scanty, not enough, too
little, too few.

insulate verb **1** *pipes must be
insulated:* **wrap,** sheathe, cover,
encase, enclose, lag,
soundproof. **2** *they were
insulated from the impact of the
war:* **protect,** save, shield,
shelter, screen, cushion,
cocoon.

insult verb **abuse,** be rude to,
call someone names, slight,
disparage, discredit, malign,
defame, denigrate, offend, hurt,
humiliate; informal bad-mouth;
Brit. informal slag off.
OPPOSITES compliment.
noun **jibe,** affront, slight, slur,
barb, indignity, abuse,
aspersions; informal dig, put-
down.

insulting adjective **abusive,**
rude, offensive, disparaging,
belittling, derogatory,
deprecating, disrespectful,
uncomplimentary; informal
bitchy, catty.

insurance noun **indemnity,**
assurance, protection, security,
cover, safeguard, warranty.

insure verb **provide insurance
for,** indemnify, cover, assure,
protect, underwrite, warrant.

intact adjective **whole,** entire,
complete, unbroken,
undamaged, unscathed,
unblemished, unmarked, in one
piece.

OPPOSITES damaged.

integral adjective **1** *an integral
part of human behaviour:*
essential, fundamental,
component, basic, intrinsic,
inherent, vital, necessary. **2** *the
dryer has an integral heat
sensor:* **built-in,** inbuilt,
integrated, inboard, fitted. **3** *an
integral approach to learning:*
unified, integrated,
comprehensive, holistic, joined-
up, all-embracing.
OPPOSITES peripheral,
supplementary, fragmented.

integrate verb **combine,**
amalgamate, merge, unite, fuse,
blend, consolidate, meld, mix,
incorporate, assimilate,
homogenize, desegregate.
OPPOSITES separate.

integrity noun **1** *I never doubted
his integrity:* **honesty,** probity,
rectitude, honour, sincerity,
truthfulness, trustworthiness.
2 *the integrity of the federation:*
unity, coherence, cohesion,
solidity. **3** *the structural
integrity of the aircraft:*
soundness, strength,
sturdiness, solidity, durability,
stability, rigidity.
OPPOSITES dishonesty, division,
fragility.

intellect noun **mind,** brain(s),
intelligence, reason, judgement,
grey matter, brain cells.

intellectual adjective **1** *his
intellectual capacity:* **mental,**
rational, conceptual,
theoretical, analytical, logical.
2 *an intellectual man:* **learned,**
cerebral, academic, erudite,
bookish, highbrow, scholarly.
OPPOSITES physical, stupid.

intelligence noun **1** *a man of
great intelligence:* **cleverness,**
intellect, brainpower,
judgement, reasoning, acumen,

i

wit, insight, perception.
2 *intelligence from our agents:*
information, facts, details,
particulars, data, knowledge;
informal info.

intelligent adjective **1** *an intelligent woman:* **clever,**
bright, quick-witted, smart,
astute, insightful, perceptive;
informal **brainy. 2** *intelligent machines:* **self-regulating,**
capable of learning, smart.
OPPOSITES unintelligent, dumb.

intelligible adjective
comprehensible,
understandable, accessible,
digestible, user-friendly, clear,
coherent, plain, unambiguous.

intend verb **plan,** mean, have in
mind, aim, propose, hope,
expect, envisage.

intense adjective **1** *intense heat:*
extreme, great, acute, fierce,
severe, high, exceptional,
extraordinary, harsh, strong,
powerful; informal serious. **2** *a very intense young man:*
passionate, impassioned,
zealous, vehement, earnest,
eager, committed.
OPPOSITES mild, apathetic.

intensify verb **escalate,**
increase, step up, raise,
strengthen, reinforce, pick up,
build up, heighten, deepen,
extend, expand, amplify,
magnify, aggravate, exacerbate,
worsen, inflame, compound.
OPPOSITES abate.

intensity noun **1** *the intensity of the sun:* **strength,** power, force,
severity, ferocity, fierceness,
harshness. **2** *his eyes had a glowing intensity:* **passion,**
ardour, fervour, vehemence,
fire, emotion, eagerness.

intensive adjective **thorough,**
thoroughgoing, in-depth,
rigorous, exhaustive, vigorous,

detailed, minute, meticulous,
painstaking, methodical,
extensive.
OPPOSITES cursory.

intent noun *he tried to divine his father's intent:* **aim,** intention,
purpose, objective, goal.
adjective **1** *he was intent on proving his point:* **bent,** set,
determined, insistent, resolved,
hell-bent, keen, committed to,
determined to. **2** *an intent expression:* **attentive,** absorbed,
engrossed, fascinated,
enthralled, rapt, focused,
preoccupied.
OPPOSITES distracted.

intention noun **aim,** purpose,
intent, objective, goal.

intentional adjective
deliberate, done on purpose,
wilful, calculated, conscious,
intended, planned, meant,
knowing.

inter verb **bury,** lay to rest,
consign to the grave, entomb.
OPPOSITES exhume.

intercept verb **stop,** head off,
cut off, catch, seize, block,
interrupt.

intercourse noun **1** *social intercourse:* **dealings,** relations,
relationships, contact,
interchange, communication.
2 *she did not consent to intercourse:* **sexual intercourse,**
sex, sexual relations, mating,
coupling, copulation.

interdict noun **prohibition,** ban,
bar, veto, embargo,
moratorium, injunction.
OPPOSITES permission.

interest noun **1** *we listened with interest:* **attentiveness,**
attention, regard, notice,
curiosity, enjoyment, delight.
2 *this will be of interest:*
concern, consequence,
importance, import,

significance, note, relevance, value. **3** *her interests include reading:* **hobby,** pastime, leisure pursuit, amusement, recreation, diversion, passion. **4** *a financial interest in the firm:* **stake,** share, claim, investment, involvement, concern.
OPPOSITES boredom.
verb *a topic that interests you:* **appeal to,** be of interest to, attract, intrigue, amuse, divert, entertain, arouse someone's curiosity, whet someone's appetite; informal tickle someone's fancy.
OPPOSITES put off.

interested adjective **1** *an interested crowd:* **attentive,** fascinated, riveted, gripped, captivated, agog, intrigued, curious, keen, eager. **2** *the government consulted with interested bodies:* **concerned,** involved, affected.

interesting adjective absorbing, engrossing, fascinating, riveting, gripping, compelling, captivating, engaging, enthralling, appealing, amusing, entertaining, stimulating, diverting, intriguing.

interfere verb *she tried not to interfere:* **butt in,** barge in, intrude, meddle, tamper, encroach; informal poke one's nose in, stick one's oar in.
■ **interfere with** impede, obstruct, stand in the way of, hinder, inhibit, restrict, constrain, hamper, handicap, disturb, disrupt, influence, affect, confuse.

interference noun **1** *they resent state interference:* **intrusion,** intervention, involvement, meddling, prying. **2** *radio interference:* **disruption,**

disturbance, static, noise.

interior adjective **1** *the house has interior panelling:* **inside,** inner, internal. **2** *the interior deserts of the US:* **inland,** upcountry, inner, central. **3** *the country's interior affairs:* **internal,** home, domestic, national, state, civil, local. **4** *an interior monologue:* **inner,** mental, spiritual, psychological, private, personal, secret.
OPPOSITES exterior, border, coastal, foreign.
noun **1** *the interior of the castle:* **inside,** depths, recesses, bowels, belly, heart. **2** *the country's interior:* **centre,** heartland.
OPPOSITES exterior, borders, coast.

intermediary noun mediator, go-between, negotiator, arbitrator, peacemaker, middleman, broker.

intermediate adjective **halfway,** in-between, middle, mid, midway, intervening, transitional.

intermittent adjective **sporadic,** irregular, fitful, spasmodic, discontinuous, isolated, random, patchy, scattered, occasional, periodic.
OPPOSITES continuous.

internal adjective **1** *an internal courtyard:* **inner,** interior, inside, central. **2** *the state's internal affairs:* **domestic,** home, interior, civil, local, national, state.
OPPOSITES external, foreign.

international adjective **global,** worldwide, world, intercontinental, universal, cosmopolitan, multiracial, multinational.
OPPOSITES national, local.

interpret verb **1** *the rabbis*

i

interpret the Jewish law: **explain,** elucidate, expound, clarify. **2** *the remark was interpreted as an invitation:* **understand,** construe, take (to mean), see, regard. **3** *the symbols are difficult to interpret:* **decipher,** decode, translate, understand.

interpretation noun **1** *the interpretation of the Bible's teachings:* **explanation,** elucidation, exposition, clarification, analysis. **2** *she did not care what interpretation he put on her haste:* **meaning,** understanding, explanation, inference. **3** *his interpretation of Mozart:* **rendition,** execution, presentation, performance, reading, playing, singing.

interrupt verb **1** *she opened her mouth to interrupt:* **cut in (on),** break in (on), barge in (on), intrude, intervene; informal butt in (on), chime in (on); Brit. informal chip in (on). **2** *the band had to interrupt their tour:* **suspend,** adjourn, break off, stop, halt; informal put on ice.

interruption noun **1** *he was not pleased at her interruption:* **cutting in,** barging in, interference, intervention, intrusion; informal butting in. **2** *an interruption of the power supply:* **suspension,** breaking off, cutting.

interval noun **intermission,** interlude, break, recess, time out.

intervene verb **intercede,** involve oneself, get involved, step in, interfere, intrude.

interview noun *all applicants will be called for an interview:* **meeting,** discussion, interrogation, cross-examination, debriefing, audience, talk, chat; informal grilling.
verb *we interviewed seventy subjects for the survey:* **talk to,** question, quiz, interrogate, cross-examine, debrief, poll, canvass, sound out; informal grill, pump.

interviewer noun **questioner,** interrogator, examiner, assessor, journalist, reporter, inquisitor.

intimacy noun **closeness,** togetherness, rapport, attachment, familiarity, friendliness, affection, warmth. OPPOSITES formality.

intimate[1] adjective **1** *an intimate friend:* **close,** bosom, dear, cherished, fast, firm. **2** *an intimate atmosphere:* **friendly,** warm, welcoming, hospitable, relaxed, informal, cosy, comfortable. **3** *intimate thoughts:* **personal,** private, confidential, secret, inward. **4** *an intimate knowledge:* **detailed,** thorough, exhaustive, deep, in-depth, profound. OPPOSITES distant, formal, cold, public, sketchy.

intimate[2] verb **1** *he intimated his decision:* **announce,** state, proclaim, make known, make public, disclose, reveal, divulge. **2** *her feelings were subtly intimated:* **imply,** suggest, hint at, indicate.

intimidate verb **frighten,** menace, scare, terrorize, threaten, browbeat, bully, harass, hound; informal lean on.

intricate adjective **complex,** complicated, convoluted, tangled, elaborate, ornate, detailed. OPPOSITES simple.

intrigue verb *her answer*

intrigued him: **interest,** fascinate, arouse someone's curiosity, attract, engage.
noun *the cabinet was a nest of intrigue:* **plotting,** conniving, scheming, machination, double-dealing, subterfuge.

intriguing adjective **interesting,** fascinating, absorbing, engaging.

introduce verb **1** *he has introduced a new system:* **institute,** initiate, launch, inaugurate, establish, found, bring in, set in motion, start, begin, get going. **2** *she introduced Lindsey to the young man:* **present,** make known, acquaint with. **3** *introducing nitrogen into canned beer:* **insert,** inject, put, force, shoot, feed. **4** *she introduced a note of seriousness:* **instil,** infuse, inject, add.
OPPOSITES end, remove.

introduction noun **1** *the introduction of democratic reforms:* **institution,** establishment, initiation, launch, inauguration, foundation. **2** *an introduction to the king:* **presentation,** meeting, audience. **3** *the introduction to the book:* **foreword,** preface, preamble, prologue, prelude; informal intro.
OPPOSITES ending, epilogue.

introductory adjective **1** *the introductory chapter:* **opening,** initial, starting, initiatory, first, preliminary. **2** *an introductory course:* **elementary,** basic, rudimentary, entry-level.
OPPOSITES final, advanced.

intrude verb **encroach,** impinge, trespass, infringe, invade, violate, disturb, disrupt.

intruder noun **trespasser,** interloper, invader, infiltrator, burglar, housebreaker; informal gatecrasher.

intuition noun **1** *he works by intuition:* **instinct,** feeling, insight, sixth sense. **2** *this confirms an intuition I had:* **hunch,** feeling in one's bones, inkling, sneaking suspicion, premonition; informal gut feeling.

intuitive adjective **instinctive,** innate, inborn, inherent, natural, unconscious, subconscious; informal gut.

invade verb **1** *the island was invaded:* **occupy,** conquer, capture, seize, take (over), annex, overrun, storm. **2** *someone had invaded our privacy:* **intrude on,** violate, encroach on, infringe on, trespass on, disturb, disrupt.
OPPOSITES leave, liberate.

invader noun **attacker,** raider, marauder, occupier, conqueror, intruder, trespasser.

invalid[1] adjective *her invalid husband:* **ill,** sick, ailing, infirm, incapacitated, bedridden, frail, sickly, poorly.
OPPOSITES healthy.
verb *an officer invalided by a chest wound:* **disable,** incapacitate, hospitalize, put out of action, lay up.

invalid[2] adjective **1** *the law was invalid:* **void,** null and void, not binding, illegitimate, inapplicable. **2** *the whole theory is invalid:* **false,** fallacious, spurious, unsound, wrong, untenable.
OPPOSITES binding, in force, true.

invaluable adjective **indispensable,** irreplaceable, all-important, crucial, vital, worth its weight in gold.
OPPOSITES dispensable.

invariably adverb **always,** at all

times, without fail, without exception, consistently, habitually, unfailingly.
OPPOSITES sometimes, never.

invasion noun **1** *the invasion of the islands:* occupation, conquering, capture, seizure, annexation, takeover. **2** *an invasion of my privacy:* violation, infringement, interruption, encroachment, disturbance, disruption, breach.
OPPOSITES withdrawal, liberation.

invent verb **1** *he invented television:* originate, create, design, devise, contrive, develop. **2** *they invented the story:* make up, fabricate, concoct, hatch, dream up; informal cook up.

invention noun **1** *the invention of the telescope:* origination, creation, development, design, discovery. **2** *medieval inventions:* innovation, creation, contraption, contrivance, device, gadget. **3** *a journalistic invention:* fabrication, concoction, (piece of) fiction, story, tale, lie, untruth, falsehood, fib.

inventive adjective **1** *the most inventive composer of his time:* creative, original, innovative, imaginative, resourceful. **2** *a fresh, inventive comedy:* original, innovative, unusual, fresh, novel, new, groundbreaking, unorthodox, unconventional.
OPPOSITES unimaginative, hackneyed.

inventor noun originator, creator, designer, deviser, developer, author, architect, father.

inventory noun list, listing, catalogue, record, register, checklist, log, archive.

invest verb *they invested £18 million:* put in, plough in, put up, advance, expend, spend; informal lay out.
■ **invest in** put money into, sink money into, plough money into, fund, back, finance, underwrite.

investigate verb enquire into, look into, go into, probe, explore, scrutinize, analyse, study, examine; informal check out, suss out.

investigation noun examination, enquiry, study, inspection, exploration, analysis, research, scrutiny, probe, review.

investigator noun researcher, examiner, analyst, inspector, scrutineer, detective.

investment noun **1** *investment in industry:* investing, speculation, outlay, funding, backing, financing, underwriting, buying shares. **2** *an investment of £305,000:* stake, payment, outlay, venture, proposition.

invisible adjective unseen, imperceptible, undetectable, inconspicuous, unnoticed, unobserved, hidden, out of sight.
OPPOSITES visible.

invitation noun request, call, summons; informal invite.

invite verb **1** *they invited us to lunch:* ask, summon, have someone over/round. **2** *applications are invited for the post:* ask for, request, call for, appeal for, solicit, seek. **3** *airing such views invites trouble:* cause, induce, provoke, ask for, encourage, lead to, bring on oneself, arouse.

inviting adjective tempting,

enticing, alluring, attractive, appealing, appetizing, mouth-watering, intriguing, seductive.
OPPOSITES repellent.

involve verb 1 *the inspection involved a lot of work:* **entail,** require, necessitate, demand, call for. 2 *I try to involve everyone in key decisions:* **include,** bring in, consult.
OPPOSITES preclude, exclude.

involved adjective 1 *social workers involved in the case:* **associated,** connected, concerned. 2 *he had been involved in burglaries:* **implicated,** caught up, mixed up. 3 *a long and involved story:* **complicated,** intricate, complex, convoluted. 4 *they were totally involved in their work:* **engrossed,** absorbed, immersed, caught up, preoccupied, intent.
OPPOSITES unconnected, straightforward.

involvement noun 1 *his involvement in the plot:* **participation,** collaboration, collusion, complicity, association, connection, entanglement. 2 *emotional involvement:* **attachment,** friendship, intimacy, commitment.

inwards adverb inside, towards the inside, into the interior, inward, within.

iron adjective 1 *an iron bar:* **ferric,** ferrous. 2 *an iron will:* **uncompromising,** unrelenting, unyielding, unbending, rigid, steely.
OPPOSITES flexible.
■ **iron something out 1** *John had ironed out all the minor snags:* resolve, straighten out, sort out, clear up, put right, solve, rectify; informal fix. 2 *ironing out*

differences in national systems: eliminate, eradicate, reconcile, resolve.

ironic adjective 1 *Edward's tone was ironic:* **sarcastic,** sardonic, dry, caustic, scathing, acerbic, bitter, trenchant, mocking, derisive, scornful; Brit. informal sarky. 2 *it's ironic that I've ended up writing:* **paradoxical,** funny, strange; informal typical.
OPPOSITES sincere.

irony noun 1 *that note of irony in her voice:* **sarcasm,** bitterness, mockery, ridicule, derision, scorn; Brit. informal sarkiness. 2 *the irony of the situation:* **paradox.**
OPPOSITES sincerity.

irrational adjective **unreasonable,** illogical, groundless, baseless, unfounded, unjustifiable.
OPPOSITES logical.

irregular adjective 1 *an irregular coastline:* **uneven,** crooked, misshapen, lopsided, asymmetrical, twisted. 2 *irregular surfaces:* **rough,** bumpy, uneven, pitted, rutted, lumpy, knobbly, gnarled. 3 *an irregular heartbeat:* **inconsistent,** unsteady, uneven, fitful, patchy, variable, varying, changeable, inconstant, erratic, unstable, spasmodic, intermittent. 4 *irregular financial dealings:* **improper,** illegitimate, unethical, unprofessional; informal shady, dodgy. 5 *an irregular army:* **guerrilla,** underground, paramilitary, partisan, mercenary, terrorist.
OPPOSITES regular, above board.
noun *gun-toting irregulars:* **guerrilla,** paramilitary, resistance fighter, partisan, mercenary, terrorist.

i

OPPOSITES regular.

irrelevant adjective **beside the point,** immaterial, unconnected, unrelated, peripheral, extraneous.

irresistible adjective **1** *her irresistible smile:* **captivating,** enticing, alluring, enchanting. **2** *an irresistible impulse:* **uncontrollable,** overwhelming, overpowering, ungovernable.

irresponsible adjective **reckless,** rash, careless, unwise, imprudent, ill-advised, injudicious, hasty, impetuous, foolhardy, foolish, unreliable, undependable, untrustworthy. OPPOSITES responsible.

irritable adjective **bad-tempered,** short-tempered, irascible, tetchy, testy, grumpy, grouchy. OPPOSITES good-humoured.

irritate verb **1** *his tone irritated her:* **annoy,** bother, vex, make cross, exasperate, infuriate, anger, madden; Brit. rub up the wrong way; informal aggravate, peeve, rile, needle, get (to), bug, hack off; Brit. informal nark, get on someone's wick; N. Amer. informal tee off, tick off, burn up. **2** *some sand irritated my eyes:* **inflame,** hurt, chafe, scratch, scrape, rub. OPPOSITES delight, soothe.

irritation noun **annoyance,** exasperation, vexation, indignation, anger, displeasure, chagrin. OPPOSITES delight.

island noun **isle,** islet, atoll; Brit. holm; (**islands**) archipelago.

isolate verb **separate,** segregate, detach, cut off, shut away, alienate, distance, cloister, seclude, cordon off, seal off, close off, fence off.

OPPOSITES integrate.

isolated adjective **1** *isolated communities:* **remote,** out of the way, outlying, off the beaten track, in the back of beyond, godforsaken, inaccessible, cut-off; informal in the middle of nowhere, in the sticks; N. Amer. informal jerkwater, in the tall timbers; Austral./NZ informal beyond the black stump. **2** *he lived a very isolated existence:* **solitary,** lonely, secluded, reclusive, hermit-like; N. Amer. lonesome. **3** *an isolated incident:* **unique,** lone, solitary, unusual, exceptional, untypical, freak; informal one-off. OPPOSITES accessible, sociable, common.

isolation noun **1** *their feeling of isolation:* **solitariness,** loneliness, friendlessness. **2** *the isolation of some mental hospitals:* **remoteness,** inaccessibility. OPPOSITES contact.

issue noun **1** *the committee discussed the issue:* **matter,** question, point at issue, affair, case, subject, topic, problem, situation. **2** *the latest issue of our magazine:* **edition,** number, instalment, copy. **3** *the issue of a special stamp:* **issuing,** release, publication. verb **1** *the minister issued a statement:* **release,** put out, deliver, publish, broadcast, circulate, distribute. **2** *the captain issued the crew with guns:* **supply,** provide, furnish, arm, equip, fit out, rig out, kit out; informal fix up. OPPOSITES withdraw, collect in. ■ **take issue with someone/ something** disagree with, challenge, dispute, (call into) question.

itch noun **1** *I have an itch on my back:* tingling, irritation, itchiness, prickle. **2** (informal) *the itch to travel:* longing, yearning, craving, ache, hunger, thirst, urge, hankering.
verb **1** *my chilblains really itch:* tingle, be irritated, be itchy, sting, hurt, be sore. **2** (informal) *he itched to do something to help:* long, yearn, ache, burn, crave, hanker for/after, hunger, thirst, be eager, be desperate; informal be dying, be gagging.

item noun **1** *an item of farm equipment:* thing, article, object, piece, element, constituent, component, ingredient. **2** *the meeting discussed the item:* issue, matter, affair, case, subject, topic, question, point. **3** *a news item:* report, story, article, piece, write-up, bulletin, feature, review.

itinerary noun route, plan, schedule, timetable, programme.

Jj

jab verb & noun poke, prod, dig, nudge, thrust, stab, push.

jacket noun wrapping, wrapper, sleeve, coat, cover, covering, sheath.

jagged adjective spiky, barbed, ragged, rough, uneven, irregular, serrated.
OPPOSITES smooth.

jail noun *he was thrown into jail:* prison, lock-up, detention centre; N. Amer. penitentiary, jailhouse, correctional facility; informal clink, cooler, the slammer, inside; Brit. informal nick; N. Amer. informal can, pen, slam, pokey.
verb *she was jailed for killing her husband:* send to prison/jail, put in prison/jail, imprison, incarcerate, lock up, put away, detain; informal send down, put behind bars, put inside; Brit. informal bang up.
OPPOSITES acquit, release.

jam verb **1** *he jammed a finger in each ear:* stuff, shove, force, ram, thrust, press, push, stick, cram. **2** *hundreds of people jammed into the hall:* crowd, pack, pile, press, squeeze, cram, throng, mob, fill, block, clog, congest. **3** *the rudder had jammed:* stick, become stuck, catch, seize (up). **4** *dust can jam the mechanism:* immobilize, paralyse, disable, clog, block; informal bung up.
noun *a traffic jam:* tailback, hold-up, queue, congestion, bottleneck; N. Amer. gridlock; informal snarl-up.

jar¹ noun *a jar of honey:* pot, container, crock.

jar² verb **1** *each step jarred my whole body:* jolt, jerk, shake, vibrate. **2** *her shrill voice jarred on him:* grate, set someone's teeth on edge, irritate, annoy, get on someone's nerves. **3** *the verse jars with the words that follow:* clash, conflict, contrast, be incompatible, be at variance, be at odds, be inconsistent.

jargon noun slang, idiom, cant, argot, patter, gobbledegook; informal lingo, -speak, -ese.

jaws plural noun mouth, maw,

muzzle; informal chops.

jealous adjective **1** *jealous of his brother*: **envious**, covetous, resentful, grudging, green with envy. **2** *a jealous lover*: **suspicious**, distrustful, possessive, proprietorial, overprotective. **3** *jealous of their rights*: **protective**, vigilant, watchful, mindful, careful.
OPPOSITES proud, trusting, careless.

jealousy noun **envy**, resentment, bitterness.

jeer verb *the demonstrators jeered the police*: **taunt**, mock, scoff at, ridicule, sneer at, deride, insult, abuse, heckle, catcall (at), boo (at), whistle at; Brit. barrack.
OPPOSITES applaud, cheer.
noun *the jeers of the crowd*: **taunt**, sneer, insult, shout, jibe, boo, catcall, derision, teasing, scoffing, abuse, scorn, heckling, catcalling; Brit. barracking.
OPPOSITES applause, cheer.

jeopardize verb **threaten**, endanger, imperil, risk, put in danger/jeopardy, compromise, prejudice.
OPPOSITES safeguard.

jeopardy noun **danger**, peril, risk.

jerk noun **1** *she gave the reins a jerk*: **yank**, tug, pull, wrench. **2** *he let the clutch in with a jerk*: **jolt**, lurch, bump, judder, jump, bounce, shake.
verb **1** *she jerked her arm free*: **yank**, tug, pull, wrench, wrest, drag, snatch. **2** *the car jerked along*: **jolt**, lurch, bump, judder, bounce.

jet noun **1** *a jet of water*: **stream**, spurt, spray, spout, gush, surge, burst. **2** *carburettor jets*: **nozzle**, head, spout.

jettison verb **dump**, drop, ditch, throw out, get rid of, discard, dispose of, scrap.
OPPOSITES retain.

jewel noun **1** *priceless jewels*: **gem**, gemstone, (precious) stone; informal sparkler, rock. **2** *the jewel of his collection*: **showpiece**, pride (and joy), cream, crème de la crème, jewel in the crown, prize, pick.

jewellery noun **jewels**, gems, gemstones, precious stones, regalia, finery, ornaments, trinkets.

jibe noun *cruel jibes*: **snide remark**, taunt, sneer, jeer, insult, barb; informal dig, put-down.

jilt verb **leave**, walk out on, throw over, finish with, break up with, stand up, leave standing at the altar; informal chuck, ditch, dump, drop, run out on, give someone the push/elbow, give someone the big E.

jingle noun & verb **clink**, chink, tinkle, jangle, ring.

jinx noun *the jinx struck six days later*: **curse**, spell, the evil eye, black magic, voodoo, bad luck; N. Amer. hex.
verb *the family is jinxed*: **curse**, cast a spell on, put the evil eye on; Austral. point the bone at; N. Amer. hex.

job noun **1** *my job involves a lot of travelling*: **position**, post, situation, appointment, occupation, profession, trade, career, work, vocation, calling. **2** *this job will take three months*: **task**, piece of work, assignment, project, chore, undertaking, venture, operation. **3** *it's your job to protect her*: **responsibility**, duty, charge, task, role, function, mission; informal department.

jobless adjective **unemployed**, out of work, out of a job, unwaged, redundant, laid off; Brit. informal on the dole, resting; Austral./NZ informal on the wallaby track.

OPPOSITES employed.

jog verb **1** *he jogged along the road:* **run**, trot, lope. **2** *a hand jogged his elbow:* **nudge**, prod, poke, push, bump, jar.
noun *he set off at a jog:* **run**, trot, lope.

join verb **1** *the two parts of the mould are joined with clay:* **connect**, unite, couple, fix, affix, attach, fasten, stick, glue, fuse, weld, amalgamate, bond, link, merge, secure, make fast, tie, bind. **2** *here the path joins a major road:* **meet**, touch, reach. **3** *I'm off to join the search party:* **help in**, participate in, get involved in, contribute to, enlist in, join up, sign up, band together, get together, team up.
OPPOSITES separate, leave.

joint noun *a leaky joint:* **join**, junction, intersection, link, connection, weld, seam.
adjective *a joint effort:* **common**, shared, communal, collective, mutual, cooperative, collaborative, concerted, combined, united.
OPPOSITES separate.

jointly adverb **together**, in partnership, in cooperation, cooperatively, in conjunction, in combination, mutually.
OPPOSITES separately.

joke noun **1** *telling jokes:* **funny story**, jest, witticism, quip, pun; informal gag, wisecrack, crack, funny, one-liner; N. Amer. informal boffola. **2** *playing stupid jokes:* **trick**, prank, stunt, hoax, jape; informal leg-pull, spoof, wind-up.

3 (informal) *he soon became a joke:* **laughing stock,** figure of fun, object of ridicule. **4** (informal) *the present system is a joke:* **farce,** travesty, waste of time; informal shambles; N. Amer. informal shuck.
verb *she joked with the guests:* **tell jokes**, jest, banter, quip; informal wisecrack, josh.

joker noun **comedian,** comedienne, comic, humorist, wit, jester, prankster, practical joker, clown.

jolly adjective **cheerful,** happy, cheery, good-humoured, jovial, merry, sunny, joyful, light-hearted, in high spirits, bubbly, genial; informal chipper, chirpy, perky, bright-eyed and bushy-tailed.
OPPOSITES miserable.

jolt verb **1** *the train jolted the passengers to one side:* **push**, thrust, jar, bump, knock, bang, shake, jog. **2** *the car jolted along:* **bump**, bounce, jerk, rattle, lurch, shudder, judder. **3** *she was jolted out of her reverie:* **startle**, surprise, shock, stun, shake; informal rock, knock sideways.
noun **1** *a series of sickening jolts:* **bump**, bounce, shake, jerk, lurch. **2** *he woke up with a jolt:* **start**, jerk, jump. **3** *the sight of the dagger gave him a jolt:* **fright**, shock, scare, surprise; informal turn.

jostle verb **1** *she was jostled by noisy students:* **push**, shove, elbow, barge. **2** *people jostled for the best position:* **struggle**, vie, jockey, scramble, fight.

journal noun **1** *a medical journal:* **periodical**, magazine, gazette, review, newsletter, news-sheet, bulletin, newspaper, paper, daily, weekly, monthly, quarterly. **2** *he keeps a*

j

journal: **diary,** log, logbook, chronicle, history, yearbook; N. Amer. daybook.

journalist noun **reporter,** correspondent, newspaperman, newspaperwoman, newsman, newswoman, columnist; informal news hound, hack, hackette, stringer, journo; N. Amer. informal newsie.

journey noun *his journey round the world:* **trip,** expedition, tour, trek, voyage, cruise, ride, drive, crossing, passage, flight, odyssey, pilgrimage.
verb *they journeyed south:* **travel,** go, voyage, sail, cruise, fly, hike, trek, ride, drive, make one's way.

jovial adjective **cheerful,** jolly, happy, cheery, good-humoured, convivial, genial, good-natured, affable, outgoing, smiling, merry, sunny.
OPPOSITES miserable.

joy noun **delight,** pleasure, jubilation, triumph, exultation, rejoicing, happiness, gladness, elation, euphoria, bliss, ecstasy, rapture.
OPPOSITES misery.

joyful adjective **1** *his joyful mood:* **cheerful,** happy, jolly, merry, sunny, joyous, cheery, smiling, mirthful, jubilant, gleeful, jovial. **2** *joyful news:* **pleasing,** happy, good, cheering, gladdening, welcome, heart-warming.
OPPOSITES sad.

jubilant adjective **overjoyed,** exultant, triumphant, joyful, cock-a-hoop, elated, thrilled, gleeful, euphoric, ecstatic; informal over the moon.
OPPOSITES despondent.

jubilee noun **anniversary,** commemoration, celebration, festival.

judge noun **1** *the judge sentenced him to five years:* **justice,** magistrate, recorder, sheriff, His/Her/Your Honour; N. Amer. jurist; Brit. informal beak. **2** *a panel of judges will select the winner:* **adjudicator,** referee, umpire, arbiter, assessor, examiner, moderator, scrutineer.
verb **1** *I judged that she was exhausted:* **conclude,** decide, consider, believe, think, deduce, infer, gauge, estimate, guess, surmise, conjecture, regard as, rate as, class as; informal reckon, figure. **2** *she was judged innocent:* **pronounce,** decree, rule, find. **3** *the competition will be judged by Alan Amey:* **adjudicate,** arbitrate, moderate, referee, umpire. **4** *entries were judged by a panel of experts:* **assess,** appraise, evaluate, examine, review.

judgement noun **1** *an error of judgement:* **sense,** discernment, perception, discrimination, understanding, powers of reasoning, reason, logic. **2** *his beliefs affect his judgement of Milton:* **opinion,** view, estimate, appraisal, conclusion, diagnosis, assessment, impression, conviction, perception, thinking. **3** *a court judgement:* **verdict,** decision, adjudication, ruling, pronouncement, decree, finding, sentence.

judicious adjective **wise,** sensible, prudent, shrewd, astute, canny, discerning.
OPPOSITES ill-advised.

jug noun **pitcher,** ewer, crock, jar, urn, carafe, flask, flagon, decanter; N. Amer. creamer.

juice noun **liquid,** fluid, sap, milk, gum, extract, concentrate, essence.

juicy adjective **succulent**, tender, moist, ripe.
OPPOSITES dry.

jumble noun *the books were in a jumble:* **heap**, muddle, mess, tangle, confusion, disarray, chaos, hotchpotch; N. Amer. hodgepodge; informal shambles.
verb *the photographs are all jumbled up:* **mix up**, muddle up, disorganize, disorder, tangle.

jump verb 1 *the cat jumped off his lap:* **leap**, spring, bound, hop, skip, caper, dance, prance, frolic, cavort. 2 *he jumped the fence:* **vault (over)**, leap over, clear, sail over, hop over. 3 *pre-tax profits jumped:* **rise**, go up, shoot up, soar, surge, climb, increase; informal skyrocket. 4 *the noise made her jump:* **start**, jolt, flinch, recoil, shudder.
noun 1 *the short jump across the gully:* **leap**, spring, bound, hop, skip. 2 *a jump in profits:* **rise**, leap, increase, upsurge, upswing; informal hike. 3 *I woke up with a jump:* **start**, jerk, spasm, shudder.

jumper noun (Brit.) **sweater**, pullover, jersey; informal woolly.

junction noun **crossroads**, intersection, interchange, T-junction, turn, turn-off, exit; Brit. roundabout; N. Amer. turnout, cloverleaf.

junior adjective 1 *the junior members of the family:* **younger**, youngest. 2 *a junior minister:* **minor**, subordinate, lower, lesser, low-ranking, secondary.
OPPOSITES senior, older.

junk noun (informal) **rubbish**, clutter, odds and ends, bits and pieces, bric-a-brac, refuse, litter, scrap, waste, debris; N. Amer. trash; Austral./NZ mullock.

just adjective 1 *a just society:* **fair**, fair-minded, equitable, even-handed, impartial, unbiased, objective, neutral, disinterested, unprejudiced, honourable, upright, decent, principled. 2 *a just reward:* **deserved**, well deserved, well earned, merited, rightful, due, proper, fitting, appropriate.
OPPOSITES unfair, undeserved.
adverb 1 *I just saw him:* **a moment ago**, a short time ago, very recently, not long ago. 2 *she's just right for him:* **exactly**, precisely, absolutely, completely, totally, entirely, perfectly, utterly, thoroughly; informal dead. 3 *we just made it:* **narrowly**, only just, by a hair's breadth, by the skin of one's teeth, barely, scarcely, hardly; informal by a whisker. 4 *she's just a child:* **only**, merely, simply, (nothing) but, no more than.
OPPOSITES hardly, easily.

justice noun 1 *I appealed to his sense of justice:* **fairness**, justness, fair play, fair-mindedness, equity, right, even-handedness, honesty, morality. 2 *the justice of his case:* **validity**, justification, soundness, well-foundedness, legitimacy. 3 **judge**, magistrate, recorder, sheriff; N. Amer. jurist.

justifiable adjective **valid**, legitimate, warranted, well founded, justified, just, reasonable, defensible.
OPPOSITES unjustifiable.

justification noun **grounds**, reason, basis, rationale, premise, vindication, explanation, defence, argument, case.

justify verb 1 *directors must justify the expenditure:* **give grounds for**, give reasons for,

j

explain, account for, defend, vindicate, excuse, exonerate.
2 *the situation justified further investigation:* **warrant,** be good reason for, be a justification for.

juvenile adjective **1** *juvenile offenders:* **young,** teenage, adolescent, junior, pubescent.

2 *juvenile behaviour:* **childish,** immature, puerile, infantile, babyish.
OPPOSITES adult, mature.
noun *many victims are juveniles:* **young person,** youngster, child, teenager, adolescent, minor, junior; informal kid.
OPPOSITES adult.

Kk

keen adjective **1** *his publishers were keen to capitalize on his success:* **eager,** anxious, intent, impatient, determined; informal raring, itching, dying. **2** *a keen birdwatcher:* **enthusiastic,** avid, eager, ardent, fervent, conscientious, committed, dedicated. **3** *a girl he was keen on:* **attracted to,** passionate about, interested in, fond of, taken with, smitten with, enamoured of, infatuated with; informal struck on, gone on, mad about. **4** *a keen cutting edge:* **sharp,** well-honed, razor-sharp. **5** *a keen mind:* **acute,** penetrating, astute, incisive, sharp, perceptive, piercing, razor-sharp, shrewd, discerning, clever, intelligent, brilliant, bright, smart, wise, insightful. **6** *a keen sense of duty:* **intense,** acute, fierce, passionate, burning, fervent, ardent, strong, powerful.
OPPOSITES reluctant, unenthusiastic, dull.

keep verb **1** *you should keep all the old forms:* **retain (possession of),** hold on to, not part with, save, store, put by/ aside, set aside; N. Amer. set by; informal hang on to. **2** *I tried to*

keep calm: **remain,** stay, carry on being. **3** *he keeps going on about the murder:* **persist in,** keep on, carry on, continue, insist on. **4** *I shan't keep you long:* **detain,** keep waiting, delay, hold up, slow down. **5** *most people kept the rules:* **comply with,** obey, observe, conform to, abide by, adhere to, stick to, heed, follow, carry out, act on, make good, honour, keep to, stand by. **6** *keeping the old traditions:* **preserve,** keep alive/up, keep going, carry on, perpetuate, maintain, uphold. **7** *where is her umbrella kept?* **store,** house, stow, put (away), place, deposit. **8** *he stole to keep his family:* **provide for,** support, feed, maintain, sustain, take care of, look after. **9** *she keeps rabbits:* **breed,** rear, raise, farm, own. **10** *his parents kept a shop:* **manage,** run, own, operate.
OPPOSITES throw away, break, abandon.
noun *money to pay for his keep:* **maintenance,** upkeep, sustenance, board (and lodging), food, livelihood.
■ **keep off** avoid, steer clear of, stay away from, not go near.

keeper noun **curator,** custodian, guardian, administrator, overseer, steward, caretaker, attendant.

keeping noun **care,** custody, charge, guardianship, possession, trust, protection.
■ **in keeping with** consistent with, in harmony with, in accord with, in agreement with, in line with, in character with, compatible with, appropriate to, befitting, suitable for.

key noun **1** *the key to the mystery:* **answer,** clue, solution, explanation, basis, foundation. **2** *the key to success:* **means,** way, route, path, passport, secret, formula.
adjective *a key figure:* **crucial,** central, essential, indispensable, pivotal, critical, dominant, vital, principal, prime, major, leading, main, important.
OPPOSITES peripheral.

kick verb *kick the ball:* **boot,** punt.
noun (informal) *I get a kick out of driving:* **thrill,** excitement, stimulation, tingle, frisson; informal buzz, high; N. Amer. informal charge.
■ **kick off** (informal) start, commence, begin, get going, get off the ground, get under way, open, start off, set in motion, launch, initiate, introduce, inaugurate. ■ **kick someone out** (informal) expel, eject, throw out, oust, evict, get rid of, dismiss, discharge; informal chuck out, send packing, boot out, sack, fire.

kid noun (informal) **child,** youngster, little one, baby, toddler, tot, infant, boy, girl, young person, minor, juvenile, adolescent, teenager, youth, stripling; Scottish bairn; informal kiddie, nipper, kiddiewink; Brit. informal sprog; N. Amer. informal rug rat; Austral./NZ ankle-biter; derogatory brat.

kidnap verb **abduct,** carry off, capture, seize, snatch, take hostage.

kill verb **1 murder,** take the life of, assassinate, eliminate, terminate, dispatch, finish off, put to death, execute, slaughter, exterminate; informal bump off, do away with, do in, top, take out, blow away; N. Amer. informal rub out, waste; literary slay. **2** (informal) *Congress killed the bill:* **veto,** defeat, vote down, rule against, reject, throw out, overturn, put a stop to.

killer noun **murderer,** assassin, butcher, serial killer, gunman, terminator, executioner; informal hit man.

killing noun **murder,** assassination, homicide, manslaughter, execution, slaughter, massacre, butchery, bloodshed, extermination.

kind[1] noun *all kinds of gifts:* **sort,** type, variety, style, form, class, category, genre.

kind[2] adjective *a kind and caring person:* **kindly,** good-natured, kind-hearted, warm-hearted, caring, affectionate, loving, warm, considerate, obliging, compassionate, sympathetic, understanding, benevolent, benign; Brit. informal decent.
OPPOSITES unkind.

kindly adjective *a kindly old lady:* **benevolent,** kind, kind-hearted, warm-hearted, generous, good-natured, gentle, warm, compassionate, caring, loving, benign, well meaning, considerate.

k

OPPOSITES unkind, cruel.
adverb *he looked at her kindly:* **nicely,** warmly, affectionately, tenderly, lovingly, compassionately, considerately, obligingly, generously.
OPPOSITES unkindly, harshly.

kindness noun kindliness, affection, warmth, gentleness, concern, care, consideration, altruism, compassion, sympathy, benevolence, generosity.
OPPOSITES unkindness.

king noun **ruler,** sovereign, monarch, Crown, His Majesty, emperor, prince, potentate.

kingdom noun **realm,** domain, dominion, country, empire, land, territory, nation, (sovereign) state, province.

kiss verb **1** *he kissed her:* informal **peck,** smooch, canoodle, neck, pet; Brit. informal snog; N. Amer. informal buss. **2** *the ball just kissed the crossbar:* **brush (against),** caress, touch, stroke, skim.
noun informal peck, smack, smacker, smooch; Brit. informal snog; N. Amer. informal buss.

kit noun **1** *the dental kit for the hospital:* **equipment,** tools, implements, instruments, gadgets, utensils, appliances, gear, tackle, hardware, paraphernalia; informal things, stuff; Military accoutrements. **2** (Brit. informal) *their football kit:* **clothes,** clothing, garments, outfit, dress, costume, attire, garb; informal gear, get-up, rig-out. **3** *a tool kit:* **set,** selection, collection, pack.
■ **kit someone/something out** equip, fit (out/up), furnish, supply, provide, issue, dress, clothe, attire, rig out, deck out; informal fix up.

knack noun **1** *a knack for making money:* **gift,** talent, flair, genius, instinct, ability, capability, capacity, aptitude, bent, facility, trick; informal the hang of something. **2** *he has a knack of getting injured:* **tendency,** habit, liability, propensity.

knickers plural noun (Brit.) **underpants,** briefs; Brit. pants; informal panties, undies; Brit. informal knicks, smalls; dated drawers; historical bloomers.

knife noun **blade,** cutter.
verb *he was knifed in the back:* **stab,** hack, gash, slash, lacerate, cut, bayonet.

knit verb **1** *disparate regions began to knit together:* **unite,** unify, come together, bond, fuse, coalesce, merge, meld, blend. **2** *we expect broken bones to knit:* **heal,** mend, join, fuse. **3** *Marcus knitted his brows:* **furrow,** contract, gather, wrinkle.

knob noun **lump,** bump, protrusion, bulge, swelling, knot, boss.

knock verb **1** *he knocked on the door:* **bang,** tap, rap, thump, pound, hammer, beat, strike, hit. **2** *she knocked her knee on the table:* **bump,** bang, hit, strike, crack, injure, hurt, bruise; informal bash, whack. **3** *he knocked into an elderly man:* **collide with,** bump into, bang into, run into, crash into, smash into, plough into; N. Amer. impact; informal bash into.
noun **1** *a knock at the door:* **tap,** rap, rat-tat, knocking, bang, banging, pounding, hammering, thump, thud. **2** *the casing can withstand knocks:* **bump,** blow, bang, jolt, jar, shock, collision, crash, smash, impact.

■ **knock someone down** fell, floor, flatten, bring down, knock to the ground, knock over, run over/down. ■ **knock something down** demolish, pull down, tear down, destroy, raze (to the ground), level, flatten, bulldoze. ■ **knock someone out** knock unconscious, knock senseless, floor, prostrate; informal lay out, KO, fell.

knot noun *a knot of people:* **cluster,** group, band, huddle, bunch, circle, ring.
verb *a scarf knotted round her throat:* **tie,** fasten, secure, bind, do up.

knotted adjective **tangled,** matted, snarled, unkempt, tousled; informal mussed up.

know verb **1** *she doesn't know I'm here:* **be aware,** realize, be conscious. **2** *do you know the rules:* **be familiar with,** be conversant with, be acquainted with, be versed in, have mastered, have a grasp of, understand, comprehend; informal be clued up on. **3** *I don't know many people here:* **be acquainted with,** have met, be familiar with; Scottish ken.

know-how noun (informal) **expertise,** skill, proficiency, knowledge, understanding, mastery, technique; informal savvy.

knowing adjective **significant,** meaningful, expressive, suggestive, superior.

knowledge noun **1** *his knowledge of history:* **understanding,** comprehension, grasp, command, mastery; informal know-how. **2** *people anxious to display their knowledge:* **learning,** erudition, education, scholarship, schooling, wisdom. **3** *he slipped away without my knowledge:* **awareness,** consciousness, realization, cognition, apprehension, perception, appreciation. **4** *a knowledge of the countryside:* **familiarity,** acquaintance, conversance, intimacy.
OPPOSITES ignorance.

knowledgeable adjective **1** *a knowledgeable old man:* **well informed,** learned, well read, (well) educated, erudite, scholarly, cultured, cultivated, enlightened. **2** *he is knowledgeable about modern art:* **conversant with,** familiar with, well acquainted with, au fait with, up on, up to date with, abreast of; informal clued up on.
OPPOSITES ignorant.

known adjective *a known criminal:* **recognized,** well known, widely known, noted, celebrated, notable, notorious, acknowledged.

k

Wordfinder

Contents

Animals

Amphibians

axolotl	fire	frog	natterjack	salamander
bullfrog	salamander	horned toad	toad	toad
cane toad	flying frog	marsh frog	newt	tree frog

Birds

albatross	blackcap	buzzard	cockatiel	dipper
Arctic tern	black swan	Canada	cockatoo	dodo
auk	bluebird	goose	condor	dotterel
avocet	blue tit	canary	coot	dove
barnacle	booby	capercaillie	cormorant	duck
goose	bowerbird	caracara	corncrake	dunlin
barn owl	brambling	cassowary	crane	dunnock
Bewick's swan	budgerigar	chaffinch	crossbill	eagle
bird of	bullfinch	chicken	crow	eagle owl
paradise	bunting	chiffchaff	cuckoo	egret
bittern	bustard	chough	curlew	eider duck
blackbird	butcher-bird	coal tit	dabchick	

Animals

emperor
 penguin
emu
falcon
fantail
fieldfare
finch
flamingo
flycatcher
fulmar
gannet
goldcrest
golden eagle
goldfinch
goose
goshawk
great tit
grebe
green
 woodpecker
greenfinch
grouse
guillemot
guineafowl
gull
harrier

hawfinch
hawk
hen
heron
hobby
hoopoe
hornbill
house martin
hummingbird
ibis
jackdaw
jay
kestrel
kingfisher
kite
kittiwake
kiwi
kookaburra
lammergeier
lapwing
lark
linnet
lovebird
lyrebird
macaw
magpie

mallard
martin
merlin
moa
mockingbird
moorhen
mynah bird
nightingale
nightjar
nuthatch
osprey
ostrich
ouzel
owl
oystercatcher
parakeet
parrot
partridge
peacock
peewit
pelican
penguin
peregrine
 falcon
petrel
pheasant

pigeon
pipit
plover
ptarmigan
puffin
quail
raven
red kite
redpoll
redstart
redwing
rhea
ring ouzel
roadrunner
robin
rook
sandpiper
seagull
shag
shearwater
shelduck
shrike
skua
skylark
snipe
sparrow

sparrowhawk
spoonbill
starling
stonechat
stork
storm petrel
sunbird
swallow
swan
swift
tern
thrush
tit
toucan
turkey
vulture
wagtail
warbler
waxwing
weaver bird
woodcock
woodlark
woodpecker
wren
yellow-
 hammer

Crustaceans

barnacle
crab
crawfish
crayfish
crevette

fiddler crab
ghost crab
goose
 barnacle
hermit crab

horseshoe
 crab
king prawn
krill
land crab

langoustine
lobster
prawn
shrimp
spider crab

woodlouse

Dinosaurs

allosaurus
ankylosaur
apatosaurus
brachiosaurus
brontosaurus
carnosaur

coelurosaur
deinonychus
diplodocus
dromaeosaur
duck-billed
 dinosaur

hadrosaur
iguanodon
megalosaurus
pliosaur
protoceratops
pteranodon

pterodactyl
raptor
saurischian
sauropod
seismosaurus
stegosaurus

theropod
triceratops
tyrannosaurus
velociraptor

Fish

anchovy
angelfish
anglerfish
archerfish

barbel
barracouta
barracuda
basking shark

bass
beluga
blenny
bluefin

boxfish
bream
brill
brisling

bullhead
butterfly fish
carp
catfish

charr
chub
clownfish
cod
coelacanth
coley
conger eel
dab
dace
damselfish
dogfish
dorado
dory
Dover sole
eel
electric eel
electric ray
fighting fish
filefish
flatfish
flathead
flounder
flying fish
garfish
goby
goldfish

gourami
grayling
great white
  shark
grouper
gudgeon
gulper eel
guppy
gurnard
haddock
hake
halfbeak
halibut
hammerhead
herring
hoki
huss
John Dory
koi carp
lamprey
lanternfish
lemon sole
loach
lumpsucker
lungfish
mackerel

mako
manta
marlin
megamouth
minnow
monkfish
moray eel
mudskipper
mullet
needlefish
nurse shark
oarfish
orfe
parrotfish
perch
pike
pilchard
pilotfish
pipefish
piranha
plaice
pollack
porbeagle
porcupine fish
puffer fish
rabbitfish

rainbow trout
ray
roach
sailfish
salmon
sardine
sawfish
scorpionfish
sea horse
shad
shark
skate
skipjack tuna
skipper
smelt
snapper
sockeye
  salmon
sole
sprat
stargazer
stickleback
stingray
stonefish
sturgeon
sunfish

surgeonfish
swordfish
swordtail
tench
tetra
thresher
tiger shark
tope
triggerfish
trout
tuna
tunny
turbot
weever
whaler
whale shark
whitebait
whitefish
whiting
wobbegong
wrasse
zander

Insects

ant
ant lion
aphid
assassin bug
bark beetle
bedbug
bee
beetle
blackfly
blowfly
bluebottle
boll weevil
bombardier
  beetle
borer
botfly
bumblebee
butterfly
caddis fly
carpet beetle
chafer
chigger

cicada
click beetle
cockchafer
cockroach
Colorado
  beetle
crane fly
cricket
daddy-long-
  legs
damselfly
death-watch
  beetle
devil's coach-
  horse
dragonfly
dung beetle
earwig
firefly
flea
fluke
fly

froghopper
fruit fly
furniture
  beetle
gadfly
gall wasp
glow-worm
gnat
goliath beetle
grasshopper
greenbottle
greenfly
honeybee
hornet
horsefly
housefly
hoverfly
lacewing
ladybird
leafcutter ant
leafhopper
leaf miner

leatherjacket
leech
locust
louse
mantis
mason bee
May bug
mayfly
mealy bug
midge
mosquito
moth
pond skater
praying mantis
rhinoceros
  beetle
robber fly
sandfly
sawfly
scale insect
scarab
scorpion fly

sexton beetle
silverfish
springtail
stag beetle
stick insect
stink bug
termite
thrips
thunderbug
thunderfly
tsetse fly
warble fly
wasp
water beetle
water
  boatman
weevil
whirligig
whitefly
witchetty
  grub

Wordfinder

Mammals

aardvark
alpaca
angora
anteater
antelope
ape
armadillo
ass
aurochs
baboon
badger
baleen whale
Barbary ape
bat
beaked whale
bear
beaver
beluga
bison
blue whale
boar
bobcat
bottlenose
  dolphin
bottlenose
  whale
bowhead
  whale
buffalo
bushbaby
camel
capuchin
  monkey
capybara
caribou
cat
chamois
cheetah
chimpanzee
chinchilla
chipmunk

civet
coati
colobus
cougar
cow
coyote
coypu
deer
dingo
dog
dolphin
donkey
dormouse
dromedary
duck-billed
  platypus
dugong
echidna
eland
elephant
elephant seal
elk
ermine
fallow deer
fennec
ferret
fin whale
flying fox
fox
fur seal
gazelle
gemsbok
gerbil
gibbon
giraffe
gnu
goat
gopher
gorilla
grampus
grizzly bear

guinea pig
hamster
hare
harp seal
hartebeest
hedgehog
hippopotamus
hog
horse
howler
  monkey
humpback
  whale
hyena
hyrax
ibex
impala
jackal
jaguar
killer whale
kinkajou
Kodiak bear
kudu
langur
laughing
  hyena
lemming
lemur
leopard
leopard seal
lion
llama
loris
lynx
macaque
manatee
mandrill
margay
marmoset
marsupial
marten

meerkat
mink
minke whale
mole
mongoose
monkey
moose
mouse
mule
muntjac
musk deer
musk ox
narwhal
ocelot
okapi
opossum
orang-utan
orca
oryx
otter
ox
panda
pangolin
panther
peccary
pig
pilot whale
pine marten
pipistrelle
platypus
polar bear
polecat
porcupine
porpoise
possum
potto
puma
rabbit
raccoon
rat
reindeer

rhinoceros
roe deer
rorqual
sea cow
seal
sea lion
serval
sheep
shrew
skunk
sloth
snow leopard
sperm whale
spider
  monkey
spiny anteater
springbok
squirrel
squirrel
  monkey
stoat
tapir
tiger
vampire bat
vervet
  monkey
vole
walrus
wapiti
warthog
waterbuck
water buffalo
weasel
whale
wild boar
wildcat
wildebeest
wolverine
yak
zebra

Reptiles

adder
alligator
anaconda
axolotl
basilisk

boa
  constrictor
bushmaster
caiman
chameleon

cobra
  constrictor
coral snake
corn snake
crocodile

diamondback
  terrapin
galliwasp
garter snake
gecko

gharial
Gila monster
glass lizard
grass snake
horned toad

iguana
Komodo
  dragon
leatherback
lizard

loggerhead
  turtle
mamba
moloch
monitor lizard
pit viper

puff adder
python
rattlesnake
reticulated
  python
rinkhals

sidewinder
skink
slow-worm
smooth snake
snake
taipan

terrapin
tortoise
turtle
viper
whip snake

Shellfish and Other Molluscs

abalone
argonaut
auger shell
cephalopod
clam
cockle
conch

cowrie
cuttlefish
limpet
mitre
murex
mussel
nautilus

nerite
nudibranch
octopus
ormer
oyster
paua
pearl oyster

periwinkle
piddock
quahog
ramshorn
snail
razor shell
scallop

sea slug
slug
snail
squid
triton
whelk
winkle

Spiders and Other Arachnids

bird-eating
  spider
black widow
camel spider
chigger

crab spider
funnel-web
  spider
harvestman
harvest mite

jigger
mite
money spider
raft spider
redback

red spider
  mite
scorpion
spider mite
tarantula

tick
trapdoor
  spider
whip scorpion
wolf spider

Male and Female Animals

antelope: *buck,
  doe*
badger: *boar, sow*
bear: *boar, sow*
bird: *cock, hen*
buffalo: *bull, cow*
cat: *tom, queen*
cattle: *bull, cow*
chicken: *cock,
  hen*
deer: *stag, doe*
dog: *dog, bitch*

donkey: *jackass,
  jenny*
duck: *drake, duck*
elephant: *bull,
  cow*
ferret: *jack, gill*
fish: *cock, hen*
fox: *dog, vixen*
goat: *billy goat,
  nanny*
goose: *gander,
  goose*

hare: *buck, doe*
horse: *stallion,
  mare*
kangaroo: *buck,
  doe*
leopard: *leopard,
  leopardess*
lion: *lion, lioness*
otter: *dog, bitch*
pheasant: *cock,
  hen*
pig: *boar, sow*

rabbit: *buck, doe*
seal: *bull, cow*
sheep: *ram, ewe*
swan: *cob, pen*
tiger: *tiger, tigress*
whale: *bull, cow*
wolf: *dog, bitch*
zebra: *stallion,
  mare*

Young Animals

calf (*antelope,
  buffalo, camel,
  cattle, elephant,
  elk, giraffe,
  rhinoceros, seal,
  whale*)

chick (*chicken,
  hawk, pheasant*)
colt (*male horse*)
cub (*badger, bear,
  fox, leopard,
  lion, tiger,
  walrus, wolf*)

cygnet (*swan*)
duckling (*duck*)
eaglet (*eagle*)
elver (*eel*)
eyas (*hawk*)
fawn (*caribou,
  deer*)

filly (*female horse*)
foal (*horse, zebra*)
fry (*fish*)
gosling (*goose*)
joey (*kangaroo,
  wallaby,
  possum*)

kid (*goat, roe deer*)
kit (*beaver, ferret, fox, mink, weasel*)

kitten (*cat, cougar, rabbit, skunk*)
lamb (*sheep*)
leveret (*hare*)
owlet (*owl*)

parr (*salmon*)
piglet (*pig*)
pup (*dog, rat, seal, wolf*)
puppy (*coyote, dog*)

smolt (*salmon*)
squab (*pigeon*)
tadpole (*frog, toad*)
whelp (*dog, wolf*)

Collective Names for Animals

band (*gorillas*)
bask (*crocodiles*)
bellowing (*bullfinches*)
bevy (*roe deer, quails, larks, pheasants*)
bloat (*hippopotami*)
brood (*chickens*)
bury (*rabbits*)
busyness (*ferrets*)
charm (*finches*)
cloud (*gnats*)
covey (*partridges*)
crash (*rhinoceros*)
cry (*hounds*)
descent (*woodpeckers*)
down (*hares*)
drove (*bullocks*)

exaltation (*larks*)
flight (*birds*)
flock (*sheep*)
gaggle (*geese on land*)
herd (*cattle, elephants*)
hive (*bees*)
hover (*trout*)
kennel (*dogs*)
kindle (*kittens*)
knot (*toads*)
labour (*moles*)
leap (*leopards*)
litter (*kittens, pigs*)
mob (*kangaroos*)
murder (*crows*)
murmuration (*starlings*)

muster (*peacocks, penguins*)
obstinacy (*buffalo*)
pack (*hounds, grouse*)
pandemonium (*parrots*)
parade (*elephants*)
parliament (*owls*)
pod (*seals*)
pride (*lions*)
rookery (*rooks*)
safe (*ducks*)
school (*whales, dolphins, porpoises*)
shoal (*fish*)
shrewdness (*apes*)
siege (*herons*)

skein (*geese in flight*)
skulk (*foxes*)
sloth (*bears*)
span (*mules*)
stare (*owls*)
string (*horses*)
stud (*mares*)
swarm (*bees, flies*)
tiding (*magpies*)
trip (*goats*)
troop (*baboons*)
turmoil (*porpoises*)
turn (*turtles*)
unkindness (*ravens*)
watch (*nightingales*)
yoke (*oxen*)
zeal (*zebras*)

Chemical Elements

*Metal

*actinium (Ac)
*aluminium (Al)
*americium (Am)
*antimony (Sb)
argon (Ar)
arsenic (As)
astatine (At)
*barium (Ba)
*berkelium (Bk)
*beryllium (Be)
*bismuth (Bi)
bohrium (Bh)
boron (B)

bromine (Br)
*cadmium (Cd)
*caesium (Cs)
*calcium (Ca)
*californium (Cf)
carbon (C)
*cerium (Ce)
chlorine (Cl)
*chromium (Cr)
*cobalt (Co)
*copper (Cu)
*curium (Cm)
darmstadtium (Ds)

dubnium (Db)
*dysprosium (Dy)
einsteinium (Es)
*erbium (Er)
*europium (Eu)
*fermium (Fm)
fluorine (F)
*francium (Fr)
*gadolinium (Gd)
*gallium (Ga)
germanium (Ge)
*gold (Au)
*hafnium (Hf)

hassium (Hs)
helium (He)
*holmium (Ho)
hydrogen (H)
*indium (In)
iodine (I)
*iridium (Ir)
*iron (Fe)
krypton (Kr)
*lanthanum (La)
*lawrencium (Lr)
*lead (Pb)
*lithium (Li)

*lutetium (Lu)
*magnesium (Mg)
*manganese (Mn)
meitnerium (Mt)
*mendelevium (Md)
*mercury (Hg)
*molybdenum (Mo)
*neodymium (Nd)
neon (Ne)
*neptunium (Np)
*nickel (Ni)
*niobium (Nb)
nitrogen (N)
*nobelium (No)

*osmium (Os)
oxygen (O)
*palladium (Pd)
phosphorus (P)
*platinum (Pt)
*plutonium (Pu)
*polonium (Po)
*potassium (K)
*praseodymium (Pr)
*promethium (Pm)
*protactinium (Pa)
*radium (Ra)
radon (Rn)
*rhenium (Re)

*rhodium (Rh)
roentgenium (Rg)
*rubidium (Rb)
*ruthenium (Ru)
rutherfordium (Rf)
*samarium (Sm)
*scandium (Sc)
seaborgium (Sg)
selenium (Se)
silicon (Si)
*silver (Ag)
*sodium (Na)
*strontium (Sr)
sulphur (S)
*tantalum (Ta)
*technetium (Tc)

tellurium (Te)
*terbium (Tb)
*thallium (Tl)
*thorium (Th)
*thulium (Tm)
*tin (Sn)
*titanium (Ti)
*tungsten (W)
*uranium (U)
*vanadium (V)
*xenon (Xe)
*ytterbium (Yb)
*yttrium (Y)
*zinc (Zn)
*zirconium (Zr)

Wordfinder

Clothing

Clothes

anorak
apron
ballgown
bandeau
basque
bell-bottoms
belt
Bermuda shorts
bib
bikini
blazer
bloomers
blouse
blouson
boa
bodice
body
body stocking
body warmer
bolero
bomber jacket
boot
bow tie
bra

braces
breeches
burka/burkha/ burqa
burnous
cagoule
cape
capri pants
cardigan
cargo pants
carpenter trousers
catsuit
chador
chinos
churidars
coat
combat trousers
cords
corset
cravat
crinoline
crop top
culottes
cummerbund

cut-offs
dashiki
denims
dhoti
dinner jacket
dirndl
djellaba
djibba
dolman
domino
donkey jacket
doublet
dress
dressing gown
dress shirt
duffel coat
dungarees
flannels
flares
fleece
flying jacket
frock coat
gilet
glove
gown

greatcoat
guernsey
gymslip
haik
hair shirt
hipsters
hoody/hoodie
hose
hot pants
housecoat
hula skirt
jacket
jeans
jellaba
jerkin
jersey
jibba
jilbab
jodhpurs
jogging pants
jumper
jumpsuit
kaftan
kagoul
kameez
kilt

kimono
knickers
lederhosen
leggings
leg warmers
leotard
loden
loincloth
lumberjacket
lungi
mac
mackintosh/ macintosh
maillot
mandarin jacket
mantilla
mantle
maxi
maxidress
mess jacket
midi
mini
miniskirt
mitt
mitten

Clothing

morning coat
muff
muffler
nightdress
nightshirt
oilskins
overalls
overcoat
overtrousers
palazzo pants
pantaloons
panties
pants
pantyhose
parka
pedal pushers
peignoir
pencil skirt
peplum
petticoat
pinafore
pinafore dress

plastron
plus fours
polo neck
polo shirt
poncho
pullover
pyjamas
raincoat
reefer jacket
robe
roll-neck
ruff
safari jacket
sailor suit
salopettes
sari
sarong
sash
scarf
serape/sarape
shawl
sheath dress

sheepskin
shell suit
shift
shirt dress
shirtwaister
shorts
skinny-rib
ski pants
skirt
skort
slacks
slip
smock
smoking
  jacket
sock
stirrup pants
stock
stocking
stole
suit
sundress

suspenders
sweater
sweatpants
sweatshirt
swimming
  costume
swimming
  trunks
swimsuit
T-shirt
tabard
tailcoat
tails
tank top
tee
tie
tights
toga
top
topcoat
tracksuit
trench coat

trews
trousers
trouser suit
trunks
tunic
turtleneck
tutu
tux/tuxedo
tweeds
twinset
ulster
underpants
underskirt
veil
vest
V-neck
waistcoat
waterproof
waxed jacket
windcheater
yashmak

Footwear

beetle-crusher
boot
bootee
brogue
carpet slipper
chappal
clog
court shoe
cowboy boot
deck shoe
desert boot

Dr Martens
  (trademark)
espadrille
flip-flop
galosh
gumboot
half-boot
high-low
hobnail boot
jackboot
jelly shoe

lace-up
loafer
moccasin
moon boot
mukluk
mule
overshoe
Oxford
patten
peep-toe
platform

plimsoll
pump
sabot
sandal
shoe
slingback
slip-on
slipper
sneaker
snow boot
step-in

stiletto
thong
top boot
trainer
wader
walking boot
wedge
wellington
  boot

Headgear

balaclava
bandeau
baseball cap
beanie
bearskin
beret
biretta
boater
bobble hat
bonnet
bowler

busby
cap
chaplet
circlet
cloche
cloth cap
cocked hat
coif
coolie hat
coronet
cowl

crash helmet
crown
deerstalker
derby
diadem
Dolly Varden
dunce's cap
fedora
fez
flat cap
garland

glengarry
hard hat
headband
headscarf
helmet
hijab
homburg
hood
jester's cap
jockey cap
Juliet cap

keffiyeh
kepi
mantilla
mitre
mob cap
mortar board
nightcap
panama
pillbox hat
pixie hat
pork-pie hat

sailor hat
skullcap
slouch hat
snood
sola topi
sombrero

sou'wester
Stetson
(trademark)
stovepipe hat
sun hat

tam-o'-
shanter
tarboosh
ten-gallon hat
tiara
top hat

topi
topper
toque
tricorne
trilby
turban

veil
wimple
wreath
zucchetto

Food and Drink

Bread and Bread Rolls

bagel
baguette
bannock
bap
bloomer
bridge roll
brioche
bun
chapatti

ciabatta
cob
cornbread
cottage loaf
crumpet
damper
farl
farmhouse
loaf

flatbread
focaccia
French stick
fruit loaf
granary bread
(trademark)
hoagie
malt loaf
matzo

milk loaf
muffin
nan/naan
panettone
panino
paratha
petit pain
pikelet
pitta

pone
poppadom
pumpernickel
puri
rye
soda bread
sourdough
split tin
stollen

Cakes, Biscuits, and Desserts

angel cake
apfelstrudel
baba
baked Alaska
Bakewell tart
baklava
banana split
banoffi/
banoffee pie
Bath bun
Bath Oliver
Battenberg
beignet
biscotti
Black Forest
gateau
blancmange
bombe
bourbon
brack
brandy snap
bread
pudding

bread-and-
butter
pudding
Brown Betty
brownie
bun
butterfly cake
cabinet
pudding
cassata
charlotte
charlotte
russe
cheesecake
chocolate
chip
clafoutis
cobbler
compote
cookie
cream cracker
cream puff
crème brûlée

crème
caramel
crêpe
crêpe Suzette
crispbread
croquem-
bouche
crumble
crumpet
cupcake
custard cream
custard pie
custard tart
Danish pastry
devil's food
cake
digestive
doughnut
drop scone
dumpling
Dundee cake
Eccles cake
eclair

egg custard
Eskimo pie
(trademark)
Eve's pudding
fairy cake
fancy
flapjack
Florentine
flummery
fool
fortune
cookie
frangipane
fruit cocktail
fruit salad
garibaldi
gateau
gelato
Genoa cake
gingerbread
ginger nut
ginger snap
granita

halwa
hot cross bun
ice cream
jelly
junket
Knickerbocker
Glory
kulfi
lady's finger
langue de
chat
lardy cake
macaroon
Madeira cake
madeleine
maid of
honour
marble cake
matzo
meringue
milk pudding
millefeuille
mince pie

Mississippi mud pie
mousse
muffin
Nice biscuit
oatcake
pancake
panettone
panforte
parfait
parkin
pavlova
peach Melba
petit four
plum duff
plum pudding
popover
pound cake
profiterole
queen of puddings
ratafia
rice pudding
rock cake
roly-poly
rusk
Sachertorte
sago pudding
Sally Lunn
sandwich
savarin
scone
seed cake
semolina pudding
shortbread
shortcake
simnel cake
sorbet
soufflé
sponge
sponge pudding
spotted dick
steamed pudding
stollen
streusel
strudel
summer pudding
sundae
Swiss roll
syllabub
tapioca pudding
tart
tarte Tatin
tartlet
tartufo
tipsy cake
tiramisu
torte
treacle tart
trifle
turnover
tutti-frutti
upside-down cake
Victoria sponge
waffle
water biscuit
water ice
whip
yogurt
yule log
zabaglione

Cheeses

asiago
Bel Paese (trademark)
blue vinny
Boursin (trademark)
Brie
Caerphilly
Camembert
Chaumes
Cheddar
Cheshire
chèvre
cottage cheese
cream cheese
crowdie/crowdy
curd cheese
Danish blue
Derby
Dolcelatte (trademark)
Double Gloucester
Dunlop
Edam
Emmental
feta/fetta
fontina
fromage blanc
fromage frais
Gloucester
Gorgonzola
Gouda
Gruyère
halloumi
havarti
Jarlsberg (trademark)
Lancashire
Leicester
Limburger
Manchego
mascarpone
Monterey Jack
mozzarella
paneer/panir
Parmesan
Parmigiano Reggiano
pecorino
Port Salut
provolone
quark
Red Leicester
ricotta
Romano
Roquefort (trademark)
sage Derby
scamorza
Stilton
taleggio
Tilsit
Wensleydale

Fruit and Nuts

almond
apple
apricot
avocado
banana
betel nut
bilberry
blackberry
blackcurrant
blueberry
boysenberry
Brazil nut
breadfruit
butternut
cantaloupe
Cape gooseberry
carambola
cashew
cherimoya
cherry
chestnut
Chinese gooseberry
citron
clementine
cloudberry
cobnut
coconut
cola nut
cowberry
crab apple
cranberry
currant
damson
date
elderberry
fig
filbert
galia melon
gooseberry
gourd
grape
grapefruit
greengage
groundnut
guava
hazelnut
honeydew melon
huckleberry
jackfruit
jujube
kiwi fruit
kumquat
lemon
lime
loganberry
loquat
lychee
macadamia
mandarin
mango
melon
minneola
monkey nut
mulberry
nectarine
olive
orange

ortanique
papaya
passion fruit
pawpaw
peach
peanut
pear
pecan
persimmon

pineapple
pine nut
pistachio
plum
pomegranate
pomelo
prickly pear
pumpkin
quince

rambutan
raspberry
redcurrant
salmonberry
sapodilla
satsuma
serviceberry
sharon fruit
sloe

star anise
starfruit
strawberry
tamarillo
tangerine
tayberry
tiger nut
Ugli fruit
(trademark)

walnut
water
chestnut
watermelon
whortleberry

Pasta

agnolotti
angel hair
cannelloni
capelli
capellini
cappelletti
conchiglie

ditalini
farfalle
farfalline
fettuccine
fusilli
lasagne
linguine

macaroni
noodles
orecchiette
orzo
pappardelle
penne
pipe

radiatori
ravioli
rigatoni
spaghetti
spaghettini
strozzapreti
tagliatelle

tagliolini
tortelli
tortellini
tortelloni
tortiglioni
vermicelli
ziti

Sweets and Confectionery

aniseed ball
barley sugar
bonbon
brittle
bullseye
butterscotch
candy
candyfloss
caramel
chew
chocolate
coconut ice
comfit
cracknel

crystallized
fruit
dolly mixtures
dragée
Easter egg
fondant
fruit drop
fruit gum
fruit pastille
fudge
gobstopper
gulab jamun
gumdrop
halva

humbug
jalebi
jelly
jelly baby
jelly bean
jujube
Kendal mint
cake
laddu
liquorice
liquorice
allsort
lollipop
lolly

marshmallow
marzipan
mint
nougat
pastille
pear drop
peppermint
peppermint
cream
Pontefract
cake
praline
rock
sherbet

sugared
almond
toffee
toffee apple
truffle
Turkish
delight
walnut whip
wine gum

Vegetables

aduki/adzuki
bean
alfalfa
artichoke
asparagus
aubergine
bamboo
shoots
bean
beet

beetroot
black bean
black-eyed
bean
borlotti bean
breadfruit
broad bean
broccoli
Brussels
sprout

butter bean
butternut
squash
cabbage
calabrese
cannellini
bean
capsicum
carrot
cassava

cauliflower
celeriac
celery
chard
chervil
chickpea
chicory
Chinese
leaves

corn on the
cob
cos lettuce
courgette
cress
cucumber
curly kale
eggplant
endive
fennel

flageolet
French bean
garlic
gherkin
globe
  artichoke
gourd
haricot bean
Jerusalem
  artichoke
kale
kidney bean
kohlrabi
leek
lentil

lettuce
lima bean
lollo rosso
mangetout
marrow
marrowfat
  pea
mooli
mung bean
mushroom
mustard
okra
onion
pak choi
parsnip

pea
pepper
petits pois
pimiento
pinto bean
plantain
potato
pumpkin
radicchio
radish
rocket
runner bean
salsify
samphire

savoy
  cabbage
shallot
snow pea
soybean
spinach
spinach beet
spring greens
spring onion
squash
string bean
sugar pea
sugar snap
  pea
swede

sweetcorn
sweet pepper
sweet potato
tomato
turnip
vegetable
  spaghetti
water
  chestnut
watercress
waxpod
yam
zucchini

Alcoholic Drinks

absinthe
advocaat
alcopop
ale
amaretto
amontillado
aquavit
Armagnac
barley wine
beer
bitter
bock
bourbon
brandy
brown ale
burgundy
Calvados
cassis
cava
champagne

chartreuse
cherry brandy
cider
claret
cocktail
cognac
crème de
  menthe
curaçao
fine
  champagne
fino
genever
gin
ginger wine
grappa
hock
ice beer
Irish coffee
Irish whiskey

kirsch
kümmel
kvass
lager
Liebfraumilch
light ale
liqueur
Madeira
malmsey
malt
malt whisky
manzanilla
maraschino
Marsala
mead
mescal
mild
milk stout
moscato
muscat

muscatel
oloroso
ouzo
pale ale
palm wine
pastis
perry
Pils
Pilsner/Pilsener
port
porter
poteen
raki
ratafia
retsina
rosé
rum
rye
sack
sake

schnapps
Scotch whisky
scrumpy
Sekt
shandy
sherry
single malt
slivovitz
sloe gin
Spumante
stout
tequila
Tia Maria
triple sec
vermouth
vinho verde
vodka
whiskey
whisky
wine

Non-alcoholic Drinks

barley water
bitter lemon
buttermilk
cafe au lait
caffè latte
caffè
  macchiato
camomile tea
cappuccino

cherryade
citron pressé
club soda
  (trademark)
cocoa
coffee
cola
cordial
cream soda

crush
dandelion
  and burdock
decaf
decaffeinated
  coffee
drinking
  chocolate
Earl Grey

espresso
filter coffee
fruit juice
fruit tea
ginger ale
ginger beer
green tea
gunpowder
  tea

herbal tea
horchata
hot chocolate
iced tea
Indian tea
infusion
isotonic drink
jasmine tea
lassi

latte	mineral water	prairie oyster	sherbet	St Clements
lemon tea	mint tea	pressé	smoothie	tea
lemonade	mocha	robusta	soda water	tisane
limeade	mochaccino	root beer	soya milk	tonic water
malted milk	orangeade	rosehip tea	sports drink	yerba maté
maté	peppermint	sarsaparilla	spring water	
milkshake	tea	seltzer	squash	

Phobias

air travel: *aerophobia*
American people and things: *Americophobia*
animals: *zoophobia*
beards: *pogonophobia*
beating: *mastigophobia*
bed: *clinophobia*
bees: *apiphobia*
birds: *ornithophobia*
blood: *haemophobia*
blushing: *erythrophobia*
bridges: *gephyrophobia*
burial alive: *taphephobia*
cancer: *carcinophobia*
cats: *ailurophobia*
childbirth: *tocophobia*
children: *paedophobia*
Chinese people and things: *Sinophobia*
clouds: *nephophobia*
cold: *cheimaphobia*
colour: *chromophobia*
computers: *cyberphobia*
corpses: *necrophobia*
crowds: *demophobia*
dampness: *hygrophobia*
darkness: *scotophobia*
dawn: *eosophobia*
death: *thanatophobia*
depth: *bathophobia*
dirt: *mysophobia*
disease: *pathophobia*
dogs: *cynophobia*
dreams: *oneirophobia*
drink: *potophobia*
dust: *koniophobia*
electricity: *electrophobia*

English people and things: *Anglophobia*
everything: *panophobia*, *pantophobia*
faeces: *coprophobia*
feathers: *pteronophobia*
fever: *febriphobia*
fire: *pyrophobia*
fish: *ichthyophobia*
flesh: *selaphobia*
floods: *antlophobia*
flowers: *anthophobia*
food: *cibophobia*, *sitophobia*
foreigners: *xenophobia*
French people and things: *Francophobia*, *Gallophobia*
fur: *doraphobia*
German people and things: *Germanophobia*, *Teutophobia*
germs: *spermophobia*
ghosts: *phasmophobia*
God: *theophobia*
gold: *aurophobia*, *chrysophobia*
hair: *trichophobia*
heat: *thermophobia*
heaven: *uranophobia*
hell: *hadephobia*, *stygiophobia*
high buildings: *batophobia*
high places: *hypsophobia*

home: *oikophobia*
homosexuals: *homophobia*
horses: *hippophobia*
ice: *cryophobia*
idleness: *thassophobia*
illness: *nosophobia*
imperfection: *atelophobia*
infinity: *apeirophobia*
insanity: *lyssophobia*, *maniphobia*
insects: *entomophobia*
insect stings: *cnidophobia*
Italian people and things: *Italophobia*
lakes: *limnophobia*
light: *photophobia*
lightning: *astrapophobia*
loneliness: *autophobia*, *ermitophobia*
machinery: *mechanophobia*
magic: *rhabdophobia*
marriage: *gametophobia*
men: *androphobia*
metal: *metallophobia*
mice: *musophobia*
microbes: *bacillophobia*
mites: *acarophobia*
mobs: *ochlophobia*
motion: *kinetophobia*
music: *musicophobia*
needles: *belonephobia*
new things: *neophobia*
night: *nyctophobia*

nudity: *gymnophobia*
open places: *agoraphobia*
pain: *algophobia*
pins: *enetophobia*
pleasure: *hedonophobia*
poison: *toxiphobia*
poverty: *peniaphobia*
precipices: *cremnophobia*
priests: *hierophobia*
punishment: *poinephobia*
religious works of art: *iconophobia*
responsibility: *hypegiaphobia*
rivers: *potamophobia*
robbers: *harpaxophobia*
ruin: *atephobia*
Russian people and things: *Russophobia*
Satan: *Satanophobia*
scabies: *scabiophobia*
Scottish people and things: *Scotophobia*

sex: *erotophobia*
shadows: *sciophobia*
sharpness: *acrophobia*
shock: *hormephobia*
sin: *hamartophobia*
sleep: *hypnophobia*
slime: *blennophobia*
small things: *microphobia*
smell: *olfactophobia*, *osmophobia*
smothering: *pnigerophobia*
snakes: *ophidiophobia*
snow: *chionophobia*
solitude: *eremophobia*
sourness: *acerophobia*
speech: *glossophobia*, *phonophobia*
speed: *tachophobia*
spiders: *arachnophobia*
stars: *siderophobia*
stealing: *kleptophobia*
stuttering: *laliophobia*, *lalophobia*
sun: *heliophobia*

swallowing: *phagophobia*
taste: *geumatophobia*
technology: *technophobia*
thunder: *brontophobia*, *keraunophobia*, *tonitrophobia*
time: *chronophobia*
touch: *haptophobia*
travel: *hodophobia*
venereal disease: *syphilophobia*
voids: *kenophobia*
vomiting: *emetophobia*
water: *hydrophobia*
waves: *cymophobia*
weakness: *asthenophobia*
wind: *anemophobia*
women: *gynophobia*
words: *logophobia*
work: *ergophobia*
writing: *graphophobia*

Wordfinder

Plants

Flowering Plants and Shrubs

acacia
acanthus
aconite
African violet
agapanthus
aloe
alstroemeria
alyssum
amaranth
amaryllis
anemone
aquilegia
arrowgrass
arum lily
asphodel
aspidistra

aster
astilbe
aubretia
avens
azalea
balsam
banksia
bedstraw
begonia
belladonna
bellflower
bergamot
betony
bilberry
bindweed

bird's-foot trefoil
black-eyed Susan
blackthorn
bleeding heart
bluebell
boneset
borage
bougainvillea
bramble
broom
bryony
buddleia
bugloss

bulrush
burdock
burnet
busy Lizzie
buttercup
cactus
calceolaria
calendula
camellia
camomile
campanula
campion
candytuft
Canterbury bell
carnation

catmint
ceanothus
celandine
chickweed
chicory
Chinese lantern
chives
choisya
chokeberry
Christmas cactus
Christmas rose
chrysanthemum

Plants

cicely
cinquefoil
clematis
clove pink
clover
cockscomb
coltsfoot
columbine
comfrey
convolvulus
coreopsis
cornflower
corydalis
cotoneaster
cottonweed
cow parsley
cowslip
cranesbill
crocus
crown
   imperial
crown of
   thorns
cuckoo pint
cyclamen
daffodil
dahlia
daisy
damask rose
dandelion
daphne
deadly
   nightshade
delphinium
dianthus
dill
dittany
dock
dog rose
duckweed
echinacea
edelweiss
eglantine
elder
evening
   primrose
eyebright
feverfew
figwort
firethorn
flax

forget-me-not
forsythia
foxglove
frangipani
freesia
fritillary
fuchsia
furze
gardenia
gentian
geranium
gladiolus
glory-of-the-
   snow
gloxinia
golden rod
gorse
grape
   hyacinth
groundsel
guelder rose
gypsophila
harebell
hawkweed
hawthorn
heartsease
heather
hebe
helianthemum
helianthus
heliotrope
hellebore
hemlock
heuchera
hibiscus
hogweed
holly
hollyhock
honesty
honeysuckle
hosta
hyacinth
hydrangea
iris
jacaranda
japonica
jasmine
jonquil
kingcup
knapweed
knotgrass

laburnum
lady's mantle
lady's tresses
larkspur
lavatera
lavender
lemon balm
lilac
lily
lily of the
   valley
lobelia
London pride
loosestrife
lords and
   ladies
lotus
lovage
love-in-a-mist
love-lies-
   bleeding
lungwort
lupin
madonna lily
magnolia
mahonia
mallow
mandrake
marguerite
marigold
marshwort
may
mayflower
meadow rue
meadow
   saffron
meadow-
   sweet
Michaelmas
   daisy
milfoil
mimosa
mint
mistletoe
mock orange
montbretia
morning glory
musk rose
myrtle
narcissus
nasturtium

nettle
nicotiana
nigella
night-scented
   stock
nightshade
old man's
   beard
oleander
orchid
ox-eye daisy
oxlip
pansy
Parma violet
parsley
pasque flower
passion
   flower
pelargonium
pennyroyal
penstemon
peony
peppermint
periwinkle
petunia
phlox
pimpernel
pink
pitcher plant
plantain
plumbago
poinsettia
polyanthus
poppy
potentilla
prickly pear
primrose
primula
privet
pulsatilla
pyracantha
pyrethrum
ragwort
ramsons
red-hot poker
rhododendron
rock rose
rose
rosebay
   willowherb

rose of
   Sharon
safflower
St John's wort
salvia
samphire
saxifrage
scabious
scarlet
   pimpernel
scilla
sedum
shamrock
shrimp plant
snapdragon
snow-in-
   summer
snowdrop
soapwort
sorrel
speedwell
spikenard
spiraea
spurge
spurrey
squill
starwort
stock
stonecrop
streptocarpus
sunflower
sweet pea
sweet william
tansy
teasel
thistle
thrift
toadflax
tradescantia
trefoil
tulip
valerian
Venus flytrap
verbena
veronica
vervain
vetch
viburnum
violet
viper's
   bugloss

wallflower	winter	wisteria	woodruff	yucca
water lily	jasmine	witch hazel	wormwood	zinnia
willowherb	wintergreen	wolfsbane	yarrow	

Trees and Shrubs

acacia	cassava	holly	mastic	rubber tree
acer	cassia	holm oak	may	sallow
alder	casuarina	honeysuckle	mimosa	sandalwood
almond	cedar	hornbeam	mirabelle	sapele
apple	cherimoya	horse	monkey	sapodilla
apricot	cherry	chestnut	puzzle	sassafras
araucaria	chestnut	hydrangea	mountain ash	satinwood
ash	cinnamon	ilex	mulberry	senna
aspen	citron	iroko	myrtle	sequoia
azalea	coco de mer	ironbark	nutmeg	service tree
balsa	coconut palm	ironwood	nux vomica	silver birch
balsam fir	cola	jacaranda	oak	Sitka cypress
bamboo	coolibah	jackfruit	oleaster	slippery elm
banksia	copper beech	jack pine	olive	smoke tree
banyan	cork oak	japonica	osier	soapberry
baobab	coromandel	jasmine	pagoda tree	spindle
basswood	crab apple	juniper	palm	spruce
bay tree	cypress	kalmia	papaya	star anise
beech	dogwood	kapok	paper	stinkwood
beefwood	dragon tree	kermes oak	mulberry	storax
bergamot	ebony	laburnum	paperbark	sumac
birch	elder	larch	pawpaw	sycamore
blackthorn	elm	laurel	pear	tallow tree
bottlebrush	eucalyptus	lemon	persimmon	tamarind
bottle tree	euonymus	Leyland	pine	tamarisk
bo tree	ficus	cypress	pistachio	tea
box	fig	leylandii	pitch pine	teak
box elder	filbert	lilac	plane	tea tree
bristlecone	fir	lime	plum	thuja
pine	firethorn	linden	pomegranate	tulip tree
broom	flame tree	liquidambar	pomelo	tulipwood
buckeye	frangipani	locust	poplar	umbrella tree
buckthorn	fuchsia	lodgepole	privet	viburnum
butternut	gean	pine	pussy willow	walnut
cacao	ginkgo	logwood	quassia	weeping
calabash	gorse	macadamia	quince	willow
camellia	grapefruit	magnolia	rambutan	wellingtonia
camphor tree	greengage	mahogany	red cedar	whitebeam
candelabra	guava	maidenhair	redwood	willow
tree	gum tree	tree	rhododendron	witch hazel
candleberry	hawthorn	mango	robinia	wych elm
candlenut	hazel	mangosteen	rosewood	yew
carambola	hemlock fir	mangrove	rowan	
carob	hickory	maple	rubber plant	

LI

label noun **1** *the price is clearly stated on the label:* **tag,** ticket, tab, sticker, marker, docket. **2** *a designer label:* **brand (name),** (trade) name, trademark, make, logo. **3** *the label the media came up with for me:* **designation,** description, tag, name, epithet, nickname, title.
verb **1** *label each jar with the date:* **tag,** ticket, mark, stamp. **2** *tests labelled him an underachiever:* **categorize,** classify, class, describe, designate, identify, mark, stamp, brand, call, name, term, dub.

laborious adjective **1** *a laborious job:* **arduous,** hard, heavy, difficult, strenuous, gruelling, punishing, exacting, tough, onerous, burdensome, back-breaking, trying, challenging. **2** *Doug's laborious style:* **laboured,** strained, forced, stiff, stilted, unnatural, artificial, overwrought, heavy, ponderous. OPPOSITES easy, effortless.

labour noun **1** *manual labour:* **work,** toil, exertion, industry, drudgery, effort; informal slog, grind. **2** *the conflict between capital and labour:* **workers,** employees, working people, labourers, workforce, staff, labour force. **3** *a difficult labour:* **childbirth,** birth, delivery.
OPPOSITES rest, management.
verb **1** *a project on which he had laboured for many years:* **work (hard),** toil, slave (away), grind away, struggle, strive, exert oneself; informal slog away, plug away. **2** *Newcastle laboured to break down their defence:* **strive,** struggle, endeavour, work, try hard, make every effort, do one's best, do one's utmost, do all one can, give one's all, go all out, fight, exert oneself; informal bend/lean over backwards, pull out all the stops.

laboured adjective **1** *laboured breathing:* **strained,** difficult, forced, laborious. **2** *a rather laboured joke:* **contrived,** strained, forced, unconvincing, unnatural, artificial, overdone, ponderous, over-elaborate.
OPPOSITES natural, easy.

labourer noun **workman,** worker, working man, manual worker, unskilled worker, blue-collar worker, (hired) hand, roustabout, drudge, menial; Austral./NZ rouseabout.

lace verb **1** *he laced up his running shoes:* **fasten,** do up, tie up, secure, knot. **2** *tea laced with rum:* **flavour,** mix, blend, fortify, strengthen, season, spice (up), liven up, doctor, adulterate; informal spike.
OPPOSITES untie.

lack noun *a lack of cash:* **absence,** want, need, deficiency, dearth, shortage, shortfall, scarcity, paucity, scarceness.
OPPOSITES abundance.
verb *she lacks judgement:* **be without,** be in need of, be short of, be deficient in, be low on, be pressed for; informal be strapped for.
OPPOSITES have, possess.

lad noun (informal) **1** *a young lad:*

boy, schoolboy, youth, youngster, juvenile, stripling; informal kid, nipper; Scottish informal laddie; derogatory brat. **2** *a hard-working lad:* **(young) man**; informal guy, fellow, geezer; Brit. informal chap, bloke; N. Amer. informal dude, hombre.

laden adjective **loaded,** burdened, weighed down, overloaded, piled high, full, packed, stuffed, crammed; informal chock-full, chock-a-block.

lady noun **1** *several ladies were present:* **woman,** female, girl; Scottish & N. English lass, lassie; N. Amer. informal dame. **2** *lords and ladies:* **noblewoman,** duchess, countess, peeress, viscountess, baroness.

laid-back adjective (informal) **relaxed,** easy-going, free and easy, casual, nonchalant, unexcitable, blasé, cool, calm, unconcerned, leisurely, unhurried; informal unflappable.
OPPOSITES uptight.

lake noun **pool,** pond, tarn, reservoir, lagoon, waterhole, inland sea; Scottish loch; Anglo-Irish lough; N. Amer. bayou.

lame adjective **1** *the mare was lame:* **limping,** hobbling, crippled, disabled, incapacitated; informal gammy. **2** *a lame excuse:* **feeble,** weak, thin, flimsy, poor, unconvincing, implausible, unlikely.
OPPOSITES sound, convincing.

lament verb **1** *he was lamenting the death of his daughter:* **mourn,** grieve, sorrow, weep, cry. **2** *entrepreneurs lamented the red tape:* **complain about,** bewail, bemoan, deplore, be disappointed at.
OPPOSITES celebrate, welcome.

land noun **1** *the lookout sighted land:* **dry land,** terra firma, coast, coastline, shore. **2** *Lyme Park has 1323 acres of land:* **grounds,** fields, open space, property, territory, acres, acreage, estate, lands, real estate. **3** *many people are leaving the land:* **the countryside,** the country, rural areas. **4** *Tunisia is a land of variety:* **country,** nation, state, realm, kingdom, province, region, area, domain.
verb **1** *Allied troops landed in France:* **disembark,** go ashore, debark, alight, get off. **2** *the ship landed at Le Havre:* **berth,** dock, moor, (drop) anchor, tie up, put in. **3** *their plane landed at Chicago:* **touch down,** make a landing, come in to land, come down. **4** (informal) *Nick landed the job of editor:* **get,** obtain, acquire, secure, gain, net, win, achieve, attain, bag, carry off; informal swing.
OPPOSITES embark, take off.

landlady, landlord noun **1** *the landlady had objected to the noise:* **owner,** proprietor, lessor, householder, landowner. **2** *the landlord of the pub:* **licensee,** innkeeper, owner, hotelier, restaurateur; Brit. publican.
OPPOSITES tenant.

landmark noun **1** *one of London's most famous landmarks:* **feature,** sight, monument, building. **2** *the ruling was hailed as a landmark:* **turning point,** milestone, watershed, critical point.

landscape noun **scenery,** country, countryside, topography, terrain, view, panorama.

landslide noun **1** *floods and landslides:* **landslip,** rockfall, mudslide, avalanche. **2** *the Labour landslide:* **decisive victory,** runaway triumph, overwhelming majority; informal whitewash.

lane noun **country road,** track, course, trail, street, alley, alleyway, passage.

language noun **1** *the structure of language:* **speech,** speaking, conversation, talking, talk, discourse, communication, words, writing, vocabulary, text. **2** *the English language:* **tongue,** mother tongue, native tongue, dialect; informal lingo. **3** *the booklet is written in simple, everyday language:* **wording,** phrasing, phraseology, style, vocabulary, terminology, expressions, turn of phrase, parlance; informal lingo.

languish verb **1** *the plants languished and died:* **weaken,** deteriorate, decline, go downhill, wither, droop, wilt, fade, waste away. **2** *the general is languishing in prison:* **waste away,** rot, be abandoned, be neglected, be forgotten, suffer, lie.
OPPOSITES thrive.

lap¹ verb **1** *waves lapped against the sea wall:* **splash,** wash, swish, slosh, break. **2** *the dog lapped water out of a puddle:* **drink,** lick up, sup, swallow, slurp, gulp.
■ **lap something up** relish, revel in, savour, delight in, wallow in, glory in, enjoy.

lap² noun *a race of eight laps:* **circuit,** leg, circle, revolution, round.
verb *she lapped the other runners:* **overtake,** outstrip, leave behind, pass, go past, catch up with.

lapse noun **1** *a lapse of concentration:* **failure,** slip, error, mistake, blunder, fault, omission; informal slip-up. **2** *his lapse into petty crime:* **decline,** fall, falling, slipping, deterioration, degeneration, backsliding, regression. **3** *a lapse of time:* **interval,** gap, pause, interlude, lull, hiatus, break.
verb **1** *the planning permission has lapsed:* **expire,** become void, become invalid, run out. **2** *do not let friendships lapse:* **(come to an) end,** cease, stop, terminate, pass, fade, wither, die. **3** *she lapsed into silence:* **revert,** relapse, drift, slide, slip, sink.

lapsed adjective **1** *a lapsed Catholic:* **non-practising,** backsliding, apostate. **2** *a lapsed season ticket:* **expired,** void, invalid, out of date.
OPPOSITES practising, valid.

large adjective **big,** great, sizeable, substantial, considerable, extensive, voluminous, vast, huge, immense, enormous, colossal, massive, heavy, mammoth, gigantic, giant, fat, stout, bulky.
OPPOSITES small.

largely adverb **mostly,** mainly, to a large/great extent, chiefly, predominantly, primarily, principally, for the most part, in the main, typically, commonly.

lash verb **1** *rain lashed the window panes:* **beat against,** dash against, pound, batter, strike, drum. **2** *the tiger lashed his tail:* **swish,** flick, twitch, whip. **3** *two boats were lashed together:* **fasten,** bind, tie (up), tether, hitch, knot, rope.
noun *he brought the lash down*

upon the prisoner's back: **whip**, scourge, flail, birch, cane; historical cat-o'-nine-tails, cat.

■ **lash out 1** *the president lashed out at the opposition:* criticize, attack, disparage, condemn, run down; informal lay into, dis; Brit. informal slag off, have a go at. **2** *Norman lashed out with a knife:* hit out at, strike, let fly at, take a swing at, set upon/about, turn on, round on, attack; informal lay into, pitch into.

last[1] adjective **1** *Rembrandt's last years:* **final**, closing, concluding, end, terminal, later, latter. **2** *the last woman in the queue:* **rearmost**, hindmost, endmost, furthest (back), ultimate. **3** *last year:* **previous**, preceding, prior, former. **4** *the last edition:* **latest**, most recent.
OPPOSITES first, next.
adverb *the candidate coming last is eliminated:* **at the end**, at/in the rear, bringing up the rear, at the back.
OPPOSITES first.

■ **at last** finally, in the end, eventually, ultimately, at long last, after a long time, in time, in (the fullness of) time.

last[2] verb **1** *the hearing lasted for six days:* **continue**, go on, carry on, keep on/going, take. **2** *how long will he last as manager?* **survive**, endure, hold on/out, keep going, persevere, persist, stay, remain; informal stick it out, hang on, go the distance. **3** *the car is built to last:* **endure**, wear well, stand up, bear up; informal go the distance.
OPPOSITES end, wear out.

lasting adjective **enduring**, long-lasting, long-lived, abiding, continuing, long-term, permanent, durable, stable, secure, long-standing, eternal, undying, everlasting, unending, never-ending.
OPPOSITES ephemeral.

late adjective **1** *the train was late:* **behind schedule**, tardy, overdue, delayed. **2** *her late husband:* **dead**, departed, lamented, passed on/away; formal deceased. **3** *some late news:* **recent**, fresh, new, up to date, latter-day, current.
OPPOSITES punctual, early, living, old.
adverb *she had arrived late:* **behind schedule**, belatedly, tardily, at the last minute.

lately adverb **recently**, not long ago, of late, latterly, in recent times.

later adjective *a later chapter:* **subsequent**, following, succeeding, future, upcoming, to come, ensuing, next.
OPPOSITES earlier, preceding.
adverb *later, the film rights were sold:* **subsequently**, eventually, then, next, later on, after this/that, afterwards, at a later date, in the future, in due course, by and by, in a while, in time; formal thereafter.

latest adjective **most recent**, newest, just out, up to the minute, state-of-the-art, current; informal in, with it, trendy, hip, hot, happening, cool.
OPPOSITES old.

latitude noun **freedom**, scope, leeway, (breathing) space, flexibility, liberty, independence, free rein, licence, slack.
OPPOSITES restriction.

latter adjective **1** *the latter half of the season:* **later**, closing, end, concluding, final. **2** *the latter option:* **last-mentioned**, second, last, final.

OPPOSITES earlier, former.

laugh verb *he started to laugh:*
chuckle, chortle, guffaw, giggle,
titter, snigger, roar, hoot with
laughter, split one's sides;
informal be in stitches, be rolling
in the aisles, crease up, fall
about, crack up; Brit. informal kill
oneself.
noun **1** *he gave a short laugh:*
chuckle, chortle, guffaw, giggle,
titter, snigger, roar, hoot,
shriek. **2** (informal) *I entered the
contest for a laugh:* **joke**, prank,
bit of fun, jest; informal lark,
hoot, scream.
■ **laugh at** ridicule, mock,
deride, scoff at, jeer at, sneer
at, jibe at, make fun of, poke
fun at; informal take the mickey
out of; Austral./NZ informal poke
mullock at. ■ **laugh something
off** dismiss, make a joke of,
make light of, shrug off, brush
aside, scoff at; informal pooh-
pooh.

laughter noun **1** *the laughter
subsided:* **laughing**, chuckling,
chortling, guffawing, giggling,
tittering, sniggering. **2** *a source
of laughter:* **amusement**,
entertainment, humour, mirth,
merriment, gaiety, hilarity,
jollity, fun.

launch verb **1** *a chair was
launched at him:* **propel**, throw,
hurl, fling, pitch, lob, let fly,
fire, shoot; informal chuck, heave,
sling. **2** *the government
launched a new campaign:*
start, begin, initiate, put in
place, set up, inaugurate,
introduce; informal kick off.

lavatory noun **toilet**, WC,
convenience, privy, latrine; Brit.
cloakroom; N. Amer. washroom,
bathroom, rest room, men's/
ladies' room, comfort station;
informal little girls'/boys' room,

smallest room; Brit. informal loo,
bog, the Ladies, the Gents,
khazi; N. Amer. informal can, john;
Austral./NZ informal dunny.

lavish adjective **1** *a lavish
apartment:* **sumptuous**,
luxurious, gorgeous, costly,
expensive, opulent, grand,
splendid, rich, fancy; informal
posh. **2** *he was lavish with his
hospitality:* **generous**, liberal,
bountiful, unstinting,
unsparing, free, munificent,
extravagant, prodigal. **3** *lavish
praise:* **extravagant**, excessive,
wasteful, prodigal, fulsome,
effusive. **4** *lavish amounts of
champagne:* **abundant**, copious,
plentiful, liberal, prolific,
generous; literary plenteous.
OPPOSITES meagre, mean, frugal.
verb *she lavished money on her
children:* **shower**, heap, pour,
deluge, throw at, squander,
dissipate.
OPPOSITES begrudge, stint.

law noun **1** *the law:* **legislation**,
constitution, rules, regulations,
legal code. **2** *a new law:*
regulation, statute, act, bill,
decree, edict, rule, ruling,
dictum, command, order,
directive, dictate, diktat, fiat,
by-law; N. Amer. formal ordinance.
3 *the laws of the game:* **rule**,
regulation, principle,
convention, instruction,
guideline. **4** *a moral law:*
principle, rule, precept,
commandment, belief, creed,
credo, maxim, tenet, doctrine,
canon.

lawyer noun **legal adviser**, legal
representative, solicitor,
barrister, advocate, counsel,
Queen's Counsel, QC; N. Amer.
attorney, counselor(-at-law);
informal brief, legal eagle.

lay¹ verb **1** *Curtis laid the*

newspaper on the table: **put (down)**, place, set (down), deposit, rest, position, shove; informal stick, dump, park, plonk; Brit. informal bung. **2** *I'd lay money on it:* **bet**, wager, gamble, stake. **3** *we laid plans for the next voyage:* **devise**, arrange, prepare, work out, hatch, design, plan, scheme, plot, conceive, put together, draw up, produce, develop, formulate; informal cook up.

■ **lay something down 1** *they laid down their weapons:* relinquish, surrender, give up, abandon. **2** *the ground rules have been laid down:* formulate, set down, draw up, frame, prescribe, ordain, dictate, decree, enact, pass, decide, determine. ■ **lay something in** stock up with/on, stockpile, store (up), amass, hoard, stow (away), put aside/away/by, garner, squirrel away; informal salt away, stash away. ■ **lay off** (informal) give up, stop, refrain from, abstain from, desist from, cut out; informal pack in, leave off, quit. ■ **lay someone off** make redundant, dismiss, let go, discharge, give notice to; informal sack, fire. ■ **lay something on** provide, supply, furnish, line up, organize, prepare, produce, make available; informal fix up. ■ **lay someone out** (informal) knock out/down, knock unconscious, fell, floor, flatten; informal KO, kayo; Brit. informal knock for six.

lay² adjective **1** *a lay preacher:* **non-ordained**, non-clerical. **2** *a lay audience:* **non-expert**, non-professional, non-specialist, non-technical, amateur, unqualified, untrained.

layer noun **sheet**, stratum, level, tier, seam, coat, coating, film, covering, blanket, skin.

layout noun **arrangement**, design, plan, formation, format, configuration, composition, organization, geography, structure.

laze verb **idle**, relax, unwind, do nothing, loaf (around/about), lounge (around/about), loll (around/about), lie (around/about), take it easy; informal hang around/round, veg (out).

lazy adjective **1** *a lazy worker:* **idle**, indolent, slothful, bone idle, work-shy, shiftless. **2** *a lazy stream:* **slow**, slow-moving, languid, leisurely, lethargic, sluggish.

OPPOSITES industrious, fast.

lead verb **1** *Michelle led them into the house:* **guide**, conduct, show (the way), usher, escort, steer, shepherd, accompany, see, take. **2** *he led us to believe they were lying:* **cause**, induce, prompt, move, persuade, drive, make. **3** *she led a coalition of radicals:* **control**, preside over, head, command, govern, run, manage, rule, be in charge of; informal head up. **4** *Rangers were leading at half-time:* **be ahead**, be winning, be (out) in front, be in the lead, be first. **5** *the champion was leading the field:* **be ahead of**, head, outrun, outstrip, outpace, leave behind, outdo, outclass, beat. **6** *I just want to lead a normal life:* **live**, have, spend, follow, pass, enjoy.

OPPOSITES follow.

noun **1** *I was in the lead early on:* **first place**, winning position, vanguard. **2** *Newcastle built up a 3-0 lead:* **margin**, advantage, gap, edge, interval. **3** *sixth-formers should give a lead to younger pupils:* **example**, model, pattern,

standard, guidance, direction, role model. **4** *playing the lead:* **leading role,** star/starring role, title role, principal role. **5** *a dog on a lead:* **leash,** tether, rope, chain. **6** *detectives were following up a new lead:* **clue,** pointer, hint, tip, tip-off, suggestion, indication, sign.
adjective *the lead position:* **leading,** first, top, foremost, front, pole, head, chief, principal, premier.
■ **lead to** result in, cause, bring on/about, give rise to, create, produce, occasion, effect, generate, contribute to, promote, provoke, stir up, spark off.

leader noun chief, head, principal, commander, captain, controller, superior, chairman, chair, director, manager, superintendent, supervisor, overseer, master, mistress, prime minister, president, premier, governor, ruler, monarch, sovereign; informal boss, skipper, gaffer, guv'nor, number one.
OPPOSITES follower, supporter.

leadership noun **1** *the leadership of the Party:* **control,** rule, command, dominion, headship, directorship, premiership, chairmanship, governorship, captaincy. **2** *firm leadership:* **guidance,** direction, authority, management, supervision, government.

leading adjective main, chief, top, front, major, prime, principal, foremost, key, central, dominant, most powerful, most important, greatest, pre-eminent, star.
OPPOSITES subordinate, minor.

leaf noun *a folder of loose leaves:* **page,** sheet, folio.

verb *he leafed through the documents:* **flick,** flip, thumb, skim, browse, glance, riffle, scan, run one's eye over, peruse.

leaflet noun pamphlet, booklet, brochure, handbill, circular, flyer, handout; N. Amer. folder, dodger.

league noun **1** *a league of nations:* **alliance,** confederation, confederacy, federation, union, association, coalition, consortium, affiliation, cooperative, partnership, fellowship, syndicate. **2** *the store is not in the same league:* **class,** group, category, level, standard.
■ **in league** collaborating, cooperating, in alliance, allied, conspiring, hand in glove; informal in cahoots.

leak verb **1** *oil was leaking from the tanker:* **seep,** escape, ooze, drip, dribble, drain, run. **2** *civil servants leaking information:* **disclose,** divulge, reveal, make public, tell, expose, release, bring into the open.
noun **1** *check that there are no leaks in the bag:* **hole,** opening, puncture, perforation, gash, slit, break, crack, fissure, rupture, tear. **2** *a gas leak:* **escape,** leakage, discharge, seepage. **3** *leaks to the media:* **disclosure,** revelation, exposé.

lean¹ verb **1** *Polly leaned against the door:* **rest,** recline. **2** *trees leaning in the wind:* **slant,** incline, bend, tilt, slope, tip, list. **3** *he leans towards existentialist philosophy:* **tend,** incline, gravitate, have a preference for, have an affinity with. **4** *someone to lean on:* **depend,** rely, count, bank, trust in.

l

lean² adjective **1** *a tall, lean man:* **slim,** thin, slender, spare, spindly, wiry, lanky. **2** *a lean harvest:* **meagre,** sparse, poor, mean, inadequate, insufficient, paltry.
OPPOSITES fat, abundant.

leaning noun **inclination,** tendency, bent, propensity, penchant, preference, predisposition, predilection.

leap verb **1** *he leapt over the gate:* **jump,** vault, spring, bound, hop, clear. **2** *profits leapt by 55%:* **rise,** jump, soar, rocket, skyrocket, shoot up.
noun *a leap of 33%:* **rise,** surge, upsurge, upswing, upturn.

learn verb **1** *learn a foreign language:* **acquire,** grasp, master, take in, absorb, assimilate, digest, familiarize oneself with, be taught; informal get the hang of. **2** *she learnt the poem:* **memorize,** learn by heart, commit to memory, learn parrot-fashion, get off/down pat. **3** *he learned that the school would be closing:* **discover,** find out, become aware, be informed, hear, understand, gather; informal get wind of the fact.

learned adjective **scholarly,** erudite, knowledgeable, widely read, cultured, intellectual, academic, literary, bookish, highbrow; informal brainy.
OPPOSITES ignorant.

learner noun **beginner,** novice, starter, trainee, apprentice, pupil, student, fledgling.
OPPOSITES expert, veteran.

learning noun **study,** knowledge, education, schooling, tuition, teaching, scholarship, erudition, research, understanding, wisdom.
OPPOSITES ignorance.

lease verb **1** *the film crew leased a large hangar:* **rent,** hire, charter. **2** *they leased the mill to a reputable family:* **rent (out),** let (out), hire (out), charter (out), loan (out).

leave¹ verb **1** *I left the hotel:* **go away from,** depart from, withdraw from, retire from, take oneself off from, take one's leave of, pull out of, quit, escape from, flee, abandon, desert, vacate; informal push off, shove off, clear out/off, split, make tracks. **2** *the next morning we left for Leicester:* **set off,** head, make, set sail, get going. **3** *he's left his wife:* **abandon,** desert, jilt, leave in the lurch, leave high and dry, throw over; informal dump, ditch, walk/run out on. **4** *he left his job in November:* **resign from,** retire from, step down from, withdraw from, pull out of, give up; informal quit, jack in. **5** *she left her handbag on a bus:* **leave behind,** forget, lose, mislay. **6** *I thought I'd leave it to the experts:* **entrust,** hand over, pass on, refer, delegate. **7** *he left her £100,000:* **bequeath,** will, endow, hand down.
OPPOSITES arrive.
■ **leave someone/something out 1** *Adam left out the address:* **miss out,** omit, overlook, forget, skip, miss. **2** *he was left out of the England squad:* **exclude,** omit, drop, pass over.

leave² noun **1** *the judge granted leave to appeal:* **permission,** consent, authorization, sanction, dispensation, approval, clearance, blessing, agreement, assent; informal the go-ahead, the green light. **2** *he was on leave:* **holiday,** vacation, break, furlough, sabbatical, leave of absence; informal vac.

lecture noun **1** *a lecture on children's literature:* **speech,** talk, address, discourse, presentation, oration. **2** *Dave got a severe lecture:* **reprimand,** scolding, rebuke, reproach; informal dressing-down, telling-off, talking-to, tongue-lashing.
verb **1** *he lectures on drugs:* **talk,** speak, discourse, hold forth, teach; informal spout, sound off. **2** *he was lectured by the headmaster:* **reprimand,** scold, rebuke, reproach, take to task; informal tell off, bawl out; Brit. informal tick off, carpet.
OPPOSITES praise.

leeway noun **freedom,** scope, latitude, space, room, liberty, flexibility, licence, free hand, free rein.

left adjective **left-hand,** sinistral; Nautical port.
OPPOSITES right, starboard.

left-wing adjective **socialist,** communist, leftist, Labour; informal Commie, lefty, red, pinko.
OPPOSITES right-wing, conservative.

leg noun *the first leg of a European tour:* **part,** stage, section, phase, stretch, lap.

legacy noun **1** *a legacy from a great aunt:* **bequest,** inheritance, endowment, gift, birthright, estate, heirloom. **2** *the legacy of the war:* **consequence,** effect, repercussion, aftermath, by-product, result.

legal adjective **1** *a legal tax-avoidance scheme:* **lawful,** legitimate, within the law, legalized, valid, permissible, permitted, allowable, allowed, above board, acceptable, constitutional; informal legit. **2** *the legal profession:* **judicial,**

juridical, forensic.
OPPOSITES illegal.

legend noun **1** *the Arthurian legends:* **myth,** saga, epic, folk tale, folk story, fable, lore, folklore, mythology, folk tradition. **2** *pop legends:* **celebrity,** star, superstar, icon, phenomenon, luminary, giant, hero; informal celeb, megastar. **3** *the wording of the legend:* **caption,** inscription, dedication, slogan, heading, title.

legendary adjective **1** *legendary kings:* **fabled,** heroic, traditional, fairy-tale, storybook, mythical, mythological. **2** *a legendary figure in the trade-union movement:* **famous,** celebrated, famed, renowned, acclaimed, illustrious, esteemed, honoured, exalted, venerable, distinguished, great, eminent.
OPPOSITES historical, insignificant.

legion noun **horde,** throng, multitude, crowd, mass, mob, gang, swarm, flock, herd, army.

legislation noun **law,** rules, rulings, regulations, acts, bills, statutes; N. Amer. formal ordinances.

legitimate adjective **1** *legitimate gambling:* **legal,** lawful, authorized, permitted, sanctioned, approved, licensed; informal legit. **2** *the legitimate heir:* **rightful,** lawful, genuine, authentic, real, true, proper. **3** *legitimate grounds for unease:* **valid,** sound, admissible, acceptable, well founded, justifiable, reasonable, sensible, just, fair, bona fide.
OPPOSITES illegal, invalid.

leisure noun **free time,** spare time, time off, rest, recreation, relaxation.

OPPOSITES work.

leisurely adjective **unhurried,** relaxed, easy, gentle, sedate, comfortable, restful, undemanding, slow.
OPPOSITES hurried.

lend verb **1** *I'll lend you my towel:* **loan,** let someone use, advance; Brit. informal sub. **2** *these examples lend weight to his assertions:* **add,** impart, give, bestow, confer, provide, supply, furnish, contribute.
OPPOSITES borrow.

length noun **1** *the whole length of the valley:* **extent,** distance, span, reach, area, expanse, stretch, range, scope. **2** *a considerable length of time:* **period,** duration, stretch, span. **3** *a length of blue silk:* **piece,** strip.
■ **at length 1** *he spoke at length:* for a long time, for ages, for hours, interminably, endlessly, ceaselessly, unendingly. **2** *his search led him, at length, to Seattle:* eventually, in time, finally, at (long) last, in the end, ultimately.

lengthen verb **1** *he lengthened his stride:* **elongate,** make longer, extend, expand, widen, broaden, enlarge. **2** *you'll need to lengthen the cooking time:* **prolong,** make longer, increase, extend, expand, protract, stretch out.
OPPOSITES shorten.

lengthy adjective **(very) long,** long-lasting, protracted, extended, long-drawn-out, prolonged, interminable, time-consuming, long-winded.
OPPOSITES short.

lenient adjective **merciful,** forgiving, forbearing, tolerant, charitable, humane, indulgent, magnanimous.

OPPOSITES severe.

lessen verb **1** *exercise lessens the risk of heart disease:* **reduce,** make less/smaller, minimize, decrease, attenuate, narrow, moderate. **2** *the pain began to lessen:* **grow less,** grow smaller, decrease, diminish, decline, subside, slacken, abate, fade, die down, let up, ease off, tail off, drop (off/away), dwindle, ebb, wane, recede.
OPPOSITES increase.

lesser adjective **1** *a lesser offence:* **less important,** minor, secondary, subsidiary, peripheral. **2** *you look down at us lesser mortals:* **subordinate,** minor, inferior, second-class, subservient, lowly, humble.
OPPOSITES greater, superior.

lesson noun **1** *a maths lesson:* **class,** session, seminar, tutorial, lecture, period. **2** *Stuart's accident should be a lesson to all parents:* **warning,** deterrent, caution, example, message, moral.

let verb **1** *let him sleep for now:* **allow,** permit, give permission to, give leave to, authorize, license, empower, enable, entitle. **2** *they've let their flat:* **rent (out),** let out, lease, hire (out).
OPPOSITES prevent, prohibit.
■ **let someone down** fail, disappoint, disillusion, abandon, desert, leave in the lurch. ■ **let go** release (one's hold on), loose one's hold on, relinquish. ■ **let something off** detonate, discharge, explode, set off, fire (off), launch. ■ **let someone off 1** (informal) *I'll let you off this time:* pardon, forgive, acquit, absolve, exonerate, clear, vindicate; informal let someone off the

hook. **2** *he let me off work:* excuse from, exempt from, spare from. ■ **let something out 1** *I let out a cry of triumph:* utter, emit, give (vent to), produce, issue, express, voice, release. **2** *she let out that he'd given her a lift home:* reveal, make known, tell, disclose, mention, divulge, let slip, give away, let it be known, blurt out. ■ **let someone out** release, liberate, (set) free, let go, discharge, set/turn loose. ■ **let up** (informal) **1** *the rain has let up.* See **LESSEN** sense 2. **2** *you never let up, do you?* relax, ease up/off, slow down, pause, break (off), take a break, rest, stop.

lethal adjective **fatal**, deadly, mortal, terminal, life-threatening, murderous, poisonous, toxic, noxious, venomous, dangerous.
OPPOSITES harmless, safe.

letter noun **1** *capital letters:* **character**, sign, symbol, figure. **2** *she received a letter:* **message**, note, line, missive, dispatch, communication, correspondence, post, mail.

level adjective **1** *a smooth and level surface:* **flat**, smooth, even, uniform, plane, flush, horizontal. **2** *he kept his voice level:* **steady**, even, uniform, regular, constant. **3** *the scores were level:* **equal**, even, drawn, tied, all square, neck and neck, level pegging, on a par, evenly matched; informal even-stevens. **4** *his eyes were level with hers:* **at the same height**, on a level, in line.
OPPOSITES uneven, unsteady, unequal.
noun **1** *the post is at a senior level:* **rank**, position, degree, grade, stage, standard, class,

group, set, classification. **2** *a high level of employment:* **quantity**, amount, extent, measure, degree, volume.
verb **1** *tilt the tin to level the mixture:* **even off/out**, flatten, smooth (out). **2** *bulldozers levelled the building:* **raze (to the ground)**, demolish, flatten, bulldoze, destroy. **3** *Carl levelled the score:* **equalize**, equal, even (up), make level. **4** *he levelled his pistol at me:* **aim**, point, direct, train, focus, turn.
■ **on the level** (informal) genuine, straight, honest, above board, fair, true, sincere, straightforward; informal upfront; N. Amer. informal on the up and up.

lever noun *the lid can be removed with a lever:* **handle**, arm, switch, crowbar, bar, jemmy.
verb *he levered the door open:* **prise**, force, wrench; N. Amer. pry; informal jemmy.

leverage noun **1** *the long handles provide increased leverage:* **force**, purchase, grip, hold, anchorage. **2** *they have significant leverage in negotiations:* **influence**, power, authority, weight, sway, pull, control, say, advantage, pressure; informal clout, muscle, teeth.

levy verb **impose**, charge, exact, raise, collect.
noun **tax**, tariff, toll, excise, duty.

liability noun **1** *they have big liabilities:* **obligations**, debts, arrears, dues, commitments. **2** *he's become a bit of a liability:* **hindrance**, encumbrance, burden, handicap, nuisance, inconvenience, embarrassment, impediment, disadvantage,

millstone.
OPPOSITES asset.

liable adjective **1** *they are liable for negligence:* **responsible,** accountable, answerable, chargeable, blameworthy, at fault, culpable, guilty. **2** *my income is liable to fluctuate wildly:* **likely,** inclined, tending, apt, prone, given. **3** *areas liable to flooding:* **exposed,** prone, subject, susceptible, vulnerable, in danger of, at risk of.

liaise verb **cooperate,** collaborate, communicate, network, interface, link up.

liaison noun **1** *the branches work in close liaison:* **cooperation,** contact, association, connection, collaboration, communication, alliance, partnership. **2** *Dave was my White House liaison:* **intermediary,** mediator, middleman, contact, link, go-between. **3** *a secret liaison:* **love affair,** relationship, romance, attachment, fling.

liar noun **fibber,** deceiver, perjurer, dissembler, faker, hoaxer, impostor.

libel noun *she sued two newspapers for libel:* **defamation (of character),** character assassination, calumny, misrepresentation, scandalmongering, aspersions, malicious gossip, slur, smear; informal mud-slinging.
verb *she claimed the magazine had libelled her:* **defame,** malign, blacken someone's name, sully someone's reputation, smear, cast aspersions on, drag someone's name through the mud/mire, denigrate; N. Amer. slur.

liberal adjective **1** *the values of a liberal society:* **tolerant,** unprejudiced, broad-minded, open-minded, enlightened, permissive, free (and easy), easy-going, libertarian, indulgent, lenient. **2** *a liberal social agenda:* **progressive,** advanced, modern, forward-looking, forward-thinking, enlightened, reformist, radical; informal go-ahead. **3** *a liberal interpretation of divorce laws:* **flexible,** broad, loose, rough, free, non-literal. **4** *liberal coatings of paint:* **abundant,** copious, ample, plentiful, generous, lavish. **5** *they were liberal with their cash:* **generous,** open-handed, unsparing, unstinting, lavish, free, munificent.
OPPOSITES reactionary, strict, miserly.

liberate verb **(set) free,** release, let out, let go, set loose, save, rescue, emancipate, enfranchise.
OPPOSITES imprison, enslave.

liberty noun **freedom,** independence, immunity, self-determination, autonomy, emancipation, sovereignty, self-government, self-rule, self determination, civil liberties, human rights.
OPPOSITES constraint, slavery.
■ **at liberty 1** *he was at liberty for three months:* **free,** loose, on the loose, at large, on the run, out. **2** *I am not at liberty to say:* **free,** able, entitled, permitted.

licence noun **1** *a driving licence:* **permit,** certificate, document, documentation, authorization, warrant, credentials, pass, papers. **2** *they manufacture footwear under licence:* **franchise,** consent, sanction, warrant, charter, concession. **3** *the army have too much* *licence:* **freedom**, liberty, free rein, latitude, independence, scope, carte blanche; *informal* a blank cheque. **4** *poetic licence:* **disregard**, inventiveness, invention, creativity, imagination, fancy, freedom.

license verb **permit**, allow, authorize, grant/give authority to, grant/give permission to, certify, empower, entitle, enable, sanction.
OPPOSITES ban.

lid noun **cover**, top, cap, covering.

lie¹ noun *it was a lie:* **untruth**, falsehood, fib, fabrication, deception, invention, (piece of) fiction, falsification, white lie; *informal* tall story, whopper; *humorous* terminological inexactitude.
OPPOSITES truth.
verb *he had lied to the police:* **tell a lie**, tell an untruth, fib, dissemble, tell a white lie, perjure oneself.

lie² verb **1** *he was lying on the bed:* **recline**, lie down/back, be recumbent, be prostrate, be supine, be prone, be stretched out, sprawl, rest, repose, lounge, loll. **2** *her handbag lay on the chair:* **be**, be situated, be positioned, be located, be placed, be found, be sited, be arranged, rest.
OPPOSITES stand.

life noun **1** *the joy of giving life to a child:* **existence**, being, living, animation, sentience, creation, viability. **2** *life on Earth:* **living beings/creatures**, human/animal/plant life, fauna, flora, the ecosystem, the biosphere, the ecosphere. **3** *an easy life:* **way of life**, lifestyle, situation, fate, lot. **4** *the last nine months of his life:* **lifetime**, lifespan, days, time

(on earth), existence. **5** *the life of a Parliament:* **duration**, lifetime, existence. **6** *he is full of life:* **vitality**, animation, liveliness, vivacity, verve, high spirits, exuberance, zest, enthusiasm, energy, vigour, dynamism, elan, gusto, bounce, spirit, fire. **7** *a life of Chopin:* **biography**, autobiography, life story/history, chronicle, account, memoirs, diary.
OPPOSITES death.

lifestyle noun **way of life**, life, situation, conduct, behaviour, ways, habits, mores.

lifetime noun **lifespan**, life, days, time (on earth), existence, career.

lift verb **1** *lift the pack on to your back:* **raise**, hoist, heave, haul up, heft, raise up/aloft, elevate, hold high, pick up, grab, take up, winch up, jack up; *informal* hump. **2** *the fog had lifted:* **clear**, rise, disperse, dissipate, disappear, vanish, dissolve. **3** *the ban has been lifted:* **cancel**, remove, withdraw, revoke, rescind, end, stop, terminate.
OPPOSITES drop, put down.
noun **1** *give me a lift up:* **push**, hand, heave, thrust, shove. **2** *he gave me a lift to the airport:* **ride**, run, drive. **3** *that goal will give his confidence a real lift:* **boost**, fillip, impetus, encouragement, spur, push; *informal* shot in the arm.
■ **lift off** take off, become airborne, be launched, take to the air, blast off.

light¹ noun **1** *the light of the candles:* **illumination**, brightness, shining, gleam, brilliance, radiance, glow, blaze, glare. **2** *there was a light on in the hall:* **lamp**, lantern, torch,

beacon, candle, bulb. **3** *we'll be driving in the light:* **daylight,** daytime, day, natural light, sunlight.
OPPOSITES darkness.
adjective **1** *a light bedroom:* **bright,** well lit, sunny. **2** *light blue:* **pale,** pastel, delicate, subtle, insipid, faint.
OPPOSITES dark.

light² adjective **1** *it's light and compact:* **lightweight,** portable, underweight. **2** *a light cotton dress:* **flimsy,** lightweight, thin, floaty, gauzy, diaphanous. **3** *she is light on her feet:* **nimble,** agile, lithe, graceful, quick, sprightly. **4** *a light dinner:* **small,** modest, simple, insubstantial, quick. **5** *light duties:* **easy,** simple, undemanding, untaxing; informal cushy. **6** *light reading:* **entertaining,** lightweight, diverting, undemanding, middle-of-the-road, mainstream, frivolous, superficial, trivial. **7** *a light touch:* **gentle,** delicate, dainty, soft, faint, careful, sensitive, subtle.
OPPOSITES heavy.

lighten¹ verb **1** *the sky was beginning to lighten:* **become/ grow/get lighter,** brighten. **2** *the first touch of dawn lightened the sky:* **brighten,** make brighter, light up, illuminate. **3** *he used lemon juice to lighten his hair:* **make lighter,** whiten, bleach, blanch.
OPPOSITES darken.

lighten² verb **1** *lightening the burden of taxation:* **reduce,** lessen, decrease, diminish, ease, alleviate, relieve. **2** *an attempt to lighten her mood:* **cheer (up),** brighten, gladden, lift, boost, buoy (up), revive, restore,

revitalize.
OPPOSITES increase, depress.

lightly adverb **1** *Maisie kissed him lightly on the cheek:* **softly,** gently, faintly, delicately. **2** *season very lightly:* **sparingly,** sparsely, moderately, delicately, subtly. **3** *her views are not to be dismissed lightly:* **carelessly,** airily, readily, heedlessly, uncaringly, unthinkingly, thoughtlessly, flippantly.
OPPOSITES hard, heavily, seriously.

lightweight adjective **1** *a lightweight jacket:* **thin,** light, flimsy, insubstantial, summery. **2** *lightweight entertainment:* **trivial,** insubstantial, superficial, shallow, undemanding, frivolous.
OPPOSITES heavy, serious.

like¹ verb **1** *I like him:* **be fond of,** have a soft spot for, think well/highly of, admire, respect, be attracted to, fancy, find attractive, be keen on, be taken with; informal rate. **2** *she likes gardening:* **enjoy,** have a taste for, have a liking for, be partial to, find/take pleasure in, be keen on, appreciate, love, adore, relish; informal have a thing about, be into, be mad about/for, be hooked on. **3** *feel free to say what you like:* **choose,** please, wish, want, see/ think fit, care to, will.
OPPOSITES hate.

like² preposition **1** *you're just like a teacher:* **similar to,** the same as, identical to, akin to, resembling. **2** *the figure landed like a cat:* **in the manner of,** in the same way/manner as, in a similar way to. **3** *big cities, like Birmingham:* **such as,** for example, for instance, in particular, namely, viz.

4 *Richard sounded mean, which isn't like him:* **characteristic of,** typical of, in character with.
OPPOSITES unlike.

likelihood noun **probability,** chance, prospect, possibility, odds, risk, threat, danger, hope, promise.

likely adjective **1** *it seemed likely that a scandal would break:* **probable,** (distinctly) possible, odds-on, plausible, imaginable; informal on the cards. **2** *a likely explanation:* **plausible,** reasonable, feasible, acceptable, believable, credible, tenable.
OPPOSITES improbable, unbelievable.

liken verb **compare,** equate, set beside.
OPPOSITES contrast.

likeness noun **1** *her likeness to Anne is quite uncanny:* **resemblance,** similarity, correspondence. **2** *a likeness of the president:* **representation,** image, depiction, portrayal, picture, drawing, sketch, painting, portrait, photograph, study.
OPPOSITES dissimilarity.

likewise adverb **1** *an ambush was out of the question, likewise poison:* **also,** equally, in addition, too, as well, to boot, besides, moreover, furthermore. **2** *encourage your family and friends to do likewise:* **the same,** similarly, correspondingly.
OPPOSITES differently.

liking noun **fondness,** love, affection, penchant, attachment, taste, passion, preference, partiality, predilection.
OPPOSITES dislike.

limb noun **arm,** leg, wing, appendage; archaic member.

limelight noun **attention,** interest, scrutiny, the public eye/gaze, the glare of publicity, prominence, the spotlight, fame, celebrity.
OPPOSITES obscurity.

limit noun **1** *the city limits:* **boundary (line),** border, frontier, edge, perimeter, margin. **2** *a limit of 4,500 supporters:* **maximum,** ceiling, upper limit.
verb *the pressure to limit costs:* **restrict,** curb, cap, (hold in) check, restrain, regulate, control, govern.

limitation noun **1** *a limitation on the number of newcomers:* **restriction,** curb, restraint, control, check. **2** *he is aware of his own limitations:* **imperfection,** flaw, defect, failing, shortcoming, weak point, deficiency, frailty, weakness.
OPPOSITES strength.

limited adjective **restricted,** finite, small, tight, slight, in short supply, short, meagre, scanty, sparse, inadequate, insufficient, paltry, poor, minimal.
OPPOSITES limitless, ample.

limp[1] verb *she limped out of the house:* **hobble,** hop, lurch, stagger, shuffle, shamble.

limp[2] adjective *a limp handshake:* **soft,** flaccid, loose, slack, lax, floppy, drooping, droopy, sagging.
OPPOSITES firm.

line noun **1** *he drew a line through the name:* **stroke,** dash, score, underline, underscore, slash, stripe, strip, band, belt; Brit. oblique. **2** *there were lines round her eyes:* **wrinkle,** furrow, crease, crinkle, crow's foot. **3** *the classic lines of the*

I

Bentley: **contour,** outline, configuration, shape, design, profile. **4** *the county line:* **boundary,** limit, border, frontier, touchline, margin, perimeter. **5** *the clothes line:* **cord,** rope, cable, wire, thread, string. **6** *a line of soldiers:* **file,** rank, column, string, train, procession, row, queue; Brit. informal crocodile. **7** *their line of flight:* **course,** route, track, path, trajectory.
verb **1** *her face was lined with age:* **furrow,** wrinkle, crease. **2** *the driveway was lined by poplars:* **border,** edge, fringe, bound.
■ **in line 1** *standing in line for food:* in a queue, in a row, in a file. **2** *the adverts are in line with the editorial style:* in agreement, in accord, in accordance, in harmony, in step, in compliance. **3** *in line with the goal:* aligned, level, alongside, abreast, side by side. ■ **in line for** a candidate for, in the running for, due for; informal up for. ■ **line up** form a queue/line, queue up, fall in. ■ **line someone/something up** assemble, get together, organize, prepare, arrange, fix up, lay on, book, schedule, timetable.

lined[1] adjective **1** *lined paper:* **ruled,** feint, striped, banded. **2** *his lined face:* **wrinkled,** wrinkly, furrowed, wizened.
OPPOSITES plain, smooth.

lined[2] adjective *lined curtains:* **covered,** backed, padded, insulated, sealed.

line-up noun **1** *a star-studded line-up:* **cast,** bill, programme. **2** *United's line-up:* **team,** squad, side, configuration.

linger verb **1** *the crowd lingered:*

wait (around), stand (around), remain, loiter; informal stick around, hang around/round. **2** *the infection can linger for years:* **persist,** continue, remain, stay, endure, carry on, last.
OPPOSITES vanish.

lining noun **backing,** facing, padding, insulation.

link noun **1** *the links between transport and the environment:* **connection,** relationship, association, linkage, tie-up. **2** *their links with the labour movement:* **bond,** tie, attachment, connection, association, affiliation.
verb **1** *four boxes were linked together:* **join,** connect, fasten, attach, bind, secure, fix, tie, couple, yoke. **2** *the evidence linking him with the body:* **associate,** connect, relate, bracket.
OPPOSITES separate.

lip noun *the lip of the crater:* **edge,** rim, brim, border, verge, brink.

liquid noun *a vat of liquid:* **fluid,** moisture, liquor, solution, juice, sap.
OPPOSITES solid.
adjective *liquid fuels:* **fluid,** liquefied, melted, molten, thawed, dissolved.
OPPOSITES solid.

liquor noun **1** *alcoholic liquor:* **alcohol,** spirits, (alcoholic) drink; informal booze, the hard stuff, hooch, moonshine. **2** *strain the liquor into the sauce:* **stock,** broth, bouillon, juice, liquid.

list[1] noun *a list of the world's wealthiest people:* **catalogue,** inventory, record, register, roll, file, index, directory, checklist.
verb *the accounts are listed*

below: **record,** register, enter, itemize, enumerate, catalogue, file, log, minute, categorize, inventory, classify, group, sort, rank, index.

list² verb *the boat listed to one side:* **lean (over),** tilt, tip, heel (over), pitch, incline, slant, slope, bank.

listen verb **1** *are you listening?* **pay attention,** be attentive, attend, concentrate, keep one's ears open, prick up one's ears; informal be all ears. **2** *policymakers should listen to popular opinion:* **heed,** take heed of, take notice/ note of, bear in mind, take into consideration/account.

literal adjective **strict,** technical, concrete, original, true. OPPOSITES figurative.

literary adjective **1** *literary works:* **artistic,** poetic, dramatic. **2** *her literary friends:* **scholarly,** intellectual, academic, bookish, erudite.

literate adjective **(well) educated,** well read, widely read, scholarly, learned, knowledgeable, cultured, cultivated, well informed. OPPOSITES ignorant.

literature noun **1** *English literature:* **writing,** poetry, drama, prose. **2** *the literature on prototype theory:* **publications,** reports, studies, material. **3** *election literature:* **documentation,** material, publicity, blurb, propaganda, advertising; informal bumf.

litigation noun **legal/judicial proceedings,** legal action, lawsuit, legal dispute, legal case, prosecution, indictment.

litter noun **1** *never drop litter:* **rubbish,** refuse, junk, waste, debris; N. Amer. trash, garbage. **2** *the litter of glasses around*

her: **clutter,** jumble, muddle, mess, heap; informal shambles. verb *clothes littered the floor:* **cover,** clutter up, pepper.

little adjective **1** *a little writing desk:* **small,** compact, miniature, tiny, toy, baby, undersized, dwarf, midget; Scottish wee; informal teeny-weeny; Brit. informal titchy, dinky; N. Amer. informal vest-pocket. **2** *a little man:* **short,** small, slight, petite, diminutive, tiny; Scottish wee; informal teeny-weeny, pint-sized. **3** *my little sister:* **young,** younger, baby. **4** *a little while:* **brief,** short, quick, hasty, cursory. **5** *a few little problems:* **minor,** unimportant, insignificant, trivial, trifling, petty, paltry, inconsequential. OPPOSITES big, large, elder, major.

determiner *they have little political influence:* **hardly any,** not much, scant, limited, restricted, modest, little or no, minimal, negligible. OPPOSITES considerable.

adverb **1** *he is little known as a teacher:* **hardly,** barely, scarcely, not much, only slightly. **2** *this disease is little seen nowadays:* **rarely,** seldom, infrequently, hardly (ever), scarcely ever, not much. OPPOSITES well, often.

■ **a little 1** *add a little water:* some, a bit of, a touch of, a dash of, a taste of, a spot of, a hint of, a dribble of, a splash of, a pinch of, a sprinkling of, a speck of; informal a smidgen of, a tad of. **2** *after a little, Oliver came in:* a short time, a while, a bit, an interval, a short period, a minute, a moment, a second, an instant; informal a sec, a mo, a jiffy. **3** *this reminds me a little* of the Adriatic: slightly, somewhat, a little bit, quite, to some degree.

live[1] verb **1** *the greatest mathematician who ever lived:* **exist,** be alive, be, have life, breathe, draw breath, walk the earth. **2** *I live in London:* **reside,** have one's home, lodge, inhabit, occupy, populate; Scottish stay. **3** *she had lived a difficult life:* **experience,** spend, pass, lead, have, go through, undergo. **4** *Freddy lived by scavenging:* **survive,** make a living, eke out a living, subsist, support oneself, sustain oneself, make ends meet, keep body and soul together.
OPPOSITES die, be dead.

live[2] adjective **1** *live bait:* **living,** alive, conscious. **2** *a live rail:* **electrified,** charged, powered up, active, switched on. **3** *a live grenade:* **unexploded,** explosive, active, primed. **4** *a live issue:* **topical,** current, controversial, burning, pressing, important, relevant.
OPPOSITES dead, inanimate.

livelihood noun **(source of) income,** means of support, living, subsistence, bread and butter, job, work, employment, occupation.

lively adjective **1** *a lively young woman:* **energetic,** active, animated, dynamic, full of life, outgoing, spirited, high-spirited, vivacious, enthusiastic, vibrant, buoyant, exuberant, effervescent, cheerful; informal full of beans. **2** *a lively bar:* **busy,** crowded, bustling, buzzing, vibrant, boisterous, jolly. **3** *a lively debate:* **heated,** vigorous, animated, spirited, enthusiastic, forceful. **4** *a lively portrait of the local community:* **vivid,** colourful, striking, graphic. **5** *he bowled at a lively pace:* **brisk,** quick, fast, rapid, swift, speedy, smart.
OPPOSITES quiet, dull, slow.

livid adjective (informal) **very angry,** enraged, furious, infuriated, irate, incensed, fuming, ranting, raving, seething, beside oneself, outraged; informal hopping mad, wild.

living noun **1** *she cleaned floors for a living:* **livelihood,** (source of) income, means of support, subsistence, keep, daily bread, bread and butter, job, work, employment, occupation. **2** *healthy living:* **way of life,** lifestyle, life, conduct, behaviour, activities, habits.
adjective **1** *living organisms:* **alive,** live, animate, sentient, breathing, existing. **2** *a living language:* **current,** contemporary, active.
OPPOSITES dead, extinct.

load noun **1** *MacDowell's got a load to deliver:* **cargo,** freight, consignment, delivery, shipment, goods, pack, bundle, parcel. **2** *a heavy teaching load:* **commitment,** responsibility, duty, obligation, burden.
verb **1** *we quickly loaded the van:* **fill (up),** pack, lade, charge, stock, stack. **2** *Larry loaded boxes into the jeep:* **pack,** stow, store, stack, bundle, place, deposit, put away. **3** *loading the committee with responsibilities:* **burden,** weigh down, saddle, charge, overburden, overwhelm, encumber, tax, strain, trouble, worry. **4** *he loaded a gun:* **prime,** charge, set up, prepare. **5** *load the cassette into the camcorder:* **insert,** put, place, slot, slide.

loaded adjective **1** *a loaded freight train:* **full,** filled, laden, packed, stuffed, crammed, brimming, stacked; informal chock-full, chock-a-block. **2** *a politically loaded word:* **charged,** emotive, sensitive, delicate.

loaf verb **laze,** lounge, loll, idle; informal hang around/round; Brit. informal hang about, mooch about/around; N. Amer. informal bum around.

loan noun **credit,** advance, mortgage, overdraft, Brit. informal sub.

loath adjective **reluctant,** unwilling, disinclined, averse, opposed, resistant.
OPPOSITES willing.

loathe verb **hate,** detest, abhor, not be able to bear/stand.
OPPOSITES love.

loathing noun **hatred,** hate, abhorrence, antipathy, dislike, hostility, animosity, malice, enmity, repugnance.

loathsome adjective **hateful,** detestable, abhorrent, repulsive, odious, repugnant, repellent, disgusting, revolting, sickening, abominable, despicable, contemptible, reprehensible, vile, horrible, nasty, obnoxious, gross, foul; informal horrid; literary noisome.

lobby noun **1** *the hotel lobby:* **entrance (hall),** hallway, hall, vestibule, foyer, reception area. **2** *the anti-hunt lobby:* **pressure group,** interest group, movement, campaign, crusade, faction, camp.
verb **1** *readers are urged to lobby their MPs:* **approach,** contact, importune, sway, petition, solicit, appeal to, pressurize. **2** *a group lobbying for better rail services:* **campaign,**

crusade, press, push, ask, call, demand, promote, advocate, champion.

local adjective **1** *the local council:* **community,** district, neighbourhood, regional, town, municipal, provincial, village, parish. **2** *a local restaurant:* **neighbourhood,** nearby, near, at hand, close by, handy, convenient. **3** *a local infection:* **confined,** restricted, contained, localized.
OPPOSITES national, widespread.
noun *complaints from the locals:* **local person,** native, inhabitant, resident, parishioner.
OPPOSITES outsider.

locate verb **1** *spotter planes located the submarines:* **find,** pinpoint, track down, unearth, sniff out, smoke out, search out, uncover. **2** *a company located near Pittsburgh:* **situate,** site, position, place, base, put, build, establish, station.

location noun **position,** place, situation, site, locality, locale, spot, whereabouts, scene, setting, area, environment, venue, address.

lock[1] noun *the lock on the door:* **bolt,** catch, fastener, clasp, hasp, latch.
verb **1** *he locked the door:* **bolt,** fasten, secure, padlock, latch, chain. **2** *the police locked arms:* **join,** interlock, link, engage, combine, connect, couple. **3** *the wheels locked:* **become stuck,** stick, jam, seize. **4** *he locked her in an embrace:* **clasp,** clench, grasp, embrace, hug, squeeze.
OPPOSITES unlock, open, separate, divide.
■ **lock someone up** imprison, jail, incarcerate, intern, send to prison, put behind bars, put

under lock and key, cage, pen, coop up; informal send down, put away, put inside.

lock² noun *a lock of hair*: **tuft**, tress, curl, ringlet, hank, strand, wisp, coil.

locker noun **cupboard**, cabinet, chest, safe, box, case, coffer, storeroom.

lodge noun **1** *the porter's lodge*: **gatehouse**, cottage. **2** *a hunting lodge*: **house**, cottage, cabin, chalet. **3** *a Masonic lodge*: **section**, branch, wing, hall, clubhouse, meeting room; N. Amer. chapter.
verb **1** *William lodged at our house*: **reside**, board, stay, live, stop; N. Amer. room. **2** *the government lodged a protest*: **submit**, register, enter, put forward, advance, lay, present, tender, proffer, put on record, record, table, file. **3** *the money was lodged in a bank*: **deposit**, put, bank, stash, store, stow, put away. **4** *the bullet lodged in his back*: **become embedded**, get/become stuck, stick, catch, become caught, wedge.

lodging noun **accommodation**, rooms, chambers, living quarters, a roof over one's head, housing, shelter; informal digs; formal residence, dwelling.

lofty adjective **1** *a lofty tower*: **tall**, high. **2** *lofty ideals*: **noble**, exalted, high, high-minded, worthy, grand, fine, elevated. **3** *lofty disdain*: **haughty**, arrogant, disdainful, supercilious, condescending, scornful, contemptuous, self-important, conceited, snobbish; informal stuck-up, snooty; Brit. informal toffee-nosed.
OPPOSITES low, short, base, lowly, modest.

log noun *a log of phone calls*:

record, register, logbook, journal, diary, minutes, chronicle, record book, ledger, account, tally.
verb **1** *all complaints are logged*: **register**, record, note, write down, put in writing, enter, file. **2** *the pilot had logged 95 hours*: **attain**, achieve, chalk up, make, do, go, cover, clock up.

logic noun **1** *this case appears to defy all logic*: **reason**, judgement, rationality, wisdom, sense, good sense, common sense, sanity. **2** *the logic of their argument*: **reasoning**, line, rationale, argument.

logical adjective **1** *information displayed in a logical fashion*: **reasoned**, rational, sound, cogent, valid, coherent, clear, systematic, orderly, methodical, analytical, consistent. **2** *the logical outcome*: **natural**, reasonable, sensible, understandable, predictable, unsurprising, likely.
OPPOSITES illogical, unlikely.

lone adjective **1** *a lone police officer*: **solitary**, single, solo, unaccompanied, sole, isolated. **2** *a lone parent*: **single**, unmarried, separated, divorced, widowed.

loneliness noun **1** *his loneliness was unbearable*: **isolation**, friendlessness, abandonment, rejection; N. Amer. lonesomeness. **2** *the enforced loneliness of a prison cell*: **solitariness**, solitude, aloneness, separation, seclusion.
OPPOSITES popularity, company.

lonely adjective **1** *I felt very lonely*: **isolated**, alone, friendless, with no one to turn to, abandoned, rejected, unloved, unwanted; N. Amer. lonesome. **2** *a lonely road*:

deserted, uninhabited, desolate, solitary, isolated, remote, out of the way, secluded, in the back of beyond, godforsaken; informal in the middle of nowhere.
OPPOSITES popular, crowded.

long[1] adjective *a long silence:* **lengthy,** extended, prolonged, protracted, long-lasting, drawn-out, endless, lingering, interminable.
OPPOSITES short, brief.

long[2] verb *I longed for the holidays:* **yearn,** pine, ache, hanker for/after, hunger, thirst, itch, be eager, be desperate, crave, dream of; informal be dying.

longing noun **yearning,** craving, ache, burning, hunger, thirst, hankering; informal yen, itch.

long-standing adjective **well established,** long-established, time-honoured, traditional, abiding, enduring.
OPPOSITES new, recent.

look verb **1** *Mrs Wright looked at him:* **glance,** gaze, stare, gape, peer, peep, peek, watch, observe, view, regard, examine, inspect, eye, scan, scrutinize, survey, study, contemplate, take in, ogle; informal take a gander, rubberneck, get a load of; Brit. informal gawp; N. Amer. informal eyeball. **2** *they looked shocked:* **seem (to be),** appear (to be), come across/over as.
OPPOSITES ignore.
noun **1** *have a look at this report:* **glance,** examination, study, inspection, scrutiny, peep, peek, glimpse; informal eyeful, once-over, squint. **2** *the look on her face:* **expression,** mien. **3** *that rustic look:* **appearance,** air, aspect, manner, mien, demeanour, impression, effect,

ambience. **4** *this season's look:* **fashion,** style; informal thing.
■ **look after** take care of, care for, attend to, minister to, tend, mind, keep an eye on, keep safe, be responsible for, protect, nurse, babysit, childmind. ■ **look down on** disdain, scorn, look down one's nose at, sneer at, despise. ■ **look for** search for, hunt, try to find, seek, cast about/ around/round for, try to track down, forage for. ■ **look forward to** await with pleasure, eagerly anticipate, lick one's lips over, be unable to wait for, count the days until. ■ **look into** investigate, enquire into, go into, probe, explore, follow up, research, study, examine; informal check out; N. Amer. informal scope out. ■ **look like** resemble, bear a resemblance to, look similar to, take after, remind one of, make one think of; informal be the (spitting) image of, be a dead ringer for. ■ **look out** beware, watch out, mind out, be on one's guard, be alert, be wary, be vigilant, be careful, take care, be cautious, pay attention, keep one's eyes open/peeled, keep an eye out, watch one's step. ■ **look something over** inspect, examine, scrutinize, cast an eye over, take stock of, vet, view, peruse, read through; informal give something a/the once-over; N. Amer. check out; N. Amer. informal eyeball. ■ **look up** improve, get better, pick up, come along/on, progress, make progress, make headway, perk up, rally, take a turn for the better. ■ **look someone up** (informal) visit, pay a visit to, call on, go to see, look in on; N. Amer. visit with, go see; informal drop in on. ■ **look up to** admire, have

a high opinion of, think highly of, hold in high regard, regard highly, respect, esteem, venerate, idolize.

lookout noun 1 *the lookout sighted sails:* **watchman,** watch, guard, sentry, sentinel, observer. 2 (Brit. informal) *that's your lookout:* **problem,** concern, business, affair, responsibility, worry; informal pigeon.
■ **be on the lookout** keep watch, keep an eye out, keep one's eyes peeled, be alert.

loom verb 1 *ghostly shapes loomed out of the fog:* **emerge,** appear, materialize, reveal itself. 2 *the church loomed above him:* **soar,** tower, rise, rear up, hang, overshadow. 3 *without reforms, disaster looms:* **be imminent,** be on the horizon, impend, threaten, brew, be just around the corner.

loop noun *a loop of rope:* **coil,** ring, circle, noose, spiral, curl, bend, curve, arc, twirl, whorl, twist, helix.
verb 1 *Dave looped rope around their hands:* **coil,** wind, twist, snake, spiral, curve, bend, turn. 2 *he looped the cables together:* **fasten,** tie, join, connect, knot, bind.

loophole noun flaw, discrepancy, inconsistency, ambiguity, omission, excuse; Brit. get-out.

loose adjective 1 *a loose floorboard:* **not secure,** unsecured, unattached, detached, wobbly, unsteady, dangling, free. 2 *she wore her hair loose:* **untied,** free, down. 3 *there's a wolf loose:* **free,** at large, at liberty, on the loose. 4 *a loose interpretation:* **vague,** imprecise, approximate, broad, general, rough, liberal. 5 *a loose jacket:* **baggy,** generously cut, slack, roomy, oversized, shapeless, sloppy.
OPPOSITES secure, literal, narrow, tight.
verb 1 *the hounds have been loosed:* **free,** let loose, release, untie, unchain, unfasten, unleash. 2 *the fingers loosed their hold:* **relax,** slacken, loosen.
OPPOSITES confine, tighten.

loosen verb 1 *you simply loosen two screws:* **undo,** slacken, unfasten, detach, release, disconnect. 2 *her fingers loosened:* **slacken,** become loose, let go, ease. 3 *Philip loosened his grip:* **weaken,** relax, slacken, loose.
OPPOSITES tighten.

loot noun *a bag full of loot:* **booty,** spoils, plunder, stolen goods, contraband, informal swag.
verb *troops looted the cathedral:* **plunder,** pillage, ransack, sack, rifle, rob, strip, gut.

lord noun 1 *lords and ladies:* **noble,** nobleman, peer, aristocrat. 2 *it is my duty to obey my lord's wishes:* **master,** ruler, leader, chief, superior, monarch, sovereign, king, emperor, prince, governor, commander.
OPPOSITES commoner, servant, inferior.

lose verb 1 *I've lost my watch:* **mislay,** misplace, be unable to find, lose track of. 2 *he lost his pursuers:* **escape from,** evade, elude, dodge, avoid, give someone the slip, shake off, throw off, leave behind, outdistance, outrun. 3 *you've lost your opportunity:* **waste,** squander, let pass, miss; informal pass up, blow. 4 *they always lose at football:* **be defeated,**

be/get beaten; informal come a
cropper, go down.
OPPOSITES find, seize, win.

loser noun (informal) **failure,**
underachiever, dead loss, write-
off, has-been, informal also-ran,
non-starter, no-hoper.
OPPOSITES success.

loss noun **1** *the loss of the papers:*
mislaying, misplacement,
destruction, theft. **2** *loss of
earnings:* **forfeiture,**
diminution, erosion, reduction,
depletion. **3** *the loss of her
husband:* **death,** demise,
passing away, end. **4** *British
losses in the war:* **casualty,**
fatality, victim, dead. **5** *a loss of
£15,000:* **deficit,** debit, debt.
OPPOSITES recovery, profit.
■ **at a loss** baffled, nonplussed,
mystified, puzzled, perplexed,
bewildered, confused, stumped,
stuck; informal flummoxed,
beaten.

lost adjective **1** *her lost keys:*
missing, mislaid, misplaced,
stolen. **2** *I think we're lost:* **off
course,** going round in circles,
adrift, at sea. **3** *a lost
opportunity:* **missed,** wasted,
squandered, gone by the board;
informal down the drain. **4** *lost
traditions:* **bygone,** past,
former, old, vanished,
forgotten, dead. **5** *lost species
and habitats:* **extinct,** died out,
defunct, vanished, gone,
destroyed, wiped out,
exterminated. **6** *lost in thought:*
engrossed, absorbed, rapt,
immersed, deep, intent,
engaged, wrapped up.
OPPOSITES current, living, saved.

lot pronoun *a lot of money | lots of
friends:* **a large amount,** a
good/great deal, an abundance,
a wealth, a profusion, plenty,
many, a great many, a large

number, a considerable
number; informal hundreds,
loads, masses, heaps, piles,
stacks, tons; Brit. informal a
shedload, lashings.
OPPOSITES a little, a few.
adverb *I work in pastels a lot:* **a
great deal,** a good deal, much,
often, frequently, regularly.
OPPOSITES a little.
noun **1** (informal) *what do your lot
think?* **group,** crowd, circle,
crew; informal bunch, gang, mob.
2 *an auction lot:* **item,** article,
batch, group, bundle, parcel.
3 *his lot in life:* **fate,** destiny,
fortune, situation,
circumstances, plight,
predicament.

lotion noun **ointment,** cream,
balm, rub, moisturizer,
lubricant, embrocation.

lottery noun **raffle,** (prize)
draw, sweepstake, sweep,
tombola, lotto, pools.

loud adjective **1** *loud music:*
noisy, blaring, booming,
deafening, roaring, thunderous,
ear-splitting, powerful,
stentorian; Music forte,
fortissimo. **2** *loud complaints:*
vociferous, clamorous,
insistent, vehement, emphatic.
3 *a loud T-shirt:* **garish,** gaudy,
lurid, showy, ostentatious,
vulgar, tasteless; informal flashy.
OPPOSITES quiet, gentle, sober,
tasteful.

loudly adverb **at high volume,** at
the top of one's voice, noisily,
stridently, vociferously, shrilly.
OPPOSITES quietly.

lounge verb *lounging around:*
laze, lie, loll, recline, relax, rest,
take it easy, sprawl, slump,
slouch, loaf, idle, do nothing.
noun *sitting in the lounge:* **living
room,** sitting room, front room,
drawing room.

lout noun hooligan, ruffian, thug, boor, oaf, rowdy; informal tough, bruiser; Brit. informal yob, yobbo.
OPPOSITES gentleman.

love noun **1** *a friendship that blossomed into love:* **infatuation,** adoration, attachment, devotion, fondness, tenderness, warmth, intimacy, passion, desire, lust, yearning, besottedness. **2** *her love of fashion:* **liking,** taste, passion, zeal, zest, enthusiasm, keenness, fondness, weakness, partiality, predilection, penchant. **3** *their love for their fellow human beings:* **compassion,** care, regard, concern, altruism, unselfishness, philanthropy, benevolence, humanity. **4** *he was her one true love:* **beloved,** loved one, dearest, darling, sweetheart, sweet, angel, honey.
OPPOSITES hatred.
verb **1** *she loves him dearly:* **be in love with,** be infatuated with, be smitten with, adore, idolize, worship, think the world of, be devoted to, dote on, care for, hold dear; informal be mad/crazy/nuts/wild/potty about, carry a torch for. **2** *Laura loved painting:* **like,** delight in, enjoy, have a passion for, take pleasure in, have a weakness for, be partial to, be taken with; informal have a thing about, be mad/crazy/nuts/wild/potty about, be hooked on.
OPPOSITES hate.

love affair noun relationship, affair, romance, liaison, fling, entanglement, involvement; Brit. informal carry-on.

lovely adjective **1** *a lovely young woman:* **beautiful,** pretty, attractive, good-looking, handsome, adorable, enchanting, gorgeous, alluring, ravishing, glamorous; Scottish & N. English bonny; Brit. informal fit; N. Amer. informal cute, foxy. **2** *a lovely view:* **scenic,** picturesque, pleasing, magnificent, stunning, splendid. **3** (informal) *we had a lovely day:* **delightful,** very pleasant, very nice, marvellous, wonderful, sublime, superb; informal terrific, fabulous, heavenly, divine, amazing, glorious.
OPPOSITES ugly, horrible.

lover noun **1** *she had a secret lover:* **boyfriend, girlfriend,** beloved, sweetheart, mistress, partner; informal bit on the side, fancy man, fancy woman. **2** *a dog lover:* **devotee,** admirer, fan, enthusiast, aficionado; informal buff, nut, ...head.

loving adjective affectionate, fond, devoted, adoring, doting, caring, tender, warm, close, amorous, passionate.
OPPOSITES cold, cruel.

low adjective **1** *a low fence:* **short,** small, little, squat, stubby, stunted. **2** *low prices:* **cheap,** economical, moderate, reasonable, affordable, modest, bargain, bargain-basement, rock-bottom. **3** *supplies were low:* **scarce,** scant, meagre, sparse, few, little, reduced, depleted, diminished. **4** *low quality:* **inferior,** substandard, poor, low-grade, unsatisfactory. **5** *a low voice:* **quiet,** soft, faint, gentle, muted, subdued, muffled, hushed. **6** *a low note:* **bass,** low-pitched, deep, rumbling, booming, sonorous.

7 *she was feeling low:*
depressed, dejected,
despondent, downhearted,
downcast, down, miserable,
dispirited, flat; informal fed up,
down in the dumps, blue.
OPPOSITES high, expensive,
plentiful, superior, loud,
cheerful, lively.

lower¹ adjective **1** *the lower
house of parliament:*
subordinate, inferior, lesser,
junior, minor, secondary,
subsidiary, subservient. **2** *her
lower lip:* **bottom,** bottommost,
nether, under. **3** *a lower price:*
cheaper, reduced, cut.
OPPOSITES upper, higher,
increased.

lower² verb **1** *she lowered the
mask:* **let down,** take down,
drop, let fall. **2** *lower your
voice:* **soften,** modulate,
quieten, hush, tone down,
muffle, turn down. **3** *they are
lowering their prices:* **reduce,**
decrease, lessen, bring down,
cut, slash.
OPPOSITES raise, increase.

lowly adjective **humble,** low,
low-ranking, common, ordinary,
plain, modest, simple, obscure.
OPPOSITES aristocratic, exalted.

loyal adjective **faithful,** true,
devoted, constant, steadfast,
staunch, dependable, reliable,
trustworthy, trusty, patriotic.
OPPOSITES disloyal.

loyalty noun **allegiance,**
faithfulness, obedience,
adherence, devotion,
steadfastness, staunchness,
dedication, commitment,
patriotism.
OPPOSITES disloyalty.

lucid adjective **rational,** sane, in
possession of one's faculties,
compos mentis, clear-headed,
sober; informal all there.

OPPOSITES confused.

luck noun **1** *with luck you'll make
it:* **good fortune,** good luck,
stroke of luck; informal lucky
break. **2** *I wish you luck:*
success, prosperity, good
fortune, good luck. **3** *it is a
matter of luck whether it hits or
misses:* **fortune,** fate,
serendipity, chance, accident, a
twist of fate.
OPPOSITES bad luck, misfortune.

luckily adverb **fortunately,**
happily, providentially, by good
fortune, as luck would have it,
mercifully, thankfully.
OPPOSITES unluckily.

lucky adjective **1** *the lucky
winner:* **fortunate,** in luck,
favoured, charmed, successful;
Brit. informal jammy. **2** *a lucky
escape:* **providential,** fortunate,
timely, opportune,
serendipitous, chance,
fortuitous, accidental.
OPPOSITES unlucky.

lucrative adjective **profitable,**
gainful, remunerative,
moneymaking, well paid,
rewarding, worthwhile.
OPPOSITES unprofitable.

ludicrous adjective **absurd,**
ridiculous, farcical, laughable,
risible, preposterous, mad,
insane, idiotic, stupid, asinine,
nonsensical; informal crazy.
OPPOSITES sensible.

luggage noun **baggage,** bags,
suitcases, cases.

lukewarm adjective **1** *lukewarm
coffee:* **tepid,** warmish, at room
temperature. **2** *a lukewarm
response:* **indifferent,** cool,
half-hearted, apathetic,
unenthusiastic, tepid, offhand.
OPPOSITES hot, cold, warm.

lull verb *the sound of the bells
lulled us to sleep:* **soothe,** calm,
hush, rock to sleep.

OPPOSITES waken, arouse.
noun 1 *a lull in the fighting:* **pause,** respite, interval, break, suspension, breathing space; informal let-up, breather. **2** *the lull before the storm:* **calm,** stillness, quiet, tranquillity, peace, silence, hush.
OPPOSITES agitation, activity.

lumber¹ verb *elephants lumbered past:* **trundle,** stumble, lurch, shamble, shuffle, trudge, clump.

lumber² verb (Brit. informal) *she was lumbered with debt:* **burden,** saddle, encumber, land.
OPPOSITES free.

lumbering adjective clumsy, awkward, slow, blundering, bumbling, ponderous; informal clodhopping.
OPPOSITES nimble, agile.

lump noun 1 *a lump of coal:* **chunk,** hunk, piece, block, wedge, slab, ball, knob, clod. **2** *a lump on his head:* **swelling,** bump, bulge, protuberance, protrusion, growth, tumour.
verb *it is convenient to lump them together:* **combine,** put, group, bunch, throw.

lunatic noun *he drives like a lunatic:* **maniac,** madman, madwoman, fool, idiot; informal loony, nutcase; Brit. informal nutter; N. Amer. informal screwball.
adjective *a lunatic idea:* **stupid,** foolish, idiotic, absurd, ridiculous, ludicrous, preposterous; informal crazy, mad; Brit. informal barmy, daft.
OPPOSITES sensible.

lunge noun *Darren made a lunge at his attacker:* **thrust,** dive, rush, charge, grab.
verb *he lunged at Finn with a knife:* **thrust,** dive, spring, launch oneself, rush.

lurch verb 1 *he lurched into the kitchen:* **stagger,** stumble, sway, reel, roll, totter. **2** *the car lurched to the left:* **swing,** list, roll, pitch, veer, swerve.

lure verb *consumers are frequently lured into debt:* **tempt,** entice, attract, induce, coax, persuade, inveigle, seduce.
OPPOSITES deter, put off.
noun *the lure of the stage:* **temptation,** attraction, pull, draw, appeal, inducement, allure, fascination, interest, glamour.

lurk verb skulk, loiter, lie in wait, hide.

lush adjective 1 *lush vegetation:* **profuse,** rich, abundant, luxuriant, riotous, vigorous, dense, thick, rampant. **2** *a lush apartment:* **luxurious,** sumptuous, palatial, opulent, lavish, elaborate, extravagant, fancy; informal plush, posh, swanky; Brit. informal swish; N. Amer. informal swank.
OPPOSITES sparse, shrivelled, austere.

lust noun 1 *his lust for her:* **desire,** longing, passion, libido, sex drive, sexuality, lechery, lasciviousness; informal horniness; Brit. informal randiness. **2** *a lust for power:* **greed,** desire, craving, eagerness, longing, yearning, hunger, thirst, appetite, hankering.
OPPOSITES dread, aversion.
■ **lust after someone** *he lusted after his employer's wife:* desire, be consumed with desire for; informal fancy, have a thing about/for, drool over. ■ **lust for/ after something** *she lusted after adventure:* crave, desire, want, long for, yearn for, dream of, hanker for/after, hunger for,

thirst for, ache for.

luxurious adjective **opulent,**
sumptuous, grand, palatial,
magnificent, extravagant, fancy;
Brit. upmarket; informal plush,
posh, classy, swanky; Brit. informal
swish; N. Amer. informal swank.
OPPOSITES plain, basic.

luxury noun **1** *we'll live in
luxury:* **opulence,**
sumptuousness, grandeur,
magnificence, splendour,
affluence. **2** *a TV is his only
luxury:* **indulgence,**
extravagance, treat, extra, frill.
OPPOSITES simplicity, necessity.

lying noun *she was no good at
lying:* **dishonesty,** fabrication,
fibbing, perjury,
untruthfulness, mendacity,
misrepresentation, deceit,
duplicity.
OPPOSITES honesty.
adjective *he was a lying
womanizer:* **dishonest,** false,
untruthful, mendacious,
deceitful, duplicitous, double-
dealing, two-faced.
OPPOSITES honest.

lyrical adjective **1** *a subtle, lyrical
film:* **expressive,** emotional,
deeply felt, personal,
passionate. **2** *she was lyrical
about her success:* **enthusiastic,**
effusive, rapturous, ecstatic,
euphoric.
OPPOSITES unenthusiastic.

Mm

machine noun **1 device,**
appliance, apparatus, engine,
gadget, mechanism. **2** *an
efficient publicity machine:*
organization, system,
structure, machinery; informal
set-up.

machinery noun **1 equipment,**
apparatus, plant, hardware,
gear, gadgetry, technology.
2 *the machinery of local
government:* **workings,**
organization, system, structure,
institution; informal set-up.

macho adjective **manly,** male,
masculine, virile, red-blooded;
informal butch, laddish.
OPPOSITES wimpish.

mad adjective **1** *he was killed by
his mad brother:* **insane,** out of
one's mind, deranged,
demented, crazed, lunatic,
unbalanced, unhinged; informal
crazy, mental, off one's head,
round the bend; Brit. informal
barmy, crackers, barking (mad),
potty, round the twist.
2 (informal) *I'm still mad at him:*
angry, furious, infuriated,
enraged, fuming, incensed,
beside oneself; informal livid,
spare; N. Amer. informal sore.
3 *some mad scheme:* **foolish,**
insane, stupid, lunatic, idiotic,
absurd, silly, asinine, wild;
informal crazy, crackpot; Brit.
informal daft. **4** (informal) *he's mad
about jazz:* **passionate,**
fanatical, ardent, fervent,
devoted to, infatuated with, in
love with; informal crazy, dotty,
nuts, wild, hooked on; Brit.
informal potty; N. Amer. informal
nutso. **5** *it was a mad dash to
get ready:* **frenzied,** frantic,
frenetic, feverish, hysterical,
wild, hectic, manic.
OPPOSITES sane, pleased,

sensible, indifferent, calm.

madden verb infuriate, exasperate, irritate, incense, anger, enrage, provoke, make someone see red; informal aggravate, make someone's blood boil; Brit. informal nark; N. Amer. informal tee off, tick off.
OPPOSITES calm.

madly adverb **1** *she was smiling madly:* **insanely,** wildly; informal crazily. **2** *it was fun, hurtling madly downhill:* **furiously,** hurriedly, speedily, energetically; informal like mad, like crazy. **3** (informal) *he loved her madly:* **intensely,** fervently, wildly, to distraction. **4** (informal) *his job isn't madly exciting:* **very,** tremendously, wildly, all that, hugely; informal awfully, terribly.
OPPOSITES sanely, slowly, slightly.

madman, madwoman noun **lunatic,** maniac, psychotic, psychopath; informal loony, nut, nutcase, head case; Brit. informal nutter; N. Amer. informal screwball.

madness noun **1** *today madness is called mental illness:* **insanity,** mental illness, dementia, derangement, lunacy, mania, psychosis. **2** *it would be madness to do otherwise:* **folly,** foolishness, idiocy, stupidity, insanity, lunacy. **3** *it's absolute madness in here:* **bedlam,** mayhem, chaos, pandemonium, uproar, turmoil, all hell broken loose; N. Amer. three-ring circus.
OPPOSITES sanity, sense.

magazine noun **journal,** periodical, supplement, colour supplement; informal glossy, mag, 'zine.

magic noun **1** *do you believe in magic?* **sorcery,** witchcraft, wizardry, necromancy, enchantment, the supernatural, occultism, the occult, black magic, the black arts, voodoo. **2** *he does magic at children's parties:* **conjuring (tricks),** illusion, sleight of hand; formal prestidigitation. **3** *the magic of the stage:* **allure,** excitement, fascination, charm, glamour. **4** *the old Liverpool magic:* **brilliance,** skill, accomplishment, expertise, art, finesse, talent.

magical adjective **1** *magical powers:* **supernatural,** magic, mystical, other-worldly. **2** *the news had a magical effect:* **extraordinary,** remarkable, incredible, amazing, astonishing, astounding, staggering, miraculous. **3** *this magical island:* **enchanting,** entrancing, spellbinding, bewitching, fascinating, captivating, alluring, enthralling, charming, lovely, delightful, beautiful; informal heavenly, gorgeous.
OPPOSITES predictable, boring.

magician noun **1** **sorcerer,** sorceress, witch, wizard, warlock, enchanter, enchantress, necromancer. **2** **conjuror,** illusionist; formal prestidigitator.

magnetic adjective **attractive,** irresistible, seductive, charismatic, hypnotic, alluring, fascinating, captivating.
OPPOSITES repellent.

magnificent adjective **1** *a magnificent view:* **splendid,** spectacular, impressive, striking, glorious, superb, majestic, awe-inspiring, breathtaking. **2** *a magnificent apartment:* **sumptuous,** grand, impressive, imposing, monumental, palatial, opulent,

luxurious, lavish, rich, dazzling, beautiful; informal posh, classy; Brit. informal swish.
OPPOSITES uninspiring, modest, tawdry.

magnify verb **enlarge**, increase, augment, extend, expand, boost, enhance, maximize, amplify, intensify; informal blow up.
OPPOSITES reduce, minimize, understate.

mail noun **1** *the mail arrived:* **post**, letters, correspondence, email. **2** *we sent it by mail:* **post**, postal system, postal service, post office; informal snail mail; N. Amer. the mails.
verb *we mailed the parcels:* **send**, post, dispatch, forward, ship, email.

maim verb **injure**, wound, cripple, disable, incapacitate, mutilate, disfigure, mangle.

main adjective **principal**, chief, leading, foremost, most important, major, dominant, central, focal, key, prime, primary, first, fundamental, predominant, pre-eminent.
OPPOSITES subsidiary, minor.

mainly adverb **mostly**, for the most part, in the main, on the whole, largely, by and large, to a large extent, predominantly, chiefly, principally, primarily.

maintain verb **1** *they wanted to maintain peace:* **preserve**, conserve, keep, retain, keep going, prolong, perpetuate, sustain, carry on, continue. **2** *the council maintains the roads:* **look after**, service, care for, take care of. **3** *the costs of maintaining a family:* **support**, provide for, keep, sustain. **4** *he maintains that he is innocent:* **insist**, declare, assert, protest,

affirm, profess, claim, contend, argue.
OPPOSITES break, discontinue, neglect, deny.

maintenance noun **1** *the maintenance of peace:* **preservation**, conservation, keeping, carrying on, prolongation, continuation. **2** *car maintenance:* **servicing**, service, repair(s), running repairs, care. **3** *the maintenance of his children:* **support**, keeping, upkeep, sustenance, nurture. **4** *absent fathers are forced to pay maintenance:* **financial support**, child support, alimony, upkeep.
OPPOSITES breakdown, discontinuation, neglect.

majestic adjective **stately**, dignified, distinguished, solemn, magnificent, grand, splendid, glorious, impressive, noble, awe-inspiring, monumental, palatial, imposing.
OPPOSITES modest, wretched.

majesty noun **stateliness**, dignity, solemnity, magnificence, pomp, grandeur, grandness, splendour, glory, impressiveness, nobility.
OPPOSITES modesty, wretchedness.

major adjective **1** *the major English poets:* **greatest**, best, finest, most important, chief, main, prime, principal, leading, foremost, outstanding, pre-eminent. **2** *a major factor:* **crucial**, vital, important, big, significant, considerable, weighty, serious, key, utmost, great, paramount, prime.
OPPOSITES minor, trivial.

majority noun **1** *the majority of cases:* **most**, bulk, mass, larger part/number, best/better part,

m

more than half, lion's share, (main) body, preponderance, predominance. **2** *a majority in the election:* (**winning**) **margin**, landslide, whitewash.
OPPOSITES minority.

make verb **1** *he makes models:* **construct**, build, assemble, put together, manufacture, produce, fabricate, create, form, fashion, model, improvise. **2** *she made me drink it:* **force**, compel, coerce, press, drive, pressurize, oblige, require; informal railroad, steamroller. **3** *don't make such a noise:* **cause**, create, produce, generate, effect. **4** *she made a little bow:* **perform**, execute, give, do, accomplish, achieve, bring off, carry out. **5** *they made him chairman:* **appoint**, designate, name, nominate, select, elect, vote in. **6** *he's made a lot of money:* **acquire**, obtain, gain, get, secure, win, earn. **7** *he made tea:* **prepare**, get ready, put together, concoct, cook, dish up, throw together, whip up, brew; informal fix.
OPPOSITES destroy, lose.
noun **brand**, marque, label.
■ **make for** contribute to, be conducive to, produce, promote, facilitate, foster.
■ **make it 1** *he never made it as a singer:* **succeed**, be a success, make good; informal make the grade, arrive. **2** *she's very ill—is she going to make it?* **survive**, pull through, get better, recover. ■ **make off** run away/off, take to one's heels, flee, take off, take flight, bolt; informal clear off/out, beat it, split, scram; Brit. informal scarper, do a runner; N. Amer. informal take a powder; Austral./NZ informal shoot through. ■ **make something out**

1 *I could just make out a figure in the distance:* see, discern, distinguish, detect, observe, recognize. **2** *he couldn't make out what she was saying:* understand, grasp, follow, work out, make sense of, interpret, decipher, make head or tail of, catch. **3** *she made out that he was violent:* allege, claim, suggest, imply, hint, insinuate, indicate, intimate. ■ **make up 1** *let's kiss and make up:* be friends again, bury the hatchet, make peace, forgive and forget, shake hands, settle one's differences. **2** *she tried to make up for what she'd said:* atone, make amends, compensate.
■ **make something up 1** *exports make up 42% of earnings:* comprise, form, compose, constitute, account for. **2** *he made up an excuse:* invent, fabricate, concoct, think up; informal cook up. ■ **make up for** *job satisfaction can make up for low pay:* offset, counterbalance, counteract, compensate for, cancel out.

maker noun **creator**, manufacturer, constructor, builder, producer.

makeshift adjective **temporary**, provisional, stopgap, standby, rough and ready, improvised, ad hoc.
OPPOSITES permanent.

make-up noun **1** *she used too much make-up:* **cosmetics**; informal warpaint, slap. **2** *the cellular make-up of plants:* **composition**, constitution, structure, configuration, arrangement. **3** *jealousy isn't part of his make-up:* **character**, nature, temperament, personality, mentality, persona.

makings plural noun **qualities**,

characteristics, ingredients, potential, capacity, capability, stuff.

male adjective **masculine,** manly, virile, macho.
OPPOSITES female.

malfunction verb *the computer has malfunctioned:* **crash,** go wrong, break down, fail, stop working; informal conk out, go kaput; Brit. informal play up, pack up.

malicious adjective **spiteful,** malevolent, vindictive, vengeful, resentful, malign, nasty, hurtful, cruel.
OPPOSITES benevolent.

maltreat verb **ill-treat,** mistreat, abuse, ill-use, mishandle, persecute, molest.

man noun **1** *a handsome man:* **male,** adult male, gentleman, youth; informal guy, fellow, gent; Brit. informal bloke, chap, lad; N. Amer. informal dude, hombre. **2** *all men are mortal:* **human being,** human, person, mortal, individual, soul. **3** *the evolution of man:* **the human race,** the human species, Homo sapiens, humankind, humanity, human beings, humans, people, mankind.
verb **1** *the office is manned from 9 to 5:* **staff,** crew, occupy, people. **2** *firemen manned the pumps:* **operate,** work, use.

manage verb **1** *she manages a staff of 80:* **be in charge of,** run, head, direct, control, preside over, lead, govern, rule, command, supervise, oversee, administer; informal head up. **2** *how much work can you manage this week?* **accomplish,** achieve, carry out, perform, undertake, deal with, cope with, get through. **3** *will you be able to manage without him?*

cope, get along/on, make do, do all right, carry on, survive, get by, muddle through/along, make ends meet; informal make out, hack it.

management noun **1** *he's responsible for the management of the firm:* **administration,** running, managing, organization, direction, leadership, control, governance, rule, command, supervision, guidance, operation. **2** *workers are in dispute with the management:* **managers,** employers, directors, board, directorate, executive, administration; informal bosses.
OPPOSITES employees, workforce.

manager noun **executive,** head, supervisor, principal, director, superintendent, foreman, forewoman, overseer, organizer, administrator; informal boss, chief, governor; Brit. informal gaffer, guv'nor.

mandate noun **1** *he sought a mandate for his policies:* **authority,** approval, ratification, endorsement, sanction, authorization. **2** *a mandate from the UN:* **instruction,** directive, decree, command, order, injunction.

mandatory adjective **obligatory,** compulsory, binding, required, requisite, necessary.
OPPOSITES optional.

mania noun **obsession,** compulsion, fixation, fetish, fascination, preoccupation, passion, enthusiasm, desire, urge, craving, craze, fad, rage; informal thing.

maniac noun **lunatic,** madman, madwoman, psychopath; informal loony, nutcase, nut, head case, headbanger, sicko; Brit. informal

m

nutter; N. Amer. informal screwball.

manifest verb display, show, exhibit, demonstrate, betray, present, reveal.
OPPOSITES hide.
adjective obvious, clear, plain, apparent, evident, patent, distinct, definite, blatant, overt, transparent, conspicuous, undisguised.
OPPOSITES secret.

manifestation noun 1 *the manifestation of anxiety:* display, demonstration, show, exhibition, presentation. 2 *manifestations of global warming:* sign, indication, evidence, symptom, testimony, proof, mark, reflection, example, instance.

manipulate verb 1 *he manipulated some levers:* operate, work, turn, pull, push, twist, slide. 2 *the government tried to manipulate the situation:* control, influence, use to one's advantage, exploit, twist.

mankind noun the human race, humankind, humanity, human beings, humans, Homo sapiens, people, man, men and women.

manly adjective virile, masculine, strong, all-male, red-blooded, muscular, muscly, strapping, well built, rugged, tough, powerful, brawny; informal hunky.
OPPOSITES effeminate.

man-made adjective artificial, synthetic, manufactured, imitation, ersatz, simulated, mock, fake.
OPPOSITES natural, real.

manner noun 1 *it was dealt with in a very efficient manner:* way, fashion, mode, means, method, system, style, approach, technique, procedure, process.

2 *her rather unfriendly manner:* behaviour, attitude, demeanour, air, aspect, bearing, conduct. 3 *the life and manners of Victorian society:* customs, habits, ways, practices, conventions, usages. 4 *you ought to teach him some manners:* etiquette, social graces, protocol, politeness, decorum, propriety, civility, Ps and Qs.

mannerism noun idiosyncrasy, quirk, oddity, foible, trait, peculiarity, habit, characteristic.

manoeuvre verb 1 *I manoeuvred the car into the space:* steer, guide, drive, negotiate, navigate, pilot, direct, manipulate, move, work. 2 *he manoeuvred things to suit himself:* manipulate, contrive, manage, engineer, fix, organize, arrange, orchestrate, choreograph, stage-manage; informal wangle.
noun 1 *a tricky parking manoeuvre:* operation, exercise, move, movement, action. 2 *diplomatic manoeuvres:* stratagem, tactic, gambit, ploy, trick, dodge, ruse, scheme, device, plot, machination, artifice, subterfuge, intrigue.

mansion noun country house, stately home, hall, manor house; informal palace, pile.
OPPOSITES hovel.

manual adjective 1 *manual work:* physical, labouring, blue-collar. 2 *a manual typewriter:* hand-operated, hand.
noun *a training manual:* handbook, instructions, guide, companion, ABC, guidebook; informal bible.

manufacture verb 1 *the company manufactures laser*

printers: **make**, produce, mass-produce, build, construct, assemble, put together, turn out. **2** *a story manufactured by the press:* **make up**, invent, fabricate, concoct, hatch, dream up, think up, contrive; informal cook up.
noun *the manufacture of aircraft engines:* **production**, making, manufacturing, mass production, construction, building, assembly.

manufacturer noun **maker**, producer, builder, constructor, industrialist.

many determiner & adjective **numerous**, a lot of, plenty of, countless, innumerable, scores of, untold, copious, abundant; informal lots of, umpteen, loads of, masses of, stacks of, heaps of, a slew of; Brit. informal a shedload of; Austral./NZ informal a swag of; literary **myriad**.
OPPOSITES few.

map noun **plan**, chart, A to Z, atlas.
verb *the region was mapped from the air:* **chart**, plot, draw, record.

mar verb **1** *an ugly bruise marred his features:* **spoil**, impair, disfigure, blemish, scar. **2** *the celebrations were marred by violence:* **spoil**, ruin, damage, wreck, taint, tarnish.
OPPOSITES enhance.

march verb **1** *the men marched past:* **stride**, walk, troop, step, pace, tread, slog, tramp, hike, trudge, parade, file. **2** *she marched in without even knocking:* **stride**, stalk, strut, flounce, storm, stomp, sweep.
noun **1** *a 20-mile march:* **walk**, trek, slog, route march, hike. **2** *police sought to ban the march:* **parade**, procession,

cortège, demonstration; informal demo. **3** *the march of technology:* **progress**, advance, development, evolution, passage.

margin noun **1** *the margin of the lake:* **edge**, side, verge, border, perimeter, brink, brim, rim, fringe, boundary, periphery, extremity. **2** *there's no margin for error:* **leeway**, latitude, scope, room, space, allowance. **3** *they won by a narrow margin:* **gap**, majority, amount.

marginal adjective **1** *the difference is marginal:* **slight**, small, tiny, minute, insignificant, minimal, negligible. **2** *a very marginal case:* **borderline**, disputable, questionable, doubtful.
OPPOSITES considerable, clear-cut.

marine adjective **1** *marine plants:* **seawater**, sea, saltwater, aquatic. **2** *a marine insurance company:* **maritime**, nautical, naval, seafaring, seagoing, ocean-going.

mariner noun **sailor**, seaman, seafarer.

marital adjective **matrimonial**, married, wedded, conjugal, nuptial, marriage, wedding.

maritime adjective **naval**, marine, nautical, seafaring, seagoing, sea, ocean-going.

mark noun **1** *a dirty mark:* **blemish**, streak, spot, fleck, blot, stain, smear, speck, smudge; informal splodge. **2** *a punctuation mark:* **symbol**, sign, character, accent, diacritic. **3** *the mark of a well-known bookseller:* **logo**, seal, stamp, symbol, emblem, device, insignia, badge, brand, trademark, monogram, hallmark. **4** *a mark of respect:*

m

sign, token, symbol, indication, symptom, proof. **5** *the mark of a civilized society:* **characteristic,** feature, trait, attribute, quality, hallmark, indicator. **6** *he got a good mark for maths:* **grade,** grading, rating, score, percentage.
verb **1** *be careful not to mark the paintwork:* **discolour,** stain, smear, smudge, streak, dirty; informal splodge. **2** *her possessions were clearly marked:* **label,** identify, flag, initial, name. **3** *I've marked the relevant passages:* **indicate,** label, tick, identify, highlight. **4** *a festival to mark the town's 200th anniversary:* **celebrate,** observe, recognize, acknowledge, keep, honour, commemorate, remember. **5** *these incidents marked a new phase:* **represent,** signify, indicate, herald. **6** *his style is marked by simplicity:* **characterize,** distinguish, identify, typify. **7** *I have a pile of essays to mark:* **assess,** evaluate, appraise, correct; N. Amer. grade.

marked adjective noticeable, pronounced, decided, distinct, striking, clear, unmistakable, obvious, conspicuous, notable.
OPPOSITES imperceptible.

market noun shopping centre, marketplace, mart, bazaar, souk, fair.
verb *the product was marketed worldwide:* **sell,** retail, merchandise, trade, advertise, promote.

marriage noun **1** *a proposal of marriage:* **matrimony,** wedlock. **2** *the marriage took place at St Margaret's:* **wedding,** wedding ceremony, nuptials, union, match. **3** *a marriage of jazz,*

pop, and gospel: **union,** fusion, mixture, mix, blend, amalgamation, combination, hybrid.
OPPOSITES divorce, separation.

marry verb **1** *the couple married last year:* **get/be married,** wed, be wed, become man and wife; informal tie the knot, walk down the aisle, get spliced, get hitched, say 'I do'. **2** *John wanted to marry her:* **wed;** informal make an honest woman of. **3** *the show marries poetry with art:* **join,** unite, combine, fuse, mix, blend, merge, amalgamate.
OPPOSITES divorce, separate.

marsh noun swamp, marshland, bog, swampland, morass, mire, quagmire, slough, fen.

marshal verb assemble, gather (together), collect, muster, call together, draw up, line up, array, organize, group, arrange, deploy, position, summon, round up.

martial adjective military, soldierly, army, warlike, fighting, militaristic; informal gung-ho.

marvel verb *she marvelled at their courage:* **be amazed,** be astonished, be in awe, wonder; informal be gobsmacked.
noun *a marvel of technology:* **wonder,** miracle, sensation, spectacle, phenomenon.

marvellous adjective excellent, splendid, wonderful, magnificent, superb, glorious, sublime, lovely, delightful; informal super, great, amazing, fantastic, terrific, tremendous; Brit. informal smashing, brilliant.
OPPOSITES commonplace, awful.

masculine adjective **1** *a masculine trait:* **male,** man's, men's, male-oriented. **2** *a*

m

powerfully masculine man:
virile, macho, manly, all-male,
muscular, muscly, strong,
strapping, well built, rugged,
robust, brawny, powerful, red-
blooded, vigorous; informal
hunky. **3** *a rather masculine
woman:* **mannish,** unfeminine,
unladylike; informal butch.
OPPOSITES feminine, effeminate.

mask noun *a mask of
respectability:* **pretence,**
semblance, veil, screen, front,
facade, veneer, disguise, cover,
cloak, camouflage.
verb *poplar trees masked the
factory:* **hide,** conceal, disguise,
cover up, obscure, screen,
cloak, camouflage.

mass noun **1** *a soggy mass of
fallen leaves:* **pile,** heap,
accumulation, mess, mat,
tangle. **2** *a mass of cyclists:*
crowd, horde, throng, host,
troop, army, herd, flock, swarm,
mob, pack, flood, multitude.
3 *the mass of the population:*
majority, greater part/number,
best/better part, major part,
bulk, main body.
adjective *mass hysteria:*
widespread, general, extensive,
large-scale, wholesale,
universal, indiscriminate.
verb *they began massing troops
in the region:* **assemble,** gather
together, collect, rally.

massacre noun *a cold-blooded
massacre:* **slaughter,** mass
killing, mass murder, mass
execution, ethnic cleansing,
genocide, holocaust,
annihilation, liquidation,
extermination, carnage,
butchery, bloodbath,
bloodletting.
verb *thousands were massacred:*
slaughter, butcher, murder,
kill, annihilate, exterminate,

execute, liquidate, eliminate,
mow down, cut to pieces.

massage noun **rub,** rub-down,
kneading.
verb **1** *he massaged her tired
muscles:* **rub,** knead,
manipulate, pummel, work.
2 *the statistics have been
massaged:* **alter,** tamper with,
manipulate, doctor, falsify,
juggle, fiddle with, tinker with,
distort, rig; informal cook, fiddle.

massive adjective **huge,**
enormous, vast, immense,
mighty, great, colossal,
tremendous, gigantic,
mammoth, monumental, giant,
mountainous; informal monster,
whopping, astronomical; Brit.
informal whacking, ginormous.
OPPOSITES tiny.

master noun **1** (historical) *he
acceded to his master's wishes:*
lord, ruler, sovereign, monarch.
2 *a chess master:* **expert,**
genius, maestro, virtuoso,
authority; informal ace, wizard,
whizz, hotshot; Brit. informal dab
hand; N. Amer. informal maven,
crackerjack. **3** *the geography
master:* **teacher,** schoolteacher,
schoolmaster, tutor, instructor.
4 *their spiritual master:* **guru,**
teacher, leader, guide, mentor.
OPPOSITES servant, amateur,
pupil.
verb **1** *I managed to master my
fears:* **overcome,** conquer, beat,
quell, suppress, control,
triumph over, subdue,
vanquish, subjugate, curb,
check, defeat, get the better of;
informal lick. **2** *it took ages to
master the technique:* **learn,**
become proficient in, pick up,
grasp, understand; informal get
the hang of.
OPPOSITES succumb to.
adjective *a master craftsman:*

m

expert, adept, proficient, skilled, skilful, deft, dexterous, adroit, practised, experienced, masterly, accomplished; informal crack, ace; N. Amer. informal crackerjack.
OPPOSITES amateur.

masterful adjective **commanding,** powerful, imposing, authoritative.
OPPOSITES weak.

masterly adjective **expert,** adept, skilful, skilled, adroit, proficient, deft, dexterous, accomplished, polished, consummate.
OPPOSITES inept.

mastermind noun *the mastermind behind the project:* **genius,** intellect, informal brain, brains.
verb *he masterminded the whole campaign:* **plan,** control, direct, be in charge of, run, conduct, organize, arrange, preside over, orchestrate, stage-manage, engineer, manage, coordinate.

masterpiece noun **magnum opus,** chef-d'œuvre, masterwork, pièce de résistance, tour de force, classic.

mastery noun **1** *her mastery of the language:* **proficiency,** ability, capability, knowledge, understanding, comprehension, command, grasp. **2** *man's mastery over nature:* **control,** domination, command, supremacy, superiority, power, authority, jurisdiction, dominion, sovereignty.

mat noun **1** *the hall mat:* **rug,** carpet, doormat. **2** *a thick mat of hair:* **mass,** tangle, mop, thatch, shock, mane.

match noun **1** *a football match:* **contest,** competition, game, tournament, tie, fixture, meet, friendly, (local) derby, bout, fight. **2** *the vase was an exact match of hers:* **lookalike,** double, twin, duplicate, mate, companion, counterpart, pair, replica, copy; informal spitting image, dead ringer.
verb **1** *the curtains matched the duvet cover:* **go with,** coordinate with, complement, suit, set off. **2** *did their statements match?* **correspond,** tally, agree, match up, coincide, square. **3** *no one can match him at chess:* **equal,** compare with, be in the same league as, touch, rival, compete with; informal hold a candle to.

matching adjective **corresponding,** equivalent, parallel, complementary, paired, twin, identical, alike.
OPPOSITES different, clashing.

mate noun **1** (Brit. informal) *he's gone out with his mates:* **friend,** companion, schoolmate, classmate, workmate; informal pal, chum; N. Amer. informal buddy, amigo, compadre. **2** *she's finally found her ideal mate:* **partner,** husband, wife, spouse, consort, lover; informal better half; Brit. informal other half. **3** *a plumber's mate:* **assistant,** helper, apprentice.
verb *pandas rarely mate in captivity:* **breed,** couple, pair.

material noun **1** *organic material:* **matter,** substance, stuff. **2** *the materials for a new building:* **constituent,** raw material, component, supplies. **3** *cleaning materials:* **things,** items, articles, stuff, supplies; Brit. informal gubbins. **4** *curtain material:* **fabric,** cloth, textiles. **5** *material for a magazine article:* **information,** data, facts, facts and figures,

statistics, evidence, details, particulars, background, notes; informal info.
adjective 1 *the material world:* **physical,** corporeal, tangible, mundane, worldly, earthly, secular, temporal, concrete, real. **2** *she was too fond of material pleasures:* **sensual,** physical, carnal, corporal, fleshly, bodily. **3** *information that could be material to the enquiry:* **relevant,** pertinent, applicable, germane, vital, essential, key.
OPPOSITES spiritual, aesthetic, irrelevant.

maternal adjective **motherly,** protective, caring, nurturing, maternalistic.

matted adjective **tangled,** knotted, tousled, dishevelled, uncombed, unkempt, ratty.

matter noun **1** *vegetable matter:* **material,** stuff, substance. **2** *a serious matter:* **affair,** business, situation, concern, incident, episode, subject, topic, issue, question, point at issue, case.
verb *it doesn't matter what you wear:* **be important,** make any difference, be of consequence, be relevant, count.

matter-of-fact adjective **unemotional,** practical, down-to-earth, sensible, realistic, unsentimental, pragmatic, businesslike, commonsensical, level-headed, hard-headed, no-nonsense, straightforward.

mature adjective **1** *a mature woman:* **adult,** grown, fully grown, in one's prime. **2** *he's very mature for his age:* **grown-up,** sensible, responsible, adult, level-headed. **3** *mature cheese:* **ripe,** mellow, rich, strong, flavoursome, full-bodied.

OPPOSITES immature.
verb **1** *kittens mature when they are about a year old:* **become fully grown,** come of age, reach adulthood, reach maturity. **2** *he's matured since he left home:* **grow up,** blossom. **3** *leave the cheese to mature:* **ripen,** mellow, age. **4** *their friendship didn't have time to mature:* **develop,** grow, evolve, bloom, blossom, flourish, thrive.

maturity noun **1** *her progress from childhood to maturity:* **adulthood,** coming of age, manhood, womanhood. **2** *he displayed a maturity beyond his years:* **responsibility,** sense, level-headedness.

maul verb **savage,** attack, claw, scratch, lacerate, mangle, tear.

maverick noun **individualist,** nonconformist, free spirit, original, eccentric, rebel, dissenter, dissident.
OPPOSITES conformist.

maximum adjective *the maximum amount:* **greatest,** highest, biggest, largest, top, most, utmost.
OPPOSITES minimum.
noun *production levels are near their maximum:* **upper limit,** limit, utmost, greatest, most, peak, height, ceiling, top.
OPPOSITES minimum.

maybe adverb **perhaps,** possibly, for all one knows; N. English happen; literary perchance.

mayhem noun **chaos,** havoc, bedlam, pandemonium, uproar, turmoil, a riot, anarchy; informal a madhouse.

maze noun **labyrinth,** network, warren, web, tangle, confusion, jungle.

meadow noun **field,** paddock, pasture; literary lea.

m

mean[1] verb **1** *flashing lights mean the road is blocked:* **signify,** denote, indicate, show, express, spell out, stand for, represent, symbolize, imply, suggest, intimate. **2** *she didn't mean to break it:* **intend,** aim, plan, have in mind, set out, want. **3** *this will mean war:* **entail,** involve, necessitate, lead to, result in, give rise to, bring about, cause, engender, produce.

mean[2] adjective **1** *he's too mean to leave a tip:* **miserly,** niggardly, parsimonious, penny-pinching, cheese-paring; informal tight-fisted, stingy, tight; N. Amer. informal cheap. **2** *a mean trick:* **unkind,** nasty, unpleasant, spiteful, malicious, unfair, shabby, despicable, contemptible, obnoxious, vile, loathsome, base, low; informal horrible, rotten.
OPPOSITES generous, kind.

meaning noun **1** *the meaning of his remark:* **significance,** sense, signification, import, gist, thrust, drift, implication, message. **2** *the word has several different meanings:* **definition,** sense, explanation, interpretation.

meaningful adjective **1** *a meaningful remark:* **significant,** relevant, important, telling. **2** *a meaningful relationship:* **sincere,** deep, serious, earnest, significant, important. **3** *a meaningful glance:* **expressive,** eloquent, pointed, pregnant, revealing, suggestive.
OPPOSITES inconsequential, insincere.

meaningless adjective **unintelligible,** incomprehensible, incoherent.

means plural noun **1** *the best*

means to achieve your goal: **method,** way, manner, course, procedure. **2** *she doesn't have the means to support herself:* **money,** resources, capital, income, finance, funds, cash, the wherewithal, assets, wealth, riches, affluence, fortune.

meanwhile, meantime adverb **1** *meanwhile, I'll stay here:* **for now,** for the moment, for the present, for the time being, in the meanwhile, in the meantime, in the interim. **2** *cook for a further half hour; meanwhile, make the stuffing:* **at the same time,** simultaneously, concurrently.

measure verb **quantify,** gauge, size, count, weigh, evaluate, assess, determine, calculate, compute.
noun **1** *cost-cutting measures:* **action,** act, course of action, deed, procedure, step, expedient, initiative, programme. **2** *the Senate passed the measure:* **statute,** act, bill, law. **3** *use a measure to check the size:* **ruler,** tape measure, gauge, meter, scale, level. **4** *sales are the measure of the company's success:* **yardstick,** test, standard, barometer, touchstone, benchmark.

measured adjective **1** *his measured tread:* **regular,** steady, even, rhythmic, unfaltering, slow, dignified, stately, sedate, leisurely, unhurried. **2** *his measured tones:* **thoughtful,** careful, considered, deliberate, restrained.

measurement noun
1 *measurement of the effect is difficult:* **quantification,** evaluation, assessment, calculation, computation. **2** *all measurements are in metric*

m

units: **size,** dimension, proportions, value, amount, quantity.

mechanical adjective **1** *a mechanical device:* **mechanized,** machine-driven, automated, automatic. **2** *a mechanical response:* **automatic,** knee-jerk, unthinking, instinctive, habitual, routine, unemotional, unfeeling.
OPPOSITES manual, thoughtful.

mechanism noun **1** *an electrical mechanism:* **apparatus,** machine, appliance, device, instrument, contraption, gadget; informal gizmo. **2** *the train's safety mechanism:* **machinery,** gear, system, equipment. **3** *a complaints mechanism:* **procedure,** process, system, method, means, medium, channel.

mediate verb **1** *Austria tried to mediate between the two sides:* **arbitrate,** conciliate, moderate, make peace, intervene, intercede, act as an intermediary, liaise. **2** *a tribunal was set up to mediate disputes:* **resolve,** settle, arbitrate in, umpire, reconcile, referee, mend, clear up; informal patch up.

mediation noun arbitration, conciliation, reconciliation, intervention, intercession, negotiation, shuttle diplomacy.

mediator noun arbitrator, arbiter, negotiator, conciliator, peacemaker, go-between, middleman, intermediary, moderator, honest broker, liaison officer, umpire, referee, adjudicator, judge.

medicine noun medication, drug, prescription, treatment, remedy, cure, nostrum, panacea, cure-all.

mediocre adjective average, ordinary, undistinguished, uninspired, indifferent, unexceptional, unexciting, unremarkable, run-of-the-mill, pedestrian, prosaic, lacklustre, forgettable, amateurish; informal so-so.
OPPOSITES excellent.

meditate verb contemplate, think, consider, ponder, muse, reflect, deliberate, ruminate, brood, mull over.

medium noun *a medium of expression:* **means,** method, avenue, channel, vehicle, organ, instrument, mechanism.
adjective *he is of medium build:* **average,** middling, medium-sized, middle-sized, moderate, normal, standard.

meet verb **1** *I met an old friend on the train:* **encounter,** come face to face with, run into, run across, come across/upon, chance on, happen on, stumble across; informal bump into. **2** *she first met Paul at a party:* **get to know,** be introduced to, make the acquaintance of. **3** *the committee met on Saturday:* **assemble,** gather, come together, get together, congregate, convene. **4** *the place where three roads meet:* **converge,** connect, touch, link up, intersect, cross, join.

meeting noun **1** *he stood up to address the meeting:* **gathering,** assembly, conference, congregation, convention, summit, rally; informal get-together. **2** *she demanded a meeting with the minister:* **consultation,** audience, interview. **3** *he intrigued her on their first meeting:* **encounter,** contact, appointment, assignation, rendezvous. **4** *the*

m

meeting of land and sea: **convergence,** coming together, confluence, conjunction, union, intersection, crossing. **5** *an athletics meeting:* **event,** tournament, meet, rally, competition, match, game, contest.

melancholy adjective *a melancholy mood:* **sad,** sorrowful, unhappy, gloomy, despondent, glum, miserable, morose; informal down in the dumps, blue.
OPPOSITES cheerful.
noun *a feeling of melancholy:* **sadness,** sorrow, unhappiness, depression, despondency, gloom, misery; informal the blues.
OPPOSITES happiness.

mellow adjective **1** *she loved the mellow tone of his voice:* **sweet-sounding,** dulcet, soft, smooth, warm, full, rich. **2** *a mellow wine:* **full-bodied,** mature, full-flavoured, rich, smooth. **3** *a mellow mood:* **genial,** affable, amiable, good-humoured, good-natured, pleasant, relaxed, easy-going.
OPPOSITES harsh, rough, irritable.

melody noun **tune,** air, strain, theme, song, refrain.

melt verb **1** *the snow was beginning to melt:* **liquefy,** thaw, defrost, soften, dissolve. **2** *his anger melted away:* **vanish,** disappear, fade, dissolve, evaporate.
OPPOSITES freeze, grow.

member noun **subscriber,** associate, supporter, fellow, representative.

memoir noun **1** *a touching memoir of her childhood:* **account,** history, record, chronicle, narrative, story, portrayal, depiction, portrait,

profile. **2** *he published his memoirs in 1955:* **autobiography,** life story, journal, diary.

memorable adjective **unforgettable,** indelible, catchy, haunting, momentous, significant, historic, notable, noteworthy, outstanding, arresting.

memorial noun **1** *the war memorial:* **monument,** cenotaph, mausoleum, statue, plaque, cairn, shrine. **2** *the festival is a memorial to his life's work:* **tribute,** testimonial, remembrance, memento.
adjective *a memorial service:* **commemorative,** remembrance.

memorize verb **commit to memory,** remember, learn (by heart), become word-perfect in.

memory noun **1** *happy memories of her childhood:* **recollection,** remembrance, reminiscence. **2** *the town built a statue in memory of him:* **commemoration,** remembrance, honour, tribute, recognition, respect.

menace noun **1** *an atmosphere full of menace:* **threat,** intimidation, malevolence, oppression. **2** *a menace to society:* **danger,** peril, risk, hazard, threat. **3** *that child is a menace:* **nuisance,** pest, troublemaker, mischief-maker; informal bad news.
verb **1** *the elephants are still menaced by poaching:* **threaten,** endanger, put at risk, jeopardize, imperil. **2** *a gang of skinheads menaced local residents:* **intimidate,** threaten, terrorize, frighten, scare, terrify.

menacing adjective

m

threatening, ominous, intimidating, frightening, forbidding, hostile, sinister, baleful.
OPPOSITES friendly.

mend verb **repair**, fix, restore, sew (up), stitch, darn, patch, renew, renovate, fill in; informal patch up.
OPPOSITES break.

mental adjective **1** *mental faculties:* **intellectual**, cerebral, rational, cognitive. **2** *a mental disorder:* **psychiatric**, psychological, behavioural.
OPPOSITES physical.

mentality noun **way of thinking**, mind set, mind, psychology, attitude, outlook, make-up.

mentally adverb **psychologically**, intellectually, in one's mind, in one's head, inwardly, internally.

mention verb **1** *don't mention the war:* **allude to**, refer to, touch on/upon, bring up, raise, broach. **2** *Jim mentioned that he'd met them before:* **state**, say, indicate, let someone know, disclose, divulge, reveal.
noun **reference**, allusion, comment, citation; informal namecheck, plug.

mentor noun **adviser**, counsellor, guide, guru, consultant, confidant(e), trainer, teacher, tutor, instructor.

menu noun **bill of fare**, tariff, carte du jour, set menu, table d'hôte.

merchandise noun **goods**, wares, stock, commodities, produce, products.

merchant noun **trader**, tradesman, dealer, wholesaler, broker, agent, seller, retailer, supplier, buyer, vendor, distributor.

mercy noun **pity**, compassion, leniency, clemency, charity, forgiveness, forbearance, kindness, sympathy, indulgence, tolerance, generosity, magnanimity.
OPPOSITES ruthlessness, cruelty.

merely adverb **only**, purely, solely, simply, just, but.

merge verb **1** *the company merged with a European firm:* **join (together)**, join forces, amalgamate, unite, affiliate, team up. **2** *the two organizations were merged:* **amalgamate**, bring together, join, consolidate, conflate, unite, unify, combine, incorporate, integrate. **3** *the two colours merged:* **mingle**, blend, fuse, mix, intermix, intermingle, coalesce.
OPPOSITES separate.

merger noun **amalgamation**, combination, union, fusion, coalition, affiliation, unification, incorporation, consolidation, link-up, alliance.
OPPOSITES split.

merit noun **1** *composers of outstanding merit:* **excellence**, quality, calibre, worth, value, distinction, eminence. **2** *the merits of the scheme:* **good point**, strong point, advantage, benefit, value, asset, plus.
OPPOSITES inferiority, fault, disadvantage.
verb *the accusation did not merit a response:* **deserve**, warrant, justify, earn, rate, be worthy of, be entitled to, have a right to, have a claim to/on.

merry adjective **cheerful**, cheery, in high spirits, sunny, smiling, light-hearted, lively, carefree, joyful, joyous, jolly, convivial, festive, gleeful, happy,

m

laughing; informal chirpy.
OPPOSITES miserable.

mesh noun *wire mesh:* **netting,**
net, grille, screen, lattice,
gauze.
verb **1** *one gear meshes with the
input gear:* **engage,** connect,
lock, interlock. **2** *our ideas just
do not mesh:* **harmonize,** fit
together, match, dovetail,
connect, interconnect.

mess noun **1** *please clear up the
mess:* **untidiness,** disorder,
disarray, clutter, muddle, chaos;
informal shambles; Brit. informal tip.
2 *I've got to get out of this mess:*
plight, predicament, tight spot,
tight corner, difficulty, trouble,
quandary, dilemma, problem,
muddle, mix-up; informal jam, fix,
pickle, hole.
■ **mess about/around** potter
about, fiddle about/around,
footle about/around, play
about/around, fool about/
around, fidget, toy, trifle,
tamper, tinker, interfere,
meddle, monkey (about/
around); Brit. informal muck
about/around. ■ **mess
something up** dirty, clutter up,
jumble, dishevel, rumple; N.
Amer. informal muss up.

message noun **1** *are there any
messages for me?*
communication, news, note,
memo, email, letter, missive,
report, bulletin, communiqué,
dispatch. **2** *the message of his
teaching:* **meaning,** sense,
import, idea, point, thrust,
moral, gist, essence,
implication.

messenger noun **courier,**
postman, runner, dispatch
rider, envoy, emissary, agent,
go-between.

messy adjective **1** *messy clothes:*
dirty, filthy, grubby, soiled,

grimy, mucky, muddy, stained,
smeared, smudged, dishevelled,
scruffy, unkempt, rumpled,
matted, tousled; informal yucky.
2 *a messy kitchen:* **untidy,**
disordered, in a muddle,
chaotic, confused, disorganized,
in disarray, cluttered, in a
jumble; informal like a bomb's hit
it; Brit. informal shambolic. **3** *a
messy legal battle:* **complex,**
tangled, confused, convoluted,
unpleasant, nasty, bitter,
acrimonious.
OPPOSITES clean, tidy.

metaphor noun **figure of
speech,** image, trope, analogy,
comparison, symbol.

method noun **1** *they use very
old-fashioned methods:*
procedure, technique, system,
practice, routine, modus
operandi, process, strategy,
tactic, approach. **2** *there's no
method in his approach:* **order,**
organization, structure, form,
system, logic, planning, design,
consistency.
OPPOSITES disorder.

methodical adjective **orderly,**
well ordered, well organized,
(well) planned, efficient,
businesslike, systematic,
structured, logical, disciplined,
consistent, scientific.

meticulous adjective **careful,**
conscientious, diligent,
scrupulous, punctilious,
painstaking, thorough,
studious, rigorous, detailed,
perfectionist, fastidious.
OPPOSITES careless.

midday noun **noon,** twelve
noon, high noon, noonday.
OPPOSITES midnight.

middle noun **1** **centre,** midpoint,
halfway point, dead centre,
hub, eye, heart, core, kernel.
2 *he had a towel round his*

middle: **midriff,** waist, belly, stomach; informal tummy.
OPPOSITES edge.
adjective *the middle point:* **central,** mid, mean, medium, median, midway, halfway.

might noun **strength,** force, power, vigour, energy, brawn.

mighty adjective **powerful,** forceful, hard, heavy, violent, vigorous, hefty.
OPPOSITES feeble.

migrant noun *economic migrants:* **immigrant,** emigrant, nomad, itinerant, traveller, transient, wanderer, drifter.
adjective *migrant workers:* **travelling,** mobile, wandering, drifting, nomadic, itinerant, transient.

migrate verb **1** *rural populations migrated to towns:* **relocate,** resettle, move (house), emigrate, go abroad. **2** *wildebeest migrate across the Serengeti:* **roam,** wander, drift, rove, travel.

mild adjective **1** *a mild tone of voice:* **gentle,** tender, soft, sympathetic, peaceable, quiet, reasonable. **2** *a mild punishment:* **lenient,** light. **3** *he was eyeing her with mild interest:* **slight,** faint, vague. **4** *mild weather:* **warm,** balmy, temperate, clement. **5** *a mild curry:* **bland,** light, insipid.
OPPOSITES harsh, strong, cold, severe, hot.

militant adjective *militant workers:* **hard-line,** extreme, active, extremist, committed, zealous, fanatical, radical.
noun *a confrontation with militants:* **activist,** extremist, radical, zealot.

military adjective **fighting,** service, army, armed, defence, martial.
OPPOSITES civilian.
noun *the military took power:* **(armed) forces,** services, militia, army, navy, air force, marines.

militate
■ **militate against** work against, hinder, discourage, be prejudicial to, be detrimental to.

milk verb *milking rich clients:* **exploit,** take advantage of, suck dry; informal bleed, squeeze, fleece.

mill noun *a steel mill:* **factory,** plant, works, workshop, shop, foundry.
verb *the wheat is milled into flour:* **grind,** pulverize, powder, granulate, pound, crush, press.
■ **mill around/about** wander, drift, swarm, crowd, pack, fill.

mimic verb **imitate,** copy, impersonate, do an impression of, ape, caricature, parody; informal send up, take off.
noun **impersonator,** impressionist; informal copycat.

mince verb **grind,** chop up, cut up, dice, crumble; N. Amer. hash.

mind noun **1** *a good teacher must stretch pupils' minds:* **brain,** intelligence, intellect, brains, brainpower, wits, understanding, reasoning, judgement, sense, head; informal grey matter; N. Amer. informal smarts. **2** *he kept his mind on the job:* **attention,** thoughts, concentration. **3** *the tragedy affected her mind:* **sanity,** mental faculties, senses, wits, reason, reasoning, judgement. **4** *a great mind:* **intellect,** thinker, brain, scholar.
verb **1** *do you mind if I smoke?* **object,** care, be bothered, be

annoyed, be upset, take offence, disapprove, look askance; informal give/care a damn. **2** *mind the step!* **be careful of,** watch out for, look out for, beware of. **3** *mind you wipe your feet:* **make sure,** see, remember to, don't forget to. **4** *her husband was minding the baby:* **look after,** take care of, keep an eye on, attend to, care for.

mine noun **1** *a coal mine:* **pit,** colliery, excavation, quarry. **2** *a mine of information:* **store,** storehouse, reservoir, repository, gold mine, treasure house, treasury.
verb *the iron ore was mined from shallow pits:* **quarry,** excavate, dig, extract.

mingle verb **1** *fact and fiction are mingled:* **mix,** blend, intermingle, intermix, interweave, interlace, combine, merge, fuse, unite, join, amalgamate. **2** *guests mingled in the marquee:* **socialize,** circulate, associate, fraternize, get together; informal hobnob.
OPPOSITES separate.

miniature adjective **small,** mini, little, small-scale, baby, toy, pocket, diminutive; Scottish wee; N. Amer. vest-pocket.
OPPOSITES giant.

minimal adjective **very little/small,** minimum, the least (possible), nominal, token, negligible.
OPPOSITES maximum.

minimize verb **1** *the aim is to minimize costs:* **keep down,** keep to a minimum, reduce, decrease, cut (down), lessen, curtail, prune; informal slash. **2** *we should not minimize his contribution:* **belittle,** make light of, play down, underrate,

downplay, undervalue.
OPPOSITES maximize, exaggerate.

minimum noun *costs will be kept to the minimum:* **lowest level,** lower limit, rock bottom, least, lowest, slightest.
OPPOSITES maximum.
adjective *with the minimum effort:* **minimal,** least, smallest, least possible, slightest, lowest, minutest.
OPPOSITES maximum.

minister noun **1** *a government minister:* **member of the government,** member of the cabinet, secretary of state. **2** *a minister of religion:* **clergyman,** clergywoman, cleric, pastor, vicar, rector, priest, parson, curate; informal reverend, padre.
verb *doctors were ministering to the injured:* **tend,** care for, take care of, look after, nurse, treat, attend to, see to, help.

ministry noun **1** *the ministry for foreign affairs:* **department,** bureau, agency, office. **2** *he's training for the ministry:* **the priesthood,** holy orders, the cloth, the church.

minor adjective **1** *a minor problem:* **slight,** small, unimportant, insignificant, inconsequential, negligible, trivial, trifling, paltry, petty; N. Amer. nickel-and-dime; informal piffling. **2** *a minor poet:* **little known,** unknown, lesser, unimportant, insignificant, obscure; N. Amer. minor-league; informal small-time; N. Amer. informal two-bit.
OPPOSITES major, important.
noun *the accused was a minor:* **child,** infant, youth, adolescent, teenager, boy, girl; informal kid.
OPPOSITES adult.

mint verb **coin,** stamp, strike, cast, manufacture.

minute | mislead

minute¹ noun **1** *it'll only take a minute:* **moment**, short time, little while, second, instant; informal sec, jiffy; Brit. informal tick, mo, two ticks. **2** *at that minute, Tony walked in:* **point (in time)**, moment, instant, second, juncture. **3** *their objection was noted in the minutes:* **record(s)**, proceedings, log, notes, transcript, summary.

minute² adjective **1** *minute particles:* **tiny**, minuscule, microscopic, miniature; Scottish wee; informal teeny, teeny-weeny; Brit. informal titchy, tiddly. **2** *a minute chance of success:* **negligible**, slight, infinitesimal, minimal. **3** *in minute detail:* **exhaustive**, painstaking, meticulous, rigorous, thorough. OPPOSITES huge.

miracle noun **wonder**, marvel, sensation, phenomenon.

miraculous adjective **amazing**, astounding, remarkable, extraordinary, incredible, unbelievable, sensational, phenomenal.

mirror noun **1** *a quick look in the mirror:* **looking glass**; Brit. glass. **2** *the Frenchman's life was a mirror of his own:* **reflection**, replica, copy, match, parallel. verb *pop music mirrored the mood of desperation:* **reflect**, match, reproduce, imitate, copy, mimic, echo, parallel.

misbehave verb **behave badly**, be naughty, be disobedient, get up to mischief, get up to no good, be rude, informal carry on, act up.

miscellaneous adjective **various**, varied, different, assorted, mixed, sundry, diverse, disparate.

mischief noun **1** *the boys are always getting up to mischief:* **naughtiness**, bad behaviour, misbehaviour, misconduct, disobedience. **2** *the mischief in her eyes:* **impishness**, roguishness, glint, twinkle.

miser noun **penny-pincher**, Scrooge; informal skinflint, cheapskate; N. Amer. informal tightwad. OPPOSITES spendthrift.

miserable adjective **1** *I'm too miserable to eat:* **unhappy**, sad, sorrowful, dejected, depressed, down, despondent, disconsolate, wretched, glum, forlorn; informal blue, down in the dumps. **2** *their miserable surroundings:* **dreary**, dismal, gloomy, drab, wretched, depressing, grim, cheerless, bleak, desolate. OPPOSITES cheerful, lovely.

misery noun **unhappiness**, distress, wretchedness, suffering, anguish, anxiety, angst, torment, pain, grief, heartache, heartbreak, despair, despondency, dejection, depression, gloom, sorrow; informal the blues. OPPOSITES contentment, pleasure.

misfortune noun **problem**, difficulty, setback, trouble, adversity, (stroke of) bad luck, misadventure, mishap, blow, failure, accident, disaster.

misguided adjective **unwise**, ill-advised, ill-judged, ill-considered, injudicious, imprudent, unsound, mistaken, misplaced. OPPOSITES wise.

mislay verb **lose**, misplace, be unable to find. OPPOSITES find.

mislead verb **deceive**, delude, take in, lie to, fool, hoodwink, misinform; informal lead up the

m

garden path; N. Amer. informal give someone a bum steer.

misleading adjective **deceptive,** confusing, deceiving, equivocal, false.
OPPOSITES clear, honest, straightforward.

miss verb **1** *the shot missed her by inches:* **go wide of,** fall short of, pass, overshoot. **2** *I left early to miss the traffic:* **avoid,** beat, evade, escape, dodge, sidestep, elude, circumvent, bypass. **3** *she missed him when he was away:* **pine for,** yearn for, ache for, long for. **4** *she never missed a meeting:* **fail to attend,** be absent from, play truant from, cut, skip, omit; Brit. informal skive off.
OPPOSITES hit, catch, attend.
noun *one hit and three misses:* **failure,** omission, slip, error, mistake.
■ **miss someone/something out** leave out, exclude, miss (off), fail to mention, pass over, skip, omit, ignore.

missing adjective **1** *his wallet is missing:* **lost,** mislaid, misplaced, absent, gone (astray), unaccounted for. **2** *passion was missing from her life:* **absent,** lacking, gone, wanting.
OPPOSITES present.

mission noun **1** *a mercy mission to Romania:* **assignment,** commission, expedition, journey, trip, undertaking, operation, project. **2** *her mission in life:* **vocation,** calling, goal, aim, quest, purpose, function, task, job, labour, work, duty.

missionary noun **evangelist,** apostle, proselytizer, preacher.

mist noun **haze,** fog, smog, murk, cloud, vapour, steam, spray, condensation.

mistake noun *it was all a mistake:* **error,** fault, inaccuracy, omission, slip, blunder, miscalculation, misunderstanding, oversight, misinterpretation, gaffe, faux pas; informal slip-up, boo-boo, howler; Brit. informal boob, clanger; N. Amer. informal goof.
verb **1** *men are apt to mistake their own feelings:* **misunderstand,** misinterpret, get wrong, misconstrue, misread. **2** *children often mistake pills for sweets:* **confuse with,** mix up with, take for.
■ **make a mistake** make an error etc., go wrong, err, blunder, miscalculate.

mistaken adjective **1** *such a mistaken view:* **inaccurate,** wrong, erroneous, incorrect, off beam, false, fallacious, unfounded, misguided. **2** *you are mistaken there:* **misinformed,** wrong, in error, under a misapprehension, barking up the wrong tree.
OPPOSITES correct.

mistimed adjective **ill-timed,** badly timed, inopportune, inappropriate, untimely.
OPPOSITES opportune.

mistrust verb **be suspicious of,** be sceptical of, be wary of, be chary of, distrust, have doubts about, have misgivings about, have reservations about, suspect.

misunderstand verb **misapprehend,** misinterpret, misconstrue, misconceive, mistake, misread, be mistaken, get the wrong idea; informal get (hold of) the wrong end of the stick.

misunderstanding noun **1** *a*

misunderstanding of juvenile crime: **misinterpretation,** misreading, misapprehension, misconception, false impression. **2** we have had some misunderstandings: **disagreement,** difference (of opinion), dispute, falling-out, quarrel, argument, clash.

misuse verb misusing public funds: **embezzle,** misappropriate, abuse, waste, squander.
noun a misuse of company assets: **embezzlement,** fraud, squandering, waste.

mix verb **1** mix all the ingredients together: **blend,** mingle, combine, jumble, fuse, unite, join, amalgamate, incorporate, meld, homogenize; technical admix; literary commingle. **2** she mixes with all sorts: **associate,** socialize, keep company, consort, mingle, circulate; Brit. rub shoulders; N. Amer. rub elbows; informal hang out/around, hobnob.
OPPOSITES separate.
noun a mix of ancient and modern: **mixture,** blend, combination, compound, fusion, union, amalgamation, medley, selection, assortment, variety.

mixed adjective **1** a mixed collection: **assorted,** varied, variegated, miscellaneous, disparate, diverse, diversified, motley, sundry, jumbled, heterogeneous. **2** mixed reactions: **ambivalent,** equivocal, contradictory, conflicting, confused, muddled.
OPPOSITES homogeneous.

mixture noun **1** the pudding mixture: **blend,** mix, brew, combination, concoction, composition, compound, alloy, amalgam. **2** a strange mixture of people: **assortment,** miscellany, medley, blend, variety, mixed bag, mix, diversity, collection, selection, hotchpotch, ragbag; N. Amer. hodgepodge.

mix-up noun **confusion,** muddle, misunderstanding, mistake, error.

moan verb **1** he moaned in agony: **groan,** wail, whimper, sob, cry. **2** (informal) you're always moaning about the weather: **complain,** grouse, grumble, whine, carp; informal gripe, grouch, bellyache, bitch, beef, whinge.

mob noun troops dispersed the mob: **crowd,** horde, multitude, rabble, mass, throng, gathering, assembly.
verb the Chancellor was mobbed: **surround,** crowd round, besiege, jostle.

mobile adjective **1** both patients are mobile: **able to move (around),** able to walk, walking; informal up and about. **2** a mobile library: **travelling,** transportable, portable, movable, itinerant, peripatetic.
OPPOSITES immobilized, fixed.

mobilize verb **1** the government mobilized the troops: **marshal,** deploy, muster, rally, call up, assemble, mass, organize, prepare. **2** mobilizing support for the party: **generate,** arouse, awaken, excite, stimulate, stir up, encourage, inspire, whip up.

mock verb the local children mocked the old people: **ridicule,** jeer at, sneer at, deride, make fun of, laugh at, scoff at, tease, taunt; informal take the mickey out of; N. Amer. informal goof on, rag on; Austral./NZ informal chiack, sling off at.
adjective mock leather:

m

imitation, artificial, man-made, simulated, synthetic, ersatz, fake, reproduction, false, counterfeit; informal pretend.
OPPOSITES genuine.

mocking adjective **sneering,** derisive, contemptuous, scornful, sardonic, ironic, sarcastic.

mode noun **1** *an informal mode of policing:* **manner,** way, means, method, system, style, approach. **2** *the camera is in manual mode:* **function,** position, operation, setting, option.

model noun **1** *a working model:* **replica,** copy, representation, mock-up, dummy, imitation, duplicate, reproduction, facsimile. **2** *the American model of airline deregulation:* **prototype,** archetype, type, version, mould, template, framework, pattern, design, blueprint. **3** *a top model:* **fashion model,** supermodel, mannequin; informal clothes horse.
adjective **1** *model trains:* **replica,** toy, miniature, dummy, imitation, duplicate, reproduction, facsimile. **2** *a model teacher:* **ideal,** perfect, exemplary, classic, flawless, faultless.

moderate adjective **1** *moderate success:* **average,** modest, medium, middling, tolerable, passable, adequate, fair; informal OK, so-so, bog-standard, fair-to-middling. **2** *moderate prices:* **reasonable,** acceptable, affordable, inexpensive, fair, modest. **3** *moderate views:* **middle-of-the-road,** non-extremist, liberal, pragmatic.
OPPOSITES great, unreasonable, extreme.

verb **1** *the wind has moderated:* **die down,** abate, let up, calm down, lessen, decrease, diminish, recede, weaken, subside. **2** *you can help her moderate her temper:* **curb,** control, check, temper, restrain, subdue, tame, lessen, decrease, lower, reduce, diminish, alleviate, allay, appease, ease, soothe, calm, tone down.
OPPOSITES increase.

moderately adverb **somewhat,** quite, fairly, reasonably, comparatively, relatively, to some extent, tolerably, adequately; informal pretty.

modern adjective **1** *modern times:* **present-day,** contemporary, present, current, twenty-first-century, latter-day, recent. **2** *her clothes are very modern:* **fashionable,** up to date, trendsetting, stylish, chic, à la mode, the latest, new, newest, newfangled, advanced; informal trendy, cool, in.
OPPOSITES past, old-fashioned.

modest adjective **1** *she was modest about her poetry:* **humble,** self-deprecating, self-effacing, unassuming, shy, diffident, reserved, coy. **2** *modest success:* **moderate,** fair, limited, tolerable, passable, adequate, satisfactory, acceptable, unexceptional. **3** *a modest house:* **small,** ordinary, simple, plain, humble, inexpensive, unostentatious, unpretentious. **4** *her modest dress:* **demure,** decent, seemly, decorous, proper.
OPPOSITES conceited, great, grand, indecent.

modesty noun **humility,** self-effacement, shyness, bashfulness, self-consciousness, reserve.

modification noun change, adjustment, alteration, adaptation, refinement, revision, amendment; informal tweak.

modify verb **1** *their economic policy has been modified:* change, alter, adjust, adapt, amend, revise, refine; informal tweak. **2** *he modified his more extreme views:* moderate, temper, soften, tone down, qualify.

moist adjective **1** *the air was moist:* damp, steamy, humid, muggy, clammy, dank, wet, soggy, sweaty, sticky. **2** *a moist fruitcake:* succulent, juicy, soft, tender.
OPPOSITES dry.

moisten verb dampen, wet, damp, water, humidify.

moisture noun wetness, wet, water, liquid, condensation, steam, vapour, dampness, damp, humidity.

moment noun **1** *he thought for a moment:* little while, short time, bit, minute, instant, (split) second; informal sec, jiffy; Brit. informal tick, mo, two ticks. **2** *just at that moment:* point (in time), stage, juncture, instant, time, hour, second, minute, day.

momentary adjective brief, short, short-lived, fleeting, passing.
OPPOSITES lengthy.

momentous adjective important, significant, historic, critical, crucial, decisive, pivotal, consequential, far-reaching; informal earth-shattering.
OPPOSITES insignificant.

momentum noun impetus, energy, force, power, strength, thrust, speed, velocity.

monarch noun sovereign, ruler,
Crown, crowned head, potentate, king, queen, emperor, empress, prince, princess.

monastery noun monastic community, friary, abbey, priory, cloister.

monetary adjective financial, fiscal, pecuniary, money, cash, capital, economic, budgetary.

money noun cash, hard cash, means, wherewithal, funds, capital, finances, notes, coins, change, currency; informal dough, bread, loot; Brit. informal dosh, brass, lolly; N. Amer. informal dinero, mazuma.

monitor noun **1** *monitors covered all entrances:* detector, scanner, recorder, sensor, security camera, CCTV. **2** *UN monitors:* observer, watchdog, overseer, supervisor, scrutineer. **3** *a computer monitor:* screen, display, VDU.
verb *his movements were closely monitored:* observe, watch, track, keep an eye on, keep under surveillance, record, note, oversee; informal keep tabs on.

monster noun **1** *legendary sea monsters:* giant, mammoth, demon, dragon, colossus, leviathan, creature. **2** *her husband is a monster:* fiend, animal, beast, devil, demon, barbarian, savage, brute; informal swine.

monstrous adjective **1** *a monstrous creature:* grotesque, hideous, ugly, ghastly, gruesome, horrible, horrific, horrifying, grisly, disgusting, repulsive, dreadful, frightening, terrible, terrifying. **2** *monstrous acts of violence:* appalling, wicked, abominable, terrible, horrible, dreadful, vile,

m

outrageous, unspeakable, despicable, vicious, savage, barbaric, inhuman.
OPPOSITES lovely, kind.

monument noun memorial, statue, pillar, cairn, column, obelisk, cross, cenotaph, tomb, mausoleum, shrine.

monumental adjective **1** *a monumental task:* huge, enormous, gigantic, massive, colossal, mammoth, immense, tremendous, mighty, stupendous. **2** *his monumental career:* significant, important, majestic, memorable, noteworthy, momentous, defining, grand, awe-inspiring, heroic, epic.
OPPOSITES tiny, insignificant.

mood noun **1** *she's in a good mood:* frame of mind, state of mind, humour, temper. **2** *he's obviously in a mood:* bad mood, temper, bad temper, sulk, low spirits, the doldrums, the blues; Brit. informal paddy. **3** *the mood of the film:* atmosphere, feeling, spirit, ambience, aura, character, flavour, feel, tone.

moody adjective temperamental, emotional, volatile, capricious, sullen, sulky, morose, glum, depressed, dejected, despondent, doleful.
OPPOSITES cheerful.

moon noun satellite.
verb **1** *stop mooning about:* waste time, loaf, idle, mope; Brit. informal mooch; N. Amer. informal lollygag. **2** *he's mooning over her photograph:* mope, pine, brood, daydream.

moor[1] verb *a boat was moored to the quay:* tie (up), secure, make fast, berth, dock.

moor[2] noun *a walk on the moor:* upland, heath, moorland; Brit. fell, wold.

mop noun *her tousled mop of hair:* shock, mane, tangle, mass.
verb *a man was mopping the floor:* wash, clean, wipe, sponge.

moral adjective **1** *moral issues:* ethical. **2** *a very moral man:* good, virtuous, righteous, upright, upstanding, high-minded, principled, honourable, honest, just, noble. **3** *moral support:* psychological, emotional, mental.
OPPOSITES dishonourable, practical.
noun **1** *the moral of the story:* lesson, message, meaning, significance, import, point, teaching. **2** (morals) moral code, code of ethics, values, principles, standards, (sense of) morality, scruples.

morale noun confidence, self-confidence, self-esteem, spirit(s), team spirit, motivation.

morality noun **1** *the morality of nuclear weapons:* ethics, rights and wrongs, whys and wherefores. **2** *a sharp decline in morality:* virtue, good behaviour, righteousness, uprightness, morals, principles, honesty, integrity, propriety, honour, decency. **3** *Christian morality:* morals, standards, ethics, principles, mores.

morbid adjective ghoulish, macabre, unhealthy, gruesome, unwholesome; informal sick.
OPPOSITES wholesome.

more determiner *some more clothes:* extra, further, added, additional, supplementary, increased, new.
OPPOSITES less, fewer.

moreover adverb besides, furthermore, what's more, in addition, also, as well, too, to boot, additionally, on top of that, into the bargain.

morning noun **1** *I've got a meeting this morning:* **before lunch(time),** a.m.; literary **morn;** Nautical & N. Amer. **forenoon. 2** *morning is on its way:* **dawn,** daybreak, sunrise, first light; N. Amer. **sunup.**

mortal adjective **1** *all men are mortal:* **perishable,** physical, bodily, corporeal, human, fleshly, earthly, impermanent, transient, ephemeral. **2** *a mortal blow:* **deadly,** fatal, lethal, death-dealing, murderous, terminal.
OPPOSITES eternal.
noun *we are mere mortals:* **human (being),** person, man, woman, earthling.

mortuary noun **morgue,** funeral parlour; Brit. **chapel of rest.**

mostly adverb **1** *the other passengers were mostly businessmen:* **mainly,** for the most part, on the whole, in the main, largely, chiefly, predominantly, principally, primarily. **2** *I mostly wear jeans:* **usually,** generally, in general, as a rule, ordinarily, normally, customarily, typically, most of the time, almost always.

mother noun informal **ma;** Brit. informal **mum, mummy;** N. Amer. informal **mom, mommy;** Brit. informal, dated **mater.**
verb *her colleagues mothered her:* **look after,** care for, take care of, nurse, protect, tend, raise, rear, pamper, coddle, cosset, fuss over.
OPPOSITES neglect.

motherly adjective **maternal,** maternalistic, protective, caring, loving, affectionate, nurturing.

motif noun **1** *a colourful tulip motif:* **design,** pattern, decoration, figure, shape, device, emblem. **2** *a recurring motif in Pinter's work:* **theme,** idea, concept, subject, topic, leitmotif.

motion noun **1** *a planet's motion around the sun:* **movement,** locomotion, progress, passage, transit, course, travel, orbit. **2** *a motion of the hand:* **gesture,** movement, signal, sign, indication, wave, nod, gesticulation. **3** *the motion was passed:* **proposal,** proposition, recommendation.
verb *he motioned her to sit down:* **gesture,** signal, direct, indicate, wave, beckon, nod.

motivate verb **1** *motivated by greed:* **prompt,** drive, move, inspire, stimulate, influence, activate, impel, propel, spur (on). **2** *the teacher must motivate the child:* **inspire,** stimulate, encourage, spur (on), excite, incentivize, fire (with enthusiasm).

motivation noun **motive,** motivating force, incentive, stimulus, stimulation, inspiration, inducement, incitement, spur.

motive noun **reason,** motivation, motivating force, rationale, grounds, cause, basis.

motto noun **slogan,** maxim, saying, proverb, aphorism, adage, saw, axiom, formula, catchphrase.

mould noun **1** *a clay mould:* **cast,** die, form, matrix, shape, template, pattern, frame. **2** *an actress in the traditional Hollywood mould:* **pattern,** form, type, style, tradition, school.
verb **1** *a figure moulded from clay:* **shape,** form, fashion,

m

model, work, construct, make, create, sculpt, cast. **2** *the ideas that mould US policy:* **determine,** direct, control, guide, influence, shape, form, fashion, make.

mound noun **1** *a mound of books:* **heap,** pile, stack, mountain. **2** *high on the mound:* **hillock,** hill, knoll, rise, hummock, hump; Scottish brae.

mount verb **1** *he mounted the stairs:* **go up,** ascend, climb (up), scale. **2** *they mounted their horses:* **get on to,** bestride, climb on to, leap on to, hop on to. **3** *the museum is mounting an exhibition:* **put on,** present, install, organize, stage, set up, prepare, launch, set in motion. **4** *their losses mounted rapidly:* **increase,** grow, rise, escalate, soar, spiral, shoot up, rocket, climb, accumulate, build up, multiply.
OPPOSITES descend, dismount, fall.
noun *a picture mount:* **setting,** backing, support, mounting, frame, stand.

mountain noun **1** *climb a mountain:* **peak,** summit; (**mountains**) range, massif, sierra; Scottish ben. **2** *a mountain of work:* **lot;** informal heap, pile, stack, slew, lots, loads, tons, masses.

mourn verb **1** *Isobel mourned her husband:* **grieve for,** sorrow over, lament for, weep for. **2** *he mourned the loss of the beautiful buildings:* **deplore,** bewail, bemoan, rue, regret.

mourning noun **grief,** grieving, sorrowing, lamentation.

mouth noun **1** **lips,** jaws, muzzle; informal trap, chops, kisser; Brit. informal gob; N. Amer. informal puss, bazoo. **2** *the mouth*

of the cave: **entrance,** opening. **3** *the mouth of the river:* **estuary,** delta, firth, outlet, outfall.

move verb **1** *she moved to the door | don't move!:* **go,** walk, step, proceed, progress, advance, budge, stir, shift, change position. **2** *he moved the chair closer to the fire:* **carry,** transfer, shift, push, pull, lift, slide. **3** *things were moving too fast:* **go,** progress, advance, develop, evolve, change, happen. **4** *he urged the council to move quickly:* **act,** take steps, do something, take measures; informal get moving. **5** *she's moved to Cambridge:* **relocate,** move house, move away/out, change address, go (away), decamp. **6** *I was deeply moved by the story:* **affect,** touch, impress, shake, upset, disturb. **7** *she was moved to find out more about it:* **inspire,** prompt, stimulate, motivate, provoke, influence, rouse, induce, incite. **8** *I move that we adjourn:* **propose,** submit, suggest, advocate, recommend, urge.
noun **1** *his eyes followed her every move:* **movement,** motion, action, gesture. **2** *his recent move to London:* **relocation,** change of house/ address, transfer, posting. **3** *the latest move in the war against drugs:* **initiative,** step, action, measure, manoeuvre, tactic, stratagem. **4** *it's your move:* **turn,** go; Scottish shot.

movement noun **1** *Rachel made a sudden movement:* **motion,** move, gesture, sign, signal, action. **2** *the movement of supplies:* **transportation,** shifting, conveyance, moving, transfer. **3** *a political movement:* **group,** party, faction, wing, lobby, camp. **4** *a movement to declare war on poverty:* **campaign,** crusade, drive, push, initiative.

movie noun **film,** picture, feature film; informal flick.

moving adjective **1 in motion,** operating, operational, working, on the move, active, movable, mobile. **2** *a moving book:* **affecting,** touching, poignant, heart-warming, heart-rending, emotional, inspiring, inspirational, stimulating, stirring.
OPPOSITES stationary, fixed.

mow verb **cut,** trim, crop, clip, shear.

much determiner *is there much food?* **a lot of,** a great/good deal of, a great/large amount of, plenty of, ample, abundant, plentiful; informal lots of, loads of, heaps of, masses of, tons of, stacks of.
OPPOSITES little.
adverb **1** *it didn't hurt much:* **greatly,** a great deal, a lot, considerably, appreciably.
2 *does he come here much?* **often,** frequently, many times, regularly, habitually, routinely, usually, normally, commonly; informal a lot.
pronoun *he did much for our team:* **a lot,** a great/good deal, plenty; informal lots, loads, heaps, masses, tons.

muck noun **1** *I'll just clean off the muck:* **dirt,** grime, filth, mud, mess; Brit. informal gunge; N. Amer. informal guck. **2** *spreading muck on the fields:* **dung,** manure, excrement, droppings.

mud noun **dirt,** sludge, ooze, silt, clay, mire, soil.

muddle verb **1** *the papers have got muddled up:* **confuse,** mix up, jumble (up), disarrange, disorganize, disorder, mess up. **2** *it would only muddle you:* **bewilder,** confuse, bemuse, perplex, puzzle, baffle, nonplus, mystify.
noun **mess,** confusion, jumble, tangle, chaos, disorder, disarray, disorganization.

muddy adjective **1** *muddy ground:* **marshy,** boggy, swampy, waterlogged, squelchy, squishy, mucky, slimy, wet, soft. **2** *muddy boots:* **dirty,** filthy, mucky, grimy, soiled. **3** *muddy water:* **murky,** cloudy, turbid.
OPPOSITES clean, clear.

muffle verb **1** *everyone was muffled up in coats:* **wrap (up),** swathe, enfold, envelop, cloak. **2** *the sound of their footsteps was muffled:* **deaden,** dull, dampen, mute, soften, quieten, mask, stifle, smother.

mug noun *a china mug:* **beaker,** cup, tankard, glass, stein.
verb (informal) *he was mugged by youths:* **assault,** attack, set upon, beat up, rob; informal jump.

multiple adjective **numerous,** many, various, different, diverse, several, manifold.
OPPOSITES single.

multiply verb **increase,** grow, accumulate, proliferate, mount up, mushroom, snowball.
OPPOSITES decrease.

mumble verb **mutter,** murmur, talk under one's breath.

mundane adjective **humdrum,** dull, boring, tedious, monotonous, tiresome, unexciting, uninteresting, uneventful, unremarkable, routine, ordinary.
OPPOSITES extraordinary.

municipal adjective **civic,** civil, metropolitan, urban, city, town, borough, council.
OPPOSITES private, rural.

m

murder noun *a brutal murder:* **killing,** homicide, assassination, extermination, execution, slaughter, butchery, massacre, manslaughter; literary slaying.
verb *someone tried to murder him:* **kill,** put/do to death, assassinate, execute, butcher, slaughter, massacre, wipe out; informal **bump off;** N. Amer. informal ice, waste; literary slay.

murderer, murderess noun **killer,** assassin, serial killer, butcher; informal **hit man,** hired gun.

murderous adjective **homicidal,** brutal, violent, savage, ferocious, fierce, vicious, bloodthirsty, barbarous, barbaric, fatal, lethal, deadly.

murky adjective **1** *a murky winter afternoon:* **dark,** gloomy, grey, leaden, dull, dim, overcast, cloudy, clouded, sunless, dismal, dreary, bleak. **2** *murky water:* **dirty,** muddy, cloudy, turbid.
OPPOSITES bright, clear.

murmur noun **1** *his voice was a murmur:* **whisper,** mutter, mumble. **2** *the murmur of bees:* **hum,** buzz, drone.
verb *he heard them murmuring in the hall:* **mutter,** mumble, whisper, talk under one's breath.

muscle noun **1** *he had muscle but no brains:* **strength,** power, brawn; informal **beef,** beefiness. **2** *financial muscle:* **influence,** power, strength, might, force, forcefulness, weight; informal clout.
■ **muscle in** (informal) interfere, force one's way in, impose oneself, encroach; informal horn in.

muscular adjective **strong,** brawny, muscly, well built, burly, strapping, sturdy, powerful, athletic; informal hunky, beefy.

muse verb **ponder,** consider, think over/about, mull over, reflect on, contemplate, turn over in one's mind, chew over.

musical adjective **tuneful,** melodic, melodious, harmonious, sweet-sounding.
OPPOSITES discordant.

must verb **ought to,** should, have (got) to, need to, be obliged to, be required to, be compelled to.

muster verb **1** *they mustered 50,000 troops:* **assemble,** mobilize, rally, raise, summon, gather, mass, call up, call to arms, recruit, conscript; US draft. **2** *reporters mustered outside her house:* **congregate,** assemble, gather (together), come together, collect, convene, mass, rally. **3** *she mustered her courage:* **summon (up),** screw up, call up, rally.

mutation noun **1** **alteration,** change, transformation, metamorphosis, transmutation. **2** *a genetic mutation:* **mutant,** freak (of nature), deviant, monstrosity, monster.

mute adjective **1** *Yasmin remained mute:* **silent,** speechless, dumb, unspeaking, tight-lipped, taciturn; informal mum. **2** *a mute appeal:* **wordless,** silent, dumb, unspoken.
OPPOSITES voluble, spoken.

muted adjective **1** *the muted hum of traffic:* **muffled,** faint, indistinct, quiet, soft, low, distant, faraway. **2** *muted tones:* **subdued,** pastel, delicate, subtle, understated, restrained.

mutilate verb **1** *the bodies had been mutilated:* **mangle,** maim, disfigure, dismember, slash, hack. **2** *the carved screen had been mutilated:* **vandalize,** damage, slash, hack, deface, violate, desecrate.

mutiny noun *a naval mutiny:* **insurrection,** rebellion, revolt, riot, uprising, insurgence, insubordination.
verb *the crew mutinied:* **rise up,** rebel, revolt, riot, strike.

mutter verb **1** *a group of men stood muttering:* **talk under one's breath,** murmur, mumble, whisper. **2** *residents muttered about the charge:* **grumble,** complain, grouse, carp, whine; informal moan, whinge.

mutual adjective **reciprocal,** reciprocated, requited, returned, common, joint, shared.

mysterious adjective
1 *mysterious circumstances:* **puzzling,** strange, peculiar, curious, funny, odd, weird, bizarre, mystifying, inexplicable, baffling, perplexing. **2** *he was being very mysterious:* **secretive,** inscrutable, enigmatic, reticent, evasive, furtive, surreptitious. OPPOSITES straightforward.

mystery noun **1** *his death remains a mystery:* **puzzle,** enigma, conundrum, riddle, secret, paradox. **2** *her past is shrouded in mystery:* **secrecy,** obscurity, uncertainty, mystique.

mystic, mystical adjective **spiritual,** religious, transcendental, paranormal, other-worldly, supernatural, occult, metaphysical.

myth noun **1** *ancient Greek myths:* **folk tale,** folk story, legend, fable, saga, lore, folklore. **2** *the myths surrounding childbirth:* **misconception,** fallacy, old wives' tale, fairy story, fiction; informal cock and bull story.

m

n

Nn

nag verb **1** *she's constantly nagging me:* **harass,** keep on at, go on at, badger, chivvy, hound, criticize, find fault with, moan at, grumble at, henpeck; informal hassle; N. Amer. informal ride. **2** *this has been nagging me for weeks:* **trouble,** worry, bother, plague, torment, niggle, prey on one's mind; informal bug.

nail noun *fastened with nails:* **tack,** pin, brad, clout, spike, staple.
verb *a board was nailed to the wall:* **fasten,** attach, fix, affix, secure, tack, hammer, pin.

naive adjective **innocent,** unsophisticated, artless, inexperienced, unworldly, trusting, gullible, credulous, immature, callow, raw, green; informal wet behind the ears. OPPOSITES worldly.

naked adjective **nude,** bare, in the nude, stark naked, having nothing on, stripped, unclothed, undressed; informal without a stitch on, in one's birthday suit, in the raw/buff, in the altogether; Brit. informal starkers; N. Amer. informal buck naked.

OPPOSITES clothed.

name noun *her name's Gemma:* **title,** honorific, designation, tag, epithet, label; informal moniker, handle.
verb **1** *they named the child Pamela:* **call,** dub, label, style, term, title, baptize, christen. **2** *he has named his successor:* **nominate,** designate, select, pick, decide on, choose.

namely adverb **that is (to say),** to be specific, specifically, viz., to wit, in other words.

nap noun **sleep,** catnap, siesta, doze, lie-down, rest; informal snooze, forty winks, shut-eye; Brit. informal kip.

narcotic noun *illegal narcotics:* **drug,** sedative, opiate, painkiller, analgesic, palliative.
adjective *a narcotic effect:* **soporific,** sedative, calming, sleep-inducing, opiate, painkilling, pain-relieving, analgesic, anodyne.

narrate verb **tell,** relate, recount, describe, chronicle, report, present.

narrative noun **account,** chronicle, history, description, record, report, story, tale.

narrator noun **storyteller,** relater, chronicler, commentator, presenter, author.
OPPOSITES listener, audience.

narrow adjective **1** *her narrow waist:* **slender,** slim, small, slight, spare, attenuated, tapering, thin, tiny. **2** *a narrow space:* **confined,** cramped, tight, restricted, limited, constricted, small, tiny. **3** *a narrow range of products:* **limited,** restricted, small, inadequate, insufficient, deficient.
OPPOSITES wide, broad.
verb *narrowing the gap between*

rich and poor: **become/make narrower,** become/make smaller, taper, diminish, decrease, reduce, contract, shrink, constrict.
OPPOSITES widen.

narrowly adverb **(only) just,** barely, scarcely, hardly, by a hair's breadth; informal by a whisker.

narrow-minded adjective **intolerant,** illiberal, reactionary, conservative, parochial, provincial, insular, small-minded, petty, blinkered, inward-looking, narrow, hidebound, prejudiced, bigoted.
OPPOSITES tolerant.

nasty adjective **1** *a nasty smell:* **unpleasant,** disagreeable, disgusting, vile, foul, abominable, revolting, repulsive, repellent, obnoxious, unsavoury, noxious, foul-smelling, smelly, stinking, rank; informal ghastly, horrid, yucky; N. Amer. informal lousy. **2** *she can be really nasty:* **unkind,** unpleasant, unfriendly, disagreeable, rude, spiteful, malicious, mean, vicious, malevolent, hurtful. **3** *a nasty accident:* **serious,** dangerous, bad, awful, dreadful, terrible, severe, painful, ugly.
OPPOSITES nice, slight.

nation noun **country,** state, land, realm, people, race, tribe, clan.

national adjective **1** *national politics:* **state,** public, federal, governmental. **2** *a national strike:* **nationwide,** countrywide, state, general, widespread.
OPPOSITES local, international.
noun *a French national:* **citizen,** subject, native, resident, inhabitant, voter, passport holder.

n

nationalism noun patriotism, allegiance, xenophobia, chauvinism, jingoism.

nationwide adjective national, countrywide, state, general, widespread, extensive.
OPPOSITES local.

native noun *a native of Sweden:* inhabitant, resident, local, citizen, national, countryman.
OPPOSITES foreigner.
adjective **1** *the native population:* indigenous, original. **2** *native produce:* domestic, home-grown, home-made, local, indigenous. **3** *her native tongue:* mother, home, local, vernacular.
OPPOSITES immigrant, imported.

natural adjective **1** *a natural occurrence:* normal, ordinary, everyday, usual, regular, common, commonplace, typical, routine, standard. **2** *natural products:* unprocessed, organic, pure, unrefined, additive-free, green, GM-free. **3** *Alex is a natural leader:* born, instinctive, congenital, pathological. **4** *his natural instincts:* innate, inborn, inherent, native, hereditary, inherited, inbred. **5** *she seemed very natural:* unaffected, spontaneous, uninhibited, relaxed, unselfconscious, genuine, open, artless, guileless, unpretentious. **6** *it was quite natural to think she admired him:* reasonable, logical, understandable, (only) to be expected, predictable.
OPPOSITES abnormal, artificial, affected.

naturally adverb **1** *he's naturally shy:* by nature, by character, inherently, innately, congenitally, pathologically.
2 *try to act naturally:* normally, in a natural manner, spontaneously, genuinely, unpretentiously; informal natural. **3** *naturally, they wanted everything kept quiet:* of course, as might be expected, needless to say, obviously, clearly, it goes without saying.
OPPOSITES self-consciously.

nature noun **1** *the beauty of nature:* the natural world, the environment, the universe, the cosmos, wildlife, the countryside, the land, the landscape. **2** *the very nature of such crimes:* essence, inherent features, character, complexion. **3** *nastiness was not in her nature:* character, personality, disposition, temperament, make-up, psyche. **4** *experiments of a similar nature:* kind, sort, type, variety, category, genre, order; N. Amer. stripe.

naughty adjective **1** *a naughty boy:* badly behaved, disobedient, bad, wayward, defiant, unruly, insubordinate, wilful, delinquent, undisciplined, disruptive, mischievous, impish. **2** *naughty jokes:* indecent, risqué, rude, racy, vulgar, dirty, filthy, smutty, crude, coarse.
OPPOSITES well behaved, clean.

nausea noun sickness, biliousness, queasiness, vomiting, retching.

nautical adjective maritime, marine, naval, seafaring, boating, sailing.

navigate verb **1** *he navigated the yacht across the Atlantic:* steer, pilot, guide, direct, captain; informal skipper. **2** *I'll drive—you can navigate:* map-read, give directions.

navy noun fleet, flotilla, armada, squadron, task force.

near adjective **1** *the house is quite near:* **close,** nearby, (close/near) at hand, a stone's throw away, within reach, accessible, handy, convenient; informal within spitting distance. **2** *the final judgement is near:* **imminent,** in the offing, (close/near) at hand, (just) around the corner, on its way, coming, impending, looming.
OPPOSITES far, distant.

nearby adjective **not far away/off,** close at hand, close by, near, within reach, neighbouring, local, accessible, handy, convenient.
OPPOSITES faraway.

nearly adverb **almost,** just about, more or less, practically, virtually, all but, as good as, not far off, to all intents and purposes, not quite; informal pretty well.

neat adjective **1** *the bedroom was neat and clean:* **tidy,** orderly, well ordered, in (good) order, spick and span, uncluttered, straight, trim. **2** *he's very neat:* **smart,** spruce, dapper, trim, well groomed, well turned out; informal natty. **3** *her neat handwriting:* **clear,** regular, precise, elegant; informal easy to read. **4** *this neat little gadget:* **compact,** well designed, handy; Brit. informal dinky, nifty. **5** *his neat footwork:* **skilful,** deft, dexterous, adroit, adept, expert; informal nifty. **6** *a neat solution:* **clever,** ingenious, inventive, imaginative. **7** *neat gin:* **undiluted,** straight, unmixed; N. Amer. informal straight up.
OPPOSITES untidy.

necessarily adverb **as a consequence,** as a result, automatically, as a matter of course, certainly, incontrovertibly, inevitably, unavoidably, inescapably, of necessity.

necessary adjective **1** *planning permission is necessary:* **obligatory,** requisite, required, compulsory, mandatory, imperative, needed. **2** *a necessary consequence:* **inevitable,** unavoidable, inescapable, inexorable.

necessity noun **1** *the VCR is now regarded as a necessity:* **essential,** requisite, prerequisite, necessary, basic; informal must-have. **2** *political necessity forced him to resign:* **force of circumstance,** obligation, need, call, exigency.

need verb **1** *do you need money?* **require,** be in/have need of, want, be crying out for, be desperate for, demand, call for, necessitate, entail, involve, lack, be without, be short of. **2** *do I need to come?* **have to,** be meant to, be supposed to, be expected to.
noun **1** *there's no need to apologize:* **necessity,** requirement, call, demand. **2** *basic human needs:* **requirement,** necessity, want, requisite, prerequisite. **3** *my hour of need:* **difficulty,** trouble, distress, crisis, emergency, urgency, extremity.

needed adjective **necessary,** required, called for, wanted, desired, lacking.
OPPOSITES optional.

needless adjective **unnecessary,** unneeded, uncalled for, gratuitous, pointless, superfluous, redundant, excessive.
OPPOSITES necessary.

needy adjective **poor,** deprived, disadvantaged, underprivileged,

in need, needful, hard up, poverty-stricken, impoverished, destitute, penniless; informal broke, strapped (for cash); Brit. informal skint.
OPPOSITES wealthy.

negative adjective **1** *a negative reply:* **opposing,** opposed, contrary, anti-, dissenting, in the negative. **2** *stop being so negative:* **pessimistic,** defeatist, gloomy, cynical, fatalistic, dismissive, unenthusiastic, apathetic, unresponsive. **3** *a negative effect on the economy:* **harmful,** bad, adverse, damaging, detrimental, unfavourable, disadvantageous.
OPPOSITES positive, optimistic, favourable.

neglect verb **1** *she neglected the children:* **fail to look after,** leave alone, abandon. **2** *he's neglecting his work:* **pay no attention to,** let slide, not attend to, be remiss about, be lax about, leave undone. **3** *I neglected to inform her:* **fail,** omit, forget.
OPPOSITES cherish, heed, remember.
noun **1** *the place had an air of neglect:* **disrepair,** dilapidation, shabbiness, disuse, abandonment. **2** *her doctor was guilty of neglect:* **negligence,** dereliction (of duty), carelessness, laxity, slackness, irresponsibility.
OPPOSITES care.

neglected adjective **1** *neglected animals:* **uncared for,** abandoned, mistreated, maltreated. **2** *a neglected cottage:* **derelict,** dilapidated, tumbledown, ramshackle, untended. **3** *a neglected masterpiece:* **disregarded,** forgotten, overlooked, ignored,

unrecognized, unnoticed, unsung, underrated.
OPPOSITES cared for, maintained, well regarded.

negligent adjective **neglectful,** remiss, careless, lax, irresponsible, inattentive, thoughtless, unmindful, forgetful, slack, sloppy; N. Amer. derelict.
OPPOSITES dutiful.

negligible adjective **trivial,** trifling, insignificant, unimportant, minor, inconsequential, minimal, small, slight, infinitesimal; informal minuscule.
OPPOSITES significant.

negotiate verb **1** *she refused to negotiate:* **discuss (terms),** talk, consult, confer, debate, compromise, bargain, haggle. **2** *he negotiated a new contract:* **arrange,** broker, work out, thrash out, agree on. **3** *I negotiated the obstacles:* **get round,** get past, get over, clear, cross, surmount, overcome, deal with, cope with.

negotiation noun **1** *the negotiations resume next week:* **discussion(s),** talks, conference, debate, dialogue, consultation. **2** *the negotiation of a deal:* **arrangement,** brokering, settlement, conclusion, completion.

negotiator noun **mediator,** arbitrator, go-between, middleman, intermediary, representative, spokesperson, broker.

neighbourhood noun **1** *a quiet neighbourhood:* **district,** area, locality, locale, quarter, community; N. Amer. informal hood, nabe. **2** *in the neighbourhood of Canterbury:* **vicinity,** environs.

neighbouring adjective

n

adjacent, adjoining, bordering, connecting, next-door, nearby. OPPOSITES remote.

neighbourly adjective **obliging,** helpful, friendly, kind, considerate, amicable, sociable, hospitable, companionable, civil, cordial. OPPOSITES unfriendly.

nerve noun **1** *the match will be a test of nerve:* **confidence,** assurance, courage, bravery, determination, will power, spirit, grit; informal guts; Brit. informal bottle; N. Amer. informal moxie. **2** *he had the nerve to chat her up:* **audacity,** cheek, effrontery, gall, temerity, presumption, impudence, impertinence, arrogance; informal face, front, brass neck, chutzpah. **3** (nerves) **anxiety,** tension, nervousness, stress, worry, cold feet, apprehension; informal butterflies (in one's stomach), collywobbles, jitters.

nervous adjective **1** *a nervous woman:* **highly strung,** anxious, edgy, nervy, tense, excitable, jumpy, neurotic. **2** *he was so nervous he couldn't eat:* **anxious,** worried, apprehensive, on edge, edgy, tense, stressed, agitated, uneasy, restless, worked up, keyed up, overwrought; informal jittery, twitchy, in a state, uptight, wired, in a flap; Brit. informal having kittens; N. Amer. informal squirrelly. OPPOSITES relaxed, calm.

nestle verb **snuggle,** cuddle, huddle, nuzzle, settle, burrow.

net[1] noun *a dress of green net:* **netting,** mesh, tulle, fishnet, lace. verb *they netted some big criminals:* **catch,** capture, trap, snare; informal nab, bag, collar,

bust; Brit. informal nick.

net[2] adjective **1** *net earnings: after tax,* after deductions, take-home, clear, final; informal bottom line. **2** *the net result:* **final,** end, ultimate, closing, overall, actual, effective. OPPOSITES gross. verb *she netted £50,000:* **earn,** make, clear, take home, bring in, pocket, realize, be paid.

network noun **1** *a network of arteries:* **web,** lattice, net, matrix, mesh, criss-cross, grid. **2** *a network of lanes:* **maze,** labyrinth, warren, tangle.

neurotic adjective **overanxious,** oversensitive, nervous, tense, highly strung, paranoid, obsessive, fixated, hysterical, overwrought, irrational. OPPOSITES stable, calm.

neutral adjective **1** *she's neutral on this issue:* **impartial,** unbiased, unprejudiced, objective, open-minded, non-partisan, even-handed, disinterested, dispassionate, detached. **2** *Switzerland remained neutral:* **unaligned,** non-aligned, unaffiliated, uninvolved. **3** *a neutral topic of conversation:* **inoffensive,** bland, unobjectionable, unexceptional, anodyne, uncontroversial, safe, harmless, innocuous. **4** *a neutral background:* **pale,** light, colourless, indeterminate, drab, insipid, nondescript, dull. OPPOSITES biased, partisan, provocative, colourful.

new adjective **1** *new technology:* **recent,** up to date, the latest, current, state-of-the-art, contemporary, advanced, cutting-edge, modern. **2** *is your boat new?* **unused,** brand new, pristine, fresh. **3** *new*

neighbours moved in: **different**, another, alternative, unfamiliar, unknown, strange. **4** *they had a new classroom built:* **additional**, extra, supplementary, further, another, fresh. **5** *I came back a new woman:* **reinvigorated**, restored, revived, improved, refreshed, regenerated.
OPPOSITES old, hackneyed, second-hand, present.

newcomer noun **1** *a newcomer to the village:* **new arrival**, immigrant, incomer, settler, stranger, outsider, foreigner, alien; informal new kid on the block; Austral. informal blow-in. **2** *photography tips for the newcomer:* **beginner**, novice, learner, trainee, apprentice, probationer; N. Amer. tenderfoot; informal rookie, newbie.

newly adverb recently, only just, lately, freshly, not long ago, a short time ago.

news noun report, story, account, announcement, press release, communication, communiqué, bulletin, intelligence, disclosure, revelation, gossip; informal scoop.

next adjective **1** *the next chapter:* **following**, succeeding, upcoming, to come. **2** *the next house in the street:* **neighbouring**, adjacent, adjoining, next-door, bordering, connected, closest, nearest.
OPPOSITES previous.
adverb *where shall we go next?* **then**, after, afterwards, after this/that, later, subsequently; formal thereafter.
OPPOSITES before.

nice adjective **1** *have a nice time:* **enjoyable**, pleasant, agreeable, good, satisfying, entertaining, amusing; informal lovely, great; N. Amer. informal neat. **2** *nice people:*

pleasant, likeable, agreeable, personable, congenial, amiable, affable, genial, friendly, charming, delightful, engaging, sympathetic. **3** *nice manners:* **polite**, courteous, civil, refined, polished, genteel, elegant. **4** *that's a rather nice distinction:* **subtle**, fine, delicate, precise, strict, close, careful, meticulous, scrupulous. **5** *it's a nice day:* **fine**, pleasant, agreeable, dry, sunny, warm, mild.
OPPOSITES unpleasant, nasty, rough.

niche noun **1** *a niche in the wall:* **recess**, alcove, nook, cranny, hollow, bay, cavity, cubbyhole, pigeonhole. **2** *he found his niche in life:* **(ideal) position**, slot, place, function, vocation, calling, métier, station, job, level.

nick noun *a slight nick in the blade:* **cut**, scratch, incision, notch, chip, dent, indentation.
verb *I nicked the edge of the table:* **cut**, scratch, graze, chip, dent.

nickname noun pet name, diminutive, endearment, tag, label, sobriquet, epithet; informal moniker.

night noun night-time, (hours of) darkness, dark.
OPPOSITES day.

nightly adjective **1** *nightly raids:* **every night**, night after night. **2** *his nightly wanderings:* **nocturnal**, night-time.
adverb *a band plays there nightly:* **every night**, each night, night after night.

nightmare noun ordeal, trial, hell, misery, agony, torture, murder, purgatory, disaster; informal the pits.

nil noun nothing, none, nought,

n

zero; Tennis **love;** Cricket a duck.

nimble adjective **1** *he was nimble on his feet:* **agile,** sprightly, light, spry, quick, lithe, skilful, deft, dexterous, adroit; informal nippy. **2** *a nimble mind:* **quick,** alert, lively, astute, perceptive, penetrating, discerning, shrewd, sharp, intelligent, bright, smart, clever, brilliant; informal quick on the uptake.
OPPOSITES clumsy, dull.

nip verb & noun **bite,** nibble, peck, pinch, tweak.

no adverb **absolutely not,** definitely not, of course not, under no circumstances, not at all, negative, never; informal nope, no way, not a chance; Brit. informal no fear; archaic nay.
OPPOSITES yes.

noble adjective **1** *a noble family:* **aristocratic,** blue-blooded, high-born, titled. **2** *a noble cause:* **worthy,** righteous, virtuous, good, honourable, worthwhile. **3** *a noble pine forest:* **magnificent,** splendid, grand, stately, imposing, dignified, proud, striking, majestic.
OPPOSITES humble, base, unimpressive.
noun *Scottish nobles:* **aristocrat,** nobleman, noblewoman, lord, lady, peer (of the realm), peeress; informal aristo.
OPPOSITES commoner.

nod verb **1** *she nodded her head:* **incline,** bob, bow, dip. **2** *he nodded to me to start:* **signal,** gesture, gesticulate, motion, sign, indicate.
noun **1** *a nod of his head:* **inclination,** bob, bow, dip. **2** *she gave a nod to the manager:* **signal,** indication, sign, cue, gesture.

noise noun **sound,** din, hubbub,

clamour, racket, uproar, tumult, commotion; informal hullabaloo; Brit. informal row.
OPPOSITES silence.

noisy adjective **1** *a noisy crowd:* **rowdy,** raucous, clamorous, boisterous, chattering, talkative, vociferous, shouting, screaming. **2** *noisy music:* **loud,** blaring, booming, deafening, thunderous, ear-splitting, piercing, strident, cacophonous.
OPPOSITES quiet, soft.

nominal adjective **1** *the nominal head of the campaign:* **in name only,** titular, formal, official, theoretical, supposed, ostensible, so-called. **2** *a nominal rent:* **token,** symbolic, minimal; Brit. peppercorn.
OPPOSITES real, considerable.

nominate verb **1** *any member may nominate a candidate:* **propose,** put forward, put up, submit, present, recommend, suggest. **2** *the President nominated her to the Supreme Court:* **appoint,** designate, assign, select, choose, decide on, promote.

non-existent adjective **imaginary,** imagined, unreal, fictional, fictitious, made up, invented, fanciful, mythical, illusory.
OPPOSITES real.

nonsense noun **1** *he was talking nonsense:* **rubbish,** gibberish, claptrap, garbage; informal baloney, tripe, drivel, gobbledegook, twaddle; Brit. informal cobblers, codswallop, double Dutch; Scottish & N. English informal havers; N. Amer. informal flapdoodle, bushwa, applesauce. **2** *she stands no nonsense:* **mischief,** messing about, misbehaviour, funny business; informal tomfoolery, monkey

business, shenanigans; Brit. informal monkey tricks, jiggery-pokery. **3** *the whole thing is a nonsense:* **joke,** farce, travesty, insanity, madness.
OPPOSITES sense, wisdom.

non-stop adjective *non-stop entertainment:* **continuous,** constant, continual, incessant, ceaseless, uninterrupted, perpetual, round-the-clock, unremitting, relentless, persistent.
OPPOSITES intermittent, occasional.
adverb *we worked non-stop:* **continuously,** continually, incessantly, ceaselessly, all the time, constantly, perpetually, round the clock, steadily, relentlessly, persistently; informal 24-7.
OPPOSITES intermittently, occasionally.

noon noun midday, twelve o'clock, twelve hundred hours, twelve noon, high noon, noonday.

norm noun **1** *norms of behaviour:* **standard,** convention, criterion, yardstick, benchmark, touchstone, rule, formula, pattern. **2** *such teams are now the norm:* **normal,** usual, the rule, standard, typical, average, par for the course, expected.

normal adjective **1** *they issue books in the normal way:* **usual,** standard, ordinary, customary, conventional, habitual, accustomed, typical, common, regular, routine, traditional. **2** *a normal couple:* **ordinary,** average, typical, run-of-the-mill, middle-of-the-road, common, conventional, mainstream; N. Amer. garden-variety; Brit. informal common or

garden, bog-standard. **3** *the man was not normal:* **sane,** in one's right mind, right in the head, of sound mind, compos mentis; informal all there.
OPPOSITES unusual, insane.

normally adverb **1** *she wanted to be able to walk normally:* **naturally,** conventionally, properly, like everyone else. **2** *normally we'd keep quiet about this:* **usually,** ordinarily, as a rule, generally, in general, mostly, for the most part, by and large, mainly, most of the time, on the whole, typically, traditionally.

nose noun **1** snout, muzzle, proboscis, trunk; informal beak, conk, schnozz, schnozzle, hooter. **2** *a nose for scandal:* **instinct,** feeling, sixth sense, intuition, insight, feel.
verb **1** *she's nosing into my business:* **pry,** enquire, poke about/around, interfere (in), meddle (in), be a busybody, stick/poke one's nose in; informal be nosy (about), snoop; Austral./NZ informal stickybeak. **2** *he nosed the car into the traffic:* **ease,** inch, edge, move, manoeuvre, steer, guide.

nostalgia noun reminiscence, remembrance, recollection, wistfulness, regret, sentimentality.

nostalgic adjective wistful, romantic, sentimental, emotional, homesick, regretful, dewy-eyed, maudlin.

notable adjective **1** *notable examples of workmanship:* **noteworthy,** remarkable, outstanding, important, significant, memorable, marked, striking, impressive. **2** *a notable author:* **prominent,** important, well known, famous,

n

famed, noted.
OPPOSITES unremarkable, unknown.

noun *movie stars and other notables:* **celebrity,** public figure, VIP, dignitary, luminary, star, superstar, big name; informal celeb, bigwig, megastar.
OPPOSITES nonentity.

notably adverb **1** *other countries, notably the USA:* **in particular,** particularly, especially, primarily, principally. **2** *these are notably short-lived birds:* **remarkably,** especially, exceptionally, singularly, particularly, peculiarly, distinctly, significantly, unusually, uncommonly, conspicuously.

notch noun **nick,** cut, incision, score, scratch, slit, snick, slot, groove.

note noun **1** *a note in her diary:* **record,** entry, reminder; informal memo. **2** *notes of the meeting:* **minutes,** record, details, report, account, transcript, summary. **3** *notes in the margins:* **annotation,** footnote, comment. **4** *he wrote me a note:* **message,** letter, line. **5** (Brit.) *a £20 note:* **banknote;** N. Amer. bill; US informal greenback. **6** *a note of hopelessness in her voice:* **tone,** hint, indication, sign, element, suggestion, sense.
verb **1** *we will note your suggestion:* **bear in mind,** be mindful of, consider, take notice of, register, record, enter. **2** *the letter noted the ministers' concern:* **mention,** refer to, touch on, indicate, point out, make known, state. **3** *note the date in your diary:* **write down,** put down, jot down, take down, enter, mark, record, register, pencil.

notebook noun **notepad,** exercise book, register, logbook, log, diary, journal, record; Brit. jotter, pocketbook.

noted adjective **famous,** famed, well known, renowned, prominent, notable, important, eminent, acclaimed, celebrated.
OPPOSITES unknown.

nothing noun **1** *there's nothing I can do:* **not a thing,** zero; N. English nowt; informal zilch, sweet FA, not a dicky bird; Brit. informal damn all, not a sausage; N. Amer. informal zip, nada, diddly-squat. **2** *the price fell to nothing:* **zero,** nought, nil, o; Tennis love; Cricket a duck.
OPPOSITES something.

notice noun **1** *nothing escaped his notice:* **attention,** observation, awareness, consciousness, perception, regard, consideration, scrutiny. **2** *a notice on the wall:* **sign,** announcement, advertisement, poster, bill, bulletin. **3** *we will give you notice of any changes:* **notification,** (advance) warning, news, word.
verb *I noticed that the door was open:* **observe,** note, see, discern, detect, spot; Brit. informal clock.
OPPOSITES overlook.

noticeable adjective **obvious,** evident, apparent, manifest, plain, clear, conspicuous, perceptible, discernible, detectable, observable, visible, appreciable.

notify verb **inform,** tell, advise, give (advance) warning, let someone know, alert, warn.

notion noun **1** *he had a notion that something was wrong:* **idea,** impression, (funny) feeling, (sneaking) suspicion, intuition, hunch, belief, opinion. **2** *Claire had no notion of what he meant:* **understanding,** idea, clue, inkling.

notorious adjective **infamous,** scandalous, disreputable.

nought noun **nil,** zero, nothing; Tennis love; Cricket a duck; informal zilch; Brit. informal not a sausage; N. Amer. informal zip, nada.

nourish verb **1** *patients must be well nourished:* **feed,** sustain, provide for, maintain. **2** *we nourish the talents of children:* **encourage,** promote, foster, nurture, cultivate, boost, strengthen, enrich.

nourishing adjective **nutritious,** wholesome, good for one, full of goodness, healthy, health-giving, beneficial.
OPPOSITES unhealthy.

novel[1] noun *a good novel:* **story,** tale, narrative, romance.

novel[2] adjective *a novel way of making money:* **new,** original, unusual, unconventional, unorthodox, different, fresh, imaginative, innovative.
OPPOSITES traditional.

novelty noun **1** *the novelty of our approach:* **originality,** newness, freshness, unconventionality, creativity, innovation, unfamiliarity, strangeness. **2** *we sell seasonal novelties:* **knick-knack,** trinket, bauble, toy, trifle, ornament; N. Amer. kickshaw.

novice noun **beginner,** learner, newcomer, fledgling, trainee, probationer, student, pupil, apprentice; informal rookie, newie; N. Amer. informal greenhorn.
OPPOSITES expert, veteran.

now adverb **1** *I'm busy now:* **at the moment,** at present, at this moment in time, at this time, currently; N. Amer. presently.

2 *television is now the main source of news:* **nowadays,** these days, today, in this day and age. **3** *you must leave now:* **at once,** straight away, right away, this minute, this instant, immediately, instantly, directly; informal pronto, asap.

nucleus noun **core,** centre, heart, hub, middle, focal point, pivot, crux.

nude adjective **naked,** stark naked, bare, unclothed, undressed, stripped, with nothing on; informal without a stitch on, in one's birthday suit, in the raw/buff, in the altogether; Brit. informal starkers; N. Amer. informal buck naked.
OPPOSITES clothed.

nudge verb **1** *he nudged Ben:* **prod,** elbow, dig, poke, jab. **2** *the canoe nudged the bank:* **touch,** bump (against), push (against), run into. **3** *we nudged them towards a decision:* **prompt,** encourage, persuade, prod.
noun *Maggie gave him a nudge:* **prod,** dig (in the ribs), poke, jab, push.

nuisance noun **annoyance,** inconvenience, bore, bother, irritation, trial, burden, pest; informal pain (in the neck), hassle, bind, drag, headache.
OPPOSITES blessing.

numb adjective **1** *my fingers are numb:* **dead,** without sensation, without feeling, numbed, desensitized, frozen, anaesthetized. **2** *the news left me numb:* **dazed,** stunned, unfeeling, stupefied, paralysed, immobilized.
OPPOSITES sensitive.
verb **1** *the cold weather numbed his fingers:* **deaden,** desensitize, anaesthetize, immobilize,

n

freeze. **2** *the news updates numb us:* **daze**, stun, dull, stupefy, paralyse, immobilize.
OPPOSITES sensitize.

number noun **1** *a whole number:* **numeral**, integer, figure, digit, character. **2** *a large number of complaints:* **quantity**, total, aggregate, tally, quota. **3** *the wedding of one of their number:* **group**, crowd, circle, party, band, crew, set, company; informal gang. **4** *the band performed another number:* **song**, piece, tune, track, dance.
verb **1** *visitors numbered more than two million:* **add up to**, amount to, total, come to. **2** *he numbers her among his friends:* **include**, count, reckon, deem.

numerous adjective **many**, a number of, a lot of, several, plenty of, copious, an abundance of, frequent; informal umpteen.
OPPOSITES few.

nurse verb **1** *they nursed smallpox patients:* **care for**, take care of, look after, tend,

minister to. **2** *they nursed old grievances:* **harbour**, foster, bear, have, hold (on to), retain.

nurture verb **1** *she nurtured her children into adulthood:* **bring up**, care for, take care of, look after, tend, rear, support. **2** *we nurtured these plants:* **cultivate**, grow, keep, tend, raise. **3** *he nurtured my love of art:* **encourage**, promote, stimulate, develop, foster, cultivate, boost, strengthen, fuel.
OPPOSITES neglect, hinder.

nut noun **1** (informal) *some nut arrived at the office:* **maniac**, lunatic, madman, madwoman; informal loony, nutcase, head case; Brit. informal nutter; N. Amer. informal screwball. **2** (informal) *a movie nut:* **enthusiast**, fan, devotee, aficionado; informal freak, fanatic, addict, buff.

nutritious adjective **nourishing**, wholesome, good for one, full of goodness, healthy, health-giving, beneficial.

Oo

oath noun **1** *an oath of allegiance:* **vow**, pledge, promise, affirmation, word (of honour), guarantee. **2** *a stream of oaths:* **swear word**, profanity, expletive, four-letter word, dirty word, obscenity, curse.

obedient adjective **compliant**, biddable, acquiescent, good, law-abiding, deferential, governable, docile, submissive.
OPPOSITES rebellious.

obey verb **1** *I obeyed him:* **do**

what someone says, submit to, defer to, do as one is told. **2** *he refused to obey the order:* **carry out**, perform, act on, execute, discharge, implement. **3** *the rules have to be obeyed:* **comply with**, adhere to, observe, abide by, act in accordance with, conform to, respect, follow, keep to, stick to.
OPPOSITES defy, ignore.

object noun **1** *wooden objects:* **thing**, article, item, entity. **2** *the object of criticism:* **target**,

butt, focus, recipient, victim.
3 *his object was to resolve the crisis:* **objective,** aim, goal, target, purpose, end, plan, point, ambition, intention, idea.
verb *teachers objected to the scheme:* **protest about,** oppose, take exception to, take issue with, take a stand against, argue against, quarrel with, condemn, draw the line at, demur at, mind, complain about; informal kick up a fuss/ stink about.
OPPOSITES approve of, accept.

objection noun **protest,** protestation, complaint, opposition, demurral, counter-argument, disagreement, disapproval, dissent.

objective adjective **1** *try to be objective:* **impartial,** unbiased, unprejudiced, non-partisan, disinterested, neutral, uninvolved, even-handed, fair, dispassionate, detached.
2 *objective knowledge:* **factual,** actual, real, empirical, verifiable.
OPPOSITES subjective, emotional.
noun *our objective is to make a profit:* **aim,** intention, purpose, target, goal, object, idea, plan.

objectively adverb **impartially,** without bias/prejudice, even-handedly, fairly, dispassionately, with an open mind, without fear or favour.

obligation noun **1** *his professional obligations:* **commitment,** duty, responsibility, function, task, job, charge, onus, liability, requirement, debt. **2** *a sense of obligation:* **duty,** compulsion, indebtedness, necessity, pressure, constraint.

obligatory adjective **compulsory,** mandatory,

prescribed, required, statutory, enforced, binding, requisite, necessary, imperative.
OPPOSITES optional.

oblige verb **1** *we are obliged to accept the decision:* **compel,** force, require, bind, constrain.
2 *I'll be happy to oblige you:* **do someone a favour,** accommodate, help, assist, indulge, humour.

obliged adjective **thankful,** grateful, appreciative, beholden, indebted, in someone's debt.

obliging adjective **helpful,** accommodating, cooperative, agreeable, amenable, generous, kind; Brit. informal decent.
OPPOSITES unhelpful.

obscene adjective **1** *obscene literature:* **pornographic,** indecent, smutty, dirty, filthy, X-rated, explicit, lewd, rude, vulgar, coarse, scatological; informal blue, porn; euphemistic adult. **2** *an obscene amount:* **scandalous,** shocking, outrageous, immoral.
OPPOSITES clean, family.

obscure adjective **1** *his origins remain obscure:* **unclear,** uncertain, unknown, mysterious, hazy, vague, indeterminate. **2** *obscure references to Proust:* **abstruse,** oblique, opaque, cryptic, enigmatic, puzzling, perplexing, baffling, elliptical. **3** *an obscure Peruvian painter:* **little known,** unknown, unheard of, unsung, unrecognized, forgotten.
OPPOSITES clear, plain, famous.
verb **1** *clouds obscured the sun:* **hide,** conceal, cover, veil, shroud, screen, mask, cloak, block, obliterate, eclipse.
2 *recent events have obscured the issue:* **confuse,** complicate,

O

obfuscate, cloud, blur, muddy. **OPPOSITES** reveal, clarify.

observation noun 1 *detailed observation of their behaviour:* **monitoring,** watching, scrutiny, survey, surveillance, attention, study. 2 *his observations were correct:* **remark,** comment, opinion, impression, thought, reflection.

observe verb 1 *she observed that he was drunk:* **notice,** see, note, perceive, discern, spot. 2 *he had been observing her:* **watch,** look at, contemplate, view, survey, regard, keep an eye on, scrutinize, keep under surveillance, keep watch on, monitor; informal keep tabs on, keep a beady eye on. 3 *'You look tired,' she observed:* **remark,** comment, say, mention, declare, announce, state. 4 *they agreed to observe the ceasefire:* **comply with,** abide by, keep, obey, adhere to, heed, honour, fulfil, respect, follow, consent to, accept.

observer noun 1 *the casual observer:* **spectator,** onlooker, watcher, fly on the wall, viewer, witness. 2 *industry observers are worried:* **commentator,** reporter, monitor.

obsessed adjective fixated, possessed, consumed, infatuated, besotted; informal smitten, hung up; N. Amer. informal hipped.

obsession noun fixation, passion, mania, compulsion, preoccupation, infatuation, hobby horse, phobia, complex, neurosis; informal bee in one's bonnet, hang-up, thing.

obsessive adjective consuming, all-consuming, compulsive, controlling, fanatical, neurotic, excessive; informal pathological.

obsolete adjective out of date, outdated, outmoded, old-fashioned, passé, antiquated, antediluvian, anachronistic, archaic, ancient, fossilized, extinct, defunct; informal out of the ark; Brit. informal past its sell-by date. **OPPOSITES** current, modern.

obstacle noun barrier, hurdle, stumbling block, obstruction, bar, block, impediment, hindrance, snag, catch, drawback, hitch, fly in the ointment, handicap, difficulty, problem, disadvantage; Brit. spanner in the works. **OPPOSITES** advantage, aid.

obstinate adjective stubborn, pig-headed, unyielding, inflexible, unbending, intransigent, intractable, self-willed. **OPPOSITES** compliant.

obstruct verb 1 *ensure that vents are not obstructed:* **block (up),** clog (up), occlude, cut off, bung up, choke, dam up. 2 *he was obstructing the traffic:* **hold up,** bring to a standstill, stop, halt, block. 3 *they may obstruct aid distribution:* **impede,** hinder, interfere with, hamper, block, interrupt, hold up, stand in the way of, frustrate, slow down, delay. **OPPOSITES** clear, facilitate.

obstruction noun obstacle, barrier, stumbling block, impediment, hindrance, difficulty, check, restriction, blockage, stoppage, congestion, bottleneck, hold-up.

obtain verb get, acquire, come by, secure, procure, pick up, be given, gain, earn, achieve, attain; informal get hold of, lay one's hands on, land. **OPPOSITES** lose.

obtainable adjective **available**, to be had, in circulation, on the market, on offer, in season, at one's disposal, accessible; informal up for grabs, on tap.

obvious adjective **clear**, plain, evident, apparent, manifest, conspicuous, pronounced, prominent, distinct, noticeable, perceptible, visible; informal sticking out a mile.
OPPOSITES imperceptible.

obviously adverb **clearly**, plainly, evidently, patently, visibly, discernibly, manifestly, noticeably, of course, naturally, needless to say, it goes without saying.
OPPOSITES perhaps.

occasion noun **1** *a previous occasion:* **time**, instance, juncture, point, moment, experience, case. **2** *a special occasion:* **event**, affair, function, celebration, party, get-together, gathering; informal do, bash.

occasional adjective **infrequent**, intermittent, irregular, periodic, sporadic, odd; N. Amer. sometime.
OPPOSITES regular, frequent.

occasionally adverb **sometimes**, from time to time, (every) now and then, (every) now and again, at times, every so often, (every) once in a while, on occasion, periodically.
OPPOSITES often.

occult adjective **supernatural**, magic, magical, satanic, mystical, unearthly, esoteric, psychic.
■ **the occult** the supernatural, magic, black magic, witchcraft, necromancy, the black arts, occultism.

occupant noun **resident**, inhabitant, owner, householder, tenant, leaseholder, lessee; Brit.

occupier, owner-occupier.

occupation noun **1** *his father's occupation:* **job**, profession, work, line of work, trade, employment, business, career, métier, calling. **2** *among her leisure occupations is birdwatching:* **pastime**, activity, leisure activity, hobby, pursuit, interest, entertainment, recreation. **3** *the Roman occupation of Britain:* **conquest**, capture, invasion, seizure, annexation, colonization, subjugation.

occupied adjective **1** *tasks which kept her occupied:* **busy**, working, at work, active; informal tied up, hard at it, on the go. **2** *the table was occupied:* **in use**, full, engaged, taken. **3** *only two flats are occupied:* **inhabited**, lived in.
OPPOSITES free, vacant.

occupy verb **1** *Carol occupied the basement flat:* **live in**, inhabit, lodge in, move into, people, populate, settle. **2** *he occupies a post at the Treasury:* **hold**, fill, have; informal hold down. **3** *something to occupy my mind:* **engage**, busy, distract, absorb, engross, hold, interest, involve, entertain. **4** *the region was occupied by Japan:* **capture**, seize, conquer, invade, colonize, annex, subjugate.

occur verb **1** *an accident occurred at 3.30:* **happen**, take place, come about; N. Amer. informal go down. **2** *the disease occurs in the tropics:* **be found**, be present, exist, appear, develop.
■ **occur to** enter someone's head/mind, cross someone's mind, come/spring to mind, strike someone, come to

O

someone, dawn on someone, suggest itself.

occurrence noun **1** *a rare occurrence:* **event,** incident, happening, phenomenon, circumstance. **2** *the occurrence of cancer:* **existence,** instance, appearance, frequency, incidence, rate, prevalence; Statistics distribution.

odd adjective **1** *an odd man:* **strange,** peculiar, queer, funny, bizarre, eccentric, unusual, weird, quirky, zany; informal wacky, off the wall. **2** *some odd things had happened:* **unusual,** strange, peculiar, funny, curious, weird, bizarre, queer, abnormal, puzzling, mystifying, baffling, unaccountable. **3** *he does odd jobs:* **occasional,** casual, irregular, isolated, sporadic, periodic, miscellaneous, various, varied, sundry. **4** *an odd shoe:* **mismatched,** unmatched, unpaired, single, lone, solitary, extra, leftover, spare.
OPPOSITES normal, ordinary, regular.

odds plural noun **likelihood,** probability, chances.
■ **odds and ends** bits and pieces, bits and bobs, stuff, paraphernalia, things, sundries, bric-a-brac, knick-knacks, oddments; informal junk; Brit. informal odds and sods, clobber, gubbins.

odour noun **smell,** stench, stink, reek, aroma, bouquet, scent, perfume, fragrance; Brit. informal pong, whiff; N. Amer. informal funk.

odyssey noun **journey,** voyage, trip, trek, travels, quest, crusade, pilgrimage.

off adjective **1** *Kate's off today:* **away,** absent, not at work, off duty, on holiday, on leave, free;

N. Amer. on vacation. **2** *the game's off:* **cancelled,** postponed, called off. **3** *the fish was off:* **rotten,** bad, stale, mouldy, sour, rancid, turned, spoiled.
OPPOSITES in, on, good.

offence noun **1** *he has committed an offence:* **crime,** illegal act, misdemeanour, breach of the law, felony, infringement, violation, wrongdoing, sin. **2** *I do not want to cause offence:* **annoyance,** resentment, indignation, displeasure, bad feeling, animosity.

offend verb **1** *I'm sorry if I offended him:* **upset,** give offence to, affront, hurt someone's feelings, insult, hurt, wound, slight. **2** *criminals who offend repeatedly:* **break the law,** commit a crime, do wrong.

offender noun **wrongdoer,** criminal, lawbreaker, crook, villain, miscreant, felon, delinquent, culprit, guilty party.

offensive adjective **1** *offensive remarks:* **insulting,** rude, derogatory, disrespectful, personal, hurtful, upsetting, wounding, abusive. **2** *an offensive smell:* **unpleasant,** disagreeable, nasty, distasteful, objectionable, off-putting, dreadful, frightful, obnoxious, abominable, disgusting, repulsive, repellent, vile, foul, sickening, nauseating; informal ghastly, horrible, horrid, gross; Brit. informal beastly. **3** *offensive operations:* **hostile,** attacking, aggressive, invading, incursive, combative, threatening, martial, warlike, belligerent, bellicose.
OPPOSITES complimentary, pleasant, defensive.

noun *a military offensive:*
attack, assault, onslaught,
invasion, push, thrust, charge,
raid, incursion, blitz, campaign.

offer verb 1 *Frank offered a
suggestion:* **put forward,**
proffer, give, present, come up
with, suggest, propose,
advance, submit, tender. 2 *she
offered to help:* **volunteer,** step/
come forward, show willing.
3 *he offered $200:* **bid,** tender,
put in a bid/offer of.
OPPOSITES withdraw, refuse.
noun 1 *an offer of help:*
proposal, proposition,
suggestion, submission,
approach, overture. 2 *the
highest offer:* **bid,** tender,
bidding price.

offering noun **contribution,**
donation, gift, present,
sacrifice, tribute.

office noun 1 *we met at her
office:* **place of work,** place of
business, workplace, workroom.
2 *the company's Paris office:*
branch, division, section,
bureau, department. 3 *the office
of President:* **post,** position,
appointment, job, occupation,
role, situation, function.

officer noun **official,** office-
holder, committee member,
board member, functionary,
executive.

official adjective 1 *an official
enquiry:* **authorized,** approved,
validated, authenticated,
certified, accredited, endorsed,
sanctioned, licensed,
recognized, legitimate, legal,
lawful, valid, bona fide, proper;
informal kosher. 2 *an official
function:* **ceremonial,** formal,
solemn, bureaucratic.
OPPOSITES unauthorized,
informal.
noun *a union official:* **officer,**

office-holder, executive,
functionary, administrator,
bureaucrat, mandarin,
representative, agent; derogatory
apparatchik.

offset verb **counteract,** balance
(out), even out/up,
counterbalance, compensate
for, make up for, neutralize,
cancel (out).

offspring noun **children,** sons
and daughters, progeny,
youngsters, babies, infants,
brood, descendants, heirs,
successors; informal kids; Brit.
informal sprogs, brats.

often adverb **frequently,** many
times, on many/numerous
occasions, a lot, repeatedly,
again and again, regularly,
commonly, generally,
ordinarily; N. Amer. oftentimes.
OPPOSITES seldom.

oily adjective **greasy,** fatty,
buttery, rich.

ointment noun **lotion,** cream,
salve, liniment, embrocation,
rub, gel, balm, emollient,
unguent.

old adjective 1 *old people:* **elderly,**
aged, older, senior, venerable,
in one's dotage, long in the
tooth, ancient, decrepit,
doddery, senescent, senile;
informal getting on, past it, over
the hill. 2 *old clothes:* **worn,**
worn out, shabby, threadbare,
frayed, patched, tattered, moth-
eaten, ragged; informal tatty. 3 *old
cars:* **antique,** veteran, vintage,
classic. 4 *an old girlfriend:*
former, previous, earlier, past,
ex-, one-time, sometime,
erstwhile.
OPPOSITES young, new, modern
current.

old-fashioned adjective **out of
date,** outdated, dated, out of
fashion, outmoded,

o

unfashionable, passé, outworn, behind the times, archaic, obsolescent, obsolete; informal out of the ark; N. Amer. informal horse-and-buggy.
OPPOSITES modern.

ominous adjective **threatening,** menacing, baleful, forbidding, foreboding, fateful, sinister, black, dark, gloomy.
OPPOSITES promising.

omission noun **1** *the omission of certain news items:* **exclusion,** leaving out, deletion, elimination. **2** *I regret any omission on my part:* **negligence,** neglect, dereliction, oversight, lapse, failure.

omit verb **1** *they omitted his name from the list:* **leave out,** exclude, leave off, miss out, miss, cut, drop, skip. **2** *I omitted to mention this:* **forget,** neglect, fail.
OPPOSITES add, include, remember.

once adverb **1** *I only met him once:* **on one occasion,** one time. **2** *he didn't help once:* **ever,** at any time, on any occasion, at all. **3** *they were friends once:* **formerly,** previously, in the past, at one time, at one point, once upon a time, in days/times gone by, in the (good) old days, long ago.
OPPOSITES often, now.
conjunction *once she's gone:* **as soon as,** the moment, when, after.
■ **at once 1** *leave at once:* immediately, right away, right now, this moment/instant/ second/minute, straight away, instantly, directly, forthwith, without delay/hesitation, without further ado. **2** *they all arrived at once:* at the same

time, (all) together, simultaneously, as a group, in unison.

one-sided adjective **1** *a one-sided account:* **biased,** prejudiced, partisan, partial, slanted, distorted, unfair. **2** *a one-sided game:* **unequal,** uneven, unbalanced.
OPPOSITES impartial, equal.

ongoing adjective **in progress,** under way, going on, continuing, proceeding.

onlooker noun **eyewitness,** witness, observer, spectator, bystander; informal rubberneck.

only adverb **1** *only enough for two:* **at most,** at best, just, no more than, hardly, barely, scarcely. **2** *for your eyes only:* **exclusively,** solely, purely. **3** *you're only saying that:* **merely,** simply, just.
adjective *their only son:* **sole,** single, one (and only), solitary, lone, unique, exclusive.

onset noun **start,** beginning, commencement, arrival, appearance, inception, day one, outbreak.
OPPOSITES end.

onslaught noun **attack,** assault, offensive, advance, charge, blitz, bombardment, barrage.

ooze verb **1** *blood oozed from the wound:* **seep,** discharge, flow, exude, trickle, drip, dribble, drain, leak. **2** *positively oozing charm:* **exude,** gush, drip, emanate, radiate.

open adjective **1** *the door's open:* **unlatched,** unlocked, off the latch, ajar, gaping, yawning. **2** *a silk shirt, open at the neck:* **unfastened,** undone, unbuttoned, unzipped. **3** *an open packet:* **opened,** undone, unsealed, uncorked, unstoppered. **4** *open*

O

countryside | open spaces: **unenclosed,** rolling, sweeping, wide open, exposed, spacious, uncluttered. **5** *a map was open beside him:* **spread out,** unfolded, unfurled, unrolled, stretched out. **6** *the bank wasn't open:* **open for business,** open to the public, working, accessible. **7** *the position is still open:* **available,** vacant, free, unfilled; informal up for grabs. **8** *open to abuse:* **vulnerable,** subject, susceptible, liable, exposed. **9** *she was very open:* **frank,** candid, honest, forthcoming, communicative, forthright, direct, unreserved, plain-spoken, outspoken; informal upfront. **10** *open hostility:* **overt,** manifest, conspicuous, plain, undisguised, unconcealed, clear, naked, blatant, flagrant, barefaced, brazen. **11** *I'm open to suggestions:* **receptive,** amenable, willing to listen, responsive. **12** *what other options are open to us?* **available,** accessible, on hand, on offer. **13** *an open meeting:* **public,** general, unrestricted. OPPOSITES shut, fastened, enclosed, closed, filled, protected, reticent, suppressed, private.
verb **1** *she opened the front door:* **unfasten,** unlock, throw wide. **2** *Katherine opened the parcel:* **unwrap,** undo, untie. **3** *shall I open another bottle?* **uncork,** crack open. **4** *Adam opened the map:* **spread out,** unfold, unfurl, unroll, straighten out. **5** *we'll be opening next week:* **start trading,** set up shop. **6** *Bryan opened the meeting:* **begin,** start, commence, initiate, set in motion, get going, get under way, get off

the ground; informal kick off. **7** *the lounge opens on to a patio:* **give access,** lead. OPPOSITES close, shut, end.

open-air adjective **outdoor,** out-of-doors, outside, alfresco. OPPOSITES indoor.

opening noun **1** *an opening in the roof:* **hole,** gap, aperture, orifice, vent, crack, slit, chink. **2** *the opening of the session:* **beginning,** start, commencement, outset; informal kick-off. **3** *a gallery opening:* **launch,** inauguration, opening/first night, premiere.
adjective *her opening remarks:* **first,** initial, introductory, preliminary, maiden, inaugural. OPPOSITES final, closing.

openly adverb **1** *drugs were openly on sale:* **publicly,** blatantly, flagrantly, overtly. **2** *he spoke openly of his problems:* **frankly,** candidly, explicitly, honestly, sincerely, forthrightly, freely. OPPOSITES secretly, privately.

open-minded adjective **unbiased,** unprejudiced, neutral, objective, disinterested, tolerant, liberal, permissive, broad-minded. OPPOSITES prejudiced, narrow-minded.

operate verb **1** *he can operate the crane:* **work,** run, use, handle, control, manage, drive, steer, manoeuvre. **2** *the machine ceased to operate:* **function,** work, go, run. **3** *the way the law operates:* **take effect,** act, apply, work, function. **4** *we operated the mines until 1979:* **direct,** control, manage, run, be in control/charge of.

operation noun **1** *the sliders ensure smooth operation:*

O

functioning, working, running, performance, action. **2** *the operation of the factory:* **management**, running, administration, supervision. **3** *a military operation:* **action**, exercise, undertaking, enterprise, manoeuvre, campaign. **4** *their mining operation:* **business**, enterprise, company, firm.

operational adjective **running**, up and running, working, functioning, operative, in operation, in use, in action, ready for use, in working order, serviceable, functional.

operative adjective **1** *the steam railway is operative:* **running**, up and running, working, functioning, operational, in operation, in use, in action, in effect. **2** *the operative word:* **key**, significant, relevant, crucial, critical.
OPPOSITES inoperative, invalid.
noun **1** *the operatives clean the machines:* **machinist**, operator, mechanic, engineer, worker, workman, (factory) hand. **2** *a CIA operative:* **agent**, secret/undercover agent, spy, mole, plant; N. Amer. informal spook.

operator noun **1** *a machine operator:* **operative**, mechanic, handler, driver, worker, engineer, machinist. **2** *a tour operator:* **contractor**, entrepreneur, promoter.

opinion noun **belief**, thought(s), idea, way of thinking, feeling, mind, view, point of view, assessment, estimation, judgement.

opponent noun **1** *his Republican opponent:* **rival**, adversary, competitor, enemy, antagonist, combatant, contender, challenger. **2** *an*

opponent of the reforms: **critic**, objector, dissenter.
OPPOSITES ally, supporter.

opportunity noun **chance**, time, occasion, moment, opening, option, window, possibility, scope, freedom; informal shot, break, look-in.

oppose verb **be against**, object to, be hostile to, disagree with, disapprove of, resist, take a stand against, put up a fight against, fight, counter, challenge; informal be anti.
OPPOSITES support.

opposed
■ **opposed to** against, dead set against, averse to, hostile to, antagonistic to, antipathetic to; informal anti. ■ **as opposed to** in contrast with, as against, as contrasted with, rather than, instead of.

opposing adjective **1** *opposing points of view:* **conflicting**, contrasting, opposite, incompatible, irreconcilable, contradictory, clashing, at variance, at odds, opposed. **2** *opposing sides:* **rival**, opposite, enemy, competing.
OPPOSITES similar, allied.

opposite adjective **1** *they sat opposite each other:* **facing**, face to face with, across from. **2** *the opposite page:* **facing**, opposing. **3** *opposite views:* **conflicting**, contrasting, incompatible, irreconcilable, contradictory, at variance, at odds, differing. **4** *opposite sides:* **rival**, opposing, competing, enemy.
OPPOSITES same, similar, allied.
noun *the opposite was true:* **reverse**, converse, antithesis, contrary.
OPPOSITES same.

opposition noun **1** *the proposal met with opposition:* **resistance**,

hostility, antagonism, antipathy, objection, dissent, disapproval. **2** *they beat the opposition:* **opponent(s),** opposing side, other side/team, competition, rival(s), adversary, adversaries.
OPPOSITES agreement, goodwill.

oppress verb **persecute,** tyrannize, crush, repress, subjugate, subdue, keep down.

oppression noun **persecution,** abuse, ill-treatment, tyranny, repression, suppression, subjection, subjugation, cruelty, brutality, injustice.
OPPOSITES freedom.

oppressive adjective **1** *an oppressive dictatorship:* **harsh,** cruel, brutal, repressive, tyrannical, despotic, ruthless, merciless, pitiless. **2** *it was overcast and oppressive:* **muggy,** close, heavy, hot, humid, sticky, airless, stuffy, stifling, sultry.
OPPOSITES kindly, fresh.

opt verb **choose,** select, pick, decide, elect.
■ **opt for** choose, select, pick (out), decide on, go for, settle on, plump for.

optimistic adjective **1** *she felt optimistic about the future:* **positive,** confident, hopeful, sanguine, bullish, buoyant; informal upbeat. **2** *the forecast is optimistic:* **encouraging,** promising, hopeful, reassuring, favourable.
OPPOSITES pessimistic, depressing.

optimum adjective **best,** most favourable, most advantageous, ideal, perfect, prime, optimal.

option noun **choice,** preference, alternative, selection, possibility.
OPPOSITES impossibility.

optional adjective **voluntary,**

non-compulsory, elective, discretionary.
OPPOSITES compulsory.

opulent adjective **luxurious,** sumptuous, palatial, lavishly appointed, rich, splendid, magnificent, grand, fancy; informal plush; Brit. informal swish; N. Amer. informal swank.
OPPOSITES spartan.

oral adjective **spoken,** verbal, unwritten, vocal, uttered.
OPPOSITES written.

orbit noun **circuit,** course, path, track, trajectory, rotation, revolution.
verb **circle,** go round, revolve round, travel round, circumnavigate.

orchestra noun **ensemble,** group; informal band, combo.

orchestrate verb **1** *the piece was orchestrated by Mozart:* **arrange,** adapt, score, set. **2** *orchestrating a protest campaign:* **organize,** arrange, plan, set up, mobilize, mount, stage, mastermind, coordinate, direct.

ordain verb **1** *the decision to ordain women:* **confer holy orders on,** admit to the priesthood, priest, appoint, anoint, consecrate. **2** *the path ordained by God:* **determine,** predestine, preordain, predetermine, prescribe, designate.

ordeal noun **unpleasant experience,** trial, hardship, suffering, nightmare, trauma, hell, torture, torment, agony.

order noun **1** *alphabetical order:* **sequence,** arrangement, organization, system, series, succession. **2** *some semblance of order:* **tidiness,** neatness, orderliness. **3** *the police managed to keep order:* **peace,**

O

control, law and order, calm.
4 *his sense of order:*
orderliness, organization,
method, symmetry, uniformity,
regularity, routine. **5** *in good
order:* **condition,** state, repair,
shape; Brit. informal nick. **6** *I had
to obey his orders:* **command,**
instruction, directive, direction,
decree, edict, injunction. **7** *the
company has won the order:*
commission, request,
requisition. **8** *the lower orders
of society:* **class,** level, rank,
grade, caste. **9** *a religious order:*
community, brotherhood,
sisterhood. **10** *the Orange
Order:* **organization,**
association, society, fellowship,
fraternity, lodge, guild, league,
union, club.
OPPOSITES chaos.
▶ verb **1** *he ordered me to return:*
instruct, tell, command, direct,
charge, require, enjoin. **2** *he
ordered that their assets be
confiscated:* **rule,** ordain,
decree, direct. **3** *order your
tickets by phone:* **request,** apply
for, book, reserve. **4** *the
messages are ordered
chronologically:* **organize,**
arrange, sort out, lay out,
group, classify, categorize,
catalogue.
OPPOSITES forbid.

orderly adjective **1** *an orderly
desk:* **neat,** tidy, well ordered,
in order, trim, in apple-pie
order. **2** *the orderly
presentation of information:*
organized, efficient,
methodical, systematic,
coherent, structured, logical.
3 *the crowd was orderly:* **well
behaved,** law-abiding,
disciplined, peaceful, peaceable,
non-violent.
OPPOSITES untidy, disorganized,
unruly.

ordinary adjective **1** *the ordinary
course of events:* **usual,** normal,
standard, typical, common,
customary, habitual, everyday,
regular, routine, day-to-day.
2 *my life seemed very ordinary:*
average, normal, run-of-the-
mill, standard, typical, middle-
of-the-road, conventional,
unremarkable, unexceptional;
informal bog-standard; Brit. informal
common or garden; N. Amer.
informal ornery.
OPPOSITES unusual.

organ noun **newspaper,** paper,
journal, periodical, magazine,
voice, mouthpiece.

organic adjective **1** *organic
matter:* **living,** live, animate,
biological. **2** *organic vegetables:*
additive-free, chemical-free,
pesticide-free, bio-, natural. **3** *a
society is an organic whole:*
structured, organized,
coherent, integrated,
coordinated, ordered,
harmonious.

organism noun **1** *fish and other
organisms:* **living thing,** being,
creature, animal, plant, life
form. **2** *a complex political
organism:* **structure,** system,
organization, entity.

organization noun **1** *the
organization of conferences:*
planning, arrangement,
coordination, organizing,
running, management. **2** *the
overall organization of the book:*
structure, arrangement, plan,
pattern, order, form, format,
framework, composition. **3** *his
lack of organization:* **efficiency,**
order, orderliness, planning. **4** *a
large organization:* **institution,**
body, group, company, firm,
business, corporation, agency,
association, society; informal
outfit.

o

organize verb **1** *organize the information:* **order**, arrange, sort, assemble, marshal, put straight, group, classify, collate, categorize, catalogue. **2** *they organized a search party:* **arrange**, coordinate, sort out, put together, fix up, set up, lay on, orchestrate, see to, mobilize.
OPPOSITES muddle.

orient, orientate verb **1** *she found it hard to orient herself:* **acclimatize**, familiarize, adjust, accustom, find one's feet, get/find one's bearings. **2** *oriented to the business community:* **aim**, direct, pitch, design, intend. **3** *the stones are oriented from north to south:* **align**, place, position, arrange.

orientation noun **1** *the orientation of the radar station:* **positioning**, location, position, situation, placement, alignment. **2** *broadly Marxist in orientation:* **attitude**, inclination. **3** *orientation courses:* **induction**, training, initiation, briefing.

origin noun **1** *the origins of life:* **beginning**, start, genesis, birth, dawning, dawn, emergence, creation, source, basis, cause, root(s). **2** *the origin of the word:* **source**, derivation, root(s), provenance, etymology; N. Amer. provenience. **3** *his Scottish origins:* **descent**, ancestry, parentage, pedigree, lineage, line (of descent), heritage, birth, extraction, family, roots.

original adjective **1** *the original inhabitants:* **indigenous**, native, first, earliest, early. **2** *an original Rembrandt:* **authentic**, genuine, actual, true, bona fide. **3** *a highly original film:*

innovative, creative, imaginative, inventive, new, novel, fresh, unusual, unconventional, unorthodox, groundbreaking, pioneering, unique, distinctive.
noun *a copy of the original:* **prototype**, source, master.

originally adverb **at first**, in the beginning, to begin with, initially, in the first place, at the outset.

originate verb **1** *the disease originates from Africa:* **arise**, have its origin, begin, start, stem, spring, emerge, emanate. **2** *Bill originated the idea:* **invent**, create, devise, think up, dream up, conceive, formulate, form, develop, produce, mastermind, pioneer.

ornament noun **1** *cheap ornaments:* **knick-knack**, trinket, bauble; N. Amer. informal tchotchke, kickshaw. **2** *a dress with no ornament at all:* **decoration**, adornment, embellishment, ornamentation, trimming, accessories, frills.

ornamental adjective **decorative**, fancy, ornate, ornamented, for show.

ornate adjective **elaborate**, decorated, embellished, adorned, ornamented, fancy, fussy, ostentatious, showy; informal flashy.
OPPOSITES plain.

orthodox adjective **1** *orthodox views:* **conventional**, mainstream, conformist, established, traditional, traditionalist, prevalent, popular, conservative, received. **2** *an orthodox Hindu:* **conservative**, traditional, observant, devout, strict.
OPPOSITES unconventional, liberal.

O

other adjective **1** *these homes use other fuels:* **alternative**, different, distinct, separate, various. **2** *are there any other questions?* **more**, further, additional, extra, fresh, new, added, supplementary.

otherwise adverb **1** *hurry up, otherwise we'll be late:* **or (else)**, if not. **2** *she's exhausted, but otherwise she's fine:* **in other respects**, apart from that. **3** *he could not have acted otherwise:* **in any other way**, differently.

oust verb **expel**, drive out, force out, remove from office/power, eject, get rid of, depose, topple, unseat, overthrow, bring down, overturn, dismiss, dislodge.

out adjective & adverb **1** *she's out at the moment:* **not here**, not at home, not in, away, gone away, elsewhere. **2** *the secret was out:* **revealed**, (out) in the open, common/public knowledge. **3** *the roses are out:* **in flower**, flowering, in (full) bloom, blooming, in blossom, blossoming. **4** *the book should be out soon:* **available**, obtainable, to be had, in the shops, published, in print. **5** (informal) *grunge is out:* **unfashionable**, out of fashion, dated, outdated, passé; informal old hat. **6** *smoking is out:* **forbidden**, not permitted, not allowed, unacceptable; informal not on. **7** *he was slightly out in his calculations:* **mistaken**, inaccurate, incorrect, wrong, in error.
OPPOSITES in.
verb (informal) *it was not our intention to out him:* **expose**, unmask.

outbreak noun **1** *outbreaks of violence:* **eruption**, flare-up, upsurge, rash, wave, spate, burst, flurry. **2** *the outbreak of war:* **start**, beginning, commencement, onset.

outburst noun **eruption**, explosion, flare-up, storm, outpouring, surge, fit.

outcome noun **result**, end result, net result, consequence, upshot, conclusion, end product; informal pay-off.

outcry noun **protest**, protestation, complaints, objections, furore, fuss, uproar, opposition, dissent; informal hullabaloo, ructions, stink.

outdated adjective **old-fashioned**, out of date, outmoded, out of fashion, unfashionable, dated, passé, old, behind the times; informal out, old hat, square; N. Amer. informal horse-and-buggy.
OPPOSITES modern.

outdoor adjective **open-air**, out-of-doors, outside, al fresco.
OPPOSITES indoor.

outer adjective **1** *the outer layer:* **outside**, outermost, outward, exterior, external, surface. **2** *the outer islands:* **outlying**, distant, remote, faraway, far-flung, furthest.
OPPOSITES inner.

outfit noun **1** *a new outfit:* **costume**, suit, uniform, ensemble, clothes, clothing, dress, garb; informal get-up; Brit. informal kit. **2** (informal) *a local manufacturing outfit:* **organization**, enterprise, company, firm, business, group, body, team; informal set-up.

outgoing adjective **1** *he's very outgoing:* **extrovert**, uninhibited, unreserved, demonstrative, affectionate, warm, sociable, convivial, lively, gregarious. **2** *the*

outgoing president: **departing,**
retiring, leaving.
OPPOSITES introverted,
incoming.

outgoings plural noun **expenses,**
expenditure, spending, outlay,
payments, costs, overheads.

outing noun **trip,** excursion,
jaunt, expedition, day out, tour,
drive, ride, run; informal spin.

outlaw noun *a band of outlaws:*
fugitive, wanted criminal,
bandit, robber.
verb *fox-hunting has been
outlawed:* **ban,** bar, prohibit,
forbid, make illegal, proscribe.
OPPOSITES permit.

outlet noun **1** *a central-heating
outlet:* **vent,** way out, outfall,
opening, channel, conduit,
duct. **2** *an outlet for farm
produce:* **market,** retail outlet,
shop, store. **3** *an outlet for their
energies:* **means of expression,**
means of release, vent, avenue,
channel.

outline noun **1** *the outline of the
building:* **silhouette,** profile,
shape, contours, form, lines.
2 *an outline of our proposal:*
rough idea, thumbnail sketch,
rundown, summary, synopsis,
résumé, precis, main points,
gist, bare bones.
verb *she outlined the plan
briefly:* **rough out,** sketch out,
draft, give a rough idea of,
summarize, precis.

outlook noun **1** *a positive
outlook:* **point of view,**
viewpoint, way of thinking,
perspective, attitude,
standpoint, stance, frame of
mind. **2** *a lovely open outlook:*
view, vista, prospect, panorama.
3 *the outlook for the economy:*
prospects, future, expectations,
prognosis.

out of date adjective **1** *the*

design is out of date:
old-fashioned, outmoded,
outdated, dated, old, passé,
behind the times, obsolete,
antiquated, anachronistic;
informal old hat; N. Amer. informal
horse-and-buggy, clunky. **2** *your
ticket is out of date:* **expired,**
lapsed, invalid, void. **3** *your
information is out of date:*
obsolete, no longer valid/
relevant/true, incorrect,
inaccurate.
OPPOSITES fashionable, valid,
current.

output noun **production,** yield,
product, productivity, work,
result, processed data.

outrage noun **1** *public outrage:*
indignation, fury, anger, rage,
wrath. **2** *it is an outrage:*
scandal, offence, insult,
affront, disgrace, atrocity.
verb *his remarks outraged
everyone:* **enrage,** infuriate,
incense, anger, scandalize,
offend, affront, shock.

outrageous adjective
1 *outrageous behaviour:*
shocking, disgraceful,
scandalous, atrocious,
appalling, dreadful. **2** *an
outrageous claim:* **exaggerated,**
improbable, preposterous,
ridiculous, unwarranted.
3 *outrageous clothes:*
eye-catching, flamboyant,
showy, gaudy, ostentatious;
informal flashy.

outright adverb **1** *he rejected the
proposal outright:* **completely,**
entirely, wholly, totally,
categorically, absolutely,
utterly, flatly, unreservedly, out
of hand. **2** *I told her outright:*
explicitly, directly, frankly,
candidly, bluntly, plainly, to
someone's face; Brit. informal
straight up. **3** *they were killed*

o

outright: **instantly,**
instantaneously, immediately,
at once, straight away, then and
there, on the spot.
adjective **1** *an outright lie:*
complete, absolute, out-and-
out, downright, utter, sheer,
categorical. **2** *the outright
winner:* **definite,** unequivocal,
clear, unmistakable, overall.

outset noun **start,** starting
point, beginning; informal the
word go.
OPPOSITES end.

outside noun *the outside of the
building:* **exterior,** outer/
external surface, case, skin,
shell, covering, facade.
adjective **1** *outside lights:*
exterior, external, outer,
outdoor, out-of-doors. **2** *outside
contractors:* **independent,**
freelance, consultant, external.
adverb *shall we eat outside?*
outdoors, out of doors,
alfresco.
OPPOSITES inside.

outsider noun **stranger,** visitor,
non-member, foreigner, alien,
interloper, immigrant, incomer,
newcomer.

outskirts plural noun **edges,**
fringes, suburbs, suburbia,
periphery.

outspoken adjective **forthright,**
direct, candid, frank,
straightforward, open, straight
from the shoulder, plain-
spoken, blunt.

outstanding adjective **1** *an
outstanding painter:* **excellent,**
marvellous, magnificent,
superb, fine, wonderful,
superlative, exceptional; informal
great, terrific, tremendous,
super; Brit. informal brilliant; N.
Amer. informal neat. **2** *how much
work is still outstanding?* **to be
done,** undone, unfinished,

incomplete, remaining,
pending. **3** *outstanding debts:*
unpaid, unsettled, owing,
owed, to be paid, payable, due,
overdue; N. Amer. delinquent.

outward adjective **external,**
surface, superficial, seeming,
apparent, ostensible.
OPPOSITES inward.

outweigh verb **be greater than,**
exceed, be superior to, prevail
over, override, supersede,
offset, cancel out, more than
make up for, outbalance,
compensate for.

ovation noun **applause,** round
of applause, cheers, bravos,
acclaim, standing ovation;
informal (big) hand.

over preposition **1** *there was cloud
over the hills:* **above,** on top of,
higher (up) than, atop,
covering. **2** *he walked over the
grass:* **across,** on. **3** *he has three
people over him:* **superior to,**
above, higher up than, in
charge of, responsible for.
4 *over 2,000 people:* **more than,**
above, in excess of, upwards of.
5 *an argument over money:*
about, on the subject of,
concerning, with reference to,
regarding, relating to, in
connection with.
OPPOSITES under.
adverb **1** *a plane flew over:*
overhead, past, by. **2** *the
relationship is over:* **at an end,**
finished, ended, no more, a
thing of the past.

overall adjective *the overall cost:*
total, all-inclusive, gross, final,
inclusive, complete, entire.
adverb *overall, things are better:*
generally (speaking), in
general, altogether, all in all, on
balance, on average, for the
most part, in the main, on the
whole, by and large.

o

overcome verb *he overcame his pain:* conquer, defeat, beat, prevail over, control, get/bring under control, master, get the better of; informal lick, best.
adjective *she was overcome with excitement:* overwhelmed, moved, affected, speechless.

overdue adjective **1** *the ship is overdue:* late, behind schedule, behind time, delayed. **2** *overdue payments:* unpaid, unsettled, owing, owed, payable, due, outstanding, undischarged; N. Amer. delinquent.
OPPOSITES early, punctual.

overflow verb *chemicals overflowed from the tank:* spill over, flow over, brim over, well over, flood.
noun *offices to accommodate the overflow:* surplus, excess, additional people/things, extra, remainder, overspill.

overhaul verb service, maintain, repair, mend, fix up, rebuild, renovate, recondition, refit, refurbish.

overhead adverb *the sky overhead:* above, high up, in the sky, on high, above one's head.
OPPOSITES below.
adjective *overhead lines:* aerial, elevated, raised, suspended, overhanging.
OPPOSITES surface, underground.

overheads plural noun running costs, operating costs, fixed costs, expenses.

overlook verb **1** *he overlooked the mistake:* fail to notice, fail to spot, miss. **2** *his work has been overlooked:* disregard, neglect, ignore, pass over, forget. **3** *she was willing to overlook his faults:* ignore, disregard, take no notice of, make allowances for, turn a blind eye to, excuse, pardon, forgive. **4** *the lounge overlooks the garden:* have a view of, look over/across, look on to, look out on/over.

overpower verb overwhelm, get the better of, overthrow, subdue, suppress, subjugate, repress, bring someone to their knees.

overpowering adjective **1** *overpowering grief:* overwhelming, oppressive, unbearable, unendurable, intolerable, shattering. **2** *an overpowering smell:* stifling, suffocating, strong, pungent, powerful, nauseating, offensive, acrid, fetid.

overrate verb overestimate, overvalue, think too much of.
OPPOSITES underestimate.

override verb **1** *the court overrode the decision:* disallow, overrule, countermand, veto, quash, overturn, overthrow, cancel, reverse, rescind, revoke, repeal. **2** *our interests should override all others:* outweigh, supersede, take precedence over, take priority over, be more important than, cancel out, outbalance.

overrule verb countermand, cancel, reverse, rescind, repeal, revoke, disallow, override, veto, quash, overturn, overthrow.

overrun verb invade, storm, occupy, swarm into, surge into, inundate, overwhelm.

overshadow verb outshine, eclipse, surpass, exceed, outclass, outstrip, outdo, upstage; informal be head and shoulders above.

overt adjective undisguised, unconcealed, plain (to see), clear, conspicuous, obvious, noticeable, manifest, patent,

open, blatant.
OPPOSITES covert.

overtake verb **1** *a green car overtook us:* **pass,** go past, pull ahead of. **2** *Goa overtook Ibiza as the favourite destination:* **outstrip,** surpass, overshadow, eclipse, outshine, outclass, exceed, top, cap. **3** *the calamity which overtook us:* **befall,** happen to, come upon, hit, strike, overwhelm, overcome.

overthrow verb *the regime was overthrown:* **oust,** remove, bring down, topple, depose, displace, unseat, defeat, conquer.
noun *the overthrow of capitalism:* **ousting,** removal, downfall, toppling, supplanting, displacement, unseating, defeat, fall, collapse, demise.

overture noun **1** *the overture to a long debate:* **preliminary,** prelude, introduction, lead-in, precursor, start, beginning. **2** *peace overtures:* **opening move,** approach, advances, feeler, signal.

overturn verb **1** *the boat overturned:* **capsize,** turn turtle, keel over, tip over, topple over. **2** *I overturned the stool:* **upset,** tip over, topple over, turn over, knock over, upend. **3** *the Senate may overturn this ruling:* **cancel,** reverse, rescind, repeal, revoke, countermand, disallow, override, overrule, veto, quash, overthrow.

overweight adjective **fat,** obese, stout, plump, portly, chubby, pot-bellied, flabby; informal tubby; Brit. informal podgy.
OPPOSITES underweight.

overwhelm verb **1** *Spain overwhelmed Russia in the hockey:* **defeat heavily,** trounce, rout, beat hollow, conquer, be victorious over, crush; informal thrash, lick, wipe the floor with. **2** *she was overwhelmed by a sense of tragedy:* **overcome,** move, stir, affect, touch, strike, dumbfound, shake, leave speechless; informal bowl over, knock sideways, floor; Brit. informal knock/hit for six.

overwhelming adjective **1** *an overwhelming number of people:* **very large,** enormous, immense, inordinate, massive, huge. **2** *an overwhelming desire to laugh:* **very strong,** powerful, uncontrollable, irrepressible, irresistible, overpowering, compelling.

owe verb **be in debt (to),** be indebted (to), be in arrears (to), be under an obligation (to).

owing adjective *the rent was owing:* **unpaid,** to be paid, payable, due, overdue, undischarged, owed, outstanding, in arrears; N. Amer. delinquent.
OPPOSITES paid.
■ **owing to** because of, as a result of, on account of, due to, as a consequence of, thanks to, in view of.

own adjective *he has his own reasons:* **personal,** individual, particular, private, personalized, unique.
verb *I own this house:* **possess,** keep, hold, be the owner of, have to one's name.

owner noun **possessor,** holder, proprietor, homeowner, freeholder, landlord, landlady.

ownership noun **possession,** freehold, proprietorship, proprietary rights, title.

Pp

pace noun 1 *ten paces:* **step. 2** *a slow, steady pace:* **gait,** stride, walk, march. **3** *a furious pace:* **speed,** rate, velocity, tempo.
verb *she paced up and down:* **walk,** stride, march, pound.

pack noun 1 *a pack of cigarettes:* **packet,** container, package, box, carton, parcel. **2** *a pack of wolves:* **group,** herd, troop. **3** *a pack of hooligans:* **crowd,** mob, group, band, party, set, gang, rabble, horde, throng, huddle, mass, assembly, gathering, host; informal **crew,** bunch.
verb **1** *she helped pack the car:* **fill (up),** put things in, load. **2** *they packed their belongings:* **stow,** put away, store, box up. **3** *the glasses were packed in straw:* **wrap (up),** package, parcel, swathe, swaddle, encase, envelop, bundle. **4** *shoppers packed the store:* **throng,** crowd, fill, cram, jam, squash into, squeeze into.

package noun 1 *the delivery of a package:* **parcel,** packet, box. **2** *a package of services:* **collection,** bundle, combination, range, complement, raft, platform.
verb *goods packaged in recyclable materials:* **wrap,** gift-wrap, pack, box, seal.

packet noun **pack,** carton, container, case, package.

pact noun **agreement,** treaty, entente, protocol, deal, settlement, armistice, truce.

pad¹ noun **1** *a pad over the eye:* **dressing,** pack, wad. **2** *making notes on a pad:* **notebook,** notepad, writing pad, jotter; N. Amer. **scratch pad.**

pad² verb *he padded along the landing:* **creep,** sneak, steal, tiptoe, pussyfoot.

padded adjective **cushioned,** insulated, lined, quilted, stuffed, lagged.

padding noun **1** *padding around the ankle:* **wadding,** cushioning, stuffing, packing, filling, lining. **2** *a concise style with no padding:* **verbiage,** wordiness; Brit. informal **waffle.**

paddle¹ noun *use the paddles to row ashore:* **oar,** scull.
verb *we paddled around the bay:* **row,** pull, scull.

paddle² verb *children were paddling in the water:* **splash (about),** dabble, wade.

pagan noun & adjective **heathen,** infidel, non-Christian.

page¹ noun **folio,** sheet, side, leaf.

page² noun **1** *a page in a hotel:* **errand boy,** messenger boy; N. Amer. **bellboy,** bellhop. **2** *a page at a wedding:* **attendant,** pageboy, train-bearer.
verb *could you please page Mr Johnson?* **call (for),** summon, send for.

pageant noun **parade,** procession, cavalcade, tableau, spectacle, extravaganza, show.

pageantry noun **spectacle,** display, ceremony, magnificence, pomp, splendour, grandeur, show; informal **razzle-dazzle,** razzmatazz.

pain noun **1** *she endured great pain:* **suffering,** agony, torture, torment, discomfort. **2** *a pain in the stomach:* **ache,** aching,

p

soreness, throbbing, sting, twinge, stab, pang, discomfort, irritation. **3** *the pain of losing a loved one:* **sorrow,** grief, heartache, heartbreak, sadness, unhappiness, distress, misery, despair, agony, torment, torture. **4** *he took great pains to hide his feelings:* **care,** effort, bother, trouble.
verb *it pained him to watch:* **sadden,** grieve, distress, trouble, perturb, oppress, cause anguish to.

painful adjective **1** *a painful arm:* **sore,** hurting, tender, aching, throbbing. **2** *a painful experience:* **disagreeable,** unpleasant, nasty, distressing, upsetting, traumatic, miserable, sad, heartbreaking, agonizing, harrowing.

painfully adverb **distressingly,** disturbingly, uncomfortably, unpleasantly, dreadfully.

painstaking adjective **careful,** meticulous, thorough, assiduous, attentive, conscientious, punctilious, scrupulous, rigorous.
OPPOSITES slapdash.

paint noun **colouring,** colour, tint, dye, stain, pigment.
verb **1** *I painted the ceiling:* **colour,** decorate, whitewash, emulsion, gloss, spray-paint, airbrush. **2** *painting slogans on a wall:* **daub,** smear, spray-paint, airbrush. **3** *Rembrandt painted his mother:* **portray,** picture, paint a picture/portrait of, depict, represent.

painting noun **picture,** illustration, portrayal, depiction, representation, image, artwork, canvas, oil, watercolour.

pair noun *a matching pair:* **set,** brace, couple, duo, two.

verb *a cardigan paired with a matching skirt:* **match,** put together, couple, combine.

palace noun **castle,** château, mansion, stately home, residence.

pale adjective **1** *she looked pale:* **white,** pallid, pasty, wan, colourless, anaemic, washed out, peaky, ashen, sickly; informal like death warmed up. **2** *pale colours:* **light,** pastel, muted, subtle, soft, faded, bleached, washed out. **3** *the pale light of morning:* **dim,** faint, weak, feeble.
OPPOSITES rosy-cheeked, dark.
verb *he paled at the news:* **go/ turn white,** grow/turn pale, blanch, lose colour.

pamper verb **spoil,** indulge, overindulge, cosset, mollycoddle, coddle, baby, wait on someone hand and foot.

pamphlet noun **brochure,** leaflet, booklet, circular; N. Amer. mailer, folder.

pan[1] noun *a pan of water:* **saucepan,** pot, bowl, frying pan, skillet.

pan[2] verb *the camera panned to the building:* **swing (round),** sweep, move, turn.

panel noun **1** *a control panel:* **console,** instrument panel, dashboard, instruments, controls, dials, array. **2** *a panel of judges:* **group,** team, body, committee, board.

panic noun *a wave of panic:* **alarm,** anxiety, fear, fright, trepidation, dread, terror, hysteria, apprehension; informal flap, fluster, cold sweat; N. Amer. informal swivet.
OPPOSITES calm.
verb **1** *there's no need to panic:* **be alarmed,** be scared, be afraid, take fright, be

hysterical, lose one's nerve, get overwrought, get worked up; informal get in a flap, run around like a headless chicken; Brit. informal get the wind up, go into a flat spin, have kittens. **2** *talk of love panicked her*: **frighten,** alarm, scare, unnerve; Brit. informal put the wind up.
OPPOSITES stay calm, calm down.

panorama noun **view,** vista, prospect, scenery, landscape, seascape, cityscape, skyline.

pant verb **breathe heavily,** breathe hard, puff and blow, huff and puff, gasp, heave, wheeze.

pants plural noun **1** (Brit.) **underpants,** briefs, boxer shorts, boxers, knickers; N. Amer. shorts, undershorts; informal panties; N. Amer. dated step-ins. **2** (N. Amer.) **trousers,** slacks; Brit. informal trews, strides, kecks; Austral. informal daks.

paper noun **1** **newspaper,** journal, gazette, periodical, tabloid, broadsheet, daily, weekly; informal rag; N. Amer. informal tab. **2** *a three-hour paper*: **exam,** examination, test. **3** *he has written a paper on global warming*: **essay,** article, monograph, thesis, work, dissertation, treatise, study, report, analysis; N. Amer. theme. **4** *personal papers*: **document,** certificate, letter, file, deed, record, archive; (**papers**) paperwork, documentation. **5** *they asked us for our papers*: **identification,** identity card, ID, credentials.

parable noun **allegory,** moral tale, fable.

parade noun **1** *a victory parade*: **procession,** march, cavalcade, motorcade, spectacle, display, pageant, review, tattoo; Brit.

march past. **2** *she walked along the parade*: **promenade,** walkway, esplanade, mall; N. Amer. boardwalk; Brit. informal prom.
verb **1** *the teams paraded through the city*: **march,** process, file, troop. **2** *she paraded up and down*: **strut,** swagger, stride. **3** *he was keen to parade his knowledge*: **display,** exhibit, make a show of, flaunt, show (off), demonstrate.

paradise noun **1** **heaven,** the promised land, the Elysian Fields. **2** *a tropical paradise*: **Utopia,** Shangri-La, Eden, heaven, idyll. **3** *this is sheer paradise!* **bliss,** heaven, ecstasy, delight, joy, happiness, heaven on earth.
OPPOSITES hell.

paradox noun **contradiction,** self-contradiction, inconsistency, incongruity, conflict, enigma, puzzle, conundrum.

paragraph noun **section,** division, part, portion, segment, passage, clause.

parallel adjective **1** *parallel lines*: **aligned,** side by side, equidistant. **2** *parallel careers*: **similar,** analogous, comparable, corresponding, like, equivalent, matching.
OPPOSITES divergent, different.
noun **1** *an exact parallel*: **counterpart,** analogue, equivalent, match, twin, duplicate, mirror. **2** *there is an interesting parallel between these figures*: **similarity,** likeness, resemblance, analogy, correspondence, comparison, equivalence, symmetry.
OPPOSITES divergence, difference.

paralyse verb 1 *both of his legs were paralysed:* **disable**, cripple, immobilize, incapacitate; (**paralysed**) Medicine paraplegic, quadriplegic. 2 *the capital was paralysed by a strike:* **bring to a standstill**, immobilize, bring to a halt, freeze, cripple, disable.

paralysis noun 1 *the disease can cause paralysis:* **immobility**, powerlessness, incapacity; Medicine paraplegia, quadriplegia. 2 *complete paralysis of the ports:* **shutdown**, immobilization, stoppage, gridlock, standstill, blockage.

paramount adjective **most important**, supreme, chief, overriding, predominant, foremost, prime, primary, principal, main, key, central; informal number-one.

paranoid adjective **suspicious**, mistrustful, anxious, fearful, insecure, obsessive.

paraphrase verb **reword**, rephrase, express differently, rewrite, gloss.

parasite noun **hanger-on**, cadger, leech, passenger; informal sponger, scrounger, freeloader; N. Amer. informal mooch; Austral./NZ informal bludger.

parcel noun *a parcel of clothes:* **package**, packet, pack, bundle, box, case, bale.
verb *she parcelled up the papers:* **pack (up)**, package, wrap (up), gift-wrap, tie up, bundle up.

pardon noun 1 *pardon for your sins:* **forgiveness**, absolution. 2 *he offered them a full pardon:* **reprieve**, amnesty, exoneration, release, acquittal, discharge.
verb 1 *I know she will pardon me:* **forgive**, absolve. 2 *they were subsequently pardoned:* **exonerate**, acquit, reprieve; informal let off.

OPPOSITES blame, punish.

parish noun 1 *the parish of Upton:* **district**, community. 2 *the vicar scandalized the parish:* **parishioners**, churchgoers, congregation, fold, flock, community.

park noun 1 **public garden**, recreation ground, playground, play area. 2 **parkland**, grassland, woodland, garden(s), lawns, grounds, estate.
verb 1 *he parked his car:* **leave**, position, stop, pull up. 2 (informal) *park your bag by the door:* **put (down)**, place, deposit, leave, stick, shove, dump; informal plonk; Brit. informal bung.

parliament noun **legislature**, assembly, chamber, house, congress, senate, diet.

parliamentary adjective **legislative**, law-making, governmental, congressional, democratic, elected.

parochial adjective **narrow-minded**, small-minded, provincial, small-town, conservative; N. Amer. informal jerkwater.

OPPOSITES broad-minded.

parody noun 1 *a parody of the news:* **satire**, burlesque, lampoon, pastiche, caricature, imitation; informal spoof, take-off, send-up. 2 *a parody of the truth:* **distortion**, travesty, caricature, misrepresentation, perversion, corruption.

parry verb 1 *Sharpe parried the blow:* **ward off**, fend off, deflect, block. 2 *I parried her questions:* **evade**, sidestep, avoid, dodge, field.

parson noun **priest**, minister, clergyman, vicar, rector, cleric, chaplain, pastor, curate; informal reverend, padre; Austral. informal josser.

p

part noun 1 *a large part of their life:* **piece**, amount, portion, proportion, percentage, fraction; informal slice, chunk. 2 *car parts:* **component**, bit, constituent, element, module. 3 *body parts:* **organ**, limb, member. 4 *the third part of the book:* **section**, division, volume, chapter, act, scene, instalment. 5 *another part of the country:* **district**, neighbourhood, quarter, section, area, region. 6 *the part of Juliet:* **role**, character. 7 *he was jailed for his part in the affair:* **involvement**, role, function, hand, responsibility, capacity, participation, contribution; informal bit.
OPPOSITES whole.
verb 1 *the curtains parted:* **separate**, divide, split, move apart. 2 *we parted on bad terms:* **leave each other**, part company, say goodbye/farewell, say one's goodbyes/farewells, go one's separate ways, take one's leave.
OPPOSITES join, meet.
■ **part with** give away, give up, relinquish, forgo, surrender, hand over. ■ **take part** participate, join in, get involved, enter, play a part, play a role, be a participant, contribute, have a hand in; informal get in on the act.

partial adjective 1 *a partial recovery:* **incomplete**, limited, qualified, imperfect, fragmentary, unfinished. 2 *a very partial view of the situation:* **biased**, prejudiced, partisan, one-sided, slanted, skewed, coloured, unbalanced.
OPPOSITES complete, unbiased.
■ **be partial to** like, love, enjoy, be fond of, be keen on, have a soft spot for, have a taste for, have a penchant for.

partially adverb **somewhat**, to a limited extent, to a certain extent, partly, in part, up to a point, slightly.
OPPOSITES wholly.

participant noun **participator**, contributor, party, member, entrant, competitor, player, contestant, candidate.

participate verb **take part**, join, engage, get involved, share, play a part, play a role, contribute, partake, have a hand in.

particle noun **(tiny) bit**, (tiny) piece, speck, spot, fragment, sliver, splinter.

particular adjective 1 *a particular group of companies:* **specific**, certain, distinct, separate, definite, precise. 2 *an issue of particular importance:* **special**, exceptional, unusual, uncommon, notable, noteworthy, remarkable, unique. 3 *he was particular about what he ate:* **fussy**, fastidious, finicky, discriminating, selective; informal pernickety, choosy, picky; Brit. informal faddy.
OPPOSITES general, indiscriminate.
noun *the same in every particular:* **detail**, item, point, element, fact, circumstance, feature.

particularly adverb 1 *the acoustics are particularly good:* **especially**, specially, exceptionally, unusually, remarkably, outstandingly, uncommonly, uniquely. 2 *he particularly asked that I should help you:* **specifically**, explicitly, expressly, in particular, especially, specially.

parting noun *an emotional*

p

parting: **farewell,** leave-taking, goodbye, adieu, departure.

partisan noun **guerrilla,** freedom fighter, resistance fighter, underground fighter, irregular.
adjective **biased,** prejudiced, one-sided, discriminatory, partial, sectarian, factional.
OPPOSITES unbiased.

partition noun **1** *the partition of Palestine:* **division,** partitioning, separation, dividing up, splitting up, breaking up, break-up. **2** *room partitions:* **screen,** room divider, dividing wall, barrier, panel.
verb **1** *moves to partition Poland:* **divide,** separate, split up, break up. **2** *the hall was partitioned:* **subdivide,** divide (up), separate, section off, screen off.

partly adverb **in part,** partially, somewhat, a little, up to a point, in some measure, slightly, to some extent.
OPPOSITES wholly.

partner noun **1** *business partners:* **colleague,** associate, co-worker, fellow worker, collaborator, comrade, teammate; Austral./NZ informal offsider. **2** *his partner in crime:* **accomplice,** confederate, accessory, collaborator, fellow conspirator, helper; informal sidekick. **3** *your relationship with your partner:* **spouse,** husband, wife, lover, girlfriend, boyfriend, fiancé, fiancée, significant other, live-in lover, mate; Brit. informal other half.

partnership noun **1** *close partnership:* **cooperation,** association, collaboration, coalition, alliance, union, affiliation, connection. **2** *thriving partnerships:*

company, association, consortium, syndicate, firm, business, organization.

party noun **1** *150 people attended the party:* **social gathering,** function, get-together, celebration, reunion, festivity, reception, soirée, social; informal bash, do; Austral./NZ informal shivoo. **2** *a party of visitors:* **group,** company, body, gang, band, crowd, pack, contingent; informal bunch, crew, load. **3** *a left-wing party:* **faction,** group, bloc, camp, caucus, alliance.

pass verb **1** *the traffic passing through the village:* **go,** proceed, move, progress, make one's way, travel. **2** *a car passed him:* **overtake,** go past/by, pull ahead of, leave behind. **3** *time passed:* **elapse,** go by/past, advance, wear on, roll by, tick by. **4** *he passed the time reading:* **occupy,** spend, fill, use (up), employ, while away. **5** *pass the salt:* **hand,** let someone have, give, reach. **6** *her estate passed to her grandson:* **be transferred,** go, be left, be bequeathed, be handed down/on, be passed on; Law devolve. **7** *his death passed unnoticed:* **happen,** occur, take place. **8** *the storm passed:* **come to an end,** fade (away), blow over, run its course, die out/down, finish, end, cease. **9** *he passed the exam:* **be successful in,** succeed in, gain a pass in, get through; informal sail through, scrape through. **10** *the Senate passed the bill:* **approve,** vote for, accept, ratify, adopt, agree to, authorize, endorse, legalize, enact; informal OK.
OPPOSITES start, fail, reject.
noun *you must show your pass:* **permit,** warrant, authorization, licence.

■ **pass as/for** be mistaken for, be taken for, be accepted as.
■ **pass out** faint, lose consciousness, black out. ■ **pass something up** turn down, reject, refuse, decline, give up, forgo, let pass, miss (out on); informal give something a miss.

passage noun **1** *their passage through the country:* **progress,** transit, advance, journey, trip, voyage. **2** *the passage of time:* **passing,** advance, course, march. **3** *clearing a passage to the front door:* **way,** route, path. **4** *the passage to the kitchen:* **corridor,** hall, hallway. **5** *a passage between the buildings:* **alley,** alleyway, passageway, lane, path, footpath, track, thoroughfare; N. Amer. areaway. **6** *a passage from 'Macbeth':* **extract,** excerpt, quotation, quote.

passenger noun **traveller,** commuter, fare-payer, rider, fare.

passing adjective **1** *of passing interest:* **fleeting,** transient, transitory, ephemeral, brief, short-lived, temporary, momentary. **2** *a passing glance:* **hasty,** rapid, hurried, brief, quick, cursory, superficial, casual, perfunctory.
noun **1** *the passing of time:* **passage,** course, progress, advance. **2** *Jack's passing:* **death,** demise, passing away, end, loss.

passion noun **1** *the passion of activists:* **enthusiasm,** ardour, fervour, eagerness, zeal, vigour, fire, energy, spirit, fanaticism. **2** *he worked himself up into a passion:* **rage,** fit of anger, temper, tantrum, fury, frenzy; Brit. informal paddy. **3** *hot with passion:* **love,** desire, lust, ardour, lasciviousness,

lustfulness. **4** *his passion for football:* **enthusiasm,** love, mania, fascination, obsession, preoccupation, fanaticism, fixation, compulsion, appetite, addiction; informal thing.
OPPOSITES apathy, calm.

passionate adjective **1** *a passionate entreaty:* **intense,** impassioned, ardent, fervent, vehement, fiery, heated, emotional, heartfelt, excited. **2** *McGregor is passionate about sport:* **very keen,** very enthusiastic, addicted; informal mad, crazy, hooked; Austral./NZ informal shook. **3** *a passionate kiss:* **amorous,** ardent, hot-blooded, loving, sexy, sensual, erotic, lustful; informal steamy, hot, turned on.
OPPOSITES apathetic, cool.

passive adjective **1** *a passive role:* **inactive,** non-active, non-participative, uninvolved. **2** *passive victims:* **submissive,** acquiescent, unresisting, compliant, docile.
OPPOSITES active, resistant.

past adjective **1** *times past:* **gone by,** bygone, former, previous, old, of old, olden, long-ago. **2** *the past few months:* **last,** recent, preceding. **3** *a past chairman:* **previous,** former, foregoing, erstwhile, one-time, sometime, ex-.
OPPOSITES present, future.
noun *details of her past:* **history,** background, past life, life story.
preposition **1** *I drove past the cafe:* **in front of,** by. **2** *it's past 9 o'clock:* **beyond,** after, later than.
adverb *they hurried past:* **along,** by, on.

paste noun **1** *blend the ingredients to a paste:* **purée,** pulp, mush, spread, pâté.

p

2 *wallpaper paste:* **adhesive,** glue, gum; N. Amer. mucilage.
verb *a notice was pasted on the door:* **stick,** glue, gum, fix, affix.

pastel adjective **pale,** soft, light, delicate, muted.
OPPOSITES dark, bright.

pastime noun **hobby,** leisure activity, leisure pursuit, recreation, game, amusement, diversion, entertainment, interest.

pastor noun **priest,** minister, parson, clergyman, cleric, chaplain, vicar, rector, curate; informal reverend, padre; Austral. informal josser.

pastoral adjective **1** *a pastoral scene:* **rural,** country, rustic, agricultural, bucolic. **2** *his pastoral duties:* **priestly,** clerical, ecclesiastical, ministerial.
OPPOSITES urban, lay.

pasture noun **grassland,** grass, grazing, meadow, field; Austral./NZ run.

pat verb & noun **tap,** clap, touch, stroke.

patch noun **1** *a reddish patch on her wrist:* **blotch,** mark, spot, smudge, smear, stain, streak, blemish; informal splodge. **2** *a patch of ground:* **plot,** area, piece, strip, tract, parcel, bed; Brit. allotment; N. Amer. lot. **3** (Brit. informal) *going through a difficult patch:* **period,** time, spell, phase, stretch.
verb *her jeans were neatly patched:* **mend,** repair, sew up, stitch up, cover, reinforce.

patent adjective **1** *patent nonsense:* **obvious,** clear, plain, evident, manifest, conspicuous, blatant, barefaced, flagrant. **2** *patent medicines:* **proprietary,** patented, licensed, branded.

path noun **1** *the path to the beach:* **footpath,** pathway, track, trail, bridle path, lane, cycle track; N. Amer. bikeway. **2** *journalists blocked his path:* **route,** way, course. **3** *the best path to follow:* **course of action,** route, road, avenue, line, approach, tack.

pathetic adjective **1** *a pathetic sight:* **pitiful,** moving, touching, poignant, plaintive, wretched. **2** (informal) *a pathetic excuse:* **feeble,** woeful, sorry, poor, pitiful, lamentable, deplorable, contemptible.
OPPOSITES funny, plausible, commendable.

patience noun **1** *she tried everyone's patience:* **forbearance,** tolerance, restraint, equanimity, understanding, indulgence. **2** *a task requiring patience:* **perseverance,** persistence, endurance, tenacity, application, staying power, doggedness.

patient adjective **1** *I must ask you to be patient:* **forbearing,** uncomplaining, tolerant, long-suffering, accommodating, understanding, indulgent. **2** *patient research:* **persevering,** persistent, tenacious, dogged, determined.
noun *a doctor's patient:* **sick person,** case, sufferer.

patriotic adjective **nationalistic,** loyalist, loyal, chauvinistic, jingoistic, flag-waving.
OPPOSITES traitorous.

patrol noun **1** *ships on patrol in the straits:* **guard,** watch, vigil. **2** *the patrol stopped a woman:* **squad,** detachment, party, force.
verb *a guard was patrolling the estate:* **guard,** keep watch on,

police, make the rounds of, stand guard (over), defend, safeguard.

patron noun 1 *a patron of the arts:* **sponsor,** backer, benefactor, contributor, subscriber, donor, philanthropist, promoter, friend, supporter. 2 *club patrons:* **customer,** client, consumer, user, visitor, guest; informal **regular.**

patronage noun 1 *arts patronage:* **sponsorship,** backing, funding, financing, assistance, support. 2 *thank you for your patronage:* **custom,** trade, business.

patronize verb 1 *don't patronize me!* **talk down to,** treat like a child. 2 *they patronized local tradesmen:* **use,** buy from, shop at, be a customer/client of, deal with, frequent, support.

patronizing adjective **condescending,** supercilious, superior, imperious, scornful; informal **uppity,** high and mighty.

pattern noun 1 *the pattern on the wallpaper:* **design,** decoration, motif, device, marking. 2 *working patterns:* **system,** order, arrangement, form, method, structure, scheme, plan, format. 3 *this set the pattern for a generation:* **model,** example, criterion, standard, norm, yardstick, touchstone, benchmark, blueprint.

pause noun *five minutes' pause:* **break,** interruption, lull, respite, breathing space, gap, interlude, adjournment, rest, wait, hesitation; informal **let-up,** breather.
verb *let's pause here:* **stop,** break off, take a break, adjourn, rest, wait, hesitate; informal **take a**

breather.

pave verb **surface,** floor, cover, tile, flag.

pavement noun **footpath,** walkway; N. Amer. **sidewalk.**

pay verb 1 *I must pay him for his work:* **reward,** reimburse, recompense, remunerate. 2 *I paid £7 for a ticket:* **spend,** pay out; informal **lay out,** shell out, fork out, cough up; N. Amer. informal **ante up, pony up.** 3 *he paid his debts:* **discharge,** settle, pay off, clear. 4 *he made the buses pay:* **be profitable,** make money, make a profit. 5 *it may pay you to be early:* **be advantageous to,** benefit, be of advantage to, be beneficial to. 6 *he will pay for his mistakes:* **suffer (the consequences),** be punished, atone, pay the penalty/price.
noun *equal pay:* **salary,** wages, payment, earnings, remuneration, fee, reimbursement, income, revenue.
■ **pay someone back** get one's revenge on, get back at, get even with, settle the score. ■ **pay something back** repay, pay off, give back, return, reimburse, refund. ■ **pay something off** pay (in full), settle, discharge, clear, liquidate. ■ **pay off** (informal) meet with success, be successful, be effective, get results, work.

payable adjective **due,** owed, owing, outstanding, unpaid, overdue; N. Amer. **delinquent.**

payment noun 1 *discounts for early payment:* **remittance,** settlement, discharge, clearance. 2 *monthly payments:* **instalment,** premium. 3 *extra payment for good performance:*

p

salary, wages, pay, earnings, fees, remuneration, reimbursement, income.

peace noun **1** *peace at last!* **quiet,** silence, peace and quiet, hush, stillness, still. **2** *peace of mind:* **serenity,** peacefulness, tranquillity, calm, calmness, composure, ease, contentment. **3** *we pray for peace:* **order,** harmony, agreement. **4** *a lasting peace:* **treaty,** truce, ceasefire, armistice.
OPPOSITES noise, agitation, war.

peaceful adjective **1** *peaceful surroundings:* **tranquil,** calm, restful, quiet, still, relaxing. **2** *his peaceful mood:* **serene,** calm, tranquil, composed, placid, at ease, untroubled, unworried, content. **3** *peaceful relations:* **harmonious,** on good terms, amicable, friendly, cordial, non-violent.
OPPOSITES noisy, agitated, hostile.

peak noun **1** *the peaks of the mountains:* **summit,** top, crest, pinnacle, cap. **2** *the highest peak:* **mountain,** hill, height. **3** *the peak of his career:* **height,** high point, pinnacle, summit, top, climax, culmination, apex, zenith, acme.
verb *Labour support has peaked:* **reach its height,** climax, culminate.
adjective *at peak times:* **maximum,** greatest, busiest, highest.

peculiar adjective **1** *something peculiar happened:* **strange,** unusual, odd, funny, curious, bizarre, weird, eccentric, abnormal, unconventional, outlandish; informal wacky. **2** *customs peculiar to this area:* **distinctive,** exclusive, unique, characteristic, distinct,

individual, typical, special, personal.
OPPOSITES ordinary.

pedantic adjective **finicky,** fussy, fastidious, dogmatic, purist, hair-splitting, quibbling; informal nit-picking, pernickety.

peddle verb **sell,** hawk, tout, trade, deal in, traffic in.

pedestrian noun **walker,** person on foot.
OPPOSITES driver.
adjective **dull,** boring, tedious, monotonous, unremarkable, uninspired, unimaginative, unexciting, routine, commonplace, ordinary, everyday, run-of-the-mill, mundane, humdrum; informal bog-standard.
OPPOSITES exciting.

pedigree noun *a fine pedigree:* **ancestry,** lineage, line, descent, genealogy, extraction, parentage, bloodline.
adjective *a pedigree cat:* **pure-bred,** full-blooded, thoroughbred.

peel verb **1** *peel and core the fruit:* **pare,** skin, hull, shell. **2** *the wallpaper was peeling:* **flake (off),** come off, fall off.
noun *orange peel:* **rind,** skin, covering, zest.

peep verb *I peeped through the keyhole:* **peek,** look, sneak a look, glance; informal squint.
noun *I'll just take a peep:* **peek,** look, glance; informal squint.

peer¹ verb *he peered at the manuscript:* **look closely,** squint, gaze.

peer² noun **1** *hereditary peers:* **aristocrat,** lord, lady, noble, nobleman, noblewoman. **2** *his academic peers:* **equal,** fellow, contemporary.

peg noun *a tent peg:* **pin,** nail, dowel.

verb **1** *the flysheet is pegged to the ground:* **fix,** pin, attach, fasten, secure. **2** *we decided to peg our prices:* **set,** hold, fix, freeze, keep down, hold down.

pen¹ verb *he penned a number of articles:* **write,** compose, draft, dash off, scribble.

pen² noun *a sheep pen:* **enclosure,** fold, pound, compound, stockade, sty, coop; N. Amer. corral.
verb *the hostages were penned up in a basement:* **confine,** coop, cage, shut, box, lock, trap, imprison, incarcerate.

penalize verb **1** *if you break the rules you will be penalized:* **punish,** discipline. **2** *a new tax would penalize the poor:* **handicap,** disadvantage, discriminate against.
OPPOSITES reward, benefit.

penalty noun **punishment,** sanction, fine, forfeit, sentence.
OPPOSITES reward.

pending adjective **1** *nine cases were still pending:* **unresolved,** undecided, unsettled, up in the air, ongoing, outstanding; informal on the back burner. **2** *with a general election pending:* **imminent,** impending, about to happen, forthcoming, on the way, coming, approaching, looming, near, on the horizon, in the offing.
preposition *they were released on bail pending an appeal:* **awaiting,** until.

penetrate verb **1** *the knife penetrated his lungs:* **pierce,** puncture, enter, perforate, stab, gore. **2** *they penetrated enemy lines:* **infiltrate,** slip through, enter. **3** *his words finally penetrated:* **register,** sink in, become clear, fall into place; informal click.

penetrating adjective **1** *a penetrating wind:* **cold,** cutting, biting, keen, sharp, harsh, raw, freezing, chill, bitter. **2** *a penetrating voice:* **shrill,** strident, piercing, ear-splitting. **3** *her penetrating gaze:* **intent,** searching, piercing, probing, sharp, keen. **4** *a penetrating analysis:* **perceptive,** insightful, keen, sharp, intelligent, clever, smart, incisive, trenchant, astute.
OPPOSITES mild, soft, stupid.

pension noun **old-age pension,** retirement pension, superannuation, allowance, benefit, support, welfare.

pensioner noun **retired person,** old-age pensioner, OAP, senior citizen; N. Amer. senior, retiree.

people plural noun **1** *crowds of people:* **human beings,** persons, individuals, humans, mortals, living souls, personages {men, women, and children}; informal folk. **2** *the British people:* **citizens,** subjects, electors, voters, taxpayers, residents, inhabitants, public, citizenry, nation, population, populace. **3** *a man of the people:* **the common people,** the proletariat, the masses, the populace, the rank and file; derogatory the hoi polloi; informal, derogatory the proles, the plebs. **4** *her people don't live far away:* **family,** parents, relatives, relations, folk, kinsfolk, flesh and blood, nearest and dearest; informal folks. **5** (singular) *a proud people:* **race,** ethnic group, tribe, clan, nation.
verb *those who once peopled Newfoundland:* **populate,** settle (in), colonize, inhabit, live in, occupy.

pepper verb **1** *stars peppered the*

desert skies: **sprinkle,** fleck, dot, spot, stipple. **2** *gunfire peppered the area:* **bombard,** pelt, shower, rain down on, strafe, rake, blitz.

perceive verb **1** *he perceived a tear in her eye:* **see,** discern, detect, catch sight of, spot, observe, notice. **2** *he was perceived as too negative:* **regard,** look on, view, consider, think of, judge, deem.

perception noun **1** *popular perceptions about old age:* **impression,** idea, conception, notion, thought, belief. **2** *he talks with great perception:* **insight,** perceptiveness, understanding, intelligence, intuition, incisiveness.

perceptive adjective **insightful,** discerning, sensitive, intuitive, observant, penetrating, intelligent, clever, canny, keen, sharp, astute, shrewd, quick, smart, acute; informal on the ball; N. Amer. informal heads-up.
OPPOSITES obtuse.

perch verb **1** *a swallow perched on the telegraph wire:* **sit,** rest, alight, settle, land, roost. **2** *she perched her glasses on her nose:* **put,** place, set, rest, balance.

perennial adjective **lasting,** enduring, abiding, long-lasting, long-lived, perpetual, continuing, continual, recurring.
OPPOSITES ephemeral.

perfect adjective **1** *a perfect wife:* **ideal,** model, faultless, flawless, consummate, exemplary, best, ultimate, copybook. **2** *in perfect condition:* **flawless,** mint, as good as new, pristine, immaculate, optimum, prime, peak; informal tip-top, A1. **3** *a perfect copy:* **exact,** precise,

accurate, faithful, true; Brit. informal spot on; N. Amer. informal on the money. **4** *the perfect Christmas present:* **ideal,** just right, appropriate, fitting, suitable, tailor-made, very; Brit. informal spot on, just the job. **5** *she felt a perfect idiot:* **absolute,** complete, total, real, out-and-out, thorough, downright, utter; Brit. informal right; Austral./NZ informal fair.
verb *he's perfecting his style:* **improve,** polish (up), hone, refine, brush up, fine-tune.

perfection noun **the ideal,** a paragon, the last word, the ultimate; informal the tops, the bee's knees.

perfectly adverb **1** *a perfectly cooked meal:* **superbly,** superlatively, excellently, flawlessly, faultlessly, to perfection, immaculately, exquisitely, consummately; N. Amer. to a fare-thee-well; informal like a dream, to a T. **2** *we understand each other perfectly:* **absolutely,** completely, altogether, entirely, wholly, totally, fully, in every respect.
OPPOSITES badly, partly.

perform verb **1** *duties to perform:* **carry out,** do, execute, discharge, conduct, implement; informal pull off. **2** *the car performs well:* **function,** work, operate, run, go, respond, behave, act. **3** *the play was performed in Britain:* **stage,** put on, present, mount, act, produce. **4** *the band performed live:* **play,** sing, appear.
OPPOSITES neglect.

performance noun **1** *the evening performance:* **show,** production, showing, presentation, staging, concert, recital; informal gig. **2** *their* *performance was excellent:* **rendition**, interpretation, playing, acting. **3** *the performance of his duty:* **carrying out**, execution, discharge, completion, fulfilment. **4** *the performance of the processor:* **functioning**, working, operation, running, behaviour, response, economy.

performer noun actor, actress, artiste, artist, entertainer, trouper, player, musician, singer, dancer, comic, comedian, comedienne.

perfume noun **1** *a bottle of perfume:* **scent**, fragrance, eau de toilette, toilet water. **2** *the heady perfume of lilacs:* **smell**, scent, fragrance, aroma, bouquet.

perhaps adverb maybe, for all one knows, it could be, it may be, it's possible, possibly, conceivably; N. English happen.

peril noun danger, jeopardy, risk, hazard, menace, threat.
OPPOSITES safety.

perimeter noun boundary, border, limits, bounds, edge, margin, fringe(s), periphery.
OPPOSITES centre.

period noun **1** *a six-week period:* **time**, spell, interval, stretch, term, span, phase, bout; Brit. informal patch. **2** *the post-war period:* **era**, age, epoch, time, days, years.

periodic adjective regular, at fixed intervals, recurrent, recurring, repeated, cyclical, seasonal, occasional, intermittent, sporadic, odd.

periodical noun journal, magazine, newspaper, paper, review, digest, gazette, newsletter, organ; informal mag, glossy.

peripheral adjective secondary, subsidiary, incidental, tangential, marginal, minor, unimportant, ancillary.
OPPOSITES central.

perish verb **1** *millions of soldiers perished:* **die**, lose one's life, be killed, fall, be lost; informal buy it. **2** *the rubber had perished:* **go bad**, spoil, rot, decay, decompose.

perk noun fringe benefit, advantage, bonus, extra, plus; informal freebie.

permanent adjective
1 *permanent brain damage:* **lasting**, enduring, indefinite, continuing, constant, irreparable, irreversible, lifelong, indelible, standing. **2** *a permanent job:* **long-term**, stable, secure.
OPPOSITES temporary.

permanently adverb **1** *the attack left her permanently disabled:* **forever**, for all time, for good, irreversibly, incurably, irreparably, indelibly; informal for keeps. **2** *I was permanently hungry:* **continually**, constantly, perpetually, always.

permission noun authorization, consent, leave, authority, sanction, licence, dispensation, assent, agreement, approval, blessing, clearance; informal the go-ahead, the green light, say-so.
OPPOSITES ban.

permit verb *other synthetic drugs would be permitted:* **allow**, let, authorize, sanction, grant, license, consent to, assent to; informal give the go-ahead to, give the green light to.
OPPOSITES ban.
noun *a work permit:* **authorization**, licence, pass,

p

ticket, warrant, passport, visa.

perpetual adjective **1** *a perpetual state of fear:* **constant,** permanent, uninterrupted, continuous, unremitting, unending, everlasting, eternal, unceasing, without end, persistent, lasting, abiding. **2** *perpetual nagging:* **interminable,** incessant, ceaseless, endless, relentless, unrelenting, persistent, continual, continuous, non-stop, never-ending, repeated, unremitting, round-the-clock, unabating; informal eternal. OPPOSITES temporary, intermittent.

perplexing adjective puzzling, baffling, mystifying, mysterious, bewildering, confusing, disconcerting, worrying.

persecute verb **1** *they were persecuted for their beliefs:* **oppress,** abuse, victimize, ill-treat, mistreat, maltreat, torment, torture. **2** *she was persecuted by the press:* **harass,** hound, plague, badger, harry, intimidate, pick on, pester; informal hassle.

persist verb **1** *Corbett persisted with his questioning:* **persevere,** continue, carry on, go on, keep on, keep going, hammer away, keep at it; informal soldier on, plug away. **2** *if dry weather persists, water the lawn thoroughly:* **continue,** hold, carry on, last, keep on, remain, linger, stay, endure. OPPOSITES give up, stop.

persistence noun perseverance, tenacity, determination, staying power, endurance, doggedness, stamina; informal stickability; N. Amer. informal stick-to-it-iveness.

persistent adjective **1** *a very*

persistent man: **tenacious,** determined, resolute, dogged, tireless, indefatigable, insistent, unrelenting. **2** *persistent rain:* **constant,** continuous, continuing, continual, non-stop, never-ending, steady, uninterrupted, unbroken, interminable, incessant, endless, unending, unrelenting. **3** *a persistent cough:* **chronic,** nagging, frequent, repeated, habitual. OPPOSITES irresolute, intermittent.

person noun human being, individual, man, woman, human, being, living soul, mortal, creature; informal type, sort, beggar, cookie.
■ **in person** physically, in the flesh, personally, oneself.

personal adjective **1** *a highly personal style:* **distinctive,** characteristic, unique, individual, idiosyncratic. **2** *a personal appearance:* **in person,** in the flesh, actual, live, physical. **3** *his personal life:* **private,** intimate. **4** *personal remarks:* **derogatory,** disparaging, belittling, insulting, rude, disrespectful, offensive, pejorative. OPPOSITES common, public, complimentary.

personality noun **1** *her cheerful personality:* **character,** nature, disposition, temperament, make-up, psyche. **2** *she had loads of personality:* **charisma,** magnetism, character, charm, presence. **3** *a famous personality:* **celebrity,** VIP, star, superstar, big name, somebody, leading light, luminary, notable; informal celeb. OPPOSITES nobody.

personally adverb **1** *I'd like to*

p

thank him personally: **in person,** oneself. **2** *every pupil is known personally:* **individually,** specially. **3** *personally, I like it:* **for my part,** for myself, as far as I am concerned, subjectively.

personnel noun **staff,** employees, workforce, workers, labour force, manpower, human resources.

perspective noun **outlook,** view, viewpoint, point of view, standpoint, position, stand, stance, angle, slant, attitude.

persuade verb **1** *he persuaded her to go with him:* **prevail on,** talk into, coax, convince, get, induce, win over, bring round, influence, sway; informal sweet-talk. **2** *lack of money persuaded them to abandon the scheme:* **cause,** lead, move, dispose, incline.
OPPOSITES dissuade, deter.

persuasion noun **1** *Monica needed a lot of persuasion:* **coaxing,** urging, inducement, convincing, encouragement, enticement; informal sweet-talking. **2** *various religious persuasions:* **group,** grouping, sect, denomination, party, camp, side, faction, school of thought, belief, creed, faith.

persuasive adjective **convincing,** compelling, effective, telling, forceful, powerful, eloquent, impressive, sound, cogent, valid, strong, plausible, credible.
OPPOSITES unconvincing.

pertinent adjective **relevant,** to the point, apposite, appropriate, suitable, applicable, material, germane.
OPPOSITES irrelevant.

perverse adjective **1** *he is being deliberately perverse:* **awkward,** contrary, difficult,

unreasonable, uncooperative, unhelpful, obstructive, stubborn, obstinate; Brit. informal bloody-minded. **2** *a verdict that is manifestly perverse:* **illogical,** irrational, wrong-headed.
OPPOSITES accommodating, reasonable.

pervert verb *perverting the course of justice:* **distort,** warp, corrupt, subvert, twist, bend, abuse, divert.
noun *a nasty pervert:* **deviant,** degenerate; informal perv, dirty old man, sicko.

perverted adjective **unnatural,** deviant, warped, twisted, abnormal, unhealthy, depraved, perverse, aberrant, debased, degenerate; informal sick, kinky.

pessimistic adjective **gloomy,** negative, defeatist, downbeat, cynical, bleak, fatalistic, depressed.
OPPOSITES optimistic.

pest noun **nuisance,** annoyance, irritant, thorn in one's flesh/side, trial, menace, trouble, problem, worry, bother; informal pain in the neck, headache.

pester verb **badger,** hound, harass, plague, annoy, bother, harry, worry; informal hassle, bug.

pet adjective **1** *a pet lamb:* **tame,** domesticated, companion; Brit. house-trained; N. Amer. housebroken. **2** *his pet theory:* **favourite,** favoured, cherished, particular, special, personal.
verb **1** *the cats came to be petted:* **stroke,** caress, fondle, pat, tickle. **2** *couples petting in their cars:* **cuddle,** embrace, caress, kiss; informal canoodle, neck, smooch; Brit. informal snog; N. Amer. informal make out.

petition noun *2,500 people have signed a petition:* **appeal,** round robin, letter, request, entreaty,

p

application, plea.
verb *the islanders petitioned the government to help them:* **appeal to,** request, ask, call on, entreat, beg, implore, plead with, apply to, press, urge.

petty adjective **1** *petty regulations:* **trivial,** trifling, minor, insignificant, inconsequential, footling; informal piffling. **2** *a petty form of revenge:* **small-minded,** mean, shabby, spiteful.
OPPOSITES important, magnanimous.

phantom noun ghost, apparition, spirit, spectre, wraith; informal spook.

phase noun **1** *the final phase of the campaign:* **stage,** period, chapter, episode, part, step. **2** *he's going through a difficult phase:* **period,** stage, time, spell; Brit. informal patch.
■ **phase something in** introduce (gradually), ease in. ■ **phase something out** withdraw (gradually), discontinue, stop using, run down, wind down.

phenomenal adjective **remarkable,** exceptional, extraordinary, marvellous, miraculous, wonderful, outstanding, unprecedented; informal fantastic, terrific, tremendous, stupendous.
OPPOSITES ordinary.

phenomenon noun **1** *a rare phenomenon:* **occurrence,** event, happening, fact, situation, circumstance, experience, case, incident, episode. **2** *a pop phenomenon:* **marvel,** sensation, wonder, prodigy.

philosopher noun thinker, theorist, theoretician, scholar, intellectual, sage.

philosophical adjective **1** *a philosophical question:* **theoretical,** metaphysical. **2** *a philosophical mood:* **thoughtful,** reflective, pensive, meditative, contemplative, introspective. **3** *he was very philosophical about it:* **stoical,** self-possessed, serene, dispassionate, phlegmatic, long-suffering, resigned.

philosophy noun **1** *the philosophy of Aristotle:* **thinking,** thought, reasoning, logic. **2** *her political philosophy:* **beliefs,** credo, ideology, ideas, thinking, theories, doctrine, principles, views, outlook.

phobia noun fear, dread, horror, terror, aversion, antipathy, revulsion; informal hang-up.

phone noun *she spent hours on the phone:* **telephone;** Brit. informal blower.
verb *I'll phone you later:* **call,** telephone; Brit. ring, ring up, give someone a ring; informal call up, give someone a buzz; Brit. informal give someone a bell, give someone a tinkle, get on the blower to; N. Amer. informal get someone on the horn.

phoney (informal) adjective *a phoney address:* **bogus,** false, fake, fraudulent, counterfeit, forged, imitation, affected, insincere; informal pretend; Brit. informal cod.
OPPOSITES authentic.
noun **1** *he's a phoney:* **impostor,** sham, fake, fraud, charlatan; informal con artist. **2** *the diamond's a phoney:* **fake,** imitation, counterfeit, forgery.

photocopy noun *a photocopy of the letter:* **copy,** duplicate, reproduction, facsimile; trademark Xerox, photostat.
verb *I photocopied the form:* **copy,** duplicate, xerox,

p

photostat, reproduce.

photograph noun *a colour photograph:* **picture**, photo, snap, snapshot, shot, print, still. verb *he was photographed in Paris:* **take a picture/photo of**, take someone's picture, snap, shoot, film.

photographic adjective **1** *a photographic record:* **pictorial**, graphic, in photographs. **2** *a photographic memory:* **detailed**, exact, precise, accurate, vivid.

phrase noun *an elegant phrase:* **expression**, construction, term, turn of phrase, idiom, saying. verb *how did you phrase the question?* **express**, put into words, put, word, formulate, couch, frame.

physical adjective **1** *physical pleasure:* **bodily**, corporeal, carnal, fleshly, non-spiritual. **2** *physical work:* **manual**, labouring, blue-collar. **3** *the physical universe:* **material**, concrete, tangible, palpable, solid, substantial, real, actual, visible. OPPOSITES mental, spiritual.

physician noun **doctor**, medical practitioner, general practitioner, GP, clinician, specialist, consultant; informal doc, medic.

pick verb **1** *picking apples:* **harvest**, gather (in), collect, pluck. **2** *pick a time that suits you:* **choose**, select, single out, opt for, plump for, elect, decide on, settle on, fix on, name, nominate, identify. **3** *he tried to pick a fight:* **provoke**, start, cause, incite, instigate, prompt. OPPOSITES reject, avoid. noun *the pick of the crop:* **best**, finest, choice, choicest, cream, flower, crème de la crème, elite. ■ **pick on** bully, victimize,

torment, persecute, taunt, tease; informal get at, needle.
■ **pick someone/something out** see, make out, distinguish, discern, spot, perceive, detect, notice, recognize, identify, catch sight of, glimpse. ■ **pick up** improve, recover, rally, bounce back, perk up, look up, take a turn for the better, turn the corner, be on the mend, make headway, make progress.
■ **pick someone/something up 1** *he picked up the baby:* lift, take up, raise, hoist, scoop up, gather up, snatch up. **2** *I'll pick up the parcel on my way:* fetch, collect, call for. ■ **pick someone up** (informal) **1** *he was picked up by the police:* arrest, apprehend, detain, take into custody, seize; informal nab, run in; Brit. informal nick. **2** *he picked her up in a club:* meet; informal get off with, pull, cop off with. ■ **pick something up 1** *we picked it up at a flea market:* find, discover, come across, stumble across, happen on, chance on, acquire, obtain, come by, get, buy, purchase; informal get hold of, get one's hands on. **2** *he picked up the story in the 1950s:* resume, take up, start again, recommence, continue, carry/go on with. **3** *she picked up a virus:* catch, contract, get, go/come down with. **4** *all the gossip he'd picked up:* hear, hear tell, get wind of, be told, learn, glean. **5** *we're picking up a distress signal:* receive, detect, get, hear.

picket noun **1** *forty pickets were arrested:* **demonstrator**, striker, protester. **2** *they decided to organize a picket:* **demonstration**, picket line, blockade, boycott, strike. verb *workers picketed the* *factory:* **demonstrate at,** blockage, boycott.

pickup noun **improvement,** recovery, revival, upturn, upswing, rally, resurgence, renewal, turnaround.
OPPOSITES slump.

picture noun **1** *pictures in an art gallery:* **painting, drawing,** sketch, watercolour, print, canvas, portrait, illustration, depiction, likeness, representation, image. **2** *we were told not to take pictures:* **photograph,** photo, snap, snapshot, shot, frame, exposure, still, print. **3** *my picture of the ideal woman:* **concept,** idea, impression, (mental) image, vision, visualization, notion. **4** *the picture of health:* **personification,** embodiment, epitome, essence, quintessence, soul, model.
verb **1** *they were pictured playing in the snow:* **depict,** portray, show, represent, **draw,** sketch, photograph, paint. **2** *Anne still pictured Richard as he had been:* **visualize,** see (in one's mind's eye), imagine, remember.

picturesque adjective **attractive,** pretty, beautiful, lovely, scenic, charming, quaint, pleasing, delightful.
OPPOSITES ugly.

piece noun **1** *a piece of cheese:* **bit,** slice, chunk, segment, section, lump, hunk, wedge, slab, block, cake, bar, stick, length. **2** *the pieces of a clock:* **component,** part, bit, constituent, element, section, unit, module. **3** *a piece of furniture:* **item,** article, specimen. **4** *a piece of the profit:* **share,** portion, slice,

quota, part, percentage, amount, quantity, ration, fraction; Brit. informal whack. **5** *pieces from his collection:* **work (of art),** artwork, artefact, composition, opus. **6** *the reporter who wrote the piece:* **article,** item, story, report, essay, feature, review, column.

pier noun **jetty,** quay, wharf, dock, landing stage.

pierce verb **penetrate,** puncture, perforate, prick, spike, stab, drill, bore.

piercing adjective **1** *a piercing shriek:* **shrill,** ear-splitting, high-pitched, penetrating, strident. **2** *his piercing gaze:* **searching,** probing, penetrating, sharp, keen.

pigment noun **colouring,** colour, tint, dye, stain.

pile¹ noun **1** *a pile of stones:* **heap,** stack, mound, pyramid, mass, collection, accumulation, assemblage, stockpile, hoard. **2** (informal) *I've a pile of work to do:* **lot,** mountain, reams, abundance; informal load, heap, mass, slew, stack, ton; Brit. informal shedload; Austral./NZ informal swag.
verb **1** *he piled up the plates:* **heap,** stack. **2** *he piled his plate with salad:* **load,** heap, fill (up), stack, charge. **3** *we piled into the car:* **crowd,** clamber, pack, squeeze, scramble, struggle.
■ **pile up** accumulate, grow, mount up, build up, multiply, escalate, soar, spiral, rocket, increase.

pile² noun *a carpet with a short pile:* **nap,** fibres, threads.

pile-up noun **crash,** collision, smash, accident; Brit. RTA; N. Amer. wreck; Brit. informal shunt.

pilgrim noun **traveller,**

wayfarer, worshipper, devotee, believer; Islam haji, alhaji.

pilgrimage noun journey, expedition, mission, hajj, visit, trek, trip, odyssey.

pill noun tablet, capsule, pellet, lozenge, pastille.

pillar noun 1 *stone pillars:* column, post, support, upright, pier, pile, prop, stanchion, obelisk. 2 *a pillar of the community:* stalwart, mainstay, bastion, leading light, worthy, backbone, supporter, upholder, champion.

pilot noun 1 *a fighter pilot:* airman, airwoman, flyer, captain; informal skipper; N. Amer. informal jock; dated aviator. 2 *a harbour pilot:* navigator, helmsman, steersman, coxswain. 3 *a pilot for a TV series:* trial, sample, experiment.
adjective *a pilot project:* experimental, exploratory, trial, test, sample, preliminary.
verb *he piloted the jet to safety:* navigate, guide, manoeuvre, steer, control, direct, captain, fly, drive, sail; informal skipper.

pin noun 1 *fasten the hem with a pin:* tack, safety pin, nail, staple, fastener. 2 *a broken pin in the machine:* bolt, peg, rod, rivet, dowel. 3 *they wore name pins:* badge, brooch.
verb 1 *she pinned the brooch to her dress:* attach, fasten, affix, fix, join, secure, clip, nail. 2 *they pinned him to the ground:* hold, press, pinion.
■ **pin someone/something down** confine, trap, hem in, corner, close in, shut in, pen in. ■ **pin something on someone** blame for, hold responsible for, attribute to, ascribe to, lay something at someone's door;

informal stick on.

pinch verb 1 *he pinched my arm:* nip, tweak, squeeze, grasp. 2 *my new shoes pinch my toes:* hurt, squeeze, crush, cramp.
noun 1 *he gave her arm a pinch:* nip, tweak, squeeze. 2 *a pinch of salt:* bit, touch, dash, spot, trace, soupçon, speck, taste; informal smidgen, tad.

pine verb *she thinks I am pining away from love:* fade, waste away, weaken, decline, languish, wilt, sicken.
■ **pine for** long for, yearn for, ache for, sigh for, hunger for, thirst for, itch for, carry a torch for, miss, mourn.

pink adjective rose, rosy, rosé, pale red, salmon, coral, flushed, blushing.

pinnacle noun 1 *the pinnacle of his career:* height, peak, high point, top, apex, zenith, acme. 2 *pinnacles of rock:* peak, needle, crag, tor.
OPPOSITES low point.

pinpoint adjective *pinpoint accuracy:* precise, exact, strict, absolute, complete, scientific.
verb *the technology can pinpoint a cellphone's position:* identify, determine, distinguish, discover, find, locate, detect, track down, spot, diagnose, recognize, pin down, home in on.

pioneer noun 1 *the pioneers of the Wild West:* settler, colonist, colonizer, frontiersman, explorer. 2 *a pioneer of motoring:* developer, innovator, trailblazer, groundbreaker, founding father, architect, creator.
verb *he pioneered the sale of insurance:* introduce, develop, launch, instigate, initiate,

p

spearhead, institute, establish, found.

pious adjective **religious,** devout, God-fearing, churchgoing, holy, godly, saintly, reverent, righteous.
OPPOSITES irreligious.

pipe noun *a central-heating pipe:* **tube,** conduit, hose, main, duct, line, channel, pipeline, drain.
verb **1** *the beer is piped into barrels:* **feed,** siphon, channel, run, convey. **2** *programmes piped in from London:* **relay,** feed, patch, transmit.

pirate noun *pirates boarded the ship:* **raider,** hijacker, marauder, freebooter; historical privateer, buccaneer.
verb *designers may pirate good ideas:* **steal,** copy, plagiarize, poach, appropriate, bootleg; informal crib, lift, rip off.

pit noun **1** *we dug a pit:* **hole,** trough, hollow, excavation, cavity, crater, pothole. **2** *pit closures:* **coal mine,** colliery, quarry, shaft.
verb *his skin had been pitted by acne:* **mark,** pockmark, pock, scar, dent, indent.

pitch noun **1** *a football pitch:* **playing field,** ground, sports field, stadium; Brit. park. **2** *her voice rose in pitch:* **tone,** key, modulation, frequency. **3** *the pitch of the roof:* **gradient,** slope, slant, angle, tilt, incline. **4** *at fever pitch:* **level,** intensity, point, degree, height, extent. **5** *his sales pitch:* **patter,** talk; informal spiel, line.
verb **1** *a kid pitched a snowball:* **throw,** toss, fling, hurl, cast, lob, flip; informal chuck, sling, heave, bung. **2** *he pitched overboard:* **fall,** tumble, topple, plunge, plummet. **3** *they pitched their tents:* **put up,** set

up, erect, raise. **4** *the boat pitched:* **lurch,** toss, plunge, roll, reel, sway, rock, list.

pitfall noun **hazard,** danger, risk, peril, difficulty, catch, snag, stumbling block, drawback.

pity noun **1** *a voice full of pity:* **compassion,** commiseration, condolence, sympathy, fellow feeling, understanding. **2** *it's a pity he never had children:* **shame,** misfortune, too bad; informal bummer.
OPPOSITES indifference, cruelty.
verb *they pitied me:* **feel sorry for,** feel for, sympathize with, empathize with, commiserate with, take pity on, be moved by, bleed for.

place noun **1** *an ideal place for dinner:* **location,** site, spot, setting, position, situation, area, region, locale, venue. **2** *foreign places:* **country,** state, area, region, town, city. **3** *a place of her own:* **home,** house, flat, apartment, accommodation, property, rooms, quarters; informal pad; Brit. informal gaff; formal residence, abode, dwelling. **4** *in your place, I'd agree:* **situation,** position, circumstances; informal shoes. **5** *a place was reserved for her:* **seat,** chair, space. **6** *I offered him a place in the company:* **job,** position, post, appointment, situation, employment. **7** *I know my place:* **status,** position, standing, rank, niche. **8** *it was not her place to sort it out:* **responsibility,** duty, job, task, role, function, concern, affair, charge.
verb **1** *books were placed on the table:* **put (down),** set (down), lay, deposit, position, plant, rest, stand, station, situate,

leave; informal stick, dump, bung, park, plonk, pop; N. Amer. informal plunk. **2** *the trust you placed in me:* **put,** lay, set, invest. **3** *a survey placed the company sixth:* **rank,** order, grade, class, classify, put. **4** *Joe couldn't quite place her:* **identify,** recognize, remember, put a name to, pin down, locate, pinpoint. **5** *we were placed with foster parents:* **accommodate,** house, home, allocate, assign.
■ **in place of** instead of, rather than, as a substitute for, as a replacement for, in exchange for, in lieu of, in someone's stead. ■ **out of place 1** *he said something out of place:* inappropriate, unsuitable, unseemly, improper, untoward, out of keeping, unbecoming. **2** *she seemed out of place in a launderette:* incongruous, out of one's element, like a fish out of water, uncomfortable, uneasy. ■ **take place** happen, occur, come about, go on, transpire; N. Amer. informal go down. ■ **take the place of** replace, stand in for, substitute for, act for, fill in for, cover for, relieve.

plague noun **1** *they died in a plague:* **pandemic,** epidemic, disease, sickness; dated contagion; archaic pestilence. **2** *a plague of fleas:* **infestation,** invasion, swarm, epidemic.
verb **1** *he was plagued by poor health:* **afflict,** trouble, torment, beset, dog, curse, bedevil. **2** *he plagued her with questions:* **pester,** harass, badger, bother, torment, harry, hound, trouble, nag, molest; informal hassle, bug; N. English informal mither; N. Amer. informal devil.

plain adjective **1** *it was plain that something was wrong:* **obvious,**

clear, evident, apparent, manifest, unmistakable. **2** *plain English:* **intelligible,** comprehensible, understandable, clear, lucid, simple, straightforward, user-friendly. **3** *plain speaking:* **candid,** frank, outspoken, forthright, direct, honest, truthful, blunt, bald, unequivocal; informal upfront. **4** *a plain dress:* **simple,** ordinary, unadorned, homely, basic, modest, unsophisticated, restrained. **5** *a plain girl:* **unattractive,** unprepossessing, ugly, ordinary; N. Amer. homely; Brit. informal no oil painting. **6** *it was plain bad luck:* **sheer,** pure, downright, out-and-out.
OPPOSITES obscure, fancy, attractive, pretentious.
noun *the plains of North America:* **grassland,** flatland, prairie, savannah, steppe, tundra, pampas, veld, plateau.

plan noun **1** *a plan for raising money:* **scheme,** idea, proposal, proposition, project, programme, system, method, strategy, stratagem, formula, recipe. **2** *her plan was to break even:* **intention,** aim, idea, objective, object, goal, target, ambition. **3** *a plan of the new office:* **map,** diagram, chart, blueprint, drawing, sketch, impression; N. Amer. plat.
verb **1** *plan your route in advance:* **organize,** arrange, work out, outline, map out, prepare, formulate, frame, develop, devise. **2** *he plans to buy a house:* **intend,** aim, propose, mean, hope. **3** *I'm planning a new garden:* **design,** draw up a plan for, sketch out, map out; N. Amer. plat.

plane¹ noun *a higher plane of achievement:* **level,** degree,

p

standard, stratum, dimension.
verb *boats planed across the water:* **skim**, glide.

plane² noun *the plane took off:* **aircraft**, airliner, jet, flying machine; Brit. aeroplane; N. Amer. airplane, ship.

plant noun 1 *garden plants:* **flower**, vegetable, herb, shrub, bush, weed; (**plants**) vegetation, greenery, flora. 2 *a CIA plant:* **spy**, informant, informer, secret agent, mole, infiltrator, operative; N. Amer. informal spook. 3 *a chemical plant:* **factory**, works, facility, refinery, mill. 4 *investment in new plant:* **machinery**, machines, equipment, apparatus, appliances, gear.
verb 1 *plant the seeds:* **sow**, scatter. 2 *he planted his feet on the ground:* **place**, put, set, position, situate, settle; informal plonk. 3 *she planted the idea in his mind:* **instil**, implant, put, place, introduce, fix, establish, lodge.

plaster noun 1 *the plaster covering the bricks:* **plasterwork**, stucco. 2 *a statuette made of plaster:* **plaster of Paris**, gypsum. 3 *waterproof plasters:* **sticking plaster**, adhesive dressing; trademark Elastoplast, Band-Aid.
verb 1 *bread plastered with butter:* **spread**, smother, smear, cake, coat. 2 *his hair was plastered down with sweat:* **flatten (down)**, smooth down, slick down.

plastic adjective 1 *at high temperatures the rocks become plastic:* **soft**, pliable, pliant, flexible, malleable, workable, mouldable; informal bendy. 2 *a plastic smile:* **artificial**, false, fake, bogus, insincere; informal

phoney, pretend.
OPPOSITES rigid, genuine.

plate noun 1 *a dinner plate:* **dish**, platter, salver; historical trencher; archaic charger. 2 *a plate of spaghetti:* **plateful**, helping, portion, serving. 3 *steel plates:* **panel**, sheet, slab. 4 *a brass plate on the door:* **plaque**, sign, tablet. 5 *the book has colour plates:* **picture**, print, illustration, photograph, photo.
verb *the roof was plated with steel:* **cover**, coat, overlay, laminate, veneer, armour, gild, chrome.

plateau noun **upland**, mesa, highland, tableland.

platform noun 1 *he made a speech from the platform:* **stage**, dais, rostrum, podium, stand. 2 *the Democratic Party's platform:* **programme**, manifesto, policies, principles, party line.

plausible adjective **credible**, believable, reasonable, likely, possible, conceivable, imaginable, convincing, persuasive.
OPPOSITES unlikely.

play verb 1 *the children played with toys:* **amuse oneself**, entertain oneself, enjoy oneself, have fun, relax, occupy oneself, frolic, romp; informal mess about/around. 2 *I used to play football:* **take part in**, participate in, be involved in, compete in, do. 3 *Liverpool play Oxford on Sunday:* **compete against**, take on, meet. 4 *he was to play Macbeth:* **act the part of**, take the role of, appear as, portray, perform.
noun 1 *work and play:* **amusement**, relaxation, recreation, diversion, leisure, enjoyment, pleasure, fun. 2 *a*

Shakespeare play: **drama,** theatrical work, piece, comedy, tragedy, production, performance. **3** *there was no play in the rope:* **movement,** slack, give.
■ **play something down** make light of, make little of, gloss over, downplay, understate, soft-pedal, diminish, trivialize.
■ **play up** (Brit. informal) **1** *the boys really did play up:* misbehave, be bad, be naughty. **2** *the boiler's playing up:* malfunction, not work, be defective, faulty; informal be on the blink, act up. **3** *his leg was playing up:* be painful, hurt, ache, be sore; informal kill someone, give someone gyp.

player noun **1** *a tournament for young players:* **participant,** contestant, competitor, contender, sportsman, sportswoman. **2** *the players in the orchestra:* **musician,** performer, artist, virtuoso, instrumentalist. **3** *the players of the Royal Shakespeare Company:* **actor, actress,** performer, thespian, entertainer, artiste, trouper.

playful adjective **1** *a playful mood:* **frisky,** lively, full of fun, frolicsome, high-spirited, exuberant, mischievous, impish; informal full of beans. **2** *a playful remark:* **light-hearted,** jokey, teasing, humorous, jocular, facetious, frivolous, flippant.
OPPOSITES serious.

plea noun appeal, entreaty, supplication, petition, request, call.

plead verb *she pleaded ignorance:* **claim,** use as an excuse, assert, allege, argue.
■ **plead with** beg, implore,

entreat, appeal to, ask.

pleasant adjective **1** *a pleasant evening:* **enjoyable,** pleasurable, nice, agreeable, entertaining, amusing, delightful, charming; informal lovely, great. **2** *the staff are pleasant:* **friendly,** charming, agreeable, amiable, nice, delightful, sweet, genial, cordial, good-natured, personable, hospitable, polite.
OPPOSITES unpleasant.

please verb **1** *he'd do anything to please her:* **make happy,** give pleasure to, make someone feel good, delight, charm, amuse, satisfy, gratify, humour, oblige. **2** *do as you please:* **like,** want, wish, desire, see fit, think fit, choose, will, prefer.
OPPOSITES annoy.

pleased adjective happy, glad, delighted, gratified, grateful, thankful, content, contented, satisfied, thrilled; informal over the moon, on cloud nine; Brit. informal chuffed; N. English informal made up; Austral. informal wrapped.
OPPOSITES unhappy.

pleasing adjective **1** *a pleasing result:* **good,** agreeable, pleasant, pleasurable, satisfying, gratifying, great. **2** *her pleasing manner:* **friendly,** amiable, pleasant, agreeable, affable, nice, genial, likeable, charming, engaging, delightful; informal lovely.
OPPOSITES poor, unfriendly.

pleasure noun **1** *she smiled with pleasure:* **happiness,** delight, joy, gladness, glee, satisfaction, gratification, contentment, enjoyment, amusement. **2** *his greatest pleasure in life:* **joy,** amusement, diversion, recreation, pastime, treat, thrill. **3** *don't mix business and pleasure:* **enjoyment,** fun,

p

entertainment, recreation, leisure, relaxation.
OPPOSITES unhappiness, trial, duty, work.

pledge noun *his election pledge:* **promise,** vow, undertaking, word, commitment, assurance, oath, guarantee.
verb *he pledged to root out corruption:* **promise,** vow, undertake, swear, commit oneself, declare, affirm.

plentiful adjective **abundant,** copious, ample, profuse, rich, lavish, generous, bountiful, bumper, prolific; informal galore.
OPPOSITES scarce.

plenty pronoun *there are plenty of books:* **a lot of,** many, a great deal of, a plethora of, enough and to spare, no lack of, a wealth of; informal loads of, heaps of, stacks of, masses of.
noun *times of plenty:* **prosperity,** affluence, wealth, opulence, comfort, luxury, abundance.

plight noun **predicament,** difficult situation, dire straits, trouble, difficulty, bind; informal tight corner, tight spot, hole, pickle, jam, fix.

plod verb **trudge,** walk heavily, clump, stomp, tramp, lumber, slog.
OPPOSITES stride, skip.

plot noun **1** *a plot to overthrow him:* **conspiracy,** intrigue, stratagem, plan. **2** *the plot of her novel:* **storyline,** story, scenario, action, thread, narrative. **3** *a three-acre plot:* **piece of ground,** patch, area, tract, acreage; Brit. allotment; N. Amer. lot, plat; N. Amer. & Austral./NZ homesite.
verb **1** *he plotted their downfall:* **plan,** scheme, arrange, organize, contrive. **2** *his brother was plotting against him:* **conspire,** scheme, intrigue, connive. **3** *the points were plotted on a graph:* **mark,** chart, map.

plough verb **1** *the fields were ploughed:* **till,** furrow, harrow, cultivate, work. **2** *the car ploughed into a wall:* **crash,** smash, career, plunge, bulldoze, hurtle, cannon.

ploy noun **ruse,** tactic, move, device, stratagem, scheme, trick, gambit, plan, manoeuvre, dodge, subterfuge; Brit. informal wheeze.

pluck verb **1** *he plucked a thread from his lapel:* **remove,** pick, pull, extract. **2** *she plucked at his T-shirt:* **pull,** tug, clutch, snatch, grab, catch, tweak, jerk; informal yank. **3** *she plucked the guitar strings:* **strum,** pick, thrum, twang.
noun *it took a lot of pluck:* **courage,** bravery, nerve, daring, spirit, grit; informal guts; Brit. informal bottle; N. Amer. informal moxie.

plug noun **1** *she pulled out the plug:* **stopper,** bung, cork, connector; N. Amer. stopple. **2** (informal) *a plug for his new book:* **advertisement,** promotion, commercial, recommendation, mention, good word; informal hype, push, puff.
verb **1** *plug the holes:* **stop,** seal, close, block, fill. **2** (informal) *she plugged her new film:* **publicize,** promote, advertise, mention, bang the drum for, draw attention to; informal hype, push.

plumb verb *an attempt to plumb her psyche:* **explore,** probe, delve into, search, examine, investigate, fathom, penetrate, understand.
adverb (informal) *it went plumb*

through the screen: **right,** exactly, precisely, directly, dead, straight; informal (slap) bang.

plummet verb **1** *the plane plummeted to the ground:* **plunge,** dive, drop, fall, hurtle. **2** *share prices plummeted:* **fall steeply,** plunge, tumble, drop rapidly, slump; informal **crash,** nosedive.
OPPOSITES soar.

plump adjective **fat,** chubby, rotund, ample, round, stout, portly, overweight; informal tubby, roly-poly, pudgy; Brit. informal podgy; N. Amer. informal zaftig, corn-fed.
OPPOSITES thin.

plunder verb **1** *they plundered the countryside:* **pillage,** loot, rob, raid, ransack, rifle, strip, sack. **2** *money plundered from pension funds:* **steal,** seize, thieve, pilfer, embezzle.
noun *huge quantities of plunder:* **booty,** loot, stolen goods, spoils, ill-gotten gains; informal swag.

plunge verb **1** *Joy plunged into the sea:* **dive,** jump, throw oneself. **2** *the aircraft plunged to the ground:* **plummet,** nosedive, drop, fall, tumble, descend. **3** *the car plunged down an alley:* **charge,** hurtle, career, plough, tear; N. Amer. informal barrel. **4** *oil prices plunged:* **fall sharply,** plummet, drop, tumble, slump; informal crash, nosedive. **5** *he plunged the dagger into her back:* **thrust,** stab, sink, stick, ram, drive, push, shove, force. **6** *plunge the pears into water:* **immerse,** submerge, dip, dunk. **7** *the room was plunged into darkness:* **throw,** cast.
OPPOSITES soar.
noun **1** *a plunge in the pool:* **dive,** jump, dip. **2** *a plunge in*

profits: **fall,** drop, slump; informal nosedive, crash.
OPPOSITES rise.

plus preposition *four novels plus various poems:* **as well as,** together with, along with, in addition to, and, added to, not to mention.
OPPOSITES minus.
noun *one of the pluses of the job:* **advantage,** good point, asset, pro, benefit, bonus, attraction; informal perk.
OPPOSITES disadvantage.

plush adjective (informal) **luxurious,** luxury, de luxe, sumptuous, opulent, magnificent, rich, expensive, fancy; Brit. upmarket; informal posh, classy; Brit. informal swish; N. Amer. informal swank.
OPPOSITES austere.

ply verb **1** *he plied a profitable trade:* **engage in,** carry on, pursue, conduct, practise. **2** *ferries ply between all lake resorts:* **travel,** shuttle, go back and forth. **3** *she plied me with scones:* **provide,** supply, shower. **4** *he plied her with questions:* **bombard,** assail, pester, plague, harass; informal hassle.

poach verb **1** *he's been poaching salmon:* **hunt illegally,** catch illegally, steal. **2** *workers were poached by other firms:* **steal,** appropriate, headhunt; informal nab, swipe; Brit. informal nick, pinch.

pocket noun **1** *a bag with two pockets:* **pouch,** compartment. **2** *pockets of resistance:* **area,** patch, region, cluster.
adjective *a pocket dictionary:* **small,** little, miniature, mini, compact, concise, abridged, portable, travel; N. Amer. vest-pocket.
verb **1** *he pocketed $4m for a*

p

few months' work: **acquire**, obtain, gain, get, secure, win, make, earn. **2** *they were pocketing money supposed to be used for repairs:* **steal**, appropriate, purloin, misappropriate, embezzle.

pod noun **shell**, husk, hull, case; N. Amer. shuck.

podium noun **platform**, stage, dais, rostrum, stand.

poem noun **verse**, rhyme, lyric, piece of poetry.

poetic adjective **expressive**, figurative, symbolic, flowery, artistic, imaginative, creative.

poetry noun **poems**, verse, versification, rhyme.

poignant adjective **touching**, moving, sad, affecting, pitiful, pathetic, plaintive.

point noun **1** *the point of a needle:* **tip**, (sharp) end, extremity, prong, spike, tine, nib, barb. **2** *points of light:* **pinpoint**, dot, spot, speck. **3** *a meeting point:* **place**, position, location, site, spot. **4** *this point in her life:* **time**, stage, juncture, period, phase. **5** *the tension had reached such a high point:* **level**, degree, stage, pitch, extent. **6** *an important point:* **detail**, item, fact, thing, argument, consideration, factor, element, subject, issue, topic, question, matter. **7** *get to the point:* **heart of the matter**, essence, nub, core, crux; informal nitty-gritty. **8** *what's the point of this?* **purpose**, aim, object, objective, goal, intention, use, sense, value, advantage. **9** *he had his good points:* **attribute**, characteristic, feature, trait, quality, property, aspect, side. verb *she pointed the gun at him:* **aim**, direct, level, train.

■ **point something out** identify, show, draw attention to, indicate, specify, detail, mention. ■ **point to something** indicate, suggest, evidence, signal, signify, denote.

pointed adjective **1** *a pointed stick:* **sharp**, spiky, spiked, tapering, barbed; informal pointy. **2** *a pointed remark:* **cutting**, biting, incisive, acerbic, caustic, scathing, venomous, sarcastic; informal **sarky**; N. Amer. informal snarky.

pointer noun **1** *the pointer moved to 100rpm:* **indicator**, needle, arrow, hand. **2** *a pointer to the outcome of the election:* **indication**, indicator, clue, hint, sign, signal, evidence. **3** *I can give you a few pointers:* **tip**, hint, suggestion, guideline, recommendation.

pointless adjective **senseless**, futile, hopeless, unavailing, aimless, idle, worthless, valueless.
OPPOSITES valuable.

poise noun **1** *poise and good deportment:* **grace**, gracefulness, elegance, balance, control. **2** *in spite of the setback she retained her poise:* **composure**, equanimity, self-possession, aplomb, self-assurance, self-control, sangfroid, dignity; informal cool.

poised adjective **1** *she was poised on one foot:* **balanced**, suspended, motionless, hanging, hovering. **2** *he was poised for action:* **prepared**, ready, braced, geared up, all set, standing by.

poison noun **toxin**, venom. verb **1** *her mother poisoned her:* **give poison to**, murder. **2** *the Amazon is being poisoned:* **pollute**, contaminate, taint, spoil. **3** *they poisoned his mind:*

twist, warp, corrupt.

poisonous adjective **1** *a poisonous snake:* **venomous,** deadly. **2** *a poisonous chemical:* **toxic,** noxious, deadly, fatal, lethal, mortal. **3** *a poisonous glance:* **malicious,** malevolent, hostile, spiteful, bitter, venomous, malign.
OPPOSITES harmless, non-toxic, benevolent.

poke verb **1** *she poked him in the ribs:* **prod,** jab, dig, elbow, nudge, shove, jolt, stab, stick. **2** *leave the cable poking out:* **stick out,** jut out, protrude, project, extend.
noun *Carrie gave him a poke:* **prod,** jab, dig, elbow, nudge.

poky adjective **small,** little, tiny, cramped, confined, restricted, boxy.
OPPOSITES spacious.

pole noun **post,** pillar, stanchion, stake, support, prop, stick, paling, staff.

police noun **police force, police service,** police officers, policemen, policewomen; Brit. constabulary; informal the cops, the fuzz, the law, the boys in blue; Brit. informal the (Old) Bill; N. Amer. informal the heat.
verb **1** *we must police the area:* **guard,** watch over, protect, defend, patrol. **2** *the regulations will be policed by the ministry:* **enforce,** regulate, oversee, supervise, monitor, observe, check.

police officer noun **policeman, policewoman;** Brit. constable; N. Amer. patrolman, trooper, roundsman; informal cop; Brit. informal rozzer; N. Amer. informal uniform.

policy noun **plans,** approach, code, system, guidelines, theory, line, position, stance.

polish verb **1** *I polished his shoes:* **shine,** wax, buff, rub up/down, gloss, burnish. **2** *polish up your essay:* **perfect,** refine, improve, hone, enhance, brush up, revise, edit, correct, rewrite, go over, touch up.
noun *his poetry has clarity and polish:* **sophistication,** refinement, urbanity, suaveness, elegance, style, grace, finesse; informal class.

polished adjective **1** *a polished table:* **shiny,** glossy, gleaming, lustrous, glassy, waxed, buffed, burnished. **2** *a polished performance:* **expert,** accomplished, masterly, skilful, adept, adroit, dexterous, consummate, superb, superlative.
OPPOSITES dull, inexpert.

polite adjective **1** *a very polite girl:* **well mannered,** civil, courteous, respectful, well behaved, well bred, gentlemanly, ladylike, genteel, gracious, tactful, diplomatic. **2** *polite society:* **civilized,** refined, cultured, sophisticated.
OPPOSITES rude, uncivilized.

politic adjective **wise,** prudent, sensible, judicious, expedient, advantageous, beneficial, profitable.
OPPOSITES unwise.

political adjective **governmental,** government, constitutional, ministerial, parliamentary, diplomatic, legislative, administrative.

politician noun **legislator,** Member of Parliament, MP, representative, minister, statesman, stateswoman, senator, congressman, congresswoman; informal politico.

politics noun **1** *a career in politics:* **government,** affairs of

p

state, public affairs, diplomacy.
2 *he studies politics:* **political science,** civics. **3** *what are his politics?* **political views,** political leanings. **4** *office politics:* **power struggles,** machinations, manoeuvring, realpolitik.

poll noun **1** *the poll to elect a new leader:* **vote,** ballot, show of hands, referendum, plebiscite, election. **2** *a poll to investigate holiday choices:* **survey,** opinion poll, market research, census.
verb **1** *most of those polled supported him:* **canvass,** survey, ask, question, interview, ballot. **2** *she polled 119 votes:* **get,** gain, register, record, return.

pollute verb **contaminate,** taint, poison, foul, dirty, soil, infect.
OPPOSITES purify.

pollution noun **contamination,** impurity, dirt, filth, infection.

pompous adjective **self-important,** overbearing, sententious, grandiose, affected, pretentious, puffed up, haughty, proud, conceited, supercilious, condescending, patronizing.
OPPOSITES modest.

ponder verb **think about,** contemplate, consider, review, reflect on, mull over, meditate on, muse on, dwell on.

pool[1] noun **1** *pools of water:* **puddle,** pond, lake. **2** *the hotel has a pool:* **swimming pool,** baths; Brit. swimming baths; N. Amer. natatorium.

pool[2] noun **1** *a pool of skilled labour:* **supply,** reserve(s), reservoir, fund, store, bank, stock, cache. **2** *a pool of money for emergencies:* **fund,** reserve, kitty, pot, bank, purse.
verb *they pooled their skills:*

combine, group, join, unite, merge, share.

poor adjective **1** *a poor family:* **poverty-stricken,** penniless, impoverished, impecunious, needy, destitute; Brit. on the breadline; informal hard up, strapped, on one's uppers. **2** *poor workmanship:* **substandard,** bad, deficient, defective, faulty, imperfect, inferior, unsatisfactory, shoddy, crude, inadequate, unacceptable; informal crummy, rubbishy, rotten; Brit. informal ropy, duff, rubbish, dodgy. **3** *a poor crop:* **meagre,** scanty, scant, paltry, reduced, modest, sparse, spare, deficient, insubstantial, skimpy, lean; informal measly, stingy. **4** *the poor thing:* **unfortunate,** unlucky, unhappy, hapless, wretched.
OPPOSITES rich, superior, abundant, lucky.

poorly adverb *the text is poorly written:* **badly,** imperfectly, incompetently, crudely, shoddily, inadequately.
adjective *she felt poorly:* **ill,** unwell, not very well, ailing, indisposed, out of sorts, under par, peaky; Brit. off colour; informal under the weather, rough; Brit. informal ropy, grotty; Scottish informal wabbit; Austral./NZ informal crook.

pop verb **1** *champagne corks popped:* **go bang,** go off, crack, snap, burst, explode. **2** *I'm just popping home:* **go;** informal tootle, whip; Brit. informal nip. **3** *pop a bag over the pot:* **put,** place, slip, throw, slide, stick, set, lay, position.
noun *the balloons burst with a pop:* **bang,** crack, snap, explosion, report.

popular adjective **1** *the*

restaurant is very popular: **well liked,** sought-after, in demand, commercial, marketable, fashionable, in vogue, all the rage, hot; informal in, cool, big. **2** *popular science books:* **non-specialist,** non-technical, amateur, lay person's, general, middle-of-the-road, accessible, simplified, understandable, mass-market. **3** *popular opinion:* **widespread,** general, common, current, prevailing, standard, ordinary, conventional. OPPOSITES unpopular, specialist, restricted.

population noun **inhabitants,** residents, people, citizens, public, community, populace, society, natives, occupants.

pornographic adjective **obscene,** indecent, dirty, smutty, filthy, erotic, titillating, sexy, risqué, X-rated, adult.

port noun **harbour,** docks, marina, haven, seaport.

portable adjective **transportable,** movable, mobile, battery, wireless, lightweight, compact, handy, convenient.

porter[1] noun *a porter helped with the bags:* **carrier,** bearer; N. Amer. redcap, skycap.

porter[2] noun (Brit.) *the college porter:* **doorman,** doorkeeper, commissionaire, gatekeeper, concierge, security officer.

portion noun **1** *the upper portion of the chimney:* **part,** piece, bit, section, segment. **2** *her portion of the allowance:* **share,** slice, quota, ration, allocation, tranche; Brit. informal whack. **3** *a portion of cake:* **helping,** serving, plateful, slice, piece.

portrait noun **1** *a portrait of the King:* **picture,** likeness,

painting, drawing, photograph, image. **2** *a vivid portrait of Italy:* **description,** portrayal, representation, depiction, impression, account, profile.

portray verb **1** *he always portrays Windermere in sunny weather:* **paint,** draw, sketch, picture, depict, represent, illustrate, render, show. **2** *the man portrayed by Waugh:* **describe,** depict, characterize, represent. **3** *he portrays her as a doormat:* **represent,** depict, characterize, describe, present. **4** *the actor portrays a spy:* **play,** act the part of, take the role of, represent, appear as.

portrayal noun **1** *her portrayal of adolescence:* **description,** representation, characterization, depiction, evocation. **2** *Brando's portrayal of Corleone:* **performance as,** representation, interpretation, rendering.

pose verb **1** *pollution poses a threat to health:* **constitute,** present, offer. **2** *the question posed earlier:* **raise,** ask, put, submit, advance, propose. **3** *the guys posing at the bar:* **posture,** attitudinize, put on airs; informal show off, ponce about. noun **1** *a formal pose:* **posture,** position, stance, attitude. **2** *her pose of aggrieved innocence:* **act,** affectation, show, display, posture, expression.
■ **pose as** pretend to be, impersonate, pass oneself off as, masquerade as.

posh adjective **1** (informal) *a posh hotel:* **smart,** stylish, fancy, high-class, fashionable, chic, luxurious, luxury, exclusive; Brit. upmarket; informal classy, plush, flash; Brit. informal swish; N. Amer. informal swank, tony. **2** (Brit.

p

informal) *a posh accent:*
upper-class, aristocratic.

position noun **1** *the aircraft's position:* **location,** place, situation, spot, site, locality, setting, area, whereabouts, bearings. **2** *a standing position:* **posture,** stance, attitude, pose. **3** *our financial position:* **situation,** state, condition, circumstances, predicament, plight. **4** *their position in society:* **status,** place, level, rank, standing, stature, prestige, reputation. **5** *a secretarial position:* **job,** post, situation, appointment, opening, vacancy, placement. **6** *the government's position on the matter:* **viewpoint,** opinion, outlook, attitude, stand, standpoint, stance, perspective, thinking, policy, feelings.
verb *he positioned a chair between them:* **put,** place, locate, situate, set, site, stand, station, plant, stick; informal plonk, park.

positive adjective **1** *a positive response:* **affirmative,** favourable, good, enthusiastic, supportive, encouraging. **2** *say something positive:* **constructive,** useful, productive, helpful, worthwhile, beneficial. **3** *she seems a lot more positive:* **optimistic,** hopeful, confident, cheerful, sanguine, buoyant; informal upbeat. **4** *positive economic signs:* **favourable,** good, promising, encouraging, heartening, propitious, auspicious. **5** *positive proof:* **definite,** certain, reliable, concrete, tangible, clear-cut, explicit, firm, decisive, real, actual. **6** *I'm positive he's coming back:* **certain,** sure, convinced, confident, satisfied.

OPPOSITES negative, pessimistic, doubtful, unsure.

positively adverb **1** *I could not positively identify the voice:* **confidently,** definitely, firmly, categorically, with certainty, conclusively. **2** *he was positively livid:* **absolutely,** utterly, downright, simply, virtually; informal plain.

possess verb **1** *the only hat she possessed:* **own,** have (to one's name), be in possession of. **2** *he did not possess a sense of humour:* **have,** be blessed with, be endowed with, enjoy, boast. **3** *an evil force possessed him:* **take control of,** take over, bewitch, enchant, enslave.

possession noun **1** *the estate came into their possession:* **ownership,** control, hands, keeping, care, custody, charge. **2** *she packed her possessions:* **belongings,** things, property, worldly goods, personal effects, stuff, bits and pieces; informal gear, junk; Brit. informal clobber.

possibility noun **1** *a possibility that he might be alive:* **chance,** likelihood, probability, potentiality, hope, risk, hazard, danger, fear. **2** *buying a smaller house is one possibility:* **option,** alternative, choice, course of action, solution. **3** *the idea has distinct possibilities:* **potential,** promise, prospects.

possible adjective **1** *it's not possible to check the figures:* **feasible,** practicable, viable, attainable, achievable, workable; informal on, doable. **2** *a possible reason for his disappearance:* **likely,** plausible, imaginable, believable, potential, probable, credible. **3** *a possible future leader:* **potential,** prospective, likely,

probable.
OPPOSITES unlikely.

possibly adverb **1** *possibly he took her with him:* **perhaps**, maybe, it is possible. **2** *you can't possibly refuse:* **conceivably**, under any circumstances, by any means. **3** *could you possibly help me?* **please**, kindly, be so good as to.

post[1] noun *wooden posts:* **pole**, stake, upright, shaft, prop, support, picket, strut, pillar.
verb **1** *the notice posted on the wall:* **affix**, attach, fasten, display, pin up, put up, stick up. **2** *the group posted a net profit:* **announce**, report, make known, publish.

post[2] noun (Brit.) **1** *the winners will be notified by post:* **mail**; informal snail mail. **2** *did we get any post?* **letters**, correspondence, mail.
verb (Brit.) *post the order form today:* **send (off)**, mail, put in the post/mail, get off.
■ **keep someone posted** keep informed, keep up to date, keep in the picture.

post[3] noun **1** *there were seventy candidates for the post:* **job**, position, appointment, situation, place, vacancy, opening. **2** *back to your posts:* **assigned position**, station, place, base.
verb **1** *he'd been posted to Berlin:* **send**, assign, dispatch. **2** *armed guards were posted:* **put on duty**, mount, station.

poster noun **notice**, placard, bill, sign, advertisement, playbill.

postpone verb **put off**, put back, delay, defer, hold over, reschedule, adjourn, shelve; informal put on ice, put on the back burner.
OPPOSITES bring forward.

posture noun **1** *a kneeling posture:* **position**, pose, attitude, stance. **2** *good posture:* **bearing**, carriage, stance, comportment; Brit. deportment. **3** *trade unions adopted a militant posture:* **attitude**, stance, standpoint, point of view, opinion, position.
verb *Keith postured, flexing his biceps:* **pose**, strike an attitude, strut.

pot noun **1** *a pot of soup:* **pan**, saucepan, casserole. **2** *Neolithic pots:* **vessel**, bowl, earthenware, pottery.

potent adjective **1** *a potent political force:* **powerful**, strong, mighty, formidable, influential, dominant. **2** *a potent argument:* **forceful**, convincing, cogent, compelling, persuasive, powerful, strong. **3** *a potent drug:* **strong**, powerful, effective; formal efficacious.
OPPOSITES weak.

potential adjective *a potential source of conflict:* **possible**, likely, prospective, future, probable.
noun *he has great potential:* **possibilities**, potentiality, prospects, promise, capability, capacity.

potter verb **amble**, wander, meander, stroll, saunter; informal mosey, tootle, toddle; N. Amer. informal putter.

pottery noun **ceramics**, crockery, earthenware, terracotta, stoneware, china, porcelain.

pounce verb **jump**, spring, leap, dive, lunge, swoop, attack.

pound[1] verb **1** *the two men pounded him with their fists:* **beat**, strike, hit, batter, thump, pummel, punch, rain blows on,

p

belabour, hammer; informal bash, clobber, wallop. **2** *waves pounded the seafront:* **beat against**, crash against, batter, dash against, lash, buffet. **3** *gunships pounded the capital:* **bombard**, bomb, shell. **4** *pound the garlic to a paste:* **crush**, grind, pulverize, mash, pulp. **5** *I heard him pounding along the gangway:* **stomp**, stamp, clomp, clump, tramp, lumber. **6** *her heart was pounding:* **throb**, thump, thud, hammer, pulse, race.

pound² noun *a dog pound:* **enclosure**, compound, pen, yard, corral.

pour verb **1** *blood was pouring from his nose:* **stream**, flow, run, gush, course, jet, spurt, surge, spill. **2** *Amy poured wine into his glass:* **tip**, splash, spill, decant; informal slosh, slop. **3** *it was pouring:* **rain heavily/hard**, teem down, pelt down, tip down, rain cats and dogs; informal be chucking it down; Brit. informal bucket down; N. Amer. informal rain pitchforks. **4** *people poured off the train:* **crowd**, throng, swarm, stream, flood.

poverty noun **1** *abject poverty:* **pennilessness**, destitution, penury, impoverishment, neediness, hardship, impecuniousness. **2** *the poverty of choice:* **scarcity**, deficiency, dearth, shortage, paucity, absence, lack. **3** *the poverty of her imagination:* **inferiority**, mediocrity, sterility.
OPPOSITES wealth, abundance, fertility.

powdery adjective **fine**, dry, fine-grained, powder-like, dusty, chalky, floury, sandy, crumbly, friable.

power noun **1** *the power of*
speech: **ability**, capacity, capability, potential, faculty. **2** *the union has enormous power:* **control**, authority, influence, dominance, sway, leverage; informal clout; N. Amer. informal drag. **3** *the power to stop and search:* **authority**, right, authorization. **4** *a major European power:* **state**, country, nation. **5** *he hit the ball with as much power as he could:* **strength**, might, force, vigour, energy; Brit. informal welly. **6** *the power of his arguments:* **forcefulness**, powerfulness, strength, force, cogency, persuasiveness. **7** *the new engine has more power:* **driving force**, horsepower, acceleration, torque; informal oomph, poke. **8** *generating power from waste:* **energy**, electricity.
OPPOSITES inability, weakness.

powerful adjective **1** *powerful shoulders:* **strong**, muscular, muscly, sturdy, strapping, robust, brawny, burly, athletic, manly, well built, solid; informal beefy. **2** *a powerful drink:* **intoxicating**, hard, strong, stiff. **3** *a powerful blow:* **violent**, forceful, hard, mighty. **4** *he felt a powerful urge to kiss her:* **intense**, keen, fierce, strong, irresistible, overpowering, overwhelming. **5** *a powerful nation:* **influential**, strong, important, dominant, commanding, formidable. **6** *a powerful critique:* **cogent**, compelling, convincing, persuasive, forceful.
OPPOSITES weak, gentle.

powerless adjective **impotent**, helpless, ineffectual, ineffective, useless, defenceless, vulnerable.

practicable adjective **realistic**,

feasible, possible, viable, reasonable, sensible, workable, achievable; informal doable.

practical adjective **1** *practical experience:* **empirical,** hands-on, actual. **2** *there are no practical alternatives:* **feasible,** practicable, realistic, viable, workable, possible, reasonable, sensible; informal doable. **3** *practical clothes:* **functional,** sensible, utilitarian. **4** *try to be more practical:* **realistic,** sensible, down-to-earth, businesslike, commonsensical, hard-headed, no-nonsense; informal hard-nosed. **5** *a practical certainty:* **virtual,** effective, near.
OPPOSITES theoretical, impractical.

practically adverb **1** *the cinema was practically empty:* **almost,** very nearly, virtually, just about, all but, more or less, as good as, to all intents and purposes; informal pretty nearly, pretty well. **2** *'You can't afford it,' he pointed out practically:* **realistically,** sensibly, reasonably, rationally, matter-of-factly.

practice noun **1** *the practice of radiotherapy:* **application,** exercise, use, operation, implementation, execution. **2** *it is common practice:* **custom,** procedure, policy, convention, tradition. **3** *the team's final practice:* **training,** rehearsal, repetition, preparation, dummy run, run-through; informal dry run. **4** *the practice of medicine:* **profession,** career, business, work. **5** *a small legal practice:* **business,** firm, office, company; informal outfit.

practise verb **1** *he practised the songs every day:* **rehearse,** run

through, go over/through, work on/at, polish, perfect. **2** *the performers were practising:* **train,** rehearse, prepare, go through one's paces. **3** *we still practise these rituals today:* **carry out,** perform, observe. **4** *she practises medicine:* **work at/in,** pursue a career in.

practised adjective **expert,** experienced, seasoned, skilled, skilful, accomplished, proficient, talented, able, adept.

pragmatic adjective **practical,** matter of fact, sensible, down-to-earth, commonsensical, businesslike, hard-headed, no-nononsense; informal hard-nosed.
OPPOSITES impractical.

praise verb **commend,** applaud, pay tribute to, speak highly of, compliment, congratulate, sing the praises of, rave about.
OPPOSITES criticize.
noun **approval,** acclaim, admiration, approbation, plaudits, congratulations, commendation, accolade, compliment, a pat on the back, eulogy.
OPPOSITES criticism.

preach verb **1** *he preached to a large congregation:* **give a sermon,** sermonize, address, speak. **2** *preaching the gospel:* **proclaim,** teach, spread, propagate, expound. **3** *they preach toleration:* **advocate,** recommend, advise, urge, teach, counsel.

precarious adjective **insecure,** uncertain, unpredictable, risky, parlous, hazardous, dangerous, unsafe, unstable, unsteady, shaky; informal dicey, iffy; Brit. informal dodgy.
OPPOSITES safe.

precaution noun **safeguard,** preventive measure, safety

p

measure, insurance; informal backstop.

precede verb **1** *adverts preceded the film:* **go/come before,** lead up to, pave the way for, herald, introduce, usher in. **2** *Catherine preceded him into the studio:* **go ahead of,** go in front of, lead the way.
OPPOSITES follow.

precedent noun **model,** exemplar, example, pattern, paradigm, criterion, yardstick, standard.

precinct noun **district,** zone, sector, quarter, area.

precious adjective **1** *precious works of art:* **valuable,** costly, expensive, invaluable, priceless. **2** *her most precious possession:* **valued,** cherished, treasured, prized, favourite, dear, beloved, special. **3** *his precious manners:* **affected,** pretentious; informal la-di-da; Brit. informal poncey.

precipitate verb **1** *the incident precipitated a crisis:* **bring about/on,** cause, lead to, give rise to, instigate, trigger, spark off, touch off, provoke. **2** *they were precipitated down the mountain:* **hurl,** catapult, throw, plunge, launch, fling, propel.
adjective *their actions were precipitate:* **hasty,** overhasty, rash, hurried, rushed, impetuous, impulsive, precipitous, incautious, imprudent, injudicious, ill-advised, reckless.

precipitous adjective **1** *a precipitous drop:* **steep,** sheer, perpendicular, abrupt, sharp, vertical. **2** *his precipitous fall from power:* **sudden,** rapid, swift, abrupt, headlong, speedy, quick, fast.

precise adjective **1** *precise measurements:* **exact,** accurate, correct, specific, detailed, explicit, careful, meticulous, strict, rigorous. **2** *at that precise moment:* **exact,** particular, very, specific.
OPPOSITES inaccurate.

precisely adverb **1** *at 2 o'clock precisely:* **exactly,** sharp, on the dot, promptly, on the stroke of ...; informal bang (on); Brit. informal spot on; N. Amer. informal on the button. **2** *precisely the man I am looking for:* **exactly,** just, in all respects; informal to a T. **3** *fertilization can be timed precisely:* **accurately,** exactly. **4** *'So you knew?' 'Precisely.':* **yes,** exactly, absolutely, (that's) right, quite so.

precision noun **exactness,** accuracy, exactitude, correctness, care, meticulousness, scrupulousness, punctiliousness, rigour.

predecessor noun **1** *the Prime Minister's predecessor:* **forerunner,** precursor, antecedent. **2** *our Victorian predecessors:* **ancestor,** forefather, forebear, antecedent.
OPPOSITES successor, descendant.

predicament noun **difficulty,** mess, plight, quandary, muddle, dilemma; informal hole, fix, jam, pickle.

predict verb **forecast,** foretell, prophesy.

predictable adjective **foreseeable,** to be expected, anticipated, likely, foreseen, unsurprising, reliable; informal inevitable.
OPPOSITES unpredictable.

prediction noun **forecast,** prophecy, prognosis, prognostication.

predominantly adverb mainly, mostly, for the most part, chiefly, principally, primarily, in the main, on the whole, largely, by and large, typically, generally, usually.

prefer verb like better, would rather (have), would sooner (have), favour, be more partial to, choose, select, pick, opt for, go for, plump for.

preferable adjective better, best, more desirable, more suitable, advantageous, superior, preferred, recommended.

preferably adverb ideally, if possible, for preference, from choice.

preference noun **1** *her preference for gin:* liking, partiality, fondness, taste, inclination, leaning, bent, penchant, predisposition. **2** *preference was given to female applicants:* priority, favour, precedence, preferential treatment.

pregnant adjective **1** *she is pregnant:* expecting, expectant, carrying a child; informal in the family way, preggers. **2** *a pregnant pause:* meaningful, significant, suggestive, expressive, charged.

prejudice noun **1** *male prejudices about women:* preconceived idea, preconception. **2** *they are motivated by prejudice:* bigotry, bias, partiality, intolerance, discrimination, unfairness, inequality.
verb **1** *the article could prejudice the jury:* bias, influence, sway, predispose, make partial, colour. **2** *this could prejudice his chances:* damage, be detrimental to, be prejudicial

to, injure, harm, hurt, spoil, impair, undermine, compromise.

prejudiced adjective biased, bigoted, discriminatory, partisan, intolerant, narrow-minded, unfair, unjust, inequitable, coloured.
OPPOSITES impartial.

preliminary adjective *at a preliminary stage:* preparatory, introductory, initial, opening, early, exploratory.
OPPOSITES final.
noun *he began without any preliminaries:* introduction, preamble, preface, opening remarks, formalities.

prelude noun preliminary, overture, opening, preparation, introduction, lead-in, precursor.

premature adjective **1** *his premature death:* untimely, too early, before time, unseasonable. **2** *such a step would be premature:* rash, overhasty, hasty, precipitate, impulsive, impetuous; informal previous.
OPPOSITES overdue.

premier adjective *Germany's premier rock band:* leading, foremost, chief, principal, head, top-ranking, top, prime, primary, first, highest, pre-eminent, senior, outstanding; N. Amer. ranking.
noun *the British premier:* head of government, prime minister, PM, president, chancellor.

premiere noun first performance, first night, opening night, debut.

premise noun proposition, assumption, hypothesis, thesis, presupposition, supposition, presumption, assertion.

premises plural noun building(s), property, site,

p

office, establishment.

premium noun **1** *monthly premiums of £30:* (**regular**) **payment,** instalment. **2** *you must pay a premium for organic fruit:* **surcharge,** additional payment, extra.
■ **at a premium** scarce, in great demand, hard to come by, in short supply, thin on the ground.

preoccupation noun
obsession, fixation, concern, passion, enthusiasm, hobby horse; informal bee in one's bonnet.

preoccupied adjective **1** *he's preoccupied with work:* **obsessed,** fixated, concerned, absorbed, engrossed, involved, wrapped up. **2** *she looked preoccupied:* **lost in thought,** deep in thought, oblivious, pensive, distracted.

preparation noun **1** *the preparation of a plan:* **devising,** putting together, drawing up, construction, composition, production, getting ready, development. **2** *preparations for the party:* **arrangements,** planning, plans, groundwork, provisions. **3** *a preparation to kill mites:* **mixture,** compound, concoction, solution, medicine, potion.

prepare verb **1** *I will prepare a report:* **make/get ready,** put together, draw up, produce, arrange, assemble, construct, compose, formulate. **2** *the meal is easy to prepare:* **cook,** make, get, put together, concoct; informal fix, rustle up; Brit. informal knock up. **3** *preparing for war:* **get ready,** make preparations, arrange things, make provision. **4** *athletes preparing for the Olympics:* **train,** get into shape,

practise, get ready, warm up, limber up. **5** *prepare yourself for a shock:* **brace,** ready, tense, steel, steady.

prepared adjective **1** *prepared for action:* **ready,** (all) set, equipped, primed, waiting, poised. **2** *I'm prepared to negotiate:* **willing,** ready, disposed, (favourably) inclined, of a mind, minded.

prescribe verb **1** *a doctor may prescribe antibiotics:* **advise,** recommend, advocate, suggest. **2** *rules prescribing your duty:* **stipulate,** lay down, dictate, order, direct, specify, determine.

presence noun **1** *the presence of an intruder:* **existence. 2** *I requested the presence of a lawyer:* **attendance,** appearance. **3** *a woman of great presence:* **aura,** charisma, personality.
OPPOSITES absence.
■ **presence of mind** composure, self-possession, level-headedness, self-assurance, calmness, alertness, quick-wittedness; informal cool, unflappability.

present¹ adjective **1** *a doctor must be present:* **in attendance,** here, there, near, nearby, at hand, available. **2** *organic compounds are present:* **in existence,** detectable, occurring, here, there. **3** *the present economic climate:* **current,** present-day, existing, extant.
OPPOSITES absent.
noun *think about the present:* **now,** today, the present time, the here and now, modern times.
OPPOSITES past, future.
■ **at present** at the moment, just

now, right now, at the present time, currently, at this moment in time.

present² verb **1** *Eddy presented a cheque to the winner:* **hand over**, give (out), confer, bestow, award, grant, accord. **2** *the committee presented its report:* **submit**, set forth, put forward, offer, tender, table. **3** *may I present my wife?* **introduce**, make known, acquaint someone with. **4** *she presents a TV show:* **host**, introduce, compère; N. Amer. informal emcee. **5** *they present him as a criminal:* **represent**, describe, portray, depict.

present³ noun *a birthday present:* **gift**, donation, offering, contribution, gratuity, tip, hand-out; informal prezzie.

presentation noun **1** *the presentation of his certificate:* **awarding**, presenting, giving, handing over, bestowal, granting. **2** *the presentation of food:* **appearance**, arrangement, packaging, layout. **3** *a sales presentation:* **demonstration**, talk, lecture, address, speech, show, exhibition, display, introduction, launch, launching, unveiling.

presently adverb **1** *I shall see you presently:* **soon**, shortly, quite soon, in a short time, in a little while, at any moment/minute/second, before long; N. Amer. momentarily; Brit. informal in a mo. **2** *he is presently abroad:* **at present**, currently, at the/this moment.

preservation noun **1** *wood preservation:* **conservation**, protection, care. **2** *the preservation of the status quo:* **continuation**, conservation, maintenance, upholding,

sustaining, perpetuation.

preserve verb **1** *oil preserves the wood:* **conserve**, protect, maintain, care for, look after. **2** *the wish to preserve the status quo:* **continue (with)**, conserve, keep going, maintain, uphold, sustain, perpetuate, prolong. **3** *preserving him from harm:* **guard**, protect, keep, defend, safeguard, shelter, shield.
OPPOSITES attack, abandon.
noun **1** *the preserve of the rich:* **domain**, area, field, sphere, orbit, realm, province, territory; informal turf, bailiwick. **2** *a game preserve:* **sanctuary**, (game) reserve, reservation.

preside

▪ **preside over** be in charge of, be responsible for, head, manage, administer, control, direct, chair, conduct, officiate at, lead, govern, rule, command, supervise, oversee; informal head up.

press verb **1** *press the paper down firmly:* **push (down)**, press down, depress, hold down, force, thrust, squeeze, compress. **2** *his shirt was pressed:* **iron**. **3** *she pressed the child to her bosom:* **clasp**, hold close, hug, cuddle, squeeze, clutch, grasp, embrace. **4** *the crowd pressed round:* **cluster**, gather, converge, congregate, flock, swarm, crowd. **5** *the government pressed its claim:* **plead**, urge, advance, present, submit, put forward. **6** *they pressed him to agree:* **urge**, put pressure on, pressurize, force, push, coerce, dragoon, steamroller, browbeat; informal lean on, put the screws on, twist someone's arm, railroad, bulldoze. **7** *they pressed for a ban:* **call**, ask, clamour, push,

p

campaign, demand.
noun **1** *the freedom of the press:*
the media, the newspapers,
journalism, reporters; Brit. dated
Fleet Street. **2** *the company had
some bad press:* **(press) reports,**
press coverage, press articles,
press reviews.

pressing adjective **1** *a pressing
problem:* **urgent,** critical,
crucial, acute, desperate,
serious, grave, life-and-death.
2 *a pressing engagement:*
important, high-priority,
critical, crucial, unavoidable.

pressure noun **1** *atmospheric
pressure:* **force,** load, stress,
thrust, compression, weight.
2 *there was pressure to conform:*
persuasion, intimidation,
coercion, compulsion, duress,
harassment, nagging,
badgering. **3** *she had a lot of
pressure at work:* **strain,** stress,
tension, trouble, difficulty,
burden; informal hassle.
verb *they pressured him into
resigning:* **coerce,** push,
persuade, force, bulldoze,
hound, nag, badger, browbeat,
bully, intimidate, dragoon,
twist someone's arm; informal
railroad, lean on; N. Amer. informal
hustle.

pressurize verb *he pressurized
us into selling:* **coerce,** pressure,
push, persuade, force, bulldoze,
hound, nag, badger, browbeat,
bully, bludgeon, intimidate,
dragoon, twist someone's arm;
informal railroad, lean on; N. Amer.
informal hustle.

prestige noun **status,** standing,
kudos, cachet, stature,
reputation, repute, renown,
honour, esteem, importance,
prominence.

prestigious adjective **reputable,**
distinguished, respected, high-
status, esteemed, eminent,
highly regarded, renowned,
influential.
OPPOSITES disreputable, obscure.

presumably adverb **I presume,**
I expect, I assume, I take it, I
imagine, I dare say, doubtless,
no doubt, apparently, probably.

presume verb **1** *I presume it
was once an attic:* **assume,**
suppose, surmise, imagine, take
it, expect. **2** *I wouldn't presume
to advise you:* **dare,** venture,
have the effrontery, be so bold
as, go so far as, take the liberty
of.

pretence noun **1** *cease this
pretence:* **make-believe,** acting,
faking, play-acting, posturing,
deception, trickery. **2** *he made a
pretence of being concerned:*
(false) show, semblance,
affectation, (false) appearance,
outward appearance,
impression, guise, facade.
OPPOSITES honesty.

pretend verb **1** *they pretend to
listen:* **make as if,** act like,
affect, go through the motions,
fake it. **2** *I'll pretend to be the
dragon:* **make believe,** play at,
act, impersonate.
adjective (informal) **mock,** fake,
sham, simulated, artificial,
false, pseudo; informal phoney.

pretty adjective *a pretty girl:*
attractive, good-looking, nice-
looking, personable, fetching,
prepossessing, appealing,
charming, delightful, cute;
Scottish & N. English bonny.
OPPOSITES plain, ugly.
adverb (informal) *it's pretty cold:*
quite, rather, somewhat, fairly.

prevail verb **1** *common sense
will prevail:* **win (out/
through),** triumph, be
victorious, carry the day, come
out on top, succeed, rule, reign.

2 *the conditions that prevailed in the 1950s:* **exist,** be present, be the case, occur, be prevalent, be in force.

prevailing adjective **current,** existing, prevalent, usual, common, general, widespread.

prevalent adjective **widespread,** frequent, usual, common, current, popular, general.
OPPOSITES rare.

prevent verb **stop,** avert, nip in the bud, foil, inhibit, thwart, prohibit, forbid.
OPPOSITES allow.

previous adjective **1** *the previous five years:* **preceding,** foregoing, prior, past, last. **2** *her previous boyfriend:* **former,** preceding, old, earlier, ex-, past, last, sometime, one-time, erstwhile. **3** (informal) *I was a bit previous:* **overhasty,** hasty, premature; informal ahead of oneself.
OPPOSITES next.

previously adverb **formerly,** earlier (on), before, hitherto, at one time, in the past.

prey noun **1** *the lions' prey:* **quarry,** kill. **2** *con men choose their prey carefully:* **victim,** target, dupe; informal **sucker**; Brit. informal **mug.**
OPPOSITES predator.

price noun **1** *the purchase price:* **cost,** charge, fee, fare, amount, sum; informal **damage. 2** *the price of success:* **consequence,** result, cost, penalty, toll, sacrifice, downside, drawback, disadvantage, minus.

priceless adjective **invaluable,** beyond price, irreplaceable, expensive, costly.
OPPOSITES worthless, cheap.

prick verb *prick the potatoes:* **pierce,** puncture, stab, perforate, spike, penetrate, jab.

noun *a prick in the leg:* **jab,** sting, pinprick, stab, pinhole, wound.

prickly adjective **spiky,** spiked, thorny, barbed, spiny, bristly.

pride noun **1** *a source of pride:* **self-esteem,** dignity, honour, self-respect. **2** *pride in a job well done:* **pleasure,** joy, delight, gratification, fulfilment, satisfaction, sense of achievement. **3** *he refused out of pride:* **arrogance,** vanity, self-importance, hubris, conceitedness, egotism, snobbery.
OPPOSITES shame, humility.

priest noun **clergyman,** clergywoman, minister, cleric, pastor, vicar, rector, parson, churchman, churchwoman, father, curate; Scottish **kirkman**; N. Amer. **dominie**; informal **reverend, padre.**

primarily adverb **1** *he was primarily a singer:* **first and foremost,** firstly, essentially, in essence, fundamentally, principally, predominantly. **2** *work is done primarily for large institutions:* **mostly,** for the most part, chiefly, mainly, in the main, on the whole, largely, principally, predominantly.

primary adjective **main,** chief, key, prime, central, principal, foremost, first, most important, predominant, paramount; informal **number-one.**
OPPOSITES secondary.

prime[1] adjective **1** *his prime reason for leaving:* **main,** chief, key, primary, central, principal, foremost, first, most important, paramount, major; informal **number-one. 2** *prime agricultural land:* **top-quality,** top, best, first-class, superior,

p

choice, select, finest; informal tip-top, A1.
OPPOSITES secondary, inferior.
noun *he is in his prime:* **heyday,** peak, pinnacle, high point/spot, zenith, flower, bloom, flush.

prime² verb *Lucy had primed him carefully:* **brief,** fill in, prepare, advise, instruct, coach, drill, train.

primitive adjective 1 *primitive times:* **ancient,** earliest, first, prehistoric, primordial, primeval. 2 *primitive tools:* **crude,** simple, rough (and ready), basic, rudimentary, makeshift.
OPPOSITES modern, sophisticated.

prince noun ruler, sovereign, monarch, crowned head.

principal adjective **main,** chief, primary, leading, foremost, first, most important, predominant, dominant, pre-eminent, highest, top; informal number-one.
OPPOSITES minor.
noun **head teacher,** headmaster, headmistress, head, dean, rector, master, mistress, chancellor, vice-chancellor, president, provost, warden; N. Amer. informal **prexy.**

principally adverb **mainly,** mostly, chiefly, for the most part, in the main, on the whole, largely, predominantly, primarily.

principle noun 1 *a basic principle of science:* **truth,** concept, idea, theory, fundamental, essential, precept, rule, law. 2 *the principle of laissez-faire:* **doctrine,** belief, creed, credo, code, ethic. 3 *a woman of principle:* **morals,** morality, ethics, ideals, standards, integrity, virtue,

probity, honour, decency, conscience, scruples.
■ **in principle 1** *there is no reason, in principle, why not:* in theory, theoretically, on paper, ideally. 2 *he accepted the idea in principle:* in general, in essence, on the whole, in the main.

print verb 1 *when was the book printed?* **publish,** issue, release, circulate, run off, copy, reproduce. 2 *patterns were printed on the cloth:* **imprint,** impress, stamp, mark.
noun 1 *large print:* **type,** printing, letters, lettering, characters, typeface, font. 2 *a print of his left hand:* **impression,** handprint, fingerprint, footprint. 3 *sporting prints:* **picture,** engraving, etching, lithograph, woodcut. 4 *prints and negatives:* **photograph,** photo, snap, snapshot, picture, still, enlargement, copy, reproduction.

prior adjective **earlier,** previous, preceding, advance, pre-existing.
OPPOSITES subsequent.
■ **prior to** before, until, up to, previous to, preceding, earlier than, in advance of.

priority noun 1 *safety is our priority:* **prime concern,** main consideration. 2 *giving priority to education:* **precedence,** preference, pre-eminence, predominance, primacy. 3 *oncoming traffic has priority:* **right of way,** precedence, supremacy, seniority.

prison noun jail, penal institution; N. Amer. jailhouse, penitentiary, correctional facility; informal clink, slammer; Brit. informal nick; N. Amer. informal can, pen.

■ **in prison** behind bars; informal inside, doing time; Brit. informal doing porridge.

prisoner noun **1** *a prisoner serving a life sentence:* convict, detainee, inmate; informal jailbird, con; Brit. informal lag; N. Amer. informal yardbird. **2** *the army took many prisoners:* prisoner of war, POW, internee, captive, hostage.

pristine adjective immaculate, perfect, in mint condition, as new, spotless, unspoilt.
OPPOSITES dirty, spoilt.

privacy noun seclusion, solitude, isolation.

private adjective **1** *his private plane:* personal, own, special, exclusive. **2** *private talks:* confidential, secret, classified. **3** *private thoughts:* intimate, personal, secret, innermost, undisclosed, unspoken, unvoiced. **4** *a very private man:* reserved, introverted, self-contained, reticent, retiring, unsociable, withdrawn, solitary, reclusive. **5** *somewhere private to talk:* secluded, undisturbed, remote, isolated. **6** *in a private capacity:* unofficial, personal. **7** *private industry:* independent, non-state, privatized, commercial, private-enterprise.
OPPOSITES public, open, extrovert, busy, crowded, official, state, nationalized.
noun *a private in the army:* private soldier, trooper; Brit. sapper, gunner; US GI; Brit. informal Tommy, squaddie.

■ **in private** in secret, secretly, privately, behind closed doors, in camera.

privilege noun **1** *senior pupils have certain privileges:*

advantage, benefit, prerogative, entitlement, right, concession, freedom, liberty. **2** *it was a privilege to meet her:* honour, pleasure.

privileged adjective **1** *a privileged background:* wealthy, rich, affluent, prosperous. **2** *I feel very lucky and privileged:* honoured, advantaged, favoured, valued, appreciated. **3** *privileged information:* confidential, private, secret, restricted, classified, not for publication, off the record, inside; informal hush-hush.
OPPOSITES underprivileged, disadvantaged, snubbed, public.

prize noun *an art prize:* award, reward, trophy, medal, cup, winnings, purse, honour.
adjective **1** *a prize bull:* champion, award-winning, top, best. **2** *a prize idiot:* utter, complete, total, absolute, real, perfect; Brit. informal right.
OPPOSITES second-rate.

probability noun **1** *the probability of winning:* likelihood, prospect, expectation, chance(s), odds. **2** *relegation is a distinct probability:* prospect, possibility.

probable adjective likely, odds-on, expected, anticipated, predictable; informal on the cards, a safe bet.
OPPOSITES improbable, unlikely.

probably adverb in all likelihood, in all probability, as likely as not, ten to one, the chances are, doubtless.

probation noun trial, trial period, test period, apprenticeship, training.

probe noun *a probe into city hall corruption:* investigation, enquiry, examination, inquest, study.

verb 1 *their long beaks are suited to probing the ground:* **prod**, poke, dig into, delve into, explore, feel around in, examine. **2** *an enquiry probed the cause of the disaster:* **investigate**, enquire into, look into, go into, study, examine, explore.

problem noun **1** *there's a problem:* **difficulty**, worry, complication, snag, hitch, drawback, stumbling block, obstacle, hiccup, setback, catch; informal dilemma, headache. **2** *I don't want to be a problem:* **nuisance**, bother; informal drag, pain. **3** *arithmetical problems:* **puzzle**, question, poser, riddle, conundrum; informal brain-teaser.

problematic adjective **difficult**, troublesome, tricky, awkward, controversial, ticklish, complicated, complex, knotty.
OPPOSITES easy, straightforward.

procedure noun **course of action**, method, system, strategy, way, approach, formula, mechanism, technique, routine, drill, practice.

proceed verb **1** *she was uncertain how to proceed:* **begin**, make a start, get going, move. **2** *he proceeded down the road:* **go**, make one's way, advance, move, progress, carry on, press on, push on. **3** *we should proceed with the talks:* **go ahead**, carry on, go on, continue, keep on, get on.
OPPOSITES stop.

proceedings plural noun **1** *the evening's proceedings:* **events**, activities, happenings, goings-on. **2** *the proceedings of the meeting:* **report**, transactions, minutes, account, story, record(s). **3** *legal proceedings:* **legal action**, litigation, lawsuit, case, prosecution.

proceeds plural noun **profits**, earnings, receipts, returns, takings, income, revenue, profit, yield; Sport gate (money); N. Amer. take.

process noun **1** *investigation is a long process:* **procedure**, operation, action, activity, exercise, affair, business, job, task, undertaking. **2** *a new canning process:* **method**, system, technique, means, practice, way, approach.
verb *applications are processed rapidly:* **deal with**, attend to, see to, sort out, handle, take care of.

procession noun **parade**, march, march past, cavalcade, motorcade, cortège, column, file; Brit. informal crocodile.

proclaim verb **declare**, announce, pronounce, state, make known, give out, advertise, publish, broadcast, trumpet.

prod verb **1** *Cassie prodded him in the chest:* **poke**, jab, stab, dig, nudge, elbow. **2** *the Department was prodded into action:* **spur**, stimulate, prompt, push, galvanize, persuade, urge, chivvy, remind.
noun **1** *a sharp prod in the ribs:* **poke**, jab, stab, dig, nudge, elbow. **2** *he might need a prod to get him to come:* **urging**, stimulus, push, prompt, reminder, chivvying.

prodigal adjective **wasteful**, extravagant, spendthrift.
OPPOSITES thrifty.

prodigy noun **genius**, mastermind, virtuoso,

wunderkind; informal whizz-kid, whizz.
OPPOSITES dunce, amateur.

produce verb **1** *the company produces furniture:* **manufacture**, make, construct, build, fabricate, put together, assemble, turn out, create, mass-produce. **2** *the vineyards produce excellent wines:* **yield**, grow, give, supply, provide, furnish, bear. **3** *she produced ten puppies:* **give birth to**, bear, deliver, bring forth, bring into the world. **4** *he produced five novels:* **create**, fashion, turn out, compose, write, pen, paint. **5** *she produced an ID card:* **pull out**, extract, fish out, present, offer, proffer, show. **6** *that will produce a reaction:* **cause**, bring about, give rise to, occasion, generate, lead to, result in, provoke, precipitate, spark off, trigger. **7** *James produced the play:* **stage**, put on, mount, present, exhibit.
noun *local produce:* **food**, foodstuff(s), products, crops, fruit and vegetables.

producer noun **1** *a car producer:* **manufacturer**, maker, builder, constructor. **2** *coffee producers:* **grower**, farmer. **3** *the producer of the show:* **impresario**, manager, administrator, promoter, director.

product noun **1** *household products:* **artefact**, commodity; (products) goods, ware(s), merchandise, produce. **2** *a product of experience:* **result**, consequence, outcome, effect, upshot.

production noun **1** *the production of cars:* **manufacture**, making, construction, building, fabrication, assembly, creation, mass production. **2** *the production of literary works:* **creation**, origination, fashioning, composition, writing. **3** *agricultural production:* **output**, yield, productivity. **4** *a theatre production:* **performance**, staging, presentation, show, piece, play.

productive adjective **1** *a productive artist:* **prolific**, inventive, creative. **2** *productive talks:* **useful**, constructive, profitable, fruitful, valuable, effective, worthwhile, helpful. **3** *productive land:* **fertile**, fruitful, rich, fecund.
OPPOSITES unproductive.

productivity noun **efficiency**, work rate, output, yield, production.

profess verb **1** *he professed his love:* **declare**, announce, proclaim, assert, state, affirm, maintain, protest. **2** *she professed to loathe publicity:* **claim**, pretend, purport, affect, make out.

professed adjective **1** *their professed independence:* **claimed**, supposed, ostensible, self-styled, apparent, pretended, purported. **2** *a professed Christian:* **declared**, self-acknowledged, self-confessed, confessed, sworn, confirmed.

profession noun **career**, occupation, calling, vocation, métier, line of work, job, business, trade, craft.

professional adjective **1** *professional occupations:* **white-collar**, non-manual, graduate, qualified, chartered. **2** *a professional cricketer:* **paid**, salaried. **3** *a very professional*

p

job: **expert,** accomplished, skilful, masterly, fine, polished, skilled, proficient, competent, able, businesslike, deft. **4** *not a professional way to behave:* **appropriate,** fitting, proper, honourable, ethical.
OPPOSITES manual, amateur, amateurish, inappropriate, unethical.
noun *she was a real professional:* **expert,** virtuoso, old hand, master, maestro, past master; informal pro, ace.
OPPOSITES amateur.

profile noun **1** *his handsome profile:* **outline,** silhouette, side view, contour, shape, form, lines. **2** *a profile of the organization:* **description,** account, study, portrait, rundown, sketch, outline.

profit noun **1** *the firm made a profit:* **financial gain,** return(s), yield, proceeds, earnings, winnings, surplus; informal pay dirt, bottom line. **2** *there was little profit in going on:* **advantage,** benefit, value, use, good; informal mileage.
OPPOSITES loss, disadvantage.
verb 1 *we will not profit from the deal:* **make money,** earn; informal rake it in, clean up, make a killing; N. Amer. informal make a fast buck. **2** *how will that profit us?* **benefit,** be advantageous to, be of use to, do someone good, help, be of service to, serve.
OPPOSITES lose, disadvantage.

profitable adjective **1** *a profitable company:* **moneymaking,** profit-making, paying, lucrative, commercial, successful, money-spinning, gainful. **2** *profitable study:* **beneficial,** useful, advantageous, valuable, productive, worthwhile, rewarding, fruitful, illuminating, informative, well spent.
OPPOSITES unprofitable, loss-making, fruitless, useless.

profound adjective **1** *profound relief:* **heartfelt,** intense, keen, extreme, acute, severe, sincere, earnest, deep, deep-seated, overpowering, overwhelming. **2** *a profound change:* **far-reaching,** radical, extensive, sweeping, exhaustive, thoroughgoing. **3** *a profound analysis:* **wise,** learned, intelligent, scholarly, discerning, penetrating, perceptive, astute, thoughtful, insightful.
OPPOSITES superficial, mild, slight.

programme noun **1** *our programme for the day:* **schedule,** agenda, calendar, timetable, order, line-up. **2** *the government's reform programme:* **scheme,** plan, package, strategy, initiative, proposal. **3** *a television programme:* **broadcast,** production, show, presentation, transmission, performance; informal prog. **4** *a programme of study:* **course,** syllabus, curriculum.
verb *they programmed the day well:* **arrange,** organize, schedule, plan, map out, timetable, line up; N. Amer. slate.

progress noun **1** *snow made progress difficult:* **(forward) movement,** advance, going, headway, passage. **2** *scientific progress:* **development,** advance, advancement, headway, step forward, improvement, growth.
OPPOSITES regression.

p

verb **1** *they progressed slowly down the road:* **go,** make one's way, move, proceed, advance, go on, continue, make headway, work one's way. **2** *the school has progressed rapidly:* **develop,** make progress, advance, make headway, take steps forward, move on, get on, gain ground, improve, get better, come on, come along, make strides; informal be getting there.
OPPOSITES regress, lapse.
■ **in progress** under way, going on, ongoing, happening, occurring, taking place, proceeding, continuing.

progression noun **1** *progression to the next stage:* **progress,** advancement, movement, passage, development, evolution, growth. **2** *a progression of peaks on the graph:* **succession,** series, sequence, string, stream, chain, train, row, cycle.

progressive adjective **1** *progressive deterioration:* **continuing,** continuous, ongoing, gradual, step-by-step, cumulative. **2** *progressive views:* **modern,** liberal, advanced, forward-thinking, enlightened, pioneering, reforming, reformist, radical; informal go-ahead.
OPPOSITES sporadic, conservative, reactionary.

prohibit verb **1** *state law prohibits gambling:* **forbid,** ban, bar, proscribe, make illegal, outlaw, disallow. **2** *a cash shortage prohibited the visit:* **prevent,** stop, rule out, preclude, make impossible.
OPPOSITES allow.

prohibition noun ban, bar, veto, embargo, boycott, injunction, moratorium.

project noun **1** *an engineering project:* **scheme,** plan, programme, enterprise, undertaking, venture, proposal, idea, concept. **2** *a history project:* **assignment,** piece of work, piece of research, task.
verb **1** *profits are projected to rise:* **forecast,** predict, expect, estimate, calculate, reckon. **2** *his projected book:* **intend,** plan, propose. **3** *balconies projected over the lake:* **stick out,** jut (out), protrude, extend, stand out, bulge out. **4** *the sun projected his shadow on the wall:* **cast,** throw, send, shed, shine.

projection noun **1** *a sales projection:* **forecast,** prediction, prognosis, expectation, estimate. **2** *tiny projections on the cliff face:* **outcrop,** outgrowth, overhang, ledge, shelf, prominence, protrusion, protuberance; informal sticky-out bit.

proliferate verb increase, grow, multiply, rocket, mushroom, snowball, burgeon, spread, expand, run riot.
OPPOSITES decrease, dwindle.

prolific adjective **1** *a prolific crop of tomatoes:* **plentiful,** abundant, bountiful, profuse, copious, luxuriant, rich, lush, fruitful. **2** *a prolific composer:* **productive,** fertile, creative, inventive.
OPPOSITES meagre, unproductive.

prolong verb lengthen, extend, drag out, draw out, protract, spin out, carry on, continue, keep up, perpetuate.
OPPOSITES shorten.

prominence noun **1** *his rise to prominence:* **fame,** celebrity, eminence, importance,

p

distinction, greatness, prestige, stature, standing. **2** *the press gave prominence to the reports:* **wide coverage,** importance, precedence, weight, a high profile, top billing.

prominent adjective **1** *a prominent surgeon:* **important,** well known, leading, eminent, distinguished, notable, noteworthy, noted, illustrious, celebrated, famous, renowned; N. Amer. major-league. **2** *prominent cheekbones:* **jutting (out),** protruding, projecting, protuberant, standing out, sticking out, proud, bulging. **3** *a prominent feature of the landscape:* **conspicuous,** noticeable, obvious, unmistakable, eye-catching, pronounced, salient, striking, dominant, obtrusive.
OPPOSITES unimportant, unknown, flat, inconspicuous.

promise noun **1** *you broke your promise:* **word (of honour),** assurance, pledge, vow, guarantee, oath, bond, undertaking, agreement, commitment, contract. **2** *he shows promise:* **potential,** ability, talent, aptitude, possibility.
verb **1** *she promised to go:* **give one's word,** swear, pledge, vow, undertake, guarantee, warrant, contract, give an assurance, commit oneself. **2** *the skies promised sunshine:* **indicate,** lead one to expect, point to, be a sign of, give hope of, augur, herald, portend.

promising adjective **1** *a promising start:* **good,** encouraging, favourable, hopeful, auspicious, propitious, bright, rosy, heartening. **2** *a promising actor:* **with**

potential, gifted, talented, budding, up-and-coming, rising, coming, in the making.
OPPOSITES unfavourable, hopeless.

promote verb **1** *she's been promoted:* **upgrade,** give promotion to, elevate, advance, move up. **2** *an organization promoting justice:* **encourage,** further, advance, foster, develop, boost, stimulate, work for. **3** *she is promoting her new film:* **advertise,** publicize, give publicity to, beat/bang the drum for, market, merchandise; informal push, plug, hype; N. Amer. informal flack.
OPPOSITES demote, obstruct, play down.

promotion noun **1** *her promotion at work:* **upgrading,** preferment, elevation, advancement, step up (the ladder). **2** *the promotion of justice:* **encouragement,** furtherance, furthering, advancement, contribution to, fostering, boosting, stimulation; N. Amer. boosterism. **3** *the promotion for her new film:* **advertising,** marketing, publicity, campaign, propaganda; informal hard sell, plug, hype, puff.

prompt verb **1** *curiosity prompted him to look:* **induce,** make, move, motivate, lead, dispose, persuade, incline, encourage, stimulate, prod, impel, spur on, inspire. **2** *the statement prompted a hostile reaction:* **give rise to,** bring about, cause, occasion, result in, lead to, elicit, produce, precipitate, trigger, spark off, provoke. **3** *the actors needed prompting:* **remind,** cue, feed, help out, jog someone's

p

memory.
OPPOSITES deter, avoid.
adjective *a prompt reply:* **quick,**
swift, rapid, speedy, fast, direct,
immediate, instant, early,
punctual, in good time, on
time.
OPPOSITES slow, late.
adverb *at 3.30 prompt:* **exactly,**
precisely, sharp, on the dot,
dead, punctually; informal bang
on; N. Amer. informal on the button,
on the nose.

promptly adverb **1** *William
arrived promptly at 7.30:*
punctually, on time; informal on
the dot, bang on; Brit. informal
spot on; N. Amer. informal on the
button, on the nose. **2** *I expect
the matter to be dealt with
promptly:* **without delay,**
straight/right away, at once,
immediately, now, as soon as
possible, quickly, swiftly,
rapidly, speedily, fast; informal
pronto, asap.
OPPOSITES late, slowly.

prone adjective **1** *softwood is
prone to rotting:* **susceptible,**
vulnerable, subject, open,
liable, given, predisposed,
likely, disposed, inclined, apt.
2 *his prone body:* **lying face
down,** on one's stomach/front,
lying flat, lying down,
horizontal, prostrate.
OPPOSITES resistant, immune,
upright.

pronounce verb **1** *his name is
difficult to pronounce:* **say,**
enunciate, utter, voice, sound,
vocalize, get one's tongue
round. **2** *the doctor pronounced
her fit for work:* **declare,**
proclaim, judge, rule, decree.

pronounced adjective
noticeable, marked, strong,
conspicuous, striking, distinct,
prominent, unmistakable,

obvious.
OPPOSITES slight.

proof noun **evidence,**
verification, corroboration,
demonstration, authentication,
confirmation, certification,
documentation.
adjective **resistant,** immune,
unaffected, impervious.

prop noun **1** *the roof is held up
by props:* **pole,** post, support,
upright, brace, buttress, stay,
strut. **2** *a prop for the economy:*
mainstay, pillar, anchor,
support, cornerstone.
verb *he propped his bike against
the wall:* **lean,** rest, stand,
balance.
■ **prop something up 1** *this post
is propping the wall up:* hold
up, shore up, buttress, support,
brace, underpin. **2** *they prop up
loss-making industries:*
subsidize, underwrite, fund,
finance.

propaganda noun **information,**
promotion, advertising,
publicity, disinformation;
informal hype.

propel verb **1** *a boat propelled
by oars:* **move,** power, push,
drive. **2** *the impact propelled
him into the street:* **throw,**
thrust, toss, fling, hurl, pitch,
send, shoot.

proper adjective **1** *he's not a
proper scientist:* **real,** genuine,
actual, true, bona fide; informal
kosher. **2** *the proper channels:*
right, correct, accepted,
conventional, established,
official, regular, acceptable,
appropriate. **3** *they were
terribly proper:* **formal,**
conventional, correct, orthodox,
polite, punctilious, respectable.
OPPOSITES fake, inappropriate,
wrong, unconventional.

property noun **1** *lost property:*

p

possessions, belongings, things, effects, stuff, goods; informal gear. **2** *private property:* **building(s),** premises, house(s), land; N. Amer. real estate. **3** *healing properties:* **quality,** attribute, characteristic, teature, power, trait, hallmark.

prophecy noun **prediction,** forecast, prognostication, prognosis, divination.

prophesy verb **predict,** foretell, forecast, foresee, prognosticate.

prophet, prophetess noun **forecaster,** seer, soothsayer, fortune teller, clairvoyant, oracle.

proportion noun **1** *a proportion of the land:* **part,** portion, amount, quantity, bit, piece, percentage, fraction, section, segment, share. **2** *the proportion of water to alcohol:* **ratio,** distribution, relative amount/number, relationship. **3** *a sense of proportion:* **balance,** symmetry, harmony, correspondence, correlation, agreement. **4** *men of huge proportions:* **size,** dimensions, magnitude, measurements, mass, volume, bulk, expanse, extent.

proportional, proportionate adjective **corresponding,** comparable, in proportion, pro rata, commensurate, equivalent, consistent.
OPPOSITES disproportionate.

proposal noun **scheme,** plan, idea, project, programme, motion, proposition, suggestion, submission.

propose verb **1** *he proposed a solution:* **put forward,** suggest, submit, advance, offer, present, move, come up with. **2** *do you propose to go?* **intend,** mean,

plan, have in mind, aim. **3** *he proposed to her!* **ask someone to marry you,** ask for someone's hand in marriage; informal pop the question.
OPPOSITES withdraw.

proposition noun **1** *a business proposition:* **proposal,** scheme, plan, project, idea, programme. **2** *doing it for real is a very different proposition:* **task,** job, undertaking, venture, activity, affair.

proprietor, proprietress noun **owner,** possessor, holder, householder, master, mistress, landowner, landlord, landlady, shopkeeper.

prosecute verb **charge,** take to court, take legal action against, sue, try, bring to trial, put on trial, put in the dock, indict; N. Amer. impeach.
OPPOSITES defend, let off.

prospect noun **1** *there is little prospect of success:* **likelihood,** hope, expectation, chance, odds, probability, possibility, promise, lookout, fear, danger. **2** *her job prospects:* **possibilities,** potential, expectations, outlook. **3** *a daunting prospect:* **vision,** thought, idea, task, undertaking.
verb *prospecting for oil:* **search,** look, explore, survey, scout, hunt, dowse.

prospective adjective **potential,** possible, probable, likely, future, eventual, -to-be, soon-to-be, in the making, intending, aspiring, would-be.

prospectus noun **brochure,** syllabus, curriculum, catalogue, programme, list, schedule.

prosper verb **flourish,** thrive, do well, bloom, blossom, burgeon, progress, do all right for oneself, get ahead, get on

(in the world), be successful;
informal go places.
OPPOSITES fail, flounder.

prosperity noun success,
affluence, wealth, ease, plenty.
OPPOSITES hardship, failure.

prosperous adjective thriving,
flourishing, successful, strong,
vigorous, profitable, lucrative,
expanding, booming,
burgeoning, **affluent,** wealthy,
rich, moneyed, well off, well-to-
do; informal in the money.
OPPOSITES ailing, poor.

prostitute noun whore, sex
worker, call girl, rent boy;
informal working girl; Brit. informal
tom; N. Amer. informal hooker,
hustler.
verb they prostituted their art:
betray, sacrifice, sell, sell out,
debase, degrade, demean,
devalue, cheapen, lower, shame,
misuse.

protect verb keep safe, keep
from harm, guard, defend,
shield, save, safeguard,
preserve, cushion, insulate,
shelter, screen, keep, look after.
OPPOSITES expose, neglect,
attack, harm.

protection noun 1 protection
against frost: defence, security,
safeguard, safety, sanctuary,
shelter, refuge, immunity,
indemnity. 2 the protection of
the Church: safe keeping, care,
charge, umbrella, guardianship,
support, aegis, patronage. 3 a
good protection against noise:
barrier, buffer, shield, screen,
cushion, bulwark, armour,
insulation.

protective adjective 1 protective
clothing: special, safety, thick,
heavy, insulated, ...-proof,
...-resistant. 2 he felt protective
towards her: solicitous, caring,
defensive, paternal, maternal,

overprotective, possessive,
jealous.

protector noun 1 a protector of
the environment: defender,
preserver, guardian, champion,
patron, custodian. 2 ear
protectors: guard, shield,
buffer, cushion, pad, screen.

protest noun 1 a storm of
protest: objection, complaint,
challenge, dissent, demurral,
remonstration, fuss, outcry.
2 the women staged a protest:
demonstration, rally, vigil, sit-
in, occupation, work-to-rule,
stoppage, strike, walkout,
mutiny, picket, boycott; informal
demo.
OPPOSITES support, approval.
verb 1 residents protested at the
plans: object, express
opposition, dissent, take issue,
take a stand, put up a fight,
take exception, complain,
express disapproval, disagree,
make a fuss, speak out; informal
kick up a fuss. 2 he protested
his innocence: insist on,
maintain, assert, affirm,
announce, proclaim, declare,
profess.
OPPOSITES acquiesce, support,
deny.

protocol noun etiquette,
convention, formalities,
custom, the rules, procedure,
ritual, decorum, the done
thing.

prototype noun original,
master, template, pattern,
sample.

protracted adjective prolonged,
extended, long-drawn-out,
lengthy, long.
OPPOSITES short.

proud adjective 1 the proud
parents: pleased, glad, happy,
delighted, thrilled, satisfied,
gratified. 2 a proud day:

p

pleasing, gratifying, satisfying, cheering, heart-warming, happy, glorious. **3** *he is too proud to admit to being in the wrong:* **arrogant,** conceited, vain, self-important, full of oneself, overbearing, bumptious, presumptuous, overweening, haughty, high and mighty; informal big-headed, too big for one's boots, stuck-up.
OPPOSITES ashamed, shameful, humble, modest.

prove verb **1** *that proves I'm right:* **show (to be true),** demonstrate (the truth of), provide proof, substantiate, verify, validate, authenticate. **2** *the rumour proved to be correct:* **turn out,** be found.
OPPOSITES disprove.

proverb noun **saying,** adage, saw, maxim, axiom, motto, aphorism, epigram.

provide verb **1** *we will provide funds:* **supply,** give, furnish, come up with, dispense, produce, yield, deliver, donate, contribute; informal fork out, lay out. **2** *he was provided with tools:* **equip,** furnish, issue, supply, fit out, rig out, kit out, arm, provision; informal fix up. **3** *the test may provide the answer:* **offer,** present, afford, give, add, bring, yield, impart, reveal.
OPPOSITES refuse, withhold, deprive, neglect.

■ **provide for** feed, nurture, nourish, support, maintain, keep, sustain.

provided, providing conjunction **if,** on condition that, provided that, presuming (that), assuming (that), as long as, with/on the understanding that.

provider noun **supplier,** donor, giver, contributor, source.

province noun **1** *a province of the Roman Empire:* **territory,** region, state, department, canton, area, district, sector, zone, division. **2** (**the provinces**) **the regions,** the rest of the country, rural areas/districts, the countryside; informal the sticks, the middle of nowhere; N. Amer. informal the boondocks. **3** *that's outside my province, I'm afraid:* **domain,** area, department, responsibility, sphere, world, realm, field, discipline, territory; informal bailiwick.

provincial adjective **1** *the provincial government:* **regional,** state, territorial, district, local, county. **2** *provincial areas:* **rural,** country, rustic, small-town, outlying, backwoods, backwater; informal one-horse. **3** *they're so dull and provincial:* **unsophisticated,** narrow-minded, parochial, small-town, suburban, insular, inward-looking; N. Amer. informal corn-fed.
OPPOSITES national, metropolitan, cosmopolitan, sophisticated, broad-minded.

provision noun **1** *the provision of weapons to guerrillas:* **supply,** giving, donation, equipping, furnishing, distribution. **2** *limited provision for young children:* **facilities,** services, amenities, resource(s), arrangements, means, funds, assistance. **3** (**provisions**) *provisions for the trip:* **supplies,** food and drink, stores, groceries, foodstuff(s), rations. **4** *the provisions of the Act:* **term,** requirement, specification, stipulation.

provisional adjective **interim,** temporary, transitional, changeover, stopgap, short-term, fill-in, acting, working.
OPPOSITES permanent, definite.

provocation noun **goading,** prodding, incitement, pressure, harassment, teasing, taunting, torment; informal hassle, aggravation.

provocative adjective **annoying,** irritating, maddening, galling, insulting, offensive, inflammatory, incendiary; informal aggravating.
OPPOSITES soothing, calming.

provoke verb **1** *the plan has provoked outrage:* **arouse,** produce, evoke, cause, give rise to, excite, spark off, touch off, kindle, generate, engender, instigate, result in, lead to, bring on, precipitate, prompt, trigger. **2** *he was provoked into replying:* **goad,** spur, prick, sting, prod, incite, rouse, stimulate. **3** *he's dangerous if provoked:* **annoy,** anger, enrage, irritate, madden, nettle; Brit. rub up the wrong way; informal aggravate, rile, needle, get/put someone's back up; Brit. informal wind up.
OPPOSITES allay, deter, pacify, appease.

prowess noun **skill,** expertise, mastery, ability, capability, capacity, talent, aptitude, dexterity, proficiency, finesse; informal know-how.
OPPOSITES inability, ineptitude.

prowl verb **steal,** slink, skulk, sneak, stalk, creep; informal snoop.

proxy noun **deputy,** representative, substitute, delegate, agent, surrogate, stand-in, go-between.

prudent adjective **1** *it is prudent to obtain consent:* **wise,** sensible, politic, judicious, shrewd, advisable. **2** *a prudent approach to borrowing:* **cautious,** careful, provident, far-sighted, judicious, shrewd, circumspect, thrifty, economical.
OPPOSITES unwise, reckless, extravagant.

prune verb **1** *I pruned the roses:* **cut back,** trim, clip, shear, shorten, thin, shape. **2** *staff numbers have been pruned:* **reduce,** cut (back/down), pare (down), slim down, trim, downsize, axe, shrink; informal slash.
OPPOSITES increase.

psychiatrist noun **psychotherapist,** psychoanalyst, analyst; informal shrink.

psychic adjective **1** *psychic powers:* **supernatural,** paranormal, other-worldly, metaphysical, extrasensory, magic(al), mystic(al), occult. **2** *I'm not psychic:* **clairvoyant,** telepathic.
OPPOSITES normal.
noun *she is a psychic:* **clairvoyant,** fortune teller, medium, spiritualist, telepath, mind-reader.

psychological adjective **1** *his psychological state:* **mental,** emotional, inner, cognitive. **2** *her pain was psychological:* **(all) in the mind,** psychosomatic, emotional, subjective, subconscious, imaginary, irrational.
OPPOSITES physical.

psychology noun *the psychology of the road user:* **mind,** thought processes, way of thinking, mentality, psyche, attitude(s), make-up, character,

p

temperament; informal what makes someone tick.

pub noun (Brit.) **bar,** inn, tavern, hostelry; Brit. public house; Austral./NZ hotel; informal watering hole; Brit. informal local, boozer; N. Amer. historical saloon.

public adjective **1** *public affairs:* **state,** national, government, constitutional, civic, civil, official, social, municipal, community, nationalized. **2** *by public demand:* **popular,** general, common, communal, collective, shared, joint, universal, widespread. **3** *a public figure:* **prominent,** well known, important, leading, eminent, distinguished, celebrated, household, famous; N. Amer. major-league. **4** *public places:* **open (to the public),** communal, available, free, unrestricted, community. **5** *the news became public:* **known,** published, publicized, open, obvious.
OPPOSITES private, obscure, unknown, restricted, secret.
noun **1** *the British public:* **people,** citizens, subjects, electors, electorate, voters, taxpayers, residents, inhabitants, citizenry, population, populace, community, society, country, nation, everyone. **2** *his adoring public:* **audience,** spectators, followers, following, fans, devotees, admirers.

publication noun **1** *the author of this publication:* **book,** volume, title, opus, tome, newspaper, paper, magazine, periodical, newsletter, bulletin, journal, report. **2** *the publication of her new book:* **issuing,** publishing, printing, distribution, spreading, appearance.

publicity noun **1** *the blaze of publicity:* **public attention/ interest,** media attention/ interest, exposure, glare, limelight. **2** *publicity should boost sales:* **promotion,** advertising, propaganda, boost, push; informal hype, ballyhoo, puff, build-up, plug.

publish verb **1** *we publish novels:* **issue,** bring out, produce, print. **2** *he ought to publish his views:* **make known,** make public, publicize, announce, broadcast, issue, put out, distribute, spread, promulgate, disseminate, circulate, air.

pudding noun **dessert,** sweet, last course; Brit. informal afters, pud.

puff noun **1** *a puff of wind:* **gust,** blast, flurry, rush, draught, waft, breeze, breath. **2** *he took a puff at his cigar:* **pull;** informal drag, toke.
verb **1** *he walked fast, puffing a little:* **breathe heavily,** pant, blow, gasp. **2** *she puffed at her cigarette:* **smoke,** draw on, drag on, suck at/on, inhale; informal toke on.

pull verb **1** *he pulled the box towards him:* **tug,** haul, drag, draw, tow, heave, jerk, wrench; informal yank. **2** *she pulled a muscle:* **strain,** sprain, wrench, tear. **3** *race day pulled big crowds:* **attract,** draw, bring in, pull in, lure, seduce, entice, tempt.
OPPOSITES push, repel.
noun **1** *give the chain a pull:* **tug,** jerk, heave; informal yank. **2** *she took a pull at her beer:* **gulp,** draught, drink, swallow, mouthful, slug; informal swig. **3** *a pull on a cigarette:* **puff;** informal

drag, toke. **4** *the pull of the theatre:* **attraction**, draw, lure, magnetism, fascination, appeal, allure.

■ **pull something off** achieve, fulfil, succeed in, accomplish, bring off, carry off, clinch, fix. ■ **pull out** withdraw, resign, leave, retire, step down, bow out, back out, give up; informal quit. ■ **pull through** get better, get well again, improve, recover, rally, come through, recuperate.

pulp noun **1** *he ground it into a pulp:* **mush**, mash, paste, purée, slop, slush, mulch. **2** *the sweet pulp on cocoa seeds:* **flesh**, marrow, meat.
verb *pulp the gooseberries:* **mash**, purée, cream, crush, press, liquidize.

pulse noun **1** *the pulse in her neck:* **heartbeat**, heart rate. **2** *the pulse of the engine:* **rhythm**, beat, tempo, pounding, throbbing, thudding, drumming. **3** *pulses of ultrasound:* **burst**, blast, surge.
verb *music pulsed through the building:* **throb**, pulsate, vibrate, beat, pound, thud, thump, drum, reverberate, echo.

pump verb **1** *they pumped air down the tube:* **force**, drive, push, inject, suck, draw. **2** *she pumped up the tyre:* **inflate**, blow up, fill up, swell, enlarge, distend, expand, dilate, puff up. **3** *blood was pumping from his leg:* **spurt**, spout, squirt, jet, surge, spew, gush, stream, flow, pour, spill, well, cascade.

punch¹ verb **1** *Jim punched him in the face:* **hit**, strike, thump, jab, smash; informal sock, slug, biff, bop; Brit. informal stick one on, slosh; N. Amer. informal boff, bust;

Austral./NZ informal quilt.
noun *a punch on the nose:* **blow**, hit, knock, thump, box, jab, clip; informal sock, slug, biff, bop; N. Amer. informal boff, bust.

punch² verb *he punched her ticket:* **perforate**, puncture, pierce, prick, hole, spike, skewer.

punctual adjective **on time**, prompt, on schedule, in (good) time; informal on the dot.
OPPOSITES late.

punctuate verb **break up**, interrupt, intersperse, pepper, sprinkle, scatter.

puncture noun **1** *the tyre developed a puncture:* **hole**, perforation, rupture, cut, gash, slit, leak. **2** *my car has a puncture:* **flat tyre**; informal flat.
verb *he punctured the balloon:* **prick**, pierce, stab, rupture, perforate, cut, slit, deflate.

punish verb **1** *they punished their children:* **discipline**, penalize, correct, sentence, teach someone a lesson; informal come down on (like a ton of bricks), have someone's guts for garters; dated chastise. **2** *higher charges would punish the poor:* **disadvantage**, handicap, hurt, penalize.

punishing adjective **arduous**, demanding, taxing, strenuous, rigorous, stressful, trying, heavy, difficult, tough, exhausting, tiring, gruelling.
OPPOSITES easy.

punishment noun **penalty**, sanction, penance, discipline, forfeit, sentence.

punitive adjective **penal**, disciplinary, corrective, retributive, retaliatory.

puny adjective **1** *a puny boy:* **small**, weak, feeble, slight, undersized, stunted; informal

p

weedy. **2** *their puny efforts:*
pitiful, pitiable, miserable,
sorry, meagre, paltry; informal
pathetic, measly.
OPPOSITES sturdy, substantial.

pupil noun **1** *former pupils of the
school:* **student,** scholar,
schoolchild, schoolboy,
schoolgirl. **2** *the guru's pupils:*
disciple, follower, student,
protégé, apprentice, trainee,
novice.
OPPOSITES teacher.

puppet noun **1** *a show with
puppets:* **marionette,** glove
puppet, finger puppet. **2** *a
puppet of the government:*
pawn, tool, instrument, cat's
paw, poodle, mouthpiece,
stooge.

purchase verb *we purchased
new software:* **buy,** acquire,
obtain, pick up, procure, pay
for, invest in; informal get hold
of, score.
OPPOSITES sell.
noun **1** *he's happy with his
purchase:* **acquisition,** buy,
investment, order, bargain,
shopping, goods. **2** *he could get
no purchase on the wall:* **grip,**
grasp, hold, foothold, toehold,
anchorage, support, traction,
leverage.
OPPOSITES sale.

pure adjective **1** *pure gold:*
unadulterated, undiluted,
sterling, solid, 100%. **2** *the air
is so pure:* **clean,** clear, fresh,
sparkling, unpolluted,
uncontaminated, untainted.
3 *pure in body and mind:*
virtuous, moral, good,
righteous, honourable,
reputable, wholesome, clean,
honest, upright, upstanding,
exemplary, chaste, decent,
worthy, noble; informal squeaky
clean. **4** *three hours of pure*

magic: **sheer,** utter, absolute,
out-and-out, complete, total,
perfect.
OPPOSITES adulterated, polluted,
immoral, practical.

purely adverb **entirely,** wholly,
exclusively, solely, only, just,
merely.

purge verb **1** *this purges the
system of impurities:* **cleanse,**
clear, purify, rid, empty, strip,
scour. **2** *the founders were
purged from the firm:* **remove,**
get rid of, eliminate, clear out,
sweep out, expel, eject, evict,
dismiss, sack, oust, axe, depose,
root out, weed out.
noun **removal,** elimination,
expulsion, ejection, exclusion,
eviction, dismissal, sacking,
ousting.

purify verb **clean,** cleanse,
refine, decontaminate, filter,
clear, freshen, deodorize,
sanitize, disinfect, sterilize.

purity noun **1** *the purity of our
tap water:* **cleanness,** freshness,
cleanliness, wholesomeness.
2 *they sought purity in a foul
world:* **virtue,** morality,
goodness, righteousness, piety,
honour, honesty, integrity,
decency, innocence.

purpose noun **1** *the purpose of
his visit:* **motive,** motivation,
grounds, occasion, reason,
point, basis, justification.
2 *their purpose was to subvert
the economy:* **intention,** aim,
object, objective, goal, plan,
ambition, aspiration. **3** *the
original purpose of the porch:*
function, role, use. **4** *they
started with some purpose:*
determination, resolution,
resolve, enthusiasm, ambition,
motivation, commitment,
conviction, dedication; informal
get-up-and-go.

■ **on purpose** deliberately, intentionally, purposely, wilfully, knowingly, consciously.

purposeful adjective **determined**, resolute, steadfast, single-minded, committed.
OPPOSITES aimless.

purposely adverb **deliberately**, intentionally, on purpose, wilfully, knowingly, consciously.

purse noun **1** *the money fell out of her purse:* **wallet**, money bag; N. Amer. change purse, billfold. **2** *(N. Amer.) a woman's purse:* **handbag**, shoulder bag, clutch bag; N. Amer. pocketbook. **3** *the fight will net him a $75,000 purse:* **prize**, reward, winnings, stake(s).
verb *he pursed his lips:* **press together**, compress, tighten, pucker, pout.

pursue verb **1** *I pursued him down the garden:* **follow**, run after, chase, hunt, stalk, track, trail, hound. **2** *pursue the goal of political union:* **strive for**, work towards, seek, search for, aim at/for, aspire to. **3** *she pursued a political career:* **engage in**, be occupied in, practise, follow, conduct, ply, take up, undertake, carry on, continue, take further, stick with/at.
OPPOSITES avoid, shun.

pursuit noun **1** *the pursuit of profit:* **striving for**, quest after/ for, search for. **2** *a worthwhile pursuit:* **activity**, hobby, pastime, diversion, recreation, amusement, occupation.

push verb **1** *she tried to push him away:* **shove**, thrust, propel, send, drive, force, prod, poke, nudge, elbow, shoulder, sweep, ram. **2** *she pushed her way into the flat:* **force**, shove, thrust, squeeze, jostle, elbow, shoulder, bundle, hustle, work, inch. **3** *he pushed the panic button:* **press**, depress, hold down, squeeze, operate, activate. **4** *don't push her to join in:* **urge**, press, pressure, pressurize, force, coerce, nag; informal lean on, twist someone's arm.
OPPOSITES pull.
noun **1** *I felt a push in the back:* **shove**, thrust, nudge, bump, jolt, prod, poke. **2** *the army's eastward push:* **advance**, drive, thrust, charge, attack, assault, onslaught, onrush, offensive.

put verb **1** *she put the parcel on a chair:* **place**, set, lay, deposit, position, leave, plant; informal stick, dump, park, plonk, pop; N. Amer. informal plunk. **2** *she put it bluntly:* **express**, word, phrase, frame, formulate, render, convey, state.
■ **put something across/over** communicate, convey, get across/over, explain, make clear, spell out. ■ **put someone off** deter, discourage, dissuade, daunt, unnerve, intimidate, scare off; informal turn off. ■ **put something off** postpone, defer, delay, put back, adjourn, hold over, reschedule, shelve; N. Amer. table; informal put on ice, put on the back burner. ■ **put someone out 1** *Maria was put out by the slur:* annoy, anger, irritate, offend, displease, irk, gall, upset; informal rile, miff. **2** *I don't want to put you out:* inconvenience, trouble, bother, impose on. ■ **put something out 1** *firemen put out the blaze:* extinguish, quench, douse, smother, blow out, snuff out.

p

2 *he put out a press release:* issue, publish, release, bring out, circulate, publicize, post.
■ **put someone up 1** *we can put him up for a few days:* accommodate, house, take in, give someone a roof over their head. **2** *they put up a candidate:* nominate, propose, put forward, recommend. ■ **put something up 1** *the building was put up 100 years ago:* build, construct, erect, raise. **2** *she put up a poster:* display, pin up, stick up, hang up, post. **3** *he put up most of the funding:* provide, supply, furnish, give, contribute, donate, pledge, pay; informal cough up, shell out;

N. Amer. informal ante up, pony up.
■ **put up with** tolerate, take, stand (for), accept, stomach, swallow, endure, bear; informal abide, lump it; Brit. informal stick, be doing with; formal brook.

puzzle verb *her decision puzzled me:* **baffle,** perplex, bewilder, confuse, bemuse, mystify, nonplus; informal stump, beat.
noun *the poem has always been a puzzle:* **enigma,** mystery, paradox, conundrum, poser, riddle, problem.

puzzling adjective **baffling,** perplexing, bewildering, confusing, complicated, unclear, mysterious, enigmatic.
OPPOSITES clear.

Qq

quaint adjective **1** *a quaint town:* **picturesque,** charming, sweet, attractive, old-fashioned, old-world; Brit. twee; N. Amer. cunning. **2** *quaint customs:* **unusual,** curious, eccentric, quirky, bizarre, whimsical, unconventional; informal offbeat.
OPPOSITES ugly, ordinary.

quake verb **shake,** tremble, quiver, shudder, sway, rock, wobble, move, heave, convulse.

qualification noun **1** *a teaching qualification:* **certificate,** diploma, degree, licence, document, warrant. **2** *I can't accept it without qualification:* **modification,** limitation, reservation, stipulation, alteration, amendment, revision, moderation, mitigation, condition, proviso, caveat.

qualified adjective **1** *a qualified*

engineer: **certified,** certificated, chartered, licensed, professional. **2** *qualified approval:* **limited,** conditional, restricted, contingent, circumscribed, guarded, equivocal, modified, adapted, amended, adjusted, moderated, reduced.
OPPOSITES unqualified, wholehearted.

qualify verb **1** *I qualify for free travel:* **be eligible,** meet the requirements, be entitled to, be permitted. **2** *they qualify as refugees:* **count,** be considered, be designated, be eligible. **3** *she qualified as a solicitor:* **be certified,** be licensed, pass, graduate, succeed. **4** *the course qualified them to teach:* **authorize,** empower, allow, permit, license. **5** *they qualified their findings:* **modify,** limit, restrict, make conditional, moderate, temper, modulate, mitigate.

quality noun **1** *a poor quality of signal:* **standard**, grade, class, calibre, condition, character, nature, form, rank, value, level. **2** *work of such quality:* **excellence,** superiority, merit, worth, value, virtue, calibre, distinction. **3** *her good qualities:* **feature,** trait, attribute, characteristic, point, aspect, facet, side, property.

quantity noun **amount,** total, aggregate, sum, quota, mass, weight, volume, bulk.

quarrel noun *they had a quarrel:* **argument,** disagreement, squabble, fight, dispute, wrangle, clash, altercation, feud; informal tiff, slanging match, run-in; Brit. informal row, bust-up.
OPPOSITES agreement, harmony.
verb *don't quarrel over it:* **argue,** fight, disagree, fall out, differ, be at odds, bicker, squabble, cross swords; Brit. informal row.
OPPOSITES agree, get on.
■ **quarrel with** *you can't quarrel with the verdict:* **fault,** criticize, object to, oppose, take exception to, attack, take issue with, impugn, contradict, dispute, controvert; informal knock; formal gainsay.

quarry noun **prey,** victim, object, goal, target, kill, game, prize.

quash verb **1** *he may quash the sentence:* **cancel,** reverse, rescind, repeal, revoke, retract, countermand, withdraw, overturn, overrule. **2** *we want to quash these rumours:* **stop,** put an end to, stamp out, crush, put down, check, curb, nip in the bud, squash, suppress, stifle.

OPPOSITES validate, encourage, perpetuate.

queen noun **monarch,** sovereign, ruler, head of state, Crown, Her Majesty.

queer adjective **odd,** strange, unusual, funny, peculiar, curious, bizarre, weird, uncanny, freakish, eerie, unnatural, abnormal, anomalous; informal spooky.
OPPOSITES normal.

query noun **1** *we can answer any queries:* **question,** enquiry. **2** *there was a query as to who owned the hotel:* **doubt,** uncertainty, question (mark), reservation.
verb **1** *'Why do that?' queried Isobel:* **ask,** enquire, question; Brit. informal quiz. **2** *folk may query his credentials:* **challenge,** question, dispute, doubt, have suspicions about, distrust.
OPPOSITES accept, trust.

quest noun **1** *their quest for her killer:* **search,** hunt, pursuance of. **2** *Sir Galahad's quest:* **expedition,** journey, voyage, trek, travels, odyssey, adventure, exploration, search, crusade, mission, pilgrimage.

question noun **1** *please answer my question:* **enquiry,** query, interrogation. **2** *there is no question that he is ill:* **doubt,** dispute, argument, debate, uncertainty, reservation. **3** *the political questions of the day:* **issue,** matter, topic, business, problem, concern, debate, argument, dispute, controversy.
OPPOSITES answer, certainty.
verb **1** *the magistrate questions the suspect:* **interrogate,** cross-examine, cross-question, quiz, interview, debrief, examine; informal grill, pump. **2** *she questioned his motives:* **query,**

q

challenge, dispute, cast aspersions on, doubt, suspect.
■ **out of the question** impossible, impracticable, unfeasible, unworkable, inconceivable, unimaginable, unrealizable, unsuitable; informal not on.

questionable adjective **suspicious,** suspect, dubious, irregular, odd, strange, murky, dark, unsavoury, disreputable; informal funny, fishy, shady, iffy; Brit. informal dodgy.
OPPOSITES honest.

questionnaire noun **question sheet,** survey form, opinion poll, test, quiz.

queue noun **row,** column, file, chain, string, procession, waiting list; N. Amer. line, wait list.

quick adjective **1** *a quick worker:* **fast,** swift, rapid, speedy, brisk, smart, lightning, whirlwind, whistle-stop, breakneck; informal nippy, zippy. **2** *a quick look:* **hasty,** hurried, cursory, perfunctory, desultory, superficial, brief. **3** *a quick end to the recession:* **sudden,** instantaneous, instant, immediate, abrupt, precipitate. **4** *she isn't as quick as the others:* **intelligent,** bright, clever, gifted, able, astute, sharp-witted, smart, alert, sharp, perceptive; informal brainy, on the ball.
OPPOSITES slow, long.

quicken verb **1** *she quickened her pace:* **speed up,** accelerate, step up, hasten, hurry (up). **2** *the film quickened his interest in nature:* **stimulate,** excite, arouse, rouse, stir up, activate, whet, inspire, kindle.

quickly adverb **1** *he walked quickly:* **fast,** swiftly, briskly, rapidly, speedily, at full tilt, at a gallop, at the double, post-haste, hotfoot; informal like (greased) lightning, hell for leather, like blazes, like the wind; Brit. informal like the clappers, like billy-o; N. Amer. informal lickety-split. **2** *you'd better leave quickly:* **immediately,** directly, at once, straight away, right away, instantly, forthwith; N. Amer. momentarily; informal like a shot, asap, p.d.q., pronto. **3** *he quickly inspected it:* **briefly,** fleetingly, briskly, hastily, hurriedly, cursorily, perfunctorily, superficially, desultorily.

quiet adjective **1** *the whole pub went quiet:* **silent,** still, hushed, noiseless, soundless, mute, dumb, speechless. **2** *a quiet voice:* **soft,** low, muted, muffled, faint, hushed, whispered, suppressed. **3** *a quiet village:* **peaceful,** sleepy, tranquil, calm, still, restful.
OPPOSITES loud, busy.
noun *the quiet of the countryside:* **silence,** still, hush, restfulness, calm, tranquillity, serenity, peace.

quietly adverb **1** *she read quietly:* **silently,** noiselessly, soundlessly, inaudibly. **2** *he spoke quietly:* **softly,** faintly, in a low voice, in a whisper, in a murmur, under one's breath, in an undertone.
OPPOSITES out loud, loudly.

quilt noun **duvet,** cover(s); Brit. eiderdown; N. Amer. comforter, puff; Austral. trademark Doona.

quirk noun **1** *they all know his quirks:* **idiosyncrasy,** peculiarity, oddity, eccentricity, foible, whim, vagary, habit, characteristic, trait, fad. **2** *a quirk of fate:* **chance,** fluke,

q

freak, anomaly, twist.

quirky adjective eccentric, idiosyncratic, unconventional, unorthodox, unusual, strange, bizarre, peculiar, zany; informal wacky, way-out, offbeat.
OPPOSITES conventional.

quit verb 1 *he quit the office at 12.30:* **leave,** vacate, exit, depart from. 2 (informal) *he quit his job:* **resign from,** leave, give up, hand in one's notice; informal chuck, pack in. 3 (informal) *quit living in the past:* **give up,** stop, discontinue, drop, abandon, abstain from; informal pack in, leave off.
OPPOSITES arrive at, continue, start.

quite adverb 1 *two quite different types:* **completely,** entirely, totally, wholly, absolutely, utterly, thoroughly, altogether. 2 *red hair was quite common:* **fairly,** rather, somewhat, relatively,

comparatively, moderately, reasonably; informal pretty.
OPPOSITES slightly, not at all.

quiz noun **competition,** test of knowledge.
verb *a man was quizzed by police:* **question,** interrogate, cross-examine, cross-question, interview; informal grill, pump.

quota noun **share,** allocation, allowance, ration, portion, slice; Brit. informal whack.

quotation noun 1 *a quotation from Dryden:* **extract,** quote, citation, excerpt, passage; N. Amer. cite. 2 *a quotation for the work:* **estimate,** quote, price, tender, bid, costing.

quote verb 1 *he quoted from the book:* **recite,** repeat, reproduce, retell, echo. 2 *she quoted one case in which a girl died:* **mention,** cite, refer to, name, instance, allude to, point out.
noun See **QUOTATION** senses 1, 2.

Rr

race[1] noun 1 *Dave won the race:* **contest,** competition, event, fixture, heat, trial(s). 2 *the race for naval domination:* **competition,** rivalry, contention, quest.
verb 1 *he will race in the final:* **compete,** contend, run. 2 *Claire raced after him:* **hurry,** dash, rush, run, sprint, bolt, charge, shoot, hurtle, hare, fly, speed; informal tear, belt.

race[2] noun 1 *pupils of different races:* **ethnic group,** racial type, origin, stock, blood, tribe. 2 *a bloodthirsty race:* **people,** nation.

racial adjective **ethnic,** ethnological, race-related, cultural, national, tribal, genetic.

rack noun *the boots live on that rack:* **frame,** framework, stand, holder, trestle, support, shelf.
verb *he was racked with guilt:* **torment,** afflict, torture, agonize, harrow, plague, persecute, trouble, worry.

racket noun 1 **noise,** din, hubbub, clamour, uproar, tumult, commotion, rumpus; informal hullabaloo; Brit. informal row. 2 (informal) *a gold-smuggling racket:* **fraud,** swindle, sharp practice; informal game, scam, rip-off.

radiate verb **1** *stars radiate energy:* **emit,** give off, discharge, diffuse, scatter, shed, cast. **2** *light radiated from the hall:* **shine,** beam, emanate, pour. **3** *four spokes radiate from the hub:* **fan out,** spread out, branch out/off, extend, issue.

radical adjective **1** *radical reform:* **thorough,** complete, total, comprehensive, exhaustive, sweeping, far-reaching, wide-ranging, extensive, profound, major. **2** *radical differences between the two theories:* **fundamental,** basic, essential, quintessential, structural, deep-seated. **3** *a radical political movement:* **revolutionary,** progressive, reformist, revisionist, progressivist, extreme, fanatical, militant.
OPPOSITES superficial, minor, conservative.

rage noun **1** *his rage is due to frustration:* **fury,** anger, wrath, outrage, indignation, temper, spleen, resentment, pique, annoyance, vexation, displeasure; informal grump, strop. **2** *the current rage for DIY:* **craze,** passion, fashion, taste, trend, vogue, fad, mania; informal thing.
verb *she raged silently:* **be angry,** be furious, be enraged, be incensed, seethe, be beside oneself, rave, storm, fume, spit; informal be livid, be wild, be steamed up.

ragged adjective **1** *ragged jeans:* **tattered,** torn, ripped, frayed, worn (out), threadbare, scruffy, shabby; informal tatty. **2** *a ragged coastline:* **jagged,** craggy, rugged, uneven, rough,

irregular, indented.
OPPOSITES new, smart, sound, smooth.

raid noun **1** *the raid on Dieppe:* **attack,** assault, descent, blitz, incursion, sortie, onslaught, storming. **2** *a raid on a shop:* **robbery,** burglary, hold-up, break-in, ram raid; informal smash-and-grab, stick-up; N. Amer. informal heist. **3** *a police raid:* **swoop,** search; N. Amer. informal bust, takedown.
verb **1** *they raided shipping in the harbour:* **attack,** assault, set upon, descend on, swoop on, storm. **2** *armed men raided the store:* **rob,** hold up, break into, plunder, steal from, pillage, loot, ransack; informal stick up. **3** *homes were raided by police:* **search,** swoop on; N. Amer. informal bust.

raider noun **robber,** burglar, thief, housebreaker, plunderer, pillager, looter, marauder, attacker, assailant, invader.

railing noun **fence,** fencing, rail(s), palisade, balustrade, banister.

rainy adjective **wet,** showery, drizzly, damp, inclement.
OPPOSITES dry, fine.

raise verb **1** *he raised a hand:* **lift (up),** hold aloft, elevate, uplift, hoist, haul up, hitch up; Brit. informal hoick up. **2** *they raised prices:* **increase,** put up, push up, up, mark up, inflate; informal hike (up), jack up, bump up. **3** *he raised his voice:* **amplify,** louden, magnify, intensify, boost, lift, increase. **4** *how will you raise the money?* **get,** obtain, acquire, accumulate, amass, collect, fetch, net, make. **5** *he raised several objections:* **bring up,** air, present, table, propose, submit, advance,

suggest, put forward. **6** *the disaster raised doubts about safety:* **give rise to**, occasion, cause, produce, engender, elicit, create, result in, lead to, prompt. **7** *most parents raise their children well:* **bring up**, rear, nurture. **8** *he raised cattle:* **breed**, rear, nurture, keep, tend, farm, produce.
OPPOSITES lower, reduce, demolish.

rake verb **1** *he raked the leaves into a pile:* **scrape**, collect, gather. **2** *she raked the gravel:* **smooth (out)**, level, even out, flatten, comb. **3** *I raked through my pockets:* **rummage**, search, hunt, sift, rifle.

rally verb **1** *the troops rallied and held their ground:* **regroup**, reassemble, re-form, reunite. **2** *share prices rallied:* **recover**, improve, get better, pick up, revive, bounce back, perk up, look up, turn a corner.
OPPOSITES disperse, slump.
noun **1** *a rally in support of the strike:* **(mass) meeting**, gathering, assembly, demonstration, (protest) march; informal demo. **2** *a rally in oil prices:* **recovery**, upturn, improvement, comeback, resurgence.
OPPOSITES slump.

ram verb **1** *he rammed his sword into its sheath:* **force**, thrust, plunge, stab, push, sink, dig, stick, cram, jam, stuff. **2** *a van rammed the car:* **hit**, strike, crash into, collide with, impact, smash into, butt.

ramble verb **1** *we rambled around the lanes:* **walk**, hike, tramp, trek, backpack. **2** *she does ramble on:* **chatter**, babble, prattle, blather, gabble, jabber, twitter, rattle; Brit. informal witter,

chunter, rabbit.

ramp noun **slope**, bank, incline, gradient, rise, drop.

rampage verb **riot**, run amok, go berserk, storm, charge, tear. ■ **go on the rampage** riot, go berserk, get out of control, run amok; N. Amer. informal go postal.

rampant adjective **uncontrolled**, unrestrained, unchecked, unbridled, out of control, out of hand, widespread, rife, spreading.
OPPOSITES controlled.

random adjective **unsystematic**, unmethodical, arbitrary, unplanned, chance, casual, indiscriminate, non-specific, haphazard, stray, erratic.
OPPOSITES systematic, deliberate.
■ **at random** unsystematically, arbitrarily, randomly, unmethodically, haphazardly.

range noun **1** *his range of vision:* **extent**, limit, reach, span, scope, compass, sweep, area, field, orbit, ambit, horizon, latitude. **2** *a range of mountains:* **row**, chain, sierra, ridge, massif. **3** *a range of foods:* **assortment**, variety, diversity, mixture, collection, array, selection, choice.
verb **1** *charges range from 1% to 5%:* **vary**, fluctuate, differ, extend, stretch, reach, go, run, cover. **2** *they ranged over the steppes:* **roam**, wander, travel, journey, rove, traverse, walk, hike, trek.

rank[1] noun **1** *he was elevated to ministerial rank:* **position**, level, grade, echelon, class, status, standing. **2** *a family of rank:* **high standing**, blue blood, high birth, nobility, aristocracy. **3** *a rank of riflemen:* **row**, line, file,

r

column, string, train, procession.

verb **1** *the plant is ranked as endangered:* **classify,** class, categorize, rate, grade, bracket, group, designate, list. **2** *tulips were ranked like guardsmen:* **line up,** align, order, arrange, dispose, set out, array, range.

rank² adjective **1** *rank vegetation:* **abundant,** lush, luxuriant, dense, profuse, vigorous, overgrown; informal jungly. **2** *a rank smell:* **offensive,** nasty, revolting, sickening, obnoxious, foul, fetid, high, rancid, putrid; Brit. informal pongy, humming. **3** *rank stupidity:* **downright,** utter, out-and-out, absolute, complete, sheer, blatant, arrant, thorough, unqualified.
OPPOSITES sparse, pleasant.

ransom noun **pay-off,** payment, sum, price.

rant verb **shout,** sound off, hold forth, go on, fulminate, spout, bluster; informal mouth off.

rap verb **hit,** knock, strike, smack, bang; informal whack, thwack, bash, wallop.

rapid adjective **quick,** fast, swift, speedy, express, brisk, lightning, meteoric, whirlwind, sudden, instantaneous, instant, immediate.
OPPOSITES slow.

rare adjective **1** *rare moments of privacy:* **infrequent,** scarce, sparse, few and far between, occasional, limited, odd, isolated, unaccustomed. **2** *rare stamps:* **unusual,** recherché, uncommon, thin on the ground, like gold dust, unfamiliar, atypical. **3** *a man of rare talent:* **exceptional,** outstanding, unparalleled, peerless, matchless, unique, unrivalled.
OPPOSITES common,

commonplace.

rarely adverb **seldom,** infrequently, hardly (ever), scarcely.
OPPOSITES often.

raring adjective **eager,** keen, enthusiastic, impatient, longing, desperate; informal dying, itching, gagging.

rarity noun **1** *the rarity of earthquakes in the UK:* **infrequency,** scarcity. **2** *this book is a rarity:* **curiosity,** oddity, collector's item, rare bird, wonder, nonpareil, one of a kind; Brit. informal one-off.

rash¹ noun **1** *he broke out in a rash:* **spots,** eruption, nettlerash, hives. **2** *a rash of articles in the press:* **series,** succession, spate, wave, flood, deluge, torrent, outbreak, epidemic, flurry.

rash² adjective **reckless,** impulsive, impetuous, hasty, foolhardy, incautious, precipitate, careless, heedless, thoughtless, imprudent, foolish.
OPPOSITES prudent.

rate noun **1** *a fixed rate of interest:* **percentage,** ratio, proportion, scale, standard. **2** *an hourly rate of £30:* **charge,** price, cost, tariff, fare, fee, remuneration, payment. **3** *the rate of change:* **speed,** pace, tempo, velocity.
verb **1** *they rated their ability at driving:* **assess,** evaluate, appraise, judge, weigh up, estimate, gauge. **2** *he rated only a brief mention:* **merit,** deserve, warrant, be worthy of.
■ **at any rate** in any case, anyhow, anyway, in any event, come what may.

rather adverb **1** *I'd rather you went:* **sooner,** by preference, by choice. **2** *it's rather complicated:* **quite,** a bit, a little, fairly, slightly, somewhat, relatively, comparatively; informal pretty. **3** *she seemed sad rather than angry:* **more,** as opposed to, instead of.

ratify verb **confirm,** approve, sanction, endorse, agree to, accept, uphold, authorize, formalize, sign.
OPPOSITES reject.

rating noun **grade,** classification, ranking, position, category, assessment, evaluation, mark, score.

ratio noun **proportion,** relationship, rate, percentage, fraction, correlation.

ration noun **1** *a daily ration of chocolate:* **allowance,** allocation, quota, share, portion, helping. **2** *the garrison ran out of rations:* **supplies,** provisions, food, stores.
verb *fuel supplies were rationed:* **control,** limit, restrict, conserve.

rational adjective **logical,** reasoned, sensible, reasonable, realistic, cogent, intelligent, shrewd, common-sense, sane, sound.
OPPOSITES irrational.

rationale noun **reason(s),** thinking, logic, grounds, sense.

rattle verb **1** *hailstones rattled against the window:* **clatter,** patter, clink, clunk. **2** *he rattled some coins:* **jingle,** jangle, clink, tinkle. **3** *the government was rattled by the strike:* **unnerve,** disconcert, disturb, fluster, shake, perturb, throw; informal faze.

ravage verb **lay waste,** devastate, ruin, destroy, wreak havoc on.

rave verb **1** *I raved and swore at them:* **rant,** rage, lose one's temper, storm, fume, shout; informal fly off the handle, hit the roof; Brit. informal go spare; N. Amer. informal flip one's wig. **2** *he raved about her talent:* **enthuse,** go into raptures, wax lyrical, rhapsodize, sing the praises of, acclaim, eulogize, extol; N. Amer. informal ballyhoo.
OPPOSITES criticize.

raw adjective **1** *raw carrot:* **uncooked,** fresh, natural. **2** *raw materials:* **unprocessed,** untreated, unrefined, crude, natural. **3** *raw recruits:* **inexperienced,** new, untrained, untried, untested, callow, green. **4** *his skin is raw:* **sore,** red, painful, tender, chafed.
OPPOSITES cooked, processed, experienced, sound.

ray noun **beam,** shaft, stream, streak, flash, glimmer, flicker, spark.

reach verb **1** *Travis reached out a hand:* **extend,** stretch, outstretch, thrust, stick, hold. **2** *she reached Helen's house:* **arrive at,** get to, come to, end up at. **3** *the temperature reached 94 degrees:* **attain,** get to, rise to, fall to, sink to, drop to; informal hit. **4** *the leaders reached an agreement:* **achieve,** work out, draw up, put together, negotiate, thrash out, hammer out. **5** *I have been trying to reach you all day:* **contact,** get in touch with, get through to, get, speak to; informal get hold of.
noun **1** *Bobby moved out of her reach:* **grasp,** range, stretch. **2** *small goals within your reach:* **capabilities,** capacity. **3** *beyond the reach of the law:* **jurisdiction,** authority, influence, power, scope, range,

r

compass, ambit.

react verb respond, act in response, reply, answer, behave.

reaction noun **1** *his reaction bewildered her:* **response,** answer, reply, rejoinder, retort, riposte; informal comeback. **2** *a reaction against modernism:* **backlash,** counteraction.

reactionary adjective *a reactionary policy:* **right-wing,** conservative, traditionalist, conventional.
OPPOSITES radical, progressive.
noun *an extreme reactionary:* **right-winger,** conservative, traditionalist.
OPPOSITES radical.

read verb **1** *he was reading the newspaper:* **peruse,** study, scrutinize, look through, pore over, run one's eye over, cast an eye over, leaf through, scan. **2** *he read the letter to me:* **read out/aloud,** recite, declaim. **3** *I can't read my writing:* **understand,** make out, make sense of, interpret, decipher.

readily adverb **1** *Durkin readily offered to drive:* **willingly,** unhesitatingly, ungrudgingly, gladly, happily, eagerly. **2** *the island is readily accessible:* **easily,** without difficulty.
OPPOSITES reluctantly, with difficulty.

readiness noun **1** *their readiness to accept change:* **willingness,** eagerness, keenness, enthusiasm. **2** *a state of readiness:* **preparedness.**
■ **in readiness** (at the) ready, available, on hand, accessible, handy.

reading noun **1** *a cursory reading of the page:* **perusal,** study, scanning, browse, look, glance, leaf. **2** *a man of wide reading:* **learning,** scholarship,

education, erudition. **3** *a poetry reading:* **recital,** recitation, performance. **4** *a Bible reading:* **lesson,** passage, excerpt. **5** *my reading of the situation:* **interpretation,** understanding, explanation, analysis, construction.

ready adjective **1** *are you ready?* **prepared,** all set, organized, primed; informal fit, psyched up, geared up. **2** *everything is ready:* **completed,** finished, prepared, organized, done, arranged, fixed. **3** *he's always ready to help:* **willing,** prepared, pleased, inclined, disposed, eager, keen, happy, glad; informal game. **4** *a ready supply of food:* **(easily) available,** accessible, handy, close/near at hand, to/ on hand, convenient, within reach, near, at one's fingertips. **5** *a ready answer:* **prompt,** quick, swift, speedy, fast, immediate, unhesitating, clever, sharp, astute, shrewd, keen, perceptive, discerning.
verb **prepare,** organize, gear up; informal psych up.

real adjective **1** *based on real events:* **actual,** true, non-fictional, factual, historical, material, physical, tangible, concrete. **2** *real gold:* **genuine,** authentic, bona fide; informal pukka, kosher. **3** *tears of real grief:* **sincere,** genuine, true, unfeigned, heartfelt. **4** *a real man:* **proper,** true; informal regular. **5** *you're a real idiot:* **complete,** utter, thorough, absolute, total, prize, perfect; Brit. informal right, proper.
OPPOSITES imaginary, imitation.

realism noun **1** *optimism tinged with realism:* **pragmatism,** practicality, common sense, level-headedness. **2** *a degree of*

realism: **authenticity**, accuracy, fidelity, verisimilitude, truthfulness.
OPPOSITES fancy, inauthenticity.

realistic adjective **1** *you've got to be realistic:* **practical**, pragmatic, matter-of-fact, down-to-earth, sensible, commonsensical, rational, level-headed; informal no-nonsense. **2** *a realistic aim:* **achievable**, attainable, feasible, practicable, reasonable, sensible, workable; informal doable. **3** *a realistic portrayal of war:* **authentic**, accurate, true to life, lifelike, truthful, faithful, natural, naturalistic.
OPPOSITES idealistic, impracticable, inauthentic.

reality noun **1** *distinguishing fantasy from reality:* **the real world**, real life, actuality, truth. **2** *the harsh realities of life:* **fact**, actuality, truth. **3** *the reality of the detail:* **authenticity**, verisimilitude, fidelity, truthfulness, accuracy.
OPPOSITES fantasy, inaccuracy.

realization noun **1** *a growing realization of the danger:* **awareness**, understanding, comprehension, consciousness, appreciation, recognition, discernment. **2** *the realization of our dreams:* **fulfilment**, achievement, accomplishment, attainment.

realize verb **1** *he suddenly realized what she meant:* **register**, perceive, understand, grasp, comprehend, see, recognize; informal tumble to; Brit. informal twig. **2** *they realized their dream:* **fulfil**, achieve, accomplish, make happen, bring to fruition, bring about/off. **3** *the company realized significant profits:* **make**, clear,

gain, earn, return, produce. **4** *the goods realized £30:* **be sold for**, fetch, go for, make, net.

really adverb **1** *he is really very wealthy:* **in (actual) fact**, actually, in reality, in truth. **2** *he really likes her:* **genuinely**, truly, certainly, honestly, undoubtedly, unquestionably.

realm noun **1** *peace in the realm:* **kingdom**, country, land, dominion, nation. **2** *the realm of academia:* **domain**, sphere, area, field, world, province, territory.

reap verb **1** *the corn was reaped:* **harvest**, cut, pick, gather, garner. **2** *reaping the benefits:* **receive**, obtain, get, derive, acquire, secure, realize.

rear[1] noun **1** *the rear of the building:* **back (part)**, hind part; Nautical stern. **2** *the rear of the queue:* **end**, tail (end), back (end).
OPPOSITES front, bow, head.
adjective *the rear bumper:* **back**, end, rearmost, hind, last.
OPPOSITES front.

rear[2] verb **1** *I was reared in Newcastle:* **bring up**, care for, look after, nurture; N. Amer. raise. **2** *he reared cattle:* **breed**, raise, keep. **3** *laboratory-reared plants:* **grow**, cultivate. **4** *houses reared up on either side:* **rise**, tower, soar, loom.

reason noun **1** *the main reason for his decision:* **cause**, ground(s), basis, rationale, motive, explanation, justification, defence, vindication, excuse. **2** *postmodern voices railing against reason:* **rationality**, logic, cognition. **3** *he was losing his reason:* **sanity**, mind, mental faculties, senses, wits; informal marbles.

r

verb *Scott reasoned that Annabel might be ill:* **calculate,** conclude, reckon, think, judge, deduce, infer, surmise; informal figure.
■ **reason something out** work out, think through, make sense of, get to the bottom of, puzzle out; informal figure out. ■ **reason with** talk round, bring round, persuade, prevail on, convince.

reasonable adjective **1** *a reasonable explanation:* **sensible,** rational, logical, fair, just, equitable, intelligent, wise, level-headed, practical, realistic, sound, valid, commonsensical, tenable, plausible, credible, believable. **2** *take all reasonable precautions:* **practicable,** sensible, appropriate, suitable. **3** *cars in reasonable condition:* **fairly good,** acceptable, satisfactory, average, adequate, fair, tolerable, passable; informal OK. **4** *reasonable prices:* **inexpensive,** affordable, moderate, low, cheap, budget, bargain.

reassure verb **put someone's mind at rest,** encourage, hearten, buoy up, cheer up, comfort, soothe.
OPPOSITES alarm.

rebate noun **partial refund,** partial repayment, discount, deduction, reduction.

rebel noun **1** *the rebels took control of the capital:* **revolutionary,** insurgent, insurrectionist, mutineer, guerrilla, terrorist, freedom fighter. **2** *the concept of the artist as a rebel:* **nonconformist,** dissenter, dissident, maverick.
OPPOSITES loyalist, conformist.
verb *the citizens rebelled:* **revolt,** mutiny, riot, rise up, take up arms.
OPPOSITES comply.
adjective **1** *rebel troops:* **rebellious,** insurgent, revolutionary, mutinous. **2** *rebel MPs:* **defiant,** disobedient, insubordinate, subversive, rebellious, nonconformist, maverick.
OPPOSITES loyal, compliant.
■ **rebel against** defy, disobey, kick against, challenge, oppose, resist.

rebellion noun **1** *troops suppressed the rebellion:* **revolt,** uprising, insurrection, mutiny, revolution, insurgence. **2** *an act of rebellion:* **defiance,** disobedience, insubordination, subversion, resistance.
OPPOSITES compliance.

rebellious adjective **1** *rebellious troops:* **rebel,** insurgent, mutinous, revolutionary. **2** *a rebellious adolescent:* **defiant,** disobedient, insubordinate, unruly, mutinous, obstreperous, recalcitrant, intractable; Brit. informal bolshie.
OPPOSITES loyal, compliant.

rebound verb **1** *the ball rebounded:* **bounce (back),** spring back, ricochet, boomerang. **2** *Thomas's tactics rebounded on him:* **backfire,** boomerang.

rebuff verb *his offer was rebuffed:* **reject,** turn down, spurn, refuse, decline, snub, slight, dismiss, brush off.
OPPOSITES accept.
noun *for fear of a rebuff:* **rejection,** snub, slight, refusal, spurning; informal brush-off, kick in the teeth, slap in the face.
OPPOSITES acceptance.

rebuke verb *she never rebuked him:* **reprimand,** reproach,

scold, admonish; informal tell off;
Brit. informal tick off; N. Amer. informal
chew out.
OPPOSITES praise.
noun *a severe rebuke:*
reprimand, reproach, scolding,
admonition; informal telling-off;
Brit. informal ticking-off.
OPPOSITES praise.

recall verb **1** *he recalled his
student days:* **remember,**
recollect, call to mind, think
back on/to, reminisce about.
2 *their exploits recall the days
of chivalry:* **remind someone
of,** bring to mind, call up,
conjure up, evoke. **3** *the
ambassador was recalled:* **call
back,** order home, withdraw.
OPPOSITES forget, post.
noun **1** *their recall of dreams:*
recollection, remembrance,
memory. **2** *the recall of the
ambassador:* **calling back,**
ordering home, withdrawal.

recede verb **1** *the waters
receded:* **retreat,** go back/down/
away, withdraw, ebb, subside,
abate, return, retire. **2** *fears of
violence have receded:*
diminish, lessen, dwindle, fade,
abate, subside.
OPPOSITES advance, grow.

receipt noun **1** *the receipt of a
letter:* **receiving,** getting,
obtaining, gaining. **2** *make sure
you get a receipt:* **proof of
purchase,** sales ticket, till
receipt, acknowledgement.

receive verb **1** *Tony received an
award:* **be given,** be presented
with, be awarded, be sent, be
told, hear, collect, get, obtain,
gain, acquire, be paid. **2** *he
received her suggestion with a
lack of interest:* **hear,** listen to,
respond to, react to. **3** *she
received an injury:* **experience,**
sustain, undergo, meet with,

suffer, bear.
OPPOSITES give, send, inflict.

recent adjective **new,** the latest,
current, fresh, modern, late,
contemporary, up to date, up to
the minute.
OPPOSITES old.

recently adverb **not long ago,** a
little while back, just now,
newly, freshly, of late, lately,
latterly.

reception noun **1** *a chilly
reception:* **response,** reaction,
treatment, welcome. **2** *a
wedding reception:* **party,**
function, social occasion,
celebration, get-together,
gathering, soirée; N. Amer. levee;
informal do.

recess noun **1** *two recesses fitted
with bookshelves:* **alcove,** bay,
niche, nook, corner. **2** *the
Christmas recess:* **break,**
adjournment, interlude,
interval, rest, holiday, vacation.

recession noun **downturn,**
depression, slump, slowdown.
OPPOSITES boom.

recipe noun *a recipe for success:*
formula, prescription,
blueprint.

recital noun **1** *a piano recital:*
performance, concert,
rendering, recitation, reading.
2 *her recital of Adam's failures:*
report, account, listing,
catalogue, litany.

recite verb **1** *he began to recite
the Koran:* **quote,** say, speak,
read aloud, declaim, deliver,
render. **2** *Sir John recited the
facts:* **recount,** list, detail, reel
off, relate, enumerate.

reckless adjective **rash,** careless,
thoughtless, heedless,
precipitate, impetuous,
impulsive, irresponsible,
foolhardy.
OPPOSITES cautious.

r

reckon verb **1** *the cost was reckoned at £60:* **calculate,** compute, work out, figure, count (up), add up, total; Brit. tot up. **2** *Anselm reckoned Hugh among his friends:* **include,** count, regard as, look on as. **3** *it was reckoned a failure:* **regard as,** consider, judge, think of as, deem, rate, gauge, count.
■ **reckon on/with** take into account, take into consideration, bargain for/on, anticipate, foresee, be prepared for, consider.

reckoning noun **calculation,** estimation, computation, working out, addition, count.

reclaim verb **1** *expenses can be reclaimed:* **get back,** claim back, recover, retrieve, recoup. **2** *Henrietta had reclaimed him from a life of vice:* **save,** rescue, redeem, salvage.

recline verb **lie (down/back),** lean back, relax, loll, lounge, sprawl, stretch out.

recognition noun **1** *there was no sign of recognition on his face:* **identification,** recollection, remembrance. **2** *his recognition of his lack of experience:* **acknowledgement,** acceptance, admission, confession. **3** *you deserve recognition for your work:* **appreciation,** gratitude, thanks, congratulations, credit, commendation, acclaim, acknowledgement.

recognize verb **1** *Hannah recognized him at once:* **identify,** place, know, put a name to, remember, recall, recollect; Scottish & N. English ken. **2** *they recognized Alan's ability:* **acknowledge,** accept, admit, concede, confess, realize. **3** *the Trust recognized their hard*

work: **pay tribute to,** appreciate, be grateful for, acclaim, commend.

recollect verb **remember,** recall, call to mind, think of, think back to, reminisce about. OPPOSITES forget.

recollection noun **memory,** recall, remembrance, impression, reminiscence.

recommend verb **1** *his former employer recommended him:* **advocate,** endorse, commend, suggest, put forward, propose, nominate, put up, speak favourably of, put in a good word for, vouch for; informal plug. **2** *the committee recommended a cautious approach:* **advise,** counsel, urge, exhort, enjoin, prescribe, argue for, back, support. OPPOSITES advise against.

recommendation noun **1** *the adviser's recommendations:* **advice,** counsel, guidance, suggestion, proposal. **2** *a personal recommendation:* **commendation,** endorsement, good word, testimonial, tip; informal plug.

reconsider verb **rethink,** review, revise, re-evaluate, reassess, have second thoughts, change one's mind.

reconstruct verb **1** *the building had to be reconstructed:* **rebuild,** recreate, remake, restore, reassemble. **2** *reconstructing events:* **recreate,** piece together, re-enact.

record noun **1** *written records:* **account,** document, data, file, dossier, evidence, report, annals, archive, chronicle, minutes, transactions, proceedings, transcript, certificate, deed, register, log.

2 *listening to records:* **album,** vinyl; dated LP, single. **3** *a good attendance record:* **previous conduct,** previous performance, history, reputation. **4** *a new British record:* **best performance,** highest achievement, best time, fastest time.
verb **1** *the doctor recorded her blood pressure:* **write down,** take down, note, jot down, put down on paper, document, enter, minute, register, log. **2** *the thermometer recorded a high temperature:* **indicate,** register, show, display. **3** *the recital was recorded live:* **capture on film/tape/disk,** film, photograph, tape, tape-record, video-record, videotape.

recount verb **tell,** relate, narrate, describe, report, relay, convey, communicate, impart.

recover verb **1** *he's recovering from a heart attack:* **get better,** improve, recuperate, convalesce, be on the mend, respond to treatment, heal, bounce back. **2** *later, shares recovered:* **rally,** improve, pick up, rebound, bounce back. **3** *the stolen material has been recovered:* **retrieve,** regain, get back, recoup, reclaim, repossess. **4** *gold coins recovered from a wreck:* **salvage,** save, rescue, retrieve.
OPPOSITES deteriorate, lose.

recovery noun **1** *her recovery may be slow:* **improvement,** recuperation, convalescence, rally, mend. **2** *the recovery of stolen goods:* **retrieval,** repossession, reclamation.
OPPOSITES relapse, loss.

recreation noun **1** *she cycles for recreation:* **pleasure,** leisure, relaxation, fun, enjoyment,

entertainment, amusement. **2** *his favourite recreations:* **pastime,** hobby, leisure activity.
OPPOSITES work.

recruit verb **1** *more soldiers were recruited:* **enlist,** call up, conscript; US draft. **2** *the king recruited an army:* **muster,** form, raise, mobilize. **3** *the company is recruiting staff:* **hire,** employ, take on, enrol, sign up, engage.
OPPOSITES demobilize, disband, dismiss.
noun **1** *new recruits were enlisted:* **conscript;** US draftee; N. Amer. informal yardbird. **2** *top-quality recruits:* **new member,** newcomer, initiate, joiner, beginner, novice.

recur verb **happen again,** reoccur, repeat (itself), come back, return, reappear.

recycle verb **reuse,** reprocess, reclaim, renew, salvage.

red adjective **1** *a red dress:* **scarlet,** vermilion, ruby, cherry, cerise, cardinal, carmine, wine. **2** *he was red in the face:* **flushed,** blushing, pink, rosy, florid, ruddy. **3** *red hair:* auburn, Titian, chestnut, carroty, ginger.

redeem verb **1** *redeeming sinners:* **save,** deliver from sin, absolve. **2** *Billy redeemed his drums from the pawnbrokers:* **retrieve,** regain, recover, get back, reclaim, repossess, buy back. **3** *this voucher can be redeemed at any branch:* **exchange,** convert, trade in, cash in.
OPPOSITES damn, pawn, buy.

redemption noun **1** *God's redemption of his people:* **saving,** freeing from sin, absolution. **2** *the redemption of their possessions:* **retrieval,**

recovery, reclamation, repossession, return. **3** *the redemption of vouchers:* **exchange,** conversion, trade-in, cashing in.
OPPOSITES condemnation, pawning, purchase.

redress verb **1** *we redressed the problem:* **rectify,** correct, right, compensate for, amend, remedy, make good. **2** *we aim to redress the balance:* **even up,** regulate, equalize.
noun *your best hope of redress:* **compensation,** reparation, restitution, recompense, repayment, amends.

reduce verb **1** *the aim to reduce pollution:* **lessen,** make smaller, lower, bring down, decrease, diminish, minimize, shrink, narrow, contract, shorten; informal chop. **2** *he reduced her to tears:* **bring to,** drive to.
OPPOSITES increase.

reduction noun **1** *a reduction in pollution:* **lessening,** lowering, decrease, diminution. **2** *a reduction in staff:* **cut,** cutback, axing, downsizing.

redundancy noun dismissal, sacking, lay-off, discharge, unemployment.

redundant adjective *redundant churches:* **unnecessary,** not required, unneeded, surplus (to requirements), superfluous.
OPPOSITES necessary.
■ **make someone redundant** dismiss, lay off, give someone their notice, discharge; informal sack, fire.

reel verb **1** *he reeled as the ship began to roll:* **stagger,** lurch, sway, rock, stumble, totter, wobble. **2** *the room reeled:* **go round (and round),** whirl, spin, revolve, swirl, twirl, turn, swim.

refer verb *the matter has been referred to my insurers:* **pass,** direct, hand on/over, send on, transfer, entrust, assign.
■ **refer to 1** *he referred to errors in the article:* mention, allude to, touch on, speak of/about, talk of/about, write about, comment on, point out, call attention to. **2** *these figures refer only to 2001:* apply to, relate to, pertain to, be relevant to, concern, be connected with. **3** *the constable referred to his notes:* consult, turn to, look at, have recourse to.

referee noun **1** *the referee blew his whistle:* **umpire,** judge, adjudicator; informal ref. **2** *include the names of two referees:* **supporter,** character witness, advocate.
verb *he refereed the game:* **umpire,** judge, adjudicate; informal ref.

reference noun **1** *a reference to his book:* **mention,** allusion, quotation, comment, remark. **2** *references are given in the bibliography:* **source,** citation, authority, credit. **3** *a glowing reference:* **testimonial,** recommendation, character reference, credentials.

referendum noun (popular) vote, ballot, poll, plebiscite.

refine verb **1** *refining our cereal foods:* **purify,** filter, distil, process, treat. **2** *helping students to refine their skills:* **improve,** perfect, polish (up), hone, fine-tune.

refined adjective **1** *refined sugar:* **purified,** processed, treated. **2** *a refined lady:* **cultivated,** cultured, polished, elegant, sophisticated, urbane, polite, gracious, well bred. **3** *a person of refined taste:* **discriminating,**

reflect | refuse

discerning, fastidious, exquisite, impeccable, fine. OPPOSITES crude, coarse.

reflect verb 1 *the snow reflects light:* **mirror,** send back, throw back, echo. 2 *their expressions reflected their feelings:* **indicate,** show, display, demonstrate, be evidence of, reveal, betray. 3 *he reflected on his task:* **think,** consider, review, mull, contemplate, cogitate, meditate, muse, brood.

reflection noun 1 *her reflection in the mirror:* **image,** likeness. 2 *your hands are a reflection of your well-being:* **indication,** display, demonstration, manifestation, expression, evidence. 3 *after some reflection, he turned it down:* **thought,** consideration, contemplation, deliberation, pondering, meditation, musing.

reform verb 1 *a plan to reform the system:* **improve,** better, ameliorate, correct, rectify, restore, revise, refine, adapt, revamp, redesign, reconstruct, reorganize. 2 *after his marriage he reformed:* **mend one's ways,** change for the better, turn over a new leaf.
noun *the reform of the prison system:* **improvement,** amelioration, refinement, rectification, restoration, adaptation, revision, redesign, revamp, reconstruction, reorganization.

refrain verb **abstain,** desist, hold back, stop oneself, forbear, avoid; informal swear off.

refresh verb 1 *the cool air will refresh me:* **reinvigorate,** revitalize, revive, restore, perk up, brace, freshen, wake up; informal buck up. 2 *let me refresh*

your memory: **jog,** stimulate, prompt, prod. OPPOSITES weary.

refreshing adjective 1 *a refreshing drink:* **invigorating,** revitalizing, reviving, bracing, fortifying, enlivening, stimulating. 2 *a refreshing change of direction:* **welcome,** stimulating, fresh, new, imaginative, innovative. OPPOSITES wearying.

refreshment noun **food and drink,** snacks, titbits; informal nibbles.

refuge noun 1 *homeless people seeking refuge:* **shelter,** protection, safety, security, asylum, sanctuary. 2 *a refuge for mountain gorillas:* **sanctuary,** shelter, haven, sanctum, retreat, bolt-hole, hiding place.

refugee noun **asylum seeker,** fugitive, displaced person, exile, émigré.

refund verb 1 *we will refund your money:* **repay,** give back, return, pay back. 2 *they refunded the subscribers:* **reimburse,** compensate, recompense.
noun *a full refund:* **repayment,** reimbursement, compensation, rebate.

refurbish verb **renovate,** recondition, rehabilitate, revamp, overhaul, restore, redecorate, upgrade, refit; informal do up.

refusal noun 1 *we had one refusal to our invitation:* **non-acceptance,** no, rejection, rebuff, turndown; informal knock-back. 2 *the refusal of planning permission:* **withholding,** denial. OPPOSITES acceptance, granting.

refuse[1] verb 1 *he refused the*

r

invitation: **decline,** turn down, say no to, reject, spurn, rebuff; informal pass up. **2** *the Council refused planning permission:* **withhold,** deny.
opposites accept, grant.

refuse² noun *piles of refuse:* **rubbish,** waste, litter; N. Amer. garbage, trash; informal dreck, junk.

regain verb **1** *government troops regained the capital:* **recover,** get back, win back, recoup, retrieve, repossess, take back, retake, recapture, reconquer. **2** *they regained dry land:* **return to,** get back to, reach again, rejoin.

regal adjective **1** *a regal feast.* See SPLENDID sense 1. **2** *his regal forebears:* **royal,** kingly, queenly, princely, majestic.

regard verb **1** *we regard the results as encouraging:* **consider,** look on, view, see, think of, judge, deem, estimate, assess, reckon, rate. **2** *he regarded her coldly:* **look at,** contemplate, eye, gaze at, stare at, observe, view, study, scrutinize.
noun **1** *he has no regard for life:* **consideration,** care, concern, thought, notice, heed, attention. **2** *doctors are held in high regard:* **esteem,** respect, admiration, approval, honour, estimation. **3** *his steady regard:* **(fixed) look,** gaze, stare, observation, contemplation, study, scrutiny. **4** (regards) *best wishes,* greetings, respects, compliments, best, love.

regarding preposition **concerning,** as regards, with/in regard to, with respect to, with reference to, relating to, respecting, re, about, apropos, on the subject of, in connection

with, vis-à-vis.

regardless adverb **anyway,** anyhow, in any case, nevertheless, nonetheless, despite everything, even so, all the same, in any event, come what may.
■ **regardless of** irrespective of, without reference to, without consideration of, discounting, ignoring, notwithstanding, no matter.

regime noun **1** *regime change:* **government,** administration, leadership, authority, control, rule, command. **2** *a health regime:* **system,** arrangement, scheme, policy, method, course, plan, programme.

region noun **district,** province, territory, division, area, section, sector, zone, belt, quarter.

regional adjective **1** *regional variation:* **geographical,** territorial. **2** *a regional parliament:* **local,** provincial, district, parochial, zonal.
opposites national.

register noun **1** *the register of electors:* **list,** roll, roster, index, directory, catalogue, inventory. **2** *the parish register:* **record,** chronicle, log, ledger, archive, annals, files.
verb **1** *I wish to register a complaint:* **record,** enter, file, lodge, write down, submit, report, note, minute, log. **2** *I'd like to register for the course:* **enrol,** put one's name down, enlist, sign on/up, apply. **3** *the dial registered 100mph:* **indicate,** read, record, show. **4** *her face registered anger:* **display,** show, express, exhibit, betray, reveal.

regret verb **1** *they came to regret their decision:* **be sorry about,** feel contrite about, feel

remorse for, rue. **2** *regretting the passing of youth:* **mourn**, grieve for/over, weep over, sigh over, lament, sorrow for.
OPPOSITES welcome.
noun **1** *both players expressed regret:* **remorse**, contrition, repentance, compunction.
2 *they left with genuine regret:* **sadness**, sorrow, disappointment, unhappiness, grief.
OPPOSITES satisfaction.

regular adjective **1** *plant them at regular intervals:* **uniform**, even, consistent, constant, unchanging, unvarying, fixed. **2** *the subject of regular protests:* **frequent**, repeated, continual, recurrent, periodic, constant, perpetual, numerous. **3** *his regular route to work:* **usual**, normal, customary, habitual, routine, typical, accustomed, established.
OPPOSITES erratic, occasional, unusual.

regulate verb **1** *the flow has been regulated:* **control**, adjust, manage, govern. **2** *a new act regulating businesses:* **police**, supervise, monitor, check (up on), be responsible for, control, manage, direct, govern.

regulation noun **1** *EC regulations:* **rule**, order, directive, act, law, by-law, statute, dictate, decree. **2** *the regulation of blood sugar:* **adjustment**, control, management, balancing. **3** *the regulation of financial services:* **policing**, supervision, superintendence, monitoring, control, governance, management, responsibility for.

rehearsal noun **1** practice, trial performance, read-through, run-through, drill, training, coaching; informal dry run.

rehearse verb **1** *I rehearsed the role:* **prepare**, practise, read through, run through/over, go over. **2** *he rehearsed the Vienna Philharmonic:* **train**, drill, prepare, coach. **3** *the document rehearsed all the arguments:* **list**, enumerate, itemize, detail, spell out, catalogue, recite, repeat, go over, run through; informal recap.

reign verb **1** *Robert II reigned for nineteen years:* **be king/queen**, sit on the throne, wear the crown, be supreme, rule. **2** *chaos reigned:* **prevail**, exist, be present, be the case, occur, be rife, be rampant, be the order of the day.
noun *Henry's reign:* **rule**, sovereignty, monarchy, dominion.

rein verb *they reined back costs:* **restrain**, check, curb, constrain, hold back/in, keep under control, regulate, restrict, control, curtail, limit.
■ **free rein** freedom, a free hand, leeway, latitude, flexibility, liberty, independence, licence, room to manoeuvre, carte blanche.
■ **keep a tight rein on** regulate, discipline, regiment, keep in line.

reinforce verb **1** *contractors reinforced the dam:* **strengthen**, fortify, bolster up, shore up, buttress, prop up, underpin, brace, support. **2** *reinforcing links between colleges and companies:* **strengthen**, fortify, cement, boost, deepen, enrich, enhance, intensify, improve. **3** *the need to reinforce NATO troops:* **augment**, increase, add to, supplement, boost, top up.

reinforcement noun **1** *the*

r

reinforcement of our defences: **strengthening,** fortification, bolstering, shoring up, buttressing, bracing. **2** (**reinforcements**) **additional troops,** auxiliaries, reserves, support, backup, help.

reinstate verb **restore,** put back, bring back, reinstitute, reinstall, re-establish.

reject verb **1** *the miners rejected the offer:* **turn down,** refuse, decline, say no to, spurn. **2** *Jamie rejected her:* **rebuff,** spurn, shun, snub, cast off/aside, discard, abandon, desert, turn one's back on.
OPPOSITES accept, welcome.
noun **1** *what a reject!* **failure,** loser, incompetent. **2** *it is only a reject:* **second,** discard, misshape, faulty item, cast-off.

rejection noun **1** *a rejection of the offer:* **refusal,** declining, turning down, dismissal, spurning. **2** *Madeleine's rejection of him:* **repudiation,** rebuff, spurning, abandonment, desertion; informal brush-off.
OPPOSITES agreement, acceptance, welcome.

rejoice verb **be happy,** be glad, be delighted, celebrate, make merry; informal be over the moon.
OPPOSITES mourn.
■ **rejoice in** delight in, enjoy, revel in, glory in, relish, savour.

rejoin verb **return to,** be reunited with, join again, reach again, regain.

relate verb *he related stories:* **tell,** recount, narrate, report, recite.
■ **relate to 1** *mortality is related to unemployment levels:* connect with, associate with, link with, ally with, couple with. **2** *the charges relate to other offences:* apply to, concern, pertain to, have a bearing on, involve. **3** *she cannot relate to her father:* have a rapport with, get on (well) with, feel sympathy with, identify with, empathize with, understand; informal hit it off with.

related adjective **connected,** interconnected, associated, linked, allied, corresponding, analogous, parallel, comparable, equivalent.
OPPOSITES unrelated.

relation noun **1** *the relation between church and state:* **connection,** relationship, association, link, correlation, correspondence, parallel. **2** *are you a relation of his?* **relative,** member of the family, kinsman, kinswoman; (**relations**) family, kin, kith and kin, kindred. **3** (**relations**) *improving relations with India:* **dealings,** communication, relationship, connections, contact, interaction.

relationship noun **1** *the relationship between diet and diabetes:* **connection,** relation, association, link, correlation, correspondence, parallel. **2** *their relationship to a common ancestor:* **family ties/connections,** blood relationship, kinship, affinity, common ancestry/lineage. **3** *the end of their relationship:* **romance,** affair, love affair, liaison, amour, fling.

relative adjective **1** *the relative importance of each factor:* **comparative,** respective, comparable. **2** *food required is relative to body weight:* **proportionate,** in proportion, commensurate, corresponding.

OPPOSITES disproportionate.

noun *he's a relative of mine:*
relation, member of the family,
kinsman, kinswoman;
(**relatives**) family, kin, kith and
kin, kindred.

relax verb **1** *relax after work:*
rest, loosen up, ease up/off,
slow down, de-stress, unbend,
unwind, put one's feet up, take
it easy; informal chill out; N. Amer.
informal hang loose. **2** *a walk will
relax you:* **calm,** unwind, rest,
loosen up, make less tense,
make less uptight, soothe. **3** *he
relaxed his grip:* **loosen,**
slacken, unclench, weaken,
lessen. **4** *they relaxed the
restrictions:* **moderate,** temper,
ease, loosen, lighten, dilute,
weaken, reduce, decrease;
informal let up on.

OPPOSITES tense, tighten.

relaxation noun **recreation,**
enjoyment, amusement,
entertainment, fun, pleasure,
leisure.

OPPOSITES activity, work.

relay noun *a live relay of the
performance:* **broadcast,**
transmission, showing, feed,
patch.

verb *I'd relayed the messages:*
pass on, hand on, transfer,
repeat, communicate, send,
transmit, circulate.

release verb **1** *all prisoners were
released:* **free,** set free, let go/
out, liberate, discharge. **2** *Burke
released the animal:* **untie,**
undo, loose, let go, unleash.
3 *police released the news
yesterday:* **make public,** make
known, issue, put out, publish,
broadcast, circulate, launch.

OPPOSITES imprison, tie up,
embargo.

noun **1** *the release of political
prisoners:* **freeing,** liberation,

deliverance, freedom, liberty.
2 *the release of the news:*
issuing, announcement,
publication, broadcasting,
circulation, launch.

OPPOSITES imprisonment,
embargo.

relegate verb **downgrade,**
demote, lower, put down, move
down.

OPPOSITES upgrade, promote.

relentless adjective **1** *their
relentless pursuit of quality:*
persistent, unfaltering,
unremitting, unflagging,
untiring, unwavering, dogged,
single-minded, tireless,
indefatigable. **2** *a relentless
taskmaster:* **harsh,** cruel,
remorseless, merciless, pitiless,
implacable, ruthless.

relevant adjective **pertinent,**
applicable, apposite, material,
apropos, to the point, germane.

OPPOSITES irrelevant.

reliable adjective **dependable,**
trustworthy, good, safe,
authentic, faithful, genuine,
sound, true, loyal, unfailing.

OPPOSITES unreliable.

reliance noun **1** *reliance on the
state:* **dependence.** **2** *reliance
on his judgement:* **trust,**
confidence, faith, belief,
conviction.

relic noun **artefact,** historical
object, antiquity, remnant,
vestige, remains.

relief noun **1** *a bit of relief from
work:* **freedom,** release,
liberation, deliverance,
comfort, respite, diversion.
2 *pain relief:* **alleviation,**
relieving, palliation, soothing,
easing, lessening. **3** *a little light
relief:* **respite,** amusement,
diversion, entertainment,
jollity, recreation. **4** *bringing
relief to the starving:* **help,** aid,

r

assistance, charity. **5** *his relief arrived to take over:* **replacement,** substitute, deputy, reserve, cover, stand-in, supply, locum, understudy.
OPPOSITES intensification.

relieve verb **1** *this helps relieve pain:* **alleviate,** mitigate, ease, counteract, dull, reduce. **2** *the helpers relieved us:* **replace,** take over from, stand in for, fill in for, substitute for, deputize for, cover for. **3** *this relieves the teacher of a heavy load:* **free,** release, exempt, excuse, absolve, let off.
OPPOSITES aggravate, inflict.

religion noun **faith,** belief, worship, creed, church, sect, denomination, cult.

religious adjective **1** *a religious person:* **devout,** pious, reverent, godly, God-fearing, churchgoing. **2** *religious beliefs:* **spiritual,** theological, scriptural, doctrinal, ecclesiastical, church, holy, divine, sacred. **3** *religious attention to detail:* **scrupulous,** conscientious, meticulous, punctilious, strict, rigorous.
OPPOSITES atheistic, secular, casual.

relinquish verb **1** *he relinquished control of the company:* **renounce,** give up/ away, hand over, let go of. **2** *he relinquished his post:* **leave,** resign from, stand down from, bow out of, give up; informal quit, chuck.
OPPOSITES retain, continue.

relish noun **1** *he dug into his food with relish:* **enjoyment,** gusto, delight, pleasure, glee, appreciation, enthusiasm. **2** *a hot relish:* **condiment,** sauce, dressing.
OPPOSITES distaste.

verb **1** *he was relishing his moment of glory:* **enjoy,** delight in, love, adore, take pleasure in, rejoice in, appreciate, savour, revel in, luxuriate in, glory in. **2** *I don't relish the drive:* **look forward to,** fancy.
OPPOSITES dislike.

reluctance noun **unwillingness,** disinclination, hesitation, wavering, vacillation, doubts, second thoughts, misgivings.

reluctant adjective **unwilling,** disinclined, unenthusiastic, resistant, opposed, hesitant, loath.
OPPOSITES willing, eager.

rely
■ **rely on** depend on, count on, bank on, be confident of, be sure of, have faith in, trust in; informal swear by; N. Amer. informal figure on.

remain verb **1** *the problem will remain:* **continue,** endure, last, abide, carry on, persist, stay around, survive, live on. **2** *he remained in hospital:* **stay,** stay behind, stay put, wait behind, be left, hang on; informal hang around/round. **3** *union leaders remain sceptical:* **continue to be,** stay, keep.

remainder noun **rest,** balance, residue, others, remnant(s), leftovers, surplus, extra, excess.

remains plural noun **1** *the remains of her drink:* **remainder,** residue, rest, remnant(s), leftovers. **2** *Roman remains:* **antiquities,** relics, artefacts. **3** *the saint's remains:* **corpse,** body, carcass, bones.

remark verb *'You're quiet,' he remarked:* **comment,** say, observe, mention, reflect.
noun *he made a few remarks:* **comment,** statement, utterance, observation,

reflection.

remarkable adjective
extraordinary, exceptional, outstanding, notable, striking, memorable, unusual, conspicuous, momentous.
OPPOSITES ordinary.

remedy noun **1** *herbal remedies:* **treatment,** cure, medicine, medication, medicament, drug. **2** *a remedy for all kinds of problems:* **solution,** answer, cure, fix, antidote, resolution.
verb *remedying the situation:* **put right,** set right, rectify, solve, sort out, straighten out, resolve, correct, repair, mend, fix.

remember verb **1** *remembering happy times:* **recall,** call to mind, recollect, think of, reminisce about, look back on. **2** *can you remember all that?* **memorize,** retain, learn off by heart. **3** *you must remember she's only five:* **bear in mind,** be mindful of, take into account. **4** *remember to feed the cat:* **be sure,** be certain, mind that you, make sure that you. **5** *the nation remembered those who gave their lives:* **commemorate,** pay tribute to, honour, salute, pay homage to.
OPPOSITES forget.

remembrance noun **1** *an expression of remembrance:* **recollection,** reminiscence, recall. **2** *we sold poppies in remembrance:* **commemoration,** memory, recognition.

remind verb jog someone's memory, prompt.
■ **remind someone of** make someone think of, cause someone to remember, put someone in mind of, call to mind, evoke.

reminiscent adjective **similar to,** comparable with, evocative of, suggestive of, redolent of, that reminds one of.

remnant noun **remains,** remainder, leftovers, offcut, residue, rest.

remorse noun **regret,** guilt, contrition, repentance, shame.

remote adjective **1** *a remote village:* **isolated,** faraway, distant, out of the way, off the beaten track, secluded, lonely; N. Amer. in the backwoods; informal in the middle of nowhere. **2** *a remote possibility:* **unlikely,** improbable, doubtful, dubious, faint, slight, slim, small, slender. **3** *she seems very remote:* **aloof,** distant, detached, withdrawn, unforthcoming, unapproachable, unresponsive, unfriendly, unsociable, introspective, introverted; informal stand-offish.
OPPOSITES close, distinct, friendly.

removal noun **1** *the removal of church treasures:* **taking away,** moving, carrying away, transporting. **2** *his removal from office:* **dismissal,** ejection, expulsion, ousting; N. Amer. ouster; informal sacking, firing. **3** *the removal of customs barriers:* **withdrawal,** elimination, abolition, taking away. **4** *her removal to France:* **move,** transfer, relocation.
OPPOSITES installation, appointment, imposition.

remove verb **1** *she removed the lid:* **take off,** take away, take out, pull out, withdraw, detach, undo, unfasten, disconnect. **2** *he was removed from his post:* **dismiss,** discharge, get rid of, expel, oust, depose; informal sack,

r

fire, kick out. **3** *tax relief was removed:* **abolish,** withdraw, eliminate, get rid of, do away with, stop, cut, axe.
OPPOSITES attach, insert, replace, appoint, impose.

renaissance noun revival, renewal, resurrection, reawakening, re-emergence, rebirth, reappearance, resurgence.

render verb **1** *her fury rendered her speechless:* **make,** cause to be/become, leave, turn. **2** *rendering assistance:* **give,** provide, supply, furnish, contribute. **3** *the characters are vividly rendered:* **act,** perform, play, depict, portray, interpret, represent, draw, paint, execute.

renew verb **1** *I renewed my search:* **resume,** return to, take up again, come back to, begin again, restart, recommence, continue (with), carry on (with). **2** *they renewed their vows:* **reaffirm,** repeat, reiterate, restate. **3** *something to renew her interest in life:* **revive,** regenerate, revitalize, reinvigorate, restore, resuscitate. **4** *the hotel was completely renewed:* **renovate,** restore, refurbish, revamp, remodel, modernize; informal do up; N. Amer. informal rehab.

renounce verb **1** *Edward renounced his claim to the throne:* **give up,** relinquish, abandon, surrender, waive, forego, desist from, keep off; informal say goodbye to. **2** *she renounced her family:* **reject,** repudiate, deny, abandon, wash one's hands of, turn one's back on, disown, spurn, shun.
OPPOSITES assert, continue, keep, accept.

renovate verb modernize, restore, refurbish, revamp, recondition, rehabilitate, update, upgrade, refit; informal do up; N. Amer. informal rehab.

renowned adjective famous, well known, celebrated, famed, eminent, distinguished, acclaimed, illustrious, prominent, great, esteemed.
OPPOSITES unknown.

rent noun *I can't afford to pay the rent:* **hire charge,** rental.
verb **1** *she rented a car:* **hire,** lease, charter. **2** *why don't you rent it out?* **let (out),** lease (out), hire (out), charter (out).

repair verb **1** *the car was repaired:* **mend,** fix (up), put/set right, restore (to working order), darn; informal patch up. **2** *repairing relations with other countries:* **put/set right,** mend, fix, straighten out, improve; informal patch up. **3** *she sought to repair the wrong she had done:* **rectify,** make good, (put) right, correct, make up for, make amends for.
noun **1** *in need of repair:* **restoration,** fixing (up), mending, renovation. **2** *an invisible repair:* **mend,** darn, patch. **3** *in good repair:* **condition,** working order, state, shape, fettle; Brit. informal nick.

repay verb **1** *repaying customers who have been cheated:* **reimburse,** refund, pay back, recompense, compensate. **2** *the grants have to be repaid:* **pay back,** return, refund, reimburse. **3** *I'd like to repay her generosity:* **reciprocate,** return, requite, reward.

repeal verb *the Act was repealed:* **cancel,** abolish, reverse, rescind, revoke, annul, quash.
OPPOSITES enact.

noun *the repeal of the law:* **cancellation**, abolition, reversal, rescinding, annulment.

repeat verb 1 *she repeated her story:* **say again**, restate, reiterate, go/run through again, recapitulate; informal recap. 2 *children can repeat chunks of text:* **recite**, quote, parrot, regurgitate, echo; informal trot out. 3 *Steele was invited to repeat his work:* **do again**, redo, replicate, duplicate. 4 *the episodes were repeated:* **rebroadcast**, rerun, reshow.
noun 1 *a repeat of the previous year's final:* **repetition**, replication, duplicate. 2 *repeats of his TV show:* **rerun**, rebroadcast, reshowing, replay.

repeatedly adverb **frequently**, often, again and again, over and over (again), time and (time) again, many times, persistently, recurrently, constantly, continually, regularly; N. Amer. oftentimes.

repel verb 1 *the US repelled an Iraqi attack:* **fight off**, repulse, drive back, force back, beat back, hold off; Brit. see off. 2 *the sight of the food repelled me:* **revolt**, disgust, repulse, sicken, nauseate, turn someone's stomach; informal turn off; N. Amer. informal gross out.
OPPOSITES attract, delight.

repertoire noun **collection**, range, repertory, list, store, stock, repository, supply.

repetition noun 1 *the statistics bear repetition:* **reiteration**, restatement, retelling. 2 *a repetition of the scene in the kitchen:* **recurrence**, rerun, repeat. 3 *there is some repetition:* **repetitiousness**, repetitiveness, redundancy,

tautology.

repetitive, repetitious adjective **recurring**, recurrent, repeated, unvaried, unchanging, routine, mechanical, automatic, monotonous, boring.
OPPOSITES unique, varied.

replace verb 1 *Adam replaced the receiver:* **put back**, return, restore. 2 *a new chairman came in to replace him:* **take the place of**, succeed, take over from, supersede, stand in for, substitute for, deputize for; informal step into someone's shoes/boots. 3 *she replaced the spoon with a fork:* **substitute**, exchange, change, swap.
OPPOSITES remove.

replacement noun 1 *we have to find a replacement:* **substitute**, stand-in, locum, understudy, relief, cover, successor. 2 *the wiring was in need of replacement:* **renewal**.

replica noun 1 *is it real or a replica?* **copy**, model, duplicate, reproduction, dummy, imitation, facsimile. 2 *a replica of her mother:* **perfect likeness**, double, lookalike, living image, twin, clone; informal spitting image, dead ringer.

reply verb *Rachel didn't reply:* **respond**, answer, write back, rejoin, retort, riposte, counter, come back.
noun *he waited for a reply:* **answer**, response, rejoinder, retort, riposte; informal comeback.

report verb 1 *the press reported the story:* **communicate**, announce, divulge, disclose, reveal, make public, publish, broadcast, proclaim, publicize. 2 *I reported him to the police:* **inform on**; informal shop, tell on,

r

squeal on, rat on; Brit. informal grass on. **3** *Juliet reported for duty:* **present oneself,** arrive, turn up; informal show up.
noun **1** *a full report on the meeting:* **account,** record, minutes, proceedings, transcript. **2** *reports of drug dealing:* **news,** information, word, intelligence. **3** *newspaper reports:* **story,** account, article, piece, item, column, feature, bulletin, dispatch. **4** (Brit.) *a school report:* **assessment,** evaluation, appraisal. **5** *reports of his imminent resignation:* **rumour,** whisper; informal buzz. **6** *the report of a gun:* **bang,** crack, explosion, boom.

reporter noun **journalist,** correspondent, newsman, newswoman, columnist; Brit. pressman; informal hack, stringer, journo; N. Amer. informal newsie.

represent verb **1** *a character representing a single quality:* **stand for,** symbolize, personify, epitomize, typify, embody, illustrate. **2** *Hathor is represented as a woman with cow's horns:* **depict,** portray, render, picture, delineate, show, illustrate. **3** *his solicitor represented him in court:* **appear for,** act for, speak on behalf of. **4** *the Queen was represented by Lord Lewin:* **deputize for,** substitute for, stand in for.

representation noun **1** *Rossetti's representation of women:* **portrayal,** depiction, presentation, rendition. **2** *representations of the human form:* **likeness,** painting, drawing, picture, illustration, sketch, image, model, figure, statue.

representative adjective **1** *a*

representative sample: **typical,** characteristic, illustrative. **2** *a female figure representative of Britain:* **symbolic,** emblematic.
OPPOSITES atypical.
noun **1** *a representative of the Royal Society:* **spokesperson,** spokesman, spokeswoman, agent, official, mouthpiece. **2** *a sales representative:* **salesman,** saleswoman, commercial traveller, agent, negotiator; informal rep; N. Amer. informal drummer. **3** *he acted as his father's representative:* **deputy,** substitute, stand-in, proxy, delegate, ambassador, emissary.

repress verb **1** *the rebellion was repressed:* **suppress,** quell, quash, subdue, put down, crush, extinguish, stamp out, defeat, contain. **2** *the peasants were repressed:* **oppress,** subjugate, keep down, tyrannize. **3** *these emotions may well be repressed:* **restrain,** hold back/in, suppress, keep in check, control, curb, stifle, bottle up; informal button up, keep the lid on.
OPPOSITES express.

repression noun **1** *the repression of the protests:* **suppression,** quashing, subduing, crushing, stamping out. **2** *political repression:* **oppression,** subjugation, suppression, tyranny, authoritarianism. **3** *the repression of sexual urges:* **restraint,** suppression, control, curbing, stifling, bottling up.

reprieve verb *she was reprieved:* **pardon,** spare, amnesty; informal let off (the hook).
noun *she was given a reprieve:* **pardon,** stay of execution, amnesty.

reprimand verb *he was publicly*

reprimanded: **rebuke,** reproach, scold, admonish; informal **tell off;** Brit. informal **tick off;** N. Amer. informal **chew out.**
OPPOSITES praise, pardon.
noun *a severe reprimand:* **rebuke,** reproach, scolding, admonition; informal **telling-off;** Brit. informal **ticking-off.**
OPPOSITES praise, pardon.

reproduce verb **1** *each artwork is reproduced in colour:* **copy,** duplicate, replicate, photocopy, xerox, photostat, print. **2** *this work has not been reproduced in other laboratories:* **repeat,** replicate, recreate, redo, simulate, imitate, emulate, mimic. **3** *some animals reproduce prolifically:* **breed,** procreate, propagate, multiply.

reproduction noun **1** *a reproduction of the original:* **print,** copy, reprint, duplicate, facsimile, photocopy; trademark Xerox. **2** *the process of reproduction:* **breeding,** procreation, multiplying, propagation.

repulsive adjective **disgusting,** revolting, foul, nasty, obnoxious, sickening, nauseating, stomach-churning.
OPPOSITES attractive.

reputation noun **name,** good name, character, repute, standing, stature, position, renown, esteem, prestige.

request noun **1** *requests for assistance:* **appeal,** entreaty, plea, petition, application, demand, call. **2** *Charlotte spoke, at Ursula's request:* **bidding,** entreaty, demand, insistence. **3** *indicate your requests on the form:* **requirement,** wish, desire, choice.
verb **1** *the government requested aid:* **ask for,** appeal for, call for,

seek, solicit, plead for, apply for, demand. **2** *I requested him to help:* **ask,** call on, beg, entreat, implore; literary **beseech.**

require verb **1** *the child required hospital treatment:* **need. 2** *a situation requiring patience:* **necessitate,** demand, call for, involve, entail. **3** *unquestioning obedience is required:* **demand,** insist on, call for, ask for, expect. **4** *she was required to pay costs:* **order,** instruct, command, enjoin, oblige, compel, force. **5** *do you require anything else?* **want,** desire, lack, be short of.

requirement noun **need,** necessity, prerequisite, stipulation, demand, want, essential.

rescue verb **1** *an attempt to rescue the hostages:* **save,** free, set free, release, liberate, deliver. **2** *Boyd rescued his papers:* **retrieve,** recover, salvage.
noun *the rescue of ten crewmen:* **saving,** rescuing, release, freeing, liberation, deliverance.

research noun *medical research:* **investigation,** experimentation, testing, analysis, fact-finding, examination, scrutiny.
verb *the phenomenon has been widely researched:* **investigate,** study, enquire into, look into, probe, explore, analyse, examine, scrutinize.

resemblance noun **similarity,** likeness, similitude, correspondence, congruence, conformity, comparability, parallelism.
OPPOSITES dissimilarity.

resemble verb **look like,** be similar to, remind one of, take after, approximate to, smack of,

r

correspond to, echo, mirror, parallel.
OPPOSITES differ from.

resent verb **begrudge,** feel aggrieved at/about, feel bitter about, grudge, be resentful of, take exception to, object to, take amiss, take offence at.
OPPOSITES welcome.

resentment noun **bitterness,** indignation, irritation, pique, dissatisfaction, disgruntlement, discontentment, acrimony, rancour.

reservation noun **1** *grave reservations:* **doubt,** qualm, scruple; (**reservations**) misgivings, scepticism, unease, hesitation, objection. **2** *an Indian reservation:* **reserve,** enclave, sanctuary, territory, homeland.

reserve verb **1** *ask your newsagent to reserve you a copy:* **put aside,** set aside, keep (back), save, hold back, keep in reserve, earmark. **2** *he reserved a table:* **book,** order, arrange for, secure. **3** *all rights reserved:* **retain,** keep, hold. **4** *reserve your judgement until you know him better:* **defer,** postpone, put off, delay, withhold.
noun **1** *reserves of petrol:* **stock,** store, supply, stockpile, pool, hoard, cache. **2** *the army are calling up reserves:* **reinforcements,** extras, auxiliaries. **3** *a nature reserve:* **national park,** sanctuary, preserve, conservation area. **4** *his natural reserve:* **shyness,** diffidence, timidity, taciturnity, inhibition, reticence, detachment, distance, remoteness. **5** *she trusted him without reserve:* **reservation,** qualification, condition, limitation, hesitation, doubt.

adjective *a reserve goalkeeper:* **substitute,** stand-in, relief, replacement, fallback, spare, extra.

reserved adjective **1** *Sewell is rather reserved:* **uncommunicative,** reticent, unforthcoming, quiet, silent, taciturn, withdrawn, secretive, shy, retiring, diffident, timid, introverted; informal stand-offish. **2** *that table is reserved:* **booked,** taken, spoken for, prearranged.
OPPOSITES outgoing.

reservoir noun **1** *sailing on the reservoir:* **lake,** pool, pond, basin. **2** *an ink reservoir:* **receptacle,** container, holder, tank. **3** *the reservoir of managerial talent:* **stock,** store, stockpile, reserve(s), supply, bank, pool.

residence noun (formal) **home,** house, address, quarters, lodgings; informal **pad**; formal dwelling.

resident noun *the residents of New York City:* **inhabitant,** local, citizen, native, householder, homeowner, occupier, tenant.
adjective **1** *resident in the UK:* **living,** residing; formal dwelling. **2** *a resident nanny:* **live-in.**

residue noun **remainder,** rest, remnant(s), surplus, extra, excess, remains, leftovers.

resign verb **1** *the manager resigned:* **leave,** give notice, stand down, step down; informal quit. **2** *19 MPs resigned their seats:* **give up,** leave, vacate, stand down from; informal quit, pack in.
■ **resign oneself** to reconcile oneself to, come to terms with.

resignation noun **1** *his resignation from his post:* **departure,** leaving, standing down, stepping down; informal quitting. **2** *he accepted his fate with resignation:* **patience,** forbearance, stoicism, fortitude, fatalism, acceptance.

resigned adjective **patient,** long-suffering, uncomplaining, forbearing, stoical, philosophical, fatalistic.

resist verb **1** *built to resist cold winters:* **withstand,** be proof against, combat, weather, endure, be resistant to, keep out. **2** *they resisted his attempts to change things:* **oppose,** fight against, object to, defy, kick against; informal be anti. **3** *I resisted the urge to retort:* **refrain from,** abstain from, forbear from, desist from, not give in to, restrain oneself from.
OPPOSITES welcome, submit to.

resistance noun **1** *resistance to change:* **opposition,** hostility. **2** *a spirited resistance:* **struggle,** fight, battle, stand, opposition, defiance. **3** *the body's resistance to disease:* **immunity from,** defences against. **4** *the French resistance:* **freedom fighters,** underground, partisans.

resistant adjective **1** *resistant to water:* **impervious,** immune, invulnerable, proof, unaffected. **2** *resistant to change:* **opposed,** averse, hostile, inimical, against; informal anti.
OPPOSITES vulnerable, favourable.

resolution noun **1** *her resolution not to smoke:* **intention,** resolve, decision, intent, aim, plan, commitment, pledge, promise. **2** *the committee passed the resolution:* **motion,** proposal, proposition; N. Amer. resolve. **3** *she handled the work with resolution:*

determination, purpose, resolve, single-mindedness; informal guts. **4** *a satisfactory resolution of the problem:* **solution,** answer, end, settlement, conclusion.

resolve verb **1** *this matter cannot be resolved overnight:* **settle,** sort out, solve, fix, straighten out, deal with, put right, rectify; informal hammer out, thrash out. **2** *David resolved to wait:* **determine,** decide, make up one's mind. **3** *the committee resolved that the project should proceed:* **vote,** rule, decide formally, agree.
noun *he reaffirmed his resolve:* **determination,** purpose, resolution, single-mindedness; informal guts.

resort noun *strike action is our last resort:* **option,** alternative, choice, possibility, hope, measure, step, recourse, expedient.
■ **resort to** fall back on, have recourse to, turn to, make use of, use, avail oneself of.

resound verb echo, reverberate, ring, boom, thunder, rumble, resonate.

resounding adjective **1** *a resounding voice:* **reverberating,** resonating, echoing, ringing, sonorous, deep, rich. **2** *a resounding success:* **enormous,** huge, very great, tremendous, terrific, colossal, emphatic, outstanding, remarkable, phenomenal.

resource noun **1** *your tutor is there as a resource:* **facility,** amenity, aid, help, support. **2** *a person of resource:* **initiative,** resourcefulness, enterprise, ingenuity, inventiveness. **3** (**resources**) *use your resources efficiently:* **assets,** funds, wealth, money, capital, supplies, materials, stores, stocks, reserves.

resourceful adjective **ingenious,** enterprising, inventive, creative, clever, talented, able, capable.

respect noun **1** *the respect due to a great artist:* **esteem,** regard, high opinion, admiration, reverence, deference, honour. **2** *he spoke to her with respect:* **due regard,** politeness, courtesy, civility, deference. **3** (**respects**) *paying one's respects:* **regards,** compliments, greetings, best/ good wishes. **4** *the report was accurate in every respect:* **aspect,** regard, feature, way, sense, particular, point, detail.
OPPOSITES contempt.
verb **1** *he is highly respected for his industry:* **esteem,** admire, think highly of, have a high opinion of, look up to, revere, honour. **2** *they respected our privacy:* **show consideration for,** have regard for, observe, be mindful of, be heedful of. **3** *father respected her wishes:* **abide by,** comply with, follow, adhere to, conform to, act in accordance with, obey, observe, keep (to).
OPPOSITES despise, disregard, disobey.

respectable adjective **1** *a respectable middle-class background:* **reputable,** upright, honest, honourable, trustworthy, decent, good, well bred, clean-living. **2** *a respectable salary:* **fairly good,** decent, fair-sized, reasonable, moderately good, large, sizeable, considerable.
OPPOSITES disreputable, paltry.

respectful adjective **deferential,**

reverent, dutiful, polite, well mannered, civil, courteous, gracious.
OPPOSITES rude.

respective adjective **separate,** personal, own, particular, individual, specific, special.

respite noun **rest,** break, breathing space, interval, lull, pause, time out, relief; informal breather, let-up.

respond verb **1** *they do not respond to questions:* **answer,** reply, write back, come back, rejoin, retort, riposte, counter. **2** *they were slow to respond:* **react,** reciprocate, retaliate.

response noun **1** *his response to the question:* **answer,** reply, rejoinder, retort, riposte; informal comeback. **2** *an angry response:* **reaction,** reply, retaliation; informal comeback.
OPPOSITES question.

responsibility noun **1** *it was his responsibility to find witnesses:* **duty,** task, function, job, role, business; Brit. informal pigeon. **2** *they denied responsibility for the attack:* **blame,** fault, guilt, culpability, liability. **3** *a sense of responsibility:* **trustworthiness,** (common) sense, maturity, reliability, dependability. **4** *managerial responsibility:* **authority,** control, power, leadership.
OPPOSITES irresponsibility.

responsible adjective **1** *who is responsible for prisons?* **in charge of,** in control of, at the helm of, accountable for, liable for. **2** *I am responsible for the mistake:* **accountable,** answerable, to blame, guilty, culpable, blameworthy, at fault, in the wrong. **3** *a responsible job:* **important,** powerful,

executive. **4** *a responsible tenant:* **trustworthy,** sensible, mature, reliable, dependable.
OPPOSITES irresponsible.

responsive adjective **reactive,** receptive, open to suggestions, amenable, flexible, forthcoming.
OPPOSITES unresponsive.

rest¹ verb **1** *he needed to rest:* **relax,** ease up/off, let up, slow down, have/take a break, unbend, unwind, take it easy, put one's feet up; informal take five, have/take a breather, chill out. **2** *his hands rested on the rail:* **lie,** be laid, repose, be placed, be positioned, be supported by. **3** *she rested her basket on the ground:* **support,** prop (up), lean, lay, set, stand, position, place, put.
noun **1** *get some rest:* **relaxation,** repose, leisure, respite, time off, breathing space; informal lie-down. **2** *a short rest from work:* **holiday,** vacation, break, breathing space, interval, interlude, intermission, time off/out; informal breather. **3** *she took the poker from its rest:* **stand,** base, holder, support, rack, frame, shelf. **4** *we came to rest 100 metres lower:* **a standstill,** a halt, a stop.

rest² noun *the rest of the board are appointees:* **remainder,** residue, balance, others, those left, remnant(s), surplus, excess.

restful adjective **relaxing,** quiet, calm, tranquil, soothing, peaceful, leisurely, undisturbed, untroubled.
OPPOSITES exciting.

restless adjective **1** *Maria was restless:* **uneasy,** ill at ease, fidgety, edgy, tense, worked up, nervous, nervy, agitated,

anxious; informal jumpy, jittery, twitchy, uptight. **2** *a restless night:* **sleepless,** wakeful, fitful, broken, disturbed, troubled, unsettled.

restoration noun **1** *the restoration of democracy:* **reinstatement,** reinstitution, re-establishment, reimposition, return. **2** *the restoration of derelict housing:* **repair,** fixing, mending, refurbishment, reconditioning, rehabilitation, rebuilding, reconstruction, renovation; N. Amer. informal rehab.

restore verb **1** *the aim to restore democracy:* **reinstate,** bring back, reinstitute, reimpose, reinstall, re-establish. **2** *he restored it to its rightful owner:* **return,** give back, hand back. **3** *the building has been restored:* **repair,** fix, mend, refurbish, recondition, rehabilitate, renovate; informal do up; N. Amer. informal rehab. **4** *a good sleep can restore you:* **reinvigorate,** revitalize, revive, refresh, energize, freshen.
OPPOSITES abolish, tire.

restrain verb **1** *Charles restrained his anger:* **control,** check, curb, suppress, contain, rein back/in; informal keep the lid on. **2** *she could barely restrain herself from swearing:* **prevent,** stop, keep, hold back.

restrained adjective **1** *Julie was quite restrained:* **self-controlled,** not given to excesses, sober, steady, unemotional, undemonstrative. **2** *restrained elegance:* **muted,** soft, discreet, subtle, quiet, unobtrusive, unostentatious, understated, tasteful.
OPPOSITES impetuous, ostentatious.

restraint noun **1** *a restraint on*

their impulsiveness: **constraint,** check, control, restriction, limitation, curtailment, rein, brake. **2** *the customary restraint of the police:* **self-control,** self-discipline, control, moderation, judiciousness. **3** *the room has been decorated with restraint:* **subtlety,** understatedness, taste, discretion, discrimination.
OPPOSITES impetuousness, ostentation.

restrict verb **1** *a busy job restricted his leisure activities:* **limit,** keep within bounds, regulate, control, moderate, cut down. **2** *the belt rather restricts movement:* **hinder,** interfere with, impede, hamper, obstruct, block, check, curb.

restricted adjective **1** *restricted space:* **cramped,** confined, constricted, small, narrow, tight. **2** *a restricted calorie intake:* **limited,** controlled, regulated, reduced. **3** *a restricted zone:* **out of bounds,** off limits, private, exclusive. **4** *restricted information:* **secret,** classified; informal hush-hush.
OPPOSITES generous, unlimited, public, open.

restriction noun **1** *there is no restriction on the number of places:* **limitation,** constraint, control, check, curb. **2** *the restriction of personal freedom:* **reduction,** limitation, diminution, curtailment. **3** *restriction of movement:* **hindrance,** impediment, slowing, reduction, limitation.

result noun *stress is the result of overwork:* **consequence,** outcome, upshot, sequel, effect, reaction, repercussion.
OPPOSITES cause.
verb *anger may result from an*

argument: **follow,** ensue, develop, stem, spring, arise, derive, proceed; (**result from**) be caused by, be brought about by, be produced by, originate in.
■ **result in** end in, culminate in, lead to, trigger, cause, bring about, occasion, effect, give rise to, produce.

resume verb **restart,** recommence, begin again, start again, reopen, renew, return to, continue with, carry on with.
OPPOSITES suspend, abandon.

résumé noun **summary,** precis, synopsis, abstract, outline, abridgement, overview.

resumption noun **restart,** recommencement, reopening, continuation, renewal, return, revival.

resurgence noun **renewal,** revival, renaissance, recovery, comeback, reawakening, resurrection, reappearance, re-emergence, resumption, continuation.

resurrect verb **revive,** restore, regenerate, revitalize, breathe new life into, reinvigorate, resuscitate, rejuvenate, re-establish, relaunch.

retain verb **1** *the government retained a share in the industries:* **keep (possession of),** keep hold of, hang on to. **2** *existing footpaths are to be retained:* **maintain,** keep, preserve, conserve.
OPPOSITES give up, abolish.

retaliate verb **fight back,** hit back, respond, react, reply, reciprocate, counter-attack, get back at someone, pay someone back; informal get one's own back.

retaliation noun **revenge,** vengeance, reprisal, retribution, repayment, response, reaction, reply, counter-attack.

r

retard verb **delay**, slow down/ up, hold back/up, postpone, detain, decelerate, hinder, impede, check.
OPPOSITES accelerate, bring forward.

reticent adjective **uncommunicative**, unforthcoming, unresponsive, tight-lipped, quiet, taciturn, silent, reserved.
OPPOSITES expansive.

retire verb **1** *he has retired:* **give up work**, stop work. **2** *Gillian retired to her office:* **withdraw**, go away, take oneself off, shut oneself away. **3** *everyone retired early:* **go to bed**, call it a day; informal turn in, hit the hay/sack.
OPPOSITES emerge, get up.

retired adjective *a retired teacher:* **former**, ex-, past, elderly.
noun **(the retired) (old-age) pensioners**, OAPs, senior citizens, the elderly; N. Amer. seniors.

retort verb *'Oh, sure,' she retorted:* **answer**, reply, respond, return, counter, riposte, retaliate.
noun *a sarcastic retort:* **answer**, reply, response, counter, rejoinder, riposte, retaliation; informal comeback.

retreat verb *the army retreated:* **withdraw**, retire, draw back, pull back/out, fall back, give way, give ground.
OPPOSITES advance.
noun **1** *the retreat of the army:* **withdrawal**, retirement, pullback, flight. **2** *her rural retreat:* **refuge**, haven, sanctuary, hideaway, hideout, hiding place; informal hidey-hole.

retrieve verb *I retrieved our ball from their garden:* **get back**, bring back, recover, recapture, regain, recoup.
2 *they tried to retrieve the situation:* **put/set right**, rectify, remedy, restore, sort out, straighten out, resolve.

return verb **1** *he returned to London:* **go back**, come back, arrive back, come home. **2** *the symptoms returned:* **recur**, reoccur, repeat (itself), reappear. **3** *he returned the money:* **give back**, hand back, pay back, repay. **4** *Peter returned the book to the shelf:* **restore**, put back, replace, reinstall. **5** *the jury returned a verdict:* **deliver**, bring in, hand down.
OPPOSITES keep.
noun **1** *the return of hard times:* **recurrence**, reoccurrence, repeat, repetition, reappearance. **2** *I requested the return of my books:* **giving back**, handing back, replacement, restoration, reinstatement, restitution. **3** *a quick return on investments:* **yield**, profit, gain, revenue, interest, dividend.

revamp verb **renovate**, redecorate, refurbish, remodel, refashion, redesign, restyle; informal do up, give something a facelift, give something a makeover, vamp up; Brit. informal tart up.

reveal verb **1** *the police can't reveal his whereabouts:* **disclose**, make known, make public, broadcast, publicize, circulate, divulge, tell, let slip/ drop, give away/out, blurt out, release, leak; informal let on. **2** *he revealed his new car:* **show**, display, exhibit, unveil, uncover.
OPPOSITES keep secret, hide.

revel verb *they revelled all night:*

r

celebrate, make merry; informal party, live it up, whoop it up, paint the town red.

noun *late-night revels:* **celebration,** festivity, jollification, merrymaking, party; informal rave, shindig, bash; Brit. informal rave-up; N. Amer. informal wingding, blast.

■ **revel in** enjoy, delight in, love, like, adore, take pleasure in, relish, lap up, savour; informal get a kick out of.

revelation noun 1 *revelations about his personal life:* **disclosure,** announcement, report, admission, confession. 2 *the revelation of a secret:* **disclosure,** divulging, letting slip/drop, giving away/out, leak, betrayal, publicizing.

revenge noun *she is seeking revenge:* **retaliation,** retribution, vengeance, reprisal, recrimination, an eye for an eye (and a tooth for a tooth), redress.

OPPOSITES forgiveness.

verb *he revenged his brother's murder:* **avenge,** exact retribution for, take reprisals for, get redress for, make someone pay for; informal get one's own back for.

OPPOSITES forgive.

revenue noun **income,** takings, receipts, proceeds, earnings, profit(s), gain, yield.

OPPOSITES expenditure.

revere verb **respect,** admire, think highly of, esteem, venerate, look up to, be in awe of.

OPPOSITES despise.

reverse verb 1 *the car reversed:* **back,** move back/backwards. 2 *reverse the bottle in the ice bucket:* **turn upside down,** turn over, upend, invert, turn back

to front. 3 *reverse your roles:* **swap (round),** change (round), exchange, switch (round), transpose. 4 *the umpire reversed the decision:* **alter,** change, overturn, overthrow, disallow, override, overrule, veto, revoke.

adjective *in reverse order:* **backward(s),** inverted, transposed, opposite.

noun 1 *the reverse is the case:* **opposite,** contrary, converse, inverse, antithesis. 2 *successes and reverses:* **setback,** reversal, upset, failure, misfortune, mishap, disaster, blow, disappointment, adversity, hardship, affliction, vicissitude, defeat. 3 *the reverse of the page:* **other side,** back, underside, wrong side.

OPPOSITES success, front.

revert verb **return,** go back, change back, default, relapse.

review noun 1 *the Council undertook a review:* **analysis,** evaluation, assessment, appraisal, examination, investigation, enquiry, probe, inspection, study. 2 *the rent is due for review:* **reconsideration,** reassessment, re-evaluation, reappraisal. 3 *book reviews:* **criticism,** critique, assessment, evaluation, commentary.

verb 1 *I reviewed the evidence:* **survey,** study, research, consider, analyse, examine, scrutinize, explore, look into, probe, investigate, inspect, assess, appraise; informal size up. 2 *the referee reviewed his decision:* **reconsider,** re-examine, reassess, re-evaluate, reappraise, rethink. 3 *she reviewed the play:* **comment on,** evaluate, assess, appraise, judge, criticize.

r

reviewer noun critic, commentator, judge.

revise verb **1** *she revised her opinion:* **reconsider,** review, re-examine, reassess, re-evaluate, reappraise, rethink, change, alter, modify. **2** *the editor revised the text:* **amend,** correct, alter, change, edit, rewrite, redraft, rephrase, rework. **3** (Brit.) *revise your lecture notes:* **go over,** reread, memorize, cram; informal bone up on; Brit. informal swot up (on), mug up (on).

revision noun **1** *a revision of the Prayer Book:* **alteration,** adaptation, editing, rewriting, redrafting, correction, updating. **2** *a major revision of the system:* **reconsideration,** review, re-examination, reassessment, re-evaluation, reappraisal, rethink, change, alteration, modification. **3** (Brit.) *he was doing some revision:* **rereading,** memorizing, cramming; Brit. informal swotting.

revival noun **1** *a revival in the economy:* **improvement,** rallying, picking up, turn for the better, upturn, upswing, resurgence. **2** *the revival of traditional crafts:* **comeback,** re-establishment, reintroduction, restoration, reappearance, resurrection. OPPOSITES downturn, disappearance.

revive verb **1** *attempts to revive her failed:* **resuscitate,** bring round, bring back to consciousness. **2** *the man soon revived:* **regain consciousness,** come round, wake up. **3** *a cup of tea revived her:* **reinvigorate,** revitalize, refresh, energize, reanimate. **4** *reviving old traditions:* **reintroduce,**

re-establish, restore, resurrect, bring back.

revolt verb **1** *the people revolted:* **rebel,** rise up, take to the streets, riot, mutiny. **2** *the smell revolted him:* **disgust,** sicken, nauseate, turn someone's stomach, put off, offend; informal turn off; N. Amer. informal gross out.
noun *an armed revolt:* **rebellion,** revolution, insurrection, mutiny, uprising, riot, insurgence, coup (d'état).

revolting adjective **disgusting,** sickening, nauseating, stomach-turning, repulsive, repugnant, hideous, nasty, foul, offensive; N. Amer. vomitous; informal ghastly, horrid, gross.
OPPOSITES attractive, pleasant.

revolution noun **1** *the French Revolution:* **rebellion,** revolt, insurrection, mutiny, rising, uprising, riot, insurgence, coup (d'état). **2** *a revolution in printing techniques:* **dramatic change,** sea change, metamorphosis, transformation, innovation, reorganization, restructuring; informal shake-up; N. Amer. informal shakedown. **3** *one revolution of a wheel:* **(single) turn,** rotation, circle, spin, orbit, circuit, lap.

revolutionary adjective **1** *revolutionary troops:* **rebellious,** rebel, insurgent, rioting, mutinous, renegade. **2** *a revolutionary kind of wheelchair:* **new,** novel, original, unusual, unconventional, unorthodox, newfangled, innovatory, modern, state-of-the-art, futuristic, pioneering.
noun *political revolutionaries:* **rebel,** insurgent, mutineer, insurrectionist, agitator.

r

revolve verb **1** *a fan revolved slowly:* **go round,** turn round, rotate, spin. **2** *the moon revolves around the earth:* **circle,** travel, orbit.

reward noun *a reward for long service:* **award,** honour, decoration, bonus, premium, bounty, present, gift, payment, recompense, prize; informal pay-off.
verb *they were well rewarded:* **recompense,** pay, remunerate.
OPPOSITES punish.

rewarding adjective **satisfying,** gratifying, pleasing, fulfilling, enriching, illuminating, worthwhile, productive, fruitful.

rhetoric noun **1** *a form of rhetoric:* **oratory,** eloquence, command of language, way with words. **2** *empty rhetoric:* **wordiness,** verbosity, grandiloquence, bombast, pomposity, extravagant language, purple prose, turgidity; informal hot air.

rhetorical adjective **1** *rhetorical devices:* **stylistic,** oratorical, linguistic, verbal. **2** *rhetorical exchanges in parliament:* **extravagant,** grandiloquent, high-flown, bombastic, grandiose, pompous, pretentious, overblown, oratorical, turgid, flowery; informal highfalutin.

rhyme noun **poem,** verse, ode; (rhymes) poetry, doggerel.

rhythm noun **1** *the rhythm of the music:* **beat,** cadence, tempo, time, pulse, throb, swing. **2** *poetic features such as rhythm:* **metre,** measure, stress, accent, cadence. **3** *the rhythm of daily life:* **pattern,** flow, tempo.

rich adjective **1** *rich people:* **wealthy,** affluent, moneyed, well off, well-to-do, prosperous; informal loaded, well heeled, made of money. **2** *rich furnishings:* **sumptuous,** opulent, luxurious, lavish, gorgeous, splendid, magnificent, costly, expensive, fancy; informal plush; Brit. informal swish; N. Amer. informal swank. **3** *a garden rich in flowers:* **well stocked,** well provided, abounding, crammed, packed, teeming, bursting. **4** *a rich supply of restaurants:* **plentiful,** abundant, copious, ample, profuse, lavish, liberal, generous. **5** *rich soil:* **fertile,** productive, fruitful. **6** *a rich sauce:* **creamy,** fatty, heavy, full-flavoured. **7** *rich colours:* **strong,** deep, full, intense, vivid, brilliant.
OPPOSITES poor, cheap, light.

riches plural noun **money,** wealth, funds, cash, means, assets, capital, resources; informal bread, loot; Brit. informal dosh, brass, lolly, spondulicks; N. Amer. informal bucks; US informal greenbacks.

richly adverb **1** *richly furnished:* **sumptuously,** opulently, luxuriously, lavishly, gorgeously, splendidly, magnificently. **2** *the joy she richly deserves:* **fully,** amply, well, thoroughly, completely, wholly, totally, entirely, absolutely, utterly.
OPPOSITES meanly.

rid verb *the aim was to rid the town of malaria:* **clear,** free, purge, empty, strip.
■ **get rid of** dispose of, throw away/out, clear out, discard, scrap, dump, bin, jettison, expel, eliminate; informal chuck (away), ditch, junk; Brit. informal get shot of; N. Amer. informal trash.

r

riddle noun puzzle, conundrum, brain-teaser, problem, question, poser, enigma, mystery.

ride verb 1 *she can ride a horse:* **sit on**, mount, control, manage, handle. 2 *riding round the town:* **travel**, move, proceed, drive, cycle, trot, canter, gallop. noun *he took us for a ride:* **trip**, journey, drive, run, excursion, outing, jaunt, lift; informal spin.

ridicule noun *he was subjected to ridicule:* **mockery**, derision, laughter, scorn, scoffing, jeering.
OPPOSITES respect.
verb *his theory was ridiculed:* **mock**, deride, laugh at, heap scorn on, jeer at, make fun of, scoff at, satirize, caricature, parody.
OPPOSITES respect.

ridiculous adjective 1 *that looks ridiculous:* **laughable**, absurd, comical, funny, hilarious, risible, droll, amusing, farcical. 2 *a ridiculous suggestion:* **foolish**, silly, senseless, foolhardy, stupid, idiotic. 3 *a ridiculous exaggeration:* **absurd**, preposterous, ludicrous, laughable, risible, nonsensical, outrageous.
OPPOSITES sensible.

rife adjective **widespread**, general, common, universal, extensive, ubiquitous, endemic, inescapable.
OPPOSITES unknown.

rifle verb 1 *she rifled through her wardrobe:* **rummage**, search, hunt, forage. 2 *a thief rifled her home:* **burgle**, rob, steal from, loot, raid, plunder, ransack.

rift noun 1 *a deep rift in the ice:* **crack**, split, breach, fissure, fracture, cleft, crevice, opening. 2 *the rift between them:* **breach**, division, split, quarrel, disagreement, falling-out, row, conflict, feud; Brit. informal bust-up.

rig¹ verb 1 *the boats were rigged with a single sail:* **equip**, kit out, fit out, supply, furnish, provide, arm. 2 *I rigged myself out in black:* **dress**, clothe, attire, robe, garb, get up; informal doll up. 3 *he will rig up a shelter:* **set up**, erect, assemble, put together, whip up, improvise, contrive; Brit. informal knock up.

rig² verb *they rigged the election:* **manipulate**, engineer, distort, misrepresent, pervert, tamper with, falsify, fake; informal fix; Brit. informal fiddle.

right adjective 1 *it wouldn't be right to do that:* **just**, fair, proper, good, upright, righteous, virtuous, moral, ethical, honourable, honest, lawful, legal. 2 *the right answer:* **correct**, accurate, exact, precise, proper, valid, conventional, established, official, formal; Brit. informal spot on. 3 *the right person for the job:* **suitable**, appropriate, fitting, correct, proper, desirable, preferable, ideal. 4 *you've come at the right time:* **opportune**, advantageous, favourable, good, lucky, fortunate. 5 *on my right side:* **right-hand**; Nautical starboard.
OPPOSITES wrong, bad, left, port.
adverb 1 *she was right at the limit of her patience:* **completely**, fully, totally, absolutely, utterly, thoroughly, quite. 2 *right in the middle of the village:* **exactly**, precisely, directly, immediately, just, squarely, dead; informal (slap) bang, smack, plumb. 3 *I think I heard right:* **correctly**,

r

accurately, properly, precisely, perfectly. **4** *make sure you're treated right:* **well,** properly, justly, fairly, equitably, impartially, honourably, lawfully, legally. **5** *things will turn out right:* **well,** for the best, favourably, happily, advantageously, profitably, luckily, conveniently.
OPPOSITES wrong, badly.
noun **1** *the difference between right and wrong:* **goodness,** righteousness, virtue, integrity, propriety, morality, truth, honesty, honour, justice, fairness, equity. **2** *you have the right to say no:* **entitlement,** prerogative, privilege, liberty, authority, power, licence, permission, dispensation, leave, due.
OPPOSITES wrong.
verb *we must right the situation:* **remedy,** rectify, retrieve, fix, resolve, sort out, settle, square, straighten out, correct, repair, mend, redress.

■ **right away** at once, straight away, (right) now, this (very) minute, this instant, immediately, instantly, directly, forthwith, without further ado, promptly, quickly, without delay, asap, as soon as possible; N. Amer. in short order; informal straight off, pronto.

righteous adjective good, virtuous, upright, upstanding, decent, ethical, principled, moral, honest, honourable, blameless.
OPPOSITES wicked.

right-wing adjective **conservative,** rightist, reactionary, traditionalist, conventional.
OPPOSITES left-wing.

rigid adjective **1** *a rigid container:* **stiff,** hard, firm, inflexible, unbending, unyielding. **2** *a rigid routine:* **fixed,** set, firm, inflexible, invariable, hard and fast, cast-iron. **3** *a rigid approach to funding:* **strict,** stringent, rigorous, inflexible, uncompromising, intransigent.
OPPOSITES flexible, lenient.

rigorous adjective **1** *rigorous attention to detail:* **meticulous,** conscientious, punctilious, careful, scrupulous, painstaking, exact, precise, accurate, particular, strict. **2** *the rigorous enforcement of rules:* **strict,** stringent, rigid, inflexible, draconian, intransigent, uncompromising. **3** *rigorous conditions:* **harsh,** severe, bleak, extreme, demanding.
OPPOSITES slapdash, lax, mild.

rim noun edge, brim, lip, border, side, margin, brink, boundary, perimeter, circumference, limits, periphery.

ring[1] noun **1** *a ring round the moon:* **circle,** band, halo, disc. **2** *the horses entered the ring:* **arena,** enclosure, circus, amphitheatre, bowl. **3** *a spy ring:* **gang,** syndicate, cartel, mob, band, circle, organization, association, society, alliance, league.
verb *police ringed the building:* **surround,** circle, encircle, enclose, hem in, confine, seal off.

ring[2] verb **1** *church bells rang:* **chime,** sound, peal, toll, clang, bong; literary knell. **2** *the room rang with laughter:* **resound,** reverberate, resonate, echo. **3** *I'll ring you tomorrow:* **telephone,** phone (up), call (up); informal give someone a buzz; Brit. informal give someone a bell, give someone a tinkle, get on the blower to.

rinse verb wash (out), clean, cleanse, bathe, dip, drench, splash, swill, sluice.

riot noun **1** *a riot in the capital:* **disorder**, disturbance, lawlesssness, upheaval, uproar, commotion. **2** *a riot of colour:* **mass**, sea, splash, show, profusion.
verb *the miners rioted:* **(go on the) rampage**, run wild, run amok, run riot, go berserk; informal raise hell.
■ **run riot** grow profusely, spread uncontrolled, burgeon, multiply, rocket.

rip verb **1** *he ripped the posters down:* **tug**, wrench, pull, snatch, tear, heave, drag, peel, pluck; informal yank. **2** *she ripped Leo's note into pieces:* **tear**, claw, hack, slit.

ripe adjective **1** *a ripe tomato:* **mature**, full grown. **2** *ripe for development:* **ready**, fit, suitable, right. **3** *the time is ripe for his return:* **opportune**, advantageous, favourable, auspicious, good, right.
OPPOSITES young, unsuitable, unfavourable.

rise verb **1** *the sun rose:* **climb**, come up, arise, ascend, mount, soar. **2** *the mountains rising above us:* **loom**, tower, soar. **3** *prices rose:* **go up**, increase, soar, shoot up, surge, leap, jump, rocket, escalate, spiral. **4** *living standards have risen:* **improve**, get better, advance. **5** *his voice rose:* **get higher**, grow, increase, become louder, swell, intensify. **6** *he rose from his chair:* **stand up**, get to one's feet, get up, jump up, leap up. **7** *he rises at dawn:* **get up**, stir, bestir oneself, be up and about;

informal surface.
OPPOSITES fall, sit down, go to bed.
noun **1** *a price rise:* **increase**, hike, leap, upsurge, upswing, climb. **2** *he got a rise of 4%:* **raise**, increase, hike, increment. **3** *a rise in standards:* **improvement**, advance. **4** *his rise to power:* **progress**, climb, promotion, elevation. **5** *we walked up the rise:* **slope**, incline, hill.

risk noun **1** *there is a certain amount of risk:* **chance**, uncertainty, unpredictability, instability, insecurity. **2** *the risk of fire:* **possibility**, chance, probability, likelihood, danger, peril, threat, menace, prospect.
OPPOSITES certainty, safety, impossibility.
verb *he risked his life to save them:* **endanger**, imperil, jeopardize, hazard, gamble (with), chance, put on the line.

risky adjective **dangerous**, hazardous, perilous, unsafe, insecure, precarious, touch-and-go, treacherous, uncertain, unpredictable; informal dicey; N. Amer. informal gnarly.

rite noun **ceremony**, ritual, ceremonial, custom, service, observance, liturgy, worship, office.

ritual noun *an elaborate civic ritual:* **ceremony**, rite, act, practice, custom, tradition, convention, formality, protocol.
adjective *a ritual burial:* **ceremonial**, prescribed, set, formal, traditional, conventional.

rival noun **1** *his rival for the nomination:* **opponent**, challenger, competitor, contender, adversary, antagonist, enemy. **2** *the tool*

r

has no rival: **equal**, match, peer, equivalent.
OPPOSITES ally.
verb *few countries can rival it for scenery:* **match**, compare with, compete with, vie with, equal, measure up to, touch; informal hold a candle to.
adjective *rival candidates:* **competing**, opposing.

rivalry noun **competition**, contention, opposition, conflict, feuding; informal keeping up with the Joneses.

river noun **1 stream**, brook, watercourse, rivulet, tributary; Scottish & N. English burn; N. English beck; S. English bourn; N. Amer. & Austral./NZ creek. **2** *a river of molten lava:* **stream**, torrent, flood, deluge, cascade.

riveting adjective **fascinating**, gripping, engrossing, intriguing, absorbing, captivating, enthralling, compelling, spellbinding, mesmerizing; informal unputdownable.
OPPOSITES boring.

road noun **1 street**, thoroughfare, roadway, highway, lane; Brit. motorway. **2** *on the road to recovery:* **way**, path, route, course.

roam verb **wander**, rove, ramble, drift, walk, traipse, range, travel, tramp, trek; Scottish & Irish stravaig; informal cruise, mosey.

roar noun **1** *the roars of the crowd:* **shout**, bellow, yell, cry, howl, clamour; informal holler. **2** *the roar of the sea:* **boom**, crash, rumble, roll, thunder.
verb **1** *'Get out!' roared Angus:* **bellow**, yell, shout, bawl, howl; informal holler. **2** *thunder roared:* **boom**, rumble, crash, roll, thunder.

roaring adjective *a roaring fire:*

blazing, burning, flaming.

rob verb **1** *the gang robbed a bank:* **burgle**, steal from, hold up, break into, raid, loot, plunder, pillage; N. Amer. burglarize. **2** *he robbed an old woman:* **steal from**, hold up; informal mug. **3** *he was robbed of his savings:* **cheat**, swindle, defraud; informal do out of, con out of. **4** *defeat robbed him of his title:* **deprive**, strip, deny.

robber noun **burglar**, thief, housebreaker, mugger, shoplifter, raider, looter.

robbery noun *they were arrested for the robbery:* **burglary**, theft, stealing, housebreaking, shoplifting, embezzlement, fraud, hold-up, raid; informal mugging, smash-and-grab, stick-up; N. Amer. informal heist.

robe noun **1** *the women wore black robes:* **cloak**, kaftan, djellaba, wrap, mantle, cape; N. Amer. wrapper. **2** *ceremonial robes:* **garb**, regalia, costume, finery, vestments.

robot noun **machine**, automaton, android, golem; informal bot, droid.

robust adjective **1** *a robust man:* **strong**, vigorous, sturdy, tough, powerful, solid, rugged, hardy, strapping, healthy, (fighting) fit, hale and hearty. **2** *these knives are robust:* **durable**, resilient, tough, hard-wearing, long-lasting, sturdy, strong.
OPPOSITES frail, fragile.

rock¹ noun **boulder**, stone, pebble.

rock² verb **1** *the ship rocked on the water:* **move to and fro**, sway, see-saw, roll, pitch, plunge, toss, lurch. **2** *Wall Street was rocked by the news:* **stun**, shock, stagger, astonish, startle, surprise, shake, take aback, throw, unnerve, disconcert.

rocky[1] adjective *a rocky path:* **stony,** pebbly, shingly, rough, bumpy, craggy, mountainous.

rocky[2] adjective **unsteady,** shaky, unstable, wobbly, tottery, rickety.
OPPOSITES steady, stable.

rod noun **bar,** stick, pole, baton, staff, shaft, strut, rail, spoke.

rogue noun **1** *a rogue without ethics:* **scoundrel,** rascal, good-for-nothing, wretch, villain, criminal, lawbreaker; informal crook. **2** *your boy's a little rogue:* **rascal,** imp, devil, monkey; informal scamp, scallywag.

role noun **1** *a small role in the film:* **part,** character. **2** *his role as President:* **capacity,** position, function, job, post, office, duty, responsibility.

roll verb **1** *the bottle rolled down the table:* **bowl,** turn over and over, spin, rotate, wheel, trundle. **2** *tears rolled down her cheeks:* **flow,** run, course, stream, pour, trickle. **3** *he rolled his handkerchief into a ball:* **wind,** coil, fold, curl, twist. **4** *the ship began to roll:* **rock,** sway, reel, list, pitch, plunge, lurch, toss.
noun **1** *a roll of paper:* **cylinder,** tube, scroll, reel, spool. **2** *a roll of the dice:* **throw,** toss, turn, spin. **3** *the electoral roll:* **list,** register, directory, record, file, index, catalogue, inventory. **4** *a roll of thunder:* **rumble,** reverberation, echo, boom, clap, crack, roar.

romance noun **1** *he's had many romances:* **love affair,** relationship, liaison, courtship, attachment, amour. **2** *an author of romances:* **story,** tale, legend, fairy tale. **3** *the romance of the Far East:* **mystery,** glamour, excitement, exoticism, mystique, appeal, allure, charm.

romantic adjective **1** *he's so romantic:* **loving,** amorous, passionate, tender, affectionate; informal lovey-dovey. **2** *romantic songs:* **sentimental,** hearts-and-flowers, mawkish, sickly, saccharine, syrupy; informal slushy, mushy, sloppy, schmaltzy; Brit. informal soppy. **3** *a romantic setting:* **idyllic,** picturesque, fairy-tale, beautiful, lovely, charming, pretty. **4** *romantic notions of rural communities:* **idealistic,** unrealistic, fanciful, impractical, head-in-the-clouds, starry-eyed, utopian, fairy-tale.
OPPOSITES unsentimental, realistic.
noun *an incurable romantic:* **idealist,** sentimentalist, dreamer, fantasist.
OPPOSITES realist.

romp verb **play,** frolic, frisk, gambol, skip, prance, caper, cavort.

room noun **1** *there isn't much room:* **space,** headroom, legroom, area, expanse, extent. **2** *room for improvement:* **scope,** capacity, leeway, latitude, freedom.

root noun **1** *the root of the problem:* **source,** origin, cause, reason, basis, foundation, bottom, seat. **2** (**roots**) *origins,* beginnings, family, birth, heritage.
verb *he rooted around in the cupboard:* **rummage,** hunt, search, rifle, delve, forage, dig, nose, poke.
■ **root something out** eradicate, eliminate, weed out, destroy, wipe out, stamp out, abolish,

r

end, put a stop to.

rope noun cord, cable, line, hawser, string.

rosy adjective **1** *a rosy complexion:* **pink,** roseate, reddish, glowing, healthy, fresh, radiant, blooming, blushing, flushed, ruddy. **2** *his future looks rosy:* **promising,** optimistic, auspicious, hopeful, encouraging, favourable, bright, golden.
OPPOSITES pale, bleak.

rot verb **1** *the floorboards rotted:* **decay,** decompose, disintegrate, crumble, perish. **2** *the meat began to rot:* **go bad,** go off, spoil, moulder, putrefy, fester. **3** *poor neighbourhoods have been left to rot:* **deteriorate,** degenerate, decline, decay, go to seed, go downhill; informal go to pot, go to the dogs.
OPPOSITES improve.
noun *the leaves turned black with rot:* **decay,** decomposition, mould, mildew, blight, canker.

rotate verb **1** *the wheels rotate continually:* **revolve,** go round, turn (round), spin, gyrate, whirl, twirl, swivel, circle, pivot. **2** *many nurses rotate jobs:* **alternate,** take turns, change, switch, interchange, exchange, swap.

rotation noun **1** *the rotation of the wheels:* **revolving,** turning, spinning, gyration, circling. **2** *a rotation of the Earth:* **turn,** revolution, orbit, spin. **3** *each member is chair for six months in rotation:* **sequence,** succession, alternation, cycle.

rotten adjective **1** *rotten meat:* **decaying,** bad, off, decomposing, putrid, perished, rancid, festering, fetid. **2** *he's rotten to the core:* **corrupt,** unprincipled, dishonest, dishonourable, unscrupulous, untrustworthy, immoral; informal crooked; Brit. informal bent.
OPPOSITES fresh, honourable.

rough adjective **1** *rough ground:* **uneven,** irregular, bumpy, stony, rocky, rugged, rutted, pitted. **2** *the terrier's rough coat:* **coarse,** bristly, scratchy, prickly, shaggy, hairy, bushy. **3** *rough skin:* **dry,** leathery, weather-beaten, chapped, calloused, scaly. **4** *his voice was rough:* **gruff,** hoarse, harsh, rasping, husky, throaty, gravelly. **5** *he gets rough when he's drunk:* **violent,** brutal, vicious, aggressive, belligerent, pugnacious, boisterous, rowdy, disorderly, unruly, riotous. **6** *a machine that can take rough handling:* **careless,** clumsy, inept, unskilful. **7** *rough manners:* **boorish,** loutish, oafish, brutish, coarse, crude, uncouth, vulgar, unrefined, unladylike, ungentlemanly, uncultured. **8** *rough seas:* **turbulent,** stormy, tempestuous, violent, heavy, choppy. **9** *a rough draft:* **preliminary,** hasty, quick, sketchy, cursory, basic, crude, rudimentary, raw, unpolished, incomplete, unfinished. **10** *a rough estimate:* **approximate,** inexact, imprecise, vague, estimated; N. Amer. informal ballpark.
OPPOSITES smooth, sleek, soft, dulcet, sweet, gentle, careful, refined, calm, exact.
noun *the artist's initial roughs:* **sketch,** draft, outline, mock-up.

round adjective *a round window:* **circular,** spherical, globular, cylindrical.
noun **1** *mould the dough into rounds:* **ball,** sphere, globe, orb, circle, disc, ring, hoop. **2** *a*

policeman on his rounds:
circuit, beat, route, tour. **3** *the first round of the contest:* **stage**, level, heat, game, bout, contest. **4** *an endless round of parties:* **succession**, sequence, series, cycle.
preposition 1 *the alleys round the station:* **around**, about, encircling, near, orbiting.
2 *casinos dotted round France:* **throughout**, all over.
verb *the ship rounded the point:* **go round**, travel round, skirt, circumnavigate, orbit.
■ **round something off** complete, finish off, crown, cap, top, conclude, close, end. ■ **round someone/something up** gather together, herd together, muster, marshal, rally, assemble, collect, group; N. Amer. corral.

roundabout adjective **1** *a roundabout route:* **circuitous**, indirect, meandering, serpentine, tortuous. **2** *I asked in a roundabout sort of way:* **indirect**, oblique, circuitous, circumlocutory.
OPPOSITES direct.

rouse verb **1** *he roused Ralph at dawn:* **wake (up)**, awaken, arouse; Brit. informal knock up. **2** *she roused and looked around:* **wake up**, awake, come to, get up, rise, bestir oneself. **3** *he roused the crowd:* **stir up**, excite, galvanize, electrify, stimulate, inspire, inspirit, move, inflame, agitate, goad, provoke, prompt. **4** *he's got a temper when he's roused:* **provoke**, annoy, anger, infuriate, madden, incense, vex, irk; informal aggravate.
OPPOSITES calm, pacify, allay.

rousing adjective **stirring**, inspiring, exciting, stimulating, moving, electrifying,

invigorating, energizing, exhilarating.

rout noun *the army's ignominious rout:* **defeat**, beating, retreat, flight; informal licking, hammering, thrashing, pasting, drubbing.
OPPOSITES victory.
verb *his army was routed:* **defeat**, beat, conquer, vanquish, crush, put to flight, drive off, scatter; informal lick, hammer, clobber, thrash; Brit. informal stuff.

route noun **way**, course, road, path, direction.

routine noun **1** *his morning routine:* **procedure**, practice, pattern, drill, regime, programme, schedule, plan. **2** *a stand-up routine:* **act**, performance, number, turn, piece; informal spiel, patter.
adjective 1 *a routine health check:* **standard**, regular, customary, normal, usual, ordinary, typical, everyday. **2** *a routine action movie:* **boring**, tedious, monotonous, humdrum, run-of-the-mill, pedestrian, predictable, hackneyed, unimaginative, unoriginal, banal, trite.
OPPOSITES unusual.

row¹ noun **1** *rows of children:* **line**, column, file, queue, procession, chain, string, succession; informal crocodile. **2** *the middle row of seats:* **tier**, line, rank, bank.
■ **in a row** consecutively, in succession, running, straight; informal on the trot.

row² (Brit. informal) noun **1** *have you two had a row?* **argument**, quarrel, squabble, fight, dispute; informal tiff, run-in, slanging match, spat; Brit. informal bust-up. **2** *I couldn't hear for the row:* **din**, noise, racket,

r

uproar, hubbub, rumpus; informal hullabaloo.

verb *they rowed about money:* **argue,** quarrel, squabble, bicker, fight, fall out, disagree, have words; informal scrap.

royal adjective **regal,** kingly, queenly, princely, sovereign.

rub verb **1** *Polly rubbed her arm:* **massage,** knead, stroke, pat. **2** *he rubbed sun lotion on her back:* **apply,** smear, spread, work in. **3** *my shoes rub painfully:* **chafe,** scrape, pinch.

noun 1 *she gave his back a rub:* **massage,** rub-down. **2** *I gave my shoes a rub:* **polish,** wipe, clean. ■ **rub something down** clean, sponge, wash. ■ **rub something out** erase, delete, remove, obliterate.

rubbish noun **1** *throw away that rubbish:* **refuse,** waste, litter, scrap, dross; N. Amer. garbage, trash; informal dreck, junk. **2** *she's talking rubbish:* **nonsense,** gibberish, claptrap, garbage; informal baloney, tripe, drivel, bilge, bunk, piffle, poppycock, twaddle, gobbledegook; Brit. informal codswallop, cobblers, tosh.

rude adjective **1** *a rude man:* **ill-mannered,** bad-mannered, impolite, discourteous, uncivil, impertinent, insolent, impudent, disparaging, abusive. **2** *rude jokes:* **vulgar,** coarse, smutty, dirty, filthy, crude, lewd, obscene, risqué; informal blue; Brit. informal near the knuckle. **3** *a rude awakening:* **abrupt,** sudden, sharp. OPPOSITES polite, clean, gentle.

ruffle verb **1** *he ruffled her hair:* **disarrange,** tousle, dishevel, rumple, mess up; N. Amer. informal muss up. **2** *don't let him ruffle you:* **disconcert,** unnerve,

fluster, agitate, upset, disturb, discomfit, put off, perturb, unsettle; informal faze, throw, get to. OPPOSITES smooth, calm.

rugged adjective **1** *the rugged path:* **rough,** uneven, bumpy, rocky, stony, pitted. **2** *a rugged vehicle:* **robust,** durable, sturdy, strong, tough, resilient. **3** *rugged manly types:* **well built,** burly, strong, muscular, muscly, brawny, strapping, tough, hardy, robust, sturdy, solid; informal hunky. **4** *his rugged features:* **strong,** craggy, rough-hewn, manly, masculine. OPPOSITES smooth, flimsy, weedy, delicate.

ruin noun **1** *the buildings were saved from ruin:* **disintegration,** decay, disrepair, dilapidation, destruction, demolition. **2** *the ruins of a church:* **remains,** remnants, fragments, rubble, debris, wreckage. **3** *electoral ruin for Labour:* **downfall,** collapse, defeat, undoing, failure. **4** *shopkeepers are facing ruin:* **bankruptcy,** insolvency, penury, poverty, destitution. OPPOSITES preservation, triumph, wealth.

verb 1 *don't ruin my plans:* **spoil,** wreck, blight, shatter, dash, torpedo, scotch, mess up, sabotage; informal screw up; Brit. informal scupper. **2** *the bank's collapse ruined them:* **bankrupt,** make insolvent, impoverish, pauperize, wipe out, break, cripple, bring someone to their knees. **3** *a country ruined by civil war:* **destroy,** devastate, lay waste, ravage, raze, demolish, wreck, wipe out, flatten. OPPOSITES save, rebuild.

r

rule noun **1** *health and safety rules:* **regulation,** directive, order, law, statute. **2** *church attendance on Sunday was the general rule:* **procedure,** practice, protocol, convention, norm, routine, custom, habit. **3** *moderation is the golden rule:* **principle,** precept, standard, axiom, truth, maxim. **4** *under British rule:* **government,** jurisdiction, command, power, dominion, control, administration, sovereignty, leadership.
verb **1** *El Salvador was ruled by Spain:* **govern,** preside over, control, lead, dominate, run, head, administer. **2** *Mary ruled for six years:* **reign,** be on the throne, be in power, govern. **3** *the judge ruled that they be set free:* **decree,** order, pronounce, judge, adjudge, ordain, decide, find. **4** *subversion ruled:* **prevail,** predominate, hold sway, be the order of the day, reign supreme. ■ **as a rule** usually, in general, normally, ordinarily, customarily, for the most part, on the whole, by and large, in the main, mostly, commonly, typically. ■ **rule something out** exclude, eliminate, disregard, preclude, prohibit, prevent, disallow.

ruler noun **leader,** sovereign, monarch, potentate, king, queen, emperor, empress, prince, princess, crowned head, head of state, president, premier, governor.
OPPOSITES subject.

ruling noun *the judge's ruling:* **judgement,** decision, adjudication, finding, verdict, pronouncement, resolution, decree, injunction.
adjective **1** *Japan's ruling party:* governing, controlling, commanding, supreme. **2** *football was their ruling passion:* **main,** chief, principal, major, dominating, consuming; informal number-one.

rumour noun **gossip,** hearsay, talk, tittle-tattle, speculation, word, report, story, whisper; informal the grapevine, the word on the street, the buzz.

run verb **1** *she ran across the road:* **sprint,** race, dart, rush, dash, hasten, hurry, scurry, scamper, gallop, jog, trot; informal leg it. **2** *the robbers turned and ran:* **flee,** take flight, make off, take off, take to one's heels, bolt, make one's getaway, escape; informal beat it, clear off/out, scram; Brit. informal scarper. **3** *the road runs the length of the valley:* **extend,** stretch, reach, continue. **4** *water ran from the eaves:* **flow,** pour, stream, gush, flood, cascade, roll, course, spill, trickle, drip, dribble, leak. **5** *a bus runs to Sorrento:* **travel,** shuttle, go. **6** *he runs a transport company:* **be in charge of,** manage, direct, control, head, govern, supervise, superintend, oversee. **7** *it's expensive to run a car:* **maintain,** keep, own, possess, have, use, operate. **8** *he left the engine running:* **operate,** function, work, go. **9** *the lease runs for twenty years:* **last,** continue, survive.
noun **1** *his morning run:* **jog,** sprint, dash, gallop, trot. **2** *she did the school run:* **route,** journey, circuit, round, beat. **3** *a run in the car:* **drive,** ride, turn, trip, excursion, outing, jaunt; informal spin, tootle. **4** *an unbeaten run of victories:* **series,** succession, sequence, string, streak, spate. **5** *a chicken*

r

run: **enclosure,** pen, coop. **6** *a ski run:* **slope,** track, piste; N. Amer. trail.

■ **run someone down 1** *he was run down by joyriders:* run over, knock down/over, hit. **2** *she ran him down in front of other people:* criticize, denigrate, belittle, disparage, deprecate, find fault with; informal put down, knock, bad-mouth; Brit. informal rubbish, slag off. ■ **run into 1** *a car ran into his van:* collide with, hit, strike, crash into, smash into, plough into, ram. **2** *I ran into Hugo the other day:* meet (by chance), run across, chance on, stumble on, happen on; informal bump into. **3** *we ran into a problem:* experience, encounter, meet with, be faced with, be confronted with. ■ **run out 1** *supplies ran out:* be used up, dry up, be exhausted, be finished, peter out. **2** *her contract ran out:* expire, end, terminate, finish, lapse. ■ **run over 1** *the bathwater ran over:* overflow, spill over, brim over. **2** *the project ran over budget:* exceed, go over, overshoot, overreach. **3** *he quickly ran over the story:* review, repeat, run through, go over, reiterate, recapitulate, look over, read through; informal recap on. ■ **run someone over.** See **RUN SOMEONE DOWN** sense 1.

rundown noun **summary,** synopsis, precis, run-through, review, overview, briefing, sketch, outline; informal lowdown, recap.

run down adjective **1** *a run-down area of London:* **dilapidated,** tumbledown, ramshackle, derelict, crumbling, neglected, uncared-for, slummy. **2** *she was feeling*

rather run down: **unwell,** ill, poorly, unhealthy, peaky, tired, drained, exhausted, worn out, below par, washed out; Brit. off colour; informal under the weather; Brit. informal off; Austral./NZ informal crook.

runner noun **1 athlete,** sprinter, hurdler, racer, jogger. **2** *the bookmaker employed runners:* **messenger,** courier, errand boy; informal gofer.

running noun **1** *the running of the school:* **administration,** management, organization, coordination, orchestration, handling, direction, control, supervision. **2** *the smooth running of her department:* **operation,** working, function, performance.
adjective **1** *running water:* **flowing,** gushing, rushing, moving. **2** *a running argument:* **ongoing,** continuous, incessant, ceaseless, constant, perpetual. **3** *she was late two days running:* **in succession,** in a row, in sequence, consecutively, straight, together; informal on the trot.

runny adjective **liquid,** liquefied, fluid, melted, molten, watery, thin.
OPPOSITES solid, thick.

rupture noun & verb **break,** fracture, crack, burst, split, fissure, breach.

rural adjective **country,** rustic, bucolic, pastoral, agricultural, agrarian.
OPPOSITES urban.

ruse noun **ploy,** stratagem, tactic, scheme, trick, gambit, dodge, subterfuge, machination, wile; Brit. informal wheeze.

rush verb **1** *she rushed home:* **hurry,** dash, run, race, sprint, bolt, dart, gallop, career,

charge, shoot, hurtle, hare, fly, speed, zoom, scurry, scuttle, scamper, hasten; informal tear, belt, pelt, scoot, zip, whip; Brit. informal bomb. **2** *water rushed along gutters:* **gush**, pour, surge, stream, course, cascade. **3** *the tax was rushed through parliament:* **push**, hurry, hasten, speed, hustle, press, force. **4** *they rushed the cordon of troops:* **attack**, charge, storm.
noun **1** *Tim made a rush for the exit:* **dash**, run, sprint, dart, bolt, charge, scramble. **2** *the lunchtime rush:* **hustle and bustle**, commotion, hubbub, hurly-burly, stir. **3** *a rush for tickets:* **demand**, clamour, call, request, run on. **4** *he was in no rush to leave:* **hurry**, haste, urgency. **5** *I made a sudden rush at him:* **charge**, onslaught, attack, assault.

adjective *a rush job:* **urgent**, high-priority, emergency, hurried, hasty, fast, quick, swift.

rust verb **corrode**, oxidize, tarnish.

rustic adjective **1** *a rustic setting:* **rural**, country, pastoral, bucolic, agricultural, agrarian. **2** *rustic wooden tables:* **plain**, simple, homely, unsophisticated, rough, crude.
OPPOSITES urban, ornate, sophisticated.
noun **peasant**, countryman, countrywoman, bumpkin, yokel, country cousin; N. Amer. informal hillbilly, hayseed, hick; Austral./NZ informal bushy.

ruthless adjective **merciless**, pitiless, cruel, heartless, hard-hearted, cold-hearted, cold-blooded, harsh, callous.
OPPOSITES merciful.

Ss

sabotage noun **vandalism**, wrecking, destruction, damage, obstruction, disruption; Brit. informal a spanner in the works.
verb **vandalize**, wreck, damage, destroy, incapacitate, obstruct, disrupt, spoil, ruin, undermine.

sack noun **bag**, pouch, pocket, pack.
verb (informal) **dismiss**, discharge, lay off, make redundant, let go, throw out; informal fire, give someone the sack; Brit. informal give someone their cards.
■ **the sack** (informal) dismissal, discharge, redundancy; informal the boot, the axe, the heave-ho, the push.

sacred adjective **1** *a sacred place:*

holy, hallowed, blessed, consecrated, sanctified. **2** *sacred music:* **religious**, spiritual, devotional, church, ecclesiastical.
OPPOSITES secular, profane.

sacrifice noun **1** *the sacrifice of animals:* **(ritual) slaughter**, (votive) offering. **2** *the sacrifice of privileges:* **surrender**, giving up, abandonment, renunciation.
verb **1** *two goats were sacrificed:* **offer up**, slaughter. **2** *he sacrificed his principles:* **give up**, abandon, renounce, relinquish, betray. **3** *he sacrificed his life:* **give (up)**, lay down, surrender, forfeit.

sad adjective **1** *we felt sad:*

unhappy, sorrowful, depressed, downcast, miserable, down, despondent, wretched, glum, gloomy, doleful, melancholy, mournful, forlorn, heartbroken; informal blue, down in the mouth, down in the dumps. **2** *a sad story:* **tragic,** unhappy, miserable, wretched, sorry, pitiful, pathetic, heartbreaking, heart-rending. **3** *a sad state of affairs:* **unfortunate,** regrettable, sorry, deplorable, lamentable, pitiful, shameful, disgraceful.
OPPOSITES happy, cheerful, fortunate.

sadden verb depress, dispirit, deject, dishearten, grieve, discourage, upset, get down.

saddle verb **burden,** encumber, lumber, land, impose something on.

sadness noun **unhappiness,** sorrow, dejection, depression, misery, despondency, wretchedness, gloom, gloominess, melancholy.

safe adjective **1** *the jewels are safe in the bank:* **secure,** protected, out of harm's way. **2** *the children are all safe:* **unharmed,** unhurt, uninjured, unscathed, all right, fine, well, in one piece, out of danger. **3** *a safe place:* **secure,** sound, impregnable, invulnerable, secret. **4** *a safe driver:* **cautious,** circumspect, prudent, careful, unadventurous, conservative. **5** *the drug is safe:* **harmless,** innocuous, benign, non-toxic, non-poisonous.
OPPOSITES insecure, dangerous, reckless, harmful.

safeguard noun **protection,** defence, buffer, provision, security, cover, insurance.
verb **protect,** preserve, conserve, save, secure, shield, guard, keep safe.
OPPOSITES jeopardize.

safety noun **1** *the safety of the residents:* **welfare,** well-being, protection, security. **2** *the safety of ferries:* **security,** soundness, dependability, reliability. **3** *the safety of the shore:* **shelter,** sanctuary, refuge.

sag verb **1** *he sagged back in his chair:* **sink,** slump, loll, flop, crumple. **2** *the floors all sag:* **dip,** droop, bulge, bag.

saga noun **1** *Icelandic sagas:* **epic,** legend, (folk) tale, romance, narrative, myth. **2** *the saga of how they met:* **story,** tale, yarn.

sage noun **wise man/woman,** philosopher, scholar, guru, prophet, mystic.

sail verb **1** *we sailed across the Atlantic:* **voyage,** travel, navigate, cruise. **2** *we sail tonight:* **set sail,** put to sea, leave, weigh anchor. **3** *who is sailing the ship?* **steer,** pilot, captain; informal skipper. **4** *clouds were sailing past:* **glide,** drift, float, flow, sweep, skim, coast, flit, scud.

sailor noun **seaman,** seafarer, mariner, yachtsman, yachtswoman, hand, merchant seaman.

sake noun **1** *for the sake of clarity:* **purpose(s),** reason(s). **2** *for her son's sake:* **benefit,** advantage, good, well-being, welfare.

salary noun **pay,** wages, earnings, payment, remuneration, fee(s), stipend, income.

sale noun **1** *the sale of firearms:* **selling,** dealing, trading. **2** *they make a sale every minute:* **deal,** transaction, bargain.

S

OPPOSITES purchase.

salty adjective **salt**, salted, saline, briny, brackish.

salute noun **tribute**, testimonial, homage, honour, celebration (of), acknowledgement (of).
verb **pay tribute to**, pay homage to, honour, celebrate, acknowledge, take one's hat off to.

salvage verb **rescue**, save, recover, retrieve, reclaim.

salvation noun **1** *praying for salvation*: **redemption**, deliverance. **2** *that man was her salvation*: **lifeline**, means of escape, saviour.
OPPOSITES damnation, ruin.

same adjective **1** *we stayed at the same hotel*: **identical**, selfsame, very same. **2** *they had the same symptoms*: **matching**, identical, alike, carbon-copy, twin, indistinguishable, interchangeable, corresponding, equivalent, parallel, like, comparable, similar.
OPPOSITES another, different, dissimilar, varying.
∎ **the same** unchanging, unvarying, unvaried, consistent, uniform.

sample noun **1** *a sample of the fabric*: **specimen**, example, snippet, swatch, taste, taster. **2** *a representative sample*: **cross section**, selection.
verb *we sampled the food*: **try (out)**, taste, test, put to the test, appraise, evaluate; informal check out.
adjective *a sample copy*: **specimen**, test, trial, pilot, dummy.

sanction noun **1** *trade sanctions*: **penalty**, punishment, deterrent, restriction, embargo, ban, prohibition, boycott. **2** *the scheme has the sanction of the court*: **authorization**, consent, leave, permission, authority, dispensation, assent, acquiescence, agreement, approval, endorsement, blessing; informal the thumbs up, the OK.
OPPOSITES reward, prohibition.
verb *the rally was sanctioned by the government*: **authorize**, permit, allow, endorse, approve, accept, back, support; informal OK.
OPPOSITES prohibit.

sanctuary noun **1** *the garden is our sanctuary*: **refuge**, haven, oasis, shelter, retreat, bolt-hole, hideaway. **2** *he was given sanctuary in the embassy*: **safety**, protection, shelter, immunity, asylum. **3** *a bird sanctuary*: **reserve**, park.

sane adjective **1** *he is presumed to be sane*: **of sound mind**, in one's right mind, compos mentis, lucid, rational, balanced, normal; informal all there. **2** *a sane suggestion*: **sensible**, practical, realistic, prudent, reasonable, rational, level-headed.
OPPOSITES mad, foolish.

sap noun *tree sap*: **juice**, secretion, fluid, liquid.
verb *illness sapped his energy*: **erode**, wear away/down, deplete, reduce, lessen, undermine, drain, bleed.

satanic adjective **diabolical**, fiendish, devilish, demonic, ungodly, hellish, infernal, wicked, evil, sinful.
OPPOSITES godly.

satire noun **parody**, burlesque, caricature, irony, lampoon, skit; informal spoof, take-off, send-up.

satirical adjective **mocking**, ironic, sardonic, critical, irreverent, disparaging,

S

satisfaction noun
contentment, content,
pleasure, gratification,
fulfilment, enjoyment,
happiness, pride.

satisfactory adjective **adequate**,
all right, acceptable, good
enough, sufficient, reasonable,
competent, fair, decent,
average, passable, fine, in order,
up to scratch, up to the mark.
OPPOSITES unsatisfactory.

satisfy verb **1** *a chance to satisfy
his lust:* **fulfil,** gratify, meet,
fill, indulge, appease, assuage,
quench, slake, satiate. **2** *she
satisfied herself that it was an
accident:* **convince,** assure,
reassure. **3** *products which
satisfy EC law:* **comply with,**
meet, fulfil, answer, conform
to, measure up to, come up to.
OPPOSITES frustrate.

saturate verb **1** *rain had
saturated the ground:* **soak,**
drench, waterlog. **2** *the
company has saturated the
market:* **flood,** glut, oversupply,
overfill, overload.

saturated adjective **1** *his
trousers were saturated:*
soaked, soaking (wet), wet
through, sopping (wet),
sodden, dripping, wringing wet,
drenched, soaked to the skin.
2 *the saturated pitch:*
waterlogged, flooded, boggy,
awash.
OPPOSITES dry.

sauce noun **relish,** condiment,
ketchup, dip, dressing, jus,
coulis, gravy.

savage adjective **1** *savage dogs:*
ferocious, fierce, vicious, wild,
feral. **2** *a savage assault:*
vicious, brutal, cruel, sadistic,
ferocious, fierce, violent. **3** *a
savage attack on free trade:*

fierce, blistering, scathing,
searing, stinging, devastating,
withering, virulent, vitriolic.
OPPOSITES tame, mild.
noun *she described her assailants
as savages:* **brute,** beast,
monster, barbarian, sadist,
animal.
verb **1** *savaged by a dog:* **maul,**
attack, lacerate, claw, bite.
2 *critics savaged the film:*
criticize, attack, lambaste,
condemn, denounce, pillory,
revile; informal pan; Brit. informal
slate; N. Amer. informal trash.

save verb **1** *the captain was
saved by his crew:* **rescue,** set
free, free, liberate, deliver.
2 *the house was saved from
demolition:* **preserve,** keep,
protect, safeguard, salvage,
retrieve, reclaim, rescue. **3** *start
saving old newspapers:* **put/set
aside,** put by/to one side, keep,
retain, store, hoard; informal
squirrel away. **4** *asking her
saved a lot of trouble:* **prevent,**
avoid, forestall, spare, stop,
obviate, avert.

saving noun **1** *a considerable
saving in cost:* **reduction,** cut,
decrease, economy. **2** (**savings**)
nest egg, capital, assets, funds,
resources, reserves.

saviour noun **rescuer,** liberator,
deliverer, champion, protector,
redeemer.

savour verb *she savoured every
moment:* **relish,** enjoy,
appreciate, delight in, revel in,
luxuriate in.
noun *the subtle savour of wood
smoke:* **smell,** aroma, fragrance,
scent, perfume, bouquet, taste,
flavour, tang, smack.

say verb **1** *he said her name:*
speak, utter, voice, pronounce.
2 *'I must go,' she said:* **declare,**
state, announce, remark,

disrespectful.

S

observe, mention, comment, note, add. **3** *they said a prayer:* **recite,** repeat, utter, deliver, perform. **4** *her watch said one twenty:* **indicate,** show, read.
noun *don't I have any say in the matter?* **influence,** sway, weight, voice, input.

saying noun proverb, maxim, aphorism, axiom, expression, phrase, formula, slogan, catchphrase.

scale noun **1** *opposite ends of the social scale:* **hierarchy,** ladder, ranking, pecking order, order, spectrum. **2** *the scale of the map:* **ratio,** proportion. **3** *the scale of the disaster:* **extent,** size, scope, magnitude, dimensions, range, breadth, degree.
verb *thieves scaled the fence:* **climb,** ascend, clamber up, scramble up, shin (up), mount; N. Amer. shinny (up).

scan verb **1** *Adam scanned the horizon:* **study,** examine, scrutinize, inspect, survey, search, scour, sweep, watch. **2** *I scanned the papers:* **glance through,** look through, have a look at, run one's eye over, cast one's eye over, flick through, browse through.
noun **1** *a quick scan through the report:* **glance,** look, flick, browse. **2** *a brain scan:* **examination,** screening.

scandal noun **1** *a scandal that led him to resign:* **affair,** issue, incident, outrage, skeleton in the cupboard; informal ...-gate. **2** *it's a scandal:* **disgrace,** outrage, (crying) shame, sin. **3** *a name tarnished by scandal:* **gossip,** rumour(s), slander, libel, aspersions, muckraking; informal dirt.

scant adjective **little,** little or no,

minimal, limited, negligible, meagre, insufficient, inadequate.
OPPOSITES abundant, ample.

scapegoat noun whipping boy, Aunt Sally; informal fall guy; N. Amer. informal patsy.

scar noun **1** *the scar on his arm:* **mark,** blemish, disfiguration, discoloration, pockmark, pit, lesion, stitches. **2** *psychological scars:* **trauma,** damage, injury.
verb *scarred for life:* **disfigure,** mark, blemish.

scarce adjective **1** *food was scarce:* **in short supply,** scant, meagre, sparse, hard to come by. **2** *wading birds are now scarce:* **rare,** few and far between, thin on the ground.
OPPOSITES plentiful.

scarcely adverb **1** *she could scarcely hear him:* **hardly,** barely, only just. **2** *I scarcely see her:* **rarely,** seldom, infrequently, not often, hardly ever; informal once in a blue moon. **3** *this could scarcely be an accident:* **surely not,** not, hardly.
OPPOSITES often.

scare verb *stop it, you're scaring me:* **frighten,** startle, alarm, terrify, unnerve, worry, intimidate, terrorize, cow; informal freak out; Brit. informal put the wind up; N. Amer. informal spook.
noun *you gave me a scare:* **fright,** shock, start, turn, jump.

scared adjective **frightened,** afraid, fearful, nervous, panicky, terrified; informal in a cold sweat; N. Amer. informal spooked.

scary adjective (informal) **frightening,** terrifying, hair-raising, spine-chilling, blood-curdling, eerie, sinister; informal

S

scatter | scheming

510

creepy, spine-tingling, spooky.

scatter verb **1** *scatter the seeds evenly:* **spread,** sprinkle, distribute, strew, disseminate, sow. **2** *the crowd scattered:* **disperse,** break up, disband, separate, dissolve. **3** *the floor was scattered with books:* **cover,** dot, sprinkle, spot, pepper, litter.
OPPOSITES gather, assemble.

scenario noun **1** *Walt wrote scenarios for various studios:* **plot,** outline, storyline, framework, screenplay, script. **2** *consider every possible scenario:* **situation,** chain of events, course of events.

scene noun **1** *the scene of the accident:* **location,** site, place, position. **2** *the scene is London in the 1890s:* **background,** setting, context, milieu, backdrop. **3** *scenes of violence:* **incident,** event, episode, happening. **4** *an impressive mountain scene:* **view,** vista, outlook, panorama, landscape, scenery. **5** *she made a scene:* **fuss,** exhibition of oneself, performance, tantrum, commotion, disturbance, row; informal to-do; Brit. informal carry-on. **6** *the political scene:* **arena,** stage, sphere, world, milieu, realm. **7** *a scene from a movie:* **clip,** section, segment, part, sequence, extract.

scenery noun **1** *beautiful scenery:* **landscape,** countryside, country, terrain, setting, surroundings, environment. **2** *scenery and costumes:* **set,** setting, backdrop.

scenic adjective **picturesque,** pretty, attractive, beautiful, charming, impressive, striking, spectacular, breathtaking, panoramic.

scent noun **1** *the scent of freshly cut hay:* **smell,** fragrance, aroma, perfume, savour, odour. **2** *a bottle of scent:* **perfume,** fragrance, eau de toilette, eau de cologne. **3** *the hounds picked up the scent:* **spoor,** trail, track.
verb *sharks soon scent the blood:* **smell,** nose out, detect, pick up, sense.

scented adjective **perfumed,** fragranced, fragrant, sweet-smelling, aromatic.

sceptic noun **cynic,** doubter, unbeliever, doubting Thomas.

sceptical adjective **dubious,** doubtful, doubting, cynical, distrustful, suspicious, disbelieving, unconvinced.
OPPOSITES certain, convinced.

scepticism noun **doubt,** a pinch of salt, disbelief, cynicism, distrust, suspicion, incredulity.

schedule noun **1** *our production schedule:* **plan,** programme, timetable, scheme. **2** *I have a busy schedule:* **timetable,** agenda, diary, calendar, itinerary.
verb *a meeting has been scheduled:* **arrange,** organize, plan, programme, timetable, set up, line up; N. Amer. slate.

scheme noun **1** *fund-raising schemes:* **plan,** project, programme, strategy, stratagem, tactic; Brit. informal wheeze. **2** *his schemes and plots:* **plot,** intrigue, conspiracy, ruse, ploy, stratagem, manoeuvre, subterfuge, machinations; informal racket, scam.
verb *he schemed endlessly:* **plot,** conspire, intrigue, connive, manoeuvre, plan.

scheming adjective **cunning,** crafty, calculating, devious,

conniving, wily, sly, tricky, artful.
OPPOSITES ingenuous, honest.

scholar noun academic, intellectual, learned person, man/woman of letters, authority, expert; informal egghead; N. Amer. informal pointy-head.

scholarly adjective learned, educated, erudite, academic, well read, intellectual, literary, highbrow.
OPPOSITES uneducated, illiterate.

scholarship noun 1 a centre of scholarship: learning, knowledge, erudition, education, academic study. 2 a scholarship of £2,000: grant, award, endowment; Brit. bursary.

school noun 1 the village school: college, academy, alma mater. 2 the university's School of English: department, faculty, division. 3 the Columbia school of history: tradition, approach, style, way of thinking, persuasion, creed, credo, doctrine, belief, opinion, point of view.
verb he schooled her in horsemanship: train, teach, tutor, coach, instruct, drill.

science noun the science of criminology: subject, discipline, field, branch of knowledge, body of knowledge, area of study.

scientific adjective 1 scientific research: technological, technical, evidence-based, empirical. 2 a more scientific approach: systematic, methodical, organized, ordered, rigorous, exact, precise, accurate, mathematical.

scoff verb sneer, jeer, laugh; (scoff at) mock, deride, ridicule, dismiss, belittle; informal pooh-pooh.

scoop noun a measuring scoop: spoon, ladle, dipper.
■ scoop out 1 hollow out, gouge out, dig, excavate. 2 remove, take out, spoon out, scrape out.
■ scoop up pick up, gather up, lift, take up, snatch up, grab.

scope noun 1 the scope of the investigation: extent, range, breadth, reach, sweep, span, area, sphere, realm, compass, orbit, ambit, terms of reference, remit. 2 the scope for change is limited: opportunity, freedom, latitude, leeway, capacity, room (to manoeuvre).

scorch verb 1 trees were scorched by the fire: burn, sear, singe, char, blacken, discolour. 2 grass scorched by the sun: dry up, parch, wither, shrivel.

scorching adjective hot, red-hot, blazing, flaming, fiery, burning, blistering, searing; informal boiling, baking, sizzling.
OPPOSITES freezing, mild.

score noun 1 the final score was 4–3: result, outcome, total, tally, count. 2 an IQ score of 161: rating, grade, mark, percentage.
verb 1 he's scored 13 goals this season: get, gain, chalk up, achieve, make, record, rack up, notch up; informal bag, knock up. 2 the piece was scored for horn and strings: arrange, set, adapt, orchestrate, write, compose. 3 score the wood in criss-cross patterns: scratch, cut, notch, incise, scrape, nick, gouge.
■ score something out/through cross out, strike out, delete, put a line through, obliterate.

scorn noun the scorn in his voice: contempt, derision, disdain, mockery, sneering.

S

OPPOSITES admiration, respect.
verb **1** *critics scorned the talks:* **deride**, treat with contempt, mock, scoff at, sneer at, jeer at, laugh at. **2** *they scorned my offers of help:* **spurn**, rebuff, reject, ignore, shun, snub.
OPPOSITES admire, respect.

scour[1] verb *the saucepan needs scouring:* **scrub**, rub, clean, polish, buff, shine, burnish, grind, abrade.

scour[2] verb *Christine scoured the shops:* **search**, comb, hunt through, rummage through, look high and low in, ransack, turn upside-down.

scout noun **1** *scouts reported that the Romans were advancing:* **lookout**, outrider, spy. **2** *a lengthy scout round the area:* **reconnaissance**, reconnoitre, survey, exploration, search; informal recce; Brit. informal shufti.
verb **1** *I scouted around for some logs:* **search**, look, hunt, ferret around, root around. **2** *a patrol was sent to scout out the area:* **reconnoitre**, explore, inspect, investigate, spy out, survey, scan, study; informal check out, case.

scramble verb **1** *we scrambled over the boulders:* **clamber**, climb, crawl, claw one's way, scrabble, struggle; N. Amer. shinny. **2** *the speaker can scramble the words:* **muddle**, confuse, mix up, jumble (up), disarrange, disorganize, disorder, disturb, mess up.
noun **1** *a short scramble over the rocks:* **clamber**, climb. **2** *the scramble for a seat:* **struggle**, jostle, scrimmage, scuffle, tussle, free-for-all, jockeying, competition, race.

scrap noun **1** *a scrap of paper:* **fragment**, piece, bit, snippet,

shred, oddment, remnant. **2** *there wasn't a scrap of evidence:* **bit**, shred, speck, iota, particle, ounce, jot. **3** *the foxes ate all our scraps:* **leftovers**, crumbs, remains, remnants, residue. **4** *a sculpture made from scrap:* **waste**, rubbish, refuse, debris; N. Amer. garbage, trash; informal junk.
verb **1** *old computers are scrapped:* **throw away**, throw out, dispose of, get rid of, discard, dispense with, bin, decommission, break up, demolish; informal chuck (away/out), ditch, dump, junk; Brit. informal get shot of; N. Amer. informal trash. **2** *the scheme is to be scrapped:* **abandon**, drop, abolish, withdraw, do away with, put an end to, cancel, axe; informal ditch, dump, junk.
OPPOSITES keep, preserve.

scrape verb **1** *we scraped all the paint off the windows:* **rub**, scratch, scour, grind, sand, sandpaper, abrade, file. **2** *their boots scraped along the floor:* **grate**, creak, rasp, scratch. **3** *Ellen scraped her shins on the wall:* **graze**, scratch, scuff, rasp, skin, cut, lacerate, bark, chafe.
noun **1** *the scrape of her key in the lock:* **grating**, creaking, rasp, scratch. **2** *a long scrape on his shin:* **graze**, scratch, abrasion, cut, laceration, wound.

scratch verb **1** *the paintwork was scratched:* **score**, abrade, scrape, scuff. **2** *thorns scratched her skin:* **graze**, scrape, skin, cut, lacerate, bark, chafe.
noun **1** *a scratch on the paintwork:* **score**, mark, line, scrape. **2** *he had scratches on his cheek:* **graze**, scrape, abrasion, cut, laceration.
■ **up to scratch** good enough, up to the mark, up to standard, up

scream verb & noun **shriek,** screech, yell, howl, bawl, yelp, squeal, wail, squawk.

screen noun **1** *he dressed behind the screen:* **partition,** divider, windbreak. **2** *a computer with a 15-inch screen:* **display,** monitor, visual display unit. **3** *a screen to keep out mosquitoes:* **mesh,** net, netting. **4** *the hedge acts as a screen against the wind:* **buffer,** protection, shield, shelter, guard.
verb **1** *the end of the hall had been screened off:* **partition,** divide, separate, curtain. **2** *the cottage was screened by the trees:* **conceal,** hide, veil, shield, shelter, shade, protect. **3** *all blood is screened for the virus:* **check,** test, examine, investigate, vet; informal check out. **4** *the programme is screened on Thursday:* **show,** broadcast, transmit, televise, put out, air.

screw noun **1** *four steel screws:* **bolt,** fastener. **2** *the ship's twin screws:* **propeller,** rotor.
verb **1** *he screwed the lid back on the jar:* **tighten,** turn, twist, wind. **2** *the bracket was screwed in place:* **fasten,** secure, fix, attach. **3** (informal) *she intended to screw more money out of them:* **extort,** force, extract, wrest, wring, squeeze; informal bleed.
■ **screw something up**
1 *Christina screwed up her face:* **wrinkle,** pucker, crumple, crease, furrow, contort, distort, twist. **2** (informal) *they'll screw up the whole thing:* **wreck,** ruin, destroy, damage, spoil, mess up; informal louse up, foul up; Brit. informal cock up.

scribble verb *he scribbled a note:* **scrawl,** scratch, dash off, jot (down), doodle, sketch.
noun *I can't read this scribble:* **scrawl,** squiggle(s), jottings, doodle, doodlings.

script noun **1** *her neat, tidy script:* **handwriting,** writing, hand. **2** *the script of the play:* **text,** screenplay, libretto, score, lines, dialogue, words.

scrub verb **1** *he scrubbed the kitchen floor:* **brush,** scour, rub, clean, cleanse, wash. **2** (informal) *the plans were scrubbed:* **abandon,** scrap, drop, cancel, call off, axe; informal ditch, dump, junk.

scrutinize verb **examine,** inspect, survey, study, look at, peruse, investigate, explore, probe, enquire into, go into, check.

sculpture noun **carving,** statue, statuette, figure, figurine, effigy, bust, head, model.

sea noun **1** **ocean,** waves; informal the drink; Brit. informal the briny; literary the deep. **2** *a sea of roofs:* **expanse,** stretch, area, tract, sweep, carpet, mass.
OPPOSITES land.
adjective *a sea story:* **marine,** ocean, oceanic, maritime, naval, nautical.
■ **at sea** **confused,** perplexed, puzzled, baffled, mystified, bemused, bewildered, nonplussed, dumbfounded, at a loss, lost; informal flummoxed, fazed.

seal noun *the seal round the bath:* **sealant,** adhesive, mastic, joint.
verb **1** *seal each bottle while hot:* **stop up,** seal up, cork, stopper, plug. **2** *they sealed the bargain:* **clinch,** secure, settle, conclude, complete, finalize, confirm.

S

■ **seal something off** close off, shut off, cordon off, fence off, isolate.

seam noun **1** *the seam was coming undone:* **join,** stitching, joint. **2** *a seam of coal:* **layer,** stratum, vein, lode.

seaman noun **sailor,** seafarer, mariner, boatman, hand, merchant seaman.
OPPOSITES landlubber.

sear verb **1** *the heat of the blast seared his face:* **scorch,** burn, singe, char. **2** *sear the meat:* **flash-fry,** seal, brown.

search verb **1** *I searched for the key:* **hunt,** look, seek, forage, fish, look high and low, ferret, root, rummage. **2** *he searched the house:* **look through,** scour, go through, sift through, comb, turn upside down; Austral./NZ informal fossick through. **3** *the guards searched him:* **examine,** inspect, check, frisk.
noun *we continued our search:* **hunt,** look, quest, examination, exploration.

searching adjective **penetrating,** piercing, probing, keen, shrewd, sharp, intent.

seaside noun **coast,** shore, seashore, beach, sand, sands.

season noun *the seasons of the year:* **period,** time, time of year, spell, term.
verb *a well seasoned dish:* **flavour,** add salt/pepper to, spice.

seasoned adjective **experienced,** practised, well versed, knowledgeable, established, veteran, hardened.
OPPOSITES inexperienced.

seasoning noun **flavouring,** salt and pepper, herbs, spices, condiments.

seat noun **1** *a wooden seat:* **chair,** bench, stool; (**seats**) seating.

2 *the seat of government:* **headquarters,** base, centre, nerve centre, hub, heart, location, site. **3** *the family's country seat:* **residence,** ancestral home, mansion.
verb **1** *they seated themselves round the table:* **position,** put, place, ensconce, install, settle. **2** *the hall seats 500:* **have room for,** contain, take, sit, hold, accommodate.

second¹ adjective **1** *the second day of the trial:* **next,** following, subsequent. **2** *a second pair of glasses:* **additional,** extra, alternative, another, spare, backup; N. Amer. alternate. **3** *second prize:* **secondary,** subordinate, subsidiary, lesser, inferior.
OPPOSITES first.
noun *Eva had been working as his second:* **assistant,** attendant, helper, aide, supporter, auxiliary, second in command, number two, deputy, understudy; informal sidekick.
verb *George seconded the motion:* **support,** vote for, back, approve, endorse.

second² noun *I'll be gone for a second:* **moment,** bit, little while, instant, flash; informal sec, jiffy; Brit. informal mo, tick.

secondary adjective **1** *a secondary issue:* **less important,** subordinate, lesser, minor, peripheral, incidental, subsidiary. **2** *secondary infections:* **accompanying,** attendant, concomitant, consequential, resulting, resultant.
OPPOSITES primary, main.

second-hand adjective **1** *second-hand clothes:* **used,** old, worn, pre-owned, nearly new, handed-down, hand-me-down, cast-off.

S

2 *second-hand information:* **indirect**.
OPPOSITES new, direct.
adverb *I heard this second-hand:* **indirectly**; informal on the grapevine.
OPPOSITES directly.

secondly adverb furthermore, also, moreover, second, in the second place, next.

secrecy noun confidentiality, privacy, mystery, concealment, stealth.

secret adjective **1** *a secret plan:* **confidential**, top secret, classified, undisclosed, unknown, private, under wraps; informal hush-hush. **2** *a secret drawer in the table:* **hidden**, concealed, disguised. **3** *a secret campaign:* **clandestine**, covert, undercover, underground, surreptitious, cloak-and-dagger; informal hush-hush. **4** *a secret code:* **cryptic**, mysterious, abstruse, recondite, arcane, esoteric.
OPPOSITES public, open.
noun **1** *it's a secret:* **confidential matter**, confidence, skeleton in the cupboard. **2** *the secrets of the universe:* **mystery**, enigma. **3** *the secret of their success:* **recipe**, magic formula, blueprint, key, answer, solution.
■ **in secret** secretly, in private, behind closed doors, under cover, furtively, stealthily, on the quiet, covertly.

secretive adjective **uncommunicative**, secret, unforthcoming, playing one's cards close to one's chest, reticent, tight-lipped.
OPPOSITES open, communicative.

secretly adverb in secret, in private, privately, behind closed doors, under cover, furtively, stealthily, on the quiet, covertly.

sect noun group, cult, denomination, order, splinter group, faction, camp.

section noun **1** *the separate sections of the box:* **part**, bit, portion, segment, compartment, module. **2** *the last section of the questionnaire:* **passage**, subsection, chapter, subdivision, clause. **3** *the reference section of the library:* **department**, area, division.

sector noun **1** *every sector of the industry:* **part**, branch, arm, division, area, department, field, sphere. **2** *the north-eastern sector of the town:* **district**, quarter, section, zone, region, area, belt.

secular adjective non-religious, lay, temporal, civil, worldly, earthly, profane.
OPPOSITES sacred, religious.

secure adjective **1** *check that all bolts are secure:* **fastened**, fixed, secured, done up, closed, shut, locked. **2** *a place where children feel secure:* **safe**, protected, safe and sound, out of harm's way, in safe hands, invulnerable, at ease, unworried, relaxed, happy, confident. **3** *a secure future:* **certain**, assured, reliable, dependable, settled, fixed.
OPPOSITES loose, vulnerable, uncertain.
verb **1** *secure the handle to the main body:* **fix**, attach, fasten, affix, connect, couple. **2** *the doors had been secured:* **fasten**, close, shut, lock, bolt, chain, seal. **3** *the division secured a major contract:* **obtain**, acquire, gain, get; informal land.

security noun **1** *the security of our citizens:* **safety**, protection.

S

2 *he could give her security:* **peace of mind,** stability, certainty. **3** *security at the court was tight:* **safety measures,** safeguards, surveillance, defence, protection, policing. **4** *additional security for your loan:* **guarantee,** collateral, surety, pledge, bond.
OPPOSITES insecurity.

sediment noun dregs, grounds, lees, residue, deposit, silt.

seduce verb **1** *customers are seduced by the advertising:* **attract,** allure, lure, tempt, entice, beguile, inveigle, manipulate. **2** *he tried to seduce her:* **have one's (wicked) way with,** take advantage of.

seductive adjective **tempting,** inviting, enticing, alluring, beguiling, attractive.

see verb **1** *he saw her in the street:* **discern,** spot, notice, catch sight of, glimpse, make out, pick out, spy; informal clap eyes on, clock; literary behold. **2** *I saw a programme about it:* **watch,** look at, view, catch. **3** *would you like to see the house?* **inspect,** view, look round, tour, survey, examine, scrutinize. **4** *I finally saw what she meant:* **understand,** grasp, comprehend, follow, realize, appreciate, recognize, work out, fathom; informal get, latch on to, tumble to, figure out; Brit. informal twig, suss (out). **5** *I must see what Victor is up to:* **find out,** discover, learn, ascertain, determine, establish. **6** *see that no harm comes to him:* **ensure,** make sure/certain, see to it, take care, mind. **7** *I see trouble ahead:* **foresee,** predict, forecast, prophesy, anticipate. **8** *later, I saw him in town:* **encounter,** meet, run into, come across, stumble across, happen on, chance on; informal bump into. **9** *you'd better see a doctor:* **consult,** confer with, talk to, have recourse to, call in, turn to. **10** *he's seeing someone else now:* **go out with,** date, take out, be involved with; informal go steady with; dated court.

■ **see to** attend to, deal with, see about, take care of, look after, sort out, organize, arrange.

seed noun **pip,** stone, kernel.

seek verb **1** *he is seeking work:* **search for,** try to find, look for, be after, hunt for. **2** *he sought help from a motorist:* **ask for,** request, solicit, call for, appeal for, apply for. **3** *we constantly seek to improve the service:* **try,** attempt, endeavour, strive, work, do one's best.

seem verb **appear (to be),** have the appearance/air of being, give the impression of being, look, sound, come across as, strike someone as.

seep verb **ooze,** trickle, exude, drip, dribble, flow, leak, drain, bleed, filter, percolate, soak.

seethe verb **1** *the water seethed with fish:* **teem,** swarm, boil, swirl, churn, surge, bubble, heave. **2** *I seethed at the injustice of it all:* **be angry,** be furious, be enraged, be incensed, be beside oneself, boil, rage, rant, fume; informal be livid, foam at the mouth.

segment noun **piece,** bit, section, part, portion, division, slice, wedge.

segregate verb **separate,** set apart, keep apart, isolate, quarantine, partition, divide, discriminate against.
OPPOSITES integrate.

seize verb **1** *she seized the microphone:* **grab,** grasp, snatch, take hold of. **2** *rebels seized the air base:* **capture,** take, overrun, occupy, conquer, take over. **3** *the drugs were seized by customs:* **confiscate,** impound, commandeer, requisition, appropriate, expropriate. **4** *terrorists seized his wife:* **kidnap,** abduct, take captive, take prisoner, take hostage; informal snatch.
OPPOSITES liberate, relinquish, release.

seizure noun **1** *Napoleon's seizure of Spain:* **capture,** takeover, annexation, invasion, occupation. **2** *the seizure of banned goods:* **confiscation,** appropriation, expropriation. **3** *the seizure of UN staff:* **kidnap,** abduction. **4** *the baby suffered a seizure:* **convulsion,** fit, spasm, paroxysm.
OPPOSITES liberation, release.

seldom adverb **rarely,** infrequently, hardly (ever), scarcely (ever); informal once in a blue moon.
OPPOSITES often.

select verb *select the correct tool for the job:* **choose,** pick (out), single out, sort out, take, adopt.
▸ adjective **1** *a small, select group:* **choice,** hand-picked, elite; informal top-flight. **2** *a very select area:* **exclusive,** privileged, wealthy; informal posh.
OPPOSITES inferior.

selection noun **1** *Jim made his selection:* **choice,** pick, option, preference. **2** *a wide selection of dishes:* **range,** array, diversity, variety, assortment, mixture. **3** *a selection of his poems:* **anthology,** assortment, collection, assemblage, miscellany, medley.

selective adjective **discerning,** discriminating, exacting, demanding, particular; informal choosy, picky.
OPPOSITES indiscriminate.

selfish adjective **egocentric,** egotistic, self-centred, self-absorbed, self-obsessed, wrapped up in oneself, mean, greedy; informal looking after number one.
OPPOSITES altruistic.

sell verb **1** *they are selling their house:* **put up for sale,** put on the market, auction (off), trade in. **2** *he sells cakes:* **trade in,** deal in, traffic in, peddle, retail, market.
OPPOSITES buy.

seller noun **vendor,** dealer, retailer, trader, merchant, agent, hawker, pedlar, purveyor, supplier, stockist.
OPPOSITES buyer.

send verb **1** *they sent a message to HQ:* **dispatch,** post, mail, consign, forward, transmit, convey, communicate, broadcast. **2** *the pump sent out a jet of petrol:* **propel,** project, eject, deliver, discharge, spout, fire, shoot, release, fling, cast. **3** *it's enough to send one mad:* **make,** drive, turn.
OPPOSITES receive.
■ **send someone down** (informal) send to prison, imprison, jail, incarcerate, lock up, confine, detain, intern; informal put away; Brit. informal bang up. ■ **send for** call, summon, ask for, request, order. ■ **send someone off** (Sport) order off, dismiss, show the red card; informal red-card, send for an early bath. ■ **send someone/something up** (informal) satirize, ridicule, make fun of, parody, lampoon, mock, caricature,

S

imitate, ape; informal take off, spoof, take the mickey out of.

send-off noun farewell, goodbye, adieu, leave-taking, funeral.
OPPOSITES welcome.

senior adjective **1** *senior school pupils:* older, elder. **2** *a senior officer:* superior, higher-ranking, more important; N. Amer. ranking.
OPPOSITES junior, subordinate.

sensation noun **1** *a sensation of heaviness:* feeling, sense, perception, impression. **2** *she caused a sensation:* commotion, stir, uproar, furore, scandal, impact; informal splash, to-do.

sensational adjective **1** *a sensational murder trial:* shocking, scandalous, appalling, fascinating, thrilling, interesting, dramatic, momentous, historic, newsworthy. **2** *sensational stories:* overdramatized, melodramatic, exaggerated, sensationalist, graphic, explicit, lurid; informal shock-horror, juicy. **3** (informal) *she looked sensational:* gorgeous, stunning, wonderful, superb, excellent, first-class; informal great, terrific, tremendous, fantastic, fabulous, out of this world; Brit. informal smashing.
OPPOSITES dull, understated, unremarkable.

sense noun **1** *the sense of touch:* feeling, faculty, awareness, sensation, recognition, perception. **2** *a sense of humour:* appreciation, awareness, understanding, comprehension. **3** *she had the sense to leave:* wisdom, common sense, wit, intelligence, judgement, reason, brain(s); informal gumption,

nous, horse sense, savvy; Brit. informal loaf, common; N. Amer. informal smarts. **4** *I can't see the sense in this:* purpose, point, use, value, advantage, benefit. **5** *different senses of the word:* meaning, definition, nuance, drift, gist, thrust, tenor, message.
OPPOSITES stupidity.
verb *she sensed their hostility:* detect, feel, observe, notice, recognize, pick up, be aware of, distinguish, make out; informal catch on to.

senseless adjective pointless, futile, useless, needless, meaningless, absurd, foolish, insane, stupid, idiotic, mindless, illogical.
OPPOSITES wise.

sensible adjective practical, realistic, responsible, reasonable, commonsensical, rational, logical, sound, no-nonsense, level-headed, down-to-earth, wise.
OPPOSITES foolish.

sensitive adjective **1** *she's sensitive to changes in temperature:* responsive to, reactive to, sensitized to, aware of, conscious of, susceptible to, affected by, vulnerable to. **2** *sensitive skin:* delicate, fragile, tender, sore. **3** *the matter needs sensitive handling:* tactful, careful, thoughtful, diplomatic, delicate, subtle, kid-glove. **4** *he's sensitive about his bald patch:* touchy, oversensitive, hypersensitive, easily offended, thin-skinned, defensive, paranoid, neurotic. **5** *a sensitive issue:* difficult, delicate, tricky, awkward, problematic, ticklish, controversial, emotive.
OPPOSITES impervious, resilient,

clumsy, thick-skinned, uncontroversial.

sensitivity noun 1 *the sensitivity of the skin:* **responsiveness,** sensitiveness, reactivity, susceptibility. 2 *the job calls for sensitivity:* **tact,** diplomacy, delicacy, subtlety, understanding. 3 *her sensitivity on the subject:* **touchiness,** oversensitivity, hypersensitivity, defensiveness. 4 *the sensitivity of the issue:* **delicacy,** trickiness, awkwardness, ticklishness.

sensual adjective 1 *sensual pleasure:* **physical,** carnal, bodily, fleshly, animal. 2 *a very sensual woman:* **passionate,** sexual, physical, tactile, hedonistic.
OPPOSITES spiritual, passionless.

sensuous adjective 1 *big sensuous canvases:* **rich,** sumptuous, luxurious. 2 *sensuous lips:* **voluptuous,** sexy, seductive, luscious, lush, ripe.

sentence noun 1 *the judge delivered his sentence:* **judgement,** ruling, decision, verdict. 2 *a long sentence:* **punishment,** prison term; informal time, stretch.
verb *they were sentenced to death:* **condemn,** doom, punish, convict.

sentiment noun 1 *the comments echo my own sentiments:* **view,** feeling, attitude, thought, opinion, belief. 2 *there's no room for sentiment:* **sentimentality,** emotion, softness; informal schmaltz, slush; Brit. informal soppiness; N. Amer. informal sappiness.

sentimental adjective 1 *she kept the vase for sentimental reasons:* **nostalgic,** emotional.

2 *the film is too sentimental:* **mawkish,** overemotional, cloying, sickly, romantic; Brit. twee; informal slushy, schmaltzy, corny; Brit. informal soppy; N. Amer. informal sappy.
OPPOSITES practical, gritty.

separate adjective 1 *his personal life was separate from his job:* **unconnected,** unrelated, different, distinct, discrete, detached, divorced, disconnected, independent. 2 *the infirmary was separate from the school:* **set apart,** detached, cut off, segregated, isolated, free-standing, self-contained.
OPPOSITES linked, attached.
verb 1 *they separated the two youths:* **split (up),** break up, part, pull apart. 2 *the connectors can be separated:* **disconnect,** detach, disengage, uncouple, split. 3 *the wall that separated the two estates:* **partition,** divide, keep apart. 4 *the south aisle was separated off:* **isolate,** partition off, section off, close off, shut off, cordon off. 5 *they separated at the airport:* **part (company),** go their separate ways, split up, disperse, scatter. 6 *the road separated:* **fork,** divide, branch, diverge. 7 *her parents separated:* **split up,** break up, part, divorce.
OPPOSITES unite, join, link, meet, merge, marry.

separately adverb **individually,** one by one, one at a time, singly, severally, apart, independently, alone, by oneself, on one's own.

separation noun 1 *the separation of the two companies:* **disconnection,** splitting, division, breaking up.

S

2 *her parents' separation:* **break-up**, split, estrangement, divorce; Brit. informal bust-up.

sequel noun **continuation**, further episode, follow-up.

sequence noun **1** *the sequence of events:* **succession,** order, course, series, chain, train, progression, chronology, pattern, flow. **2** *a sequence from his film:* **excerpt,** clip, extract, section.

series noun **succession,** sequence, string, chain, run, round, spate, wave, rash, course, cycle, row.

serious adjective **1** *a serious expression:* **solemn,** earnest, grave, sombre, unsmiling, stern, grim, humourless, stony. **2** *serious decisions:* **important,** significant, momentous, weighty, far-reaching. **3** *serious consideration:* **careful,** detailed, in-depth. **4** *a serious play:* **intellectual,** highbrow, heavyweight, deep, profound, literary, learned, scholarly; informal heavy. **5** *serious injuries:* **severe,** grave, bad, critical, acute, terrible, dire, dangerous. **6** *we're serious about equality:* **sincere,** earnest, genuine, wholehearted, committed, resolute, determined.
OPPOSITES light-hearted, trivial, superficial, lowbrow, minor, half-hearted.

seriously adverb **1** *Faye nodded seriously:* **solemnly,** earnestly, gravely, sombrely, sternly, grimly, humourlessly. **2** *seriously injured:* **severely,** gravely, badly, critically, dangerously. **3** *seriously, I'm very pleased:* **really,** honestly, truthfully, truly, actually; Brit. informal straight up.

sermon noun **address,** homily, talk, speech, lecture.

servant noun **attendant,** domestic, maid, housemaid, retainer, flunkey, minion, slave.

serve verb **1** *they served their masters faithfully:* **work for,** obey, do the bidding of. **2** *this job serves the community:* **benefit,** help, assist, aid, make a contribution to, do one's bit for. **3** *he served his apprenticeship in Scotland:* **carry out,** perform, do, fulfil, complete, discharge, spend. **4** *serve the soup hot:* **present,** offer, give out, distribute, dish up, provide, supply. **5** *she served another customer:* **attend to,** deal with, see to, assist, help, look after. **6** *a saucer serving as an ashtray:* **act,** function, work, perform. **7** *official forms will serve in most cases:* **suffice,** do, be good enough, be adequate, fit/fill the bill, suit.

service noun **1** *conditions of service:* **work,** employment, labour. **2** *he has done us a service:* **favour,** kindness, good turn, helping hand. **3** *the service was excellent:* **waiting,** serving, attendance, attention. **4** *products which give reliable service:* **use,** usage, functioning, operation. **5** *he took his car in for a service:* **overhaul,** check, maintenance. **6** *a marriage service:* **ceremony,** ritual, rite, liturgy. **7** *a range of local services:* **amenity,** facility, resource, utility. **8** *soldiers leaving the services:* **(armed) forces,** military, army, navy, air force.
verb *the appliances are serviced regularly:* **overhaul,** check, go over, maintain.

session noun **1** *a session of the committee:* **meeting,** sitting, assembly, conclave; N. Amer. & NZ caucus. **2** *this parliamentary session:* **period**, time, term, year.

set¹ verb **1** *Beth set the bag on the table:* **put (down)**, place, lay, deposit, position, settle, leave, stand, plant; informal stick, dump, park, plonk, pop. **2** *the fence is set in concrete:* **fix**, embed, insert, mount. **3** *a ring set with precious stones:* **adorn**, ornament, decorate, embellish. **4** *I'll set the table:* **lay**, prepare, arrange, fix. **5** *we set them some work:* **assign**, allocate, give, allot. **6** *they set a date for the election:* **arrange**, schedule, fix (on), settle on, determine, designate, name, specify. **7** *he set his watch:* **adjust**, regulate, synchronize, calibrate, put right, correct. **8** *the adhesive will set in an hour:* **solidify**, harden, stiffen, thicken, gel, cake, congeal, coagulate, clot.
OPPOSITES melt.
■ **set off/out** set out, start out, sally forth, leave, depart, embark, set sail; informal hit the road. ■ **set something up 1** *a monument was set up:* **erect**, put up, construct, build. **2** *she set up her own business:* **establish**, start, begin, institute, found, create. **3** *set up a meeting:* **arrange**, organize, fix (up), schedule, timetable, line up.

set² noun **1** *a set of postcards:* **series**, collection, group, batch, arrangement, array, assortment, selection. **2** *the literary set:* **group**, circle, crowd, crew, band, fraternity, company, ring, camp, school, clique, faction; informal gang, bunch.

set³ adjective **1** *a set routine:* **fixed**, established,

predetermined, hard and fast, unvarying, unchanging, invariable, rigid, inflexible, strict, settled. **2** *she had very set ideas:* **inflexible**, rigid, fixed, entrenched. **3** *I was all set for the evening:* **ready**, prepared, organized, equipped, primed; informal geared up, psyched up.
OPPOSITES variable, flexible, unprepared.

setback noun **problem**, difficulty, hitch, complication, upset, blow; informal glitch, hiccup.
OPPOSITES breakthrough.

setting noun **surroundings**, position, situation, environment, background, backdrop, spot, place, location, locale, site, scene.

settle verb **1** *they settled the dispute:* **resolve**, sort out, clear up, end, fix, work out, iron out, set right, reconcile; informal patch up. **2** *she settled her affairs:* **put in order**, sort out, tidy up, arrange, organize, order, clear up. **3** *they settled on a date for the wedding:* **decide on**, set, fix, agree on, name, establish, arrange, choose, pick. **4** *she went to settle her bill:* **pay**, square, clear. **5** *he settled in London:* **make one's home**, set up home, take up residence, put down roots, establish oneself, live, move to. **6** *immigrants settled much of Australia:* **colonize**, occupy, populate. **7** *a brandy will settle your nerves:* **calm**, quieten, quiet, soothe, pacify, quell. **8** *a butterfly settled on the flower:* **land**, come to rest, alight, perch.
OPPOSITES stir up, take off.

settlement noun **1** *a pay settlement:* **agreement**, deal,

S

arrangement, resolution, understanding, pact. **2** *the settlement of the dispute:* **resolution**, settling, solution, reconciliation. **3** *a frontier settlement:* **community**, colony, outpost, encampment, post, village.

settler noun **colonist**, frontiersman, pioneer, immigrant, newcomer, incomer.
OPPOSITES native.

sever verb **1** *the head was severed from the body:* **cut off**, chop off, detach, separate, amputate. **2** *a knife had severed the artery:* **cut (through)**, rupture, split, pierce. **3** *they severed diplomatic relations:* **break off**, discontinue, suspend, end, cease, dissolve.
OPPOSITES join, maintain.

several adjective **some**, a number of, a few, various, assorted.

severe adjective **1** *severe injuries:* **acute**, very bad, serious, grave, critical, dangerous, life-threatening. **2** *severe storms:* **fierce**, violent, strong, powerful. **3** *a severe winter:* **harsh**, bitter, cold, freezing, icy, arctic. **4** *severe criticism:* **harsh**, scathing, sharp, strong, fierce, savage, devastating, withering. **5** *his severe expression:* **stern**, dour, grim, forbidding, disapproving, unsmiling, unfriendly, sombre, stony, cold, frosty. **6** *a severe style of architecture:* **plain**, simple, austere, unadorned, stark, clinical, uncluttered.
OPPOSITES minor, gentle, mild, friendly, ornate.

severely adverb **1** *he was severely injured:* **badly**, seriously, critically. **2** *murderers should be treated more severely:*

harshly, strictly, sternly, rigorously. **3** *she looked severely at Harriet:* **sternly**, grimly, dourly, disapprovingly.

sew verb **stitch**, tack, seam, hem, embroider.

sex noun **1** *they talked about sex:* **sexual intercourse**, lovemaking, making love, the sex act, sexual relations, mating, copulation. **2** *adults of both sexes:* **gender**.

sexual adjective **1** *the sexual organs:* **reproductive**, genital, sex. **2** *sexual activity:* **carnal**, erotic.

sexuality noun **1** *she had a powerful sexuality:* **sensuality**, sexiness, seductiveness, eroticism, physicality, sexual appetite, passion, desire, lust. **2** *I'm open about my sexuality:* **sexual orientation**, sexual preference, leaning, persuasion.

sexy adjective **1** *she's so sexy:* **sexually attractive**, seductive, desirable, alluring; informal fanciable; Brit. informal fit; N. Amer. informal foxy. **2** *sexy videos:* **erotic**, sexually explicit, titillating, naughty, X-rated, rude, pornographic, crude; informal raunchy, steamy; euphemistic adult. **3** *they weren't feeling sexy:* **sexually aroused**, sexually excited, amorous, lustful, passionate; informal turned on; Brit. informal randy.

shabby adjective **1** *a shabby little bar:* **run down**, scruffy, dilapidated, squalid, sordid; informal crummy; Brit. informal grotty; N. Amer. informal shacky. **2** *a shabby grey coat:* **scruffy**, old, worn out, threadbare, ragged, frayed, tattered, battered, faded, moth-eaten; informal tatty; N. Amer. informal raggedy. **3** *her shabby treatment of Ben:* **mean**,

S

unkind, unfair, shameful, shoddy, unworthy, contemptible, despicable, discreditable; informal rotten.
OPPOSITES smart, decent.

shack noun **hut,** cabin, shanty, lean-to, shed, hovel; Scottish bothy.

shade noun **1** *they sat in the shade:* **shadow,** shelter, cover, cool. **2** *shades of blue:* **colour,** hue, tone, tint, tinge. **3** *shades of meaning:* **nuance,** gradation, degree, difference, variation, variety, nicety, subtlety, undertone, overtone. **4** *her skirt was a shade too short:* **little,** bit, trace, touch, modicum, tinge; informal tad, smidgen; (**a shade**) slightly, rather, somewhat. **5** *the window shade:* **blind,** curtain, screen, cover, covering, awning, canopy.
OPPOSITES light.
verb *vines shaded the garden:* **cast a shadow over,** shadow, shelter, cover, screen.

shadow noun **1** *he saw her shadow in the doorway:* **silhouette,** outline, shape, contour, profile. **2** *he emerged from the shadows:* **shade,** darkness, twilight, gloom.
verb *he is shadowing a suspect:* **follow,** trail, track, stalk, pursue; informal tail, keep tabs on.

shady adjective **1** *a shady garden:* **shaded,** shadowy, dim, dark, sheltered, leafy. **2** (informal) *shady deals:* **suspicious,** suspect, questionable, dubious, irregular, underhand; N. Amer. snide; informal fishy, murky; Brit. informal dodgy; Austral./NZ informal shonky.
OPPOSITES bright, honest.

shaft noun **1** *the shaft of a golf club:* **pole,** shank, stick, rod,

staff, handle, stem. **2** *shafts of sunlight:* **ray,** beam, gleam, streak. **3** *a ventilation shaft:* **tunnel,** passage, hole, bore, duct, well, flue, vent.

shake verb **1** *the building shook:* **vibrate,** tremble, quiver, quake, shiver, shudder, judder, wobble, rock, sway, convulse. **2** *she shook the bottle:* **jiggle,** agitate; informal wiggle, waggle. **3** *he shook his stick:* **brandish,** wave, flourish, swing, wield. **4** *what she saw shook her:* **upset,** distress, disturb, unsettle, disconcert, discompose, unnerve, throw off balance, agitate, fluster, shock, alarm, scare, worry; informal rattle.
OPPOSITES soothe.
noun **1** *camera shake:* **judder,** trembling, quivering, quake, tremor, shiver, shudder, wobble. **2** *he gave his coat a shake:* **jiggle,** joggle; informal waggle. **3** *a shake of his fist:* **flourish,** wave.

shaky adjective **1** *shaky legs:* **unsteady,** unstable, rickety, wobbly; Brit. informal wonky. **2** *I feel a bit shaky:* **faint,** dizzy, light-headed, giddy, weak, wobbly, in shock. **3** *the evidence is shaky:* **unreliable,** untrustworthy, questionable, dubious, doubtful, tenuous, suspect, flimsy, weak; informal iffy; Brit. informal dodgy.
OPPOSITES steady, stable, sound.

shallow adjective **superficial,** trivial, facile, insubstantial, lightweight, empty, trifling, surface, skin-deep, frivolous, foolish, silly.
OPPOSITES profound.

sham noun *it's all a sham:* **pretence,** act, simulation, fraud, lie, counterfeit, humbug.
adjective *a sham marriage:* **fake,**

S

pretended, feigned, simulated, false, artificial, bogus, insincere, affected, make-believe; informal pretend, put-on, phoney.
OPPOSITES genuine.
verb *he's shamming:* **pretend,** fake, malinger; informal put it on; Brit. informal swing the lead.

shambles plural noun **1** *we have to sort out this shambles:* **chaos,** muddle, jumble, confusion, disorder, havoc. **2** *the room was a shambles:* **mess,** pigsty; informal disaster area; Brit. informal tip.

shame noun **1** *a sense of shame:* **guilt,** remorse, contrition. **2** *he brought shame on the family:* **humiliation,** embarrassment, indignity, mortification, disgrace, dishonour, discredit, ignominy, disrepute, infamy, scandal. **3** *it's a shame she never married:* **pity,** sad thing, bad luck; informal crime, sin.
OPPOSITES pride, honour.
verb **1** *you shamed your family:* **disgrace,** dishonour, discredit, blacken, drag through the mud. **2** *he was shamed in public:* **humiliate,** embarrass, humble, take down a peg or two, cut down to size; informal show up; N. Amer. informal make someone eat crow.
OPPOSITES honour.

shameful adjective **1** *shameful behaviour:* **disgraceful,** deplorable, despicable, contemptible, discreditable, reprehensible, unworthy, shabby, shocking, scandalous, outrageous, abominable, atrocious, appalling, inexcusable, unforgivable. **2** *a shameful secret:* **embarrassing,** mortifying, humiliating, ignominious.
OPPOSITES admirable.

shape noun **1** *the shape of the dining table:* **form,** appearance, configuration, structure, contours, lines, outline, silhouette, profile. **2** *a spirit in the shape of a fox:* **guise,** likeness, semblance, form, appearance, image. **3** *in good shape:* **condition,** health, trim, fettle, order; Brit. informal nick.
verb **1** *the metal is shaped into tools:* **form,** fashion, make, mould, model. **2** *attitudes shaped by his report:* **determine,** form, fashion, mould, develop, influence, affect.

share noun *her share of the profits:* **portion,** part, division, quota, allowance, ration, allocation; informal cut, slice; Brit. informal whack.
verb **1** *we share the bills:* **split,** divide, go halves on; informal go fifty-fifty on. **2** *they shared out the peanuts:* **apportion,** divide up, allocate, portion out, measure out, carve up; Brit. informal divvy up. **3** *we all share in the learning process:* **participate,** take part, play a part, be involved, have a hand.

sharp adjective **1** *a sharp knife:* **keen,** razor-edged, sharpened, well-honed. **2** *a sharp pain:* **intense,** acute, severe, agonizing, excruciating, stabbing, shooting, searing. **3** *a sharp taste:* **tangy,** piquant, acidic, acid, sour, tart, pungent. **4** *a sharp wind:* **cold,** chilly, icy, bitter, biting, brisk, keen, penetrating. **5** *sharp words:* **harsh,** bitter, cutting, spiteful, hurtful, cruel. **6** *a sharp photo:* **clear,** distinct, crisp, focused. **7** *a sharp increase:* **sudden,** abrupt, rapid, steep. **8** *she was sharp and witty:* **astute,** intelligent, bright, incisive,

S

keen, quick-witted, shrewd, canny, perceptive, smart, quick; informal on the ball, quick on the uptake; N. Amer. informal heads-up.
OPPOSITES blunt, mild, sweet, soft, kind, indistinct, gradual, slow, stupid.
adverb **precisely**, exactly, promptly, prompt, punctually; informal on the dot; N. Amer. informal on the button.
OPPOSITES roughly.

sharpen verb **hone**, whet, strop, grind, file.

shatter verb **1** *the glasses shattered*: **smash**, break, splinter, crack, fracture, fragment, disintegrate. **2** *the announcement shattered their hopes*: **destroy**, wreck, ruin, dash, crush, devastate, demolish, torpedo, scotch; informal do for, put paid to; Brit. informal scupper.

shattered adjective **1** *he was shattered by the reviews*: **devastated**, shocked, stunned, dazed, traumatized. **2** (informal) *I feel too shattered to move*: **exhausted**, tired, worn out, weary, fatigued, ready to drop; informal done in, all in, dead beat; Brit. informal knackered, whacked, zonked; N. Amer. informal pooped, tuckered out.
OPPOSITES thrilled, fresh.

shave verb **1** *he shaved his beard*: **cut off**, crop, trim, barber. **2** *shave off excess wood*: **plane**, pare, whittle, scrape.

sheath noun **covering**, cover, case, casing, sleeve, scabbard.

shed[1] noun *a shed in the garden*: **hut**, lean-to, outhouse, outbuilding, cabin, shack.

shed[2] verb **1** *the trees shed their leaves*: **drop**, scatter, spill. **2** *the caterpillar shed its skin*: **throw off**, cast off, discard, slough off,

moult. **3** *we shed our clothes*: **take off**, remove, discard, climb out of, slip out of; Brit. informal peel off. **4** *the moon shed a watery light*: **cast**, radiate, emit, give out.
OPPOSITES keep, put on.

sheen noun **shine**, lustre, gloss, patina, burnish, polish, shimmer.

sheer adjective **1** *the sheer audacity of the plan*: **utter**, complete, absolute, total, pure, downright, out-and-out. **2** *a sheer drop*: **steep**, abrupt, sharp, precipitous, vertical. **3** *a sheer dress*: **thin**, fine, gauzy, diaphanous, transparent, see-through, flimsy.
OPPOSITES gradual, thick.

sheet noun **1** *a sheet of ice*: **layer**, covering, blanket, coat, film, veneer, crust, skin, surface, stratum. **2** *a sheet of glass*: **pane**, panel, slab, plate, piece. **3** *a fresh sheet of paper*: **page**, leaf, piece. **4** *a sheet of water*: **expanse**, area, stretch, sweep.

shell noun **1** *peanut shells*: **pod**, hull, husk; N. Amer. shuck. **2** *the metal shell of the car*: **body**, case, casing, framework, hull, fuselage, hulk.
verb **1** *they were shelling peas*: **pod**, hull, husk; N. Amer. shuck. **2** *rebel artillery shelled the city*: **bombard**, fire on, attack, bomb, blitz.

shelter noun **1** *the trees provide shelter for animals*: **protection**, cover, shade, safety, security, refuge. **2** *a shelter for abandoned cats*: **sanctuary**, refuge, home, haven, safe house.
OPPOSITES exposure, danger.
verb **1** *the hut sheltered him from the sun*: **protect**, shield,

S

screen, cover, shade, defend, cushion, guard, insulate. **2** *the convoy sheltered in a bay:* take **shelter**, take refuge, take cover; informal hole up.
OPPOSITES expose.

sheltered adjective **1** *a sheltered stretch of water:* **protected**, tranquil, still, shady. **2** *a sheltered life:* **protected**, cloistered, insulated, privileged, secure, safe, quiet.

shelve verb **postpone**, put off, delay, defer, put back, reschedule, hold over/off, put to one side, suspend, stay, mothball; N. Amer. put over, table; informal put on ice, put on the back burner.
OPPOSITES execute, bring forward, revive.

shepherd verb **usher**, steer, herd, lead, take, escort, guide, conduct, marshal, walk.

shield noun *a shield against radiation:* **protection**, guard, defence, cover, screen, shelter.
verb *he shielded his eyes:* **protect**, guard, defend, cover, screen, shade, shelter.
OPPOSITES expose.

shift verb **1** *he shifted some chairs:* **move**, transfer, transport, switch, relocate, reposition, rearrange. **2** *the cargo has shifted:* **move**, slide, slip, be displaced. **3** *the wind shifted:* **veer**, alter, change, turn. **4** (Brit.) *this brush really shifts the dirt:* **get rid of**, remove, get off, budge, lift.
OPPOSITES leave.
noun **1** *a shift in public opinion:* **change**, alteration, adjustment, variation, modification, revision, reversal, U-turn. **2** *they worked three shifts:* **stint**, stretch, spell.

shimmer verb *the sea*

shimmered in the sunset: **glint**, glisten, twinkle, sparkle, flash, gleam, glow, glimmer, wink.
noun *a shimmer of moonlight:* **glint**, twinkle, sparkle, flash, gleam, glow, glimmer, lustre, glitter.

shine verb **1** *the sun shone:* **beam**, gleam, radiate, glow, glint, glimmer, sparkle, twinkle, glitter, glisten, shimmer, flash. **2** *she shone her shoes:* **polish**, burnish, buff, rub up, brush, clean. **3** *they shone at university:* **excel**, stand out.
noun *linseed oil restores the shine:* **polish**, gleam, gloss, lustre, sheen, patina.

shiny adjective **glossy**, bright, glassy, polished, gleaming, satiny, lustrous.
OPPOSITES matt.

ship noun **boat**, vessel, craft.
verb *goods are shipped within 24 hours:* **deliver**, send, dispatch, transport, carry, distribute.

shiver verb *she was shivering with fear:* **tremble**, quiver, shake, shudder, quake.
noun *she gave a shiver:* **shudder**, twitch, start.

shock¹ noun **1** *the news came as a shock:* **blow**, upset, surprise, revelation, bolt from the blue, rude awakening, eye-opener. **2** *you gave me a shock:* **fright**, scare, start; informal turn. **3** *suffering from shock:* **trauma**, collapse, breakdown, post-traumatic stress disorder. **4** *the first shock of the earthquake:* **vibration**, reverberation, shake, jolt, impact, blow.
verb *the murder shocked the nation:* **appal**, horrify, outrage, scandalize, disgust, traumatize, distress, upset, disturb, stun, rock, shake.
OPPOSITES delight.

S

shock² noun *a shock of red hair:* **mass,** mane, mop, thatch, head, bush, tangle, cascade, halo.

shocking adjective **appalling,** horrifying, horrific, dreadful, awful, terrible, scandalous, outrageous, disgraceful, abominable, atrocious, disgusting, distressing, upsetting, disturbing, startling.

shoot verb **1** *they shot him in the street:* **gun down,** mow down, hit, wound, injure, shoot someone dead, kill. **2** *they shot at the police:* **fire,** open fire, snipe, let fly, bombard, shell. **3** *it can shoot bullets or grenades:* **discharge,** fire, launch, propel, release. **4** *a car shot past:* **race,** speed, flash, dash, rush, hurtle, streak, whizz, zoom, career, fly; informal belt, tear, zip, whip; Brit. informal bomb; N. Amer. informal hightail it, barrel. **5** *the film was shot in Tunisia:* **film,** photograph, take, make, record.
noun *new shoots:* **sprout,** bud, runner, tendril.

shop noun **store,** retail outlet, boutique, emporium, department store, supermarket, hypermarket, superstore, chain store; N. Amer. minimart.

shore noun **seashore,** beach, sand(s), shoreline, coast.

short adjective **1** *short people:* **small,** little, petite, tiny, diminutive, elfin; Scottish wee. **2** *a short report:* **concise,** brief, succinct, compact, pithy, abridged, abbreviated, condensed. **3** *a short visit:* **brief,** fleeting, lightning, quick, cursory. **4** *money is a bit short:* **scarce,** scant, meagre, sparse, insufficient, deficient, inadequate, lacking. **5** *he was rather short with her:* **curt,** sharp, abrupt, blunt, brusque, terse, offhand.
OPPOSITES tall, long, plentiful, courteous.
adverb *she stopped short:* **abruptly,** suddenly, sharply, all of a sudden, unexpectedly, without warning.
■ **short of** deficient in, lacking, in need of, low on, short on, missing; informal strapped for, pushed for, minus.

shortage noun **scarcity,** dearth, poverty, insufficiency, deficiency, inadequacy, famine, lack, deficit, shortfall.
OPPOSITES abundance.

shortcoming noun **fault,** defect, flaw, imperfection, deficiency, limitation, failing, drawback, weakness, weak point.
OPPOSITES strength.

shorten verb **abbreviate,** abridge, condense, contract, compress, reduce, shrink, diminish, cut (down), trim, pare (down), prune, curtail, truncate.
OPPOSITES lengthen.

shortly adverb **soon,** presently, in a little while, at any moment, in a minute, in next to no time, before long, by and by; N. Amer. momentarily; informal anon, any time now, in a jiffy; Brit. informal in a mo.

shot noun **1** *a shot rang out:* **report,** crack, bang, blast; (shots) gunfire, firing. **2** *a winning shot:* **stroke,** hit, strike, kick, throw. **3** *Mike was an excellent shot:* **marksman,** markswoman, shooter. **4** *a shot of us on holiday:* **photograph,** photo, snap, snapshot, picture, print, slide, still.

shoulder verb **1** *I shouldered the responsibility:* **take on**

S

(**oneself**), undertake, accept, assume, bear, carry. **2** *another lad shouldered him aside:* push, shove, thrust, jostle, force, bulldoze, bundle.

shout verb *I heard a shout:* yell, cry (out), call (out), roar, howl, bellow, bawl, raise one's voice; informal holler.
OPPOSITES whisper.
noun *he shouted a warning:* yell, cry, call, roar, howl, bellow, bawl; informal holler.

shove verb **1** *she shoved him back:* push, thrust, propel, drive, force, ram, knock, elbow, shoulder. **2** *she shoved past him:* push (one's way), force one's way, barge (one's way), elbow (one's way), shoulder one's way.
noun *a hefty shove:* push, thrust, bump, jolt, barge.

show verb **1** *the stitches do not show:* be visible, be seen, be in view, be obvious. **2** *he wouldn't show the picture:* display, exhibit, put on show, put on display, put on view. **3** *Frank showed his frustration:* manifest, exhibit, reveal, convey, communicate, make known, express, make plain, make obvious, disclose, betray. **4** *I'll show you how to cook:* demonstrate, explain, describe, illustrate, teach, instruct. **5** *events show this to be true:* prove, demonstrate, confirm, substantiate, corroborate, verify, bear out. **6** *she showed them to their seats:* escort, accompany, take, conduct, lead, usher, guide, direct.
OPPOSITES conceal.
noun **1** *a spectacular show of bluebells:* display, array, sight, spectacle. **2** *the motor show:* exhibition, display, fair, festival, parade; N. Amer. exhibit. **3** *a TV show:* programme, broadcast, presentation, production, episode. **4** *she's only doing it for show:* appearance, display, image. **5** *Drew made a show of looking busy:* pretence, outward appearance, (false) front, guise, pose.
■ **show off** (informal) put on airs, put on an act, swank, strut, grandstand, posture, draw attention to oneself. ■ **show something off** display, show to advantage, exhibit, demonstrate, parade, draw attention to, flaunt. ■ **show up 1** *cancers show up on X-rays:* be visible, be obvious, be seen, be revealed, appear. **2** (informal) *only two waitresses showed up:* turn up, appear, arrive, come, get here/there, put in an appearance, materialize. ■ **show someone up** (informal) humiliate, embarrass, shame, put someone to shame, mortify. ■ **show something up** expose, reveal, make obvious, highlight, emphasize, draw attention to.

showdown noun confrontation, clash, face-off.

shower noun **1** *a shower of rain:* fall, drizzle, sprinkling. **2** *a shower of missiles:* volley, hail, salvo, barrage.
verb **1** *confetti showered down on us:* rain, fall, hail. **2** *she showered them with gifts:* deluge, flood, inundate, swamp, overwhelm, snow under.

show-off noun (informal) exhibitionist, extrovert, poser, poseur, swaggerer, self-publicist.

showy adjective ostentatious, flamboyant, gaudy, garish, brash, vulgar, loud, fancy,

S

shred | sick

ornate; informal flash, flashy.
OPPOSITES restrained.

shred noun 1 *her dress was torn to shreds:* **tatter,** ribbon, rag, fragment, sliver. 2 *not a shred of evidence:* **scrap,** bit, speck, particle, ounce, jot, crumb, fragment, grain, drop, trace.
verb *shredding vegetables:* **grate,** mince, grind.

shrewd adjective **astute,** sharp, smart, intelligent, clever, canny, perceptive; informal on the ball.
OPPOSITES stupid.

shriek verb & noun **scream,** screech, squeal, squawk, roar, howl, shout, yelp.

shrink verb 1 *the number of competitors shrank:* **get smaller,** contract, diminish, lessen, reduce, decrease, dwindle, decline, fall off. 2 *he doesn't shrink from naming names:* **recoil,** shy away, flinch, be averse, be afraid, hesitate.
OPPOSITES expand, increase.

shrivel verb **wither,** shrink, wilt, dry up, dehydrate, parch, frazzle.

shroud noun *a shroud of mist:* **covering,** cover, cloak, mantle, blanket, layer, cloud, veil, winding sheet.
verb *shrouded by cloud:* **cover,** envelop, veil, cloak, blanket, screen, conceal, hide, mask, obscure.

shudder verb *the ground shuddered:* **shake,** shiver, tremble, quiver, judder.
noun *the truck's shudders and jolts:* **shake,** shiver, tremor, trembling, quivering, vibration, judder.

shuffle verb 1 *they shuffled along the passage:* **shamble,** dodder, drag one's feet. 2 *she shuffled her feet:* **scrape,** drag, scuffle. 3 *he shuffled the cards:*

mix (up), rearrange, jumble (up).

shun verb **avoid,** steer clear of, give a wide berth to, have nothing to do with; informal freeze out; Brit. informal send to Coventry.
OPPOSITES welcome.

shut verb *please shut the door:* **close,** pull to, push to, slam, fasten, put the lid on, lock, secure.
OPPOSITES open, unlock.
■ **shut down** cease activity, close (down), cease trading; informal fold. ■ **shut up** (informal) be quiet, keep quiet, stop talking, quieten down; informal shut it, shut your face/mouth/trap, belt up, give it a rest; Brit. informal shut your gob; N. Amer. informal save it. ■ **shut someone/ something up** (informal) silence, quieten down, hush, gag, muzzle.

shuttle verb **commute,** run, ply, go/travel back and forth, ferry.

shy adjective **bashful,** diffident, timid, reserved, introverted, retiring, self-effacing, withdrawn.
OPPOSITES confident.
■ **shy away from** flinch, recoil, hang back, be loath, be reluctant, be unwilling, be disinclined, hesitate, baulk at.

sick adjective 1 *the children are sick:* **ill,** unwell, poorly, ailing, indisposed; informal laid up, under the weather; Austral./NZ informal crook. 2 *he was feeling sick:* **nauseous,** queasy, bilious, green about the gills. 3 *I'm sick of this music:* **fed up,** bored, tired, weary. 4 (informal) *a sick joke:* **macabre,** tasteless, ghoulish, morbid, black, gruesome, gallows, cruel.
OPPOSITES well.

S

■ **be sick** (Brit.) vomit, heave; informal puke, throw up; N. Amer. informal barf, upchuck.

sicken verb **1** *the stench sickened him:* **nauseate**, make sick, turn someone's stomach, disgust; N. Amer. informal gross out. **2** *she sickened and died:* **fall ill**, catch something.
OPPOSITES please, recover.

sickening adjective **nauseating**, stomach-turning, repulsive, revolting, disgusting, offensive, off-putting, distasteful, obscene, gruesome, grisly; N. Amer. **vomitous**; informal gross.

sickness noun **1** *she was absent through sickness:* **illness**, disease, ailment, infection, malady, infirmity; informal bug, virus; Brit. informal lurgy; Austral. informal wog. **2** *a wave of sickness:* **nausea**, biliousness, queasiness. **3** *sickness and diarrhoea:* **nausea**, vomiting, retching; informal throwing up, puking.

side noun **1** *the side of the road:* **edge**, border, verge, boundary, margin, fringe(s), flank, bank, perimeter, extremity, periphery, limit(s). **2** *the wrong side of the road:* **half**, part, carriageway, lane. **3** *the east side of the city:* **district**, quarter, area, region, part, neighbourhood, sector, zone. **4** *one side of the paper:* **surface**, face. **5** *his side of the argument:* **point of view**, viewpoint, perspective, opinion, standpoint, position, outlook, slant, angle. **6** *the losing side:* **faction**, camp, bloc, party. **7** *the players in their side:* **team**, squad, line-up.
OPPOSITES centre, end.
adjective **1** *elaborate side pieces:* **lateral**, wing, flanking. **2** *a side issue:* **subordinate**, secondary,

minor, peripheral, incidental, subsidiary.
OPPOSITES front, central.
■ **side with** support, take someone's part, stand by, back, be loyal to, defend, champion, ally oneself with.

sideways adverb **1** *I slid sideways:* **to the side**, laterally. **2** *the expansion slots are mounted sideways:* **edgewise**, edgeways, side first, end on.
adjective **1** *sideways force:* **lateral**, sideward, on the side, side to side. **2** *a sideways look:* **indirect**, oblique, sidelong, surreptitious, furtive, covert, sly.

sift verb **1** *sift the flour into a large bowl:* **sieve**, strain, screen, filter. **2** *we sift out unsuitable applications:* **separate out**, filter out, sort out, weed out, get rid of, remove. **3** *sifting through the wreckage:* **search**, look, examine, inspect, scrutinize, pore over.

sight noun **1** *she has excellent sight:* **eyesight**, vision, eyes. **2** *her first sight of it:* **view**, glimpse, glance, look. **3** *historic sights:* **landmark**, place of interest, monument, spectacle, marvel, wonder.
verb *one of the helicopters sighted wreckage:* **glimpse**, catch sight of, see, spot, spy, make out, pick out, notice, observe.

sign noun **1** *a sign of affection:* **indication**, signal, symptom, pointer, suggestion, intimation, mark, manifestation, demonstration, token. **2** *a sign of things to come:* **warning**, omen, portent, threat, promise. **3** *signs saying 'danger':* **notice**, board, placard, signpost. **4** *the dancers were daubed with signs:*

symbol, figure, emblem, device, logo, character.
verb **1** *he signed the letter:* write one's name on, autograph, initial, countersign. **2** *the government signed the treaty:* endorse, validate, agree to, approve, ratify, adopt. **3** *he signed his name:* write, inscribe, pen.

signal noun **1** *a signal to stop:* gesture, sign, wave, cue, indication, warning, prompt, reminder. **2** *a clear signal that we're in trouble:* indication, sign, symptom, hint, pointer, clue, demonstration, evidence, proof.
verb **1** *the driver signalled to her:* gesture, sign, indicate, motion, wave, beckon, nod. **2** *they signalled their displeasure:* indicate, show, express, communicate. **3** *his death signals the end of an era:* mark, signify, mean, be a sign of, be evidence of.

significance noun importance, import, consequence, seriousness, gravity, weight, magnitude.
OPPOSITES insignificance.

significant adjective **1** *a significant fact:* notable, noteworthy, remarkable, important, of consequence. **2** *a significant increase:* large, considerable, sizeable, appreciable, conspicuous, obvious, sudden. **3** *a significant look:* meaningful, expressive, eloquent, suggestive, knowing, telling.
OPPOSITES insignificant.

signify verb mean, denote, designate, represent, symbolize, stand for.

silence noun **1** *the silence of the night:* quietness, quiet, still,

stillness, hush, tranquillity, peace. **2** *her silence was answer enough:* failure to speak, dumbness, reticence, taciturnity.
OPPOSITES sound, loquacity.
verb **1** *he silenced her with a kiss:* quieten, quiet, hush. **2** *dissidents have been silenced:* gag, muzzle, censor.

silent adjective **1** *the forest was silent:* quiet, still, hushed, noiseless, soundless, inaudible. **2** *the right to remain silent:* speechless, quiet, unspeaking, dumb, mute, taciturn, uncommunicative, tight-lipped. **3** *silent thanks:* unspoken, wordless.
OPPOSITES audible, noisy, spoken.

silhouette noun *silhouettes of aircraft:* outline, contour(s), profile, form, shape.
verb *silhouetted against the window:* outline, define.

silly adjective **1** *don't be so silly:* foolish, stupid, scatterbrained, frivolous, inane, immature, childish, empty-headed; informal dotty, scatty. **2** *that was a silly thing to do:* unwise, imprudent, thoughtless, foolish, stupid, unintelligent, idiotic, rash, reckless, foolhardy, irresponsible; informal crazy, mad; Brit. informal daft. **3** *he would worry about silly things:* trivial, trifling, frivolous, petty, small, insignificant, unimportant; informal piffling.
OPPOSITES sensible, serious.

similar adjective **1** *you two are very similar:* alike, the same; informal much of a muchness. **2** *northern India and similar areas:* comparable, like, corresponding, equivalent.
OPPOSITES different, unlike.

S

■ **similar to** like, much the same as, comparable to.

similarity noun resemblance, likeness, comparability, correspondence, parallel, equivalence, uniformity.

simmer verb 1 *the soup was simmering on the stove:* **boil gently,** cook gently, bubble. **2** *she was simmering with resentment:* **seethe,** fume, smoulder.

■ **simmer down** calm down, cool off/down.

simple adjective 1 *it's really pretty simple:* **straightforward,** easy, uncomplicated, uninvolved, undemanding, elementary. **2** *simple language:* **clear,** plain, straightforward, unambiguous, understandable, comprehensible, accessible; informal user-friendly. **3** *a simple white blouse:* **plain,** unadorned, basic, unsophisticated, no-frills, classic, understated, uncluttered, restrained. **4** *simple country people:* **unpretentious,** unsophisticated, ordinary, unaffected, unassuming, natural, straightforward; N. Amer. cracker-barrel.
OPPOSITES difficult, complex, fancy, sophisticated.

simplicity noun 1 *the simplicity of the recipes is an advantage:* **straightforwardness,** ease. **2** *the simplicity of the language:* **clarity,** plainness, intelligibility, comprehensibility, accessibility. **3** *the building's simplicity:* **austerity,** plainness, spareness, clean lines. **4** *the simplicity of their lifestyle:* **plainness,** modesty, naturalness.
OPPOSITES difficulty, complexity, adornment, sophistication.

simplify verb make simpler,

clarify, put into words of one syllable, streamline; informal dumb down.
OPPOSITES complicate.

simply adverb 1 *he always spoke simply and forcefully:* **straightforwardly,** directly, clearly, plainly, lucidly, unambiguously. **2** *she was dressed simply:* **plainly,** soberly, unfussily, classically. **3** *they lived simply:* **modestly,** plainly, quietly. **4** *they are welcomed simply because they are rich:* **merely,** just, purely, solely, only. **5** *she was simply delighted:* **utterly,** absolutely, completely, positively, just; informal plain.
OPPOSITES confusingly, elaborately.

simulate verb 1 *they simulated pleasure:* **feign,** pretend, fake, affect, put on. **2** *simulating conditions in space:* **imitate,** reproduce, replicate, duplicate, mimic.

simultaneous adjective concurrent, happening at the same time, contemporaneous, coinciding, coincident, synchronized.
OPPOSITES separate.

simultaneously adverb at the same time, at one and the same time, at once, concurrently, (all) together, in unison, in concert, in chorus.

sin noun 1 *a sin in the eyes of God:* **wrong,** act of wickedness, transgression, crime, offence, misdeed. **2** *the human capacity for sin:* **wickedness,** wrongdoing, evil, immorality, iniquity, vice, crime.
OPPOSITES virtue.
verb *I have sinned:* **transgress,** do wrong, misbehave, err, go astray.

s

sincere adjective **1** *our sincere gratitude:* **heartfelt,** wholehearted, profound, deep, true, honest. **2** *a sincere person:* **honest,** genuine, truthful, direct, frank, candid; informal straight, on the level; N. Amer. informal on the up and up.

sincerely adverb **genuinely,** honestly, really, truly, truthfully, wholeheartedly, earnestly.

sincerity noun **genuineness,** honesty, truthfulness, integrity, directness, openness, candour.

sing verb **1** *he began to sing:* **chant,** trill, intone, croon, chorus. **2** *the birds were singing:* **trill,** warble, chirp, chirrup, cheep.

singe verb **scorch,** burn, sear, char.

singer noun **vocalist,** songster, songstress, soloist, chorister, cantor.

single adjective **1** *a single red rose:* **sole,** one, lone, solitary, unaccompanied, alone. **2** *every single word:* **individual,** separate, distinct. **3** *is she single?* **unmarried,** unwed, unattached, free, a bachelor, a spinster.
OPPOSITES double, multiple, married.
■ **single someone/something out** select, pick out, choose, decide on, target, earmark, mark out, separate out, set apart.

singly adverb **one by one,** one at a time, one after the other, individually, separately.
OPPOSITES together.

sinister adjective **1** *there was a sinister undertone in his words:* **menacing,** threatening, ominous, forbidding, frightening, alarming, disturbing, dark. **2** *a sinister*

motive: **evil,** wicked, criminal, nefarious, villainous, base, malicious; informal shady.
OPPOSITES unthreatening, innocent.

sink verb **1** *the coffin sank below the waves:* **submerge,** founder, go down, be engulfed, drop, fall, descend. **2** *they sank their ships:* **scuttle;** Brit. scupper. **3** *the sun was sinking:* **set,** go down. **4** *Loretta sank into an armchair:* **lower oneself,** flop, collapse, drop, slump; informal plonk oneself. **5** *sink the pots into the ground:* **embed,** insert, drive, plant.
OPPOSITES float, rise.

sip verb *she sipped her martini:* **drink,** taste, sample, nip.
noun *have a sip:* **mouthful,** swallow, drink, drop, dram, nip; informal swig.

sit verb **1** *you'd better sit down:* **take a seat,** be seated, perch, ensconce oneself, flop; informal take the load off one's feet; Brit. informal take a pew. **2** *she sat the package on the table:* **put,** place, set, lay, deposit, rest, stand; informal stick, park. **3** *the committee sits on Saturday:* **be in session,** meet, be convened. **4** *she sits on the tribunal:* **serve on,** have a seat on, be a member of.
OPPOSITES stand.

site noun *the site of the battle:* **location,** place, position, situation, locality, whereabouts.
verb *sited in an industrial area:* **place,** put, position, situate, locate.

situation noun **1** *their financial situation:* **circumstances,** state of affairs, state, condition. **2** *I'll fill you in on the situation:* **the facts,** how things stand, the lie of the land, what's going on;

S

Brit. the state of play; N. Amer. the lay of the land; informal the score. **3** *the hotel's pleasant situation:* **location,** position, spot, site, setting, environment.

size noun **dimensions,** measurements, proportions, magnitude, largeness, area, expanse, breadth, width, length, height, depth.

■ **size someone/something up** (informal) assess, appraise, get the measure of, judge, take stock of, evaluate; Brit. informal suss out.

sizeable adjective **large,** substantial, considerable, respectable, significant, goodly. OPPOSITES small.

sizzle verb **crackle,** frizzle, sputter, hiss, spit.

sketch noun *a sketch of the proposed design:* **drawing,** outline, draft, diagram, design, plan; informal rough.
verb *he sketched the garden:* **draw,** make a drawing of, pencil, rough out, outline.

skilful adjective **expert,** accomplished, skilled, masterly, talented, deft, dexterous, handy; informal mean, crack, ace; N. Amer. informal crackerjack.
OPPOSITES incompetent.

skill noun **expertise,** accomplishment, skilfulness, mastery, talent, deftness, dexterity, prowess, competence, artistry.
OPPOSITES incompetence.

skim verb **1** *skim off the fat:* **remove,** scoop off, separate. **2** *the boat skimmed over the water:* **glide,** move lightly, slide, sail, skate. **3** *she skimmed through the newspaper:* **glance,** flick, flip, leaf, thumb, scan, run one's eye over.

skin noun **1** *leopard skins:* **hide,** pelt, fell, fleece. **2** *a banana*

skin: peel, rind. **3** *milk with a skin on it:* **film,** layer, membrane, crust, covering, coating.
verb **1** *skin the tomatoes:* **peel,** pare. **2** *he skinned his knee:* **graze,** scrape, abrade, bark, rub raw, chafe.

skinny adjective **thin,** underweight, scrawny, bony, gaunt, emaciated, skeletal, wasted, pinched, spindly, gangly; informal anorexic.

skip verb **1** *skipping down the path:* **caper,** prance, trip, dance, bound, bounce, gambol. **2** *we skipped the boring stuff:* **omit,** leave out, miss out, dispense with, pass over, skim over, disregard; informal give something a miss.

skirt verb **1** *he skirted the city:* **go round,** walk round, circle. **2** *the fields that skirt the park:* **border,** edge, flank, line. **3** *he carefully skirted round the subject:* **avoid,** evade, sidestep, dodge, pass over, gloss over; informal duck; Austral./NZ informal duck-shove.

slab noun **piece,** block, hunk, chunk, lump, cake, tablet, brick, panel, plate, sheet.

slack adjective **1** *the rope went slack:* **limp,** loose. **2** *slack skin:* sagging, flabby, flaccid, loose, saggy. **3** *business is slack:* **sluggish,** slow, quiet, slow-moving, flat, depressed, stagnant. **4** *slack procedure:* **lax,** negligent, careless, slapdash, slipshod; informal sloppy.
OPPOSITES taut, firm, busy, strict.
verb (Brit. informal) *no slacking!* **idle,** shirk, be lazy, be indolent, waste time, lounge about; Brit. informal skive; N. Amer. informal goof off.

slam verb **1** *he slammed the door:*

S

bang, shut with a bang. **2** *the car slammed into a lamp post:* **crash**, smash, plough, run, bump, collide with, hit, strike, ram; N. Amer. impact.

slant verb **1** *the floor slanted:* **slope**, tilt, incline, be at an angle, tip, lean, dip, pitch, shelve, list, bank. **2** *their findings were slanted in our favour:* **bias**, distort, twist, skew, weight.
noun **1** *the slant of the roof:* **slope**, incline, tilt, gradient, pitch, angle, camber. **2** *a feminist slant:* **point of view**, viewpoint, standpoint, stance, angle, perspective, approach, view, attitude, position, bias.

slap verb *he slapped her hard:* **smack**, strike, hit, cuff, clip, spank; informal whack.
noun *a slap across the face:* **smack**, blow, cuff, clip, spank; informal whack.

slash verb **1** *her tyres had been slashed:* **cut**, gash, slit, lacerate, knife. **2** (informal) *the company slashed prices:* **reduce**, cut, lower, bring down, mark down.
noun *a slash across his temple:* **cut**, gash, slit, laceration, incision, wound.

slaughter verb **1** *the cattle were slaughtered:* **kill**, butcher, cull, put down. **2** *civilians are being slaughtered:* **massacre**, murder, butcher, kill, exterminate, wipe out, put to death, execute; literary slay.
noun *a scene of slaughter:* **massacre**, (mass) murder, (mass) killing, (mass) execution, extermination, carnage, bloodshed, bloodletting, bloodbath; literary slaying.

slave noun *the work was done by slaves:* **servant**, lackey; Brit. informal skivvy, dogsbody; historical serf, vassal.
OPPOSITES freeman, master.
verb *we slaved away:* **toil**, labour, sweat, work like a Trojan/dog; informal kill oneself, sweat blood, slog away; Brit. informal graft; Austral./NZ informal bullock.

slavery noun **enslavement**, servitude, serfdom, bondage, captivity.
OPPOSITES freedom.

sleazy adjective **1** *sleazy politicians:* **corrupt**, immoral. **2** *a sleazy bar:* **squalid**, seedy, seamy, sordid, insalubrious.
OPPOSITES honest, reputable, upmarket.

sleek adjective **1** *his sleek dark hair:* **smooth**, glossy, shiny, shining, lustrous, silken, silky. **2** *the car's sleek lines:* **streamlined**, elegant, graceful.
OPPOSITES scruffy, crude.

sleep noun **nap**, doze, siesta, catnap; informal snooze, forty winks, shut-eye; Brit. informal kip; literary slumber.
OPPOSITES wakefulness.
verb **be asleep**, doze, take a siesta, take a nap, catnap; informal snooze, snatch forty winks, get some shut-eye; Brit. informal kip; N. Amer. informal catch some Zs; literary slumber.
OPPOSITES wake up.
■ **go to sleep** fall asleep, get to sleep; informal drop off, nod off, drift off, crash out, flake out; N. Amer. informal sack out.

sleepy adjective **1** *she felt very sleepy:* **drowsy**, tired, somnolent, heavy-eyed; informal dopey. **2** *a sleepy little village:* **quiet**, peaceful, tranquil, placid, slow-moving, dull, boring.
OPPOSITES awake, alert.

slender adjective **1** *her tall,*

S

slender figure: **slim,** lean, willowy, svelte, lissom, graceful, slight, thin, skinny. **2** *slender evidence:* **meagre,** limited, slight, scanty, scant, sparse, flimsy, insubstantial. **3** *the chances seemed slender:* **faint,** remote, tenuous, fragile, slim.

OPPOSITES plump, strong.

slice noun **1** *a slice of cake:* **piece,** portion, slab, wedge, rasher, sliver, wafer. **2** *a huge slice of public spending:* **share,** part, portion, tranche, percentage, proportion, allocation.
verb *slice the cheese thinly:* **cut,** carve, divide.

slick adjective **1** *a slick advertising campaign:* **efficient,** smooth, smooth-running, polished, well organized, well run, streamlined. **2** *a slick salesman:* **glib,** polished, assured, self-assured, smooth-talking, plausible; informal smarmy.

OPPOSITES incompetent, hesitant.
verb *his hair was slicked down:* **smooth,** plaster, sleek, grease, oil, gel.

slide verb glide, slip, slither, skim, skate, skid, slew.

slight adjective **1** *the chance of success is slight:* **small,** tiny, minute, negligible, insignificant, minimal, remote, slim, faint. **2** *Elizabeth's slight figure:* **slim,** slender, delicate, dainty, fragile.

OPPOSITES good, plump.
verb *he had been slighted:* **insult,** snub, rebuff, spurn, give someone the cold shoulder, cut (dead), scorn.

OPPOSITES respect.
noun *an unintended slight:* **insult,** affront, snub, rebuff;

informal put-down.

OPPOSITES compliment.

slightly adverb **a little,** a bit, somewhat, faintly, vaguely, a shade.

OPPOSITES very.

slim adjective **1** *tall and slim:* **slender,** lean, thin, willowy, sylphlike, svelte, lissom, trim. **2** *a slim silver bracelet:* **narrow,** slender. **3** *a slim chance:* **slight,** small, slender, faint, poor, remote.

OPPOSITES plump, wide, good.
verb *I'm trying to slim:* **lose weight,** get into shape; N. Amer. slenderize.

OPPOSITES put on weight.

slimy adjective **slippery,** slithery, greasy; informal slippy, gloopy.

OPPOSITES firm, grippy.

sling verb **1** *a hammock was slung between two trees:* **hang,** suspend, string, swing. **2** (informal) *she slung her jacket on the sofa:* **throw,** toss, fling, hurl, cast, pitch, lob, flip; informal chuck, heave, bung.

slip verb **1** *she slipped on the ice:* **slide,** skid, slither, fall (over), lose one's balance, tumble. **2** *the envelope slipped through Luke's fingers:* **fall,** drop, slide. **3** *we slipped out by a back door:* **creep,** steal, sneak, slide, sidle, slope, slink, tiptoe. **4** *she slipped the map into her pocket:* **put,** tuck, shove; informal pop, stick, stuff.
noun **1** *a single slip could send them plummeting down:* **false step,** slide, skid, fall, tumble. **2** *a careless slip:* **mistake,** error, blunder, gaffe, oversight, omission, lapse; informal slip-up, boo-boo, howler; Brit. informal boob, clanger, bloomer; N. Amer. informal goof, blooper.
■ **slip up** (informal) make a

mistake, blunder, get something wrong, make an error, err; informal make a boo-boo; Brit. informal boob, drop a clanger; N. Amer. informal goof up.

slippery adjective **1** *the roads are slippery:* **slithery**, greasy, oily, icy, glassy, smooth, slimy, wet; informal slippy. **2** *a slippery customer:* **sneaky**, sly, devious, crafty, cunning, tricky, evasive, scheming, unreliable, untrustworthy; N. Amer. snide; informal shady, shifty; Brit. informal dodgy; Austral./NZ informal shonky.

slit noun **1** *three diagonal slits:* **cut**, incision, split, slash, gash. **2** *a slit in the curtains:* **opening**, gap, chink, crack, aperture, slot.
verb *he threatened to slit her throat:* **cut**, slash, split open, slice open.

slogan noun **catchphrase**, catchline, motto, jingle; N. Amer. informal tag line.

slope noun *the slope of the roof:* **tilt**, pitch, slant, angle, gradient, incline, inclination, fall, camber; N. Amer. grade.
verb *the garden sloped down to a stream:* **tilt**, slant, incline, lean, drop/fall away, descend, shelve, camber, rise, ascend, climb.

sloping adjective **slanting**, leaning, inclined, angled, cambered, tilted.
OPPOSITES level.

sloppy adjective **1** *sloppy chicken curry:* **runny**, watery, liquid, mushy; informal gloopy. **2** *their defending was sloppy:* **careless**, slapdash, slipshod, untidy, slack, slovenly; informal slap-happy. **3** *sloppy letters:* **sentimental**, mawkish, romantic; informal slushy, schmaltzy; Brit. informal soppy;

N. Amer. informal cornball, sappy, hokey.

slot noun **1** *he slid a coin into the slot:* **aperture**, slit, crack, hole, opening. **2** *a mid-morning slot:* **time**, spot, period, niche, space; informal window.
verb *he slotted a cassette into the machine:* **insert**, slide, fit, put, place.

slow adjective **1** *their slow walk home:* **unhurried**, leisurely, steady, sedate, sluggish, plodding. **2** *a slow process:* **lengthy**, time-consuming, long-drawn-out, protracted, prolonged, gradual. **3** *he's a bit slow:* **stupid**, unintelligent, obtuse; informal dense, dim, thick, slow on the uptake, dumb, dopey; Brit. informal dozy.
OPPOSITES quick.
verb **1** *the traffic forced him to slow down:* **reduce speed**, go slower, decelerate, brake. **2** *this would slow down economic growth:* **hold back/up**, delay, retard, set back, check, curb.
OPPOSITES accelerate.

slowly adverb **1** *Rose walked off slowly:* **unhurriedly**, without hurrying, steadily, at a leisurely pace, at a snail's pace. **2** *her health is improving slowly:* **gradually**, bit by bit, little by little, slowly but surely, step by step.
OPPOSITES quickly.

sluggish adjective **lethargic**, listless, lacking in energy, lifeless, inactive, slow; N. Amer. logy.
OPPOSITES vigorous.

slum noun **hovel**; (slums) ghetto, shanty town.

slump verb **1** *he slumped into a chair:* **sit heavily**, flop, collapse, sink; informal plonk oneself. **2** *house prices slumped:* **fall**,

S

plummet, tumble, collapse, drop; informal crash, nosedive.
OPPOSITES rise, boom.
noun **1** *a slump in profits:* **fall**, drop, tumble, downturn, downswing, slide, decline, decrease; informal nosedive. **2** *an economic slump:* **recession**, decline, depression, slowdown.
OPPOSITES rise, boom.

sly adjective **1** *she's very sly:* **cunning**, crafty, clever, wily, artful, tricky, scheming, devious, underhand, sneaky. **2** *a sly grin:* **roguish**, mischievous, impish, playful, wicked, arch, knowing. **3** *she took a sly sip of water:* **surreptitious**, furtive, stealthy, covert.
OPPOSITES open, straightforward.

smack noun *she gave him a smack:* **slap**, blow, cuff, clip, spank; informal whack.
verb *he tried to smack her:* **slap**, strike, hit, cuff, clip, spank; informal whack.
adverb (informal) *smack in the middle:* **exactly**, precisely, straight, right, directly, squarely, dead, plumb; informal slap, bang; N. Amer. informal smack dab.

small adjective **1** *a small flat:* **little**, compact, tiny, miniature, mini, minute, toy, baby, poky, cramped; Scottish wee; informal tiddly; Brit. informal titchy; N. Amer. informal little-bitty. **2** *a very small man:* **short**, little, petite, diminutive, elfin, tiny; Scottish wee; informal teeny, pint-sized. **3** *a few small changes:* **slight**, minor, unimportant, trifling, trivial, insignificant, inconsequential, negligible; informal minuscule, piffling.
OPPOSITES big, tall, major.

smart adjective **1** *you look very*

smart: **well dressed**, stylish, chic, fashionable, modish, elegant, dapper; N. Amer. trig; informal natty, snappy; N. Amer. informal fly. **2** *a smart restaurant:* **fashionable**, stylish, high-class, exclusive, chic, fancy; Brit. upmarket; N. Amer. high-toned; informal trendy, classy, swanky; Brit. informal swish; N. Amer. informal swank. **3** (informal) *he's very smart:* **clever**, bright, intelligent, quick-witted, shrewd, astute, perceptive; informal brainy, quick on the uptake. **4** *a smart pace:* **brisk**, quick, fast, rapid, lively, energetic, vigorous; informal cracking.
OPPOSITES untidy, downmarket, stupid, slow, gentle.
verb **1** *her eyes were smarting:* **sting**, burn, tingle, prickle, hurt. **2** *she smarted at the accusations:* **feel hurt**, feel upset, take offence, feel aggrieved, feel indignant, be put out.

smash verb **1** *he smashed a window:* **break**, shatter, splinter, crack; informal bust. **2** *she's smashed the car:* **crash**, wreck; Brit. write off; N. Amer. informal total. **3** *they smashed into a wall:* **crash**, smack, slam, plough, run, bump, hit, strike, ram, collide with; N. Amer. impact.
noun *a motorway smash:* **crash**, collision, accident; N. Amer. wreck; informal pile-up; Brit. informal shunt.

smear verb **1** *the table was smeared with grease:* **streak**, smudge, mark. **2** *smear the meat with olive oil:* **cover**, coat, grease. **3** *she smeared sunblock on her skin:* **spread**, rub, daub, slap, smother, plaster. **4** *they are trying to smear our*

reputation: **sully,** tarnish, blacken, drag through the mud, damage, defame, malign, slander, libel; N. Amer. slur.
noun **1** *smears of blood:* **streak,** smudge, daub, dab, spot, patch, blotch, mark; informal splodge. **2** *press smears about his closest aides:* **accusation,** lie, untruth, slur, slander, libel, defamation.

smell noun *the smell of the kitchen:* **odour,** aroma, fragrance, scent, perfume, bouquet, nose, stench, stink; Brit. informal pong.
verb **1** *he smelled her perfume:* **scent,** get a sniff of, detect. **2** *the dogs smelled each other:* **sniff,** nose. **3** *the cellar smells:* **stink,** reek; Brit. informal pong.

smelly adjective **foul-smelling,** stinking, reeking, rank; informal stinky; Brit. informal pongy.

smile verb *he smiled at her:* **beam,** grin (from ear to ear), smirk, simper, leer.
OPPOSITES frown.
noun *the smile on her face:* **beam,** grin, smirk, simper, leer.

smooth adjective **1** *the smooth flat rocks:* **even,** level, flat, glassy, glossy, silky, polished. **2** *a smooth sauce:* **creamy,** fine, velvety. **3** *a smooth sea:* **calm,** still, tranquil, undisturbed, unruffled, even, flat, like a millpond. **4** *smooth operation:* **steady,** regular, uninterrupted, unbroken, straightforward, easy, effortless, trouble-free. **5** *a smooth, confident man:* **suave,** urbane, sophisticated, polished, debonair, courteous, gracious, glib, slick; informal smarmy.
OPPOSITES uneven, rough, lumpy, irregular, gauche.
verb **1** *she smoothed the soil:* **flatten,** level (out/off), even

out/off, press, roll, iron, plane. **2** *brokers smooth the passage of goods:* **ease,** facilitate, expedite, assist, aid.
OPPOSITES roughen, hinder.

smother verb **1** *she tried to smother her baby:* **suffocate,** asphyxiate, stifle, choke. **2** *we smothered the flames:* **extinguish,** put out, snuff out, douse, stamp out. **3** *we smothered ourselves with suncream:* **smear,** daub, spread, cover. **4** *she smothered a sigh:* **stifle,** muffle, strangle, suppress, hold back, fight back, swallow, conceal.

smug adjective **self-satisfied,** conceited, complacent, superior, pleased with oneself.

snack noun **light meal,** sandwich, refreshments, nibbles, titbit(s); informal bite (to eat).

snag noun *we've met a snag:* **complication,** difficulty, catch, hitch, obstacle, pitfall, problem, setback, disadvantage, drawback.
verb *thorns snagged his sweater:* **catch,** hook, tear.

snap verb **1** *the ruler snapped:* **break,** fracture, splinter, split, crack; informal bust. **2** *'Shut up!' Anna snapped:* **smear,** snarl, growl, retort. **3** *photographers snapped the royals:* **photograph,** picture, take, shoot, film, capture.
noun **1** *she closed her purse with a snap:* **click,** crack, pop. **2** *holiday snaps:* **photograph,** picture, photo, shot, snapshot, print, slide.
■ **snap something up** buy eagerly, accept eagerly, jump at, take advantage of, grab, seize (on), pounce on.

snare noun *a fox caught in a*

S

snare: **trap,** gin, wire, net, noose.

verb *game birds were snared:* **trap,** catch, net, bag, ensnare, hook.

snatch verb 1 *she snatched the microphone:* **grab,** seize, take hold of, take, pluck, grasp at, clutch at. **2** (informal) *someone snatched my bag:* **steal,** take, thieve; informal swipe, nab, lift; Brit. informal nick, pinch, whip.

noun 1 *brief snatches of sleep:* **period,** spell, time, fit, bout, interval, stretch. **2** *a snatch of conversation:* **fragment,** snippet, bit, scrap, extract, excerpt, portion.

sneak verb 1 *I sneaked out:* **creep,** slink, steal, slip, slide, sidle, tiptoe, pad. **2** *she sneaked a camera in:* **smuggle,** spirit, slip.

adjective *a sneak preview:* **furtive,** secret, stealthy, sly, surreptitious, clandestine, covert, private, quick, exclusive.

sneaking adjective 1 *a sneaking admiration for him:* **secret,** private, hidden, concealed, unvoiced. **2** *a sneaking feeling:* **niggling,** nagging, lurking, insidious, lingering, persistent.

sneaky adjective sly, crafty, cunning, wily, scheming, devious, deceitful, underhand.
OPPOSITES honest.

sneer noun 1 *a sneer on her face:* **smirk,** curled lip. **2** *the sneers of others:* **jibe,** jeer, taunt, insult; informal dig.

verb 1 *he looked at me and sneered:* **smirk,** curl one's lip. **2** *it is easy to sneer at them:* **scoff,** laugh, scorn, disdain, mock, ridicule, deride; N. Amer. slur.

sniff verb 1 *she sniffed and blew her nose:* **inhale,** snuffle. **2** *Tom*

sniffed the fruit: **smell,** scent, get a whiff of.

noun 1 *she gave a loud sniff:* **snuffle,** snort. **2** *a sniff of fresh air:* **smell,** scent, whiff, lungful.
■ **sniff something out** (informal) detect, find, discover, bring to light, track down, dig up, root out, uncover, unearth.

snigger verb & noun giggle, titter, snicker, chortle, laugh, sneer, smirk.

snobbish, snobby adjective elitist, superior, supercilious, arrogant, condescending, pretentious, affected; informal snooty, high and mighty, la-di-da, stuck-up; Brit. informal toffee-nosed.

snub verb *sponsors find themselves snubbed by politicians:* **rebuff,** spurn, cold-shoulder, cut (dead), ignore, insult, slight; informal freeze out; N. Amer. informal stiff.

noun *a very public snub:* **rebuff,** slap in the face; informal brush-off, put-down.

snug adjective 1 *our tents were snug:* **cosy,** comfortable, warm, sheltered, secure; informal comfy. **2** *a snug dress:* **tight,** skintight, close-fitting, figure-hugging.
OPPOSITES bleak, loose.

soak verb 1 *soak the beans in water:* **dip,** immerse, steep, submerge, douse, marinate, souse. **2** *we got soaked outside:* **drench,** wet through, saturate, waterlog. **3** *the sweat soaked through his clothes:* **permeate,** penetrate, impregnate, percolate, seep, spread. **4** *use towels to soak up the water:* **absorb,** suck up, blot, mop up.

soaking adjective drenched, wet (through), soaked (through), sodden, soggy, waterlogged, saturated, sopping, dripping,

S

wringing.
OPPOSITES parched.

soar verb 1 *the bird soared into the air:* rise, ascend, climb.
2 *the gulls soared on the winds:* glide, plane, float, hover. 3 *the cost of living soared:* increase, escalate, shoot up, spiral; informal go through the roof, skyrocket.
OPPOSITES plummet.

sob verb weep, cry, snivel, whimper; Scottish greet; informal blubber; Brit. informal grizzle.

sober adjective 1 *the driver was clearly sober:* clear-headed, teetotal, abstinent, dry; informal on the wagon. 2 *a sober view of life:* serious, solemn, sensible, grave, sombre, level-headed, businesslike, down-to-earth. 3 *a sober suit:* sombre, subdued, severe, quiet, drab, plain.
OPPOSITES drunk, frivolous, sensational, flamboyant.

so-called adjective supposed, alleged, presumed, inappropriately named, ostensible, reputed, self-styled.

sociable adjective friendly, amicable, affable, companionable, gregarious, cordial, warm, genial.
OPPOSITES unfriendly.

social adjective 1 *a social problem:* communal, community, collective, group, general, popular, civil, public.
2 *a social club:* recreational, leisure, entertainment.
OPPOSITES individual, professional.
noun *the club has a social once a month:* party, gathering, function, get-together, celebration; informal do.

society noun 1 *a danger to society:* **the community**, the (general) public, the people, the population, civilization,

humankind, mankind. 2 *an industrial society:* culture, community, civilization, nation, population. 3 *Lady Angela will help you enter society:* **high society**, polite society, the upper classes, the gentry, the elite, the smart set; informal the upper crust. 4 *a local history society:* **club**, association, group, circle, institute, guild, lodge, league, union, alliance. 5 *the society of others:* **company**, companionship, fellowship, friendship.

sofa noun settee, couch, divan, chaise longue, chesterfield.

soft adjective 1 *soft fruit:* mushy, squashy, pulpy, slushy, squelchy, squishy, doughy; informal gooey; Brit. informal squidgy. 2 *soft ground:* swampy, marshy, boggy, muddy, squelchy. 3 *a soft cushion:* squashy, spongy, supple, springy, elastic, resilient. 4 *soft fabric:* smooth, velvety, fleecy, downy, furry, silky. 5 *soft light:* dim, low, faint, subdued, muted. 6 *soft colours:* pale, pastel, muted, restrained, subdued, subtle. 7 *soft voices:* quiet, low, gentle, faint, muted, subdued, muffled, hushed, whispered. 8 *soft outlines:* blurred, vague, hazy, misty, foggy, nebulous, fuzzy, indistinct. 9 *soft words:* kind, gentle, sympathetic, soothing, tender, sensitive, affectionate, loving, warm, sweet, sentimental. 10 *she's too soft with her pupils:* lenient, easy-going, tolerant, forgiving, forbearing, indulgent, liberal, lax.
OPPOSITES hard, firm, rough, harsh, lurid, strident, sharp, strict.

S

soften verb *the compensation should soften the blow*: ease, alleviate, relieve, soothe, take the edge off, cushion, lessen, diminish, blunt, deaden.

soil[1] noun **1** *acid soil*: earth, dirt, clay, ground, loam. **2** *British soil*: territory, land, region, country, domain, dominion.

soil[2] verb *he soiled his tie*: dirty, stain, smear, smudge, spoil, foul.

soldier noun fighter, trooper, serviceman, servicewoman, warrior; US GI; Brit. informal squaddie.

sole adjective only, one, single, solitary, lone, unique, exclusive.

solely adverb only, simply, purely, just, merely, uniquely, exclusively, entirely, wholly, alone.

solemn adjective **1** *a solemn occasion*: dignified, ceremonial, stately, formal, majestic, imposing, splendid, magnificent, grand. **2** *he looked very solemn*: serious, grave, sober, sombre, unsmiling, stern, grim, dour, humourless. **3** *a solemn promise*: sincere, earnest, honest, genuine, firm, heartfelt, wholehearted, sworn.
OPPOSITES frivolous, light-hearted, insincere.

solid adjective **1** *the plaster was solid*: hard, rock-hard, rigid, firm, solidified, set, frozen. **2** *solid gold*: pure, unadulterated, genuine. **3** *solid houses*: well built, sound, substantial, strong, sturdy, durable. **4** *a solid argument*: well founded, valid, sound, logical, authoritative, convincing. **5** *solid support from their colleagues*: unanimous, united, consistent, undivided.
OPPOSITES liquid, alloyed, flimsy, untenable, half-hearted.

solidarity noun unanimity, unity, agreement, team spirit, accord, harmony, consensus; formal concord.

solitary adjective **1** *a solitary man*: lonely, unaccompanied, by oneself, on one's own, alone, friendless, unsociable, withdrawn, reclusive; N. Amer. lonesome. **2** *solitary farmsteads*: isolated, remote, lonely, out of the way, in the back of beyond, outlying, off the beaten track, secluded; N. Amer. in the backwoods. **3** *a solitary piece of evidence*: single, lone, sole, only, one, individual.
OPPOSITES sociable, accessible.

solution noun **1** *a solution to the problem*: answer, result, resolution, key, explanation. **2** *a solution of salt and water*: mixture, blend, compound.

solve verb answer, resolve, work out, puzzle out, fathom, decipher, decode, clear up, straighten out, get to the bottom of, unravel, explain; informal figure out, crack; Brit. informal suss out.

sombre adjective **1** *sombre clothes*: dark, drab, dull, dingy, restrained, subdued, sober, funereal. **2** *a sombre expression*: solemn, earnest, serious, grave, sober, unsmiling, stern, grim, dour, gloomy, sad, mournful, lugubrious.
OPPOSITES bright, cheerful.

somehow adverb one way or another, no matter how, by fair means or foul, by hook or by crook, come what may.

sometimes adverb occasionally, from time to time, now and then, every so often, once in a

S

while, on occasion, at times, off and on.

song noun **air**, strain, ditty, chant, number, track, melody, tune.

soon adverb **shortly**, presently, in the near future, before long, in a little while, in a minute, in a moment; Brit. informal in a tick.

sooner adverb **1** *he should have done it sooner:* **earlier**, before now. **2** *I would sooner stay:* **rather**, preferably, given the choice.

soothe verb **1** *Rachel tried to soothe him:* **calm (down)**, pacify, comfort, hush, quiet, settle (down), appease, mollify; Brit. quieten (down). **2** *an anaesthetic to soothe the pain:* **ease**, alleviate, relieve, take the edge off, allay, lessen, reduce.
OPPOSITES agitate, aggravate.

soothing adjective **relaxing**, restful, calm, calming, tranquil, peaceful.

sophisticated adjective **1** *sophisticated technology:* **advanced**, state-of-the-art, the latest, up-to-the-minute, cutting-edge, trailblazing, complex. **2** *a sophisticated woman:* **worldly**, worldly-wise, experienced, cosmopolitan, urbane, cultured, cultivated, polished, refined.
OPPOSITES crude, naive.

sophistication noun **worldliness**, experience, urbanity, culture, polish, refinement, elegance, style, poise, finesse, savoir faire.

sore adjective **1** *a sore leg:* **painful**, hurting, hurt, aching, throbbing, smarting, stinging, inflamed, sensitive, tender, raw. **2** (N. Amer. informal) *they were sore at us:* **upset**, angry, annoyed, cross, disgruntled, dissatisfied,

irritated; informal aggravated, miffed, peeved; Brit. informal narked; N. Amer. informal ticked off.

sorrow noun **1** *he felt sorrow at her death:* **sadness**, unhappiness, misery, despondency, regret, despair, desolation, heartache, grief. **2** *the sorrows of life:* **trouble**, difficulty, problem, woe, affliction, trial, tribulation, misfortune.
OPPOSITES joy.

sorry adjective **1** *I was sorry to hear about his accident:* **sad**, moved, sorrowful, distressed. **2** *he felt sorry for her:* **full of pity**, sympathetic, compassionate, moved, concerned. **3** *I'm sorry I was rude:* **regretful**, apologetic, remorseful, contrite, repentant, rueful, penitent, guilty, shamefaced, ashamed.
OPPOSITES glad, unsympathetic, unrepentant.

sort noun *what sort of book is it?* **type**, kind, variety, class, category, style, form, genre, species, make, model.
verb **1** *they sorted the books alphabetically:* **classify**, class, group, organize, arrange, order. **2** *the problem was soon sorted out:* **resolve**, settle, solve, fix, work out, straighten out, deal with, put right, set right, rectify, iron out.

soul noun **1** *his soul cried out:* **spirit**, psyche, (inner) self. **2** *their music lacked soul:* **feeling**, emotion, passion, animation, intensity, warmth, energy, vitality, spirit.

sound¹ noun **1** *the sound of a car:* **noise**, din, racket, row, resonance, reverberation. **2** *she did not make a sound:* **utterance**, cry, word, noise,

S

peep. **3** *the sound of the flute:*
tone, timbre, call, song, voice.
OPPOSITES silence.
verb **1** *the buzzer sounded:* **make
a noise**, resonate, resound,
reverberate, go off, ring, chime,
ping. **2** *drivers must sound their
horns:* **blow**, blast, toot, ring,
use, operate, activate, set off.
3 *it sounds a crazy idea:* **appear**,
look (like), seem, give every
indication of being.

sound² adjective **1** *your heart is
sound:* **healthy**, in good
condition/shape, fit, hale and
hearty, in fine fettle,
undamaged, unimpaired. **2** *a
sound building:* **well built**,
solid, substantial, strong,
sturdy, durable, stable, intact.
3 *sound advice:* **well founded**,
valid, reasonable, logical,
weighty, authoritative, reliable.
4 *a sound judge of character:*
reliable, dependable,
trustworthy, fair, good.
5 *financially sound:* **solvent**,
debt-free, in the black, in
credit, creditworthy, secure. **6** *a
sound sleep:* **deep**, undisturbed,
uninterrupted, untroubled,
peaceful.
OPPOSITES unhealthy, unsound,
unsafe, unreliable, insolvent.

sour adjective **1** *sour wine:* **acid**,
acidic, tart, bitter, sharp,
vinegary, pungent. **2** *sour milk:*
bad, off, turned, curdled,
rancid, high, fetid. **3** *a sour old
man:* **embittered**, resentful,
jaundiced, bitter, cross, crabby,
crotchety, cantankerous; informal
grouchy.
OPPOSITES sweet, fresh, amiable.
verb *the dispute soured
relations:* **spoil**, mar, damage,
harm, impair, wreck, upset,
poison, blight.
OPPOSITES improve.

source noun **1** *the source of the
river:* **spring**, origin. **2** *the
source of the rumour:* **origin**,
starting point, root, author,
originator. **3** *historical sources:*
reference, authority,
informant, document.

souvenir noun memento,
keepsake, reminder, memorial,
trophy.

sovereign noun *the sovereign's
prerogative:* **ruler**, monarch,
potentate, overlord, king,
queen, emperor, empress,
prince, princess.
adjective *a sovereign state:*
autonomous, independent,
self-governing, self-
determining, non-aligned, free.

sovereignty noun **1** *their
sovereignty over the islands:*
power, rule, supremacy,
dominion, jurisdiction,
ascendancy, domination,
authority, control. **2** *full
sovereignty was achieved in
1955:* **autonomy**, independence,
self-government, self-rule,
home rule, self-determination,
freedom.

sow verb plant, scatter, disperse,
strew, broadcast, seed.

space noun **1** *there was not
enough space:* **room**, capacity,
latitude, margin, leeway, play,
elbow room, clearance. **2** *green
spaces in London:* **area**, expanse,
stretch, sweep, tract. **3** *a space
between the timbers:* **gap**,
interval, opening, aperture,
cavity, niche. **4** *write your name
in the appropriate space:* **blank**,
gap, box, field. **5** *a space of
seven years:* **period**, span, time,
duration, stretch, course,
interval, gap. **6** *the first woman
in space:* **outer space**, deep
space, the universe.
verb *the chairs were spaced*

widely: **position,** arrange, range, array, spread, lay out, set.

spacious adjective **roomy,** capacious, commodious, voluminous, sizeable, generous. OPPOSITES cramped.

span noun **1** *a six-foot wing span:* **extent,** length, width, reach, stretch, spread, distance, range. **2** *the span of one week:* **period,** space, time, duration, course, interval.
verb **1** *an arch spanned the stream:* **bridge,** cross, traverse, pass over. **2** *his career spanned twenty years:* **last,** cover, extend, spread over.

spare adjective **1** *a spare set of keys:* **extra,** supplementary, additional, second, other, alternative, emergency, reserve, backup, relief, substitute; N. Amer. alternate. **2** *they sold off the spare land:* **surplus,** superfluous, excess, leftover, redundant, unnecessary, unwanted; informal going begging. **3** *your spare time:* **free,** leisure, own. **4** *her spare, elegant form:* **slender,** lean, willowy, svelte, lissom, thin, skinny, gaunt, lanky, spindly.
verb **1** *he couldn't spare any money:* **afford,** manage, part with, give, provide. **2** *they were spared by their captors:* **pardon,** let off, forgive, have mercy on, reprieve, release, free.

sparing adjective **thrifty,** economical, frugal, careful, prudent, cautious.
OPPOSITES lavish, extravagant.

spark noun *a spark of light:* **flash,** glint, twinkle, flicker, flare.
verb *the arrest sparked off riots:* **cause,** give rise to, occasion, bring about, start, precipitate, prompt, trigger (off), provoke, stimulate, stir up.

sparkle verb & noun **glitter,** glint, glisten, twinkle, flicker, flash, shimmer.

sparkling adjective **1** *sparkling wine:* **effervescent,** fizzy, carbonated, aerated. **2** *a sparkling performance:* **brilliant,** dazzling, scintillating, exciting, exhilarating, stimulating, invigorating, vivacious, lively, vibrant.
OPPOSITES still, dull.

spate noun **series,** succession, run, cluster, string, rash, epidemic, outbreak, wave, flurry.

speak verb **1** *she refused to speak about it:* **talk,** converse, communicate, chat, have a word, gossip, commune, say anything/something. **2** *she spoke her words carefully:* **say,** utter, state, declare, voice, express, pronounce, articulate, enunciate, verbalize. **3** *the Minister spoke for two hours:* **give a speech,** talk, lecture, hold forth; informal spout, sound off.

speaker noun **speech-maker,** lecturer, talker, orator, spokesperson, spokesman/ woman, reader, commentator, broadcaster, narrator.

S

special adjective **1** *a very special person:* **exceptional,** unusual, remarkable, outstanding, unique. **2** *our town's special character:* **distinctive,** distinct, individual, particular, specific, peculiar. **3** *a special occasion:* **momentous,** significant, memorable, important, historic. **4** *a special tool for cutting tiles:* **specific,** particular, purpose-built, tailor-made, custom-built.
OPPOSITES ordinary, general.

specialist noun expert, authority, pundit, professional, connoisseur, master, maestro; informal buff.
OPPOSITES amateur.

speciality noun 1 *his speciality was watercolours:* **strength**, strong point, forte, métier, strong suit, party piece, pièce de résistance; informal bag, thing. 2 *a speciality of the region:* **delicacy**.

species noun type, kind, sort, breed, strain, variety, class, classification, category.

specific adjective 1 *a specific purpose:* **particular**, specified, fixed, set, determined, distinct, definite. 2 *I gave specific instructions:* **detailed**, explicit, express, clear-cut, unequivocal, precise, exact.
OPPOSITES general, vague.

specification noun 1 *clear specification of objectives:* **statement**, identification, definition, description, setting out. 2 *a shelter built to their specifications:* **instruction**, guideline, parameter, stipulation, requirement, condition, order, detail.

specify verb state, name, identify, define, set out, itemize, detail, list, spell out, stipulate, lay down.

specimen noun sample, example, model, instance, illustration, demonstration.

spectacle noun 1 *his love of spectacle:* **display**, show, pageantry, performance, exhibition, pomp and circumstance, extravaganza, spectacular. 2 *they were rather an odd spectacle:* **sight**, vision, scene, prospect, picture.

spectacular adjective 1 *a spectacular view:* **striking**, picturesque, eye-catching, breathtaking, arresting, glorious; informal out of this world. 2 *a spectacular victory:* **impressive**, magnificent, splendid, dazzling, sensational, dramatic, outstanding, memorable, unforgettable.
OPPOSITES dull, unimpressive.

spectator noun watcher, viewer, observer, onlooker, bystander, witness.
OPPOSITES participant.

spectre noun ghost, phantom, apparition, spirit, wraith, presence; informal spook.

speculate verb 1 *they speculated about my private life:* **conjecture**, theorize, hypothesize, guess, surmise, wonder, muse. 2 *investors speculate on the stock market:* **gamble**, venture, wager, invest, play the market; Brit. informal punt.

speculative adjective 1 *any discussion is largely speculative:* **conjectural**, suppositional, theoretical, hypothetical, tentative, unproven, unfounded, groundless, unsubstantiated. 2 *a speculative investment:* **risky**, hazardous, unsafe, uncertain, unpredictable; informal chancy.

speech noun 1 *the power of speech:* **speaking**, talking, verbal expression, verbal communication. 2 *her speech was slurred:* **diction**, elocution, articulation, enunciation, pronunciation, delivery, words. 3 *an after-dinner speech:* **talk**, address, lecture, discourse, oration, presentation, sermon. 4 *in popular speech:* **language**, parlance, tongue, idiom, dialect, vernacular; informal lingo.

speed noun 1 *the speed of their*

progress: **rate**, pace, tempo, momentum, velocity; informal lick. **2** *the speed with which they responded:* **rapidity**, swiftness, promptness, briskness, haste, hurry.
OPPOSITES slowness.
verb **1** *I sped home:* **hurry**, rush, dash, race, sprint, career, shoot, hurtle, hare, fly, zoom, hasten; informal tear, belt, pelt; Brit. informal bomb. **2** *a holiday will speed his recovery:* **hasten**, speed up, accelerate, advance, further, promote, boost, stimulate, aid, assist, facilitate.
OPPOSITES dawdle, slow, hinder.
■ **speed up** hurry up, accelerate, go faster, get a move on, put a spurt on, pick up speed; informal step on it.

speedy adjective **fast**, swift, quick, rapid, prompt, immediate, brisk, hasty, hurried, precipitate, rushed.
OPPOSITES slow.

spell[1] verb *the drought spelled disaster:* **signal**, signify, mean, amount to, add up to, constitute.
■ **spell something out** explain, make clear, clarify, specify, detail.

spell[2] noun **1** *the witch muttered a spell:* **charm**, incantation, formula, curse; N. Amer. hex; (spells) magic, sorcery, witchcraft. **2** *she surrendered to his spell:* **influence**, charm, magnetism, charisma, magic.
■ **put a spell on** bewitch, enchant, entrance, curse, jinx, witch; N. Amer. hex.

spell[3] noun **1** *a spell of dry weather:* **period**, time, interval, season, stretch, run; Brit. informal patch. **2** *a spell of dizziness:* **bout**, fit, attack.

spend verb **1** *she spent £185 on*

shoes: **pay out**, expend; informal blow, splurge. **2** *the morning was spent gardening:* **pass**, occupy, fill, take up, while away. **3** *I've spent hours on this essay:* **put in**, devote, waste, squander.

sphere noun **1** *a glass sphere:* **globe**, ball, orb, bubble. **2** *sphere of influence:* **area**, field, compass, orbit, range, scope, extent. **3** *the sphere of foreign affairs:* **domain**, realm, province, field, area, territory, arena, department.

spice noun **1** *the spices in curry powder:* **seasoning**, flavouring, condiment. **2** *the risk added spice to their affair:* **excitement**, interest, colour, piquancy, zest, an edge.

spicy adjective **hot**, tangy, peppery, piquant, spiced, highly seasoned, pungent.
OPPOSITES bland.

spike noun **prong**, pin, barb, point, skewer, stake, spit.

spill verb **1** *Kevin spilled his drink:* **knock over**, tip over, upset, overturn. **2** *the bath water spilled on to the floor:* **overflow**, slop, slosh, splash, leak. **3** *students spilled out of the building:* **stream**, pour, surge, swarm, flood, throng, crowd.

spin verb **1** *the wheels are spinning:* **revolve**, rotate, turn, go round, whirl. **2** *she spun round to face him:* **whirl**, wheel, twirl, turn, swing, twist, swivel, pivot.
noun **1** *a spin of the wheel:* **rotation**, revolution, turn, whirl, twirl. **2** *a positive spin:* **slant**, angle, twist, bias. **3** *a spin in the car:* **trip**, jaunt, outing, excursion, journey,

S

drive, ride, run, turn; informal tootle.

spine noun 1 *he injured his spine:* **backbone**, spinal column, back. 2 *cactus spines:* **needle**, quill, bristle, barb, spike, prickle, thorn.

spiral adjective *a spiral column:* **coiled**, helical, curling, winding, twisting.
noun *a spiral of smoke:* **coil**, curl, twist, whorl, scroll, helix, corkscrew.
verb *smoke spiralled up:* **coil**, wind, swirl, twist, snake.

spirit noun 1 *body and spirit:* **soul**, psyche, inner self, inner man/woman, mind. 2 *a spirit haunts the island:* **ghost**, phantom, spectre, apparition, presence. 3 *in good spirits:* **mood**, frame/state of mind, humour, temper. 4 *team spirit:* **morale**, esprit de corps. 5 *the spirit of the age:* **ethos**, essence, atmosphere, mood, feeling, climate. 6 *they played with spirit:* **enthusiasm**, energy, verve, vigour, dynamism, dash, sparkle, exuberance, gusto, fervour, zeal, fire, passion; informal get-up-and-go. 7 *the spirit of the law:* **real meaning**, true meaning, essence, substance, idea.
OPPOSITES body, flesh.

spirited adjective **lively**, energetic, enthusiastic, vigorous, dynamic, passionate; informal feisty, gutsy; N. Amer. informal peppy.
OPPOSITES apathetic, lifeless.

spiritual adjective 1 *your spiritual self:* **inner**, mental, psychological, incorporeal, non-material. 2 *spiritual writings:* **religious**, sacred, divine, holy, devotional.
OPPOSITES physical, secular.

spit verb 1 *Cranston coughed and spat:* **expectorate**, hawk; Brit. informal gob. 2 *the fat began to spit:* **sizzle**, hiss, crackle, sputter.
noun *spit dribbled from his mouth:* **spittle**, saliva, sputum, slobber, dribble; Brit. informal gob.

spite noun *he said it out of spite:* **malice**, malevolence, ill will, vindictiveness, meanness, nastiness; informal bitchiness, cattiness.
OPPOSITES kindness.
verb *he did it to spite me:* **upset**, hurt, wound.
OPPOSITES please.
■ **in spite of** despite, notwithstanding, regardless of, in defiance of, in the face of.

splash verb 1 *splash your face with water:* **sprinkle**, spray, shower, wash, squirt, daub, wet. 2 *his boots were splashed with rain:* **spatter**, splatter, speck, smear, stain, mark. 3 *waves splashing on the beach:* **wash**, break, lap, pound. 4 *children splashed in the water:* **paddle**, wade, wallow.
noun 1 *a splash of rain:* **spot**, blob, smear, speck. 2 *a splash of lemonade:* **drop**, dash, bit, spot, soupçon, dribble; Scottish informal scoosh. 3 *a splash of colour:* **patch**, burst, streak.

splendid adjective 1 *splendid costumes:* **magnificent**, sumptuous, grand, imposing, superb, spectacular, resplendent, rich, lavish, ornate, gorgeous, glorious, dazzling, handsome, beautiful; informal plush; Brit. informal swish. 2 (informal) *a splendid holiday:* **excellent**, wonderful, marvellous, superb, glorious, lovely, delightful, first-class; informal super, great, amazing,

fantastic, terrific, tremendous; Brit. informal smashing, brilliant.
OPPOSITES simple, modest, awful.

splendour noun **magnificence,** sumptuousness, grandeur, resplendence, richness, glory, majesty.
OPPOSITES simplicity, modesty.

splinter noun *a splinter of wood:* **sliver,** chip, shard, fragment, shred; Scottish skelf.
verb *the glass splintered:* **shatter,** smash, break into smithereens, fracture, split, crack, disintegrate.

split verb **1** *the force split the wood:* **break,** cut, burst, snap, crack. **2** *the ice split under him:* **break,** fracture, rupture, burst, snap, crack, come apart, splinter. **3** *her dress was split:* **tear,** rip, slash, slit. **4** *they split the profit:* **share,** divide up, distribute, dole out, parcel out, carve up, slice up. **5** *the path split:* **fork,** divide, branch, diverge. **6** *the band split up last year:* **break up,** separate, part, part company, go their separate ways.
OPPOSITES mend, join, unite, pool, converge, get together.
noun **1** *a split in the rock face:* **crack,** fissure, cleft, crevice, break, fracture, breach. **2** *a split in the curtain:* **rip,** tear, cut, rent, slash, slit. **3** *a split in the Party:* **division,** rift, breach, schism, rupture, partition. **4** *the acrimonious split with his wife:* **break-up,** split-up, separation, parting, estrangement, rift.
OPPOSITES join, merger, marriage.

spoil verb **1** *smoking spoils your complexion:* **damage,** ruin, impair, blemish, disfigure, blight, deface, harm, destroy,

wreck. **2** *rain spoiled my plans:* **ruin,** wreck, upset, undo, mess up, sabotage, scotch, torpedo; informal muck up, screw up, do for; Brit. informal cock up, scupper. **3** *his sisters spoil him:* **overindulge,** pamper, indulge, mollycoddle, cosset, wait on someone hand and foot.
4 *stockpiled food may spoil:* **go bad,** go off, go rancid, turn, go sour, rot, perish.
OPPOSITES improve, enhance, further, neglect, be strict with, keep.

spoken adjective **verbal,** oral, vocal, unwritten, word-of-mouth.
OPPOSITES non-verbal, written.

spokesperson, spokesman, spokeswoman noun **representative,** voice, mouthpiece, agent, official; informal spin doctor.

sponsor noun **backer,** patron, promoter, benefactor, supporter, contributor.
verb **finance,** fund, subsidize, back, promote, support, contribute to; N. Amer. informal bankroll.

spontaneous adjective **1** *a spontaneous display of affection:* **unplanned,** unpremeditated, impulsive, impromptu, spur-of-the-moment, unprompted; informal off-the-cuff. **2** *a spontaneous kind of person:* **natural,** uninhibited, relaxed, unselfconscious, unaffected.
OPPOSITES planned, inhibited.

sport noun **game,** physical recreation.
verb *he was sporting a new tie:* **wear,** have on, dress in, show off, parade, flaunt.

sporting adjective **sportsmanlike,** generous,

S

considerate, fair; Brit. informal decent.
OPPOSITES dirty, unfair.

sporty adjective (informal) **athletic**, fit, active, energetic.
OPPOSITES unfit, lazy.

spot noun **1** *a grease spot:* **mark**, patch, dot, fleck, smudge, smear, stain, blotch, splash; informal splodge. **2** *a spot on his nose:* **pimple**, pustule, blackhead, boil; informal zit; Scottish informal plook; (**spots**) acne. **3** *a secluded spot:* **place**, site, position, situation, setting, location, venue.
verb *she spotted him:* **see**, notice, observe, detect, make out, recognize, identify, locate; Brit. informal clock.

spotlight noun **attention**, glare of publicity, limelight, public eye.

spotted adjective **spotty**, dotted, polka-dot, freckled, mottled.
OPPOSITES plain.

spotty adjective **1** *a spotty dress:* **polka-dot**, spotted, dotted. **2** (Brit.) *his spotty face:* **pimply**, pimpled, acned; Scottish informal plooky.

spouse noun **partner**, husband, wife, mate, consort; informal better half; Brit. informal other half.

sprawl verb **stretch out**, lounge, loll, slump, flop, slouch.

spray noun **1** *a spray of water:* **shower**, sprinkle, jet, squirt, mist, spume, foam, froth. **2** *a perfume spray:* **aerosol**, vaporizer, atomizer, sprinkler.
verb **1** *we sprayed water on the soil:* **sprinkle**, dribble, drizzle. **2** *spray the plants with weedkiller:* **water**, mist, soak, douse, drench. **3** *water sprayed into the air:* **spout**, jet, gush, spurt, shoot, squirt.

spread verb **1** *he spread the map out:* **lay out**, open out, unfurl, unroll, roll out, straighten out, fan out, stretch out, extend. **2** *the landscape spread out below:* **extend**, stretch, sprawl. **3** *papers were spread all over his desk:* **scatter**, strew, disperse, distribute. **4** *he's spreading rumours:* **circulate**, broadcast, put about, publicize, propagate, repeat. **5** *the disease spread rapidly:* **travel**, move, be borne, sweep, diffuse, reproduce, be passed on, be transmitted. **6** *she spread sun cream on her arms:* **smear**, daub, plaster, apply, rub.
OPPOSITES fold up, suppress.
noun **1** *the spread of learning:* **expansion**, proliferation, dissemination, diffusion, transmission, propagation. **2** *a spread of six feet:* **span**, width, extent, stretch, reach.

spree noun **bout**, orgy; informal binge, splurge.

spring verb **1** *the cat sprang off her lap:* **leap**, jump, bound, vault. **2** *the branch sprang back:* **fly**, whip, flick, whisk, kick, bounce. **3** *all springs from feelings:* **originate**, derive, arise, stem, emanate, evolve.
noun *the mattress has lost its spring:* **springiness**, bounce, resilience, elasticity, flexibility, stretch, stretchiness, give.

sprinkle verb **1** *he sprinkled water on the cloth:* **splash**, trickle, drizzle, spray, shower, drip. **2** *sprinkle sesame seeds over the top:* **scatter**, strew. **3** *sprinkle the cake with icing sugar:* **dredge**, dust.

sprint verb **run**, race, rush, dash, bolt, fly, charge, shoot, speed; informal hotfoot it, leg it.
OPPOSITES walk.

sprout | squeeze

sprout verb **1** *the seeds begin to sprout:* **germinate,** put/send out shoots, bud. **2** *parsley sprouted from the pot:* **spring,** come up, grow, develop, appear.

spur noun *the spur of competition:* **stimulus,** incentive, encouragement, inducement, impetus, motivation.
OPPOSITES disincentive.
verb *the thought spurred him into action:* **stimulate,** encourage, prompt, prod, impel, motivate, move, galvanize, inspire, drive.
OPPOSITES discourage.

spurn verb **reject,** rebuff, scorn, turn down, treat with contempt, disdain, look down one's nose at; informal turn one's nose up at.
OPPOSITES welcome, accept.

spy noun *a foreign spy:* **agent,** mole, plant; N. Amer. informal spook.
verb *she spied a coffee shop:* **notice,** observe, see, spot, sight, catch sight of, glimpse, make out, discern, detect.
■ **spy on** observe, keep under surveillance, eavesdrop on, watch, bug.

spying noun **espionage,** intelligence gathering, surveillance, infiltration.

squabble noun *there was a brief squabble:* **quarrel,** disagreement, row, argument, dispute, wrangle, clash, altercation; informal tiff, set-to, run-in, scrap, dust-up; Brit. informal barney, ding-dong; N. Amer. informal rhubarb.
verb *they squabbled over money:* **quarrel,** row, argue, bicker, disagree; informal scrap.

squad noun **1** *a maintenance squad:* **team,** crew, gang, force.

2 *a squad of marines:* **detachment,** detail, unit, platoon, battery, troop, patrol, squadron, commando.

squander verb **waste,** throw away, misuse, fritter away, spend like water; informal blow, go through, splurge, pour down the drain.
OPPOSITES manage, make good use of, save.

square adjective *the sides were square at half-time:* **level,** even, drawn, equal, tied, level pegging; informal even-steven(s).
OPPOSITES uneven.
verb **1** *this does not square with the data:* **agree,** tally, be in agreement, be consistent, match up, correspond, fit.
2 *Tom squared things with his boss:* **resolve,** sort out, settle, clear up, work out, iron out, straighten out, set right, rectify, remedy; informal patch up.

squash verb **1** *the fruit got squashed:* **crush,** squeeze, mash, pulp, flatten, compress, distort, pound, trample. **2** *she squashed her clothes inside the bag:* **force,** ram, thrust, push, cram, jam, stuff, pack, squeeze, wedge.

squeeze verb **1** *I squeezed the bottle:* **compress,** press, crush, squash, pinch, nip, grasp, grip, clutch. **2** *squeeze the juice from both oranges:* **extract,** press, force, express. **3** *Sally squeezed her feet into the sandals:* **force,** thrust, cram, ram, jam, stuff, pack, wedge, press, squash. **4** *we all squeezed into Steve's van:* **crowd,** crush, cram, pack, jam, squash, shove, push, force one's way.
noun **1** *he gave her hand a squeeze:* **press,** pinch, nip, grasp, grip, clutch, hug. **2** *it was*

S

quite a squeeze: **crush**, jam, squash, congestion.

stab verb *he stabbed him in the stomach:* **knife**, run through, skewer, spear, gore, spike, impale.
noun **1** *a stab of pain:* **twinge**, pang, throb, spasm, cramp, prick, flash, thrill. **2** (informal) *a stab at writing:* **attempt**, try; informal go, shot, crack, bash.

stability noun **1** *the stability of the equipment:* **firmness**, solidity, steadiness. **2** *his mental stability:* **balance (of mind)**, (mental) health, sanity, reason. **3** *the stability of their relationship:* **strength**, durability, lasting nature, permanence.

stable adjective **1** *a stable vehicle:* **firm**, solid, steady, secure. **2** *a stable person:* **well balanced**, of sound mind, compos mentis, sane, normal, rational. **3** *a stable relationship:* **secure**, solid, strong, steady, firm, sure, steadfast, established, enduring, lasting.
OPPOSITES wobbly, unbalanced, rocky, changeable.

stack noun *a stack of boxes:* **heap**, pile, mound, mountain, pyramid, tower.
verb **1** *Leo was stacking plates:* **heap (up)**, pile (up), assemble, put together, collect. **2** *they stacked the shelves:* **load**, fill (up), pack, charge, stuff, cram, stock.
OPPOSITES clear.

staff noun **1** *we'll take on new staff:* **employees**, workers, workforce, personnel, human resources, manpower, labour. **2** *a wooden staff:* **stick**, stave, pole, rod.
verb *the centre is staffed by teachers:* **man**, people, crew, work, operate.

stage noun **1** *this stage of the development:* **phase**, period, juncture, step, point, level. **2** *the last stage of the race:* **part**, section, portion, stretch, leg, lap, circuit. **3** *a raised stage:* **platform**, dais, stand, rostrum, podium.

stagger verb **1** *he staggered to the door:* **lurch**, reel, sway, teeter, totter, stumble. **2** *I was absolutely staggered:* **amaze**, astound, astonish, surprise, stun, confound, daze, take aback; informal flabbergast; Brit. informal gobsmack.

stain verb **1** *her clothing was stained with blood:* **discolour**, soil, mark, spot, spatter, splatter, smear, splash, smudge. **2** *the wood was stained:* **colour**, tint, dye, pigment.
noun **1** *a mud stain:* **mark**, spot, blotch, smudge, smear. **2** *a stain on his character:* **blemish**, taint, blot, smear, dishonour.

stake[1] noun *a stake in the ground:* **post**, pole, stick, spike, upright, support, cane.

stake[2] noun **1** *high stakes:* **bet**, wager, ante. **2** *a 40% stake in the business:* **share**, interest, ownership, involvement.
verb *he staked his week's pay:* **bet**, wager, lay, put on, gamble.

stale adjective **1** *stale food:* **old**, past its best, off, dry, hard, musty, rancid. **2** *stale air:* **stuffy**, musty, fusty, stagnant. **3** *stale beer:* **flat**, spoiled, off, insipid, tasteless. **4** *stale jokes:* **overused**, hackneyed, tired, worn out, overworked, threadbare, banal, clichéd; N. Amer. played out.
OPPOSITES fresh, original.

stalk verb **1** *he was stalking a deer:* **trail**, follow, shadow,

S

track, go after, hunt; informal tail.
2 *she stalked out:* **strut,** stride,
march, flounce, storm, stomp,
sweep.

stall noun **1** *a market stall:*
stand, table, counter, booth,
kiosk. **2** *stalls for larger
animals:* **pen,** coop, sty, corral,
enclosure, compartment.
verb **1** *quit stalling:* **delay,** play
for time, procrastinate, hedge,
drag one's feet, filibuster,
stonewall. **2** *stall him for a bit:*
delay, divert, distract, hold off.

stalwart adjective **staunch,**
loyal, faithful, committed,
devoted, dedicated, dependable,
reliable.
OPPOSITES disloyal, unfaithful,
unreliable.

stamina noun **endurance,**
staying power, energy,
toughness, determination,
tenacity, perseverance, grit.

stammer verb **stutter,** stumble
over one's words, hesitate,
falter, pause, splutter.

stamp verb **1** *he stamped on my
toe:* **trample,** step, tread, tramp,
crush, squash, flatten. **2** *John
stamped off, muttering:* **stomp,**
stump, clump. **3** *the name is
stamped on the cover:* **imprint,**
print, impress, punch, inscribe,
emboss.
noun *the stamp of authority:*
mark, hallmark, sign, seal, sure
sign, smack, savour, air.
■ **stamp something out** put an
end to, end, stop, crush, put
down, curb, quell, suppress,
extinguish, stifle, abolish, get
rid of, eliminate, eradicate,
destroy, wipe out.

stance noun **1** *a natural golfer's
stance:* **posture,** body position,
pose, attitude. **2** *a liberal
stance:* **attitude,** opinion,
standpoint, position, approach,

policy, line.

stand verb **1** *the men stood up:*
rise, get to one's feet, get up,
pick oneself up. **2** *today a house
stands on the site:* **be situated,**
be located, be positioned, be
sited, have been built. **3** *he
stood the vase on the shelf:* **put,**
set, erect, place, position, prop,
install, arrange; informal park.
4 *my decision stands:* **remain in
force,** remain in operation,
hold, hold good, apply, be the
case, exist. **5** *his heart could not
stand the strain:* **withstand,**
endure, bear, put up with, take,
cope with, handle, sustain,
resist, stand up to. **6** (informal) *I
won't stand cheek:* **put up with,**
endure, tolerate, accept, take,
abide, stand for, support,
countenance; formal brook.
OPPOSITES sit, lie down.
noun **1** *the party's stand on
immigration:* **attitude,** stance,
opinion, standpoint, position,
approach, policy, line. **2** *a stand
against tyranny:* **opposition,**
resistance. **3** *a mirror on a
stand:* **base,** support, platform,
rest, plinth, tripod, rack, trivet.
4 *a newspaper stand:* **stall,**
counter, booth, kiosk.
■ **stand by** wait, be prepared, be
in (a state of) readiness, be
ready for action, be on full
alert, wait in the wings. ■ **stand
by someone/something 1** *she
stood by her husband:* **remain/
be loyal to,** stick with/by,
remain/be true to, stand up for,
support, back up, defend, stick
up for. **2** *the government must
stand by its pledges:* **abide by,**
keep (to), adhere to, hold to,
stick to, observe, comply with.
■ **stand for** mean, be short for,
represent, signify, denote,
symbolize. ■ **stand in** deputize,
act, substitute, fill in, take over,

S

cover, hold the fort, step into the breach, replace, relieve, take over from; informal sub, step into someone's shoes; N. Amer. pinch-hit. ■ **stand out** be noticeable, be visible, be obvious, be conspicuous, stick out, attract attention, catch the eye, leap out; informal stick/stand out a mile, stick/stand out like a sore thumb.

standard noun 1 *the standard of her work:* **quality,** level, calibre, merit, excellence. 2 *a safety standard:* **guideline,** norm, yardstick, benchmark, measure, criterion, guide. 3 *a standard to live by:* **principle,** ideal; (**standards**) code of behaviour, morals, ethics. 4 *the regiment's standard:* **flag,** banner, ensign, colour(s).
adjective 1 *the standard way of doing it:* **normal,** usual, typical, stock, common, ordinary, customary, conventional, established. 2 *the standard work on the subject:* **definitive,** classic, recognized, accepted.
OPPOSITES unusual, special.

standing noun 1 *his standing in the community:* **status,** ranking, position, reputation, stature. 2 *a person of some standing:* **prestige,** rank, eminence, seniority, repute, stature, esteem, importance, account.

staple adjective **main,** principal, chief, major, primary, leading, foremost, first, most important, predominant, dominant, basic, prime; informal number-one.

star noun 1 *the sky was full of stars:* **celestial/heavenly body,** sun. 2 *the stars of the film:* **principal,** leading lady/man, lead, hero, heroine. 3 *a star of the world of chess:* **celebrity,** superstar, famous name, household name, leading light, VIP, personality, luminary; informal celeb, big shot, megastar.
OPPOSITES nobody.
adjective 1 *a star pupil:* **outstanding,** exceptional. 2 *the star attraction:* **top,** leading, greatest, foremost, major, pre-eminent.
OPPOSITES poor, minor.

stare verb **gaze,** gape, goggle, glare, ogle, peer; informal gawk; Brit. informal gawp.

stark adjective 1 *a stark silhouette:* **sharp,** crisp, distinct, clear, clear-cut. 2 *a stark landscape:* **desolate,** bare, barren, empty, bleak. 3 *a stark room:* **austere,** severe, plain, simple, bare, unadorned. 4 *stark terror:* **sheer,** utter, absolute, total, pure, downright, out-and-out, outright. 5 *the stark facts:* **blunt,** bald, bare, simple, plain, unvarnished, harsh, grim.
OPPOSITES fuzzy, indistinct, lush, ornate, disguised.
adverb *stark naked:* **completely,** totally, utterly, absolutely, entirely, wholly, fully, quite, altogether, thoroughly.

start verb 1 *the meeting starts at 7.45:* **begin,** commence, get under way, get going, go ahead; informal kick off. 2 *this was how her illness started:* **come into being/existence,** begin, commence, be born, arise, originate, develop. 3 *she started her own charity:* **establish,** set up, found, create, bring into being, institute, initiate, inaugurate, introduce, open, launch. 4 *you can start the machine:* **activate,** switch/turn on, start up, fire up, boot up. 5 *the machine started:* **begin working,** start up, get going,

S

spring into life. **6** *'Oh my!' she said, starting:* **flinch,** jerk, jump, twitch, wince.
OPPOSITES finish, stop, wind up, close down.
noun **1** *the start of the event:* **beginning,** commencement, inception. **2** *the start of her illness:* **onset,** emergence. **3** *a quarter of an hour's start:* **lead,** head start, advantage. **4** *she awoke with a start:* **jerk,** twitch, spasm, jump.
OPPOSITES end, finish.

startle verb **surprise,** frighten, scare, alarm, shock, give someone a fright, make someone jump.
OPPOSITES put at ease.

starving adjective **hungry,** undernourished, malnourished, starved, ravenous, famished.
OPPOSITES full.

state¹ noun **1** *the state of the economy:* **condition,** shape, position, predicament, plight. **2** *an autonomous state:* **country,** nation, land, kingdom, realm, power, republic. **3** *the country is divided into thirty-two states:* **province,** region, territory, canton, department, county, district; Brit. shire. **4** *the power of the state:* **government,** parliament, administration, regime, authorities.

state² verb **express,** voice, utter, put into words, declare, announce, make known, put across/over, communicate, air.

stately adjective **dignified,** majestic, ceremonious, courtly, imposing, solemn, regal, grand.
OPPOSITES undignified.

statement noun **declaration,** expression, affirmation, assertion, announcement, utterance, communication, bulletin, communiqué.

station noun **1** *a research station:* **establishment,** base, camp, post, depot, mission, site, facility, installation. **2** *a police station:* **office,** depot, base, headquarters; N. Amer. precinct, station house. **3** *a radio station:* **channel,** wavelength.
verb *the regiment was stationed at Woolwich:* **base,** post, establish, deploy, garrison.

stationary adjective **static,** parked, motionless, immobile, still, stock-still, at a standstill, at rest.
OPPOSITES moving, shifting.

stature noun **1** *small in stature:* **height,** size, build. **2** *an architect of international stature:* **reputation,** repute, standing, status, position, prestige, distinction, eminence, prominence, importance.

status noun **1** *the status of women:* **standing,** rank, position, level, place. **2** *wealth and status:* **prestige,** kudos, cachet, standing, stature, esteem, image, importance, authority, fame.

staunch¹ adjective *a staunch supporter:* **stalwart,** loyal, faithful, committed, devoted, dedicated, reliable.
OPPOSITES disloyal, unfaithful, unreliable.

staunch² verb *try to staunch the flow:* **stem,** stop, halt, check, curb; N. Amer. stanch.

stay verb **1** *he stayed where he was:* **remain (behind),** wait, linger, stick, be left, hold on, hang on; informal hang around; Brit. informal hang about. **2** *they won't stay hidden:* **continue (to be),** remain, keep, carry on being, go on being. **3** *our aunt is staying with us:* **visit,** stop (off/over), holiday, lodge;

S

N. Amer. vacation.
OPPOSITES leave, stop being.
noun *a stay at a hotel:* **visit,**
stop, stopover, break, holiday;
N. Amer. vacation.

steady adjective **1** *the ladder*
must be steady: **stable,** firm,
fixed, secure. **2** *keep the camera*
steady: **still,** motionless, static,
stationary. **3** *a steady gaze:*
fixed, intent, unwavering,
unfaltering. **4** *a steady income:*
constant, regular, consistent,
reliable. **5** *steady rain:*
continuous, continual,
unceasing, ceaseless, perpetual,
unremitting, endless. **6** *a steady*
boyfriend: **regular,** settled,
firm, committed, long-term.
OPPOSITES unstable, loose, shaky,
darting, fluctuating, sporadic,
occasional.
verb **1** *he steadied the rifle:*
stabilize, hold steady, brace,
support, balance, rest. **2** *she*
needed to steady her nerves:
calm, soothe, quieten, compose,
settle, subdue, quell.

steal verb **1** *burglars stole the*
TV: **take,** thieve, help oneself
to, pilfer, embezzle; informal
swipe, lift, filch; Brit. informal nick,
pinch, knock off; N. Amer. informal
heist. **2** *his work was stolen by*
his tutor: **plagiarize,** copy,
pirate; informal rip off, lift, pinch,
crib; Brit. informal nick. **3** *he stole*
out of the room: **creep,** sneak,
slink, slip, glide, tiptoe, slope.

stealth noun **furtiveness,**
secretiveness, secrecy,
surreptitiousness.
OPPOSITES openness.

stealthy adjective **furtive,**
secretive, secret, surreptitious,
sneaky, sly.
OPPOSITES open.

steep adjective **1** *steep cliffs:*
sheer, precipitous, abrupt,

sharp, perpendicular, vertical.
2 *a steep increase:* **sharp,**
sudden, dramatic.
OPPOSITES gentle, gradual,
reasonable.

steeped
■ **steeped in** imbued with, filled
with, permeated with, suffused
with, soaked in, pervaded by.

steer verb **guide,** direct,
manoeuvre, drive, pilot,
navigate.

stem[1] noun *a plant stem:* **stalk,**
shoot, trunk.
■ **stem from** come from, arise
from, originate from, have its
origins in, spring from, derive
from.

stem[2] verb *they stemmed the*
flow of blood: **stop,** staunch,
halt, check, curb; N. Amer. stanch.

step noun **1** *Frank took a step*
forward: **pace,** stride. **2** *she*
heard a step on the stairs:
footstep, footfall, tread. **3** *the*
top step: **stair,** tread; (**steps**)
stairs, staircase, flight of stairs.
4 *resigning is a very serious*
step: **action,** act, course of
action, measure, move,
operation. **5** *a significant step*
towards a ceasefire: **advance,**
development, move, movement,
breakthrough. **6** *the first step*
on the managerial ladder: **stage,**
level, grade, rank, degree,
phase.
verb *she stepped forward:* **walk,**
move, tread, pace, stride.
■ **step down** resign, stand
down, give up one's post/job,
bow out, abdicate; informal quit.
■ **step in** intervene, become
involved, intercede. ■ **step**
something up increase,
intensify, strengthen, escalate,
speed up, accelerate; informal up,
crank up.

stereotype noun *the stereotype*

of the woman as carer:
conventional idea, standard
image, cliché, formula.
verb *bodybuilders are
stereotyped as 'muscleheads'*:
typecast, pigeonhole,
conventionalize, categorize,
label, tag.

sterile adjective **1** *sterile desert*:
unproductive, infertile,
unfruitful, barren. **2** *sterile
conditions*: **hygienic**, clean,
pure, uncontaminated,
sterilized, disinfected, germ-
free, antiseptic.
OPPOSITES fertile, productive,
septic.

stern adjective **1** *a stern
expression*: **unsmiling**,
frowning, serious, severe,
forbidding, grim, unfriendly,
austere, dour. **2** *stern measures*:
strict, severe, stringent, harsh,
drastic, hard, tough, extreme,
draconian.
OPPOSITES genial, friendly,
lenient, lax.

stick¹ noun **1** *a fire made of
sticks*: **branch**, twig. **2** *he walks
with a stick*: **walking stick**,
cane, staff, crutch. **3** *the plants
need supporting on sticks*: **post**,
pole, cane, stake. **4** *he beat me
with a stick*: **club**, cudgel,
truncheon, baton, cane, switch,
rod; Brit. informal cosh.

stick² verb **1** *he stuck his fork
into the sausage*: **thrust**, push,
insert, jab, poke, dig, plunge.
2 *the bristles stuck into his skin*:
pierce, penetrate, puncture,
prick, stab. **3** *the mug stuck to
the mat*: **adhere**, cling. **4** *stick
the stamp there*: **attach**, fasten,
affix, fix, paste, glue, gum, tape.
5 *the wheels stuck fast*: **jam**, get
jammed, catch, get caught, get
trapped. **6** *that sticks in his
mind*: **remain**, stay, linger,

persist, continue, endure. **7** (Brit.
informal) *I can't stick it*: **tolerate**,
put up with, take, stand,
stomach, endure, bear; informal
abide.
■ **stick out 1** *his front teeth
stuck out*: protrude, jut (out),
project, stand out, extend, poke
out, bulge. **2** *they stuck out in
their new clothes*: be
conspicuous, be obvious, stand
out, attract attention, leap out;
informal stick out a mile. ■ **stick
to** abide by, keep, adhere to,
hold to, comply with, fulfil,
stand by. ■ **stick up for** support,
take someone's side, side with,
stand by, stand up for, defend.

sticky adjective **1** *sticky tape*:
adhesive, self-adhesive,
gummed. **2** *sticky clay*: **tacky**,
gluey, gummy, treacly,
glutinous; informal gooey. **3** *sticky
weather*: **humid**, muggy, close,
sultry, steamy, sweaty. **4** *a
sticky situation*: **awkward**,
difficult, tricky, ticklish,
delicate, embarrassing,
sensitive; informal hairy.
OPPOSITES dry, fresh, cool, easy.

stiff adjective **1** *stiff cardboard*:
rigid, hard, firm. **2** *a stiff paste*:
thick, firm, viscous, semi-solid.
3 *I'm stiff all over*: **aching**, achy,
painful, arthritic. **4** *a rather
stiff manner*: **formal**, reserved,
wooden, forced, strained,
stilted; informal starchy, uptight.
5 *a stiff fine*: **harsh**, severe,
heavy, stringent, drastic,
draconian; Brit. swingeing. **6** *stiff
resistance*: **vigorous**,
determined, strong, spirited,
resolute, tenacious, dogged,
stubborn. **7** *a stiff climb*:
difficult, hard, arduous, tough,
strenuous, laborious, exacting,
tiring, demanding. **8** *a stiff
breeze*: **strong**, fresh, brisk. **9** *a
stiff drink*: **strong**, potent,

S

alcoholic.
OPPOSITES flexible, limp, runny, supple, relaxed, informal, lenient, mild, half-hearted, easy, gentle, weak.

stifle verb suppress, smother, restrain, check, curb, silence, hinder, hamper, impede, prevent, inhibit.
OPPOSITES encourage, let out.

still adjective 1 *Polly lay still:* motionless, unmoving, stock-still, immobile, rooted to the spot, transfixed, static, stationary. 2 *a still night:* quiet, silent, calm, peaceful, serene, windless. 3 *the lake was still:* calm, flat, smooth, like a millpond.
OPPOSITES moving, active, noisy, rough.
adverb 1 *he's still here:* even now, yet. 2 *He's crazy. Still, he's harmless:* nevertheless, nonetheless, all the same, even so, but, however, despite that, in spite of that, for all that.
verb *he stilled the crowd:* quieten, quiet, silence, hush, calm, settle, pacify, subdue.
OPPOSITES stir up.

stimulate verb encourage, prompt, motivate, trigger, spark, spur on, galvanize, fire, inspire, excite; N. Amer. light a fire under.
OPPOSITES discourage.

stimulating adjective thought-provoking, interesting, inspiring, inspirational, lively, exciting, provocative.
OPPOSITES uninspiring, boring.

stimulus noun motivation, encouragement, impetus, prompt, spur, incentive, inspiration.
OPPOSITES deterrent, discouragement.

sting noun 1 *a bee sting:* prick, wound, injury. 2 *this cream will take the sting away:* pain, pricking, smart, soreness, hurt, irritation.
verb 1 *she was stung by a scorpion:* prick, wound. 2 *the smoke made her eyes sting:* smart, burn, hurt, be irritated, be sore. 3 *the criticism stung her:* upset, wound, hurt, pain, mortify.

stink verb *his clothes stank of sweat:* reek, smell.
noun *the stink of sweat:* stench, reek; Brit. informal pong; N. Amer. informal funk.

stint noun spell, stretch, turn, session, term, time, shift, tour of duty.

stipulate verb specify, set out, lay down, demand, require, insist on.

stir verb 1 *stir the mixture well:* mix, blend, beat, whip, whisk, fold in; N. Amer. muddle. 2 *James stirred in his sleep:* move, change one's position, shift. 3 *a breeze stirred the leaves:* disturb, rustle, shake, move, agitate. 4 *the war stirred him to action:* spur, drive, rouse, prompt, propel, motivate, encourage, urge, impel, provoke.
noun *the news caused a stir:* commotion, disturbance, fuss, excitement, sensation; informal to-do, hoo-ha.

stock noun 1 *the shop doesn't carry much stock:* merchandise, goods, wares. 2 *a stock of fuel:* store, supply, stockpile, reserve, hoard, cache, bank. 3 *farm stock:* animals, livestock, beasts, flocks, herds. 4 *his mother was of French stock:* descent, ancestry, origin(s), lineage, birth,

S

extraction, family, blood, pedigree.
adjective *the stock response:* **usual,** routine, predictable, set, standard, staple, customary, familiar, conventional, traditional, stereotyped, clichéd, hackneyed, unoriginal, formulaic.
OPPOSITES non-standard, original.
verb *we do not stock GM food:* **sell,** carry, keep (in stock), offer, supply, provide, furnish.

stomach noun **1** *a pain in my stomach:* **abdomen,** belly, gut, middle; informal tummy, insides. **2** *his fat stomach:* **paunch,** belly, beer belly, girth; informal pot, tummy, spare tyre, middle-aged spread; N. Amer. informal bay window. **3** *no stomach for a fight:* **appetite,** taste, inclination, desire, wish.
verb *they couldn't stomach it:* **tolerate,** put up with, take, stand, endure, bear; informal hack, abide; Brit. informal stick.

stone noun **1** *someone threw a stone:* **rock,** pebble, boulder. **2** *a precious stone:* **gem,** gemstone, jewel; informal rock, sparkler. **3** *a peach stone:* **kernel,** seed, pip, pit.

stoop verb *she stooped to pick up the pen:* **bend,** lean, crouch, bow, duck.
noun *a man with a stoop:* **hunch,** round shoulders.

stop verb **1** *we can't stop the decline:* **end,** halt, finish, terminate, wind up, discontinue, cut short, interrupt, nip in the bud, shut down. **2** *he stopped running:* **cease,** discontinue, desist from, break off, give up, abandon, cut out; informal quit, pack in; Brit. informal jack in. **3** *the car stopped:*

pull up, draw up, come to a stop/halt, come to rest, pull in/over. **4** *the music stopped:* **cease,** end, come to an and, halt, finish, draw to a close, be over, conclude. **5** *the police stopped her leaving:* **prevent,** obstruct, impede, block, bar, preclude, dissuade from.
OPPOSITES start, begin, continue, allow, encourage.
noun 1 *all business came to a stop:* **halt,** end, finish, close, standstill. **2** *a brief stop in the town:* **break,** stopover, stop-off, stay, visit. **3** *the next stop is Oxford Street:* **stopping place,** station, halt.
OPPOSITES start, beginning, continuation.

store noun **1** *a store of food:* **stock,** supply, stockpile, hoard, cache, reserve, bank, pool. **2** *a grain store:* **storeroom,** storehouse, repository, stockroom, depot, warehouse. **3** *ship's stores:* **supplies,** provisions, stocks, food, rations, materials, equipment, hardware. **4** *a DIY store:* **shop,** (retail) outlet, boutique, department store, supermarket, hypermarket, superstore, megastore.
verb *rabbits don't store food:* **keep,** stockpile, lay in, set aside, put aside, put away/by, save, collect, accumulate, hoard; informal squirrel away.
OPPOSITES use, discard.

storehouse noun **warehouse,** depository, repository, store, storeroom, depot.

storm noun **1** *battered by a storm:* **tempest,** squall, gale, hurricane, tornado, cyclone, typhoon, thunderstorm, rainstorm, monsoon, hailstorm, snowstorm, blizzard. **2** *there*

S

was a storm over his remarks:
uproar, outcry, fuss, furore,
rumpus, trouble; informal to-do,
hoo-ha, ructions, stink; Brit.
informal row.

verb 1 *she stormed out:* **stride,**
march, stomp, stamp, stalk,
flounce, fling. **2** *police stormed
the building:* **attack,** charge,
rush, swoop on.

stormy adjective **1** *stormy
weather:* **blustery,** squally,
windy, gusty, blowy, thundery,
wild, violent, rough, foul. **2** *a
stormy debate:* **angry,** heated,
fierce, furious, passionate,
acrimonious.

OPPOSITES calm, fine, peaceful.

story noun **1** *an adventure story:*
tale, narrative, account, history,
anecdote, saga; informal yarn.
2 *the novel has a good story:*
plot, storyline, scenario. **3** *the
story appeared in the papers:*
news, report, item, article,
feature, piece. **4** *there have
been a lot of stories going
round:* **rumour,** whisper,
allegation, speculation, gossip;
Austral./NZ informal furphy.

stout adjective **1** *a short stout
man:* **fat,** plump, portly, rotund,
dumpy, corpulent; informal tubby;
Brit. informal podgy; N. Amer. informal
zaftig, corn-fed. **2** *stout leather
shoes:* **strong,** sturdy, solid,
robust, tough, durable, hard-
wearing. **3** *stout resistance:*
determined, vigorous, forceful,
spirited, committed, brave;
informal gutsy.

OPPOSITES thin, flimsy, feeble.

straight adjective **1** *a long,
straight road:* **direct,** linear,
unswerving, undeviating. **2** *that
picture isn't straight:* **level,**
even, in line, aligned, square,
vertical, upright, perpendicular,
horizontal. **3** *we must get the*

place straight: **in order,** tidy,
neat, shipshape, orderly,
organized, arranged, sorted out,
straightened out. **4** *a straight
answer:* **honest,** direct, frank,
candid, truthful, sincere,
forthright, straightforward,
plain-spoken, blunt,
unambiguous; informal upfront.
5 *straight brandy:* **neat,**
undiluted, pure; N. Amer. informal
straight up.

OPPOSITES winding, crooked,
untidy, evasive.

adverb **1** *he looked me straight in
the eyes:* **right,** directly,
squarely, full; informal smack,
(slap) bang; N. Amer. informal
spang, smack dab. **2** *she drove
straight home:* **directly,** right.
3 *I told her straight:* **frankly,**
directly, candidly, honestly,
forthrightly, plainly, point-
blank, bluntly, flatly; Brit. informal
straight up. **4** *he can't think
straight:* **logically,** rationally,
clearly, lucidly, coherently,
cogently.

■ **straight away** at once, right
away, (right) now, this/that
(very) minute, this/that
instant, immediately, instantly,
directly, forthwith, then and
there; N. Amer. in short order;
informal straight off, pronto;
N. Amer. informal lickety-split.

straighten verb **1** *Rory
straightened his tie:* **put
straight,** adjust, arrange,
rearrange, tidy. **2** *we must
straighten things out with Viola:*
put right, sort out, clear up,
settle, resolve, rectify, remedy;
informal patch up.

straightforward adjective
1 *the process was remarkably
straightforward:*
uncomplicated, simple, plain
sailing. **2** *a straightforward
man:* **honest,** frank, candid,

open, truthful, sincere, on the level, forthright, plain-speaking, direct; informal upfront; N. Amer. informal on the up and up.
OPPOSITES complicated, devious.

strain¹ verb **1** *take care that you don't strain yourself:* **overtax**, overwork, overextend, overreach, overdo it, exhaust, wear out; informal knacker, knock oneself out. **2** *you have strained a muscle:* **injure**, damage, pull, wrench, twist, sprain. **3** *strain the mixture:* **sieve**, sift, filter, screen.
noun **1** *the rope snapped under the strain:* **tension**, tightness, tautness. **2** *muscle strain:* **injury**, sprain, wrench, twist. **3** *the strain of her job:* **pressure**, demands, burdens, stress; informal hassle. **4** *Melissa was showing signs of strain:* **stress**, (nervous) tension, exhaustion, fatigue, pressure, overwork.

strain² noun *a different strain of flu:* **variety**, kind, type, sort, breed, genus.

strained adjective **1** *relations were strained:* **awkward**, tense, uneasy, uncomfortable, edgy, difficult, troubled. **2** *a strained smile:* **forced**, unnatural, artificial, insincere, false, affected, put-on.
OPPOSITES friendly, genuine.

strait noun **1** **channel**, sound, narrows, stretch of water. **2** (**straits**) **difficulty**, trouble, crisis, mess, predicament, plight; informal hot water, jam, hole, fix, scrape.

strand noun **thread**, filament, fibre, length.

stranded adjective **1** *stranded on a desert island:* **shipwrecked**, wrecked, marooned, high and dry, grounded, aground,

beached. **2** *stranded in a strange city:* **helpless**, abandoned, lost, adrift.

strange adjective **1** *strange things have been happening:* **unusual**, odd, curious, peculiar, funny, bizarre, weird, uncanny, anomalous; informal fishy. **2** *visiting a strange house:* **unfamiliar**, unknown, new, novel.
OPPOSITES ordinary, familiar.

stranger noun **newcomer**, new arrival, visitor, guest, outsider, foreigner.

strangle verb **throttle**, choke, garrotte, asphyxiate.

strap noun *thick leather straps:* **belt**, tie, band, thong.
verb *a bag was strapped to the bicycle:* **tie**, lash, secure, fasten, bind, make fast, truss.

strapping adjective **big**, strong, well-built, brawny, burly, muscular; informal beefy.
OPPOSITES weedy.

strategic adjective **planned**, calculated, deliberate, tactical, judicious, prudent, shrewd.

strategy noun **plan**, grand design, game plan, policy, programme, scheme.

stray verb **1** *the gazelle had strayed from the herd:* **wander off**, get separated, get lost, drift away. **2** *we strayed from our original topic:* **digress**, deviate, wander, get sidetracked, go off at a tangent, get off the subject.
adjective **1** *a stray dog:* **homeless**, lost, abandoned, feral. **2** *a stray bullet:* **random**, chance, freak, unexpected.

streak noun **1** *a streak of light:* **band**, line, strip, stripe, vein, slash, ray, smear. **2** *a streak of self-destructiveness:* **element**, vein, strain, touch. **3** *a winning*

S

streak: **period,** spell, stretch, run; Brit. informal **patch.**
verb 1 *the sky was streaked with red:* **stripe,** band, fleck, smear, mark. **2** *Miranda streaked across the road:* **race,** speed, flash, shoot, dash, rush, hurtle, whizz, zoom, career, fly; informal belt, tear, zip, whip; Brit. informal bomb; N. Amer. informal barrel.

stream noun **1** *a mountain stream:* **brook,** rivulet, tributary; Scottish & N. English burn; N. English beck; S. English bourn; N. Amer. & Austral./NZ creek. **2** *a stream of boiling water:* **jet,** flow, rush, gush, surge, torrent, flood, cascade. **3** *a steady stream of visitors:* **succession,** series, string.
verb 1 *tears were streaming down her face:* **flow,** pour, course, run, gush, surge, flood, cascade, spill. **2** *children streamed out of the classrooms:* **pour,** surge, flood, swarm, pile, crowd.

streamlined adjective **1** *streamlined cars:* **aerodynamic,** smooth, sleek. **2** *a streamlined organization:* **efficient,** smooth-running, well run, slick.

street noun **road,** thoroughfare, avenue, drive, boulevard, lane; N. Amer. highway.

strength noun **1** *enormous physical strength:* **power,** muscle, might, brawn, force. **2** *Oliver began to regain his strength:* **health,** fitness, vigour, stamina. **3** *her great inner strength:* **fortitude,** resilience, spirit, backbone, courage, bravery, pluck, grit; informal guts. **4** *the strength of the retaining wall:* **robustness,** sturdiness, firmness, toughness, soundness, solidity, durability. **5** *political strength:* **power,** influence; informal clout. **6** *strength of feeling:* **intensity,** vehemence, force, depth. **7** *the strength of their argument:* **force,** weight, power, persuasiveness, soundness, cogency, validity. **8** *what are your strengths?* **strong point,** advantage, asset, forte, aptitude, talent, skill, speciality. **9** *the strength of the army:* **size,** extent, magnitude.
OPPOSITES weakness.

strengthen verb **1** *calcium strengthens growing bones:* **make strong/stronger,** build up, harden, toughen, fortify, stiffen, reinforce. **2** *the wind had strengthened:* **become strong/stronger,** gain strength, intensify, pick up.
OPPOSITES weaken.

strenuous adjective **1** *a strenuous climb:* **difficult,** arduous, hard, tough, taxing, demanding, exacting, exhausting, tiring, gruelling, back-breaking; Brit. informal knackering. **2** *strenuous efforts:* **vigorous,** energetic, forceful, strong, spirited, intense, determined, resolute, dogged.
OPPOSITES easy, half-hearted.

stress noun **1** *he's under a lot of stress:* **strain,** pressure, (nervous) tension, worry, anxiety, trouble, difficulty; informal hassle. **2** *laying greater stress on education:* **emphasis,** importance, weight.
verb 1 *they stress the need for reform:* **emphasize,** draw attention to, underline, underscore, point up, highlight. **2** *all the staff were stressed:* **overstretch,** overtax, pressurize, pressure, worry, harass; informal hassle.
OPPOSITES play down.

S

stretch verb **1** *this material stretches:* **expand,** give, be elastic, be stretchy. **2** *he stretched the elastic:* **pull (out),** draw out, extend, lengthen, elongate, expand. **3** *stretching the truth:* **bend,** strain, distort, exaggerate, embellish. **4** *she stretched out her arm:* **reach out,** hold out, extend, straighten (out). **5** *she stretched out on the sofa:* **lie down,** recline, lean back, sprawl, lounge, loll. **6** *the desert stretches for miles:* **extend,** spread, continue, go on.
OPPOSITES shorten, contract, fold up.
noun **1** *magnificent stretches of forest:* **expanse,** area, tract, belt, sweep, extent. **2** *a four-hour stretch:* **period,** time, spell, run, stint, session, shift.

strict adjective **1** *a strict interpretation of the law:* **precise,** exact, literal, faithful, accurate, careful, meticulous, rigorous. **2** *strict controls on spending:* **stringent,** rigorous, severe, harsh, hard, rigid, tough. **3** *strict parents:* **stern,** severe, harsh, uncompromising, authoritarian, firm. **4** *in strict confidence:* **absolute,** utter, complete, total.
OPPOSITES loose, liberal.

stride verb & noun **step,** pace, march.

strife noun **conflict,** friction, discord, disagreement, dissension, dispute, argument, quarrelling.
OPPOSITES peace.

strike verb **1** *the teacher struck Mary:* **hit,** slap, smack, thump, punch, beat, bang; informal clout, wallop, belt, whack, thwack, bash, clobber, bop, biff; Austral./NZ informal quilt. **2** *the car struck a tree:* **crash into,** collide with, hit, run into, bump into, smash into; N. Amer. impact. **3** *a thought struck her:* **occur to,** come to (mind), dawn on one, hit, spring to mind, enter one's head. **4** *you strike me as intelligent:* **seem to,** appear to, give someone the impression of being. **5** *train drivers are to strike:* **take industrial action,** go on strike, down tools, walk out.
noun **1** *a 48-hour strike:* **industrial action,** walkout. **2** *a military strike:* **attack,** assault, bombing.

striking adjective **1** *a striking resemblance:* **noticeable,** obvious, conspicuous, marked, unmistakable, strong, remarkable. **2** *Kenya's striking landscape:* **impressive,** imposing, magnificent, spectacular, breathtaking, marvellous, wonderful, stunning, sensational, dramatic.
OPPOSITES unremarkable.

string noun **1** *a ball of string:* **twine,** cord, yarn, thread. **2** *a string of brewers:* **chain,** group, consortium. **3** *a string of convictions:* **series,** succession, chain, sequence, run, streak. **4** *a string of wagons:* **queue,** procession, line, file, column, convoy, train, cavalcade. **5** (strings) *a guaranteed loan with no strings:* **conditions,** qualifications, provisions, provisos, caveats, stipulations, riders, limitations, restrictions; informal catches.
verb *lights were strung across the promenade:* **hang,** suspend, sling, stretch, run, thread, loop, festoon.

stringent adjective **strict,** firm, rigid, rigorous, severe, harsh,

S

tough, tight, exacting,
demanding.
OPPOSITES lax.

strip[1] verb **1** *he stripped and got
into bed:* **undress,** strip off, take
one's clothes off, disrobe.
2 *stripping the paint off the
door:* **peel,** remove, scrape,
clean. **3** *I stripped down the
engine:* **dismantle,** disassemble,
take to bits/pieces, take apart.
4 *the house had been stripped:*
empty, clear, clean out,
plunder, rob, burgle, loot,
pillage, ransack, sack.
OPPOSITES dress, reassemble.

strip[2] noun *a strip of paper:*
(narrow) piece, band, belt,
ribbon, slip, shred, stretch.

stroke noun **1** *five hammer
strokes:* **blow,** hit. **2** *light
upward strokes:* **movement,**
action, motion. **3** *broad brush
strokes:* **mark,** line. **4** *he
suffered a stroke:* **thrombosis,**
seizure, apoplexy.
verb *she stroked the cat:* **caress,**
fondle, pat, pet, touch, rub,
massage, soothe.

stroll verb & noun **walk,** amble,
wander, meander, ramble,
promenade, saunter; informal
mosey.

strong adjective **1** *a strong lad:*
powerful, sturdy, robust,
athletic, tough, rugged, lusty.
2 *she isn't very strong:* **well,**
healthy, fit. **3** *a strong
character:* **forceful,**
determined, spirited, self-
assertive, tough, formidable,
strong-minded; informal gutsy,
feisty. **4** *a strong fortress:*
secure, well built, well
fortified, well protected, solid.
5 *strong cotton bags:* **durable,**
hard-wearing, heavy-duty,
tough, sturdy, well made, long-
lasting. **6** *a strong interest in*

literature: **keen,** passionate,
fervent. **7** *strong feelings:*
intense, forceful, passionate,
ardent, fervent, deep-seated.
8 *strong arguments:* **forceful,**
compelling, powerful,
convincing, persuasive, sound,
valid, cogent, well founded. **9** *a
strong voice:* **loud,** powerful,
forceful, resonant, sonorous,
rich, deep, booming. **10** *strong
language:* **bad,** foul, obscene,
profane. **11** *a strong blue
colour:* **intense,** deep, rich,
bright, brilliant, vivid, vibrant.
12 *strong lights:* **bright,**
brilliant, dazzling, glaring.
13 *strong coffee:* **concentrated,**
undiluted. **14** *strong cheese:*
highly flavoured, mature, ripe,
piquant, tangy, spicy. **15** *strong
drink:* **alcoholic,** intoxicating,
hard, stiff.
OPPOSITES weak, gentle, mild.

stronghold noun **1** *the enemy
stronghold:* **fortress,** fort,
castle, citadel, garrison. **2** *a
Tory stronghold:* **bastion,**
centre, hotbed.

structure noun **1** *a vast Gothic
structure:* **building,** edifice,
construction, erection. **2** *the
structure of local government:*
construction, organization,
system, arrangement,
framework, form, formation,
shape, composition, anatomy,
make-up.
verb *the programme is
structured around periods of
study:* **arrange,** organize,
design, shape, construct, build.

struggle verb **1** *they struggled
to do better:* **strive,** try hard,
endeavour, make every effort.
2 *James struggled with the
raiders:* **fight,** battle, grapple,
wrestle, scuffle. **3** *she struggled
over the dunes:* **scramble,**

flounder, stumble, fight/battle one's way, labour.
noun 1 *the struggle for justice:* **striving**, endeavour, campaign, battle, crusade, drive, push. **2** *no signs of a struggle:* **fight**, scuffle, brawl, tussle, fracas; informal bust-up, ding-dong. **3** *many perished in the struggle:* **conflict**, fight, battle, confrontation, clash, hostilities, fighting, war, warfare, campaign. **4** *a struggle within the leadership:* **contest**, competition, fight, clash, rivalry, friction, feuding, conflict.

strut verb **swagger**, prance, parade, stride, sweep; N. Amer. informal sashay.
OPPOSITES slink.

stubborn adjective **1** *you're too stubborn to admit it:* **obstinate**, headstrong, wilful, strong-willed, pig-headed, inflexible, uncompromising, unbending; informal stiff-necked. **2** *stubborn stains:* **indelible**, permanent, persistent, tenacious, resistant.
OPPOSITES compliant, removable.

stuck adjective **1** *a message was stuck to his screen:* **fixed**, fastened, attached, glued, pinned. **2** *the gate was stuck:* **jammed**, immovable. **3** *if you get stuck, leave a blank:* **baffled**, beaten, at a loss; informal stumped, bogged down, flummoxed, bamboozled.

student noun **1** *a university student:* **undergraduate**, postgraduate. **2** *a former student:* **pupil**, schoolchild, schoolboy, schoolgirl, scholar. **3** *a nursing student:* **trainee**, apprentice, probationer, novice, learner.

studio noun **workshop**, workroom, atelier.

studious adjective **scholarly**, academic, bookish, intellectual, erudite, learned, donnish; informal brainy.

study noun **1** *two years of study:* **learning**, education, schooling, scholarship, tuition, research. **2** *a study of global warming:* **investigation**, enquiry, research, examination, analysis, review, survey. **3** *Bob was in the study:* **office**, workroom, studio.
verb **1** *Anne studied hard:* **work**, revise; informal swot, cram. **2** *he studied maths:* **learn**, read, be taught. **3** *Thomas studied ants:* **investigate**, research, look at, examine, analyse. **4** *she studied him thoughtfully:* **scrutinize**, examine, inspect, consider, regard, look at, observe, watch, survey; informal check out.

stuff noun **1** *suede is tough stuff:* **material**, substance, fabric, cloth. **2** *first-aid stuff:* **items**, articles, objects, goods; informal things, bits and pieces, odds and ends. **3** *all my stuff is in the suitcase:* **belongings**, possessions, effects, paraphernalia; informal gear, things, kit; Brit. informal clobber.
verb **1** *stuffing pillows:* **fill**, pack, pad, upholster. **2** *Robyn stuffed her clothes into a bag:* **shove**, thrust, push, ram, cram, squeeze, force, jam, pack, pile.

stuffing noun **padding**, wadding, filling, packing.

stuffy adjective **1** *a stuffy atmosphere:* **airless**, close, musty, stale. **2** *a stuffy young man:* **staid**, sedate, sober, priggish, strait-laced, conformist, conservative, old-fashioned; informal straight, starchy, fuddy-duddy.
OPPOSITES airy, clear, informal, modern.

S

stumble verb 1 *he stumbled and fell:* **trip,** lose one's balance, lose one's footing, slip. 2 *he stumbled back home:* **stagger,** totter, blunder, hobble.
■ **stumble across/on** find, chance on, happen on, light on, come across/upon, discover, unearth, uncover; informal dig up.

stump verb (informal) **baffle,** perplex, puzzle, confound, defeat, put at a loss; informal flummox, fox, throw, floor.

stun verb 1 *the force of the blow stunned him:* **daze,** stupefy, knock out, lay out. 2 *she was stunned by the news:* **astound,** amaze, astonish, dumbfound, stupefy, stagger, shock, take aback; informal flabbergast, knock sideways.

stunning adjective **beautiful,** lovely, glorious, wonderful, marvellous, magnificent, superb, sublime, spectacular, fine, delightful; informal fantastic, terrific, tremendous, sensational, heavenly, divine, gorgeous, fabulous, awesome.
OPPOSITES ordinary.

stunt noun **feat,** exploit, trick.

stunted adjective **small,** undersized, underdeveloped, diminutive.

stupid adjective 1 *he's really stupid:* **unintelligent,** dense, foolish, slow, idiotic, simple-minded; informal thick, dim, dumb, dopey, dozy; Brit. informal daft. 2 *a stupid idea:* **foolish,** silly, senseless, idiotic, ill-advised, ill-considered, unwise; informal crazy, half-baked, cockeyed, hare-brained; Brit. informal potty.
OPPOSITES intelligent, sensible.

sturdy adjective 1 *a sturdy lad:* **strapping,** well built, muscular, strong, hefty, brawny, powerful, solid, burly; informal beefy. 2 *sturdy boots:* **robust,** strong, well built, solid, stout, tough, durable, long-lasting, hard-wearing.
OPPOSITES feeble, flimsy.

style noun 1 *differing styles of management:* **manner,** way, technique, method, approach, system, form. 2 *dressing with style:* **flair,** elegance, taste, grace, poise, polish, sophistication, dash; informal class. 3 *Laura travelled in style:* **comfort,** luxury. 4 *modern styles:* **fashion,** trend, vogue.
verb *sportswear styled by Karl:* **design,** fashion, tailor, cut.

stylish adjective **fashionable,** modern, up to date, modish, smart, sophisticated, elegant, chic, dapper, dashing; informal trendy, natty; N. Amer. informal kicky, tony.
OPPOSITES unfashionable.

subdue verb **conquer,** defeat, vanquish, overcome, overwhelm, crush, beat, subjugate, suppress.

subdued adjective 1 *Lewis's subdued air:* **sombre,** downcast, sad, dejected, depressed, gloomy, despondent. 2 *subdued voices:* **hushed,** muted, quiet, low, soft, faint, muffled, indistinct. 3 *subdued lighting:* **dim,** muted, soft, low, mood.
OPPOSITES cheerful, loud, bright.

subject noun 1 *the subject of this chapter:* **theme,** subject matter, topic, issue, question, concern. 2 *popular university subjects:* **branch of study,** discipline, field. 3 *British subjects:* **citizen,** national, resident, taxpayer, voter.
verb *subjected to violence:* **expose to,** treat with, put through.

■ **subject to** conditional on, contingent on, dependent on.

subjective adjective **personal,** individual, emotional, biased, intuitive.
OPPOSITES objective.

submerge verb **1** *the U-boat submerged:* **go under** (water), dive, sink, plunge, blow its tanks. **2** *submerge the bowl in water:* **immerse,** plunge, sink. **3** *the farmland was submerged:* **flood,** deluge, swamp, overwhelm, inundate.
OPPOSITES surface, drain.

submission noun **1** *submission to authority:* **yielding,** capitulation, surrender, resignation, acceptance, consent, compliance, acquiescence, obedience, subjection, subservience, servility. **2** *a report for submission to the Board:* **presentation,** proffering, tendering, proposing. **3** *his original submission:* **proposal,** suggestion, proposition, entry, recommendation. **4** *the judge rejected his submission:* **argument,** assertion, contention, statement, claim, allegation.
OPPOSITES defiance, resistance.

submit verb **1** *she was forced to submit:* **yield,** give in/way, back down, cave in, capitulate, surrender. **2** *he refused to submit to their authority:* **be governed by,** abide by, comply with, accept, be subject to, agree to, consent to, conform to. **3** *we submitted an application:* **put forward,** present, offer, tender, propose, suggest, enter, put in, send in. **4** *they submitted that the judgement was incorrect:*

contend, assert, argue, state, claim.
OPPOSITES resist, withdraw.

subordinate adjective **inferior,** junior, lower-ranking, lower, supporting.
OPPOSITES superior, senior.
noun **junior,** assistant, second (in command), number two, deputy, aide, underling, minion.
OPPOSITES superior, senior.

subscribe verb *we subscribe to charity:* **contribute,** donate, give, pay.
■ **subscribe to** support, endorse, agree with, accept, go along with.

subscription noun **membership fee,** dues, annual payment, charge.

subsequent adjective **following,** ensuing, succeeding, later, future, coming, to come, next.
OPPOSITES previous.

subsequently adverb **later** (on), at a later date, afterwards, in due course, following this/that, eventually; formal thereafter.

subside verb **1** *wait until the storm subsides:* **abate,** let up, quieten down, calm, slacken (off), ease (up), relent, die down, diminish, decline. **2** *the flood has subsided:* **recede,** ebb, fall, go down, get lower. **3** *the house is gradually subsiding:* **sink,** settle, cave in, collapse, give way.
OPPOSITES intensify, rise.

subsidiary adjective *a subsidiary company:* **subordinate,** secondary, subservient, supplementary, peripheral, auxiliary.
OPPOSITES principal.
noun *the firm's Spanish*

S

subsidiary: **branch,** division, subdivision, derivative, offshoot.
OPPOSITES headquarters, holding company.

subsidize verb **finance,** fund, support, contribute to, give money to, underwrite, sponsor; informal shell out for; N. Amer. informal bankroll.

subsidy noun **finance,** funding, backing, support, grant, sponsorship, allowance, contribution, handout.

substance noun **1** *organic substances:* **material,** compound, matter, stuff. **2** *none of the objections has any substance:* **significance,** importance, import, validity, foundation. **3** *the substance of the tale is very thin:* **content,** subject matter, theme, message, essence. **4** *men of substance:* **wealth,** fortune, riches, affluence, prosperity, money, means.

substantial adjective
1 *substantial progress had been made:* **considerable,** real, significant, important, major, valuable, useful. **2** *substantial damages:* **sizeable,** considerable, significant, large, ample, appreciable.
3 *substantial Victorian villas:* **sturdy,** solid, stout, strong, well built, durable, long-lasting, hard-wearing.
OPPOSITES little, meagre, flimsy.

substitute noun *substitutes for permanent employees:* **replacement,** deputy, relief, proxy, reserve, surrogate, cover, stand-in, understudy; informal sub.
adjective *a substitute teacher:* **acting,** replacement, deputy,

relief, reserve, surrogate, stand-in.
OPPOSITES permanent.
verb **1** *curd cheese can be substituted for yogurt:* **exchange,** swap, use instead of, use as an alternative to, use in place of, replace with. **2** *the Senate was empowered to substitute for the President:* **deputize,** stand in, cover.

subtle adjective **1** *subtle colours:* **understated,** muted, subdued, delicate, soft. **2** *subtle distinctions:* **fine,** nice. **3** *a subtle change:* **gentle,** slight, gradual.
OPPOSITES gaudy, crude, dramatic.

subtlety noun **delicacy,** understatedness, refinement, mutedness, softness.

subversive adjective *subversive literature:* **disruptive,** troublemaking, insurrectionary, seditious, dissident.
noun *suspected of being a subversive:* **troublemaker,** dissident, agitator, renegade.

succeed verb **1** *Darwin finally succeeded:* **triumph,** achieve success, be successful, do well, flourish, thrive; informal make it, make the grade. **2** *the plan succeeded:* **be successful,** turn out well, work (out), be effective; informal come off, pay off. **3** *he succeeded Gladstone as Prime Minister:* **replace,** take over from, supersede.
OPPOSITES fail, precede.

success noun **1** *the success of the scheme:* **favourable outcome,** triumph. **2** *the trappings of success:* **prosperity,** affluence, wealth, riches, opulence. **3** *a box-office success:* **triumph,** best-seller, sell-out; informal hit, smash, winner.

OPPOSITES failure.

successful adjective **1** *a successful designer:* **prosperous,** affluent, wealthy, rich, famous, eminent, top, respected. **2** *successful companies:* **flourishing,** thriving, booming, buoyant, doing well, profitable, moneymaking, lucrative.

succession noun **sequence,** series, progression, chain, string, train, line, run.

successive adjective **consecutive,** in a row, sequential, in succession, running; informal on the trot.

succumb verb **1** *she finally succumbed to temptation:* **yield,** give in/way, submit, surrender, capitulate, cave in. **2** *he succumbed to the disease:* **die from/of.**
OPPOSITES resist.

suck verb **1** *they sucked orange juice through straws:* **sip,** sup, siphon, slurp, drink. **2** *Fran sucked in a deep breath:* **draw,** pull, breathe, gasp.

sudden adjective **unexpected,** unforeseen, immediate, instantaneous, instant, precipitous, abrupt, rapid, swift, quick.

suddenly adverb **all of a sudden,** all at once, abruptly, swiftly, unexpectedly, without warning, out of the blue.
OPPOSITES gradually.

sue verb **take legal action (against),** go to court, take to court.

suffer verb **1** *I hate to see him suffer:* **hurt,** ache, be in pain, be in distress, be upset, be miserable. **2** *he suffers from asthma:* **be afflicted by,** be affected by, be troubled with, have. **3** *England suffered a humiliating defeat:* **undergo,**

experience, be subjected to, receive, endure, face. **4** *our reputation has suffered:* **be impaired,** be damaged, decline.

suffering noun **hardship,** distress, misery, adversity, pain, agony, anguish, trauma, torment, torture, hurt, affliction.
OPPOSITES pleasure, joy.

sufficient adjective & determiner **enough,** adequate, plenty of, ample.
OPPOSITES inadequate.

suggest verb **1** *Ruth suggested a holiday:* **propose,** put forward, recommend, advocate, advise. **2** *evidence suggests that voters are unhappy:* **indicate,** lead to the belief, demonstrate, show. **3** *what exactly are you suggesting?* **hint,** insinuate, imply, intimate.

suggestion noun **1** *some suggestions for tackling this problem:* **proposal,** proposition, recommendation, advice, counsel, hint, tip, clue, idea. **2** *the suggestion of a smirk:* **hint,** trace, touch, suspicion, ghost, semblance, shadow, glimmer. **3** *a suggestion that he knew about the plot:* **insinuation,** hint, implication.

suggestive adjective **1** *an odour suggestive of a brewery:* **redolent,** evocative, reminiscent, characteristic, indicative, typical. **2** *suggestive remarks:* **indecent,** indelicate, improper, unseemly, sexual, sexy, smutty, dirty.

suit noun **1** *a pinstriped suit:* **outfit,** ensemble. **2** *a medical malpractice suit:* **legal action,** lawsuit, (court) case, action, (legal/judicial) proceedings, litigation.
verb **1** *blue really suits you:* **look**

S

attractive **on,** look good on, become, flatter. **2** *savings schemes to suit all pockets:* **be convenient for,** be acceptable to, be suitable for, meet the requirements of; informal fit. **3** *recipes suited to students:* **be appropriate,** tailor, fashion, adjust, adapt, modify, fit, gear, design.

suitable adjective **1** *suitable employment:* **acceptable,** satisfactory, fitting; informal right up someone's street. **2** *a drama suitable for all ages:* **appropriate,** fitting, fit, acceptable, right. **3** *music suitable for a dinner party:* **appropriate,** suited, befitting, in keeping with. **4** *they treated him with suitable respect:* **proper,** seemly, decent, appropriate, fitting, correct, due.
OPPOSITES inappropriate.

suite noun **apartment,** flat, rooms.

sum noun **1** *a large sum of money:* **amount,** quantity, price, charge, fee, cost. **2** *the sum of two numbers:* **total,** sum total, grand total, tally. **3** *the sum of his wisdom:* **entirety,** totality, total, whole, beginning and end. **4** *we did sums at school:* **calculation,** problem; (sums) arithmetic, mathematics; Brit. informal **maths;** N. Amer. informal math.
OPPOSITES difference.

■ **sum someone/something up 1** *that just about sums him up:* evaluate, describe, encapsulate, summarize, put in a nutshell. **2** *he summed up his reasons:* summarize, make/give a summary of, precis, outline, recapitulate, review; informal recap.

summarize verb **sum up,** abridge, condense, outline, put in a nutshell, precis.

summary noun *a summary of the findings:* **synopsis,** precis, résumé, abstract, outline, rundown, summing-up, overview.

summit noun **1** *the summit of Mont Blanc:* **(mountain) top,** peak, crest, crown, apex, tip, cap, hilltop. **2** *the next superpower summit:* **meeting,** conference, talk(s).
OPPOSITES base.

summon verb **1** *he was summoned to the Embassy:* **send for,** call for, request the presence of, ask, invite. **2** *they were summoned as witnesses:* **summons,** subpoena. **3** *he summoned the courage to move closer:* **muster,** gather, collect, rally, screw up.

sumptuous adjective **lavish,** luxurious, opulent, magnificent, resplendent, gorgeous, splendid; informal plush; Brit. informal swish.
OPPOSITES plain.

sunny adjective **1** *a sunny day:* **bright,** sunlit, clear, fine, cloudless. **2** *a sunny disposition:* **cheerful,** cheery, happy, bright, merry, joyful, bubbly, jolly.
OPPOSITES dull, miserable.

sunrise noun **dawn,** crack of dawn, daybreak, break of day, first light, early morning; N. Amer. sunup.

sunset noun **nightfall,** twilight, dusk, evening; N. Amer. sundown.

superb adjective **1** *a superb goal:* **excellent,** first-class, outstanding, marvellous, wonderful, splendid, admirable, fine, exceptional, glorious; informal great, fantastic, fabulous, terrific, super,

awesome, ace; Brit. informal
brilliant, smashing. **2** *a superb
house:* **magnificent**, splendid,
grand, impressive, imposing,
awe-inspiring, breathtaking,
gorgeous, beautiful.
OPPOSITES poor, unimpressive.

superficial adjective
1 *superficial burns:* **surface**,
exterior, external, outer, slight.
2 *a superficial investigation:*
cursory, perfunctory, casual,
sketchy, desultory, token,
slapdash, offhand, rushed,
hasty, hurried. **3** *a superficial
resemblance:* **apparent**,
seeming, outward, ostensible,
cosmetic, slight. **4** *a superficial
person:* **facile**, shallow, flippant,
empty-headed, trivial,
frivolous, silly, inane.
OPPOSITES deep, thorough,
strong, intelligent.

superfluous adjective surplus
(to requirements), redundant,
unneeded, unnecessary, excess,
extra, (to) spare, remaining,
unused, left over, waste.
OPPOSITES necessary.

superior adjective **1** *a superior
officer:* **senior**, higher-level,
higher-ranking, higher. **2** *the
superior candidate:* **better**,
worthier, finer, preferred.
3 *superior chocolate:*
top-quality, choice, select,
exclusive, prime, fine, excellent,
best, choicest, finest. **4** *a
superior smile:* **condescending**,
supercilious, patronizing,
haughty, disdainful; informal high
and mighty.
OPPOSITES junior, inferior,
modest.
noun *my immediate superior:*
manager, chief, supervisor,
senior, controller, foreman;
informal boss.
OPPOSITES subordinate.

superiority noun **supremacy**,
advantage, lead, dominance,
primacy, ascendancy, eminence.

supernatural adjective
1 *supernatural powers:*
paranormal, psychic, magic,
magical, occult, mystic,
mystical. **2** *a supernatural
being:* **ghostly**, phantom,
spectral, other-worldly,
unearthly.

supersede verb **replace**, take
the place of, take over from,
succeed, supplant.

supervise verb **oversee**, be in
charge of, superintend, preside
over, direct, manage, run, look
after, be responsible for,
govern, keep an eye on,
observe, monitor, mind.

supervisor noun **manager**,
director, overseer, controller,
superintendent, governor,
chief, head, foreman; informal
boss; Brit. informal gaffer.

supple adjective **1** *her supple
body:* **lithe**, lissom, willowy,
flexible, agile, acrobatic,
nimble. **2** *supple leather:*
pliable, flexible, soft, bendy,
workable, stretchy, springy.
OPPOSITES stiff, rigid.

supplement noun **1** *a dietary
supplement:* **extra**, add-on,
accessory, adjunct. **2** *a single
room supplement:* **surcharge**,
addition, increase. **3** *a
supplement to the essay:*
appendix, addendum,
postscript, addition, coda. **4** *a
special supplement with today's
paper:* **pull-out**, insert.
verb *he supplemented his income
by teaching:* **add to**, augment,
increase, boost, swell, amplify,
enlarge, top up.

supply verb **1** *they supplied
money to the rebels:* **give**,
contribute, provide, furnish,

S

donate, confer, dispense. **2** *the lake supplies the city with water:* **provide,** furnish, serve, endow, equip, arm. **3** *windmills supply their power needs:* **satisfy,** meet, fulfil, cater for.
noun **1** *a limited supply of food:* **stock,** store, reserve, reservoir, stockpile, hoard, cache, fund, bank. **2** *the supply of alcoholic liquor:* **provision,** distribution, serving. **3** (**supplies**) **provisions,** stores, rations, food, necessities.

support verb **1** *a roof supported by pillars:* **hold up,** bear, carry, prop up, keep up, brace, shore up, underpin, buttress, reinforce. **2** *he struggled to support his family:* **provide for,** maintain, sustain, keep, take care of, look after. **3** *she supported him to the end:* **stand by,** defend, back, stand/stick up for. **4** *evidence to support the argument:* **back up,** substantiate, bear out, corroborate, confirm. **5** *the money supports charitable projects:* **help,** aid, assist, contribute to, back, subsidize, fund, finance; N. Amer. informal bankroll. **6** *a candidate supported by local people:* **back,** champion, favour, be in favour of, advocate, encourage, promote, endorse, espouse.
OPPOSITES neglect, contradict, oppose.
noun **1** *bridge supports:* **pillar,** post, prop, upright, brace, buttress, foundation. **2** *I was lucky to have their support:* **encouragement,** friendship, backing, endorsement, help, assistance, comfort. **3** *thank you for your support:* **contributions,** backing, donations, money, subsidy, funding, funds, finance, capital.

OPPOSITES opposition.

supporter noun **1** *supporters of gun control:* **advocate,** backer, adherent, promoter, champion, defender, upholder, campaigner. **2** *the charity relies on its supporters:* **contributor,** donor, benefactor, sponsor, backer, patron, subscriber, well-wisher. **3** *the team's supporters:* **fan,** follower, enthusiast, devotee, admirer.

supportive adjective encouraging, caring, sympathetic, reassuring, understanding, concerned, helpful.

suppose verb **1** *I suppose he's used to it:* **assume,** presume, expect, dare say, take it, guess. **2** *suppose you had a spacecraft:* **imagine,** assume, (let's) say, hypothesize, theorize, speculate.

supposed adjective **1** *the supposed phenomena:* **alleged,** reputed, rumoured, claimed, purported. **2** *I'm supposed to meet him at 8.30:* **meant,** intended, expected, required, obliged.

suppress verb **1** *they will suppress any criticism:* **subdue,** repress, crush, quell, quash, squash, stamp out, put down, crack down on. **2** *she suppressed her irritation:* **conceal,** restrain, stifle, smother, check, curb, contain. **3** *the report was suppressed:* **censor,** keep secret, conceal, hide, hush up, gag, withhold, cover up, stifle.
OPPOSITES allow, encourage, reveal.

supremacy noun **control,** power, rule, sovereignty, dominance, superiority, predominance, primacy, dominion, authority, mastery, ascendancy.

supreme adjective **1** *the supreme commander:* **highest,** chief, head, top, foremost, principal, superior, premier, first, prime. **2** *a supreme achievement:* **extraordinary,** remarkable, phenomenal, exceptional, outstanding, incomparable, unparalleled. **3** *the supreme sacrifice:* **ultimate,** greatest, highest, extreme, final, last.
OPPOSITES subordinate, insignificant.

sure adjective **1** *I'm sure they knew:* **certain,** positive, convinced, confident, definite, satisfied, persuaded. **2** *someone was sure to find out:* **bound,** likely, destined, fated. **3** *a sure winner:* **guaranteed,** unfailing, infallible, unerring, certain, inevitable; informal sure-fire. **4** *a sure sign that he's worried:* **reliable,** trustworthy, certain, unambiguous.
OPPOSITES uncertain, unlikely.

surface noun **1** *the surface of the wall:* **outside,** exterior, top, side, finish. **2** *the surface of polite society:* **outward appearance,** facade, veneer.
OPPOSITES inside, interior.
verb **1** *a submarine surfaced:* **come to the surface,** come up, rise. **2** *the idea first surfaced in the sixties:* **emerge,** arise, appear, come to light, crop up, materialize, spring up.
OPPOSITES dive.

surge noun **1** *a surge of water:* **gush,** rush, outpouring, stream, flow. **2** *a surge in demand:* **increase,** rise, growth, upswing, upsurge, escalation, leap. **3** *a sudden surge of anger:* **rush,** storm, torrent, blaze, outburst, eruption.

verb **1** *the water surged into people's homes:* **gush,** rush, stream, flow, burst, pour, cascade, spill, sweep, roll. **2** *the Dow Jones index surged 47.63 points:* **increase,** rise, grow, leap.

surpass verb **excel,** exceed, transcend, outdo, outshine, outstrip, outclass, eclipse, improve on, top, trump, cap, beat, better, outperform.

surplus noun *food surpluses:* **excess,** surfeit, superfluity, oversupply, glut, remainder, residue, remains, leftovers.
OPPOSITES dearth.
adjective *surplus cash:* **excess,** leftover, unused, remaining, extra, additional, spare, superfluous, redundant, unwanted, unneeded, dispensable.
OPPOSITES insufficient.

surprise noun **1** *Kate looked at me in surprise:* **astonishment,** amazement, wonder, bewilderment, disbelief. **2** *the test came as a big surprise:* **shock,** bolt from the blue, bombshell, revelation, rude awakening, eye-opener.
verb **1** *I was so surprised that I dropped it:* **astonish,** amaze, startle, astound, stun, stagger, shock; informal bowl over, floor, flabbergast; Brit. informal knock for six. **2** *she surprised a burglar:* **take by surprise,** catch unawares, catch off guard, catch red-handed.

surprising adjective **unexpected,** unforeseen, astonishing, amazing, startling, astounding, staggering, incredible, extraordinary.

surrender verb **1** *the gunmen surrendered:* **give up,** give oneself up, give in, cave in,

S

capitulate, concede (defeat), submit, lay down one's arms/weapons. **2** *they surrendered power to the government:* **give up**, relinquish, renounce, cede, abdicate, forfeit, sacrifice, hand over, turn over, yield.
OPPOSITES resist, seize.
noun **1** *the surrender of the hijackers:* **capitulation**, submission, yielding. **2** *a surrender of power:* **relinquishment**, renunciation, abdication, resignation.

surround verb encircle, enclose, encompass, ring, hem in, confine, cut off, besiege, trap.

surrounding adjective **neighbouring**, enclosing, nearby, near, local, adjoining, adjacent.

surroundings plural noun **environment**, setting, background, backdrop, vicinity, locality, habitat.

survey verb **1** *he surveyed his work:* **look at**, look over, view, contemplate, regard, gaze at, stare at, eye, scrutinize, examine, inspect, scan, study; informal size up. **2** *they surveyed 4,000 drug users:* **interview**, question, canvass, poll, investigate, research, study. **3** *he was asked to survey the house:* **inspect**, assess, appraise, prospect.
noun **1** *a survey of the current literature:* **study**, review, overview, examination. **2** *a survey of sexual behaviour:* **poll**, investigation, enquiry, study, probe, questionnaire, census, research. **3** *a thorough survey of the property:* **inspection**, assessment, appraisal.

survive verb **1** *he survived by escaping through a hole:* **remain**

alive, live, sustain oneself, pull through, hold out, make it. **2** *the theatre must survive:* **continue**, remain, persist, endure, live on, persevere, abide, go on, carry on. **3** *he was survived by his sons:* **outlive**, outlast.

suspect verb **1** *I suspected she'd made a mistake:* **have a suspicion**, have a feeling, feel, be inclined to think, fancy, reckon, guess, surmise, have a hunch, fear. **2** *he had no reason to suspect me:* **doubt**, distrust, mistrust, have misgivings about, have qualms about, be suspicious of.
adjective *a suspect package:* **suspicious,** dubious, doubtful, untrustworthy; informal fishy, funny; Brit. informal dodgy.

suspend verb **1** *the court case was suspended:* **adjourn**, interrupt, break off, cut short, discontinue; N. Amer. table. **2** *he was suspended from college:* **exclude**, debar, remove, expel, eject, rusticate. **3** *lights were suspended from the ceiling:* **hang**, sling, string, swing, dangle.

suspense noun **tension**, uncertainty, doubt, anticipation, excitement, anxiety, strain.

suspicion noun **1** *she had a suspicion that he didn't like her:* **intuition**, feeling, impression, inkling, hunch, fancy, notion, idea, theory, premonition; informal gut feeling. **2** *I confronted him with my suspicions:* **misgiving**, doubt, qualm, reservation, hesitation, question.
OPPOSITES trust.

suspicious adjective **1** *she gave him a suspicious look:* **doubtful,**

unsure, dubious, wary, sceptical, mistrustful. **2** *a suspicious character:* **suspect**, dubious, unsavoury, disreputable; informal shifty, shady; Brit. informal dodgy. **3** *in suspicious circumstances:* **strange**, odd, questionable, irregular, funny, doubtful, mysterious, murky; informal fishy; Brit. informal dodgy.
OPPOSITES trusting, honest, innocent.

sustain verb **1** *her memories sustained her:* **comfort**, help, assist, encourage, support, give strength to, buoy up. **2** *they were unable to sustain a coalition:* **continue**, carry on, keep up, keep alive, maintain, preserve. **3** *she had bread and cheese to sustain her:* **nourish**, feed, nurture, keep alive, keep going. **4** *she sustained slight injuries:* **suffer**, experience, undergo, receive. **5** *the allegation was not sustained:* **confirm**, corroborate, substantiate, bear out, prove, authenticate, back up, uphold.

sustained adjective **continuous**, ongoing, steady, continual, constant, prolonged, persistent, non-stop, perpetual, relentless.
OPPOSITES sporadic.

swallow verb **eat**, drink, gulp down, consume, devour, put away, quaff, slug; informal swig, swill, down; Brit. informal scoff.

swamp noun *he got stuck in the swamp:* **marsh**, bog, fen, quagmire.
verb **1** *the rain was swamping the boat:* **flood**, inundate, deluge, fill. **2** *he was swamped by media attention:* **overwhelm**, inundate, flood, deluge, engulf, snow under.

swap verb **exchange**, trade,

barter, switch, change, replace.

swarm noun **1** *a swarm of bees:* **hive**, flock. **2** *a swarm of reporters:* **crowd**, horde, mob, throng, mass, army, herd, pack.
verb *reporters were swarming all over the place:* **flock**, crowd, throng, surge, stream.

swathe verb **wrap**, envelop, bandage, cover, shroud, drape, wind, enfold.

sway verb **1** *the curtains swayed in the breeze:* **swing**, shake, undulate, move to and fro. **2** *she swayed on her feet:* **stagger**, wobble, rock, lurch, reel, roll. **3** *we are swayed by the media:* **influence**, affect, manipulate, bend, mould.
noun **1** *the sway of her hips:* **swing**, roll, shake, undulation. **2** *a province under the sway of the Franks:* **power**, rule, government, sovereignty, dominion, control, jurisdiction, authority.

swear verb **1** *they swore to protect each other:* **promise**, vow, pledge, give one's word, undertake, guarantee. **2** *she swore she would never go back:* **insist**, declare, proclaim, assert, maintain, emphasize, stress. **3** *Kate spilled her wine and swore:* **curse**, blaspheme, use bad language; informal cuss, eff and blind.

swearing noun **bad language**, strong language, cursing, blaspheming, obscenities, expletives, swear words; informal effing and blinding, four-letter words.

sweat noun *drenched with sweat:* **perspiration**.
verb **1** *she was sweating heavily:* **perspire**. **2** *I've sweated over this book:* **work**, labour, toil, slog, slave, work one's fingers

S

to the bone.

sweep verb **1** *she swept the floor:* **brush,** clean, scrub, mop, scour. **2** *he was swept out to sea:* **carry,** pull, drag, tow. **3** *riots swept the country:* **engulf,** overwhelm, flood, spread across. **4** *she swept down the stairs:* **glide,** sail, breeze, drift, race, speed, stride.

noun **1** *a sweep of his hand:* **gesture,** stroke, wave, movement. **2** *a long sweep of golden sand:* **expanse,** tract, stretch, extent. **3** *the broad sweep of our interests:* **range,** scope, compass, reach, spread, extent.

sweeping adjective **1** *sweeping changes:* **extensive,** wide-ranging, broad, comprehensive, far-reaching, thorough, radical. **2** *sweeping statements:* **wholesale,** blanket, general, unqualified, indiscriminate, oversimplified.
OPPOSITES limited, focused.

sweet adjective **1** *sweet biscuits:* **sugary,** sweetened, sugared, honeyed, sickly, cloying. **2** *the sweet scent of roses:* **fragrant,** aromatic, perfumed. **3** *her sweet voice:* **musical,** melodious, dulcet, tuneful, soft, harmonious, silvery. **4** *life was still sweet:* **pleasant,** agreeable, delightful, nice, satisfying, gratifying, good. **5** *she has a sweet nature:* **likeable,** appealing, engaging, amiable, pleasant, agreeable, kind, thoughtful, considerate, delightful, lovely. **6** *she looks sweet:* **cute,** lovable, adorable, endearing, charming.
OPPOSITES sour, savoury, harsh, disagreeable.
noun (Brit.) **1** *sweets for the children:* **confectionery,**

bonbon; N. Amer. candy; informal sweetie. **2** *a delicious sweet for the guests:* **dessert,** pudding; Brit. informal afters, pud.

sweetheart noun **1** *you look lovely, sweetheart:* **darling,** dear, dearest, love, beloved, sweet; informal honey, sweetie, sugar, baby, poppet. **2** *my high-school sweetheart:* **lover,** love, girlfriend, boyfriend, beloved; informal steady, flame.

swell verb **1** *her lip swelled up:* **expand,** bulge, distend, inflate, dilate, bloat, puff up, balloon, fatten, fill out. **2** *the population swelled:* **grow,** enlarge, increase, expand, rise, escalate, multiply, proliferate, snowball, mushroom.
OPPOSITES shrink, decrease.
noun *a heavy swell on the sea:* **surge,** wave, roll.

swelling noun **bump,** lump, bulge, protuberance, protrusion, distension.

swift adjective **1** *a swift decision:* **prompt,** rapid, quick, sudden, immediate, instant, abrupt, hasty, hurried. **2** *swift runners:* **fast,** rapid, quick, speedy, brisk, lively.
OPPOSITES slow, leisurely.

swing verb **1** *the sign swung in the wind:* **sway,** move back and forth, oscillate, wave, rock, swivel, pivot, turn, rotate. **2** *Helen swung the bottle:* **brandish,** wave, flourish, wield. **3** *the road swings round:* **curve,** bend, veer, turn, bear, wind, twist, deviate, slew. **4** *the needle swings to the right:* **rotate,** swivel, pivot, turn.
noun **1** *a swing of the pendulum:* **oscillation,** sway, wave. **2** *the swing to the Conservatives:* **change,** move, turnaround, turnabout, reversal. **3** *mood*

S

swings: **fluctuation,** change, shift, variation, oscillation.

swirl verb **whirl,** eddy, billow, spiral, twist, twirl, circulate, revolve, spin.

switch noun **1** *the switch on top of the telephone:* **button,** lever, control. **2** *a switch from direct to indirect taxation:* **change,** move, shift, transition, transformation, reversal, turnaround, U-turn, changeover, transfer, conversion.
verb **1** *he switched sides:* **change,** shift; informal chop and change. **2** *he managed to switch the envelopes:* **exchange,** swap, interchange, change round, rotate.

swoop verb **1** *pigeons swooped down after the grain:* **dive,** descend, pounce, plunge, pitch, nosedive. **2** *police swooped on the flat:* **raid,** descend on, pounce on, attack; N. Amer. informal bust.

symbol noun **1** *the lotus is the symbol of purity:* **representation,** token, sign, emblem, figure, image, metaphor, allegory. **2** *the chemical symbol for helium:* **sign,** character, mark, letter. **3** *the Red Cross symbol:* **logo,** emblem, badge, stamp, trademark, crest, insignia, coat of arms, seal, device, monogram, hallmark, motif.

symmetrical adjective **regular,** uniform, consistent, even, equal, balanced, proportional.

sympathetic adjective **1** *a sympathetic listener:* **compassionate,** caring, concerned, understanding, sensitive, supportive. **2** *the most sympathetic character in the book:* **likeable,** pleasant, agreeable, congenial.
OPPOSITES unsympathetic, unfeeling, unlikeable.

sympathize verb **commiserate,** show concern, offer condolences; (**sympathize with**) pity, feel sorry for, feel for, identify with, understand, relate to.

sympathy noun **compassion,** care, concern, sympathetic, commiseration, pity.
OPPOSITES indifference.

symptom noun **indication,** indicator, manifestation, sign, mark, feature, trait, clue, hint, warning, evidence, proof.

synthetic adjective **artificial,** fake, imitation, mock, simulated, man-made, manufactured; informal pretend.
OPPOSITES natural.

system noun **1** *a system of canals:* **structure,** organization, arrangement, complex, network; informal set-up. **2** *a system for regulating sales:* **method,** technique, procedure, means, way, scheme, plan, policy, programme, formula, routine. **3** (**the system**) **the establishment,** the administration, the authorities, the powers that be, bureaucracy, officialdom.

systematic adjective **structured,** methodical, organized, orderly, planned, regular, routine, standardized, standard, logical, coherent, consistent.
OPPOSITES unstructured, disorganized.

S

Tt

table noun chart, diagram, figure, graphic, graph, plan, list.

taboo noun *the taboo against lying:* **prohibition,** proscription, veto, ban.
adjective *taboo language:* **forbidden,** prohibited, banned, proscribed, outlawed, off limits, unmentionable, unspeakable, unutterable; informal no go.
OPPOSITES acceptable.

tack noun *tacks held the carpet down:* **pin,** nail, staple, rivet.
verb *a photo tacked to the wall:* **pin,** nail, staple, fix, fasten, attach, secure.
■ **tack something on** add, append, attach, join on, tag on.

tackle noun **1** *fishing tackle:* **gear,** equipment, apparatus, kit, hardware; informal things, clobber. **2** *a tackle by the scrum half:* **interception,** challenge, block, attack.
verb **1** *we must tackle the problems:* **deal with,** take care of, attend to, see to, handle, manage, get to grips with, address, take on. **2** *he tackled an intruder:* **confront,** face up to, take on, challenge, attack, grab, struggle with, intercept, block, stop, bring down, floor, fell; informal have a go at.

tactful adjective **diplomatic,** discreet, considerate, sensitive, understanding, thoughtful, delicate, judicious, subtle.

tactic noun **1** *a tax-saving tactic:* **scheme,** plan, manoeuvre, method, trick, ploy. **2** (**tactics**) **strategy,** policy, campaign, game plan, planning, generalship, manoeuvres, logistics.

tactical adjective **calculated,** planned, strategic, prudent, politic, diplomatic, judicious, shrewd.

tactless adjective **insensitive,** inconsiderate, thoughtless, indelicate, undiplomatic, indiscreet, unsubtle, inept, gauche, blunt.

tag noun *a price tag:* **label,** ticket, badge, mark, tab, sticker, docket.
verb *bottles tagged with stickers:* **label,** mark, ticket, identify, flag, indicate.

tail noun *the tail of the queue:* **rear,** end, back, extremity, bottom.
OPPOSITES head, front, start.
verb (informal) *the detectives tailed him to his hide-out:* **follow,** shadow, stalk, trail, track, keep under surveillance.

tailor noun **outfitter,** couturier, costumier, dressmaker, fashion designer.
verb *services can be tailored to requirements:* **customize,** adapt, adjust, modify, change, convert, alter, mould, gear, fit, shape, tune.

taint verb **1** *the wilderness is tainted by pollution:* **contaminate,** pollute, adulterate, infect, blight, spoil, soil, ruin. **2** *fraudulent firms taint our reputation:* **tarnish,** sully, blacken, stain, blot, damage.
OPPOSITES clean, improve.

take verb **1** *she took his hand:* **grasp,** get hold of, grip, clasp,

clutch, grab. **2** *he took an envelope from his pocket:* **remove,** pull, draw, withdraw, extract, fish. **3** *a passage taken from my book:* **extract,** quote, cite, excerpt, derive, abstract, copy, cull. **4** *many prisoners were taken:* **capture,** seize, catch, arrest, apprehend, take into custody, carry off, abduct. **5** *someone's taken my car:* **steal,** remove, appropriate, make off with, pilfer, purloin; *informal* filch, swipe, snaffle; *Brit. informal* pinch, nick. **6** *take four from the total:* **subtract,** deduct, remove, discount; *informal* knock off, minus. **7** *all the seats had been taken:* **occupy,** use, utilize, fill, hold, reserve, engage; *informal* bag. **8** *he took notes:* **write,** note (down), jot (down), scribble, scrawl, record, register, document, minute. **9** *I took it back to London:* **bring,** carry, bear, transport, convey, move, transfer, shift, ferry; *informal* cart, tote. **10** *the priest took her home:* **escort,** accompany, help, assist, show, lead, guide, see, usher, convey. **11** *he took the train:* **travel on/ by,** journey on, go via, use. **12** *I can't take much more:* **endure,** bear, tolerate, stand, put up with, abide, stomach, accept, allow, countenance, support, shoulder; *formal* brook.
OPPOSITES give, free, add.
■ **take after** resemble, look like, remind one of. ■ **take something apart** dismantle, take to pieces, take apart, disassemble, break up. ■ **take someone in** deceive, delude, hoodwink, mislead, trick, dupe, fool, cheat, defraud, swindle; *informal* con. ■ **take something in** comprehend, understand, grasp, follow, absorb; *informal* get.

■ **take off 1** *the plane took off:* become airborne, take to the air, leave the ground, lift off, blast off. **2** *the idea really took off:* succeed, do well, become popular, catch on, prosper, flourish. ■ **take someone on 1** *there was no challenger to take him on:* compete against, oppose, challenge, confront, face. **2** *we took on extra staff:* engage, hire, employ, sign up. ■ **take something on** undertake, accept, assume, shoulder, acquire. ■ **take something over** assume control of, take charge of, take command of, seize, hijack, commandeer. ■ **take something up 1** *he took up abstract painting:* begin, start, commence, engage in, practise. **2** *the meetings took up all her time:* consume, fill, absorb, use, occupy. **3** *her cousin took up the story:* resume, recommence, restart, carry on, continue, pick up, return to. **4** *he took up their offer of a job:* accept, say yes to, agree to, adopt.

takeover noun buyout, purchase, acquisition, merger, amalgamation.

tale noun story, narrative, anecdote, account, history, legend, fable, myth, saga; *informal* yarn.

talent noun flair, aptitude, facility, gift, knack, technique, bent, ability, forte, genius, brilliance.

talented adjective gifted, skilful, accomplished, brilliant, expert, consummate, able; *informal* ace.
OPPOSITES untalented, inept.

talk verb **1** *I was talking to a friend:* **speak,** chat, chatter, gossip, jabber; *informal* yak; *Brit. informal* natter. **2** *they were able to talk in peace:* **converse,**

t

communicate, speak, confer,
consult, negotiate, parley;
informal have a confab.
noun 1 *he was bored with all this
talk:* **chatter**, gossip, prattle,
jabbering; informal yak; Brit. informal
nattering. **2** *she needed a talk
with Vi:* **conversation**, chat,
discussion, tête-à-tête, heart-to-
heart, dialogue; informal confab,
gossip. **3** (**talks**) negotiations,
discussions, conference,
summit, meeting, consultation,
dialogue. **4** *she gave a talk on
her travels:* **lecture**, speech,
address, discourse, oration,
presentation, report, sermon.

talkative adjective **chatty**,
garrulous, loquacious, voluble,
communicative; informal mouthy.
OPPOSITES taciturn.

tall adjective **1** *a tall man:* **big**,
large, huge, towering, gigantic,
giant, leggy, gangling. **2** *tall
buildings:* **high**, big, lofty,
towering, sky-high. **3** *a tall tale:*
unlikely, improbable,
exaggerated, far-fetched,
implausible, dubious,
unbelievable, incredible,
untrue; informal cock and bull.
4 *a tall order:* **demanding**,
exacting, difficult,
unreasonable, impossible.
OPPOSITES short, low, wide,
credible, easy.

tally noun *a tally of the score:*
running total, count, record,
reckoning, register, account,
roll.
verb *these statistics tally with
government figures:*
correspond, agree, accord,
concur, coincide, match, fit, be
consistent, conform, equate,
parallel; informal square.
OPPOSITES disagree.

tame adjective **1** *a tame elephant:*
domesticated, docile, broken,

trained, gentle, mild, pet. **2** *a
tame affair:* **unexciting**,
uninteresting, uninspiring,
dull, bland, flat, pedestrian,
humdrum, boring.
OPPOSITES wild, exciting.
verb 1 *wild rabbits can be
tamed:* **domesticate**, break,
train, master, subdue. **2** *she
learned to tame her emotions:*
subdue, curb, control, calm,
master, moderate, discipline,
suppress, temper, bridle.

tangible adjective **real**, actual,
physical, solid, palpable,
material, substantial, concrete,
visible, definite, perceptible,
discernible.
OPPOSITES abstract, theoretical.

tangle verb *the wool got tangled
up:* **entangle**, snarl, catch,
entwine, twist, knot, mat,
jumble.
noun 1 *a tangle of branches:*
snarl, mass, knot, mesh,
mishmash. **2** *the defence got
into an awful tangle:* **muddle**,
jumble, mix-up, confusion,
shambles.

tantrum noun **fit of temper**, fit
of rage, outburst, pet,
paroxysm, frenzy; informal paddy,
wobbly; N. Amer. informal hissy fit.

tap[1] noun *she turned the tap on:*
valve, stopcock; N. Amer. faucet,
spigot.
verb 1 *their telephones were
tapped:* **bug**, wiretap, monitor,
overhear, eavesdrop on. **2** *the
resources were to be tapped for
our benefit:* **draw on**, exploit,
milk, mine, use, utilize, turn to
account.

tap[2] verb *she tapped on the door:*
knock, rap, strike, beat, pat,
drum.

tape noun **1** *a package tied with
tape:* **binding**, ribbon, string,
braid, band. **2** *they made a tape*

of the concert: (**audio**) **cassette**, (**tape**) **recording**, **video**.
verb **1** *a card was taped to the box:* **bind**, stick, fix, fasten, secure, attach. **2** *police taped his confession:* **record**, tape-record, video.

target noun **1** *their profit target:* **objective**, goal, aim, mark, end, plan, intention, aspiration, ambition. **2** *she was the target for abuse:* **victim**, butt, recipient, focus, object, subject.
verb **1** *he was targeted by a gunman:* **pick out**, single out, earmark, fix on, attack, aim at, fire at. **2** *the product is targeted at a specific market:* **aim**, direct, level, intend, focus.

tariff noun **1** *import tariffs:* **tax**, duty, toll, excise, levy, charge, rate, fee. **2** *the bar tariff:* **price list**, menu.

tarnish verb **1** *gold does not tarnish easily:* **discolour**, rust, oxidize, corrode, stain, dull, blacken. **2** *it tarnished his reputation:* **sully**, blacken, stain, blemish, ruin, disgrace, mar, damage, harm.
OPPOSITES polish, enhance.
noun **1** *the tarnish on the candlesticks:* **discoloration**, oxidation, rust, verdigris. **2** *the tarnish on his reputation:* **smear**, stain, blemish, blot, taint, stigma.

tart[1] noun *a jam tart:* **pastry**, flan, quiche, tartlet, vol-au-vent, pie.

tart[2] (informal) verb **1** *she tarted herself up:* **dress up**, make up, smarten up; informal doll oneself up, titivate oneself. **2** *we must tart this place up a bit:* **decorate**, renovate, refurbish, redecorate, smarten up; informal do up, fix up.

tart[3] adjective **1** *a tart apple:*
sour, sharp, acidic, zesty, tangy, piquant. **2** *a tart reply:* **scathing**, sharp, biting, cutting, sarcastic, acrimonious, nasty, rude, vicious, spiteful.
OPPOSITES sweet, kind.

task noun **job**, duty, chore, charge, assignment, detail, mission, engagement, occupation, undertaking, exercise.

taste noun **1** *a distinctive sharp taste:* **flavour**, savour, relish, tang, smack. **2** *a taste of brandy:* **mouthful**, drop, bit, sip, nip, touch, soupçon, dash. **3** *it's too sweet for my taste:* **palate**, appetite, stomach. **4** *a taste for adventure:* **liking**, love, fondness, fancy, desire, penchant, inclination. **5** *my first taste of prison:* **experience**, impression, exposure to, contact with, involvement with. **6** *the house was furnished with taste:* **judgement**, discrimination, discernment, refinement, elegance, grace, style. **7** *the photo was rejected on grounds of taste:* **sensitivity**, decorum, propriety, etiquette, nicety, discretion.
OPPOSITES dislike.
verb **1** *Adam tasted the wine:* **sample**, test, try, savour. **2** *he could taste blood:* **perceive**, discern, make out, distinguish. **3** *a beer that tasted of cashews:* **have the flavour**, savour, smack, be reminiscent.

tasteful adjective **stylish**, refined, cultured, elegant, smart, chic, exquisite.
OPPOSITES tasteless.

tasty adjective **delicious**, palatable, luscious, mouth-watering, delectable, appetizing, tempting; informal yummy, scrumptious, moreish.

t

OPPOSITES bland.

taunt noun *the taunts of his classmates:* **jeer,** gibe, sneer, insult, barb; informal dig, put-down; (**taunts**) teasing, provocation, goading, derision, mockery.
verb *she taunted him about his job:* **jeer at,** sneer at, scoff at, poke fun at, make fun of, get at, insult, tease, torment, ridicule, deride, mock; N. Amer. ride; informal rib, needle.

tax noun *they have to pay tax:* **duty,** excise, customs, dues, levy, tariff, toll, tithe, charge.
verb *his whining taxed her patience:* **strain,** stretch, overburden, overload, overwhelm, try, wear out, exhaust, sap, drain, weary, weaken.

teach verb **educate,** instruct, school, tutor, inform, coach, train, drill.

teacher noun **educator,** tutor, instructor, schoolteacher, master, mistress, schoolmarm, governess, coach, trainer, lecturer, professor, don, guide, mentor, guru.

team noun *the sales team:* **group,** squad, company, party, crew, troupe, band, side, line-up; informal bunch, gang.
verb *ankle boots teamed with jeans:* **match,** coordinate, complement, pair up.
■ **team up** join (forces), collaborate, work together, unite, combine, cooperate, link, ally, associate, club together.

tear verb **1** *your shirt's torn:* **rip,** split, slit, pull apart, pull to pieces, shred, rupture, sever. **2** *his flesh was torn:* **lacerate,** cut (open), gash, slash, scratch, hack, pierce, stab. **3** *Gina tore the book from his hands:*

snatch, grab, seize, rip, wrench, wrest, pull, pluck; informal yank.
noun *a tear in her dress:* **rip,** hole, split, slash, slit, ladder, snag.

tease verb **make fun of,** laugh at, deride, mock, ridicule, guy, make a monkey (out) of, taunt, bait, goad, pick on; informal take the mickey out of, rag, have on, pull someone's leg; Brit. informal wind up.

technical adjective **1** *an important technical achievement:* **practical,** scientific, technological, high-tech. **2** *this might seem very technical:* **specialist,** specialized, scientific, complex, complicated, esoteric.

technique noun **1** *different techniques for solving the problem:* **method,** approach, procedure, system, way, means, strategy. **2** *I was impressed with his technique:* **skill,** ability, proficiency, expertise, artistry, craftsmanship, adroitness, deftness, dexterity.

tedious adjective **boring,** dull, monotonous, repetitive, unrelieved, unvaried, uneventful, lifeless, uninteresting, unexciting, uninspiring, lacklustre, dreary, soul-destroying; informal deadly; N. Amer. informal dullsville.
OPPOSITES exciting.

teenager noun **adolescent,** youth, young person, minor, juvenile; informal teen.

telephone noun *Sophie picked up the telephone:* **phone,** handset, receiver; informal blower; N. Amer. informal horn.
verb *he telephoned me:* **phone,** call, dial; Brit. ring (up); informal call up, give someone a buzz, get on the blower to; Brit. informal

give someone a bell, give someone a tinkle; N. Amer. informal get someone on the horn.

television noun TV; informal the small screen; Brit. informal telly, the box; N. Amer. informal the tube.

tell verb **1** *why didn't you tell me?* **inform**, notify, let know, make aware, acquaint with, advise, put in the picture, brief, fill in, alert, warn; informal clue in/up. **2** *she told the story slowly:* **relate**, recount, narrate, report, recite, describe, sketch. **3** *she told him to leave:* **instruct**, order, command, direct, charge, enjoin, call on, require. **4** *it was hard to tell what he said:* **ascertain**, determine, work out, make out, deduce, discern, perceive, see, identify, recognize, understand, comprehend; informal figure out; Brit. informal suss out. **5** *he couldn't tell one from the other:* **distinguish**, differentiate, discriminate. **6** *the strain began to tell on him:* **take its toll**, leave its mark, affect.

telling adjective **revealing**, significant, weighty, important, meaningful, influential, striking, potent, powerful, compelling.
OPPOSITES insignificant.

temper noun **1** *he walked out in a temper:* **rage**, fury, fit of pique, tantrum, bad mood, pet, sulk, huff; Brit. informal strop, paddy; N. Amer. informal hissy fit. **2** *a display of temper:* **anger**, fury, rage, annoyance, irritation, pique, petulance; Brit. informal stroppiness. **3** *she struggled to keep her temper:* **composure**, self-control, self-possession, calm, good humour; informal cool.
verb *their idealism is tempered with realism:* **moderate**, modify, modulate, mitigate, alleviate, reduce, weaken, lighten, soften.
■ **lose one's temper** get angry, fly into a rage, erupt; informal go mad, go bananas, have a fit, see red, fly off the handle, blow one's top, hit the roof, lose one's rag; Brit. informal go spare, throw a wobbly.

temperamental adjective **volatile**, excitable, emotional, unpredictable, hot-headed, quick-tempered, impatient, touchy, moody, sensitive, highly strung.
OPPOSITES placid.

temple noun **house of God**, shrine, sanctuary, church, cathedral, mosque, synagogue.

temporarily adverb **1** *they are temporarily abroad:* **for the time being**, for the moment, for now, for the present, provisionally, pro tem. **2** *he was temporarily blinded by the light:* **briefly**, for a short time, momentarily, fleetingly.
OPPOSITES permanently.

temporary adjective **1** *temporary accommodation:* **provisional**, short-term, interim, makeshift, stopgap, acting, fill-in, stand-in, caretaker. **2** *a temporary loss of self-control:* **brief**, short-lived, momentary, fleeting, passing, ephemeral.
OPPOSITES permanent, lasting.

tempt verb **1** *the manager tried to tempt me to stay:* **entice**, persuade, convince, inveigle, induce, cajole, coax, lure; informal sweet-talk. **2** *more customers are being tempted by credit:* **attract**, allure, appeal to, whet the appetite of, seduce.
OPPOSITES discourage, deter.

t

temptation noun **1** *Mary resisted the temptation to answer back:* **desire,** urge, itch, impulse, inclination. **2** *the temptations of London:* **lure,** enticement, attraction, draw, pull. **3** *the temptation of exotic travel:* **allure,** appeal, attraction, fascination.

tempting adjective **enticing,** alluring, attractive, appealing, inviting, seductive, beguiling, fascinating.
OPPOSITES off-putting, uninviting.

tenant noun **occupant,** resident, inhabitant, leaseholder, lessee, lodger; Brit. occupier.
OPPOSITES owner, freeholder.

tend[1] verb **1** *I tend to get very involved in my work:* **be inclined,** be apt, be disposed, be prone, be liable. **2** *younger voters tended towards the tabloid press:* **incline,** lean, gravitate, prefer, favour; N. Amer. trend.

tend[2] verb *she tended her cattle:* **look after,** take care of, minister to, attend to, see to, watch over, keep an eye on, mind, protect, guard.
OPPOSITES neglect.

tendency noun **inclination,** propensity, proclivity, proneness, aptness, likelihood, bent, leaning, liability.

tender[1] adjective **1** *a gentle, tender man:* **caring,** kind, kind-hearted, soft-hearted, compassionate, sympathetic, warm, gentle, mild, benevolent. **2** *a tender kiss:* **affectionate,** fond, loving, romantic, emotional; informal lovey-dovey. **3** *simmer until the meat is tender:* **soft,** succulent, juicy, melt-in-the-mouth. **4** *her ankle was swollen and tender:* **sore,** sensitive, inflamed, raw, painful, hurting, aching, throbbing. **5** *the tender age of fifteen:* **young,** youthful, impressionable, inexperienced; informal wet behind the ears.
OPPOSITES hard-hearted, callous, tough, ripe.

tender[2] verb *she tendered her resignation:* **offer,** proffer, present, put forward, propose, suggest, advance, submit, hand in.
noun *contractors were invited to submit tenders:* **bid,** offer, quotation, quote, estimate, price.

tense adjective **1** *tense muscles:* **taut,** tight, rigid, stretched, strained, stiff. **2** *Loretta was feeling tense:* **anxious,** nervous, on edge, edgy, strained, stressed, under pressure, ill at ease, uneasy, restless, worked up, keyed up, overwrought, jumpy, nervy; informal a bundle of nerves, jittery, twitchy, uptight. **3** *a tense moment:* **nerve-racking,** stressful, anxious, worrying, fraught, charged, strained, nail-biting.
OPPOSITES slack, relaxed, calm.
verb *Hebden tensed his muscles:* **tighten,** tauten, flex, contract, brace, stiffen.
OPPOSITES relax.

tension noun **1** *the tension of the rope:* **tightness,** tautness, rigidity, pull. **2** *the tension was unbearable:* **strain,** stress, anxiety, pressure, worry, nervousness, jumpiness, edginess, restlessness, suspense, uncertainty. **3** *months of tension between the military and the government:* **strained relations,** strain, ill feeling, friction, antagonism, antipathy, hostility.

t

tentative adjective **1** *tentative arrangements:* **provisional,** unconfirmed, preliminary, exploratory, experimental. **2** *he took a few tentative steps:* **hesitant,** uncertain, cautious, timid, hesitating, faltering, shaky, unsteady, halting.
OPPOSITES definite, confident.

term noun **1** *scientific terms:* **word,** expression, phrase, name, title, designation, label, description. **2** *the terms of the contract:* **condition,** stipulation, specification, provision, proviso, restriction, qualification. **3** *the President is elected for a four-year term:* **period,** length of time, spell, stint, duration, stretch, run, session.
verb *he has been termed the father of modern theology:* **call,** name, entitle, title, style, designate, describe as, dub, label, tag.

terminal adjective **1** *a terminal illness:* **incurable,** untreatable, inoperable, fatal, lethal, mortal, deadly. **2** *a terminal bonus may be payable:* **final,** last, concluding, closing, end.
OPPOSITES curable, initial.
noun **1** *a railway terminal:* **station,** last stop, end of the line, depot; Brit. terminus. **2** *a computer terminal:* **workstation,** VDU, visual display unit.

terminate verb **1** *treatment was terminated:* **bring to an end,** bring to a close, close, conclude, finish, stop, wind up, discontinue, cease, cut short, abort, axe; informal pull the plug on. **2** *the pregnancy was terminated:* **abort,** end.
OPPOSITES begin, start, continue.

terrain noun **land,** ground, territory, topography, landscape, countryside, country.

terrestrial adjective **earthly,** worldly, mundane, earthbound.

terrible adjective **1** *a terrible crime:* **dreadful,** awful, appalling, horrific, horrible, horrendous, atrocious, monstrous, sickening, heinous, vile. **2** *he was in terrible pain:* **severe,** extreme, intense, excruciating, agonizing, unbearable. **3** *the film was terrible:* **very bad,** dreadful, awful, frightful, atrocious, poor; informal pathetic, pitiful, useless, lousy, appalling; Brit. informal chronic, rubbish, pants.
OPPOSITES minor, slight, excellent.

terribly adverb **1** *he played terribly:* **very badly,** atrociously, awfully, dreadfully, appallingly, execrably; informal abysmally, pitifully. **2** (informal) *I shall miss you terribly:* **very much,** greatly, a great deal, a lot; informal loads.

terrific adjective **1** *a terrific bang:* **tremendous,** huge, massive, gigantic, colossal, mighty, considerable; informal mega, whopping; Brit. informal ginormous. **2** (informal) *a terrific game of top-quality football:* **marvellous,** wonderful, sensational, outstanding, superb, excellent, first-rate, dazzling, out of this world, breathtaking; informal great, fantastic, fabulous, super, ace, wicked, awesome; Brit. informal brilliant.

terrify verb **frighten,** horrify, petrify, scare, strike terror into, paralyse, transfix.

territory noun **1** *British overseas territories:* **region,** area,

t

enclave, country, state, land, dependency, colony, dominion. **2** *mountainous territory:* **terrain,** land, ground, countryside. **3** *the territory of biblical scholarship:* **domain,** province, department, field, preserve, sphere, arena, realm, world.

terror noun **fear,** dread, horror, fright, alarm, panic, shock.

test noun **1** *a series of scientific tests:* **trial,** experiment, check, examination, assessment, evaluation, appraisal, investigation. **2** *candidates must take a test:* **exam,** examination; N. Amer. quiz.
verb *a small-scale prototype was tested:* **try out,** trial, put through its paces, experiment with, check, examine, assess, evaluate, appraise, investigate, sample.

testify verb **swear,** attest, give evidence, state on oath, declare, assert, affirm.

testimonial noun **reference,** letter of recommendation, commendation.

testimony noun **evidence,** sworn statement, attestation, affidavit, statement, declaration, assertion.

testing adjective **difficult,** challenging, tough, hard, demanding, taxing, stressful.
OPPOSITES easy.

text noun **1** *a text which explores pain and grief:* **book,** work, textbook. **2** *the pictures relate well to the text:* **words,** content, body, wording, script, copy.

textiles plural noun **fabrics,** cloths, materials.

texture noun **feel,** touch, appearance, finish, surface, grain, consistency.

thank verb **express one's gratitude to,** say thank you to, show one's appreciation to.

thankful adjective **grateful,** relieved, pleased, glad.

thanks plural noun *they expressed their thanks and wished her well:* **gratitude,** appreciation, acknowledgement, recognition, credit.
■ **thanks to** as a result of, owing to, due to, because of, through, on account of, by virtue of.

thaw verb **melt,** unfreeze, defrost, soften, liquefy.
OPPOSITES freeze.

theatrical adjective **1** *a theatrical career:* **stage,** dramatic, thespian, show-business; informal showbiz. **2** *Henry looked over his shoulder with theatrical caution:* **exaggerated,** ostentatious, stagy, showy, melodramatic, affected.

theft noun **robbery,** stealing, larceny, shoplifting, burglary, embezzlement, raid, hold-up; informal smash-and-grab; N. Amer. informal heist.

theme noun **1** *the theme of her speech:* **subject,** topic, argument, idea, thrust, thread, motif, keynote. **2** *the first violin takes up the theme:* **melody,** tune, air, motif, leitmotif.

then adverb **1** *I was living in Cairo then:* **at that time,** in those days, at that point (in time), at that moment, on that occasion. **2** *she won the first and then the second game:* **next,** after that, afterwards, subsequently; formal thereafter.

theoretical adjective **hypothetical,** speculative, academic, conjectural, suppositional, notional, unproven.
OPPOSITES actual, real, practical.

theory noun **1** *that confirms my theory:* **hypothesis,** thesis, conjecture, supposition, speculation, postulation, proposition, premise, opinion, view, belief, contention. **2** *modern economic theory:* **principles,** ideas, concepts, philosophy, ideology, thinking.

therapeutic adjective **healing,** curative, remedial, medicinal, restorative, health-giving. OPPOSITES harmful.

therapist noun **psychologist,** psychotherapist, analyst, psychoanalyst, psychiatrist, counsellor; informal shrink.

therapy noun **1** *complementary therapies:* **treatment,** remedy, cure. **2** *he's currently in therapy:* **psychotherapy,** psychoanalysis, counselling.

therefore adverb **consequently,** because of that, for that reason, that being the case, so, as a result, hence, accordingly.

thesis noun **1** *the central thesis of his lecture:* **theory,** contention, argument, proposal, proposition, premise, assumption, hypothesis. **2** *a doctoral thesis:* **dissertation,** essay, paper, treatise, composition, study; N. Amer. theme.

thick adjective **1** *thick stone walls:* **broad,** wide, deep, stout, bulky, hefty, chunky, solid, plump. **2** *the station was thick with people:* **crowded,** full, packed, teeming, seething, swarming, crawling, crammed, thronged, bursting at the seams, solid, overflowing; informal jam-packed, chock-a-block, stuffed; Austral./NZ informal chocker. **3** *the thick vegetation:* **plentiful,** abundant, profuse, luxuriant, bushy, rich, riotous, exuberant, rank, rampant, dense; informal jungly. **4** *a thick paste:* **semi-solid,** firm, stiff, heavy, viscous, gelatinous. **5** *thick fog:* **dense,** heavy, opaque, impenetrable, soupy, murky. OPPOSITES thin, slender, sparse.

thicken verb **stiffen,** condense, solidify, set, gel, congeal, clot, coagulate.

thief noun **robber,** burglar, housebreaker, shoplifter, pickpocket, mugger, kleptomaniac; informal crook.

thieve verb **steal,** take, purloin, help oneself to, snatch, pilfer, embezzle, misappropriate; informal rob, swipe, nab, lift; Brit. informal nick, pinch, knock off; N. Amer. informal heist.

thin adjective **1** *a thin white line:* **narrow,** fine, attenuated. **2** *a thin cotton nightdress:* **lightweight,** light, fine, delicate, flimsy, diaphanous, gossamer, sheer, filmy, transparent, see-through. **3** *a tall, thin woman:* **slim,** lean, slender, willowy, svelte, sylphlike, spare, slight, skinny, underweight, scrawny, scraggy, bony, gaunt, emaciated, skeletal, lanky, spindly, gangly; informal anorexic. **4** *thin soup:* **watery,** weak, runny, sloppy. OPPOSITES thick, broad, fat.
verb **1** *some paint must be thinned down:* **dilute,** water down, weaken. **2** *the crowds were beginning to thin out:* **disperse,** dissipate, scatter. OPPOSITES thicken, gather.

thing noun **1** *the room was full of strange things:* **object,** article, item, artefact, commodity; informal doodah, whatsit, whatchamacallit, thingummy, thingy; Brit. informal gubbins.

think | thought

588

2 (**things**) *I'll collect my things:* **belongings**, possessions, stuff, property, worldly goods, effects, paraphernalia, bits and pieces, luggage, baggage; informal gear, junk; Brit. informal clobber.
3 (**things**) *his gardening things:* **equipment**, apparatus, gear, kit, tackle, stuff, implements, tools, utensils, accoutrements.

think verb **1** *I think he's gone home:* **believe**, be of the opinion, be of the view, be under the impression, expect, imagine, anticipate, suppose, guess, fancy; informal reckon, figure. **2** *his family was thought to be rich:* **consider**, judge, hold, reckon, deem, presume, estimate, regard as, view as. **3** *Jack thought for a moment:* **ponder**, reflect, deliberate, consider, meditate, muse, brood. **4** *she thought of all the visits she had made:* **recall**, remember, recollect, call to mind. **5** *I can't think how bad it must be:* **imagine**, picture, visualize, envisage.
■ **think something up** devise, dream up, come up with, invent, create, concoct, make up, hit on.

thinker noun **intellectual**, philosopher, scholar, sage, ideologist, theorist, intellect, mind; informal brain.

thinking adjective *a thinking man:* **intelligent**, sensible, reasonable, rational, logical, analytical, thoughtful.
OPPOSITES stupid, irrational.
noun *the thinking behind the campaign:* **reasoning**, idea(s), theory, thoughts, philosophy, beliefs, opinion(s), view(s).

thirst noun *his thirst for knowledge:* **craving**, desire,

longing, yearning, hunger, hankering, eagerness, lust, appetite; informal yen, itch.
■ **thirst for** crave, want, covet, desire, hunger for, lust after, hanker after, wish for, long for.

thirsty adjective **longing for a drink**, dry, dehydrated; informal parched, gasping.

thorn noun **prickle**, spike, barb, spine.

thorough adjective **1** *a thorough investigation:* **rigorous**, in-depth, exhaustive, minute, detailed, close, meticulous, methodical, careful, complete, comprehensive. **2** *he is slow but thorough:* **meticulous**, scrupulous, assiduous, conscientious, painstaking, punctilious, methodical, careful. **3** *the child is being a thorough nuisance:* **utter**, downright, absolute, complete, total, out-and-out, real, perfect, proper; Brit. informal right; Austral./NZ informal fair.
OPPOSITES superficial, cursory, careless.

though conjunction *though she smiled bravely, she looked tired:* **although**, even though, even if, despite the fact that, notwithstanding (the fact) that, for all that.
adverb *You can't always do that. You can try, though.*
nevertheless, nonetheless, even so, however, be that as it may, for all that, despite that, having said that; informal still and all.

thought noun **1** *what are your thoughts on the matter?* **idea**, notion, opinion, view, impression, feeling, theory. **2** *he gave up any thought of taking a degree:* **hope**, aspiration, ambition, dream, intention, idea, plan, design, aim. **3** *it only took a moment's thought:* **thinking,** contemplation, musing, pondering, consideration, reflection, deliberation, meditation. **4** *have you no thought for others?* **consideration,** understanding, regard, sensitivity, compassion, sympathy, care, concern.

thoughtful adjective **1** *a thoughtful expression:* **pensive,** reflective, contemplative, musing, meditative, philosophical, preoccupied. **2** *how very thoughtful of you!* **considerate,** caring, attentive, understanding, sympathetic, solicitous, concerned, helpful, obliging, accommodating, kind, compassionate.
OPPOSITES vacant, inconsiderate.

thrash verb **1** *she thrashed him with a whip:* **hit,** beat, strike, batter, thump, hammer, pound; informal belt. **2** *he was thrashing around in pain:* **flail,** writhe, thresh, jerk, toss, twist, twitch.

thread noun **1** *a needle and thread:* **cotton,** yarn, filament, fibre. **2** *she lost the thread of the conversation:* **train of thought,** drift, direction, theme, tenor.
verb **1** *he threaded the rope through a pulley:* **pass,** string, work, ease, push, poke. **2** *she threaded her way through the tables:* **weave,** inch, squeeze, navigate, negotiate.

threat noun **1** *Maggie ignored his threats:* **threatening remark,** warning, ultimatum. **2** *a possible threat to aircraft:* **danger,** peril, hazard, menace, risk. **3** *the company faces the threat of liquidation:* **possibility,** chance, probability, likelihood, risk.

threaten verb **1** *how dare you threaten me?* **menace,** intimidate, browbeat, bully, terrorize. **2** *these events could threaten the stability of Europe:* **endanger,** jeopardize, imperil, put at risk. **3** *the grey skies threatened snow:* **herald,** bode, warn of, presage, foreshadow, indicate, point to, be a sign of, signal.

threshold noun **1** *the threshold of the church:* **doorstep,** entrance, entry, gate. **2** *on the threshold of a new era:* **start,** beginning, commencement, brink, verge, dawn, inception, day one, opening, debut. **3** *the human threshold of pain:* **limit,** minimum.

thrifty adjective **frugal,** economical, sparing, careful with money, provident, prudent, abstemious, parsimonious, penny-pinching.
OPPOSITES extravagant.

thrill noun *the thrill of jumping out of an aeroplane:* **excitement,** stimulation, pleasure, tingle; informal buzz, kick; N. Amer. informal charge.
OPPOSITES boredom.
verb **1** *his words thrilled her:* **excite,** stimulate, arouse, rouse, inspire, delight, exhilarate, intoxicate, stir, electrify, move; informal give someone a buzz, give someone a kick; N. Amer. informal give someone a charge. **2** *he thrilled at the sound of her voice:* **feel excited,** tingle; informal get a buzz out of, get a kick out of; N. Amer. informal get a charge out of.
OPPOSITES bore.

thrilling adjective **exciting,** stimulating, stirring, action-packed, rip-roaring, gripping, electrifying, riveting,

t

fascinating, dramatic, hair-raising.
OPPOSITES boring.

thrive verb **flourish**, prosper, burgeon, bloom, blossom, do well, advance, succeed, boom.
OPPOSITES decline, wither.

thriving adjective **flourishing**, prospering, growing, developing, blooming, healthy, successful, booming, profitable; informal going strong.
OPPOSITES declining.

throb verb *her arms and legs throbbed with tiredness:* **pulsate**, beat, pulse, palpitate, pound, thud, thump, drum, judder, vibrate, quiver.
noun *the throb of the ship's engines:* **pulsation**, beat, pulse, palpitation, pounding, thudding, thumping, drumming, juddering, vibration, quivering.

throng noun *throngs of people blocked her way:* **crowd**, horde, mass, army, herd, flock, drove, swarm, sea, troupe, pack; informal gaggle, bunch, gang.
verb **1** *the pavements were thronged with tourists:* **fill**, crowd, pack, cram, jam.
2 *people thronged to see the play:* **flock**, stream, swarm, troop. **3** *visitors thronged round him:* **crowd**, cluster, mill, swarm, congregate, gather.

throttle verb **choke**, strangle, garrotte.

through preposition **1** *he got the job through an advertisement:* **by means of**, by way of, by dint of, via, using, thanks to, by virtue of, as a result of, as a consequence of, on account of, owing to. **2** *he worked through the night:* **throughout**, for the duration of, until/to the end of, all.

throughout preposition **1** *it had repercussions throughout Europe:* **all over**, in every part of, everywhere in. **2** *Rose had been very fit throughout her life:* **all through**, for the duration of, for the whole of, until the end of, all.

throw verb **1** **hurl**, toss, fling, pitch, cast, lob, launch, bowl; informal chuck, heave, sling, bung. **2** *he threw the door open:* **push**, thrust, fling, bang. **3** *a chandelier threw its light over the walls:* **cast**, send, give off, emit, radiate, project. **4** *his intervention threw me:* **disconcert**, unnerve, fluster, ruffle, put off, throw off balance, unsettle, confuse; informal rattle, faze.
noun **lob**, toss, pitch, bowl.
■ **throw something away/out** discard, dispose of, get rid of, scrap, dump, jettison; informal chuck (away/out), ditch, bin, junk; Brit. informal get shot of.
■ **throw someone out** expel, eject, evict, drive out, force out, oust, remove, get rid of, depose, topple, unseat, overthrow; informal boot out, kick out; Brit. informal turf out.

thrust verb **1** *a spear was thrust into the sack:* **shove**, push, force, plunge, stick, drive, ram. **2** *fame had been thrust on him:* **force**, foist, impose, inflict. **3** *he thrust his way past her:* **push**, shove, force, elbow, shoulder, barge.
noun **1** *a hard thrust:* **shove**, push, lunge, poke. **2** *a thrust by the Third Army:* **advance**, push, drive, attack, assault, onslaught, offensive. **3** *only one engine is producing thrust:* **force**, propulsion, power, impetus. **4** *the thrust of the speech:* **gist**, substance, drift,

message, import, tenor.

thug noun **ruffian**, hooligan, bully boy, hoodlum, gangster, villain; informal **tough**, bruiser, heavy; Brit. informal **rough**, bovver boy; N. Amer. informal **hood**, goon.

thump verb **1** *he thumped the policeman:* **hit**, punch, strike, smack; informal **whack**, wallop, bash, biff, bop, clobber; Brit. informal **slosh**; N. Amer. informal **slug**. **2** *her heart thumped with fright:* **throb**, pound, thud, hammer.
noun **1** *a thump in the eye:* **blow**, punch, box, cuff, smack; informal **whack**, wallop, bash, biff; Brit. informal **slosh**; N. Amer. informal **boff**, slug. **2** *she put the box down with a thump:* **thud**, clunk, clonk, crash, smack, bang.

thunder noun **rumble**, boom, roar, pounding, thud, crash, reverberation.
verb **1** *below me the surf thundered:* **rumble**, boom, roar, pound, thud, thump, bang. **2** *'Answer me!' he thundered:* **shout**, roar, bellow, bark, bawl.

thus adverb **1** *the studio handled production, thus cutting its costs:* **consequently**, so, therefore, accordingly, hence, as a result. **2** *legislation forbids such data being held thus:* **like this/that**, in this/that way, so, like so, as follows.

thwart verb **foil**, frustrate, forestall, stop, check, block, prevent, defeat, impede, obstruct, derail, snooker; informal **put paid to**, do for, stymie; Brit. informal **scupper**.
OPPOSITES help.

ticket noun **1** *a bus ticket:* **pass**, authorization, permit, token, coupon, voucher. **2** *a price ticket:* **label**, tag, sticker, tab, slip, docket.

tickle verb **1** **stroke**, pet, chuck. **2** *something tickled his imagination:* **stimulate**, interest, appeal to, arouse, excite. **3** *the idea tickled Lewis:* **amuse**, entertain, divert, please, delight.

tide noun **1** **current**, flow, stream, ebb. **2** *the tide of history:* **course**, movement, direction, trend, current, drift, run.

tidy adjective **1** *a tidy room:* **neat**, orderly, well ordered, well kept, in apple-pie order, uncluttered, straight. **2** *a very tidy person:* **organized**, neat, methodical, meticulous.
OPPOSITES messy, disorganized.
verb *I'd better tidy up the living room:* **put in order**, clear up, sort out, straighten (up), clean up, spruce up.
OPPOSITES mess up.

tie verb **1** *he tied the boat to the jetty:* **bind**, tie up, tether, hitch, strap, truss, fetter, rope, make fast, moor, lash. **2** *he bent to tie his shoelaces:* **do up**, lace, knot. **3** *women can feel tied by childcare responsibilities:* **restrict**, restrain, limit, tie down, constrain, cramp, hamper, handicap, hamstring, encumber, shackle. **4** *a pay deal tied to productivity:* **link**, connect, couple, relate, join, marry. **5** *they tied for second place:* **draw**, be equal, be even.
noun **1** *he tightened the ties of his robe:* **lace**, string, cord, fastening. **2** *family ties:* **bond**, connection, link, relationship, attachment, affiliation. **3** *pets can be a tremendous tie:* **restriction**, constraint, curb, limitation, restraint, hindrance, encumbrance, handicap, obligation, commitment. **4** *a tie*

t

for first place: **draw**, dead heat.

tier noun **1** *six tiers of seats:* **row**, rank, bank, line, layer, level. **2** *a tier of management:* **grade**, gradation, echelon, rung on the ladder.

tight adjective **1** *a tight grip:* **firm**, secure. **2** *the rope was pulled tight:* **taut**, rigid, stiff, tense, stretched, strained. **3** *tight jeans:* **close-fitting**, narrow, figure-hugging, skintight; informal **sprayed on**. **4** *a tight mass of fibres:* **compact**, compressed, dense, solid. **5** *a tight space:* **small**, tiny, narrow, limited, restricted, confined, cramped, constricted. **6** *a tight joint:* **sealed**, sound, impenetrable, impervious. OPPOSITES slack, loose, roomy, leaky.

tighten verb **1** *he tightened his grip:* **strengthen**, harden. **2** *she tightened the rope:* **stretch**, tauten, strain, stiffen, tense. OPPOSITES loosen, slacken, relax.

tilt verb *the ground seemed to tilt:* **slope**, tip, lean, list, bank, slant, incline, pitch, cant, angle. noun *a tilt of some 45°:* **slope**, list, camber, gradient, bank, slant, incline, pitch, cant, bevel, angle.

timber noun **1** *houses built of timber:* **wood**; N. Amer. lumber. **2** *the timbers of wrecked ships:* **beam**, spar, plank, batten, lath, board, joist, rafter.

time noun **1** *the best time to leave:* **moment**, point (in time), occasion, instant, juncture, stage. **2** *he worked there for a time:* **while**, spell, stretch, stint, interval, period, length of time, duration, phase. **3** *the time of the dinosaurs:* **era**, age, epoch, period, years, days. verb *the meeting is timed for*

4 o'clock: **schedule**, arrange, set, organize, fix, book, line up, timetable, plan; N. Amer. slate. ■ **all the time** constantly, the entire time, around the clock, day and night, {morning, noon, and night}, {day in, day out}, always, without a break, ceaselessly, endlessly, incessantly, perpetually, permanently, continuously, continually, eternally; informal 24-7. ■ **at times** occasionally, sometimes, from time to time, now and then, every so often, once in a while, on occasion, off and on, at intervals, periodically.

timeless adjective **lasting**, enduring, classic, ageless, permanent, perennial, abiding, unchanging, unvarying, never-changing, eternal, everlasting. OPPOSITES ephemeral.

timely adjective **opportune**, well timed, convenient, appropriate, expedient, seasonable, propitious. OPPOSITES ill-timed.

timetable noun **schedule**, programme, agenda, calendar, diary. verb **schedule**, arrange, programme, organize, fix, time, line up; Brit. diarize; N. Amer. slate.

timid adjective **fearful**, afraid, faint-hearted, timorous, nervous, scared, frightened, shy, diffident. OPPOSITES bold.

tinge verb **1** *white blossom tinged with pink:* **tint**, colour, stain, shade, wash. **2** *his optimism is tinged with realism:* **influence**, affect, touch, flavour, colour. noun **1** *a blue tinge:* **tint**, colour, shade, tone, hue. **2** *a tinge of* *cynicism:* **trace,** note, touch, suggestion, hint, flavour, element, streak, suspicion, soupçon.

tinker verb fiddle, play about, mess about, adjust, try to mend; Brit. informal muck about.

tint noun 1 *an apricot tint:* **shade,** colour, tone, hue, tinge, cast, flush, blush. 2 *a hair tint:* **dye,** colourant, colouring, wash. verb *she had her hair tinted:* **dye,** colour, tinge.

tiny adjective minute, minuscule, microscopic, very small, mini, diminutive, miniature, baby, toy, dwarf; Scottish wee; informal teeny, tiddly; Brit. informal titchy; N. Amer. informal little-bitty.
OPPOSITES huge.

tip[1] noun 1 *the tip of the spear:* **point,** end, extremity, head, spike, prong, nib. 2 *the tips of the mountains:* **peak,** top, summit, apex, crown, crest, pinnacle.
verb *mountains tipped with snow:* **cap,** top, crown, surmount.

tip[2] verb 1 *the boat tipped over:* **overturn,** turn over, topple (over), fall (over), keel over, capsize, roll over. 2 *a whale could tip over a small boat:* **upset,** overturn, topple over, turn over, push over, upend, capsize; informal roll. 3 *the car tipped to one side:* **lean,** tilt, list, slope, bank, slant, incline, pitch, cant. 4 *she tipped the water into the trough:* **pour,** empty, drain, dump, discharge, decant.
noun (Brit.) *rubbish must be taken to the tip:* **dump,** rubbish dump, landfill site.

tip[3] noun 1 *a generous tip:* **gratuity,** baksheesh, present, gift, reward. 2 *useful tips:* piece

of advice, suggestion, word of advice, pointer, hint; informal wrinkle.

tire verb 1 *he began to tire:* **get tired,** weaken, flag, droop. 2 *the journey had tired him:* **fatigue,** tire out, exhaust, wear out, drain, weary; informal knock out, take it out of; Brit. informal knacker. 3 *they tired of his difficult behaviour:* **weary,** get tired, get fed up, get sick, get bored.

tired adjective 1 *tired from travelling:* **exhausted,** worn out, weary, fatigued, ready to drop, drained; informal all in, dead beat, shattered; Brit. informal knackered, whacked; N. Amer. informal pooped, tuckered out; Austral./NZ informal stonkered. 2 *are you tired of having him here?* **fed up with,** weary of, bored with/by, sick (and tired) of; informal up to here with. 3 *tired jokes:* **hackneyed,** overused, stale, clichéd, predictable, unimaginative, unoriginal, dull, boring; informal corny.
OPPOSITES energetic, lively, fresh.

tiring adjective exhausting, wearying, taxing, draining, hard, arduous, strenuous, onerous, gruelling; informal killing; Brit. informal knackering.

title noun 1 *the title of the article:* **heading,** label, inscription, caption, subheading, legend. 2 *the title of Duke of Marlborough:* **name,** designation, form of address, rank, office, position; informal moniker, handle. 3 *an Olympic title:* **championship,** crown, first place.

toast noun 1 *he raised his glass in a toast:* **tribute,** salutation. 2 *he was the toast of the West*

t

End: **darling,** favourite, pet, heroine, hero, talk; Brit. informal blue-eyed boy/girl.

verb *we toasted the couple with champagne:* **drink (to) the health of,** salute, honour, pay tribute to.

together adverb **1** *friends who work together:* **with each other,** in conjunction, jointly, in cooperation, in collaboration, in partnership, in combination, in league, side by side; informal in cahoots. **2** *they both spoke together:* **simultaneously,** at the same time, at once, concurrently, as a group, in unison, in chorus.
OPPOSITES separately, successively.
adjective (informal) *she looks a very together young woman:* **level-headed,** well adjusted, sensible, practical, realistic, mature, stable, full of common sense, well organized, efficient, methodical, self-confident, self-assured; informal unflappable.
OPPOSITES flighty, disorganized.

toil verb **1** *she toiled all night:* **work,** labour, slave, strive; informal slog, beaver; Brit. informal graft. **2** *she began to toil up the path:* **struggle,** drag oneself, trudge, slog, plod; N. Amer. informal schlep.
OPPOSITES rest, relax.
noun *a life of toil:* **hard work,** labour, exertion, slaving, drudgery, effort, {blood, sweat, and tears}; informal slog, elbow grease; Brit. informal graft.

toilet noun **1** lavatory, WC, (public) convenience, cloakroom, powder room, latrine, privy, urinal; N. Amer. bathroom, washroom, rest room, men's/ladies' room, comfort station; Brit. informal loo, the Ladies, the Gents; N. Amer. informal can, john; Austral./NZ informal dunny.

token noun **1** *a token of our appreciation:* **symbol,** sign, emblem, badge, representation, indication, mark, expression, demonstration. **2** *a book token:* **voucher,** coupon, note.
adjective *token resistance:* **symbolic,** nominal, perfunctory, slight, minimal, superficial, emblematic, indicative.

tolerance noun **1** *an attitude of tolerance towards people:* **acceptance,** open-mindedness, broad-mindedness, forbearance, patience, charity, understanding. **2** *the plant's tolerance of pollution:* **endurance,** resilience, resistance, immunity. **3** *a 1% maximum tolerance in measurement:* **deviation,** variation, play, inaccuracy, imprecision.

tolerant adjective **open-minded,** forbearing, broad-minded, liberal, unprejudiced, unbiased, patient, long-suffering, understanding, charitable, lenient, easy-going.
OPPOSITES intolerant, strict.

tolerate verb **1** *a regime unwilling to tolerate dissent:* **allow,** permit, condone, accept, swallow, countenance. **2** *he couldn't tolerate her moods any longer:* **endure,** put up with, bear, take, stand, support, stomach; informal abide; Brit. informal stick.

toll[1] noun **1** *a motorway toll:* **charge,** fee, payment, levy, tariff, tax. **2** *the toll of dead and injured:* **number,** count, tally, total, sum. **3** *the toll on the environment has been high:*

harm, damage, hurt, injury, detriment, adverse effect, cost, price, loss.

toll² verb *I heard the bell toll:* **ring,** sound, clang, chime, strike, peal.

tomb noun **burial chamber,** vault, crypt, catacomb, sepulchre, mausoleum, grave.

tone noun **1** *the tone of the tuba:* **sound,** timbre, voice, colour, tonality. **2** *the impatient tone of his letter:* **mood,** air, feel, flavour, note, attitude, character. **3** *a dialling tone:* **note,** signal, bleep. **4** *tones of lavender and rose:* **shade,** colour, hue, tint, tinge.
verb *the shirt toned well with her cream skirt:* **harmonize,** go, blend, coordinate, team, match, suit, complement.

■ **tone something down 1** *the colour needs to be toned down:* soften, lighten, mute, subdue. **2** *the papers refused to tone down their criticism:* moderate, modify, temper, soften, modulate.

tonic noun **stimulant,** boost, restorative, refresher, fillip; informal shot in the arm, pick-me-up, bracer.

too adverb **1** *invasion would be too risky:* **excessively,** overly, unduly, immoderately, inordinately, unreasonably, extremely, very. **2** *he was unhappy, too, you know:* **also,** as well, in addition, into the bargain, besides, furthermore, moreover.

tool noun **implement,** utensil, device, apparatus, gadget, appliance, machine, contrivance, contraption; informal gizmo.

top noun **1** *the top of the cliff:* **summit,** peak, pinnacle, crest,

crown, brow, head, tip, apex. **2** *the top of the coffee jar:* **lid,** cap, cover. **3** *he was at the top of his profession:* **height,** peak, pinnacle, zenith, culmination, climax, prime.
OPPOSITES bottom, base.
adjective **1** *the top floor:* **highest,** topmost, uppermost. **2** *top scientists:* **foremost,** leading, principal, pre-eminent, greatest, best, finest, elite. **3** *the organization's top management:* **chief,** principal, main, leading, highest, ruling, commanding, most powerful, most important. **4** *a top hotel:* **prime,** premier, excellent, superior, choice, select, five-star, grade A, best, finest. **5** *at top speed:* **maximum,** greatest, utmost.
OPPOSITES bottom, lowest, minimum.
verb **1** *sales topped £1 billion:* **exceed,** surpass, go beyond, better, beat, outstrip, outdo, outshine, eclipse. **2** *their CD is currently topping the charts:* **lead,** head, be at the top of. **3** *mousse topped with cream:* **cover,** cap, coat, finish, garnish.
■ **top something up** fill, refill, refresh, freshen, replenish, recharge, resupply.

topic noun **subject,** theme, issue, matter, point, question, concern, argument, thesis.

topical adjective **current,** up to date, up to the minute, contemporary, recent, relevant, in the news.
OPPOSITES out of date.

topple verb **1** *she toppled off the chair:* **fall,** tumble, tip, overbalance, overturn, keel over, lose one's balance. **2** *protesters toppled a statue:* **knock over,** upset, push over,

t

tip over, upend. **3** *a plot to topple the government:* **overthrow,** oust, unseat, overturn, bring down, defeat, get rid of, dislodge, eject.

torment noun *emotional torment:* **agony,** suffering, torture, pain, anguish, misery, distress, trauma.
verb **1** *she was tormented by shame:* **torture,** afflict, rack, harrow, plague, haunt, distress, agonize. **2** *she began to torment the boys:* **tease,** taunt, bait, provoke, harass, bother, persecute; informal **needle.**

torn adjective **1** *a torn shirt:* **ripped,** rent, cut, slit, ragged, tattered. **2** *she was torn between the two options:* **wavering,** vacillating, irresolute, dithering, uncertain, unsure, undecided, in two minds.

tornado noun **whirlwind,** cyclone, typhoon, storm, hurricane; N. Amer. informal **twister.**

torrent noun **1** *a torrent of water:* **flood,** deluge, spate, cascade, rush. **2** *a torrent of abuse:* **outburst,** outpouring, stream, flood, volley, barrage, tide.
OPPOSITES trickle.

torture noun **1** *the torture of political prisoners:* **abuse,** ill-treatment, mistreatment, maltreatment, persecution, cruelty, atrocity. **2** *the torture of losing a loved one:* **torment,** agony, suffering, pain, anguish, misery, distress, heartbreak, trauma.
verb **1** *the forces routinely tortured suspects:* **abuse,** ill-treat, mistreat, maltreat, persecute. **2** *he was tortured by grief:* **torment,** rack, afflict,

harrow, plague, distress, trouble.

toss verb **1** *he tossed his tools into the boot:* **throw,** hurl, fling, sling, pitch, lob, launch; informal heave, chuck, bung. **2** *he tossed a coin:* **flip,** flick, spin. **3** *the ship tossed about on the waves:* **pitch,** lurch, rock, roll, plunge, reel, sway. **4** *toss the ingredients together:* **mix,** combine, stir, turn, shake.

total adjective **1** *the total cost:* **entire,** complete, whole, full, combined, aggregate, gross, overall. **2** *a total disaster:* **utter,** complete, absolute, thorough, perfect, downright, out-and-out, outright, sheer, unmitigated.
OPPOSITES partial, net.
noun *a total of £16:* **sum,** aggregate, whole, entirety, totality.
verb **1** *the prize money totalled £33,050:* **add up to,** amount to, come to, run to, make. **2** *he totalled up his score:* **add,** count, reckon, tot up, compute, work out.

totally adverb **completely,** entirely, wholly, thoroughly, fully, utterly, absolutely, perfectly, unreservedly, unconditionally, downright, one hundred per cent.
OPPOSITES partly.

touch verb **1** *his feet touched the floor:* **contact,** meet, brush, graze, come up against, be in contact with, border, abut. **2** *he touched her cheek:* **feel,** pat, tap, stroke, fondle, caress, pet, handle. **3** *sales touched twenty grand:* **reach,** attain, come to, make, rise to, soar to, sink to, plummet to; informal **hit.**
4 *nobody can touch him when he's on form:* **compare with,** be

on a par with, equal, match, rival, measure up to, better, beat; informal hold a candle to. **5** *you're not supposed to touch the computer:* **handle**, hold, pick up, move, use, meddle with, play about with, fiddle with, interfere with, tamper with, disturb. **6** *Lisa felt touched by her kindness:* **affect**, move, stir.
noun **1** *her touch on his shoulder:* **tap**, pat, contact, stroke, caress. **2** *his political touch:* **skill**, expertise, dexterity, deftness, adroitness, adeptness, ability, talent, flair, facility, proficiency, knack. **3** *there was a touch of bitterness in her voice:* **trace**, bit, suggestion, suspicion, hint, scintilla, tinge, dash, taste, spot, drop, dab, soupçon. **4** *the gas lights are a nice touch:* **detail**, feature, point, element, addition. **5** *have you been in touch with him?* **contact**, communication, correspondence.
■ **touch on/upon** refer to, mention, comment on, remark on, bring up, raise, broach, allude to, cover, deal with.

touching adjective moving, affecting, heart-warming, emotional, emotive, poignant, sad, tear-jerking.

tough adjective **1** *tough leather:* **durable**, strong, resilient, sturdy, rugged, solid, stout, robust, hard-wearing, long-lasting, heavy-duty, well built, made to last. **2** *he'll survive— he's pretty tough:* **robust**, resilient, strong, hardy, rugged, fit; informal hard. **3** *tough sentencing for offenders:* **strict**, stern, severe, stringent, rigorous, hard, firm, hard-hitting, uncompromising. **4** *the training was pretty tough:*

difficult, hard, strenuous, onerous, gruelling, exacting, arduous, demanding, taxing, tiring, exhausting, punishing. **5** *tough questions:* **difficult**, hard, knotty, thorny, tricky. OPPOSITES weak, lenient, light, easy.
noun *a gang of toughs:* **ruffian**, thug, hoodlum, hooligan, bully boy; Brit. rough; informal heavy, bruiser; Brit. informal yob.

tour noun **1** *a three-day walking tour:* **trip**, excursion, journey, expedition, jaunt, outing, trek, safari. **2** *a tour of the factory:* **visit**, inspection, walkabout.
verb **1** *this hotel is well placed for touring Devon:* **travel round**, explore, holiday in; informal do. **2** *the Prince toured a local factory:* **visit**, inspect, go round, walk round.

tourist noun holidaymaker, traveller, sightseer, visitor, backpacker, globetrotter, tripper; N. Amer. vacationer. OPPOSITES local.

tournament noun competition, contest, championship, meeting, event.

tow verb pull, haul, drag, draw, tug, lug.

towards preposition **1** *they were driving towards her flat:* **in the direction of**, to, on the way to, on the road to. **2** *towards evening dark clouds gathered:* **just before**, shortly before, near, around, approaching, getting on for. **3** *her attitude towards politics:* **with regard to**, regarding, in/with regard to, in relation to, concerning, about, apropos.

tower verb *snow-capped peaks towered over the valley:* **soar**, rise, rear, overshadow, overhang, hang over, dominate.

t

toxic adjective **poisonous**, dangerous, harmful, injurious, noxious, pernicious, deadly, lethal.
OPPOSITES harmless.

toy noun *playing with their toys:* **plaything**, game.
adjective *a toy gun:* **model**, imitation, replica, miniature.
■ **toy with 1** *I was toying with the idea:* think about, consider, flirt with, entertain the possibility of; informal kick around. **2** *Adam toyed with his glasses:* fiddle with, play with, fidget with, twiddle, finger.

trace verb **1** *police hope to trace the owner:* **track down**, find, discover, detect, unearth, turn up, hunt down, ferret out, run to ground. **2** *she traced a pattern in the sand:* **draw**, outline, mark.
noun **1** *no trace had been found of the missing plane:* **sign**, mark, indication, evidence, clue, vestige, remains, remnant. **2** *a trace of bitterness crept into her voice:* **bit**, touch, hint, suggestion, suspicion, shadow, dash, tinge; informal smidgen, tad.

track noun **1** *a gravel track:* **path**, footpath, lane, trail, route. **2** *the final lap of the track:* **course**, racecourse, racetrack, velodrome; Brit. circuit. **3** *he found the tracks of a fox:* **traces**, marks, prints, footprints, trail, spoor. **4** *the railway tracks:* **rail**, line. **5** *the album's title track:* **song**, recording, number, piece.
verb *he tracked a bear for 40 km:* **follow**, trail, pursue, shadow, stalk; informal tail.
■ **track someone/something down** discover, find, detect, hunt down, unearth, uncover, turn up, dig up, ferret out, run to ground.

trade noun **1** *the trade in stolen cattle:* **dealing**, buying and selling, commerce, traffic, business. **2** *the glazier's trade:* **occupation**, work, craft, job, career, profession, business, line (of work), métier.
verb **1** *he made his fortune trading in diamonds:* **deal**, do business, bargain, negotiate, traffic, buy and sell. **2** *the business is trading at a loss:* **operate**, run, do business, deal. **3** *I traded the old machine for a newer model:* **swap**, exchange, barter, part-exchange.

trader noun **dealer**, merchant, buyer, seller, vendor, purveyor, supplier, trafficker.

tradition noun **custom**, practice, convention, ritual, observance, way, usage, habit, institution, unwritten law; formal praxis.

traditional adjective **customary**, long-established, time-honoured, classic, wonted, accustomed, standard, regular, normal, conventional, habitual, ritual, age-old, folk.

traffic noun **1** *the increased use of railways for goods traffic:* **transport**, freight, shipping. **2** *the traffic in stolen art:* **trade**, dealing, commerce, business, buying and selling.
verb *he confessed to trafficking in ivory:* **trade**, deal, do business, buy and sell.

tragedy noun **disaster**, calamity, catastrophe, cataclysm, misfortune, adversity.

tragic adjective **1** *a tragic accident:* **disastrous**, calamitous, catastrophic, cataclysmic, devastating, terrible, dreadful, awful, appalling, horrendous, fatal. **2** *a*

tragic tale: **sad**, unhappy, pathetic, moving, distressing, painful, harrowing, heart-rending, sorry.
OPPOSITES fortunate, happy.

trail noun **1** *a trail of clues:* **series**, string, chain, succession, sequence. **2** *wolves on the trail of their prey:* **track**, spoor, path, scent, traces, marks, signs, prints, footprints. **3** *the plane's vapour trail:* **wake**, tail, stream. **4** *nature trails:* **path**, way, footpath, track, route.
verb **1** *her robe trailed along the ground:* **drag**, sweep, be drawn, dangle. **2** *the roses trailed over the banks:* **hang**, droop, fall, spill, cascade. **3** *Sharpe suspected they were trailing him:* **follow**, pursue, track, shadow, stalk, hunt; informal tail. **4** *the defending champions were trailing 10–5:* **lose**, be down, be behind, lag behind.
OPPOSITES lead.

train verb **1** *an engineer trained in remote-sensing techniques:* **instruct**, teach, coach, tutor, school, educate, prime, drill, ground. **2** *she's training to be a hairdresser:* **study**, learn, prepare, take instruction. **3** *with the Olympics in mind, athletes are training hard:* **exercise**, work out, get into shape, practise. **4** *she trained the gun on him:* **aim**, point, direct, level, focus.
noun *a bizarre train of events:* **chain**, string, series, sequence, succession, set, course.

trainer noun **coach**, instructor, teacher, tutor, handler.

trait noun **characteristic**, attribute, feature, quality, habit, mannerism, idiosyncrasy, peculiarity.

traitor noun **betrayer**, back-stabber, double-crosser, renegade, Judas, quisling, fifth columnist, turncoat, defector; informal snake in the grass.

tramp verb **1** *men were tramping through the shrubbery:* **trudge**, plod, stamp, trample, lumber; informal traipse. **2** *he spent ten days tramping through the jungle:* **trek**, walk, hike, slog, march, roam, ramble, rove; informal traipse; N. Amer. informal schlep.
noun **1** *a dirty old tramp:* **vagrant**, vagabond, homeless person, down-and-out, traveller, drifter; N. Amer. hobo; N. Amer. informal bum. **2** *the tramp of boots:* **tread**, step, footstep, footfall. **3** *a tramp round York:* **trek**, walk, hike, slog, march, roam, ramble; N. Amer. informal schlep.

trample verb **tread**, stamp, walk, squash, crush, flatten.

trance noun **daze**, stupor, hypnotic state, dream, reverie.

tranquil adjective **1** *a tranquil village:* **peaceful**, calm, restful, quiet, still, relaxing, undisturbed. **2** *Martha smiled, perfectly tranquil:* **calm**, serene, relaxed, unruffled, unperturbed, unflustered, untroubled, composed; informal unflappable.
OPPOSITES busy, excitable.

transaction noun **deal**, bargain, agreement, undertaking, arrangement, negotiation, settlement.

transfer verb **move**, take, bring, shift, convey, remove, carry, transport, relocate.

transform verb **change**, alter, convert, revolutionize, overhaul, reconstruct, rebuild, reorganize, rearrange, rework.

transition noun **change**,

t

passage, move, transformation, conversion, metamorphosis, alteration, changeover, shift, switch.

transitional adjective **1** *a transitional period:* **intermediate**, interim, changeover, changing, fluid, unsettled. **2** *the transitional government:* **interim**, temporary, provisional, pro tem, acting, caretaker.

translate verb **interpret**, convert, render, put, change, express, decipher, reword, decode, gloss, explain.

translation noun **interpretation**, rendition, conversion, change, alteration, adaptation.

transmission noun **1** *the transmission of knowledge:* **transfer**, communication, passing on, conveyance, dissemination, spread, circulation, relaying. **2** *the transmission of the film:* **broadcasting**, airing, televising. **3** *a live transmission:* **broadcast**, programme, show.

transmit verb **1** *the use of computers to transmit information:* **transfer**, communicate, pass on, hand on, convey, impart, channel, carry, relay, dispatch, disseminate, spread, circulate. **2** *the programme will be transmitted on Sunday:* **broadcast**, send out, air, televise.

transparent adjective **1** *transparent blue water:* **clear**, translucent, limpid. **2** *fine transparent fabrics:* **see-through**, sheer, filmy, gauzy, diaphanous. **3** *a transparent attempt to buy votes:* **obvious**, blatant, unambiguous, unequivocal,

clear, plain, apparent, unmistakable, manifest, conspicuous, patent. OPPOSITES opaque, obscure.

transplant verb **1** *these ideas were transplanted to America:* **transfer**, move, remove, shift, relocate, take, replant. **2** *kidneys are frequently transplanted:* **transfer**, implant, graft.

transport verb *the blocks were transported by lorry:* **convey**, carry, take, transfer, move, shift, send, deliver, bear, ship, ferry; informal cart. noun *the transport of crude oil:* **conveyance**, carriage, delivery, shipping, freight, shipment, haulage.

trap noun **1** *an animal caught in a trap:* **snare**, net, mesh, gin; N. Amer. deadfall. **2** *the question was set as a trap:* **trick**, ploy, ruse, deception, subterfuge; informal set-up. verb **1** *police trapped the men:* **snare**, entrap, capture, catch, ambush. **2** *a rat trapped in a barn:* **confine**, cut off, corner, shut in, pen in, hem in, imprison. **3** *I hoped to trap him into an admission:* **trick**, dupe, deceive, fool, hoodwink.

trash noun **1** (N. Amer.) *the entrance was blocked with trash:* **rubbish**, refuse, waste, litter, junk; N. Amer. garbage. **2** (informal) *they read trash:* **rubbish**, nonsense, trivia, pulp fiction, pap; N. Amer. garbage; informal drivel.

trauma noun **1** *the trauma of divorce:* **shock**, upheaval, distress, stress, strain, pain, anguish, suffering, upset, ordeal. **2** *trauma to the liver:* **injury**, damage, wound.

traumatic adjective **disturbing,**

shocking, distressing, upsetting, painful, agonizing, hurtful, stressful, devastating, harrowing.
OPPOSITES comforting.

travel verb **journey,** tour, take a trip, voyage, go sightseeing, globetrot, backpack, trek.
noun **(travels) travelling,** journeys, expeditions, trips, tours, excursions, voyages, treks, wanderings, jaunts.

traveller noun **tourist,** tripper, holidaymaker, sightseer, globetrotter, backpacker, passenger, commuter; N. Amer. vacationer.

tread verb **1** *he trod purposefully down the hall:* **walk,** step, stride, pace, march, tramp, plod, stomp, trudge. **2** *the snow had been trodden down by the horses:* **crush,** flatten, press down, squash, trample on, stamp on.
noun *we heard his heavy tread on the stairs:* **step,** footstep, footfall, tramp.

treason noun **treachery,** disloyalty, betrayal, sedition, subversion, mutiny, rebellion.
OPPOSITES allegiance, loyalty.

treasure noun **1** *a casket of treasure:* **riches,** valuables, jewels, gems, gold, silver, precious metals, money, cash, wealth, fortune. **2** *art treasures:* **masterpiece,** gem, pearl, jewel.
verb *I treasure the photographs:* **cherish,** hold dear, prize, set great store by, value greatly.

treasury noun **storehouse,** repository, treasure house, exchequer, fund, mine, bank, coffers, purse.

treat verb **1** *Charlotte treated him badly:* **behave towards,** act towards, use, deal with, handle. **2** *police are treating the fires as*

arson: **regard,** consider, view, look on, put down as. **3** *the book treats its subject with insight:* **deal with,** tackle, handle, discuss, explore, investigate. **4** *she was treated in hospital:* **tend,** nurse, attend to, give medical attention to. **5** *a cream used to treat sunburn:* **cure,** heal, remedy. **6** *he treated her to lunch:* **buy,** take out for, stand, give, pay for, entertain, wine and dine; informal foot the bill for. **7** *delegates were treated to dance performances:* **entertain with/to,** regale with, fête with, amuse with.
noun **1** *a birthday treat:* **celebration,** entertainment, amusement, surprise. **2** *I bought you some chocolate as a treat:* **present,** gift, titbit, delicacy, luxury, indulgence, extravagance; informal goody. **3** *it was a real treat to see them:* **pleasure,** delight, thrill, joy.

treatment noun **1** *the company's treatment of its workers:* **behaviour towards,** conduct towards, handling of, dealings with. **2** *she's responding well to treatment:* **medical care,** therapy, nursing, medication, drugs. **3** *her treatment of the topic:* **discussion,** handling, investigation, exploration, consideration, study, analysis.

treaty noun **agreement,** settlement, pact, deal, entente, concordat, accord, protocol, compact, convention; formal concord.

trek noun **journey,** trip, expedition, safari, hike, march, tramp, walk.

tremble verb **1** *Joe's hands were trembling:* **shake,** quiver, twitch. **2** *the entire building* *trembled:* **shudder,** shake, judder, vibrate, wobble, rock, move, sway.

tremendous adjective
1 *tremendous sums of money:* **huge,** enormous, immense, colossal, massive, prodigious, stupendous; informal whopping, astronomical; Brit. informal ginormous. **2** *a tremendous result:* **excellent,** first-class, outstanding, marvellous, wonderful, splendid, admirable; informal great, fantastic, fabulous, terrific, super, awesome, ace; Brit. informal brilliant, smashing.
OPPOSITES tiny, poor.

trench noun ditch, channel, trough, excavation, furrow, rut, conduit.

trend noun **1** *an upward trend in unemployment:* **tendency,** movement, drift, swing, shift, course, current, direction, inclination, leaning. **2** *the latest trend in music:* **fashion,** vogue, style, mode, craze, mania, rage; informal fad, thing.

trespass verb intrude, encroach, invade, enter without permission.

trial noun **1** *a county court trial:* **case,** lawsuit, hearing, tribunal, litigation, proceedings. **2** *the drug is undergoing clinical trials:* **test,** experiment, pilot study, examination, check, assessment, audition, evaluation, appraisal; informal dry run. **3** *trials and tribulations:* **trouble,** affliction, ordeal, tribulation, difficulty, problem, misfortune, mishap, misadventure.

tribe noun ethnic group, people, family, clan, race, dynasty, house, nation.

tribunal noun court, board,

panel, committee.

tribute noun accolade, praise, commendation, salute, testimonial, homage, congratulations, compliments, plaudits.
OPPOSITES criticism, condemnation.

trick noun **1** *a mean trick:* **stratagem,** ploy, ruse, scheme, device, manoeuvre, dodge, subterfuge, swindle, fraud; informal con, set-up, sting. **2** *he's playing a trick on us:* **practical joke,** prank; informal leg-pull, spoof, put-on. **3** *it was probably a trick of the light:* **illusion,** figment of the imagination, mirage. **4** *the tricks of the trade:* **knack,** skill, technique, secret, art.
verb *tricked by villains:* **deceive,** delude, hoodwink, mislead, take in, dupe, fool, cheat, defraud, swindle; informal con, diddle, take for a ride, shaft, do; N. Amer. informal sucker.

trickle verb *blood was trickling from two cuts:* **dribble,** drip, ooze, leak, seep, spill.
OPPOSITES pour, gush.
noun *trickles of water:* **dribble,** drip, thin stream, rivulet.

tricky adjective **1** *a tricky situation:* **difficult,** awkward, problematic, delicate, ticklish, sensitive; informal sticky. **2** *a tricky politician:* **cunning,** crafty, wily, devious, sly, scheming, calculating, deceitful.
OPPOSITES straightforward, honest.

trifle noun triviality, thing of no consequence, bagatelle, inessential, nothing, technicality; (**trifles**) trivia, minutiae.

trifling adjective trivial,

unimportant, insignificant, inconsequential, petty, minor, of little/no account, footling, incidental; informal piffling.
OPPOSITES important.

trigger verb start, set off, initiate, spark (off), activate, touch off, provoke, precipitate, prompt, stir up, cause, give rise to, lead to, set in motion, bring about.

trim verb **1** *his hair had been trimmed:* cut, crop, bob, shorten, clip, snip, shear, dock, lop off, prune, shave, pare. **2** *gloves trimmed with fake fur:* decorate, adorn, ornament, embellish, edge, border, fringe.
noun **1** *white curtains with a blue trim:* decoration, ornamentation, adornment, embellishment, border, edging, piping, fringe, frill. **2** *hair in need of a trim:* haircut, cut, clip, snip.
adjective **1** *a very trim garden:* neat, tidy, orderly, uncluttered, well kept, well maintained, immaculate, spick and span, spruce, dapper. **2** *her trim figure:* slim, slender, lean, sleek, willowy.
OPPOSITES untidy, messy.
■ **in trim** fit, in good health, in fine fettle, slim, in shape.

trimming noun **1** *a black dress with lace trimming:* decoration, ornamentation, adornment, borders, edging, piping, fringes, frills. **2** (trimmings) accompaniments, extras, frills, accessories, accoutrements, trappings, paraphernalia, garnish.

trio noun threesome, three, triumvirate, triad, troika, trinity, trilogy.

trip verb **1** *he tripped on the stones:* stumble, lose one's

footing, catch one's foot, slip, fall (down), tumble. **2** *they tripped up the steps:* skip, dance, prance, bound, spring, scamper.
noun **1** *a trip to Paris:* excursion, outing, jaunt, holiday, break, visit, tour, journey, expedition, voyage, drive, run; informal spin. **2** *trips cause many accidents:* stumble, slip, fall, misstep.

triple adjective **1** *a triple alliance:* threefold, tripartite, three-way. **2** *triple the going rate:* three times, treble.

triumph noun **1** *Napoleon's triumphs:* victory, win, conquest, success, achievement. **2** *his eyes shone with triumph:* jubilation, exultation, elation, delight, joy, happiness, glee, pride, satisfaction.
OPPOSITES defeat, disappointment.
verb *he triumphed in the Grand Prix:* win, succeed, come first, be victorious, carry the day, prevail.
OPPOSITES lose.
■ **triumph over** defeat, beat, conquer, trounce, vanquish, overcome, overpower, overwhelm, get the better of; informal lick.

triumphant adjective **1** *the triumphant team:* victorious, successful, winning, conquering. **2** *a triumphant expression:* jubilant, exultant, celebratory, elated, joyful, delighted, gleeful, proud, cock-a-hoop.
OPPOSITES unsuccessful, defeated, despondent.

trivial adjective unimportant, insignificant, inconsequential, minor, of no account, of no importance, petty, trifling,

t

footling, negligible; informal piffling.

OPPOSITES important, significant.

troop noun 1 *a troop of musicians:* **group**, party, band, gang, body, company, troupe, crowd, squad, unit. 2 (**troops**) **soldiers**, armed forces, soldiery, servicemen, servicewomen.
verb *we trooped out of the hall:* **walk**, march, file, flock, crowd, throng, stream, swarm.

trophy noun 1 *a swimming trophy:* **cup**, medal, prize, award. 2 *trophies from his travels:* **souvenir**, memento, keepsake, spoils, booty.

tropical adjective **hot**, sweltering, humid, sultry, steamy, sticky, oppressive, stifling.

OPPOSITES cold.

trot verb **run**, jog, scuttle, scurry, bustle, scamper.

trouble noun 1 *you've caused enough trouble:* **difficulty**, problems, bother, inconvenience, worry, anxiety, distress, stress, agitation, harassment, unpleasantness; informal hassle. 2 *she poured out all her troubles:* **problem**, misfortune, difficulty, trial, tribulation, woe, grief, heartache, misery, affliction, suffering. 3 *he's gone to a lot of trouble:* **bother**, inconvenience, fuss, effort, exertion, work, labour. 4 *I wouldn't want to be a trouble to her:* **nuisance**, bother, inconvenience, irritation, problem, trial, pest; informal headache, pain, drag. 5 *you're too gullible, that's your trouble:* **shortcoming**, weakness, failing, fault. 6 *he had heart trouble:* **disease**, illness, sickness, ailment, complaint, problem, disorder,

disability. 7 *the crash was due to engine trouble:* **malfunction**, failure, breakdown. 8 *a match marred by crowd trouble:* **disturbance**, disorder, unrest, fighting, scuffles, breach of the peace.
verb 1 *this matter had been troubling her for some time:* **worry**, bother, concern, disturb, upset, agitate, distress, perturb, annoy, nag, prey on someone's mind; informal bug. 2 *he was troubled by ill health:* **afflict**, burden, suffer from, be cursed with. 3 *there is nothing you need trouble about:* **worry**, upset oneself, fret, be anxious, be concerned. 4 *I'm sorry to trouble you:* **inconvenience**, bother, impose on, disturb, put out, disoblige; informal hassle.

troublesome adjective 1 *a troublesome problem:* **annoying**, irritating, exasperating, maddening, infuriating, bothersome, tiresome, nagging, difficult, awkward; N. Amer. informal pesky. 2 *a troublesome child:* **difficult**, awkward, uncooperative, rebellious, unmanageable, unruly, obstreperous, disruptive, disobedient, naughty, recalcitrant.

OPPOSITES simple, cooperative.

truce noun **ceasefire**, armistice, cessation, peace.

true adjective 1 *what I say is true:* **correct**, accurate, right, verifiable, the case, so. 2 *true craftsmanship:* **genuine**, authentic, real, actual, bona fide, proper. 3 *true repentance:* **sincere**, genuine, real, unfeigned, heartfelt. 4 *a true friend:* **loyal**, faithful, constant, devoted, trustworthy, reliable, dependable. 5 *a true reflection*

of life: **accurate,** faithful, telling it like it is, realistic, factual, lifelike.
OPPOSITES untrue, false, disloyal, inaccurate.

truly adverb **1** *tell me truly what you want:* **truthfully,** honestly, frankly, candidly, openly. **2** *I'm truly grateful:* **sincerely,** genuinely, really, indeed, heartily, profoundly. **3** *a truly dreadful song:* **really,** absolutely, simply, utterly, totally, perfectly, thoroughly, completely. **4** *this is truly a miracle:* **without (a) doubt,** unquestionably, certainly, surely, definitely, undeniably, really, actually, in fact.

trumpet verb **proclaim,** announce, declare, noise abroad, shout from the rooftops.
OPPOSITES keep quiet about.

trunk noun **1** *the trunk of a tree:* **stem,** bole, stock, stalk. **2** *his powerful trunk:* **torso,** body. **3** *an elephant's trunk:* **proboscis,** nose, snout. **4** *an enormous tin trunk:* **chest,** box, crate, coffer, case, portmanteau.

trust noun **1** *good relationships are built on trust:* **confidence,** belief, faith, certainty, assurance, conviction, credence, reliance.
OPPOSITES distrust, mistrust, doubt.
verb **1** *I should never have trusted her:* **have faith in,** have (every) confidence in, believe in, pin one's hopes/faith on. **2** *he can be trusted to carry out an impartial investigation:* **rely on,** depend on, bank on, count on, be sure of. **3** *I trust we shall meet again:* **hope,** expect, take it, assume, presume. **4** *they won't trust their money to*

strangers: **entrust,** consign, commit, give, hand over, turn over, assign.
OPPOSITES distrust, mistrust, doubt.

trusting adjective **trustful,** unsuspecting, unquestioning, naive, innocent, childlike, ingenuous, wide-eyed, credulous, gullible, easily taken in.
OPPOSITES distrustful, suspicious.

trustworthy adjective **reliable,** dependable, honest, as good as one's word, above suspicion; informal **on the level.**
OPPOSITES unreliable.

truth noun **1** *he doubted the truth of her statement:* **accuracy,** correctness, authenticity, veracity, verity. **2** *truth is stranger than fiction:* **fact(s),** reality, real life, actuality.
OPPOSITES lies, fiction, falsehood.

truthful adjective **true,** accurate, correct, factual, faithful, reliable.
OPPOSITES deceitful, untrue.

try verb **1** *try to help him:* **attempt,** endeavour, make an effort, strive, do one's best, do one's utmost, aim; informal **have a go,** go all out. **2** *try it and see what you think:* **test,** sample, taste, inspect, investigate, examine, appraise, evaluate, assess; informal **check out. 3** *Mary tried everyone's patience:* **tax,** strain, test, stretch, sap, drain, exhaust, wear out.
noun *I'll have one last try:* **attempt,** effort, endeavour; informal **go,** shot, crack, stab, bash.

trying adjective **1** *a trying day:* **stressful,** taxing, demanding,

difficult, challenging, pressured, frustrating, fraught; informal hellish. **2** *Steve was very trying:* **annoying**, irritating, exasperating, maddening, infuriating, tiresome, troublesome.
OPPOSITES easy, accommodating.

tuck verb push, insert, slip, thrust, stuff, stick, cram; informal pop.

tug verb **1** *Ben tugged at her sleeve:* **pull**, pluck, tweak, twitch, jerk, catch hold of; informal yank. **2** *she tugged him towards the door:* **drag**, pull, lug, draw, haul, heave, tow, trail.

tuition noun instruction, teaching, coaching, tutoring, tutelage, lessons, education, schooling, training.

tumble verb **1** *he tumbled over:* **fall (over/down)**, topple over, lose one's balance, take a spill, trip (up), stumble. **2** *oil prices tumbled:* **plummet**, plunge, dive, nosedive, drop, slump, slide; informal crash.
OPPOSITES rise.

tumour noun **cancer**, growth, lump, malignancy; Medicine carcinoma, sarcoma.

tune noun *she hummed a tune:* **melody**, air, strain, theme, song, jingle, ditty.
verb *a body clock tuned to the tides:* **attune**, adapt, adjust, regulate.

tunnel noun **underground passage**, underpass, subway, shaft, burrow, hole, warren, labyrinth.
verb dig, burrow, mine, bore, drill.

turbulent adjective tempestuous, stormy, unstable, unsettled, tumultuous, chaotic, anarchic, lawless.

OPPOSITES peaceful.

turmoil noun confusion, upheaval, turbulence, tumult, disorder, disturbance, ferment, chaos, mayhem.
OPPOSITES peace, order.

turn verb **1** *the wheels were still turning:* **go round**, revolve, rotate, spin, roll, circle, wheel, whirl, gyrate, swivel, pivot. **2** *I turned and headed back:* **change direction**, change course, make a U-turn, turn about/round, wheel round. **3** *the path turned to right and left:* **bend**, curve, wind, twist, meander, snake, zigzag. **4** *Emma turned red:* **become**, go, grow, get. **5** *the milk had turned:* **(go) sour**, go off, curdle, become rancid, go bad, spoil.
noun **1** *a turn of the wheel:* **rotation**, revolution, spin, whirl, gyration, swivel. **2** *a turn to the left:* **change of direction**, veer, divergence. **3** *we're approaching the turn:* **bend**, corner, junction, twist, dog-leg; Brit. hairpin bend. **4** *you'll get your turn:* **opportunity**, chance, say, stint, time, try; informal go, shot, stab, crack. **5** *she did me some good turns:* **service**, deed, act, favour, kindness, disservice, wrong.
■ **turn someone/something down 1** *his novel was turned down:* **reject**, spurn, rebuff, refuse, decline. **2** *Pete turned the sound down:* **reduce**, lower, decrease, lessen, mute. ■ **turn into** become, develop into, turn out to be, be transformed into, change into. ■ **turn something into something** convert, change, transform, make, adapt, modify. ■ **turn something off/out** switch off, shut off, put off, extinguish, deactivate; informal kill, cut. ■ **turn something on**

switch on, put on, start up, activate, trip. ■ **turn out 1** *a huge crowd turned out*: come, be present, attend, appear, turn up, arrive, assemble, gather; informal show up. **2** *it turned out that she had been abroad*: transpire, emerge, come to light, become apparent. **3** *things didn't turn out well*: happen, occur, come about, develop, work out, come out, end up; informal pan out. ■ **turn up 1** *the documents turned up*: be found, be discovered, be located, reappear. **2** *the police turned up*: arrive, appear, present oneself; informal show (up). **3** *something better will turn up*: present itself, occur, happen, crop up. ■ **turn something up 1** *she turned up the volume*: increase, raise, amplify, intensify. **2** *they turned up lots of information*: discover, uncover, unearth, find, dig up, expose.

turning noun junction, turn-off, side road, exit; N. Amer. turnout.

turning point noun watershed, critical moment, decisive moment, moment of truth, crossroads, crisis.

turnout noun **1** *the lecture attracted a good turnout*: **attendance,** audience, house, congregation, crowd, gate, gathering. **2** *his turnout was very elegant*: **outfit,** clothing, dress, garb, attire, ensemble; informal get-up.

turnover noun **1** *a turnover of £2 million*: **gross revenue,** income, yield, sales. **2** *staff turnover*: **replacement,** change, movement.

tutor noun *a history tutor*: **teacher,** instructor, coach,

educator, lecturer, trainer, mentor.
verb *he was tutored at home*: **teach,** instruct, educate, school, coach, train, drill.

twilight noun **1** *we arrived at twilight*: **dusk,** sunset, sundown, nightfall, evening, close of day. **2** *it was scarcely visible in the twilight*: **half-light,** semi-darkness, gloom.
OPPOSITES dawn.

twin noun *a sitting room that was the twin of her own*: **duplicate,** double, carbon copy, likeness, mirror image, replica, lookalike, clone, match, pair; informal spitting image, dead ringer.
adjective **1** *the twin towers of the stadium*: **matching,** identical, paired. **2** *the twin aims of conservation and recreation*: **twofold,** double, dual, related, linked, connected, parallel, complementary.
verb *the company twinned its brewing with distilling*: **combine,** join, link, couple, pair.

twinkle verb & noun glitter, sparkle, shine, glimmer, shimmer, glint, gleam, glisten, flicker, flash, wink.

twist verb **1** *the impact twisted the chassis*: **crumple,** crush, buckle, mangle, warp, deform, distort, contort. **2** *he twisted round in his seat*: **turn,** swivel, spin, pivot, rotate, revolve, twiddle. **3** *I twisted my ankle*: **sprain,** wrench, turn, rick, crick. **4** *she twisted her hair round her finger*: **wind,** twirl, coil, curl, wrap. **5** *the wires were twisted together*: **intertwine,** interlace, weave, plait, braid, coil, wind. **6** *the*

t

road twisted and turned: **wind,** bend, curve, turn, meander, weave, zigzag, snake.
noun 1 *the twist of a dial:* **turn,** twirl, spin. **2** *the twists of the road:* **bend,** curve, turn, zigzag, dog-leg. **3** *the twists of the plot:* **convolution,** complication, complexity, intricacy, surprise, revelation.

twitch verb 1 *he twitched and then lay still:* **jerk,** convulse, have a spasm, quiver, tremble, shiver, shudder. **2** *he twitched the note out of my hand:* **snatch,** tweak, pluck, pull, tug; informal **yank.**
noun 1 *a twitch of her lips:* **spasm,** convulsion, quiver, tremor, shiver, shudder, tic. **2** *he gave a twitch at his moustache:* **pull,** tug, tweak; informal **yank.**

tycoon noun magnate, mogul, businessman, captain of industry, industrialist, financier, entrepreneur; informal, derogatory **fat cat.**

type noun 1 *six types of coffee:* **kind,** sort, variety, class, category, set, genre, species, order, breed. **2** *italic type:* **print,** typeface, characters, lettering, font; Brit. **fount.**

typical adjective 1 *a typical example of art deco:* **representative,** characteristic, classic, quintessential, archetypal. **2** *a fairly typical day:* **normal,** average, ordinary, standard, regular, routine, run-of-the-mill, conventional, unremarkable; informal **bog-standard.**
OPPOSITES unusual, exceptional.

tyranny noun despotism, absolute power, autocracy, dictatorship, totalitarianism, fascism, oppression, repression, subjugation, enslavement.

Uu

ubiquitous adjective everywhere, omnipresent, all over the place, all-pervasive, universal, worldwide, global.
OPPOSITES rare.

ugly adjective 1 unattractive, unsightly, ill-favoured, hideous, plain, unprepossessing, horrible, ghastly, repellent; N. Amer. **homely;** Brit. informal **no oil painting. 2** *things got pretty ugly:* **unpleasant,** nasty, disagreeable, alarming, charged, dangerous, perilous, threatening, menacing, hostile, ominous, sinister.
OPPOSITES beautiful, pleasant.

ultimate adjective 1 *the ultimate collapse of the Empire:* **eventual,** final, concluding, terminal, end. **2** *ultimate truths:* **fundamental,** basic, primary, elementary, absolute, central, crucial, essential, pivotal. **3** *the ultimate gift for cat lovers:* **best,** ideal, greatest, supreme, quintessential.

ultimately adverb 1 *the cost will ultimately fall on us:* **eventually,** in the end, in the long run, at length, finally, in time, one day. **2** *two ultimately contradictory reasons:* **fundamentally,** basically, primarily, essentially, at heart, deep down.

t
u

umpire noun **referee,** judge, line judge, linesman, touch judge, adjudicator, arbitrator, moderator; informal ref.

unable adjective **incapable,** powerless, impotent, inadequate, incompetent, unqualified, unfit.

unanimous adjective **1** *doctors were unanimous about the effects:* **in agreement,** of one mind, in accord, united, undivided. **2** *a unanimous vote:* **uniform,** consistent, united.
OPPOSITES split.

unarmed adjective **defenceless,** unprotected, unguarded.
OPPOSITES armed.

unaware adjective **ignorant,** oblivious, unconscious, unwitting, unsuspecting, uninformed, unenlightened, innocent; informal in the dark.
OPPOSITES aware.

unbelievable adjective **incredible,** inconceivable, unthinkable, unimaginable, unconvincing, far-fetched, implausible, improbable; informal hard to swallow.
OPPOSITES believable.

unborn adjective **expected,** embryonic, fetal, in utero.

unbroken adjective **1** *the last unbroken window:* **undamaged,** unharmed, unscathed, untouched, sound, intact, whole. **2** *an unbroken chain of victories:* **uninterrupted,** continuous, endless, constant, unremitting, ongoing. **3** *his record is still unbroken:* **unbeaten,** undefeated, unsurpassed, unrivalled, unmatched, supreme.

uncanny adjective **1** *the silence was uncanny:* **eerie,** unnatural, unearthly, other-worldly, ghostly, strange, abnormal,

weird; informal creepy, spooky. **2** *an uncanny resemblance:* **striking,** remarkable, extraordinary, exceptional, incredible.

uncertain adjective **1** *the effects are uncertain:* **unknown,** debatable, open to question, in doubt, unsure, in the balance, up in the air, unpredictable, unforeseeable; informal iffy. **2** *Ed was uncertain about the decision:* **unsure,** doubtful, dubious, undecided, irresolute, hesitant, vacillating, vague, unclear, ambivalent, in two minds.
OPPOSITES certain, predictable, sure.

unclear adjective **uncertain,** unsure, unsettled, up in the air, in doubt, ambiguous, equivocal, indefinite, vague, mysterious, obscure, hazy, nebulous.
OPPOSITES clear, evident.

uncomfortable adjective **1** *an uncomfortable chair:* **painful,** awkward, lumpy, confining, cramped. **2** *I felt uncomfortable in her presence:* **uneasy,** awkward, nervous, tense, edgy, restless, embarrassed, anxious; informal rattled, twitchy.
OPPOSITES comfortable, relaxed.

uncommon adjective **unusual,** abnormal, rare, atypical, exceptional, unconventional, unfamiliar, strange, extraordinary, peculiar, scarce, few and far between, isolated, infrequent.
OPPOSITES common.

unconditional adjective **unquestioning,** unqualified, unreserved, unlimited, unrestricted, wholehearted, complete, total, entire, full, absolute, unequivocal.

unconscious adjective **1** *she*

u

made sure he was *unconscious*: **knocked out,** senseless, comatose, inert; informal out cold, out for the count. **2** *an unconscious desire:* **subconscious,** instinctive, involuntary, uncontrolled, subliminal; informal gut. **3** *blissfully unconscious of these problems:* **unaware of,** oblivious to, insensible to, impervious to, unaffected by.
OPPOSITES conscious, voluntary, aware.

uncouth adjective **uncivilized,** uncultured, rough, coarse, crude, loutish, boorish, rude, discourteous, disrespectful, bad-mannered, ill-bred.
OPPOSITES civilized.

uncover verb **1** *she uncovered the sandwiches:* **expose,** reveal, lay bare, unwrap, unveil, strip. **2** *they uncovered a plot:* **discover,** detect, come across, stumble on, chance on, find, turn up, unearth, dig up.

under preposition **1** *they hid under a bush:* **below,** beneath, underneath. **2** *the rent is under £250:* **less than,** lower than, below. **3** *branch managers are under the retail director:* **subordinate to,** answerable to, responsible to, subject to, junior to, inferior to.
OPPOSITES above, over.

undercover adjective **secret,** covert, clandestine, underground, surreptitious, furtive, cloak-and-dagger, stealthy; informal hush-hush.
OPPOSITES overt.

underestimate verb **underrate,** undervalue, miscalculate, misjudge, do an injustice to.
OPPOSITES overestimate.

undergo verb **experience,** go

through, submit to, face, be subjected to, receive, endure, brave, bear, withstand, weather.

underground adjective **1** *an underground car park:* **subterranean,** buried, sunken, basement. **2** *underground organizations:* **secret,** clandestine, surreptitious, covert, undercover, closet, cloak-and-dagger, resistance, subversive.
noun **1** *he took the underground:* **metro;** N. Amer. subway; Brit. informal tube. **2** *information from the French underground:* **resistance,** partisans, guerrillas, freedom fighters.

underline verb **1** *she underlined a phrase:* **underscore,** mark, pick out, emphasize, highlight. **2** *the programme underlines the benefits of exercise:* **emphasize,** stress, highlight, accentuate, accent, focus on, spotlight.

underlying adjective **fundamental,** basic, primary, central, essential, principal, elementary, initial.

undermine verb **weaken,** diminish, reduce, impair, mar, spoil, ruin, damage, sap, shake, threaten, subvert, compromise, sabotage.
OPPOSITES strengthen, support.

understand verb **1** *he couldn't understand anything we said:* **comprehend,** grasp, take in, see, apprehend, follow, make sense of, fathom; informal work out, figure out, make head or tail of, get; Brit. informal twig, suss. **2** *she understood how hard he'd worked:* **know,** realize, recognize, acknowledge, appreciate, be aware of, be conscious of. **3** *I understand that you wish to go:* **believe,** gather, take it, hear (tell), notice, see, learn.

understandable adjective
1 *make it understandable to the layman:* **comprehensible**, intelligible, clear, plain, unambiguous, transparent, straightforward, explicit, coherent. **2** *an understandable desire:* **unsurprising**, expected, predictable, inevitable, reasonable, acceptable, logical, rational, normal, natural, justifiable, excusable, pardonable, forgivable.
OPPOSITES incomprehensible, surprising, illogical, abnormal, unforgivable.

understanding noun **1** *test your understanding of the language:* **comprehension**, grasp, mastery, appreciation, knowledge, awareness, skill, expertise, proficiency; informal know-how. **2** *a young man of brilliant understanding:* **intellect**, intelligence, brainpower, judgement, insight, intuition, acumen, sagacity, wisdom; informal nous. **3** *it was my understanding that this was free:* **belief**, perception, view, conviction, feeling, opinion, intuition, impression. **4** *he treated me with understanding:* **sympathy**, compassion, pity, feeling, concern, consideration, kindness, sensitivity, decency, goodwill. **5** *we had a tacit understanding:* **agreement**, arrangement, deal, bargain, settlement, pledge, pact.
OPPOSITES ignorance, indifference.
adjective *an understanding friend:* **sympathetic**, compassionate, sensitive, considerate, kind, thoughtful, tolerant, patient, forbearing, lenient, forgiving.

understate verb **play down**, underrate, underplay, trivialize, minimize, diminish, downgrade, brush aside, gloss over.
OPPOSITES exaggerate.

undertake verb **1** *we undertook a survey of the site:* **set about**, embark on, go about, engage in, take on, be responsible for, get down to, get to grips with, tackle, attempt; informal have a go at. **2** *the Minister undertook to attend:* **promise**, pledge, vow, give one's word, swear, guarantee, contract, give an assurance, commit oneself.

undertaker noun **funeral director**; N. Amer. mortician.

undertaking noun **1** *a risky undertaking:* **enterprise**, venture, project, campaign, scheme, plan, operation, endeavour, effort, task. **2** *sign this undertaking to comply with the rules:* **promise**, pledge, agreement, oath, covenant, vow, commitment, guarantee, assurance.

underwater adjective **submerged**, sunken, undersea, submarine.

underwear noun **underclothes**, undergarments, underthings, lingerie; informal undies; Brit. informal smalls.

underwrite verb **sponsor**, support, back, insure, indemnify, subsidize, pay for, finance, fund; N. Amer. informal bankroll.

undesirable adjective **unpleasant**, disagreeable, nasty, unwelcome, unwanted, unfortunate.
OPPOSITES pleasant.

undo verb **1** *he undid his shirt:* **unfasten**, unbutton, unhook, untie, unlace, unlock, unbolt,

u

loosen, detach, free, open.
2 *they will undo a decision by the lords*: **cancel,** reverse, overrule, overturn, repeal, rescind, countermand, revoke, annul, invalidate, negate. **3** *she undid much of the good work*: **ruin,** undermine, overturn, scotch, sabotage, spoil, impair, mar, destroy, wreck; informal blow; Brit. informal scupper.
OPPOSITES fasten, ratify, enhance.

undoubtedly adverb doubtless, indubitably, unquestionably, indisputably, undeniably, incontrovertibly, without (a) doubt, clearly.

unearth verb **1** *workmen unearthed an artillery shell*: **dig up,** excavate, exhume, disinter, root out. **2** *I unearthed an interesting fact*: **discover,** uncover, find, come across, hit on, bring to light, expose, turn up.

uneasy adjective **1** *the doctor made him feel uneasy*: **worried,** anxious, troubled, disturbed, nervous, nervy, tense, edgy, apprehensive, fearful, uncomfortable, unsettled; informal jittery. **2** *an uneasy peace*: **tense,** awkward, strained, fraught, precarious, unstable, insecure.
OPPOSITES calm, stable.

unemployed adjective jobless, out of work, unwaged, redundant, laid off, on benefit; Brit. signing on; N. Amer. on welfare; Brit. informal on the dole, resting.

uneven adjective **1** *uneven ground*: **bumpy,** rough, lumpy, stony, rocky, rutted. **2** *uneven teeth*: **irregular,** crooked, lopsided, askew, asymmetrical. **3** *uneven quality*: **inconsistent,**

variable, fluctuating, irregular, erratic, patchy.
OPPOSITES flat, regular.

unfair adjective **1** *the trial was unfair*: **unjust,** prejudiced, biased, discriminatory, one-sided, unequal, uneven, unbalanced, partisan. **2** *his comments were unfair*: **undeserved,** unmerited, unreasonable, unjustified; Brit. informal out of order. **3** *unfair play*: **unsporting,** dirty, underhand, dishonourable, dishonest.
OPPOSITES fair, just, justified.

unfasten verb undo, open, disconnect, remove, untie, unbutton, unzip, loosen, free, unlock, unbolt.

unfit adjective **1** *the film is unfit for children*: **unsuitable,** inappropriate, not designed. **2** *unfit for duty*: **incapable of,** not up to, not equal to, unequipped, inadequate; informal not cut out for. **3** *I am unfit*: **unhealthy,** out of condition/ shape.
OPPOSITES fit, suitable, capable, healthy.

unfold verb **1** *May unfolded the map*: **open out,** spread out, flatten, straighten out, unroll. **2** *I watched the events unfold*: **develop,** evolve, happen, take place, occur.
OPPOSITES fold up.

unfortunate adjective **1** *unfortunate people*: **unlucky,** hapless, wretched, forlorn, poor, pitiful; informal down on one's luck. **2** *an unfortunate start to our holiday*: **unwelcome,** disadvantageous, unfavourable, unlucky, adverse, unpromising, inauspicious. **3** *an unfortunate remark*: **regrettable,** inappropriate,

u

unsuitable, tactless, injudicious.
OPPOSITES fortunate, lucky,
auspicious, well-chosen.

ungainly adjective **awkward,**
clumsy, graceless, inelegant,
gawky, gauche, uncoordinated.
OPPOSITES graceful.

unhappy adjective **1** *why are*
you looking so unhappy? **sad,**
miserable, sorrowful, dejected,
despondent, disconsolate,
morose, heartbroken, down,
dispirited, downhearted,
depressed, melancholy,
mournful, gloomy, glum; informal
down in the mouth, fed up,
blue. **2** *I was unhappy with the*
service: **dissatisfied,** displeased,
discontented, disappointed,
disgruntled. **3** *an unhappy*
coincidence: **unfortunate,**
unlucky, ill-starred, ill-fated,
doomed; informal jinxed.
OPPOSITES happy, pleased,
cheerful, lucky.

unhealthy adjective **1** *an*
unhealthy lifestyle: **harmful,**
detrimental, destructive,
injurious, damaging, noxious,
poisonous. **2** *he's pretty*
unhealthy: **sick,** poorly, ill,
unwell, unfit, ailing, weak,
frail, infirm, washed out, run
down. **3** *an unhealthy obsession:*
abnormal, morbid, macabre,
twisted, unwholesome, warped,
depraved, unnatural; informal
sick.

uniform adjective **1** *a uniform*
temperature: **constant,**
consistent, steady, invariable,
unchanging, stable, static,
regular, fixed, even. **2** *pieces of*
uniform size: **identical,**
matching, similar, equal, same,
like, consistent.
OPPOSITES variable.
noun *a soldier in uniform:*
costume, outfit, suit, ensemble,

livery, regalia; informal get-up,
rig, gear.

unify verb **unite,** combine, bring
together, join, merge, fuse,
amalgamate, coalesce,
consolidate.
OPPOSITES separate.

uninteresting adjective **boring,**
dull, unexciting, tiresome,
tedious, dreary, lifeless,
humdrum, colourless, bland,
insipid, banal, dry.
OPPOSITES interesting, exciting.

union noun **1** *the union of art*
and nature: **unification,**
joining, merger, fusion,
amalgamation, coalition,
combination, synthesis, blend.
2 *a trade union:* **association,**
league, guild, confederation,
federation.
OPPOSITES separation, parting.

unique adjective **1** *each town has*
its unique quality: **distinctive,**
individual, special, particular,
specific, idiosyncratic, single,
sole, lone, unrepeated, solitary,
exclusive; informal one-off. **2** *a*
unique insight into history:
remarkable, special, notable,
unequalled, unparalleled,
unmatched, unsurpassed,
incomparable.
OPPOSITES common.

unit noun **1** *the family is the*
fundamental unit of society:
component, element,
constituent, subdivision. **2** *a*
unit of currency: **quantity,**
measure, denomination. **3** *a*
guerrilla unit: **group,**
detachment, contingent,
division, cell, faction,
department, office, branch.

unite verb **1** *uniting the nation:*
unify, join, link, connect,
combine, amalgamate, fuse,
weld, bond, bring together.
2 *environmentalists and*

u

activists united: **join together,** join forces, combine, band together, ally, cooperate, collaborate, work together, team up. **3** *he sought to unite comfort with elegance:* **merge,** mix, blend, mingle, combine.
OPPOSITES divide.

unity noun **1** *European unity:* **union,** unification, integration, amalgamation, coalition, federation, confederation. **2** *unity between opposing factions:* **harmony,** accord, cooperation, collaboration, agreement, consensus, solidarity. **3** *the organic unity of the universe:* **oneness,** singleness, wholeness, uniformity, homogeneity.
OPPOSITES division, discord.

universal adjective **general,** common, widespread, ubiquitous, comprehensive, global, worldwide, international.

universally adverb **always,** without exception, by everyone, in all cases, everywhere, worldwide, globally, internationally, commonly, generally.

universe noun **cosmos,** macrocosm, space, infinity, nature, all existence.

unkind adjective **1** *everyone was being unkind to him:* **unpleasant,** disagreeable, nasty, mean, cruel, vicious, spiteful, malicious, callous, unsympathetic; informal bitchy. **2** *unkind weather:* **inclement,** intemperate, rough, severe, filthy.

unknown adjective **1** *the outcome was unknown:* **undisclosed,** unrevealed, secret, undetermined, undecided. **2** *unknown country:*

unexplored, uncharted, unmapped, undiscovered. **3** *persons unknown:* **unidentified,** unnamed, anonymous. **4** *firearms were unknown to the Indians:* **unfamiliar,** unheard of, new, novel, strange. **5** *unknown artists:* **obscure,** unheard of, unsung, minor, undistinguished.
OPPOSITES known, familiar.

unlike preposition **1** *England is totally unlike Jamaica:* **different from,** dissimilar to. **2** *unlike Lyn, Chris was a bit of a radical:* **in contrast to,** as opposed to.
OPPOSITES similar to.

unlikely adjective **improbable,** doubtful, dubious, questionable, unconvincing, implausible, far-fetched, unrealistic, incredible, unbelievable, inconceivable.
OPPOSITES probable, believable.

unload verb **1** *we unloaded the van:* **unpack,** empty. **2** *they unloaded the cases from the lorry:* **remove,** offload, discharge, dump.
OPPOSITES load.

unlucky adjective **1** *the unlucky victim:* **unfortunate,** hapless, ill-fated. **2** *an unlucky number:* **unfavourable,** inauspicious, unpropitious, ominous, jinxed.
OPPOSITES fortunate, favourable.

unnatural adjective **1** *the life of a battery hen is completely unnatural:* **abnormal,** unusual, uncommon, extraordinary, strange, unorthodox, exceptional, irregular, untypical. **2** *an unnatural colour:* **artificial,** man-made, synthetic, manufactured. **3** *her voice sounded unnatural:* **affected,** artificial, stilted,

u

forced, false, fake, insincere;
informal put on, phoney.
OPPOSITES normal, genuine.

unnecessary adjective
unneeded, inessential, not
required, uncalled for,
unwarranted, dispensable,
optional, extraneous,
expendable, redundant.
OPPOSITES necessary.

unpleasant adjective **1** *a very*
unpleasant situation:
disagreeable, irksome,
distressing, nasty, horrible,
terrible, awful, dreadful,
invidious, objectionable. **2** *an*
unpleasant man: **unlikeable,**
unlovable, disagreeable,
unfriendly, rude, impolite,
obnoxious, nasty, spiteful,
mean, insufferable,
objectionable, unbearable,
annoying, irritating. **3** *an*
unpleasant taste: **unappetizing,**
unpalatable, unsavoury,
unappealing, disgusting,
revolting, nauseating,
sickening.
OPPOSITES agreeable, likeable.

unpopular adjective **disliked,**
friendless, unloved,
unwelcome, avoided, ignored,
rejected, shunned, out of
favour.

unravel verb **1** *he unravelled the*
strands: **untangle,** disentangle,
separate out, unwind, untwist.
2 *detectives are trying to*
unravel the mystery: **solve,**
resolve, clear up, puzzle out,
get to the bottom of, explain,
clarify; informal figure out.
OPPOSITES entangle.

unreal adjective **imaginary,**
fictitious, pretend, make-
believe, made-up, dreamed-up,
mock, false, illusory, mythical,
fanciful, hypothetical,
theoretical; informal phoney.

OPPOSITES real.

unrest noun **disturbance,**
trouble, turmoil, disruption,
disorder, chaos, anarchy,
dissatisfaction, dissent, strife,
agitation, protest, rebellion,
uprising, rioting.
OPPOSITES peace, contentment.

unsafe adjective **1** *the building*
was unsafe: **dangerous,** risky,
hazardous, high-risk,
treacherous, insecure, unsound,
harmful, injurious, toxic. **2** *the*
verdict was unsafe: **unreliable,**
insecure, unsound,
questionable, doubtful,
dubious, suspect; informal iffy;
Brit. informal dodgy.
OPPOSITES safe, harmless,
secure.

unsatisfactory adjective
disappointing, displeasing,
inadequate, unacceptable, poor,
bad, substandard, weak,
mediocre, not up to par,
defective, deficient; informal
leaving a lot to be desired.

unscrupulous adjective
dishonest, deceitful, devious,
underhand, unethical, immoral,
shameless, exploitative,
corrupt, unprincipled,
dishonourable, disreputable;
informal crooked, shady.

unsettle verb **disturb,**
disconcert, unnerve, upset,
disquiet, perturb, alarm,
dismay, trouble, bother, agitate,
fluster, ruffle, shake (up),
throw; informal rattle, faze.

unsightly adjective
unattractive, ugly,
unprepossessing, hideous,
horrible, repulsive, revolting,
offensive, grotesque.
OPPOSITES attractive.

unsociable adjective **unfriendly,**
uncongenial, unneighbourly,
unapproachable, introverted,

u

reserved, withdrawn, retiring, aloof, distant, remote, detached; informal stand-offish.
OPPOSITES sociable, friendly.

unstable adjective **1** *icebergs are notoriously unstable:* **unsteady,** rocky, wobbly, rickety, shaky, unsafe, insecure, precarious. **2** *unstable coffee prices:* **changeable,** volatile, variable, fluctuating, irregular, unpredictable, erratic. **3** *he was mentally unstable:* **unbalanced,** of unsound mind, mentally ill, deranged, demented, disturbed, unhinged.
OPPOSITES stable, steady, firm.

unsuccessful adjective **1** *an unsuccessful attempt:* **failed,** abortive, ineffective, fruitless, profitless, unproductive, vain, futile. **2** *an unsuccessful business:* **unprofitable,** loss-making. **3** *an unsuccessful candidate:* **failed,** losing, beaten, unlucky.

unsuitable adjective **1** *an unsuitable product:* **inappropriate,** ill-suited, inapposite, unacceptable, unfitting, incompatible, out of place, out of keeping. **2** *an unsuitable moment:* **inopportune,** badly timed, unfortunate, difficult, infelicitous.
OPPOSITES appropriate, opportune.

u **unsure** adjective **1** *she felt very unsure:* **unconfident,** unassertive, insecure, hesitant, diffident, anxious, apprehensive. **2** *Sally was unsure what to do:* **undecided,** uncertain, irresolute, dithering, in two minds, in a quandary. **3** *some teachers are unsure about the proposed strike:* **dubious,** doubtful, sceptical,

uncertain, unconvinced.
OPPOSITES confident.

untangle verb disentangle, unravel, unsnarl, straighten out, untwist, unknot, sort out.
OPPOSITES tangle.

unthinkable adjective unimaginable, inconceivable, unbelievable, incredible, implausible, out of the question, impossible, unconscionable, unreasonable.

untidy adjective **1** *untidy hair:* **scruffy,** tousled, dishevelled, unkempt, messy, rumpled, bedraggled, uncombed, tangled, matted. **2** *the room was untidy:* **disordered,** messy, disorganized, cluttered, in chaos, haywire, in disarray; informal higgledy-piggledy.
OPPOSITES tidy, neat, orderly.

untoward adjective **unexpected,** unforeseen, surprising, unusual, inappropriate, inconvenient, unwelcome, unfavourable, adverse, unfortunate, infelicitous.

untrue adjective **false,** invented, made up, fabricated, concocted, trumped up, erroneous, wrong, incorrect, inaccurate.
OPPOSITES true, correct.

unusual adjective **1** *an unusual sight:* **uncommon,** abnormal, atypical, unexpected, surprising, unfamiliar, different, strange, odd, curious, extraordinary, unorthodox, unconventional, peculiar; informal weird, offbeat. **2** *a man of unusual talent:* **remarkable,** extraordinary, exceptional, particular, outstanding, notable, noteworthy, distinctive, striking, significant, special, unique, unparalleled, prodigious.
OPPOSITES common.

unwarranted adjective **1** *the criticism is unwarranted:* **unjustified,** indefensible, inexcusable, unforgivable, unpardonable, uncalled for, unnecessary, unjust, groundless. **2** *an unwarranted invasion of privacy:* **unauthorized,** unsanctioned, unapproved, uncertified, unlicensed, illegal, unlawful, illicit, illegitimate, criminal, actionable.
OPPOSITES justified.

unwieldy adjective **awkward,** unmanageable, unmanoeuvrable, cumbersome, clumsy, massive, heavy, hefty, bulky.

unwilling adjective **1** *unwilling conscripts:* **reluctant,** unenthusiastic, hesitant, resistant, grudging, involuntary, forced. **2** *he was unwilling to take on responsibility:* **disinclined,** reluctant, averse, loath; (**be unwilling to do something**) baulk at, demur at, shy away from, flinch from, shrink from, not have the heart to, have qualms about, have misgivings about, have reservations about.
OPPOSITES willing, keen.

upbeat adjective (informal) **cheerful,** optimistic, cheery, positive, confident, hopeful, bullish, buoyant.
OPPOSITES pessimistic, negative.

upbringing noun **childhood,** early life, formative years, teaching, instruction, rearing.

update verb **1** *security measures are continually updated:* **modernize,** upgrade, improve, overhaul. **2** *I'll update him on developments:* **brief,** bring up to date, inform, fill in, tell, notify, keep posted; informal clue in, put

in the picture, bring/keep up to speed.

upgrade verb **improve,** modernize, update, reform.
OPPOSITES downgrade.

upheaval noun **disturbance,** disruption, trouble, turbulence, disorder, confusion, turmoil.

uphill adjective **1** *an uphill path:* **upward,** rising, ascending, climbing. **2** *an uphill job:* **difficult,** hard, tough, demanding, arduous, taxing, exacting, stiff, gruelling, onerous.
OPPOSITES downhill.

uphold verb **1** *the court upheld his claim:* **confirm,** endorse, sustain, approve, support, back (up). **2** *they've a tradition to uphold:* **maintain,** sustain, continue, preserve, protect, keep, hold to, keep alive, keep going.
OPPOSITES overturn, oppose.

upkeep noun **1** *the upkeep of the road:* **maintenance,** repair(s), servicing, care, preservation, conservation, running. **2** *the child's upkeep:* (**financial**) **support,** maintenance, keep, subsistence, care.

uplifting adjective **inspiring,** stirring, inspirational, rousing, moving, touching, affecting, cheering, heartening, encouraging.

upper adjective **1** *the upper floor:* **higher,** superior, top. **2** *the upper echelons of the party:* **senior,** superior, higher-level, higher-ranking, top.
OPPOSITES lower.

upper-class adjective **aristocratic,** noble, patrician, titled, blue-blooded, high-born, elite; Brit. county; informal upper-crust, top-drawer; Brit. informal posh.

u

upright adjective **1** *an upright position:* **vertical,** perpendicular, plumb, straight (up), erect, on end, on one's feet. **2** *an upright member of the community:* **honest,** honourable, upstanding, respectable, high-minded, law-abiding, worthy, righteous, decent, good, virtuous, principled.
OPPOSITES flat, horizontal, dishonourable.

uprising noun **rebellion,** revolt, insurrection, mutiny, revolution, insurgence, rioting, coup.

uproar noun **1** *the uproar in the kitchen continued:* **commotion,** disturbance, rumpus, disorder, confusion, chaos, tumult, mayhem, pandemonium, bedlam, noise, din, clamour, hubbub, racket; informal hullabaloo; Brit. informal row. **2** *there was an uproar when he was dismissed:* **outcry,** furore, fuss, commotion, hue and cry, rumpus; informal hullabaloo, stink, ructions; Brit. informal row.
OPPOSITES calm.

upset verb **1** *the accusation upset her:* **distress,** trouble, perturb, dismay, sadden, grieve, disturb, unsettle, disconcert, disquiet, worry, bother, agitate, fluster, throw, ruffle, unnerve, shake. **2** *he upset the soup:* **knock over,** overturn, upend, tip over, topple, spill. **3** *the dam will upset the ecological balance:* **disrupt,** interfere with, disturb, throw into confusion, mess up.
OPPOSITES calm, reassure.
noun **1** *a legal dispute will cause upset:* **distress,** dismay, trouble, worry, bother, agitation, hurt, grief. **2** *a*

stomach upset: **disorder,** complaint, ailment, illness, sickness; informal bug; Brit. informal lurgy.
OPPOSITES reassurance.
adjective **1** *I was upset by the news:* **distressed,** troubled, perturbed, dismayed, disturbed, unsettled, disconcerted, worried, bothered, anxious, agitated, flustered, ruffled, unnerved, shaken, saddened, grieved; informal cut up, choked; Brit. informal gutted. **2** *an upset stomach:* **disturbed,** unsettled, queasy, bad, poorly; informal gippy.
OPPOSITES unperturbed, calm.

upside down adjective **1** *an upside-down canoe:* **upturned,** upended, wrong side up, overturned, inverted, capsized. **2** *they left the flat upside down:* **in disarray,** in disorder, jumbled up, in a muddle, untidy, disorganized, in chaos, in confusion; informal higgledy-piggledy.

up to date adjective **1** *up-to-date equipment:* **modern,** contemporary, the latest, state-of-the-art, new, up-to-the-minute, advanced. **2** *the newsletter will keep you up to date:* **informed,** up to speed, in the picture, in touch, au fait, conversant, familiar, knowledgeable, acquainted.
OPPOSITES out of date, old-fashioned.

urban adjective **town,** city, municipal, metropolitan, built-up, inner-city, suburban.
OPPOSITES rural.

urge verb **1** *she urged him to try:* **encourage,** exhort, press, entreat, implore, call on, appeal to, beg, plead with. **2** *I urge caution in interpreting these*

results: **advise,** counsel, advocate, recommend.
noun *his urge to travel:* **desire,** wish, need, compulsion, longing, yearning, hankering, craving, hunger, thirst; informal yen, itch.

urgent adjective **pressing,** acute, dire, desperate, critical, serious, grave, intense, crying, burning, compelling, extreme, high-priority, life-and-death.

usage noun **1** *energy usage:* **consumption,** use. **2** *the usage of equipment:* **use,** utilization, operation, manipulation, running, handling. **3** *English usage:* **language,** expression, phraseology, parlance, idiom.

use verb **1** *she used her key to open the door:* **utilize,** employ, avail oneself of, work, operate, wield, ply, apply, put into service. **2** *the court will use its discretion:* **exercise,** employ, bring into play, practise, apply. **3** *she was using me:* **take advantage of,** exploit, manipulate, take liberties with, impose on, abuse, capitalize on, profit from, trade on, milk; informal cash in on, walk all over. **4** *we have used up our funds:* **consume,** get/go through, exhaust, deplete, expend, spend.
noun **1** *the use of such weapons:* **utilization,** application, employment, operation, manipulation. **2** *his use of other people for his own ends:* **exploitation,** manipulation, abuse. **3** *what is the use of that?* **advantage,** benefit, good, point, object, purpose, sense, reason, service, utility, help, gain, avail, profit, value, worth.

used adjective *a used car:* **second-hand,** pre-owned,

nearly new, old, worn, hand-me-down, cast-off.
OPPOSITES new.
■ **used to** accustomed to, no stranger to, familiar with, at home with, in the habit of, experienced in, versed in, conversant with, acquainted with.

useful adjective **1** *a useful tool:* **functional,** practical, handy, convenient, utilitarian, serviceable, of service; informal nifty. **2** *a useful experience:* **beneficial,** advantageous, helpful, worthwhile, profitable, rewarding, productive, constructive, valuable, fruitful.
OPPOSITES useless, disadvantageous.

useless adjective **1** *it was useless to try:* **futile,** pointless, to no avail, vain, to no purpose, unavailing, hopeless, ineffectual, fruitless, unprofitable, unproductive. **2** (informal) *he was useless at his job:* **incompetent,** inept, ineffective, incapable, inadequate, hopeless, bad; informal a dead loss.
OPPOSITES useful, beneficial, competent.

usher verb *she ushered him to a seat:* **escort,** accompany, take, show, see, lead, conduct, guide.
noun *ushers showed them to their seats:* **guide,** attendant, escort.

usual adjective **normal,** customary, accustomed, wonted, habitual, routine, regular, standard, typical, established, set, stock, conventional, traditional, expected, familiar.
OPPOSITES unusual, exceptional.

usually adverb **normally,**

u

generally, habitually, customarily, routinely, typically, ordinarily, commonly, as a rule, in general, more often than not, mainly, mostly.

utensil noun **implement,** tool, instrument, device, apparatus, gadget, appliance, contrivance, contraption; informal gizmo.

utility noun **usefulness,** use, benefit, value, advantage, help, practicality, effectiveness, service.

utilize verb **use,** employ, avail oneself of, press into service, bring into play, deploy, draw on, exploit.

utmost adjective **greatest,** highest, maximum, most, extreme, supreme, paramount.

utter[1] adjective *that's utter nonsense:* **complete,** total, absolute, thorough, perfect, downright, out-and-out, outright, sheer, arrant, positive, prize, pure, unmitigated.

utter[2] verb **say,** speak, voice, mouth, express, articulate, pronounce, enunciate, emit, let out, give, produce.

Vv

vacancy noun **opening,** position, post, job, opportunity.

vacant adjective **1** *a vacant house:* **empty,** unoccupied, not in use, free, unfilled, uninhabited, untenanted. **2** *a vacant look:* **blank,** expressionless, unresponsive, emotionless, impassive, vacuous, empty, glazed.
OPPOSITES full, occupied, expressive.

vacate verb **1** *he was forced to vacate the premises:* **leave,** move out of, evacuate, quit, depart from. **2** *he will be vacating his post next year:* **resign from,** leave, stand down from, give up, bow out of, relinquish, retire from; informal quit.
OPPOSITES occupy, take up.

vacation noun **holiday,** trip, tour, break, leave, time off, recess.

vagrant noun **tramp,** drifter, down-and-out, beggar, itinerant, wanderer, nomad, traveller; N. Amer. hobo; N. Amer. informal bum.

vague adjective **1** *a vague shape:* **indistinct,** indefinite, indeterminate, unclear, ill-defined, hazy, fuzzy, misty, blurry, out of focus, shadowy, obscure. **2** *a vague description:* **imprecise,** rough, approximate, inexact, non-specific, ambiguous, hazy, uncertain. **3** *she was so vague in life:* **absent-minded,** forgetful, dreamy, abstracted; informal scatty, not with it.
OPPOSITES clear, precise, certain, sharp.

vain adjective **1** *their flattery made him vain:* **conceited,** proud, arrogant, boastful, cocky, immodest; informal big-headed. **2** *a vain attempt:* **futile,** useless, pointless, ineffective, fruitless, unproductive, unsuccessful, failed, abortive.
OPPOSITES modest, successful.

u
v

■ **in vain** unsuccessfully, to no avail, to no purpose, fruitlessly.

valid adjective **1** *a valid criticism:* **well founded**, sound, reasonable, rational, logical, justifiable, defensible, cogent, credible, forceful. **2** *a valid contract:* **legally binding**, lawful, official, in force, in effect.
OPPOSITES invalid.

valley noun **dale**, vale, hollow, gully, gorge, ravine, canyon, rift; Brit. combe; Scottish glen.

valuable adjective **1** *a valuable watch:* **precious**, costly, high-priced, expensive, dear, priceless. **2** *a valuable contribution:* **useful**, helpful, beneficial, invaluable, productive, worthwhile, worthy, important.
OPPOSITES cheap, worthless, useless.

valuables plural noun **precious items**, costly items, prized possessions, treasures.

value noun **1** *houses exceeding £250,000 in value:* **price**, cost, worth, market price. **2** *the value of adequate preparation:* **worth**, usefulness, advantage, benefit, gain, profit, good, help.
3 (values) **principles**, ethics, morals, standards, code of behaviour.
verb **1** *his estate was valued at £45,000:* **evaluate**, assess, estimate, appraise, price. **2** *she valued his opinion:* **think highly of**, have a high opinion of, rate highly, esteem, set great store by, respect.
OPPOSITES despise.

vanish verb **1** *he vanished into the darkness:* **disappear**, be lost to sight, become invisible, recede from view. **2** *all hope vanished:* **fade (away)**, evaporate, melt away, end, cease to exist, pass away, die out.
OPPOSITES appear, materialize.

vanity noun **conceit**, self-love, self-admiration, egotism, pride, arrogance, boastfulness, cockiness, swagger; informal big-headedness.
OPPOSITES modesty.

variable adjective **changeable**, shifting, fluctuating, irregular, inconstant, inconsistent, fluid, unstable; informal up and down.
OPPOSITES constant.

variant noun *variants of the same idea:* **variation**, form, alternative, version, adaptation, alteration, modification.
adjective *a variant spelling:* **alternative**, other, different, divergent.

variation noun **1** *regional variations in farming:* **difference**, dissimilarity, disparity, contrast, discrepancy, imbalance. **2** *opening times are subject to variation:* **change**, alteration, modification. **3** *there was very little variation from the pattern:* **deviation**, variance, divergence, departure, fluctuation.

varied adjective **diverse**, assorted, miscellaneous, mixed, sundry, wide-ranging, disparate, motley.
OPPOSITES similar, unchanging.

variety noun **1** *the lack of variety in the curriculum:* **diversity**, variation, diversification, change, difference. **2** *a wide variety of flowers:* **assortment**, miscellany, range, array, collection, selection, mixture, medley. **3** *fifty varieties of pasta:* **sort**, kind, type, class, category, style, form, make,

V

model, brand, strain, breed.
OPPOSITES uniformity.

various adjective **diverse,** different, differing, varied, assorted, mixed, sundry, miscellaneous, disparate, motley.
OPPOSITES similar.

vary verb **1** *estimates of the cost vary:* **differ,** be dissimilar, disagree. **2** *rates of interest vary over time:* **fluctuate,** rise and fall, go up and down, change, alter, shift, swing. **3** *the diaphragm is used for varying the aperture:* **modify,** change, alter, adjust, regulate, control, set.

vast adjective **huge,** extensive, broad, wide, boundless, enormous, immense, great, massive, colossal, gigantic, mammoth, giant, mountainous; informal **mega,** whopping; Brit. informal **ginormous.**
OPPOSITES tiny.

vault[1] noun **1** *the vault under the church:* **cellar,** basement, crypt, undercroft, catacomb, burial chamber. **2** *valuables stored in the vault:* **strongroom,** safe deposit.

vault[2] verb *he vaulted over the gate:* **jump,** leap, spring, bound, clear.

veer verb **turn,** swerve, swing, weave, wheel, change direction, change course, deviate.

vehicle noun **1** *a stolen vehicle:* **means of transport,** conveyance. **2** *a vehicle for the communication of ideas:* **channel,** medium, means, agent, instrument, mechanism, organ, apparatus.

veil noun *a thin veil of cloud:* **covering,** screen, curtain, mantle, cloak, mask, blanket, shroud, canopy, cloud, pall.

verb *the peak was veiled in mist:* **cover,** surround, swathe, enfold, envelop, conceal, hide, obscure, screen, shield, cloak, blanket, shroud.

vein noun **1** *veins of quartz:* **layer,** seam, lode, stratum, deposit. **2** *he closes his article in a humorous vein:* **mood,** humour, attitude, tone, spirit, character, feel, flavour, quality, atmosphere, manner, way, style.

velocity noun **speed,** pace, rate, tempo, rapidity.

vengeance noun **revenge,** retribution, retaliation, requital, reprisal, an eye for an eye.
OPPOSITES forgiveness.

venomous adjective **poisonous,** toxic, dangerous, deadly, lethal, fatal.
OPPOSITES harmless.

vent noun *an air vent:* **outlet,** inlet, opening, aperture, hole, gap, orifice, space, duct, flue, shaft, well, passage, airway.

verb *the crowd vented their fury:* **let out,** release, pour out, utter, express, air, voice.

venture noun *a business venture:* **enterprise,** undertaking, project, scheme, operation, endeavour, speculation.

verb **1** *we ventured across the moor:* **set out,** go, travel, journey. **2** *may I venture an opinion?* **put forward,** advance, proffer, offer, air, suggest, volunteer, submit, propose. **3** *I ventured to invite her:* **dare,** be so bold as, presume, have the audacity, have the nerve, take the liberty of.

verbal adjective **oral,** spoken, word-of-mouth, stated, said, unwritten.

verdict noun **judgement,**

V

adjudication, decision, finding, ruling, sentence.

verge noun 1 *the verge of the lake:* **edge,** border, margin, side, brink, rim, lip, fringe, boundary, perimeter. 2 *I was on the verge of tears:* **brink,** threshold, edge, point.
■ **verge on** approach, border on, be close/near to, resemble, be tantamount to, tend towards, approximate to.

verify verb **confirm,** prove, substantiate, corroborate, back up, bear out, justify, support, uphold, testify to, validate, authenticate.
OPPOSITES refute.

versatile adjective 1 *a versatile player:* **adaptable,** flexible, all-round, multitalented, resourceful. 2 *a versatile device:* **adjustable,** adaptable, multi-purpose, all-purpose.

verse noun 1 *Elizabethan verse:* **poetry,** lyrics. 2 *a verse he'd composed:* **poem,** lyric, rhyme, ditty, lay. 3 *a poem with sixty verses:* **stanza.**
OPPOSITES prose.

version noun 1 *his version of events:* **account,** report, statement, description, record, story, rendering, interpretation, explanation, understanding, reading, impression, side. 2 *the English version will be published next year:* **edition,** translation, impression. 3 *they have replaced coal-burning fires with gas versions:* **type,** sort, kind, form, equivalent, variety, variant, design, model, style.

vertical adjective **upright,** erect, perpendicular, plumb, on end, standing.
OPPOSITES flat, horizontal.

very adverb *that's very kind of you:* **extremely,** exceedingly,

exceptionally, extraordinarily, tremendously, immensely, acutely, abundantly, singularly, decidedly, highly, remarkably, really; informal awfully, terribly, majorly, seriously, mega, ultra; Brit. informal ever so, well, dead, jolly; N. Amer. informal real, mighty.
OPPOSITES slightly.
adjective 1 *those were his very words:* **exact,** actual, precise. 2 *the very thought of food made her feel ill:* **mere,** simple, pure, sheer.

vessel noun 1 *a fishing vessel:* **boat,** ship, craft. 2 *a cooking vessel:* **container,** receptacle, basin, bowl, pan, pot, jug.

vestige noun **remnant,** fragment, relic, echo, trace, mark, legacy, reminder.

vet verb **check up on,** screen, investigate, examine, scrutinize, inspect, look over, assess, evaluate, appraise; informal check out.

veteran noun *a veteran of many political campaigns:* **old hand,** past master, doyen, doyenne; informal old-timer; N. Amer. informal vet.
OPPOSITES novice.
adjective *a veteran diplomat:* **long-serving,** seasoned, old, hardened, practised, experienced; informal battle-scarred.

veto noun *parliament's right of veto:* **rejection,** dismissal, prohibition, proscription, embargo, ban.
OPPOSITES approval.
verb *the president vetoed the bill:* **reject,** turn down, throw out, dismiss, prohibit, forbid, proscribe, disallow, embargo, ban; informal kill.
OPPOSITES approve.

viable adjective **feasible,**

V

workable, practicable, practical, realistic, achievable, attainable; informal doable.
OPPOSITES impracticable.

vibrant adjective 1 *a vibrant performance:* spirited, lively, energetic, vigorous, storming, dynamic, passionate, fiery; informal feisty. 2 *vibrant colours:* vivid, bright, striking, brilliant, glowing, strong, rich.
OPPOSITES lifeless, pale.

vibrate verb shake, tremble, shiver, quiver, shudder, throb, pulsate.

vice noun 1 *youngsters may be driven to vice:* immorality, wrongdoing, wickedness, evil, iniquity, villainy, corruption, misconduct, sin, depravity. 2 *smoking is my only vice:* fault, failing, flaw, defect, shortcoming, weakness, deficiency, foible, frailty.
OPPOSITES virtue.

vicious adjective 1 *a vicious killer:* brutal, ferocious, savage, violent, ruthless, merciless, heartless, callous, cruel, cold-blooded, inhuman, barbaric, bloodthirsty. 2 *a vicious hate campaign:* malicious, spiteful, vindictive, cruel, bitter, acrimonious, hostile, nasty; informal catty.
OPPOSITES gentle, kindly.

victim noun sufferer, injured party, casualty, fatality, loss, survivor.

victorious adjective triumphant, conquering, vanquishing, winning, champion, successful.
OPPOSITES unsuccessful, losing.

victory noun success, triumph, conquest, win, coup; informal walkover.
OPPOSITES defeat, loss.

vie verb compete, contend,

struggle, fight, battle, jockey.

view noun 1 *the view from her flat:* outlook, prospect, panorama, vista, scene, scenery, landscape. 2 *we agree with this view:* opinion, viewpoint, belief, judgement, thinking, notion, idea, conviction, persuasion, attitude, feeling, sentiment. 3 *the church came into view:* sight, perspective, vision, visibility.
verb 1 *they viewed the landscape:* look at, observe, eye, gaze at, contemplate, regard, scan, survey, inspect, scrutinize; informal check out; N. Amer. informal eyeball. 2 *the law was viewed as a last resort:* consider, regard, look on, see, perceive, judge, deem, reckon.

viewer noun watcher, spectator, onlooker, observer; (viewers) audience, crowd.

vigilant adjective watchful, observant, attentive, alert, eagle-eyed, on the lookout, on one's guard; informal beady-eyed.
OPPOSITES inattentive.

vigorous adjective 1 *the child was vigorous:* robust, healthy, hale and hearty, strong, sturdy, fit, hardy, tough, energetic, lively, active. 2 *a vigorous defence:* strenuous, powerful, forceful, spirited, determined, aggressive, passionate; informal punchy, feisty.
OPPOSITES weak, feeble.

vigorously adverb strenuously, strongly, powerfully, forcefully, energetically, heartily, all out, fiercely, hard; informal like mad; Brit. informal like billy-o.

vigour noun health, strength, robustness, energy, life, vitality, spirit, passion, determination, dynamism, drive; informal oomph, get-up-and-go.

v

OPPOSITES lethargy.

vile adjective **foul**, nasty, unpleasant, bad, horrid, repulsive, disgusting, hateful, nauseating; informal gross.
OPPOSITES pleasant.

villain noun **criminal**, lawbreaker, offender, felon, miscreant, wrongdoer, rogue, scoundrel, reprobate; informal crook, baddy.

vindicate verb **1** *he was vindicated by the jury:* **acquit**, clear, absolve, exonerate; informal let off. **2** *our concerns were vindicated:* **justify**, warrant, substantiate, confirm, corroborate, prove, defend, support, back, endorse.
OPPOSITES incriminate.

vintage adjective **1** *vintage French wine:* **high-quality**, quality, choice, select, superior. **2** *vintage motor vehicles:* **classic**, ageless, timeless, old, antique, heritage, historic.

violate verb **1** *this violates human rights:* **contravene**, breach, infringe, break, transgress, disobey, defy, flout, disregard, ignore. **2** *the tomb was violated:* **desecrate**, profane, defile, degrade, debase, damage, vandalize, deface, destroy.
OPPOSITES respect.

violation noun **1** *a traffic violation:* **contravention**, breach, infringement, transgression, defiance, flouting, disregard. **2** *the violation of the relics:* **desecration**, defilement, damage, vandalism, destruction.

violence noun **1** *police violence:* **brutality**, savagery, cruelty, barbarity. **2** *the violence of the blow:* **force**, power, strength,

might. **3** *the violence of his passion:* **intensity**, severity, strength, force, vehemence, power, ferocity, fury.

violent adjective **1** *a violent alcoholic:* **brutal**, vicious, savage, rough, aggressive, threatening, fierce, ferocious. **2** *a violent blow:* **powerful**, forceful, hard, sharp, smart, strong, vigorous, mighty, hefty. **3** *violent jealousy:* **intense**, extreme, strong, powerful, unbridled, uncontrollable, ungovernable, consuming, passionate.
OPPOSITES gentle, weak, mild.

virgin adjective **1** *virgin forest:* **untouched**, unspoilt, untainted, pristine, spotless, unpolluted, undefiled, perfect, intact, unexplored, uncharted. **2** *virgin girls:* **chaste**, celibate, abstinent, pure, uncorrupted, undefiled, innocent, immaculate.

virtual adjective **effective**, near (enough), essential, practical, to all intents and purposes, in all but name, implied, unacknowledged.

virtually adverb **effectively**, all but, more or less, practically, almost, nearly, close to, verging on, just about, as good as, essentially, to all intents and purposes.

virtue noun **1** *the simple virtue of peasant life:* **goodness**, righteousness, morality, integrity, dignity, rectitude, honour. **2** *promptness was not one of his virtues:* **good point**, good quality, strong point, asset, forte, attribute, strength, talent. **3** *I can see no virtue in this:* **merit**, advantage, benefit, usefulness, strength.
OPPOSITES vice, failing,

V

disadvantage.

visible adjective **observable**, perceptible, noticeable, detectable, discernible, in sight, in view, on display, evident, apparent, manifest, plain.
OPPOSITES invisible.

vision noun **1** *her vision was blurred:* **eyesight**, sight, observation, eyes, view, perspective. **2** *visions of the ancestral pilgrims:* **apparition**, spectre, phantom, ghost, wraith, manifestation, hallucination, illusion, mirage; informal spook. **3** *visions of a better future:* **dream**, reverie, plan, hope, fantasy, delusion. **4** *his speech lacked vision:* **imagination**, creativity, inventiveness, innovation, inspiration, intuition, perception, insight.

visit verb **1** *I visited my uncle:* **call on**, go to see, look in on, stay with, holiday with, stop by, drop by; informal pop in on, drop in on, look up. **2** *Alex was visiting America:* **stay in**, stop over in, spend time in, holiday in, vacation in, tour, explore, see; informal do.
noun **1** *she paid a visit to her mum:* (social) **call**. **2** *a visit to the museum:* **trip**, tour of, look round, stopover, stay, holiday, break, vacation.

visitor noun **1** *I am expecting a visitor:* **guest**, caller, company. **2** *the monument attracts many visitors:* **tourist**, traveller, holidaymaker, tripper, vacationer, sightseer, pilgrim, foreigner, stranger.

vista noun **view**, scene, prospect, panorama, sight, scenery, landscape.

visual adjective **1** *visual defects:* **optical**, ocular, eye, vision,

sight. **2** *a visual indication that the alarm works:* **visible**, observable, perceptible, discernible.
OPPOSITES acoustic.

visualize verb **envisage**, conjure up, picture, call to mind, see, imagine, dream up.

vital adjective **1** *it is vital that action is taken:* **essential**, critical, crucial, indispensable, all-important, imperative, mandatory, high-priority. **2** *he is young and vital:* **lively**, energetic, active, sprightly, spirited, vivacious, exuberant, dynamic, vigorous; informal full of beans.
OPPOSITES unimportant, listless.

vitality noun **life**, energy, spirit, vivacity, exuberance, dynamism, vigour, passion, drive; informal get-up-and-go.

vivid adjective **1** *a vivid blue:* **bright**, colourful, brilliant, radiant, vibrant, strong, bold, deep, intense, rich, warm. **2** *a vivid account:* **graphic**, realistic, lifelike, faithful, authentic, striking, evocative, arresting, colourful, dramatic, memorable, powerful, stirring, moving, haunting.
OPPOSITES dull, vague.

vocal adjective **1** *vocal sounds:* **spoken**, said, voiced, uttered, articulated, oral. **2** *a vocal critic:* **vociferous**, outspoken, forthright, plain-spoken, blunt, frank, candid, passionate, vehement, vigorous.

vocation noun **calling**, life's work, mission, purpose, profession, occupation, career, job, employment, trade, craft, line (of work).

vogue noun **fashion**, trend, fad, fancy, craze, rage, enthusiasm, passion.

v

voice noun **1** *the voice of the people:* **opinion,** view, feeling, wish, desire, vote. **2** *a powerful voice for conservation:* **mouthpiece,** representative, spokesperson, agent, vehicle.
verb *they voiced their opposition:* **express,** communicate, declare, state, vent, utter, say, speak, articulate; informal come out with.

void noun *the void of space:* **vacuum,** emptiness, nothingness, blankness, (empty) space, gap, cavity, chasm, gulf.
verb *the contract was voided:* **invalidate,** annul, nullify, negate, quash, cancel, countermand, repeal, revoke, rescind, retract, withdraw, reverse.
OPPOSITES validate, fill.
adjective **1** *vast void spaces:* **empty,** vacant, blank, bare, clear, free. **2** *the election was void:* **invalid,** null, ineffective, worthless.
OPPOSITES full, valid.

volatile adjective **1** *a volatile personality:* **unpredictable,** temperamental, capricious, fickle, impulsive, emotional, excitable, turbulent, erratic, unstable. **2** *the atmosphere is too volatile for an election:* **tense,** strained, fraught, uneasy, uncomfortable, charged, explosive, inflammatory, turbulent.
OPPOSITES stable, calm.

volley noun **barrage,** cannonade, battery, bombardment, salvo, burst, storm, hail, shower, deluge, torrent.

volume noun **1** *a volume from the library:* **book,** publication, tome, work, title. **2** *a syringe of known volume:* **capacity,** mass, bulk, extent, size, dimensions. **3** *a huge volume of water:* **quantity,** amount, mass, bulk, measure. **4** *she turned the volume down:* **loudness,** sound, amplification.

voluntarily adverb **of one's own free will,** of one's own volition, by choice, by preference, spontaneously, willingly, readily, freely.
OPPOSITES compulsorily.

voluntary adjective **1** *attendance is voluntary:* **optional,** discretionary, elective, non-compulsory. **2** *voluntary work:* **unpaid,** unsalaried, for free, without charge, for nothing, honorary.
OPPOSITES compulsory, paid.

volunteer verb **1** *I volunteered my services:* **offer,** tender, proffer, put forward, put up, venture. **2** *he volunteered as a driver:* **offer one's services,** present oneself, make oneself available, come forward.
OPPOSITES withdraw, refuse.

vomit verb **1** *he needed to vomit:* **be sick,** spew, fetch up, heave, retch, gag; informal throw up, puke; N. Amer. informal barf. **2** *I vomited my breakfast:* **bring up,** regurgitate, spew up; informal throw up, puke up; Brit. informal sick up.
noun *a coat stained with vomit:* **sick;** informal puke, spew; N. Amer. informal barf.

vote noun **1** *a rigged vote:* **ballot,** poll, election, referendum, plebiscite, show of hands. **2** *in 1918 women got the vote:* **suffrage,** franchise, voting rights, voice, say.
verb *I vote we have one more game:* **suggest,** propose,

recommend, advocate, move, submit.

voucher noun coupon, token, ticket, pass, chit, slip, stub, docket; Brit. informal chitty.

vow noun *a vow of silence:* promise, pledge, oath, bond, covenant, commitment, word (of honour).
verb *I vowed to do better:* promise, pledge, swear, undertake, make a commitment, give one's word, guarantee.

voyage noun journey, trip, cruise, passage, sail, crossing, expedition.

vulgar adjective **1** *a vulgar joke:* rude, crude, dirty, filthy, smutty, naughty, indecent, obscene, coarse, risqué; informal blue. **2** *the decor was lavish but vulgar:* tasteless, crass, tawdry, ostentatious, flamboyant, showy, gaudy, garish; informal flash, tacky. **3** *it was vulgar for a woman to whistle:* impolite, ill-mannered, boorish, uncouth, unsophisticated, unrefined.
OPPOSITES clean, tasteful, decent.

vulnerable adjective **1** *a vulnerable city:* in danger, in peril, in jeopardy, at risk, unprotected, undefended, unguarded, open to attack, exposed. **2** *he is vulnerable to criticism:* exposed, open, liable, prone, prey, susceptible, subject.
OPPOSITES invulnerable, safe.

Ww

waddle verb toddle, totter, wobble, shuffle.

wade verb **1** *they waded in the water:* paddle, wallow, splash; informal splosh. **2** *I had to wade through some hefty documents:* plough, plod, trawl, labour, toil.

wag verb **1** *the dog's tail wagged:* swing, swish, switch, sway, shake; informal waggle. **2** *he wagged his stick at them:* shake, wave, wiggle, flourish, brandish.

wage noun *the workers' wages:* pay, salary, stipend, fee, remuneration, income, earnings.
verb *they waged war on the guerrillas:* engage in, carry on, conduct, execute, pursue, prosecute, proceed with.

wail noun & verb howl, cry, bawl, moan, groan, yowl, whine, lament.

wait verb **1** *we'll wait in the airport:* stay (put), remain, rest, stop, halt, pause, linger, loiter; informal stick around. **2** *she had to wait until her bags arrived:* stand by, hold back, bide one's time, mark time, kill time, waste time, kick one's heels, twiddle one's thumbs; informal hold on, hang around, sit tight. **3** *that job will have to wait:* be postponed, be delayed, be put off, be deferred; informal be put on the back burner, be put on ice.
noun *a long wait:* delay, hold-up, interval, interlude, pause, break, suspension, stoppage, halt, interruption, lull, gap.

waiter, waitress noun server,

steward, stewardess, attendant, butler, servant; N. Amer. waitperson.

waive verb **1** *he waived his right to a hearing:* **give up**, abandon, renounce, relinquish, surrender, sacrifice, turn down. **2** *the manager waived the rules:* **disregard**, ignore, overlook, set aside, forgo.

wake¹ verb **1** *at 4.30 a.m. Mark woke up:* **awake**, waken, stir, come to, come round. **2** *she woke her husband:* **rouse**, waken.
OPPOSITES go to sleep, send to sleep.
noun **vigil**, watch, funeral.
■ **wake up to** realize, become aware of, become conscious of.

wake² noun *the cruiser's wake:* **backwash**, slipstream, trail, path, track.
■ **in the wake of** in the aftermath of, after, subsequent to, following, as a result of, as a consequence of, on account of, because of.

walk verb **1** *they walked along the road:* **stroll**, saunter, amble, trudge, plod, hike, tramp, trek, march, stride, troop, wander, ramble, promenade, traipse; informal mosey, hoof it. **2** *he walked her home:* **accompany**, escort, guide, show, see, take.
noun **1** *country walks:* **ramble**, hike, tramp, march, stroll, promenade, constitutional, turn. **2** *her elegant walk:* **gait**, step, stride, tread. **3** *the riverside walk:* **path**, pathway, footpath, track, walkway, promenade, footway, pavement, trail, towpath.

walker noun rambler, hiker, trekker, stroller, pedestrian.

wallet noun purse, case, pouch, holder; N. Amer. billfold, pocketbook.

wander verb **1** *I wandered around the estate:* **stroll**, amble, saunter, walk, potter, ramble, meander, roam, range, drift; Scottish & Irish stravaig; informal traipse, mosey. **2** *we are wandering from the point:* **stray**, depart, diverge, deviate, digress, drift, get sidetracked.

wane verb **decline**, diminish, decrease, dwindle, shrink, tail off, ebb, fade, lessen, peter out, fall off, recede, slump, weaken, wither, evaporate, die out.
OPPOSITES wax, grow.

want verb **desire**, wish for, hope for, fancy, care for, like, long for, yearn for, crave, hanker after, hunger for, thirst for, cry out for, covet; informal have a yen for, be dying for.
noun **1** *his want of vigilance:* **lack**, absence, non-existence, dearth, deficiency, inadequacy, insufficiency, paucity, shortage, scarcity. **2** *a time of want:* **need**, austerity, privation, deprivation, poverty, destitution. **3** *her wants would be taken care of:* **wish**, desire, demand, longing, fancy, craving, need, requirement; informal yen.

wanting adjective **deficient**, inadequate, lacking, insufficient, imperfect, flawed, unsound, substandard, inferior, second-rate.
OPPOSITES sufficient.

wanton adjective **deliberate**, wilful, malicious, gratuitous, unprovoked, motiveless, arbitrary, unjustifiable, senseless.
OPPOSITES justifiable.

war noun **1** *the Napoleonic wars:* **conflict**, warfare, combat, fighting, action, bloodshed,

W

struggle, fight, campaign, hostilities, jihad, crusade. **2** *the war against drugs:* **campaign,** crusade, battle, fight, struggle. OPPOSITES peace.

verb *rival Emperors warred against each other:* **fight,** battle, combat, wage war, take up arms, feud, quarrel, struggle, contend, wrangle, cross swords.

ward noun **1** *the surgical ward:* **room,** department, unit, area. **2** *the most marginal ward in Westminster:* **district,** constituency, division, quarter, zone, parish. **3** *the boy is my ward:* **dependant,** charge, protégé.

warden noun **1** *the flats have a resident warden:* **superintendent,** caretaker, porter, steward, custodian, watchman, concierge, doorman, commissionaire. **2** *a game warden:* **ranger,** keeper, guardian, protector. **3** *he was handcuffed to a warden:* **prison officer,** guard, jailer, warder, keeper; informal screw. **4** (Brit.) *the college warden:* **principal,** head, governor, master, mistress, rector, provost, dean, president, director, chancellor.

warehouse noun storeroom, depot, depository, stockroom, magazine, granary; informal lock-up.

wares plural noun **goods,** merchandise, products, produce, stock, commodities.

warfare noun **fighting,** war, combat, conflict, action, hostilities.

warm adjective **1** *a warm kitchen:* **hot,** cosy, snug. **2** *a warm day:* **balmy,** summery, sultry, hot, mild, temperate. **3** *warm water:* **tepid,** lukewarm. **4** *a warm sweater:* **thick,** chunky, thermal, winter, woolly. **5** *a warm welcome:* **friendly,** cordial, amiable, genial, kind, pleasant, fond, welcoming, hospitable, hearty. OPPOSITES cold, chilly, light, hostile.

verb *warm the soup in that pan:* **heat (up),** reheat. OPPOSITES chill.

warmth noun **1** *the warmth of the fire:* **heat,** cosiness, snugness. **2** *the warmth of their welcome:* **friendliness,** amiability, geniality, cordiality, kindness, tenderness, fondness.

warn verb **1** *David warned her that it was too late:* **inform,** notify, tell, alert, apprise, make someone aware, remind; informal tip off. **2** *police are warning galleries to be alert:* **advise,** exhort, urge, counsel, caution.

warning noun **1** *the earthquake came without warning:* **(advance) notice,** alert, hint, signal, sign, alarm bells; informal a tip-off. **2** *a health warning:* **caution,** notification, information, exhortation, advice. **3** *a warning of things to come:* **omen,** premonition, foreboding, prophecy, prediction, forecast, token, portent, signal, sign. **4** *his sentence is a warning to other drunk drivers:* **example,** deterrent, lesson, caution, message, moral. **5** *a written warning:* **reprimand,** caution, remonstrance, admonition, censure; informal dressing-down, talking-to, telling-off.

warp verb **1** *timber which is too dry will warp:* **buckle,** twist, bend, distort, deform, curve, bow, contort. **2** *he warped the mind of her child:* **corrupt,** twist, pervert, deprave.

W

OPPOSITES straighten.

warrant noun **1** *a warrant for his arrest:* **authorization**, order, writ, mandate, licence, permit, summons. **2** *a travel warrant:* **voucher**, chit, slip, ticket, coupon, pass.
verb **1** *the charges warranted a severe sentence:* **justify**, deserve, vindicate, call for, sanction, permit, authorize, excuse, account for, legitimize, support, license, merit, qualify for, rate. **2** *we warrant that the texts do not infringe copyright:* **guarantee**, promise, affirm, swear, vouch, vow, pledge, undertake, declare, testify.

warranty noun **guarantee**, assurance, promise, commitment, undertaking, pledge, agreement, covenant.

warrior noun **fighter**, soldier, serviceman, combatant.

wary adjective **1** *he was trained to be wary:* **cautious**, careful, circumspect, on one's guard, chary, alert, on the lookout, attentive, heedful, watchful, vigilant, observant. **2** *we are wary of strangers:* **suspicious**, chary, leery, careful, distrustful. **OPPOSITES** inattentive, trustful.

wash verb **1** *he washed in the bath:* **clean oneself**, bathe, shower. **2** *she washed her hands:* **clean**, cleanse, scrub, wipe, shampoo, lather, sluice, swill, douse, swab, disinfect. **3** *she washed off the blood:* **remove**, expunge, eradicate, sponge off, scrub off, wipe off, rinse off. **4** *the women were washing clothes:* **launder**, clean, rinse. **5** *waves washed against the hull:* **splash**, lap, dash, break, beat, surge, ripple, roll. **6** *the wreckage was washed downriver:* **sweep**, carry, convey, transport, deposit. **OPPOSITES** dirty.
noun **1** *that shirt should go in the wash:* **laundry**, washing. **2** *the wash of a motor boat:* **backwash**, wake, trail, path. ■ **wash something away** erode, abrade, wear away, eat away, undermine.

waste verb **1** *he doesn't like to waste money:* **squander**, misspend, misuse, fritter away, throw away, lavish, dissipate; informal blow, splurge. **2** *kids are wasting away in the streets:* **grow weak**, grow thin, shrink, wilt, fade, flag, deteriorate. **3** *the disease wasted his legs:* **emaciate**, atrophy, wither, shrivel, shrink, weaken. **OPPOSITES** conserve, thrive.
adjective **1** *waste material:* **unwanted**, excess, superfluous, left over, scrap, unusable, unprofitable. **2** *waste ground:* **uncultivated**, barren, desert, arid, bare, desolate.
noun **1** *a waste of money:* **misuse**, misapplication, abuse, extravagance, lavishness. **2** *household waste:* **rubbish**, refuse, litter, debris, junk, sewage, effluent; N. Amer. garbage, trash. **3** (**wastes**) **desert**, wasteland, wilderness, emptiness, wilds.

wasteful adjective **prodigal**, profligate, uneconomical, extravagant, lavish, excessive, imprudent, improvident, spendthrift. **OPPOSITES** frugal.

watch verb **1** *she watched him as he spoke:* **observe**, view, look at, eye, gaze at, peer at, contemplate, inspect, scrutinize, scan; informal check out, get a load of, recce, eyeball. **2** *he was being watched*

by the police: **spy on,** keep in sight, keep under surveillance, track, monitor, tail; informal keep tabs on, stake out. **3** *we stayed to watch the boat:* **guard,** mind, protect, look after, keep an eye on, take care of, shield, defend.
OPPOSITES ignore, neglect.
noun **1** *Bill looked at his watch:* **wristwatch,** timepiece, chronometer. **2** *we kept watch on the yacht:* **guard,** vigil, lookout, an eye, observation, surveillance.

watchdog noun ombudsman, monitor, scrutineer, inspector, supervisor.

water verb **1** *water the plants:* **sprinkle,** moisten, dampen, wet, spray, splash. **2** *my mouth watered:* **moisten,** become wet, salivate.
■ **water something down 1** *staff had watered down the drinks:* **dilute,** thin (out), weaken, adulterate. **2** *the proposals were watered down:* tone down, temper, mitigate, moderate, soften, tame.

waterfall noun falls, cascade, cataract, rapids.

wave verb **1** *he waved his flag:* **flap,** wag, shake, swish, swing, brandish, flourish, wield. **2** *the grass waved in the breeze:* **ripple,** flutter, undulate, stir, flap, sway, shake, quiver. **3** *the waiter waved them closer:* **gesture,** signal, beckon, motion.
noun **1** *she gave him a friendly wave:* **signal,** sign, motion, gesture. **2** *he surfs the big waves:* **breaker,** roller, comber, boomer, ripple; (**waves**) swell, surf. **3** *a wave of emigration:* **rush,** flow, surge, flood, stream, tide, deluge, spate. **4** *a wave of self-pity:* **surge,** rush, stab, upsurge, sudden feeling.

waver verb **1** *the candlelight wavered in the draught:* **flicker,** quiver. **2** *his voice wavered:* **falter,** wobble, tremble, quaver. **3** *he wavered between the choices:* **hesitate,** dither, be irresolute, be undecided, vacillate, blow hot and cold; Brit. haver, hum and haw; informal shilly-shally, sit on the fence.

way noun **1** *a way of reducing the damage:* **method,** process, procedure, technique, system, plan, strategy, scheme, means, mechanism, approach. **2** *she kissed him in her brisk way:* **manner,** style, fashion, mode. **3** *I've changed my ways:* **practice,** wont, habit, custom, convention, routine, trait, attribute, peculiarity, idiosyncrasy, conduct, behaviour, manner, style. **4** *which way leads home?* **route,** course, direction, track, path, access, gate, exit, entrance, door. **5** *a short way downstream:* **distance,** length, stretch, journey. **6** *April is a long way away:* **time,** stretch, span, duration. **7** *a car coming the other way:* **direction,** bearing, course, orientation, line, tack. **8** *in some ways, he may be better off:* **respect,** regard, aspect, facet, sense, detail, point, particular. **9** *the country is in a bad way:* **state,** condition, situation, circumstances, position, predicament, plight; informal shape.
■ **give way 1** *the government gave way and passed the bill:* **yield,** back down, surrender, concede defeat, give in, submit; informal throw in the towel/sponge, cave in. **2** *the door gave way:* **collapse,** give, cave in, fall in, come apart, crumple.

weak adjective **1** *they are too weak to move:* **feeble,** frail, delicate, fragile, infirm, debilitated, decrepit, exhausted; informal weedy. **2** *bats have weak eyes:* **inadequate,** poor, feeble, defective, faulty, deficient, imperfect, substandard. **3** *a weak excuse:* **unconvincing,** tenuous, implausible, unsatisfactory, poor, inadequate, feeble, flimsy, lame, hollow; informal pathetic. **4** *a weak bridge:* **fragile,** frail, rickety, insubstantial, wobbly, unstable, ramshackle, jerry-built, shoddy. **5** *I was too weak to be a rebel:* **spineless,** craven, cowardly, timid, irresolute, indecisive, ineffectual, meek, tame, soft, faint-hearted; informal yellow, gutless. **6** *a weak light:* **dim,** pale, wan, faint, feeble, muted. **7** *a weak voice:* **indistinct,** muffled, muted, hushed, faint, low. **8** *weak coffee:* **watery,** dilute, watered down, thin.
OPPOSITES strong, powerful, convincing, solid, resolute, bright, loud.

weaken verb **1** *the virus weakened him:* **enfeeble,** debilitate, incapacitate, sap, tire, exhaust. **2** *our morale weakened:* **decrease,** dwindle, diminish, wane, ebb, subside, peter out, fizzle out, tail off, decline, falter. **3** *the move weakened her authority:* **impair,** undermine, compromise, lessen.
OPPOSITES strengthen, bolster.

weakness noun **1** *with old age came weakness:* **frailty,** feebleness, fragility, delicacy, debility, incapacity, decrepitude; informal weediness. **2** *he has worked on his weaknesses:* **fault,** flaw, defect, deficiency, failing, shortcoming, imperfection, Achilles heel. **3** *a weakness for champagne:* **fondness,** liking, partiality, love, penchant, predilection, inclination, taste. **4** *the President was accused of weakness:* **timidity,** cravenness, cowardliness, indecision, irresolution, ineffectuality, ineffectiveness, impotence. **5** *the weakness of this argument:* **inadequacy,** implausibility, poverty, untenability, transparency, flimsiness, hollowness.

wealth noun **1** *a gentleman of wealth:* **affluence,** prosperity, riches, means, fortune, money, cash, capital, treasure, finance; informal wherewithal, dough, bread. **2** *a wealth of information:* **abundance,** profusion, plethora, mine, store; informal lot, load, mountain, stack, ton; Brit. informal shedload.
OPPOSITES poverty, dearth.

wealthy adjective **rich,** affluent, moneyed, well off, well-to-do, prosperous; informal well heeled, rolling in it, made of money, loaded, flush.
OPPOSITES poor.

wear verb **1** *he wore a suit:* **dress in,** be clothed in, have on, sport. **2** *Barbara wore a smile:* **bear,** have (on one's face), show, display, exhibit, give, put on, assume. **3** *the bricks have been worn down:* **erode,** abrade, rub away, grind away, wash away, crumble (away), eat away (at). **4** *the tyres are wearing well:* **last,** endure, hold up, bear up.
noun **1** *you won't get much wear out of that:* **use,** service, value; informal mileage. **2** *evening wear:*

W

clothes, garments, dress, attire, garb, wardrobe; informal get-up, gear, togs; Brit. informal kit, clobber. **3** *the varnish will withstand wear:* **damage,** friction, abrasion, erosion.
■ **wear off** *the novelty soon wore off:* fade, diminish, lessen, dwindle, decrease, wane, peter out, fizzle out, pall, disappear, vanish. ■ **wear out** deteriorate, become worn, fray, become threadbare, go into holes.
■ **wear someone out** tire out, fatigue, weary, exhaust, drain, sap, enervate; informal whack, poop, shatter, do in; Brit. informal knacker.

wearing adjective tiring, exhausting, wearying, fatiguing, enervating, draining, sapping, demanding, exacting, taxing, gruelling, punishing.

weary adjective **1** *he was weary after cycling:* **tired,** worn out, exhausted, fatigued, sapped, spent, drained; informal done in, ready to drop, bushed, shattered; Brit. informal knackered, whacked; N. Amer. informal pooped. **2** *a weary journey:* **tiring,** exhausting, fatiguing, enervating, draining, sapping, demanding, taxing, arduous, gruelling.
OPPOSITES fresh, keen, refreshing.

weather noun *what's the weather like?* **conditions,** climate, elements, forecast, outlook.
verb *we weathered the recession:* **survive,** come through, ride out, pull through, withstand, endure, rise above; informal stick out.

weave[1] verb **1** *flowers were woven into their hair:* **entwine,** lace, twist, knit, braid, plait.

2 *he weaves colourful plots:* **invent,** make up, fabricate, construct, create, spin.

weave[2] verb *he had to weave his way through the crowds:* **thread,** wind, wend, dodge, zigzag.

web noun **1** *a spider's web:* **mesh,** net, lattice, lacework, gauze, gossamer. **2** *a web of friendships:* **network,** nexus, complex, tangle, chain.

wedded adjective **1** *wedded bliss:* **married,** matrimonial, marital, conjugal, nuptial. **2** *he is wedded to his work:* **dedicated,** devoted, attached, fixated.

wedding noun marriage (service), nuptials, union.

wedge noun **1** *the door was secured by a wedge:* **chock,** stop. **2** *a wedge of cheese:* **triangle,** segment, slice, section, chunk, lump, slab, hunk, block, piece. verb *she wedged her case between two bags:* **squeeze,** cram, jam, ram, force, push, shove; informal stuff, bung.

weep verb cry, shed tears, sob, snivel, whimper, wail, bawl, keen; Scottish greet; informal boohoo, blub.
OPPOSITES rejoice.

weigh verb **1** *she weighs the vegetables:* **put on the scales. 2** *he weighed 118 kg:* **tip the scales at. 3** *he has to weigh up the possibilities:* **consider,** contemplate, think about, mull over, chew over, reflect on, ruminate about, muse on, assess, examine, review, explore, take stock of. **4** *they need to weigh benefit against risk:* **balance,** evaluate, compare, juxtapose, contrast.

weight noun **1** *the weight of the book:* **mass,** heaviness, load, burden. **2** *his recommendation*

will carry great weight:
influence, force, leverage, sway, pull, power, authority; informal clout. **3** *a weight off her mind:* **burden,** load, millstone, trouble, worry. **4** *the weight of the evidence is against him:* **most,** bulk, majority, preponderance, body, lion's share.

weird adjective **1** *weird apparitions:* **uncanny,** eerie, unnatural, supernatural, unearthly, other-worldly, ghostly, mysterious, strange, abnormal, unusual; informal creepy, spooky, freaky. **2** *a weird sense of humour:* **bizarre,** odd, curious, strange, quirky, outlandish, eccentric, unconventional, unorthodox, idiosyncratic, surreal, crazy, absurd, grotesque, peculiar; informal wacky, freaky; N. Amer. informal wacko.
OPPOSITES normal, conventional.

welcome noun *a welcome from the vicar:* **greeting,** salutation, reception, hospitality, the red carpet.
verb **1** *welcome your guests in their own language:* **greet,** salute, receive, meet, usher in. **2** *we welcomed their decision:* **be pleased by,** be glad about, approve of, applaud, appreciate, embrace.
OPPOSITES resent, object to.
adjective *welcome news:* **pleasing,** agreeable, encouraging, gratifying, heartening, promising, favourable, pleasant.
OPPOSITES unwelcome.

weld verb fuse, bond, stick, join, attach, seal, splice, melt, solder.

welfare noun **1** *the welfare of children:* **well-being,** health, comfort, security, safety,

protection, success, interest, good. **2** *we cannot claim welfare:* **social security,** benefit, public assistance, pension, credit, support, sick pay, unemployment benefit; Brit. informal the dole.

well[1] adverb **1** *please behave well:* **satisfactorily,** nicely, correctly, properly, fittingly, suitably, appropriately. **2** *they get on well together:* **amicably,** agreeably, pleasantly, nicely, happily, harmoniously, amiably, peaceably; informal famously. **3** *he plays the piano well:* **skilfully,** ably, competently, proficiently, adeptly, deftly, expertly, excellently. **4** *treat your employees well:* **decently,** fairly, kindly, generously. **5** *mix the ingredients well:* **thoroughly,** completely, effectively, rigorously, carefully. **6** *I know her quite well:* **intimately,** thoroughly, deeply, profoundly, personally. **7** *they studied the car market well:* **carefully,** closely, attentively, rigorously, in depth, exhaustively, in detail, meticulously, scrupulously, methodically, comprehensively, fully, extensively. **8** *they speak well of him:* **admiringly,** highly, approvingly, favourably, appreciatively, warmly, enthusiastically, glowingly. **9** *she lives well:* **comfortably,** in luxury, prosperously. **10** *you may well be right:* **quite possibly,** conceivably, probably. **11** *he is well over forty:* **considerably,** very much, a great deal, substantially, easily, comfortably, significantly. **12** *she could well afford it:* **easily,** comfortably, readily, effortlessly.
OPPOSITES badly, negligently,

W

disparagingly, barely.
adjective 1 *she was completely well again:* **healthy,** fine, fit, robust, strong, vigorous, blooming, thriving, in fine fettle; informal in the pink. **2** *all is not well:* **satisfactory,** all right, fine, in order, as it should be, acceptable; informal OK, hunky-dory.
OPPOSITES poorly, unsatisfactory.
■ **as well** too, also, in addition, into the bargain, besides, furthermore, moreover, to boot.
■ **as well as** together with, along with, besides, plus, and, with, on top of, not to mention.

well² noun *she drew water from the well:* **borehole,** spring, waterhole, shaft.
verb *tears welled from her eyes:* **flow,** spill, stream, gush, roll, cascade, flood, spout, burst, issue.

wet adjective **1** *wet clothes:* **damp,** moist, soaked, drenched, saturated, sopping, dripping, soggy, waterlogged, squelchy. **2** *it was cold and wet:* **rainy,** pouring, teeming, showery, drizzly. **3** *the paint is still wet:* **sticky,** tacky.
OPPOSITES dry, fine.
verb *wet the clothes before ironing them:* **dampen,** moisten, sprinkle, spray, splash, soak, saturate, flood, douse, drench.
OPPOSITES dry.

wharf noun **quay,** pier, dock, berth, landing, jetty, harbour, dockyard.

wheel verb **1** *she wheeled the trolley away:* **push,** trundle, roll. **2** *the flock of doves wheeled round:* **turn,** go round, circle, orbit.

whereabouts noun **location,** position, site, situation, spot, point, home, address, neighbourhood.

while noun *we chatted for a while:* **time,** spell, stretch, stint, span, interval, period; Brit. informal patch.
verb *tennis helped to while away the time:* **pass,** spend, occupy, use up, kill.

whim noun **impulse,** urge, notion, fancy, caprice, vagary, inclination.

whine verb **1** *a child was whining:* **wail,** whimper, cry, mewl, moan, howl, yowl. **2** *the lift began to whine:* **hum,** drone, beep. **3** *he's always whining about something:* **complain,** grouse, grouch, grumble, moan, carp; informal gripe, bellyache, whinge.

whip noun *he used a whip on his dogs:* **lash,** scourge, strap, belt.
verb **1** *he whipped the boy:* **flog,** lash, scourge, strap, belt, thrash, beat. **2** *then whip the cream:* **whisk,** beat. **3** *he whipped his listeners into a frenzy:* **rouse,** stir up, excite, galvanize, electrify, stimulate, inspire, fire up, inflame, provoke.

whirl verb **1** *leaves whirled in the wind:* **rotate,** circle, wheel, turn, revolve, orbit, spin, twirl. **2** *they whirled past:* **hurry,** race, dash, rush, run, sprint, bolt, career, charge, shoot, hurtle, hare, fly, speed; informal tear, belt; Brit. informal bomb. **3** *his mind was whirling:* **spin,** reel, swim.
noun **1** *a whirl of dust:* **swirl,** flurry, eddy. **2** *the mad social whirl:* **hurly-burly,** activity, round, bustle, rush, flurry. **3** *Laura's mind was in a whirl:* **spin,** daze, muddle, jumble, confusion; informal dither.

whisk verb **1** *the cable car will*

whisk you to the top: **speed,** hurry, rush, sweep, hurtle, shoot. **2** *she whisked the cloth away:* **pull,** snatch, pluck, tug, jerk; informal whip, yank. **3** *whisk the egg yolks:* **whip,** beat, mix.
noun *an egg whisk:* **beater,** mixer, blender.

whisper verb *Alison whispered in his ear:* **murmur,** mutter, mumble, speak softly, breathe.
OPPOSITES shout.
noun **1** *she spoke in a whisper:* **murmur,** mutter, mumble, low voice, undertone. **2** *I heard a whisper that he's left town:* **rumour,** story, report, gossip, speculation, suggestion, hint; informal buzz.
OPPOSITES shout.

white adjective *her face went white:* **pale,** pallid, wan, ashen, chalky, pasty, peaky, washed out, ghostly, deathly.

whole adjective **1** *the whole report:* **entire,** complete, full, unabridged, uncut. **2** *the eggs emerge whole:* **intact,** in one piece, unbroken, undamaged, flawless, unmarked, perfect.
OPPOSITES incomplete.
noun **1** *a single whole:* **entity,** unit, body, ensemble. **2** *the whole of the year:* **all,** every part, the lot, the sum.
■ **on the whole** overall, all in all, all things considered, for the most part, in the main, in general, by and large, normally, usually, almost always, typically, ordinarily.

wholehearted adjective **unqualified,** unreserved, unconditional, complete, full, total, absolute.
OPPOSITES half-hearted.

wholesale adverb *the images were removed wholesale:* **extensively,** on a large scale, comprehensively, indiscriminately, without exception.
OPPOSITES selectively.
adjective *wholesale destruction:* **extensive,** widespread, large-scale, wide-ranging, comprehensive, total, mass, indiscriminate.
OPPOSITES partial.

wholly adverb **completely,** totally, absolutely, entirely, fully, thoroughly, utterly, downright, in every respect; informal one hundred per cent.

wicked adjective **1** *wicked deeds:* **evil,** sinful, immoral, wrong, bad, iniquitous, corrupt, base, vile, villainous, criminal, nefarious; informal crooked. **2** *a wicked sense of humour:* **mischievous,** playful, naughty, impish, roguish, puckish, cheeky.
OPPOSITES virtuous.

wide adjective **1** *a wide river:* **broad,** extensive, spacious, vast, spread out. **2** *a wide range of opinion:* **comprehensive,** ample, broad, extensive, large, exhaustive, all-inclusive. **3** *his shot was wide:* **off target,** off the mark, inaccurate.
OPPOSITES narrow.
adverb **1** *he opened his eyes wide:* **fully,** to the fullest/furthest extent, as far/much as possible. **2** *he shot wide:* **off target,** wide of the mark/target, inaccurately.

widen verb **broaden,** open up/out, expand, extend, enlarge.

widespread adjective **general,** extensive, universal, common, global, worldwide, omnipresent, ubiquitous, across the board, predominant, prevalent, rife, broad.
OPPOSITES limited.

W

width noun breadth, thickness, span, diameter, girth.

wield verb 1 *he was wielding a sword:* **brandish**, flourish, wave, swing, use, employ, handle. 2 *he has wielded power since 1972:* **exercise**, exert, hold, maintain, command, control.

wife noun **spouse**, partner, mate, consort, bride; informal better half, missus; Brit. informal other half.

wild adjective 1 *wild animals:* **untamed**, undomesticated, feral, fierce, ferocious, savage. 2 *wild flowers:* **uncultivated**, native, indigenous. 3 *wild hill country:* **uninhabited**, unpopulated, uncultivated, rugged, rough, inhospitable, desolate, barren. 4 *a wild night:* **stormy**, squally, tempestuous, turbulent, boisterous. 5 *wild behaviour:* **uncontrolled**, unrestrained, undisciplined, unruly, rowdy, disorderly, riotous. 6 *Bill's wild schemes:* **foolish**, ridiculous, ludicrous, stupid, foolhardy, idiotic, madcap, absurd, silly, impractical, impracticable, unworkable; informal crazy, crackpot. 7 *a wild guess:* **random**, arbitrary, haphazard, uninformed.
OPPOSITES tame, cultivated, calm, disciplined.

wilderness noun 1 *the Siberian wilderness:* **wilds**, wastes, desert. 2 *a litter-strewn wilderness:* **wasteland**.

wilful adjective 1 *wilful destruction:* **deliberate**, intentional, premeditated, planned, conscious. 2 *a wilful child:* **headstrong**, strong-willed, obstinate, stubborn, pig-headed, recalcitrant, uncooperative; Brit. informal bloody-minded, bolshie.
OPPOSITES accidental, amenable.

will noun 1 *the will to succeed:* **determination**, strength of character, resolve, single-mindedness, drive, commitment, dedication, doggedness, tenacity, staying power. 2 *they stayed against their will:* **desire**, wish, preference, inclination, intention. 3 *God's will:* **wish**, desire, decision, choice, decree, command.
verb 1 *do what you will:* **want**, wish, please, see fit, think fit/best, like, choose, prefer. 2 *God willed it:* **decree**, order, ordain, command.

willing adjective 1 *I'm willing to give it a try:* **ready**, prepared, disposed, inclined, minded, happy, glad, pleased, agreeable, amenable; informal game. 2 *willing help:* **readily given**, ungrudging.
OPPOSITES reluctant.

willingly adverb **voluntarily**, of one's own free will, of one's own accord, readily, without reluctance, ungrudgingly, cheerfully, happily, gladly, with pleasure.
OPPOSITES reluctantly.

willingness noun **readiness**, inclination, will, wish, desire.
OPPOSITES reluctance.

wilt verb 1 *the roses had begun to wilt:* **droop**, sag, become limp, flop. 2 *we were wilting in the heat:* **languish**, flag, droop, become listless.
OPPOSITES flourish.

win verb 1 *Steve won the race:* **come first in**, take first prize in, triumph in, be successful in. 2 *she was determined to win:* **come first**, be victorious, carry/

win the day, come out on top, succeed, triumph, prevail. **3** *he won a cash prize:* **earn,** gain, secure, collect, pick up, walk away/off with, carry off; informal land, net, bag, scoop.
OPPOSITES lose.
noun *a 3–0 win:* **victory,** triumph, conquest.
OPPOSITES defeat.

wince verb **grimace,** pull a face, flinch, blench, start.

wind¹ noun **1** *the trees were swaying in the wind:* **breeze,** current of air, gale, hurricane, gust, draught; informal blow; literary zephyr. **2** *Jez got his wind back:* **breath;** informal puff.

wind² verb **1** *the road winds up the mountain:* **twist (and turn),** bend, curve, loop, zigzag, weave, snake. **2** *he wound a towel around his waist:* **wrap,** furl, entwine, lace. **3** *Anne wound the wool into a ball:* **coil,** roll, twist, twine.
■ **wind something up 1** *Richard wound up the meeting:* **conclude,** bring to an end/close, terminate; informal wrap up. **2** *the company has been wound up:* **close (down),** dissolve, put into liquidation.

windfall noun **bonanza,** jackpot, pennies from heaven, godsend.

windy adjective **breezy,** blowy, fresh, blustery, gusty, wild, stormy, squally.
OPPOSITES still.

wing noun **1** *the east wing of the house:* **part,** section, side, annexe, extension. **2** *the radical wing of the party:* **faction,** camp, caucus, arm, branch, group, section, set.
verb **1** *a seagull winged its way over the sea:* **fly,** glide, soar. **2** *she was shot at and winged:* **wound,** graze, hit.

wink verb **1** *he winked an eye at her:* **blink,** flutter, bat. **2** *the diamond winked in the moonlight:* **sparkle,** twinkle, flash, glitter, gleam, shine, scintillate.

winner noun **victor,** champion, conqueror, vanquisher, medallist; informal champ, top dog.
OPPOSITES loser.

winning adjective **1** *the winning team:* **victorious,** successful, triumphant, undefeated, conquering, first, top. **2** *a winning smile:* **engaging,** charming, appealing, endearing, sweet, cute, winsome, attractive, prepossessing, fetching, disarming, captivating.

winnings plural noun **prize money,** gains, booty, spoils, proceeds, profits, takings, purse.

wipe verb **1** *Beth wiped the table:* **rub,** mop, sponge, swab, clean, dry, polish. **2** *he wiped the marks off the window:* **rub off,** clean off, remove, erase, efface.

wisdom noun **1** *we questioned the wisdom of the decision:* **understanding,** intelligence, sagacity, sense, common sense, shrewdness, astuteness, judgement, prudence, circumspection, logic, rationale, soundness, advisability. **2** *the wisdom of the East:* **knowledge,** learning, erudition, scholarship, philosophy, lore.
OPPOSITES folly.

wise adjective *a wise old man:* **sage,** sagacious, intelligent, clever, learned, knowledgeable, enlightened, astute, smart, shrewd, sharp-witted, canny, knowing, sensible, prudent, discerning, perceptive.

W

OPPOSITES foolish.

wish verb **1** *they can do as they wish:* **want**, desire, feel inclined, feel like, care, choose, please, think fit. **2** *I wish you to send them a message:* **want**, desire, require.
noun **1** *his wish to own a Mercedes:* **desire**, longing, yearning, whim, craving, hunger, hope, aspiration, aim, ambition, dream; informal hankering, yen. **2** *her parents' wishes:* **request**, requirement, bidding, instruction, direction, demand, order, command, want, desire, will.
■ **wish for** desire, want, hope for, covet, dream of, long for, yearn for, crave, hunger for, aspire to, set one's heart on, seek, fancy, hanker after; informal have a yen for.

wit noun **1** *he needed all his wits to escape:* **intelligence**, shrewdness, astuteness, cleverness, canniness, sense, judgement, acumen, insight, brains, mind; informal nous. **2** *my sparkling wit:* **wittiness**, humour, drollery, repartee, badinage, banter, wordplay, jokes, witticisms, quips, puns. **3** *she's such a wit:* **comedian**, humorist, comic, joker; informal wag.

witch noun **1** *the witch cast a spell:* **sorceress**, enchantress, hex, Wiccan. **2** (informal) *she's a right old witch:* **hag**, crone, harpy, harridan, she-devil; informal battleaxe.

witchcraft noun **sorcery**, (black) magic, wizardry, spells, incantations, necromancy, Wicca.

withdraw verb **1** *she withdrew her hand from his:* **remove**, extract, pull out, take out, take back. **2** *the ban on advertising was withdrawn:* **abolish**, cancel, lift, set aside, end, stop, remove, reverse, revoke, rescind, repeal, annul. **3** *she withdrew the allegation:* **retract**, take back, go back on, recant, repudiate, renounce, back down, climb down, backtrack, back-pedal, do a U-turn, eat one's words. **4** *the troops withdrew from the city:* **retreat**, pull out of, evacuate, quit, leave. **5** *his partner withdrew from the project:* **pull out of**, back out of, bow out of. **6** *they withdrew to their rooms:* **retire**, retreat, adjourn, decamp, leave, depart, absent oneself; formal repair.
OPPOSITES insert, introduce, deposit, enter.

withdrawal noun **1** *the withdrawal of subsidies:* **removal**, abolition, cancellation, discontinuation, termination, elimination. **2** *the withdrawal of the troops:* **departure**, pull-out, exit, exodus, evacuation, retreat.

wither verb **1** *the flowers withered in the sun:* **shrivel (up)**, dry up, wilt, droop, go limp, fade, perish. **2** *the muscles in his leg withered:* **waste (away)**, shrivel (up), shrink, atrophy. **3** *her confidence withered:* **diminish**, dwindle, shrink, lessen, fade, wane, evaporate, disappear.
OPPOSITES thrive, grow.

withering adjective **scornful**, contemptuous, scathing, stinging, devastating, humiliating, mortifying.
OPPOSITES admiring.

withhold verb **1** *he withheld the information:* **hold back**, keep back, refuse to give, retain,

hold on to, hide, conceal, keep secret; informal sit on. **2** *she could not withhold her tears:* **suppress,** repress, hold back, fight back, choke back, control, check, restrain, contain.
OPPOSITES release.

withstand verb **resist,** weather, survive, endure, cope with, stand, tolerate, bear, defy, brave, hold out against.

witness noun *witnesses claimed that he started the fight:* **observer,** onlooker, eyewitness, spectator, viewer, watcher, bystander, passer-by.
verb **1** *who witnessed the incident?* **see,** observe, watch, view, notice, spot, be present at, attend. **2** *the will is correctly witnessed:* **countersign,** sign, endorse, validate.

witty adjective **humorous,** amusing, droll, funny, comic, jocular, sparkling, scintillating, entertaining, clever, quick-witted.

wizard noun **1** *the wizard cast a spell:* **sorcerer,** warlock, magus, (black) magician, enchanter. **2** *a financial wizard:* **genius,** expert, master, virtuoso, maestro, marvel; informal hotshot, whizz-kid; Brit. informal dab hand; N. Amer. informal maven.

wobble verb **1** *the table wobbled:* **rock,** teeter, jiggle, sway, see-saw, shake. **2** *he wobbled across to the door:* **teeter,** totter, stagger, lurch. **3** *her voice wobbled:* **tremble,** shake, quiver, quaver, waver.

wobbly adjective **1** *a wobbly table:* **unsteady,** unstable, shaky, rocky, rickety, unsafe, precarious; informal wonky. **2** *her legs were a bit wobbly:* **shaky,** quivery, weak, unsteady; informal like jelly.

OPPOSITES stable.

woe noun **1** *a tale of woe:* **misery,** sorrow, distress, sadness, unhappiness, heartache, heartbreak, despair, adversity, misfortune, disaster, suffering, hardship. **2** *financial woes:* **trouble,** difficulty, problem, trial, tribulation, misfortune, setback, reverse.
OPPOSITES joy.

woman noun **lady,** female; Scottish & N. English lass; Irish colleen; informal chick; N. Amer. informal sister, dame, broad; Austral./NZ informal sheila; literary damsel.

womanly adjective **1** *womanly virtues:* **feminine,** female. **2** *her womanly figure:* **voluptuous,** curvaceous, shapely, ample, buxom, full-figured; informal curvy, busty.
OPPOSITES manly, boyish.

wonder noun **1** *she was speechless with wonder:* **awe,** admiration, fascination, surprise, astonishment, amazement. **2** *the wonders of nature:* **marvel,** miracle, phenomenon, sensation, spectacle, beauty, curiosity.
verb **1** *I wondered what was on her mind:* **ponder,** think about, meditate on, reflect on, muse on, speculate about, conjecture, be curious about. **2** *people wondered at such bravery:* **marvel,** be amazed, be astonished, stand in awe, be dumbfounded; informal be flabbergasted.

wonderful adjective **marvellous,** magnificent, superb, glorious, sublime, lovely, delightful; informal super, great, fantastic, terrific, tremendous, sensational, fabulous, awesome, magic,

W

wicked; Brit. informal smashing, brilliant; N. Amer. informal peachy, dandy, neat; Austral./NZ informal beaut, bonzer.

woo verb **1** *Richard wooed Joan:* **pay court to**, pursue, chase (after); dated court, romance, seek the hand of. **2** *the party wooed voters with promises:* **seek**, pursue, curry favour with, try to win, try to attract, try to cultivate. **3** *an attempt to woo him out of retirement:* **entice**, tempt, coax, persuade, wheedle, seduce; informal sweet-talk.

wood noun **1** *polished wood:* **timber**, planks, logs; N. Amer. lumber. **2** *a walk through the woods:* **forest**, woodland, trees, copse, coppice, grove; Brit. spinney.

wooded adjective **forested**, afforested, tree-covered; literary sylvan.

wooden adjective **1** *a wooden door:* **wood**, timber. **2** *wooden acting:* **stilted**, stiff, unnatural, awkward, flat, stodgy, lifeless, soulless. **3** *her face was wooden:* **expressionless**, impassive, poker-faced, emotionless, blank, vacant, unresponsive.

wool noun **fleece**, hair, coat.

word noun **1** *the Italian word for 'ham':* **term**, name, expression, designation. **2** *his words were meant kindly:* **remark**, comment, observation, statement, utterance. **3** *I've got three weeks to learn my words:* **script**, lines, lyrics, libretto. **4** *I give you my word:* **promise**, assurance, guarantee, undertaking, pledge, vow, oath, bond. **5** *I want a word with you:* **talk**, conversation, chat, tête-à-tête, heart-to-heart, one-to-one, discussion; informal confab.

6 *there's no word from the hospital:* **news**, information, communication, intelligence, message, report, communiqué, dispatch, bulletin.
verb *the question was carefully worded:* **phrase**, express, put, couch, frame, formulate, style.

wording noun **phrasing**, phraseology, language, words, expression, terminology.

wordy adjective **long-winded**, verbose, lengthy, rambling, garrulous, voluble; informal windy; Brit. informal waffly.
OPPOSITES succinct.

work noun **1** *a day's work in the fields:* **labour**, toil, slog, drudgery, exertion, effort; informal grind, sweat; Brit. informal graft. **2** *I'm looking for work:* **employment**, job, post, position, situation, occupation, profession, career, vocation, calling. **3** *haven't you got any work?* **tasks**, jobs, duties, assignments, projects, chores. **4** *works of literature:* **composition**, piece, creation, opus. **5** *this is the work of a radical faction:* **handiwork**, doing, act, deed. **6** *a lifetime spent doing good works:* **deeds**, acts, actions, turns. **7** *the complete works of Shakespeare:* **writings**, oeuvre, canon, output. **8** *a car works:* **factory**, plant, mill, workshop, facility. **9** *the works of a clock:* **mechanism**, machinery, workings, parts, movement, action; informal insides.
OPPOSITES leisure, pleasure.
verb **1** *staff worked late into the night:* **labour**, toil, exert oneself, slave (away); informal slog (away), beaver away; Brit. informal graft. **2** *he worked in education for years:* **be**

employed, have a job, earn one's living, do business.
3 *farmers worked the land:* **cultivate,** farm, till, plough.
4 *his car was working perfectly:* **function,** go, run, operate; informal behave. **5** *how do I work this machine?* **operate,** use, handle, control, manipulate, run. **6** *their ploy worked:* **succeed,** turn out well, go as planned, get results, be effective; informal come off, pay off, do the trick. **7** *blusher can work miracles:* **achieve,** accomplish, bring about, produce, perform. **8** *he worked the crowd into a frenzy:* **stir (up),** excite, drive, move, rouse, fire, galvanize; whip up, agitate.
9 *work the mixture into a paste:* **knead,** squeeze, form; mix, stir, blend. **10** *he worked the blade into the padlock:* **manipulate,** manoeuvre, guide, squeeze, edge. **11** *he worked his way through the crowd:* **manoeuvre,** make, thread, wind, weave, wend, elbow.
OPPOSITES rest, fail.

■ **work something out 1** *work out what you can afford:* calculate, compute, reckon up, determine. **2** *I'm trying to work out what she meant:* understand, comprehend, puzzle out, sort out, make sense of, get to the bottom of, make head or tail of, unravel, decipher, decode; informal figure out; Brit. informal suss out. **3** *they worked out a plan:* devise, formulate, draw up, put together, develop, construct, arrange, organize, contrive, concoct; hammer out, negotiate.

worker noun **employee,** member of staff, workman, labourer, hand, operator,

operative, agent, wage-earner, breadwinner, proletarian.

workshop noun **1** *an ideal set of tools for a workshop:* **workroom,** studio, factory, works, plant, industrial unit.
2 *a workshop on combating stress:* **study group,** discussion group, seminar, forum, class.

world noun **1** *he travelled the world:* **earth,** globe, planet, sphere. **2** *the academic world:* **sphere,** society, circle, arena, milieu, province, domain, preserve, realm, field. **3** (**the world**) *the world would hear of her achievements:* **everyone,** people, mankind, humankind, humanity, the public, all and sundry.

worldly adjective **1** *worldly pursuits:* **earthly,** terrestrial, temporal, mundane, mortal, human, material, physical. **2** *a worldly man:* **sophisticated,** experienced, worldly-wise, knowledgeable, knowing, enlightened, mature, seasoned, cosmopolitan, urbane, cultured.
OPPOSITES spiritual, naive.

worldwide adjective **global,** international, intercontinental, universal, ubiquitous.
OPPOSITES local.

worn adjective **shabby,** worn out, threadbare, in tatters, falling to pieces, ragged, frayed, moth-eaten, scruffy, having seen better days.
OPPOSITES new, smart.

worried adjective **anxious,** troubled, bothered, concerned, uneasy, fretful, agitated, nervous, edgy, tense, apprehensive, fearful, afraid, frightened; Brit. informal in a stew, in a flap.
OPPOSITES carefree.

worry verb **1** *she worries about*

W

his health: **be anxious,** be concerned, fret, agonize, brood, panic, lose sleep, get worked up; informal get in a flap, get in a state. **2** *is something worrying you?* **trouble,** bother, make anxious, disturb, distress, upset, concern, unsettle, perturb, scare, prey on someone's mind; informal bug, get to.
noun **1** *I'm beside myself with worry:* **anxiety,** distress, concern, unease, disquiet, nerves, agitation, edginess, tension, apprehension, fear, misgiving; informal butterflies. **2** *the rats are a worry:* **problem,** cause for concern, nuisance, pest, trial, trouble, bane, bugbear; informal pain, headache, hassle.
OPPOSITES peace of mind.

worsen verb **1** *insomnia can worsen a patient's distress:* **aggravate,** add to, intensify, increase, compound, magnify, heighten, inflame, exacerbate. **2** *the recession worsened:* **deteriorate,** degenerate, decline; informal go downhill.
OPPOSITES improve.

worship noun **1** *the worship of saints:* **reverence,** veneration, adoration, glorification, exaltation, devotion, praise, thanksgiving, homage, honour. **2** *morning worship:* **service,** rite, prayer, praise, devotion, observance.
verb **1** *they worship pagan gods:* **revere,** pray to, pay homage to, honour, adore, venerate, praise, glorify, exalt. **2** *he absolutely worshipped her:* **love,** cherish, treasure, hold dear, esteem, adulate, idolize, deify, hero-worship, lionize; informal put on a pedestal.
OPPOSITES mock, despise, shun.

worth noun **1** *evidence of the rug's worth:* **value,** price, cost, valuation, estimate. **2** *the intrinsic worth of education:* **benefit,** good, advantage, use, value, virtue, desirability, sense.

worthless adjective **1** *the item was worthless:* **valueless. 2** *a mountain of worthless information:* **useless,** pointless, meaningless, senseless, inconsequential, ineffective, ineffectual, fruitless, unproductive, unavailing, valueless. **3** *his worthless son:* **good-for-nothing,** ne'er-do-well, useless, despicable, contemptible, degenerate; informal no-good, lousy.
OPPOSITES valuable, useful, worthy.

worthwhile adjective **valuable,** useful, of service, beneficial, rewarding, advantageous, positive, helpful, profitable, gainful, fruitful, productive, constructive, effective.

worthy adjective *a worthy citizen:* **good,** righteous, virtuous, moral, ethical, upright, respectable, upstanding, high-minded, principled, reputable, decent.
OPPOSITES disreputable.
noun *local worthies:* **dignitary,** personage, grandee, VIP, notable, pillar of society, luminary, leading light; informal bigwig.
OPPOSITES nobody.

would-be adjective **aspiring,** budding, promising, prospective, potential, hopeful, keen, eager, ambitious; informal wannabe.

wound noun **1** *a chest wound:* **injury,** cut, gash, laceration, graze, scratch, abrasion,

W

puncture, lesion; Medicine
trauma. **2** *the wounds inflicted
by the media:* **insult,** blow,
slight, offence, affront, hurt,
damage, injury.
verb **1** *he was critically
wounded:* **injure,** hurt, harm,
lacerate, cut, graze, gash, stab,
slash, wing. **2** *her words had
wounded him:* **hurt,** insult,
slight, offend, affront, distress,
grieve, pain, sting.

wrap verb **1** *she wrapped herself
in a towel:* **enclose,** enfold,
envelop, encase, cover, fold,
wind, swathe, bundle, swaddle.
2 *I wrapped the vase carefully:*
pack, package, parcel up,
bundle (up), gift-wrap.
noun *he put a wrap round her:*
shawl, stole, cloak, cape,
mantle, scarf.

wrath noun **anger,** rage, temper,
fury, outrage, spleen,
resentment, (high) dudgeon,
indignation.
OPPOSITES happiness.

wreath noun **garland,** circlet,
chaplet, crown, festoon, lei,
ring, loop, circle.

wreathe verb **1** *a pulpit
wreathed in holly:* **festoon,**
garland, drape, cover, deck,
decorate, ornament, adorn.
2 *blue smoke wreathed
upwards:* **spiral,** coil, loop,
wind, curl, twist, snake.

wreck noun **1** *salvage teams
landed on the wreck:*
shipwreck, sunken ship, hull.
2 *the wreck of a stolen car:*
wreckage, debris, ruins,
remains, burnt-out shell.
verb **1** *he had wrecked her car:*
destroy, break, demolish, crash,
smash up, write off; N. Amer.
informal trash, total. **2** *the crisis
wrecked his plans:* **ruin,** spoil,
disrupt, undo, put a stop to,

frustrate, blight, crush, dash,
destroy, scotch, shatter,
devastate, sabotage; informal
mess up, screw up, put paid to,
stymie; Brit. informal scupper.

wrench noun **1** *she felt a wrench
on her shoulders:* **tug,** pull, jerk,
jolt, heave; informal yank. **2** *hold
the piston with a wrench:*
spanner. 3 *leaving was an
immense wrench:* **blow,** ache,
trauma, pang.
verb **1** *he wrenched the gun from
her:* **tug,** pull, jerk, wrest,
heave, twist, force, prise; N. Amer.
pry; informal yank. **2** *she
wrenched her ankle:* **sprain,**
twist, turn, strain, rick, crick.

wrestle verb **grapple,** fight,
struggle, scuffle, tussle, brawl;
informal scrap.

wretched adjective **1** *I felt so
wretched without you:*
miserable, unhappy, sad,
heartbroken, grief-stricken,
distressed, desolate, devastated,
disconsolate, downcast,
dejected, depressed,
melancholy, forlorn. **2** *wretched
living conditions:* **harsh,** hard,
grim, difficult, poor, pitiful,
piteous, pathetic, tragic,
miserable, bleak, cheerless,
hopeless, sorry, sordid; informal
crummy.
OPPOSITES cheerful, comfortable.

wriggle verb *she tried to hug
him but she wriggled:* **squirm,**
writhe, wiggle, thresh,
flounder, flail, twitch, twist and
turn, snake, worm.
■ **wriggle out of** avoid, shirk,
dodge, evade, sidestep; escape;
informal duck.

wrinkle noun *fine wrinkles
around her mouth:* **crease,** fold,
pucker, line, crinkle, furrow,
ridge, groove; informal crow's
feet.

W

verb *his coat tails wrinkled up:* **crease,** pucker, gather, crinkle, crumple, rumple, ruck up, scrunch up.

write verb **1** *he wrote her name in the book:* **put in writing,** put down, jot down, note (down), take down, record, inscribe, sign, scribble, scrawl, pen, pencil. **2** *I wrote a poem:* **compose,** draft, think up, formulate, compile, pen, dash off, produce. **3** *he promised to write:* **correspond,** communicate, get in touch, keep in contact; informal drop someone a line.

writer noun **author,** wordsmith; informal scribbler, scribe, pen-pusher, hack.

writing noun **1** *I can't read his writing:* **handwriting,** hand, script, calligraphy, lettering, print, printing; informal scribble, scrawl. **2** *this fear did not show in her writing:* **written work,** compositions, books, publications, papers, articles, essays, oeuvre.

wrong adjective **1** *the wrong answer:* **incorrect,** mistaken, erroneous, inaccurate, inexact, imprecise; informal off beam, out. **2** *he knew he had said the wrong thing:* **inappropriate,** unsuitable, ill-advised, ill-considered, ill-judged, unwise, infelicitous; informal out of order. **3** *I've done nothing wrong:* **bad,** dishonest, illegal, unlawful, illicit, criminal, corrupt, unethical, immoral, wicked, sinful, iniquitous, nefarious, reprehensible; informal crooked. **4** *there's something wrong with the engine:* **amiss,** awry, out of order, not right, faulty, defective.
OPPOSITES right, correct, appropriate, legal.
adverb *she guessed wrong:* **incorrectly,** wrongly, inaccurately, erroneously, mistakenly.
noun **1** *the difference between right and wrong:* **immorality,** sin, wickedness, evil, illegality, unlawfulness, crime, corruption, villainy, dishonesty, injustice, misconduct, transgression. **2** *an attempt to make up for past wrongs:* **misdeed,** offence, injury, crime, transgression, sin, injustice, outrage, atrocity.
OPPOSITES right.
verb *she was determined to forget the man who had wronged her:* **mistreat,** ill-use, ill-treat, do an injustice to, abuse, harm, hurt, injure.

wrongdoer noun **offender,** lawbreaker, criminal, felon, delinquent, villain, culprit, evil-doer, sinner, transgressor, malefactor, miscreant, rogue, scoundrel; informal crook, wrong 'un.

Xx

xenophobic adjective **jingoistic,** chauvinistic, flag-waving, nationalistic, isolationist, prejudiced, bigoted, intolerant.

Yy

yank verb & noun (informal) **jerk,** pull, tug, wrench.

yarn noun **thread,** cotton, wool, fibre, filament.

yawning adjective **gaping,** wide, cavernous, deep, huge, vast.

yearly adjective **annual.** adverb **annually,** once a year, per annum, each/every year.

yearn verb **long,** pine, crave, desire, want, wish, hanker, covet, hunger, thirst, ache; informal **itch.**

yell verb *he yelled in agony:* **shout,** cry out, howl, wail, scream, shriek, screech, yelp, squeal, roar, bawl.
noun *a yell of rage:* **shout,** cry, howl, scream, shriek, screech, yelp, squeal, roar.

yellow adjective **golden,** gold, blonde, fair, flaxen.

yes adverb **certainly,** very well, of course, by all means, sure, all right, absolutely, indeed, affirmative, agreed, roger; Scottish & N. English, aye; Nautical aye aye; informal yeah, yep, uh-huh, okay, OK; Brit. informal righto, righty-ho; N. Amer. informal surely.
OPPOSITES no.

yet adverb **1** *he hasn't made up his mind yet:* **so far,** as yet, up to now, up till now. **2** *don't celebrate just yet:* **(right) now,** at this time, already, so soon. **3** *he did nothing, yet he seemed happy:* **nevertheless,** nonetheless, even so, but, however, still, notwithstanding, despite that, in spite of that, for all that, all the same, just the same, at the same time. **4** *yet more advice:* **even,** still.

yield verb **1** *such projects yield poor returns:* **produce,** bear, give, provide, afford, return, bring in, earn, realize, generate, deliver, pay out. **2** *Duke was forced to yield:* **surrender,** capitulate, submit, admit defeat, back down, give in.
OPPOSITES withhold, resist.
noun *we expected a higher yield:* **profit,** gain, return, dividend, earnings.
■ **yield to** give in to, give way to, submit to, comply with, agree to, consent to, go along with, grant, permit, allow; informal cave in to; formal accede to.

yob, yobbo noun (Brit. informal) **lout,** thug, hooligan, tearaway, vandal, ruffian, troublemaker; Austral. **larrikin;** informal tough, bruiser; Brit. informal lager lout; Scottish informal ned.

young adjective **1** *young people:* **youthful,** juvenile, junior, adolescent, teenage. **2** *she's very young for her age:* **immature,** childish, inexperienced, naive, green. **3** *a young industry:* **fledgling,** developing, budding, in its infancy, emerging.
OPPOSITES old, mature.
noun **1** *a robin feeding its young:* **offspring,** progeny, family, babies, litter, brood. **2** *the young don't care nowadays:* **young people,** children, boys and girls, youngsters, youth, the younger generation, juveniles, minors; informal kids.
OPPOSITES old.

y

youngster noun **child,** teenager, adolescent, youth, juvenile, minor, junior, boy, girl; Scottish & N. English lass, lassie; informal lad, kid, whippersnapper, teen.

youth noun **1** *he was a fine athlete in his youth:* **early years,** teens, teenage years, adolescence, boyhood, girlhood, childhood, minority. **2** *local youths:* **young man,** boy, juvenile, teenager, adolescent, junior, minor; informal lad, kid. **3** *the youth of the nation:* **young people,** young, younger generation, next generation; informal kids.
OPPOSITES adulthood, old age, elderly.

youthful adjective **young,** boyish, girlish, fresh-faced, young-looking, spry, sprightly, vigorous, active.
OPPOSITES elderly.

Zz

zany adjective **eccentric,** odd, unconventional, bizarre, weird, mad, crazy, comic, madcap, quirky, idiosyncratic; informal wacky, oddball, off the wall; Brit. informal daft; N. Amer. informal kooky, wacko.
OPPOSITES conventional, sensible.

zeal noun **enthusiasm,** passion, ardour, fervour, fire, devotion, gusto, vigour, energy.
OPPOSITES apathy.

zero noun **1** *the answer is zero:* **nought,** nothing, nil, o. **2** *there was absolutely zero I could do about it:* **nothing (at all),** nil, none; N. English nowt; informal zilch, not a dicky bird; Brit. informal damn all, not a sausage; N. Amer. informal zip, nada.

zigzag verb **twist,** meander, snake, wind, weave, swerve.

zone noun **area,** sector, section, belt, stretch, region, territory, district, quarter, neighbourhood.

zoom verb (informal) *he zoomed off:* **hurry,** rush, dash, race, speed, sprint, career, shoot, hurtle, hare, fly; informal tear, belt; Brit. informal bomb.

y

z